Contemporary Theatre, Film, and Television

A Note About
Contemporary Theatre, Film, and Television
and
Who's Who in the Theatre

Contemporary Theatre, Film, and Television is a continuation of *Who's Who in the Theatre*, expanded to include film and television personalities. The editors believe this change in coverage of the series makes for a more representative and useful reference tool.

To provide continuity with *Who's Who in the Theatre*, the cumulative index at the back of this volume interfiles references to *Contemporary Theatre, Film, and Television*, Volumes 1-3, with references to *Who's Who in the Theatre*, 1st-17th Editions, and, beginning with this volume, *Who Was Who in the Theatre*.

ISSN 0749-064X

Contemporary Theatre, Film, and Television

A Biographical Guide Featuring Performers, Directors, Writers, Producers, Designers, Managers, Choreographers, Technicians, Composers, Executives, Dancers, and Critics in the United States and Great Britain

A Continuation of
Who's Who in the Theatre

Monica M. O'Donnell, Editor

Foreword by Lynne Stuart

Volume 3

Includes Cumulative Index Containing References to
Who's Who in the Theatre and *Who Was Who in the Theatre*

GALE RESEARCH COMPANY • BOOK TOWER • DETROIT, MICHIGAN 48226

STAFF

Monica M. O'Donnell, *Editor*

Timothy L. Schuman, *Assistant Editor*

J. Peter Bergman, Mel Cobb, James R. Kirkland, *Sketchwriters*
Thomas M. Bachmann, Darryl W. Bridson, Vincent Henry,
Tracie Morris, Mia Perkin-Jensen, *Editorial Assistants*

Peter Dolgenos, *Contributing Editor*

Mary Beth Trimper, *Production Supervisor*
Dorothy Kalleberg, *Senior Production Associate*
Roger D. Hubbard, *Layout Artist and Graphic Arts Coordinator*
Charles M. Hunt, *Cameraman and Keyliner*
Arthur Chartow, *Art Director*

Special acknowledgment is due to the
Contemporary Authors staff members who
assisted in the preparation of this volume.

Frederick G. Ruffner, *Publisher*
Dedria Bryfonski, *Editorial Director*
Ellen Crowley, *Associate Editorial Director*
Christine Nasso, *Director, Literature Division*
Linda Hubbard, *Senior Editor*

Copyright © 1986 by GALE RESEARCH COMPANY

Library of Congress Catalog Card Number 84-649371
ISBN 0-8103-2066-5
ISSN 0749-064X

Computerized photocomposition by
Roberts/Churcher
Brooklyn, New York

Contents

Foreword

By Lynne Stuart

Today's advanced technology is changing all forms of entertainment. The theatre as we once knew it has changed—changed so much in even these last twenty years as to be in some ways unrecognizable. Today's skyrocketing costs are a major factor, resulting in fewer shows and smaller casts. In the mid-sixties, when three shows could be produced for a million dollars, independent producers used to have two or three shows ready to go into production at the same time. One season, for example, producer David Merrick had five shows playing at once, and producer-director Hal Prince had two playing with another two or three ready to go! With the astronomical prices of the mid-eighties, a production can cost anywhere from half a million dollars for a play, to over four or five million dollars for a musical. The Consumer Price Index has risen 233 percent in these past twenty years, but alarmingly, over the same period theatre costs and ticket prices have risen almost 600 percent in some categories. No wonder the public doesn't have the expendable income for an evening at the theatre. Even if it were the case, as some theatre people insist, that theatre ticket prices have risen in direct proportion to other prices, the truth of the matter is this: if the public perceives theatre to be too expensive, then theatre is too expensive.

More and more producers now depend on the less risky regional, college, small community theatre, or Off-Broadway run to help mount a production. Then if it looks good and everything goes well, the show moves to Broadway. The *Othello* production of a few seasons ago came from the American Shakespeare Theatre in Connecticut; *Crucifer of Blood* began at the Studio Arena in Buffalo; the prize-winning *Da* by Hugh Leonard originated at the Off-Broadway Hudson Guild Theatre; and *Big River* started at the La Jolla Playhouse in California.

Now, I am not going to bemoan the loss of the "good ole days," but I *do* bemoan the fact that so many of us who are theatre professionals stand around like ostriches with our heads in the sand, pretending theatre has not changed, pretending that things can continue being done the way they have always been done because that is the way they have always been done! I bemoan the fact that a large part of the former theatre-going public has been cut off from this source of entertainment because ticket prices exceed their budgets for "non-essentials" like theatre.

I remember a college professor of mine talking about the prime achievers of history. These were people, "movers and shakers," who had the courage and the strong intellectual, physical, emotional, and spritual beliefs and standards to overcome overwhelming obstacles (including the overwhelming obstacle of the status quo) and set an example for others. If we in the entertainment industry will not be afraid to challenge tradition, to realize that change is the only constant, we will be able to learn from the past and then let it go.

There are still those dreamers today, movers and shakers, who have been thinking in a positive way. There was the owner of a small Connecticut theatre who dabbled in gadgets and set up a method, in the 1960's, to accommodate the overflow audience that did not fit into his tiny theatre. He rigged up a sort of closed-circuit television broadcast of the play that he showed simultaneously with the production that was under way in an adjoining room. And, though it took twenty years, in May of 1986 that idea reappeared at the Public Theatre in New York City with the announcement that the overflow theatre patrons of its new show could purchase tickets for a live, closed-circuit television broadcast.

The impact of new technology is hitting every part of the industry. The Musicians Union recently presented to its membership a synthesizer symposium on the use of emulators (machines that make sound effects and can reproduce anything from human-like voices to musical instruments) in theatres and concerts halls. And composer Andrew Lloyd Webber's *Song and Dance* was brought to Broadway from London because RCA/Columbia Video offered to make a home-video version of the show. The original theatre piece was markedly transformed for the home videocassette recorder (VCR) market.

In a similar dual-market production, *National Lampoon* and World Wide Film Services have planned a number of original *Lampoon* comedy revues to be done in a New York theatre and taped for the home VCR market. These revues, like *Song and Dance*, won't be staged specifically for video, but the video market is the major reason for their existence. The point is that a good, affordable show will draw people. So the stage, screen, and video markets don't necessarily compete with each other but are able to enhance one another.

Today's climate gives all of us in theatre, film, and/or television expanded fields in which to work. The average American is said to watch more than fifty hours of television per week. Children spend probably twice as much time being educated by television as by school. And VCRs are more and more becoming a permanent piece of electrical equipment in living rooms across the nation. We certainly live in an electronic age.

And what an exciting time it is to be part of these fabulous industries! There is no reason to cry, "The VCRs are ruining the theatre just like talkies ruined vaudeville." VCR owners simply need to be instructed that they no longer have to miss the excitement of seeing live drama and live musicals because their favorite television shows are on. They can really have it all. Just set the timing device, record that favorite television show while at the theatre or a movie, and make a special event of watching the recorded program at a convenient time.

What a far cry this technology is from the early days of television when I began as a production coordinator for a one-hour show five nights a week at CBS in Los Angeles. Those were the days when producers, directors, and even performers were more involved in the technical aspects of putting on a show. Today it's harder to have that involvement because of our technological advancements, but we can make it our business to be aware of and know something about those other areas. And how far we've come from the days when I was hostess of my own television show in Tampa, Florida, and did thirteen live commercials every show, all memorized because there was no such thing as a TelePrompTer.

Look at the endless possibilities our technologies can bring us. We've only begun to tap the resources of videotape and videodisc and interfacing these with the personal computer. A whole new means of entertaining, teaching, learning, observing, and absorbing is before us. What a treasure chest of riches we can record and preserve of the philosophies, ideas, creativity, and personal thoughts of some of our own movers and shakers, the living legends of today, the geniuses of our time. As our own "giant step" away from theatre as we had always known it, my partner, Richard Horner, and I have just produced a how-to video on the work of one such genius, the realist painter Philip Pearlstein, in the formats of a ninety-minute videocassette, a thirty-minute television show, and a laserbeam videodisc. The presentations are called "Philip Pearlstein Draws the Artist's Model."

The newest of the three formats, the laserdisc, looks like a twelve-inch record except for its silver color, which comes from the protective layer of aluminum coating and silver that encases the laser-imbued information micro-dots on the plastic. Another difference is that the disc holds pictures or text in addition to sound. With a capacity of fifty-four thousand still photographic frames per side, over one hundred thousand frames per disc, a single disc can hold the entire *Encyclopaedia Britannica*. Since it is read by a laser beam, not played by a needle, there is no wear on the disc. How fabulous if we had been able to use that technology to preserve the thoughts and works of performers and creative artists like Sarah Bernhardt, Frank Lloyd Wright, Marc Chagall, Arturo Toscanini, or Max Reinhardt.

Never has there been an era of such exciting possibilities. Today's writers, producers, and performers now have the opportunity to crisscross the boundaries of the entertainment world, working on a commercial, a soap opera, or a sitcom during the day and doing a live show in the evening. With more and more television and film work coming back to New York from the West Coast, we no longer have to hop on a plane and make an either/or decision—now we can do it all. Directors and performers are producing, writers and producers are directing, and we are all exploring not just one craft relating to the theatre but all the crafts of show business—of theatre, film, and television. As a theatre professional, I say to my colleagues, let's make the most of it. Let's take the initiative. Let's read all those new scripts the playwrights are writing; let's use imagination and courage and give the public shows that it wants to see. Let there be variety in the theatre again as there is variety in television and film. Let's urge the media to present the theatre in a positive light, encouraging people to decide for themselves what is good and what they want, rather than trying to tell them. Let's get the people back to the theatre who never go anymore because they're tired of being told something is terrific that really isn't terrific—just expensive. Let's get people into the theatre who have never been to live theatre and show them it can be as vital and even more thrilling than a car chase on a television show. Let's face it, Irving Berlin said it best with "There's No Business Like Show Business!" and today show business is theatre—on stage, on videocassette, on television, and on film.

Lynne Stuart appeared on Broadway and on television before she began producing plays. With her partner, Richard Horner, she is president of Interactive Media, a video and laserdisc production company.

Preface

The worlds of theatre, film, and television hold an undeniable appeal, and the individuals whose careers are devoted to these fields are subjects of great interest. The people both behind the scenes and in front of the lights and cameras—writers, directors, producers, performers, and others—all have a significant impact on our lives, for they enlighten us as they entertain.

Contemporary Theatre, Film, and Television
Continues and Improves
Who's Who in the Theatre

Contemporary Theatre, Film, and Television (CTFT), a comprehensive new biographical guide, is designed to meet the need for information on theatre, film, and television personalities. Existing biographical sources covering entertainment figures are generally limited in scope, focusing only on theatre, for example, as was the case with *Who's Who in the Theatre (WWT)*. For more than seventy years *WWT* provided reliable information on theatre people. However, when the editors began reviewing names for inclusion in a proposed supplement to the seventeenth edition of *WWT*, they recognized that they were eliminating large numbers of people who, though not active in the theatre, make significant contributions to other entertainment media. Thus, the editors believe that expanding the scope of *WWT* to encompass not only theatre notables but film and/or television figures as well provides a more useful reference tool.

In addition to its expanded scope, *CTFT* improves upon *WWT* in other important ways. *WWT* was published in *editions,* with the majority of the biographies in every edition being updated and included in subsequent editions. Since entries were dropped from one edition to the next only when listees had been inactive for a sustained period or when active listees died, the number of new entries it was possible to include in each *WWT* edition was governed in part by how many old ones were dropped. *CTFT,* however, is published annually in *volumes,* and each volume covers primarily new, entirely different personalities. Thus *CTFT*'s coverage is not limited by the number of entries that can be listed in a single volume, and the cumulative index makes the entries in all *CTFT* volumes easily accessible.

Entry format, discussed in greater detail later in this preface, has also been improved in *CTFT.* Instead of presenting information with minimal paragraphing, as was the case in *WWT,* the editors have divided *CTFT* entries into numerous clearly labeled sections to make it easier to locate specific facts quickly. And the inclusion of hundreds of photographs of the personalities listed in *CTFT* adds a useful visual dimension to *CTFT* missing from *WWT.*

Scope

CTFT is a biographical series covering not only performers, directors, writers, and producers but also designers, managers, choreographers, technicians, composers, executives, dancers, and critics from the United States and Great Britain. With over 700 entries in *CTFT* Volume 3, the series now provides biographies for more than 2,500 people involved in all aspects of the theatre, film, and television industries.

Primary emphasis is given to people who are currently active. *CTFT* includes major, established figures whose positions in entertainment history are assured, such as dancer, choreographer, and actor Mikhail Baryshnikov; entertainer Bob Hope; actor, producer, director, and writer Paul Newman; television producer Aaron Spelling; actress Sylvia Syms; and actress Joanne Woodward. New and highly promising individuals who are beginning to make their mark are represented in *CTFT* as well—people such as actor and comedian Jim Belushi, who rose to prominence as a regular performer on television's *Saturday Night Live* and is now branching out to act in such feature films as *Salvador;* actor Dennis Christopher, who has had featured roles on stage and television as well as in the films *Breaking Away* and *Chariots of Fire;* actress Demi Moore, one of the young stars of the motion picture *St. Elmo's Fire;* and Susan Seidelman, director of both the underground film *Smithereens* and the commercially successful movie *Desperately Seeking Susan.*

CTFT also includes sketches on people no longer professionally active who have made significant contributions to their fields and whose work remains of interest today. This volume, for example, contains entries on actor and dancer Ray Bolger, choreographer Agnes de Mille, actor and businessman Douglas Fairbanks, Jr., and actress Myrna Loy. Selected sketches also record the achievements of theatre, film, and television personalities deceased since 1960. Among such notables with listings in this volume are Anne Baxter, James Cagney, Simone Signoret, and Orson Welles.

With its broad coverage and detailed entries, *CTFT* is designed to assist a variety of users—a student preparing for a class, a teacher drawing up an assignment, a researcher seeking a specific fact, a librarian searching for the answer to a question, or a general reader looking for information about a favorite personality.

Compilation Methods

Every effort is made to secure information directly from biographees. The editors consult industry directories, biographical dictionaries, published interviews, feature stories, and film, television, and theatre reviews to identify people not previously covered in *WWT* or *CTFT*. Questionnaires are mailed to prospective listees or, when addresses are unavailable, to their agents, and sketches are compiled from the information they supply. The editors also select major figures included in *WWT* whose entries require updating and send them copies of their previously published entries for revision. *CTFT* sketches are then prepared from the new information submitted by these well-known personalities or their agents. Among the notable figures whose *WWT*, seventeenth edition, entries have been completely revised for this volume of *CTFT* are Carol Channing, Israel Horovitz, Trevor Nunn, and Gwen Verdon. If people of special interest to *CTFT* users are deceased or fail to reply to requests for information, materials are gathered from reliable secondary sources. Sketches prepared solely through research are clearly marked with an asterisk (*) at the end of the entries.

The emphasis in future volumes will remain on people currently active in theatre, film, and television who are not already covered in *WWT* or *CTFT*. To insure *CTFT*'s timeliness and comprehensiveness, future volumes will continue to include updated *WWT* entries and will also provide revisions of *CTFT* sketches that have become outdated.

Format

CTFT entries, modeled after those in the Gale Research Company's highly regarded *Contemporary Authors* series, are written in a clear, readable style with few abbreviations and no limits set on length. So that a reader needing specific information can quickly focus on the pertinent portion of an entry, typical *CTFT* listings are clearly divided into the following sections:

> **Entry heading**—Cites the form of the name by which the listee is best known followed by birth and death dates, when available.

> **Personal**—Provides the biographee's full or original name if different from the entry heading, date and place of birth, family data, and information about the listee's education (including professional training), politics, religion, and military service.

> **Vocation**—Highlights the individual's primary fields of activity in the entertainment industry.

> **Career**—Presents a comprehensive listing of principal credits or engagements. The career section lists theatrical debuts (including New York and London debuts), principal stage appearances, and major tours; film debuts and principal films; television debuts and television appearances; and plays, films, and television shows directed and produced. Related career items, such as professorships and lecturing, are also included as well as non-entertainment career items.

> **Writings**—Lists published and unpublished plays, screenplays, and scripts along with production information. Published books and articles, often with bibliographical data, are also listed.

> **Recordings**—Cites album and single song releases with recording labels, when available.

> **Member**—Highlights professional, union, civic, and other association memberships, including official posts held.

> **Awards**—Notes theatre, film, and television awards and nominations as well as writing awards, military and civic awards, and fellowships and honorary degrees received.

Sidelights—Cites favorite roles, recreational activities, and hobbies. Frequently this section provides portions of agent-prepared biographies or personal statements from the listee.

Addresses—Notes home, office, and agent addresses, when available. (In those instances where an individual prefers to withhold his or her home address from publication, the editors make every attempt to include at least one other address in the entry.)

Enlivening the text in many instances are large, clear photographs. Often the work of theatrical photographers, these pictures are supplied by the biographees to complement their sketches. This volume, for example, contains over 270 such portraits received from various individuals profiled in the following pages.

Brief Entries

CTFT users have indicated that having some information, however brief, on individuals not yet in the series would be preferable to waiting until full-length sketches can be prepared as outlined above under "Compilation Methods." Therefore, *CTFT* includes abbreviated listings on notables who presently do not have sketches in *CTFT*. These short profiles, identified by the heading "Brief Entry," highlight the person's career in capsule form.

Brief entries are not intended to replace sketches. Instead, they are designed to increase *CTFT*'s comprehensiveness and thus better serve *CTFT* users by providing pertinent and timely information about well-known people in the entertainment industry, many of whom will be the subjects of full sketches in forthcoming volumes.

This volume, for example, includes brief entries on such up-and-coming people as Whoopi Goldberg, Tom Hulce, Madonna, and Patrick Swayze.

Cumulative Index

To facilitate locating sketches on the thousands of notables profiled in *CTFT* as well as in *WWT*, the *CTFT* cumulative index at the back of this volume interfiles references to *CTFT*, Volumes 1 through 3, with references to *WWT*, first through seventeenth editions, and *Who Was Who in the Theatre*. For entertainment figures listed in *CTFT*, the index directs users to the appropriate *CTFT* volume. For theatrical personalities whose *WWT* sketches have not yet been updated and included in *CTFT*, the index cites the latest edition of *WWT* containing their entries. And the index refers users to *Who Was Who in the Theatre* for listings on inactive or deceased individuals whose initial entries were contained in the first fifteen editions of *WWT*. Thus by consulting only one source— the *CTFT* cumulative index—users have easy access to the tens of thousands of biographical sketches in *CTFT*, *WWT*, and *Who Was Who in the Theatre*.

Suggestions are Welcome

If readers would like to suggest people to be covered in future *CTFT* volumes, they are encouraged to send these names (along with addresses, if possible) to the editor. Other suggestions and comments are also most welcome and should be addressed to: The Editor, *Contemporary Theatre, Film, and Television*, 150 E. 50th Street, New York, NY 10022.

Contemporary Theatre, Film, and Television

Contemporary Theatre, Film, and Television

* Indicates that a listing has been compiled from secondary sources believed to be reliable.

ACKERMAN, Harry S.   1912-

PERSONAL: Born November 17, 1912, in Albany, NY; son of Harold (an automobile executive) and Ann (Flannery) Ackerman; married second wife, Elinor Donahue (an actress), April 21, 1961; children: (first marriage) Susan, Stephen; (second marriage) Brian, Peter, James, Christopher. EDUCATION: Dartmouth College, A.B., 1935.

VOCATION: Producer.

CAREER: PRINCIPAL TELEVISION WORK—Executive producer, CBS, 1948; director of network programs in Hollywood, CBS, 1948; vice president in charge of network radio programs, CBS, 1950; vice president in charge of network television programs in Hollywood, CBS, 1951; executive director of special programs, CBS, 1956; vice president and executive producer, Screen Gems Inc., 1958-73; with Paramount; president, Harry Ackerman Productions.

While executive producer with CBS in New York, Ackerman supervised development, writing, and casting of all CBS New York based shows such as *Studio One* and *Suspense.*

As vice president of CBS programs in Hollywood, he supervised all production elements of the following series: *Gunsmoke* (also developed and cast this for radio, and later recast for television); *I Love Lucy* (also developed concept with Jess Oppenheimer, Lucille Ball, and Desi Arnaz); *The Jack Benny Show; Burns and Allen; Amos and Andy* (both the radio series and later the film series); *Our Miss Brooks* (also co-creator); *The Edgar Bergen Show; Climax; Yours Truly, Johnny Dollar* (also created).

Ackerman was executive producer of such specials as *The Day Lincoln Was Shot; Blither Spirit; Twentieth Century; A Bell for Adano; The Caine Mutiny Court Martial.*

Independently, he developed and produced *Bachelor Father* and *Leave It to Beaver.*

With Screen Gems, he was executive producer for *Dennis the Menace; The Donna Reed Show; Tightrope; My Sister Eileen; The Farmer's Daughter; Hazel; Love on a Rooftop* (also co-creator); *Occasional Wife; The Wackiest Ship in the Army; Gidget; Bewitched* (also co-creator); *The Flying Nun* (also creator); *The Paul Lynde Show; Temperature's Rising;* also produced three "Movie of the Week" features.

With Paramount, Ackerman produced the ninety minute special *Paramount Presents.*

As president of Harry Ackerman Productions, he was responsible for *The Sky's No Limit,* CBS; "Welcome Home, Jellybean," *Schoolbreak Special,* CBS; *Gidget's Summer Reunion,* 1985; and is currently preparing twenty-two episodes of a new "Gidget" television series.

HARRY S. ACKERMAN

RELATED CAREER—With Young and Rubicam Advertising Agency, NY: Director, radio operations, 1936-42, then head of radio productions, 1942-45, then vice president of program operations, 1946-48.

MEMBER: American Academy of Television Arts and Sciences (was president for two terms), Motion Picture and Television Fund (trustee), Television Academy Foundation (chairman of programs board); Dartmouth Club, Manuscript Society.

ADDRESSES: HOME—North Hollywood, CA. OFFICE—315 S. Beverly Drive, Beverly Hills, CA 90212.

*   *   *

ADAMS, Don   1926-

PERSONAL: Born April 13, 1926, in New York, NY.

VOCATION: Comedian and actor.

CAREER: PRINCIPAL TELEVISION APPEARANCES—Series: One of the "Kraft Music Hall Players," *The Perry Como Show*, NBC, 1961-63; Byron Glick, *The Bill Dana Show*, NBC, 1963-65; Maxwell Smart (Agent 86), *Get Smart*, NBC, 1968-69, then CBS, 1970; host, *The Hollywood Palace*, ABC; host and director, *Don Adams' Screen Test*, syndicated, 1975; Detective Lennie Crooke, *The Partners*, NBC, 1971-72; Howard Bannister, *Check It Out!*, syndicated, 1986.

Guest: Voice, *Wait Till Your Father Gets Home*, syndicated cartoon show, 1972; *Celebrity Challenge of the Sexes*, CBS, 1978; *Hooray for Hollywood; Three Times Daley; Billy; The Tonight Show*.

PRINCIPAL FILM APPEARANCES—Maxwell Smart, *The Nude Bomb*, Universal, 1980.

RELATED CAREER—Comedian and impressionist in cabaret and night clubs.

AWARDS: Outstanding Continued Performance by an Actor in a Leading Role in a Comedy Series, Emmys, 1967-68, 1968-69, both for *Get Smart*.

MEMBER: American Federation of Television and Radio Artists, Screen Actors Guild.

SIDELIGHTS: CTFT learned Don Adams won the Arthur Godfrey talent contest at the beginning of his career.

ADDRESSES: AGENT—David Licht, 9171 Wilshire Blvd., Beverly Hills, CA 90210.*

*   *   *

ADAMS, Edie

PERSONAL: Born Edith Adams Enke, April 16, in Kingston, PA; daughter of Sheldon and Ada (Adams) Enke; married Ernie Kovacs (died, 1962); maried Marty Mills (a photographer; divorced); mar-

ried Pete Candoli (an entertainer), 1972 (divorced); children (first marriage) Mia Susan (died, 1981). EDUCATION: Attended Juilliard School of Music and Columbia University; trained in design at the Traphagen School of Fashion Design.

VOCATION: Actress.

CAREER: TELEVISION DEBUT—*Arthur Godfrey's Talent Scouts*. PRINCIPAL TELEVISION APPEARANCES—Series: *Ernie in Kovacsland*, NBC, 1951; *The Ernie Kovacs Show*, CBS, 1952-53, then NBC, 1956; *The Chevy Show*, NBC, 1958; *Take a Good Look*, ABC, 1960-61; *The Edie Adams Show* (also known as *Here's Edie*), ABC, 1963-64; Rosanne, *As the World Turns*, CBS.

Episodic: *U.S. Steel Hour; Hooray for Hollywood*, CBS, 1970.

Specials: *Cinderella*, 1959; *Ernie Kovacs: Television's Original Genius*, cable, 1982.

Movie: *Shooting Stars*, ABC, 1983.

PRINCIPAL FILM APPEARANCES—*The Apartment*, United Artists, 1960; *Lover, Come Back*, Universal, 1962; *Under the Yum-Yum Tree*, Columbia, 1963; *It's a Mad Mad Mad World*, United Artists, 1963; *Love with the Proper Stranger*, Paramount, 1964; *The Best Man*, United Artists, 1964; *Made in Paris*, Metro-Goldwyn-Mayer, 1966; *The Oscar*, Embassy, 1966; *The Honey Pot*, United Artists, 1967; also, *Anyone for Venice*.

STAGE DEBUT—*Blithe Spirit*, Chapel Theatre, Ridgewood, NJ, 1947. NEW YORK DEBUT—Eileen, *Wonderful Town*, Winter Garden Theatre, 1953. PRINCIPAL STAGE APPEARANCES—Daisy Mae, *Li'l Abner*, St. James Theatre, NY, 1956; *Sweet Bird of Youth*, 1960; *Free as a Bird*, 1960; Sadie Thompson, *Rain*, Packard Music Hall, Warren, OH, 1963; title role, *La Perichole*, Opera House, Seattle, WA, 1972; *Best Little Whorehouse in Texas*, Falmouth Playhouse, ME, 1983; *The Merry Widow*, Long Beach Civic Light Opera, CA, 1986.

MAJOR TOURS—*The Merry Widow*, 1959; Reno Sweeney, *Anything Goes*, 1974; Lovely Lowell, *The Cooch Dancer*, 1975; also, *Where's Charley?*

CABARET—*It's a Bird, It's a Plane, It's Edie and Peter*, 1973; *Broadway, My Way*, St. Regis Hotel, NY, 1982.

AWARDS: Antoinette Perry Award, 1956, for *Li'l Abner*.

SIDELIGHTS: RECREATIONS—Dressmaking, interior decoration.

ADDRESSES: AGENT—c/o Lillian Micel, Diamond Artists, 9200 Sunset Blvd., Suite 909, Los Angeles, CA 90069; Henri Bollinger Public Relations, 9200 Sunset Blvd., Suite 601, Los Angeles, CA 90069.*

*   *   *

ADELMAN, Sybil   1942-

PERSONAL: Born March 15, 1942, in Winnipeg, Canada; daughter of Abraham (a supermarket operator) and Mina (Kagan) Adelman; married Martin Sage (a writer), May 4, 1980; children: Maurice Nicholas "Nicky." EDUCATION: New York University, A.B., 1963.

VOCATION: Television writer.

WRITINGS: TELEVISION—(With Barbara Gallagher) *The Mary Tyler Moore Show*, CBS, 1972; (with Barbara Gallagher) *Maude*, CBS, 1973; *Lily* (Lily Tomlin special), 1973; *Alice*, CBS, 1978; (with Martin Sage), episode of *Magnum, P.I.*, CBS, 1985; (with Martin Sage), *Growing Pains*, ABC, 1985.

AWARDS: Writers Guild of America Award and Alan King Comedy Award, both 1973, for *Lily*.

ADDRESSES: AGENT—Leading Artists, 445 N. Bedford Drive, Beverly Hills, CA 90210.

*   *   *

ADJANI, Isabelle   1955-

PERSONAL: Born June 27, 1955, in Germany.

VOCATION: Actress.

CAREER: PRINCIPAL FILM APPEARANCES—Title role, *The Story of Adele H.*, New World Pictures, 1975; *The Slap*, Silver Screen (French), 1976; *The Tenant*, Paramount, 1976; *The Driver*, Twentieth Century-Fox, 1978; *Nosferatu, the Vampire*, Twentieth Century-Fox, 1979; *The Bronte Sisters*, French, 1979; *Quartet*, New World Pictures, 1981; *Possession*, 1981; *One Deadly Summer*, Universal, 1984; *Subway*, Island Alive, 1985; also, *Faustine; Barocco; Next Year If All Goes Well*.

ADDRESSES: AGENT—M. Israel, 56 Rue de Passy, Paris, France 75016.*

*   *   *

ADLER, Jerry   1929-

PERSONAL: Born February 4, 1929, in Brooklyn, NY; son of Philip (a general manager of the Group Theatre) and Pauline Adler; married Dolores Parker (divorced); married Cathy Rice (a dancer and choreographer). EDUCATION: Attended Syracuse University, NY; trained as a director with Sawyer Falk and Ervin Piscator.

VOCATION: Director, producer, and production supervisor.

CAREER: FIRST STAGE WORK—Assistant stage manager, *Gentlemen Prefer Blondes*, Ziegfeld Theatre, NY, 1950. PRINCIPAL STAGE WORK—Production supervisor, Broadway productions: *Who's Who in Hell; Anna Christie; I Remember Mama; A Time for Singing; At the Drop of Another Hat; Little Murders; The Homecoming; The Unknown Soldier and His Wife; Halfway Up the Tree; My Fair Lady*, 1956; *Coco; The Apple Tree; Oh! What a Lovely War*, 1964; *Camelot*, New York State Theatre, NY, 1980.

Stage manager, Broadway productions: *Of Thee I Sing*, 1952; *My Fair Lady*, 1956; *Lunatics and Lovers*, 1964; *The Girl Who Came to Supper*, 1964; *Oh! What a Lovely War*, 1964.

Director, Broadway productions: *Fun City*, 1972; *Good Evening*, 1973; *Words and Music*, John Golden Theatre, 1974; *My Fair Lady*, 1975; *We Interrupt This Program*, 1975; *Checking Out; Hellzapoppin*, 1976; *Play Me a Country Song*, Virginia Theatre, NY, 1982.

Director, Off-Broadway, Regional and Stock productions: *All My Sons*, Lenox Hill Playhouse, NY, 1957; *Conflict of Interest*, 1972; *That Championship Season*, 1977; *California Suite*, 1978; also, *Light Up the Sky; A View from the Bridge; The Ofay Watchers; Charlie Was Here and Now He's Gone; A Conflict of Interest*.

Produced on Broadway: *Orson Welles' Moby Dick*, 1962; *Drat! The Cat!*, 1965.

MAJOR TOURS—Directed: *Good Evening*, 1975; *Words and Music*, 1975-76; *My Fair Lady*, 1977-78.

PRINCIPAL TELEVISION WORK—Production assistant: Tony Award Presentations (Antoinette Perry Awards), 1957-63; *Mark Twain Tonight*, CBS.

MEMBER: Society of Stage Directors and Choreographers (executive board).

ADDRESSES: OFFICE—c/o Society of Stage Directors and Choreographers, 1501 Broadway, 31st Fl., New York, NY 10036.*

*   *   *

ADLER, Stella   1902-

PERSONAL: Born 1902, in New York, NY; daughter of Jacob P. (an actor and producer) and Sarah (an actress and producer; maiden name, Lewis) Adler; married Horace Eleaschreff (divorced); married Harold Clurman (divorced); married Mitchell Wilson (died February 26, 1973). EDUCATION: Attended New York University; trained for the stage at the American Laboratory Theatre with her father, Jacob, Maria Ouspenskaya, and Richard Boleslavsky; also studied with Constantin Stanislavsky in Europe.

VOCATION: Actress, director, and teacher of acting.

CAREER: STAGE DEBUT—*Broken Hearts*, Grand Theatre, NY, 1906. LONDON DEBUT—Naomi, *Elisha Ben Avi*, Pavilion, Mile End, 1919. PRINCIPAL STAGE APPEARANCES—Appeared in her father's repertory company continuously in plays by Shakespeare, Tolstoy, Jacob Gordon, as well as other classical and modern plays, including *The Merchant of Venice* and *The Lower Depths*. Appeared in *Martinique, The Man of the Mountains* and (as Lola Adler) *The World We Live In*, NY, 1920; played one season of vaudeville on the Orpheum Circuit.

Baroness Creme de la Creme, *The Straw Hat*, American Laboratory Theatre, NY, 1926; Elly, *Big Lake*, 1927; played a season at the Living Place Theatre, 1928; appeared in a series of leading roles with Maurice Schwartz and Samuel Golendenberg at the Yiddish Art Theatre, Second Avenue, NY, including: *Kiddish Hashem; The God of Vengeance; The Witch of Castile; The Lower Depths; The Living Corpse; He Who Gets Slapped; Liliom; Jew Suss;* played over one hundred parts from 1927-31.

Joined the Group Theatre, 1931, and with it appeared in the following: Geraldine, *The House of Connelly*, Martin Beck Theatre, NY, 1931, then Mansfield Theatre, NY, 1931; Dona Josefa, *Night Over Taos*, 48th Street Theatre, NY, 1932; Sarah Glassman, *Success Story*, Maxine Elliott Theatre, NY, 1932; Myra Bonney, *Big Night*, Maxine Elliott Theatre, NY, 1933; Hilda, *Hilda Cassidy*, Martin Beck Theatre, NY, 1933; Gwyn Ballantyne, *Gentlewoman*, Cort Theatre, NY, 1934; Adah Menken, *Gold-Eagle Guy*, Morosco

Theatre, NY, 1934; Bessie Berger, *Awake and Sing,* Belasco Theatre, NY, 1935; Clara, *Paradise Lost,* Longacre Theatre, NY, 1935; Catherine Carnick, *Sons and Soldiers,* Morosco Theatre, NY, 1943; Clotilde, *Pretty Little Parlor,* National Theatre, NY, 1944; Zinaida, *He Who Gets Slapped,* Booth Theatre, NY, 1946.

Also appeared as Madame Rosepettle, *Oh Dad, Poor Dad, Mama's Hung You in the Closet and I'm Feelin' So Sad,* Lyric Theatre, Hammersmith, London, 1961; Madame Arkadina, *The Three Sisters,* Yale School of Drama, New Haven, CT, 1967; also appeared in *A Guide for the Bedevilled.*

MAJOR TOURS—Appeared with her father's repertory company in cities throughout the U.S. at the beginning of her career; played in a repertory of plays in cities throughout the U.S., South America, and Paris, Antwerp and Brussels, 1930.

TEACHING POSTITIONS—Head of the acting department under Erwin Piscator, dramatic workshop, New School for Social Research, NY, 1940-42; director and teacher, Stella Adler Conservatory of Acting, NY (formerly the Stella Adler Theatre Studio), 1949—; adjunct professor of acting, Yale University, New Haven, CT, 1966-67; head of undergraduate department of drama, New York University.

PRINCIPAL STAGE WORK—Director: *Golden Boy,* Group Theatre, San Francisco, 1938; *Manhattan Nocturne,* Forrest Theatre, NY, 1943; *Polonaise,* Alvin Theatre, NY, 1945; *Sunday Breakfast,* Coronet Theatre, NY, 1952; *Johnny Johnson,* Carnegie Hall Playhouse, NY, 1956.

FILM DEBUT—*Love on Toast,* 1938. PRINCIPAL FILM APPEARANCES—*Shadow of the Thin Man,* Metro-Goldwyn-Mayer, 1941; *My Girl Tisa,* 1948.

SIDELIGHTS: "The teacher has to inspire. The teacher has to agitate," explained Stella Adler in a 1984 *New York Times* interview with Samuel G. Freedman. "You cannot teach acting. You can only stimulate what's already there." For nearly half of a century, this world famous acting teacher and actress has been stimulating and inspiring students using the "Stanislavsky Method" of acting, a technique that encourages actors to tap into their own sense memories, emotion memories, and imaginations to bring their characters to life. Over the years, her students, most notably at the Stella Adler Conservatory of Acting established in 1949, have included such stars as Marlon Brando (who called Adler "a genius" in a 1979 *Times* article), Warren Beatty, and Robert De Niro.

Adler, who acquired her basic theories of acting in Paris in 1937 from the great Russian director and teacher Constantin Stanislavsky himself, began her own theatrical career at age four under the tutelage of two of the stars of the turn-of-the-century Yiddish theatre, her parents, Jacob and Sarah Adler. "In my family," she told a New York *Herald-Tribune* reporter in 1946, "immediately you could barely speak, you were put on the stage." The young actress spent twelve years in her father's company, appearing in Yiddish translations of Shakespeare's *The Merchant of Venice* and *The Lower Depths* by turn-of-the-century Russian author Maxim Gorky. In the early 1920's, she began to take parts in English-language Broadway plays, the first being Josef and Karel Capek's *The World We Live In.*

Just after the Capek play closed, Adler, whose father had instilled in her a respect for European theatrical tradition, undertook her first formal acting study, with Richard Boleslavsky, a former student of

Stanislavsky's, at the American Laboratory Theatre (ALT). In 1931 she, along with several other former ALT students, founded the Group Theatre, which became one of the most innovative theatrical companies of the 1930's, specializing in experimental and socially conscious plays. She remained with the organization until it dissolved in 1941, taking some time off to act in Hollywood films.

During and immediately after World War II, Adler devoted much of her energy to fund-raising benefits for the Emergency Committee to Save the Jewish People of Europe and the American League for a Free Palestine. Adler actively supported these causes by purchasing guns and forging passports and visas for people wishing to immigrate to Palestine.

Following the establishment of the state of Israel, Adler turned her attention to teaching rather than performing and since founding her acting school in 1949, Adler has appeared on stage herself only on rare occasions. On one such occasion, when she played Madame Arkadina in the Yale School of Drama's 1967 production of Checkov's *The Three Sisters,* Robert Brustein, the school's dean, said, "This marks the return of one of the great figures of the theatre to the American stage." Brustein also called Adler "the greatest teacher of acting in America."

ADDRESSES: OFFICE—130 W. 56th Street, New York, NY 10019.*

*   *   *

AIDEM, Betsy   1957-

PERSONAL: Born October 28, 1957; daughter of Howard P. (a physician) and Roberta D. (Turek) Aidem. EDUCATION: Attended Mills College for one year; New York University, B.F.A.

BETSY AIDEM

VOCATION: Actress.

CAREER: PRINCIPAL STAGE APPEARANCES—Shelby, *The Trading Post*, WPA Theatre, NY, 1981; Jean, *A Different Moon*, WPA Theatre, NY, 1983; *Crossing the Bar*, Center Stage Theatre, Baltimore, MD, 1983; Kay, *Balm in Gilead*, Circle Repertory Theatre, then Minetta Lane Theatre, NY, 1984; Brandy, *Battery*, New York Theatre Workshop, 1985; Virginia, *The Golden Age*, Dorset Theatre, 1985; Sally, *A Lie of the Mind*, Promenade Theatre, NY, 1986; also, Miss Scoons, *Angel City* and Maria, *Back Bog Beast Bait*, both at Syracuse Stage; three seasons with the Williamstown Theatre Festival, MA.

TELEVISION DEBUT—Movie: Elyssa, *Kojack: The Belarus File*, CBS, 1985.

PRINCIPAL FILM APPEARANCE—*Dottie*, independent, 1986.

MEMBER: Actors' Equity Association, Screen Actors Guild, American Federation of Television and Radio Artists.

ADDRESSES: HOME—New York, NY. AGENT—Ann Wright Representatives, 136 E. 57th Street, New York, NY 10022.

*   *   *

ALDA, Alan   1936-

PERSONAL: Born Alphonso D'Abruzzo, January 28, 1936, in New York, NY; son of Alphonso Roberto (an actor and singer; stage name, Robert Alda) and Joan (Browne) D'Abruzzo; married Arlene Weiss (a clarinetist and artist), 1957; children: Eve, Elizabeth, Beatrice. EDUCATION: Fordham University, B.S., 1956; attended Paul Sills Improvisational Workshop.

VOCATION: Actor, writer, and director.

CAREER: DEBUT—At the Hollywood Canteen with his father performing Abbott-and-Costello-style sketches, 1951. NEW YORK DEBUT—Clarence McShame (understudy), *The Hot Corner*, Golden Theatre, 1956. PRINCIPAL STAGE APPEARANCES—Jack Chesney, *Charley's Aunt*, Barnesville, PA, 1953; Leo Davis, *Room Service*, Teatro del Eliseo, Rome, Italy, 1955; Wade, *Roger the Sixth*, Artie, *Compulsion*, Irwin Trowbridge, *Three Men on a Horse*, Horace, *The Little Foxes*, all in stock, 1957; Billy, *Tuck in Nature's Way*, 1958; *The Book of Job*, David Williams, *Who Was That Lady I Saw You With?*, Toni, *To Dorothy, a Son*, all at the Cleveland Playhouse, 1958-59; Sky Masterson, *Guys and Dolls*, stock, 1959; telephone man, *Only in America*, Cort Theatre, NY, 1959.

Title role, *L'il Abner*, stock, 1960; revue, *Darwin's Theories*, Madison Avenue Playhouse, NY, 1960; David, *The Woman with Red Hair*, Teatro del Servi, Rome, Italy, 1961; Fergie Howard, *Golden Fleecing*, stock, 1961; Fleider, *Anatol*, Boston Arts Center, Boston, MA, 1961; Charlie Cotchipee, *Purlie Victorious*, Cort Theatre, NY, 1962; *Compass Improvisational Revue*, Hyannisport, MA, 1962; Howard Mayer, *A Whisper in God's Ear*, Cricket Theatre, NY, 1962; Willie Alvarez, *Memo*, Shubert Theatre, New Haven, CT, 1963; *Second City at Square East*, NY, 1963; Benny Bennington, *Fair Game for Lovers*, Cort Theatre, NY, 1963; Dr. Gilbert, *Cafe Crown*, Martin Beck Theatre, NY, 1964; F. Sherman, *The Owl and the Pussycat*, American National Theatre and Academy (ANTA), NY, 1964; Adam, Captain Sanjar, and Flip the Prince Charming, *The Apple Tree*, Shubert Theatre, NY, 1966.

ALAN ALDA

FILM DEBUT—Charlie Cotchipee, *Gone Are the Days!*, Hammer Films, 1963. PRINCIPAL FILM APPEARANCES—George Plimpton, *Paper Lion*, United Artists, 1968; *The Extraordinary Seaman*, Metro-Goldwyn-Mayer, 1969; *Jenny*, Cinerama, 1970; *The Moonshine War*, 1970; *The Mesphisto Waltz*, Twentieth Century-Fox, 1971; *To Kill a Clown*, Twentieth Century-Fox, 1972; *California Suite*, Columbia, 1978; *Same Time, Next Year*, Universal, 1979; title role, *The Seduction of Joe Tynan*, Universal, 1979; *The Four Seasons*, Universal, 1981; *Sweet Liberty*, Universal, 1986.

PRINCIPAL FILM WORK—Director: *The Seduction of Joe Tynan*, Universal, 1979; *The Four Seasons*, Universal, 1981; *Sweet Liberty*, Universal, 1986.

PRINCIPAL TELEVISION APPEARANCES—Regular, *That Was the Week That Was*, NBC, 1964; Capt. Benjamin Franklin (Hawkeye) Pierce, *M*A*S*H*, CBS, 1972-1983.

Episodic: *The Four Seasons*, CBS, 1984.

Guest: *The David Frost Revue*, syndicated, 1971; *Carol Burnett Show*, CBS, 1974.

Movies: *The Glass House*, 1972; *6 Rms Riv Vu*, 1974; Caryl Chessman, *Kill Me If You Can*, 1977.

Specials: *Free to Be . . . You and Me;* others.

PRINCIPAL TELEVISION WORK—Director, episodes of *M*A*S*H;* producer, *The Four Seasons*, CBS, 1984.

WRITINGS: SCREENPLAYS—*The Seduction of Joe Tynan,* Universal, 1979; *The Four Seasons,* Universal, 1981; *Sweet Liberty,* Universal, 1986.

TELEVISION—Episodes of *M*A*S*H;* creator of the television series, *We'll Get By,* CBS, 1975.

RECORDINGS: ALBUMS—*The Apple Tree,* original cast recording, Columbia Records.

AWARDS: Theatre World Award, 1963, for *Fair Game for Lovers;* Actor of the Year—Series and Best Lead Actor in a Comedy Series, Emmys, both 1973-74, for *M*A*S*H;* Outstanding Directing in a Comedy Series (Single Episode), Emmy, 1976-77, for "Dear Sigmund," *M*A*S*H;* Outstanding Writing in a Comedy or Comedy-Variety Show (Single Episode), Emmy, 1978-79, for "Inga," *M*A*S*H;* Outstanding Lead Actor in a Comedy Series, Emmy, 1981-82; for *M*A*S*H;* Humanitas Award for Writing; Writers Guild Award; two Directors Guild Awards; five Golden Globe Awards for Best Comedy Actor; seven People's Choice Awards.

ADDRESSES: OFFICE—Martin Bregman Productions, 641 Lexington Avenue, New York, NY 10022.

*   *   *

ALDA, Robert   1914-1986

PERSONAL: Born Alphonso Giovanni Giuseppe Roberto D'Abruzzo, February 26, 1914, in New York, NY; died in Los Angeles, May 3, 1986; son of Anthony (a barber) and Frances (Tumillo) D'Abruzzo; married Joan Browne (divorced); married Flora Marino (an architectural draughtsman); children: Alan (the actor). EDUCATION: Attended New York University.

VOCATION: Actor.

CAREER: STAGE DEBUT—Singer, *Charlie Ahearn and His Millionaires,* RKO Theatre, NY, 1933. BROADWAY DEBUT—Sky Masterson, *Guys and Dolls,* 46th Street Theatre, 1950. PRINCIPAL STAGE APPEARANCES—Appeared in stock engagements in the Catskills, 1935-40, in such plays as: *Waiting for Lefty; Golden Boy; Of Mice and Men; Men in White; Three Men on a Horse; Love from a Stranger; Tobacco Road; Boy Meets Girl; Room Service; The Jazz Singer; The Postman Always Rings Twice; The Time of Your Life.*

There Goes the Bride, La Jolla Playhouse, CA, 1947; *The Male Animal,* Beverly, MA, 1948; Sky Masterson, *Guys and Dolls,* Royal Nevada Hotel, Las Vegas, NV, 1955; Chris, *Harbor Lights,* Playhouse, NY, 1956; Al Manheim, *What Makes Sammy Run,* 54th Street Theatre, NY, 1964; Arthur Gordon, *My Daughter, Your Son,* Booth Theatre, NY, 1969; Walter Burns, *The Front Page,* Ethel Barrymore Theatre, NY, 1970; Benjamin Stone, *Follies,* Westchester Country Playhouse, NY, 1973.

MAJOR TOURS—Singer, *Charlie Ahearn and His Millionaires,* RKO vaudeville circuit, U.S. cities, 1934; burlesque houses, U.S. cities, 1935-40; *A Hollywood Review,* U.S. cities, 1949-50; *La Padrona di Raggio di Luna,* Italian, Sicilian cities, 1955-56; *Roger the VI,* U.S. cities, 1957; *Fair Game* and *Three Men on a Horse,* U.S. cities, 1958; *Can-Can,* U.S. cities, 1963; Benjamin Stone, *Follies,* U.S. cities, 1973; *The Sunshine Boys,* U.S. cities, 1974-75; *Burlesque, U.S.A.,* U.S. cities, 1980-81.

FILM DEBUT—George Gershwin, *Rhapsody in Blue,* 1945. PRINCIPAL FILM APPEARANCES—*The Beast with Five Fingers,* 1946; *The Man I Love,* 1946; Tommy Jones, *Cinderella Jones,* 1946; *Cloak and Dagger,* 1946; *Nora Prentiss,* 1947; *April Showers,* 1948; *Homicide,* 1949; *Tarzan and the Slave Girl,* 1950; *Two Gals and a Guy,* 1951; *Mr. Universe,* 1951; *Beautiful but Dangerous,* Twentieth Century-Fox, 1958; *Imitation of Life,* Universal, 1959; *Cleopatra's Daughter,* 1960; *The Girl Who Knew too Much,* 1969; *Night Flight from Moscow* (also known as *The Serpent*), 1973; *House of Exorcism,* 1975; *I Will, I Will . . . For Now,* Twentieth Century-Fox, 1976; *Bittersweet Love,* Avco Embassy, 1976; also, *Toto e Peppino divisi a Berlino; Paura; Cagliostro; Hollywood Varieties.*

TELEVISION DEBUT—*Alda and Henry,* 1937. PRINCIPAL TELEVISION APPEARANCES—Series: *By Popular Demand,* CBS, 1950; *The Milton Berle Show,* 1950-51; *What's Your Bid,* Dumont, 1953; *Personality Puzzle,* ABC, 1953; *The Robert Alda Show,* 1953; *Can-Do,* NBC, 1956; Dr. Dan Lewis, *Supertrain,* NBC, 1976; also, *Secret File; U.S.A. 5.*

Episodic: *Your Story Theatre,* Dumont, 1951; *M*A*S*H,* CBS; *The Invisible Man,* NBC; *Rhoda,* CBS; *Fame,* syndicated; *Code Red,* ABC; *Days of Our Lives,* 1981; *Police Story.*

Movie: *Perfect Gentlemen,* 1978.

PRINCIPAL RADIO APPEARANCES—Appeared regularly on radio between 1934-38.

WRITINGS: BOOKS—(With Flora Marino) *99 Ways to Cook Pasta,* 1980.

AWARDS: Antoinette Perry Award, Donaldson Award, Variety New York Drama Critics Award, all 1950 for *Guys and Dolls;* Golden Wing Award, Italy, 1956 for *La Padrona di Raggio di Luna.**

*   *   *

ALDRICH, Richard   1902-1986

PERSONAL: Born August 17, 1902, in Boston, MA; died in Williamsburg, VA, March 31, 1986; married Gertrude Lawrence (the actress), 1940 (died, 1952); married Elizabeth Boyd; children: Richard, David, Susan, Mary. EDUCATION: Attended Harvard University. MILITARY: U.S. Navy, World War II, U.S. Naval Reserve, Korean conflict.

VOCATION: Producer, manager, and author.

CAREER: FIRST STAGE WORK—Producer, *Art and Mrs. Bottle,* 1930. PRINCIPAL STAGE WORK—Producer, Broadway productions: *La Gringa; Lean Harvest; Springtime for Henry; Three Cornered Moon; By Your Leave; Pure in Heart; Petticoat Fever; Fresh Fields; Aged 26; Tide Rising; Be So Kindly; Lorelei; The Importance of Being Earnest; My Dear Children; The Devil and Daniel Webster; Margin for Error; Cue for Passion; Plan M; Pygmalion; The Playboy of the Western World; It Takes Two; Macbeth; Volpone; The Alchemists; Goodbye My Fancy; Caesar and Cleopatra; The Guardsman; Four Twelves Are 48; The Moon Is Blue; The Gypsies Wore High Hats; The Love of Four Colonels; A Girl Can Tell; Dear Charles; Sailor's Delight; Little Glass Clock;* sponsored U.S. performances of The Old Vic Theatre Company of London, England, Habimah Players from Tel Aviv, Israel, Dublin Gate Theatre Company, Dublin, Ireland.

PRINCIPAL FILM WORK—Advisor, *Star!*, Twentieth Century-Fox, 1968.

RELATED CAREER—Founder, The Jitney Players, Harvard University; manager, Richard Boleslavsky's American Laboratory Theater, 1926-28; producing manager, Cape Playhouse, Dennis, MA, 1935-55; director, Central City Colorado Summer Festival, 1937-38; producing manager, Falmouth Playhouse, Coonamessett, MA 1949-55; producing manager, Cape Cod Melody Tent, Hyannis, MA, 1950-55.

WRITINGS: BOOKS—*Gertrude Lawrence as Mrs. A: An Intimate Biography of a Great Star*, Greystone Press, 1955.

MEMBER: American National Theatre and Academy (board of directors), Cape Playhouse (trustee), Dennis, MA; Dramatic Club (student president), Harvard University.

SIDELIGHTS: Richard Aldrich was director of the Economic Aid Mission and minister of the embassy for Economic Affairs in Madrid, Spain, from 1955-62; he was also U.S. aid director to Morocco, 1962-65.*

*   *   *

ALDRIDGE, Michael   1920-

PERSONAL: Born September 9, 1920, in Glastonbury, Somerset, England; son of Frederick James and Kathleen Michaela Marietta (White) Aldridge; married Kirsteen Rowntree. EDUCATION: Attended Gresham's School, Holt, Norfolk, England.

VOCATION: Actor and director.

CAREER: STAGE DEBUT—Kenneth, *French without Tears*, Palace Theatre, Watford, UK, 1939. LONDON DEBUT—Prologue, Mechanic, *This Way to the Tomb*, Garrick Theatre, 1946. PRINCIPAL STAGE APPEARANCES—Appeared with the Nottingham Theatre Trust, 1948-49; joined the Birmingham Repertory Company, 1949; title role, *Othello*, Embassy Theatre, 1949.

With the Old Vic Theatre Company, London, 1949: Ferdinand, *Love's Labour's Lost;* Hastings, *She Stoops to Conquer;* Valere, *The Miser;* Horatio, *Hamlet*, repeated this role at Elsinore Castle, 1950.

With the Bristol Old Vic Theatre Company, 1951-52: Macbeth, *Macbeth;* Launce, *Two Gentlemen of Verona;* Lenny, *Of Mice and Men.*

Peter Henderson, *Escapade*, St. James's Theatre, London, 1953; *Salad Days*, Vaudeville Theatre, London, 1954; Lord Paul Posthumous, *Free as Air*, Savoy Theatre, London, 1957; Theseus, *Phedre*, Theatre in the Round, London, 1957; Philip Lowrie, *Tenebrae*, Repertory Players, Lyric Theatre, London, 1958; James Tyrone, *A Moon for the Misbegotten*, Arts Theatre, London, 1960.

Aubrey Tanqueray, *The Second Mrs. Tanqueray*, Pembroke Theatre, Croydon, 1961; James O'Shaughnessy, *State of Emergency*, Pembroke Theatre, Croydon, 1962; Lord Steyne, *Vanity Fair*, Queen's Theatre, London, 1962; Major Frederick Lowndes, *Home and Beauty*, Ashcroft Theatre, Croydon, 1964; Gorse, *The Man Who Let It Rain*, Theatre Royal, Stratford, 1964; Father Kahn, *The Third Picture*, Empire Theatre, Sunderland, 1965.

MICHAEL ALDRIDGE

With the Chichester Festival: Baron Henry Belazor, *The Fighting Cock*, 1966 (also performed in this at the Duke of York's Theatre, London, 1966); Churdles Ash, *The Farmer's Wife*, 1967; Hector Hushabye, *Heartbreak House*, 1967 (also performed in this at the Lyric Theatre, London, 1967); Nonancourt, *An Italian Straw Hat*, 1967; Banquo, *Macbeth*, 1967; Enemy Leader, *The Unknown Soldier and His Wife*, Edward, *The Cocktail Party*, 1968 (also performed in this at Wyndham's Theatre and the Haymarket Theatre, London, 1969); Stephano, *The Tempest*, 1968; Lawyer, *Caucasian Chalk Circle*, Captain Horatio Vale, *The Magistrate* (also performed in this at the Cambridge Theatre, London, 1969), Enobarbus, *Antony and Cleopatra*, 1969.

Lord Minto, *A Bequest to the Nation*, Haymarket Theatre, London, 1970.

With the Chichester Festival: Cravatar, *Dear Antoine*, Rufio, *Caesar and Cleopatra*, Anton Krug, *Reunion in Vienna*, all 1971 (also performed in this at the Piccadilly Theatre, London, 1972); Lockit, *The Beggars' Opera*, Cutler Walpole, *The Doctor's Dilemma*, Hebble Tyson, *The Lady's Not for Burning*, all 1972.

Mr. Black, *Who's Who*, Arnaud Theatre, Guildford, 1972; Ronald, *Absurd Person Singular*, Criterion Theatre, London, 1973; Prospero, *The Tempest*, and Serebriakov, *Uncle Vanya*, both at The Other Place, Stratford-Upon-Avon, 1973; Jeeves, *Jeeves*, Her Majesty's Theatre, London, 1975; Sir Richard Jackson, *Lies!*, Albery Theatre, London, 1975; Victor, *The Bed Before Yesterday*, Lyric

Theatre, London, 1975; Dr. Kroll, *Rosmersholm,* Haymarket Theatre, London, 1977; Duff, *The Old Country,* Queen's Theatre, London, 1978; Victor, *Bedroom Farce,* National Theatre, London, 1978; Selsdon Mowbray, *Noises Off,* Lyric Theatre, Hammersmith, then Savoy Theatre, London, 1982.

MAJOR TOURS—The Arts Council Midland Theatre Company, U.K. cities, 1946-48.

PRINCIPAL STAGE WORK—Director, *King Lear,* Empire Theatre, Sunderland, 1964.

FILM DEBUT—*Nothing Venture,* 1946. PRINCIPAL FILM APPEARANCES—*Bullshot,* Island Alive, 1985.

SIDELIGHTS: RECREATIONS—Sailing.

ADDRESSES: HOME—Eleven Crooms Hill, Greenwich SE10, England; South Bell House, Bell Land, Birdham, Sussex, England.

*			*			*

ANDRESS, Ursula   1936-

PERSONAL: Born 1936 in Berne, Switzerland; married John Derek (divorced).

VOCATION: Actress.

CAREER: PRINCIPAL FILM APPEARANCES—*Dr. No,* United Artists, 1963; *Four for Texas,* Warner Brothers, 1963; *Fun in Acapulco,* Paramount, 1963; *She,* Metro-Goldwyn-Mayer, 1965; *The Tenth Victim,* Embassy, 1965; *What's New Pussycat?,* United Artists, 1965; *Casino Royale,* Columbia, 1967; *The Southern Star,* Columbia, 1969; *Perfect Friday,* Chevron, 1970; *The Red Sun,* National General, 1972; *Clash of the Titans,* United Artists, 1981; also: *Toys for Christmas; Chinese Adventures in China; Scaramouche.*

PRINCIPAL TELEVISION APPEARANCES—Mini-Series: *Peter the Great,* NBC, 1986.

ADDRESSES: AGENT—c/o Mike Greenfield, Charter Management, 9000 Sunset Blvd., Suite 1112, Los Angeles, CA 90069.*

*			*			*

ANDREWS, Tige

PERSONAL: Born with surname of Androwas; son of George E. (a shopkeeper) and Selma (Shaleesh) Androwas; married Norma Nadine Thornton (a ballerina); children: John, Barbara, Gina, Steven, Jole, Anthony. EDUCATION: Graduate, American Academy of Dramatic Arts; studied acting with Jellinger. POLITICS: Democrat. RELIGION: Greek Orthodox. MILITARY: U.S. Army, Second Lieutenant, 4th Division.

VOCATION: Actor and singer.

CAREER: NEW YORK DEBUT—Beadseller, Minaret singer, assistant stage manager, *Hidden Horizon,* 47th Street Theatre, 1946.

PRINCIPAL STAGE APPEARANCES—*Ticklish Acrobat,* Off-Broadway production; *Mr. Roberts,* Alvin Theatre, NY, 1951; streetsinger, also played Mack the Knife for twenty performances, *The Threepenny Opera,* Theatre De Lys, NY, 1951; *Heartbreak House,* Westwood Playhouse, Los Angeles.

FILM DEBUT—Wylie, *Mr. Roberts,* Warner Brothers, 1954. PRINCIPAL FILM APPEARANCES—Onionhead, *Until They Sail,* 1957; *China Doll,* United Artists, 1958; *A Private Affair,* Twentieth Century-Fox, 1959; *The Last Tycoon,* Paramount, 1977.

TELEVISION DEBUT—Policeman, *Seven Keys to Baldpate.* PRINCIPAL TELEVISION APPEARANCES—Series: *The Phil Silvers Show,* CBS, 1954; Lt. John Russo, *The Detectives, Starring Robert Taylor,* ABC, 1959-61, NBC, 1961-62; Captain Adam Greer, *The Mod Squad,* ABC, 1968-73.

MEMBER: Screen Actors Guild, American Federation of Television and Radio Artists, Actors' Equity Association.

AWARDS: Emmy Award nomination, Golden Globe Award, Best Supporting Actor in a Drama, both for Captain Greer, *The Mod Squad.*

SIDELIGHTS: Tige Andrews tells *CTFT* that he has written six scripts with collaborator J. Marlando which have yet to be produced. His favorite role is that of the Streetsinger in *The Threepenny Opera.* He speaks French and Italian and enjoys painting.

ADDRESSES: HOME—Encino, CA. AGENT—Alex Brewis Agency, 8721 Sunset Blvd., Suite 104, Los Angeles, CA 90069.

*			*			*

ANNAUD, Jean-Jacques   1943-

PERSONAL: Born January 10, 1943; son of Pierre and Madeleine (Tripoz) Annaud; married Monique Rossignol (divorced, 1980); children: Mathilde, Juliette. EDUCATION: Attended Ecole Nationale de Photo et Cinema, Paris, France, and the Institut des Hautes Etudes Cinematographiques, Sorbonne, Paris.

VOCATION: Writer and director.

CAREER: FILM DEBUT—Writer and director, *Black and White in Color,* Allied Artists, 1977. PRINCIPAL FILM WORK—Writer and director: *Hot Head,* 1979; *Quest for Fire,* Twentieth Century-Fox, 1982; *The Name of the Rose,* 1986.

PRINCIPAL TELEVISION WORK—Director for over 500 commercials.

AWARDS: Best Foriegn Film, Academy Award, 1977, for *Black and White in Color;* Best Film, Caesar Award, France, 1982, *Quest for Fire;* numerous Clio Awards and Silver Lion Awards for commercials.

SIDELIGHTS: CTFT learned that Jean-Jacques Annaud started as an 8mm filmmaker at age eleven. He speaks French and English is his second language.

ADDRESSES: AGENT—c/o Jeff Berg, International Creative Management, 8899 Beverly Blvd., Los Angeles, CA 90048.

Photograph by Gamma

JEAN-JACQUES ANNAUD

*   *   *

ANN-MARGRET   1941-

PERSONAL: Born Ann-Margret Olsson, April 28, 1941, in Valso-byn, Jamtland, Sweden; daughter of Gustav and Anna (Aronson) Olsson; married Roger Smith (an actor, director, and producer), 1967; children: (step-children) Jordan, Tracey, Dallas Thomas. EDUCATION: Northwestern University.

VOCATION: Actress and entertainer.

CAREER: FILM DEBUT—Louise, *Pocketful of Miracles*, United Artists, 1961. PRINCIPAL FILM APPEARANCES—Emily, *State Fair*, Twentieth Century-Fox, 1962; Kim, *Bye, Bye Birdie*, Columbia, 1963; *Viva Las Vegas*, Metro-Goldwyn-Mayer, 1964; *Kitten with a Whip*, Universal, 1964; *Bus Riley's Back in Town*, Universal, 1965; *The Cincinnati Kid*, Metro-Goldwyn-Mayer, 1965; *Once a Thief*, Metro-Goldwyn-Mayer, 1965; *The Pleasure Seekers*, Twentieth Century-Fox, 1965; *The Swinger*, Paramount, 1966; Dallas, *Stagecoach*, Twentieth Century-Fox, 1966; *Murderer's Row*, Columbia, 1966; *Made in Paris*, Metro-Goldwyn-Mayer, 1966; *The Tiger and the Pussycat*, Embassy, 1967; *The Train Robbers*, Warner Brothers, 1967.

C.C. and Company, Avco Embassy, 1970; *R.P.M.*, Columbia, 1970; Bobbi Templeton, *Carnal Knowledge*, Avco Embassy, 1971; *The Outside Man*, United Artists, 1973; mother, *Tommy*, Columbia, 1975; *The Twist* (also known as *Folies Bourgeoisie*), 1976; *The Last Remake of Beau Geste*, Universal, 1977; *Joseph Andrews*, 1977; *The Cheap Detective*, Columbia, 1978; *Magic*, Twentieth Century-Fox, 1978; *The Villain*, Columbia, 1979; *Middle Age Crazy*, Twen-

tieth Century-Fox, 1980; *Lookin' to Get Out*, Paramount, 1982; *I Ought to Be in Pictures*, 1982; *The Return of the Soldier*, European Classics, 1985; *Twice in a Lifetime*, independent, 1985; also, *Andante; The Prophet; The Puzzle*.

PRINCIPAL TELEVISION APPEARANCES—Episodic: *The Jack Benny Show*, CBS, 1960; Ann-Margrock (voice only), *The Flintstones*, ABC.

Movies: *Who Will Love My Children?*, 1983; Blanche Du Bois, *A Streetcar Named Desire*, 1984.

Specials: Ruby, *Dames at Sea; When You're Smiling*, NBC; *Ann-Margret: Hollywood Movie Girls*, ABC, 1979.

NIGHTCLUB AND CONCERT APPEARANCES—With George Burns, at the Sahara Hotel, Las Vegas, 1960; clubs in Las Vegas, Lake Tahoe, Atlantic City, others.

RECORDINGS: ALBUMS—*Bye, Bye Birdie*, original soundtrack recording, Victor; *Ann-Margret*, Victor; *Vivacious One*, Victor; *Love Rush*, MCA Records.

AWARDS: Golden Globe Award and Best Supporting Actress, Academy Award nomination, both 1971, for *Carnal Knowledge;* Golden Globe Award and Best Actress, Academy Award nomination, both 1975, for *Tommy;* United Motion Pictures Association, Female Star of the Year Award (three times); Theatre Owners of America Outstanding Box-Office Star of the Year (two times); *Photoplay* Magazine's Gold Medal Award, Most Popular Actress,

Photograph by Harry Langdon

ANN-MARGRET

1971, 1972; Citation for outstanding performances (tours of Vietnam and the Far East) from President Lyndon B. Johnson; Royal Command Performance for Queen Elizabeth II of England; Italian Motion Picture Industry award.

SIDELIGHTS: From material supplied by her agent, *CTFT* learned that in 1972, while performing her elaborate nightclub show in Lake Tahoe, Ann-Margret fell off the set, plunging twenty-two feet and seriously injuring her face which had to be rebuilt. Two months later, she was back on stage in Las Vegas. She gives much of the credit for her continued success to her husband-manager Roger Smith. She and Smith now live in the home that once belonged to Humphrey Bogart and Lauren Bacall.

ADDRESSES: OFFICE—435 N. Bedford Drive, Beverly Hills, CA 90210. AGENT—Creative Artists Agency, 1888 Century Park E., Los Angeles, CA 90067.

*   *   *

ANSARA, Michael   1927-

PERSONAL: Born April 15, 1927, in Lowell, MA. EDUCATION: Studied at the Pasadena Playhouse. MILITARY: U.S. Army.

VOCATION: Actor.

CAREER: PRINCIPAL TELEVISION APPEARANCES—Series: Cochise, *Broken Arrow,* ABC, 1956-60; Deputy U.S. Marshal Sam Buckhart, *Law of the Plainsman,* NBC, 1959-60, ABC, 1962 (also packaged as *The Westerners,* in syndication); Kane, *Buck Rogers in the 25th Century,* NBC, 1979-80.

Mini-Series: Lame Beaver, *Centennial,* NBC, 1979.

PRINCIPAL FILM APPEARANCES—*Soldiers Three,* 1951; *Only the Valiant,* 1951; *The Robe,* 1953; *Julius Caesar,* 1953; *Sign of the Pagan,* 1954; *Bengal Brigade,* 1954; *New Orleans Uncensored,* Columbia, 1955; *Diane,* Metro-Goldwyn-Mayer, 1956; *Lone Ranger,* Warner Brothers, 1956; *Sol Madrid,* Metro-Goldwyn-Mayer, 1968; *Daring Game,* Paramount, 1968; *The Bears and I,* Buena Vista, 1974; *Mohammad, Messenger of God,* Tarik Film Distributors, 1977; *The Manitou,* Avco Embassy, 1978; *Knights of the City,* New World Pictures, 1986.

ADDRESSES: AGENT—Comtemporary-Korman, 132 Lasky Drive, Beverly Hills, CA 90212.*

*   *   *

ANSPACH, Susan

PERSONAL: Born in New York, NY. EDUCATION: Attended Catholic University of America.

VOCATION: Actress.

CAREER: PRINCIPAL FILM APPEARANCES—*Five Easy Pieces,* Columbia, 1970; *The Landlord,* United Artists, 1970; *Play It Again Sam,* Paramount, 1972; *Blume in Love,* Warner Brothers, 1973; *The Big Fix,* Universal, 1979; *Running,* Universal, 1979; *The Devil and Max Devlin,* Buena Vista, 1981; *Gas,* Paramount, 1981; *Misunderstood,* Metro-Goldwyn-Mayer, 1984.

PRINCIPAL TELEVISION APPEARANCES—Series: Grace McKenzie, *The Yellow Rose,* NBC, 1983.

Mini-Series: *Space,* CBS, 1985.

PRINCIPAL STAGE APPEARANCES—Performed in Off-Broadway productions in early career; *A Coupla White Chicks Sitting Around Talking,* Hollywood Playhouse, Los Angeles, 1985.

MEMBER: Actors' Equity Association, American Federation of Television and Radio Artists, Screen Actors Guild.

ADDRESSES: AGENT—Phil Gersh Agency, 222 N. Canon Drive, Suite 204, Beverly Hills, CA 90210.*

*   *   *

ANTILLE, Lisa

PERSONAL: Born in Los Angeles, CA.

VOCATION: Actress.

CAREER: PRINCIPAL TELEVISION APPEARANCES—Series: Lisa, *The Ted Knight Show,* syndicated, 1985—.

Episodic: *The A-Team,* NBC; *Happy Days,* ABC; *Gimme a Break,* NBC.

Specials: *J.O.B.,* PBS; *Pals,* PBS.

PRINCIPAL FILM APPEARANCES—*Valley Girls,* Atlantic, 1983.

LISA ANTILLE

PRINCIPAL STAGE APPEARANCES—*Othello; Butterflies Are Free; The Treasure of Sierra Madre,* Los Angeles.

RELATED CAREER—Professional model.

ADDRESSES: AGENT—Sumski, Green, and Company, 8380 Melrose Avenue, Suite 200, Los Angeles, CA 90069.

*   *   *

ANTON, Susan   1951-

PERSONAL: Born October 12, 1951, in Yucaipa, CA; daughter of Wally (a detective) and Lou Anton. EDUCATION: Attended Bernadino College.

VOCATION: Actress and entertainer.

CAREER: PRINCIPAL FILM APPEARANCES—*Goldengirl,* Avco Embassy, 1979; *Spring Fever,* 1983; *Cannonball Run II,* Warner Brothers, 1984.

PRINCIPAL TELEVISION APPEARANCES—Series: Susan Williams, *Stop Susan Williams* (part of the *Cliff Hangers* series), NBC, 1979; *Presenting Susan Anton,* NBC, 1979.

Guest: *Bob Hope Special; David Copperfield Special; Anthony Newley Special; Merv Griffin Show; The Tonight Show.*

©*Charles William Bush*

SUSAN ANTON

STAGE DEBUT—A musical nightclub act in Las Vegas. PRINCIPAL STAGE APPEARANCES—*They're Playing Our Song;* Darlene, *Hurlyburly,* on Broadway, 1985.

MAJOR TOURS—*They're Playing Our Song,* U.S. cities; toured the country with Kenny Rogers' concert tour.

RECORDINGS: ALBUM—*The First Time* (country and western). SINGLES—*Killin' Time; Foxy* (country and western).

MEMBER: Actor's Equity Association, Screen Actors Guild, American Federation of Television and Radio Artists.

SIDELIGHTS: Susan Anton was Miss California in 1969 and tied for second runner-up in the 1970 Miss America pageant. She began her professional entertaining career with a musical Las Vegas night club act, and she won the role of the "Muriel Cigar" girl in 1976, competing against 400 others.

ADDRESSES: AGENT—c/o Jacqueline Burnham, Burnham-Callaghan Associates, 9123 Sunset Blvd., Los Angeles, CA 90069; Michael Levine Public Relations Co., 9123 Sunset Blvd., Los Angeles, CA 90069.

*   *   *

APPLE, Gary   1955-

PERSONAL: Born August 21, 1955, in New York, NY; son of Jerry and Beverly (Schlenoff) Apple. EDUCATION: State University of New York at Brockport, B.S., 1976.

VOCATION: Playwright.

WRITINGS: PLAYS, PRODUCED—*It,* published by Samuel French Inc.; *Do,* published by Samuel French, Inc.; *Black & White,* published by Samuel French, Inc.; *When God Comes to Breakfast, You Don't Burn the Toast,* published by Samuel French Inc.; *D.C.T.,* produced at Astoria Arts Center, Stagewrights, NY, 1986.

MEMBER: Dramatist Guild, American Federation of Television and Radio Artists, Stagewrights, Inc. (founding member), NY, 1983-86.

SIDELIGHTS: Gary Apple informs *CTFT* that he is changing focus and plans to write for film and television.

ADDRESSES: HOME—411 E. 85th Street, New York, NY 10028. OFFICE—165 W. 47th Street, New York, NY 10036.

*   *   *

ARANHA, Ray

PERSONAL: EDUCATION: Florida A & M University, B.A., dramatic arts, 1961; studied at the American Academy of Dramatic Arts in New York, 1961-62.

VOCATION: Playwright, actor, director, and teacher.

CAREER: PRINCIPAL STAGE APPEARANCES—With the Hartford Stage Company, CT, 1974: Bill Lewis, *Hot L Baltimore,* Frederick Douglas, *One Wore Blue: One Wore Grey,* farmworker, *On the Season,* one man show, *I Am Black,* a mexican, *Folklorico* (chil-

RAY ARANHA

dren's show); title role, *Purlie Victorious,* Waldo-Astoria Dinner Theatre, 1974; Johnson, *The Brownsville Raid,* O'Neill Theatre Centre, Waterford, CT, 1975; Eddie/Daddy, *My Sister, My Sister,* Milwaukee Repertory Theatre, 1976; Kgaravu, *The Dozens,* Tiffany's Attic Dinner Theatre, 1976; Benjamin Banneker, *The Estate,* Hartford Stage Company, 1976; title role, *Macbeth,* Champlain Shakespeare Festival, 1977; Galactic Jack, *Tooth of Crime,* Stage West, 1977; title role, *Othello,* Champlain Shakespeare Festival, 1978; Joe, *The Shadow Box,* Alliance Theatre, Atlanta, 1978; with the Folger Theatre Group, Washington, DC, 1979: Dandelion, *Benefit of a Doubt,* Corin/Hymen, *As You Like It,* Duncan, *Macbeth,* Farmer Banks, *Wild Oats.*

Reuben, *Zooman and the Sign,* Negro Ensemble Company, 1980; Lt. Colonel Frank Harrow, *Appear and Show Cause,* Cleveland Playhouse, 1982; Steve, *A Lesson from Aloes,* South Jersey Repertory Theatre, 1983; Verrazano Narrows (a wino), *Dimion's Dance,* South Jersey Repertory Theatre, 1984; Professor/Panhandler, *City Lights,* People's Light and Theatre Company, 1984; Jim Bono, *Fences,* Yale Repertory Theatre, New Haven, CT, 1985.

MAJOR TOURS—*I Am Black,* one man show, Midwest cities, 1971-72; Willie, *Master Harold and the Boys,* national, 1983-84.

PRINCIPAL STAGE WORK—Director: *Lizzie,* Rites and Reason

Theatre, Brown University, 1982; *Sons and Fathers of Sons* and *Fugue on a Funny House,* both Alliance Theatre, Atlanta, 1982.

RELATED CAREER—Director, originator, and organizer, the Miami Summer Players, FL, 1958; teacher and director of drama, Dade County Public Schools, Miami, FL, 1961-64; teacher and director, Fine Arts Conservatory, Miami, 1964-66; director, originator, and organizer, the SRO Players, Miami, 1964; director, originator, and organizer, the Production Class, Miami, 1966; workshop director, the Acorn Players, Miami Beach, FL, 1967; director and writer, Channel 3 Educational Television, Miami, 1967; actor and lighting master, President Eisenhower's Cultural Exchange Program to seven African countries, 1967; director of the work release drama program, Rikers' Island inmates, Theatre for the Forgotten, 1973; workshop director of acting and playwriting, Housatonic Regional High School, Falls Village, CT, 1974-75; workshop director of acting and playwriting, Milwaukee Repertory Theatre, 1976; literary manager, Alliance Theatre, 1981-82.

WRITINGS: PLAYS, PRODUCED—*I Am Black,* one man show, toured Iowa, Kansas, Nebraska, Oklahoma, Wisconsin, Michigan, 1971-72; *My Sister, My Sister,* Hartford Stage Company, CT, 1973, Urgent Theatre, 1974, and the Little Theatre, NY, 1974, published by Samuel French Inc., 1974; *The Clowns' Corner Concert* (one act children's play), Hartford Stage Company, CT, 1974, Baltimore Center Stage, 1976; *Way Back When* (one act children's play) Hartford Stage Company, 1975, Baltimore Center Stage, 1976; *The Estate,* Hartford Stage Company, 1976, Afro-American Total Theatre, 1978, optioned for public television by the Minority Cultural Project, 1978; *Akosu'a of the First and Final Day,* staged reading, Stage West, 1977; *Holidays (New Years)* (ten minute play for dramatic anthology series entitled *Holidays),* Actors Theatre of Louisville, KY, 1979.

Snow-Pressings, Virginia Polytechnical University, 1980, O'Neill Playwrights Conference, 1981; *Remington* (one act), commissioned by the Actors Theatre of Louisville, produced, 1980, published by Theatre Communications Group, Plays-in-Progress, 1980; *Sons and Fathers of Sons,* O'Neill Playwrights Conference, 1981, Alliance Theatre, Atlanta, 1982, and Negro Ensemble Company, NY, 1983; *Fugue on a Funny House,* staged reading, Alliance Theatre, 1982; *Lizzie,* Rites and Reason Theatre, Brown University, 1982.

RADIO—"The Antique Bearers," *Earplay,* PBS, 1978. TELEVISION—*The Gift of the Magi,* adapted for Channel 2, Educational Television, 1967; *Lizzie,* commissioned by Visions, Community Television of Southern California, KCET, 1977; *The Soul,* commissioned and produced by Infinity Factory, PBS, 1977.

PLAYS, UNPRODUCED—"The Nature of Violence," commissioned by the Actors Theatre of Louisville, 1979; "Creedmore" (one act), commissioned by the Actors Theatre of Louisville, 1980; "The Visions of Fire-Eater" (one act), commissioned by the Actors Theatre of Louisville, 1981; "Orphans and Cannibals," 1984.

MEMBER: Actors' Equity Association, Screen Actors Guild, American Federation of Television and Radio Artists, Dramatists Guild, Authors League of America, Writers Guild of America; New Playwrights Grant Committee, National Endowment for the Arts (panelist), 1980-81; New Playwrights' Grant Committee, CAPS Program New York State, (panelist), 1981-82; Maryland Commission on the Arts (panelist), 1985-86.

AWARDS: Drama Desk Award, 1974, for *My Sister, My Sister;* Rockefeller Playwright-in-Residence Grants, 1974 and 1975; National Endowment for the Arts Creative Writing Fellowship, 1977-78; Literature Award Grant, Connecticut Commission on the Arts, 1984.

ADDRESSES: OFFICE—G.P.O. Box 1743, New York, NY 10001.

* * *

ARDEN, Eve   1912-

PERSONAL: Born Eunice Quedens, April 30, 1912, in Mill Valley, CA; daughter of Charles Peter and Lucille (Frank) Quedens; married Edward G. Bergen (divorced); married Brooks West (an actor and artist), 1951 (died, 1984); children: (adopted, with first husband) Liza, Constance; (second marriage) Douglas Brooks (adopted, with second husband) Duncan Paris. EDUCATION: Tamalpais High School; trained for the stage with the Henry Duffy Stock Company, Alcazar Theatre, San Francisco, 1928-29.

VOCATION: Actress.

CAREER: NEW YORK DEBUT—*The Ziegfeld Follies,* Winter Garden, 1934. PRINCIPAL STAGE APPEARANCES—*Low and Behold,* Pasadena Playhouse, CA, 1933; *Parade,* Guild Theatre, NY, 1935; *The Ziegfeld Follies,* Winter Garden, NY, 1936; Winnie Spofford, *Very Warm for May,* Alvin Theatre, NY, 1939; *Two for the Show,* Booth Theatre, NY, 1940; Maggie Watson, *Let's Face It,* Imperial Theatre, NY, 1941; in summer stock she played Paula Wharton, *Over 21,* 1950; Mary Hilliard, *Here Today,* Olney Theatre, MD, 1951; *Marriage-Go-Round,* Grist Mill Playhouse, 1961; Dolly Gallagher Levi, *Hello, Dolly!,* Shubert Theatre, Chicago, IL, 1966; Mrs. Banks, *Barefoot in the Park,* Atlanta Municipal Theatre, Atlanta, GA, 1967; Stephanie, *Cactus Flower,* Coconut Grove Playhouse, Miami, FL, 1968; Mrs. Baker, *Butterflies Are Free,* Huntington Hartford Theatre, Los Angeles, CA, 1970; *Under Papa's Picture,* San Diego, CA, 1973; *The Most Marvelous News,* Chicago, 1977; Marion, *Absurd Person Singular,* Ahmanson Theatre, Los Angeles, CA, 1978; Hedda Holloway, *Moose Murders* (for two preview performances), Eugene O'Neill Theatre, NY, 1983; also, *She Couldn't Say No,* Palace, Los Angeles.

MAJOR TOURS—Matilda, *On Approval,* Amanda Prynne, *Private Lives,* both with the Bandbox Repertory, U.S. cities, 1933; Mame, *Auntie Mame,* West Coast cities, 1958; Charlie, *Goodbye, Charlie,* U.S. cities, 1960; *Beekman Place,* U.S. cities, 1965; Mrs. Baker, *Butterflies Are Free,* U.S. cities, 1970; Jessica Brandenburg, *Natural Ingredients,* U.S. cities, 1971; *Silverplate,* U.S. cities, 1971.

FILM DEBUT—*Oh, Doctor,* 1937. PRINCIPAL FILM APPEARANCES—*Stage Door,* 1937; *Cocoanut Grove,* 1938; Cora, *Letter of Introduction,* Universal, 1938; *Eternally Yours,* 1939; *At the Circus,* 1939; *The Women,* 1939; *Slightly Honorable,* 1940; *Comrade X,* 1940; *Ziegfeld Girl,* 1941; *Whistling in the Dark,* 1941; *Obliging Young Lady,* 1941; *Bedtime Story,* 1941; *Manpower,* 1941; *Change of Heart* (also known as *Hit Parade of 1943*), 1943; *Let's Face It,* 1943; *Cover Girl,* 1944; *The Doughgirls,* 1944; *Mildred Pierce,* 1945; *The Kid from Brooklyn,* 1946; *My Reputation,* 1946; *Night and Day,* 1946; *Voice of the Turtle,* 1947; *Tea for Two,* 1950; *Three Husbands,* 1950; *Goodbye My Fancy,* 1951; *We're Not Married,* 1952; *Anatomy of a Murder,* Columbia, 1959; *Dark at the Top of the Stairs,* Warner Brothers, 1960; *Sergeant Deadhead,* American International, 1965; *The Strongest Man in the World,* Buena Vista, 1975; *Grease,* Paramount, 1978; *Under the Rainbow,* Warner

Brothers, 1981; *Grease II,* Paramount, 1982; *Pandemonium,* 1982; also, *Lottie; Having a Wonderful Time;* Susan Warren, *Big Town Czar; Sing for Your Supper; Last of the Duanes; San Antonio Rose; She Knew All the Answers.*

PRINCIPAL RADIO APPEARANCES—Connie Brooks, *Our Miss Brooks,* 1948-56.

PRINCIPAL TELEVISION APPEARANCES—Series: Connie Brooks, *Our Miss Brooks,* CBS, 1952-56; Liza Hammond, *The Eve Arden Show,* CBS, 1957-58; Eve Hubbard, *The Mothers-in-Law,* NBC, 1967-69.

Special: *Meet Cyd Charisse,* NBC, 1959.

Episodic: *Starlight Theatre,* CBS; "Mother of the Bride," *ABC Afternoon Playbreak,* ABC, 1974; "Secret Cinema," *Amazing Stories,* NBC, 1985.

Movie: *A Very Missing Person,* ABC, 1972; *Alice in Wonderland,* CBS, 1985.

WRITINGS: AUTOBIOGRAPHY—*Three Phases of Eve,* St. Martin's Press, 1985.

MEMBER: Actors' Equity Association, Screen Actors Guild, American Federation of Television and Radio Artists.

AWARDS: Best Female Star of a Regular Series, Emmy, 1953, for *Our Miss Brooks;* Actress of the Year, Sarrah Siddons Award, 1967-68, for *Hello, Dolly!*

ADDRESSES: AGENT—Glenn Rose, 9665 Wilshire Blvd., Beverly Hills, CA 90210.*

* * *

ARELL, Sherry H.   1950-

PERSONAL: Born August 4, 1950, in Quincy, MA; daughter of Albert Armand (a maintenance supervisor) and Eleanor C. (Morse) Arell; married Hugh Karraker, (an actor), June 3, 1978. EDUCATION: Attended summer workshops at Emerson College and Massachusetts Institute of Technology; studied at the Stage One Drama Workshop for two years with Kaleel Sakakeeny and Stephen Snow.

VOCATION: Actress.

CAREER: STAGE DEBUT—Jill, *Butterflies Are Free,* Encore Playhouse, West Dover, VT, 1974. NEW YORK DEBUT—Sharon, *One Night Stand,* Vandam Theatre, 1982. PRINCIPAL STAGE APPEARANCES—Fleur Stein, *And Miss Reardon Drinks a Little* and Bonnie, *Applause,* both Encore Playhouse; Candy, *One Flew Over the Cuckoo's Nest,* Southbury Playhouse; Ma Perkins, *Only an Orphan Girl,* Worcester Theatre; Mother/guest, *Everyman* and Sea Captain/ Curio, *Twelfth Night,* both West-Park Theatre; the maid, *Stone Soup,* Direct Theatre, NY; Ann, *The Guillotine,* Theatre for the New City, NY; Ida, *Becca,* Brooklyn Academy of Music; Sandy, *Missionary Ridge,* La Mama E.T.C.; Hannah, *Icebound,* Meat & Potatoes Company, NY; Helen, *Union Dues,* Stonewall Repertory.

PRINCIPAL FILM APPEARANCES—Appeared in student films at the University of California and New York University.

SHERRY H. ARELL

PRINCIPAL TELEVISION APPEARANCES—New York University's Dramalab.

MEMBER: Actors' Equity Association, Screen Actors Guild, American Federation of Television and Radio Artists.

SIDELIGHTS: RECREATIONS—Tennis, platform tennis, bowling, and cross country skiing.

ADDRESSES: HOME—150 W. 82nd Street, New York, NY, 10024.

*   *   *

ARIS, Ben   1937-

PERSONAL: Full name, Benjamin Patrick Aris; born March 16, 1937, in London; son of John Woodbridge (an insurance executive) and Joyce Mary (a painter; maiden name, Williams) Aris; married Yemaiel Oven (a ballet dancer), July 3, 1966; children: Rachel, Jonathan. EDUCATION: Attended Arts Educational School, London, and the General Academic and Training School. MILITARY: National Service, 1955-57.

VOCATION: Actor.

CAREER: STAGE DEBUT—Child actor, dancer, *Christmas Party/ Sauce Tatare*, Cambridge Theatre, London, 1949. NEW YORK DEBUT—Rosencrantz, *Hamlet*, Lunt-Fontanne Theatre, 1969. PRINCIPAL STAGE APPEARANCES—Acted extensively in children's

theatre, musicals, and revues in the West End district of London including: *The Boy Friend; Pieces of Eight; One Over the Eight; Funny Thing; Code of Woosters; Otherwise Engaged*, South Africa; *Hamlet; I, Claudius; The Second Mrs. Tanqueray*, National Theatre.

MAJOR TOURS—*Stepping Out; Hamlet.*

FILM DEBUT—*Tom Brown's Schooldays*, 1950. PRINCIPAL FILM APPEARANCES—*The Charge of the Light Brigade*, United Artists, 1967; *If*, Paramount, 1968; *The Music Lovers*, United Artists, 1969; *Oh Lucky Man*, 1972; *Juggernaut*, United Artists, 1974; *Tommy*, Columbia, 1974; *The Voyage of the Damned*, Avco Embassy, 1976; *The Ritz*, Warner Brothers, 1976; *Sir Henry at Rawlingson Ends*, 1979; *Hussy*, 1980.

PRINCIPAL TELEVISION APPEARANCES—Played many roles during childhood; since has appeared in series like: *To the Manor Born; Bergerac; Hi De Hi; Shine on Harvey Moon; By the Sword Divided; Chance in a Million; Star Quality; Call Me Mister; Assassination Run*, BBC; *Hazell*, Thames; *Clouds of Glory*, Granada; *The Diplomatic Clerk*, BBC; *Masterspy*, ATV.

MEMBER: Royal General and Theatrical Fund Association (board of directors, 1973—).

SIDELIGHTS: RECREATIONS—Ben Aris wrote *CTFT* that he is a "keen amateur naturalist, particularly birdwatching," and he enjoys music, wine, and travel.

ADDRESSES: AGENT—c/o Barry Brown, Barry Brown Management, 47 W. Square, London SE 11, England.

Photograph by Louanne Richards

BEN ARIS

ARKOFF, Samuel Z.   1918-

PERSONAL: Born June 12, 1918, in Fort Dodge, IA; married Hilda Rusoff. EDUCATION: Attended the University of Colorado, University of Iowa; Loyola University, J.D., 1948. MILITARY: U.S. Army Air Force, World War II.

VOCATION: Producer and executive.

CAREER: PRINCIPAL FILM WORK—Producer, American International Releases: *Master of the World*, 1961; *The Pit and the Pendulum*, 1961; *Premature Burial*, 1962; *Panic in the Year Zero*, 1962; *The Raven*, 1963; *Haunted Palace*, 1963; *Beach Party*, 1963; *Comedy of Terrors*, 1964; *Pajama Party*, 1964; *Bikini Beach*, 1964; *Masque of the Red Death*, 1964; *Muscle Beach Party*, 1964; *Tomb of Ligeria*, 1965; *The Wild Angels*, 1966; *The Trip*, 1967; *Wild in the Streets*, 1968; *Three in the Attic*, 1968; *The Oblong Box*, 1969; *Scream and Scream Again*, 1970; *Cry of the Banshee*, 1970; *Bloody Mama*, 1970; *Wuthering Heights*, 1971; *Murders in the Rue Morgue*, 1971; *Dr. Phibes*, 1972; *Frogs*, 1972; *Blacula*, 1972; *Dillinger*, 1973; *Heavy Traffic*, 1973; *Hennessy*, 1975; *Cooley High*, 1975; *Futureworld*, 1975; *A Matter of Time*, 1975; *Food of the Gods*, 1976; *Great Scout and Cathouse Thursday*, 1976; *At Earth's Core*, 1976; *Empire of the Ants*, 1977; *The Island of Dr. Moreau*, 1977; *Our Winning Season*, 1978; *Force Ten from Navrone*, 1978; *Love at First Bite*, 1979; *California Dreaming*, 1979; *Something Short of Paradise*, 1979; *Meteor*, 1979; *The Amityville Horror*, 1979; *How to Beat the High Cost of Living*, 1980; *Dressed to Kill*, 1980; *The Earthling*, 1981; *Underground Aces*, 1981.

RELATED CAREER—Co-founder, American Releasing, 1954; Co-founder, American International Pictures, 1955; president, chairman of the board, American International Pictures, 1955-79; president, chairman, Samuel Z. Arkoff Company, 1980—; president, Arkoff International Pictures, 1981—.

AWARDS: Producer of the Year Award, Allied States Association of Motion Picture Theatre Owners, 1963; Master Showman of the Decade Award, Theatre Owners of America, 1964; Commendatore of the Order of Merit Award, Italy, 1970; Pioneer of the Year Award, Foundation of the Motion Picture Pioneers, 1971; International Ambassador, Variety Clubs International.

MEMBER: Loyola-Marymount University (trustee), Los Angeles, CA.

ADDRESSES: OFFICE—9200 Sunset Blvd., Penthouse 3, Los Angeles, CA 90069.*

*   *   *

ARNAZ, Desi   1917-

PERSONAL: Full name Desiderio Alberto Arnaz; born March 2, 1917, in Santiago, Cuba; married Lucille Ball, November 30, 1940 (divorced, 1960); children: Lucie Desiree, Desiderio Alberto IV (Desi Jr.). EDUCATION: Attended Colegio Dolores, Jesuit Preparatory School, Santiago, Cuba. MILITARY: U.S. Army Medical Corps, sergeant.

VOCATION: Actor, singer, producer, and writer.

CAREER: PRINCIPAL FILM APPEARANCES—*Father Takes A Wife*, 1941; *The Navy Comes Through*, 1942; *Bataan*, 1943; *Four Jacks and a Jill*, 1944; *Cuban Pete*, 1950; *The Long Long Trailer*,

Metro-Goldwyn-Mayer, 1953; *Holiday in Havana*, 1955; *Forever Darling*, Metro-Goldwyn-Mayer, 1955; *The Escape Artist*, Warner Brothers, 1982.

PRINCIPAL TELEVISION APPEARANCES—Series: Ricky Ricardo, *I Love Lucy*, CBS, 1951-57; host and performer, *Westinghouse Desilu Playhouse*, CBS, 1958-60; Ricky Ricardo, *The Lucy-Desi Comedy Hour*, CBS, ran as summer shows in 1962-65 and 1967.

PRINCIPAL FILM WORK—Producer, *Forever Darling*, 1956.

PRINCIPAL TELEVISION WORK—Producer: *I Love Lucy*, CBS; *Westinghouse-Desilu Playhouse*, CBS; *The Mothers-in-Law*, NBC, 1967-79.

RELATED CAREER—President, Desilu Productions, Inc., 1962; president, Desi Arnaz Productions, Inc., 1965.

SIDELIGHTS: CTFT notes that Desi Arnaz is the owner of the Corona Breeding Farm.

ADDRESSES: OFFICE—c/o Chateau Marmont, 8221 Sunset Blvd., Los Angeles, CA 90046.*

*   *   *

ARNESS, James   1923-

PERSONAL: Born May 26, 1923, in Minneapolis, MN; son of Rolf C. and Ruth (Duesler) Arness; married Virginia Chapman, February 12, 1948; children: Craig, Jenny Lee, Rolf. EDUCATION: Attended Beloit College. MILITARY: U.S. Army.

VOCATION: Actor.

CAREER: PRINCIPAL TELEVISION APPEARANCES—Series: Marshal Matt Dillon, *Gunsmoke*, CBS, 1955-1975; Zeb Macahan, *How the West Was Won*, ABC, 1978-79; Detective Jim McClain, *McClain's Law*, NBC, 1981-82.

Movies: *The Macahans*, ABC, 1976.

FILM DEBUT—*Farmer's Daughter*, 1947. PRINCIPAL FILM APPEARANCES—*Battleground*, 1948; *The Thing*, 1951; *People Against O'Hara*, 1951; *The Iron Man*, 1951; *Big Jim McClain*, 1952; *Horizon's West*, 1952; *Lone Hand*, 1953; *Island in the Sky*, 1953; *Veils of Bagdad*, 1953; *Her Twelve Men*, 1954; *Them*, 1954; *Many Rivers to Cross*, Metro-Goldwyn-Mayer, 1955; *Sea Chase*, Warner Brothers, 1955; *Gun the Man Down*, United Artists, 1956; *Flame of the Islands*, Republic, 1958; also, *Hellgate*.

NON-RELATED CAREER—Advertising executive; real estate salesman.

MEMBER: American Federation of Television and Radio Artists, Screen Actors Guild.

ADDRESSES: HOME—P.O. Box 223, Santa Susana, CA 93062.*

*   *   *

ARNOLD, Danny   1925-

PERSONAL: Born Arnold Rothmann, January 23, 1925, in New York, NY; son of Abraham and Esther (Colker) Rothmann; married

Donna Cooke, February 16, 1961; children: David, Dannel.

VOCATION: Writer, director, producer, and former actor.

CAREER: PRINCIPAL TELEVISION APPEARANCES—*Martin and Lewis Show,* 1947-51.

PRINCIPAL TELEVISION WORK—Series: Producer, writer, and director, *The Real McCoys,* ABC, 1961-62; *Bewitched,* ABC, 1963-64; *Wackiest Ship in the Army,* NBC, 1964-65; *That Girl,* ABC, 1967-69; *My World and Welcome to It,* NBC, 1969-70; *Barney Miller,* ABC, 1973-82.

PRINCIPAL FILM APPEARANCES—*Breakthrough,* 1950; *Inside the Walls of Folsom Prison,* 1951; *Sailor Beware,* 1951; *Jumping Jacks,* 1952; *Scared Stiff,* 1953; *Stars Are Singing,* 1953.

RELATED CAREER—Nightclub and vaudeville entertainer; film sound effects editor, 1944-46; president, Four D. Productions, Inc., 1958—.

WRITINGS: FILMS—*The Caddy,* 1953; *Desert Sands,* United Artists, 1955; *Fort Yuma,* United Artists, 1955; *Rebel in Town,* United Artists, 1956; *Outside the Law,* Universal, 1956.

TELEVISION—*Tennesee Ernie Ford Show,* NBC; *Martin and Lewis Comedy Hour,* 1953.

MEMBER: Directors Guild of America, Writers Guild of America West, Screen Actors Guild, American Federation of Television and Radio Artists.

AWARDS: Outstanding Comedy Series, Emmy Awards, 1969-70, for *My World and Welcome to It,* and 1981-82, for *Barney Miller.*

ADDRESSES: OFFICE—1293 Sunset Plaza Drive, Los Angeles, CA 90069.*

*   *   *

ARNOTT, Peter   1936-

PERSONAL: Born November 21, 1936, in Ipswich, England; son of George William (a civil servant) and Audrey (Smith) Arnott; married Eva Schenkel, July 26, 1958; children: Catherine, Christopher, Jennifer. EDUCATION: University of Wales, B.A., M.A., Ph.D., 1948-58; University of Oxford, M.A., 1953. POLITICS: Republican. RELIGION: Episcopalian.

VOCATION: Historian and puppeteer.

CAREER: Professor of drama, University of Iowa, 1958-69; professor of drama, Tufts University, 1969—.

RELATED CAREER—Producer, director, *Marionette Theatre of Peter Arnott,* tours from Boston across the U.S. performing Greek plays.

MEMBER: Active in the Boy Scouts of America; National Model Railroad Association.

AWARDS: Honorary doctor of humane letters, Suffolk University, 1978; Shaw Medal, Boston College, 1984.

PETER ARNOTT

ADDRESSES: HOME—Six Herrick Street, Winchester, MA 01890. OFFICE—Drama Department, Tufts University, Medford, MA 02153.

*   *   *

ARRAMBIDE, Mario   1953-

PERSONAL: Born March 1, 1953, in San Antonio, TX; son of Oscar Aleman and Maria Santos (Ocampo) Arrambide. EDUCATION: Trained for the stage at the Royal Academy of Dramatic Art, London, 1979-81, and for stage combat with B. H. Barry, 1982. RELIGION: Roman Catholic. MILITARY: U.S. Army, 1971-74.

VOCATION: Actor.

CAREER: STAGE DEBUT—Gratiano, *The Merchant of Venice,* Folger Theatre, Washington, DC, 1982. NEW YORK DEBUT—Spirit of the Golem, *The Golem,* Public Theatre, 1984. LONDON DEBUT—Raimondo, *Aunt Dan and Lemon,* Royal Court Theatre, 1985.

PRINCIPAL STAGE APPEARANCES—At the Folger Theater, Washington, DC: Lord, *All's Well That Ends Well;* Second Shepard, *Second Shepard's Play;* Sir Charles Marlow, *She Stoops to Conquer;* Palamede, *Marriage a la Mode.*

At the McCarter Theatre, Princeton, NJ: Mr. Pugh, Utah Watkins, Mr. Waldo, and Mog Edwards, *Under Milkwood;* Don Juan, *Faustus in Hell;* second narrator, *A Christmas Carol;* Sgt. Major Vaskov, *The Dawns Are Quiet Here.*

Also, Mog Edwards, *Under Milkwood,* Virginia Museum Theatre, Richmond, VA; the Duke, *Measure for Measure,* American Theatre Alliance, NY; Raimondo, *Aunt Dan and Lemon,* New York Shakespeare Festival, Public Theatre, NY, 1985.

MEMBER: Actors' Equity Association.

AWARDS: Amanda Steel Scholarship to Royal Academy of Dramatic Art; Royal Academy of Dramatic Art Awards: Dame Flora Robsom Award, Best Classical Performance, for *The Maid's Tragedy;* Derek Ware Award, Best Stage Fight from a Set Text, for *Richard III.*

ADDRESSES: HOME—1239 37th Street, N.W., Washington, DC 20007. AGENT—Ann Wright Representatives, 136 E. 57th Street, New York, NY 10022.

*   '*   ⊥

ASQUITH, Ward

PERSONAL: Born in Philadelphia, PA; son of Harold A. and Elsie (Ritter) Asquith. EDUCATION: University of Pennsylvania, B.A.; Columbia University, one year graduate work; studied for the theatre with Michael Shurtleff, Maria Greco, Karen Kayser, David Kerry Heefner, others. MILITARY: U.S. Army, Artillery Division.

VOCATION: Actor.

CAREER: STAGE DEBUT—Petey, *The Birthday Party,* NY, 1976.

WARD ASQUITH

PRINCIPAL STAGE APPEARANCES—Scroop and Exton, *Richard II;* Candy, *Of Mice and Men;* Bert, *To Bury a Cousin;* Marchand, *Incident at Vichy,* Jewish Repertory Company, NY; Lee Brown, *After the Rise,* Astor Place Theatre, NY, 1979; the old man, *Fool for Love,* regional theatre production.

MAJOR TOURS—Bonno, *Amadeus,* national.

PRINCIPAL FILM APPEARANCES—Studio head, *Zelig,* Warner Brothers, 1983; Jimmy, *The Snows,* Independent Feature.

PRINCIPAL TELEVISION APPEARANCES—Series: Assistant District Attorney Paul Carlin, *Ryan's Hope;* taxi driver, *The Guiding Light;* Captain Chase, *Love of Life;* Kirkwood, *Somerset;* also, announcer, WNET, NY.

Episodic: *Kojak,* CBS.

Mini-Series: *Woman of Valor,* NBC.

RELATED CAREER—Editor, NBC Television, NY; assistant to vice president for radio, National Association of Broadcasters, Washington, DC; editor, CBS Television, NY.

ADDRESSES: HOME—484 W. 43rd Street Apt. 44-P, New York, NY 10036.

*   *   *

ASSEYEV, Tamara

PERSONAL: EDUCATION: Marymount College, B.A.; UCLA, M.A., theatre arts.

VOCATION: Producer.

CAREER: PRINCIPAL FILM WORK—Production assistant, *The Pit and Pendulum,* American-International, 1961; production assistant, *The Saint Valentine's Day Massacre,* Twentieth Century-Fox, 1967; production assistant, *The Devil's Angels,* American International, 1967; associate producer, *The Wild Racers,* American International, 1967; production assistant, *Targets,* Paramount, 1968; associate producer, *Paddy,* Allied Artists, 1968; associate producer, *Sweet Kill* (also known as *The Arousers* and *A Kiss from Eddie*), New World Films, 1970; co-producer, *Drive-In,* Columbia, 1976; co-producer, *I Wanna Hold Your Hand,* Universal, 1978; co-producer, *Big Wednesday,* Warner Brothers, 1978; co-producer, *Norma Rae,* Twentieth Century-Fox, 1979; also produced documentary: *A History of Atlantic Records.*

MEMBER: Producers Guild of America, Academy of Motion Picture Arts and Sciences (board of governors, producers' branch).

AWARDS: Best Picture, Academy Award nomination, Golden Globe Award nomination, Christopher Award, all 1979, for *Norma Rae.*

SIDELIGHTS: Tamara Asseyev has worked with producer Roger Corman on eight films. Beginning with 1976's *Drive-In,* her co-producer has been Alex (Alexandra) Rose. She is presently working under a television and feature film production agreement with New World Pictures. In a press release, Asseyev lists among her other current activities serving as the West Coast scout for publisher E.P.

Dutton and working as a member of the Costume Council of the Los Angeles City Museum. She is a founding member of the Los Angeles Museum of Contemporary Art and is a member of the Amazing Blue Ribbon for the Los Angeles Music Center.

ADDRESSES: OFFICE—New World Pictures, 1888 Century Park East, Fifth Floor, Los Angeles, CA 90067.

*   *   *

ASTAIRE, Fred   1899-

PERSONAL: Born Frederic Austerlitz, May 10, 1899, in Omaha, NE; son of Frederic and Ann (Geilus) Austerlitz; married Phyllis Baker, July 12, 1933 (died, 1954); married Robyn Smith, 1980; children: (first marriage) Fred, Ava, (stepson) Peter Potter. RELIGION: Episcopalian.

VOCATION: Actor, dancer, and singer.

CAREER: STAGE DEBUT—Formed partnership with sister Adele, 1905. NEW YORK DEBUT—*Over the Top*, 44th Street Roof Theatre, 1917. LONDON DEBUT—*Stop Flirting*, Shaftesbury Theatre, 1923. PRINCIPAL STAGE APPEARANCES—*The Passing Show of 1918*, Winter Garden Theatre, NY, 1918; *The Love Letter*, Globe Theatre, NY, 1921; *For Goodness Sake*, Lyric Theatre, NY, 1922; *The Bunch and Judy*, Globe Theatre, NY, 1922; *Lady, Be Good!*, Liberty Theatre, NY, 1924; *Funny Face*, Alvin Theatre, NY, 1927, then Prince's Theatre, London, 1928; *Smiles*, Ziegfeld Theatre, NY, 1930; *The Band Wagon*, New Amsterdam Theatre, NY, 1931; *Gay Divorce*, Barrymore Theatre, NY, 1932, then Palace Theatre, London, 1933.

FILM DEBUT—*Dancing Lady*, Metro-Goldwyn-Mayer, 1933. PRINCIPAL FILM APPEARANCES—*Flying Down to Rio*, RKO, 1933; *The Gay Divorcee* (adapted from the stage production *Gay Divorce*), RKO, 1934; *Top Hat*, RKO, 1935; *Follow the Fleet*, RKO, 1936; *Swing Time*, RKO, 1936; *Shall We Dance?*, RKO, 1937; *A Damsel in Distress*, RKO, 1937; *Carefree*, RKO, 1938; *The Story of Vernon and Irene Castle*, RKO, 1939.

Broadway Melody of 1940, Metro-Goldwyn-Mayer, 1940; *Second Chorus*, Paramount, 1940; *You'll Never Get Rich*, Columbia, 1941; *Holiday Inn*, Paramount, 1942; *You Were Never Lovelier*, Columbia, 1942; *The Sky's the Limit*, RKO, 1943; *Yolanda and the Thief*, Metro-Goldwyn-Mayer, 1945; *Blue Skies*, Paramount, 1946; *Ziegfeld Follies*, Metro-Goldwyn-Mayer, 1948; *Easter Parade*, Metro-Goldwyn-Mayer, 1948; *The Barkleys of Broadway*, Metro-Goldwyn-Mayer, 1949.

Three Little Words, Metro-Goldwyn-Mayer, 1950; *Let's Dance*, Paramount, 1950; *Royal Wedding*, Metro-Goldwyn-Mayer, 1951; *The Belle of New York*, Metro-Goldwyn-Mayer, 1952; *The Band Wagon*, Metro-Goldwyn-Mayer, 1953; *Daddy Long Legs*, Twentieth Century-Fox, 1955; *Funny Face*, Paramount, 1957; *Silk Stockings*, Metro-Goldwyn-Mayer, 1957; *On the Beach*, United Artists, 1959.

The Pleasure of His Company, Paramount, 1961; *The Notorious Landlady*, Columbia, 1962; *Finian's Rainbow*, Warner Brothers, 1968; *The Midas Run*, Cinerama, 1969; *That's Entertainment!*, Metro-Goldwyn-Mayer, 1974; *The Towering Inferno*, Twentieth Century Fox/Warner Brothers, 1974; *The Amazing Dobermans*,

Golden Films, 1976; *That's Entertainment, Part II*, Metro-Goldwyn-Mayer, 1976; *Un Taxi Mauve (The Purple Taxi)*, Sofracima-Rizzola, 1977; *Ghost Story*, Universal, 1981; *That's Dancing!*, Metro-Goldwyn-Mayer/United Artists, 1985.

PRINCIPAL TELEVISION APPEARANCES—Series: *Fred Astaire's Alcoa Premiere Theatre*, ABC: "Mr. Easy," 1962, "Moment of Decision," 1962, "Guest in the House," 1962, "Mr. Lucifer," 1962, "Blues for a Hanging," 1962, also served as host, 1961-63. Host and entertainer, *Hollywood Palace*, ABC, 1965-66; Alister Mundy, *It Takes a Thief*, ABC, 1969-70.

Episodic: "Imp on a Cobweb Leash," 1958, and "Man on a Bicycle," 1959, both *General Electric Theatre*, CBS; "Think Pretty," *Bob Hope's Chrysler Theatre*, NBC, 1964; *Dr. Kildare*, four part drama, NBC, 1965; *Battlestar Galactica*, 1978.

Specials: *An Evening with Fred Astaire*, NBC, 1958; *Another Evening with Fred Astaire*, NBC, 1959; *Astaire Time*, 1960; *The Fred Astaire Show*, NBC, 1968; voice, *Santa Claus Is Coming to Town*, cartoon, 1971; *'S' Wonderful, 'S' Marvelous, 'S' Gershwin*, NBC, 1972; *Fred Astaire, Change Partners and Dance*, PBS, 1980.

Movies: *The Over the Hill Gang Rides Again*, ABC, 1970; *A Family Upside Down*, NBC, 1978; seven characters, *The Man in the Santa Claus Suit*, 1978.

WRITINGS: BOOKS—*Steps in Time*, 1959.

MEMBER: The Lambs Club, The Brook Club, Racquet and Tennis Club.

AWARDS: Special Academy Award, for raising the standards of all musicals, 1949; Outstanding Performance in a Variety or Musical Program or Series, Emmy, 1960-61, for *Astaire Time;* Outstanding Lead Actor in a Special, Emmy, 1978, for *A Family Upside Down;* Best Supporting Actor, Academy Award nomination, 1974, for *Towering Inferno;* American Film Institute Lifetime Achievement Award, 1981.

SIDELIGHTS: As a dancer, film star, singer, and symbol of elegance, Fred Astaire set the standards for an entire generation, assessed Patrick Dennis in his novel *Auntie Mame*. "Our only god was Fred Astaire," wrote Dennis. "He was everything we wanted to be: smooth, suave, debonair, dapper, intelligent, adult, witty, and wise. We saw his pictures over and over, played his records until they were gray and blurred, [and] dressed as much like him as we dared."

The man whom choreographer George Balanchine called "the greatest dancer who ever lived" began dancing professionally in 1905 with his sister, Adele. The Astaires, as they came to be known professionally, spent much of their childhood and adolescence working in vaudeville and then graduated to featured parts in Broadway shows. Reversing the usual procedure for American performers, they first became stars in London following the 1923 premiere of the musical *Stop Flirting*, a revised version of the 1922 *For Goodness Sake* which had been only a moderate hit for them in New York. The Astaires' next two starring vehicles, *Lady, Be Good!* and *Funny Face*, written especially for them by George and Ira Gershwin, were hits on both sides of the Atlantic. Following *The Band Wagon* in 1931, Adele left the act to get married.

After scoring a stage triumph on his own in 1932 in *Gay Divorce*, Astaire moved to films. A studio executive reacted to Astaire's screen test for RKO Radio Pictures with the now-famous words: "Can't act. Slightly bald. Also dances." The studio, however, signed him anyway at the insistence of its production chief, David O. Selznick. In his first RKO film, *Flying Down to Rio* in 1933, Astaire received fifth billing behind such now-faded stars as Dolores Del Rio and Gene Raymond, but he and his new dancing partner, Ginger Rogers, stole the show with their "Carioca" number, in which they made several turns while their heads touched.

For their next film, *The Gay Divorcee*, Astaire was billed first and Rogers second. The pair went on to make seven more films between 1934 and 1939, the most famous of which, *Top Hat*, took its title from part of Astaire's trademark costume—top hat, white tie, and tails. The Astaire-Rogers team split up after *The Story of Vernon and Irene Castle*, but were reunited in 1949 for *The Barkleys of Broadway*.

Over the years, Astaire has danced with Eleanor Powell (in *Broadway Melody of 1940*), Rita Hayworth (*You'll Never Get Rich* and *You Were Never Lovelier*), Judy Garland (*Easter Parade*), Cyd Charisse (*The Band Wagon* and *Silk Stockings*), and Gene Kelly (*Ziegfeld Follies*). Trick photography enabled him to dance with a hat rack ("Sunday Jumps" in *Royal Wedding*) and an array of flying shoes ("Shoes with Wings On" in *The Barkleys of Broadway*); on the walls and ceiling ("You're All the World to Me," also in *Royal Wedding*); and in front of a line of Fred Astaires ("Puttin' on the Ritz" in *Blue Skies*).

Although Astaire was primarily a dancer, he also achieved success as a singer. Many of America's greatest songwriters, including Irving Berlin, Cole Porter, George Gershwin, and Jerome Kern, considered him their favorite performer and asked him to introduce some of their tunes, among them Porter's "Night and Day" and Berlin's "Cheek to Cheek." Astaire himself wrote several songs, the most popular of which was "I'm Building Up to an Awful Let-down."

Astaire gave up the rigors of film musicals in the late 1950's, and since 1959 when he starred as a nuclear physicist in his first non-musical picture, *On the Beach*, all of his screen appearances, except *Finian's Rainbow* and in his hosting duties in the compilation film *That's Entertainment, Part II*, have been in straight dramatic parts.

Astaire's long career was honored by the American Film Institute in 1981. At that time, President Ronald Reagan sent him this message: "There is nobody like you, and while they say that every generation has its own style, your style reaches and delights us all."

ADDRESSES: AGENT—International Creative Management, 8899 Beverly Blvd., Los Angeles, CA 90048.*

*　　*　　*

ATKINSON, Barbara　1926-

PERSONAL: Born January 8, 1926, in Manchester, England; daughter of Charles Stuart and Dorothy Carol (Lyons) Atkinson. EDUCATION: Attended Chatelard; trained for the stage at the Birmingham Repertory Theatre.

VOCATION: Actress.

CAREER: STAGE DEBUT—Mr. Fox, *Toad of Toad Hall*, Birmingham Repertory, 1945. LONDON DEBUT—Mary Williams, *Serious*

BARBARA ATKINSON

Charge, Garrick Theatre, 1955. PRINCIPAL STAGE APPEARANCES—Appeared in repertory at Swindon, Wigan, Wednesbury, Oxford, Birmingham, Nottingham; Fanny, *Annie and Fannie*, Octagon Theatre, Bolton, England, 1967; Mincing, *The Way of the World*, National Theatre Company, London, 1969-70; Mrs. Higgins, *Pygmalion*, and *Tonight at 8:30*, Birmingham Repertory, then at the Ravinia Festival, Chicago, IL, 1970; Gertrude, *Hamlet*, Leeds Playhouse, UK, 1971; Honorable Margaret Wyndham, *Crown Matrimonial*, Theatre Royal, then Haymarket Theatre, London, 1972; played repertory at Sheffield, Watford, and Leeds, 1975-77, including *The Wedding Feast*, 1977 and Mrs. Malaprop, *The Rivals;* Lady Markby, *An Ideal Husband*, Greenwich Theatre, London, 1978; Eve, *Molly*, Comedy, Theatre, London, 1978; performed at Birmingham, Colchester, Coventry, and Watford, 1980; guest performer at Guildford, 1980; at the Savoy Theatre, London, 1981; in Newcastle, Leeds, and Ipswich, 1982-84.

PRINCIPAL TELEVISION APPEARANCES—*Emergency Ward 10; Secret Orchards; Prince Regent; Cyrano de Bergerac; Miracles; Tender Is the Night.*

PRINCIPAL RADIO WORK—Numerous BBC dramatic presentations.

SIDELIGHTS: RECREATIONS—Travel.

ADDRESSES: AGENT—Roger Storey, 71 Westbury Road, London N12 7PB, England.

AUBREY, James   1947-

PERSONAL: Born James Aubrey Tregidgo, August 28, 1947, in Klagenfurt, Austria; son of Aubrey James (an army officer) and Edna May (Boxall) Tregidgo; married Agnes Kristin Hallander (divorced). EDUCATION: Trained for the stage at the Drama Centre, London, 1967-70.

VOCATION: Actor.

CAREER: STAGE DEBUT—Philip, *Isle of Children*, Wilmington Playhouse, DE, 1962. NEW YORK DEBUT—Philip, *Isle of Children*, Cort Theatre, 1962. LONDON DEBUT—Constable, *Magnificence*, Royal Court Theatre, 1973. PRINCIPAL STAGE APPEARANCES—Aguecheek, *Twelfth Night*, Theridamas, *Tamburlaine*, Flamineo, *The White Devil*, Pozzo, *Waiting for Godot*, Claire, *The Maids*, all at Citizens Theatre, Glasgow, Scotland, 1970-72; Theridamas, *Tamburlaine*, Edinburgh Festival, 1972; Mick, *Bird Child*, Theatre Upstairs, 1974; Sebastian, *The Tempest*, Confessor and Froth, *Measure for Measure*, Jeff, *Afore Night Come*, all with the Royal Shakespeare Company, Stratford, 1974-75; Ralph, *Hitting Town*, Bush Theatre, London, 1975; Dennis, *Loot*, Royal Court, Theatre, London, 1975; Orlando, *As You Like It*, Birmingham Repertory, England, 1975.

Rex, *City Sugar*, Comedy Theatre, London, 1976; Terry, *Army and the Price of Cotton*, Theatre Upstairs, 1976; Tom, *The Glass Menagerie*, Shaw, Theatre, London, 1977; Ritchie, *Streamers*, Round House, 1978; Faulkland, *The Rivals*, Edgar, *King Lear*, both at Prospect Theatre, Old Vic, 1978; Faustus, *Dr. Faustus*, Lyric Studio, Hammersmith, 1980.

MAJOR TOURS—Aguecheek, *Twelfth Night*, Diggory, *She Stoops to Conquer*, both with Cambridge Theatre Company, U.K. cities, 1973-74; Mark, *The Shadow Box*, Tony, *From the Greek*, both with Cambridge Theatre Company, U.K. cities, 1979.

FILM DEBUT—*Lord of the Flies*, Continental, 1963. PRINCIPAL FILM APPEARANCES—*Home Before Midnight*, 1979; *The Great Rock 'n' Swindle*, 1980.

PRINCIPAL TELEVISION APPEARANCES—*A Bouquet of Barbed Wire; Danton's Death; Saint Joan*, 1979.

ADDRESSES: HOME—95 Barnsbury Street, London N1, England.*

*   *   *

AVALON, Frankie   1940-

PERSONAL: Full name Francis Thomas Avalone; born September 18, 1940, in Philadelphia, PA. EDUCATION: Attended public schools in Philadelphia.

VOCATION: Singer and actor.

CAREER: PRINCIPAL FILM APPEARANCES—*Guns of the Timberland*, Warner Brothers, 1960; *The Alamo*, United Artists, 1960; *Voyage to the Bottom of the Sea*, 1961; *Sail a Crooked Ship*, Columbia, 1962; *Panic in the Year Zero*, American International, 1962; *Bikini Beach*, American International, 1964; *Beach Blanket Bingo*, American International, 1965; *Jet Set*, 1965; *I'll Take Sweden*, United Artists, 1965; *Sergeant Deadhead*, American Inter-

national, 1965; *The Take*, Columbia, 1974; *Grease*, Paramount, 1978.

PRINCIPAL TELEVISION APPEARANCES—Series: *Easy Does It . . . Starring Frankie Avalon*, CBS, 1976.

Episodic: *The Patty Duke Show*, ABC, 1966; *Hullabaloo*, NBC, 1966; *Off to See the Wizard*, ABC, 1967; *$weepstake$*, NBC, 1979; *Happy Days*, ABC.

Guest: *The Ed Sullivan Show; The Perry Como Show; The Pat Boone Show; Arthur Murray's Houseparty; American Bandstand; The Milton Berle Show; Golden Circle Spectacular; The Dinah Shore Show; The Steve Allen Show.*

RELATED CAREER—Cabaret and nightclub entertainer.

RECORDINGS: Signed to Chancellor Records, 1957. SINGLES—"Venus." ALBUMS—*Swingin' on a Rainbow*.

AWARDS: Gold Record, 1957, for "Venus;" Gold Album, 1959, for *Swingin' on a Rainbow*.

SIDELIGHTS: CTFT has learned that Frankie Avalon was considered a trumpet playing prodigy at the age of nine.

ADDRESSES: AGENT—Burton Moss Agency, 113 N. San Vincente, Suite 202, Beverly Hills, CA 90211.*

*   *   *

AXTON, Hoyt   1938-

PERSONAL: Full name, Hoyt Wayne Axton; born March 25, 1938, in Duncan, OK; son of John Thomas and N. Mae (Boren) Axton; married Kathy Roberts, 1963 (divorced, 1973); married Donna; children: Mark Roberts, Michael Stephen, April Laura, Matthew. EDUCATION: Attended Oklahoma State University. POLITICS: Democrat. MILITARY: U.S. Navy, 1958-62.

VOCATION: Actor, composer, and singer.

CAREER: PRINCIPAL TELEVISION APPEARANCES—Series: Cactus Jack Slade, *Rousters*, NBC, 1983-84; Rip Steele, *Domestic Life*, CBS, 1984.

Episodic: *Bonanza*, 1964; *I Dream of Jeannie*, 1964; *Chrysler Theatre*, 1965; *Bionic Woman*, 1975; *McCloud*, 1976; *Dukes of Hazard*, 1981; Coop Johnson, *Seven Brides for Seven Brothers*, CBS, 1983; *Trapper John, M.D.*, 1985; *Dallas; Glitter; Flo; WKRP in Cincinnati.*

Guest: *Smothers Brothers Show*, 1975; *Midnight Special*, 1975-77; *Dinah Shore Show*, 1975-77; *The Tonight Show*, 1976-77; *Hee Haw*, 1977; *Nashville on the Road*, 1980-81; *Barbara Mandrell Show*, 1981.

Specials: *The Hoyt Axton Country Western, Boogie Woogie, Gospel, Rock and Roll Show*, 1975; *The Hoyt Axton Show*, NBC.

PRINCIPAL FILM APPEARANCES—*The Story of a Folk Singer*, 1963; *Smoky*, Twentieth Century-Fox, 1966; *Act of Vengeance*,

HOYT AXTON

1974; *Black Stallion*, United Artists, 1980; *Junk Man*, 1981; *Liar's Moon*, 1981; *Endangered Species*, Metro-Goldwyn-Mayer/United Artists, 1982; *Heart Like a Wheel*, Twentieth Century-Fox, 1983; *Gremlins*, Warner Brothers, 1984.

PRINCIPAL STAGE APPEARANCES—*Grand Ole Opry*, Nashville, TN, 1974-76, 1980; *Ernest Tubb Record Shop*, Nashville, 1974-75; Inaugural Ball for President Jimmy Carter, 1977.

RELATED CAREER—Chairman, Jeremiah Records, 1979—.

WRITINGS: SONGS—"Greenback Dollar," 1962; "The Pusher," 1964; "Snowblind Friend," 1967; "Joy to the World," 1971; "Never Been to Spain," 1972; "Ease Your Pain," 1973; "Less Than the Song," 1973; "When the Morning Comes," 1974; "Boney Fingers," 1974; "Lion in the Winter," 1974; "The No, No Song," 1975; "Fearless Free Sailin'"; "Life Machine"; "My Griffin Is Gone"; "Southbound"; "Evangelina"; "Wild Bull Rider."

MUSICALS—*The Happy Song*, 1972.

FILM SOUNDTRACKS—*Outlaw Blues*, 1977.

BOOKS—*Line Drawings, Volumes I-V*, 1974-78.

SONGBOOKS—*Life Machine*, 1973; *Southbound*, 1974; *Less Than the Song*, 1977.

RECORDINGS: ALBUMS—*Hoyt Axton Live*, Jeremiah Records; *Rusty Old Halo*, Jeremiah Records; *Pistol Packin' Mama*, Jeremiah Records; *Fearless*, A & M; *Free Sailin'*, MCA; *Heartbreak Hotel*, Accord; *Life Machine*, A & M; *Road Songs*, A & M; *Snowblind Friend*, MCA.

MEMBER: Screen Actors Guild, American Federation of Television and Radio Artists, American Federation of Musicians, Country Music Association, Broadcast Music Inc.; American Heart Association (spokesman, 1975), UNICEF; Oklahoma Cattlemen's Association.

SIDELIGHTS: CTFT learned from press material from his agent that Hoyt Axton has been active in the political campaigns of Eugene McCarthy, George McGovern, Edmund Brown, and David Borean.

ADDRESSES: OFFICE—Jeremiah Records, P.O. Box 1077, Henersonville, TN, 37075. AGENT—Charles Stern Agency, 9220 Sunset Blvd., Los Angeles, CA 90069.

*   *   *

AYRES, Lew   1908-

PERSONAL: Born December 28, 1908, in Minneapolis, MN; married Lola Lane, 1931 (divorced, 1933); married Ginger Rogers, 1933 (divorced, 1939); married Diana Hall, 1964; children: Justin Bret. MILITARY: Conscientious objector, served with U.S. Army, as medical corpsman and assistant chaplain in World War II.

VOCATION: Actor, musician, director, and producer.

CAREER: FILM DEBUT—*The Kiss*, Metro-Goldwyn-Mayer, 1929. PRINCIPAL FILM APPEARANCES—*The Sophomore*, Pathe, 1929; *All Quiet on the Western Front*, Universal, 1930; *Common Clay*, Twentieth Century-Fox, 1930; *East Is West*, Universal, 1930; *Doorway to Hell*, Twentieth Century-Fox, 1930; *Many a Slip*, Universal, 1931; *Iron Man*, Universal, 1931; *Up for Murder*, Universal, 1931; *Spirit of Notre Dame*, Universal, 1931; *Heaven on Earth*, Universal, 1931; *Okay America!*, Universal, 1932; *Impatient Maiden*, Universal, 1932; *Night World*, Universal, 1932; *State Fair*, Twentieth Century-Fox, 1933; *Don't Bet on Love*, Universal, 1933; *My Weakness*, Twentieth Century-Fox, 1933; *Cross Country Cruise*, Universal, 1934; *Let's Be Ritzy*, Universal, 1934; *She Learned About Sailors*, Twentieth Century-Fox, 1934; *Servants' Entrance*, Twentieth Century-Fox, 1934; *Lottery Lover*, Twentieth Century-Fox, 1935; *Silk Hat Kid*, Twentieth Century-Fox, 1935; *The Leathernecks Have Landed*, Republic, 1936; *Panic on the Air*, Columbia, 1936; *Shakedown*, Columbia, 1936; *Murder with Pictures*, Paramount, 1936; *The Crime Nobody Saw*, Paramount, 1937; *Lady Be Careful*, Paramount, 1937; *Last Train from Madrid*, Paramount, 1937; *Hold 'em Navy*, Paramount, 1937; *King of the Newsboys*, Republic, 1938; *Scandal Sheet*, Paramount, 1938; *Holiday*, 1938; *Rich Man, Poor Girl*, Metro-Goldwyn-Mayer, 1938; title role, *Young Dr. Kildare*, Metro-Goldwyn-Mayer, 1938; *Spring Madness*, Metro-Goldwyn-Mayer, 1938; *Ice Follies of 1939*, Metro-Goldwyn-Mayer, 1939; *Broadway Serenade*, Metro-Goldwyn-Mayer, 1939; title role, *Calling Dr. Kildare*, Metro-Goldwyn-Mayer, 1939; *These Glamour Girls*, Metro-Goldwyn-Mayer, 1939; *Remember?*, Metro-Goldwyn-Mayer, 1939; title role, *The Secret of Dr. Kildare*, Metro-Goldwyn-Mayer, 1939; *These Glamour Girls*, Metro-Goldwyn-Mayer, 1939.

Title role, *Dr. Kildare's Strange Case*, Metro-Goldwyn-Mayer, 1940; title role, *Dr. Kildare Goes Home*, Metro-Goldwyn-Mayer, 1940; title role, *Dr. Kildare's Crisis*, Metro-Goldwyn-Mayer, 1940; *The Golden Fleecing*, Metro-Goldwyn-Mayer, 1940; *Maisie Was a Lady*, Metro-Goldwyn-Mayer, 1940; title role, *The People vs. Dr. Kildare*, Metro-Goldwyn-Mayer, 1941; title role, *Dr. Kildare's Wedding Day*, Metro-Goldwyn-Mayer, 1941; title role, *Dr. Kil-*

dare's Victory, Metro-Goldwyn-Mayer, 1941; *Fingers at the Window,* Metro-Goldwyn-Mayer, 1942; *Dark Mirror,* Universal, 1946; *The Unfaithful,* Warner Brothers, 1947; *Johnny Belinda,* Warner Brothers, 1948.

The Capture, RKO, 1950; *New Mexico,* United Artists, 1951; *No Escape,* United Artists, 1953; *Donovan's Brain,* United Artists, 1954; *Advise and Consent,* Columbia, 1962; *The Carpetbaggers,* Paramount, 1964; *Earth II,* Metro-Goldwyn-Mayer, 1971; *Last Generation,* 1971; *Biscuit Eater,* Buena Vista, 1972; *The Man,* Paramount, 1972; *Battle for the Planet of the Apes,* Twentieth Century-Fox, 1973; *Damien, Omen—II,* Twentieth Century-Fox, 1978; *Battlestar Galatica,* Universal, 1979.

PRINCIPAL FILM WORK—Director, *Hearts of Bondage;* writer, director, and producer, *Altars of the East,* 1955, revised and released as *Altars of the World,* 1977.

PRINCIPAL TELEVISION APPEARANCES—Series: Host, *Frontier Justice,* CBS, 1958.

Movie: *Under Siege,* NBC, 1986.

WRITINGS: NON-FICTION—*Altars of the East.*

AWARDS: Best Actor, Academy Award nomination, 1948, for *Johnny Belinda;* Best Documentary, Golden Globe, 1977.

SIDELIGHTS: Beginning his film career as a silent screen actor in 1929, Lew Ayres gained stardom the following year with his first talking role, that of a young German soldier in the now classic anti-war movie *All Quiet on the Western Front.* The following years brought him numerous parts but it was with his performances as the young physician Dr. Kildare in nine films released by Metro-Goldwyn-Mayer between 1938 and 1941 that Ayres' career fully established itself. The actor's career suffered a serious reversal after the outbreak of World War II, however, when he refused to take up arms and entered a labor camp as the country's most famous conscientious objector. In an era of superpatriotism, Ayres became an object of derision—denigrated by the press, shunned by the entertainment industry, abandoned by his fans—and many theatre owners refused even to show his films. Eventually permitted to serve his country as a noncombatant in the Army Medical Corps, Ayres twice earned decorations for valor under fire, thus recapturing the respect of his critics. Still, he never regained his former stature as a motion picture star, acting primarily in low budget movies thereafter. One notable exception came in 1948, when Ayres, once again playing a doctor, won an Academy Award nomination for his performance in *Johnny Belinda.*

In 1953, Ayres temporarily retired from the screen to pursue an interest in philosophy and world religions; and in 1955 he released *Altars of the East,* a documentary movie on Middle and Far Eastern religions. He wrote, produced, directed and financed the film, and later published a book of the same title. A revised version of the film, *Altars of the World,* won the Golden Globe Award for best documentary film in 1977.

ADDRESSES: AGENT—William Morris Agency, 151 El Camino Drive, Beverly Hills, CA 90212.*

B

BACHARACH, Burt   1929-

PERSONAL: Born May 12, 1929, in Kansas City, MO; son of Bert and Irma (Freeman) Bacharach; married Paula Stewart (a singer; marriage ended); married Angie Dickinson (an actress) in 1965 (divorced); children: (second marriage) Lea ''Nikki.'' EDUCATION: Attended McGill University; New School for Social Research, Mannes School of Music, NY; Music Academy of the West, Santa Barbara, CA; studied with composers Darius Milhaud, Henry Cowell, and Bohuslav Martinu.

VOCATION: Composer, conductor, arranger, and performer.

CAREER: PRINCIPAL FILM WORK—Composer: *The Man Who Shot Liberty Valance,* Paramount, 1962; *Wives and Lovers,* Paramount, 1963; *Send Me No Flowers,* Universal, 1964; *A House Is Not a Home,* Embassy Pictures, 1964; *Who's Been Sleeping in My Bed?,* Paramount, 1964; *What's New Pussycat?,* United Artists, 1965; *Promise Her Anything,* Paramount, 1966; *Alfie,* Paramount, 1966; *Casino Royale,* Columbia, 1967; *The April Fools,* National General Films, 1969; *Butch Cassidy and the Sundance Kid,* Twentieth Century-Fox, 1969; *Lost Horizon,* Columbia, 1973.

PRINCIPAL STAGE WORK—Composer, *Promises, Promises,* Majestic Theatre, NY, 1969.

RELATED CAREER—Accompanist for Vic Damone, 1952, Polly Bergen, Georgia Gibbs, and the Ames Brothers. Conductor for Joel Gray and Marlene Dietrich.

RECORDINGS: ALBUMS—Composer: *What's New Pussycat?,* original soundtrack recording, United Artists Records; *Casino Royale,* original soundtrack recording, Colgems Records; *Promises, Promises,* original cast recording, United Artists Records; *The April Fools,* original soundtrack recording; *Butch Cassidy and the Sundance Kid,* original soundtrack recording, A & M Records; (also producer) *Lost Horizon,* original soundtrack recording, Bell Records.

Composer, songs, recorded: ''Raindrops Keep Fallin' on My Head,'' ''Moments,'' ''The Story of My Life,'' ''Don't Make Me Over,'' ''Walk on By,'' ''Trains and Boats and Planes,'' ''Close to You,'' ''Anyone Who Had a Heart,'' ''What the World Needs Now,'' ''I'll Never Fall in Love Again,'' ''Do You Know the Way to San Jose?,'' ''The Look of Love,'' ''One Less Bell to Answer,'' ''Alfie,'' ''This Guy's in Love with You,'' others.

Performer: *Burt Bacharach,* ''Futures,'' A & M Records; *Man! His Songs,* Kapp Records.

WRITINGS: BOOKS—(With Hal David) *The Bacharach-David Song Book,* 1970.

AWARDS: Best Score for a Musical, Antoinette Perry Award, 1969, for *Promises, Promises;* Best Original Score (Not a Musical), Academy Award, 1969, for *Butch Cassidy and the Sundance Kid,* Best Song, Academy Award, 1969, for ''Raindrops Keep Fallin' on My Head,'' from the same film; Best Song, Academy Award nominations, 1965, for *What's New Pussycat?,* 1966, for *Alfie,* 1967, for ''The Look of Love,'' from *Casino Royale.*

SIDELIGHTS: Bacharach's chief collaborators and lyricists have been Hal David, Mack David, Bob Hilliard, and Jack Wolfe.*

*   *   *

BAIN, Barbara

PERSONAL: Married Martin Landau (divorced); children: Susan, Juliet. EDUCATION: University of Illinois, B.A., sociology; studied acting at the Actors Studio and the Neighborhood Playhouse.

BARBARA BAIN

CAREER: PRINCIPAL TELEVISION APPEARANCES—Series: Karen Wells, *Richard Diamond, Private Detective,* CBS, 1959; Cinnamon Carter, *Mission: Impossible,* CBS, 1966-69; Dr. Helena Russell, *Space: 1999,* syndication, 1974-76.

Episodic: *Ben Casey; Dick Van Dyke Show; Smothers Brothers Show; Kraft Music Hall; Mickey Spillane's Mike Hammer; Moonlighting,* others.

PRINCIPAL STAGE APPEARANCES—*Long Day's Journey into Night,* Intiman Theatre, Seattle, WA, 1984; *Wings,* Odessey Theatre, Los Angeles, CA, 1985.

MEMBER: Actors' Equity Association, American Federation of Television and Radio Artists, Screen Actors Guild, Actors Studio.

AWARDS: Outstanding Continued Performances by an Actress in a Leading Role in a Dramatic Series, Emmy Awards, 1966-67, 1967-68, 1968-69, for *Mission: Impossible;* Dramalogue Award, *LA Weekly* Award, Los Angeles Drama Critics Circle Award nomination, all 1985, for *Wings.*

ADDRESSES: AGENT—The Agency, 10351 Santa Monica Blvd., Suite 211, Los Angeles, CA 90025.

*   *   *

BAKER, George   1931-

PERSONAL: Born April, 1931; married; children: five daughters. EDUCATION: Attended Lancing College, Sussex.

VOCATION: Actor, director, producer, and writer.

CAREER: LONDON DEBUT—Arthur Wells, *Aren't We All?,* Hay-

GEORGE BAKER

market Theatre, 1953. NEW YORK DEBUT—Phillipe de Croze, *Look After Lulu,* Henry Miller Theatre, 1959. PRINCIPAL STAGE APPEARANCES—Nevile Strange, *Towards Zero,* St. James's Theatre, London, 1956; Florent and France, *Restless Heart,* St. James's Theatre, London, 1957.

With the Old Vic Company, London: Henry Bolingbroke, *Richard II,* and Page, *The Merry Wives of Windsor,* both 1959; Earl of Warwick, *Saint Joan,* and David Wylie, *What Every Woman Knows,* both 1960.

Buddy, *The Glad and the Sorry Season,* Piccadilly Theatre, London, 1962; Rawdon Crawley, *Vanity Fair,* Queen's Theatre, London, 1962; Paul Sevigne, *A Shot in the Dark,* Lyric Theatre, London, 1963; Eliot Barlow, *Portrait of Murder,* Savoy Theatre, London, 1963; Gentleman Caller, *The Glass Menagerie,* Yvonne Arnaud Theatre, Guildford, then Haymarket Theatre, London, 1965; Son, *Days in the Trees,* Aldwych Theatre, London, 1968; Regent, *The Sleeping Prince,* St. Martin's Theatre, London, 1968; Gene Garrison, *I Never Sang for My Father,* Duke of York's Theatre, London, 1970.

With the Royal Shakespeare Company, 1975: Worcester and Clarence, *Henry IV, Part I,* Memorial Theatre, London, and Claudius, *Hamlet,* Clarence, *Richard III,* at The Other Place, Stratford, 1975.

Claudius, *Hamlet,* Round House Theatre, London, 1976; Worcester, *Henry IV, Part I,* Aldwych Theatre, London, 1975; Austin Proctor, *Cousin Vladimir,* Aldwych Theatre, London, 1978; The Duke, *Measure for Measure,* Riverside Studios, Hammersmith, 1979.

MAJOR TOURS—John Worthing, *The Importance of Being Earnest,* Third Witch and Porter, *Macbeth,* Warwick, *Saint Joan,* Antonio, *The Merchant of Venice,* all with the Old Vic Company, U.K. and Soviet cities, 1961; Thomas Mendip, *The Lady's Not for Burning,* U.K. cities, 1971.

PRINCIPAL STAGE WORK—Producer, *The Critic,* Ember's Playhouse, London, 1966; director, *The Sleeping Prince,* St. Martin's Theatre, London, 1968; director, *The Lady's Not for Burning,* Old Vic Theatre, London, 1978.

FILM DEBUT—*The Intruder,* 1953. PRINCIPAL FILM APPEARANCES—*Dam Busters,* Warner Brothers, 1955; *Ship That Died of Shame,* Continental, 1956; *A Hill in Korea* (also known as *Hell in Korea*), Hal Roach, 1956; *Tread Softly Stranger,* Bentley Films, 1956; *Lancelot and Guinivere,* Universal, 1963; *Curse of the Fly,* Avco Embassy, 1965; *Justine,* Twentieth Century-Fox, 1969; *Goodbye Mr. Chips,* Metro-Goldwyn-Mayer, 1969; *On Her Majesty's Secret Service,* United Artists, 1969; *The Executioner,* Columbia, 1970; *A Warm December,* National General, 1973; *The Spy Who Loved Me,* United Artists, 1977; *The Thirty Nine Steps,* 1978; *A Nightingale Sang in Berkeley Square,* 1979; *Hopscotch,* 1980. Also appeared in: *Woman for Joe, Extra Day, Feminine Touch, No Time for Tears, These Dangerous Years, Mister Ten Percent, The Fire Fighters, North Sea Hijack.*

TELEVISION DEBUT—1957. PRINCIPAL TELEVISION APPEARANCES—Episodic and Specials: (Mostly on British television) *Fan Show; Ron Raudell Show; Guinea Pig; Death of a Salesman; The Last Troubadour; The Square Ring; Nick of the River; Mary Stuart; Probation Officers; Far Away Music; It Happened Like This; Boule de Fuif; Maigret; Zero One; Rupert Henzau; Miss Memory; Any Other Business; The Navigators; Common Ground; Alice; The*

Queen and Jackson; The Big Man Coughed and Died; Up and Down; Call My Bluff; The Baron; St. Patrick; Love Life; Seven Deadly Virtues; The Prisoner; The Sex Games; Z Cars; Paul Temple; Candida; Fenn Street; Man Outside; The Persuaders; Main Chance; Ministry of Fear; Voyage in the Dark; Dial M for Murder; Zodiac; The Survivors; Medea; I, Claudius; Print Out; Goodbye, Darling; Chinese Detective; Triangle; Minder; Hart to Hart; Goodbye Mr. Chips; If Tomorrow Comes; Dead Head; The Bird Fancier; Robin of Sherwood; The Canterville Ghost; Time After Time; Room at the Bottom.

Mini-series: *A Woman of Substance,* 1985.

RELATED CAREER—Artistic director of Candida Plays, 1966, where productions included *Charley's Aunt, Ghosts, Private Lives, Gigi, School for Scandal,* and *The Constant Wife.*

WRITINGS: TELEVISION—*The Fatal Spring, Imaginary Friends, Just a Hunch; The Hopkins; Going for Broke; The Marches of Wales; Sister, Dear Sister.*

SIDELIGHTS: RECREATIONS—Horseback riding.

ADDRESSES: AGENT—(Acting) International Creative Management, 388/396 Oxford Street, London W1N 9HE, England; (writing) c/o Terence Baker, Hatton and Baker, 18 Jermyn Street, London W1, England.

*   *   *

BALDWIN, James   1924-

PERSONAL: Born August 2, 1924, in New York, NY; son of David (a minister) and Berdis (Jones) Baldwin. EDUCATION: Attended public schools in New York.

VOCATION: Novelist, essayist, playwright, and director.

CAREER: PRINCIPAL STAGE WORK—Director, *Fortune and Men's Eyes,* Istanbul, Turkey, 1970.

PRINCIPAL FILM WORK—Director, *The Inheritance,* 1973.

WRITINGS: NOVELS—*Go Tell It on the Mountain,* Alfred Knopf, 1953, reissued in hardcover by Dial Press, 1963; *Giovanni's Room,* Dial, 1956, reprinted by Transworld, 1977; *Another Country,* Dial, 1962; *Tell Me How Long the Train's Been Gone,* Dial, 1968; *If Beale Street Could Talk,* Dial, 1974; *Little Man, Little Man: A Story of Childhood* (juvenile), M. Joseph, 1976, then Dial, 1977; *Just Above My Head,* Dial Press, 1979.

ESSAYS—*Notes of a Native Son,* Beacon Press, 1955; *Nobody Knows My Name: More Notes of a Native Son,* Dial, 1961; *The Fire Next Time,* Dial, 1963; *Black Anti-Semitism and Jewish Racism* (with others), R. W. Baron, 1969; *Menschenwuerde und Gerechtigkeit* (with Kenneth Kaunda; essays delivered at the fourth assembly of the World Council of Churches), edited and introduced by Carl Ordnung, Union-Verl, 1969; *No Name in The Streets,* Dial Press, 1972; *The Devil Finds Work,* 1976.

OTHER WORKS—*Autobiographical Notes,* Alfred Knopf, 1953; *Nothing Personal* (author of text; photography portraits by Richard Avedon), Atheneum, 1964; *Going to Meet the Man* (short stories), Dial Press, 1965; *This Morning, This Evening, So Soon* (short story), edited by Johannes Schuetze, Diesterweg, 1967; *A Rap on Race* (with Margaret Mead), Lippincott, 1971; *A Dialogue* (with Nikki Giovanni), Lippincott, 1973; *Cesar: Compressions d'or* (with Francoise Giroud), Hachette, 1973. Work anthologized in *American Negro Short Stories,* edited by John Henrik Clarke, Hill and Wang, 1966. Contributor of numerous magazines in the United States and abroad, including *Harper's, Nation, Esquire, Partisan Review, Mademoiselle,* and *New Yorker.*

PLAYS—*The Amen Corner,* produced at Howard University, 1953, Los Angeles, 1964, at the Ethel Barrymore Theatre, NY, 1965, Europe and the Far East, 1965, Chicago, IL, 1979, and at the Black Theatre Festival, Lincoln Center, NY, 1979, was published by Dial Press, 1968; *Giovanni's Room* (based on novel of same name), produced at Actors Studio workshop, 1958; *Blues for Mister Charlie,* American National Theatre and Academy (ANTA), 1964, published by Dial Press, 1964; *A Deed from the King of Spain,* first produced at American Center for Stanislavsky Theatre Art, NY, 1974.

SCREENPLAYS—*One Day, When I Was Lost: A Scenario* (based on *The Autobiography of Malcolm X*), 1973.

MEMBER: Authors League, International PEN, Dramatists Guild, National Institute of Arts and Letters, Actors Studio, National Committee for a Sane Nuclear Policy.

AWARDS: Eugene F. Saxton Memorial Trust award, 1945; Rosenwald Fellowship, 1948; Guggenheim Fellowship, 1954; National Institute of Arts and Letters grant in literature, 1956; *Partisan Review* Fellowship, 1956; Ford Foundation Grant-in-Aid, 1959; National Conference of Christians and Jews Brotherhood Award, 1962, for *Nobody Knows My Name;* George Polk Award, 1963; Foreign Drama Critics Award, 1964; National Association of Independent Schools Award, 1964, for *The Fire Next Time;* D. Litt., University of British Columbia, 1964; American Book Award nomination, 1980, for *Just Above My Head;* Dial Press has initiated the James Baldwin Prize, presented at irregular intervals to new or previously unrecognized black writers of unusual talent.

SIDELIGHTS: From James Baldwin's publicity biography, *CTFT* notes that he was a child preacher at the Fireside Pentecostal Assembly from the time he was fourteen until he turned seventeen. At seventeen, he embarked upon his literary career. He gained international prominence as a leader and spokesman for the civil rights movement, although he prefers to call himself a witness to that movement. He has spoken passionately before audiences of thousands urging recognition of the rights of all. Still a frequent speaker at colleges and universities, Baldwin was Regent's Lecturer during a month-long visit at the University of California at Berkeley in 1979. He addressed the American Booksellers Convention in Los Angeles, in May of that same year. He spends his time between his homes in New York City and southern France.

ADDRESSES: HOME— New York, NY; France. OFFICE—c/o Holt, Rinehart and Winston, CBS Inc., 521 Fifth Avenue; New York, NY 10175.

BALL, Lucille 1911-

PERSONAL: Born August 11, 1911, in Jamestown, NY; daughter of Henry D. and Desiree (Hunt) Ball; married Desiderio Alberto (Desi) Arnaz, November 30, 1940 (divorced, 1960); married Gary Morton, November 19, 1961; children (first marriage) Lucie Desiree, Desiderio Alberto IV (Desi, Jr.). EDUCATION: Attended Chautauqua Institute of Music and John Murray Anderson Drama School.

VOCATION: Actress and producer.

CAREER: STAGE DEBUT—*Rio Rita.* PRINCIPAL STAGE APPEARANCES—Broadway: *Hey Diddle, Diddle; Dream Girl; Wildcat.*

FILM DEBUT—*Roman Scandals,* 1933. PRINCIPAL FILM APPEARANCES—*Roberta,* 1935; *Stage Door,* 1937; *Room Service,* 1938; *Big Street,* 1942; *Du Barry Was a Lady,* Metro-Goldwyn-Mayer, 1943; *Best Foot Forward,* Metro-Goldwyn-Mayer, 1943; *Meet the People,* Metro-Goldwyn-Mayer, 1944; *Ziegfeld Follies,* Metro-Goldwyn-Mayer, 1945; *Bud Abbott and Lou Costello in Hollywood,* Metro-Goldwyn-Mayer, 1945; *Without Love,* Metro-Goldwyn-Mayer, 1945; *Dark Corner,* Twentieth Century-Fox, 1946; *Two Smart People,* Metro-Goldwyn-Mayer, 1946; *Easy to Wed,* 1946; *Lured,* 1947; *Sorrowful Jones,* 1949; *Easy Living,* 1949; *Miss Grant Takes Richmond,* 1949; *Fuller Brush Girl,* 1950; *Fancy Pants,* 1950; *Magic Carpet,* 1951; *The Long, Long Trailer,* Metro-Goldwyn-Mayer, 1953; *Forever Darling,* Metro-Goldwyn-Mayer, 1955; *Facts of Life,* United Artists, 1960; *Critics Choice,* Warner Brothers, 1963; *Yours, Mine, and Ours,* United Artists, 1968; *Mame,* Warner Brothers, 1974.

PRINCIPAL RADIO WORK—*My Favorite Husband,* late 1940's.

PRINCIPAL TELEVISION APPEARANCES—Series: Lucy Ricardo, *I Love Lucy,* CBS, 1951-57; Lucy Ricardo, *Lucy-Desi Comedy Hour,* CBS, ran as summer shows in 1962-65 and 1967; Lucy Carmichael, *The Lucy Show,* CBS, 1962-68; Lucy Carter, *Here's Lucy,* CBS, 1968-74; *Lucy,* ABC, 1986—.

Episodic: *The Danny Thomas Show; David Frost Revue; Ed Wynn Show; Milton Berle Show;* "K.O. Kitty," and "Westinghouse Lucille Ball-Desi Arnaz Shows," *Westinghouse Desilu Playhouse; Inside U.S.A. with Chevrolet; The Tonight Show; Mary Tyler Moore Hour; Body Language.*

Movie: *Stone Pillow,* NBC, 1985.

RELATED CAREER—Entertainer, Stage Canteen, World War II; president, Desilu Productions, Inc., 1962-67; executive producer, *The Lucy Show,* 1962-68; president, Lucille Ball Productions, 1967—.

AWARDS: Motion Picture Daily Awards: Most Promising Star, 1951, Best Performer, 1952, Best Comedy Team, 1954, Best Comedienne, 1952, 1954-55, and 1957; Emmy Awards: Best Comedienne, 1952, for *I Love Lucy,* Best Actress in a Continuing Performance, 1955, for *I Love Lucy,* Outstanding Continued Performance by an Actress in a Leading Role in a Comedy Series, 1966-67, for *The Lucy Show,* Outstanding Continued Performance By an Actress in a Leading Role in a Comedy Series, 1967-68, for *The Lucy Show;* Golden Apple Award, 1973; Ruby Award, 1974; Entertainer of the Year Award, 1975; inducted into the Television Academy Hall of Fame, 1984.

SIDELIGHTS: Although Lucille Ball had been fairly popular as a film actress and on radio, nothing in her early career foreshadowed

the phenomenal success she would achieve as Lucy Ricardo, the scatterbrained wife of Cuban bandleader Ricky Ricardo (played by her then real-life husband, Desi Arnaz) in her first television series, *I Love Lucy.* Within a few months of its October 1951 premiere, *I Love Lucy* became the top-rated television show in the country, and it held that position for four of its six years on the air.

Describing *I Love Lucy* in the cover story of the May 26, 1952 issue, a writer for *Time* magazine wrote, "What televiewers see on their screens is the sort of cheerful rowdiness that has been rare in the U.S. since the days of the silent movies' Keystone Comedies." Ball says that she learned a great deal about comedy from the great silent comedian Buster Keaton when they were both under contract to Metro-Goldwyn-Mayer in the forties.

When Ball became pregnant before the start of *I Love Lucy*'s second season, her "expectancy" was written into the show. In their book *Watching TV* (McGraw-Hill, 1982), Harry Castleman and Walter J. Podrazik described January 19, 1953, the day on which both the real and fictional Lucys gave birth, as "the point at which television became synonymous with American popular culture." Forty-four million viewers watched *I Love Lucy* that night—more than twice the number that saw President Eisenhower's inauguration the next day.

After the initial run of *I Love Lucy* ended, Ball and Arnaz played the Ricardos in one-hour specials for three years. The couple divorced in 1960, and in 1962, Ball returned to the regular-series schedule on her own in *The Lucy Show.* The title character, Lucy Carmichael, was still essentially the same scatterbrained person as Lucy Ricardo, and the show featured the same brand of wacky slapstick comedy as *I Love Lucy.* Ball's third comedy series, *Here's Lucy,* broadcast from 1968 to 1974, in which she played Lucy Carter, a worker for an employment agency, again drew on these same elements for its laughs.

Ball's first show had been produced by Desilu, the company she and Arnaz had formed. A month after her second series, *The Lucy Show,* went on the air, Ball purchased Arnaz's interest in Desilu and became the first female president of a major production company. By that time, Desilu had become one of the country's largest television production companies, responsible for such popular programs as *Make Room for Daddy* and *The Untouchables* as well as *The Lucy Show.* Ball remained as the firm's head until 1967, when she sold her interest in Desilu to Gulf and Western for $10 million.

Adding to Ball's considerable wealth are the syndication rights to her series, all of which—especially *I Love Lucy*—have been major hits in reruns. In New York in 1977, what Terrence O'Flaherty of *TV Guide* estimated was the "face seen by more people, more often, than the face of any human being who ever lived" could be seen four times each weekday and once on Saturday. Her enduring popularity was marked in 1984, when Lucille Ball became one of the first seven inductees in the Television Academy Hall of Fame.

ADDRESSES: OFFICE—c/o ABC Public Relations, 4151 Prospect Avenue, Los Angeles, CA 90027; Twentieth Century-Fox, P.O. Box 900, Beverly Hills, CA 90213.*

*   *   *

BALLANTYNE, Paul 1909-

PERSONAL: Born July 18, 1909, in Moorhead, IA; son of James Carl and Inez Mae (Adams) Ballantyne. EDUCATION: Sherwood

Music School, Chicago, IL, teacher's certificate, 1931; trained for the stage with Luella Canterbury and served apprenticeship with Eva Le Gallienne's Civic Repertory Company. MILITARY: U.S. Army, 1940-46.

VOCATION: Actor.

CAREER: NEW YORK DEBUT—Eight of Hearts, *Alice in Wonderland,* 1932. PRINCIPAL STAGE APPEARANCES—Fred, *Talent,* Cape Playhouse, Dennis, MA, 1934; Captain Jack Absolute, *The Rivals,* title role, *Everyman,* Young Marlowe, *She Stoops to Conquer,* all with WPA's Federal Theatre Project, 1935-37; Heinrich Wertheimer, *Mrs. O'Brien Entertains,* and Johann, *Brown Danube,* both at Lyceum Theatre, NY, 1939; Student, *The Unconquered,* and Kurt, *Goodbye in the Night,* both at Biltmore Theatre, NY, 1940; Charles Owen, *Suzanna and the Elders,* Morosco Theatre, NY, 1940.

Brutus, *Julius Caesar,* Ferrovius, *Androcles and the Lion,* Frank, *The Little Blue Light,* Reverend Davidson, *Rain,* Northumberland, *Henry IV, Part 2,* Tchebutykin, *The Three Sisters,* the Burglar, *Heartbreak House,* Costard, *Love's Labour's Lost,* Cleante, *Tartuffe,* all at the Brattle Theatre, Cambridge, MA, 1950-51.

William Clark, S.J., *The Strong Are Lonely,* Broadhurst Theatre, NY, 1953; Brackenbury, *Richard III,* City Center Theatre, NY, 1953.

At the Guthrie Theatre, Minnesota Theatre Company, MN: Marcellus, *Hamlet,* La Fleche, *The Miser,* Charley, *The Death of a Salesman,* all 1963; Williams, *Henry V,* de Stogumber, *Saint Joan,* first avocatore, *Volpone,* both 1964; *The Way of the World, Richard III, The Cherry Orchard, The Caucasian Chalk Circle,* all 1965; *The Dance of Death, As You Like It, SS Glencairn,* all 1966; *House of Atreus, Shoemaker's Holiday, Thieves' Carnival, Harper's Ferry, She Stoops to Conquer, Tango, Man with a Flower in His Mouth,* all 1967; *Twelfth Night, Serjeant Musgrave's Dance, The Resistible Rise of Arturo Ui, The Houe of Atreus,* all 1968.

Chorus leader, *The House of Atreus,* and Hindborough, *The Resistible Rise of Arturo Ui,* both with the Minnesota Theatre Company at the Billy Rose Theatre, NY, 1968.

Also at the Guthrie: *The Beauty Part,* title role, *Uncle Vanya,* General St. Pe, *Ardele,* all 1969; *The Venetian Twins, The Tempest,* Galy Gay, in *A Man's a Man,* and *A Play by Alexander Solzhenitsyn,* all 1970.

Murderous Angels, Mark Taper Forum, Los Angeles, CA, 1970; Crysalde, *School for Wives,* Lyceum Theatre, NY, 1971.

Again at the Guthrie: *Misalliance,* 1971-72; Candy, *Of Mice and Men,* 1972; *The Government Inspector,* 1973; Gloucester, *King Lear,* Deputy Governor Danforth, *The Crucible,* all 1974.

Andre Wyke, *Sleuth,* and Arvide Abnerathy, *Guys and Dolls,* both at the Chanhassen Theatre, Minneapolis, 1975; Nat Miller, *Ah, Wilderness!,* and Captain Andy, *Showboat,* both at the Chanhassen, 1976; returned to the Guthrie to portray the Count in *La Ronde,* and Diggory in *She Stoops to Conquer,* both 1977; Al Lewis, *The Sunshine Boys,* Merlin, *Camelot,* Starkeeper, *Carousel,* all at the Chanhassen, 1979-80; Serebriakov, *Uncle Vanya,* Arizona Theatre Company, 1983; Andie, *And a Nightingale Sang . . . ,* Arizona Theatre Company, 1984.

MAJOR TOURS—*Dark Tower,* Cape Playhouse, Dennis, MA, 1934; Bing, *Brother Rat,* U.S. cities, 1937-38; Kurt, *Biography,* U.S. cities, 1940; de Baudricourt, *Saint Joan,* U.S. cities, 1954; Fred Bailey, *The Skin of Our Teeth,* European cities for U.S. State Department, 1961; Earl of Shrewsbury, *Mary Stuart,* and Sir Walter Raleigh, *Elizabeth the Queen,* both with National Repertory Theatre, U.S. cities, 1961-62.

PRINCIPAL FILM APPEARANCES—Lt. Smith (a movie made for soldiers during World War II), RKO; *The Andromeda Strain,* Universal, 1971.

TELEVISION DEBUT—*Family Honor,* NBC, 1939. PRINCIPAL TELEVISION APPEARANCES—*Hallmark Hall of Fame; You Are There; The Play of the Week.*

SIDELIGHTS: FAVORITE ROLES—Vanya, General St. Pe, Galy Gay.

ADDRESSES: HOME—1912 Dupont Avenue South, Minneapolis, MN 55403.*

*   *   *

BALLARD, Kaye   1926-

PERSONAL: Born Catherine Gloria Balotta, November 20, 1926, in Cleveland, OH; daughter of Vincent and Lena (Nacarato) Balotta.

VOCATION: Actress, singer, comedienne, and writer.

KAYE BALLARD

CAREER: STAGE DEBUT—*Stage Door Canteen,* USO production, Cleveland, OH, 1941. NEW YORK DEBUT—*Three to Make Ready,* revue, Adelphi Theatre, 1946. LONDON DEBUT—*Touch and Go,* revue, Prince of Wales Theatre, 1950. PRINCIPAL STAGE APPEARANCES—RKO vaudeville circuit with Spike Jones, Vaughn Monroe, Stan Kenton, 1943-45; *That's the Ticket,* Shubert Theatre, Philadelphia, 1948; Helen of Troy, *The Golden Apple,* Phoenix Theatre, NY, 1954; Countess, *Reuben, Reuben,* Shubert Theatre, Boston, 1955.

The Ziegfeld Follies, Alexandra Theatre, Toronto, Canada, 1967; Incomparable Rosalie, *Carnival,* Imperial Theatre, NY, 1961; Rose, *Gypsy,* State Fair Music Hall, Dallas, TX, 1962; Ruth, *Wonderful Town,* City Center Theatre, NY, 1963; *The Beast in Me,* Plymouth Theatre, NY, 1963; *The Decline and Fall of the Entire World as Seen Through the Eyes of Cole Porter Revisited,* Square East Theatre, NY, 1965; Molly Goldberg, *Molly,* Alvin Theatre, NY, 1973; Lola Delaney, *Sheba,* First Chicago Center, 1974; *I'll Stake My Life,* Crystal Palace, Dallas, TX, 1975; Ruth, *Pirates of Penzance,* Uris Theatre, NY, 1981; *Hey Ma . . . Kaye Ballard,* Promenade Theatre, NY, 1984; *She Stoops to Conquer,* Roundabout Theatre, NY, 1985; Madame Arcarti, *High Spirits,* Berkshire Theatre Festival, MA, 1985; also has appeared at the Burt Reynolds Theatre in Florida.

MAJOR TOURS—*Annie Get Your Gun; Wonderful Town; Look Ma, I'm Dancing; Out of This World; Top Banana; Minnie's Boys; Gypsy.*

CABARET—The Bowery, Detroit; Mister Kelly's, Chicago, 1972; St. Regis Hotel, NY, 1973; Hyatt Regency, Chicago, 1975; Persian Room, Plaza Hotel, NY, 1975-76; Michael's Pub, NY, 1985.

FILM DEBUT—*The Girl Most Likely,* Universal, 1958. PRINCIPAL FILM APPEARANCES—*A House Is Not a Home,* Embassy, 1964; *The Ritz,* Warner Brothers, 1976; *Freaky Friday,* Buena Vista, 1977; *Falling in Love Again,* 1980.

TELEVISION DEBUT—*The Mel Torme Show,* 1951. PRINCIPAL TELEVISION APPEARANCES—Series: Regular, *Henry Morgan's Great Talent Hunt,* NBC, 1951; Kraft Music Hall player, *The Perry Como Show,* NBC, 1961-63; Kaye Buell, *The Mothers-in-Law,* NBC, 1967-69; Angie Palucci, *The Doris Day Show,* CBS, 1970-71; cast, *The Steve Allen Comedy Hour,* NBC, 1980-81.

Episodic: *The Montefuscos; The Patty Duke Show; Love American Style; The Love Boat; Fantasy Island; Police Story; Alice.*

Guest: *The Jack Paar Show; The Tonight Show, Starring Johnny Carson; Hollywood Squares; The Merv Griffin Show; Dinah; What's My Line; The Muppet Show; Welcome to Las Vegas.*

Specials: *Cinderella,* Rodgers and Hammerstein's original version; *Hello Kaye Ballard.*

WRITINGS: PLAYS—*Hey, Ma . . . Kaye Ballard,* produced at the Promenade Theatre, NY, 1984.

RECORDINGS: ALBUM— *The Golden Apple,* Broadway cast album; *The Ladies Who Wrote the Lyrics.*

MEMBER: Actors' Equity Association, Screen Actors Guild, American Federation of Television and Radio Artists, American Guild of Variety Artists.

AWARDS: The Italian American award; Best Actress, Dallas State Fair Award, for *Gypsy.*

SIDELIGHTS: Kaye Ballard has informed *CTFT* that she began her apprenticeship ushering at a movie theatre in Cleveland, seeing each movie over and over, absorbing the art of acting and sharpening her sense of mimicry. She now maintains an apartment on New York's upper East side and is dedicated to the love and care of animals. She is the proud possessor of three uncut, apricot French poodles named Pockets, Punky, and Shirley.

ADDRESSES: HOME—New York, NY. AGENT—c/o Jerry Hogan, Henderson-Hogan Agency, 405 W. 44th Street, New York, NY 10036.

* * *

BAMMAN, Gerry 1941-

PERSONAL: Born September 18, 1941, in Independence, KS; son of Harry W. (a salesman) and Mary M. (Farrell) Bamman; married Emily Mann (writer and director), August 12, 1981; children: Nicholas. EDUCATION: Xavier University, B.S., Cincinnati, OH; New York University, M.F.A. MILITARY: U.S. Army, 1964-65.

VOCATION: Actor and writer.

CAREER: STAGE DEBUT—Fag, *The Rivals,* Edgecliff Theatre, Cincinnati, OH, 1965; NEW YORK DEBUT—March Hare and White Knight, *Alice in Wonderland,* Virginia Theatre, 1970. PRINCIPAL STAGE APPEARANCES—*As You Like It,* American Repertory Thea-

GERRY BAMMAN

tre, Cambridge, MA, 1980; Thomas, *The Recruiting Officer* and Dr. Relling, *The Wild Duck*, Brooklyn Academy of Music (BAM) Theatre Company, 1981; understudy, *The Good Parts*, Astor Place Theatre, NY, 1982; title role, *Macbeth*, Cincinnati Playhouse, OH, 1982; *Rip Van Winkle or "The Works,"* Yale Repertory Theatre, New Haven, CT, 1982; Buckingham, *Richard III*, Delacorte Theatre, NY, 1983; Jack, *All Night Long*, McGinn/Cazale Theatre, NY, 1984; Norman, *Execution of Justice*, Virginia Theatre, NY, 1986; also performed in *Accidental Death of an Anarchist; Dwarfman.*

FILM DEBUT—*Lightning Over Water*. PRINCIPAL FILM APPEARANCES—Mr. Sloan, *Old Enough*, Midwest Films, 1984.

TELEVISION DEBUT—*Concealed Enemies*, PBS, 1984. PRINCIPAL TELEVISION APPEARANCES—Malouf, *Saigon*, Thames TV (England), 1985.

RELATED CAREER—Co-founder, Manhattan Project; acting teacher, New York University, 1983-85.

WRITINGS: PLAYS—*A Thousand Nights and a Night*, Theatre of the Open Eye, NY, 1978; *Ecco!*, Portland Stage Company, Portland, ME, 1983.

AWARDS: CBS/Dramatists Guild National Award, 1983, for *Ecco!*

ADDRESSES: AGENT—c/o Harris Spylios, Spylios Agency, 250 W. 57th Street, New York, NY 10107.

*   *   *

BANERJEE, Victor

PERSONAL: Born in Calcutta, India; married Maya; children: two daughters. EDUCATION: Taught by Irish Christian Brothers; M.A., comparative literature.

VOCATION: Actor.

CAREER: FILM DEBUT—*The Chess Players*. PRINCIPAL FILM APPEARANCES—In India: *Hullabaloo; Madhurban; Tanaya; Pratidan; Prarthana; Dui Prithri; Kalyug; Arohan.* In Germany, *Jaipur Junction*. Worldwide: Dr. Aziz, *Passage to India*, Columbia, 1985; *The Home and the World*, 1985.

STAGE DEBUT—*Pirates of Penzance*. PRINCIPAL STAGE APPEARANCES—*Desert Song*; Jesus, *Godspell.*

PRINCIPAL STAGE WORK—Director, *An August Requium*, 1981.

AWARDS: Best Actor, National Critics Association Award, for *Pratidan;* Best Actor, National Board of Review, International Star of the Year Award, National Association of Theatre Owners of Texas Award, United Motion Picture Association Award, all 1985, for *Passage to India;* National Debate Champion Award, India.

SIDELIGHTS: RECREATIONS—Tennis, swimming, hockey, and soccer.

CTFT learned from material supplied by his agent that Victor Banerjee debuted in *Pirates of Penzance* at age 5. In 1984, he was instrumental in forming the first Screen Extras Union in India, of which he is presently founding secretary.

ADDRESSES: AGENT—Rogers and Cowan, Inc., 10000 Santa Monica Blvd., Los Angeles, CA 90067.

VICTOR BANERJEE

*   *   *

BANNER, Bob   1921-

PERSONAL: Born August 15, 1921, in Ennis, TX; son of Robert James and Viola (Culbertson) Banner; married Alice Jane Baird, January 14, 1946; children: Baird Allen, Robert James, Charles Moore. EDUCATION: Southern Methodist University, B.A., 1943; Northwestern University, M.A., 1948. MILITARY: U.S. Naval Reserve, 1943-46. RELIGION: Presbyterian.

VOCATION: Producer and director.

CAREER: PRINCIPAL TELEVISION WORK—Series: Director, *Garroway at Large*, NBC, 1949-50; produced and directed all of the following: *Fred Waring Show*, CBS, 1950-53; *Nothing but the Best*, NBC, 1953; *Omnibus*, CBS, 1953-54; *Dave Garroway Show*, NBC, 1953-54; *Dinah Shore Show*, NBC, 1954-57; *Don Ho Show*, 1976; *Solid Gold*, syndicated, 1980—.

Executive producer—*Garry Moore Show*, CBS, 1950-51, 1958-67; *Candid Camera; Jimmy Dean Show*, ABC, 1963-66; *Kraft Summer Music Hall*, 1966; *Carol Burnett Show*, CBS, 1969.

Specials: Executive producer—*Carnegie Hall Salutes Jack Benny*, 1961; *Julie and Carol at Carnegie Hall*, 1962; *Carol and Company*, 1963; *Calamity Jane*, 1964; *Once Upon a Mattress*, 1964; *The Entertainers*, 1965; *Carol x 2*, 1966; *Carol & Company*, 1969; *Ice Follies*, 1969; *Peggy Fleming at Madison Square Garden*, 1967; *John Davidson at Notre Dame*, 1971; *Here's Peggy Fleming*, 1971; *Peggy Fleming at Sun Valley*, 1971; *The American West of John*

Ford, 1971; "Love! Love! Love!," *Hallmark Hall of Fame*, 1972; *To Europe with Love*, 1972.

Specials: Director—*Peggy Fleming Visits the Soviet Union; Perry Como's Lake Tahoe Holiday '75; Perry Como's Christmas in Mexico '75; Perry Como's Hawaiian Holiday '76; Perry Como's Spring in New Orleans '76; Perry Como Las Vegas Style*, 1976; *Perry Como's Christmas in Austria*, 1976; *Almost Anything Goes*, 1976; *All Star Anything Goes*, 1977; *Peggy Fleming and Holiday on Ice at Madison Square Garden*, 1976; *Julie Andrews*, 1978; *One Step into Spring*, 1978; *Leapin' Lizards*, 1978; *Liberace*, 1978; *Perry Como's Easter by the Sea*, 1978.

Movies: Producer—*The Last Survivors; Journey from Darkness; Warning Shot.*

PRINCIPAL FILM WORK—Producer: *My Sweet Charlie*, Universal, 1970; *Mongo's Back in Town*, 1971.

RELATED CAREER—Faculty, Northwestern University, 1948-50; staff director, NBC, Chicago, 1949-50.

MEMBER: Academy of Television Arts and Sciences.

AWARDS: Emmy Award, Best Direction, for *Solid Gold.*

ADDRESSES: OFFICE—Pacific Design Center, 8687 Melrose Avenue, Suite M20, Los Angeles, CA 90069.*

*   *   *

BARDOT, Brigitte   1934-

PERSONAL: Born September 28, 1934, in Paris, France; daughter of Louis and Anne-Marie (Mucel) Bardot; married Roger Vadim (director), 1952 (divorced); married Jacques Charrier (divorced); married Gunther Sachs, 1966 (divorced, 1969). EDUCATION: Paris Conservatory.

VOCATION: Actress.

CAREER: PRINCIPAL FILM APPEARANCES—*Manina: La fille sans voile; Le fils de Caroline cherie; Futures vedettes; Les grandes manoeuvres; La Lumiere d'en face; Cette sacree gamine; La mariee est top belle; En effeuillant la marguerite; Une parisienne; Les bijoutiersdu clair de lune; En cas de malheur; La femme et le pantin; Babette s'en va-t-en guerre; Voulez-vous danser avec moi? La verite; Le mepris; Le repos du guerrier; Une ravissante idiote; Viva Maria; A coeur joie*, 1967; *Shalako*, 1968; *Les femmes*, 1969; *Les novices*, 1970; *Boulevard du rhum*, 1971; *Les petroleuses*, 1971; *Don Juan*, 1973; *L'Histoire tres bonne et tres joyeuse de Colinot trousse-chemise*, 1973.

Helen of Troy, Warner Brothers, 1956; *Doctor at Sea*, Republic, 1956; *Two Weeks in September*, Paramount, 1967; *A Very Private Affair*, Metro-Goldwyn-Mayer, 1962; *Spirits of the Dead*, American International Pictures, 1969. Also: *Please Not Now; The Bride Is Much Too Beautiful; Moonlight Jewelers; And God Created Woman; Love Is My Profession.*

PRINCIPAL STAGE APPEARANCES—*L'invitation au chateau*, Paris.

AWARDS: Legion d'honneur, 1985.

ADDRESSES: AGENT—Olga Horstig-Primuz, 78 Champs Elysee, Paris, France.

BARNES, Clive   1927-

PERSONAL: Born May 13, 1927, in London; son of Arthur Lionel and Freda Marguerite (Garratt) Barnes; married Patricia Amy Evelyn Winckley. EDUCATION: Oxford University, B.A., 1951.

VOCATION: Drama and dance critic.

WRITINGS: PERIODICALS—Music, dance, drama, and film critic, *Daily Express*, London, 1956-65; dance critic, *The Spectator*, London, 1959-65; dance critic, *New York Times*, 1965-78; drama critic, *New York Times*, 1967-77; drama and dance critic, *New York Post*, 1978—.

BOOKS—*Ballet in Britain Since the War*, 1953; *Frederick Ashton and His Ballets*, 1961; (with others) *Ballet Here and Now*, 1961; *Dance Scene USA*, 1967; *Nureyev*, Helene Obolensky Ent., 1982; *Inside American Ballet Theatre*, Da Capo, 1983.

Edited: *Best American Plays: Seventh Series*, Crown, 1975; *Best American Plays: Eighth Series*, Crown, 1983.

RELATED CAREER—Co-editor, *Arabesque*, 1950; assistant editor, *Dance and Dancers*, 1950-58, executive editor, 1961-65, New York editor, 1965—; adjunct associate professor, department of journalism, New York University, 1968—.

MEMBER: Critics Circle (past secretary), New York Drama Critics Circle (president 1973-75, chairman of ballet section).

ADDRESSES: OFFICE—*New York Post*, 210 South Street, New York, NY 10002.*

*   *   *

BARRIE, Barbara   1931-

PERSONAL: Born Barbara Ann Berman, May 23, 1931, in Chicago, IL; daughter of Louis and Frances Rose (Boruszak) Berman; married Jay Malcolm Harnick (an artistic director), July 23, 1964; children: Jane Caroline, Aaron Louis. EDUCATION: University of Texas at Austin, B.F.A., 1953; trained for the stage at Herbert Berghof Studio with Uta Hagen and Walt Whitcover. RELIGION: Jewish.

VOCATION: Actress.

CAREER: NEW YORK DEBUT—*The Wooden Dish*, 1955. PRINCIPAL STAGE APPEARANCES—Elizabeth Proctor, *The Crucible*, NY, 1958; Hermia, *A Midsummer Night's Dream*, Diana, *All's Well That Ends Well*, Anne Page, *The Merry Wives of Windsor*, Player Queen, *Hamlet*, Dorcas, *The Winter's Tale*, all American Shakespeare Festival, Stratford, CT, 1958-59; Bianca, *The Taming of the Shrew*, New York Shakespeare Festival, Delacorte Theatre, NY, 1960; *Conversations in the Dark*, Theatre Guild, NY, 1964; Helena, *All's Well That Ends Well*, New York Shakespeare Festival, Delacorte, NY, 1966; *Happily Never After*, NY, 1966; *Horseman, Pass By*, NY, 1966.

Viola, *Twelfth Night*, New York Shakespeare Festival, Delacorte Theatre, NY, 1969; Sarah, *Company*, NY, 1970; Birdie, *The Little Foxes*, Westwood Playhouse, Los Angeles, CA, 1971; *The Selling of the President*, NY, 1972; *The Prisoner of Second Avenue*, NY,

BARBARA BARRIE

1972; *The Killdeer,* Public Theatre, NY, 1974; *California Suite,* Los Angeles, then NY, 1976; Lotte, *Big and Little,* Phoenix Theatre, then Marymount Playhouse, NY, 1979; Tasha Blumberg, *Isn't It Romantic,* Lucille Lortel Theatre, NY, 1984; *A Backer's Audition* (workshop), Manhattan Theatre Club, NY, 1984.

MAJOR TOURS—Annie Sullivan, *The Miracle Worker,* Theater Guild, European and Middle Eastern cities, 1961.

PRINCIPAL TELEVISION APPEARANCES—Series: Norma Brodnik, *Diana,* NBC, 1973; Elizabeth Miller, *Barney Miller,* ABC, 1975-76; Evelyn Stohler, *Breaking Away,* ABC, 1980; Ellen Hobbs, *Tucker's Witch,* CBS, 1982; Elizabeth Potter, *Reggie,* ABC, 1983; *Double Trouble,* NBC, 1984-85; also, *Love of Life.*

Episodic: *Ben Casey,* ABC; *The Fugitive,* ABC; *Dr. Kildare,* NBC; *The Virginian,* NBC; *Rawhide,* CBS; *Naked City,* ABC; *Route 66,* CBS; *Mr. Novak,* NBC; *Alfred Hitchcock Presents; The Defenders,* CBS; *Ironside,* NBC; *The Invaders,* ABC; *Mary Tyler Moore Show,* CBS; *Lou Grant,* CBS; *Trapper John, M.D.,* CBS.

Movies: *To Be Young, Gifted and Black,* 1972; *79 Park Avenue,* 1977; *Summer of My German Soldier,* 1978; *Roots, Part II,* 1978; *Tell Me My Name,* 1978; *To Race the Wind,* 1979; Mamie Eisenhower, *Backstairs at the White House,* 1979; *Working,* PBS; *Barefoot in the Park,* HBO, 1981; *Two of a Kind,* 1983; *An American Romance,* 1983; *The Execution,* NBC, 1985.

PRINCIPAL FILM APPEARANCES—*Giant,* Warner Brothers, 1956; *The Caretakers,* United Artists, 1963; *One Potato, Two Potato,*

Cinema V, 1964; *The Bell Jar,* Avco Embassy, 1979; Evelyn Stohler, *Breaking Away,* Twentieth Century-Fox, 1979; Mrs. Benjamin, *Private Benjamin,* Warner Brothers, 1980.

MEMBER: Actors' Equity Association, American Federation of Television and Radio Artists, Screen Actors Guild.

AWARDS: Best Actress, Cannes Film Festival Award, 1964, for *One Potato, Two Potato;* Best Supporting Actress in a Musical, Antoinette Perry Award nomination, 1970, for *Company;* Los Angeles Drama Critics Award nomination, 1971, for *The Little Foxes;* Obie Award, Drama Desk Award, 1974, for *The Killdeer;* Best Supporting Actress, Academy Award nomination, 1980, for *Breaking Away.*

ADDRESSES: AGENT—c/o Ed Robbin, William Morris Agency, 1350 Avenue of the Americas, New York, NY 10019.

*   *   *

BART, Lionel   1930-

PERSONAL: Born August 1, 1930, in London, England.

VOCATION: Composer, lyricist, and playwright.

CAREER: FIRST STAGE WORK—Composer and lyricist, *Fings Ain't Wot They Used T' Be,* Theatre Royal, Stratford, 1959, then Garrick Theatre, London, 1960. PRINCIPAL STAGE WORK—Lyricist, *Lock Up Your Daughters!,* 1959, Mermaid Theatre, London, 1969; composer, lyricist, and bookwriter, *Oliver!,* London, 1960, then Imperial Theatre, NY, 1963, revived at Mark Hellinger Theatre, NY, 1983; composer, lyricist, co-director, and co bookwriter, *Blitz,* 1962; composer and lyricist, *Merry Roosters Panto,* 1963; composer and lyricist, *Maggie May,* 1964; composer and lyricist, *Twang!,* 1965; composer and lyricist, *La Strada,* NY, 1969; composer, *The Londoners,* 1972; composer, *Costa Packet,* 1972; musical supervisor, *So You Want to Be in Pictures,* 1973.

PRINCIPAL FILM WORK—Film scores: *Rock Around the World* (also known as *The Tommy Steele Story*), American International, 1957; *Sparrows Can't Sing,* Janus, 1963; *From Russia with Love,* United Artists, 1963; *Man in the Middle,* Twentieth Century-Fox, 1964. Also: *Serious Charge; In the Nick; Heart of a Man; Let's Get Married; Light Up the Sky; The Duke Wore Jeans; Tommy the Toreador.*

RELATED CAREER—President, Lionel Bart, Ltd., 1957-72.

WRITINGS: (In addition to above stage and screen work) PLAYS—(Uncompleted) ''Quasimodo.'' SCREENPLAYS—(Uncompleted) ''Ruggles of Red Gap;'' ''The Josephine Baker Story;'' ''The Man Who Could Work Miracles.'' SONG—''Rock with the Caveman,'' 1955.

AWARDS: Ivor Novello Awards for: *Lock Up Your Daughters!, Oliver!* and *Blitz;* Best Musical, Antoinette Perry Award, and Best Album Sales, Gold Disc Award, both 1963, for *Oliver!;* Ivor Novello Award, Jimmy Kennedy Award, both 1986.

SIDELIGHTS: In 1955, Tommy Steele recorded Lionel Bart's song, ''Rock with the Caveman.'' The song was a sensation, Steele became a teen idol, and Bart continued on to write the score for seven films with Steele as the lead.

ADDRESSES: AGENT—c/o Patricia McNaughton, MLR, 200 Fulham Road, London SW10, England.

*   *   *

BARYSHNIKOV, Mikhail   1948-

PERSONAL: Born January 28, 1948, in Riga, Latvia; became naturalized U.S. citizen, July 3, 1986; son of Nicholai and Alexandra (Kisselov) Baryshnikov; children: Alexandra. EDUCATION: Trained for the dance at Ballet School of Riga and the Kirov Ballet School, Leningrad, Soviet Union.

VOCATION: Dancer, choreographer, and artistic director.

CAREER: PRINCIPAL STAGE APPEARANCES—Principal dancer: Kirov Ballet Company, 1966-74; American Ballet Theatre, 1974-78; New York City Ballet Company, 1978-79.

Guest artist: National Ballet of Canada; Royal Ballet; Hamburg Ballet; Ballet Victoria; Australia Ballet; Stuttgart Ballet; Covent Garden Ballet; Spoleto Festival.

Dancer: *Medea,* Spoleto Festival, 1975; *Awakening,* American Ballet Theatre, NY, 1975; *Push Comes to Shove,* American Ballet Theatre, NY, 1976; *Connotations on Hamlet,* American Ballet Theatre, NY, 1976; *Pas de Duke,* Alvin Ailey Company, NY, 1976; *Other Dances,* Metropolitan Opera House, NY, 1976; *Once More Frank,* American Ballet Theatre, NY, 1976; *Variations on America,* Eliot Feld Company, NY, 1977; *Pique Dame,* Ballets de Marseilles, Paris, 1978; *Four Seasons,* New York City Ballet, 1979; *Eatin' Rain*

MIKHAIL BARYSHNIKOV

in Space, International Dance Festival, Chicago, 1979; *Rhapsody,* Royal Ballet, 1980; *Configurations, The Wild Boy,* both John F. Kennedy Center for the Performing Arts, Washington, DC, 1981; *Follow the Feet,* 1982; *The Little Ballet,* Kennedy Center, 1982; *Sinatra Suite,* Kennedy Center, 1983.

FILM DEBUT—Yuri, *The Turning Point,* Twentieth Century-Fox, 1977. PRINCIPAL FILM APPEARANCES—Narrator, *That's Dancing!,* Metro-Goldwyn-Mayer/United Artists, 1985; *White Nights,* Columbia, 1985.

PRINCIPAL TELEVISION APPEARANCES—*In Performance at Wolf Trap, An Evening with Mikhail Baryshnikov,* PBS, 1976; "Giselle," *Live from Lincoln Center,* PBS, 1977; "Theme and Variations," *Live from Lincoln Center,* PBS, 1978; "Prodigal Son," "The Steadfast Tin Soldier," "Tchaikovsky Pas de Deux," "Other Dances," all *Dance in America, PBS; Baryshnikov at the White House,* PBS, 1979; *The Nutcracker,* CBS, 1977; *Don Quixote,* PBS, 1978; *Baryshnikov on Broadway,* ABC, 1980; *Baryshnikov in Hollywood,* CBS, 1982; also, *Baryshnikov Dances Tharp,* PBS; *Bob Hope on the Road to China,* NBC; *Carmen,* France; *Baryshnikov: The Dancer and the Dance,* PBS.

PRINCIPAL STAGE WORK—Ballet choreographer: *The Nutcracker Suite,* John F. Kennedy Center for the Performing Arts, Washington, DC, 1976; *Don Quixote,* Kennedy Center, DC, 1978; *Cinderella,* Kennedy Center, 1983. Artistic director of the American Ballet Theatre, NY, beginning in 1980.

WRITINGS: NON-FICTION—*Baryshnikov at Work: Mikhail Baryshnikov Discusses His Roles,* Knopf, 1976; *Baryshnikov in Color,* Abrams, 1980.

AWARDS: Gold Medal Award, Varna Competition, Bulgaria, 1966; First Prize Award, International Ballet Competition, Moscow, Soviet Union, 1968; Nijinsky Prize Award, International Ballet Competition, Paris Academy, France, 1968; Best Supporting Actor, Academy Award nomination, 1976, for *The Turning Point; Dance Magazine* Award, 1978; Emmy Award, 1979 for *Baryshnikov at the White House;* honorary degree, Yale University, D.F.A., 1979.

SIDELIGHTS: Dancer Mikhail Baryshnikov, whose presence has created a sensation on the stage, screen, and television, performed with the Soviet Union's Kirov Ballet from 1966 to 1974 and attracted an international following even before his highly publicized defection to the West in 1974. He said that he defected for artistic rather than political reasons, suggesting that he might have remained in Russia "if only the Kirov had permitted me to dance with other companies in the West so that I could have absorbed new styles. If only they had asked foreign choreographers to compose works for us in which the Western contemporary approach to ballet is explored."

Once in the West, Baryshnikov immigrated to the United States joined the American Ballet Theatre (ABT) as a principal dancer and immediately thrilled audiences and critics alike with his ability to perform the "double tour en l'air," a difficult maneuver in which the dancer executes two full revolutions in midair. In 1978 Baryshnikov moved to the New York City Ballet in order to work with the world-renowned choreographer George Balanchine, but in September of 1980 he returned to the ABT as its artistic director.

In addition to his work with the ABT and his numerous stage appearances, Baryshnikov has danced on several television specials. He choreographed and appeared in a 1977 broadcast of *The*

Nutcracker, and later he starred in the special *Baryshnikov on Broadway*, a production featuring excerpts from such musicals as *Fiddler on the Roof*, *Guys and Dolls*, and *Can-Can*. At the time, the dancer noted that he had been a fan of American movie musicals during his youth.

In 1977 the artist brought his dancing to the Hollywood screen. In his first film, *The Turning Point*, released in 1977, Baryshnikov played Yuri, a member of a ballet company modeled after the ABT. *New Yorker* critic, Pauline Kael disliked the film in general but said, "When Baryshnikov is in motion, [the director and cinematographer] certainly know they've captured pure joy up there on the screen." Kael also described Baryshnikov's acting as "lightly understated."

Baryshnikov's dancing was also widely regarded as the best aspect of his second film, 1985's *White Nights*, in which he played an emigre dancer whose plane crashes in Siberia. David Ansen wrote in *Newsweek*, "Mikhail Baryshnikov's first starring role leaves no doubt that he has both the charm and the sexual charisma of a major star."

ADDRESSES: AGENT—Edgar Vincent, 124 E. 40th Street, New York, NY 10016.

*   *   *

BAXTER, Anne   1923-1985

PERSONAL: Born May 7, 1923, in Michigan City, IN; died of a stroke in New York City, December 12, 1985; daughter of Kenneth Stuart and Catherine (Wright) Baxter; married John Hodiak, 1946 (divorced, 1953); married Randolph Galt (divorced, 1967); married David Klee, 1977 (died, 1978); children: (first marriage) Katrina Vonditter; (second marriage) Melissa Galt, Maginel Galt. EDUCATION: Attended Theodora Irvine's School of Theatre, 1934-36; studied acting with Maria Ouspenskaya in New York, 1936-39.

VOCATION: Actress.

CAREER: NEW YORK DEBUT—*Seen But Not Heard*, Henry Miller's Theatre, 1936. LONDON DEBUT—*The Joshua Tree*, 1958. PRINCIPAL STAGE APPEARANCES—*There's Always a Breeze*, on Broadway, 1938; *Madame Capet*, on Broadway, 1938; *Susan and God*, Cape Playhouse, Dennis, MA, 1938; *Spring Meeting*, Cape Playhouse, 1939; *The Square Root of Wonderful*, on Broadway, 1957; *Suite in Two Keys*, on Broadway, 1958; *Light Up the Sky*, on Broadway, 1958; Margo, *Applause*, Palace Theatre, NY, 1971.

MAJOR TOURS—*John Brown's Body*, National tour, 1953.

FILM DEBUT—*Twenty Mule Team*, Metro-Goldwyn-Mayer, 1940. PRINCIPAL FILM APPEARANCES—*The Great Profile*, Twentieth Century-Fox, 1940; *Charley's Aunt*, Twentieth Century-Fox, 1941; *Swamp Water*, 1941; *The Magnificent Ambersons*, RKO, 1942; *The Pied Piper*, 1942; *Crash Dive*, 1943; *Five Graves to Cairo*, 1943; *Guest in the House*, 1944; *A Royal Scandal*, 1944; *The North Star*, 1944; *The Sullivans*, 1944; *The Eye of St. Mark*, 1944; *Sunday Dinner for a Soldier*, 1944; *Smokey*, 1946; *Angel on My Shoulder*, 1946; Sophie, *The Razor's Edge*, 1946; *Blaze of Noon*, 1947; *Homecoming*, Metro-Goldwyn-Mayer, 1948; *The Walls of Jericho*, 1948; *The Luck of the Irish*, 1948; *Yellow Sky*, 1948; *You're My Everything*, 1949.

A Ticket to Tomahawk, 1950; Eve Harrington, *All About Eve*, 1950; *Follow the Sun*, 1951; *The Outcasts of Poker Flat*, 1952; *My Wife's*

Best Friend, 1952; *O. Henry's Full House*, 1952; *I Confess*, Warner Brothers, 1953; *Blue Gardenia*, Warner Brothers, 1953; *Carnival Story*, 1954; *Bedevilled*, Metro-Goldwyn-Mayer, 1955; *One Desire*, Universal, 1955; *The Spoilers*, Universal, 1955; *The Come On*, Allied Artists, 1956; *Nefertiti*, *The Ten Commandments*, Paramount, 1956; *Three Violent People*, Paramount, 1956; *Chase a Crooked Shadow*, Warner Brothers, 1957.

Cimarron, Metro-Goldwyn-Mayer, 1960; *Season of Passion*, United Artists, 1961; *Mix Me a Person*, 1962; *A Walk on the Wild Side*, 1962; *The Family Jewels*, Paramount, 1965; *Tall Women*, Allied Artists, 1967; *The Busy Body*, Paramount, 1967; *Fools Parade*, Columbia, 1971; *The Late Liz*, 1971; *Lapin 360*, 1971; *Jane Austen in Manhattan*, Merchant Ivory, 1980.

PRINCIPAL TELEVISION APPEARANCES—Series: Myra Sherwood, *Marcus Welby, M.D.*, ABC, 1969-70; Victoria Cabot, *Hotel*, ABC, 1983-85.

Episodic: *Playhouse 90*; *CBS-Television Theatre*; *General Electric Theatre*; *The Name of the Game*, 1969.

Movies: *Stranger on the Run*, Universal Television, 1969; *Companions in Nightmare*, Universal Television; *The Challengers*, Universal Television; *The Ritual of Evil*, Universal Television; *The Catcher*, Universal Television; *If Tomorrow Comes*, Universal Television; *Marcus Welby, M.D.*, Universal Television; *Lisa, Bright and Dark*, 1973; *Nero Wolfe*, 1977; *Little Mo*, 1978.

Mini-Series: *The Moneychangers*, 1978; *East of Eden*.

Specials: *Blake: A Marriage of Heaven and Hell;* narrator, *The Architecture of Frank Lloyd Wright*, (documentary); narrator, *The Thrill of Genius* (Italian documentary on Alfred Hitchcock).

WRITINGS: AUTOBIOGRAPHY—*Intermisson: A True Story*, 1976.

AWARDS: Best Supporting Actress, Academy Award and Golden Globe, both 1946, for Sophie, in *The Razor's Edge;* Best Actress nomination, Academy Award, 1950, for Eve Harrington, in *All About Eve;* 1950; Emmy nomination, 1969, *The Name of the Game*.

SIDELIGHTS: Anne Baxter's grandfather was the noted architect Frank Lloyd Wright.

In *All About Eve*, the film for which she is best remembered, Baxter portrayed an aspiring actress who ingratiates herself with, and eventually supplants, an aging star (Bette Davis). Both Davis and Baxter received Academy Award nominations, but because Baxter insisted on being nominated for Best Actress instead of Best Supporting Actress, they split the votes in the former category, allowing Judy Holliday to win. Twenty years later, Baxter appeared on Broadway in *Applause*, the musical version of *All About Eve*, this time as the character Davis had originally played.

Between 1960 and 1963, Baxter abandoned her career to live with her second husband, Randolph Galt, on a ranch in the remote Australian outback. She described the experience in her book, *Intermission: A True Story*.

The December 18, 1985, edition of *Variety* published an obituary and noted, "Although she never gained superstardom, Baxter was a survivor and had the reputation of being a dedicated and reliable worker, living up to her favorite motto: 'See into life—just don't look at it.'"*

BAYLER, Terence   1930-

PERSONAL: Born January 24, 1930, in Wanganui, New Zealand; son of Harold (a stagehand) and Amy (Allomes) Bayler; married Bridget Armstrong, 1958 (divorced, 1978); children: Michael, Lucy. EDUCATION: Attended Wanganui Technical College; graduated from London University, dramatic art; attended the Royal Academy of Dramatic Art, London.

VOCATION: Actor.

CAREER: STAGE DEBUT—Narrator, *Hiawatha,* Royal Albert Hall, London, 1953. PRINCIPAL STAGE APPEARANCES—Dion, *Critic's Choice,* Vaudeville Theatre, London, 1961; Forster, *The Right Honourable Gentleman,* Her Majesty's Theatre, London, 1964; Hopper, *Lady Windermere's Fan,* Phoenix Theatre, London, 1966; Nicholas, *Sign Here Please,* Whitehall Theatre, London, 1967; Giles, *The Mousetrap,* Ambassadors Theatre, London, 1968; Narrator, *The Rocky Horror Show,* Kings Road Theatre, London, 1974; Slater, *Pass the Butler,* Globe Theatre, London, 1982; Willis, *Ratepayer's Iolanthe,* Phoenix Theatre, London, 1984.

FILM DEBUT—Tom, *Broken Barrier,* Pacific Films, 1952. PRINCIPAL FILM APPEARANCES—Macduff, *Macbeth,* Columbia, 1972; Gregory, *Monty Python's Life of Brian,* Warner Brothers, 1979; Rochfort, *Pictures,* Pacific Films, 1981; Lucien, *Time Bandits,* Handmade Films, 1981.

TERENCE BAYLER

TELEVISION DEBUT—Robert *Building of Jalna,* BBC, 1955. PRINCIPAL TELEVISION APPEARANCES-Movies: Leggy Mountbatten, *The Rutles,* NBC; *Peer Gynt; The Snow Queen; The Hunchback of Notre Dame; Murder Not Proven; The Light Princess; This Office Life; Artists and Models.*

ADDRESSES: HOME—Five Graham Road, London SW19 3SW, England. AGENT—Barry Brown Management, 47 West Square, London SE11, England.

*   *   *

BEAN, Orson   1928-

PERSONAL: Born Dallas Frederick Burrows, July 22, 1928, in Burlington, VT; son of George F. and Marian Ainsworth (Pollard) Burrows; married Jacqueline de Sibour (stage name, Rain Winslow), July 2, 1956 (divorced, 1962); married Carolyn Maxwell (a custom-order fashion designer), October 3, 1965; children: (first marriage) one daughter; (second marriage) two sons, one daughter, Michelle. EDUCATION: Attended Cambridge Latin School. MILITARY: U.S. Army, 1946-47.

VOCATION: Actor and comedian.

CAREER: STAGE DEBUT—*The Spider,* Cambridge Summer Theatre, MA, 1945. NEW YORK DEBUT—Edgar Grasthal, *Men of Distinction,* 48th Street Theatre, 1953. PRINCIPAL STAGE APPEARANCES—*Goodbye Again,* 1948; *Josephine,* 1953; Careless, *The School for Scandal,* Theatre de Lys, NY, 1953; *John Murray Anderson's Almanac Review,* Imperial Theatre, NY, 1953; *The Scarecrow,* 1953; *Men of Distinction,* 1953; George MacCauley, *Will Success Spoil Rock Hunter?,* Belasco Theatre, NY, 1955; Ensign Pulver, *Mr. Roberts,* City Center Theatre, NY, 1956; Billy Turk, *Nature's Way,* Coronet Theatre, NY, 1957; Jack Jordan, *Say Darling,* City Center Theatre, NY, 1959.

Charlie Smith, *Subways Are for Sleeping,* St. James Theatre, NY, 1961; Charlie, *Never Too Late,* Playhouse Theatre, NY, 1962; Rather Shenanigan, *Home Movies,* Provincetown Playhouse, NY, 1964; in summer stock played Arthur, *Warm Heart, Cold Feet,* 1964; Tom Considine, *I Was Dancing,* Lyceum Theatre, NY, 1964; Cocky, *The Roar of the Grease Paint, the Smell of the Crowd,* Shubert Theatre, NY, 1965; Homer Thrace, *Ilya Darling,* Mark Hellinger Theatre, NY, 1967; *A Round with Ring Revue,* Theatre de Lys, NY, 1969.

Make Someone Happy, St. Regis Hotel, NY, 1980; John Caroon, *Rockaway,* Vineyard Theatre, NY, 1982; Scrooge, *A Christmas Carol,* Perry Street Theatre, NY, 1982-83; title roles, *The Strange Case of Dr. Jeckyll and Mr. Hyde,* Apple Corps Theatre, NY, 1983; also, *I'm Getting My Act Together and Taking It on the Road; Forty-Deuce.*

MAJOR TOURS—Sonny Dorrance, *Josephine,* U.S. cities, 1953; Chuck Baxter, *Promises, Promises,* Australian cities, 1970-71.

CABARET: Blue Angel nightclub, 1952.

FILM DEBUT—*How to Be Very, Very Popular,* 1955. PRINCIPAL FILM APPEARANCES—*Anatomy of a Murder,* Columbia, 1959; *Lola* (also known as *Twinky*), 1969; *Skateboard,* 1977.

PRINCIPAL TELEVISION APPEARANCES—Series: Regular, *I've Got a Secret,* CBS, 1952; host, *The Blue Angel,* CBS, 1954;

Pantomime Quiz,; Keep Talking, CBS, 1959-60; *To Tell the Truth,* CBS, 1964-67; Reverend Brim, *Mary Hartman, Mary Hartman,* syndicated, 1977-78.

Episodic: "Arsenic and Old Lace," *Best of Broadway,* CBS, 1955; "The Star Wagon," *NET Playhouse,* 1966; *Philco Playhouse; Celebrity Time; Nothing but the Truth; The Arthur Murray Show; The Mel Torme Show; Broadway TV Playhouse; Playhouse 90; Studio One; Kraft Television Theatre; Omnibus; The Play of the Week; Ed Sullivan Show; Steve Allen Show; Jack Parr Show; Laugh Line; Password; Match Game;* also, video adaptations of *Mircle on 34th Street* and *The Man in the Dog Suit.*

Specials: Voice, *The Hobbitt* (cartoon), 1979; host, *New Year's in New York;* host, *The Golden Age of Movie Seriels;* host, *The Bean Show.*

NON-RELATED CAREER—Founder, administrative director, 15th Street School, NY.

WRITINGS: PLAY—(Adaptation)*A Christmas Carol.* BOOKS—*Me and the Orgone,* 1971.

MEMBER: Actors' Equity Association, Screen Actors Guild, American Federation of Television and Radio Artists.

SIDELIGHTS: CTFT learned Orson Bean made his first cabaret appearance as a magician in New York at the Blue Angel in 1952.

ADDRESSES: AGENT—William Morris Agency, 1350 Sixth Avenue, New York, NY 10019.*

*   *   *

BEATTY, Warren   1938-

PERSONAL: Born March 30, 1938, in Richmond, VA; son of Ira O. and Kathlyn (McLean) Beatty. EDUCATION: Northwestern University, 1956; studied acting at the Stella Adler Theatre School, 1957. POLITICS: Democrat.

CAREER: PRINCIPAL FILM APPEARANCES—*Splendor in the Grass,* Warner Brothers, 1961; *The Roman Spring of Mrs. Stone,* Warner Brothers, 1961; *All Fall Down,* Metro-Goldwyn-Mayer, 1962; *Lilith,* Columbia, 1963; *Mickey One,* Columbia, 1965; *Promise Her Anything,* Paramount, 1966; *Kaleidoscope,* Warner Brothers, 1968; *Bonnie and Clyde,* Warner Brothers/Seven Arts, 1967; *The Only Game in Town,* Twentieth Century-Fox, 1970; *McCabe and Mrs. Miller,* 1971; *Dollars,* Columbia, 1971; *The Parallax View,* Paramount, 1974; *The Fortune,* Columbia, 1975; *Shampoo,* Columbia, 1975; *Heaven Can Wait,* Paramount, 1978; *Reds,* Paramount, 1981.

PRINCIPAL FILM WORK—Producer, *Bonnie and Clyde,* Warner Brothers/Seven Arts, 1967; producer, co-screenwriter, *Shampoo,* Columbia, 1975; producer, co-director, co-screenwriter, *Heaven Can Wait,* Paramount, 1978; producer, director, co-writer, *Reds,* Paramount, 1981.

PRINCIPAL TELEVISION APPEARANCES—Milton Armitage, *The Many Loves of Dobie Gillis,* CBS, 1959-60.

NEW YORK STAGE DEBUT—*A Loss of Roses,* 1960. PRINCIPAL STAGE APPEARANCES—*Compulsion,* North Jersey Playhouse.

MEMBER: Screen Actors Guild, Writers Guild of America, Directors Guild of America.

AWARDS: Best Actor, Best Director, Best Screenplay, Best Picture, Academy Award nominations, 1978, all for *Heaven Can Wait;* Best Director, Academy Award, 1981, for *Reds;* Best Actor, Best Screenplay, Best Picture, Academy Award nominations, 1981, all for *Reds.*

SIDELIGHTS: The brother of actress Shirley MacLaine, Warren Beatty, before becoming an actor, worked as a rat-catcher at Washington's National Theatre, sandhog on the Lincoln Tunnel, construction worker and bricklayer's assistant. His first movie, *Splendor in the Grass,* established him as a star, with critics hailing him as the successor to Marlon Brando and James Dean.

When *Bonnie and Clyde,* his first film as a producer, opened to disappointing box-office business, Beatty, in the words of his biographer Suzanne Munshower, "singlehandedly mounted his own campaign to resell his movie and get it rereviewed and noticed." Largely through his efforts, the picture became a major hit, especially with the 1960's "youth generation," and spawned a fad for 1930's clothing. A later Warner Brothers press release called *Bonnie and Clyde* "the entertainment event of its time."

Beatty's next two self-produced films, *Shampoo* and *Heaven Can Wait,* were also highly successful financially. In *Shampoo,* he satirized his own offscreen image as on of Hollywood's most famous playboys, about which he once commented, "If I tried to even keep up with what was said about me . . . I would be, as (Frank) Sinatra once said, speaking to you from a jar in the University of Chicago medical center." *Time* magazine put Beatty on the cover of its July 3, 1978 issue, with the tag "Mister Hollywood."

With *Heaven Can Wait,* Beatty became the first person ever to earn Oscar nominations in four separate categories—Best Picture (as the film's director), Best Actor, Best Director, and Best Screenplay—for a single movie. He repeated the feat in 1982, with *Reds.*

A prominent liberal Democrat, Beatty has been active on behalf of such candidates as Robert Kennedy and George McGovern and such causes as gun control. Colorado Senator Gary Hart credits Beatty with inventing the political concert for the McGovern campaign.

ADDRESSES: OFFICE—JRS Produtions, 5555 Melrose Avenue, Los Angeles, CA 90038. AGENT—William Morris Agency, 151 El Camino Drive, Beverly Hills, CA 90212.*

*   *   *

BECK, Michael

PERSONAL: Born in Chicago, IL. EDUCATION: Millsap College; three years at Central School of Speech and Drama, London.

VOCATION: Actor.

CAREER: FILM DEBUT—*Madman,* 1977. PRINCIPAL FILM APPEARANCES—*The Warriors,* Paramount, 1977; *Xanadu,* Universal, 1980; *Megaforce,* Twentieth Century-Fox, 1982; *The Golden Seal.*

PRINCIPAL TELEVISION APPEARANCES—Mini-Series: *Holocaust; Mayflower: The Pilgrim Adventure; Celebrity.*

Movies: *Alcatraz: The Whole Shocking Story,* 1980; *Blackout,* HBO, 1985; *Clarence Carnes.*

PRINCIPAL STAGE APPEARANCES—Chance Wayne, *Sweet Bird of Youth*, Haymarket Theatre, London, 1985.

MAJOR TOURS—English Repertory Companies, U.K. cities, 1974-76.

SIDELIGHTS: Michael Beck attended Millsap College on a football scholarship.

ADDRESSES: AGENT—McCartt, Oreck, Barrett, 9200 Sunset Blvd., Suite 1009, Los Angeles, CA 90026.*

* * *

BEDELIA, Bonnie 1950-

PERSONAL: Born Bonnie Culkin, March 25, 1950, in New York, NY; daughter of Philip Harley (a journalist) and Marian Ethel (a writer and editor; maiden name, Wagner) Culkin; married Kenneth Luber, April 15, 1969 (divorced, 1980); children: Uri, Jonah. EDUCATION: Professional Children's School, New York; attended Hunter College; studied for the theatre at Herbert Berghof Studios with Uta Hagen and at the Actors Studio with Lee Strasberg.

VOCATION: Actress, singer, and former dancer.

CAREER: STAGE DEBUT—Jackie, *Dr. Praetorius*, North Jersey Playhouse, 1957. NEW YORK DEBUT—Kathy, *Isle of Children*, Cort Theatre, 1962. PRINCIPAL STAGE APPEARANCES—Dancer, *Medea*, New York City Ballet, NY, 1958-60; Wanda, *Enter Laughing*, Henry Miller's Theatre, NY, 1963; Pauline, *The Playroom*, Brooks Atkinson Theatre, NY, 1965; Sarah Mills, *Happily Never After*, Eugene O'Neill Theatre, NY, 1966; Marlene Chambers, *My Sweet Charlie*, Longacre Theatre, NY, 1967; Laura, *The Glass Menagerie*, Nina, *The Seagull*, Helena, *A Midsummer Night's Dream*, all Los Angeles Repertory Theatre, 1967-69.

MAJOR TOURS—National tour, with New York City Opera, 1960-61; summer stock tours.

PRINCIPAL FILM APPEARANCES—*The Gypsy Moths*, Metro-Gold-

BONNIE BEDELIA

wyn-Mayer, 1969; Ruby, *They Shoot Horses, Don't They?* ABC-Palomar, 1969; *Lovers and Other Strangers*, ABC Pictures, 1970; title role, *The Strange Vengeance of Rosalie*, Cinecrest Films, London, 1971; *Between Friends* (Canadian), 1973; *The Big Fix*, Universal, 1976; Shirley Muldowney, *Heart Like a Wheel*, Twentieth Century-Fox, 1983; *Violets Are Blue*, Columbia, 1986; *The Boy Who Could Fly*, Lorimar-Fox, 1986.

TELEVISION DEBUT—Clara, ''The Nutcracker,'' *Playhouse 90*, CBS, 1958. PRINCIPAL TELEVISION APPEARANCES—Series: Anna Larsen, *The New Land*, ABC, 1974.

Episodic: Over one hundred appearances on live television shows between 1958 and 1966 including *U.S. Steel Hour; Armstrong Circle Theatre*, CBS, and *Hallmark Hall of Fame;* also, *The Defenders, Naked City, East-Side/West-Side; Bonanza.*

Movies: *A Message to My Daughter*, 1973; *Hawkins on Murder*, 1973; *A Question of Love*, 1978; *Salems Lot*, 1979; *Fighting Back*, 1980; *Lady from Yesterday*, CBS, 1985; *Alex, The Life of a Child;* others.

RECORDINGS: SONG—''The Best Things in Life Are Free,'' from *They Shoot Horses, Don't They?*, original soundtrack recording, ABC Records.

AWARDS: Theatre World Award, *My Sweet Charlie*, 1967; Golden Globe Award nomination, *Heart Like a Wheel*, 1983; scholarship to study with George Balanchine at the New York City Ballet, 1957-62.

ADDRESSES: OFFICE—Jamner, Pariser and Meschures, 760 N. La Cienega, Blvd., Los Angeles, CA 90069. AGENT—c/o Michael Black, International Creative Management, 8899 Beverly Blvd., Los Angeles, CA 90048.

* * *

BEERY, Noah 1916-

PERSONAL: Born August 10, 1916, in New York, NY; son of Noah (an actor) and Marguerite Beery; married Lisa; children: Maxine, Melissa, Bucklind, and three stepchildren. EDUCATION: Urban and Harvard Military Academy.

VOCATION: Actor.

CAREER: STAGE DEBUT—Child, *The Mark of Zorro*, stock, 1920.

PRINCIPAL FILM APPEARANCES—*Father and Son; Road Back*, 1937; *Only Angels Have Wings*, 1939; *Doolins of Oklahoma*, 1949; *Davy Crockett, Indian Scout*, 1950; *Savage Horde; Rocketship XM*, 1950; *Two Flags West*, 1950; *Last Outpost*, 1951; *Cimarron Kid*, 1951; *Wagons West; Story of Will Rogers*, 1952; *Wings of the Hawk*, 1953; *War Arrow*, 1953; *Tropic Zone*, 1953; *The Yellow Tomahawk*, 1954; *Black Dakotas*, 1954; *White Feather*, Twentieth Century-Fox, 1955; *Jubal*, Columbia, 1956; *Fastest Gun Alive*, Metro-Goldwyn-Mayer, 1956; *Journey to Shiloh*, Universal, 1968; *Heaven with a Gun*, Metro-Goldwyn-Mayer, 1969; *Walking Tall*, Cinerama, 1973; *The Spikes Gang*, United Artists, 1974; *The Best Little Whorehouse in Texas*, Universal, 1982.

PRINCIPAL TELEVISION APPEARANCES—Series: Joey, the Clown, *Circus Boy*, NBC, 1956-57, ABC, 1958; Bill Blake, *Riverboat*, NBC, 1960-61; Buffalo Baker, *Hondo*, ABC, 1967; Barney Weeks,

Doc Elliot, ABC, 1973-74; Joseph "Rocky" Rockford, *Rockford Files*, NBC, 1974-80; Art Henley, *The Quest*, ABC, 1982; Luther Dillard, *Yellow Rose*, NBC, 1983-84.

Mini-Series: *The Bastard*, 1978.

Movies: *Savages*, 1974; *Francis Gary Powers*, 1976; Luther Dillard, *Yellow Rose*.

SIDELIGHTS: CTFT learned Noah Beery toured with his parents in stock companies when he was a child.

ADDRESSES: AGENT—Mishkin Agency, 9255 Sunset Blvd., Los Angeles, CA 90069.*

*   *   *

BEL GEDDES, Barbara   1922-

PERSONAL: Born October 31, 1922, in New York, NY; daughter of Norman and Helen Belle (Sneider) Bel Geddes; married Carl Schreuer, January 24, 1944 (divorced, 1951); married Windsor Lewis, April 15, 1951 (deceased); children: (first marriage) Susan; (second marriage) Betsy. EDUCATION: Attended Buxton Country School, Putney School and Andrebrook.

VOCATION: Actress.

CAREER: STAGE DEBUT—*School for Scandal*, Clinton Playhouse, Clinton, CT, 1940. NEW YORK DEBUT—Dottie Coburn, *Out of the Frying Pan*, Windsor Theatre, 1941. PRINCIPAL STAGE APPEARANCES—Cynthia Brown, *Little Darling*, Biltmore Theatre, NY, 1942; Alice, *Nine Girls*, Longacre Theatre, NY, 1943; Wilhelmina, *Mrs. January and Mr. X*, Belasco Theatre, NY, 1955; Genevra Langdon, *Deep Are the Roots*, Fulton Theatre, NY, 1945; Mordeen, *Burning Bright*, Broadhurst Theatre, NY, 1950; Patty O'Neill, *The Moon Is Blue*, Henry Miller's Theatre, NY, 1951; Rose Pemberton, *The Living Room*, Henry Miller's Theatre, NY, 1954; Maggie, *Cat on a Hot Tin Roof*, Morosco Theatre, NY, 1955; Mary, *The Sleeping Prince*, Coronet Theatre, NY, 1956; Katherine Johnson, *Silent Night*, Morosco Theatre, NY, 1959; Mary, *Mary, Mary*, Helen Hayes Theatre, NY, 1961; Ellen Manville, *Luv*, Booth Theatre, NY, 1966; Jenny, *Everything in the Garden*, Plymouth Theatre, NY, 1967; Katy Cooper, *Finishing Touches*, Plymouth Theatre, NY, then Ahmanson Theatre, Los Angeles, CA, 1973.

Appeared frequently in stock in such productions as *Claudia, Lilian, Born Yesterday, Voice of the Turtle, Wait Until Dark* and *Tobacco Road*.

MAJOR TOURS—Judy, *Junior Miss*, USO, U.S. Army installations, 1942; Katy Cooper, *Finishing Touches*, U.S. cities, 1974; *Ah! Wildnerness*, U.S. cities, 1975.

FILM DEBUT—*The Long Night*, 1947. PRINCIPAL FILM APPEARANCES—*I Remember Mama*, 1948; *Blood on the Moon*, 1948; *Caught*, Metro-Goldwyn-Mayer, 1949; *Panic in the Streets*, 1950; *Fourteen Hours*, 1951; *The Five Pennies*, Columbia, 1959; *Five Branded Women*, Paramount, 1960; *By Love Posessed*, United Artists, 1961; *The Todd Killings* (also known as *A Dangerous Friend*), National General, 1971; *Summertree*, Columbia, 1971.

PRINCIPAL TELEVISION APPEARANCES—Series: Eleanor Southworth (Miss Ellie) Ewing, *Dallas*, CBS, 1978-84, 1985—.

Episodic: "Molly Morgan," *Nash Airflyte Theater*, CBS, 1951.

AWARDS: Best Lead Actress in a Drama Series (for a Continuing or Single Performance in a Regular Series), Emmy, 1979-80, for *Dallas*.

SIDELIGHTS: RECREATIONS—Painting and animals.

CTFT learned Barbara Bel Geddes designs greeting cards for George Caspari, Inc.

ADDRESSES: OFFICE—c/o Dallas, CBS Television, 7800 Beverly Blvd., Los Angeles, CA 90036.*

*   *   *

BELUSHI, Jim   1954-

PERSONAL: Born May 15, 1954; son of Adam (a restaurateur and bartender) and Agnes (a cashier); married; children: Robert. EDUCATION: Attended College of DuPage; graduated, Southern Illinois University.

VOCATION: Actor and writer.

CAREER: PRINCIPAL TELEVISION APPEARANCES—Series: Bert Gunkel, *Who's Watching the Kids*, NBC, 1978; Ernie O'Rourke, *Working Stiffs*, CBS, 1979; *Saturday Night Live*, NBC, 1983-85.

Episodic: *Laverne and Shirley*, ABC; "Pinocchio," *Faerie Tale Theatre*, Showtime.

Movie: *Best Legs in the Eighth Grade*, HBO.

PRINCIPAL FILM APPEARANCES—*Thief*, United Artists, 1981; *Trading Places*, Paramount, 1983; *The Man with One Red Shoe*, Twentieth Century-Fox, 1985; *Salvador*, Hemdale, 1986; Bernie,

JIM BELUSHI

About Last Night . . . (formerly *Sexual Perversity in Chicago*), Tri-Star, 1986; *Number One with a Bullet,* Cannon (upcoming).

PRINCIPAL STAGE APPEARANCES—At College of DuPage, IL: *Under Milkwood, Born Yesterday, Dumbwaiter; Second City Revue,* Chicago, IL, 1977-78; Bernie, *Sexual Perversity in Chicago,* Apollo Theatre, Chicago, IL, 1979; *Baal in the Twenty-First Century,* Goodman Theatre, Chicago, 1980; Pirate King, *Pirates of Penzance,* Uris Theatre, NY, 1982; Lee, *True West,* Cherry Lane Theatre, NY, 1983.

WRITINGS: SCREENPLAY—(Co-author) *Number One with a Bullet.*

MEMBER: Actors' Equity Association, Screen Actors Guild, American Federation of Television and Radio Artists, Writers Guild of America, Professional Stuntman's Association (booster member).

SIDELIGHTS: In material supplied by Jim Belushi's agent, *CTFT* learned that Belushi would like to become a professional wrestler.

ADDRESSES: AGENT—Brillstein Company, 9200 Sunset Blvd., Suite 428, Los Angeles, CA 90069.

* * *

BENEDICT, Paul

PERSONAL: Son of Mitchell M. (a doctor) and Alma M. (a journalist; maiden name, Loring) Benedict. EDUCATION: Boston College High School; Suffolk University, Boston. MILITARY: U.S. Marine Corps (Reserve), 1956-62.

VOCATION: Actor and director.

CAREER: STAGE DEBUT—Chaplain, *The Lady's Not for Burning,* Image Theatre, Boston, 1962, for forty performances. NEW YORK DEBUT—Sailor Shawnee, *Live Like Pigs,* Actor's Playhouse, 1964 for approximately one hundred four performances. PRINCIPAL STAGE APPEARANCES—*Little Murders,* Circle in the Square Theatre, NY, 1969; *The White House Murder Case,* Circle in the Square Theatre, NY, 1970; *Bad Habits,* Astor Place Theatre, NY, 1974; also appeared with Theatre Company of Boston, Trinity Square Repertory Company, Providence, RI, and the American Repertory Theatre, Cambridge, MA; at Arena Stage, Washington, DC, Playhouse in the Park, Cincinnati, OH, and Center Stage, Baltimore, MD.

PRINCIPAL STAGE WORK—Director: *Beyond Therapy* and *Geniuses,* both Los Angeles Public Theatre; *It's Only a Play,* Artists and Directors Theatre, NY; *Crimes of the Heart,* Trinity Square Playhouse, Providence, RI.

FILM DEBUT—Zen Buddhist, *Cold Turkey,* Tandem Productions, 1969. PRINCIPAL FILM APPEARANCES—Ben, *Taking Off,* Universal, 1970; Reverend Lindquist, *Jeremiah Johnson,* Warner Brothers, 1972; Plunkett, *The Front Page,* Universal, 1974; Mark Bodine, *The Goodbye Girl,* 1977.

TELEVISION DEBUT—The mad painter, *Sesame Street,* Children's Television Workshop/National Educational Television, 1969. PRINCIPAL TELEVISION APPEARANCES—Series: Harry Bentley, *The Jeffersons,* CBS, 1974-85; Calvin Klinger, *Mama Malone,* CBS, 1982.

Episodic: *Kojak; Harry-O; Maude;* others.

PAUL BENEDICT

PRINCIPAL TELEVISION WORK—Director, "The Truth Hurts," *The Jeffersons,* CBS, 1985.

ADDRESSES: AGENT—Irv Schechter Company, 9300 Wilshire Blvd., Suite 410, Beverly Hills, CA 90212.

* * *

BENJAMIN, Allan   1949-

PERSONAL: Born Allan Benjamin Goldstein, March 19, 1949, in New York, NY; son of Irwin (a court reporter) and Annette Renee (a medical secretary; maiden name, Farber) Goldstein; married Annette Mayo (an actress) June 7, 1980. EDUCATION: Attended University of Denver; University of Copenhagen, B.A., 1971; studied for the theatre with Jo Bellamo, Jutta Rose, Stella Adler, and Terry Schreiber. RELIGION: Jewish.

VOCATION: Actor.

CAREER: STAGE DEBUT—Man, *Moon,* Changing Scene Theatre, Denver, CO, January, 1972, for eight performances. NEW YORK DEBUT—Minor roles and assistant stage manager, *Battle of Angels,* Circle Repertory Company, 1974, for twenty-one performances. PRINCIPAL STAGE APPEARANCES—*Hay Fever,* Dorset Playhouse, Dorset, VT; waiter, *Scapino,* Buffalo Studio Arena, Buffalo, NY; *Mr. Runaway,* Riverside Church, NY; *Curse of the Zombie* and *A Trinity,* both West End Theatre, NY; David, *Minesa Pudica* and *If Men Played Cards as Women Do,* both at the Terry Schreiber Festival of One-Act plays, NY, January, 1986.

ALLAN BENJAMIN

PRINCIPAL FILM APPEARANCES—*The Justice System.*

PRINCIPAL TELEVISION APPEARANCES—*Johnny Carson Presents Television's Greatest Commercials, Part I,* NBC; also commercials.

MEMBER: Actors' Equity Association, Screen Actors Guild, American Federation of Television and Radio Artists.

AWARDS: Omikron Delta Kappa, 1971, for involvement with theatre in community and schools.

SIDELIGHTS: Allan Benjamin told *CTFT* that he attended Denver Bartending School; he appears occasionally in that capacity. He has been an on-air reader for "In Touch" Network Radio. With the Performing Arts League, he has played shortstop in softball tournaments.

Writing to *CTFT,* Benjamin confessed that at age nine, he wanted to be Jerry Lewis. He spent a year in Denmark when he was twenty. He attended much ballet and opera and realized at that time that theatre was a legitimate profession.

ADDRESSES: HOME—36-16 30th Street, Long Island City, NY 11106.

*   *   *

BENSON, George   1911-1983

PERSONAL: Born January 11, 1911, in Cardiff, South Wales; died June 17, 1983; son of Leslie Bernard Gilpin and Isita Lenora (Waddington) Benson; married Jane Ann Sterndale Bennett (divorced); married Pamela White. EDUCATION: Attended Blundell's School; trained for the stage at the Royal Academy of Dramatic Art. MILITARY: Royal Artillary, 1940-46.

VOCATION: Actor and director.

CAREER: STAGE DEBUT—Roman soldier, *Caesar and Cleopatra,* Malvern Festival, U.K. LONDON DEBUT—Various roles, *Charlot's Masquerade,* Cambridge Theatre, 1930. NEW YORK DEBUT— Desmond Curry, *The Winslow Boy,* Empire Theatre, 1947.

PRINCIPAL STAGE APPEARANCES—Willie, *Wonder Bar,* Savoy Theatre, London, 1930; George Pelham, *Faces,* Comedy Theatre, London, 1932; Ben and Trapland, *Love for Love,* Faculty of Arts Theatre, London, 1932; Sam Gerridge, *Caste,* Embassy Theatre, London, 1932; *Please,* Savoy Theatre, London, 1933; Courtier, *The Golden Toy,* Coliseum Theatre, London, 1934; Snyde, *Mary Read,* His Majesty's Theatre, London, 1934; *Shall We Reverse?,* Comedy Theatre, London, 1935; *Stop—Go!,* Vaudeville Theatre, London, 1935; King Hildebrand, *What a Witch!,* 1935; *The Town Talks,* 1936; Socrates, *No More Peace,* Gate Theatre, London, 1936; Edward Gill, *The Two Bouquets,* Ambassadors' Theatre, London, 1936; Dromio of Ephesus, *The Comedy of Errors,* Open Air Theatre, London, 1937; Vlas Fillipovich, *Distant Point,* Gate Theatre, London, 1937; *Nine Sharp Revue,* Little Theatre, London, 1938; Gus Michaels, *Paradise Lost,* Wyndham's Theatre, London, 1938; Tony Lumpkin, *She Stoops to Conquer,* Old Vic Theatre, London, 1939; *The Little Revue,* Little Theatre, London, 1939.

Diversion, Wyndham's Theatre, London, 1940; *Better Late,* Garrick Theatre, London, 1946; *Between Ourselves Revue,* Playhouse, London, 1946.

For the Old Vic Company in London, 1949-50 season, played: Costard, *Love's Labour's Lost,* Bolshinstov, *A Month in the Country,* Jacques, *The Miser,* Marcellus and first Gravedigger, *Hamlet.*

Poupart, *Music at Midnight,* His Majesty's Theatre, London, 1950; *The Lyric Revue,* Lyric Theatre, Hammersmith, then Globe Theatre, London, 1951; Pasqualino, *The Impresario from Smyrna,* Arts Theatre, London, 1954; Mr. Pooter, *The Diary of a Nobody,* Arts Theatre, London, 1954; Duke of Epping, *Jubilee Girl,* Victoria Palace, London, 1956; Mr. Gilbey, *Fanny's First Play,* Lyceum Theatre, Edinburgh Festival, Scotland, 1956; Sibilot, *Nekrassov,* Lyceum Theatre, Edinburgh Festival, Scotland, then Royal Court Theatre, London, 1957; Magistrate, *Lysistrata,* Royal Court Theatre, London, 1957; Wellington Potts, *Caught Napping,* Piccadilly Theatre, London, 1959; Arthur Groomkirby, *One Way Pendulum,* Royal Court Theatre, London, 1959, then Criterion Theatre, London, 1960.

Dr. Crippen, *Belle, or the Ballad of Dr. Crippen,* Strand Theatre, London, 1961; Mr. Bolt, *August for the People,* Edinburgh Festival, Scotland, then Royal Court Theatre, London, 1961; Boss Mangan, *Heartbreak House,* Oxford Playhouse, U.K., then Wyndham's Theatre, London, 1961; Rupert Tilling, *The Tulip Tree,* Haymarket Theatre, London, 1962; Henry Carter, *The Excursion,* Ashcroft Theatre, Croydon, 1964; Thring, *The Man Who Let It Rain,* Theatre Royal, Stratford, 1964; Earl of Loam, *Our Man Crichton,* Shaftesbury Theatre, London, 1964; Count Bodo, *The Marriage of Mr. Mississippi,* Hampstead Theatre Club, U.K., 1965; Dudley, *A Family and a Fortune,* Yvonne Arnaud Theatre, Guildford, U.K., 1966; Lord Pilco, *The Last of Mrs. Cheyney,* and Simon, Fred, Reginald, *The Adventures of Tom Random,* both at Yvonne Arnaud Theatre, Guildford, U.K., 1967; Steward, Carpenter, January, *Canterbury Tales,* Phoenix Theatre, London, 1968-70.

Justice Shallow, *Henry IV, Part II*, Gonzalo, *The Tempest*, and Inquisitor, *St. Joan*, all at the Mermaid Theatre, London, 1970; Dean Judd, *Dandy Dick*, Birmingham Repertory, U.K., 1972; Reverend Harold Davison, *The Vicar of Soho*, Gardner Centre, Brighton, U.K., 1972; Christopher Glowrey, *Nightmare Abbey*, Arnaud Theatre, Guildford Theatre, U.K., 1972; Squire Trelawney, *Treasure Island*, Mermaid Theatre, London, 1972; Polonius, *Hamlet*, Theatre Royal, Windsor, U.K., 1973.

MAJOR TOURS—Nicholas Hannell and Athene Seylker's Company, Egyptian and Australian cities, 1932-33; *Nine Sharp*, U.K. cities, 1940; Desmond Curry, *The Winslow Boy*, U.S. and Canadian cities, 1948; Launcelot Gobbo, Prince of Arragon, *The Merchant of Venice*, Grumio, *The Taming of the Shrew*, Pompey, *Measure for Measure*, all with the Old Vic Company, Australian cities, 1955; Dudley, *A Family and a Fortune*, U.K. cities, 1966; Waiter, *You Never Can Tell*, Cambridge Theatre Company, U.K. cities, 1973.

PRINCIPAL STAGE WORK—Director: *In Town Again*, Criterion Theatre, London, 1940; *Diversion*, Wyndham's Theatre, London, 1940.

PRINCIPAL FILM APPEARANCES—*Keep Fit*, 1937; *The Man in the White Suite*, 1951; *Doctor in the House*, 1954; *Value for Money*, Rank, 1957; *A Home of Your Own*, 1965.

MEMBER: Society for Theatre Research (chairman, 1968-72).

AWARDS: Keasts Medal Award, Blundell's School, 1927, 1928; Silver Medal Award, Royal Academy of Dramatic Art, 1930.*

* * *

BENTON, Robert   1932-

PERSONAL: Full name Robert Douglass Benton; born September 29, 1932, in Waxahachie, TX; son of Ellery Douglass and Dorothy (Spaulding) Benton; married Sally Rendigs, October 20, 1964; children: John. EDUCATION: University of Texas, B.F.A., 1953. MILITARY: U.S. Army, 1954-56.

VOCATION: Writer and director.

CAREER: PRINCIPAL FILM WORK—Director: *Bad Company*, Paramount, 1972; *The Late Show*, Warner Brothers, 1977; *Kramer vs. Kramer*, Columbia, 1979; *Still of the Night*, Metro-Goldwyn-Mayer/United Artists, 1982.

WRITINGS: SCREENPLAYS—(all with David Newman except as indicated) *Bonnie and Clyde*, Warner Brothers, 1967; *There Was a Crooked Man*, Warner Brothers, 1970; *Bad Company*, Paramount, 1972; (and Buck Henry) *What's Up Doc?*, Warner Brothers, 1972; (sole author) *The Late Show*, Warner Brothers, 1977; (and Mario Puzo and Leslie Newman) *Superman*, Warner Brothers, 1978; *Kramer vs. Kramer*, Columbia, 1979; *Still of the Night*, Metro-Goldwyn-Mayer/United Artists, 1982; *Places in the Heart*, Tri-Star, 1984; also, *Money's Tight*.

PLAYS—Libretto: *It's a Bird . . . It's a Plane . . . It's Superman*. Sketch: *Oh! Calcutta*.

BOOKS—(With Harvey Schmidt) *The In and Out Book*, Viking, 1959; *Little Brother, No More*, Knopf, 1960; (with Schmidt) *The Worry Book*, Viking, 1962; (with David Newman) *Extremism: A Non-Book*, Viking, 1964; *Don't Ever Wish for a Seven Foot Bear*, illustrations by wife, Sally Rendigs, Knopf, 1972.

MAGAZINES—Writer and art director, *Esquire;* author of column with Newman, "Man Talk," *Mademoiselle;* contributor to numerous magazines.

AWARDS: New York Film Critics, National Society of Film Critics, Writers Guild awards for best original screenplay and best drama, and Academy Award nomination for best story and screenplay, all 1967, for *Bonnie and Clyde;* Academy Award nomination for best story and screenplay, 1977, for *The Late Show;* Directors Guild of America, Academy Awards for best screenplay and best director, all 1979, for *Kramer vs. Kramer;* Best Screenplay, New York Film Critics, 1984, *Places in the Heart*.

ADDRESSES: AGENT—c/o Sam Cohn, International Creative Management, 40 W. 57th Street, New York, NY 10019.*

* * *

BERENGER, Tom   1950-

PERSONAL: Born May 31, 1950, in Chicago, IL. EDUCATION: Attended University of Missouri.

VOCATION: Actor.

CAREER: FILM DEBUT—*Beyond the Door*, Film Ventures International, 1975. PRINCIPAL FILM APPEARANCES—*The Sentinel*, Universal, 1977; *Looking for Mr. Goodbar*, Paramount, 1977; *In Praise of Older Women*, Avco Embassy, 1979; *Butch and Sundance: The Early Days*, Twentieth Century-Fox, 1979; *The Dogs of War*, United Artists, 1981; *The Big Chill*, Columbia, 1983; *Eddie and the Cruisers*, Embassy, 1983; *Firstborn*, Paramount, 1984; *Fear City*, Chevy Chase Co., 1984; *Rustler's Rhapsody*, Paramount, 1985.

PRINCIPAL TELEVISION APPEARANCES—Series: *One Life to Live*.

Movies: *Johnny We Hardly Knew Ye*, 1977; *Flesh and Blood*, 1979.

PRINCIPAL STAGE APPEARANCES—Has appeared in Regional and Off-Broadway productions of *The Rose Tatoo; Electra; Streetcar Named Desire; End as a Man*.

ADDRESSES: AGENT—Bill Treusch, 853 Seventh Avenue, New York, NY 10019.*

* * *

BERENSON, Stephen   1953-

PERSONAL: Born March 29, 1953, in New York, NY. EDUCATION: Attended Carnegie Mellon University for two years; Drake University, B.F.A.; studied with Linda Lavin, Lee Breuer, and Teri Ralston.

VOCATION: Actor, director, and teacher.

CAREER: DEBUT—Blifil, *Tom Jones*, Hartman Theatre, Stamford, CT, February, 1976. NEW YORK DEBUT—Pontdue, *High Button Shoes*, St. Clement's Theatre, October, 1977. PRINCIPAL STAGE APPEARANCES—Bunthorne, *Patience*, Minor Latham Playhouse, NY; Androcles, *Androcles and the Lion*, Changing Space, NY; Milty, *Dead End* and First King, *The Butterfingers Angel*, both Quaigh Theatre, NY; Stephen, *Close Enough for Jazz*, Wonderhorse Theatre, NY.

STEPHEN BERENSON

Borachio, *Much Ado About Nothing*, Weathervane Theatre, NH; Bob, *Green Julia*, Harmon Center, Des Moines, IA; title role, *Gimpel the Fool*, O'Neill Theatre Center, CT; Bottom, *A Midsummer Night's Dream* and Bernard, *Death of a Salesman*, both Hartman Theatre, Stamford, CT; Chip, *On the Town*, Lake Placid Theatre Company, Lake Placid, NY; Feste, *Twelfth Night*, Bread Loaf Theatre, Middlebury, VT; Young Scrooge, *A Christmas Carol*, Trinity Rep Company, Providence, RI.

MAJOR TOURS—Ram Dass, *Sara Crewe*, Performing Arts Repertory Theatre, Kennedy Center, Washington, DC, then Brooklyn Academy of Music, Brooklyn, NY, and Town Hall, NY.

FILM APPEARANCES—*Frank's Folly*, film short.

TELEVISION APPEARANCES—*Introduction to Television*, ABC.

SIDELIGHTS: Stephen Berenson has also worked in the industrial theatre market, performing for Pathmark, Mead Paper, Gallow Wine and United Features. He has been seen in commercials. Since January of 1985, he has worked at Trinity Rep Company in Providence, Rhode Island, as an actor, teacher, and director of the summer conservatory as well as holding the post of director of the extension program.

ADDRESSES: HOME—340 E. 86th Street, New York, NY 10028.

*   *   *

BERGEN, Candice   1946-

PERSONAL: Born May 9, 1946, in Beverly Hills, CA; daughter of Edgar (the ventriloquist, comedian, and actor) and Frances (Wester-

man) Bergen; married Louis Malle, September 27, 1980; children: Chloe. EDUCATION: Attended the University of Pennsylvania.

VOCATION: Actress, photographer, and writer.

CAREER: DEBUT—As a guest on her father Edgar Bergen's radio program, 1952.

FILM DEBUT—Lakey, *The Group*, United Artists, 1966. PRINCIPAL FILM APPEARANCES—*The Sand Pebbles*, Twentieth Century-Fox, 1966; *The Day the Fish Came Out*, International Classics, 1967; *Live for Life*, United Artists, 1967; *The Magus*, Twentieth Century-Fox, 1969; *The Adventurers*, Paramount, 1970; *Getting Straight*, Columbia, 1970; *Soldier Blue*, Avco Embassy, 1970; Susan, *Carnal Knowledge*, Avco Embassy, 1971; *The Hunting Party*, United Artists, 1971; *T.R. Baskin*, 1971; *11 Harrowhouse*, Twentieth Century-Fox, 1974; *Bite the Bullet*, Columbia, 1975; *The Wind and the Lion*, United Artists/Metro-Goldwyn-Mayer, 1975; *The Domino Principle*, Avco Embassy, 1977; *The End of the World in Our Usual Bed in a Night Full of Rain*, Warner Brothers, 1978; *Oliver's Story*, Paramount, 1978; *Starting Over*, Paramount, 1979; *Rich and Famous*, 1981; *Gandhi*, Columbia, 1982; *Stick*, Universal, 1985.

PRINCIPAL TELEVISION APPEARANCES—Episodic: Commentator, *Today Show*, NBC, 1975; guest host, *Saturday Night Live*, NBC.

Mini-Series: *Hollywood Wives*, ABC, 1985.

Movies: *Arthur the King*, CBS, 1985; *Murder by Reason of Insanity*, CBS, 1985.

PRINCIPAL STAGE APPEARANCES—Darlene, *Hurlyburly*, Ethel Barrymore Theatre, NY, 1985.

WRITINGS: PLAYS—*The Freezer*, Best Short Plays of 1968. AUTOBIOGRAPHY—*Knock Wood*, Linden Press, 1984, reprinted by G.K. Hall and Ballantine. ARTICLES—Photojournalist, contributing articles to *Life*, *Playboy*, *Esquire*, and others.

AWARDS: Best Supporting Actress nomination, Academy Award, 1979, for *Starting Over*.

SIDELIGHTS: As a child, Candice Bergen was dubbed "Charlie's sister" by the press, a reference to her ventriloquist father Edgar Bergen's famous dummy Charlie McCarthy. And although she got an early start in her career, it was not until years later, when she began modeling while a student at the University of Pennsylvania, that Bergen made a name for herself.

Considered a striking beauty, Bergen became a top fashion model and appeared on the covers of several major magazines. Her good looks and high visability attracted the attention of the film industry, and by the time Bergen left college at the end of her sophomore year, she had already been offered her first film role, as the lesbian Lakey in *The Group*.

In an article in *Life* magazine just after *The Group* was released, critic Pauline Kael remarked that Bergen "is like some mythological creature . . . so inordinately beautiful that at first one is awe-struck just looking at (her)." Kael, however, was unimpressed by Bergen's acting: "She doesn't know how to move, she cannot say her lines so that one sounds different from the one before. As an actress, her only flair is in her nostrils." A similar mixture of admiration for Bergen's looks and disdain for her acting skills marked much of the critical response to her early films. She herself admitted, in her auto-biography *Knock Wood,* that at age twenty-five, "I had still not studied acting, and it showed."

Bergen's performance in director Mike Nichol's 1971 film *Carnal Knowledge,* however, earned critical praise. Kathleen Carroll of the New York *Daily News* called Susan, the Smith coed whom Bergen "plays this campus queen with touching sincerity." In *Knock Wood,* Bergen recalled the making of *Carnal Knowledge* as "a perfect experience."

Of her later films, Bergen said in her autobiography that she was proudest of her performances in two comedies, *Starting Over,* for which she received an Academy Award nomination, and *Rich and Famous.* "I had been afraid that people would laugh at me," she wrote about playing Burt Reynolds' "vain and venal" wife in *Starting Over.* "Instead, I found the joy of making people laugh."

Early in her acting career, Bergen also pursued an interest in photojournalism that began when she did a piece on the making of *The Group,* entitled "What I Did Last Summer," for *Esquire.* She went on to contribute photo articles to such magazines as *Life* (including the cover story on silent film great Charlie Chaplin's return to America) and *Playboy* and, for a brief period beginning in 1975, to display and comment on her photographs on NBC's *Today Show.* For a time she considered herself a photojournalist who acted as a sideline. When she reached her early thirties, however, she gave up professional photography, feeling that "if I wasn't going to make the commitment to master the profession, I had no business taking assignments I didn't deserve."

Reflecting on this and other decisions in her life, Bergen ended her autobiography: "It takes a long time to become a person. Longer than they tell you. Longer than I thought. I am grateful for my past; it has given me the present. I want to do well by the future."

ADDRESSES: AGENT—Creative Artists Agency, 1888 Century Park E., Suite 1400, Los Angeles, CA 90069.*

*   *   *

BERGMAN, Ingmar   1918-

PERSONAL: Born July 14, 1918, in Uppsala, Sweden; married Ingrid Karlebovon Rosen; children: eight. EDUCATION: Attended the University of Stockholm.

VOCATION: Director and writer.

CAREER: PRINCIPAL FILM WORK—Director: *Kris,* 1946; *Night Is My Future,* 1947; *Port of Call,* 1948; *Summer Interlude* (also known as *Illicit Interlude*), 1951; *Three Strange Loves,* 1951; *Summer with Monika,* 1952; *The Naked Light,* 1953; *A Lesson in Love,* 1954; *Smiles of a Summer Night,* Rank, 1955; *The Seventh Seal,* Janus, 1956; *Wild Strawberries,* 1957; *Brink of Life,* 1958; *The Magician,* 1959; *The Virgin Spring,* 1959; *The Devil's Eye,* 1960; *Through a Glass, Darkly,* 1962; *Winter Light,* 1962; *The Silence,* Janus, 1964; *All These Women,* Janus, 1964; *Persona,* Lopert, 1967; *Hour of the Wolf,* Lopert, 1969; *Shame,* Lopert, 1969.

The Passion of Anna, United Artists, 1970; *Cries and Whispers,* New World Pictures, 1973; *Scenes from a Marriage,* Cinema, 1974; *Face to Face,* Paramount, 1976; *The Serpents Egg,* Paramount, 1978; *Autumn Sonata,* New World Pictures, 1979; *Fanny and Alexander,* Embassy, 1983; *After the Rehearsal,* Triumph, 1984.

Also: *Det Regnar Pa Var Karlek; Skepp Till Indialand; Till Gladje; High Tension; Bris* (soap ads); *Secrets of Women; Dreams; Sista Paret Ut; Life of the Marionettes.*

PRINCIPAL STAGE WORK—Director, *Macbeth,* 1940; (also writer) *Death of Punch,* 1940.

PRINCIPAL TELEVISION WORK—Director, *These Blessed Two,* Swedish television, 1985.

RELATED CAREER—Writer, director, Svensk Film Industries, 1942—; chief of production, Civic Malmo, 1956-60; director, Swedish National Theatre.

AWARDS: Best Foreign Film, Academy Award, 1959, for *The Virgin Spring.*

ADDRESSES: OFFICE—c/o Press Relations, New World Pictures, 11600 San Vincente Blvd., Los Angeles, CA 90069.*

*   *   *

BERKSON, Susan

PERSONAL: Daughter of Myron Edward (a psychiatrist) and Muriel (Rosner) Berkson. EDUCATION: Attended Princeton University; Macalester College, St. Paul, MN, B.A.; University of Minnesota, Minneapolis, M.F.A.; studied for the theatre with Elizabeth Parrish, Dick Andros, Margot Moser, and others including the Dudley Riggs Brave New Workshop and an internship with the Minnesota Opera Company.

SUSAN BERKSON

VOCATION: Actress.

CAREER: PRINCIPAL STAGE APPEARANCES—Cheryl, *John*, Playwrights Lab, Minneapolis; Bloody Mary, *South Pacific*, Chimera Theatre, St. Paul; Ruth, *Pirates of Penzance*, Cha Cha, *Grease*, both at Theatre by the Sea, Matunuck; Ghost of Christmas Past, *A Christmas Carol*, Fegan Productions, Dallas; Agnes, *I Do, I Do*, Dunes Summer Theatre, IN; hostess, *That Jones Boy*, ASCAP Workshop, NY; Wendy, *John*, Stageworks, NY; Margaret, *The Other Cinderella*, 78th Street Theatre Lab, NY; Lola, *Crossroads Cafe*, 18th Street Playhouse, NY; Harriet, *Valentine*, New Arts Theatre, NY; Hag Annie, *The Prince and the Pauper*, Lambs Theatre, NY; Sophenia Holmes, *The Winds of Change*, Amas Repertory Theatre, NY; Maggie, *What the Hell, Nell*, workshop production, NY; Edith, *Nymph Errant*, Equity Library Theatre, NY.

PRINCIPAL FILM APPEARANCE—Mental patient, *Committed*.

SIDELIGHTS: Berkson has also appeared in commercials and industrial shows.

ADDRESSES: AGENT—Eleanor Moore, 1610 W. Lake Street, Minneapolis, MN 55408.

*   *   *

BERLE, Milton   1908-

PERSONAL: Born Milton Berlinger, July 12, 1908, in New York, NY; son of Moses and Sarah (Glantz) Berlinger; married Joyce Mathews (divorced); remarried Joyce Mathews (divorced again); married Ruth Gosgrove Rosenthal, December 9, 1953; children: (first marriage) two children; (second marriage) Vicki, Billy. EDUCATION: Professional Children's School.

VOCATION: Comedian and actor.

CAREER: STAGE DEBUT—*Floradora*, Globe Theatre, Atlantic City, NJ, 1920. NEW YORK DEBUT—*Floradora*, Century Theatre, 1920. PRINCIPAL STAGE APPEARANCES—*Earl Carroll Vanities*, NY, 1932; Windy Walker, *Saluta*, Imperial Theatre, NY, 1934; Arthur Lee, *See My Lawyer*, Biltmore Theatre, NY, 1939; Max Silverman, *The Goodbye People*, Ethel Barrymore Theatre, NY, 1968; Noah, *Two by Two*, State Fair Music Hall, Dallas, TX, 1971; *The Milton Berle Show*, Westbury Music Fair, Long Island, NY, 1971; Barney Cashman, *Last of the Red Hot Lovers*, Westbury Music Fair, Long Island, NY, 1971; Ben Chambers, *Norman, Is That You?*, Westchester Country Playhouse, NY, 1973; *The Best of Everybody*, Studebaker Theatre, Chicago, IL, 1975; *The Sunshine Boys*, Arlington Park, IL, 1976.

Appeared in vaudeville for many years with E.F. Wolf, then with Elizabeth Kennedy, finally touring with his own company; also with the Ziegfeld Follies in 1936 and at the Winter Garden, NY, in 1943; extensive appearances in cabaret revues at the Desert Inn, 1964, 1972, Caesar's Palace, 1972, Frontier Hotel, 1974, The Sands Hotel, 1974, all in Las Vegas, NV; and Playboy Plaza, Miami Beach, FL, 1972, Hyatt Regency O'Hare, Chicago, IL, 1975.

MAJOR TOURS—*Life Begins at 8:40*, U.S. cities, 1935; Walter Gribble, *Spring in Brazil*, U.S. cities, 1945; Jerry Biffle, *Top Banana*, U.S. cities, 1963; Barney Cashman, *Last of the Red Hot Lovers*, U.S. cities, 1970; Ben Chambers, *Norman, Is That You?*, U.S. cities, 1975.

PRINCIPAL STAGE WORK—Producer: (with Clifford Hayman) *I'll Take the High Road*, Ritz Theatre, NY, 1943; (with Sammy Lambert and Bernie Foyer) *Seventeen*, Broadhurst Theatre, NY, 1951.

FILM DEBUT—Played children's roles for Biograph films. PRINCIPAL FILM APPEARANCES—*Tall, Dark, and Handsome*, 1941; *Sun Valley Serenade*, 1941; *Over My Dead Body*, 1942; *Margin for Error*, 1943; *Always Leave Them Laughing*, 1949; *Let's Make Love*, Twentieth Century-Fox, 1960; *It's a Mad, Mad, Mad World*, United Artists, 1963; *The Loved One*, Metro-Goldwyn-Mayer, 1965; *The Oscar*, Embassy, 1966; *The Happening*, 1967; *Who's Minding the Mint*, Columbia, 1967; *Where Angels Go, Trouble Follows*, 1968; *Can Hieronymus Merkin Ever Forget Mercy Humppe and Find True Happiness?*, Regional, 1969; *Lepke*, Warner Brothers, 1975; *The Muppet Movie*, Associated Films, 1979; *Broadway Danny Rose*, Orion, 1984.

PRINCIPAL RADIO WORK—*Texaco Star Theatre*, 1948.

PRINCIPAL TELEVISION APPEARANCES—Series: *Texaco Star Theatre*, NBC, 1948-56; *Milton Berle Starring in the Kraft Music Hall*, NBC, 1958-59; *The Milton Berle Show*, ABC, 1966-67.

Episodic: *Max Liebman Presents*, NBC, 1955; *The Music Shop*, NBC, 1959; "Dear Charlie," *The Barbara Stanwyck Show*, NBC, 1961; guest host, *Hollywood Palace*, ABC; *The Big Valley*, ABC; Wise Owl, *F Troop*, ABC; "Celebrity Roast," *Kraft Music Hall*, NBC; *Love, American Style*, ABC; *The Muppet Show*, syndicated; *Make Room for Granddaddy*, ABC, 1971; *Johnny Mann's Stand Up and Cheer*, syndicated; *Don Adams' Screen Test*, syndicated, 1975; guest host, *Saturday Night Live*, NBC.

WRITINGS: BOOKS—*Laughingly Yours*, 1939; *Out of My Trunk*, 1945; *Milton Berle*, 1974. SONG LYRICS—*Sam, You Made the Pants Too Long; I'm So Happy I Could Cry; Leave the Dishes in the Sink, Ma*.

AWARDS: Humanitarian Award, Yiddish Theatrical Alliance, 1951; National Academy of Arts and Sciences Award, Man of the Year, 1959.

SIDELIGHTS: Milton Berle's comedy-variety series *Texaco Star Theatre*, which aired from 1948 to 1956, Tuesday nights at eight o'clock, played a primary role in establishing television as a major entertainment medium. The year it went on the air, critic Jack Gould wrote that "Berle's rapid gags, broad clowning, versatility, and hard work added up to video's first smash hit." Les Brown, in his *Encyclopedia of Television*, asserted that "The program, beginning in a time when TV was a luxury enjoyed chiefly by the wealthier families, helped to spur the sale of television sets to working-class homes."

Because of the phenomenal popularity of the *Texaco Star Theatre*, Berle became known as "Mr. Television." He also gained another nickname, along with family status in thousands of American homes, when one night on the show he told children to heed their parents and go to bed on time: "Now listen to your Uncle Miltie . . ." To this day he remains "Uncle Miltie" in the minds of millions of television viewers.

Berle developed the successful comic technique he used on *Texaco Star Theatre* over a performing career that began at age five, when he won a contest for Charlie Chaplin imitators. He spent much of his childhood working in vaudeville, first as a member of E. W. Wolf's children's acts, then joining with Elizabeth Kennedy to form the team of "Kennedy and Berle," and finally as a solo performer.

In the 1930's, Berle often worked as a master of ceremonies at vaudeville and movie houses. During this period, he also began his radio career, which included stints as a regular comedian on several different shows. It was the success of Berle's 1948 radio version of *Texaco Star Theatre* that convinced Texaco and NBC to let him transfer the show to television.

Since *Texaco Star Theatre* went off the air in 1956, Berle recounted in his 1974 autobiography that he has made guest appearances on nearly every major television comedy or dramatic show. He has also appeared in two more of his own television shows, several movies, in nightclubs, and on stage in touring versions of several plays.*

*   *   *

BERLINER, Ron   1958-

PERSONAL: Born October 13, 1958, in Coral Gables, FL; son of M. J. and Marilyn (Morris) Berliner. EDUCATION: New York University, B.F.A., drama; attended the summer program of the Royal Academy of Dramatic Arts in London, England; studied acting with Stella Adler for four years; studied with Jerzy Grotowski and Harold Clurman at Columbia University.

VOCATION: Actor and writer.

CAREER: STAGE DEBUT—Francis Flute, *A Midsummer Night's Dream*, Miami Beach Shakespeare Festival, 1972. NEW YORK DEBUT—Antonius/Plebian, *Julius Caesar*, Brooklyn Academy of Music, 1978. PRINCIPAL STAGE APPEARANCES—Snobby Price,

RON BERLINER

Major Barbara, Troupe Theatre, NY, 1979; Rodas, *The Royal Hunt of the Sun*, Riverwest Theatre, NY, 1983; Andre, *Pictures at an Exhibition*, No Smoking Playhouse, NY, 1983; The Guide, *Vatzlav*, Quaigh Theatre, NY, 1984; Arnold, *Nighthawks*, South Street Theatre, NY, 1985; Dr. Gold, *Cellmates*, Gene Frankel Theatre, NY, 1985; also, Lelio the Liar, *Peer Gynt*.

MAJOR TOURS—The Fool, *King Lear*, European tour, 1985.

FILM DEBUT—Barnes, *The World According to Garp*, Warner Brothers, 1982. PRINCIPAL FILM APPEARANCES—Roy, *The Manhattan Project*, 1985; Private Nelson, Woody Allen's "Fall project," 1985.

TELEVISION DEBUT—Ted, *Ryan's Hope*, ABC, 1983. PRINCIPAL TELEVISION APPPEARANCES—Episodic: *The Equalizer*, NBC, 1985; *Rockabye*, 1985.

RELATED CAREER—Impressionist, performed in Miami Beach; personal secretary to Joshua Logan, Bertha Klausner and Dr. Maria Ley-Piscator; editor of Maria Ley-Piscator's personal memoirs.

MEMBER: Actors' Equity Association, American Federation of Television and Radio Artists, Screen Actors Guild.

SIDELIGHTS: FAVORITE ROLES—Lelio the Liar in *Peer Gynt* and the Fool in *King Lear*.

ADDRESSES: OFFICE—c/o American Federation of Television and Radio Artists, 1350 Sixth Avenue, New York, NY 10019.

*   *   *

BERNSTEIN, Leonard   1918-

PERSONAL: Born August 25, 1918, in Lawrence, MA; son of Samuel J. and Jennie (Resnick) Bernstein; married Felicia Montealegre Cohn, December 9, 1951 (died June, 1978); children: Jamie, Nina, Alexander. EDUCATION: Boston Latin School; Harvard University, B.A., 1939; studied music at the Curtis Institute of Music; also studied with Walter Piston, Edward Burlingame Hill, Fritz Reiner, A. Tillman Merritt, Helen Coates, Heinrich Gebhard, Isabelle Vengerova, Randall Thompson; studied with Serge Koussevitzky at the Berkshire Music Center. RELIGION: Jewish.

VOCATION: Composer, conductor, pianist, lecturer, and writer.

CAREER: STAGE DEBUT—Conductor, with New York Philharmonic Orchestra, 1943. PRINCIPAL STAGE APPEARANCES—Assistant conductor to Serge Koussevitzky, 1942; conductor, New York Philharmonic Orchestra, 1943-44; conductor, New York City Symphony Orchestra, 1945-48; conductor, *Facsimile,* Ballet Theatre, Broadway Theatre, NY, 1946; conductor, Israel Philharmonic, 1947-57; music advisor, Israel Philharmonic, 1948-49; co-conductor, New York Philharmonic, 1957-1958; musical director, New York Philharmonic, 1958-69.

Conducted all of the following: *Medea*, La Scala, Milan, Italy, December 10, 1953; *La Sonnambula*, La Scala, Milan, March 5, 1955; *La Boheme*, La Scala, Milan; *Falstaff*, Metropolitan Opera, NY, March-April, 1964; *Kaddish Symphony*, Boston and NY, April, 1964; conducted and played a policeman and a reporter, *The Cradle Will Rock*, Philharmonic Hall, NY, April, 1964; *Chichester Psalms*, Philharmonic Hall, NY, May, 1965, then Chichester, Sussex, England, summer, 1965; *Falstaff*, Vienna State Opera,

Vienna, Austria, 1966; *Der Rosenkavalier*, Vienna State Opera, Vienna, 1968; *Fidelio*, Vienna State Opera, Vienna, 1970; *Cavalleria Rusticana*, Metropolitan Opera, NY, 1970; *Carmen*, Metropolitan Opera, NY, 1974; guest conductor with many well-known orchestras.

TELEVISION DEBUT—Conductor and lecturer on a episode on the works of Ludwig von Beethoven, *Omnibus*, CBS, 1952. PRINCIPAL TELEVISION APPEARANCES—Musical director and conductor, *New York Philharmonic Young People's Concerts*, CBS, 1957-1971; *The Unanswered Question*, a series of lectures on music, 1976.

RELATED CAREER: Professor of Music, Brandeis University, 1951-56.

WRITINGS: MUSICAL SCORES, DANCE—*Fancy Free*, 1944; *Facsimile*, 1946; *The Age of Anxiety*, 1949; *The Dybbuk*, 1974.

MUSICAL SCORES, THEATRE—(With Betty Comden and Adolph Green) *On the Town*, Adelphi Theatre, NY, 1944; incidental music and songs, including lyrics, *Peter Pan*, Imperial Theatre, NY, 1950; music and texts, *Trouble in Tahiti*, Festival of Creative Arts, Brandeis University, Waltham, MA, 1952, later Broadway run, 1955; (with Comden and Green) *Wonderful Town*, Alvin Theatre, NY, 1953; (with Richard Wilbur, John LaTouche, Dorothy Parker, Lillian Hellman and additional lyrics by Bernstein) *Candide*, Martin Beck Theatre, NY, 1956, revised version presented at the Brooklyn Academy of Music, later Broadway, 1973-74; *The Lark*, 1955; (with Stephen Sondheim) *West Side Story*, Winter Garden Theatre, NY, 1957; incidental music and songs, *The First-Born*, 1958; (with Stephen Schwartz) *Mass*, Kennedy Center, Washington, DC, 1971, then Metropolitan Opera House, 1972; (with Alan Jay Lerner) *1600 Pennsylvania Avenue*, Mark Hellinger Theatre, NY, 1976; *A Quiet Place*, 1984.

MUSICAL SCORES, FILM—*On the Waterfront*, Columbia, 1954; *West Side Story*, United Artists, 1961.

MUSICAL SCORES, ORCHESTRAL—*Symphony No. 1* ("*Jeremiah*"), 1942; *Symphony No. 2* ("*The Age of Anxiety*"), 1944; *Serenade for Violin Solo, Strings, and Percussion*, 1952; *Symphony No. 3* ("*Kaddish*"), 1964; *Chichester Psalms* (with chorus), 1965.

MUSICAL SCORES, INSTRUMENTAL—*Sonata for Clarinet*, 1941; *Prelude, Fugue, and Riffs for Jazz Combo*, 1950.

BOOKS—*The Joy of Music*, 1959; *Leonard Bernstein's Young People's Concerts*, 1962; *The Infinite Variety of Music*, 1966; *The Unanswered Question*, 1976.

RECORDINGS: As composer, or composer and conductor: *On the Town*, Columbia; *Peter Pan*, Columbia; *Wonderful Town*, Decca; *Candide*, Columbia, (revival) Columbia; *West Side Story* (both stage and film versions), Columbia; *Mass*, Columbia; *Trouble in Tahiti*, Columbia, Heliodor, and others; *Serenade for Violin Solo, Strings and Percussion*, Columbia; *Chichester Psalms*, Columbia; *Dybbuk*, Columbia; *Symphony No. 1*, Columbia; *Symphony No. 2*, Columbia; *Symphony No. 3*, Columbia; the complete symphonies can be found on Columbia; *Prelude, Fugue, and Riffs*, Columbia; *On the Waterfront: Symphonic Suite*, Columbia; *Fancy Free*, Columbia; *Facsimile*, Columbia; *Sonata for Clarinet*, Odyssey; others.

As pianist and accompanist: (With Betty Comden, Adolph Green, Judith Tuvim [Judy Holliday], and others) *The Revuers: The Girl with*

Two Left Feet/Sonja Henie Fan Club, Musicraft, 1940; *A Recital of Mahler Songs with Dietrich Fischer-Dieskau*, Columbia; others.

As conductor: *Marc Blitzstein's "Symphony: The Airborne"* (with the New York City Symphony) Victor (78rpm only); *Carmen*, Metropolitan Opera production, Deutsche Gramaphone; *Der Rosenkavalier*, Columbia; *Beethoven: The Nine Symphonies* (with the New York Philharmonic) Columbia; *Tchaikovsky: Symphonies 1, 2 and 3* (with the New York Philharmonic) Columbia; *Bernstein Conducts Wagner* (with New York Philharmonic) Columbia; *William Tell—Favorite Overtures* (with New York Philharmonic) Columbia; many others.

As lecturer: *What Is Jazz?*, Columbia; *Leonard Bernstein at Harvard—The Norton Lectures 1973*, Columbia; *The Unanswered Question, Vols. 1-6* complete, Columbia; others.

MEMBER: American Society of Composers Authors and Publishers (since 1944); Berkshire Music Center (faculty, since 1948); National Institute of Arts and Letters.

AWARDS: Best Score, Academy Award nomination, 1954, for *On the Waterfront;* New York Theatre Critics Award, 1956, for *Candide;* Einstein Commemorative Award; Newspaper Guild of New York Page One Award and Citation; Peabody Award; Emmy Award, for *Young People's Concerts;* Alice M. Ditson awards; Sonning Prize, Denmark; decorated by the governments of Chile, Finland, France, Austria, and Italy.

SIDELIGHTS: As a teenager, Leonard Bernstein played jazz piano with a high school band. During his college years he composed for college societies and performed with a Works Progress Administration orchestra. Later, he worked for a Tin Pan Alley publishing house under the name Lenny Amber. In 1941, he opened a piano studio of his own in Boston. In 1964, he served as musical consultant for a revival of *The Cradle Will Rock*, at Theatre Four in New York; this production was later recorded.

His *Young People's Concerts* have been televised throughout the United States and have also been seen by children and adults in twenty-nine other countries. At the Berkshire Music Center, Bernstein served as head of the conducting department in 1951. He was the first American to conduct at the La Scala Opera House in Milan working on two new productions for soprano Maria Callas. There have been two biographies of Bernstein as well as two musical revues based on his works, *Leonard Bernstein's Theatre Songs*, 1965; *By Bernstein*, 1975.

With the New York Philharmonic answering to the beat of his baton, Bernstein has released more than one hundred recordings and has played over nine hundred concerts.

ADDRESSES: OFFICE—ASCAP, One Lincoln Plaza, New York, NY 10023.*

*   *   *

BERTINELLI, Valerie 1960-

PERSONAL: Born April 23, 1960, in Wilmington, DE; married Eddie Van Halen (a musician) April 11, 1981. EDUCATION: Studied at the Tami Lynn Academy of Artists, CA.

VOCATION: Actress and producer.

VALERIE BERTINELLI

CAREER: PRINCIPAL TELEVISION APPEARANCES—Series: Barbara Cooper Royer, *One Day at a Time*, CBS, 1975-84.

Episodic: *Apple's Way*, CBS.

Movies: *Young Love, First Love*, 1979; *The Promise of Love*, 1980; *The Princess and the Cabbie*, 1981; *I Was a Mail Order Bride*, 1982; *The Seduction of Gina*, 1984; *Shattered Vows*, NBC, 1984; *Silent Witness*, NBC, 1985; *Rockabye*, CBS, 1986; *Aladdin and His Magic Lamp*, Showtime (upcoming).

Specials: *The Secret of Charles Dickens; The Magic of David Copperfield.*

RELATED CAREER—Owner, Bertinelli, Inc., (a production company to acquire properties for herself).

ADDRESSES: OFFICE—P.O. Box 1409, Beverly Hills, CA 90213. AGENT—c/o Alan Iezman, William Morris Agency, 151 El Camino Drive, Beverly Hills, CA 90212; c/o Heidi Schaeffer, PMK Public Relations, 8436 W. Third Street, Suite 650, Los Angeles, CA 90048.

*   *   *

BIXBY, Bill   1934-

PERSONAL: Born January 22, 1934, in San Francisco, CA; married Brenda Bennett (died); children: one (died). EDUCATION: Attended University of California at Berkeley.

VOCATION: Actor.

CAREER: PRINCIPAL TELEVISION APPEARANCES—Series: Tim O'Hara, *My Favorite Martian*, CBS, 1963-64; Tom Corbett, *The Courtship of Eddie's Father*, ABC, 1969-72; panelist, *Masquerade Party*, syndicated, 1974-75; David Bruce Banner, *The Incredible Hulk*, CBS, 1978-82; Matt Cassidy, *Goodnight, Beantown*, CBS, 1983-84.

Episodic: *Dobie Gillis; Danny Thomas Show; Joey Bishop Show; Andy Griffith Show.*

Movie: *International Airport*, ABC, 1985.

PRINCIPAL FILM APPEARANCES—*Lonely Are the Brave*, Universal, 1962; *Irma La Douce*, United Artists, 1963; *Under the Yum Yum Tree*, Columbia, 1963; *Ride Beyond Vengeance*, Columbia, 1966; also, *This Way Out Please.*

PRINCIPAL STAGE APPEARANCES—*Under the Yum Yum Tree.*

MAJOR TOURS—*The Fantasticks*, U.S. cities.

RELATED CAREER—Has done industrial films for General Motors and Chrysler; spokesman for Radio Shack.*

*   *   *

BLAIR, Linda   1959-

PERSONAL: Born January 22, 1959, in St. Louis, MO; daughter of James Frederick and Elinore Blair.

VOCATION: Actress.

CAREER: PRINCIPAL FILM APPEARANCES—*The Way We Live Now*, United Artists, 1969; *The Sporting Club*, Avco Embassy, 1970; Regan, *The Exorcist*, Warner Brothers, 1973; *Airport '75*, Universal, 1974; *Sweet Hostage*, 1975; *Exorcist Part II: The Heretic*, Warner Brothers, 1977; *Roller-Boogie*, 1979; *Hell Night*, 1981; *Chained Heat*, 1983; *Night Patrol*, New World, 1985; *Savage Streets*, Motion Picture Marketing, 1985.

PRINCIPAL TELEVISION APPEARANCES—Movies: *Born Innocent*, 1974; *Sarah T.—Portrait of a Teenage Alcoholic*, 1974; *Victory at Entebbe*, 1976.

RELATED CAREER—Model and commercials actress.

MEMBER: Screen Actors Guild, American Federation of Television and Radio Artists; American Horse Shows Association.

AWARDS: Golden Globe Award, People's Choice Award, both 1974, for *The Exorcist;* Favorite Actress, three *Bravo Magazine* Awards; Favorite Actress Award, South America, 1977.

ADDRESSES: AGENT—Michael Levine Public Relations, 967 N. La Cienga Blvd., Los Angeles, CA 90069.*

*   *   *

BLAISDELL, Nesbitt   1928-

PERSONAL: Born December 6, 1928, in New York, NY; son of Donald C. (a government-employed diplomat and teacher) and Dorothea (a linguist and hostess; maiden name, Chambers) Blaisdell; married Marlene DeKay, May 26, 1956 (divorced, 1975);

NESBITT BLAISDELL

married Ann Mathews (a stage manager), October 29, 1984; children: (first marriage) Geoffrey, Andrew, Robert, Jenny. EDUCATION: Amherst College, B.A., 1951; Columbia University, M.F.A., 1958; attended the University of Iowa, 1965-68; studied at the Paul Mann Actors Workshop. MILITARY: U.S. Marine Corps., 1951-54.

VOCATION: Actor and teacher.

CAREER: STAGE DEBUT—Abe Lincoln, *Abe Lincoln in Illinois,* New Salem, IL, as part of the Illinois Sesquisentenial celebration, 1968. NEW YORK DEBUT—Count d'Orssini, *Moliere in Spite of Himself,* 1978. PRINCIPAL STAGE APPEARANCES—Dogberry, *Much Ado About Nothing,* Court Theatre, Chicago, IL, 1975; Seth Beckwith, *Mourning Becomes Electra* and Howie Newsom, *Our Town,* both Goodman Theatre, Chicago, 1975; Friar Lawrence, *Romeo and Juliet,* Court Theatre, Chicago, 1976; Bill Skittles, *Sitcom,* St. Nicholas Theatre Company, Chicago, IL, 1976; *Old Man Joseph and His Family,* Chelsea Theatre, NY, 1977; Sergeant Blecher, *Guests of the Nation,* Max Abramson, *Ballroom in St. Patrick's Cathedral,* and one-eyed Musketeer, *Moliere in Spite of Himself* all at the Colonnades Theatre Lab, NY, 1977-81; Sea Captain, *Twelfth Night* and Soothsayer, *Julius Caesar,* American Shakespeare Festival, Stratford, CT, 1979.

Gibbet, *Beaux Strategem,* Hartford Stage Company, 1980; Slim, *Of Mice and Men,* Phildelphia Drama Guild, 1981; Bennie, *Getting Out* and Major Reno, *Custer,* both A Contemporary Theatre, Seattle, WA, 1981; D.J. Thomas, *A Child's Christmas in Wales,* Great Lakes Shakespeare Festival, Cleveland, OH, 1982; Major Brigg, *Savages,* Center Stage, Baltimore, MD, 1982; Peter Stockmann, *An Enemy of the People,* Alaska Repertory Theatre, 1982;

psychiatrist, *Invitation from the Asylum,* Citadel Theatre, Edmonton, Alberta, Canada, 1983; Peter Shirley, *Major Barbara,* Alaska Repertory Theatre, 1983; Abner Spragg, *Custom of the Country,* Shakespeare & Co., Lennox, MA, 1984; Big Daddy, *Cat on a Hot Tin Roof,* Certre Stage, Toronto, Canada, 1984; Reverend Charlie Bowers, *Ballad of Soapy Smith,* New York Shakespeare Festival, Public Theatre, 1984; Abner Spragg, *Custom of the Country,* Second Stage Theatre, NY, 1985; Duncan, *Macbeth* and Inspector Thomas, *The Unexpected Guest,* both American Stage Festival, Milford, NH, 1985; Candy, *Of Mice and Men,* Actors Theatre of Louisville, 1985; Old Man, *Fool for Love,* Citadel Theatre, 1986; Huck Finn, *Boys in Autumn,* Indiana Repertory Theatre, 1986.

FILM DEBUT—Sheriff Nighblick, *Eddie Macon's Run,* Universal, 1982.

TELEVISION DEBUT—Lyndon Johnson, *Kennedy,* NBC, 1983. PRINCIPAL TELEVISION APPEARANCES—Sergeant Belcher, "Guests of the Nation," *Great Performances,* PBS, 1981.

RELATED CAREER—Taught academic courses at the college level, 1960-75; associate professor of theatre, University of Wisconsin, Green Bay, 1970-75.

MEMBER: Actors' Equity Association, American Federation of Television and Radio Artists, Screen Actors Guild, Canadian Actors' Equity Association; Sierra Club.

ADDRESSES: HOME—71 Second Avenue, New York, NY 10003. AGENT—Writers & Artists, 162 W. 56th Street, New York, NY 10019.

*   *   *

BLAKE, Robert   1933-

PERSONAL: Born September 18, 1933, in Nutley, NJ; married Sondra Kerry (an actress).

VOCATION: Actor.

CAREER: PRINCIPAL TELEVISION APPEARANCES—Series: Detective Tony Baretta, *Baretta,* ABC, 1975-78; Father Noah "Hardstep" Rivers, *Hell Town,* NBC, 1985.

Movie: Joe Dancer, *Big Black Pill,* NBC, 1981; Jimmy Hoffa, *Blood Feud,* syndicated, 1983.

PRINCIPAL FILM APPEARANCES—As a child actor in the "Our Gang" series; title role, *Mokey,* Metro-Goldwyn-Mayer, 1942; *Andy Hardy's Double Life,* Metro-Goldwyn-Mayer, 1942; *Lost Angel,* Metro-Goldwyn-Mayer, 1943; *Town without Pity,* United Artists, 1961; *PT-109,* Warner Brothers, 1963; *The Greatest Story Ever Told,* United Artists, 1965; *This Property Is Condemned,* Paramount, 1966; *In Cold Blood,* Columbia, 1968; *Tell Them Willie Boy Is Here,* Universal, 1970; *Electra-Glide in Blue,* United Artists, 1973; *Busting,* United Artists, 1974; *Coast to Coast,* Paramount, 1980; *Second Hand Hearts,* Paramount, 1981; also, *The Connection; Corky.*

STAGE DEBUT—*Hatful of Rain,* Gallery Theater.

RELATED CAREER—Stuntman, *Rumble on the Docks; The Tijuana Story.**

LINDSAY BLOOM

BLOOM, Lindsay   1955-

PERSONAL: Born 1955, in Omaha, NE; married Mayf Nutter (an actor). EDUCATION: Attended the University of Utah; studied acting with Charles Conrad and Sandford Meisner in Los Angeles.

VOCATION: Actress.

CAREER: PRINCIPAL TELEVISION APPEARANCES—Series: One of the "Ding-a-Ling Sisters," *The Dean Martin Show*, NBC, 1972; Maybelle Tillingham, *The Dukes of Hazzard*, CBS; Rocket, *Vega$*, ABC; Bonnie Robertson, *Dallas*, CBS, 1982; Velda, *Mickey Spillane's Mike Hammer*, CBS, 1984-85, 1986—.

Mini-Series: Pam Singleton, *The Lone Star Bar*, Showtime.

Episodic: *The New Love American Style*, ABC; *Hollywood Beat*, ABC; *Police Story*, NBC; *Trapper John, M.D.*, CBS; *Switch*, CBS; *Emergency*, NBC; *The Love Boat*, ABC; *Rhoda*, CBS; *Sanford and Son*, NBC; *The Dick Van Dyke Show*, CBS; *Laverne and Shirley*, ABC.

Movies: Elaine Gardner, *A Bridge Across Time*, NBC, 1985; Velda, *The Return of Mike Hammer*, CBS, 1986.

Specials: *Circus of the Stars*, CBS.

PRINCIPAL FILM APPEARANCES—*Six Pack Annie*, 1975; *H.O.T.S.*, 1979; Jean Harlow, *Hughes and Harlow, Angels in Hell; Cycling Through China*, World Pacific Pictures.

AWARDS: Miss Arizona, Miss U.S.A., 1972.

ADDRESSES: AGENT—Sumski, Green, and Company, 8380 Melrose Avenue, Suite 200, Los Angeles, CA 90069.

*   *   *

BLUMENFELD, Robert   1943-

PERSONAL: Born February 26, 1943, in New York, NY; son of Max David (a chemist and bacteriologist) and Ruth (Korn) Blumenfeld. EDUCATION: Rutgers University, B.A., French, 1964; Columbia University, M.A., French, 1967; studied acting with Alice Spivak and Uta Hagen at the Herbert Berghof Studio in New York.

VOCATION: Actor.

CAREER: STAGE DEBUT—*The American Savoyards*, Jan Hus Playhouse, NY, 1965. PRINCIPAL STAGE APPEARANCES—Malvolio, *Twelfth Night* and Lepidus, *Antony and Cleopatra*, both with the American Shakespeare Theatre, Stratford CT, 1970-72; Van Helsing, *Dracula*, Equity Library Theatre, NY, 1978; Lieber, *Portage to San Cristobal*, Jonas and Dolan, *The Great Magoo*, and Kulygin, *The Three Sisters*, all Hartford Stage Company; Feydak, *Biography*, Sexton, *The Tenth Man*, and Sam Lewis, *Gossip*, all PAF Playhouse, Long Island, NY; Furtado, *King of Schnorrers*, George Street Playhouse, New Brunswick, NJ; Telyeghin, *Uncle Vanya*, A.C.T., Aldelphi Universtity; Kammerling, *Going Hollywood*, Broadway Workshop; Venetian Senator, *Othello*, American National Theatre and Academy (ANTA), NY; Felix, *House Music*, American Jewish Theatre, NY; Herb, *Free Ride*, Wonderhorse Theatre, NY; The Pope and Coach, *Nature and Purpose of the Universe*, Direct Theatre, NY; Osher, *The Dybbuk*, New York Shakespeare Festival; Furtado, *Tatterdemalion*, Douglas Fairbanks Theatre, NY; Barry, *Boys & Girls, Men & Women*, American Place

ROBERT BLUMENFELD

Theatre, NY; Norman, *The Dresser*, A Contemporary Theatre, Seattle, WA, 1983; first voice, *Under Milkwood*, McCarter Theatre, Princeton, NJ, 1985.

FILM DEBUT—Patrick, *One Woman or Two*, Orion, 1985.

TELEVISION DEBUT—*Sesame Street*, PBS, 1977. PRINCIPAL TELEVISION APPEARANCES—*Festival of Hands*, WGBH, PBS; *Nova*, WGBH, PBS; Wilhite, *The Equalizer*, CBS, 1985.

MEMBER: Actors' Equity Association, Screen Actors Guild, American Federation of Television and Radio Artists, Dramatists Guild.

AWARDS: American Shakespeare Festival's William Hart Benton Award, 1971, for Malvolio, *Twelfth Night*.

SIDELIGHTS: About his career, Robert Blumenfeld tells *CTFT*, "I love acting and felt I could contribute to people's understanding of life and relationships through my art." He speaks French, Italian, and German fluently and has travelled extensively.

ADDRESSES: HOME—321 W. 105th Street, New York, NY 10025. AGENT—Abrams Artists and Associates, 420 Madison Avenue, New York, NY 10019.

*   *   *

BOGARD, Travis   1918-

PERSONAL: Born January 25, 1918; son of Verner E. and Gertrude T. Bogard; married Jane Malmgren, June 21, 1947; children: John G., Sara Snow. EDUCATION: University of California, Berkeley, A.B., 1939, M.A., 1940; Princeton University, Ph.D., 1947. MILITARY: Army Service Force, 1941-44.

VOCATION: Writer.

CAREER: RELATED CAREER—Professor, Dramatic Art, University of California, Berkeley, CA, 1947-present.

WRITINGS: BOOKS—*The Tragic Satire of John Webster*, University of California Press, 1955; *The Theatre We Worked For: The Correspondence of Eugene O'Neill and Kenneth Macgowan*, Yale University Press, 1982; *Contour in Time: The Plays of Eugene O'Neill*, Oxford University Press, 1977.

AWARDS: Guggenheim Fellowship, 1958; Silver Medal Award, Commonwealth Club of California, 1977; Gold Medal Award, Theatre Committee for Eugene O'Neill, 1984.

ADDRESSES: OFFICE—Department of Dramatic Art, University of California, Berkeley, CA 94720.

*   *   *

BOHAY, Heidi

PERSONAL: Born in Bound Brook, NJ.

VOCATION: Actress.

CAREER: PRINCIPAL TELEVISION APPEARANCES—Series: Megan Kendal, *Hotel*, ABC, 1983—.

HEIDI BOHAY

Episodic: *Finder of Lost Loves; Happy Days; Quincy; CHiPs; The Devlin Connection; Buck Rogers; Here's Boomer; Teachers Only*.

Movies: *The Grace Kelly Story; Thursday's Child*, 1983.

PRINCIPAL FILM APPEARANCES—*Superstition; Those Golden Years*.

MEMBER: American Federation of Television and Radio Artists; National March of Dimes Association.

ADDRESSES: HOME—Los Angeles, CA. AGENT—Michael Levine Public Relations, 9123 Sunset Blvd., Los Angeles, CA 90069.

*   *   *

BOLGER, Ray   1904-

PERSONAL: Born January 10, 1904, in Dorchester, MA; son of James Edward and Anne (Wallace) Bolger; married Gwendolyn Rickard. EDUCATION: Dorchester High School.

VOCATION: Actor and dancer.

CAREER: STAGE DEBUT—With the Bob Ott Musical Comedy Repertory Company, Boston, 1922. NEW YORK DEBUT—*The Merry World*, Imperial Theatre, June 8, 1926. PRINCIPAL STAGE APPEARANCES—*A Night in Paris*, Casino de Paris, NY, 1926; *Ritz-Carlton Nights*, Palace Theatre, NY, 1926; Georgie, *Heads Up*, Alvin Theatre, NY, 1929; *George White's Scandals*, Apollo

RAY BOLGER

Theatre, NY, 1931; *Life Begins at 8:40,* Winter Garden Theatre, NY, 1934; Phil Dolan III, *On Your Toes,* Imperial Theatre, NY, 1936; *Keep Off the Grass,* Broadhurst Theatre, NY, 1940; Sapiens, *By Jupiter,* Shubert Theatre, NY, 1942; *Three to Make Ready,* Adelphi Theatre, NY, 1946; Charlie Wykeham, *Where's Charley?* St. James Theatre, NY, 1948-51; Professor Fodorski, *All American,* Winter Garden Theatre, NY, 1962; Phineas Sharp, *Come Summer,* Lunt-Fontanne Theatre, NY, 1969.

MAJOR TOURS—Vaudeville tour, 1924-26; *The Passing Show of 1926,* 1926; *Ritz-Carlton Nights,* 1927-28; USO Camp shows, 1943-45; *Where's Charley?,* national, 1951; *The Ray Bolger Show,* summer, 1965.

CONCERT AND CLUB APPEARANCES—Empire Room, Waldorf-Astoria, NY, February 1967; cabaret appearance, March, 1968; Von Wenzell Hall, Sarasota, FL, January, 1980.

FILM APPEARANCES—As himself, *The Great Ziegfeld,* Metro-Goldwyn-Mayer, 1936; Bill Delroy, *Rosalie,* Metro-Goldwyn-Mayer, 1937; Happy Moore, *The Girl of the Golden West* (cut from release print), Metro-Goldwyn-Mayer, 1938; Hans, the Dancer, *Sweethearts,* Metro-Goldwyn-Mayer, 1938; Hunk (Scarecrow), *The Wizard of Oz,* Metro-Goldwyn-Mayer, 1939; *Sunny,* Metro-Goldwyn-Mayer, 1941; *The Harvey Girls,* Metro-Goldwyn-Mayer, 1946; *Look for the Silver Lining,* Warner Brothers, 1949; Charley Wykeham, *Where's Charley?,* Warner Brothers, 1952; *April in Paris,* Warner Brothers, 1953; Toymaker, *Babes in Toyland,* Buena Vista, 1961; *The Daydreamer,* Embassy, 1966; *The Runner Stumbles,* Twentieth Century-Fox, 1979.

TELEVISION APPEARANCES—Series: Raymond Wallace, *The Ray Bolger Show* (original title: *Where's Raymond*), ABC, 1953-55.

Guest: *The Colgate Comedy Hour,* CBS, 1950-51; *The Bell Telephone Hour,* NBC, 1960; *The Judy Garland Show,* CBS, 1963.

Episodic: *The Partridge Family; The Love Boat.*

Specials: *Washington Square; The Entertainer,* 1976.

Mini-Series: *Captains and Kings.*

RECORDINGS: ALBUMS—*The Wizard of Oz,* film soundtrack, Metro-Goldwyn-Mayer; "Once in Love with Amy," from *Where's Charley?; All American,* original cast album, Columbia Special Products.

AWARDS: Newpaper Guild Page One Award, 1943; Best Musical Comedy Performance, Drama Critics Poll, 1946, for *Three to Make Ready;* Antoinette Perry Award and Donaldson Award, both 1949, for *Where's Charley?;* Decency in Entertainment, Notre Dame Club, Chicago, 1967; Medallion of Valor, Israel, 1970; Theatrical Hall of Fame, 1980.

SIDELIGHTS: Prior to breaking into the ranks of professional theatre, Bolger worked on the amateur boards in New England. Best known for his "rubbery" style of dancing, which was exemplified by his "elastic" performance as the scarecrow in the Metro-Goldwyn-Mayer spectacular, *The Wizard of Oz,* his career has been an active one, encompassing all the aspects of popular entertainment.

ADDRESSES: HOME—618 N. Beverly Drive, Beverly Hills, CA 90210.

*   *   *

BOLOGNA, Joseph   1938-

PERSONAL: Born 1938, in Brooklyn, NY; married Renee Taylor (an actress, comedian, and writer), 1965. EDUCATION: Attended Brown University. MILITARY: U.S. Marine Corps.

VOCATION: Actor and writer.

CAREER: PRINCIPAL FILM APPEARANCES—*Lovers and Other Strangers,* Cinerama, 1970; *Made for Each Other,* Twentieth Century-Fox, 1971; *Cops and Robbers,* United Artists, 1973; *Mixed Company,* United Artists, 1974; *The Big Bus,* Paramount, 1976; *Chapter Two,* Columbia, 1979; *My Favorite Year,* Metro-Goldwyn-Mayer, 1982; *Blame It on Rio,* Twentieth Century-Fox, 1984; *The Woman in Red,* Orion, 1984; *Transylvania 6-5000,* New World Pictures, 1985.

PRINCIPAL TELEVISION APPEARANCES—Episodic: *Calucci's Department,* CBS, 1973.

Specials: *Acts of Love and Other Comedies,* ABC, 1973; *Paradise,* 1979.

Movies: *Honor Thy Father,* 1973; *Torn Between Two Lovers,* 1979.

PRINCIPAL STAGE APPEARANCES—*Lovers and Other Strangers,* Brooks Atkinson Theatre, NY, 1968; *It Had to Be You,* 1985.

WRITINGS: PLAYS—(with Renee Taylor) *Lovers and Other Strangers* (four one-acts), Brooks Atkinson Theatre, NY, 1968, published by Samuel French, 1968.

SCREENPLAYS—(Both with Renee Taylor) *Lovers and Other Strangers,* Cinerama, 1970; *Made for Each Other,* Twentieth Century-Fox, 1971.

TELEVISION—Series: (Contributor) *Calucci's Department,* CBS, 1973; *The Great American Dream Machine,* PBS.

Specials: *Benny*, PBS, 1971; *Acts of Love and Other Comedies*, ABC, 1973.

AWARDS: Outstanding Writing Achievement in Comedy, Variety, or Music Special, Emmy Award, 1972-73, for *Acts of Love and Other Comedies*.

ADDRESSES: AGENT—c/o Jim Costa, The Artists Agency, 10,000 Santa Monica Blvd., Suite 305, Los Angeles, CA 90067.*

*   *   *

BOLT, Jonathan   1935-

PERSONAL: Born September 22, 1935, in Statesville, NC; son of John Abner (a textile worker) and Lila Mae (a dietician; maiden name, Smith) Bolt; married Gigi Gibson (divorced, 1983); children: Julie Elizabeth. EDUCATION: Attended Elon College, Elon, NC, 1952-53; attended Richmond Professional Institute of the College of William and Mary, 1955-57, art major; studied for the theatre with Mary Welch and Sanford Meisner.

VOCATION: Actor, director, and playwright.

CAREER: STAGE DEBUT—As a scenic designer, Myrtle Beach Playhouse, SC, 1956. NEW YORK DEBUT—Eugene Gant, *Look Homeward, Angel*, Ethel Barrymore Theatre, 1958. PRINCIPAL STAGE APPEARANCES—Resident with Myrtle Beach Playhouse, SC, 1956; resident actor, Hyde Park Playhouse, Hyde Park, NY, 1957; Biff, *Death of a Salesman*, Moorestown Summer Theatre, 1965; *Don't Drink the Water*, Morosco Theatre, NY, 1966; *Love in E Flat*, Brooks Atkinson Theatre, NY, 1967.

As resident with Cleveland Playhouse, Cleveland, OH: Atahualpa, *Royal Hunt of the Sun*, Vladimir, *Waiting for Godot*, Gentleman Caller, *The Glass Menagerie*, Mortimer Brewster, *Arsenic and Old Lace*, Mitch, *Luv*, Andrew, *In Celebration*, the man, *Woman in the Dunes*, Anderson, *The Devil's Disciple*, Mangiacavallo, *The Rose Tattoo*, McCann, *The Birthday Party*, John Buchannan, *Summer and Smoke*, Horner, *The Country Wife*, Aston, *The Caretakers*, Hamm, *Endgame*, Jay, *All the Way Home*, Pantalone, *The Liar*, Starbuck, *Moby Dick Rehearsed*, Etienne, *A Flea in Her Ear*, David Greenglass, *The United States versus Julius and Ethel Rosenberg*, all between 1967-73.

Oedipus Rex, Oedipus at Colonus, Antigone, Woyzeck, Gille de Rais, Leonce and Lena, all for the Classic Stage Company, NY, 1980-81; *The Great Great Grandson of Jedediah Kohler, Richard II, Black Angel*, and with the Dramatists Guild Young Playwrights Festival, all at Circle Repertory Company, NY; *The Rimers of Eldritch*, La Mama Experimental Theatre Club, NY; Sir Toby Belch, *Twelfth Night*, Maryland Shakespeare Festival; *Out of Order, Family Album, The Only Woman Awake, Simon of Cyrene*, all as guest artist with Theatre in the Works, University of MA; *Passion*, Longacre Theatre, NY, 1983; Edward Muybridge, *The Photographer*, Brooklyn Academy of Music, NY, 1983; *What the Butler Saw*, Theatre by the Sea, Portsmouth, NH, 1985; *Foxfire*, Guthrie, Minneapolis, MN, 1985; Robert Oppenheimer, *No Mercy*, Actors Theatre of Louisville, 1986.

MAJOR TOURS—Eugene Gant, *Look Homeward, Angel*, national, 1959-60; Phil Romano, *That Championship Season*, national, 1973-74; Edward Muybridge, *The Photographer*, spring tour, 1984; *Foxfire*, 1985.

PRINCIPAL STAGE WORK—Director: *The Midnight Caller*, The Dancers, both at Pico Playhouse, Los Angeles, CA, 1965; *The Kilgo Run*, Los Angeles, 1965; *Bus Stop* and *Sunday in New York*, both dinner theatre tour, 1966.

At the Cleveland Playhouse, OH: *Mornings at Seven*, 1968, *The Effect of Gamma Rays on Man-in-the-Moon Marigolds*, 1969, *Gallows Humor*, 1970, *Except for Susie Finkle*, 1970, *The Promise*, 1971, *The Price*, 1972, *Forty Carats*, 1972, *The Showoff*, 1972, *Johnny No-Trump*, 1972, *Light Up the Sky*, 1974, *The Owl and the Pussycat*, 1974, *No Hard Feelings*, 1974, *A Shot in the Dark*, 1974, *Generation*, 1974, *Poor Richard*, 1974, *Champagne Complex*, 1974, *Cat on a Hot Tin Roof*, 1974, *The Hot L Baltimore*, 1975, *Bingo*, 1975, *Great Expectations*, 1977, *Threads*, Cleveland Playhouse, 1979, *The Archbishop's Ceiling*, 1984.

The Effect of Gamma Rays on Man-in-the-Moon Marigolds, PAF Playhouse, Huntington, NY, 1975; *The Great Magoo*, Kingston, RI, 1976; *Luv*, Advent Theatre, Nashville, TN, 1977; *The Bright and Golden Land*, PAF Playhouse, Huntington, NY, 1977; *The Male Animal*, Asolo State Theatre, Sarasota, FL, 1982.

FILM DEBUT—Rocking chair soldier, *Captain Newman, MD*, Universal, 1963. PRINCIPAL FILM APPEARANCES—Seward, *The Eyes of Amaryllis*, 1982.

TELEVISION DEBUT—*The Verdict Is Yours*, CBS, 1960. PRINCIPAL TELEVISION APPEARANCES—*Death Valley Days; Combat;*

JONATHAN BOLT

The Twilight Zone; Wanted Dead or Alive; The Detectives; Stagecoach West; Channing; Wyatt Earp; The Tom Ewell Show; The Gertrude Berg Show; The Guiding Light; Another World; Search for Tomorrow; One Life to Live; The Adams Chronicles; Loving.

RELATED CAREER—Associate artistic director, Cleveland Playhouse, Cleveland, OH, 1971-73; company playwright, Circle Repertory Company, New York, 1980—.

WRITINGS: PLAYS, PRODUCED—*Threads,* O'Neill Center, Cleveland Playhouse, Playmakers Repertory, Circle Repertory, 1978, published 1981; *Eye and the Hands of God,* Fordham University, Cleveland State University, 1980; (with composer Tom Tierney and lyricist John Forester) *Teddy Roosevelt,* Theatreworks, USA, national tours, 1980-1984; (with composer Tom Tierney and lyricist John Forester) *First Lady,* Theatreworks, USA, national tour, Promenade Theatre, NY, 1984; *Plotline,* Pioneer Square Theatre, Seattle, WA, 1985; *To Culebra,* Actors Theatre of Louisville Humana Festival, 1986.

PLAYS, UNPRODUCED—"Running Time."

SCREENPLAY, UNPRODUCED—"Alamance Summer."

MEMBER: Dramatists Guild, Actors' Equity Association, Screen Actors Guild, American Federation of Television and Radio Artists, Society of Stage Directors and Choreographers.

AWARDS: New York State Creative Arts Public Service Grant for Playwriting, 1979; Drama League of New York Award for Playwriting, 1985, for *To Culebra.*

ADDRESSES: HOME—345 W. 86th Street, New York, NY 10024.

*   *   *

BOND, Gary   1940-

PERSONAL: Born February 7, 1940, in Alton, Hampshire, England; son of James Ker and Violet Clara (Brett) Bond. EDUCATION: Attended Churcher's College; trained for the stage at the Central School of Speech and Drama.

VOCATION: Actor.

CAREER: STAGE DEBUT—Worthing, *Not in the Book,* Connaught Theatre, 1963. LONDON DEBUT—Pip, *Chips with Everything,* Royal Court Theatre, 1963. NEW YORK DEBUT—Pip, *Chips with Everything,* Plymouth Theatre, 1963. PRINCIPAL STAGE APPEARANCES—Simon Sparrow, *Doctor in the House,* Connaught Theatre, 1963; Frank, *Mrs. Warren's Profession,* Hampstead Theatre, 1965; Joe, *On the Level,* Saville Theatre, London, 1966; John Shand, *What Every Woman Knows,* Arnaud Theatre, Guildford, 1967; Giles Cadwallader, *The Man Most Likely To . . . ,* Royal Windsor Theatre, 1967.

Benedick, *Much Ado About Nothing* and title role, *The Lord Byron Show,* both Open Air Theatre, Regents Park, London, 1970; Karl Sandys, *We Were Dancing,* George Pepper, *Red Peppers,* and Jasper Featherways, *Family Album,* all Hampstead Theatre, 1970; triple bill, *Tonight at 8:30,* transferred from Hampstead Theatre to the Fortune Theatre, London, 1971; Antipholus, *Comedy of Errors,* Young Vic Company, London, 1972; title role, *Joseph and the Amazing Technicolor Dreamcoat,* Young Vic Company, Edinburgh Festival, 1972, then Roundhouse Theatre, London, 1972, and

Albery Theatre, London, 1973; Simon, *More Stately Mansions,* Greenwich Theatre, 1974; Barnet, *The National Health,* Hurst, *Serjeant Musgrave's Dance,* Edward, *Old Flames,* and Johnny Hobnails, *Afore Night Come,* all Bristol Old Vic Company, 1975-76; Hevern, *The Zykovs,* Royal Shakespeare Company, 1976; Willie Oban, *The Iceman Cometh,* Royal Shakespeare Company, 1976; Damien Foxworth, *Getting Away with Murder,* Comedy Theatre, London, 1976; Brutus, *Julius Caesar* and title role, *The Lord Byron Show,* Chichester, 1977; Toby, *Alice's Boys,* Savoy Theatre, London, 1978; Che, *Evita,* Prince Edward Theatre, London, 1978.

MAJOR TOURS—Sebastian, *Twelfth Night,* Pete Swan, *No Man's Land,* and Sergius, *Arms and the Man,* with Prospect Theatre Company, 1968; Oswald Alving, *Ghosts,* with the Cambridge Theatre Company, 1972; *The Scenario,* Alexandra Theatre, Toronto, 1976.

FILM DEBUT—*Zulu,* Embassy, 1964. PRINCIPAL FILM APPEARANCES—*Anne of the Thousand Days,* 1970; *The Outback,* United Artists, 1971.

PRINCIPAL TELEVISION APPEARANCES—British: *Great Expectations; The Main Chance; The Duchess of Malfi; Wings of Sons.*

ADDRESSES: AGENT—Larry Dalzell Associates, Three Goodwin's Court, St. Martin's Lane, London WC2, England.*

*   *   *

BOTTOMS, Timothy   1951-

PERSONAL: Born August 30, 1951, in Santa Barbara, CA.

VOCATION: Actor.

CAREER: FILM DEBUT—*Johnny Got His Gun,* Marketing and Distributing Co., 1971. PRINCIPAL FILM APPEARANCES—*The Last Picture Show,* Columbia, 1971; *Love and Pain (and the Whole Damn Thing),* Columbia, 1973; *The Paper Chase,* Twentieth Century-Fox, 1973; *White Dawn,* Paramount, 1974; *The Crazy World of Julius Vrooder,* Twentieth Century-Fox, 1974; *Operation Daybreak,* 1974; *A Small Town in Texas,* American-International, 1976; *Rollercoaster,* Universal, 1977; *The Other Side of the Mountain, Part II,* Universal, 1978; *Hurricane,* Paramount, 1979; *The First Hello,* 1979; *Hambone and Hillie,* 1984.

PRINCIPAL TELEVISION APPEARANCES—Movies: *David,* 1976; *Escape,* 1979; *A Shining Season,* 1979.

Mini-Series: *The Moneychangers,* 1976; *East of Eden,* 1980.

PRINCIPAL STAGE APPEARANCES—*West Side Story,* Santa Barbara, CA.

MAJOR TOURS—With the Santa Barbara Madrigal Society, European tour, 1967.

MEMBER: Screen Actors Guild, American Federation of Television and Radio Artists.

ADDRESSES: HOME—Santa Barbara, CA.*

BOWIE, David   1947-

PERSONAL: Born David Robert Jones, January 8, 1947, in Brixton, South London, England; married Angela (divorced, 1970); children: Zowie.

VOCATION: Singer, songwriter, and actor.

CAREER: PRINCIPAL FILM APPEARANCES—Title role, *Ziggy Stardust and the Spiders from Mars*, 1973 (not released in U.S. until 1983); *The Man Who Fell to Earth* (British), 1976; *Just a Gigolo* (West German), 1979; *Wir Kinder von Bahnhof* (West German), 1981; *Cat People*, Universal, 1983; title role, *Merry Christmas, Mr. Lawrence*, 1983; *The Hunger*, Metro-Goldwyn-Mayer/United Artists, 1983; *Absolute Beginners*, Orion, 1986; *Labyrinth* (upcoming).

PRINCIPAL STAGE APPEARANCES—Title role, *The Elephant Man*, Booth Theatre, NY, 1980.

PRINCIPAL TELEVISION APPEARANCES—Guest: *Christmas with Bing Crosby; The Midnight Special*, NBC.

RECORDINGS: ALBUMS—*Aladdin Sane*, RCA; *Bertolt Brecht's "Baal,"* RCA; *Changesonebowie*, RCA; *Changestwobowie*, RCA; *David Live*, RCA; *Diamond Dogs*, RCA; *Fame and Fashion: All-Time Greatest Hits*, RCA; *Golden Years*, RCA; *Heroes*, RCA; *Hunky Dory*, RCA; *Let's Dance*, EMI; *Lodger*, RCA; *Love You Till Tuesday*, London; *Low*, RCA; *The Man Who Sold the World*, RCA; *Pin Ups*, RCA; *Scary Monsters*, RCA; *Space Oddity*, RCA; *Starting Point*, RCA; *Station to Station*, RCA; *Tonight*, Capitol; *Young Americans*, RCA; *Ziggy Stardust*, RCA.

ADDRESSES: AGENT—William Morris Agency, 151 El Camino Drive, Beverly Hills, CA 90212; Rogers and Cowan, 122 E. 42nd Street, New York, NY 10168.*

*   *   *

BOXLEITNER, Bruce   1950-

PERSONAL: Born May 12, 1950, in Elgin, IL.

VOCATION: Actor.

CAREER: PRINCIPAL TELEVISION APPEARANCES—Series: Luke Macahan, *How the West Was Won*, ABC, 1978; Frank Buck, *Bring 'em Back Alive*, CBS, 1982-83; Lee Stetson (Scarecrow), *Scarecrow and Mrs. King*, CBS, 1983—.

Movies: *Kiss Me, Kill Me*, 1976; *Happily Ever After*, 1978; *Zuma Beach*, 1978; *Kenny Rogers as The Gambler*, 1980; *Fly Away Home*, 1981; *The Gambler, Part II: The Adventure Continues*, 1983; *Passion Flower*, 1986.

Mini-Series: *How the West Was Won; The Last Convertible*, NBC, 1979; *East of Eden*, 1980; *Bare Essence*.

PRINCIPAL FILM APPEARANCES—*The Baltimore Bullet*, Avco Embassy, 1980; *Tron*, Buena Vista, 1982.

MEMBER: American Federation of Television and Radio Artists, Screen Actors Guild.

ADDRESSES: OFFICE—CBS, 7800 Beverly Blvd., Los Angeles, CA 90036.*

BOYLE, Peter   1933-

PERSONAL: Born 1933 in Philadelphia, PA; married Lorraine Alterman, October, 1977. EDUCATION: Attended LaSalle College, Philadelphia.

VOCATION: Actor.

CAREER: FILM DEBUT—Title role, *Joe*, Cannon, 1970. PRINCIPAL FILM APPEARANCES—*T.R. Baskin*, 1972; Lucas, *The Candidate*, Warner Brothers, 1972; *Steelyard Blues*, Warner Brothers, 1973; *Slither*, Metro-Goldwyn-Mayer, 1973; *The Friends of Eddie Coyle*, Paramount, 1973; *Kid Blue*, Twentieth Century-Fox, 1973; *Crazy Joe*, Columbia, 1974; the monster, *Young Frankenstein*, Twentieth Century-Fox, 1974; *Taxi Driver*, Columbia, 1976; *Swashbuckler*, Universal, 1976; *F.I.S.T.*, United Artists, 1978; *The Brink's Job*, Universal, 1978; *Hardcore*, Columbia, 1979; *Beyond the Poseidon Adventure*, Warner Brothers, Columbia, 1979; *In God We Trust*, Universal, 1980; *Where the Buffalo Roam*, 1980; *Hammett*, 1980; *Outland*, Warner Brothers, 1981; *Yellowbeard*, Orion, 1983; *Joe II*, Cannon, 1984; *Turk 182!*, Twentieth Century-Fox, 1985.

PRINCIPAL TELEVISION APPEARANCES—Series: Regular, *Comedy Tonight*, CBS, 1970.

Movies: Senator Joseph McCarthy, *Tail-Gunner Joe*, 1977.

Mini-Series: Fatso Judson, *From Here to Eternity*, NBC, 1979.

PRINCIPAL STAGE APPEARANCES—With Second City Company, Chicago; others.

MEMBER: Screen Actors Guild, Actors' Equity Association, American Federation of Television and Radio Artists.

SIDELIGHTS: Peter Boyle was a monk in the Christian Brothers Order.

ADDRESSES: AGENT—Abrams Artists and Associates, 420 Madison Avenue, New York, NY 10017.*

*   *   *

BRACKEN, Eddie   1920-

PERSONAL: Born February 7, 1920, in Astoria, NY; son of Joseph L. and Catherine Bracken; married Connie Nickerson. EDUCATION: Attended the Professional School for Actors.

VOCATION: Actor and director.

CAREER: FILM DEBUT—Rich boy, *Our Gang* (series), 1920's. PRINCIPAL FILM APPEARANCES—Series: *Kiddie Trouper*, 1920's; *Many Girls*, 1940; *Life with Henry*, 1941; *Fleet's In*, 1942; *Star Spangled Rhythm*, 1942; *Young and Willing*, 1943; *Happy Go Lucky*, 1943; *The Miracle of Morgan's Creek*, 1944; *Hail the Conquering Hero*, 1944; *Summer Stock*, 1950; *Two Tickets to Broadway*, 1951; *About Face*, 1952; *We're Not Married*, 1952; *A Slight Case of Larceny*, 1953; *Shinbone Alley* (animated), Allied Artists, 1971; *National Lampoon's Vacation*, Warner Brothers, 1983. Also: *The Sweater Girl; From Jones Beach*.

TELEVISION DEBUT—Panelist, *I've Got a Secret*, CBS, 1952. PRINCIPAL TELEVISION APPEARANCES—Panelist, *Make the Connection*, NBC, 1955; *Front Row Center*, 1956; moderator, *Masquerade Party*, NBC, 1957; *Archie and Mehitabel;* voice, *The Wind in the Willows*, ABC, 1985.

STAGE DEBUT—Purser, *The Good Ship Leviathan*, Knights of Columbus, Astoria, NY. NEW YORK DEBUT—Western Union Boy, *The Man on Stilts*, Plymouth Theatre, 1931. PRINCIPAL STAGE APPEARANCES—Hank Parkes, *The Lady Refuses*, Bijou Theatre, NY, 1933; a boy, *The Drunkard*, American Music Hall, NY, 1934; Alfred, *Life's Too Short*, Broadhurst Theatre, NY, 1935; Cadet Brown, *So Proudly We Hail*, 46th Street Theatre, NY, 1935; a plumber, *Iron Men*, Longacre Theatre, NY, 1936; Billy Randolph, *Brother Rat*, Biltmore Theatre, NY, 1937; Hal, *What a Life*, Biltmore Theatre, NY, 1938; Jo Jo Jordan, *Too Many Girls*, Imperial Theatre, NY, 1939.

Richard Sherman, *The Seven Year Itch*, Fulton Theatre, NY, 1955; Archy, *Shinbone Alley*, Broadway Theatre, NY, 1957; Erwin Trowbridge, *Three Men on a Horse*, Drury Lane, London, 1957; Charles Wykeham, *Where's Charley?*, Music Theatre, Columbus, OH, 1958; Kreton, *Visit to a Small Planet*, Grist Mill Playhouse, Andover, NJ, 1958; Pistol, *Beg, Borrow or Steal*, Martin Beck Theatre, NY, 1960; Howard Bevins, *Hot September*, Shubert Theatre, Boston, MA, 1965; Felix, *The Odd Couple*, Plymouth Theatre, NY, 1966; Harry Lamert, *Never Too Late*, Country Dinner Playhouse, Dallas, TX, 1973; *Hot Line to Heaven*, Country Dinner Playhouse, Dallas, TX, 1975; Horace Vandergelder, *Hello, Dolly!*, Lunt-Fontanne Theatre, NY, 1978, then Theatre Royal, Drury Lane, London, 1979, then Shaftesbury Theatre, London, 1980; *Show Boat*, Paper Mill Playhouse, Milburn, NJ, 1985.

MAJOR TOURS—Henry Aldrich, *What a Life*, U.S. cities, 1939; entertainer, USO, U.S. Army installations, South Pacific and U.S.

In U.S. cities: Richard Sherman, *The Seven Year Itch*, Charlie Reader, *The Tender Trap*, George MacCauley, *Will Success Spoil Rock Hunter?*, 1953-54; Sakini, *The Teahouse of the August Moon*, 1956; Richard Sherman, *The Seven Year Itch*, Charlie Reader, *The Tender Trap*, George MacCauley, *Will Success Spoil Rock Hunter?*, 1956; Augie Poole, *The Tunnel of Love*, 1958; Jack Jordan, *Say Darling*, Richard Sherman, *The Seven Year Itch*, 1959; Fergie Howard, *The Golden Fleecing*, Og the Leprechaun, *Finian's Rainbow*, Ensign Pulver, *Mr. Roberts*, 1960; Richard Pawling, George, Chuck, *You Know I Can't Hear You When the Water's Running*, 1967-68; *The Girl in the Freudian Slip*, 1972; *Born Yesterday*, 1974; *The Sunshine Boys*, 1975; Horace Vandergelder, *Hello, Dolly!*, 1977-80.

PRINCIPAL STAGE WORK—Producer: *Beg, Borrow or Steal*, Martin Beck Theatre, NY, 1960.

Director: *What a Life*, 1939; *How to Make a Man*, Brooks Atkinson Theatre, NY, 1961.

RELATED CAREER—Co-owner, Staircase Theatre, NY, 1970.

WRITINGS: RADIO—*Bob Hope Show*, 1934-36.

SIDELIGHTS: CTFT learned Eddie Bracken also wrote a syndicated column for the Sunrise Press called *Crackin with Bracken*, in 1963.*

BRAGG, Bernard

PERSONAL: EDUCATION: Gallaudet College, B.A., 1952; San Francisco Stage College, M.A., 1959; studied theatre arts at New York University between 1952 and 1959; studied mime with Marcel Marceau, Paris as well as with Marceau's teacher, Etienne Decroux; studied acting with Joe Chaikin at the O'Neill Center, Waterford, Connecticut.

VOCATION: Actor, mime, producer, director, writer, and teacher.

CAREER: STAGE DEBUT—Guest actor, *Sign Me Alice*, Chicago Theatre of the Deaf, Chicago, IL, 1975. PRINCIPAL STAGE APPEARANCES—Artist-in-Residence, Moscow Theatre of Mimicry and Gesture, 1973; guest actor, *The Merchant Gentleman*, National Technical Institute for the Deaf, April, 1978; *The White Hawk*, Annenberg Theatre Center, University of Pennsylvania, Philadelphia, 1981; solo improvisational mime, *Second City*, Chicago, 1983; *Disabled Genius*, Chicago, 1983.

MAJOR TOURS—Europe and America, 1957-66; with National Theatre of the Deaf, Europe and America, 1967-77; lecture, performance tour, 38 cities around the world, September 1977-February 1978.

TELEVISION DEBUT—*The Quiet Man*, KQED, San Francisco, 1959-61. PRINCIPAL TELEVISION APPEARANCES—*What's New?*, syndicated, 1961-68; *Aesop's Fables in Mime*, BBC, London, 1962; *NBC Experiment in TV*, 1967; *David Frost Show*, 1972; *A Child's Christmas in Wales*, BBC, London, 1973; Paul, *And Your Name Is Jonah*, CBS, 1978; *Thinkabout*, PBS, 1979-80; title role, *Captain Marvelous*, WGBH, Boston, 1981; *The Disabled Genius*, PBS, 1981; *Can Anybody Hear Me?*, 1981-82; numerous television commercials; others.

PRINCIPAL FILM WORK—Producer, *That Makes Two of Us*, videotape for schools, 1981; producer and director, *It's Your Choice*, 1983; *Gallaudet College Is Ready for You*, producer and director, 1983.

PRINCIPAL STAGE WORK—Director: Workshop in kentic imagery, Loeb Theatre, Harvard University, 1974; workshop for the Danish Theatre of the Deaf, Copenhagen, Denmark, 1979; *Tales from a Clubroom*, Cincinnati, OH, 1980; *That Makes Two of Us*, Gallaudet College Theatre, Washington, DC, 1980.

RELATED CAREER—Academic and drama instructor, California School for the Deaf, Berkeley, 1952-59; taught sign-mime at the annual summer school of the National Theatre of the Deaf, Waterford, CT, 1967-79; taught total communication, Montana State University, summers, 1973-75; visiting professor, Gallaudet College, 1978; taught drama of visual language, Wesleyan University, Middletown, CT, 1979; assistant professor, Gallaudet College, 1980; drama instructor, program for gifted hearing impaired youth at Boys Town, Omaha, NE, 1982; consultant (artist associate), public relations division, Gallaudet College, 1983.

Also appeared as mime in night clubs and in numerous television commercials; appeared on television in Zagreb, Yugoslavia, 1962; participated in workshops with Peter Brook, International Theatre Research Institute, Paris, 1970, and with Jean-Louis Barrault at the O'Neill Theatre Center, 1974; directed a workshop at the Tyst Theatre, Sweden, 1973, and another at the Danish School for the Deaf in Copenhagen, 1979; has been a consultant, technical advisor, and special coach for hearing actors; has written and published poetry as well as a wide variety of articles on the theatre and the hearing impaired.

WRITINGS: PLAYS, PRODUCED—(With Eugene Bergman) *Tales from a Clubroom,* 1979, published by Gallaudet College Press, 1981; *That Makes Two of Us,* 1980. SHORT STORIES—(Roz Rosen) *A Handful of Stories,* Gallaudet College Press, 1981.

AWARDS: Knight of Flying Fingers, National Association of the Deaf, 1967; Special "Tony" (Antoinette Perry Award) for his ten-year service to the National Theatre of the Deaf; Alumnus of the Year Award, Kappa Gamma Fraternity, 1972; La Decoration au Merite Social International—Premiere Class, World Federation of the Deaf, 1975; Man of the Year Award, Alpha Sigme Pi Fraternity, 1978; various plaques commending his work for the deaf in the the the Theatre, 1971, 1983, 1978, 1979; The Teegarden Award for Creative Poetry, 1952.

SIDELIGHTS: In material supplied by Bernard Bragg's agent, *CTFT* learned that in 1966, Bernard Bragg joined forces with David Hays to found the National Theatre of the Deaf. He has since performed with them throughout the United States and Europe including at least two Broadway engagements. He has performed the duties of actor, teacher, director, lecturer, and administrator for the company.

He became a founding member of the Little Theatre of the Deaf in 1968.

In September 1983 Bragg was included among twenty outstanding national artists and arts administration personnel whose lives and careers were highlighted in a publication sponsored by the National Endowment for the Arts and the President's Committee on Employment of the Handicapped.

ADDRESSES: OFFICE—Gallaudet College, Kendall Green, Washington, DC 20002.

*   *   *

BRANDO, Marlon   1924-

PERSONAL: Born April 3, 1924, in Omaha, NE; son of Marlon and Dorothy Pennebaker (Myers) Brando; married Anna Kashfi, 1957 (divorced); married Movita (divorced); children: (first marriage) Christian; (second marriage) one child. EDUCATION: Attended Shattuck Military Academy; attended the Dramatic Workshop, New York.

VOCATION: Actor and director.

CAREER: PRINCIPAL STAGE APPEARANCES—Appeared in stock productions in Sayville, NY; on Broadway appeared in: *Truckline Cafe,* 1946; *A Flag Is Born,* 1946; *A Streetcar Named Desire,* 1947; also appeared on Broadway in *I Remember Mama; Candida.*

FILM DEBUT—*The Men,* 1950. PRINCIPAL FILM APPEARANCES—Stanley Kowalski, *A Streetcar Named Desire,* Warner Brothers, 1951; *Viva Zapata!,* 1952; *The Wild One,* 1953; Marc Anthony, *Julius Caesar,* 1953; Napoleon, *Desiree,* 1954; Terry Malloy, *On the Waterfront,* Columbia, 1954; Sky Masterson, *Guys and Dolls,* Metro-Goldwyn-Mayer, 1955; *Teahouse of the August Moon,* Metro-Goldwyn-Mayer, 1956; *Sayonara,* Warner Brothers, 1957; *The Young Lions,* Twentieth Century-Fox, 1958; *Fugitive Kind,* United Artists, 1959.

One Eyed Jacks, Paramount, 1961; Fletcher Christian, *Mutiny on the Bounty,* Metro-Goldwyn-Mayer, 1962; *The Ugly American,* Universal, 1963; *Bedtime Story,* Universal, 1964; *The Saboteur: Code Name Morituri* (also known as *Morituri*), Twentieth Century-Fox, 1965; *The Chase,* Columbia, 1966; *Appaloosa,* Universal, 1966; *A Countess from Hong Kong,* Universal, 1967; *Reflections in a Golden Eye,* Warner Brothers, 1967; *Candy,* Cinerama, 1968; *Queimada!,* 1968; *Night of the Following Day,* Universal, 1969; *Burn!,* United Artists, 1970; *The Nightcomers,* Avco Embassy, 1972; Don Vito Corleone, *The Godfather,* Paramount, 1972; Paul, *Last Tango in Paris,* United Artists, 1972; *The Missouri Breaks,* 1976; Jarel, *Superman,* Warner Brothers, 1978; Kurtz, *Apocalypse Now,* United Artists, 1979; *The Formula,* United Artists, 1980; Jor-El, *Superman II,* Warner Brothers, 1981.

PRINCIPAL FILM WORK—Director, *One Eyed Jacks,* Paramount, 1961.

PRINCIPAL TELEVISION APPEARANCES—George Lincoln Rockwell, *Roots: The Next Generation,* ABC, 1979.

PRINCIPAL TELEVISION WORK—Director, a segment of *Roots: The Next Generation,* ABC, 1979.

AWARDS: One of the top ten money making stars, *Motion Picture Herald-Fame* Poll, 1954-55; Best Actor, Academy Award nominations, 1951, for *A Streetcar Named Desire* 1952, for *Viva Zapata!,* and 1953, for *Julius Caesar;* Best Actor, Academy Awards, 1954, for *On the Waterfront* and 1972, for *The Godfather.*

SIDELIGHTS: Considered one of the most influential actors of his time, Marlon Brando first attracted attention with a bit part in Maxwell Anderson's play *Truckline Cafe* in 1946. It was, however, his dynamic characterization of the brutal Stanley Kowalski in the 1947 production of Tennessee Williams' classic drama *A Streetcar Named Desire,* his only Broadway starring role, that garnered critical kudos. Brando's performance as Kowalski "threatened, for a moment, to make all his contemporaries obsolete," as critic Molly Haskell recalled in a 1973 *Village Voice* article. His first screen appearances, as a disabled veteran in *The Men* (for which he prepared by living with paraplegics in a hospital for a month) and then in the movie version of *Streetcar,* had a similar impact on film critics and audiences. As his biographer Bob Thomas put it in *Marlon: Portrait of the Rebel as an Artist,* Brando "brought a realism and intensity that had never been seen on the screen before."

In the wake of his success, a generation of young actors emulated Brando's acting style—from his "mumbling" manner of speech to his reliance on the internal techniques of acting (the so-called "Method") he had learned from the teacher Stella Adler and at the Actors Studio. In his personal life, Brando also influenced fads by wearing T-shirts and jeans, riding a motorcycle, and adopting a rebellious attitude towards the Hollywood business and social scene and the established power structure in general. These traits carried to the screen, most notably in the motorcycle gang leader whom Brando played in *The Wild One,* the 1953 movie that established the actor as a favorite with youthful filmgoers.

After earning Academy Award nominations three years in a row for *Streetcar, Viva Zapata!,* and *Julius Caesar,* Brando became the youngest man ever to win the Oscar for best actor for his portrayal of Terry Malloy, a small-time boxer turned mob stooge, in the 1954 *On the Waterfront.* His lines, "I could have been somebody, instead of a bum, which is what I am," became watchwords, along with "What have you got?," his response in *The Wild One* to the question, "What are you rebelling against?"

Refusing to be typecast, in 1955 Brando demonstrated his acting range by starring in the musical *Guys and Dolls* and playing an Oriental in the 1956 comedy *The Teahouse of the August Moon*. After he scored two more hits with *Sayonara* and *The Young Lions*, his career entered a period of decline. Not only were most of his films made during the sixties commercial and critical failures, but Brando himself was accused of escalating the costs of many of them by causing delays in filming and engaging in other "difficult" behavior. This charge was made particularly in connection with his appearance as Fletcher Christian in the lavish 1962 Metro-Goldwyn-Mayer remake of *Mutiny on the Bounty*.

Because of Brando's reputation for creating problems, Paramount Pictures executives were at first reluctant to cast him as Don Vito Corleone in the 1972 film about organized crime, *The Godfather*. Director Francis Ford Coppola persuaded the actor to make a screen test, a rare thing for a figure of Brando's stature. An aging Brando, apparently transformed by makeup and a vivid performance, went unrecognized by studio executives viewing the test. Studio production head Robert Evans said, "He looks Italian, fine. But who is he?" Evans consented to casting Brando in the part, but only after the actor agreed to work for a small salary (variously reported between $50,000 and $250,000) plus a percentage of the profits, which brought him over a million dollars as the film smashed all box-office records. Brando received his second Academy Award for his performance in *The Godfather*, but in keeping with his longtime social activism, the actor refused it as a protest against Hollywood's treatment of American Indians.

Following *The Godfather*, Brando starred in Bernardo Bertolucci's 1972 film, *Last Tango in Paris*, one of the most sexually explicit films ever to feature a major international star. According to David Thompson in *A Biographical Dictionary of Film* (Morrow, 1981), much of Brando's own life history was written into his *Last Tango* character, and the actor improvised some of his own dialogue.

Since 1972, Brando has appeared on screen only in relatively small parts in such movies as *Apocalypse Now* and *Superman*, reportedly receiving up to $3.5 million for each of them. In 1979, he made his television min-series debut playing in *Roots: The Next Generation* American Nazi leader George Lincoln Rockwell. He also directed the segment in which he starred.

An intensely private man, Brando, between films, lives an isolated existence on the South Pacific island of Tetiaroa, near Tahiti. He explained to a *Life* magazine reporter in 1972, "Being in Tahiti gives me a sense of the one-to-one ratio of things. You have the coconut in the tree, the fish in the water, and if you want something to eat, you have to get it."

ADDRESSES: HOME—Tetiaroa Island, Tahiti. AGENT—c/o Norton Brown, Brown, Kraft Company, 11940 San Vincente Blvd., Suite 200, Los Angeles, CA 90049.*

*   *   *

BRANDT, Yanna Kroyt   1933-

PERSONAL: Born Yanna Kroyt, September 6, 1933; daughter of Boris (a concert artist) and Sonya (Blumin) Kroyt; married Nathan H. Brandt, Jr. (an editor and writer) April 5, 1955; children: Anthony Kroyt, Ariane Leonovna and (step-child) Kevin. EDUCATION: Attended University of Michigan, 1951-52; Vassar College, A.B., 1953; Columbia School of Journalism, M.S., 1954; also studied at Mills College, American Theatre Wing.

YANNA KROYT BRANDT

VOCATION: Writer, producer, and director.

CAREER: PRINCIPAL TELEVISION WORK—Producer and writer, *Budapest String Quartet at the Frick Collection*, WCBS, NY; producer and writer, *New York Wonderland*, WPIX, NY; producer and writer, *Problems of Everyday Living*, WPIX, NY; program associate, *Concept*, CBS, all for Metropolitan Educational TV Association, 1957-59; writer of special projects, *CBS News*, 1960-61; producer and writer, *Playwright at Work, This Is Opera, Great Decisions: Spain, Astronomy for You, Nationalism and Colonialism, International Essay*, and special news events during the Cuban Crisis and 1962 elections, all for National Educational Television and Channel 13, 1960-64.

Producer and writer, *The Maltreated Child, Icons: Images of God*; writer, *A Challenge to Medical Care*; associate producer, *New York Night, New Voices in the Wilderness, The Unemployables, A Matter of Life, We Are All Policemen, The Abundant Land, The New Left Bank, The Big Apple, Hollywood on the Hudson, Light Across the Shadow, City of Ships, Man in the Middle*, all for WNBC Public Affairs, NY, 1964-1970; producer, director, and writer, *Vibrations*, WNET National Programming Division, 1970-72; Producer, director, and writer, *UN Day Concert with Pablo Casals*, 1971, *Boulez: A Portrait in Three Movements*, 1971, *Sonny Brown and the Fallen Sparrows*, 1972, WNET National Programming Division.

Producer and writer, *Choices for '76*, 1972-73; producer, *Hello New Place*, pilot for unsold series, 1973; executive producer, *Vegetable Soup*, NBC and public television, 1973-1977; producer and writer, *FYI with Hal Linden*, ABC; producer and writer, *The Nutcracker with Mikhail Baryshnikov*, CBS and PBS; producer, writer, and creator, *High Feather*, NBC, PBS; producer, *A House Divided*, PBS (segments seen on *American Playhouse*); other projects in development.

PRINCIPAL FILM WORK—Writer, *Foxfire*, 1973.

PRINCIPAL STAGE WORK—Director, *Charlie's Wedding Day,* staged reading.

MEMBER: Writers Guild of America East, National Television Academy, New York Women in Film (committee head), Columbia Journalism Alumnae Council, Writers Guild of America Awards Committee; National Academy of Television Arts and Sciences (Emmy blue ribbon panelist).

AWARDS: Recipient of seven Emmy Awards between 1980 and 1983 and more than sixty other awards including the George Polk Award in 1962 for the election coverage and the Robert E. Sherwood Award for the CBS program, *Concept.*

SIDELIGHTS: Yanna Kroyt Brandt's career in television began in 1954, as an assistant on the foreign news desk at CBS News. She has written for *Redbook, Readers Digest* and *The New York Times* in the fields of medicine, psychiatry, welfare, and travel, as well as editing *World Week* magazine from 1955-57, a weekly for high school current events classes. She speaks Russian, French, and Spanish.

ADDRESSES: HOME—Twelve E. Twelfth Street, New York, NY 10011. AGENT—c/o Robert Partnoy, Cohn-Glickstein, 1370 Avenue of the Americas, New York, NY 10019.

*   *   *

BRENNER, Randy   1955-

PERSONAL: Born October 4, 1955, in Philadelphia, PA; son of Joseph Carol (a contracting manager) and Edythe Bertha (Schwartz) Brenner. EDUCATION: Temple University, B.S. and B.A.; studied with Uta Hagen at the Herbert Berghof Studios, New York.

VOCATION: Actor and singer.

CAREER: STAGE DEBUT—Boy Number Two, *All the Way Home,* Plays and Players Theatre, Philadelphia, 1965, for one hundred performances. PRINCIPAL STAGE APPEARANCES—Harry Jolson, *Joley,* Northstage Dinner Theatre, 1979; *New Faces of '52* (revival), Equity Library Theatre, NY, 1982; Little Earl, *Found a Peanut,* WPA Theatre, NY, 1983; Sergeant, *Dynamite Tonight,* Cultural Affairs Building, NY, 1984; also, *Tintypes,* St. Louis Repertory Theatre; troll, *Sleeping Beauty,* Municipal Opera of St. Louis; Benson, *Shine,* Virginia Museum Theatre; *Lovers and Other Strangers,* Bucks County Theatre.

PRINCIPAL TELEVISION APPEARANCES—Octopus, *Safe at Home,* Turner Broadcasting Station (TBS), 1985; wimp, *Rocky Road,* TBS, 1986.

RELATED CAREER—Mime instructor, Neshaminy High School, 1980-81; acting instructor, Greenwich House of Music, 1983-84.

WRITINGS: PLAYS, UNPRODUCED—(With Mitchell Greenberg) "Hyde and Seek," 1985; (with Mark Norby and Rusty Steiger, "The Jackie Gilbert Story."

MEMBER: Actors' Equity Association, Screen Actors Guild, American Federation of Television and Radio Artists; Center for Environmental Education.

AWARDS: Best Actor, Bucks County Theatre Festival, for *Lovers and Other Strangers;* Best Actor in a Musical, Phoebe Award, 1982, for *Tintypes.*

ADDRESSES: HOME—7260 Hillside Avenue, Apt. 205, Los Angeles, CA 90046. AGENT—Abrams, Rubaloff, and Lawrence, 8075 W. Third Street, Suite 101B, Los Angeles, CA 90069; Ann Wright Representatives, 136 E. 57th Street, New York, NY 10022.

*   *   *

BRESSACK, Celia   1956-

PERSONAL: Born December 28, 1956, in New York, NY; daughter of Alfred and Harriette Beatrice (a teacher; maiden name, Nesin) Bressack. EDUCATION: Attended the High School of Music and Art, 1973; Herbert H. Lehman College, City College of New York, B.A., music, 1978; studied acting with Stephen Strimpell and Aaron Frankel at the Herbert Berghof Studios.

VOCATION: Actress.

CAREER: STAGE DEBUT—Kate, *The Taming of the Shrew,* 13th Street Theatre, NY, 1980. PRINCIPAL STAGE APPEARANCES—Ritsy, *The Cutting Room* and Graffiti Kid, *Biting the Apple,* featured performer, *New Wave Follies,* all Off Center Theatre, NY; Isabella, *The Company of Wayward Saints,* Royal Court Theatre; the manager, *It Wasn't the Coke,* 13th Street Theatre, NY; Elizabeth, *Frankenstein,* Lincoln Center Festival, NY; Sophia, *Graven Images,* Shandol Theatre; Ceclia, *Fefu and Her Friends,* Sticks and Bones Theatre; Harriet, *Barefoot in the Park,* Barbara, *No Sex Please, We're British* and featured performer, *What's a Nice Country Like You Doing In a State Like This?,* all Host Farm Resort Dinner Theatre, PA; Molly, *Benjamin Banneker,* Sultana, *Sinbad the Sailor,* both part of a children's festival, Lincoln Center, NY; sister, *Beauty and the Beast,* children's show, Off Center Theatre; Queen and Witch, *The Snow White Show,* 13th Street Theatre; Gretel and Witch, *Hansel and Gretel,* Courtyard Playhouse.

CELIA BRESSACK

FILM DEBUT—Lucy, *The Gig*, The Gig Company, 1985. PRINCIPAL FILM APPEARANCES—Information clerk, *Jetlag*, Figaro Films; Rachel, *Awake*, Picker Films; woman in cafe, *Echoes*, Independent.

PRINCIPAL TELEVISION APPEARANCES—Episodic: *Ryan's Hope*, ABC; *As the World Turns*, NBC; *F.Y.I. (For Your Information)*, ABC.

MEMBER: Actors' Equity Association, American Federation of Television and Radio Artists, Off Center Theatre.

ADDRESSES: HOME—157 E. Third Street, New York, NY 10019.

*   *   *

BRETT, Jeremy   1933-

PERSONAL: Born Jeremy Huggins, November 3, 1933, in Berkswell Grange, Warwickshire, England; son of H.W. (a military colonel) and Elizabeth Edith Cadbury (Butler) Huggins; married Anna Massey, May, 1958 (divorced); married Joan Wilson, 1977 (a television producer; died July, 1985); children: (first marriage) David; (second marriage) one child. EDUCATION: Attended Eton; studied at the Central School of Speech and Drama.

VOCATION: Actor and director.

CAREER: LONDON DEBUT—Patriclus, *Troilus and Cressida*, Old Vic Theatre, 1956. NEW YORK DEBUT—Duke of Aumerle, *Richard II*, Winter Garden Theatre, 1956. PRINCIPAL STAGE APPEARANCES—Mercury, *Amphytrion 38* and Duke of Aumerle, *Richard II*, both Library Theatre, Manchester, England, 1954; Malcolm, *Macbeth*, Paris, *Romeo and Juliet*, Duke of Aumerle, *Richard II*, and above London Debut, all old Vic, 1956, with all roles repeated at the Winter Garden Theatre, except that he played Troilus in a modern dress version of *Troilus and Cressida*, NY, 1956; Roderick, *Meet Me by Moonlight*, Aldwych Theatre, London, 1957; Ron, *Variations on a Theme*, Globe Theatre, London, 1958; William McFly, *Mr. Fox of Venice*, Piccadilly Theatre, London, 1959; Archie Forsythe, *Marigold*, Savoy Theatre, London, 1959; Sebastian, *The Edwardians*, Saville Theatre, London, 1959.

Reverend Richard Highfield, *Johnny the Priest*, Princes Theatre, London, 1960; title role, *Hamlet*, Strand Theatre, London, 1961; Peter, *The Kitchen*, Royal Court Theatre, London, 1961; Dunois, *Saint Joan* and Maurice Sweetman, *The Workhouse Donkey*, both Chichester Festival, 1963; Father Riccardo Fontana, *The Deputy*, Brooks Atkinson Theatre, NY, 1964; Gilbert, *A Measure of Cruelty*, Birmingham Repertory, England, 1965; Beliaev, *A Month in the Country*, Cambridge Theatre, London, 1965; Ronnie, *Any Just Cause*, Adeline Genee Theatre, East Grinstead, England, 1967. With the National Theatre Company: Orlando, *As You Like It* and Valere, *Tartuffe*, both 1967; Kent, *Edward II* and Berowne, *Love's Labour's Lost*, both 1968; Che Guevara, *Macrune's Guevara*, 1969 (also seen at the Jeannetta Cochrane).

Bassinio, *The Merchant of Venice*, Old Vic Theatre, London, 1970; George Tesman, *Hedda Gabler*, 1970; the son, *A Voyage Round My Father*, Haymarket Theatre, London, 1971; Thorndike, *Leatherhead*, 1972; Gaston, *Traveller without Luggage*, 1972; John Rosmer, *Rosmersholm*, Greenwich Theatre, London, 1973; Otto, *Design for Living*, Phoenix Theatre, London, 1973; Mirabell, *The Way of the World*, Stratford Shakespeare Festival, Ontario, Canada, 1976; Theseus and Oberon, *A Midsummer Night's Dream*; Robert Browning, *Robert and Elizabeth* and title role, *Dracula*, Ahmanson

Theatre, Los Angeles, 1978; offstage narrator, *Song*, Martha Graham's Ballet, 1982; Honorable William Tatham, *Aren't We All*, Brooks Atkinson Theatre, NY, 1985.

MAJOR TOURS—Duke of Aumerle, *Richard II*, Malcolm, *Macbeth*, Paris, *Romeo and Juliet*, Troilus, *Troilus and Cressida*, U.S. and Canada, 1957.

PRINCIPAL STAGE WORK—Director, *The Tempest*, Canada, 1982.

PRINCIPAL TELEVISION APPEARANCES—Plays and Movies: Paris, *Romeo and Juliet*, NBC, 1957; Malcolm, *Macbeth*, NBC, 1961; *Florence Nightingale*, NBC, 1985; Bryan Foxworth, *Deceptions*, NBC, 1985; also appeared in *Jennie, Katherine Mansfield*, and as Danilo in *The Merry Widow*, all for the BBC; as the host of *Picadilly Circus*, Max de Winter, "Rebecca," *Mystery*, as the title role in "The Adventures of Sherlock Holmes," *Mystery*, 1985-86, all on PBS. He has also been seen as the title role, *Picture of Dorian Gray*, Jacques, *Dinner with Family*, and Joseph Surface, *The School for Scandal*.

Episodic: *Hart to Hart*, ABC.

PRINCIPAL FILM APPEARANCES—Nicholas, *War and Peace*, Paramount, 1956; Freddie Eynsford, *My Fair Lady*, Warner Brothers, 1964.

ADDRESSES: AGENT—William Morris Agency, Ltd., 147 Wardour Street, London W1V 3TB, England.*

*   *   *

BRIDGES, Beau   1941-

PERSONAL: Born Lloyd Vernet Bridges, III, December 9, 1941, in Los Angeles, CA; son of Lloyd Vernet (the actor) and Dorothy (Simpson) Bridges; married Julie; children: Casey. EDUCATION: Attended University of California, Los Angeles, and University of Hawaii.

VOCATION: Actor.

CAREER: FILM DEBUT—*The Incident*, 1967. PRINCIPAL FILM APPEARANCES—*For Love of Ivy*, Cinerama, 1968; *Gaily, Gaily*, United Artists, 1969; *The Landlord*, United Artists, 1970; *Adam's Woman*, 1971; *The Christian Licorice Store*, National General, 1971; *Hammersmith Is Out*, Cinerama, 1972; *Child's Play*, Paramount, 1972; *Your Three Minutes Are Up*, Cinerama, 1973; *Lovin' Molly*, Columbia, 1974; *The Other Side of the Mountain*, Universal, 1975; *One Summer Love* (also known as *Dragonfly*), American International, 1976; *Swashbuckler*, Universal, 1976; *Two Minute Warning*, Universal, 1976; *Greased Lightning*, Warner Brothers, 1977; *Norma Rae*, Twentieth Century-Fox, 1979; *The Runner Stumbles*, Twentieth Century-Fox, 1979; *The Fifth Musketeer*, Austrian, 1979; *Honky Tonk Freeway*, Universal, 1980; *Night Crossing*, Buena Vista, 1982; *Love Child*, Warner Brothers, 1982; *Heart Like a Wheel*, Twentieth Century-Fox, 1983; *The Hotel New Hampshire*, Orion, 1984.

PRINCIPAL TELEVISION APPEARANCES—Series: Seaman Howard Spicer, *Ensign O'Toole*, NBC, 1962-63, ABC, 1963-64; Richard Chapin, *United States*, NBC, 1980.

Episodic: *Sea Hunt; Ben Casey; Dr. Kildare; Mr. Novak; Combat; Eleventh Hour*.

Movies: *The Man without a Country,* 1973; *The Whirlwind,* 1974; *The Four Feathers,* 1978; Thad Taylor, *A Fighting Choice,* ABC, 1986.

Mini-Series: *Space,* CBS, 1985.

ADDRESSES: AGENT—Creative Artists Agency, 1888 Century Park E., Suite 1400, Los Angeles, CA 90067.*

*   *   *

BRIDGES, Jeff 1951-

PERSONAL: Born in 1951; son of Lloyd Vernet (the actor) and Dorothy (Simpson) Bridges; married; children: three. EDUCATION: Studied with Uta Hagen in New York.

VOCATION: Actor.

CAREER: PRINCIPAL FILM APPEARANCES—*Silent Night, Lonely Night,* 1969; *The Last Picture Show,* Columbia, 1971; *Fat City,* Columbia, 1972; *Bad Company,* Paramount, 1972; *Lolly Madonna (XXX),* Metro-Goldwyn-Mayer, 1973; *The Last American Hero,* Twentieth Century-Fox, 1973; *The Iceman Cometh,* AFT Distributing, 1973; *Thunderbolt and Lightfoot,* United Artists, 1974; *Rancho Deluxe,* United Artists, 1975; *Hearts of the West,* United Artists, 1975; *Stay Hungry,* United Artists, 1976; *King Kong,* Paramount, 1976; *Somebody Killed Her Husband,* Columbia, 1978; *Winter Kills,* Avco Embassy, 1979; *Heaven's Gate,* United Artists, 1980; *Cutter's Way* (also known as *Cutter and Bone*), United Artists, 1981; *Tron,* Buena Vista, 1982; *Kiss Me Goodbye,* Twentieth Century-Fox, 1982; *Against All Odds,* Columbia, 1984; *Starman,* Columbia, 1984; *Jagged Edge,* Columbia, 1985; *8 Million Ways to Die,* Tri-Star, 1986.

PRINCIPAL TELEVISION APPEARANCES—Episodic: *Sea Hunt; The Lloyd Bridges Show.*

PRINCIPAL STAGE APPEARANCES—Toured New England when he was fourteen years old with his father in a stock production of *Anniversary Waltz.*

ADDRESSES: AGENT—Creative Artists Agency, 1888 Century Park E., Suite 1400, Los Angeles, CA 90067.*

*   *   *

BRIDGES, Lloyd 1913-

PERSONAL: Full name, Lloyd Vernet Bridges II; born January 15, 1913, in San Leandro, CA; son of Lloyd and Harriet (Brown) Bridges; married Dorothy Simpson; children: Lloyd Vernet III (Beau), Jeff, Lucinda. EDUCATION: Attended University of California, Los Angeles.

VOCATION: Actor.

CAREER: PRINCIPAL TELEVISION APPEARANCES—Series: Mike Nelson, *Sea Hunt,* syndicated, 1957-61; Adam Shepherd and various others, *The Lloyd Bridges Show,* CBS, 1962-63; William Colton, *The Loner,* CBS, 1965-66; Jim Conrad, *San Francisco International Airport,* NBC, 1970-71; title role, *Joe Forrester,* NBC, 1975-76; Grant Harper, *Paper Dolls,* ABC, 1984.

Episodic: "A Man's First Debt," *Bigelow Theatre,* CBS, 1950;

Summer Night Theatre, Dumont, 1953; *Kraft Suspense Theatre,* NBC, 1963; "Return of Joe Forrester," *Police Story,* NBC, 1974; also, *Footlights Theatre,* CBS; "Wild Bill Hickok—The Legend and the Man," *The Great Adventure,* CBS; "Her Last Adventure," *Suspense,* CBS; *Undercurrent,* CBS.

Mini-series: Evan Brent, *Roots,* ABC, 1977; *The Blue and the Gray,* NBC, 1984.

Movies: *Disaster on the Coastliner,* 1979; Johnny Hyde, "This Year's Blonde" (retitled "The Secret Love of Marilyn Monroe"), *Movieola,* NBC, 1980; *East of Eden,* 1981.

PRINCIPAL FILM APPEARANCES—*Trouble with Women,* 1942; *Miss Susie Slagle's,* 1945; *Abilene Town,* 1946; *Canyon Passage,* 1946; *Ramrod,* 1947; *Calamity Jane and Sam Bass,* 1949; *Trapped,* 1949; *Colt .45,* 1950; *Rocket Ship X M,* 1950; *Sound of Fury* (retitled *Try and Get Me*), 1951; *Whistle at Eaton Falls,* 1951; *Plymouth Adventure,* 1952; *High Noon,* 1952; *Apache Woman,* American International, 1955; *Wichita,* Allied Artists, 1955; *The Rainmaker,* 1958; *The Goddess,* 1958; *Daring Game,* 1968; *Happy Ending,* 1969; *Silent Night, Lonely Night,* 1969; *The Fifth Musketeer,* 1979; *Airplane!,* Paramount, 1980; *Airplane II,* Paramount, 1983; also appeared in, *Hideout; Three Steps North; Last of the Comanches; Walk in the Sun; Home of the Brave; White Tower; Tall Texan; Kid from Left Field; City of Bad Men; Limping Man; Pride of the Blue Grass; Deadly Game; Wetbacks.*

PRINCIPAL STAGE APPEARANCES—Appeared in stock productions, including *Anniversary Waltz,* New England, 1955.*

*   *   *

BRIDGES, Robert 1937-

PERSONAL: Born September 10, 1937, in San Francisco, CA; son of Frank Frazer and Margaret (O'Neill) Bridges. EDUCATION: Attended San Francisco State College, Sacramento State College, and University of the Pacific; studied at the San Francisco Actor's Workshop with Jules Irving and with De Marcus Brown at the University of the Pacific. MILITARY: U.S. Air Force, 1954-58.

VOCATION: Director and actor.

CAREER: FIRST STAGE WORK—Director, *The Biggest Thief in Town,* Tokyo Playhouse, Tokyo, Japan, 1955. NEW YORK DEBUT—Director, *The Patrick Pearse Motel,* Riverwest Theatre, 1984. PRINCIPAL STAGE WORK—Director: *Don Quixote,* Caravan Theatre, MA, 1969; *The York Mystery Cycle,* Three Boards Playhouse, MA, 1973; *The Gin Game,* TheatreWest, CA, 1983; *The Patrick Pearse Motel,* Los Gatos Acting Company, CA, 1984; *Deathtrap,* Equity Library Theatre, NY, 1985; *She Loves Me,* Equity Library Theatre, NY, 1985; *Light Up the Sky,* Jewish Repertory Theatre, NY, 1986.

Also directed *A Man's a Man* and *The White Devil,* Theatre Intime, Princeton University, Princeton, NJ; *Hedda Gabler* and *As You Like It,* University of the Pacific; *The Beautiful People,* Keio University, Tokyo, Japan; also directed new scripts at Theatre Guinevere and RiverWest Theatre, NY.

PRINCIPAL STAGE APPEARANCES—Seasons at the San Francisco Actor's Workshop; McCarter Theatre, Princeton, NJ; Oregon Shakespeare Festival; Colorado Shakespeare Festival; Canal Fulton Summer Arena.

ROBERT BRIDGES

MAJOR TOURS—*Da*, First National Company.

RELATED CAREER—Staff director, Tokyo Playhouse, Tokyo, Japan, 1955-57; staff director, Canal Fulton Summer Arena, 1965; two seasons, Sacramento Civic Theatre, CA; three seasons, Children's Theatre of the West, CA; guest director, at Tobay Players, NY, Concord Players, MA, and Fallon House Summer Theatre, CA.

MEMBER: Society of Stage Directors and Choreographers, Actors' Equity Association, Screen Actors Guild, American Federation of Television and Radio Artists.

SIDELIGHTS: Mr. Bridges is a painter and graphic artist whose canvases and prints have been exhibited at the Boston Public Library and the Institute of Contemporary Art in Boston.

ADDRESSES: HOME—Five Ninth Avenue, New York, NY 10014.

*   *   *

BRONSON, Charles   1920-

PERSONAL: Born in 1920, in Ehrenfeld, PA; married Harriet Tendler (divorced); married Jill Ireland (the actress), 1969; children: (first marriage) two children; (second marriage) Zuleika (daughter), two stepchildren. MILITARY: U.S. Army, 1943-46.

VOCATION: Actor.

CAREER: FILM DEBUT—*You're in the Navy Now*, 1951. PRINCIPAL FILM APPEARANCES—*The Mob*, 1951; *Red Skies of Montana*, 1952; *My Six Convicts*, 1952; *Pat and Mike*, 1952; *House of Wax*, 1953; *Miss Sadie Thompson*, 1953; *Crime Wave*, 1954; *Tennessee Champ*, 1954; *Apache*, 1954; *Drumbeat*, 1954; *Vera Cruz*, 1954; *Big House, U.S.A.*, United Artists, 1955; *Jubal*, Columbia, 1956; Blue Buffalo, *Run of the Arrows*, Universal, 1957; *Machine Gun Kelly*, American International, 1958; *Never So Few*, Metro-Goldwyn-Mayer, 1959.

The Magnificent Seven, United Artists, 1960; *A Thunder of Drums*, Metro-Goldwyn-Mayer, 1961; *Kid Galahad*, United Artists, 1962; *Lonely Are the Brave*, Universal, 1962; *The Great Escape*, United Artists, 1963; *4 for Texas*, Warner Brothers, 1963; *The Battle of the Bulge*, Warner Brothers, 1965; *The Sandpiper*, Metro-Goldwyn-Mayer, 1965; *This Property Is Condemned*, Paramount, 1966; *The Dirty Dozen*, Metro-Goldwyn-Mayer, 1967; *Guns for San Sebastian*, Metro-Goldwyn-Mayer, 1967; *Adieu, L'Ami (Farewell, Friend)*, 1968; *Villa Rides*, Paramount, 1968; *Once Upon a Time in the West*, Paramount, 1969; *Twinky*, 1969; *Le Passager de la Pluie*, 1969.

Rider in the Rain, Avco Embassy, 1970; *You Can't Win Them All*, Columbia, 1970; *Cold Sweat*, 1970; *Someone Behind the Door*, Cinerama, 1971; *Chato's Land*, United Artists, 1971; *Red Sun*, National General, 1972; *The Valachi Papers*, 1972; *The Mechanic*, United Artists, 1972; *Valdez the Halfbreed/Chino*, 1973; *Stone Killer*, Columbia, 1973; *Mr. Majestyk*, United Artists, 1974; *Death Wish*, Paramount, 1974; *Breakout*, 1975; *Hard Times*, Columbia, 1975; *Breakheart Pass*, 1976; *St. Ives*, Warner Brothers, 1976; *From Noon Till Three*, United Artists, 1976; *Telefon*, United Artists, 1977; *The White Buffalo*, 1977; *Love and Bullets*, 1979; *Cabo Blanco*, 1979.

Borderline, Associated Films Distributors, 1980; *Death Hunt*, Twentieth Century-Fox, 1981; *Deathwish II*, Filmways, 1982; *The Evil That Men Do*, Tri-Star, 1984; *Deathwish III*, Cannon, 1985; Jack Murphy, *Murphy's Law*, Cannon, 1986.

PRINCIPAL TELEVISION APPEARANCES—Series: Mike Kovac, *Man with a Camera*, ABC, 1958-60; Paul Moreno, *Empire*, NBC, 1963; Linc Murdoch, *The Travels of Jamie McPheeters*, ABC, 1963-64.

Episodic: *Meet McGraw; Redigo; Twilight Zone; Pepsi-Cola Playhouse; Treasury Men in Action; The Line-up; The Legend of Jesse James; Sheriff of Cochise; The Big Valley; The FBI.*

Movies: *Raid on Entebbe*, 1977; *Yablonsky*, HBO, 1986.

ADDRESSES: AGENT—Paul Kohner-Michael Levy Agency, 9169 Sunset Blvd., Los Angeles, CA 90069.*

*   *   *

BROOKS, Charles David, III   1939-

PERSONAL: Born September 28, 1939, in New York, NY; son of Charles David II and Ruth Cornelia (Butler) Brooks; married wife Wilson (an educator), January 1, 1978; children: Charles David IV, Solomon Michael. EDUCATION: University of California at Los Angeles, B.A., 1974, M.F.A., 1976; post graduated work done at Columbia University Teachers College, 1984-86; trained for the stage with Jerry Blount. POLITICS: Independent. RELIGION: Baptist. MILITARY: U.S. Air Force, 1959.

CHARLES DAVID BROOKS III

VOCATION: Director, producer, writer, and actor.

CAREER: STAGE DEBUT—Captain, *Harambee*, Pasadena Civic Theater, Pasadena, 1969, for twelve performances. NEW YORK DEBUT—David, *Building a Nation*, Walter Bruno Auditorium, Lincoln Center, 1979, for four performances. PRINCIPAL STAGE WORK—Director, producer, and playwright, *Search*, Lincoln Center, NY; producer, director, and playwright, *Ifrique and Lifestyles*, Los Angeles; producer, director, and playwright, *Love*, Los Angeles, 1974; actor, *The Great White Hope*, Los Angeles; director, *No Place to Be Somebody*, Los Angeles; actor, *Dracula*, Los Angeles; actor, *Garbage Hustler*, Los Angeles; actor, *Conspiracy*, Los Angeles; actor, *The Awful Pit*, Los Angeles; actor, *Our Lan'*, Los Angeles, CA.

PRINCIPAL FILM APPEARANCES—*The Great White Hope*, Twentieth Century-Fox, 1970; also appeared in *Emma Mae; Welcome Home, Brother Charles; Bush Mama; The Robert Small Story*.

PRINCIPAL TELEVISION APPEARANCES—Host, *Charles Brooks Show*, cable.

RELATED CAREER—Director, Watts Repertory Company, CA; director, Community Theatre Workshop; program director, Community Services Commission; artistic director, Mafundi Institute; president, film and television, Gigantic Enterprises; community outreach co-ordinator, Theatre for the Forgotten; teacher, University of California at Los Angeles Experimental College; drama instructor, citywide, NY; New York City Board of Education, 1980-85; financial aid administrator, Teachers College, Columbia University, NY, 1985.

AWARDS: John Golden Award, 1979 and 1980, for *Search;* Arts Managers Fellowship Award, National Endowment for the Arts.

MEMBER: Society of Stage Directors and Choreographers, Dramatists' Guild, National Endowment for the Arts, International Platform Association, Broadcast Music Inc.

ADDRESSES: HOME—400 W. 43rd Street, Apt. 18D, New York, NY 10036. OFFICE—c/o Director of Performing Arts, JHS 117K, 300 Willoughby Avenue, Brooklyn, NY 11205.

*   *   *

BROOKS, James L.   1940-

PERSONAL: Born May 9, 1940, in Brooklyn, NY; son of Edward M. and Dorothy Helen (Sheinheit) Brooks; married Marianne Catherine Morrissey, July 7, 1964 (divorced); married Holly Beth Holmberg, July 23, 1978; children: (first marriage) Amy Lorriane. EDUCATION: Attended New York University, 1958-60.

VOCATION: Screenwriter, producer, director, and actor.

CAREER: PRINCIPAL TELEVISION WORK—Episodic: Story editor and co-creator, *Room 222*, ABC, 1968-69; executive producer and co-creater, *Mary Tyler Moore Show*, CBS, 1970-77; producer, *Paul Sand in Friends and Lovers*, CBS, 1974; co-creator and co-executive producer, *Rhoda*, CBS, 1974-75; writer, *The New Lorenzo Music Show*, CBS, 1976; co-executive producer, *Lou Grant*, CBS, 1977; co-creator and executive producer, *Taxi*, ABC, 1978-80; co-creator and executive producer, *The Associates*, ABC, 1979.

Movies: Writer, producer, *Thursday's Game*, 1974; executive producer, co-writer, *Cindy*, 1978.

PRINCIPAL FILM WORK—Writer and co-producer, *Starting Over*, Paramount, 1979; actor, Columbia, *Modern Romance*, 1981; co-producer, writer, and director, *Terms of Endearment*, Paramount, 1983; producer, co-writer, and director, *Perfect!*, 1985; producer, *Between Friends*, Orion, 1986.

RELATED CAREER: Writer, *CBS News*, NY, 1964-66; writer and producer of documentaries for Wolper Productions, Los Angeles, CA, 1966-67; guest lecturer, Stanford Graduate School of Communications.

AWARDS: (With Allan Burns) Outstanding Writing Achievement in Comedy (Series), Emmy, 1970-71, for "Support Your Local Mother," *Mary Tyler Moore Show;* (with Allan Burns) Outstanding Comedy Series, Emmys, 1974-75, 1975-76, and 1976-77, for *Mary Tyler Moore Show;* (with others) Outstanding Writing in a Comedy Series (Single Episode), Emmy, 1976-77, for "The Final Show," *Mary Tyler Moore Show;* Achievement in a Comedy Series, TV Critics Circle Award, 1976-77 for *Mary Tyler Moore Show*.

Peabody Awards, 1977 and 1978, for *Lou Grant;* (with others) Outstanding Comedy Series, Emmys, 1978-79, 1979-80, and 1980-81, for *Taxi;* Best Comedy Series, Golden Globe Awards, 1978, 1979, and 1980, for *Taxi;* Humanities Prize Award, 1979, for "Blind Date," *Taxi;* Outstanding Comedy Script, Writers Guild Award, 1978, for *Cindy;* Best Film, Best Director, and Best Screenplay, Academy Award, 1984, for *Terms of Endearment*.*

DAVID BROWN

BROWN, David   1916-

PERSONAL: Born July 28, 1916; son of Edward Fisher and Lillian (Baren) Brown; married Liberty LeGacy, April 15, 1940 (divorced, 1951); married Wayne Clark, May 25, 1951 (divorced, 1957); married Helen Gurley (an editor), September 25, 1959; children: (first marriage) Bruce LeGacy. EDUCATION: Stanford University, A.B., 1936; Columbia University, M.S., 1937. MILITARY: U.S. Army, World War II.

VOCATION: Film producer, writer, and journalist.

CAREER: PRINCIPAL FILM WORK—Producer: *The Sting,* Universal, 1973; *SSSSSSS,* Universal, 1973; *The Sugarland Express,* Universal, 1974; *The Black Windmill,* Universal, 1974; *Willie Dynamite,* Universal, 1974; *The Girl from Petrovka,* Universal, 1974; *Jaws,* Universal, 1975; *The Eiger Sanction,* Universal, 1975; *MacArthur,* Universal, 1977; *Jaws 2,* Universal, 1978; *The Island,* Universal, 1980; *The Verdict,* Warner Brothers, 1982; *Neighbors,* Warner Brothers, 1985; *Cocoon,* Twentieth Century-Fox, 1985; *Target,* Warner Brothers, 1985.

RELATED CAREER—Apprentice, *San Francisco News;* apprentice, *Wall Street Journal,* 1936; night editor and assistant drama critic, Fairchild Publications, 1937-39; editorial director, Milk Research Council, 1939-40; associate editor, Street & Smith Publications, 1940-43; associate editor, executive editor, and editor-in-chief, *Liberty Magazine,* 1943-49; editorial director, national campaign, American Medical Association, 1949; associate editor and managing editor, *Cosmopolitan,* magazine, 1949-52; managing editor, story editor, and head of scenario department, Twentieth Century-Fox Film Corporation, 1952-56; studio executive committee, Twentieth Century-Fox, 1956-60; producer, executive story editor, and head of scenario department, Twentieth Century-Fox, 1956-60; editorial vice-president, New American Library of World Literature, Inc., 1963-64; vice-president and director of story operation, Twentieth Century-Fox, 1964-69; executive vice-president of creative operations, Twentieth Century-Fox, 1969-70.

Executive vice-president, Warner Brothers, 1970-72; partner and director, Zanuck/Brown Company, Universal Pictures, 1972-80; producer, Twentieth Century-Fox, 1980-83; producer, Warner Brothers, 1983—.

WRITINGS: MAGAZINE STORIES AND ARTICLES—*American Magazine; Collier's; Harper's; Readers Digest; American Mercury; The Saturday Evening Post; Saturday Review of Literature; Cosmopolitan; Journalists in Action.*

AWARDS: National Association of Theatre Owners of America, Producer of the Year, 1974 and 1985; Best Picture, Academy Award, 1974, for *The Sting;* Best Picture, Academy Award nominations, 1975, for *Jaws,* and 1982, for *The Verdict.*

MEMBER: American Film Institute (trustee, member of executive committee); Commission on Film, Museum of Modern Art, NY (trustee); National Academy of Motion Picture Arts and Sciences; The Century Club, Players Club, Overseas Press Club, Dutch Treat, National Press Club.

ADDRESSES: HOME—One W. 81st Street, New York, NY 10024. OFFICE—200 W. 57th Street, New York, NY 10019.

*   *   *

BRUCE, Susan   1957-

PERSONAL: Born Susan Titman, March 10, 1957, in New York, NY; daughter of John D. (works for HBO) and Narcissa (a choir director; maiden name, Hargroves) Titman. EDUCATION: University of Michigan, B.A., theatre, 1980; New York University professional training program, M.F.A., 1983.

SUSAN BRUCE

VOCATION: Actress.

CAREER: PRINCIPAL STAGE APPEARANCES—Paula, *End of Summer* and Puck, *A Midsummer Night's Dream*, both Michigan Repertory Theatre; Emily, *Our Town*, Blacksheep Repertory Theatre, MI; Mag, *Winners*, Hermia, *A Midsummer Night's Dream*, Susan, *Loose Ends*, all New York University; Robin, *Godspell*, Gallery Players, NY; She, *Loveliest Afternoon of the Year*, Double Image Theatre, NY; Fern, *Charlotte's Web*, Lincoln Center, NY; Elizabeth, *Frankenstein* and Gerd, *Brand*, both City Stage Company; Lady Anne (understudy), *Richard III*, New York Shakespeare Festival.

PRINCIPAL TELEVISION APPEARANCES—Phyllis, *Edge of Night*, ABC; Trudy, *Another World*, NBC.

RELATED CAREER—Movement and voice teacher, Northwestern University, 1985.

MEMBER: Actors' Equity Association, American Federation of Television and Radio Artsts.

ADDRESSES: HOME—c/o Guerrero, 147 Montague Street, Brooklyn, NY 11201.

*   *   *

BRYNNER, Yul   1920-1985

PERSONAL: Born Taidje Kahn, July 11, 1920, in Sakhalin, an island north of Japan; died of cancer in New York, NY, on October 10, 1985; married Virgnia Gilmore, September 6, 1944 (divorced); married Doris Kleiner (divorced); married Jacqueline de Croisset (divorced); married Kathy Lee, 1983; children: (first marriage) Rock. EDUCATION: Attended the Sorbonne, Paris.

VOCATION: Actor.

CAREER: NEW YORK DEBUT—*Twelfth Night* (as Youl Bryner), Little Theater, 1941. PRINCIPAL STAGE APPEARANCES—Broadway: *Lute Song*, 1945-46; *Dark Eyes*, 1947-48; King of Siam, *The King and I*, 1951-54, 1977-85 (for a total of 4,625 performances); Odysseus, *Home Sweet Homer*, 1975.

FILM DEBUT—*Port of New York*, 1949. PRINCIPAL FILM APPEARANCES—*The Ten Commandments*, Paramount, 1956; King of Siam, *The King and I*, Twentieth Century-Fox, 1956; *Anastasia*, Twentieth Century-Fox, 1956; *The Brothers Karamazov*, Metro-Goldwyn-Mayer, 1958; *The Buccaneer*, Paramount, 1958; *Solomon and Sheba*, United Artists, 1959; *The Sound and the Fury*, Twentieth Century-Fox, 1959; *The Journey*, Metro-Goldwyn-Mayer, 1959.

The Magnificent Seven, United Artists, 1960; *Once More with Feeling*, Columbia, 1960; *Taras Bulba*, United Artists, 1962; *Escape from Zahrain*, Paramount, 1962; *Kings of the Sun*, United Artists, 1963; *Flight from Ashiya*, United Artists, 1964; *Invitation to a Gunfighter*, United Artists, 1964; *Morituri*, Twentieth Century-Fox, 1965; *Cast a Giant Shadow*, United Artists, 1966; *Return of the Seven*, United Artists, 1966; *The Double Man*, Warner Brothers, 1967; *The Long Duel*, Paramount, 1967; *Villa Rides*, Paramount, 1968; *The Madwoman of Chaillot*, Warner Brothers, 1969; *The File of the Golden Goose*, United Artists, 1969.

Romance of a Horsethief, Allied Artists, 1971; *Adios Sabota*, 1971; *Light at the Edge of the World*, National General, 1971; *The Battle of*

YUL BRYNNER

Neretra, American International, 1971; *Catlow*, United Artists, 1971; *Fuzz*, United Artists, 1972; *Westworld*, Metro-Goldwyn-Mayer, 1973; *The Serpent*, 1973; *The Ultimate Warrior*, 1975; *Death Rage*, 1976; *Future World*, American International, 1976.

TELEVISION DEBUT—As an actor, producer, and director on the first NBC talk show, 1948. PRINCIPAL TELEVISION APPEARANCES—Series: King of Siam, *Anna and the King*, CBS, 1972.

Episodic: "Friend of the Family," *Fireside Theatre*, NBC, 1949; "Flowers from a Stranger," *Studio One*, CBS, 1949; *Omnibus*, CBS, 1953.

PRINCIPAL TELEVISION WORK—Director, "Footprints in the Jungle," *Somerset Maugham Theatre*, CBS, 1950; producer and director, *Life with Snarky Parker*, CBS, 1950; director, *Danger*, CBS, 1950-54.

PRINCIPAL RADIO APPEARANCES—Announcer (in French), Office of War Information, 1942-46.

WRITINGS: BOOKS—*Bring Forth the Children*.

MEMBER: United Nations High Commission for Refugees.

AWARDS: Donaldson Award, Best Actor, 1951; Best Actor, Academy Award, 1956, for *The King and I;* National Board of Review Motion Pictures Award, Best Performance, for *The King and I;* Antoinette Perry Award; Critics Circle Award.

SIDELIGHTS: Yul Brynner told several conflicting stories about his birth and early years; at various times, he gave his birthdate as 1915, 1917, 1920, and 1922. According to his obituaries in *The New York Times* and *Variety*, he was the son of a Mongolian-Swiss mining engineer and a Rumanian gypsy woman, grew up in Peking and Paris, and worked as a circus acrobat and clown during his teens.

Unknown at the time, Brynner was cast as the King of Siam in *The King and I* only after several better-known actors turned the role down. Originally, Gertrude Lawrence, who appeared opposite him as Anna, received star billing, while Brynner's name was listed in smaller type below the title. He remained with the show throughout its original three-year New York run, and subsequently played the King in two successful Broadway revivals, several extensive road tours, the 1956 film, and a short-lived television series. Reviewing Brynner's 1985 "farewell engagement" in the musical, Frank Rich of *The New York Times* wrote, "Man and role have long since merged into a fixed image that is as much a part of our collective consciousness as the Statue of Liberty."

Brynner's bald head, which he originally shaved for *The King and I*, became his trademark.

A year before his death from lung cancer, Brynner, who at one time had smoked five packs of cigarettes a day, stated in a radio interview, "I'm talking to you now that I'm gone, and I'm telling you right now . . . that you must stop smoking." By prearrangement, the interview was broadcast after he died.*

*   *   *

BUJOLD, Genevieve   1942-

PERSONAL: Born July 1, 1942, in Montreal; daughter of Firmin and Laurette (Cavanaugh) Bujold; married Paul Almond (a television producer); children: Matther James. EDUCATION: Montreal Drama Conservatory.

VOCATION: Actress.

CAREER: PRINCIPAL FILM APPEARANCES—*La Guerre est Finie*, Brandon, 1966; *King of Hearts*, Lopert, 1967; *Isabel*, Paramount, 1968; Anne Boleyn, *Anne of a Thousand Days*, 1970; *The Act of the Heart*, Universal, 1970; *The Journey*, Canadian, 1972; *Earthquake*, Universal, 1974; *Swashbuckler*, Universal, 1976; *Obsession*, Columbia, 1976; *Alex and the Gypsy*, 1976; *Another Man, Another Chance*, United Artists, 1977; *Coma*, United Artists, 1978; *Murder by Decree*, Avco-Embassy, 1979; *The Last Flight of Noah's Ark*, Buena Vista, 1980; *Final Assignment*, 1980; *Monsignore*, Twentieth Century-Fox, 1982; *Tightrope*, Warner Brothers, 1984; *Choose Me*, Island Alive, 1984; *Trouble in Mind*, Island Alive, 1986; also, *La Fleur de L'Age; Entre La Mer et L'eau Douce; The Thief; Kamouraska*.

TELEVISION DEBUT—*St. Joan*. PRINCIPAL TELEVISION APPEARANCES—*Anthony and Cleopatra*.

STAGE DEBUT—*St. Joan*. PRINCIPAL STAGE APPEARANCES—*The Barber of Seville; A Midsummer Night's Dream; A House . . . A Day*.

AWARDS: Susan Bianchetti Award, 1966, for *La Guerre est Fini*; Best Actress, Carthagenia Film Festival Award, Golden Globe Award, Earle Grey Award, 1972, all for *Anne of a Thousand Days*.

ADDRESSES: HOME—Los Angeles, CA 90069. AGENT—Traubner and Flynn, 1849 Sawtelle Blvd., Suite 500, Los Angeles, CA 90025.*

*   *   *

BULLOCK, Donna   1955-

PERSONAL: Born December 11, 1955, in Dallas, TX; daughter of Jack (a real estate agent) and Shirley Ann (a secretary; maiden name, Black) Bullock. EDUCATION: Attended Southern Methodist University, 1979. RELIGION: Episcopalian.

VOCATION: Actress.

CAREER: STAGE DEBUT—*Heaven Can Wait*, Kenley Players, Warren, OH, 1977. NEW YORK DEBUT—Katie Yoder, *Plain and Fancy*, Equity Library Theatre, 1980. PRINCIPAL STAGE APPEARANCES—Ensemble, *Noel*, Goodspeed Opera House, CT, 1980; Raven, *The Evangelist*, Wonderhorse Theatre, NY, 1982; Jenny, *Portrait of Jenny*, Henry Street Settlement, NY, 1982; Liz, *Billy Liar*, Westside Mainstage, 1982; Jeanine, Win, Waitress, *Top Girls*, New York Shakespeare Festival, Public Theatre, 1983; Nancy, *Stem of a Briar*, Kenyon Festival, OH, 1983; Fiona Kelly, *Shot Thru the Heart*, Birmingham Theatre, MI, 1983; *The Dining Room*, Plaza Theatre, Dallas, TX, 1983-84.

MAJOR TOURS—Jenny, *The Umbrellas of Cherbourg*, West Coast, 1980; *A Christmas Carol*, Baltimore, MD, New Orleans, LA, 1981-82.

TELEVISION DEBUT—*Dallas*, CBS, 1978. PRINCIPAL TELEVISION APPEARANCES—Kim McGuire, *All My Children*, ABC.

MEMBER: Actors' Equity Association, American Federation of Television and Radio Artists; New York Arts Group.

AWARDS: Obie Award, 1983, for the ensemble, *Top Girls*.

ADDRESSES: HOME—210 W. 89th Street, New York, NY 10024. AGENT—Leverton/Sames Associates, 1650 Broadway, New York, NY 10019.

*   *   *

BURNS, George   1896-

PERSONAL: Born Nathan Birnbaum, January 20, 1896, in New York, NY; married Gracie Allen, January 7, 1926 (died, August, 1964); children: (adopted) Sandra Jean, Ronald John.

VOCATION: Comedian and actor.

CAREER: STAGE DEBUT—Dancer, singer, and comedian, Keith Vaudeville Circuit. PRINCIPAL STAGE APPEARANCES—*Burns and Allen*, Keith Vaudeville Circuit, 1923. MAJOR TOURS—*Burns and Allen*, U.S. and European cities.

FILM DEBUT—1932. PRINCIPAL FILM APPEARANCES—*The Big Broadcast*, 1932; *International House*, 1933; *Love in Bloom*, 1933; *College Humor*, 1933; *Six of a Kind*, 1934; *We're Not Dressing*, 1934; *College Holiday*, 1936; *The Big Broadcast*, 1936, *A Damsel in Distress*, 1937; *The Big Broadcast*, 1937; *College Swing*, 1938; *Many Happy Returns*, 1939; *Honolulu*, 1939; *Two Girls and a Sailor*, 1944; *The Sunshine Boys*, United Artists, 1975; title role, *Oh, God!*, Warner Brothers, 1977; *Sgt. Pepper's Lonely Hearts Club Band*, Universal, 1978; *Just You and Me, Kid*, Columbia, 1979; title role, *Oh, God! Book II*, Warner Brothers, 1980; title roles, *Oh, God! You, Devil!*, Warner Brothers, 1985.

PRINCIPAL TELEVISION APPEARANCES—Series: As himself, *Burns and Allen Show*, CBS, 1950-58; as himself, *George Burns Show*, NBC, 1958-59; as himself, *Wendy and Me*, ABC, 1964-65; host, *George Burns Comedy Week*, CBS, 1985.

Episodic: "Tin Pan Alley Today," *Kraft Music Hall*, NBC; *The Muppet Show*, syndicated; *Startime*, NBC; *That's Life*, ABC, *Wayne and Shuster Take an Affectionate Look*, CBS.

Movie: *Two of a Kind*, 1982.

Specials: Numerous of his own and as a guest.

PRINCIPAL TELEVISION WORK—Producer, *Meet Mona McClusky*, NBC, 1965.

WRITINGS: BOOKS—*I Love Her, That's Why!*, 1955; *Living It Up, or They Still Love Me in Altoona*, 1976; *How to Live to be One Hundred or More*, Putnam, 1983; *Dear George: Advice and Answers from America's Leading Expert on Everything from A to B*, Putnam, 1985; *Dr. Burn's Prescription for Happiness*, Putnam, 1985.

RECORDINGS: COMEDY—*I Wish I Was Eighteen Again*, Mercury, 1980; *George Burns in Nashville*, 1981.

AWARDS: Best Supporting Actor, Academy Award, 1976, for *The Sunshine Boys*.

ADDRESSES: OFFICE—c/o Putnam Publishing Group, 200 Madison Avenue, New York, NY 10016.*

*   *   *

BURR, Raymond   1917-

PERSONAL: Born May 21, 1917, in New Westminster, BC, Canada. EDUCATION: Studied at Stanford, the University of California, Columbia University, and the University of Chungking.

CAREER. PRINCIPAL TELEVISION APPEARANCES—Series: Title role, *Perry Mason*, CBS, 1957-66; narrator, *Actuality Specials*, NBC, 1962-68; Robert Ironside, *Ironside*, NBC, 1967-75; R.B. Kingston, *Kingston: Confidential*, NBC, 1977.

Episodic: *ABC Dramatic Shorts*, 1952-53; "Dragnet," *Chesterfield Sound Off Time*, NBC, 1951; *Stars Over Hollywood*, NBC, 1951; "How Much Land Does a Man Need?," *Favorite Story*, syndicated, 1952; "The Ordeal of Dr. Sutton," *Schlitz Playhouse of Stars*, CBS; *Undercurrent*, CBS; *The Loveboat*, ABC.

Movies: *Kingston: The Power Play*, NBC, 1976; *Mallory: Circumstantial Evidence*, 1976; *79 Park Avenue*, 1977; *Disaster on a Coastliner*, 1979; title role, *Perry Mason Returns*, NBC, 1985; Perry Mason, *The Case of the Notorious Nun*, NBC, 1986.

Mini-Series: Bockweiss, *Centennial*, NBC, 1978.

PRINCIPAL FILM APPEARANCES—*Pitfall*, 1948; *Raw Deal*, 1948; *Criss Cross*, 1949; *Key to the City*, 1950; *His Kind of Woman*, 1951; *Place in the Sun*, 1951; *New Mexico*, 1951; *Mara Maru*, 1952; *Meet Danny Wilson*, 1952; *Horizons West*, 1952; *Blue Gardenia*, 1953; *Fort Algiers*, 1953; *Casanova's Big Night*, 1954; *Gorilla at Large*, 1954; *Khyber Patrol*, 1954; *Rear Window*, 1954; *They Were So Young*, Lippert, 1955; *You're Never Too Young*, Paramount, 1955; *A Man Alone*, Republic, 1955; *Count Three and Pray*, Columbia, 1955; *Please Murder Me*, Distributors Corp. of America, 1956; *Godzilla King of the Monsters*, Embassy, 1956; *Great Day in the Morning*, 1956; *Secret of Treasure Mountain*, Columbia, 1956; *Cry in the Night*, Warner Brothers, 1956; *P.J.*, Universal, 1968; *Airplane II: The Sequel*, Paramount, 1980; *Godzilla '85*, 1985.

PRINCIPAL STAGE APPEARANCES—*Night Must Fall; Mandarin; Crazy with the Heat; Duke in Darkness;* Burr has performed on stage in many countries.

PRINCIPAL STAGE WORK—Director, Pasadena Community Playhouse, CA, 1943.

AWARDS: Best Actor in a Leading Role (Continuing Character) in a Dramatic Series, Emmys, 1958-59 and 1960-61, for *Perry Mason*.

ADDRESSES: AGENT—David Shapira and Associates, 15301 Ventura Blvd., Suite 345, Sherman Oaks, CA 91403.*

*   *   *

BURROUGHS, Robert C.   1923-

PERSONAL: Born March 1, 1923, in Milwaukee, WI, son of S. Dillon (a sales manager) and Matta (Smith) Burroughs; married Patricia Genematas (a costume designer) December 29, 1951; children: Robert, Christopher. EDUCATION: Hanover College, B.A., 1943; Iowa State University, M.A., 1947; studied for three summers at Cornell University, 1951-53. POLITICS: Democrat. RELIGION: Methodist. MILITARY: U.S. Army, Sergeant, 1943-46.

VOCATION: Educator, director, designer, and actor.

CAREER: PRINCIPAL EDUCATIONAL APPOINTMENTS—Temporary instructor of drama, Hanover College, IN, 1942-43; instructor of theatre, San Diego State University, 1948; instructor of speech and drama, University of Alabama, 1949-50; instructor, University of Arizona's High School fine arts camp, 1954; instructor in theatre, U.S. Army Special Services, Fort Huachuca, Arizona, 1961-62; professor of drama, University of Arizona, 1947—; head of drama department, College of Fine Arts, University of Arizona, 1978—.

ROBERT C. BURROUGHS

PRINCIPAL STAGE WORK—Director at the University of Arizona: *Follies; Over Here; Dear Liar; Charley's Aunt; The Imaginary Invalid; The Clown Who Ran Away; The Little Foxes; A Doll's House; Pinocchio; The Heiress; Born Yesterday; The Steadfast Tin Soldier; Who'll Save the Ploughboy; Absence of a Cello; Misalliance; I Never Sang for My Father; The Prime of Miss Jean Brodie; Indians; Under Two Flags; The Taming of the Shrew; Playboy of the Western World; The Pursuit of Happiness; Hotel Paradiso; The Guardsman;* also directed plays at the National Music Camp, Interlochen Center for the Arts, MI; Arizona Theatre Company, Tucson, AZ; Imperial Players, Cripple Creek, CO.

Designer, University of Arizona: *An Evening with Lincoln; Girl Crazy; The Guardsman; Gigi; The Pursuit of Happiness; Peer Gynt; Hello, Dolly!; Hamlet; Mourning Becomes Electra; Playboy of the Western World; King Lear; Henry IV, Part I; Othello; Antony and Cleopatra; Misalliance;* designed plays at the University of Alabama, summer seasons, 1949-50; designed *She Stoops to Conquer, Joan of Lorraine,* and *The Dove and the Duck,* all at the University of Iowa, 1946-47; designed *The Doughgirls,* U.S.O., Alaska, 1944; designed *Take a Break,* U.S. Army Special Services Overseas Touring production, 1944-45; designed at the Tucson Children's Theatre, 1950-70.

PRINCIPAL STAGE APPEARANCES—With the Town Hall Players, Brewster-on-the-Cape, MA, 1948; Wagon Wheel Theatre, Rockton, IL, 1954; University of Arizona, 1947—; University of Alabama, 1949-50; narrator, San Xavier Fiesta, Tucson Festival Society, 1958—; narrator, Tucson Symphony, 1983.

MAJOR TOURS—*Take a Break,* U.S. Army Special Services Overseas production, 1944-45.

WRITINGS: PUBLICATIONS—(with Professor J.E. Lafferty) *Syllabus for Stagecraft and Stage Lighting,* 1960; *A Bibliography of Interest to Theatre Workers,* American Educational Theatre·Association Inc., 1961; "Some New Solutions for Old Problems," *The Arizona Journal of Speech and Drama,* 1961; *Athenian Theatre: 2000 Years Later, Drama at Calgary,* International Theatre Publication, 1969; "Plays and Awards," *Arizona Speech and Drama Journal,* 1964.

MEMBER: Dramatists Guild, American Theatre Association, (chairman, scene design and technical development committee, 1959-63), Speech Communications Association, United States Institute of Theatre Technology, Western Speech Association, Childrens Theatre Conference, National Collegiate Players, University Players (faculty advisor, 1947-72); Arizona Communication and Theatre Association, Arizona Speech and Drama Association (president, 1960-62), Arizona Alliance for Arts Education, Arizona Education Collaborative; Sigma Chi; The North Tucson Exchange Club.

AWARDS: Scholarship in R.C. Burroughs name established by Corson Foundation at National Music Camp, 1967; regional and national winner, American College Theatre Festival, University of Arizona, 1969, for *Misalliance;* Citation of Merit, American College Theatre Festival, Pacific South Region II, University of Arizona, 1977, for *Hotel Paradiso;* grants from the Arizona Foundation to establish a permanent collection of professional scene and costume designs and to aid in organizing a touring exhibit of theatre designs of R.C. Burroughs and Dennis Sporre.

ADDRESSES: HOME—5810 N. Williams Drive, Tucson, AZ, 85704. OFFICE—Department of Drama, University of Arizona, Tucson, AZ, 85721.

BUTLEROFF, Helen 1950-

PERSONAL: Born August 15, 1950, in New York, NY; daughter of Boris B. (a dancer) and Helen Mae (a dancer; maiden name, Rosler) Butleroff; married Joe Bruscino (a physicist) April 19, 1969 (divorced). EDUCATION: Queens College, New York, B.A., speech and theatre; graduate studies at Hunter College in theatre.

VOCATION: Director, choreographer, and performer.

CAREER: PRINCIPAL STAGE APPEARANCES—Dancer, as a Rockette and with the Ballet Company, Radio City Music Hall; dancer, with June Taylor Dancers, in *Around the World in Eighty Days* and *Mardi Gras,* both at the Jones Beach Memorial Theatre, Long Island, NY; dance captain and swing dancer, *Mack & Mabel,* Palace Theatre, NY, 1974.

PRINCIPAL STAGE WORK—Director: *The Blind,* NY; *The Decline and Fall of the Entire World as Seen Through the Eyes of Cole Porter,* Stony Brook, NY; *Funny Girl, No, No Nanette,* and *Mack & Mabel,* all at the Music Theatre of Wichita, Wichita, KS; *Hair,* Kansas City Starlight Theatre, Kansas City, MO; *Aquarius,* New York Hilton, NY; *Las Americanitas,* Caracas, Venezuela; *Joshua Logan's Musical Moments,* Reno Sweeney's, NY; *Times of Your Life, Strictly USA,* and *The Carol Lawrence Show,* all Sheraton Lakeview Theatre.

Choreographer: *When the Cookie Crumbles,* Town Hall, NY; *Oh, What a Wedding,* Anderson Theatre, NY; *Woyzeck,* The Production Company, NY; *The Entertainer,* Joseph Jefferson Theatre, Chicago; *Gay Divorce,* Equity Library Theatre, NY; *Dragons,* City Center Theatre, NY; *The Wizard of Oz,* Westbury Music Fair/Valley Forge Music Fair; *Swing Shift,* Theatre by the Sea, Portsmouth, NH; *Gay Divorce,* Goodspeed Opera House, East Haddam, CT; *The Boyfriend,* Theatre by the Sea, Matunuck, RI; *Company* and *Funny Girl,* Lakewood Musical Playhouse, Lakewood, PA; *Carousel,* Club Bene, Sayerville, NJ; *1776, Showboat, Hello, Dolly!,* and *The Music Man,* all for Little Theatre on the Square; *Camelot, Good News, I Do I Do, Funny Girl, The Red Mill, Cabaret, Fanny, Sweet Charity, Naughty Marietta, Paint Your Wagon, No, No Nanette,* and *My Fair Lady,* all for the Pittsburgh Civic Light Opera, Pittsburgh, PA; *The Music Man, Jesus Christ Superstar, Annie Get Your Gun, The Wizard of Oz, Cabaret, Camelot,* and *Oliver!,* all for Kansas City Starlight Theatre.

MEMBER: Actors' Equity Association, Society of Stage Directors and Choreographers, American Guild of Variety Artists, Screen Actors Guild; United University Professors.

SIDELIGHTS: Butleroff has also directed and/or choreographed industrial shows for Dairy Queen, Kraft, Hamilton Beach, Gitano Jeans, Hart Schaffner and Marx and others. She has done commercials as well.

ADDRESSES: OFFICE—P.O. Box 553, Grace Station, New York, NY 10028.

*　　*　　*

BUZZI, Ruth 1939-

PERSONAL: Born July 24, 1939, in Westerly, RI; daughter of Angelo Peter (a stone sculptor) and Rena Pauline (Macchi) Buzzi; married second husband, Kent Perkins, December 10, 1979. EDUCATION: Trained for the stage at the Pasadena Playhouse, 1954-57.

RUTH BUZZI

VOCATION: Actress.

CAREER: PRINCIPAL TELEVISION APPEARANCES—Series: *The Days of Our Lives*, NBC; *The Entertainers*, CBS, 1964-65; *The Steve Allen Comedy Hour*, CBS, 1967; Margie "Pete" Peterson, *That Girl*, ABC, 1967-68; *Rowan and Martin's Laugh-In*, NBC, 1968-73; *Book of Lists*, CBS, 1982; *The Lost Saucer*, ABC.

Movies: *In Name Only*, 1969; *The Entertainers; Aloha Paradise*.

Episodic: *Love American Style; Trapper John, M.D.; Medical Center; Alice; Loveboat; Comedy Break; Down to Earth; Emergency; Fridays; The Muppet Show; Here's Lucy; Masquerade; Lotsa Luck; Gunshy; The Monkees; Snowjob; Madam's Place; Rhoda.*

Guest: *Garry Moore Show; Dean Martin Roasts; The Donny and Marie Show; The Dean Martin Show; The Tonight Show; Kroft's Superstars; Gladys and Tyrone; Carol Burnett and Friends; The Flip Wilson Show; Tony Orlando and Dawn; The Dean Martin Variety Hour; Leslie Uggams Show; Epcot Magazine*, Disney Channel; *Sonny and Cher Show; Cher; The Mac Davis Show; Hee Haw; Jonathan Winters Improv Series; Evening at the Improv; Pat Boone U.S.A.; Jack Burns and Avery Schreiber Show; The Jim Nabors Show; The Bobby Vinton Show; That's Life; The Donna Fargo Show; Marty Robbins Spotlight; The Ralph Emery Show; Pop Goes the Country; Here's Julie; The Rene Simard Show; Betsy Lee's Ghost Town Jamboree; Whatever Turns You On.*

Here's Flip; Bob Hope's Women I Love; Beautiful but Funny; Gene Kelly and Fifty Girls Count 'Em Fifty; Dom Deluise and Friends; Sandy in Disneyland; Here's Goldie; The Dean Martin Christmas Special; Salute to Jerry Lee Lewis; The Gift of Music; The Brothers Grim; The Wayne Newton Special; The Wayne Newton Sea World Special; David Copperfield Magic Special; Here Comes Didi; You Oughta Be in Pictures; NBC Comedy Special; Milton Berle's Magic of Stars; Super Heros; CBN Special; Superbowl '77; Rolf Harris in Seoul; Wind Surf World; Anne Murray in Jamaica; Saturday Afternoon Special; Fun in Las Vegas; The Celebrity Love Cruise; Saturday Morning Special.

PRINCIPAL FILM APPEARANCES—*Freaky Friday*, Buena Vista, 1977; *Skatetown, U.S.A.*, Rastar, 1977; *The Villain*, Rastar, 1979; *The North Avenue Irregulars*, Buena Vista, 1979; *Chu Chu and the Philly Flash*, Twentieth Century-Fox, 1981; *Surf Two*, International Film Marketing, 1984; *The Being*, Best Film, 1985; *The Bad Guys*, Tomorrow Entertainment, 1986; also, *The Apple Dumpling Gang Rides Again*, Buena Vista; *Easter Sunday; Record City; The Trouble with Hello.*

PRINCIPAL STAGE APPEARANCES—Broadway: *Sweet Charity*.

Off-Broadway: *A Man's a Man; Little Mary Sunshine; Babe's in the Woods; Misguided Tour.*

Stock: *The Ruth Buzzi Show*, Las Vegas, NV; Pasadena Playhouse, CA.

MEMBER: Screen Actors Guild, American Federation of Television and Radio Artists, Academy of Motion Picture Arts and Sciences, American Guild of Variety Artists, American Society of Composers, Authors, and Publishers.

AWARDS: Four Emmy Award nominations; Golden Globe Award; Variety Artist of the Year, American Guild of Variety Artists Award, 1977; Rhode Island Hall of Fame Award; Pasadena Playhouse Achievement Award, 1979; Presidential Commendation Award, Outstanding Artist in the Field of Entertainment, 1980; National Association for the Advancement of Colored People's Image Award.

ADDRESSES: AGENT—Barry Freed Company, 9255 Sunset Blvd., Los Angeles, CA 90069; Sutton, Barth, and Vennari, 8322 Beverly Blvd., Los Angeles, CA 90048.

C

CAESAR, Adolph 1934-1986

PERSONAL: Born 1934, in Harlem, NY; died of an apparent heart attack in Los Angeles, CA, March 6, 1986; children: three.

VOCATION: Actor.

CAREER: PRINCIPAL STAGE APPEARANCES—*The River Niger,* Square Root of the Soul, and *The Brownsville Raid,* all for the Negro Ensemble Company, NY, beginning 1970; Sgt. Vernon Walters, *A Soldier's Play,* Negro Ensemble Company, NY, 1981-82; appeared with the Oregon Shakespeare Festival, the American Shakespeare Company, the Minnesota Theatre Company, the Center Theatre Group at the Mark Taper Forum, Los Angeles, the New York Shakespeare Festival, and the Lincoln Center Repertory Company.

MAJOR TOURS—Sgt. Vernon Walters, *A Soldier's Play,* national.

PRINCIPAL FILM APPEARANCES—*Che!,* Twentieth Century-Fox, 1969; *The Hitter,* 1978; Sgt. Vernon Walters, *A Soldier's Story,* Columbia, 1984; *The Color Purple,* Warner Brothers, 1985; *Club Paradise,* Warner Brothers, 1985; *Tough Guys* (incomplete at time of death), Touchstone (upcoming).

PRINCIPAL TELEVISION APPEARANCES—''Getting Even,'' *ABC After School Special,* 1985.

AWARDS: Obie Award, New York Drama Desk Award, both for *A Soldier's Play;* Best Supporting Actor, Academy Award nomination, 1984, for *A Soldier's Story;* Image Award, National Association for the Advancement of Colored People.*

*   *   *

CAGNEY, James 1899-1986

PERSONAL: Full name James Francis Cagney, Jr.; born July 17, 1899, in New York, NY; died of a circulatory ailment in Stanfordville, NY, March 30, 1986; son of James (a bartender and saloon owner) and Carolyn (Nelson) Cagney; married Frances Willard ''Willie'' Vernon (an actress, singer, and dancer), 1922; children: (adopted) James Jr. (died, 1984), Cathleen. EDUCATION: Graduate, Stuyvesant High School, New York, NY; attended Columbia University. POLITICS: Democrat.

VOCATION: Actor, singer, dancer, producer, director, and author.

CAREER: STAGE DEBUT—As a ''chorus girl'' in a female impersonation act, vaudeville, 1919. PRINCIPAL STAGE APPEARANCES—

Chorus, specialty dancer, *Pitter Patter,* NY, 1920; *Penny Arcade,* NY, 1930; *Outside Looking In,* NY, 1931; *Women Go on Forever,* NY, 1931.

FILM DEBUT—*Sinners Holiday,* Warner Brothers, 1930. PRINCIPAL FILM APPEARANCES—*Doorway to Hell,* Warner Brothers, 1930; *Other Men's Women,* Warner Brothers, 1931; *The Millionaire,* Warner Brothers, 1931; *The Public Enemy,* Warner Brothers, 1931; *Smart Money,* 1931; *Blonde Crazy,* Warner Brothers, 1931; *Taxi!,* 1932; *The Crowd Roars,* Warner Brothers, 1932; *Winner Take All,* 1932; *Hard to Handle,* 1933; *Picture Snatcher,* 1933; *The Mayor of Hell,* 1933; *Footlight Parade,* 1933; *Lady Killer,* Warner Brothers, 1933; *Jimmy the Gent,* 1934; *He Was Her Man,* 1934; *Here Comes the Navy,* 1934; *The St. Louis Kid,* 1934; *Devil Dogs of the Air,* 1935; *G-Men,* 1935; *The Irish in Us,* 1935; Bottom, *A Midsummer Night's Dream,* Warner Brothers, 1935; *Frisco Kid,* 1935; *Ceiling Zero,* 1935; *Great Guy,* 1936; *Something to Sing About,* 1937; *Boy Meets Girl,* 1938; *Angels with Dirty Faces,* Warner Brothers, 1938; *The Oklahoma Kid,* 1939; *Each Dawn I Die,* 1939; *The Roaring Twenties,* 1939.

The Fighting 69th, 1940; *Torrid Zone,* 1940; *City for Conquest,* 1941; *The Strawberry Blonde,* 1941; *The Bride Came C.O.D.,* 1941; *Captain of the Clouds,* 1942; George M. Cohan, *Yankee Doodle Dandy,* Warner Brothers, 1942; *Johnny Come Lately,* United Artists, 1943; *Blood on the Sun,* United Artists, 1945; *13 Rue Madeleine,* Twentieth Century-Fox, 1946; *The Time of Your Life,* 1948; *White Heat,* Warner Brothers, 1949.

The West Point Story, 1950; *Kiss Tomorrow Goodbye,* 1950; *Come Fill the Cup,* 1951; *Starlift,* 1951; *What Price Glory,* 1952; *A Lion Is in the Streets,* 1953; *Run for Cover,* Paramount, 1955; *Love Me or Leave Me,* Metro-Goldwyn-Mayer, 1955; the Captain, *Mister Roberts,* Warner Brothers, 1955; *The Seven Little Foys,* Paramount, 1955; *Tribute to a Bad Man,* Metro-Goldwyn-Mayer, 1956; *These Wilder Years,* Metro-Goldwyn-Mayer, 1956; *Man of a Thousand Faces,* Universal, 1957; *Short Cut to Hell,* Paramount, 1957; *Never Steal Anything Small,* Universal, 1958; *Shake Hands with the Devil,* United Artists, 1959.

The Gallant Hours, United Artists, 1960; *One, Two, Three,* United Artists, 1961; Rheinlander Waldo, *Ragtime,* Paramount, 1981.

PRINCIPAL FILM WORK—Producer, in partnership with his brother, William, as Cagney Productions: *Johnny Come Lately,* United Artists, 1943; *Blood on the Sun,* United Artists, 1945; *The West Point Story,* United Artists, 1950; *Kiss Tomorrow Goodbye,* 1950; *Come Fill the Cup,* 1951; *Starlift,* 1951; *A Lion Is in the Streets,* 1953; director, *Short Cut to Hell,* Paramount, 1957.

PRINCIPAL TELEVISION APPEARANCES—Episodic: "Soldier from the War Returning," *Robert Montgomery Presents*, NBC, 1956.

Guest: Scenes from *Mister Roberts*, on the *Ed Sullivan Show*, 1955; *This Is Your Life*, tribute to William Wellman, NBC; *Night of One Hundred Stars*, 1982; *NBC Magazine with David Brinkley*, NBC.

Movies: *Terrible Joe Moran*, 1984.

WRITINGS: AUTOBIOGRAPHY—*Cagney by Cagney*, 1976.

AWARDS: Voted one of the best ten Money-Making Stars in *Motion Pictures Herald-Fame* Poll, 1935, 1939, 1940, 1941, 1942, 1943; Best Actor, New York Film Critics and Academy Award nomination, both 1938, for *Angels with Dirty Faces;* Best Actor, Academy Award, 1942, for George M. Cohan, *Yankee Doodle Dandy;* Best Actor, Academy Award nomination, 1955, for *Love Me or Leave Me;* American Film Institute's Life Achievement Award, 1974; citation for career achievement, Kennedy Center Honors, 1980; United States Government's Medal of Freedom, 1984.

MEMBER: Screen Actors Guild (president, 1942-43); National Victory Committee, (chairman, actors group), World War II.

SIDELIGHTS: From his obituary in *The New York Times*, *CTFT* learned that after his retirement in 1961, James Cagney enjoyed his upstate New York farm where he raised Morgan horses, wrote verse, became a successful farmer, sailed, painted, and played classical guitar. "Absorption in things other than self," he observed, "is the secret of a happy life."*

*   *   *

CALLAHAN, James T.   1930-

PERSONAL: Born October 4, 1930, in Grand Rapids, MI; son of William Thomas (a salesman) and Elenora Gert (a saleslady; maiden name, MacDonald) Callahan. POLITICS: Democrat. RELIGION: Roman Catholic. MILITARY: U.S. Army, 1951-53.

VOCATION: Actor.

CAREER: STAGE DEBUT—Rocky, *Damn Yankees*, Starlite Theatre, Seattle, WA. NEW YORK DEBUT—Dan Brophy, *Children of the Wind*, Belasco Theatre. PRINCIPAL STAGE APPEARANCES—Bill Maitland, *Inadmissible Evidence*, Broadway production.

MAJOR TOURS—*Forty Carats*, East Coast and Midwest cities.

FILM DEBUT—Reg Johnson, *Battle of the Coral Sea*, Columbia, 1961. PRINCIPAL FILM APPEARANCES—Reg Hanley, *Lady Sings the Blues*, Paramount, 1971; Garland Dupre, *Outlaw Blues*, Warner Brothers, 1973; General Almond, *Inchon*, independent, 1977.

PRINCIPAL TELEVISION APPEARANCES—Series: Danny Adams, *Wendy and Me*, ABC, 1964-65; Lt. Dick O'Connell, *Convoy*, NBC, 1965; George Callison, *The Governor & J.J.*, CBS, 1969-72; Sgt. Hal Grady *The Runaways*, NBC, 1978-79.

MEMBER: Actors' Equity Association, Screen Actors Guild, American Federation of Television and Radio Artists.

AWARDS: Best Supporting Actor, Belgian Grand Prize, Belgian Film Festival, 1974, for Garland Dupre, *Outlaw Blues*.

SIDELIGHTS: James Callahan informs *CTFT* that he has appeared in over four hundred television programs and sixty films.

ADDRESSES: HOME—2125 W. 21st Street, Los Angeles, CA 90018. AGENT—Harry Gold, 12725 Ventura Blvd., Studio City, CA 91604.

*   *   *

CAMERON, James   1954-

BRIEF ENTRY: Born August 16, 1954, in Kapuskasing, Ontario, Canada. Screenwriter and director. Cameron lived there for five years before his father, an electrical engineer for a paper company, moved his family to Niagra Falls, and then Orange County, California. Cameron majored in physics at California State University at Fullerton, and after graduating, he supported himself as a truck driver while writing screenplays. His first film work was with Roger Corman's production company, New World Pictures, as a miniature set builder, process projection supervisor, and art director on *Battle Beyond the Stars*. In 1982, he left New World Pictures to co-script and direct *Piranha II: The Spawning*. He has since directed *The Terminator*, a critically acclaimed adventure film, and is currently directing *Aliens*, the sequel to *Alien*. In addition to his directing credits, Cameron co-wrote *Rambo: First Blood, Part II*, with Sylvester Stallone.*

*   *   *

CANNON, Dyan   1937-

PERSONAL: Born January 4, 1937, in Tacoma, WA; married Cary Grant (the actor, divorced); children: Jennifer. EDUCATION: Attended University of Washington; studied acting with Sanford Meisner in New York.

VOCATION: Actress.

CAREER: PRINCIPAL STAGE APPEARANCES—*The Fun Couple*, Broadway; *Ninety-Day Mistress*, Broadway.

MAJOR TOURS—*How to Succeed in Business Without Really Trying*, National tour.

PRINCIPAL FILM APPEARANCES—*Bob and Carol and Ted and Alice*, Columbia, 1969; *The Anderson Tapes*, Columbia, 1971; *Such Good Friends*, Paramount, 1971; *The Love Machine*, Columbia, 1971; *Doctors' Wives*, Columbia, 1971; *The Burglars*, Columbia, 1972; *The Last of Sheila*, Warner Brothers, 1973; *Shamus*, Columbia, 1973; *Revenge of the Pink Panther*, United Artists, 1978; *Child Under a Leaf*, 1978; *Heaven Can Wait*, Paramount, 1978; *Coast to Coast*, Paramount, 1980; *Honeysuckle Rose*, Warner Brothers, 1980; *Deathtrap*, Warner Brothers, 1982.

PRINCIPAL TELEVISION APPEARANCES—Episodic: "Diane's Adventure," *Playhouse 90*, CBS.

Movies: *Virginia Hill Story*, 1974; *Lady of the House*, 1978; *Master of the Game*, 1981; *Jenny's War*, 1984; *Arthur the King*, CBS, 1985.

RELATED CAREER—Professional model.

AWARDS: Best Supporting Actress, Academy Award nomination, 1969, for *Bob and Carol and Ted and Alice;* Best Actress of the Year, National Association of Theatre Owners, 1970, for *Bob and Carol and Ted and Alice.*

ADDRESSES: AGENT—Creative Artists Agency, Inc., 1888 Century Park E., Suite 1400, Los Angeles, CA 90048.*

* * *

CAPECCE, Victor

PERSONAL: EDUCATION: Ithaca College, B.F.A., 1972; Yale University, M.F.A., 1975.

VOCATION: Designer, scenic artist, and producer.

CAREER: NEW YORK DEBUT—Scenic and costume designer, *L'Histoire du Soldat,* New York City Opera, New York State Theatre, 1977. PRINCIPAL STAGE WORK—Scenic and costume designer, *Nukata,* Tokyo Parco-Seibu Theatre; scenic designer for: *Blood Memories,* Alvin Ailey Dance Theatre; *Miss Liberty* and *Lock Up Your Daughters,* both Goodspeed Opera House, East Haddam, CT.

Associate producer, Clinton Summer Theatre, Clinton, NJ, 1971-73; associate producer, *A Midsummer Night's Dream,* Peregrine Productions, 1983.

PRINCIPAL FILM WORK—Scenic artist, *Tattoo,* Twentieth Century-Fox, 1981; *Ghostbusters,* Columbia, 1984; *The Manhattan Project,* Twentieth Century-Fox.

PRINCIPAL TELEVISION WORK—Scenic artist, *Saturday Night Live, Another World, Texas, David Brinkley's Magazine,* all on NBC, 1979-81; chargeman scenic artist, *Tomorrow Show,* NBC; art director, *Enough Is Enough,* PBS; art director, Macy's Broadcast Division, 1981-83; scenic artist, *Death of a Salesman,* 1985. Also worked on commercials for "Jordache on Broadway," "IBM's Over Size," and "Hallmark Cards Valentine's Day Cards."

RELATED CAREER—Artist in residence, New Jersey Institute of Technology, Newark, NJ, 1983-85; artist in residence, Albright College, Reading, PA, 1985-86.

MEMBER: United Scenic Artists, Local 829 (International Brotherhood of Painters and Allied Trades); Lancaster Chamber of Commerce and Industry, National Small Business Association.

SIDELIGHTS: Capecce informed *CTFT* that he has worked for ". . . eleven years as a designer and artist for the stage, motion pictures, and television" and served as "associate producer for summer theatres and Off-Broadway productions and art director for commercials." His hobbies are weights training, magic, and puppetry. He is also adept at trompe l'oiel painting and silk screening techniques, stop-motion animation and various forms of video production. He has his own business, Renn-Art Associates, located in Lancaster, Pennsylvania.

ADDRESSES: OFFICE—Renn-Art Associates, 434 N. Water Street, Lancaster, PA 17603.

CAPLIN, Jeremy O.   1955-

PERSONAL: Born March 17, 1955, in Charlottesville, VA; son of Mortimer Maxwell (an attorney) and Ruth (a psychologist; maiden name, Sacks) Caplin. EDUCATION: Wesleyan University, B.A., theatre, 1977; University of Virginia, M.F.A., acting and directing, 1980.

VOCATION: Actor.

CAREER: STAGE DEBUT—Thomas, *The Philadelphia Story,* Heritage Repertory Theatre, Charlottesville, VA, June, 1976, for twenty-four performances. NEW YORK DEBUT—Agent, Studio Head, Photographer (understudy), *Marilyn: An American Fable,* Minksoff Theatre, November, 1983. PRINCIPAL STAGE APPEARANCES—Tevya, *Fiddler on the Roof* and Little John, *Robin Hood,* both CPCC Summer Theatre, 1978; Dr. Watson, *Sherlock Holmes,* Antipholus of Syracuse, *The Comedy of Errors,* and Bogart, *Play It Again, Sam,* all Lake Erie Repertory Theatre, 1979; Gravedigger and Marcellus, *Hamlet* and Starveling, Snout, *A Midsummer Night's Dream,* both National Shakespeare Company, 1980.

Gonzalo, *The Tempest* and Cobbler, Cinna, and Lucilius, *Julius Caesar,* both Virginia Shakespeare Festival, 1981; Dangerfield, *The Ginger Man,* seven roles, *The Good Doctor,* Leslie Lizard, *Seascape,* and Colm Primrose, *Sea Marks,* all for Florida State Theatre, 1981; Alfred P. Doolittle, *My Fair Lady,* Haymarket Dinner Theatre, 1982; Matt Friedman, *Talley's Folly* and Jerry, *Betrayal,* both Florida Studio Theatre, 1982; Harold Hill, *The Music Man,* Swift Creek Mill Playhouse, Richmond, VA, 1983; Van Helsing, *Dracula,* Charlie Martin, *On Golden Pond,* Dr. Carelli, *Black Coffee,* and Felix, *The Owl and the Pussycat,* all at the

JEREMY O. CAPLIN

Wayside Theatre, 1983; Horner, *The Country Wife,* Sweet Briar College, VA, 1983; Don, *American Buffalo,* Paul, *Absent Friends,* Miguel, *El Grande de Coca Cola,* and Phillip Carter, *Relatively Speaking,* all at the Florida State Theatre, 1984; Santa Anna, *The Lone Star* and the Judge, *Hello, Dolly!,* both M.M. Northern Amphitheatre, 1985; bailiff, Frediani, and riot cop, *Execution of Justice,* Virginia Theatre, NY, 1986.

MEMBER: Actors' Equity Association, Screen Actors Guild, American Federation of Television and Radio Artists.

AWARDS: Phoebe Award, 1983, for Harold Hill, *The Music Man.*

SIDELIGHTS: FAVORITE ROLES—Matt in *Talley's Folly,* Harold Hall in *The Music Man,* and the first gravedigger in *Hamlet.*

*   *   *

CAPRA, Frank, Jr.

PERSONAL: Son of Frank (a film director) and Lucille (Warner) Capra.

VOCATION: Producer.

CAREER: PRINCIPAL FILM WORK—Associate producer, *Planet of the Apes,* Twentieth Century-Fox, 1968; associate producer, *Marooned,* Columbia, 1969; associate producer, *Play It Again, Sam,* Paramount, 1972; producer, *Born Again,* Avco Embassy, 1978; producer, *The Black Marble,* Avco Embassy, 1980; producer, *An Eye for An Eye,* Embassy, 1981.

PRINCIPAL TELEVISION WORK—Series: Producer—*Dick Powell's Zane Grey Theatre,* CBS; *Gunsmoke,* CBS; *The Rifleman,* ABC.

RELATED CAREER: Vice-president of worldwide production, Avco Embassy Picture, 1981; president, Avco Embassy Pictures, 1981-82.

ADDRESSES: OFFICE—P.O. Box 98, La Quinta, CA 92253.*

*   *   *

CARIOU, Len   1939-

PERSONAL: Full name, Leonard Cariou; born September 30, 1939, in St. Boniface, Manitoba, Canada; son of George Marius (a salesman) and Molly Estelle (Moore) Cariou; children: Laurel Freedy. EDUCATION: Attended Holy Cross School and St. Paul's College, Winnipeg, Canada; studied for the theatre with Kristin Linklater, Fran Bennett, Judith Liebowitz, and Paul Gavert and at the Stratford Shakespeare Festival, Ontario, Canada and the Guthrie Theatre in Minneapolis.

VOCATION: Actor, singer, director, and administrator.

CAREER: STAGE DEBUT—Chorus, *Damn Yankees,* Rainbow Theatre, Winnipeg, Canada, 1959. NEW YORK DEBUT—Orestes, *The House of Atreus,* Billy Rose Theatre, 1968. PRINCIPAL STAGE APPEARANCES—Walter Sugarsop, *The Taming of the Shrew, The Tempest, Macbeth,* and *Cyrano de Bergerac,* all with the Stratford Shakespeare Festival, Canada, 1962; Margrelon, *Troilus and Cres-*

sida, Macbeth, Cyrano de Bergerac, and *The Comedy of Errors,* all with the Stratford Shakespeare Festival, 1963; Longaville, *Love's Labour's Lost,* Chichester, England, 1964; Sir John Bushy, *Richard II,* Cleante, *Le Bourgeous Gentilhomme,* and in *The Country Wife,* all with the Stratford Shakespeare Festival, Canada, 1964; Orlando, *As You Like It, The Skin of Our Teeth,* and *S.S. Glencairn,* all at the Guthrie Theatre, Minneapolis, MN, 1966; Orestes, *The House of Atreus,* Feste, *Twelfth Night,* and title role, *Sergeant Musgrave's Dance,* all at the Guthrie Theatre, 1968; title role, *Henry V, Much Ado About Nothing,* and *The Three Sisters,* all with the American Shakespeare Festival, Stratford, CT, 1969; Henry, *Henry V,* American National Theatre and Academy (ANTA), NY, 1969.

Bill Sampson, *Applause,* Palace Theatre, NY, 1970; Christian, *Cyrano de Bergerac* and *The Taming of the Shrew,* both at the Guthrie Theatre, 1971; John Wheeler, *Night Watch,* Morosco Theatre, NY, 1972; Oberon, *A Midsummer Night's Dream,* Guthrie Theatre, 1972; title role, *Oedipus the King,* Guthrie Theatre, 1973; Frederick Egerman, *A Little Night Music* and *Sondheim: A Musical Tribute,* both at the Shubert Theatre, NY, 1973; title role, *King Lear,* Guthrie Theatre, 1974; *Equus* and *Cyrano de Bergerac,* both at the Manitoba Theatre Center, Winnipeg, Canada, 1975; monodrama, *A Sorrow Beyond Dreams,* Marymount Manhattan Theatre, NY, then Guthrie Theatre, 1977; Richard Landau, *Cold Storage,* Lyceum Theatre, NY, 1977; title role, *Sweeney Todd,* Uris (now Gershwin) Theatre, NY, 1979; Harry, *Dance a Little Closer,* Minskoff Theatre, NY, 1983; title role, *Coriolanus,* Petruchio, *The Taming of the Shrew,* Sergius, *Arms and the Man,* Brutus, *Julius Caesar,* and Prospero, *The Tempest,* all with the Stratford Shakespeare Festival, Canada, 1984-85; Sam, *Traveler in the Dark,* Mark Taper Forum, Los Angeles, 1985; Stalin, *Master Class,* Roundabout Theatre, NY, 1986.

LEN CARIOU

Has also appeared in: *Mr. Roberts, Mother Courage,* and *Who's Afraid of Virginia Woolf?,* at the Manitoba Theatre Center; *Timon of Athens* and *Mahagonny,* with the Stratford Shakespeare Festival, Canada; *The Skin of Our Teeth* and *Diary of a Scroundrel,* Guthrie Theatre; Iago, *Othello,* Chicago, IL; *The Physicists,* Kennedy Center for the Performing Arts, Washington, DC.

PRINCIPAL STAGE WORK—Director: *Of Mice and Men,* Guthrie Theatre, 1972, also at the Manitoba Theatre Center; *The Petrified Forest,* Guthrie Theatre, also Off-Broadway production, 1974; *The Crucible,* Guthrie Theatre, 1974; *Don't Call Back,* Broadway production, 1979; *Cold Storage,* Jewish Repertory Theatre, NY, 1985.

PRINCIPAL FILM APPEARANCES—*A Little Night Music,* 1978; *The Four Seasons,* Universal, 1981; *One Man,* National Film Board of Canada.

TELEVISION DEBUT—Ragnar Brovik, *The Master Builder,* 1965. PRINCIPAL TELEVISION APPEARANCES—Specials: *Juno and the Paycock.*

Movies: *Applause; Who'll Save Our Children,* CBS; *Surviving,* 1985.

RELATED CAREER—Associate director, Guthrie Theatre, 1971-73; artistic director, Manitoba Theatre Center, 1974-75; associate director, Citadel Theatre, Edmonton, Alberta, Canada, 1986.

MEMBER: Actors' Equity Association, Canadian Actors' Equity Association, Screen Actors Guild; Friars Foundation (board of governors), Friars Club.

AWARDS: Best Actor in a Musical, Antoinette Perry Award, 1979, for *Sweeney Todd;* Antoinette Perry Award nominations, for *Applause* and *A Little Night Music;* honorary doctorate, University of Windsor, Canada.

SIDELIGHTS: Len Cariou told *CTFT* that when not working onstage, he enjoys baseball, golf, tennis, and gymnastics. Prior to his stage career he worked as a salesman for farm machinery and men's clothing.

ADDRESSES: AGENT—STE Representation, 888 Seventh Avenue, New York, NY 10019; Don Buchwald Associates, Ten E. 44th Street, New York, NY 10017.

*   *   *

CARLISLE, Kitty   1914-

PERSONAL: Born Catherine Conn, September 3, 1914, in New Orleans, LA; daughter of Dr. Joseph and Hortense (Holzman) Conn; married Moss Hart (playwright, producer, and director), August 10, 1946 (died, 1961); children: Christopher, Catherine. EDUCATION: Chateau Mont-Choisi, Lausanne, Switzerland; private schools in London, Paris, Rome; studied for the theatre at the Royal Academy of Dramatic Art, London, England and at the Theatre de l'Atelier in Paris with Dullin.

VOCATION: Actress and singer.

KITTY CARLISLE

CAREER: DEBUT—Title role, *Rio Rita,* tabloid version of show, Capitol Theatre, NY, 1932. PRINCIPAL STAGE APPEARANCES—Prince Orlofsky, *Champagne Sec,* Morosco Theatre, NY 1933; Katarina, *White Horse Inn,* Center Theatre, NY, 1936; Marie Hiller, Charlotte, Franzi, *Three Waltzes,* Majestic Theatre, NY, 1937; Diana Lake, *French without Tears* and Karen Andre, *Night of January 16th,* Ridgeway Theatre, White Plains, NY, 1938; Pamela Gibson, *Walk with Music,* Ethel Barrymore Theatre, NY, 1940; *Show Time,* NY, 1942; Sonia, *The Merry Widow,* Boston Opera House, Boston, MA, 1943; Gilda, *Design for Living,* Cleveland, OH, 1943; Leonora, *There's Always Juliet,* Philadelphia, PA, 1944; Lucretia, *The Rape of Lucretia,* Ziegfeld Theatre, NY, 1948.

Alice Walters, *Anniversary Waltz,* Broadhurst Theatre, NY, 1954; Katherine, *Kiss Me Kate,* New York City Center, NY, 1956; Prince Orlovsky, *Die Fledermaus,* Metropolitan Opera House, NY, 1966-67; Duchess of Krackenthorp, *La Fille du Regiment,* Boston Opera Company, Boston, MA, 1973; Prince Orlovsky, *Die Fledermaus,* Metropolitan Opera House (summer season) June, 1973; Peggy, *On Your Toes,* Virginia Theatre, NY, 1984.

MAJOR TOURS—*A Successful Calamity,* summer tour, 1939; *Tonight or Never,* summer tour, 1939 and again in 1946; Maggie Cutler, *The Man Who Came to Dinner,* summer tour, 1949; Content Lowell, *The Marriage-Go-Round,* summer tour including Elitch Gardens, Denver, CO, 1965; Prince Orlovsky, *Die Fledermaus,* Metropolitan Opera tour, 1967; Irene Livingston, *Light Up the Sky,* national tour, 1970-71 and again 1972; *Don't Frighten the Horses,* summer tour, 1973; *You Never Know,* summer tour, 1975.

PRINCIPAL FILM APPEARANCES—*Murder at the Vanities,* Paramount, 1934; Midge Mercer, *She Loves Me Not,* Paramount, 1934; Princess Alexandra, *Here Is My Heart,* Paramount, 1934; Rosa Carlotti, *A Night at the Opera,* Metro-Goldwyn-Mayer, 1935; *Hollywood Canteen,* Warner Brothers, 1945.

PRINCIPAL TELEVISION APPEARANCES—Game shows: Guest panelist, *Who Said That?,* NBC, 1948-55; panelist, *I've Got a Secret,* CBS, 1952-53; panelist, *What's Going On?* ABC, 1954; panelist, *To Tell the Truth,* CBS, 1956-1967.

CONCERT APPEARANCES—With the Philadelphia Orchestra, Saratoga Performing Arts Center, Saratoga, NY, 1967; *Kurt Weill Memorial Concert,* Philharmonic Hall, NY.

RELATED CAREER—Former chairman, New York State Council for the Arts; lecturer with *First Person Singular;* chairman, Governor Rockefeller's Conference on Women, NY, May, 1966; former special consultant to the governor of New York on women's opportunities.

WRITINGS: COLUMN—"Kitty's Calendar," for *Women's Unit News.*

MEMBER: Visiting committee of the Board of Overseers of Harvard University for the music department; visiting committee on the arts, Massachusetts Institute of Technology.

AWARDS: Elected associated fellow, Yale University; Doctor of Humane Letters: New Rochelle College, Hartwick College, Marymount College.

ADDRESSES: OFFICE—80 Centre Street, New York, NY 10013. AGENT—c/o Keedick Lecture Bureau, 850 Boylston Street, Boston, MA 02167.

*   *   *

CARNE, Judy   1939-

PERSONAL: Born Joyce A. Botterill, April 27, 1939, in Northampton, England; daughter of Harold (a greengrocer) and Kathleen (a greengrocer; maiden name, Cambell) Botterill; married Burt Reynolds, June, 1963, (divorced, 1966). EDUCATION: Attended Bush-Davies Theatrical Boarding School, East Grinstead Sussex, England; studied with Noreen Bush at the Total Theatre. POLITICS: Conservative. RELIGION: Church of England.

VOCATION: Actress and comedienne.

CAREER: STAGE DEBUT—*For Amusement Only,* revue, Apollo Theatre, London, England, 1956. NEW YORK DEBUT—Polly, *The Boyfriend,* Ambassador Theatre, 1970. MAJOR TOURS—Sally Bowles, *Cabaret,* 1975; *Absurd Person Singular,* national, 1976; *Blithe Spirit,* England, 1980; *Happy Birthday,* England, 1981; also toured in *The Owl and the Pussycat* and *There's a Girl in My Soup.*

FILM DEBUT—Juanita, *Danger Man,* ITC Productions, 1959.

TELEVISION DEBUT—*The Rag Trade,* BBC, 1959. PRINCIPAL TELEVISION APPEARANCES—Series: Heather, *Fair Exchange,* CBS, 1962-63; Barbara Wyntoon, *The Baileys of Balboa,* CBS, 1964-65; Julie Willis, *Love on a Rooftop,* ABC, 1966-67; *Rowan and Martin's Laugh-In,* NBC, 1968-70.

JUDY CARNE

WRITINGS: AUTOBIOGRAPHY—*Laughing on the Outside, Crying on the Inside,* Rawson and Associates, 1985.

ADDRESSES: HOME—Carne Lodge, Church Brampton, England. AGENT—c/o Mitch Douglas, International Creative Management, 40 W. 57th Street, New York, NY 10019.

*   *   *

CARON, Leslie   1931-

PERSONAL: Full name Leslie Claire Margaret Caron; born November 4, 1931, in Paris, France; daughter of Claude (a chemist) and Margaret (Petit) Caron; married George Hormel (a meat packer) 1951 (divorced, 1954); married Peter Hall (a producer and director) 1956 (divorced, 1966); children: (second marriage) Christopher, Jennifer. EDUCATION: Convent of the Assumption, Paris; National Conservatory of Dance, Paris.

VOCATION: Dancer and actress.

CAREER: STAGE DEBUT—As a dancer, Paris. PRINCIPAL STAGE APPEARANCES—Featured soloist, *Ballet des Champs Elysee,* Paris. MAJOR TOURS—*On Your Toes,* U.S. cities, 1985.

FILM DEBUT—Lise Bourvier, *An American in Paris,* Metro-Goldwyn-Mayer, 1951. PRINCIPAL FILM APPEARANCES—*The Man with a Cloak*, Metro-Goldwyn-Mayer, 1951; *Glory Alley*, Metro-Goldwyn-Mayer, 1952; *The Story of Three Loves*, Metro-Goldwyn-Mayer, 1953; title role, *Lili*, Metro-Goldwyn-Mayer, 1953; Julie, *Daddy Long Legs*, Twentieth Century-Fox, 1955; Cinderella, *The Glass Slipper*, Metro-Goldwyn-Mayer, 1955; title role, *Gaby*, Metro-Goldwyn-Mayer, 1956; title role, *Gigi*, Metro-Goldwyn-Mayer, 1958; Mrs. Dubedat, *The Doctor's Dilemma*, Metro-Goldwyn-Mayer, 1958; *The Man Who Understood Women*, Twentieth Century-Fox, 1959.

The Subterraneans, Metro-Goldwyn-Mayer, 1960; title role, *Fanny*, Warner Brothers, 1961; *Guns of Darkness*, Warner Brothers, 1962; *The L-Shaped Room* Columbia, 1963; Catherine Freneau, *Father Goose*, Universal-International, 1964; *A Very Special Favor*, Universal, 1965; *Promise Her Anything*, Paramount, 1966; Francoise Labe, *Is Paris Burning?*, Paramount, 1966; the nun, *Madron*, Metro-Goldwyn-Mayer/Four Star Excelsior Films, 1970; *Chandler*, Metro-Goldwyn-Mayer, 1971; Alla Nazimova, *Valentino*, United Artists, 1977. Also, *Head of the Family; The Beginners; Purple Night*.

PRINCIPAL TELEVISION APPEARANCES—Mini-Series: *Master of the Game*.

RECORDINGS: ALBUMS—Original soundtrack recording, *An American in Paris*, Metro-Goldwyn-Mayer; original soundtrack recording, *Gigi*, Metro-Goldwyn-Mayer. SINGLE—"Hi Lili Hi Lo," from *Lili*, Metro-Goldwyn-Mayer.

Photograph by J.P. Guilloteau/KIPA

LESLIE CARON

AWARDS: Best Actress, Academy Award nominations, 1953, for *Lili*, and 1963, for *The L-Shaped Room*.

SIDELIGHTS: Leslie Caron was a sixteen-year old dancer with the Ballet des Champs-Elysees in Paris when actor-dancer Gene Kelly first saw her perform and chose her to star opposite him in the movie *An American in Paris*. The hit film, particularly the young dancer's performance in its climactic ballet, launched Caron's early career as the ingenue lead in a number of fifties musicals, including the popular *Lili* and *Gigi*. Caron's "elfin charm," according to some critics, lent itself well to playing adolescents or young women learning to deal with love and the adult world. Later in her motion picture career, Caron gave up musicals to concentrate on straight dramatic roles. She has since won acclaim for her work in such films as *The L-Shaped Room*.

ADDRESSES: AGENT—The Blake Agency, 409 N. Camden Drive, Suite 202, Beverly Hills, CA 90210.

*   *   *

CARR, Allan   1941-

PERSONAL: Born Allan Solomon, May 27, 1941, in Chicago, IL; son of Albert and Ann (Neimitz) Solomon. EDUCATION: Lake Forest College, B.A., 1962.

VOCATION: Film producer and celebrity representative.

CAREER: PRINCIPAL FILM WORK—Assistant to producer, *King of Kings*, Metro-Goldwyn-Mayer, 1961; producer, *The First Time*, United Artists, 1969; producer, *C.C. and Company*, Avco Embassy, 1970; creative consultant, *Tommy*, Columbia, 1975; co-producer, *Survive*, Paramount, 1976; producer, *Can't Stop the Music*, Associated Film Distributors, 1980; producer, *Grease II*, Paramount, 1982; creative consultant, *Bugsy Malone* Paramount, 1976; producer, *Where the Boys Are*, Tri-Star, 1984.

PRINCIPAL STAGE WORK—Co-producer, *Grease*, 1977; producer, *La Cage Aux Folles*, NY and Los Angeles, 1983; co-producer, *Much Ado About Nothing* and *Cyrano de Bergerac*, Royal Shakespeare Company, Gershwin Theatre, NY, 1984-85; has produced plays at the Civic Theatre, Chicago.

PRINCIPAL TELEVISION WORK—Co-executive producer, *Ann-Margret Special*, 1977; co-creator, *Playboy-Penthouse* television series.

RELATED CAREER—Has been artist's representative for Ann-Margret, Petula Clark, Marlo Thomas, Peter Sellers, Marvin Hamlisch, Nancy Walker, Melina Mercouri, Stockard Channing, Frankie Valli. Creative consultant, Robert Stigwood Organization; president of Allan Carr Enterprises; vice-president, Caloric Productions; vice-president, Rogalian Productions.

MEMBER: National Association of Christians and Jews.*

*   *   *

CARRADINE, Robert   1954-

PERSONAL: Full name, Robert Reed Carradine; born March 24, 1954; son of John (the actor) and Sonia (Sorel) Carradine.

VOCATION: Actor.

CAREER: PRINCIPAL FILM APPEARANCES—*The Cowboys,* Warner Brothers, 1972; *Joyride,* Allied Artists, 1977; *Orca,* Paramount, 1977; *Blackout,* 1978; *Coming Home,* United Artists, 1978; *The Long Riders,* United Artists, 1980; *The Big Red One,* United Artists, 1980; *Wavelength,* New World Pictures, 1983; *Just the Way You Are,* Metro-Goldwyn-Mayer/United Artists, 1984.

PRINCIPAL TELEVISION APPEARANCES—Slim, *The Cowboys,* ABC, 1974; *The Last Convertible;* title role, ''Aladdin,'' *Faerie Tale Theatre,* Showtime, 1985.

Movie: *The Sun Also Rises,* NBC, 1984.

ADDRESSES: AGENT—Mishkin Agency, 9255 Sunset Blvd., Suite 610, Los Angeles, CA 90069.*

*   *   *

CARROLL, Diahann   1935-

PERSONAL: Born July 17, 1935, in Bronx, NY; daughter of John and Mabel (Faulk) Johnson; married Monte Kay (divorced); married Fredde Glusman (a Las Vegas clothier; divorced); married Robert Deleon (a magazine managing editor), 1975 (died, 1977). EDUCATION: Attended New York University.

VOCATION: Actress and singer.

CAREER: STAGE DEBUT—*House of Flowers,* Broadway production, 1954. PRINCIPAL STAGE APPEARANCES— *No Strings,* Broadway production; *Same Time, Next Year,* Broadway production; Dr. Martha Livingston, *Agnes of God,* Music Box Theatre, NY, 1983.

FILM DEBUT—*Carmen Jones,* Twentieth Century-Fox, 1955. PRINCIPAL FILM APPEARANCES—*Porgy and Bess,* Columbia, 1959; *Hurry Sundown,* Paramount, 1967; *Paris Blues,* United Artists, 1961; *Claudine,* Twentieth Century-Fox, 1974.

TELEVISION DEBUT—*Chance of a Lifetime,* 1953. PRINCIPAL TELEVISION APPEARANCES—Series: Julia Baker, *Julia,* NBC, 1968-71; *Diahann Carroll Show,* CBS, 1976; Dominique Deveraux, *Dynasty,* ABC, 1984—.

Guest host: *On Parade,* NBC, 1964.

AWARDS: Best Actress, Academy Award nomination, 1974, for *Claudine.*

SIDELIGHTS: The distinguished singer-actress Diahann Carroll grew up in Harlem and was a member of the choir at the Abyssinian Baptist Church. She began working in nightclubs while still a student at the High School of Music and Art in New York. During her only year at New York University (NYU), Carroll's singing brought her three thousand dollars in prizes on the television talent show *Chance of a Lifetime,* and she then left NYU to take her first film role, in *Carmen Jones.*

Later that same year, Carroll appeared in her first Broadway show, Harold Arlen's musical *House of Flowers.* William Hawkins of the New York *World-Telegram and Sun* called her ''a great find'' and added, ''She has a rich, lovely, easy voice, and great freshness of personality.''

DIAHANN CARROLL

Composer Richard Rodgers wrote Carroll's second Broadway musical, *No Strings,* especially for her after watching her sing as a guest on Jack Paar's television show. In his autobiography, *Musical Stages* (Random House, 1975), Rodgers tells the story: ''Her singing and her appearance immediately gave me the idea of starring her in a musical in which she would play a chic, sophisticated woman of the world. She would not represent a cause or be a symbol of her race, but a believable human being, very much a part of a stratum of society that the theatre thus far had never considered for a black actress.'' *No Strings,* and especially Carroll's performance in it, were highly praised by the critics; George Oppenheimer wrote in *Newsday,* ''She is beguiling and lithe and graceful and endowed with that star quality that is encountered all too seldom in these days when glamour seems to have become a vanished commodity.'' The musical ran for 580 performances.

Carroll worked both on Broadway and in films during the mid-1960's. When she took the part of widowed nurse Julia Baker on *Julia* in 1968, she became the first black performer to star in a television comedy series playing a non-stereotypical character. Because *Julia* was set in a middle-class millieu rather than the ghetto, some critics felt it was not ''relevant'' enough, to which a reporter for the New York *Daily News* replied: ''For years we've been looking at escapist television, so why, when a Negro actress is starred in the same kind of a series does she suddenly have to carry the weight of the whole racial question around her shoulders? . . . It's enough that an attractive, talented actress has been cast in the part and is doing a good job.'' Audiences were evidently not disturbed by *Julia*'s failure to deal with social issues, as the series ranked in the top ten in the Nielsen ratings during its first season and remained on the air for three years.

Carroll has moved from the portrayal of a middle-class working woman to that of a wealthy jet-setter in her latest television role, that of Dominique Deveraux on the nighttime serial *Dynasty*. The actress described her role in a New York *Post* interview as ''the first black bitch on television.'' She said that she conceived of the character herself ''because people are afraid to cast blacks in unsympathetic roles.''

ADDRESSES: OFFICE—Aaron Spelling Productions, 1041 N. Formosa Avenue, Los Angeles, CA 90046. AGENT—Roy Gerber Associates, 9200 Sunset Blvd., Suite 620, Los Angeles, CA 90069.

*   *   *

CARROLL, Pat   1927-

PERSONAL: Born May 5, 1927, in Shreveport, LA; daughter of Maurice Clifton and Kathryn Angela (Meagher) Carroll; children: Sean, Kerry, Tara. EDUCATION: Attended Immaculate Heart College, 1944-47; graduated from Catholic University, 1950. MILITARY: U.S. Army, ''civilian actress technician.''

VOCATION: Actress.

CAREER: PRINCIPAL TELEVISION APPEARANCES—Series: Regular, *Red Buttons Show*, CBS, 1952-53; regular, *Saturday Night Revue*, NBC, 1953-54; Alice Brewster, *Caesar's Hour*, NBC, 1956-57; panelist, *Masquerade Party*, CBS, 1958; regular, *Keep Talking*, CBS, 1958-60; panelist, *You're in the Picture*, CBS, 1961; Bunny Halper, *Danny Thomas Show*, CBS, 1961-63; Rita Simon, *Getting Together*, ABC, 1971-72; Pearl Markowitz, *Busting Loose*, CBS, 1977.

Episodic: *George Gobel Show; Jimmy Durante Show; Mickey Rooney Show; Max Liebman Presents; Studio 57.*

STAGE DEBUT—*A Goose for the Gander*, 1947. NEW YORK DEBUT—*Catch a Star*, Broadway, 1955. PRINCIPAL STAGE APPEARANCES—Title role, *Gertrude Stein, Gertrude Stein*, 1979; *The Last Resort*, 1979; Madeline Bernard, *Dancing in the End Zone*, Ritz Theatre, NY, 1985.

MAJOR TOURS—Title role, *Getrude Stein, Getrude Stein*, Arena Stage, Washington, DC, Cleveland Playhouse, McCarter Theatre, Princeton, NJ, and other U.S. cities, 1980-81.

CABARET DEBUT—Le Ruban Bleu, NY, 1950.

PRINCIPAL FILM APPEARANCES—*With Six You Get Eggroll*, National General, 1968.

RELATED CAREER—Hyde Park Theatre, Hyde Park, NY (board of directors); president, Sea-Ker, Inc., Beverly Hills, 1979—.

MEMBER: Actors' Equity Association, American Federation of Television and Radio Artists, Screen Actors Guild, Academy of Television Arts and Sciences (trustee, 1958-59); Center of Films for Children (president, 1971-73); District Attorney's Citizens Committee, Los Angeles, 1970-75; Immaculate Heart College (board of

regents); American Youth Hostels; Delaware and Hudson Canal Historical Society; George Heller Memorial Foundation.

AWARDS: Best Supporting Actress, Emmy, 1956, for *Caesar's Hour.*

ADDRESSES: AGENT—Janice S. Morgan Communications, 301 W. 53rd Street, New York, NY 10019.*

*   *   *

CARSON, Johnny   1925-

PERSONAL: Born October 23, 1925, in Corning, IA; son of Homer and Ruth (Hook) Carson; married Jody Wolcott, 1948 (divorced, 1963), married Joanne Copeland, August, 1963 (divorced); married Joanna Holland, 1972 (divorced); children: (first marriage) Chris, Ricky, Cory. EDUCATION: University of Nebraska, B.A., 1949. MILITARY: U.S. Naval Reserve, World War II.

VOCATION: Talk show host, producer, comedian, former actor.

CAREER: PRINCIPAL TELEVISION APPEARANCES—Host: *Carson's Cellar*, 1951; emcee, *Earn Your Vacation*, CBS, 1954; guest host, *The Red Skelton Show*, CBS; *The Johnny Carson Show*, CBS, 1955-56; emcee, *Who Do You Trust?*, CBS, 1957-62; ''Queen of the Orange Bowl,'' *U.S. Steel Hour*, CBS, 1960; ''Johnny Come Lately'' (unproduced pilot), shown on *New Comedy Showcase*, CBS, 1960; *Tonight Show*, NBC, 1962—; ''Friar's Club Roast,'' *Kraft Music Hall*, NBC; substitute host, *The Sammy Davis, Jr. Show*, NBC, 1966; *Joys!*, 1976. host, Academy Award ceremonies, 1979-82, 1984

PRINCIPAL TELEVISION WORK—Producer, *Tonight Show*, NBC; *TV's Bloopers and Practical Jokes*, NBC, 1984-85.

PRINCIPAL RADIO WORK—Announcer: KFAB, Lincoln, NE, 1948; WOW, Omaha, NE; KNXT, Los Angeles, CA, 1950.

RELATED CAREER—President, Carson Productions.

WRITINGS: TELEVISION—Series: *Red Skelton Show.*

BOOKS—*Happiness Is a Dry Martini*, 1965.

AWARDS: Entertainer of the Year Award; Outstanding Program Achievement, Emmy, 1977-78 and 1979-80, for *Tonight Show.*

SIDELIGHTS: Considered America's most durable television personality, comedian Johnny Carson has hosted the NBC talk show *Tonight* since 1962, when he replaced Jack Paar. Carson's audience, an estimated 7.5 million when he took the job, has increased steadily and by 1978 had reached 17.3 million viewers, ''a feat that,'' Kenneth Tynan asserted in *The New Yorker* of February 20, 1978, ''in its blend of staying power and mounting popularity, is without precedent in the history of television.'' In 1983, Pierson G. Mapes, the president of NBC's television network said, ''By any count that matters, he [Carson] is now what he has been from the beginning—America's most popular, best loved late-night entertainer.''

Carson began hs show business career as a radio comedy writer while still a student at the University of Nebraska. After graduating he worked as an television announcer on WOW in Omaha, Nebraska, before moving to California, where he became an all-purpose announcer with a Los Angeles television station. Within a short time he had his own show, a half-hour comedy program aired on Sunday afternoons as *Carson's Cellar*. Comedians Groucho Marx and Fred Allen were among the show's fans and made guest appearances without pay. The show lasted for only thirty weeks, but having attracted comic Red Skelton as a viewer, it earned Carson a job as a writer on Skelton's television show. One night, after Skelton injured himself two hours before air time, Carson substituted for the ailing star. He so impressed network officials that they gave him his own prime-time show. *The Johnny Carson Show* failed after thirty-nine weeks and Carson moved to New York where in 1957 he signed on as the host of the daytime game show *Who Do You Trust?* The show, which featured Carson's humorous repartee with guest contestants, became ABC's top daytime program and led NBC to offer Carson the *Tonight Show* when Paar quit in 1962.

By 1967 Carson was "an institution," reported a May 19 *Time* cover story that year. Over the years since, his popularity has remained undiminished. Carson's phenomenal success during nearly a quarter-of-a-century as *Tonight*'s host has been attributed to his comic charm and to his ability to make guests and audiences alike feel comfortable. As *Time* put it: "Carson is a master of the cozy pace and mood that he believes are appropriate for the muzzy midnight hours . . . he avoids meet-the-press style interviewing, and never goes beyond his intellectual depth. Neither does he use his terrible swift wit to cut down guests." Celebrities praise Carson's ability to bring out the best in them; they particularly appreciate his role as straight man and the fact that he never competes with his guests for laughs.

In 1979, only two years after negotiating a landmark contract with an annual salary of $3 million, Carson threatened to quit NBC. At that time, the *Tonight Show* accounted for approximately 17 percent of the network's profits, or $23 million annually. Carson, whose contracts over the years have earned him increasing sums of money while at the same time reducing his *Tonight* work schedule, reportedly was miffed at a network executive who commented that the host should spend more time on the show. Carson's action earned him a new contract in 1980 that further lessened Carson's work time, shortening the show from ninety minutes to one hour, and increased his pay check to $5 million a year. Now earning more than $15 million a year, including personal appearances and such business ventures as Johnny Carson Apparel, Carson recently signed a contract with NBC which, according to NBC Entertainment president Brandon Tartikoff will keep him on the network at least through 1987. Carson is uncontested as the highest paid television personality in history.

ADDRESSES: OFFICE—NBC, 3000 W. Alameda Avenue, Burbank, CA 91505.*

*　　*　　*

CARTER, Nell   1948-

PERSONAL: Born Nell Hardy, September 13, 1948, in Birmingham, AL; daughter of Horace L. and Edna M. Hardy; married. EDUCATION: Attended Bill Russell School of Drama, 1970-73. POLITICS: Democrat. RELIGION: Presbyterian.

VOCATION: Actress and singer.

CAREER: PRINCIPAL TELEVISION APPEARANCES—Series: Sergeant Hildy Jones, *Lobo*, NBC, 1980-81; Nell Harper, *Gimme a Break*, NBC, 1981—.

Episodic: *The Big Show*, NBC, 1980.

Specials: *Baryshnikov on Broadway; Ain't Misbehavin'*, NBC, 1981; *Nell Carter, Never too Old to Dream*, NBC, 1986.

PRINCIPAL STAGE APPEARANCES—*Hair; Dude; Don't Bother Me, I Can't Cope; Jesus Christ Superstar; Bury the Dead; Rhapsody in Gershwin; Blues Is a Woman; Black Broadway; Ain't Misbehavin'*.

PRINCIPAL FILM APPEARANCES—*Hair*, United Artists, 1979; *Modern Problems*, Twentieth Century-Fox, 1981; *Back Roads*, Warner Brothers, 1981.

RELATED CAREER—Numerous radio and television appearances in Alabama; numerous club and concert appearances, including with the Los Angeles Philharmonic.

MEMBER: Actors' Equity Association, Screen Actors Guild, American Federation of Television and Radio Artists; National Association for the Advancement of Colored People.

AWARDS: Antoinette Perry Award, Obie Award, Drama Desk Award, *Soho News* Award, all for *Ain't Misbehavin'*; Outstanding Individual Achievement (Special Class), Emmy, 1981, for *Ain't Misbehavin'*.

ADDRESSES: AGENT—c/o John Kimble, Triad Artists, 10100 Santa Monica Blvd., 16th Floor, Los Angeles, CA 90067; c/o Laurie Jonas, Rogers and Cowan, 10,000 Santa Monica Blvd., Suite 400, Los Angeles, CA 90067.

*　　*　　*

CARVER, James C.   1932-

PERSONAL: Born January 30, 1932, in Kalamazoo, MI; son of Norman F. (a theatre manager) and Helen Louise (an actress; maiden name, Blackaller) Carver; married Nancy Organ (a teacher), March 5, 1955; children: Scott, Stephen. EDUCATION: Michigan State University, B.A., television, 1954, M.A., theatre, 1959. MILITARY: U.S. Army.

VOCATION: Director, manager, and adminstrator.

CAREER: STAGE DEBUT—Appeared in children's theatre production as a child. PRINCIPAL STAGE APPEARANCES—Has appeared in such roles as Harold Hill, *The Music Man*, title role, *Macbeth*, Pseudolus, *A Funny Thing Happened on the Way to the Forum*, Foxwell Sly, *Sly Fox*, Martin Dysart, *Equus*, and more than seventy others.

PRINCIPAL STAGE WORK—Has directed more than one hundred productions, including *Fools*.

RELATED CAREER—With the Kalamazoo Civic Players: production assistant, 1959-61; assistant business manager, 1961-68, business manager, 1968-74, managing director, 1974—; manager, Civic Auditorium, Kalamazoo, 1968—.

JAMES C. CARVER

Carver has worked in print advertising, industrial films, commercials for television and radio as well as directing for television at WNEM-TV, Michigan; also, adjunct associate professor and chairman of theatre department, Nazareth College, 1960-77; guest lecturer, Western Michigan University, 1977-78.

MEMBER: Michigan Council for the Arts (theatre advisory committee, 1966-79); Festival of American Community Theatre Association (national chairman, 1981); American Theatre Association (1960—); American Community Theatre Association (board of directors; president, 1985-86).

AWARDS: Dionysus Award, American Community Theatre Association; national award winner, director, for *Fools*.

SIDELIGHTS: "My grandparents and my parents were professional theatre people and my son, Stephen, is an actor," James Carver informed *CTFT*. He went on to say that he had "judged theatre festivals and conducted festivals and theatre workshops throughout the United States. I have represented the U.S. at International Amateur Theatre Association Congresses in Bulgaria in 1979, and Monaco in 1981."

Carver is vice president of the "Save our Roadside Environment" group.

ADDRESSES: HOME—5624 Lovers Lane, Kalamazoo, MI 49002. OFFICE—329 S. Park Street, Kalamazoo, MI 49007. AGENT--Jo Hickey, Abbey's People, 115 Wanondoger Court, Battle Creek, MI, 49017.

CASADY, Cort   1947-

PERSONAL: Born April 22, 1947, in McAllen, TX; son of Simon (an editor and publisher) and Virginia Kent (Boon) Casady; married Barbara Mercer Kellard (an interior designer), December 28, 1982. EDUCATION: Harvard University, B.A., 1968.

VOCATION: Writer, producer, and composer.

CAREER: PRINCIPAL TELEVISION WORK—Series: Writer, *The Jim Nabors Show,* syndication, 1978-79; *Barbara Mandrell and the Mandrell Sisters,* NBC, 1981-82; *Star Search,* 1984.

Movie: *Kenny Rogers as the Gambler,* CBS, 1980

Episodic: *Saturday Night Live* (Pamela Sue Martin show), NBC, 1985.

Specials: *A Special Kenny Rogers,* CBS, 1979; *The Eddie Rabbitt Special,* NBC, 1980; *John Schneider: Back Home,* CBS, 1980; *Kenny Rogers and the American Cowboy,* CBS, 1980; writer and producer, *Third Annual ''Music City News'' Top Country Hits,* 1983; *Ronnie Milsap: In Celebration,* 1984; *Wembley Music Festival: Country Goes to England,* 1984; *Fifth Annual National Songwriters' Awards,* 1985; *Through the Years: The Osmonds' Twenty-Fifth Anniversary,* 1985; *Sixth Annual National Songwriters' Awards,* 1986.

RELATED CAREER—Partner, Cannon and Casady Creative.

WRITINGS: BOOKS—*The Singing Entertainer,* Alfred, 1980.

CORT CASADY

SCREENPLAYS—*Underground; A Full House; President Under Glass.*

MUSIC—Composed for television: *Nichols and Dymes*, NBC; *One Night Band*, CBS; *First Time, Second Time*, CBS; *The First; Rick and Bob's America.*

MEMBER: Writers Guild of America West, American Federation of Television and Radio Artists, Signature, American Film Institute.

ADDRESSES: OFFICE—1543 Sunset Plaza Drive, Los Angeles, CA, 90069. AGENT—c/o Aaron Cohen, William Morris Agency, 151 El Camino Drive, Beverly Hills, CA 90212.

*   *   *

CASS, Peggy   1926-

PERSONAL: Full name, Mary Margaret Cass; born May 21, 1926, in Boston, MA; daughter of Raymond James and Margaret (Loughlin) Cass; married Carl Fisher (divorced); married Martin Feeney (an accountant), 1980. EDUCATION: Attended Cambridge Latin School; trained for the stage with Uta Hagen, Mira Rostova, and Tamara Daykarhanova.

VOCATION: Actress.

CAREER: FIRST STAGE APPEARANCES—*The Doughgirls*, Australian cities, 1945. NEW YORK DEBUT—Maisie, *Burlesque*, Belasco Theatre, 1948. PRINCIPAL STAGE APPEARANCES—*Touch and Go Revue*, Broadhurst Theatre, NY, 1949; Emily Clayton, *House on the Cliff*, Shubert Theatre, New Haven, CT, 1950; Liz Fargo, *The Live Wire*, Playhouse, NY, 1950; the Woman Scorned, "Burlesque," *ANTA Album*, Ziegfeld Theatre, NY, 1951; Helen, *Bernadine*, Playhouse, NY, 1952; *Phoenix '55 Revue*, Phoenix Theatre, NY, 1955; Bianca, *Othello*, Mistress Quickley, *Henry IV, Part I*, both City Center Theatre, NY, 1955; Agnes Gooch, *Auntie Mame*, Broadhurst Theatre, NY, 1956-58; *A Thurber Carnival*, American National Theatre and Academy (ANTA), NY, 1960; Vera von Stobel, *Children from Their Games*, Morosco Theatre, NY, 1963; Marion Hollander, *Don't Drink the Water*, Morosco Theatre, NY, 1967; Mollie Malloy, *The Front Page*, Ethel Barrymore Theatre, NY, 1969; *Plaza Suite*, Plymouth Theatre, NY, 1969, then Westbury Music Fair, Long Island, NY, 1971; *Last of the Red Hot Lovers*, Westbury Music Fair, Long Island, NY, 1972; *The Torch-Bearers*, McCarter Theatre, Princeton, NJ, 1978; Mother Basil, *Once a Catholic*, Helen Hayes Theatre, NY, 1979; Maggie Jones, *Forty-Second Street*, Majestic Theatre, NY, 1981, then again in 1985; Lil, *The Octette Bridge Club*, Music Box Theatre, NY, 1985.

Appeared in summer musicals at the Dallas State Fair, TX: *Do Re Mi*, 1962 and *Bells Are Ringing*, 1963.

MAJOR TOURS—Mildred Turner, *Oh, Men! Oh, Women!*, U.S. cities, 1954-55; Madame Zelda, *The Amazing Adele*, U.S. cities, 1955-56; Alix Carpenter, *A Community of Two*, U.S. cities, 1974; *Cheaters*, national, 1980; Mother Miriam Ruth, *Agnes of God*, midwestern tour, 1984.

PRINCIPAL FILM APPEARANCES—*The Marrying Kind*, 1952; *Auntie Mame*, Warner Brothers, 1958; *Gidget Goes Hawaiian*, Columbia, 1961; *If It's Tuesday, This Must be Belgium*, United Artists, 1969; *Paddy*, Allied Artists, 1970.

PRINCIPAL TELEVISION APPEARANCES—Series: Regular, *Keep Talking*, CBS, 1958-59, then ABC, 1959-60; semi-regular, *The Jack Paar Show*, NBC, 1958-62; Elinore Hathaway, *The Hathaways*, ABC, 1961-62; regular panelist, *To Tell the Truth*, CBS, 1964-67; *Cheaters*, cable, 1981.

Episodic: "Call Me Annie," *The Barbara Stanwyck Show*, NBC, 1960; *The Garry Moore Show*.

AWARDS: Antoinette Perry Award, 1956, for *Auntie Mame;* Best Supporting Actress, Academy Award nomination, 1958, for *Auntie Mame.*

SIDELIGHTS: FAVORITE ROLES—Agnes Gooch, *Auntie Mame.*

Peggy Cass is the subject of a song called "I'm in Love with Peggy Cass," written by Gary Senick in 1978.

ADDRESSES: OFFICE—200 E. 62nd Street, New York, NY 10021.*

*   *   *

CASSAVETES, John   1929-

PERSONAL: Born December 9, 1929, in New York, NY; married Gena Rowlands, March 19, 1958. EDUCATION: Attended Mohawk College, Colgate University, and the Academy of Dramatic Arts.

VOCATION: Actor and director.

CAREER: FILM DEBUT—*Taxi*, 1953. PRINCIPAL FILM APPEARANCES—*Night Holds Terror*, Columbia, 1955; *Crime in the Streets*, Allied Artists, 1956; *Edge of the City*, Metro-Goldwyn-Mayer, 1957; *Devil's Angels*, American International, 1967; *The Dirty Dozen*, Metro-Goldwyn-Mayer, 1967; *Rosemary's Baby*, Paramount, 1968; *Faces*, Continental, 1968; *Husbands*, Columbia, 1970; *Machine Gun McCain*, Columbia, 1970; Nicky, *Mikey and Nicky*, Paramount, 1976; *Two Minute Warning*, Universal, 1976; *The Fury*, Twentieth Century-Fox, 1978; *Brass Target*, United Artists, 1978; *Whose Life Is It Anyway?*, United Artists, 1981; *Tempest*, Columbia, 1982; *Incubus*, 1982; *Marvin and Tige*, Lorimar, 1983; *Big Trouble*, 1984; *Love Streams*, Cannon, 1985; also, *Fever Tree.*

PRINCIPAL FILM WORK—Director: *Shadows*, 1960; *Too Late Blues*, Paramount, 1962; *A Child Is Waiting*, United Artists, 1963; *Faces*, Continental, 1968; *Husbands*, Columbia, 1970; *Minnie & Moskowitz*, Universal, 1971; *A Woman Under the Influence*, 1974; *Killing of a Chinese Bookie*, Faces Distribution Corp., 1976; *Opening Night*, 1977; *Gloria*, Columbia, 1980; *Love Streams*, Cannon, 1985.

PRINCIPAL TELEVISION APPEARANCES—Series: Title role, *Johnny Staccato*, NBC, 1959.

Episodic: *Omnibus; Danger; Alcoa Theatre; Bob Hope Presents the Chrysler Theatre; Elgin TV Hour.*

Movies: *Flesh and Blood*, 1979.

PRINCIPAL STAGE WORK—Broadway: assistant stage manager, *Fifth Season;* appeared in stock productions.

WRITINGS: SCREENPLAYS—*Too Late Blues*, 1962; *Faces*, 1968; *Husbands;* 1970; *Minnie & Moskowitz*, 1971; *Killing of a Chinese*

Bookie, 1976; *Opening Night,* 1977; *Gloria,* 1980; *Love Streams,* 1985.

AWARDS: Golden Lion Award, Venice Film Festival Award, 1980, for *Gloria.*

ADDRESSES: AGENT—Esme Chandee, 9056 Santa Monica Blvd., Suite 201, Los Angeles, CA 90069.*

*   *   *

CASSIDY, Shaun   1958-

PERSONAL: Born September 27, 1958, in Los Angeles, CA; son of Jack (an actor) and Shirley (an actress and singer; maiden name, Jones) Cassidy. EDUCATION: Beverly Hills High School.

VOCATION: Singer, composer, and actor.

CAREER: PRINCIPAL TELEVISION APPEARANCES—Series: Joe Hardy, *Hardy Boys Mysteries,* ABC, 1977-79; Dave Stohler, *Breaking Away,* ABC, 1980-81.

Movie: Roger, *Like Normal People,* 1979.

Guest: *Don Kirshner's Rock Concert,* syndicated.

PRINCIPAL FILM APPEARANCES—*Born of Water.*

PRINCIPAL STAGE APPEARANCES—*Mass Appeal,* U.S. cities, 1984.

MAJOR TOURS—As a singer, has toured U.S., Europe, and Australia.

RECORDINGS: ALBUMS—*Born Late;* others.*

*   *   *

CASSUTT, Michael   1954-

PERSONAL: Born April 13, 1954, in Owatonna, MN; son of Florian Francis (a teacher and athletic's coach) and Joyce (a teacher; maiden name, Williams) Cassutt; married Cynthia Lee Stratton (a magazine editor) August 19, 1978; children: Ryan Spencer. EDUCATION: University of Arizona in Tucson, B.A., radio and television, 1975.

VOCATION: Writer.

CAREER: PRINCIPAL RADIO WORK—Program director, KHYT Radio, Tucson, AZ, 1975-78.

PRINCIPAL TELEVISION WORK—Program executive, CBS Television, Hollywood, CA, 1979-85.

WRITINGS: TELEVISION—Episodes of *Alice,* CBS; *The Twilight Zone,* CBS; *Simon & Simon,* CBS; others.

MAGAZINES—In *Omni* (magazine of fantasy and science fiction); others.

NOVELS—*The Star Country,* Doubleday, 1986.

MEMBER: Writers Guild of America West, Science Fiction Writers of America, American Film Institute; National Space Institute.

ADDRESSES: HOME—5523 Ranchito Avenue, Van Nuys, CA 91401. AGENT—(Television and film) Robinson, Weintraub, Gross, 8428 Melrose Place Suite C, Los Angeles, CA 90069; (print) Richard Curtis Associates, 164 E. 64th Street, New York, NY 10021.

*   *   *

CAULFIELD, Maxwell   1959-

BRIEF ENTRY: Born in 1959, in Derbyshire, England. Actor. Caulfield moved to Kensington, London with his family at the age of two. At age fifteen, after attending several schools and numerous family arguments, he moved out of his parents' home and got his first job as a nude dancer to Led Zepplin and Pink Floyd music at a London nightclub. He left England for America in 1978, with $300 and a copy of Jack Kerouac's *On the Road* in his pocket. His first theatrical job in New York was running the concession stand at the Truck and Warehouse Theatre, where he lived, sleeping on the stage. His big break came when he portrayed an East End thug in *Class Enemy,* for which he won a *Theatre World* Award, and the title role in *Entertaining Mr. Sloane* in an Off-Broadway production. Caulfield met his future wife, the actress Juliet Mills, while playing John Merrick in *The Elephant Man* in a production in Florida. In the Public Theatre, New York, production of *Salonika* with Jessica Tandy, he spent most of the play lying nude on the sand onstage. *Grease II* was Caulfield's first major role in films, and he more recently co-starred in the independently released *Boys Next Door.* On television, he has been seen opposite Rosanna Arquette in the movie *The Parade,* and is currently portraying Miles Colby on *Dynasty II: The Colbys.**

*   *   *

CHANNING, Carol   1921-

PERSONAL: Born January 31, 1921, in Seattle, WA; daughter of George and Adelaide (Glaser) Channing; married Theodore Nadish (divorced); married Al Carson (divorced); married Charles F. Lowe, September 5, 1956; children: (second marriage) Channing. EDUCATION: Attended Bennington College.

VOCATION: Actress.

CAREER: NEW YORK DEBUT—Singer, *No for an Answer,* Center Theatre, 1941. LONDON DEBUT—*Carol Channing and Her Stouthearted Men,* Drury Lane Theatre, 1971. PRINCIPAL STAGE APPEARANCES—*Let's Face It,* Imperial Theatre, NY, 1941; Steve, *Proof Through the Night,* Morosco Theatre, NY, 1942; *Lend an Ear,* National Theatre, NY, 1948; Lorelei Lee, *Gentlemen Prefer Blondes,* Ziegfeld Theatre, NY, 1949, then Palace Theatre, Chicago, 1951; Ruth, *Wonderful Town,* Winter Garden Theatre, NY, 1953; Flora Weems, *The Vamp,* Winter Garden Theatre, NY, 1955; *Show Business,* Curran Theatre, San Francisco, CA, 1959; *Show Girl,* Eugene O'Neill Theatre, NY, 1961; Dolly Gallagher Levi, *Hello, Dolly!,* St. James Theatre, NY, 1964-65, then Shubert Theatre, NY, 1966, then Lunt-Fontanne Theatre, NY, 1978, then Shaftesbury Theatre, London, 1980; *Four on a Garden,* Broadhurst Theatre, NY, 1971; *Carol Channing and Her Gentlemen Prefer Blondes,* Princess Theatre, Melbourne, Australia and Regent Thea-

CAROL CHANNING

tre, Sydney, Australia, 1972; Lorelei Lee, *Lorelei, or Gentlemen Still Prefer Blondes,* Palace Theatre, NY, 1974; as Lorelei Lee, *Parade of Stars Playing the Palace,* Palace Theatre, NY, 1983; *Legends,* Los Angeles, CA, 1985.

MAJOR TOURS—U.S. cities: Lorelei Lee, *Gentlemen Prefer Blondes,* 1951-52; Eliza Doolittle, *Pygmalion,* 1953; Ruth, *Wonderful Town,* 1954; *Show Business,* 1959; *Show Girl Revue,* 1961; *George Burns-Carol Channing Musical Revue,* 1962; Dolly Gallagher Levi, *Hello, Dolly!,* 1965-66, 1967, 1977-80, 1983; *The Carol Channing Show,* 1971; Lorelei Lee, *Lorelei or Gentlemen Still Prefer Blondes,* 1975; Alma, *The Bed Before Yesterday,* Florida cities, 1976; *Jerry's Girls,* pre-Broadway in Florida cities, 1984; *Legends,* select national cities, 1985-86.

CABARET—Tropicana Hotel, Las Vegas, NV, 1957; President Johnson's Inaugural Gala, Washington, DC, 1965; Nugget Hotel, Reno, NV, 1972; Palmer House, Chicago, IL, 1972.

PRINCIPAL FILM APPEARANCES—*The First Traveling Saleslady,* Universal, 1956; *Thoroughly Modern Millie,* Universal, 1967; *Skidoo,* Paramount, 1968; *Archie and Mehitabel.*

PRINCIPAL TELEVISION APPEARANCES—Has appeared as a guest on more than fifty television programs and in a number of her own specials.

Movie: White Queen, *Alice in Wonderland,* CBS, 1986.

MEMBER: Actors' Equity Association.

AWARDS: New York Drama Critics Award, 1948, for *Lend an Ear;* New York Drama Critics Award, Antoinette Perry Award, 1964, for *Hello Dolly!;* Best Supporting Actress, Golden Globe, 1967, for *Thoroughly Modern Millie;* London Critics Award, 1970, for *Carol Channing and Her Ten Stout-Hearted Men.*

ADDRESSES: AGENT—c/o Tony Fantozzi, William Morris Agency, 151 El Camino Drive, Beverly Hills, CA, 90212; c/o Dawn Bridges, Solters, Roskin, Friedman, Inc., 5455 Wilshire Blvd., Suite 2200, Los Angeles, CA 90036.

*   *   *

CHAPLIN, Geraldine   1944-

PERSONAL: Born 1944 in Santa Monica, CA; daughter of Charles (the actor and director) and Oona (O'Neill) Chaplin; children: Shane. EDUCATION: Studied at the Royal Ballet School, London.

VOCATION: Actress.

CAREER: PRINCIPAL FILM APPEARANCES—*Doctor Zhivago,* Metro-Goldwyn-Mayer, 1965; *I Killed Rasputin,* French-Italian, 1967; *The Hawaiians,* United Artists, 1970; *Zero Population Growth,* 1970; *Innocent Bystanders,* Paramount, 1973; *The Three Musketeers,* Twentieth Century-Fox, 1974; *Nashville,* Paramount, 1975; *Stranger in the House,* Warner Brothers, 1975; *Buffalo Bill and the Indians,* United Artists, 1976; *Welcome to L.A.,* Lions Gate, 1977; *Roseland,* Cinema Shares, 1977; *Remember My Name,* 1978; *The Mirror Crack'd,* Associated Film Distributors, 1980; *Hidden Talent,* 1984.

PRINCIPAL TELEVISION APPEARANCES—Movies: *The Corsican Brothers,* CBS, 1985.

SIDELIGHTS: CTFT notes that Geraldine Chaplin has starred in many European films including seven with Spain's leading filmmaker, Carlos Saura.

ADDRESSES: AGENT—William Morris Agency, 151 El Camino Drive, Beverly Hills, CA 90212.*

*   *   *

CHARTOFF, Robert

PERSONAL: Born in New York, NY; son of William and Bessie Chartoff; married Vanessa Howard, July 3, 1970; children: Jenifer, William, Julie, Charley. EDUCATION: Union College, A.B., 1955; Columbia Law School, L.L.B., 1958.

VOCATION: Producer.

CAREER: PRINCIPAL FILM WORK—Co-Producer (all with Irwin Winkler): *Double Trouble,* Metro-Goldwyn-Mayer, 1967; *Point Blank,* Metro-Goldwyn-Mayer, 1967; *The Split,* Metro-Goldwyn-Mayer, 1968; *Leo the Last,* United Artists, 1969; *They Shoot Horses, Don't They,* Cinerama, 1969; *The Strawberry Statement,* Metro-Goldwyn-Mayer, 1970; *The Gang That Couldn't Shoot Straight,* Metro-Goldwyn-Mayer, 1971; *Believe in Me,* Metro-Goldwyn-Mayer, 1971; *The New Centurions,* Columbia, 1972; *The Mechanic,* United Artists, 1972; *Up the Sandbox,* National General,

1972; *S*P*Y*S,* Twentieth Century-Fox, 1974; *Busting,* United Artists, 1974; *Peeper,* Twentieth Century-Fox, 1975; *The Gambler,* Paramount, 1975; *Breakout,* 1975; *Rocky,* United Artists, 1976; *Nickelodeon,* Columbia, 1976; *New York, New York,* United Artists, 1977; *Valentino,* 1977; *Comes a Horseman,* United Artists, 1978; *Uncle Joe Shannon,* United Artists, 1978; *Rocky II,* United Artists, 1979; *Raging Bull,* United Artists, 1980; *True Confessions,* United Artists, 1981; *Rocky III,* Metro-Goldwyn-Mayer/United Artists, 1982; *The Right Stuff,* Warner Brothers, 1983; *Rocky IV,* Metro-Goldwyn-Mayer/United Artists, 1985.

AWARDS: (Shared with Irwin Winkler) Best Picture, Academy Award, 1976, for *Rocky;* (shared with Irwin Winkler) Best Picture, Academy Award nomination, 1980, for *Raging Bull.*

ADDRESSES: OFFICE—Chartoff-Winkler Productions, Inc., 10125 W. Washington Blvd., Culver City, CA 90230.

*   *   *

CHASE, Chevy   1943-

PERSONAL: Born Cornelius Crane, October 8, 1943, in New York, NY; son of Edward Tinsley and Cathalene (Widdoes) Crane; married Jacqueline Carlin, December 4, 1976 (divorced, 1980); married Jayni; children: (second marriage) Cydney Cathalene, Caley Leigh. EDUCATION: Bard College, B.A., English, 1967; Massachusetts Institute of Technology, M.A.; studied Audio Research at CCS Institute. POLITICS: Democrat.

VOCATION: Actor, writer, and comedian.

CAREER: PRINCIPAL FILM APPEARANCES—*Foul Play,* Paramount, 1978; *Oh Heavenly Dog,* Twentieth Century-Fox, 1980; *Caddyshack,* Warner Brothers, 1980; *Seems Like Old Times,* Columbia, 1980; *Under the Rainbow,* Warner Brothers, 1981; *Modern Problems,* Twentieth Century-Fox, 1981; *National Lampoon's Vacation,* Warner Brothers, 1983; *Deal of the Century,* Warner Brothers, 1983; *Fletch,* Universal, 1985; *National Lampoon's European Vacation,* Warner Brothers, 1985; *Follow That Bird,* Warner Brothers, 1985; *Spies Like Us,* Warner Brothers, 1985; *The Three Amigos,* Orion, 1986.

PRINCIPAL TELEVISION APPEARANCES—Series: Not Ready for Prime Time Player, *Saturday Night Live,* NBC, 1975-76.

Specials: Chase has had several of his own specials on NBC.

WRITINGS: TELEVISION—Series: Staff writer, *Saturday Night Live,* NBC, 1975-76.

Specials: *The Paul Simon Special;* several of his own specials.

PLAYS, PRODUCED—(With Kenny Shapiro and Lane Sarahnson) *Groove Tube,* Off-Broadway, NY, 1973.

SCREENPLAY—*Groove Tube,* Levitt-Pickman Films, 1974.

RELATED CAREER—Artist, Metro-Goldwyn-Mayer Records, 1968; artist, *Mad* magazine, 1969.

AWARDS: Outstanding Single or Continuing Performance by a Supporting Actor in Variety or Music, Emmy Award, 1975-76, for *Saturday Night Live;* (with Anne Beatts, Tom Davis, Al Franken,

Lorne Michaels, Marilyn Suzanne Miller, Michael O'Donoghue, Herb Sargent, Tom Schiller, Rosie Schuster, and Alan Zweibel) Outstanding Writing in a Comedy-Variety or Music Series (a single episode of a regular or limited series), Emmy Award, 1975-76, for *Saturday Night Live;* (with Tom Davis, Al Franken, Charles Grodin, Lorne Michaels, Paul Simon, Lily Tomlin, and Alan Zweibel), Outstanding Writing in a Comedy-Variety or Music Special, Emmy Award, 1977-78, for *The Paul Simon Special.*

MEMBER: National Academy of Television Arts and Sciences, Actors' Equity Association, American Federation of Television and Radio Artists, American Federation of Musicians, Screen Actors Guild.

ADDRESSES: AGENT—William Morris Agency, 151 El Camino Drive, Beverly Hills, CA 90212.

*   *   *

CHELSOM, Peter   1956-

PERSONAL: Born April 20, 1956, in Blackpool, England; EDUCATION: Wrekin College Public School, Shropshire; studied acting at the Central School of Speech and Drama, London. RELIGION: Church of England.

VOCATION: Actor.

CAREER: PRINCIPAL STAGE APPEARANCES—With the Royal Lyceum Theatre Company, Edinburgh: Edmund, *Edward II,* 1978-79; *All Ayre and Fire,* 1978-79; the son, *Bingo,* 1978-79; Charley, *Charley's Aunt,* 1978-79.

Title role, *The Gingerbread Man,* Leeds Playhouse Company, 1979-80; Harcourt, *The Country Wife,* Thorndike Theatre, Leatherhead, 1980.

PETER CHELSOM

With the Royal Shakespeare Company, London and Stratford, 1980-82: as Nick Croucher in *Television Times,* as Ralph in *The Accrington Pals,* as Florizel in *The Winter's Tale,* as Valentine in *Two Gentlemen of Verona,* in *Titus Andronicus* and *All's Well That Ends Well,* and as Nicky Hutchinson in *Our Friends in the North.*

Joe Conran, *Ourselves Alone,* Royal Court Theatre, London, 1982.

PRINCIPAL FILM APPEARANCES—Mitchell, *The Ringer,* 1978.

PRINCIPAL TELEVISION APPEARANCES—Movies: Bernard Wilsher, *Cream in My Coffee,* 1980; Houseman, *Intensive Care,* BBC, 1982; Kenny Winters, *Not That Kind of People,* 1982; Giles, *An Englishman Abroad,* BBC, 1983; Nigel Playfare, *Christmas Present;* Alan, *Time and the Conways,* BBC; Bryan Snow, *Star Quality,* BBC.

Mini-Series: Edwin, *A Woman of Substance,* 1984.

Series: Christopher Sorrell, *Sorrell and Son* (six episodes), Yorkshire TV, 1983; also appeared in *Alcohol,* Granada TV, 1979.

PRINCIPAL RADIO BROADCAST—Horatio, *A Hard Night in Elsinore,* BBC, 1978-79.

MEMBER: British Actors' Equity Association.

SIDELIGHTS: Mr. Chelsom informs *CTFT* that he is fluent in French and German and that he is best known in the United States for his appearance in *A Woman of Substance.* He travels to this country often.

*ADDRESSES:*HOME—London, England. AGENT—James Sharkey Associates, 15 Golden Square, Third Floor, London W1R 3AG, England; c/o Susan Smith, Smith-Freedman Assoc., 123 N. San Vincente Blvd., Beverly Hills, CA 90211.

*   *   *

CHER   1946-

PERSONAL: Born Cherilyn Sarkisian, May 20, 1946; daughter of John and Georgia (Holt) Sarkisian; married Sonny Bono, 1964 (divorced); married Gregg Allman, 1975 (divorced); children: (first marriage) Chastity; (second marriage) Elijah Blue. EDUCATION: Trained for the stage with Jeff Corey.

VOCATION: Actress and singer.

CAREER: PRINCIPAL FILM APPEARANCES—*Good Times,* Columbia, 1967; *Chastity,* American International, 1969; *Come Back to the Five and Dime, Jimmy Dean, Jimmy Dean,* 1982; *Silkwood,* Twentieth Century-Fox, 1983; *Mask,* Universal, 1985.

PRINCIPAL TELEVISION APPEARANCES—Series: *The Sonny and Cher Comedy Hour,* CBS, 1971-74; *Cher,* CBS, 1975-76; *The Sonny and Cher Show,* CBS, 1976-77.

Guest: *Shindig,* ABC, 1964.

NEW YORK DEBUT—Sissy, *Come Back to the Five and Dime, Jimmy Dean, Jimmy Dean,* Martin Beck Theatre, NY, 1982.

RECORDINGS: SINGLES—(With Sonny Bono) *I Got You Babe;*

CHER

Baby Don't Go; You Better Sit Down Kids. (Solo) *Gypsies, Tramps and Thieves; Dark Lady; Take Me Home; Half Breed,* MCA.

AWARDS: Best Supporting Actress, Academy Award nomination, 1983, for *Silkwood.*

ADDRESSES: AGENT—Creative Artists Agency, 1888 Century Park E., Suite 1400, Los Angeles, CA 90069; Bill Sammeth Organization, 9200 Sunset Blvd., Suite 1001, Los Angeles, CA 90069.

*   *   *

CHEW, Lee

PERSONAL: Full name, Robert Lee Chew, III; born February 8, in Roanoke, VA; son of Robert Lee (a Virginia state trooper) and Ruby Pearl (a beautician; maiden name, Bevins) Chew. EDUCATION: Attended Virginia Western Community College, 1967-68; Virginia Commonwealth University, B.F.A., 1972.

VOCATION: Actor.

CAREER: STAGE DEBUT—Jerry Johnson, *Silent Night, Lonely Night,* Showtimers, Salem, VA, 1962. NEW YORK DEBUT—Hercule, *Can-Can,* Equity Library Theatre, 1978. PRINCIPAL STAGE APPEARANCES—First murderer, *Macbeth,* Virginia Museum Theatre, 1972; Mr. Carol, *Shenandoah,* Carousel Theatre and Canal Fulton Theatre, 1978; Moon, *The Real Inspector Hound,* Stage Works, NY, 1979; Timothy Hogarth, *Room Service,* Folly Theatre, Kansas City, MO, 1981; Georg Nowack, *She Loves Me,* Pocono Playhouse, PA, 1982; Humpy Grogan, *Eileen,* New Amsterdam Theatre Company, Town Hall Theatre, NY, 1982; Georg Nowack, *She Loves Me,* Equity Library Theatre, NY, 1985; Peter Sloan, *Light Up the Sky,* Jewish Repertory Theatre, NY, 1986.

LEE CHEW

MAJOR TOURS—Chip Salisbury, *Woman of the Year*, national, 1984; Cornelius Hackl, *Hello Dolly!*, East Coast, 1985.

MEMBER: Actors' Equity Association.

ADDRESSES: HOME—400 W. 43rd Street, New York, NY 10036. AGENT—Alan Willig Associates, 165 W. 46th Street, New York, NY 10036.

*   *   *

CHRISTIE, Julie   1941-

PERSONAL: Full name, Julie Frances Christie; born April 14, 1941, in Chukur, Assam, India; daughter of Frank St. John and Rosemary (Ramsden) Christie. EDUCATION: Central School of Dramatic Arts, London; Brighton Technical College.

VOCATION: Actress.

CAREER: PRINCIPAL STAGE APPEARANCES—Appeared with Birmingham Repertory Company, England, 1963, and the Royal Shakespeare Company, 1964; *Uncle Vanya*, all-star production, NY, 1973.

FILM DEBUT—*Crooks Anonymous*, Anglo-Amalgamated Films, 1962. PRINCIPAL FILM APPEARANCES—*The Fast Lady*, Rank Films, 1962; *Billy Liar*, Vic Films, 1963; *Young Cassidy*, Metro-Goldwyn-Mayer, 1964; *Darling*, Anglo-Amalgamated/Vic/Appia Films, 1965; Lara, *Dr. Zhivago*, Metro-Goldwyn-Mayer, 1965; *Fahrenheit 451*, Rank Films, 1966; Bathsheba Everdene, *Far from the Madding Crowd*, EMI/Vic/Appia, 1967; title role, *Petulia*,

Warner Brothers, 1968; *In Search of Gregory*, Universal, 1969; *The Go-Between*, EMI, 1970; Mrs. Miller, *McCabe and Mrs. Miller*, Warner Brothers, 1971; *Don't Look Now*, Paramount, 1974; *Shampoo*, Columbia, 1975; *Demon Seed*, United Artists, 1977; *Heaven Can Wait*, Paramount, 1978; *Memoirs of a Survivor*, 1980; *Gold*, 1980; *Les Quarantiemes Rugissants*, 1981; *Heat and Dust*, Universal, 1983; *The Gold Diggers*, 1984; *The Return of the Soldier*, European Classics, 1985; *Power*, 1985.

TELEVISION DEBUT—*A is for Andromeda*, British Television.

AWARDS: Best Actress, Academy Award, New York Film Critics Award, 1965, for *Darling*; Donatello Award, 1965, for *Dr. Zhivago*; Best Dramatic Actress, Laurel Award and *Herald* Award, 1967; Best Actress, Academy Award nomination, 1971, for *McCabe and Mrs. Miller*.

ADDRESSES: AGENT—International Creative Management. 40 W. 57th Street, New York, NY 10019.*

*   *   *

CHRISTOPHER, Dennis   1955-

PERSONAL: Born December 2, 1955, in Philadelphia, PA. EDUCATION: Attended Temple University; studied acting with Tracy Roberts, Charles Conrad, Florence Riggs, David Craig, Stella Adler, and Peggy Feury in Los Angeles; studied with Austin Pendleton and Michael Howard in New York.

VOCATION: Actor.

CAREER: NEW YORK DEBUT—*Yentl the Yeshiva Boy*, Chelsea Theatre Center, 1974. PRINCIPAL STAGE APPEARANCES—*Dr. Needle and the Infectious Laughter Epidemic*, Circle Repertory Theatre, NY; *Butterflies Are Free*, Burt Reynolds Theatre, FL; *Balm in Gilead*, Pan Andreas Theatre, LA; *The Slab Boys*, Back Alley Theatre, LA; Leo Hubbard, *The Little Foxes*, Parker Playhouse, FL, Kennedy Center for the Performing Arts, Washington, DC, then Martin Beck Theatre, NY, 1981; Tommy, *Brothers*, Colonial Theatre, Boston, MA, Forrest Theatre, Philadelphia, PA, Music Box Theatre, NY, 1983; *The Triplet Collection*, Matrix Theatre, LA.

FILM DEBUT—*Blood and Lace*, American International, 1971. PRINCIPAL FILM APPEARANCES—*Fellini's Roma*, United Artists, 1972; *Salome*, Italian, 1972; *Three Women*, Twentieth Century-Fox, 1977; *September 30, 1955*, Universal, 1978; *A Wedding*, Twentieth Century-Fox, 1978; *California Dreaming*, Orion, 1979; *The Last Word*, Goldwyn Studios, 1979; Dave Stohler, *Breaking Away*, Twentieth Century-Fox, 1979; *Fade to Black*, American Cinema, 1980; *Chariots of Fire*, Warner Brothers, 1981; *Don't Cry, It's Only Thunder*, Sanrio/Lorimar, 1982; *The Falling*, American Distributors, Inc. 1983; *Flight of the Spruce Goose*, 1984; *Jake Speed*, New World Pictures, 1986.

PRINCIPAL TELEVISION APPEARANCES—Episodic: "A Safe Place," *Cagney & Lacey*, CBS; "The Lady in the Iron Mask," *Moonlighting*, ABC; "Promises, Promises," *Trapper John M.D.*, CBS; "Jack and the Beanstalk," *Faerie Tale Theatre*, Showtime Cable; "Number Eight," *Tales of the Unexpected*, NBC; "Bernice Bobs Her Hair," *The American Short Story*, PBS.

Movies: *The Oregon Trail*, NBC, 1976.

DENNIS CHRISTOPHER

MEMBER: Actors' Equity Association, Screen Actors Guild, American Federation of Television and Radio Artists; Hollywood Arts Council (board of trustees); Writer's Lab, Los Angeles, CA.

AWARDS: Hollywood Drama-Logue Award, for *Balm in Gilead;* British Academy Award, Hollywood Women's Photo and Press Club Youth in Film award, and Golden Globe nomination, all 1979, for *Breaking Away;* Bronze Mask of Polifemo, Italy's Taorimina International Film Festival, 1980, for *Fade to Black.*

SIDELIGHTS: Dennis Christopher told *CTFT* that he worked with The Living Theatre in Paris, participating in street theatre and experimental films.

ADDRESSES: AGENT—c/o Barbara Gale, William Morris Agency, 151 El Camino Drive, Beverly Hills, CA 90212.

*   *   *

CHURCHILL, Caryl   1938-

PERSONAL: Born September 3, 1938, in London, England; married David Harter, 1961; children: three sons. EDUCATION: Trafalgar School, Montreal, Canada; Lady Margaret Hall, Oxford, B.A., 1960.

VOCATION: Playwright.

WRITINGS: PLAYS, PRODUCED—*Downstairs,* Oxford, England, 1958, then London, 1959; *Having a Wonderful Time,* London, 1960; *Easy Death,* Oxford, 1962; *Schreber's Nervous Illness,*

King's Head Theatre, London, 1972; *Owners,* Royal Court Theatre, Upstairs, London, 1972, then NY, 1973; *Perfect Happiness,* London, 1974; *Moving Clocks Go Slow,* London, 1975; *Objections to Sex and Violence,* London, 1975; *Light Shining in Buckinghamshire,* 1975; *Vinegar Tom,* London, 1976; *Traps,* 1977; *Cloud Nine,* 1979; *Three More Sleepless Nights,* 1980; *Top Girls,* London, 1982; *Fen,* London, 1983; *Softcops,* London, 1984.

REVUE SKETCHES—For *Floorshow,* 1977.

RADIO SCRIPTS—*The Ants,* 1962; *Lovesick,* 1967; *Identical Twins,* 1968; *Abortive,* 1971; *Not, Not, Not, Not, Not Enough Oxygen,* 1972; *Henry's Past,* 1972; *Perfect Happiness,* 1973.

TELEVISION SCRIPTS—*The Judge's Wife,* 1972; *Turkish Delight,* 1974; *The After Dinner Joke,* 1978; *The Legion Hall Bombing,* 1978; *Crimes,* 1981.

ADDRESSES: HOME—London, England. AGENT—Margaret Ramsay Ltd., 14A Goodwin's Court, London WC2N 4LL, England.

*   *   *

CICCONE, Madonna
See MADONNA

*   *   *

CLARK, B. D.   1945-

PERSONAL: Born Bruce Clark, June 29, 1945, in Christchurch, New Zealand. EDUCATION: University of California at Los Angeles, M.F.A., 1971.

VOCATION: Director, producer, and writer.

CAREER: PRINCIPAL FILM WORK—Director and co-writer, *Naked Angels,* New World, 1969; director and co-writer, *Ski Bum,* Avco Embassy, 1971; director, *Hammer,* United Artists, 1973; director and co-writer, *Galaxy of Terror,* New World, 1980.

PRINCIPAL TELEVISION WORK—Director and co-writer, *Games Affair,* 1976; producer and director, *Stories from the Magic Cave,* 1982.

MEMBER: Writers Guild of America West.

ADDRESSES: OFFICE—P. O. Box 212, Deer Harbor, WA 98243.

*   *   *

CLARK, Dick   1929-

PERSONAL: Full name, Richard Wagstaff Clark; born November 30, 1929, in Mt. Vernon, NY; son of Richard Augustus and Julia Clark; married Barbara Mallery, 1952 (divorced); married Loretta Martin, 1962 (divorced); married Kari Wigton; children: (first marriage) Richard Augustus, II; (second marriage) Duane, Cindy. EDUCATION: Syracuse University, 1951.

VOCATION: Producer, television host, actor, and writer.

CAREER:PRINCIPAL TELEVISION APPEARANCES—Announcer, WKTV, Utica, NY, 1951; staff announcer, *Paul Whiteman's TV Teen Club*, ABC, 1952; host, *American Bandstand*, ABC daytime edition, 1952-64, evening edition, 1957; guest, *Open Hearing* (public affairs talk show), ABC, 1957-58; host, *The Dick Clark Show*, ABC, 1958-60 (derived from above); host, *Dick Clark's World of Talent*, ABC, 1959; host *The $25,000 Pyramid* (later, the *$50,000 Pyramid*), daytime version, CBS, 1973-74, ABC, 1974-80, CBS, 1982—; host, *Dick Clark Presents the Rock and Roll Years*, ABC, 1973-74; host, *Dick Clark's Live Wednesday*, NBC, 1978; host, *The Krypton Factor* (quiz show), ABC, 1981; *Inside America*, ABC, 1982; co-host (with Ed McMahon), *TV's Bloopers and Practical Jokes*, NBC, 1984-85; host, *32nd Annual Emmy Awards Show*; also, *The Dick Clark Beechnut Show; The Object Is; Missing Links; Record Years*.

PRINCIPAL TELEVISION WORK—Series: Producer—*Dick Clark Presents the Rock and Roll Years*, ABC, 1973-74; *Dick Clark's Live Wednesday*, NBC, 1978; *Inside America*, ABC, 1982; *TV's Bloopers and Practical Jokes*, NBC, 1984-85.

Specials: *TV's Censored Bloopers*, NBC, 1981-83; *Dick Clark's Rock 'n' Roll Revue; Dick Clark's Nifty 50's; Natalie Cole Special; Where the Action Is; Swinging Country; Happening; Get It Together; Shebang; Record Years; Academy of Country Music Awards; American Music Awards; The 'Golden Globe Awards; Celebrities: Where Are They Now?; Dick Clark's Rockin' New Year's Eve*, others.

Movies: Producer—*The Man in the Santa Claus Suit*, 1978; *The Birth of the Beatles*, 1979; *Elvis*, 1979; *Murder in Texas*, 1981; *The Demon Murder Case* (also known as *The Rhode Island Murders*), 1983; *The Woman Who Willed a Miracle*, 1984; *Copacabana*, 1985.

PRINCIPAL FILM APPEARANCES—*Because They're Young*, Columbia, 1960; Dr. Alexander, *The Young Doctors*, United Artists, 1961; as himself, *Wild in the Streets*, American International Pictures, 1968.

PRINCIPAL FILM WORK—Producer: *Psych-Out*, American International Pictures, 1968; *The Savage Seven*, American International Pictures, 1968; *Killers Three*, American International Pictures, 1969; *The Dark*, 1979; *Remo Williams: The Adventure Begins*, 1985.

PRINCIPAL STAGE WORK—Producer, *Rock and Roll: The First Thousand Years*, Broadway production.

PRINCIPAL RADIO WORK—Staff announcer, WOLF, Syracuse, 1950; announcer, WRUN, Utica, NY, 1950; announcer, WFIL, Philadelphia, 1952; numerous syndicated programs, including *Countdown America* and *Rock, Roll, and Remember*.

WRITINGS: BOOKS, PUBLISHED—*Your Happiest Years*, Random House, 1959; *To Goof or Not to Goof*, Bernard Geis, 1963; *Rock, Roll, and Remember*, T.Y. Crowell, 1976; *Looking Great, Staying Young*, 1981; *Dick Clark's First 25 Years of Rock 'n' Roll*, 1981; *The History of American Bandstand*, 1985; *Dick Clark's Easygoing Guide to Good Grooming*, 1986.

ARTICLES—Contributor of articles on teenage problems to national publications.

ADDRESSES: OFFICE—Dick Clark Productions, 3003 W. Olive Avenue, Burbank, CA 91505.

CLARK, Susan   1944-

PERSONAL: Born Nora Golding, March 8, 1944, in Sarnia, Ontario, Canada; daughter of George Raymond and Eleanor Almond (McNaughton) Clark; married Alex Karras (an actor and former professional football player). EDUCATION: Attended Children's Players, Toronto, 1956-59; attended the Royal Academy of Dramatic Arts, London.

VOCATION: Actress and producer.

CAREER: FILM DEBUT—*Banning*, Universal, 1967. PRINCIPAL FILM APPEARANCES—*Madigan*, Universal, 1968; *Coogan's Bluff*, Universal, 1968; *Skullduggery*, Universal, 1970; *Colossus: The Forbin Project*, Universal, 1970; *Tell Them Willie Boy Is Here*, Universal, 1970; *Skin Game*, Warner Brothers, 1971; *Valdez Is Coming*, United Artists, 1971; *Showdown*, Universal, 1973; *Midnight Man*, Universal, 1974; *Airport '75*, Universal, 1974; *Night Moves*, Warner Brothers, 1975; *The Apple Dumpling Gang*, Buena Vista, 1975; *Murder by Decree*, Avco Embassy, 1979; *City on Fire*, Avco Embassy, 1979; *Promises in the Dark*, Warner Brothers, 1979; *The North Avenue Irregulars*, Buena Vista, 1979; *Double Negative*, Canadian, 1980; *Porky's*, Twentieth Century Fox, 1982.

PRINCIPAL FILM WORK—Producer: *Jimmy B. and Andre*, 1979; *Word of Honor*, 1980; *Maid in America*, 1982.

PRINCIPAL TELEVISION APPEARANCES—Series: Katherine Calder-Young Papadapolis, *Webster*, ABC, 1983—.

Episodic: *Columbo*, NBC.

Plays (Canada): *Heloise and Abelard; Hedda Gabler; Taming of the Shrew*.

Movies: Babe Didrickson Zaharias, *Babe*, CBS, 1975; title role, *Amelia Earhart*, 1976; *The Choice*, 1981; *Sherlock Holmes*, HBO, 1981.

PRINCIPAL STAGE APPEARANCES—*Poor Bitos*, London; *Sherlock Holmes*, Williamstown Theater Festival, MA; *Getting Out*, Mark Taper Forum, Los Angeles, CA, 1978; *Silk Stockings;* has also performed with the London Shakespeare Festival Company and the British Repertory Company.

RELATED CAREER—Partner, Georgian Bay Productions.

MEMBER: Screen Actors Guild, American Federation of Television and Radio Artists, American Film Institute; American Civil Liberties Union.

AWARDS: Outstanding Lead Actress in a Drama or Comedy Special, Emmy Award, 1975-76, for *Babe;* Outstanding Lead Actress in a Drama or Comedy Special, Emmy Award nomination, 1976-77, for *Amelia Earhart*.

ADDRESSES: OFFICE—Georgian Bay Productions, 3620 Fredonia Drive, Hollywood, CA 90068.*

*   *   *

CLOSE, Glenn   1947-

PERSONAL: Born March 19, 1947, in Greenwich, CT. EDUCATION: Attended College of William and Mary.

VOCATION: Actress.

CAREER: NEW YORK DEBUT—*Love for Love, The Member of the Wedding, Rules of the Game,* all with the Phoenix Repertory Company. PRINCIPAL STAGE APPEARANCES—*Rex,* Broadway production; *Crucifer of Blood,* Broadway production, 1978; Charity Barnum, *Barnum,* St. James Theatre, 1980; *Uncle Vanya,* Yale Repertory, New Haven, CT, 1981; title role, *The Singular Life of Albert Nobbs,* Manhattan Theatre Club, Downstage Theatre, NY, 1982; Annie, *The Real Thing,* Plymouth Theatre, NY, 1984; Actress, *Childhood,* Samuel Beckett Theatre, NY, 1985; title role, *Joan of Arc at the Stake,* York Theatre Company, Church of the Heavenly Rest Theatre, NY, May 5, 1985; Jane, *Benefactors,* Brooks Atkinson Theatre, NY, 1985-86; also, *Wine Untouched,* Off-Broadway production; *The Winter Dancers,* Off-Broadway production; *A Streetcar Named Desire,* McCarter Theatre, Princeton, NJ; *King Lear,* Milwaukee Repertory Theatre; *The Rose Tatoo,* Long Warf Theatre, New Haven, CT; *Uncommon Women and Others,* Phoenix Repertory Co., NY.

MAJOR TOURS—Charity Barnum, *Barnum,* Golden Gate Theatre, San Francisco and Pantages Theatre, Los Angeles, 1981-82.

FILM DEBUT—Jenny, *The World According to Garp,* Warner Brothers, 1982. PRINCIPAL FILM APPEARANCES—Sarah, *The Big Chill* Columbia, 1983; *The Natural,* Tri-Star, 1984; *The Stone Boy,* Twentieth Century-Fox, 1984; title role, *Maxie,* Orion, 1985; *Jagged Edge,* Columbia, 1985.

PRINCIPAL TELEVISION APPEARANCES—Movies: *The Orphan Train,* 1979 (released to theatres in 1982); Gail Bennett, *Something About Amelia,* 1984.

RECORDINGS: ALBUMS—*Barnum,* original cast recording; *The Real Thing,* original cast recording.

MEMBER: Actors' Equity Association, Screen Actors Guild, American Federation of Television and Radio Artists, American Society of Composers, Authors, and Publishers (ASCAP).

AWARDS: Antoinette Perry Award nomination, 1980, for *Barnum;* Obie Award, 1982, for *The Singular Life of Albert Nobbs;* Best Supporting Actress, Academy Award nominations, 1982, for *The World According to Garp,* 1983, for *The Big Chill,* and 1984, for *The Natural;* Best Actress, Antoinette Perry Award, 1984, for *The Real Thing;* Emmy and Golden Globe nominations, both 1984, for *Something About Amelia;* Golden Globe nomination, 1985, for *Maxie;* Grammy nomination, 1984, for the recording of *The Real Thing;* graduated from William and Mary Phi Beta Kappa.

ADDRESSES: AGENT—c/o Fred Specktor, Creative Artists Agency, 1888 Century Park E., Suite 1400, Los Angeles, CA 90067.

*　　*　　*

COATES, Carolyn

PERSONAL: Born April 29, in Oklahoma City, OK; daughter of Glenn Clinton and Jessica Amanda (Owen) Coates; married James Noble. EDUCATION: University of California at Los Angeles; studied for the theatre with Lee Strasberg and with Paul Curtis of the American Mime Theatre.

VOCATION: Actress.

CAREER: DEBUT—Title role, *A Modern Cinderella,* Children's Theatre, Santa Monica, CA, 1939. NEW YORK DEBUT—Miss Jessell, *The Innocents,* Gramercy Arts Theatre, 1959. LONDON DEBUT—The Woman, *A Whitman Portrait,* Open Space Theatre, 1969.

PRINCIPAL STAGE APPEARANCES—Madame Irma, *The Balcony,* Circle in the Square Downtown, NY, 1961; Hecuba, *The Trojan Women* (played this role for eighteen months after replacing actress Mildred Dunnock), Circle in the Square, NY, 1964; Miss Alithea, *The Country Wife,* 1965, Johanna, *The Condemned of Altona,* 1966, various roles, *The Caucasian Chalk Circle,* all three with the Repertory Theatre of Lincoln Center, Vivian Beaumont Theatre, NY; Madame Arkadina, *The Seagull,* Madame Ranevskaya, *The Cherry Orchard,* both Williamstown, MA, 1965-66; The Woman, *A Whitman Portrait,* Gramercy Arts Theatre, NY, 1966; Helen Radamacher, *The Party on Greenwich Avenue,* Cherry Lane Theatre, NY, 1967; Agnes, *A Delicate Balance,* Studio Arena, Buffalo, NY, 1967; Elmira Ruggles, *The Club Bedroom,* Theatre de Lys, NY, 1967; title role, *Phaedra,* Studio Theatre, Theatre Company of Boston, 1968; second nurse, *The Death of Bessie Smith,* Mrs. Barker, *The American Dream* (double bill), Billy Rose Theatre, NY, 1968; Elinor, *The Lion in Winter,* Studio Arena, Buffalo, NY, 1968; Lorna, *Fire!,* Longacre Theatre, NY, 1969; Agnes, *A Scent of Flowers,* Martinique Theatre, NY, 1969.

Ophelia Beans, Dirty Gertie, and Nicotine Flightpath, *The Disintegration of James Cherry,* Lincoln Center Repertory Theatre, Forum Theatre, NY, 1970; Marge, *Other People,* Berkshire Theatre Festival, Stockbridge, MA, 1970; Beatrice, *The Effect of Gamma Rays on Man-in-the-Moon Marigolds,* New Theatre, NY, 1971; Agnes, *A Delicate Balance,* Mary Tyrone, *A Long Day's Journey into Night,* Kate, *Old Times,* all Cincinnati Playhouse, Cincinnati, OH, 1973; Aimee Semple McPherson, *Alive and Well in Argentina,* St. Clement's Church, NY, 1974; Regina, *The Little Foxes,* Indiana Repertory Company, Indianapolis, IN, 1974.

Queen Margaret, *Richard III,* Long Wharf Theatre, New Haven, CT, 1975; Hester, *Equus,* Coconut Grove Playhouse, FL, 1975; Hesione Hushabye, *Heartbreak House,* Arena Stage, Washington, DC, 1976; Constance, *The Autumn Garden,* Long Wharf Theatre, New Haven, 1976; Louise, *Five Finger Exercise,* Ruth, *Blithe Spirit,* both Walnut Street Theatre, Philadelphia, 1977; Mrs. Eastman-Cuevas, *In the Summerhouse,* Manhattan Theatre Club, NY, 1977; Hester, *Equus,* Playhouse in the Park, Philadelphia, 1977; *Three Plays by Thornton Wilder,* McCarter Theatre, Princeton, NJ, 1977; Gertrude, *Hamlet,* Playmakers Repertory, NC, 1978; *Coward in Two Keys,* Studio Arena, Buffalo, 1978; Myra, *Deathtrap,* Parker Playhouse, Ft. Lauderdale, FL, 1978; Lyda, *The Road to the Graveyard,* as part of Marathon '85, Ensemble Studio Theatre, NY, 1985.

MAJOR TOURS—Standby for Geraldine Page (the Princess Cosmonopolis), *Sweet Bird of Youth,* national tour, 1960.

PRINCIPAL FILM APPEARANCES—*The Hustler,* Twentieth Century-Fox, 1961; *The Effect of Gamma Rays on Man-in-the-Moon Marigolds,* Twentieth Century-Fox, 1973.

TELEVISION DEBUT—As a mime, 1957. PRINCIPAL TELEVISION APPEARANCES—Episodic: *Knots Landing; Dallas.*

MEMBER: American Mime Theatre.

SIDELIGHTS: Carolyn Coates has appeared in new play readings and performances for six seasons at the O'Neill Playwrights Conference in Waterford, CT.*

COBURN, James 1928-

PERSONAL: Born August 31, 1928, in Laurel, NE; married; children: James IV, Lisa. EDUCATION: Los Angeles City College, B.A., drama. MILITARY: U.S. Army.

VOCATION: Actor and producer.

CAREER: PRINCIPAL FILM APPEARANCES—*Face of a Fugitive*, Columbia, 1959; *Ride Lonesome*, Columbia, 1959; *The Magnificent Seven*, United Artists, 1960; *Hell Is for Heroes*, Paramount, 1962; *The Great Escape*, United Artists, 1963; *Charade*, Universal, 1964; *The Americanization of Emily*, Metro-Goldwyn-Mayer, 1964; *The Loved One*, Metro-Goldwyn-Mayer, 1965; *A High Wind in Jamaica*, Twentieth Century-Fox, 1965; *Major Dundee*, Columbia, 1965; *Our Man Flint*, Twentieth Century-Fox, 1966; *What Did You Do In the War, Daddy?*, United Artists, 1966; *Dead Heat on a Merry-Go-Round*, Columbia, 1966; *In Like Flint*, Twentieth Century-Fox, 1967; *The President's Analyst*, Paramount, 1967; *Waterhole No. 3*, Paramount, 1967; *Candy*, Cinerama, 1968; *Hard Contract*, 1969.

Last of the Mobile Hot Shots, Warner Brothers, 1970; *The Carey Treatment*, Metro-Goldwyn-Mayer, 1972; *The Honkers*, United Artists, 1972; *Duck, You Sucker*, United Artists, 1972; *Harry in Your Pocket*, United Artists, 1973; *Pat Garrett and Billy the Kid*, Metro-Goldwyn-Mayer, 1973; *The Last of Sheila*, Warner Brothers, 1973; *A Reason to Live, a Reason to Die* (also know as *Massacre at Fort Hamilton*), 1974; *The Internecine Project*, British, 1974; *Bite the Bullet*, Columbia, 1975; *Hard Times*, Columbia, 1975; *Sky Riders*, Twentieth Century-Fox, 1976; *The Last Hard Men*, Twentieth Century-Fox, 1976; *Midway*, 1976; *Cross of Iron*, Avco Embassy, 1977; *The Muppet Movie*, Associated Film Distributors, 1979; *Fire Power*, Associated Film Distributors, 1979; *Golden Girl*, Avco Embassy, 1979; *Loving Couples*, Twentieth Century-Fox, 1980; *The Baltimore Bullet*, Avco Embassy, 1980; *High Risk*, 1981; *Looker*, Warner Brothers, 1981; *Martin's Day*, Metro-Goldwyn-Mayer/United Artists, 1985; *Death of a Soldier*, Scotti Brothers/Suatu Film, 1986.

PRINCIPAL FILM WORK—Producer: *The President's Analyst*, Paramount, 1967; *Waterhole No. 3*, Paramount, 1967.

PRINCIPAL TELEVISION APPEARANCES—Series: Jeff Durain, *Klondike*, NBC, 1960-61; Gregg Miles, *Acapulco*, NBC, 1961; host, *Darkroom*, ABC, 1981-82.

Episodic: *Studio One; G.E. Theatre; Robert Montgomery Presents; Bronco;* "Safari," *The Dick Powell Show; Games People Play*.

Movies: *Draw*, HBO, 1984; *Sins of the Fathers*, NBC, 1985.

Mini-Series: *The Dane Curse.*

PRINCIPAL STAGE APPEARANCES—*Billy Budd;* appeared in summer stock productions.

RELATED CAREER—Owner, Panpiper Productions, Hollywood.

MEMBER: Screen Actors Guild.

ADDRESSES: AGENT—International Creative Management, 8899 Beverly Blvd., Los Angeles, CA 90048.*

JAMES COCO

COCO, James 1929-

PERSONAL: Born March 21, 1929, in New York, NY; son of Feliche (a shoemaker) and Ida (Detestes) Coco. EDUCATION: Trained for the stage at the Herbert Berghof Studio with Uta Hagen.

VOCATION: Actor.

CAREER: STAGE DEBUT—*Old King Cole*, Clare Tree Majors Theater. NEW YORK DEBUT—Tabu, *Hotel Paradiso*, Henry Miller's Theatre, 1957. PRINCIPAL STAGE APPEARANCES—*Darwin's Theories*, Madison Avenue Playhouse, NY, 1960; Tausch, *The Moon in the Yellow River*, East End Theatre, NY, 1961; Doctor, *Everybody Loves Opal*, Longacre Theatre, NY, 1961; Mr. Hammidullah, *A Passage to India*, Ambassador Theatre, NY, 1962; O'Casey, *Arturo Ui*, Lunt-Fontanne Theatre, NY, 1963; Leslie Edwards, *The Sponge Room*, Stanley Mintey, *Squat Betty*, both East End Theatre, NY, 1964; The First, *That 5 AM Jazz*, Astor Place Theatre, NY, 1964; Roger Varnum, *Lovey*, Cherry Lane Theatre, NY, 1965; A Sewerman, *The Devils*, Broadway Theatre, NY, 1965; Barber, *Man of La Mancha*, Washington Square Theatre, NY, 1966; Inspector Rogers, *The Astrakhan Coat*, Helen Hayes Theatre, NY, 1967; Lee, *Here's Where I Belong*, Billy Rose Theatre, NY, 1968; Window Washer, *Witness*, Gramercy Arts Theatre, NY, 1968; Marion Cheever, *Next*, Greenwich Mews Theatre, NY, then Mark Taper Forum, Los Angeles, CA, 1969; Barney Cashman, *Last of the Red Hot Lovers*, Eugene O'Neill Theatre, NY, 1969; Benno Blimpie, *The Transfiguration of Benno Blimpie*, Astor Place Theatre, NY, 1977; *Little Me*, NY, 1982; *You Can't Take It with You*, NY, 1983.

FILM DEBUT—*Ensign Pulver*, Warner Brothers, 1964. PRINCIPAL FILM APPEARANCES—*Generation*, Avco Embassy, 1969; *End of the Road*, Allied Artists, 1970; *The Strawberry Statement*, Metro-Goldwyn-Mayer, 1970; *Tell Me That You Love Me, Junie Moon*, Paramount, 1970; *A New Leaf*, Paramount, 1971; *Such Good*

Friends, Paramount, 1971; *Man of La Mancha,* United Artists, 1972; *The Wild Party,* American International, 1975; *Murder by Death,* Columbia, 1976; *Charleston,* 1978; *Bye Bye Monkey; The Cheap Detective,* Columbia, 1978; *Scavenger Hunt,* Twentieth Century-Fox, 1979; Wholly *Moses,* Columbia, 1980; *Only When I Laugh,* Columbia, 1981; *The Muppets Take Manhattan,* Tri-Star, 1984.

PRINCIPAL TELEVISION APPEARANCES—Series: Joe Calucci, *Calucci's Department,* CBS, 1974; Joe Dumpling, *The Dumplings,* NBC, 1976.

Episodic: "Cora and Arnie," *St. Elsewhere,* NBC, 1983.

Guest: *Johnny Carson Show; Raquel Welch Special.*

Movies: *The French Atlantic Affair,* 1979; *Diary of Anne Frank,* 1980.

MEMBER: Actors' Equity Association, American Federation of Television and Radio Artists, Screen Actors Guild.

AWARDS: Obie Award, 1961, for *Moon in the Yellow River;* Obie Award, 1967, for *Fragments;* Obie Award, 1977, for *Benno Blimpie;* Academy Award nomination, People's Choice Award, Entertainer of the Year Award, Film Exhibitors Award, 1982, all for *Only When I Laugh;* Outstanding Supporting Actor, Emmy Award, 1983-84, for "Cora and Arnie," *St. Elsewhere.*

WRITINGS: BOOKS—*The James Coco Diet Book,* 1984.

ADDRESSES: AGENT—c/o Paul H. Wolfowitz, 59 E. 54th Street, New York, NY 10022.

*   *   *

PETER COE

COE, Peter   1929-

PERSONAL: Born April 18, 1929, in London, England; son of Leonard and Gladys (Firth) Coe; married Maria Caday (divorced); married Tsai Chin (divorced); married Suzanne Fuller (an actress; divorced); married Ingeborg. EDUCATION: Attended Latymer Upper School, College of St. Mark and St. John; studied for the theatre at the London Academy of Music and Dramatic Art.

VOCATION: Director and playwright.

CAREER: PRINCIPAL STAGE WORK—Director: (London, unless otherwise noted) *Lock Up Your Daughters,* 1959; *The World of Susie Wong,* 1959; *Treasure Island,* 1959; *Twelfth Night,* in India, 1959; *Oliver!,* 1960; *The Miracle Worker,* 1961; *Julius Caesar,* in Israel, 1961; *Oliver!,* in Australia, 1961; *Castle in Sweden,* 1962; *Macbeth,* in Canada, 1962; *Oliver!,* New York City, 1962; *Pickwick,* 1963; *The Rehearsal,* New York City, 1963; *Next Time I'll Sing to You,* New York City, 1963; *Caligula,* 1964; *In White America,* 1964; *Golden Boy,* New York City, 1964; *Pickwick,* New York City, 1965; *Oliver!,* Israel, 1965; *The King's Mare,* 1966; *In the Matter of J. Robert Oppenheimer,* 1966; *On a Clear Day You Can See Forever,* New York City, 1966; *The Silence of Lee Harvey Oswald,* Hampstead, England, 1966; *World War 2 1/2,* 1967; *The Four Musketeers,* 1967; *An Italian Straw Hat,* Chichester, England, 1967; *The Skin of Our Teeth,* Chichester, 1968; *The Causacian Chalk Circle,* Chichester, 1969; *A Doll's House,* 1970; *Peer Gynt,* Chichester, 1970; *The Hero,* Edinburgh, Scotland, 1970; *Kiss Me Kate,* Sadlers Wells, London, England, 1970.

Six, New York City, 1971; *Fish Out of Water,* 1971; *The Marquis,* 1971; *Woman of the Dunes,* New York City, 1971; *The Black Macbeth,* 1972; *Tom Brown's Schooldays,* 1972; *Hamlet,* 1972; *Games,* 1973; *Storytheatre,* India, 1973; *Decameron '73,* 1973; *Treasure Island,* Chichester, 1973; *Tonight We Improvise,* Chichester, 1974; *Candida,* Vienna, Austria, 1974; *The Trials of Oscar Wilde,* Oxford, England, 1974; *Poets to the People,* Mermaid Theatre, London, 1974; *Kingdom of the Earth,* Vienna, 1975; *Romeo and Jeannette,* Guildford, England, 1975; *The Exorcism,* 1975; *Cages, Storytheatre, The Great Exhibition, The Trial of Marie Stopes,* all for Bubble Theatre, London, 1975; *Lucy Crown,* 1976; *Ride! Ride!,* 1976; *Richard III,* Denmark, 1976; *Macbeth,* Arts Council tour, 1976; *Tonight We Improvise,* India, 1977; *Jericho,* Young Vic, London, 1976; *Romeo and Juliet,* Arts Council tour, 1977; *The Corn Is Green,* tour, 1978; *Harold and Maude,* Canada, 1978; *Richard III,* Canada, 1978; *Flowers for Algernon,* Canada, 1978; *Cause Celebre,* Canada, 1979; *Flowers for Algernon,* Queen's Theatre, London, 1979; *Hamlet,* Canada, 1979; *Mister Lincoln,* Morosco Theatre, New York City, 1979.

On the Twentieth Century, London, 1980; *Hey Marilyn, A Life, Groucho at Large,* and *Ballerina,* all in Canada, 1980; *Barnum,* London, 1981; *Feasting with Panthers,* Chichester, 1981; *Henry V* and *Othello,* both at American Shakespeare Festival, Stratford, CT, 1981; *Othello,* Winter Garden Theatre, New York City, 1982; *Henry IV* and *Hamlet,* both at Stratford, CT, 1982; *Oliver!,* tour, 1983; *Tartuffe* and *Murder, Dear Watson,* both Churchill Theatre, Bromley, 1983; *The Sleeping Prince,* Chichester, 1983; *Oliver,* London, 1983; *Hello, Dolly!,* London, 1983; *Ballerina,* New York City, 1984; *Oliver,* New York City, 1984; *The Fly and the Fox,*

Churchill Theatre, 1984; *The Doctor's Dilemma,* tour, 1984; *Great Expectations,* Old Vic, London, 1984; *Barnum,* London, 1984; *The Waiting Room,* Churchill Theatre, 1985; *A View from the Bridge,* tour, 1985; *Season's Greetings,* tour, 1985; *The Miser,* Churchill Theatre, 1986; *Jane Eyre,* Chichester Festival, 1986.

PRINCIPAL OPERA WORK—Director: *The Love of Three Oranges,* Saddler's Wells Opera Company, London, England, 1963; *The Angel of Fire,* Saddler's Wells, London, 1965; *Ernani,* Saddler's Wells, London, 1967; *The Love of Three Oranges,* Coliseum Theatre, London, 1969.

PRINCIPAL FILM WORK—Director: *Lock Up Your Daughters,* Columbia, 1969.

WRITINGS: PLAYS, PRODUCED—*Woman of the Dunes,* New York City, 1971; *Storytheatre,* India, 1973; (co-adaptor) *Treasure Island,* Chichester, 1973; (devised) *The Trials of Oscar Wilde,* Oxford, 1974; *Cages, The Great Exhibition,* and *The Trial of Marie Stopes,* all at the Bubble Theatre, London, 1975; *Lucy Crown,* 1976.

SIDELIGHTS: Peter Coe began his career in 1957, as artistic director of the Arts Theatre in Ipswich, England. He went on, the following year, to become the artistic director for the Queen's Theatre, Hornchurch, and was the first resident director of London's Mermaid Theatre which opened in 1959, with his production of *Lock Up Your Daughters.* In 1975, he became the artistic director of the Bubble Theatre in London and in 1978, he was appointed artistic director of the Citadel Theatre in Edmonton, Alberta, Canada. Subsequently, he held similar positions with the American Shakespeare Theatre in Stratford, Connecticut (1981-82), and the Churchill Theatre, Bromley, England (since 1983).

ADDRESSES. HOME—The Old Barn, East Clandon, Surrey, England.

*   *   *

COLEMAN, Cy   1929-

PERSONAL: Born June 14, 1929, in New York, NY. EDUCATION: High School of Music and Art; New York College of Music; studied music with Rudolph Gruen and Adele Marcus.

VOCATION: Composer and pianist.

CAREER: STAGE DEBUT—Piano recital, Steinway Hall, NY, 1935. PRINCIPAL STAGE APPEARANCES—Piano recitals, Town Hall, NY; others.

PRINCIPAL TELEVISION APPEARANCES—With the Cy Coleman Trio, *Starlit Time,* Dumont, 1950; as orchestra conductor, *ABC's Nightlife,* ABC, 1965.

WRITINGS: SCORES, THEATRICAL—Songs, *John Murray Anderson's Almanac,* NY, 1954; background score, *Compulsion,* NY, 1957; (with Carolyn Leigh) *Wildcat,* Alvin Theatre, NY, 1960; (with Carolyn Leigh) *Little Me,* Lunt-Fontanne Theatre, NY, 1962; (with Dorothy Fields) *Sweet Charity,* Palace Theatre, NY, 1966; *Seesaw,* Uris Theatre (now Gershwin), NY, 1973; (with Michael Stewart) *I Love My Wife,* Ethel Barrymore Theatre, NY, 1977; (with Betty Comden and Adolph Green) *On the Twentieth Century,* St. James Theatre, NY, 1978; (with Michael Stewart) *Barnum,* St. James Theatre, NY, 1980; *Little Me* (revised version), Neil Simon Theatre, NY, 1983.

SCORES, FILM—*Spartacus,* Universal, 1960; *The Troublemaker,* Janus, 1964; *Father Goose,* Universal, 1965; *The Art of Love,* 1965; *Sweet Charity,* Universal, 1969.

SCORES, TELEVISION—Specials for Shirley MacLaine, including *If They Could See Me Now;* others.

SONGS (NON-THEATRICAL), PUBLISHED, RECORDED, ETC.—"I Walk a Little Faster," "Firefly," "Witchcraft," "You Fascinate Me So," "Playboy Theme," others.

RECORDINGS: ALBUMS—*The Piano Artistry of Cy Coleman,* Seeco; *If My Friends Could See Me Now,* Columbia; *The Party's On,* RCA.

MEMBER: American Society of Composers and Publishers (since 1953), Dramatists Guild.

AWARDS: Antoinette Perry Award, 1980, for *Barnum;* Academy Award nomination, Best Score of a Motion Picture (original or adaptation), 1969, for *Sweet Charity;* (with Bob Wells and John Bradford) Outstanding Writing in a Comedy-Variety or Music Special, Emmy, 1974-75, for *Shirley MacLaine: If They Could See Me Now.*

SIDELIGHTS· As a pianist, Cy Coleman has led his own trio, performed as a soloist in nightclubs, hotels and on television, and concertized. He is the president of his own publishing firm, Notable Music Company, and has worked, within his company, to find and promote young talent. Among his chief collaborators (not named above) are Joseph Allen McCarthy, Bob Hilliard, and Peggy Lee.

ADDRESSES: AGENT—c/o ASCAP, One Lincoln Plaza, New York, NY 10023.

*   *   *

COLEMAN, Dabney   1932-

PERSONAL: Full name, Dabney W. Coleman; born January 3, 1932, in Austin, TX; son of Melvin Randolph and Mary (Johns) Coleman; married Ann Courtney Harrell, December 21, 1957 (divorced, 1959); married Carol Jean Hale, December 11, 1961 (divorced); children: Kelly Johns, Randolph, Mary. EDUCATION: Virginia Military Institute, 1949-51; University of Texas, 1951-57; studied for the theatre at the Neighborhood Playhouse School, 1958-60. MILITARY: U.S. Army, 1953-55. RELIGION: Episcopalian.

VOCATION: Actor.

CAREER: PRINCIPAL FILM APPEARANCES—Salesman, *This Property Is Condemned,* Paramount, 1966; *The Slender Thread,* Paramount, 1966; *The Scalp Hunters,* United Artists, 1968; *The Other Side of the Mountain,* Universal, 1975; *Rolling Thunder,* American International, 1977; *Viva Kneivel!,* Warner Brothers, 1977; *North Dallas Forty,* Paramount, 1979; *Nothing Personal* (Canadian), 1980; *How to Beat the High Cost of Living,* Filmways, 1980; *Melvin and Howard,* Universal, 1980; Franklyn Hart, *Nine to Five,* Twentieth Century-Fox, 1980; *Tootsie,* Columbia, 1982; *Wargames,* Metro-Goldwyn-Mayer/United Artists, 1983; *Cloak and Dagger,* Universal, 1984; *The Man with One Red Shoe,* Twentieth Century-Fox, 1985; also, *The Black Streetfighter.*

PRINCIPAL TELEVISION APPEARANCES—Series: Dr. Leon Bessemer, *That Girl,* ABC, 1966-67; Merle Jeeter, *Mary Hartman,*

Mary Hartman, syndicated, 1975-78; ''Fast Eddie'' Murtaugh, *Apple Pie,* ABC, 1978; Bill Bittinger, *Buffalo Bill,* NBC, 1983-84.

Episodic: *Forever Fernwood,* syndicated; *The Mary Tyler Moore Show,* CBS; others.

Movies: *When She Was Bad,* 1979.

WRITINGS: TELEVISION—Two scripts, *Bright Promise,* NBC, 1972.

AWARDS: Best Actor in a Comedy-Variety Series, Emmy Award nomination, 1983, for *Buffalo Bill.*

MEMBER: Phi Delta Theta.*

*   *   *

COLEMAN, Gary   1968-

PERSONAL: Born February 8, 1968, in Zion, IL.

VOCATION: Actor.

CAREER: PRINCIPAL TELEVISION APPEARANCES—Series: Arnold Jackson, *Diff'rent Strokes,* NBC, 1978-85, then ABC, 1985-86.

Episodic: *The Little Rascals; Good Times,* CBS; *The Jeffersons,* CBS; *Lucy Moves to NBC; The Big Show; America 2-Night; Tonight Show, Starring Johnny Carson.*

Movies: *The Kid from Left Field,* 1979; *Scout's Honor,* 1980; *Playing with Fire,* 1984.

GARY COLEMAN

PRINCIPAL FILM APPEARANCES—*On the Right Track,* 1981; *Jimmy the Kid,* 1983; title role, *The Fantastic World of D.C. Collins,* 1983.

ADDRESSES: AGENT—Victor Perillo Agency, 9229 Sunset Blvd., Suite 611, Los Angeles, CA 90069.

*   *   *

COLLINS, Stephen

PERSONAL: Born October 1, in Des Moines, IA; son of Cyrus S. (an airline executive) and Madeleine (Robertson) Collins; married Faye Grant (an actress), April 21, 1985. EDUCATION: Amherst College, B.A., cum laude, 1969.

VOCATION: Actor.

CAREER: STAGE DEBUT—Title role, *Baal,* Island Repertory Theatre, Edgartown, MA, 1968. NEW YORK DEBUT—Valentine, *Twelfth Night,* New York Shakespeare Festival, Delacorte Theatre, 1969. PRINCIPAL STAGE APPEARANCES—In Broadway productions: Dick in *Moonchildren,* Detective Michael Brick in *The Ritz,* in *Censored Scenes from Hong Kong,* as the title role in *The Loves of Anatol.*

Off-Broadway: Bruce, *Beyond Therapy,* Phoenix Theatre; Macduff, *Macbeth* and in *More Than You Deserve,* both New York Shakespeare Festival, Lincoln Center.

The Last Days of British Honduras and as Christian in *Cyrano de Bergerac,* both at Williamstown Theatre Festival; appeared in *The New York Idea,* as Andrei in *The Three Sisters,* and in *The Play's the Thing,* all at the Brooklyn Academy of Music.

MAJOR TOURS—*Forty Carats,* First National Company.

FILM DEBUT—Hugh Sloan, *All the President's Men,* Warner Brothers, 1976. PRINCIPAL FILM APPEARANCES—*Between the Lines,* Midwest Film Productions, 1977; *Fedora,* United Artists, 1978; *The Promise,* Universal, 1979; Decker, *Star Trek: The Motion Picture,* Paramount, 1979; *Loving Couples,* Twentieth Century-Fox, 1980; *Brewster's Millions,* Universal, 1985; *On Dangerous Ground,* Warner Brothers, 1986; *Jumpin' Jack Flash,* Twentieth Century-Fox, 1986.

TELEVISION DEBUT—*Dan August,* CBS, 1970. PRINCIPAL TELEVISION APPEARANCES—Series: Jake Cutter, *Tales of the Gold Monkey,* ABC, 1982-83.

Episodic: *The Waltons,* CBS; *Barnaby Jones,* CBS; *Good Heavens,* CBS; *Jigsaw John,* NBC; ''Visit from a Dead Man,'' *ABC Wide World of Mystery; The Hitchhiker,* HBO, 1984.

Movies: *Summer Soltice,* ABC; Teddy Roosevelt, *The Best of Families,* PBS; *Edith Wharton: Looking Back,* PBS; *Chiefs,* CBS; David Spaulding, *The Rhinemann Exchange,* NBC, 1977; *The Henderson Monster,* CBS, 1980; *Inside the Third Reich,* ABC, 1982; *Threesome,* CBS, 1984; *The Dark Mirror,* ABC, 1984.

Guest: *George Burns Comedy Week,* CBS.

MEMBER: Actors' Equity Association, Screen Actors Guild, American Federation of Television and Radio Artists; American

Association for Unified Field Based Rehabilitation; Institute for Social Rehabilitation (board of directors).

SIDELIGHTS: Stephen Collins informs *CTFT* that his favorite roles have been Hugh Sloan in *All the President's Men*, Michael Brick in *The Ritz*, and Macduff in *Macbeth*.

ADDRESSES: AGENT—c/o Johnnie Planco, William Morris Agency, 1350 Sixth Avenue, New York, NY 10019.

*   *   *

CONNELL, Jane   1925-

PERSONAL: Born Jane Sperry Bennett, October 27, 1925, in Oakland, CA; daughter of Louis Wesley and Mary (Sperry) Bennett; married William Gordon Connell (an actor and musician); children: Melissa, Margaret. EDUCATION. Anna Head School, Berkeley, CA; University of California at Berkeley.

VOCATION: Actress.

CAREER: DEBUT—Revue performer, *Straw Hat Revue*, Lafayette, CA, 1947 (through 1953). NEW YORK DEBUT—Revue performer, *Shoestring Revue* (replacing Beatrice Arthur), President Theatre, 1955. LONDON DEBUT—Princess Winnifred, *Once Upon a Mattress*, Adelphi Theatre, 1960. PRINCIPAL STAGE APPEARANCES—Revue performer, *New Faces of 1952*, Music Circus, Sacramento, CA, 1954; Mrs. Peachum, *The Threepenny Opera*, Theatre de Lys, NY, 1955; revue performer, *New Faces of 1956*, Ethel Barrymore Theatre, NY, 1956; revue performer at Tamiment Music Camp, 1957; cabaret revue performer, *Demi-Dozen*, Upstairs at the Downstairs, NY, 1957; Kate, *Girl Crazy*, Katisha, *The Mikado*, Aunt Eller, *Oklahoma!*, Maud, *Happy Hunting*, Lady Jane, *Rose Marie*, all in stock at Flint, MI, and Detroit, MI, music tents, 1958; Adelaide, *Guys and Dolls*, Mammy Yokum, *L'il Abner*, Agnes Gooch, *Auntie Mame*, Lalume, *Kismet*, Sue, *Bells Are Ringing*, all at the Music Circus, Sacramento, CA, 1959.

Mrs. Spencer, *The Oldest Trick*, Martinique Theatre, NY, 1961; Christina, *Fortuna*, Maidman Theatre, NY, 1962; Lovey Mars, *The Golden Apple*, York Theatre, NY, 1962; Mae Peterson, *Bye Bye Birdie*, Mrs. Spofford, *Gentlemen Prefer Blondes*, Sue, *Bells Are Ringing*, all at Music Circus, Sacramento, 1962; Mme. Dubonnet, *The Boy Friend*, Sheraton Plaza, San Francisco, CA, 1962; revue performer, *Put It in Writing*, Theatre de Lys, NY, 1963; Miss Ramphere, *The Peacock Season*, Playhouse on the Mall, Paramus, NJ, 1964; Queen Frederika, *Royal Flush*, Shubert Theatre, New Haven, CT, 1964; Matilda Van Guilder, *Drat! The Cat!*, Martin Beck Theatre, NY, 1965; Agnes Gooch, *Mame*, Winter Garden Theatre, NY, 1966; Gabrielle, *Dear World*, Mark Hellinger Theatre, NY, 1969.

Agnes Gooch, *Mame*, Huntington Hartford Theatre, Los Angeles, CA, 1970, and at the Dallas Summer Musical Theatre, 1970; Mrs. Hardcastle, *She Stoops to Conquer*, Roundabout Theatre, NY, 1971; Widow Merryweather and General Arden Clobber, *Drat!*, McAlpin Rooftop Theatre, NY, 1971; Mother, *After Magritte*, Mrs. Drudge, *The Real Inspector Hound*, double bill, Theatre Four, NY, 1972; Gamma, *Lysistrata*, Brooks Atkinson Theatre, NY, 1972; *Cyrano de Bergerac*, Ahmanson Theatre, Los Angeles, CA, 1973; Mrs. Malaprop, *The Rivals*, Roundabout Stage One, NY, 1975; Miss Prism, *The Importance of Being Earnest*, Mark Taper Forum, Los Angeles, CA, 1977; actress, *A History of the American Film*, Mark Taper Forum, Los Angeles, CA, 1977; *Peculiar Pastimes*,

JANE CONNELL

Beverly Hills Playhouse, Los Angeles, CA, 1977; Mrs. Rice, *The Rise and Rise of Daniel Rocket*, Playwrights Horizons, NY, 1982; Edith, *Dog Eat Dog*, Hartford Stage Company, Hartford, CT, 1983; Agnes Gooch, *Mame*, Gershwin Theatre, NY, 1983; Mama, *The Guardsman*, Paper Mill Playhouse, NJ, 1984; Alice, "Goodbye, Howard," and May Ford, "F.M.," as part of *Laughing Stock*, Manhattan Punchline, then Lion Theatre, NY, 1984; one woman show, *The Singular Dorothy Parker*, Actors Playhouse, NY, 1985; Duchess of Hareford, *Me and My Girl*, Dorothy Chandler Pavilion, Los Angeles, Marquis Theatre, NY, 1986.

MAJOR TOURS—Revue performer, *Straw Hat Revue*, toured New England, California and Honolulu, Hawaii, 1947-53; Agnes Gooch, *Mame*, West Coast tour, 1968; Miss Hannigan, *Annie*, National Company and West Coast tours, 1978-82; Betty, *The Foreigner*, 1985-86.

PRINCIPAL FILM APPEARANCES—*Ladybug, Ladybug*, United Artists, 1963; Agnes Gooch, *Mame*, Warner Brothers, 1974; *Rabbit Test*, 1978.

PRINCIPAL TELEVISION APPEARANCES—Series: Jane, *Stanley*, NBC, 1956-57; Bridget McKenna, *The Dumplings*, NBC, 1976.

Guest: *Kraft Music Hall; The Garry Moore Show; The Jack Paar Show*, others.

Episodic: *Bewitched; All in the Family; Maude; Mary Hartman, Mary Hartman; Tales from the Dark Side*.

PRINCIPAL RADIO APPEARANCES—For NBC Radio, San Francisco, 1946-53; Standard School broadcasts, 1955-60.

CABARET AND NIGHT CLUB APPEARANCES—Debut, with husband, Gordon Connell at the Ruban Bleu, NY, 1954, then One Fifth Avenue, NY, 1955; club act with husband at the Purple Onion, San Francisco, 1954; revue artist, Julius Monk shows (including *Demi-Dozen,* see above), Upstairs at the Downstairs, 1955-60; Hungry i, San Francisco, 1956; revue performer, Plaza 9, NY, 1963.

ADDRESSES: AGENT—Gage Group, 1650 Broadway, New York, NY 10019.

*   *   *

CONNERY, Sean   1930-

PERSONAL: Born August 25, 1930, in Edinburgh, Scotland; son of Joseph and Euphamia C. Connery; married Diane Cilento, 1962 (divorced); married Micheline Roquebrune, 1979; children: (first marriage) one son; (second marriage) one stepdaughter. MILITARY: British Royal Navy.

VOCATION: Actor.

CAREER: STAGE DEBUT—*South Pacific,* 1953.

PRINCIPAL STAGE WORK—Director, *I've Seen You Cut Lemons,* London.

FILM DEBUT—*No Road Back,* 1957. PRINCIPAL FILM APPEARANCES—*Action of the Tiger,* Metro-Goldwyn-Mayer, 1957; *Another Time, Another Place,* Paramount, 1958; *Hell Drivers,* Rank Film Distributors of America, 1958; *Tarzan's Greatest Adventure,* Paramount, 1959; *Darby O'Gill and the Little People,* Buena Vista, 1959; *The Longest Day,* Twentieth Century-Fox, 1962; *The Frightened City,* Allied Artists, 1962; James Bond, *Doctor No,* United Artists, 1963; James Bond, *From Russia with Love,* United Artists, 1964; James Bond, *Goldfinger,* United Artists, 1964; *Woman of Straw,* United Artists, 1964; *Marnie,* Universal, 1964; James Bond, *Thunderball,* United Artists, 1965; *The Hill,* Metro-Goldwyn-Mayer, 1965; *Operation Snafu* (also known as *On the Fiddle*), American International, 1965; *A Fine Madness,* Warner Brothers, 1966; James Bond, *You Only Live Twice,* United Artists, 1967; *Shalako,* Cinerama, 1968.

The Molly Maguires, Paramount, 1970; *The Red Tent,* Paramount, 1971; *The Anderson Tapes,* Columbia, 1971; James Bond, *Diamonds Are Forever,* United Artists, 1971; *The Offence,* United Aritsts, 1973; *Zardoz,* Twentieth Century-Fox, 1974; *Ransom,* 1974; *Murder on the Orient Express,* Paramount, 1974; *The Wind and the Lion,* Metro-Goldwyn-Mayer, 1975; *The Man Who Would Be King,* Allied Artists/Columbia, 1975; Robin Hood, *Robin and Marian,* Columbia, 1976; *The Next Man,* Allied Artists, 1976; *A Bridge Too Far,* United Artists, 1977; *The Great Train Robbery,* United Artists, 1979; *Meteor,* American International, 1979; *Cuba,* United Artists, 1979; *Outland,* Warner Brothers, 1981; *Time Bandits,* Embassy, 1981; *Wrong Is Right,* Columbia, 1982; *Sword of the Valiant,* 1982; *Five Days One Summer,* Warner Brothers, 1982; James Bond, *Never Say Never Again,* Warner Brothers, 1983; *The Highlander,* Twentieth Century-Fox, 1986.

PRINCIPAL FILM WORK—Producer and director, *The Bowler and the Bonnet* (documentary); producer, *Something Like the Truth.*

PRINCIPAL TELEVISION APPEARANCES—Movies: *Requiem for a Heavyweight; Anna Christie; Boy with the Meataxe; Women in Love; The Crucible; Riders to the Sea; Colombe; Adventure Story; Anna Karenina; Macbeth* (Canadian).

Guest: host, *Sammy and Company.*

RELATED CAREER: Director, Tantallon Films Ltd., 1972—.

ADDRESSES: AGENT—Creative Artists Agency, 1888 Century Park E., Suite 1400, Los Angeles, CA 90067.*

*   *   *

CONRAD, Robert   1935-

PERSONAL: Born Conrad Robert Falk, March 1, 1935, in Chicago, IL; children: Christian, Shane. EDUCATION: Attended public schools in Chicago; attended Northwestern University.

VOCATION: Actor.

CAREER: STAGE DEBUT—Cabaret performance, Chicago, IL.

PRINCIPAL TELEVISION APPEARANCES—Series: Tom Lopaka, *Hawaiian Eye,* ABC, 1959-63; James T. West, *The Wild, Wild West,* CBS, 1965-70; Deputy District Attorney Paul Ryan, *The D.A.,* NBC, 1971-72; Jake Webster, *Assignment Vienna,* ABC, 1972-73; Major Gregory "Pappy" Boyington, *Baa Baa Black Sheep,* NBC, 1976-78; Oscar "Duke" Ramsey, *The Duke,* NBC, 1979; Thomas Remington Sloane, III, *A Man Called Sloane,* NBC, 1979-80.

Episodic: *Lawman,* ABC; *Maverick,* ABC; *77 Sunset Strip,* ABC.

Mini-Series: Pasquinel, *Centennial,* NBC, 1980.

Specials: *Battle of the Network Stars,* ABC.

Movies: *Wild, Wild West Revisited,* 1979; *More Wild, Wild West,* 1980; *Breaking Up is Hard to Do,* 1980; title role, *Will: G. Gordon Liddy,* 1982; *Confessions of a Married Man,* 1983; *Hard Knox,* 1984; *Two Fathers' Justice,* NBC, 1985; *Sullivan,* 1985; *Assassin,* CBS, 1986; title role, *Charley Hannah,* ABC, 1986.

FILM DEBUT—*Thundering Jets,* Twentieth Century-Fox, 1958. PRINCIPAL FILM APPEARANCES—*Palm Springs Weekend,* Warner Brothers, 1963; *Young Dillinger,* Allied Artists, 1965; *Murph the Surf,* American International, 1975; *Sudden Death,* 1975; *Wrong Is Right,* Columbia, 1982; *The Woman in Red,* Orion, 1984; *Moving Violations,* Twentieth Century-Fox, 1985; *Uncommon Courage,* 1985.

RELATED CAREER: President, Robert Conrad Productions, 1966—.

ADDRESSES: AGENT—David Shapira, 15301 Ventura Blvd., Sherman Oaks, CA 91403.*

*   *   *

CONTI, Tom   1941-

PERSONAL: Born November 22, 1941; son of Alfonso and Mary (McGoldrick) Conti; married Kara Wilson, 1967; children: one daughter. EDUCATION: Attended the Royal Scottish Academy, Glasgow, Scotland.

VOCATION: Actor and director.

CAREER: STAGE DEBUT—*The Roving Boy,* Citizen's Theatre, Glasgow, Scotland, 1959. LONDON DEBUT—Carlos, *Savages,* Comedy Theatre, 1973. NEW YORK DEBUT—Ken Harrison, *Whose*

TOM CONTI

Life Is It Anyway?, Trafalgar Theatre, 1979. PRINCIPAL STAGE APPEARANCES—Harry Vine, *The Black and White Minstrels*, Edinburgh Festival, 1972; Ben, *Let's Murder Vivaldi*, King's Head Theatre, Islington, 1972; Harry Vine, *The Black and White Minstrels*, Enrico Zamati, *Other People*, both Hampstead Theatre, London, 1974; title role, *Don Juan*, Hampstead Theatre, London, 1976; Dick Dudgeon, *The Devil's Disciple*, Royal Shakespeare Company, at the Aldwych Theatre, London, 1976; Ken Harrison, *Whose Life Is It Anyway?*, Mermaid Theatre, London, 1978, then the Savoy Theatre, London, 1978; *They're Playing Our Song*, London, 1980; *Romantic Comedy*, London, 1982.

PRINCIPAL FILM APPEARANCES—*Galileo*, AFT, 1975; *Full Circle*, British, Canadian, 1976; *The Duellists*, Paramount, 1978; *Blade on the Feather*, 1981; *Merry Christmas Mr. Lawrence*, 1982; *Reuben, Reuben*, Twentieth Century Fox, 1983; *American Dreamer*, 1983; *Saving Grace*, 1984; also, *Flame*.

PRINCIPAL TELEVISION APPEARANCES—*Mother of Men*, 1959; *The Glittering Prizes; Madame Bovary; Treats; The Norman Conquests*.

PRINCIPAL STAGE WORK—Director: *Last Licks*, Longacre Theatre, NY, 1979; *Before the Party*, Oxford Playhouse, Queen's Theatre, London, 1980.

AWARDS: Best Actor, Academy Award nomination, 1983, for *Reuben, Reuben;* Variety Club of Great Britian, 1978, for *Whose Life Is It Anyway?;* Best Actor, Antoinette Perry Award, 1979, for *Whose Life Is It Anyway?;* West End Theatre Managers Award; Royal Television Society Award.

SIDELIGHTS: CTFT notes that Tom Conti enjoys playing flamenco guitar.

ADDRESSES: AGENT—Chatto and Linnit, Prince of Wales Theatre, Coventry Street, London W1V 7FE, England.

* * *

CONVERSE, Frank   1938-

PERSONAL: Born May 22, 1938, in St. Louis, MO. EDUCATION: Attended Carnegie Mellon University; studied acting in New York.

VOCATION: Actor.

CAREER: BROADWAY DEBUT—*First One Asleep, Whistle*, 1966. PRINCIPAL STAGE APPEARANCES—*The Philadelphia Story*, Circle in the Square, NY, 1980; *House of Blue Leaves*, Off-Broadway production, 1982; *Brothers*, Music Box Theatre, NY, 1983; Otto, *Design for Living*, Circle in the Square, NY, 1984-85; two seasons with the American Shakespeare Festival, Stratford, CT; *The Seagull; Death of a Salesman; The Night of the Iguana; A Man for All for All Seasons; Arturo Ui*.

PRINCIPAL FILM APPEARANCES—*Hurry Sundown*, Paramount, 1967; *Hour of the Gun*, United Artists, 1967.

PRINCIPAL TELEVISION APPEARANCES—Series: Michael Alden, *Coronet Blue*, CBS, 1967; Detective Johnny Corso, *N.Y.P.D.*, ABC, 1967-69; Will Chandler, *Movin' On*, NBC, 1974-76.

Episodic: *The Mod Squad*, ABC; *Medical Center*, CBS; *The Bold Ones*, NBC; *The Guest House*.

Movies: *Dr. Cook's Garden*, 1970, *The Tattered Web*, 1971; *The Rowdyman; Shadow of a Gunman; The Widowing of Mrs. Holyrod*.

ADDRESSES: OFFICE—P.O. Box 3101, Belden Island, Stony Creek, CT 06405.*

* * *

CONWAY, Tim   1933-

PERSONAL: Born December 15, 1933, in Willoughby, OH; married Mary Anne, 1961; children: Kelly Ann, Timothy, Patrick, Jaime, Corey, Seann. EDUCATION: Attended Bowling Green State University. MILITARY: U.S. Army, two years.

VOCATION: Actor, comedian, and writer.

CAREER: PRINCIPAL TELEVISION APPEARANCES—Series: Regular, *The Steve Allen Show*, CBS, 1961; Ensign Charles Parker, *McHale's Navy*, ABC, 1962-66; regular, *The John Gary Show*, CBS, 1966; title role, *Rango*, ABC, 1967; host, *Turn-On*, ABC, 1969; Spud Barrett, *The Tim Conway Show*, CBS, 1970; regular, *The Carol Burnett Show*, CBS, 1975-78, ABC, 1978-79; star, *The Tim Conway Comedy Hour*, CBS, 1980-81; title role, *Ace Crawford, Private Eye*, CBS, 1983.

Guest: *Operation: Entertainment*, ABC, 1968; *Hollywood Palace*, ABC; *The Garry Moore Show*, CBS; *That's Life*, ABC; *The Dean Martin Show*, NBC; *The Red Skelton Show*, CBS; *The Danny Kaye Show*, CBS; *Cher*, CBS; *The Doris Day Show*, CBS.

PRINCIPAL FILM APPEARANCES—*McHale's Navy,* Universal, 1964; *McHale's Navy Joins the Air Force,* Universal, 1965; *The World's Greatest Athlete,* Buena Vista, 1973; *The Apple Dumpling Gang,* Buena Vista, 1975; *Gus,* Buena Vista, 1976; *The Shaggy D.A.,* Buena Vista, 1976; *They Went That-a-Way and That-a-Way,* 1978; *Billion Dollar Hobo,* 1978; *Cannonball Run II,* Warner Brothers, 1984; *The Longshot,* Orion, 1984.

RELATED CAREER—Night club performer.

WRITINGS: SCREENPLAYS—*Billion Dollar Hobo,* 1978; *They Went That-a-Way and That-a-Way,* 1978.

TELEVISION—Writer and director, KWY-TV, Cleveland, OH; episodes and skits, *The Carol Burnett Show,* CBS.

AWARDS: Emmy Awards: Outstanding Achievement by a Supporting Performer in a Music or Variety Show, 1972-73, for *The Carol Burnett Show;* Outstanding Continuing Performance by a Supporting Actor in a Variety or Music Show, 1976-77 and 1977-78, for *The Carol Burnett Show;* Outstanding Writing in a Comedy-Variety or Music Series, 1977-78, for *The Carol Burnett Show.*

SIDELIGHTS: CTFT learned that Tim Conway auditioned for Steve Allen while working for KWY-TV in Cleveland and became a regular on the *Steve Allen Show.*

ADDRESSES: OFFICE—425 S. Beverly Drive, Beverly Hills, CA 90212.*

*   *   *

COOK, Barbara   1927-

PERSONAL: Born October 25, 1927, in Atlanta, GA; daughter of Charles Bunyan and Nell (Harwell) Cook; married David LeGrant (divorced).

VOCATION: Actress and singer.

CAREER: NEW YORK DEBUT—Sandy, *Flahooley,* Broadhurst Theatre, 1951. PRINCIPAL STAGE APPEARANCES—Ado Annie, *Oklahoma!,* New York City Center, NY, 1953; Hilda Miller, *Plain and Fancy,* Mark Hellinger Theatre, NY, 1955; Cunegonde, *Candide,* Martin Beck Theatre, NY, 1956; Julie Jordan, *Carousel,* New York City Center, NY, 1957; Marian Paroo, *The Music Man,* Majestic Theatre, NY, 1957; Anna Leonowens, *The King and I,* New York City Center, NY, 1960; Liesl Brandel, *The Gay Life,* Shubert Theatre, NY, 1961; Amalia Balish, *She Loves Me,* Eugene O'Neill Theatre, NY, 1963; Carol Deems, *Something More!,* Eugene O'Neill Theatre, NY, 1964; Ellen Gordon, *Any Wednesday* (replaced Sandy Dennis), Music Box Theatre, NY, 1965; Magnolia, *Show Boat,* American Musical Theatre, New York State Theatre, Lincoln Center, NY, 1966; Patsy Newquist, *Little Murders,* Broadhurst, NY, 1967; Dolly Talbo, *The Grass Harp,* Martin Beck Theatre, NY, 1972; Kleopatra, *Enemies,* Vivian Beaumont Theatre, Lincoln Center, NY, 1973; *"Follies" in Concert,* Avery Fischer Hall, Lincoln Center, NY, 1985.

MAJOR TOURS—Ado Annie, *Oklahoma!,* 1954; Molly Brown, *The Unsinkable Molly Brown,* national tour, 1964; Fanny Brice, *Funny Girl,* summer tour, 1967; *The Gershwin Years,* 1973.

CABARET—Brothers and Sisters, NY, July, 1974; Carnegie Hall, NY, January 27, 1975; Maisonette, St. Regis Hotel, NY, March 1975; Michael's Pub; many others.

PRINCIPAL TELEVISION APPEARANCES—Episodic: *Alfred Hitchcock Presents; The U.S. Steel Hour; The Perry Como Show; The Ed Sullivan Show,* others.

Specials: Gretel, *Hansel and Gretel,* NBC, 1958; Evelina, *Bloomer Girl; The Yeoman of the Guard; It's Better with a Band,* others.

RECORDINGS: ALBUMS—*Flahooley,* original cast recording; *Plain and Fancy,* original cast recording, Capitol; *Candide,* original cast recording, Columbia; *The Music Man,* original cast recording, Capitol; *The Gay Life,* original cast recording, Capitol; *She Loves Me,* original cast recording, Metro-Goldwyn-Mayer; *Show Boat,* original cast recording, RCA; *The Grass Harp,* original cast recording, Painted Smiles; *Hansel and Gretel,* original television cast recording, Metro-Goldwyn-Mayer; *Show Boat* (1962 recording), Columbia; *"Follies" in Concert,* original cast recording; *Barbara Cook: Today,* Columbia; *Ben Bagley's George Gershwin Revisited,* Painted Smiles; *Ben Bagley's Jerome Kern Revisited,* Painted Smiles; *It's Better with a Band;* others.

AWARDS: Antoinette Perry Award, 1960, for *The Music Man.**

*   *   *

COOK, James   1937-

PERSONAL: Born March 7, 1937, in New York, NY; son of Merill L. (worked for New York Telephone) and Winifred A. (worked for New York Telephone; maiden name, Kane) Cook. EDUCATION: Attended Fairfield University (pre-medical) for one year. MILITARY: U.S. Army Security Agency, 1956-59. RELIGION: Catholic.

VOCATION: Actor.

JAMES COOK

CAREER: NEW YORK DEBUT—The Mute, *The Fantasticks*, Sullivan Street Playhouse, 1962. PRINCIPAL STAGE APPEARANCES—Tom, *That Championship Season*, Cincinnati Playhouse in the Park, 1976; Dr. Loubser, *The Biko Inquest*, Off-Broadway production, 1979; Nana, *Peter Pan*, St. James Theatre, NY, 1981.

MAJOR TOURS—The Mute, *The Fantasticks*, midwest tour, 1966; Nana, *Peter Pan*, national tour, 1982.

PRINCIPAL STAGE WORK—Director, *The Fantasticks*, in three stock productions.

FILM DEBUT—Vack, *Bananas*, United Artists, 1971. PRINCIPAL FILM APPEARANCES—*Blade*, Joseph Green Pictures, 1973.

TELEVISION DEBUT—A district attorney, *The Andros Targets*, CBS, 1977.

Movie: Dr. Flowers, *The Man Who Wouldn't Die*, ABC.

SIDELIGHTS: RECREATIONS—Golf, sailing, photography, sculpture, and making ships in bottles.

ADDRESSES: HOME—New York, NY. AGENT—Manning, Selvage, and Lee, Inc., 99 Park Avenue, New York, NY 10016.

*   *   *

COOK, Linda

PERSONAL: Born June 8; married Patrick Mann (a designer), May 8, 1976. EDUCATION: Studied acting with Michael Howard in New York.

LINDA COOK

VOCATION: Actress.

CAREER: STAGE DEBUT—Louise, *Carousel*, Atlanta, GA. NEW YORK DEBUT—Honor, *The Wager*, Eastside Playhouse, 1974. PRINCIPAL STAGE APPEARANCES—Minnie Powell, *Shadow of a Gunman*, Classic Theatre; Charlene, *The Workingman* and *Merry-Go-Round*, both 78th Street Theatre Lab; Mo, *Saigon Rose*, A.P.C., NY; Joy, *Be My Father*, St. Clements Theatre, NY; Nina, *Splendour Harmonies*, Ensemble Studio Theatre, NY; Roxy, *Ghosts of the Loyal Oaks*, W.P.A. Theatre, NY; Carrie, *Lunch Hour*, Mississippi Repertory Theatre; Candy Starr, *One Flew Over the Cuckoo's Nest*, Coconut Grove Playhouse, Coconut Grove, FL; Dora, *Night Must Fall*, Royal Poinciana Playhouse, FL; multiple roles, *Under Milkwood* and Lissa, *Arthur*, both Theatre Atlanta; Nancy, *Angel Street*, New Orleans Repertory Company.

Phoebe and Audrey, *As You Like It*, New Orleans Repertory Company; Alexandra, *The Little Foxes*, Mickey, *Marathon '33*, and Luciana, *Comedy of Errors*, all Alliance Theatre, Atlanta, GA; Ghost of Christmas Past and Mrs. Dilber, *A Christmas Carol* and Elizabeth Smart, *By Grand Central, I Sat Down and Wept*, both Loretto Hilton Repertory Company, St. Louis, MO; Claire, *First Stage, Last Looks*, Center Stage, Baltimore, MD; Sabine, *The Flying Doctor*, Virginia Stage Company, Norfolk, VA; Magdelon, *The Ridiculous Young Ladies* and Shelly, *Buried Child*, both Virginia Stage Company; *Romantic Arrangements*, Equity Library Theatre, NY, 1984; Karen, *Home Front*, Royale Theatre, NY, 1985.

MAJOR TOURS—Meg, *Crimes of the Heart*, national.

PRINCIPAL TELEVISION APPEARANCES—Episodic: Mrs. Hyams, *Nurse*, CBS; Laurie Dallas, *The Edge of Night*, NBC; Lacy Hunter, *As the World Turns*, CBS.

Special: Singer, *Give Me Liberty*, NBC.

MEMBER: Actors' Equity Association, American Federation of Television and Radio Artists, Screen Actors Guild.

ADDRESSES: AGENT—Smith-Freedman Associates, 850 Seventh Avenue, New York, NY 10019.

*   *   *

COOK, T.S.   1947-

PERSONAL: Full name Thomas S. Cook; born August 25, 1947, in Cleveland, OH; son of Horace William and Betty Marion (Thompson) Cook; married Marie Monique de Varennes; children: Katherine, Christopher. EDUCATION: Dennison University, B.A., 1969; University of Iowa, M.F.A., 1973.

VOCATION: Writer and producer.

CAREER: PRINCIPAL TELEVISION WORK—Supervision producer, *Airwolf*, Universal, 1984-85.

RELATED CAREER—Lecturer, University of Nevada, Las Vegas, continuing education program, 1984—.

WRITINGS: TELEVISION—Movies: *Out of Darkness*, CBS, 1978; *Attack on Fear*, CBS; *Scared Straight—Another Story*, CBS, 1980; *Red Flag—The Ultimate Game*, CBS, 1981; *We're Fighting Back*, CBS, 1981.

Series: (Episodes) *Baretta; The Paper Chase; Project UFO; Airwolf.*

SCREENPLAY—*The China Syndrome,* Columbia, 1979.

AWARDS: Best Screenplay, American Movie Award, Writers Guild Award, Christopher, Academy Award nomination and British Academy Award nomination, all 1979, for *The China Syndrome;* Golden Globe nomination, 1980; Scott Newman Drug Abuse Prevention Award, 1981; Writers Guild Award, 1983.

ADDRESSES: AGENT—c/o Michael Werner, Morton Agency, 1105 Glendon, Los Angeles, CA 90024.

*   *   *

COOPER, T.G.   1939-

PERSONAL: Full name, Theodore G. Cooper; born August 14, 1939; son of Theodore Gladstone Cooper and Ruth Theresa (Brown) Cooper Greene; married Maudine Rice, May 13, 1960 (divorced, 1971); married Valerie Mills, December 22, 1982; children: (first marriage) Maria Teresa, Irene Ruth. EDUCATION: Howard University, B.F.A.; University of Miami, M.A., directing and theatre management; certificate in stocks and insurance, financial program, Denver, Colorado; completed course requirements toward doctorate in multidisciplinary studies, Laurence University.

VOCATION: Producer, director, educator, writer, and actor.

CAREER: PRINCIPAL STAGE WORK—Director and producer: *The Trial of Mary Dugan; Lysistrata, 2002; God's Trombones; Purlie Victorious; Medea; The River Niger; Carmen Jones; My Fair Lady;*

T.G. COOPER

The Great White Hope; Amen Corner; You're a Good Man Charlie Brown.

PRINCIPAL STAGE APPEARANCES—Jason, *Medea;* Edwards, *Fear;* Scrooge, *A Christmas Carol;* Holley, *Of Being Hit;* Cliff Dawson, *In the Wine Time;* Lee Mack, *A Town Called Tobyville;* Creon, *Antigone;* Jesse McOdd, *Portrait of a Woman;* Morose, *Crucificado.*

RELATED CAREER—Chairman, producer, and artistic director, Howard University drama department, 1972-78; professor of drama, Howard University, 1972—; consulting artists for the state of Virginia, Project REINFORCE; workshops in Southampton County Schools, 1977; workshops on religious drama, Shiloh Baptist Church; evaluator, IBM Film, *America on Stage;* workshops on theatre management, Madison College, VA; evaluator of black films for media center, Federal City College; moderator for the Frank Silvera's Playwriting Workshop, NY, 1974-76; workshops, theatre management, Virginia State College; national consultant to the Center for the Study of Southern Culture, University of Mississippi; developed New Wave Communications, Washington, DC; grants and research for the Martin Luther King Boulevard Development Corporation, Miami, FL; stockbroker and district manager, Financial Programs of Denver, CO; founder and director, Soul Book International, Washington, DC; community organizer for the Office for Equal Opportunity, Washington, DC, 1961-70.

WRITINGS: PLAYS, PRODUCED—*Strawman,* Howard University, 1970; *A Town Called Tobyville,* University of Miami, 1972; *Portrait of a Woman,* Playboy Plaza, Miami Beach, 1972, then Howard University, 1973; *Goodnight Mary Beck,* Howard University, 1976; *Find Yourself a Dream,* Howard University, 1977; *Chickenbone Special,* Howard University, 1983.

PLAYS, UNPRODUCED—"Queen's Chillum," "Chocolate Boy," "Have You Seen Mommy Lately," "Obeah."

BOOKS—Novels: *Obeah: God of Voodoo,* Nuclassics and Science Publishing Company, 1978. Textbook: *Onstage in America,* Drama Jazz House, 1984.

ARTICLES—In such periodicals as: *New Directions; On Stage Magazine; Priority Magazine; Urban Journalism Workshop.*

MEMBER: American College Theatre Festival, region II (chairman, playwriting committee); associate, Danforth Foundation, 1980-86; advisory board, Center for Ethnic Music, Howard University.

AWARDS: Certificate for distinguished service, University without Walls, Howard University; plaque in recognition and appreciation, the Armour J. Blackburn University Center, Howard University; certificate of appreciation for contribution to programs and objectives, Smithsonian Institution; certificate of appreciation in recognition of cooperative interest and support from University of the District of Columbia College of Liberal and Fine Arts, 1982; certificate of recognition, Annapolis Best, City of Annapolis, MD; certificate of excellence in community service, Walter Reed Army Medical Center; certificate, National Zeta Phi Eta Award Prize, for excellence in children's theatre.

My hobbies are reading plays and viewing movies. I have traveled all over the United States and Nassau."

SIDELIGHTS: T.G. Cooper informs *CTFT* that "my major motivation was my godfather's brother, who is Sidney Poitier. My favorite roles are Creon in *Antigone,* and Scrooge in *A Christmas Carol.* The most important thing in my career is motivating young people in the art of theatre and helping them to develop into strong individuals. My hobbies are reading plays and viewing movies. I have traveled all over the United States and Nassau.''

ADDRESSES: OFFICE—Department of Drama, College of Fine Arts, Howard University, Washington, DC, 20001.

*   *   *

COSBY, Bill   1937-

PERSONAL: Born July 12, 1937, in Philadelphia, PA; son of William (in the U.S. Navy) and Anna Cosby; married Camille Hanks, January 25, 1964; children: Erika Ranee, Erinn Chalene, Ensa Camille, Evin Harrah, Ennis William. EDUCATION: Attended Temple University; M.A. 1972, Ed.D., 1977, University of Massachusetts. MILITARY: U.S. Navy Medical Corps.

VOCATION: Comedian, actor, producer, writer.

CAREER: STAGE DEBUT—Comedian, at ''The Underground,'' in a room called ''The Cellar,'' Philadelphia, PA. PRINCIPAL STAGE APPEARANCES—Comedian, ''The Gaslight,'' New York; *An Evening with Bill Cosby,* Radio City Music Hall, NY, 1986; also headliner at major clubs and hotels.

TELEVISION DEBUT—Alexander Scott, *I Spy,* NBC, 1965-68. PRINCIPAL TELEVISON APPEARANCES—Series: Chet Kincaid, *The Bill Cosby Show,* NBC, 1969-71; regular, *COS,* ABC, 1976; star, *The New Bill Cosby Show,* CBS, 1972-73; Dr. Heathcliff ''Cliff'' Huxtable, *The Cosby Show,* NBC, 1984—.

Children's Shows: *Children's Theatre,* NBC; *The Electric Company,* PBS; host, ''Picture Pages,'' *Captain Kangaroo's Wake Up,* CBS; *The Fat Albert Show; Fat Albert and the Cosby Kids.*

Specials: *The First Bill Cosby Special; The Second Bill Cosby Special.*

Guest: *People,* CBS, 1978; *The Tonight Show,* NBC.

FILM DEBUT—*Man and Boy,* Levitt-Pickman, 1972. PRINCIPAL FILM APPEARANCES—*Hickey and Boggs,* United Artists, 1972; *Uptown Saturday Night,* Warner Brothers, 1974; *Let's Do It Again,* Warner Brothers, 1975; *Mother, Jugs and Speed,* 1976; *Aesop's Fables* (animated feature); *A Piece of the Action,* Warner Brothers, 1977; *California Suite,* Columbia, 1978; *The Devil and Max Devlin,* Buena Vista, 1981; *Bill Cosby Himself,* HBO Pictures, 1985.

PRINCIPAL RADIO APPEARANCES—*The Bill Cosby Radio Program.*

RELATED CAREER—Spokesman for Jell-O Pudding (General Foods Incorporated), Coca Cola, Ford Motor Company, Texas Instruments Corporation.

WRITINGS: BOOKS—*The Wit and Wisdom of Fat Albert,* 1973; *Bill Cosby's Personal Guide to Power Tennis.*

RECORDINGS: COMEDY ALBUMS—*Bill Cosby Is a Very Funny Fellow . . . Right?; I Started Out as a Child; Why Is There Air?; Wonderfulness; Revenge; To Russell, My Brother, Whom I Slept With; 200 MPH; It's True, It's True; 8:15, 12:15; Bill Cosby Himself.*

MUSIC ALBUMS—*Silverthroat; Hooray for the Salvation Army Band.*

BILL COSBY

VIDEO—Children's pre-school cassette on home video by Disney.

AWARDS: Emmy Awards: Outstanding Continued Performance by an Actor in a Leading Role in a Dramatic Series, 1965-66, 1966-67, and 1967-68, *I Spy;* Grammy awards, Best Comedy Albums, 1964, 1965, 1966, 1967, 1969; seven Recording Industry Association of America Gold Records; Outstanding Children's Program, International Film and Television Festival, Gold Award, 1981; honorary degree, Brown University; People's Choice Award, 1986.

MEMBER: Temple University (trustee).

SIDELIGHTS: In publicity materials submitted to *CTFT* for this volume, we note that *The Cosby Show,* NBC, has achieved the highest Nielsen ratings ''week after week,'' making it the number one show on television for 1985-86. *Life* magazine comments on his show, ''Cosby's success may have changed the game as well as the scores. Before his show hit the air, many viewers had rejected prime-time television as an electronic guignol of crime, slime, glitz and glands . . . What Cosby offered instead was a gentle, whimsical, warm-hearted sitcom about family life that found humor in the little things that happen in every home.'' On the evolution of his own style of comedy, ''Cosby states that he was drawn at an early age to the master of jazz: Charlie Parker, Louis Armstrong, Charlie Mingus and Miles Davis. Through their musical example, Cosby learned to emulate in comedy their ability to take an idea and continually find new and innovative ways of expressing the same theme.''

ADDRESSES: OFFICE—The Brokaw Company, 9255 Sunset Blvd., Los Angeles, CA 90069.

COSTABILE, Richard   1947-

PERSONAL: Born July 16, 1947, in Bronx, NY; son of Joseph (a machinist) and Anna Maria (an executive medical secretary; maiden name, Mogerauer) Costabile; married Carol J. Kerner, June 28, 1975 (divorced, 1982). EDUCATION: Fordham University, B.A., mathematics; studied for the theatre at the Neighborhood Playhouse with Sanford Meisner and Bill Esper.

VOCATION: Actor and stage manager.

CAREER: STAGE DEBUT—Det. Sgt. Trotter, *The Mousetrap,* Fort Salem Summer Theatre, Salem, NY, July, 1975. NEW YORK DEBUT—Menelaus, *Troilus and Cressida,* Changing Space, September, 1978, for twelve performances. PRINCIPAL STAGE APPEARANCES—Joseph Hewes, *1776,* Carter-Barron Amphitheatre, Washington, DC, 1980; Claude, *The Workroom,* South Street Theatre, NY, 1982.

PRINCIPAL STAGE WORK—Assistant stage manager, *The Workroom,* South Street Theatre, NY, 1982; production stage manager, *Marathon '83,* Ensemble Studio Theatre, NY, 1983; production stage manager, *To Gillian on Her 37th Birthday,* Ensemble Studio Theatre and Circle in the Square Downtown, NY, 1983-84; production stage manager, *The Grand Hysteric, The Box,* and *A Fool's Errand,* Theatre Workshop New Directors Project at Perry Street Theatre, NY, 1984; production stage manager, *She Also Dances* and *Miss Julie,* Theatre of the Open Eye, NY, 1985; stage manager, *Tomorrow's Monday,* Circle Repertory, 1985; production stage manager, *Self-Torture and Strenuous Exercise* and *Out at Sea,* Drama League at Circle Repertory, NY, 1985.

MAJOR TOURS—Stage manager: *Plaza Suite, The Odd Couple,* and *Lovers and Other Strangers,* around the world cruise, S.S. Rotterdam, January-April, 1981.

FILM DEBUT—Ptl. Ferguson, *Prince of the City,* Warner Brothers, 1981. PRINCIPAL FILM APPEARANCES—Tim Shaw, *Without a Trace,* Twentieth Century-Fox, 1982; Jerry Williams, *Trading Places,* Paramount, 1983.

TELEVISION DEBUT—Doctor, *All My Children,* ABC, 1979. PRINCIPAL TELEVISION APPEARANCES—Wayne Eggles, *Nurse,* CBS, 1982.

PRINCIPAL TELEVISION WORK—Floor manager and stage manager, *Independent Study,* Big Run, Ltd., 1985.

ADDRESSES: HOME—33-09 31st Avenue, Astoria, NY 11106.

* * *

CRAWFORD, Michael   1942-

PERSONAL: Born January 19, 1942, in Salisbury, England. EDUCATION: St. Michael's College, Bexley; Oakfield School, Dulwich.

VOCATION: Actor.

CAREER: LONDON DEBUT—Buddy, *Come Blow Your Horn,* Prince of Wale's Theatre, 1962. NEW YORK DEBUT—Tom, *White Lies* and Brindsley Miller, *Black Comedy,* a double bill, Ethel Barrymore Theatre, 1967. PRINCIPAL STAGE APPEARANCES—Arnold Champion, *Travelling Light,* Prince of Wales Theatre, 1965; Tom, *The Anniversary,* Duke of York's Theatre, London, 1966;

Brian Runnicles, *No Sex Please, We're British,* Strand Theatre, London, 1971; Bill Fisher, *Billy,* Drury Lane Theatre, London, 1974; George, *Same Time Next Year,* Prince of Wales Theatre, London, 1976; Charlie Gordon, *Flowers for Algernon,* Queens Theatre, London, 1979; title role, *Barnum,* Palladium, London, 1981-83, Manchester Opera House, 1984-85, then at the Victoria Palace Theatre, London, 1984-86.

PRINCIPAL FILM APPEARANCES—*Soap Box Derby,* 1950; *Blow Your Own Trumpet,* 1954; *Two Living One Dead,* 1962; *The War Lover,* Columbia, 1962; *Two Left Feet,* 1963; *The Knack . . . And How to Get It,* United Artists, 1965; Hero, *A Funny Thing Happened on the Way to the Forum,* United Artists, 1966; *The Jokers,* United Artist, 1967; *How I Won the War,* United Artiss, 1967; Cornelius Hackel, *Hello, Dolly!,* Twentieth Century-Fox, 1969; *The Games,* Twentieth Century-Fox, 1970; *Hello-Goodbye,* Twentieth Century-Fox, 1970; *Alice's Adventures in Wonderland,* 1972; *Condorman,* Buena Vista, 1981.

PRINCIPAL TELEVISION APPEARANCES—Series: *Sir Francis Drake,* 1962; *Chalk and Cheese; Some Mothers Do 'ave 'em.*

Episodic: *Still Life; Destiny; Byron; Move After Checkmate; Three Barrelled Shotgun; Home Sweet Honeycomb; Private View.*

Plays: *Sorry; BBC Play for Today; Barnum,* 1986.

RECORDINGS: ALBUMS—*Billy,* original cast recording, Columbia, CBS; *A Funny Thing Happened on the Way to the Forum,* original soundtrack recording, United Artists; *Hello, Dolly!,* original soundtrack recording, Twentieth Century-Fox; *Flowers for Algernon,* original cast recording.

ADDRESSES: AGENT—Duncan Heath Associated, Ltd., Paramount House, 162/170 Wardour Street, London W1, England.

* * *

CRENNA, Richard   1927-

PERSONAL: Born November 30, 1927, in Los Angeles, CA. EDUCATION: Attended the University of Southern California.

VOCATION: Actor.

CAREER: PRINCIPAL TELEVISION APPEARANCES—Series: Walter Denton, *Our Miss Brooks,* CBS, 1952-55; Luke McCoy, *The Real McCoys,* ABC, 1957-62, CBS, 1962-63; James Slattery, *Slattery's People,* CBS, 1964-65; Richard C. Barrington, *All's Fair,* CBS, 1976-77; Dr. Sam Quinn, *It Takes Two,* ABC, 1982-83.

Mini-Series: Colonel Frank Skimmerhorn, *Centennial,* NBC, 1978-80.

Movies: *Double Indemnity,* 1973; *Passions,* CBS, 1984; *The Rape of Richard Beck,* ABC, 1985; *Doubletake,* CBS, 1985; *Switch,* CBS, 1986; *A Case of Deadly Force,* CBS, 1986.

PRINCIPAL FILM APPEARANCES—*Pride of St. Louis,* 1952; *It Grows on Trees,* 1952; *Red Skies Over Montana,* 1952; *John Goldfarb, Please Come Home,* Twentieth Century-Fox, 1965; *The Sand Pebbles,* Twentieth Century-Fox, 1966; *Made in Paris,* Metro-Goldwyn-Mayer, 1966; *Wait Until Dark,* Warner Brothers, 1967; *Star!,* Twentieth Century-Fox, 1968; *Marooned,* Columbia, 1969.

Red Sky at Morning, Universal, 1970; *The Deserter,* Paramount, 1971; *Doctors' Wives,* Columbia, 1971; *Catlow,* United Artists, 1971; *Dirty Money,* French, 1972; *A Man Called Noon,* National General, 1973; *Breakheart Pass,* 1976; *Death Ship,* Canadian, 1980; *Body Heat,* Warner Brothers, 1981; *First Blood,* Orion, 1982; *Table for Five,* Warner Brothers, 1983; *The Flamingo Kid,* Twentieth Century-Fox, 1984; *Rambo: First Blood Part II,* Tri-Star, 1985; *Summer Rental,* Paramount, 1985; also *Five Against Texas; Pendick Enterprises.*

PRINCIPAL RADIO PERFORMANCES—*Boy Scout Jambouree; A Date With Judy; The Great Gildersleeve; Johnny Dollar; Our Miss Brooks.*

MEMBER: Screen Actors Guild, Directors Guild of America.

ADDRESSES: AGENT—Henderson/Hogan, 247 S. Beverly Drive, Suite 306, Beverly Hills, CA 90212.*

*   *   *

CRISTOFER, Michael   1945-

PERSONAL: Born Michael Procaccino, January 28, 1945, in Trenton, NJ; son of Joseph Peter and Mary (Muccioli) Procaccino. EDUCATION: Attended Catholic University, 1962-65; attended American University, Beirut, 1968-69.

VOCATION: Actor and playwright.

CAREER: NEW YORK DEBUT—Trofimov, *The Cherry Orchard,* Vivian Beaumont Theatre, Lincoln Center, 1977. PRINCIPAL STAGE APPPEARANCES—Repertory actor with Arena Stage, Washington, DC, 1967-68, Theatre of the Living Arts, Philadelphia, 1968, and Beirut Repertory Co., 1968-69; *The Tooth of Crime,* Mark Taper Forum, Music Center, Los Angeles, CA, 1973; *Confessions of a Female Disorder,* Mark Taper Forum, Los Angeles, 1973; Carlos, *Savages,* Mark Taper Forum, Los Angeles, 1974; Colin, *Ashes,* Mark Taper Forum, Los Angeles, 1976; Charlie, *Conjuring an Event,* American Place Theatre, NY, 1978; also appearances at A Contemporary Theatre (ACT), Seattle, WA, Long Wharf, New Haven, CT, others.

PRINCIPAL FILM APPEARANCES—*An Enemy of the People,* 1978.

PRINCIPAL TELEVISION APPEARANCES—*The Last of Mrs. Lincoln,* PBS; *The Andros Targets.*

WRITINGS: PLAYS, PRODUCED—*Americommedia* (street theatre), 1972; *Plot Counter Plot,* 1972; *The Mandala,* Theatre of the Living Arts, Philadelphia, PA, 1975; *The Shadow Box,* Mark Taper Forum, Los Angeles, Long Wharf Theatre, New Haven, 1975; *Ice,* 1976; *The Shadow Box,* Morosco Theatre, NY, 1977; *Black Angel,* 1978, Circle Repertory Theatre, NY, 1982-83; *The Lady and the Clarinet,* Mark Taper Forum, Los Angeles, CA, 1980, Long Wharf Theatre, New Haven, CT, 1983, and Lucille Lortel Theatre, NY, 1983.

AWARDS: Los Angeles Drama Critics Award, 1973; Best Play, Antoinette Perry Award, Pulitzer Prize for Drama, both 1977, for *The Shadow Box;* 1977, *Theatre World* Award.

ADDRESSES: AGENT—c/o Michael Peretzian, William Morris Agency, 151 El Camino Drive, Beverly Hills, CA 90212.*

CRONIN, Jane   1936-

PERSONAL: Born April 4, 1936, in Boston, MA. EDUCATION: Attended Boston University School of Theatre; trained for the stage with David Pressman and Peter Kass.

VOCATION: Actress.

CAREER: STAGE DEBUT—Willie, *This Property Is Condemned,* Charles Playhouse, Boston, MA, 1957. NEW YORK DEBUT—Five roles, *Postmark Zero,* Brooks Atkinson Theatre, 1956. PRINCIPAL STAGE APPEARANCES—Nurse Ratched, *One Flew Over the Cuckoo's Nest,* Mercer Arts Theatre, NY, 1971; April, *The Hot L Baltimore,* Circle in the Square, NY, 1973; Lizavetta, *A Month in the Country,* Roundabout Theatre, NY, 1979.

Off-Broadway: Celia, *The Exhaustion of Our Son's Love;* Marie, *The Bald Soprano;* Belle, *Needs;* Mary Elizabeth, *The Elephant in the House;* Paula, *Catsplay;* Judith, *Hayfever;* Claudia, *The Trading Post;* Lil, *The Gathering;* Maggie, *Cracks.* Also appeared in *Absurd Person Singular,* at The Whole Theater.

Regional: Gertrude, *Hamlet,* Celia, *As You Like It,* Eleanor, *King John,* all at the Old Globe Theatre, San Diego, CA; Estelle, *No Exit,* Dolly, *The Grass Harp,* The Actress, *La Ronde,* Carol Cutrere, *Orpheus Descending,* all Charles Playhouse, Boston, MA; Eleanor, *Lion in Winter,* lead, *Plaza Suite,* Titania, *Midsummer Night's Dream,* Naughty Nancy, *Little Mary Sunshine,* Hannah, *Night of the Iguana,* all at the Barter Theatre, Abingdon, VA; Nora, *A Touch of the Poet,* Williamstown Theatre Festival, MA; Countess Rosine, *The Marriage of Figaro,* McCarter Theatre, Princeton, NJ; Rummy, *Major Barbara,* Florrie, *Porcelaintime,* Mrs. Coffman, *Come*

JANE CRONIN

Back Little Sheba, all at the Berkshire Theatre Festival, Stockbridge, MA; *The Workroom, The Guardsman,* both at the Long Wharf Theatre, New Haven, CT. Also appeared as Jenny, in *Everything in the Garden.*

MAJOR TOURS—*Desire Under the Elms,* 1964; *The Sign in Sidney Brustein's Window,* 1965.

TELEVISION DEBUT—*The Best of Families.* PRINCIPAL TELEVISION APPEARANCES—Episodic: *As the World Turns; The Edge of Night; One Life to Live; Search for Tomorrow;* "Needs," *Andros Targets,* CBS.

PRINCIPAL FILM APPEARANCES—*Private Sessions; Sigo's Choice.*

MEMBER: Actors' Equity Association, Screen Actors Guild, American Federation of Television and Radio Artists.

ADDRESSES: HOME—439 W. 21st Street, New York, NY 10011.

*   *   *

CROTHERS, Scatman   1910-

PERSONAL: Full name, Benjamin Sherman Crothers; born May 23, 1910, in Terre Haute, IN; married Helen Sullivan, 1937; children: Donna.

VOCATION: Actor and nightclub musician.

CAREER: FILM DEBUT—*Meet Me at the Fair,* 1949. PRINCIPAL FILM APPEARANCES—*Hello Dolly,* Twentieth Century-Fox, 1969; *The Great White Hope,* Twentieth Century-Fox, 1970; *Lady Sings the Blues,* Paramount, 1972; *The King of Marvin Gardens,* Columbia, 1972; *One Flew Over the Cuckoo's Nest,* United Artists, 1975; *The Fortune,* Columbia, 1975; *The Shootist,* Paramount, 1976; *Silver Streak,* Twentieth Century-Fox, 1977; *Scavenger Hunt,* Twentieth Century-Fox, 1979; *Bronco Billy,* Warner Brothers, 1980; *The Shining,* Warner Brothers, 1980; *Zapped,* Embassy, 1982; *The Rats* (also known as *Deadly Eyes*), 1982; "Kick the Can," *Twilight Zone, The Movie,* Warner Brothers, 1983; *Two of a Kind,* Twentieth Century-Fox, 1983; *The Journey of Natty Gann,* Buena Vista, 1985.

PRINCIPAL TELEVISION APPEARANCES—Series: Louie, *Chico and The Man,* NBC, 1974-78; Bernard Solomon, *One of the Boys,* NBC, 1982; Sam, *Casablanca,* NBC, 1983; Excell, *Morning Star, Evening Star,* CBS, 1986; also performed voiceovers for cartoons.

Mini-Series: Mingo, *Roots,* ABC, 1977-78.

ADDRESSES: AGENT—Don Schwartz & Associates, 8721 Sunset Blvd., Los Angeles, CA 90069.*

*   *   *

CRUISE, Tom

PERSONAL: Born in Syracuse, NY.

VOCATION: Actor.

CAREER: PRINCIPAL FILM APPEARANCES—*Endless Love,* Universal, 1981; David Shawn, *Taps,* Twentieth Century-Fox, 1981; *Losin' It,* Embassy, 1983; Stephen Randall, *The Outsiders,* Warner Brothers, 1983; Joel Goodsen, *Risky Business,* Warner Brothers, 1983; Stef Djordevic, *All the Right Moves,* Warner Brothers, 1983; Jack o' the Green, *Legend,* Universal, 1986; Maverick, *Top Gun,* Paramount, 1986; *The Color of Money,* Buena Vista (upcoming).

PRINCIPAL STAGE APPEARANCES—*Godspell.*

SIDELIGHTS: According to material supplied to *CTFT* by his agent, Tom Cruise participated in acting workshops set up by Francis Ford Coppola as a means of casting *The Outsiders.*

ADDRESSES: AGENT—c/o Andrea Jaffe, Inc., 9229 Sunset Blvd., Suite 401, Los Angeles, CA 90069.

*   *   *

CRYSTAL, Billy   1947-

PERSONAL: Born March 14, 1947, on Long Island, NY; son of Jack (a jazz concert promoter, part owner of Commodore recording label) and Helen Crystal; married Janice; children: Jennifer, Lindsay. EDUCATION: Attended Marshall University and Nassau Community College; graduated New York University.

VOCATION: Comedian and actor.

CAREER: PRINCIPAL TELEVISION APPEARANCES—Series: Jodie Dallas, *Soap,* ABC, 1977-81; host, *The Billy Crystal Comedy Hour,* NBC, 1982; regular, *Saturday Night Live,* NBC, 1984-85.

Guest: *That Was the Year That Was.*

Special: *Comic Relief,* benefit for the homeless, HBO, 1986.

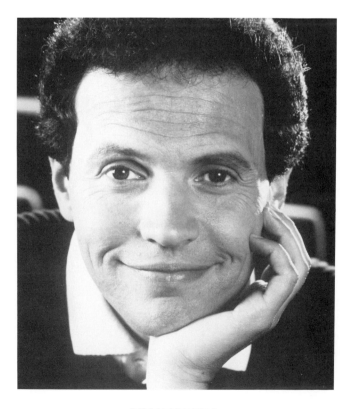

BILLY CRYSTAL

Movies: *Breaking Up Is Hard to Do,* 1979; *Enola Gay: The Men, The Mission, the Atomic Bomb,* NBC, 1980; also appeared in *Death Flight.*

PRINCIPAL FILM APPEARANCES—*Rabbit Test,* 1978; *Running Scared,* Metro-Goldwyn-Mayer, 1986.

ADDRESSES: OFFICE—Rollins, Joffe, Morra, and Brezner, 5555 Melrose Avenue, Los Angeles, CA 90038; Arnold Lipsman, 8961 Sunset Blvd., Suite 2E, Los Angeles, CA 90069.

*   *   *

CULP, Robert   1930-

PERSONAL: Born August 16, 1930, in Oakland, CA; married Nancy Wilner (divorced, 1967); married France Nuyen (divorced, 1969); children: (first marriage) four. EDUCATION: Attended College of the Pacific, Washington University, and San Francisco State College; studied at the Herbert Berghof Studios.

VOCATION: Actor and writer.

CAREER: PRINCIPAL FILM APPEARANCES—*PT 109,* Warner Brothers, 1963; *Sammy,* 1963; *The Raiders,* 1964; *Sunday in New York,* Metro-Goldwyn-Mayer, 1964; *Rhino,* Metro-Goldwyn-Mayer, 1964; *The Hanged Man,* 1969; *Bob & Carol & Ted & Alice,* Columbia, 1969; *The Grove,* 1972; *Hannie Caulder,* 1972; *Hickey and Boggs,* United Artists, 1972; *Sky Riders,* Twentieth Century-Fox, 1976; *The Great Scout and Cathouse Thursday,* American International, 1976; *Breaking Point,* 1976; *Inside Out,* Warner Brothers, 1976; *Turk 182!,* Twentieth Century-Fox, 1985.

PRINCIPAL TELEVISION APPEARANCES—Series: Hoby Gilman, *Trackdown,* CBS, 1957; Kelly Robinson, *I Spy,* NBC, 1965-68; Bill Maxwell, *The Greatest American Hero,* ABC, 1981-83.

Episodic: "Dead Man's Walk," *Chevy Mystery Show; Rawhide; Wagon Train; Bob Hope Presents the Chrysler Theatre; Rifleman; Cain's Hundred; The Dick Powell Show; Accused; American Profile; Kaiser Aluminum Hour; Star Tonight.*

Movies: *A Cold Night's Death,* 1973; *Outrage,* 1973; *Strange Homecoming,* 1974; *Houston, We've Got a Problem,* 1974; *Cry for Help,* 1975; *Flood!,* 1976; *Her Life as a Man,* 1984; also, *The Calendar Girl Murders; Brothers in Law.*

Mini-Series: *From Sea to Shining Sea,* 1974-75; *The Key to Rebecca,* Taft Entertainment, syndicated, 1985.

PRINCIPAL STAGE APPEARANCES—Off-Broadway: *The Prescott Proposals; He Who Gets Slapped; A Clearing in the Woods.*

WRITINGS: TELEVISION—*The Rifleman.*

AWARDS: Best Actor, Obie Award, for *He Who Gets Slapped.*

ADDRESSES: AGENT—William Morris Agency, 151 El Camino Drive, Beverly Hills, CA 90212.*

*   *   *

CUNNINGHAM, Sarah   1919-1986

PERSONAL: Born in Greenville, SC, 1919; died of an asthmatic attack while attending the Academy Award ceremonies at the Dorothy Chandler Pavilion in Los Angeles, CA, March 24, 1986; married John Randolph (an actor) 1946.

VOCATION: Actress.

CAREER: STAGE DEBUT—First appeared on stage in Greenville, SC. PRINCIPAL STAGE APPEARANCES—Broadway productions: *The Visit; Mme. Colombe; Toys in the Attic; The Respectful Prostitute; Fair Game; My Sweet Charlie.*

PRINCIPAL FILM APPEARANCES—*The Cowboys,* Warner Brothers, 1972; *Fun with Dick and Jane,* Columbia, 1977; *Frances,* Universal, 1982; *Jagged Edge,* Columbia, 1985.

PRINCIPAL TELEVISION APPEARANCES—Episodic: *The Rookies,* ABC; *Police Woman,* NBC; *Baretta,* ABC; *Starsky & Hutch,* ABC; *Trapper John M.D.,* CBS; *Dallas,* CBS.

RELATED CAREER—With her husband, John Randolph, founded the Ensemble Theater in New York which later moved to Los Angeles.*

*   *   *

CURTIN, Jane   1947-

PERSONAL: Full name, Jane Therese Curtin; born September 6, 1947 in Cambridge, MA; daughter of John Joseph and Mary Constance (Farrell) Curtin; married Patrick F. Lynch, April 31, 1975. EDUCATION: Elizabeth Seton Junior College, A.A., 1967; attended Northwestern University, 1967-68.

VOCATION: Actress and writer.

CAREER: PRINCIPAL TELEVISION APPEARANCES—Series: A Not Ready for Prime Time Player, *Saturday Night Live,* NBC, 1975-80; Allie Lowell, *Kate & Allie,* CBS, 1984—.

Episodic: *What Really Happened to the Class of '65,* NBC, 1978.

Movies: *Divorce Wars: A Love Story,* 1982.

PRINCIPAL STAGE APPEARANCES—*Pretzels,* Off-Broadway production, 1974-75; Prossy, *Candida,* Circle in the Square, NY, 1981.

MAJOR TOURS—*The Last of the Red Hot Lovers,* national.

PRINCIPAL FILM APPEARANCES—*Mr. Mike's Mondo Video,* 1979; *How to Beat the High Cost of Living,* Filmways, 1980.

RELATED CAREER: Company member, "The Proposition" comedy group, 1968-72.

WRITINGS: PLAY—Contributor, *Pretzels,* 1974.

AWARDS: Outstanding Lead Actress in a Comedy Series, Emmys, 1983-84 and 1984-85, both for *Kate & Allie.*

ADDRESSES: AGENT—Creative Artists Agency, 1888 Century Park E., Suite 1400, Los Angeles, CA 90067.*

CURTIS, Tony 1925-

PERSONAL: Born Bernard Schwartz, June 1, 1925, in New York, NY; son of Manuel Mond (an actor) and Helen (Klein) Schwartz; married Janet Leigh (an actress), June 4, 1951 (divorced, 1963); married Christine Kaufman (an actress), February 8, 1963 (divorced, 1967); married Leslie Allen, 1968; children: (first marriage) Kelly Lee, Jamie Leigh; (second marriage) Alexandra, Allegra; (third marriage) Nicholas, Benjamin. EDUCATION: Seward Park High School. MILITARY: U.S. Navy.

VOCATION: Actor.

CAREER: PRINCIPAL FILM APPEARANCES—*Criss Cross*, Universal, 1948; *City Across the River*, Universal, 1949; *The Lady Gambles*, Universal, 1949; *Johnny Stool Pigeon*, Universal, 1949; (as Anthony Curtis) Captain Jones, *Francis*, Universal, 1949; *I Was a Shoplifter*, Universal, 1950; *Winchester '73*, Universal, 1950; *The Prince Who Was a Thief*, Universal, 1951; *Flesh and Fury*, Universal, 1952; *No Room for the Groom*, Universal, 1952; *Son of Ali Baba*, Universal, 1952; title role, *Houdini*, Paramount, 1953; *The All American*, Universal, 1953; *Forbidden*, Universal, 1953; *Beachhead*, United Artists, 1954; *The Black Shield of Falworth*, Universal, 1954; *Johnny Dark*, Universal, 1954; *So This Is Paris*, Universal, 1954; *The Purple Mask*, Universal, 1954.

Six Bridges to Cross, Universal, 1955; *The Square Jungle*, Universal, 1955; Tino Orsini, *Trapeze*, United Artists, 1956; *The Rawhide Years*, Universal, 1956; *Mister Cory*, Universal, 1957; *The Midnight Story*, Universal, 1957; *Sweet Smell of Success*, United Artists, 1957; Eric, *The Vikings*, United Artists, 1958; *Kings Go Forth*, United Artists, 1958; John "Joker" Jackson, *The Defiant Ones*, United Artists, 1958; *The Perfect Furlough*, Universal, 1958; Joe (Josephine), *Some Like It Hot*, United Artists, 1959; Lieutenant Nick Holden, *Operation Petticoat*, Universal, 1959; unbilled guest appearance, *Pepe*, Columbia, 1960; *Who Was That Lady?*, Columbia, 1960; Pete Hammond, Jr., *The Rat Race*, Paramount, 1960; Antonius, *Spartacus*, Universal, 1960; DeMara, *The Great Imposter*, Universal, 1960.

The Outsider, Universal, 1961; *40 Pounds of Trouble*, Universal, 1962; *Taras Bulba*, United Artists, 1962; *The List of Adrian Messenger*, Universal, 1963; Corporal Jackson Laibowitz, *Captain Newman, M.D.*, Universal, 1963; *Paris When It Sizzles*, Paramount, 1964; *Wild and Wonderful*, Universal, 1964; *Goodbye, Charlie*, Twentieth Century-Fox, 1964; *Sex and the Single Girl*, Warner Brothers, 1964; The Great Leslie, *The Great Race*, Warner Brothers, 1964.

Boeing-Boeing, Paramount, 1965; *Not with My Wife, You Don't*, Warner Brothers, 1966; unbilled guest appearance, *Chamber of Horrors*, Warner Brothers, 1966; *Arrividerci, Baby*, Paramount, 1966; *Don't Make Waves*, Metro-Goldwyn-Mayer, 1967; *The Chastity Belt*, Warner Brothers/Seven Arts, 1967; *The Boston Strangler*, Twentieth Century-Fox, 1968; *On My Way to the Crusades I Met a Girl Who—*, Warner Brothers, 1969; *Those Daring Young Men in Their Jaunty Jalopies*, Paramount, 1969; *Suppose They Gave a War and Nobody Came*, ABC Films, 1969; *You Can't Win 'em All*, Columbia, 1970; title role, *Lepke*, Warner Brothers, 1974; *The Last Tycoon*, Paramount, 1976; *The Manitou*, Avco Embassy, 1978; *The Bad News Bears Go to Japan*, Paramount, 1978; *Sextette*, independent, 1978; *Little Miss Marker*, 1980; *The Mirror Crack'd*, Associated Film Distributors, 1980; *Insignificance*, Island Alive Films, 1985; also appeared in *Monte Carlo or Bust, The Dubious Patriots*.

PRINCIPAL TELEVISION WORK—Series: Danny Wilde, *The Persuaders*, ABC, 1971-72; title role, *McCoy*, NBC, 1975-76; Philip Roth, *Vega$*, ABC, 1978-81.

Movies: *The Users*, 1978; "The Scarlet O'Hara War," *Moviola*, 1980; *The Million Dollar Face*, 1981; *The Second Girl on the Right; Half Nelson*, NBC, 1985; *Mafia Princess*, ABC, 1986.

Episodic: "The Stone," *General Electric Theatre*, CBS; *Good Company*, ABC, 1967; others.

AWARDS: Best Actor, Academy Award nomination, 1958, for *The Defiant Ones*.

WRITINGS: NOVEL—*Kid Andrew Cody and Julie Sparrow*, 1977.

ADDRESSES: AGENT—c/o Jerry Zeitman, The Agency, 10351 Santa Monica Blvd., Suite 211, Los Angeles, CA 90025.*

D

DAILEY, Irene 1920-

PERSONAL: Born September 12, 1920, in New York, NY; daughter of Daniel James and Helen Theresa (Ryan) Dailey. EDUCATION: Mother Cabrini High School; studied for the theatre at the Actors Studio with Lee Strasberg; also studied with Uta Hagen and Herbert Berghof, 1951-61, Mira Rostova, Robert Lewis, and Jane White; studied dance with Anna Sokolow. RELIGION: Unitarian.

VOCATION: Actress, writer, and teacher.

CAREER: DEBUT—*Out of the Frying Pan,* Red Barn Theatre, Locust Valley, NY, 1941. NEW YORK DEBUT—*Girls.* LONDON DEBUT—Jasmine Adair, *Tomorrow—With Pictures,* Lyric Theatre, Hammersmith, then Duke of York's Theatre. PRINCIPAL STAGE APPEARANCES—*Room Service,* Red Barn Theatre, Locust Valley, NY, 1941; Shotput, *Nine Cards,* Longacre Theatre, 1943; Angie, *Truckline Cafe,* Belasco Theatre, NY, 1946; Shirley, *Idiot's Delight,* New York City Center, NY, 1951; Mrs. Shin, *The Good Woman of Setzuan,* Phoenix Theatre, NY, 1956; Adele Farnum, *Miss Lonely-Hearts,* Music Box Theatre, NY, 1957; Irene, *Idiot's Delight,* Equity Library Theatre, NY, 1957; Eloise, *Uncle Wiggly in Connecticut,* HB Studio, NY, 1959.

Valeria, *Daughter of Silence,* Erlanger Theatre, Philadelphia, PA, 1961; Abbie, *Desire Under the Elms,* McCarter Theatre, Princeton, NJ, 1961; Clara, *Winterkill,* Playhouse in the Park, Philadelphia, 1962; Senora, *Andorra,* Biltmore Theatre, NY, 1963; Hannah Jelkes, *The Night of the Iguana,* Playhouse in the Park, Philadelphia, 1963; Pamela Pew-Pickett, *Tchin-Tchin,* Playhouse in the Park, Philadelphia, 1963, also at Sombrero Playhouse, Phoenix, AZ, 1964; Nettie Cleary, *The Subject Was Roses,* Royale Theatre, NY, 1964; Miss Quincey, *Better Luck Next Time,* Mrs. Henry, *A Walk in Dark Places* (a double bill), Cherry Lane Theatre, NY, 1966; Beatrice, *The Effect of Gamma Rays on Man-in-the-Moon Marigolds,* White Barn Theatre, Westport, CT, 1966; *Rooms,* 1966-67; various roles, *You Know I Can't Hear You When the Water's Running* (replacing Eileen Heckart), Ambassador Theatre, NY, 1968.

Beatrice, *The Effect of Gamma Rays on Man-in-the-Moon Marigolds,* Ivanhoe Theatre, Chicago, IL, 1971; *Buying Out,* Studio Arena, Buffalo, NY, 1971; Banannas, *The House of Blue Leaves,* Ivanhoe Theatre, Chicago, 1972; Mme. Arkadina, *The Seagull,* McCarter Theatre, Princeton, NJ, 1973; Mary Tyrone, *Long Day's Journey into Night,* Loeb Theatre, Purdue, IN, 1973; *Lotsa Ladies,* WPA Theatre, NY, 1976; *Rio Grande,* Playwrights Horizons, NY, 1976; Cass, *The Loves of Cass Maguire,* Three Muses Theatre, Hotel Ansonia, NY, 1979; *On Bliss Street in Sunnyside,* Actors Studio, NY, 1981.

MAJOR TOURS—Caroline, *Laughing Water,* 1944; *Skylark,* 1952.

IRENE DAILEY

PRINCIPAL FILM APPEARANCES—*Daring Game,* Paramount, 1968; *No Way to Treat a Lady,* Paramount, 1968; *Five Easy Pieces,* Columbia, 1970; *The Grissom Gang,* National General, 1971; *The Amityville Horror,* American International, 1979; also, *The Last Two Weeks.*

PRINCIPAL TELEVISION APPEARANCES—*Robert Montgomery Presents,* 1951; also, *The Defenders; The Twilight Zone; Dr. Kildare; Another World,* others.

RELATED CAREER—Founder, artistic director, teacher, School of the Actors Company, NY, 1961-73.

WRITINGS: PLAYS—*Waiting for Mickey and Ava.*

RECORDINGS: ALBUM—*The Subject Was Roses,* Columbia.

MEMBER: Actor's Equity Association, Screen Actors Guild, American Federation of Television and Radio Artists, National Academy of Television Arts and Sciences, Ensemble Studio Theatre, American Educational Association..

AWARDS: London Magazine Critics Award, 1960, for *Tomorrow—With Pictures;* Sarah Siddons Award, Best Actress in Chicago, *The Effect of Gamma Rays on Man-in-the-Moon Marigolds,* 1971; Joseph Jefferson nomination, 1972, for *House of Blue Leaves;* Emmy Award, *Another World,* 1979.

SIDELIGHTS: As an escape from acting, Irene Dailey enjoys reading, charcoal sketching, watercolor painting, and various sports.

ADDRESSES: OFFICE—P.O. Box 385, Sheffield, MA 01257.

*   *   *

DALE, Jim   1935-

PERSONAL: Born Jim Smith, August 15, 1935, in Rothwell, Northantshire, England; son of William Henry and Miriam Jean (Wells) Smith; married Patricia Gardiner. EDUCATION: Attended Kettering and District Grade School; trained for the ballet for six years.

VOCATION: Actor.

CAREER: STAGE DEBUT—Comedian, Savoy Theatre, Kettering, England. PRINCIPAL STAGE APPEARANCES—William Dowton, *The Wayward Way,* Lyric Theatre, Hammersmith, England, 1954; Autolycus, *The Winter's Tale,* Edinburgh Festival, Scotland, then Cambridge, England, 1966; Burglar, *The Burglar,* Vaudeville Theatre, London, 1967; Bottom, *A Midsummer Night's Dream,* Edinburgh Festival, Scotland, then Saville Theatre, London, 1967. With the National Theatre Company, Old Vic, London: Barnet, *The National Health,* 1969, Nicholas, *The Travails of Sancho Panza,* 1969, Costard, *Love's Labour's Lost,* 1970, Launcelot Gobbo, *The Merchant of Venice,* 1970; at the Young Vic, London: Scapino, *The Cheats of Scapino,* 1970, Petruchio, *The Taming of the Shrew,* 1970.

Old Vic, London: The Architect, *The Architect and the Emperor of Assyria,* 1971, Mr. Lofty, *The Good-Natured Man,* 1971, and Kalle, *The Captain of Kopenick,* 1971. Denry Machin, *The Card,* Queen's Theatre, London, 1973; Petruchio, *The Taming of the Shrew,* Young Vic Company, Brooklyn Academy of Music, NY, 1974; title role, *Scapino,* Brooklyn Academy of Music, NY, Circle in the Square, NY, and Ambassador Theatre, NY, 1974; Gethin Price, *Comedians,* Mark Taper Forum, Los Angeles, CA, 1977; Terri Dennis, *Privates on Parade,* Long Wharf Theatre, New Haven, CT, 1979; title role, *Barnum,* St James Theatre, NY, 1979-81; *A Day in the Death of Joe Egg,* Promenade Theatre, NY, 1984, then Longacre Theatre, NY, 1985.

MAJOR TOURS—Petruchio, *The Taming of the Shrew,* European cities, 1972; title role, *The Music Man,* U.S. cities, 1984.

PRINCIPAL STAGE WORK—Director, *Scapino,* Brooklyn Academy of Music, NY, Circle in the Square, NY, and Ambassador Theatre, NY, 1974.

PRINCIPAL FILM APPEARANCES—*Raising the Wind,* 1961; *Carry on Spying,* Governor, 1965; *Carry on Cleo,* Governor, 1965; *Lock Up Your Daughters!,* 1969; *Digby—The Biggest Dog in the World,* 1974; *Joseph Andrews,* 1977; *Pete's Dragon,* Buena Vista, 1977; *The Unidentified Flying Oddball,* Buena Vista, 1979; *Scandalous,* Orion, 1984; also, *The Big Job; Carry on Cowboy; Carry on Screaming; The National Health.*

PRINCIPAL TELEVISION APPEARANCES—Movies: The Duke, *The Adventures of Huckleberry Finn,* PBS, 1985; *Circus,* CBS, 1986.

WRITINGS: MUSIC—"Georgy Girl;" score, *Scapino,* Brooklyn Academy of Music, NY, Circle in the Square, NY, and Ambassador Theatre, NY, 1974.

AWARDS: Best Original Song, Academy Award nomination, 1966, for *Georgy Girl;* Best Actor, Drama Desk Award, Outer Critics Circle Award, Antoinette Perry Award nomination, 1974, for *Scapino;* Best Actor in a Musical, Drama Desk Award, Antoinette Perry Award, 1979, for *Barnum.*

SIDELIGHTS: FAVORITE ROLES—Scapino and Petruchio.

ADDRESSES: AGENT—Harold Schiff, 555 Fifth Avenue, New York, NY 10017.

*   *   *

DANGERFIELD, Rodney   1922-

PERSONAL: Born Jack Roy, 1922, in Babylon, NY; married Joyce Indig (died).

VOCATION: Comedian, actor, and author.

CAREER: PRINCIPAL TELEVISION APPEARANCES—Series: *The Dean Martin Show,* NBC, 1972-73.

Guest: *The Ed Sullivan Show; On Broadway Tonight; The Tonight Show,* host, *Saturday Night Live.*

Specials: Three on ABC, 1982, 1984, and 1985; one on HBO, 1985.

PRINCIPAL FILM APPEARANCES—*The Projectionist,* Ted Maron Films, 1971; *Caddyshack,* Warner Brothers, 1980; *Easy Money,* Orion, 1983.

RELATED CAREER—Nightclub owner, Dangerfields, New York, NY.

WRITINGS: SCREENPLAYS—(with others) *Caddyshack,* Warner Brothers, 1980; (with others) *Back to School,* Orion, 1986.

BOOKS—*I Couldn't Stand My Wife's Cooking So I Opened a Restaurant,* 1972; *I Don't Get No Respect,* 1973.

RECORDINGS: COMEDY ALBUMS—*The Loser; I Don't Get No Respect; No Respect; Rappin' Rodney.*

MEMBER: Screen Actors Guild, American Federation of Television and Radio Artists, Writers Guild of America, National Academy of Recording Arts and Sciences, Broadcast Music, Inc., American Society of Composers, Authors and Publishers.

RODNEY DANGERFIELD

AWARDS: Best Comedy Album, Grammy Award.

ADDRESSES: OFFICE—Dangerfields, 1118 First Avenue, New York, NY 10021. AGENT—c/o Kathy Lymberopoulos, Endler Associates, 3920 Sunny Oak Road, Sherman Oaks, CA 91403.

*   *   *

DANIELEWSKI, Tad

PERSONAL: The "W" in the surname is pronounced as a "V"; born in Poland; children: Christopher, Mark, Anne. EDUCATION: Ohio University, B.F.A., 1950; State University of Iowa, graduate work, 1950-51; Johns Hopkins University, graduate work, 1953-56; studied for the theatre at the Royal Academy of Dramatic Art, London, 1946-48.

VOCATION: Director and writer.

CAREER: PRINCIPAL STAGE WORK—Director: Numerous regional theatre productions as well as New York, London, and Los Angeles productions of the works of a widely divergent group of playwrights from Shakespeare to Neil Simon.

PRINCIPAL FILM WORK—Director: Productions in Africa, Argentina, Japan, India, and Spain for English language as well as European markets, including: *The Big Wave*, Allied Artists, 1960; *No Exit; The Guide; Open Door; Africa; Copernicus;* others.

PRINCIPAL TELEVISION WORK—Director: Specials, as well as series work, for such programs as *Omnibus*, 1954; *Robert Montgomery Presents; Hamlet; Africa*, ABC; *Eddie Fisher Show; Matinee Theatre, Wide, Wide World;* CBS daytime dramas; NBC bicentennial shows; produced and directed a series of dramatic shows on WWAM in cooperation with NBC, 1953-54; others.

WRITINGS: SCREENPLAYS—*The Guide*, Stratton, 1965; (co-writer) *Imperial Woman; Spain; Copernicus* (English version).

MEMBER: Academy of Motion Picture Arts and Sciences, Directors Guild of America, Society of Stage Directors and Choreographers, National Academy of Television Arts and Sciences (governor); Dramatic Workshop (NBC, New York and Los Angeles; director).

AWARDS: Emmy Award, 1967, for *Africa* (documentary); others.

ADDRESSES: AGENT—Irv Schechter Agency, 9300 Wilshire Blvd., Beverly Hills, CA 90212.

*   *   *

DANIELS, Danny   1924-

PERSONAL: Born Daniel Giagni, Jr., October 25, 1924, in Albany, NY; son of Daniel (a salesman) and Mary (Bucci) Giagni; married Bernice Grant (a former dancer), November 29, 1947; children: Annamary, Daniel, Peter. EDUCATION: Attended Hollywood High School; studied dance with Thomas Sternfield, Edith Jane, Jack Potteiger, Vincenzo Celli, Mme. Anderson, and Vilzak. RELIGION: Catholic. MILITARY: U.S. Army Signal Corps.

VOCATION: Choreographer, dancer, and director.

CAREER: PRINCIPAL STAGE APPEARANCES—Dancer, Broadway shows: *Best Foot Forward*, 1941; *Count Me In*, 1942; *Billion Dollar Baby*, 1945; *Make Mine Manhattan*, 1948; *Kiss Me Kate*, 1950.

MAJOR TOURS—*Tap Dance Concerto*, Boston Symphony, Brandeis University; has danced with the Los Angeles Symphony, Hollywood Bowl; New York Philharmonic, Lewison Stadium; Little Orchestra Society, Town Hall, NY; Berlin Symphony, Germany; New York Philharmonic, Lincoln Center; soloist, *Agnes de Mille Dance Theatre*, national tour, 1953-54; *Danny Daniels Dance America Company*.

PRINCIPAL STAGE WORK—Choreographer, Broadway productions: *Boys Against the Girls; All American; High Spirits; Annie Get Your Gun; Walking Happy; I Remember Mama; The Tap Dance Kid*. Off-Broadway productions: *The Littlest Revue; Shoestring Revue, '57; Best Foot Forward*. In Los Angeles: *Love Match; 1491; Wonderful Town; On a Clear Day You Can See Forever*. Also, choreographed *High Spirits* in London and *Ciao, Rudy* in Rome.

PRINCIPAL FILM WORK—Choreographer: *The Night They Raided Minsky's*, United Artists, 1968; *Piaf*, 1974; *Pennies from Heaven*, United Artists, 1981; *Indiana Jones and the Temple of Doom*, Paramount, 1984; *Richard; Stilletto*. Directed *Best Foot Forward*.

PRINCIPAL TELEVISION WORK—Choreographer, Series: *The Martha Raye Show*, NBC, 1955-56; *The Ray Bolger Show*, ABC, 1953; *The Patrice Munsel Show*, ABC, 1957; *The Firestone Hour; The Revlon Revue*, CBS, 1960; *The Perry Como Show*, NBC; *The Judy Garland Show*, CBS.

Specials: *The Fabulous Fifties, 25 Years of Life*, 1960; *Bing Crosby Special; Danny Kaye Special; Milton Berle Special; Arthur Godfrey Special; Gene Kelly Specials; Mitzi Gaynor Special; Dick Van Dyke Special; John Denver Special;* "The Presidency," *CBS News*.

PRINCIPAL CABARET WORK—Choreographer for Arthur Godfrey, Leslie Uggams, George Gobel, Gene Kelly, Mitzi Gaynor. Also choreographed *The Milliken Breakfast Show,* for two years.

RELATED CAREER—Founder, director, teacher, Danny Daniels Dance America School, Santa Monica, CA, 1974-81.

MEMBER: Founding member, Society of Stage Directors and Choreographers (president, 1968-71).

AWARDS: Emmy Awards, 1960, for *The Fabulous Fifties* and 1976, for *The John Denver Special;* Antoinette Perry and Astaire Awards, both 1984, for *The Tap Dance Kid;* six Antoinette Perry Award nominations for work as dancer and choreographer.

SIDELIGHTS: Danny Daniels worked directly with composer Morton Gould on the creation of *Tap Dance Concerto,* which he premiered in Rochester, NY, 1952.

ADDRESSES: AGENT—c/o Clifford Stevens, STE Representation, 888 Seventh Avenue, New York, NY 10019.

*   *   *

DANIELS, William   1927-

PERSONAL: Born March 31, 1927, in Brooklyn, NY. EDUCATION: Attended Northwestern University.

VOCATION: Actor.

CAREER: PRINCIPAL FILM APPEARANCES—*A Thousand Clowns,* United Artists, 1965; *Two for the Road,* Twentieth Century-Fox, 1967; *Marlowe,* Metro-Goldwyn-Mayer, 1969; John Adams, *1776,* Columbia, 1972; *The Parallax View,* Paramount, 1974; *Black Sunday,* Paramount, 1977; *Oh God!,* Warner Brothers, 1977; *Sunburn,* Paramount, 1979; *The Blue Lagoon,* Columbia, 1980.

PRINCIPAL TELEVISION APPEARANCES—Series: Carter Nash/title role, *Captain Nice,* NBC, 1967; Lt. Commander Kenneth Kittredge, *The Nancy Walker Show,* ABC, 1976; District Attorney Walter W. Cruikshank, *Freebie and the Bean,* CBS, 1980-81; voice of KITT, *Knight Rider,* NBC, 1982—; Dr. Mark Craig, *St. Elsewhere,* NBC, 1982—.

Episodic: "Heaven on Earth," *Comedy Theatre,* NBC.

Movies: *A Case of Rape,* 1974; *Blind Ambition.*

Mini-Series: *The Adams Chronicles,* PBS.

STAGE DEBUT—*Life with Father.* PRINCIPAL STAGE APPEARANCES—*A Thousand Clowns; On a Clear Day You Can See Forever; 1776; Dear Me, The Sky Is Falling; A Little Night Music.*

MEMBER: Actors' Equity Association, Screen Actors Guild, American Federation of Television and Radio Artists.

ADDRESSES: AGENT—Jack Fields and Associates, 9255 Sunset Blvd., Suite 1105, Los Angeles, CA 90069.*

DARBY, Kim   1948-

PERSONAL: Born Derby Ferby, July 8, 1948, in Hollywood, CA. EDUCATION: Studied at the Desilu Workshop in Hollywood.

VOCATION: Actress.

CAREER: PRINCIPAL FILM APPEARANCES—*Bus Riley's Back in Town,* Universal, 1965; *True Grit,* Paramount, 1969; *Generation,* Avco Embassy, 1969; *Norwood,* Paramount, 1970; *The Strawberry Statement,* Metro-Goldwyn-Mayer, 1970; *The Grissom Gang,* National General, 1971; *The One and Only,* Paramount, 1978; also appeared in *Better Off Dead,* CBS Theatrical Films.

TELEVISION DEBUT—*Mr. Novak.* PRINCIPAL TELEVISION APPEARANCES—Episodic: *Eleventh Hour; Gunsmoke.*

Movies: *Don't Be Afraid of the Dark,* 1973; *Flesh and Blood,* 1979; *Embassy,* ABC, 1985; *First Steps,* CBS, 1985.

Mini-Series: Virginia Calder, *Rich Man, Poor Man, Book I,* ABC, 1976; Ann Rowan, *The Last Convertible,* NBC, 1979.

MEMBER: Screen Actors Guild, American Federation of Television and Radio Artists.*

*   *   *

DARREN, James   1936-

PERSONAL: Born June 8, 1936, in Philadelphia, PA. EDUCATION: Studied acting with the Stella Adler Group.

VOCATION: Actor.

CAREER: FILM DEBUT—*Rumble on the Docks,* Columbia, 1956. PRINCIPAL FILM APPEARANCES—*The Brothers Rico,* Columbia, 1957; *Guns of Navarone,* Columbia, 1961; *Gidget Goes Hawaiian,* Columbia, 1961; *The Lively Set,* Universal, 1964; *633 Squadron,* United Artists, 1964; *Venus in Furs,* American International, 1970.

PRINCIPAL TELEVISION APPEARANCES—Series: Dr. Tony Newman, *The Time Tunnel,* ABC, 1966-67; Officer Jim Corrigan, *T.J. Hooker,* CBS, 1983-85, ABC, 1985—.

Episodic: *The Web,* NBC, 1957.

Movie: Officer Jim Corrigan, *Blood Sport,* CBS, 1986.

MEMBER: Screen Actors Guild, American Federation of Television and Radio Artists.

ADDRESSES: OFFICE— P.O. Box 1088, Beverly Hills, CA 90213.*

*   *   *

DAVENPORT, Nigel   1928-

PERSONAL: Born May 23, 1928, in Shelford, Cambridge, England; son of Arthur Henry and Katherine Lucy (Meiklejohn) Davenport; married Helena Margaret White (died); married Maria Aitken (divorced). EDUCATION: St. Peter's, Seaford; Cheltenham College; Trinity College, Oxford.

NIGEL DAVENPORT

VOCATION: Actor.

CAREER: STAGE DEBUT—Bottom, *A Midsummer Night's Dream,* OUDS, Oxford. LONDON DEBUT—Hon. Peter Ingleton, *Relative Values* (had been understudy), Savoy Theatre, 1952. NEW YORK DEBUT—Peter, *A Taste of Honey,* Lyceum Theatre, 1960. PRINCIPAL STAGE APPEARANCES—Cardinal, *The Duchess of Malfi,* OUDS, Oxford; Horner, *The Country Wife,* Theatre Royal, Stratford, U.K., 1955.

With English Stage Company, Royal Court Theatre, London: Captain Walcott, *The Mulberry Bush,* Thomas Putnam, *The Crucible,* sculptor/Alfredo, *Don Juan,* Anthony Lissenden, *The Death of Satan,* Jellicoe, *Cards of Identity,* policeman, *The Good Woman of Setzuan,* Quack, *The Country Wife,* all for the 1956 season; Bro Paradock, *A Resounding Tinkle* (trial production), 1957; Barney Evans, *Epitaph for George Dillon,* Bro Paradock, *A Resounding Tinkle,* Mr. Jackson, *Live Like Pigs,* all for the 1958 season; Peter, *A Taste of Honey,* Theatre Royal, Stratford, then at the Criterion Theatre, London, 1959; Mr. Marango, *The Kitchen* (trial production), 1959; King of Frankland, *One Leg Over the Wrong Wall* (trial production), 1960.

Peter, *A Taste of Honey* (pre-Broadway), Biltmore Theatre, Los Angeles, 1960; Pittakos, *Sappho,* Edinburgh Festival, Edinburgh, Scotland, 1961; Odilon, *Bonne Soupe,* Comedy Theatre, London, 1961, then Wyndham's Theatre, London, 1962; Charles, *The Perils of Scobie Prilt,* New Theatre, Oxford, 1963; *A Taste of Honey,* Broadway production, 1963; Monceau, *Incident at Vichy,* Phoenix Theatre, London, 1966; C. J. Shine, *Breakdown,* Gate Theatre, Dublin, Ireland, 1966; Jim North, *Notes on a Love Affair,* Globe Theatre, London, 1972; Verskinin, *The Three Sisters,* Cambridge Theatre, 1976.

PRINCIPAL FILM APPEARANCES—*Peeping Tom,* 1959; *In the Cool of the Day,* Metro-Goldwyn-Mayer, 1963; Frederick Thornton, *A High Wind in Jamaica,* Twentieth Century-Fox, 1965; *Sands of Kalahari,* Paramount, 1965; Parkington, *Where the Spies Are,* Metro-Goldwyn-Mayer, 1966; *A Man for All Seasons,* Columbia, 1966; *Sinful Davey,* United Artists, 1967; *The Virgin Soldiers,* Columbia, 1968; *The Royal Hunt of the Sun,* National General, 1968; *Play Dirty,* United Artists, 1968; *No Blade of Grass,* Metro-Goldwyn-Mayer, 1970; *Villain,* Metro-Goldwyn-Mayer, 1971; *Mary, Queen of Scots,* Universal, 1971; *Living Free,* Columbia, 1972; *Stand Up, Virgin Soldiers,* Columbia, 1977; *Island of Dr. Moreau,* American International, 1977; *Zulu Dawn,* 1979; *Nighthawks,* Universal, 1981; *Chariots of Fire,* Warner Brothers, 1981; *Greystoke, the Legend of Tarzan, Lord of the Apes,* Warner Brothers, 1984; *Caravaggio,* British Film Institute, 1986.

PRINCIPAL TELEVISION APPEARANCES—*South Riding; The Apple Cart; Oil Strike North; The Prince Regent; The Picture of Dorian Gray; A Midsummer Night's Dream; The Ordeal of Doctor Mudd; Mountbatten, the Last Viceroy,* others from 1952—.

MEMBER: British Actors' Equity Association (former vice president); Shakespeare Memorial Theatre Company, 1953-54; Chesterfield Civic Theatre Company (played over seventy-five roles) 1954-55.

SIDELIGHTS: Nigel Davenport has expressed a special fondness for his role of Bro Paradock in the play *A Resounding Tinkle* which he helped develop with the English Stage Company. Among classic repertory, he has expressed a personal penchant for the roles of Othello and Verskinin.

ADDRESSES: AGENT—Michael Whitehall, Ltd., 125 Gloucester Road, London SW7 4TE, England.

*   *   *

DAVIS, Ann B.   1926-

PERSONAL: Full name, Ann Bradford Davis; born May 5, 1926, in Schenectady, NY; daughter of Cassius Miles and Marguerite (Stott) Davis. EDUCATION: University of Michigan, B.A., 1948.

VOCATION: Actress.

CAREER: PRINCIPAL STAGE APPEARANCES—Apperared in stock productions in Erie, PA, 1948-49, Porterville, CA, 1949-51, Yosemite, CA, 1950-51, Monterey, CA, 1952-53, and Hollywood, CA, 1954-55.

MAJOR TOURS—USO tour, Asia, South Pacific, Korea, 1967-70; *No, No Nanette,* national, 1972-73.

PRINCIPAL TELEVISION APPEARANCES—Series: Charmaine "Shultzy" Schultz, *The Bob Cummings Show* (also known as *Love That Bob*), NBC, 1955, CBS, 1955-57, NBC, 1957-59, and ABC, 1959-61; regular, *The Keefe Braselle Show,* CBS, 1963; Miss Wilson, *The John Forsythe Show,* NBC, 1965-66; Alice Nelson, *The Brady Bunch,* ABC, 1969-74; Alice, *The Brady Bunch Hour,* ABC, 1977.

AWARDS: Best Continuing Supporting Performance by an Actress in a Dramatic or Comedy Series, Emmy Awards, 1957, 1958, and 1959, for *The Bob Cummings Show.*

MEMBER: American Federation of Television and Radio Artists; Girls Friday of Showbiz; Spotlighters.

ADDRESSES: AGENT—Contemporary-Korman, 132 Lasky Drive, Beverly Hills, CA 90212.*

*   *   *

DAVIS, Clayton   1948-

PERSONAL: Born Norman Frederick Davis, May 18, 1948, in Pensacola, FL; son of Clay Savelle (an accountant) and Norma Helen (a computer systems analyst; maiden name, Clenney) Davis. EDUCATION: Princeton University, B.S.E., aerospace and mechanical sciences; Florida State University, M.F.A., acting; studied for the theatre at the Asolo Conservatory at Florida State; also studied with Neal Kenyon, Henry LeTang, Laura Thomas, Dennis Buck, April Adams, and others. MILITARY: U.S. Navy, 1970-75 (achieved rank of Lieutenant, Naval Flight Officer).

VOCATION: Actor.

CAREER: STAGE DEBUT—Ben, *The Remarkable Mr. Pennypacker*, Pensacola Little Theatre, Pensacola, FL, 1955. NEW YORK DEBUT—Ensemble, *Oklahoma!*, Equity Library Theatre, 1979, for thirty-two performances. PRINCIPAL STAGE APPEARANCES—Oscar, *Another Part of the Forest*, Ligniere, *Cyrano de Bergerac*, Dinsdale, *The Ruling Class*, all at Asolo Repertory Co., FL; *Troilus and Cressida*, McCarter Repetory Theatre, Princeton, NJ; Walt, *George M!* and

CLAYTON DAVIS

priest and apostle, *Jesus Christ Superstar*, both at Artpark Theatre, NY; Jamie, *My Fair Lady*, Theatre of the Stars; Marcel, *The Boyfriend*, Golden Apple Dinner Theatre; Ike Skidmore, *Oklahoma!*, Village and Pineville Dinner Theatres; Ambrose Kemper, *Hello, Dolly!*, Artpark Theatre, NY; Philip, *The Lion in Winter*, Golden Apple Dinner Theatre; cockney soldier, *Oh, Johnny*, Players Theatre, NY, 1982; Jack Chesney, *Where's Charley?*, Equity Library Theatre, NY, 1983; others.

MAJOR TOURS—Revue performer, *Sham on Wry*, national; revue performer, *Call a Spade a Shovel*, national; revue performer, *A Different Kick*, national; also numerous music revues aboard ships of the Holland America Line.

PRINCIPAL FILM APPEARANCES—*It's My Turn*, Columbia, 1980; *Nighthawks*, Universal, 1981; *The Fan*, 1981; *Ragtime*, Paramount, 1981; *Prince of the City*, Warner Brothers, 1981; *Zelig*, Warner Brothers, 1983; also U.S. Army training films: *The Search for Meaning* and *Loneliness: Taking Care of Our Own*.

PRINCIPAL TELEVISION APPEARANCES—Episodic: "Flora, the Red Menace," *Camera Three*, CBS, 1980; *The Guiding Light; The Doctors; Ryan's Hope; Nurse*.

MEMBER: Actors' Equity Association, Screen Actors Guild, American Federation of Television and Radio Artists.

ADDRESSES: HOME—New York, NY.

*   *   *

DAVIS, Luther   1921-

PERSONAL: Born August 29, 1921, in New York, NY; son of Charles Thomas (a manufacturer of surgical supplies) and Henrietta (Roesler) Davis; married Dorothy de Milhau, November 3, 1943 (divorced, 1961); children: Noelle, Laura Duval. EDUCATION: Yale University, B.A., 1938. MILITARY: U.S. Army Air Force, 1942-45.

VOCATION: Writer and producer.

CAREER: PRINCIPAL TELEVISION WORK—Series: Writer and producer—*Bus Stop; Kraft Suspense Theatre; Run for Your Life; The Silent Force*.

WRITINGS: SCREENPLAYS—*The Hucksters* (adapted from the novel by Frederic Wakeman), Metro-Goldwyn-Mayer, 1947; *B.F.'s Daughter* (adapted from the novel by John P. Marquand), Metro-Goldwyn-Mayer, 1948; *The Black Hand*, Metro-Goldwyn-Mayer, 1950; *A Lion Is in the Streets*, (adapted from the novel by Adria Locke Langley), Warner Brothers, 1953; (contributor) *New Faces*, Twentieth Century-Fox, 1954; (with Charles Lederer) *Kismet*, Metro-Goldwyn-Mayer, 1955; *The Gift of Love* (adapted from "The Little Horse," a short story by Nelia Gardner White), Twentieth Century-Fox, 1958; *Holiday for Lovers* (adapted from the play by Ronald Alexander), Twentieth Century-Fox, 1959; *The Wonders of Aladdin*, Metro-Goldwyn-Mayer, 1961; (also producer) *Lady in a Cage*, Paramount, 1964; *Across 110th Street*, United Artists, 1972.

TELEVISION MOVIES—*End of the World, Baby*, 1964; *Daughter of the Mind* (adapted from the novel *The Hand of Mary Constable* by Paul Gallico), ABC, 1966; *Arsenic and Old Lace* (adapted from the play by Joseph Kesselring), ABC, 1969; *The Old Man Who Cried Wolf*, ABC, 1970.

PLAYS, PRODUCED—*Kiss Them for Me,* Belasco Theatre, NY, 1945; book (with Charles Lederer), *Kismet* (based on the play of the same title by Edward Knoblock), Ziegfeld Theatre, NY, 1953; *Timbuktu* (based on *Kismet*), Mark Hellinger Theatre, NY, 1978.

MEMBER: Dramatists Guild, Writers Guild of America West, League of New York Theatres and Producers, Producers Guild of America, New York Athletic Club.

AWARDS: Best American Play, Clarence Derwent Award, 1945, for *Kiss Them for Me;* Best Screenplay, Fame Award, 1946, for *The Hucksters;* Best Musical, Antoinette Perry Award, 1954, for *Kismet;* Edgar Allan Poe Awards from Mystery Writers of America, 1963, for *End of the World, Baby,* and 1970, for *Daughter of the Mind;* Best Musical, Antoinette Perry Award, 1979, for *Timbuktu.*

ADDRESSES: OFFICE—Pictures, Inc., 18 W. 55th Street, New York, NY 10019.

*   *   *

DAVIS, Mac   1942-

PERSONAL: Born January 21, 1942, in Lubbock, TX; son of T.J. and Edith Irene (Lankford) Davis; married; children: Joel Scott. EDUCATION: Attended Emory University and Georgia State College.

VOCATION: Actor, singer, and songwriter.

CAREER: PRINCIPAL FILM APPEARANCES—*North Dallas Forty,* Paramount, 1979; *Cheaper to Keep Her,* 1980; *The Sting II,* Universal, 1983.

PRINCIPAL TELEVISION APPEARANCES—Specials: *You Put Music in My Life,* 1978.

RELATED CAREER—District sales manager, Liberty Records, 1965; manager, Metric Music, 1966-68.

RECORDINGS: ALBUMS—*Little Touch of Love,* Accord; *Till I Made It with You,* MCA; *Greatest Hits,* Canaan; *Very Best and More,* Casablanca; *Who's Loving You,* Columbia.

SIDELIGHTS: Mac Davis worked as a ditch digger, service station attendant, laborer, and probation officer before he became a professional singer and actor.

ADDRESSES: AGENT—Katz, Gallin, and Morey Enterprises, Inc., 9255 Sunset Blvd., Suite 1115, Los Angeles, CA 90069.

*   *   *

DEAN, Laura   1963-

BRIEF ENTRY: Born May 27, 1963, in Smithtown, NY. Actress. Dean's first major role was as Lisa Monroe in *Fame,* the film about the students who attend the High School of Performing Arts in New York City, of which Dean is herself a graduate. The next role to win Dean critical acclaim was Boopsie, the cheerleader in the Broadway production of *Doonesbury.* For her performance in this, she won a *Theatre World Award.* Dean's acting debut had come long before these successes, however, when she was cast at age seven in a touring production of *The Sound of Music.* Between the ages of ten and fifteen, she performed with the New York City Opera in such productions as *Carmen* and *La Boheme.* With that same company,

Dean was the soloist, Flora, in Benjamin Britten's *Turn of the Screw.* Dean made her Off-Broadway debut in 1973 in *The Secret Life of Walter Mitty* and was also seen Off-Broadway in the Public Theatre's critically acclaimed production of John Guare's *Landscape of the Body.* In addition to her numerous commercial appearances, Dean was seen on television in the final six months of the daytime serial *Love of Life.* Dean pursues her musical interests by performing with the band "The Wrecking Crew."*

*   *   *

DEERING, Olive   1919-1986

PERSONAL: Born 1919, in New York, NY; died in New York of cancer, March 22, 1986. EDUCATION: Studied at the Professional Children's School.

VOCATION: Actress.

CAREER: NEW YORK DEBUT—*Girls in Uniform,* Booth Theatre, 1933. PRINCIPAL STAGE APPEARANCES—*Growing Pains,* Ambassador Theatre, NY, 1933; *Picnic,* National Theatre, NY, 1934; *Searching for the Sun,* 58th Street Theatre, NY, 1936; *Daughters of Atreus,* 44th Street Theatre, NY, 1936; *The Eternal Road,* Manhattan Opera House, 1937; *Richard II,* St. James Theatre, NY, 1937; *Medicine Show,* New Yorker Theatre, NY, 1940; *No for an Answer,* Mecca Theatre, NY, 1941; *They Walk Alone,* Shubert Theatre, NY, 1941; *Nathan the Wise,* Belasco Theatre, NY, 1942; Regina Gordon, *Counselor-at-Law,* Royale Theatre, NY, 1942; Ruth, *Winged Victory,* 44th Street Theatre, NY, 1943; *Yellow Jack,* Broadway production, 1944; Francey, *Skydrift,* Belasco Theatre, NY, 1945; Mollie Malloy, *The Front Page,* Royale Theatre, NY, 1946; Rose Perozzi, *Dark Legend,* President Theatre, NY, 1952; *The Trojan Women,* 1957; Bianca, *Othello,* American Shakespeare Festival, Stratford, CT, 1957.

Contessa, *The Devil's Advocate,* Billy Rose Theatre, NY, 1961; Eve Adamanski, *Marathon '33,* American National Theatre and Academy (ANTA), 1963; Woman of Canterbury, *Murder in the Cathedral,* American Shakespeare Festival, 1966; appeared with the Theatre Company of Boston, 1966-67; Madame Arkadina, *The Seagull,* Brandeis University Theatre Arts, Waltham, MA, 1966; Emma, *Ceremony of Innocence,* American Place Theatre, NY, 1967; *After the Fall,* Manitoba Theatre Center, Winnipeg, Canada, 1970; Charlotte Shade, *The Sun and the Noon,* 1972; appeared in *Mr. McMannis, What Time Is It?,* Cubiculo Theatre, NY, 1976; Mrs. Wayne, *Vieux Carre,* St. James Theatre, NY, 1977; also in *The Young Elizabeth* and *Garden District.* Also appeared in *Suddenly Last Summer,* in Los Angeles.

PRINCIPAL FILM APPEARANCES—*Sampson and Delilah,* 1949; *Caged,* 1950; *The Ten Commandments,* Paramount, 1956; *Shock Treatment,* Twentieth Century-Fox, 1964.

PRINCIPAL TELEVISION APPEARANCES—*Philco Summer Playhouse,* NBC; Desdemona, *Othello.*

PRINCIPAL RADIO APPEARANCES—*True Story; Against the Storm.**

*   *   *

de LAPPE, Gemze   1922-

PERSONAL: Born February 28, 1922, in Portsmouth, VA; daughter of Birch Wood (an actor and teacher) and Maureen (an actress and drummer; maiden name, McDonough) de Lappe; married John Carisi (a musician), May 22, 1959; children: Peter, Jonathan. EDUCATION: Attended the High School of Music and Art in New York, NY; trained for the stage at the Isadora Duncan School with Irma Duncan and at the Michael Fokine Ballet Company.

VOCATION: Dancer, choreographer, and actor.

CAREER: STAGE DEBUT—Dancer, *Michael Fokine Ballet,* Lewisohn Stadium, NY, 1932. BROADWAY DEBUT—King Simon of Legree, *The King and I,* St. James Theatre, 1951. LONDON DEBUT—Dream Ballet Laurey, *Oklahoma!,* Drury Lane Theatre, 1947. PRINCIPAL STAGE APPEARANCES—Yvonne, *Paint Your Wagon,* Shubert Theatre, NY, 1952; the Maid, *The Gorey Stories,* Booth Theatre, NY; also appeared in *Brigadoon;* Lizzie Borden, *Fall River Legend;* French Ballerina, *Gala Performance; Billy the Kid; Fancy Free.*

PRINCIPAL STAGE WORK—Choreographer: *Oklahoma!,* Australia; The Takarazuka Company, Japan; Antwerp and Munich Volsoper.

PRINCIPAL TELEVISION APPEARANCES—*Conversations About the Dance; Musical Comedy Tonight.*

PRINCIPAL FILM APPEARANCES—King Simon of Legree, *The King and I,* Twentieth Century-Fox, 1956.

RELATED CAREER: Artist in residence, Smith College, Northampton, MA.

AWARD: Donaldson Award, 1952, for *Paint Your Wagon.*

MEMBER: Actor's Equity Association, Screen Actors Guild, Society of Stage Directors and Choreographers, American Guild of Musical Artists.

ADDRESSES: HOME—Williamsburg, MA. OFFICE—Dance Department, Smith College, Northampton, MA 01096. AGENT—c/o Milton Goldman, International Creative Management, 40 W. 57th Street, New York, NY 10019.

*   *   *

de MILLE, Agnes   1905-

PERSONAL: Born 1905, in New York, NY; daughter of William C. (an author and producer) and Anna (George) de Mille; married Walter Foy Prude, June 14, 1943; children: Jonathan. EDUCATION: University of California, B.A., cum laude; studied dance in London with Marie Rambert, Antony Tudor and Tamara Karsavina, and in Los Angeles with Koslov.

VOCATION: Choreographer, dancer, dance director, stage director, and author.

CAREER: NEW YORK DEBUT—Dancer, *La Finta Giardiniera,* 1927. LONDON DEBUT—The priggish virgin, *Three Virgins and the Devil,* cowgirl, *Rodeo,* both Royal Opera House, Covent Garden, London, 1956. PRINCIPAL STAGE APPEARANCES—In concert, Republic Theatre, NY, 1928; *The Rehearsal,* Royal Winnipeg Ballet, Winnipeg, Canada, 1965; *Conversations About the Dance,* Hunter College, NY, 1974.

MAJOR TOURS—As dancer, throughout the United States, England,

AGNES de MILLE

France, and Denmark, 1928-42; with her own companies, 1953-54, and with Heritage Dance Theatre, 1973-74.

PRINCIPAL STAGE WORK—Choreographer: (also dancer) *The Black Crook,* Hoboken, NJ, 1929; *Nymph Errant,* Adelphi Theatre, London, 1933; *Leslie Howard's Hamlet,* Broadway production, 1936; *Hooray for What,* Broadway production, NY, 1937; *Swingin' the Dream,* Broadway production, 1939; *Obeah, Ballet Joors, Black Ritual, Three Virgins and the Devil,* and *Rodeo,* all for Ballet Theatre, NY, 1939-42; *The American Legend,* 1941; *Drum Sounds in Hackensack* (ballet), 1941; *Oklahoma!,* St. James Theatre, NY, 1943; *One Touch of Venus,* Imperial Theatre, NY, 1943; *Bloomer Girl,* NY, 1944; *Tally Ho* (ballet), 1944; *Carousel,* Majestic Theatre, NY, 1945; *Brigadoon,* Ziegfeld Theatre, NY, 1947; *Fall River Legend* (ballet), 1948; *Allegro,* Majestic Theatre, NY, 1948; *Gentlemen Prefer Blondes,* Majestic Theatre, NY, 1949; *Out of This World,* New Century Theatre, NY, 1950; *Paint Your Wagon,* Shubert Theatre, NY, 1951; *The Harvest According* (ballet), 1952; *The Girl in Pink Tights,* Mark Hellinger Theatre, NY, 1954.

Goldilocks, Lunt-Fontanne Theatre, NY, 1958; *Juno,* Winter Garden Theatre, NY, 1959; *Bitter Weird,* Royal Winnipeg Ballet Co., Winnipeg, 1961; *Kwamina,* Broadway production, 1961; *110 in the Shade,* 46th Street Theatre, NY, 1963; *The Wind in the Mountains* (ballet), 1965; *The Four Marys* (ballet), 1965; *Carousel,* 1965; *Where's Charley?,* national company, 1966; *The Golden Age* (ballet), 1967; *A Rose for Miss Emily* (ballet), 1970; *Come Summer,* Broadway production, 1971; *Texas 4th* (ballet), 1977; *Oklahoma!,* Palace Theatre, NY, 1979; *A Bridegroom Called Death* (ballet), 1980.

Choreographer for Ballet Russe de Monte Carlo; Royal Winnipeg Ballet; American Ballet Theatre.

Choreographer and director, *Allegro,* 1947.

Director: *Rape of Lucrecia,* 1949; *Out of This World,* New Century Theatre, New York, 1950; *Come Summer,* Broadway production, 1971.

PRINCIPAL FILM WORK—Choreographer: *Romeo and Juliet,* Metro-Goldwyn-Mayer, 1937; *Oklahoma!,* Magna, 1955.

WRITINGS: BOOKS—*Dance to the Piper* (autobiography), Da Capo, 1951, reprinted 1980; *And Promenade Home* (autobiography), Da Capo, 1956, reprinted 1980; *To a Young Dancer,* 1962; *The Book of Dance,* 1963; *Dance in America,* 1970' *Russian Journals,* 1970; *Speak to Me, Dance with Me,* 1974; *Where the Wings Grow,* 1978; *America Dances,* 1980; *Reprieve,* 1981.

ARTICLES—Contributor to numerous magazine articles and book chapters.

MEMBER: Ballet Theatre (since 1939), Society of Stage Directors and Choreographers (president, 1965-66), National Council of the Performing Arts (since 1965).

AWARDS: Antoinette Perry Awards, 1947, for *Brigadoon,* 1961, for *Kwamina;* numerous Donaldson Awards; numerous *Variety* New York Critics Poll Awards; Lord and Taylor Award; Dancing Masters of Merit Award; *Dance* Magazine Award; Capezio Award; Handel Award from the Mayor of New York; Kennedy Award; Woman of the Year Award, American Newspaper Women's Guild; named to Theatre Hall of Fame, 1973.

Honorary degrees from Smith College, Western College, Hood College, Goucher College, Northwestern University, California University, Clarke University, Mills College, Russell Sage College, Franklin and Marshall, Western Michigan University, Nasson College, Dartmouth College, Duke University, University of North Carolina, New York University.

SIDELIGHTS: Agnes de Mille's extensive collection of films and videotapes of her work has been deposited with the Dance Collection of the Performing Arts Research Center in the New York Public Library at Lincoln Center for use by scholars of the dance with special permission granted for such use by Miss de Mille. She has copyrights on her dances for her Rodgers and Hammerstein musicals (most especially for *Oklahoma!* and *Carousel*) and a much touted, unpublished agreement with the Rodgers and Hammerstein office which demands that all professional productions of these shows include her copyrighted choreography.

She has choreographed numerous ballets for leading dance companies and given several television interviews on her life and her work. Her uncle was Cecil B. de Mille, the motion picture producer and director.

In 1975, the North Carolina School of Arts at Winston-Salem named a theatre in her honor.

ADDRESSES: OFFICE—Harold Ober Associates, 40 E. 49th Street, New York, NY 10017.

*   *   *

De MORNAY, Rebecca   1962-

PERSONAL: Born in 1962, in Santa Rosa, CA. EDUCATION: Graduated High School Kitzbuhel, Austria; trained for the stage at the Lee Strasberg Theatre Institute, Los Angeles, CA and with Sandra Seacat and Geraldine Page; also apprenticed with Francis Ford Coppola's Zoetrope Studio, 1981.

VOCATION: Actress.

CAREER: FILM DEBUT—*One from the Heart,* Columbia, 1982. PRINCIPAL FILM APPEARANCES—*Risky Business,* Warner Brothers, 1983; *Testament,* Paramount, 1983; *The Sluggers Wife,* Columbia, 1985; *The Trip to Bountiful,* Island Alive, 1985; *Runaway Train,* Cannon, 1985.

SIDELIGHTS: Rebecca De Mornay told *CTFT* that before she began her acting career she lived in Austria, England, France, Italy, East Germany, Mexico, and Jamaica. She speaks fluent French and German.

ADDRESSES: AGENT—c/o Paula Wagner, Creative Artists Agency, 1888 Century Park E., Suite 1400, Los Angeles, CA 90067; Andrea Jaffe, Inc., 9229 Sunset Blvd., Suite 401, Los Angeles, CA 90069.

*   *   *

DENHAM, Maurice   1909-

PERSONAL: Born December 23, 1909, in Beckenham, Kent, England; son of Norman and Eleanor Winifred (Lillico) Denham; married Margaret Dunn (died). EDUCATION: Attended the Tonbridge School. MILITARY: British Army, World War II.

VOCATION: Actor.

MAURICE DENHAM

CAREER: STAGE DEBUT—Hubert, *The Marquise*, Little Theatre, Hull, England, 1934. LONDON DEBUT—George Furness, *Rain Before Seven*, Arts Theatre, 1936. PRINCIPAL STAGE APPEARANCES—(All London unless otherwise indicated) George, *Busman's Honeymoon*, Comedy Theatre, 1936; George Lumb, *Flying Blind*, Arts Theatre, 1937; Eddie Norman, *Heaven and Charing Cross*, Player's Theatre, 1938; Peter Mansky, *A Room in Red, White, and Blue*, Repertory Players at the Savoy Theatre, 1938; Fletcher, *The Heart Was Not Burned*, Gate Theatre, 1938; Henry Gow, *Fumed Oak* and Willy Banbury, *Fallen Angels*, both Ambassadors Theatre, 1949; Shaw Festival of one-act plays, Arts Theatre, 1951; Ilam Carve, *The Great Adventure*, Arts Theatre, 1951; Sam and George Titmarsh, *The House at Bury Hill*, Queens Theatre, 1952; Stefan, *Satellite Story*, Whitehall Theatre, 1954; Sir Mark Evershed, *Shadow of Fear*, Wyndhams Theatre, 1956; double bill, Fowle, *The Dock Brief*, Arthur Loudin, *What Shall We Tell Caroline?*, Lyric Theatre, Hammersmith, Garrick Theatre, London, 1958; Arthur Crabb, *Who's Your Father?*, Cambridge Theatre, 1958.

Henry Wirtz, *The Andersonville Trial*, Mermaid Theatre, 1961; title role, *King John*, the Old Vic Theatre Company at the Edinbrugh Festival, and at the Old Vic Theatre, London, 1961; title role, *Macbeth*, Old Vic Theatre, 1961; Stone, *The Sky Is Green*, Ashcroft Theatre, Croydon, 1963; Dr. Neuross, *Do You Know the Milky Way?*, Hampstead Theatre Club, 1964; title role, *Nathan the Wise*, Mermaid Theatre, 1967; Proteus, *The Apple Cart*, Mermaid Theatre, 1970; Pierre Lannes, *The Lovers of Viorne*, Royal Court Theatre, 1971; Serebryakov, *Uncle Vanya*, Hampstead Theatre, 1979; *Incident at Tulse Hill*, Hampstead Theatre, 1981.

PRINCIPAL FILM APPEARANCES—*Barnacle Bill*, 1941; *Blanche Fury*, 1948; *London Belongs to Me* (also known as *Dulcimer Street*), 1948; *It's Not Cricket*, 1948; *Traveller's Joy*, 1949; *Landfall*, 1949; *The Spider and the Fly*, 1949; *Quartette*, 1949; *The Set Up*, 1949; *The King's Breakfast*, 1949; *Penang*, 1949; *No Highway in the Sky*, 1951; *The Net*, 1951; *Eight O'Clock Walk*, 1952; *Both Sides of the Law* (also known as *Street Corner*), 1954; *The Man with a Million* (also known as *Million Pound Note*), 1954; *Purple Plain*, 1955; *Doctor at Sea*, 1955; *Court Martial* (also known as *Carrington, V.C.*), 1955; *Checkpoint*, 1955; *The Night of the Demon*, 1955; *Man with a Dog*, 1955; *Simon and Laura*, 1956; *23 Paces to Baker Street*, 1956.

The Captain's Table, 1960; *Our Man in Havana*, 1960; *Sink the Bismark*, 1960; *Two-Way Stretch*, 1960; *The Mark*, 1961; *Loss of Innocence* (also know as *Greengage Summer*), 1961; *H.M.S. Defiant*, 1961; *Time Bomb*, 1961; *The Very Edge*, 1963; *Paranoiac*, 1963; *Downfall*, 1964; *Hysteria*, 1964; *The Uncle*, 1964; *Operation Crossbow*, 1965; *The Nanny*, 1965; *Those Magnificent Men in Their Flying Machines*, 1965; *Heroes of Telemark*, 1965; *The Legend of Dick Turpin*, 1965; *After the Fox*, 1966; *The Alphabet Murders*, 1966; *The Long Duel*, 1967; *The Eliminator*, 1967; *Danger Route*, 1968; *Negatives*, 1968; *Attack on the Iron Coast*, 1968; *The Torture Garden*, 1968; *The Best House in London*, 1969; *The Midas Run*, 1969; *Some Girls Do*, 1969; *The Touch of Love*, 1969; *The Virgin and the Gypsy*, 1970; *Sunday, Bloody Sunday*, 1971; *Nicholas and Alexandra*, 1971; *Countess Dracula*, 1972; *The Day of the Jackal*, 1973; *Luther*, 1974; *The Night Callers*, 1975; *Shout at the Devil*, 1976; *Julia*, 1977; *The Recluse*, 1978; *From a Far Country: Pope John Paul II*, 1981; *Mr. Love*, 1981; *84 Charing Cross Road*, 1985.

PRINCIPAL TELEVISION APPEARANCES—(All in England) *Uncle Harry; Day of the Monkey; Miss Nabel; Angel Pavement; The Paraguayan Harp; The Wild Bird; Soldier Soldier; Changing Values;*

Maigret; The Assassins; Saturday Spectacular; Vanishing Act; A Chance in Life; Virtue; Somerset Maugham; Three of a Kind; Sapper; Pig in the Middle; Their Obedient Servants; Long Past Glory; Devil in the Wind; Any Other Buisiness; The Retired Colourman; Sherlock Holmes; Blackmail; Knock on Any Door; Danger Man; Dr. Finley's Casebook; How to Get Rid of Your Husband; Talking to a Stranger; A Slight Ache; From Chekhov with Love; Home Sweet Honeycomb; St. Joan; Julius Caesar; Golden Days; Marshall Petain; The Lotus Eaters; Fall of Eagles; Carnforth Practice; The Unofficial Rose; Omnibus; Balzac; Love's Labour's Lost; Angels; Huggy Bear; The Portrait; The Crumbles Murder; A Chink in the Wall; Porridge; For God's Sake; Bosch; Marie Curie; Upchat Line; Secret Army; My Son, My Son; Edward and Mrs. Simpson; Gate of Eden; Potting Shed; Double Dealer; Minder; Agatha Christie Hour; Chinese Detective; The Old Men at the Zoo; The Hope and the Glory; Luther; Love Song.

MEMBER: Garrick Club.

SIDELIGHTS: RECREATION—Golf.

ADDRESSES: HOME—44 Brunswick Gardens, Flat 2, London W8, England.

*   *   *

DENNISON, Sally   1941-

PERSONAL: Born November 9, 1941, in Evanston, IL; daughter of James T. and Nancy W. Dennison. EDUCATION: Attended Carnegie Institute of Technology.

VOCATION: Casting director.

CAREER: PRINCIPAL FILM WORK—Casting director: *Zabriski Point*, Metro-Goldwyn-Mayer, 1970; *Bound for Glory*, United Artists, 1977; *Close Encounters of the Third Kind*, Columbia, 1977; (with Lynn Stallmaster) *Coming Home*, United Artists, 1978; *The China Syndrome*, Columbia, 1979; *Meatballs*, Paramount, 1979; *1941*, Universal, 1979; *Players*, Paramount, 1979; *Fame*, United Artists, 1980; *Tom Horn*, Warner Brothers, 1980; *Used Cars*, Columbia, 1980; *Endless Love*, Universal, 1981; *Hard Feelings*, Polygram, 1981.

With Julie Selzer: *Grease II*, Paramount, 1982; *Heart Like a Wheel*, Twentieth Century-Fox, 1983; *Whoopee Boys*, Paramount; *USA Today* (upcoming); *Robocop* (upcoming).

PRINCIPAL TELEVISION WORK—Movies: Casting director—*White Water Rebels*, CBS, 1983; *Quarterback Princess*, CBS, 1983; *Last of the Great Survivors*, CBS, 1984; *A Touch of Scandal*, CBS, 1984; *My Wicked, Wicked Ways: The Legend of Errol Flynn*, CBS, 1985; also, *Homeroom*, ABC.

Series: *Powers of Matthew Star*, NBC, 1982-83.

PRINCIPAL STAGE WORK—Producer: *Runaways; When You Comin' Back Red Ryder; G.R. Point; Wrestlers*, all in Los Angeles.

MEMBER: Casting Society of America.

ADDRESSES: OFFICE—Laird Mansion, Laird Studios, 9336 W. Washington Blvd., Culver City, CA 90230. AGENT—c/o Mike Menchel, Creative Artists Agency, 1888 Century Park E., Suite 1400, Los Angeles, CA 90067.

DEREK, Bo   1956-

PERSONAL: Born Mary Cathleen Collins, November 20, 1956, in Torrance, CA; married John Derek (an actor, producer, and director).

VOCATION: Actress.

CAREER: FILM DEBUT—*Orca, the Killer Whale*, Paramount, 1977. PRINCIPAL FILM APPEARANCES—*10*, Warner Brothers, 1979; *Change of Seasons*, Twentieth Century-Fox, 1980; *Tarzan, the Ape Man*, United Artists, 1981; *Bolero*, Cannon, 1984.

ADDRESSES: AGENT—Creative Artists Agency, Inc., 1888 Century Park E., Suite 1400, Los Angeles, CA 90067.

*   *   *

DEREK, John   1926-

PERSONAL: Born August 12, 1926, in Hollywood, CA; married Ursula Andress (an actress; divorced); married Linda Evans (an actress; divorced); married Mary Cathleen Collins (an actress; professional name, Bo Derek).

VOCATION: Actor, producer, director, and writer.

CAREER: FILM DEBUT—*I'll Be Seeing You*, 1945. PRINCIPAL FILM APPEARANCES—*Knock on Any Door*, 1949; *All the King's Men*, 1949; *Mask of the Avenger*, 1951; *Scandal Sheet*, 1952; *Mission Over Korea*, 1953; *The Adventures of Haji Baba*, 1954; *Prince of Players*, 1955; *Run for Cover*, Paramount, 1955; *The Leather Saint*, Paramount, 1956; *The Ten Commandments*, Paramount, 1956; *Omar Khayyam*, Paramount, 1957; *Prisoner of the Volga*, Paramount, 1960; *Exodus*, United Artists, 1960; *Nightmare in the Sun*, Zodiac, 1963.

PRINCIPAL FILM WORK—Producer and director, *Nightmare in the Sun*, Zodiac, 1963; producer and director, *Once Before I Die*, 1965; producer, director, screenwriter, and cinematographer for *A Boy . . . a Girl*, Cinema J, 1969, *Childish Things*, Filmworld, 1969, and also, *Once Upon a Time;* director, *Tarzan, the Ape Man*, United Artists, 1981; director, *Bolero*, Cannon, 1984.

ADDRESSES: AGENT—c/o Martin Baum, Creative Artists Agency, 1888 Century Park E., Suite 1400, Los Angeles, CA 90067.*

*   *   *

DERN, Bruce   1936-

PERSONAL: Full name, Bruce MacLeish Dern; born June 4, 1936 in Chicago, IL; son of John and Jean (MacLeish) Dern; married Diane Ladd (an actress; divorced); married Andrea Beckett, October 20, 1969; children: (first marriage) Laura Elizabeth. EDUCATION: Attended University of Pennsylvania; studied for the theatre with Gordon Phillips and has been a member of the Actors Studio since 1959.

VOCATION: Actor.

CAREER: NEW YORK DEBUT—*Shadow of a Gunman*, 1959. PRINCIPAL STAGE APPEARANCES—Chance Wayne, *Sweet Bird of Youth;* F. Scott Fitzgerald, *Strangers,* New York production, 1979; also appeared in *Orpheus Descending.*

FILM DEBUT—*Wild River*, Twentieth Century-Fox, 1960; *John, Hush, Hush Sweet Charlotte*, Twentieth Century-Fox, 1964; *Marnie*, Universal, 1964; Loser, *The Wild Angels*, American International, 1966; *The Trip*, American International, 1967; *The War Wagon*, Universal, 1967; *Waterhole No. 3*, Paramount, 1967; *Will Penny*, Paramount, 1968; *Number One*, United Artists, 1969; *Support Your Local Sheriff*, United Artists, 1969; *Castle Keep*, Columbia, 1969; *Bloody Mama*, American International, 1970; *They Shoot Horses, Don't They?*, Cinerama, 1970; *Drive, He Said*, Columbia, 1971; *The Cowboys*, Warner Brothers, 1972; *Silent Running*, Universal, 1972; *King of Marvin Gardens*, Columbia, 1972; *The Laughing Policeman*, Twentieth Century-Fox, 1973; Tom Buchanan, *The Great Gatsby*, Paramount, 1974; *Smile*, United Artists, 1975; *Posse*, Paramount, 1975; *Family Plot*, Universal, 1976; *Won Ton Ton, the Dog Who Saved Hollywood*, Paramount, 1976; *Black Sunday*, Paramount, 1977; *Coming Home*, United Artists, 1978; *The Driver*, Twentieth Century-Fox, 1978; *Middle Age Crazy*, Twentieth Century-Fox, 1980; *Tattoo*, Twentieth Century-Fox, 1981; *That Championship Season*, Cannon Films, 1982; *On the Edge*, New Front Films, 1986.

PRINCIPAL TELEVISION APPEARANCES—Series: E.J. Stocker, *Stoney Burke*, ABC, 1962-63.

Mini-Series: *Space*, CBS, 1985.

Movie: *Toughlove*, ABC, 1985.

AWARDS: National Society of Film Critics Award, 1971, for *Drive He Said;* Actor of the Year, Pacific Archives Award, Berkeley, California, 1972; Best Supporting Actor, Golden Globe nomination, 1974, for *The Great Gatsby;* Best Supporting Actor, Academy Award nomination, People's Choice Award, both 1978, for *Coming Home.*

MEMBER: Actors' Equity Association, Screen Actors Guild; Santa Monica Track Club.

ADDRESSES: AGENT—Creative Artists Agency, 1888 Century Park E., Suite 1400, Los Angeles, CA 90067.*

*   *   *

DERN, Laura   1967-

BRIEF ENTRY: Full name, Laura Elizabeth Dern; born in 1967, in Santa Monica, CA. Actress. Laura Dern is in the position to be considered one of the "brat pack" (which includes such young actors as Emilo Estevez, Demi Moore, Ali Sheedy, and Rob Lowe), but her film appearances are proof that she wishes to maintain an individuality from the commercial successes of her peers. In 1984, she played a student considering abortion after being impregnated by a teacher in *Teachers*. In the 1985 film, *Mask*, she portrayed a blind girl who falls in love with a facially deformed boy. Her latest role, in *Smooth Talk*, is that of a young woman whose promiscuity leads to an almost violent sexual awakening. Dern's acting career began at the age of seven when she had to eat nineteen ice cream cones in a row before the actual scene was shot in the film *Alice Doesn't Live Here Anymore*, which co-starred her mother, Diane Ladd. The young actress also appeared as an extra in several films of her father, the actor, Bruce Dern. Laura Dern is currently filming David Lynch's *Blue Velvet.**

DEVANE, William   1937-

PERSONAL: Born September 5, 1937, in Albany, NY; married Eugenie; children: Josh, Jake. EDUCATION: Attended American Academy of Dramatic Arts, New York.

VOCATION: Actor.

CAREER: PRINCIPAL FILM APPEARANCES—*Marathon Man,* 1976; *Family Plot,* Universal, 1976; *Rolling Thunder,* American International, 1977; *The Bad News Bears in Breaking Training,* Paramount, 1977; *Butch and Sundance: The Early Years,* Twentieth Century-Fox, 1979; *Yanks,* Universal, 1979; *Honky Tonk Freeway,* Universal, 1980; *Testament,* Paramount, 1983; *Hadley's Rebellion,* CBS Theatrical, 1985.

PRINCIPAL TELEVISION APPEARANCES—Series: Gregory Sumner, *Knot's Landing,* CBS, 1983—.

Movies: John F. Kennedy, *The Missiles of October; The Snoop Sisters,* 1972; *Shirts/Skins,* 1973; *Crime Club,* 1973; *The Bait,* 1973; *Fear on Trial,* 1975; *With Intent to Kill,* CBS, 1984; also appeared in *Black Beauty.*

Mini-Series: Master Sergeant Milt Warden, *From Here to Eternity,* NBC, 1979.

Specials: *Judgement: The Court Martial of the Tiger of Malaya—General Yamashita.*

Episodic: *Medical Center; Ironside; Hawaii Five-0; Insight.*

PRINCIPAL STAGE APPEARANCES—*One Flew Over the Cuckoo's Nest.*

PRINCIPAL STAGE WORK—Director, *G.R. Point,* Playhouse Theatre, NY.

MEMBER: Actors' Equity Association, Screen Actors Guild, American Federation of Television and Radio Artists.

ADDRESSES: AGENT—Agency for the Performing Arts, 9000 Sunset Blvd., Suite 315, Los Angeles, CA 90069.

*   *   *

DEVINE, Loretta

BRIEF ENTRY: Born August 21, in Houston, TX. Actress and singer. Lorretta Devine worked as a teacher for disadvantaged but gifted children and as an actress, director, and producer for several productions at Houston's Black Arts Center before finding national acclaim. Since leaving Houston, she has worked in over fifteen Off-Broadway plays and made her Broadway debut in the revival of *Hair.* Her roles in the Broadway productions of *Comin' Uptown* and *A Broadway Musical* brought her to the attention of director and choreographer Michael Bennett, who cast her as Lorrell Robinson in *Dreamgirls,* a role she portrayed for two years on Broadway. Devine's performance of ''Ain't No Party'' from the show has become her trademark and she often opens her nightclub act with it. In 1984, the performer received the Citizen Advocates for Justice award for performing a forty-five minute show at three New York State penitentiaries. Currently, Devine is winning acclaim as the leading actress in Bob Fosse's new Broadway musical, *Big Deal.**

ELIZABETH DIGGS

DIGGS, Elizabeth   1939-

PERSONAL: Born August 6, 1939, in Tulsa, OK; daughter of James B. (an attorney) and Virginia Francis Diggs; children: Jennifer Mackenzie. EDUCATION: Brown University, B.A., 1961; Columbia University, M.A., Ph.D., comparative literature.

VOCATION: Writer.

WRITINGS: PLAYS—*Goodbye Freddy,* SouthCoast Repertory, Costa Mesa, CA, 1983, Portland Stage Company, Portland, ME, 1984, Arizona Theatre Company, 1985, Manhattan Punch Line, NY, 1985, Capitol Repertory Company, Albany, NY, 1986; *Close Ties,* Capitol Repertory Company, 1980, Long Wharf Theatre, New Haven, CT, 1981, Victory Gardens, Chicago, IL, 1982, Los Angeles Public Theatre, 1982, Alley Theatre, 1982, American Theatre Company, Tulsa, OK, 1984; *Dumping Ground,* Ensemble Studio Theatre, NY, 1981, Fourth Estate Theatre, Los Angeles, CA, 1982, Ensemble Studio Theatre, NY, 1982.

PLAYS PUBLISHED—*Close Ties,* Doubleday (book club edition), 1981, Dramatists Play Service, 1981; *Dumping Ground,* Dramatists Play Service, 1981.

SCREENPLAYS—*Dumping Ground,* Zoetrope, 1984.

TELEVISION—''Tweety and Ralph,'' *St. Elsewhere,* 1982.

RELATED CAREER: Assistant professor of English, co-ordinator of women's studies program, Jersey City State College, 1972-77; lecturer in English at Queens College, City University of New York, and Manhattan Community College.

AWARDS: Los Angeles DramaLogue, for *Close Ties;* CBS/FDG Prize, for *Goodbye Freddy;* SouthCoast Repertory commission for play *American Beef.*

MEMBER: Ensemble Studio Theatre, NY (board of directors); Dramatists Guild.

SIDELIGHTS: Elizabeth Diggs told *CTFT,* "I was born and grew up in Tulsa, and have lived in New York since I was graduated from Brown in 1961. I write plays full time."

ADDRESSES: OFFICE—33 Bleeker Street, New York, NY 10012. AGENT—c/o George Lane, William Morris Agency, 1350 Avenue of the Americas, New York, NY 10019.

*　　*　　*

DILLER, Barry　1942-

PERSONAL: Born February 2, 1942, in San Francisco, CA; son of Michael and Reva (Addison) Diller.

VOCATION: Film and television executive.

CAREER: PRINCIPAL TELEVISION WORK—Assistant to vice-president of programming, ABC, 1966; executive assistant, vice-president of programming and directing of feature films, ABC, 1968; vice-president, feature films and program development, east coast, ABC, 1969; vice-president, feature films and Circle Entertainment, ABC, 1971-73, during which time he was responsible for selecting, producing, and scheduling the *Tuesday Movie of the Week, Wednesday Movie of the Week,* and Circle Film original features for airing on ABC, as well as acquisition and scheduling of theatrical features for airing on *ABC Sunday Night Movie* and *ABC Monday Night Movie;* vice-president, prime time television, ABC Entertainment, 1973.

PRINCIPAL FILM WORK—Board chairman and chief executive officer, Paramount Pictures, 1974; president, Gulf and Western Entertainment and Communications Group, 1983-84; board chairman and chief executive officer, Twentieth Century-Fox, 1984—.

MEMBER: American Film Institute, Academy of Motion Picture Arts and Sciences, Hollywood Radio and Television Society; Variety Clubs International; American Civil Liberties Union, National Conference of Christians and Jews.

ADDRESSES: OFFICE—Twentieth Century-Fox Film Corp., 10201 W. Pico Blvd., Los Angeles, CA 90035.*

*　　*　　*

DILLMAN, Bradford　1930-

PERSONAL: Born April 14, 1930, in San Francisco, CA; son of Dean and Josephine (Moore) Dillman; married Frieda Harding, 1956 (divorced, 1962); married Suzy Parker (an actress and model), 1963; children: (first marriage) Jeffrey, Pamela; (second marriage) Dinah, Christopher Parker; (step-daughter) Georgina Belle La Salle. EDUCATION: Yale University, B.A., 1951; studied for the

theatre at the Actors Studio. MILITARY: U.S. Marine Corps, 1951-53.

VOCATION: Actor.

CAREER: STAGE DEBUT—Title role, *The Scarecrow,* New York production, 1953. PRINCIPAL STAGE APPEARANCES—*Third Person,* New York production, 1955; Edmund Tyrone, *Long Day's Journey into Night,* New York production, 1956; *The Fun Couple,* New York production, 1962.

FILM DEBUT—*A Certain Smile,* Twentieth Century-Fox, 1958. PRINCIPAL FILM APPEARANCES—*In Love and War,* Twentieth Century-Fox, 1958; Artie Straus, *Compulsion,* Twentieth Century-Fox, 1959; *Crack in the Mirror,* Twentieth Century-Fox, 1960; *Circle of Deception,* Twentieth Century-Fox, 1961; *Sanctuary,* Twentieth Century-Fox, 1961; title role, *Francis of Assisi,* Twentieth Century-Fox, 1961; *A Rage to Live,* United Artists, 1965; *Jigsaw,* Beverly Pictures, 1965; *Sergeant Ryker,* Universal, 1968; *The Bridge at Remagen,* United Artists, 1969.

Suppose They Gave a War and Nobody Came, Cinerama, 1970; *The Mephisto Waltz,* Twentieth Century-Fox, 1971; *Brother John,* Columbia, 1971; *Escape from the Planet of the Apes,* Twentieth Century-Fox, 1971; *The Iceman Cometh,* AFT Distributing, 1973; J.J., *The Way We Were,* Columbia, 1973; *Chosen Survivors,* Columbia, 1974; *Gold,* Allied Artists, 1974; *99 and 44/100% Dead,* Twentieth Century-Fox, 1974; *Bug,* Paramount, 1975; *The Enforcer,* Warner Brothers, 1976; *The Swarm,* Warner Brothers, 1978; *Piranha,* New World Films, 1978; *The Amsterdam Kill,* Columbia, 1978.

Guyana: Cult of the Damned, 1980; *Sudden Impact,* Warner Brothers, 1983; *Treasure of the Amazon,* 1985; also appeared in *A Black Ribbon for Deborah, One Away, The Lincoln Conspiracy, Love and Bullets,* and *Running Scared.*

PRINCIPAL TELEVISION APPEARANCES—Series: Capt. David Young, *Court-Martial,* ABC, 1966; Paul Hollister, *King's Crossing,* ABC, 1982; Darryl Clayton, *Falcon Crest,* CBS, 1982-83.

Episodic: *Wide World of Mystery;* others.

Movies: *Black Water Gold,* 1970; *Revenge,* 1972; *Deliver Us from Evil,* 1973; *Murder of Mercy,* 1974; *Disappearance of Flight 412,* 1974; *Force Five,* 1975; *Widow,* 1976; *The Covenant,* NBC, 1985.

AWARDS: Theatre World Award, 1957, for *Long Days Journey into Night;* Best Actor, Cannes Film Festival, 1959, for *Compulson.*

ADDRESSES: AGENT—Contemporary-Korman, 132 Lasky Drive, Beverly Hills, CA 90212.*

*　　*　　*

DILLON, Melinda

VOCATION: Actress.

CAREER: FILM DEBUT—*The April Fools,* National General, 1969. PRINCIPAL FILM APPEARANCES—*Bound for Glory,* United Artists, 1976; *Slap Shot,* Universal, 1977; *Close Encounters of the Third Kind,* Columbia, 1977; *F.I.S.T.,* United Artists, 1978; *Absence of Malice,* Columbia, 1981; *A Christmas Story,* Metro-Goldwyn-Mayer/United Artists, 1983; *Songwriter,* Tri-Star, 1984.

PRINCIPAL TELEVISION APPEARANCES—Mini-series: *Space,* CBS, 1985.

PRINCIPAL STAGE APPEARANCES—Honey, *Who's Afraid of Virginia Woolf?,* Broadway production.

ADDRESSES: AGENT—Belson and Klass, 211 S. Beverly Drive, Beverly Hills, CA 90212.*

*   *   *

DiVITO, Joanne   1941-

PERSONAL: Born March 10, 1941, in Chicago, IL; daughter of Uldrich Vincenzo (a naprapath) and Genevieve (a naprapath; maiden name, Gulizia) DiVito; married Chick Yennera (an actor), May 15, 1970 (divorced 1982); children: Nicole. EDUCATION: Attended Amundsen Junior College; studied dance at the Ballet Russe with Anatole Vilzak; studied at the Ballet Theatre with William Dollar; studied choreography with Jaime Rogers and Anthony Tudor.

VOCATION: Choreographer, director, and dancer.

CAREER: PRINCIPAL STAGE WORK—Choreographer: *Jockeys,* 1976; *Gangs,* 1978; *Flashdance Fever,* Marina Hotel, 1983-84; *Growing Pains,* NY, 1985.

PRINCIPAL FILM WORK—Choreographer: *Almost Summer,* Universal, 1977; *Thank God It's Friday* (also known as *TGIF*), Colum-

JOANNE DiVITO

bia, 1978; *Eddie and the Cruisers,* Aurora Productions, 1980; *Little Treasures,* Tri-Star Productions, 1982-83.

Director, *Body Rock,* New World Productions, 1984; *Once Bitten,* Nite-Life Productions, 1985; *Bad Guys,* Tomorrow Entertainment, 1985.

PRINCIPAL TELEVISION WORK—Choreographer: *First Annual Cheerleading Championship,* CBS, 1977; *Second Annual Cheerleading Championship,* CBS, 1978; *Fourth Annual Cheerleading Champanionship,* CBS, 1980.

Videos: *San Say,* Hiroshima, 1983; *Street Beat* (fashion), Norma Kamali, 1983; *You Are,* Lionel Richie, 1983; *Human Touch,* Rick Springfield, 1983; *Supernatural Love,* Donna Summer, 1984; *Swear,* Sheena Easton, 1984; *I Feel for You,* Chaka Khan, 1984; *Like a Surgeon,* Weird Al Yankovic, 1985; also directed, *Bad Guys,* Precious Metal, 1985.

STAGE DEBUT—Ababu Princess, *Kismet,* New York State Theatre, 1965-67.

PRINCIPAL STAGE APPEARANCES—Minnie Minerva, *By Jupiter,* Goodspeed Opera House, East Haddam, CT, 1967; dancer, *Annie Get Your Gun,* New York State Theatre, 1967-68; *West Side Story,* South Shore Music Circus, MA, 1968; Molly Yanoff, *The Education of Hyman Kaplan,* Alvin Theatre, NY, 1969; Ababu Princess, *Kismet,* Dorothy Chandler Pavilion, 1976-77.

MAJOR TOURS—Ababu Princess, *Kismet,* National tour, 1966-67; dancer, *Annie Get Your Gun,* National tour, 1967-68; Wicked Witch, *Disney on Parade,* Canada, U.S., 1970-72; dancer, *Really Raquel,* Las Vegas, 1972-73.

PRINCIPAL TELEVISION APPEARANCES—Movies: *79 Park Avenue,* NBC, 1977; *Amateur Night at the Dixie Bar and Grill,* NBC, 1978; *Jayne Mansfield Story,* CBS, 1979.

Episodic: *Goodtime Girls,* ABC, 1979; *Dreams,* CBS, 1984; *Santa Barbara,* NBC, 1985.

Guest: *Dance Fever,* CBS, 1978.

RELATED CAREER—Owner, DiVito Productions, production company serving corporate and industry entertainment.

AWARDS: American Video Award nomination, 1985, for Chaka Khan's *I Feel for You,*.

MEMBER: Society of Stage Directors and Choreographers (Los Angeles area representative), Screen Actors Guild.

ADDRESSES: AGENT—Christopher Nassif Agency and Associates, 8721 Sunset Blvd., Suite 202, Los Angeles, CA 90069.

*   *   *

DOBSON, Kevin

PERSONAL: Married Susan; children: three. EDUCATION: Attended New York University; studied acting at the Neighborhood Playhouse with Sanford Meisner.

VOCATION: Actor.

KEVIN DOBSON

CAREER: STAGE DEBUT—*The Impossible Years,* National tour, 1970. PRINCIPAL STAGE APPEARANCES—Stanley (understudy), *A Streetcar Named Desire,* Los Angeles.

PRINCIPAL FILM APPEARANCES—*Love Story,* Paramount, 1970; *Klute,* Warner Brothers, 1971; *The French Connection,* Twentieth Century-Fox, 1971.

PRINCIPAL TELEVISION APPEARANCES—Series: *The Mod Squad,* ABC; Detective Bobby Crocker, *Kojak,* CBS, 1973-78; Detective Jack Shannon, *Shannon,* CBS, 1981-82; Patrick MacKenzie, *Knots Landing,* CBS, 1982—.

Movies: *Transplant,* 1979; *Orphan Train,* 1979; *Hardhat and Legs,* 1980; *Reunion,* 1980; *Mark, I Love You,* 1980; *Mickey Spillane's Margin for Murder,* 1981; *Sweet Revenge,* CBS, 1984; also, "Help Wanted," *CBS Afternoon Special.*

AWARDS: United States Jaycees Outstanding Young Man of America award for Professional Achievement and Community Service.

MEMBER: Actors' Equity Association, Screen Actors Guild, American Federation of Television and Radio Artists.

SIDELIGHTS: Kevin Dobson worked as an engineer on the Long Island Railroad, a fireman on the Santa Fe Railroad and as a cab driver, bartender and waiter while in school studying to be an actor. His publicity material informs *CTFT* that his favorite charities are Retinitis Pigmentosa, Muscular Dystrophy and Easter Seals. He enjoys baseball, tennis, golf, skiing and basketball.

ADDRESSES: AGENT—Sutton & Freeman, 8961 Sunset Blvd., Second Floor, Los Angeles, CA 90069.

DONNELLY, Donal   1931-

PERSONAL: First name pronounced "*Doe*-null;" born July 6, 1931, in Bradford, England; son of James (a doctor) and Nora (a teacher; maiden name, O'Connor) Donnelly; married Patricia May Porter (a dancer); children: Damian, Jonathan. EDUCATION: Syng Street Christian Brothers, Dublin, Ireland; studied for the theatre at the Dublin Gate Theatre.

VOCATION: Actor.

CAREER: DEBUT—Robin, *Dr. Faustus,* Dublin Gate Theatre, 1952, for twenty-four performances. NEW YORK DEBUT—Garreth O'Donnell (Gar Private), *Philadelphia, Here I Come,* Helen Hayes Theatre, 1966, for 352 performances. LONDON DEBUT—Tommy Owens, *Shadow of a Gunman,* Lyric Hammersmith Theatre, 1958, for forty-eight performances. PRINCIPAL STAGE APPEARANCES— Sparky, *Sergeant Musgrave's Dance,* Royal Court Theatre, London, 1959; Christy Mahon, *The Playboy of the Western World,* Piccadilly Theatre, then St. Martin's Theatre, London, 1960; Jemmo Fitzgerald, *The Scatterin',* Theatre Royal, Stratford, England, 1962; Ayamonn Breydon, *Red Roses for Me,* Mermaid Theatre, London, 1962; *Philadelphia, Here I Come,* Lyric Theatre, London, 1967; Bri, *Joe Egg,* Brooks Atkinson Theatre, NY, 1968; Milo Tindle, *Sleuth,* St. Martin's Theatre, London, 1970, then Music Box Theatre, NY, 1972, and Ahmanson Theatre, Los Angeles, 1972; George Bernard Shaw, *My Astonishing Self* (one-man show), Dublin Festival, 1976; Dr. Frederick Treves, *The Elephant Man,* Booth Theatre, NY, 1979; Teddy, *The Faith-Healer,* Longacre Theatre, NY, 1979; Maitland, *The Chalk Garden,* Roundabout

DONAL DONNELLY

Theatre, NY, 1982; George Bernard Shaw, *My Astonishing Self,* Players Theatre, NY, 1983; Byrne, *Big Maggie,* Douglas Fairbanks Theatre, NY, 1983; Scrooge, *A Christmas Carol,* Ford's Theatre, Washington, DC, 1984; Coroner Stephens, Harry Britt, Dr. Blinder, *Execution of Justice,* Virginia Theatre, NY, 1986.

MAJOR TOURS—Milo Tindle, *Sleuth,* U.S. and Britain, 1975; *The Last of Mrs. Cheyney,* U.S. 1978; *84 Charing Cross Road,* U.S. and Canadian tour; *My Astonishing Self,* world tour.

FILM DEBUT—Rebel, *Rising of the Moon,* Four Province/John Ford, 1957. PRINCIPAL FILM APPEARANCES—*Gideon's Day* (also known as *Gideon of Scotland Yard*), Columbia, 1958; Willie Cafferty, *Shakes Hands with the Devil,* Pennebaker Productions/United Artists, 1959; *Young Cassidy,* Metro-Goldwyn-Mayer, 1965; *The Knack,* United Artists, 1965; *Up Jumped a Swagman,* 1968; *The Mind of Mr. Soames,* Columbia, 1970; *Waterloo,* Paramount, 1971.

TELEVISION DEBUT—Johnny Boyle, *Juno and the Paycock,* BBC, 1958. PRINCIPAL TELEVISION APPEARANCES—Plays: *Home Is the Hero,* BBC; *The Venetian Twins,* BBC; *The Plough and the Stars,* ITV; *Playboy of the Western World,* ITV; *Sergeant Musgrave's Dance,* ITV.

Series: *Yes—Honestly,* ITV.

AWARDS: Best Actor, Outer Critics Circle Award, Antoinette Perry Award nomination, both 1966, for *Philadelphia, Here I Come;* Best Supporting Actor, Drama Desk Award, *The Faith-Healer,* 1979.

MEMBER: Actors' Equity Association, Screen Actors Guild, American Federation of Television and Radio Artists.

SIDELIGHTS: Donal Donnelly's favorite roles, to date, have been Christy Mahon in *Playboy of the Western World* and Gareth O'Donnell in *Philadelphia, Here I Come.*

ADDRESSES: HOME—Westport, CT. AGENT—William Morris Agency, 1350 Avenue of the Americas, New York, NY 10019.

*   *   *

DOOLEY, Paul   1928-

PERSONAL: Born Paul Brown, February 22, 1928; son of Peter James (a factory worker) and Ruth Irene Brown; married Winifred Holzman (a writer and actress) November 18, 1984; children: (previous marriage) Robin, Adam, Peter, Savannah. EDUCATION: West Virginia University, B.A., speech and drama, 1948-52. MILITARY: U.S. Navy, 1946-48.

VOCATION: Actor and writer.

CAREER: STAGE DEBUT—The Butler, *Holiday,* Mt. Gretna, PA, 1951. NEW YORK DEBUT—Walt Dreary, *The Threepenny Opera,* Off-Broadway. PRINCIPAL STAGE APPEARANCES—Elwood P. Dowd, *Harvey,* Jackson, WY, 1954; Second City Revue; *The Odd Couple,* Broadway; *Adaptation/Next, The White House Murder Case, Hold Me, 'Toinette, Dr. Willy Nilly, The Amazin' Casey Stengel,* all Off-Broadway.

FILM DEBUT—Television reporter, *What's So Bad About Feeling Good,* Universal, 1968. PRINCIPAL FILM APPEARANCES—*The*

PAUL DOOLEY

Out of Towners, Paramount, 1970; *Gravy Train,* Columbia, 1974; *Death Wish,* Paramount, 1974; *Slap Shot,* Universal, 1977; *A Wedding,* Twentieth Century-Fox, 1978; Alex, *A Perfect Couple,* Twentieth Century-Fox, 1979; *Rich Kids,* United Artists, 1979; Ray Stohler, *Breaking Away,* Twentieth Century-Fox, 1979; Wimpy, *Popeye,* Paramount, 1980; *Paternity,* Paramount, 1981; *Endangered Species,* Metro-Goldwyn-Mayer/United Artists, 1982; *Kiss Me Goodbye,* Twentieth Century-Fox, 1982; *Health,* Twentieth Century-Fox, 1982; *Strange Brew,* Metro-Goldwyn-Mayer/United Artists, 1983; *Going Berserk,* Universal, 1983; *Sixteen Candles,* Universal, 1984; *Little Shop of Horrors,* Universal, 1986; *O.C. and Stiggs,* Metro-Goldwyn-Mayer (upcoming); *Big Trouble* (upcoming).

WRITINGS: TELEVISION—*The Electric Company,* PBS. SCREENPLAY—(With Robert Altman and Frank Barhyte) *Health,* Twentieth Century-Fox, 1982.

AWARDS: D.W. Griffith Best Supporting Actor, 1979, for *Breaking Away.*

MEMBER: Actors' Equity Association, Screen Actors Guild, American Federation of Television and Radio Artists.

SIDELIGHTS: Paul Dooley told *CTFT* that his favorite roles are Ray Stohler in *Breaking Away,* Wimpy in *Popeye,* and Alex in *A Perfect Couple.*

ADDRESSES: HOME—New York, NY. AGENT—c/o Sam Cohn, International Creative Management, 40 W. 57th Street, New York, NY 10019.

DORN, Harding   1923-

PERSONAL: Born August 1, 1923, in New York, NY; son of Morris (a designer) and Celia Dorn.

VOCATION: Director, choreographer, producer, and dancer.

CAREER: STAGE DEBUT—Benjamin, *Jacob and his Brother,* Juilliard School of Music, NY, 1936, for fifteen performances. PRINCIPAL STAGE APPEARANCES—In seasons with the Ballet Russe de Monte Carlo, 1948-55: Dance master, *Gaite Parisienne,* prince's friend, *Swan Lake,* cowhand and caller, *Rodeo,* Czardas and Pas de Classique Hongrois, *Raymonda,* head mistress, *Graduation Ball,* Waltz of the Flowers, *Nutcracker,* Sailor, *Frankie and Johnny,* Shepherd Divertissment, *Night Shadow,* Harlequin, *Coppelia,* Bird and the Man, *Seventh Symphony.* Also danced in the ballets: *Virginia Sampler, Le Beau Danube, Rouge et Noir, Ballet Imperial, Madronos, Serenade, The Snow Maiden, Prince Igor, Baiser de la Fee, Giselle.*

At theatres throughout the U.S., Canada and Australia danced in musicals: Simon of Legree, *The King and I;* Harry Beaton, *Brigadoon;* Indian dancer, *Annie Get Your Gun;* dancer, *Lend an Ear;* head dressmaker, *Arabian Nights;* Tommy Djilis, *The Music Man;* dancer, *Merry Widow;* mayor and shriner, *Bye, Bye Birdie;* the Admiral, *Fannie;* various roles, *Little Me.*

PRINCIPAL STAGE WORK—Director, choreographer, and associate producer: *George M; Sweet Charity; The Music Man; Damn Yankees;*

HARDING DORN

My Fair Lady; 70 Girls 70; West Side Story; The Boy Friend; Hello, Dolly!; Fiddler on the Roof; Molly Brown; How to Succeed in Business without Really Trying; Funny Girl; On a Clear Day; I Do, I Do; La Deuce.

Choreographer: *Calamity Jane; Cinderella; Around the World in 80 Days; Tom Sawyer; On a Clear Day; Call Me Madam; Can Can; Peter Pan; Wildcat; Carousel; 110 in the Shade; Camelot; South Pacific; Little Me; Tovarich; West Side Story; Rose Marie; Firefly; Merry Widow; Sound of Music; Funny Girl; Milk and Honey; Gypsy; The King and I; Annie; Mr. President; Bells Are Ringing; Bye, Bye Birdie; Carnival; Oklahoma; Superman; Panama Game; Student Prince; Wizard of Oz; Meet Me in St. Louis.*

Also: Choreographer, director, and co-producer, *Los Pretty Americanos,* Puerto Rico Sheraton, San Juan; choreographer and musical staging, *Little Me,* Mineola Playhouse, NY; choreographer and musical staging, *Mr. Scrooge,* Crest, Toronto, Canada; choreographer and musical staging, *The Music Man,* Melbourne, Australia; director, choreographer, and writer, *The Wyatt Earp Western Review,* Melbourne, Australia; choreographer and musical staging, *The King and I, My Fair Lady, Merry Widow, Brigadoon,* and *Carmen,* all at the St. Paul Civic Opera; choreographer and musical staging, *Die Fledermaus;* director and choreographer, *Revue,* Royal Alexander, Toronto, Canada; creator, *Purely for Pleasure;* choreographer and musical staging, *Lend an Ear, The Day Before Spring, Brigadoon,* all at the Royal Poinciana Playhouse, Palm Beach, FL.

PRINCIPAL FILM WORK—Casting director: *Death Wish,* Paramount, 1974; *Three Days of the Condor,* Paramount, 1975; *Report to the Commissioner,* United Artists, 1975; *The Stepford Wives,* Columbia, 1975; *The Reincarnation of Peter Proud,* American International, 1975; *Aaron Loves Angela,* Columbia, 1975.

PRINCIPAL TELEVISION WORK—Casting director: Movies *Kojack; Queen of the Stardust Ballroom; Life of Ralph Waldo Emmerson.*

RELATED CAREER—Teacher: Studio of Dance Arts, Woodmere, Long Island, NY, 1955-60; Master Classes, Kansas City, MO, 1963-71; University of Missouri, Kansas City, MO; Butler University, Indianapolis, IA; Poughkeepsie Civic Ballet, NY; Showcase Studios and Broadway Arts Studios, NY, 1976-77.

MEMBER: Actors' Equity Association, Society of Stage Directors and Choreographers.

ADDRESSES: HOME—206 E. 67th Street, New York, NY 10021. OFFICE—c/o Jerome Cargill Productions, 97 Reade Street, New York, NY 10013.

*   *   *

DOTRICE, Roy   1925-

PERSONAL: Born May 26, 1925, in Guernsey, Channel Islands, England; son of Louis and Neva (Wilton) Dotrice; married Kay Newman (an actress), August 8, 1947; children: Michele, Karen, Yvette. EDUCATION: Attended Dayton Academy and State of Guernsey Intermediate College. POLITICS: Conservative. RELIGION: Church of England. MILITARY: Royal Air Force, 1940-45.

VOCATION: Actor and director.

CAREER: STAGE DEBUT—Began acting while a prisoner of war in Stalagluft Three, Silesia, Germany, during World War II. LONDON

ROY DOTRICE

DEBUT—*Back Home Revue,* Stoll Theatre, London, 1945, for forty-eight performances. NEW YORK DEBUT—John Aubrey, *Brief Lives,* Golden, 1967, for thirty-five performances. PRINCIPAL STAGE APPEARANCES—Liverpool Repertory, Manchester Repertory, and Oldham Repertory, 1945-55; founded the Guernsey Repertory Theatre Company as an actor and director, 1955-57.

With the Shakespeare Memorial Theatre Company from 1958-60, and when it became the Royal Shakespeare Company, Stratford on Avon, in 1961, he contracted with them from 1961-65. Among the roles he played during that entire period: Egeus, *A Midsummer Night's Dream,* and Duke of Burgundy, *King Lear,* both 1959; Vincentio, *The Taming of the Shrew,* and Antenor, *Troilus and Cressida,* both 1960; Father Ambrose, *The Devils,* and Firs, *The Cherry Orchard,* both 1961; Simon Chachava, *The Caucasian Chalk Circle,* William Marshall, *Curtmantle,* and Ajax, *Troilus and Cressida,* 1962; Caliban, *The Tempest,* title role, *Julius Caesar,* and as the Duke of Bedford, *Henry VI,* title role, *Edward IV,* and Edward IV, *Richard III,* in performances collectively titled *The Wars of the Roses,* 1963; John of Gaunt, *Richard II,* Hotspur, *Henry IV, Part I,* Shallow, *Henry IV, Part II,* and repeated his roles in *The War of the Roses,* 1964.

Repeated above roles in *The Wars of the Roses,* Aldwych Theatre, London, 1964; Jan Puntila, *Squire Puntila and His Servant Matti,* and in a concert reading of *The Investigation,* both at the Aldwych Theatre, London, 1965; John Aubrey, *Brief Lives* (one man play), Hampstead Theatre Club, London, 1967; Man, *World War 2 1/2,* New Theatre, London, 1967; John Morley, *The Latent Heterosexual,* and William Clark Brackman, *God Bless,* both with the

Royal Shakespeare Company at the Aldwych Theatre, London, 1968; John Aubrey, *Brief Lives,* Criterion Theatre, 1969; Peer, *Peer Gynt,* Chichester Festival, 1970; Matthew Cragg, *The Hero,* Lyceum Theatre, Edinburgh, 1970.

James Blanch, *One at Night,* Royal Court Theatre, London, 1971; Adam, *Mother Adam,* Arts Theatre, London, 1971; Dr. Arnold, *Tom Brown's Schooldays,* Cambridge Theatre, London, 1972; title role, *Gomes,* Queen's Theatre, London, 1973; Stranger, *The Dragon Variation,* Duke of York's Theatre, London, 1977; Boanerges, *The Apple Cart,* Phoenix Theatre, London, 1977; Professor Van Helsing, *The Passion of Dracula,* Queen's Theatre, London, 1978; Fagin, *Oliver!,* Albery Theatre, London, 1979; title role, *Mister Lincoln,* Capital Theatre, Edmonton, Alberta, Canada, 1979, then at the Morosco Theatre, NY, 1980.

Fortune, NY, 1981; *A Life,* Morosco Theatre, NY, 1981, Falstaff, *Henry IV* and Polonius, *Hamlet,* both with the American Shakespeare Festival, Stratford, CT, 1982-83; *Kingdoms,* Cort Theatre, NY, 1983; title role, *Churchill,* Ford's Theatre, Washington, DC, then Huntington Hartford Theatre, Los Angeles, CA, 1983; *The Genius,* Mark Taper Forum, Los Angeles, CA, 1984; *Down an Alley Filled with Cats,* Plaza Theatre, Dallas, TX, 1984; Dr. Stockman, *Enemy of the People,* Roundabout Theatre, NY, 1985; *Great Expectations,* Old Vic Theatre, London, 1985; David Bliss, *Hayfever,* Music Box Theatre, NY, 1985-86, the Kennedy Center for the Performing Arts, Washington, DC, 1986.

MAJOR TOURS—*Move Over Mrs. Markham,* Australian cities, 1972; Oliver Crown, *Lucy Crown,* UK cities, 1976; Sir Anthony Eden, *Suez,* UK cities, 1977; Iago, *Othello,* Australian cities, 1978.

FILM DEBUT—*Heroes of Telemark,* Columbia, 1964. PRINCIPAL FILM APPEARANCES—*A Twist of Sand,* United Artists, 1968; *Lock Up Your Daughters,* Columbia, 1969; *Buttercup Chain,* Columbia, 1971; *Nicholas and Alexandra,* Columbia, 1971; *Tomorrow,* 1972; *One of Those Things,* 1972; *Cheech and Chong's The Corsican Brothers,* Orion, 1984; and as Leopold Mozart, *Amadeus,* Orion, 1984; *The Eliminators,* 1986; *Shaka Zulu* (upcoming).

PRINCIPAL TELEVISION APPEARANCES—Specials: *Dear Liar; The Caretaker; Brief Lives; Imperial Palace; Misleading Cases; Clochemerle; Dickens of London; Family Reunion.*

Episodic: *Magnum P.I.; Remington Steele; Hart to Hart; Tales of the Gold Monkey.*

MEMBER: Actor's Equity Association, Screen Actors Guild, Garrick Club, Players Club.

AWARDS: Emmy Award, 1965, for *The Caretaker;* Television Actor of the Year, BBC, 1968, for *Brief Lives;* Best Actor, Antoinette Perry Award nomination, 1981, for *A Life;* Dramalogue Award, 1982 and 1984.

SIDELIGHTS: CTFT learned that while he was serving his country durning World War II as an air gunner for the Royal Air Force, Dotrice was captured by the Germans and was held a prisoner of war from 1942-45. Roy Dotrice's London debut, the revue *Back Home,* was performed as a benefit for the Red Cross by former prisoners of war.

Dotrice holds the world record for longest running performance (over four hundred) for his portrayal of John Aubrey in *Brief Lives.*

ADDRESSES: HOME—London. AGENT—c/o Ann Hutton, Hutton Management, 200 Fulham Road, London SW 10, England; c/o Robert Lantz, Lantz Office, 888 Seventh Avenue, New York, NY 10106.

*   *   *

DRUMMOND, Alice   1928-

PERSONAL: Born Alice Ruyter, May 21, 1928, in Providence, RI; daughter of Arthur (an auto mechanic) and Sarah Irene (a secretary; maiden name, Alker) Ruyter; married Paul Drummond, March 3, 1951 (divorced, 1975). EDUCATION: Brown University, B.A.

VOCATION: Actress.

CAREER: PRINCIPAL STAGE APPEARANCES—Broadway productions: *You Can't Take It with You; The Ballad of the Sad Cafe;* Eloisa Brace, *Malcolm;* Mrs. Lee, *The Chinese and Dr. Fish; Thieves; Summer Brave; Some of My Best Friends.* Off-Broadway productions: Mrs. Carpenter, *The Carpenters;* Anne of Cleves, *Royal Gambit;* Marion, *Go Show Me a Dragon;* Lucy and Martha, *Gallows Humor;* Bea, *A Toy for the Clowns;* Isabel, *The Blue Boy in Black;* Boudicca, *The Giants Dance;* Mrs. Barker, *The American Dream;* Persephone, *Enter a Free Man; Boy Meets Girl* and *Secret Service,* both Phoenix Theatre Company; *A Memory of Two Mondays; Endgame,* Samuel Beckett Theatre.

Sweet Bird of Youth, Haymarket Theatre, London, England, 1985.

PRINCIPAL FILM APPEARANCES—*Where's Poppa,* United Artists,

ALICE DRUMMOND

1970; *Man on a Swing,* Paramount, 1974; *Thieves,* Paramount, 1977; *King of the Gypsies,* Paramount, 1978; *Hide in Plain Sight,* United Artists, 1980; *Eyewitness,* Twentieth Century-Fox, 1981; *Ghostbusters,* Columbia, 1984; *Animal Behavior.*

PRINCIPAL TELEVISION APPEARANCES—Series: Frances Heine, *Park Place,* CBS, 1981; *The Best of Families.*

Episodic: *Where the Heart Is; The Guiding Light; Search for Tomorrow; Love of Life; Dark Shadows; As the World Turns; Father Brown, Detective.*

Specials: *Secret Service,* PBS; Mrs. Ewing, *Particular Men,* PBS; Mommy, *The Sandbox,* PBS.

Movie: Mrs. Milligan, *The Milligan Case.*

MEMBER: Actors' Equity Association, Screen Actors Guild, American Federation of Television and Radio Artists.

AWARDS: Antoinette Perry Award nomination, for *The Chinese and Dr. Fish;* Drama Desk award nomination, for *A Memory of Two Mondays.*

ADDRESSES: HOME—New York, NY 10022. AGENT—STE Representation Ltd., 888 Seventh Avenue, New York, NY 10106.

*   *   *

DUELL, William

PERSONAL: Born August 30, in Corinth, NY; son of Leon George (an employee of International Paper Company) and E. Janet (Harrington) Duell. EDUCATION: Illinois Wesleyan University, B.A., 1949; Yale School of Drama, M.F.A., 1952. MILITARY: U.S. Navy.

VOCATION: Actor.

CAREER: STAGE DEBUT—Filch, messenger, *The Threepenny Opera,* Theater de Lys, NY, 1954 (continued in role through 1961, for 2,474 performances). PRINCIPAL STAGE APPEARANCES—Flute, *A Midsummer Night's Dream,* Wollman Arena, Central Park, Delacorte Mobile Theatre, NY, 1961; Cook, *A Cook for Mr. General,* Playhouse, NY, 1961; Willie, *The Barroom Monks,* McCann, *A Portrait of the Artist as a Young Man,* Martinique Theatre, NY, 1962; Horace Wells and Merlie Ryan, *The Ballad of the Sad Cafe,* Martin Beck Theatre, NY, 1963; Nym, *Henry V,* Biondello, *The Taming of the Shrew,* both at Delacorte Mobile Theatre, NY, 1965; Garbage, *Illya Darling,* Mark Hellinger Theatre, NY, 1967; Peter Thumb, *The Memorandum,* Public Theatre, NY, 1968; Peter, *Romeo and Juliet,* Delacorte Theatre, NY, 1968; Earl Williams, *The Front Page,* Plumstead Playhouse, Mineola, NY, 1968; Congressional Custodian Andrew McNair, *1776,* 46th Street Theatre, NY, 1969.

Barber, *Man of La Mancha,* Parker Playhouse, Fort Lauderdale, FL, 1972; Jake, *Threepenny Opera,* Vivian Beaumont Theatre, 1976, then Delacorte Theatre, NY, 1977; various roles, *Stages,* Belasco Theatre, NY, 1978; Bobchinsky, *The Inspector General,* Circle in the Square, NY, 1978; Billy, *That's It, Folks,* Playwrights Horizons, NY, 1983; Alcott and Lonesome Charley, *Romance Language,* Playwrights Horizons, NY, 1984; Pedant, *The Taming of the Shrew,* American Shakespeare Festival, Stratford, CT, 1985; Antonio, *The Marriage of Figaro,* Circle in the Square, NY, 1985.

WILLIAM DUELL

TELEVISION DEBUT—Court Clerk, "The Trial of Charlie Christmas," *Gulf Playhouse*, NBC, 1952. PRINCIPAL TELEVISION APPEARANCES—Episodic: Obie, "A Touch of Summer," *Kraft Television Theatre*, NBC, 1954; various roles, *Kraft Television Theatre*, NBC, 1954-57; Eli Bence, "The Trial of Lizzie Borden," *Omnibus*, ABC, 1957; Riordan, "American Trial by Jury," *Omnibus*, NBC, 1957; messboy, "Billy Budd," *Dupont Show of the Month*, CBS, 1959; pirate, "Treasure Island," *Dupont Show of the Month*, CBS, 1960; hoodlum, *Pontiac Star Parade*, NBC, 1960; Master Harringate, "The Three Musketeers," *Family Classics*, CBS, 1960.

Hotel Clerk, "A Very Cautious Boy," *Naked City*, ABC, 1961; Coyle, "The Cruel Hook," *The Defenders*, CBS, 1963; actor, "The Maze," *Look Up and Live*, CBS, 1964; medical examiner, "What Can Go Wrong?," *Trials of O'Brien*, CBS, 1965; bellboy, "Ulysses and the Republic," *Hawk*, ABC, 1966; Walt, "Fast Gun," *N.Y.P.D.*, ABC, 1967; Earl Williams, *Front Page*, WNEW, NY, 1970; Howard Ace, "Meet Mr. Meat," *On Our Own*, CBS, 1977.

Movies: Sam, *Big Henry and the Polka Dot Kid*, NBC, 1976; Mayor Holderness, *Summer of My German Soldier*, NBC, 1978; Rooster, *My Old Man*, CBS, 1979; Bob Daly, *Casey Stengel*, PBS, 1981; Parsons, *Sherlock Holmes*, HBO, 1981.

Series: Johnny the Snitch, *Police Squad*, ABC, 1982.

FILM DEBUT—A hustler, *The Hustler*, Twentieth Century-Fox,

1961. PRINCIPAL FILM APPEARANCES—Gas station boss, *Black Like Me*, Walter Read-Sterling, 1964; Andrew McNair, *1776*, Columbia, 1972; meek man, *The Happy Hooker*, Cannon, 1975; Sefelt, *One Flew Over the Cuckoo's Nest*, United Artists, 1975; polygraph operator, *Without a Trace*, Twentieth Century-Fox, 1983; Lenny, *Mrs. Soffel*, Twentieth Century-Fox, 1984; Mr. Jenkins, *Grace Quigley*, Cannon, 1985.

ADDRESSES: AGENT—Triad Artists, Inc., 888 Seventh Avenue, Suite 1602, New York, NY 10036.

*   *   *

DUFFY, Patrick   1949-

PERSONAL: Born March 17, 1949, in Townsend, Montreal, Canada; married Carlyn; children: two sons. EDUCATION: Attended the University of Washington.

VOCATION: Actor.

CAREER: PRINCIPAL TELEVISION APPEARANCES—Series: Mark Harris, *The Man from Atlantis*, NBC, 1977-78; Bobby Ewing, *Dallas*, CBS, 1978-85; 1986—.

Movies: *Hurricane*, 1973; *Enola Gay: The Men, the Mission, the Atomic Bomb*, 1980; *Cry for the Strangers*, 1982; *Strong Medicine*, syndicated, 1986; also appeared in *The Man Who Looks Like Me*.

Specials: *The Last of Mrs. Lincoln*.

Episodic: *Switch*.

PRINCIPAL STAGE APPEARANCES—Has appeared with the San Diego Shakespeare Festival and in off-Broadway productions.

RELATED CAREER—Teacher of mime and movement, Seattle, WA.

ADDRESSES: OFFICE—c/o *Dallas*, CBS Television City, 7800 Beverly Blvd., Los Angeles, CA 90036.*

*   *   *

DUKE, Patty   1946-

PERSONAL: Full name, Anna Marie Duke; born December 14, 1946, in New York, NY; daughter of John P. and Frances (McMahon) Duke; married John Astin (an actor), 1973 (divorced); married Michael Pearce, March 15, 1986; children: (first marriage) Mackenzie (a son). EDUCATION: Graduated from Quintano's School for Young Professionals.

VOCATION: Actress.

CAREER: PRINCIPAL FILM APPEARANCES—*I'll Cry Tomorrow*, Metro-Goldwyn-Mayer, 1955; *Somebody Up There Likes Me*, Metro-Goldwyn-Mayer, 1957; *The Goddess*, Columbia, 1958; *Happy Anniversary*, 1959; Helen Keller, *The Miracle Worker*, United Artists, 1962; *Billie*, United Artists, 1965; *Valley of the Dolls*, 1967; *My Sweet Charlie* (originally a television movie), Universal, 1970; *Me, Natalie*, National General, 1969; *You'll Like My Mother*, Universal, 1972; *The Swarm*, Warner Brothers, 1978; *By Design*, Canadian, 1981; *Willy Nilly*, 1984.

PRINCIPAL TELEVISION APPEARANCES—Series: Patty/Cathy Lane, *Patty Duke Show,* ABC, 1963-66; Molly Quinn, *It Takes Two,* ABC, 1982-83; *Hail to the Chief,* ABC, 1985.

Episodic: *Armstrong Circle Theatre,* 1955; *U.S. Steel Hour,* 1959; *All's Fair,* CBS, 1982.

Movies: *The Prince and the Pauper,* 1957; *Wuthering Heights,* 1958; *Swiss Family Robinson,* 1958; *Meet Me in St. Louis,* 1959; *The Power and the Glory,* 1961; *My Sweet Charlie,* 1970; Annie Sullivan, *The Miracle Worker,* 1979; *Before and After,* 1979; *The Baby Sitter,* 1980; *The Women's Room,* 1980; *Something So Right,* 1982; also appeared in *Women in White.*

Mini-Series: Bernadette Hennessey Armagh, *Captains and the Kings,* NBC, 1976-77; Martha Washington, *George Washington,* CBS, 1984.

PRINCIPAL STAGE APPEARANCES—Helen Keller, *The Miracle Worker,* 1959-61; *Isle of Children,* 1962.

WRITINGS: BOOKS—(Co-author) *Surviving Sexual Assault,* 1983.

MEMBER: Screen Actors Guild (president, 1985—), American Federation of Television and Radio Artists.

AWARDS: Theatre World Award, 1959-60; Best Supporting Actress, Academy Award, 1963, for *The Miracle Worker;* Best Actress, Golden Globe, 1970, for *Me, Natalie;* Outstanding Single Performance by an Actress in a Leading Role, Emmy, 1970, for *My Sweet Charlie;* Outstanding Lead Actress in a Limited Series, Emmy, 1976, for *Captains and the Kings;* Outstanding Lead Actress in a Limited Series or Special, Emmy, 1979, for *The Miracle Worker.*

ADDRESSES: AGENT—Creative Artists Agency, 1888 Century Park E., Suite 1400, Los Angeles, CA 90067.*

*   *   *

DURANG, Christopher   1949-

PERSONAL: Born January 2, 1949, in Montclair, NJ; son of Francis Ferdinand (an architect) and Patricia (a secretary) Durang. EDUCATION: Harvard University, B.A., 1971; Yale University, School of Drama, M.F.A., 1974.

VOCATION: Playwright and actor.

CAREER: PRINCIPAL STAGE APPEARANCES—At the Yale School of Drama: Gustaf, *Urlicht,* 1971; Darryl, *Better Dead Than Sorry,* 1972; performer, *The Life Story of Mitzi Gaynor, or Gyp,* 1973; Bruce, *Happy Birthday, Montpelier Pizz-zazz,* 1974; Emcee, *When Dinah Shore Ruled the Earth,* 1975.

At the Yale Repertory Theatre: Chorus, *The Frogs,* 1974; student, *The Possessed,* 1974; Alyosha, *The Idiots Karamazov,* 1974; performer, *I Don't Generally Like Poetry But Have You Read "Trees?,"* NY, 1973; performer, *Das Lusitania Songspiel,* 1976, 1980.

Also, young cashier, *Hotel Play,* NY, 1981; Wallace, *The Birthday Present,* Circle Rep, NY, 1983.

WRITINGS: PLAYS PUBLISHED, PRODUCED—*The Nature and Purpose of the Universe,* Northampton, MA, 1971, NY, 1975; *'dentity Crisis,* Cambridge, MA, 1971, New Haven, CT, 1975;

CHRISTOPHER DURANG

Better Dead Than Sorry, New Haven, CT, 1972, NY, 1975; (with Albert Innaurato) *I Don't Generally Like Poetry But Have You Read "Trees?,"* New Haven, CT, 1972, Manhattan Theatre Club, 1973; (with Albert Innaurato) *The Life Story of Mitzi Gaynor, or Gyp,* New Haven, CT, 1973; *The Marriage of Bette and Boo,* New Haven, CT, Yale Theatre, 1973, revised NY, 1979; (with Albert Innaurato) *The Idiots Karamazov,* Yale Theatre, New Haven, CT, 1974; *Titanic,* New Haven, CT, 1974, NY, 1976; *Death Comes to Us All, Mary Agnes,* New Haven, CT, 1975; (with Wendy Wasserstein) *When Dinah Shore Ruled the Earth,* New Haven, CT, 1975; *Das Lusitania Songspiel,* NY, 1976, 1980; *A History of the American Film,* Hartford Stage Company, CT, 1976, NY, 1978; *The Vietnamization of New Jersey,* New Haven, CT, 1977, NY, 1978.

Sister Mary Ignatius Explains It All for You and *The Actor's Nightmare,* Westside Arts Theatre, NY, 1982; *Beyond Therapy,* Brooks Atkinson Theatre, NY, 1982, Gate at the Latchmere Theatre, London, 1983; *Baby with the Bath Water,* American Repertory Theatre, Cambridge, MA, 1983-84; *Marriage of Bette and Boo,* Public, NY, 1985.

MEMBER: Dramatists Guild, Writers Guild, Actors' Equity Association, American Society of Composers, Authors and Publishers.

AWARDS: CBS fellowship, 1975; Rockefeller grant, 1976; Guggenheim playwriting fellowship, 1979; Kenyon Festival Playwriting Award, 1983; Obie Award, 1984, for *Sister Mary Ignatius Explains It All for You.*

ADDRESSES: HOME—New York, NY. AGENT—c/o Helen Merrill, Helen Merrill Agency, 337 W. 22nd Street, New York, NY 10011.

DUTTON, Charles S.   1951-

BRIEF ENTRY: Actor. In 1985, Charles S. Dutton received critical acclaim as Levee, the explosive trumpet player who fatally wounds a member of his band in the Broadway production of *Ma Rainey's Black Bottom*. Just prior to this role, Dutton had been making a name for himself as an important actor in plays ranging from Shakespeare to Brecht, but his role as Levee comes closest to who the actor is. Born and raised in a Baltimore housing project, Dutton dropped out of school at age thirteen and found himself in jail at age seventeen after being convicted of murder. Seven years later he was released, but was behind bars again within five months for possession of a weapon. The sentence for this crime was three years. An additional eight years was added to this sentence when he was accused of being the ring leader in a prison riot. During this time, he received a copy of Douglas Turner Ward's *A Day of Absence* and with the help of a social studies instructor, Dutton formed a drama group and performed the play for the prison. Shortly after this, a near fatal stabbing in the neck disabled Dutton for nearly two years. In his own opinion, his choice not to take revenge on his attacker has helped him to be where he is today. After recovery, Dutton was allowed to attend the nearby Hagerstown Junior College after passing a high school equivalency test and when he was released in 1976, he enrolled at Towson State University, Maryland, where he majored in theatre. He graduated in 1978 and with the help of his mentor, Paul Berman, he received a scholarship to the Yale School of Drama.*

DUVALL, Shelley   1949-

PERSONAL: Born 1949, in Houston, TX; daughter of Robert and Bobby Duvall.

VOCATION: Actress and producer.

CAREER: FILM DEBUT—*Brewster McCloud*, Metro-Goldwyn-Mayer, 1970. PRINCIPAL FILM APPEARANCES—*McCabe and Mrs. Miller*, Warner Brothers, 1971; *Thieves Like Us*, United Artists, 1974; *Nashville*, Paramount, 1975; *Buffalo Bill and the Indians, or Sitting Bull's History Lesson*, United Artists, 1976; *Three Women*, Twentieth Century-Fox, 1977; *Annie Hall*, United Artists, 1977; Olive Oyl, *Popeye*, Paramount, 1979; *The Shining*, Warner Brothers, 1980; *Time Bandits*, Embassy, 1981.

PRINCIPAL TELEVISION APPEARANCES—*Bernice Bobs Her Hair*, PBS, 1977.

PRINCIPAL TELEVISION WORK—Executive producer, *Faerie Tale Theatre*, Showtime, 1983—; executive producer, *Tall Tales and Legends*, Showtime, 1985—.

MEMBER: Screen Actors Guild.

ADDRESSES: AGENT—Creative Artists Agency, 1888 Century Park E., Suite 1400, Los Angeles, CA 90067.*

E

EBSEN, Buddy   1908-

PERSONAL: Full name, Christian Ebsen, Jr.; born April 2, 1908; married; children: Bonnie. EDUCATION: Attended University of Florida, Rollins College.

VOCATION: Actor and dancer.

CAREER: STAGE DEBUT—Dancer, *Whoopee*, 1928. PRINCIPAL STAGE APPEARANCES—*Flying Colors*, Broadway production, 1932; *Ziegfeld Follies*, Broadway production, 1934; *Good Night, Ladies*, Chicago, 1942; *The Male Animal*, Broadway production, 1952; *Take Her, She's Mine; Our Town*.

FILM DEBUT—*Broadway Melody of 1936*, Metro-Goldwyn-Mayer, 1935. PRINCIPAL FILM APPEARANCES—*Born to Dance*, Metro-Goldwyn-Mayer, 1936; *Captain January*, 1936; *Banjo on My Knee*, 1936; *Broadway Melody of 1938*, Metro-Goldwyn-Mayer, 1938; *Yellow Jack*, Metro-Goldwyn-Mayer, 1938; *The Girl of the Golden West*, Metro-Goldwyn-Mayer, 1938; *Four Girls in White*, Metro-Goldwyn-Mayer, 1938; *My Lucky Star*, 1938; *The Kid from Texas*, Metro-Goldwyn-Mayer, 1939; *They Met in Argentina*, RKO, 1941; *Parachute Battalion*, RKO, 1941; *Sing Your Worries Away*, RKO, 1942; *Under Mexicali Stars*, Republic, 1950; *Thunder in God's Country*, Republic, 1951; *Silver City Bonanza*, Republic, 1951; *The Rodeo King and the Senorita*, Republic, 1951; *Utah Train Wagon*, Republic, 1951; *Night People*, Twentieth Century-Fox, 1954; *Red Garters*, 1954; George Russel, *Davy Crockett, King of the Wild Frontier*, Buena Vista, 1955; George Russel, *Davy Crockett and the River Pirates*, Buena Vista, 1956; *Attack*, United Artists, 1956; *Fury River*, Metro-Goldwyn-Mayer, 1959; *Breakfast at Tiffany's*, Paramount, 1961; *Mail Order Bride*, Metro-Goldwyn-Mayer, 1963; *The One and Only Genuine Original Family Band*, Buena Vista, 1968.

PRINCIPAL TELEVISION APPEARANCES—Series: Sgt. Hunk Marriner, *Northwest Passage*, NBC, 1958-59; Jed Clampett, *The Beverly Hillbillies*, CBS, 1962-71; title role, *Barnaby Jones*, CBS, 1973-80; Roy Houston, *Matt Houston*, ABC, 1984-85.

Episodic: *ABC Drama Shorts;* George Russel, "Davy Crockett," *Disneyland*, ABC, 1954-55; *Hawaii Five-0; Gunsmoke;* others.

RELATED CAREER—Dancer, entertainer, nightclubs and tours.

SIDELIGHTS: CTFT learned that Buddy Ebsen partnered with his sister Vilma when he danced in nightclubs and on tour in the United States.

ADDRESSES: AGENT—James McHugh Agency, 8150 Beverly Blvd., Suite 206, Los Angeles, CA 90048.*

ECKART, Jean   1921-

PERSONAL: Born Jean Levy, August 18, 1921 in Glencoe, IL; daughter of Herbert and Catharyn (Rubel) Levy; married William J. Eckart (a designer and producer). EDUCATION: Attended Tulane University and Yale University.

VOCATION: Set, lighting, and costume designer and producer.

CAREER: PRINCIPAL STAGE WORK—Set and lighting designer (in collaboration with her husband; all Broadway productions unless otherwise noted): *Glad Tidings*, 1951; *To Dorothy, a Son*, 1951; *Gertie*, 1952; *Maya*, 1953; *The Scarecrow*, 1953; *The Little Clay Cart*, 1953; *Dear Pigeon*, 1953; *Oh Men! Oh Women!*, 1953; *The Golden Apple*, Phoenix Theatre, NY, 1954; *Wedding Breakfast*, 1954; *Portrait of a Lady*, 1954; *Damn Yankees*, 1955; *Reuben, Reuben*, 1955; *Mister Johnson*, 1956; *L'il Abner*, St. James Theatre, NY, 1956; *Damn Yankees*, London production, 1957; *Livin' the Life*, 1957; *Copper and Brass*, NY, 1957; *The Body Beautiful*, NY, 1958; *Once Upon a Mattress*, Phoenix Theatre, then Winter Garden Theatre, NY, 1959; *Fiorello!*, Broadhurst Theatre, NY, 1960; *Viva Madison Avenue!*, 1960; *Once Upon a Mattress*, London production, 1960.

The Happiest Girl in the World, Martin Beck Theatre, NY, 1961; *Let It Ride!*, Eugene O'Neill Theatre, NY, 1961; *Take Her, She's Mine*, NY, 1961; *Oh Dad, Poor Dad, Mama's Hung You in the Closet and I'm Feelin' So Sad*, NY, 1962; *Never Too Late*, NY, 1962; *She Loves Me*, Eugene O'Neill Theatre, NY, 1963; *Never Too Late*, London production, 1963; *Here's Love*, Shubert Theatre, NY, 1963; *Too Much Johnson*, 1964; *Anyone Can Whistle*, Majestic Theatre, NY, 1964; *She Loves Me*, London production, 1964; *All About Elsie*, New York World's Fair, 1964; *Fade Out—Fade In*, Mark Hellinger Theatre, NY, 1964; *A Sign of Affection*, 1965; *Flora, the Red Menace*, Alvin Theatre, NY, 1965; *The Zulu and the Zayda*, Cort Theatre, NY, 1965; *Oh Dad, Poor Dad, Mama's Hung You in the Closet and I'm Feelin' So Sad*, London production, 1965.

Mame, Winter Garden Theatre, NY, 1966; *Agatha Sue, I Love You*, NY, 1966; *A Midsummer Night's Dream*, American Shakespeare Festival, Stratford, CT, 1967; *Hallelujah, Baby*, NY, 1967; *The Education of H*Y*M*A*N* K*A*P*L*A*N*, 1968; *Maggie Flynn*, NY, 1968; *A Mother's Kisses*, NY, 1968; *The Fig Leaves are Falling*, NY, 1969; *A Way of Life*, NY, 1969; *Mame*, London production, 1969; *Norman, Is That You?*, NY, 1970; *Sensations*, Off-Broadway production, NY, 1970; *Of Mice and Men*, NY, 1974; *Mame* (based on original design by Jean and William Eckart), Gershwin Theatre, NY, 1983.

Costume designer: *Damn Yankees*, 1955; *Mister Johnson*, 1956; *Fiorello!*, 1960.

MAJOR TOURS—Set and lighting designer: *Where's Charley?*, 1966.

PRINCIPAL FILM WORK—Costume designer, *The Pajama Game*, Warner Brothers, 1957; set and costume designer, *Damn Yankees*, Warner Brothers, 1958; set and costume designer, *The Night They Raided Minsky's*, United Artists, 1968.

PRINCIPAL TELEVISION WORK—Has worked in television as a designer since 1950.

ADDRESSES: OFFICE—Fourteen St. Luke's Place, New York, NY 10014.

*   *   *

EDEN, Barbara   1934-

PERSONAL: Born Barbara Jean Huffman, August 23, 1934, in Tucson, AZ; daughter of Harrison Connor and Alice Mary (Franklin) Huffman; married Michael Ansara (an actor), January 17, 1958 (divorced, 1974); married Charles Donald Ferget (a publishing executive), September, 1977 (divorced, 1982); children: (first marriage) Michael. EDUCATION: Attended San Francisco City College; studied at the San Francisco Conservatory of Music and the Elizabeth Holloway School of Theatre.

VOCATION: Actress.

CAREER: TELEVISION DEBUT—*The West Point Story*, 1956. PRINCIPAL TELEVISION APPEARANCES—Series: Title role, *I Dream of Jeannie*, NBC, 1965-70; Stella Johnson, *Harper Valley PTA*, 1980-82.

Episodic: *I Love Lucy*.

Movies: *The Feminist and the Fuzz*, ABC, 1971; *Guess Who's Sleeping in My Bed*, 1973; *The Stranger Within*, 1974; *Let's Switch*, 1975; *How to Break Up a Happy Divorce*, 1976; *I Dream of Jeannie: Twenty Years Later*, NBC, 1986; also appeared in *How to Marry a Millionaire*.

PRINCIPAL FILM APPEARANCES—*Back from Eternity*, Universal, 1956; *Twelve Hours to Kill*, Twentieth Century-Fox, 1960; *Flaming Star*, Twentieth Century-Fox, 1960; *Voyage to the Bottom of the Sea*, 1961; *Five Weeks in a Balloon*, Twentieth Century-Fox, 1962; *Wonderful World of the Brothers Grimm*, Metro-Goldwyn-Mayer, 1963; *Seven Faces of Dr. Lao*, Metro-Goldwyn-Mayer, 1964; *The Brass Bottle*, Universal, 1964; *Ride the Wild Surf*, Columbia, 1964; *The New Interns*, Columbia, 1964; *Harper Valley PTA*, Metro-Goldwyn-Mayer, 1978.*

*   *   *

EDWARDS, Ralph

PERSONAL: Full name, Ralph Livingston Edwards; born in Merino, CO; son of Henry Livingston and Minnie Mae (Browns) Edwards; married Barbara Jean Sheldon, September 19, 1939; children: Christine Alison, Gary Livingston, Lauren Avery. EDUCATION: University of California, A.B., 1935; RELIGION: Presbyterian.

VOCATION: Television and radio producer, program creator, master of ceremonies, writer, announcer, and actor.

CAREER: PRINCIPAL RADIO WORK—Writer, actor, producer, and announcer, KROW, Oakland, CA, 1929-35; actor, producer, announcer, and writer, KFSO and KFRC, Oakland and San Francisco 1935-36; announcer, CBS and NBC, NY, 1936-40; creator, producer, and master of ceremonies, *Mr. Hush and Walking Man* (charity contests), NY, 1940-54; creator and master of ceremonies, *Truth or Consequences;* master of ceremonies, *This Is Your Life,* 1948-50; creator, producer, *Place the Face*.

PRINCIPAL TELEVISION WORK—Creator and producer, *It Could Be You* (also known as *The Bill Gwin Show, This Could Be You,* and *This Is My Song*), ABC, 1951-52; producer, creator, and master of ceremonies, *This Is Your Life*, NBC, 1952-61; master of ceremonies, *Ralph Edwards Show*, NBC, 1952; creator and producer, *Place the Face*, NBC, 1953, CBS, 1954, NBC, 1954; creator and producer, *The End of the Rainbow*, NBC, 1958; creator and producer, *About Faces*, 1959; producer, *The Wide Country*, NBC, 1961; producer, *Who in the World*, CBS, 1962; producer, *Woody Woodbury Show*, 1969; producer, *Name That Tune*, NBC, 1974-81; producer, *The Cross-Wits*, syndicated, 1975-81; producer, *Knockout*, 1977; executive producer, *The People's Court*, syndicated, 1981—.

PRINCIPAL FILM APPEARANCES—*Seven Days Leave*, 1945.

PRINCIPAL RADIO APPEARANCES—*Radio Stars in Parade*, 1947; *Bamboo Blonde*, 1948; *Beat the Band*, 1949.

MEMBER: Berkeley Fellows, University of California; Robert Gordon Sproul Association (founder and chairman, 1965-66); Bohemian Club; Los Angeles Country Club; Los Angeles 100 Club; American Cancer Society (national crusade chairman); National Easter Seal Society (chairman), 1973.

AWARDS: Eisenhower Award for highest E bond salesman, 1946; Best Game and Audience Participation Show, Emmy, 1951, for *Truth or Consequences;* Best Audience Participation, Quiz, or Panel Show, Emmy, 1954, for *This Is Your Life;* Carbon Mike Award, Pacific Pioneer Broadcasters; Alumnus of the Year, University of California, 1965; honorary awards: LL.D., Pepperdine University and LH.D., St. Mary of the Plains College.

ADDRESSES: OFFICE—1717 Highland Avenue, Los Angeles, CA 90028.*

*   *   *

ELLIOTT, Sam   1944-

PERSONAL: Born August 9, 1944; married Katharine Ross (an actress). EDUCATION: Attended University of Oregon.

VOCATION: Actor.

CAREER: PRINCIPAL TELEVISION APPEARANCES—Movies: *The Challenge*, 1970; *Assault on the Wayne*, 1970; *The Blue Knight*, 1975; *I Will Fight No More Forever*, 1975; *The Sacketts*, 1978; *Shadow Riders*, 1982; *A Death in California*, ABC, 1985; also, *Once an Eagle; Aspen*.

Series: Chance McKenzie, *Yellow Rose*, NBC, 1983-84.

PRINCIPAL FILM APPEARANCES—*The Games*, Universal, 1970; *Frogs*, American International, 1972; *Molly and Lawless John*, 1972; *The Lifeguard*, Paramount, 1976; *The Legacy*, Universal, 1979; *Mask*, Lorimar, 1985.

ADDRESSES: AGENT—Creative Artists Agency, 1888 Century Park E., Suite 1400, Los Angeles, CA 90067.*

*   *   *

ELLIS, Anita 1920-

PERSONAL: Born Anita Kert, April 12, 1920, in Montreal, Canada; daughter of Harry and Lillian Pearson (Peretz) Kert; married Frank Ellis, (Colonel, U.S. Air Force) 1943 (divorced 1946, died 1957); married Mortimer F. Shapiro (a neurologist). July 31, 1960. EDUCATION: Graduate, Hollywood High School; attended University of California at Los Angeles and the College of Music of Cincinnati; studied voice with Leone Kruse at the Cincinnati Conservatory of Music; studied with Glen Raikes in California and Marion Manderen in New York.

VOCATION· Singer

CAREER: PRINCIPAL CONCERT APPEARANCES—Libby Holman Center for the Arts, Stamford, CT, 1973; musical salute to Ira Gershwin, Avery Fisher Hall, NY, 1975; *Anita Ellis Sings,* Town Hall, NY, 1975; American Cinematheque Benefit, *By George . . . By Ira,* Carnegie Hall, NY, 1978; musical salute to Cole Porter, Avery Fisher Hall, NY, 1979; *Anita Ellis Sings,* Alice Tully Hall, Lincoln Center, NY, 1979; *Lyrics and Lyricists, Harburg in Hollywood,* 92nd Street YHMA, NY, 1982; *Great Ladies of Jazz,* Metropolitan Museum of Art, 1983.

PRINCIPAL CABARET APPEARANCES—The Colony, London, England; Riviera Hotel, Havana, Cuba; Fiesta Room, Empire Club, Toronto, Canada; Balinese Room, Hotel Galvez, Galveston, TX; Zephyr Room, Cleveland, OH; Old New Orleans Club, Washington, DC; New York: La Vie en Rose, The Village Vanguard, The Blue Angel, Bon Soir, all NY, 1952-57; Michael's Pub, NY, 1975-75.

ANITA ELLIS

PRINCIPAL FILM WORK—Sang for Rita Hayworth in *Gilda,* Columbia, 1946, *The Loves of Carmen,* Columbia, 1948, *The Lady from Shanghai,* Columbia, 1948, and *Down to Earth,* Columbia, 1948; sang for Vera-Ellen in *Three Little Words,* Metro-Goldwyn-Mayer, 1950 and *The Belle of New York,* Metro-Goldwyn-Mayer, 1952; sang for Jeanne Crain in *Gentlemen Marry Brunettes,* Metro-Goldwyn-Mayer, 1955.

PRINCIPAL FILM APPEARANCES—*Dancing Coeds,* Metro-Goldwyn-Mayer, 1938; *Babes in Arms,* Metro-Goldwyn-Mayer, 1939; *Forty Little Mothers,* Metro-Goldwyn-Mayer, 1940; *Strike Up the Band,* Metro-Goldwyn-Mayer, 1940; *The Joe Louis Story,* 1953; *Pull My Daisy,* 1953; *Anita Ellis: For the Record,* Filmex Film Festival, Aquarius Theatre, Los Angeles, 1981.

PRINCIPAL TELEVISION APPEARANCES—Guest: Girl of the Week, *Today Show,* NBC, 1958; inaugural broadcast, Channel 13, WNET, NY, 1961; *Dinah! & Friends,* NBC, 1980.

Special: *Skyline—Anita Ellis: For the Record,* PBS, 1979.

PRINCIPAL RADIO APPEARANCES—Guest: *The Chesterfield Show; The Andy Russell Show; The Jack Carson Show; The Edgar Bergen Show; The Red Skelton Show.*

Series: *Anita Ellis Sings,* WOR; *Songs Overseas,* CBS; *Personal Album,* Armed Forces Network; *American Popular Song,* National Public Radio, 1978.

PRINCIPAL STAGE APPEARANCES—Lucy Brown, *The Threepenny Opera* (concert version), First American Music Festival, NY, 1952; understudy, *Flower Drum Song,* Broadway production, 1958; special guest appearance, *Urameshia (The Ghost),* Phoenix Theatre, 1960.

RECORDINGS: SINGLES—*Anniversary Song; Man with a Horn; The Old Lamplighter; Either It's Love or It Isn't; Golden Earrings; Love for Love; I'm Yours; Ask Anyone Who Knows.*

SOUNDTRACK ALBUMS—*Three Little Words,* Metro-Goldwyn-Mayer; *The Belle of New York,* Metro-Goldwyn-Mayer; *Gentlemen Marry Brunettes,* Coral.

ALBUMS—*I Wonder What Became of Me,* Epic, 1953; *Hims,* Epic, 1954; *The World in My Arms,* Elektra, 1960; *Anita Ellis—Echoes,* Michael's Pub, 1979; *Anita Ellis with Ellis Larkins: A Legend Sings,* Orion Master Recordings, 1979.

AWARDS: National Endowment for the Arts Grant, 1981.

SIDELIGHTS: RECREATIONS—Wilderness travels, walking, swimming, sailing, skindiving, skiing, cooking and reading.

ADDRESSES: HOME—New York, NY.

*   *   *

ENGEL, Susan 1935-

PERSONAL: Born March 25, 1935 in Vienna, Austria; daughter of Fritz and Anni (Stefansky) Engel; married Sylvester Morand. EDUCATION: Attended the Sorbonne, Paris, and Bristol University; studied for the theatre at the Bristol Old Vic School.

VOCATION: Actress.

SUSAN ENGEL

CAREER: DEBUT—*Pantomime*, Bristol Old Vic, England, 1959. LONDON DEBUT—Mrs. Phineus, *The Happy Haven*, Royal Court Theatre, 1960. PRINCIPAL STAGE APPEARANCES—Mrs. Noah, *The Wakefield Mystery Cycle*, Mermaid Theatre, London, 1961; Alice Arden, *Arden of Faversham*, Arts Theatre, Cambridge, England, 1962; Calpurnia, *Julius Caesar*, Royal Shakespeare Company, Stratford, England then Aldwych Theatre, London, 1963; Queen Elizabeth, *The War of the Roses*, Royal Shakespeare Company, Stratford then Aldwych Theatre, London, 1963-64; Doll Tearsheet, *Henry IV*, Royal Shakespeare Company, Stratford then Aldwych Theatre, London, 1964; Adriana, *The Comedy of Errors*, Royal Shakespeare Company, Stratford then Aldwych Theatre, London, 1965; Lucille Harris, *Adventures in the Skin Trade*, Hampstead Theatre, London, 1966; Lady Macduff, *Macbeth* and Lady Macbeth, *Macbeth*, both Royal Court Theatre, London, 1966; Amy, *The Hotel in Amsterdam*, Royal Court Theatre, then the New Theatre, London, 1968.

Esther, *Friends*, Round House Theatre, London, 1970; Amelia Evans, *Ballad of the Sad Cafe*, Thorndike Theatre, Leatherhead, England, 1971; old woman, *Passion*, Alexandra Park Racecourse, England, 1971; Rosa, *The Old Ones*, Royal Court Theatre, London, 1972; Frau Gabor, *Spring Awakening*, Old Vic, for the National Theatre, London, 1974; Olga, *The Three Sisters*, Cambridge Theatre, London, 1976; Gulschan, *The Ascent of Mount Fuji*, Hampstead Theatre, London, 1977; Katya, *Cousin Vladimir*, Royal Shakespeare Company, Aldwych Theatre, London, 1978; company, *The Private Life of the Third Reich*, Open Space Theatre, London, 1979; Elaine Navazio, *The Last of the Red Hot Lovers*, Criterion Theatre, London, 1979.

Sara, *Watch on the Rhine*, National Theatre, London, 1980; Gertrude, *Hamlet*, Warehouse Theatre, London, then Piccadilly Theatre, London, 1982; *Shortlist*, Hampstead Theatre, London, 1982;

Madame Ranvesky, *The Cherry Orchard*, Haymarket Theatre, Leichester, 1984; *A Kind of Alaska*, Duchess Theatre Theatre, London, 1985.

PRINCIPAL FILM APPEARANCES—*Charlie Bubbles*, Regional Films, 1968; *King Lear*, 1971; *Butley*, AFT Distributing, 1974; *Ascendancy*, BFI Films.

PRINCIPAL TELEVISION APPEARANCES—*The War of the Roses; The Lotus Eaters; Exiles; Doctor Who; We'll Meet Again*, LWT; *A Kind of Alaska*, Central, 1985.

ADDRESSES: HOME—Fifteen Compayne Gardens, London NW6, England.

*   *   *

EPPS, Sheldon   1952-

PERSONAL: Born November 15, 1952, in Los Angeles, CA; son of St. Paul (a minister) and Kathryn (a teacher; maiden name, Gilliam) Epps. EDUCATION: Carnegie Mellon University, B.F.A., 1973.

VOCATION: Director and actor.

CAREER: PRINCIPAL STAGE WORK—Director: *Disgustingly Rich, Incandescent Tones*, and *A Midsummer Night's Dream*, all at the Production Company, NY; *And I Ain't Finished Yet*, Manhattan Theatre Club; *Bravo: A Musical Portrait of Edith Piaf*, Mayfair Theatre, Los Angeles, CA, then Apollo Theatre Center, Chicago, IL; *Scenes and Revelations*, Circle in the Square, NY, 1981; *Blues in the Night*, Rialto Theatre, NY, 1982; *Dark of the Moon*, Asolo State Theatre, Sarasota, FL, 1983; has also directed for the Phoenix Theatre and McCarter Theatre.

MAJOR TOURS—*Broadway Rhythm* and *The Best of Broadway*, international tours as part of the "I Love New York," commercial campaign; *Blues in the Night*, National tour.

RELATED CAREER—Co-founder of the Production Company in New York.

MEMBER: Society of Stage Directors and Choreographers, Actors' Equity Association, Screen Actors Guild.

SIDELIGHTS: CTFT learned from Sheldon Epps' agent that he began his career as an actor appearing in theatres in New York and across the country, including the Brooklyn Academy of Music's Theatre Company, Indiana Repertory Company, Alley Theatre, Houston, TX, Civic Light Opera of Pittsburgh and the Production Company in New York.

ADDRESSES: OFFICE—165 Van Buski Road, Teaneck, NJ 07666. AGENT—c/o George Lane, William Morris Agency, 1350 Avenue of the Americas, New York, NY 10019.

*   *   *

ESSEX, David   1947-

PERSONAL: Born David Cook, July 23, 1947, in London, England; son of Albert and Doris Cook; married Maureen Neal. EDUCATION: Shipman Secondary School.

VOCATION: Actor, singer, and composer.

CAREER: STAGE DEBUT—Matt, *The Fantasticks,* Festival Hall, Paignton, England. LONDON DEBUT—Revue performer, *Ten Years' Hard,* May Fair Theatre, 1970. PRINCIPAL STAGE APPEARANCES—*The Magic Carpet,* Arnaud Theatre, Guildford, England, 1968; Jesus, *Godspell,* Roundhouse Theatre, London, 1971, then Wyndham's Theatre, London, 1972; in his own variety revue, Palladium Theatre, London, 1973; Che Guevara, *Evita,* Prince Edward Theatre, London, 1978; Lord Byron, *Childe Byron,* Young Vic, London, 1983-84; Fletcher Christian, *Mutiny!* (also composer), Piccadilly Theatre, London, 1985.

MAJOR TOURS—Duke of Durham, *Oh, Kay!,* 1968.

PRINCIPAL FILM APPEARANCES—*Assault* (also known as *In the Devil's Garden* and *Tower of Terror*), British, 1971; *All Coppers Are . . . ,* British, 1971; *That'll Be the Day,* British, 1973; *Stardust,* Columbia, 1975; *Silver Dream Racer,* British, 1980.

TELEVISION DEBUT—*Five O'Clock Club,* 1966. PRINCIPAL TELEVISION APPEARANCES—*American Bandstand; Midnight Special; Don Kirshner's Rock Concert; A.M. America; Phil Everly in Session; The Cher Show; Merv Griffin;* guest of variety shows in the United Kingdom, the United States, France, Germany, Spain, Denmark, Australia, and Japan.

RECORDINGS: ALBUMS—*Rock On,* 1974; *All the Fun of the Fair; Out on the Street,* 1976; *Gold and Ivory,* 1977; (with Cat Stevens) *From Alpha to Omega,* 1978; *Imperial Wizard,* 1979; *Hot Love,* 1980; *Be Bop the Future,* 1981; *Stage Struck,* 1982; *The Whisper,* 1983; *This One's for You,* 1984; (with Jeff Wayne, Richard Burton, and others) *The War of the Worlds.*

MEMBER: Save the Children Funds, Roundabout Club, Act Club (former president).

AWARDS: Most Promising Newcomer, Variety Club Award, 1973, for *That'll Be the Day;* Best Male Singer and Outstanding Music Personality, *Daily Mirror* Poll, 1976; Show Business Personality of the year, Variety Club, 1978; numerous gold and silver records for albums and singles in Europe and the United States, including Grammy nomination for *Rock On.*

SIDELIGHTS: Beginning his career as a singer and drummer, David Essex moved into the worlds of the legitimate stage, television, and film while maintaining a busy concert schedule in twenty-one different countries. He enjoys horses, motorcycling, flying and tennis, and attends the theatre regularly. Prior to entering show business he was an apprentice engineer.

ADDRESSES: MANAGER—Derek Bowman, 109 Eastbourne Mews, London W2, England.

*   *   *

ESTEVEZ, Emilio

PERSONAL: Born in New York, NY; son of Martin (an actor; original surname, Estevez) and Janet Sheen. EDUCATION: Attended Santa Monica High School, CA.

VOCATION: Actor, writer, and director.

CAREER: FILM DEBUT—Johnny Collins, *Tex,* Buena Vista, 1982. PRINCIPAL FILM APPEARANCES—Two-Bit Matthews, *The Outsiders,* Zoetrope, 1983; *Nightmares,* 1983; Otto, *Repo Man;* An-

drew, *Breakfast Club,* Columbia, 1985; *St. Elmo's Fire,* Columbia, 1985; Mark Jennings, *That Was Then . . . This Is Now,* 1985; *Wisdom,* Twentieth Century-Fox, 1987; Bill Robinson, *Maximum Overdrive* (upcoming).

PRINCIPAL FILM WORK—Director, *Wisdom,* Twentieth Century-Fox, 1987.

TELEVISION DEBUT—"Seventeen, Going on Nowhere," *ABC Afterschool Special,* ABC. PRINCIPAL TELEVISION APPEARANCES—*To Climb a Mountain; Making the Grade; In the Custody of Strangers.*

STAGE DEBUT—*Echoes of an Era,* Santa Monica High School, Los Angeles, CA. PRINCIPAL STAGE APPEARANCES—*Mister Roberts,* Burt Reynold's Theatre, FL.

WRITINGS: PLAYS, PRODUCED—*Echoes of an Era,* Santa Monica High School, CA.

SCREENPLAYS—*That Was Then . . . This Is Now,* 1985; *Wisdom,* Twentieth Century-Fox, 1987.

SIDELIGHTS: From material supplied by his agent, *CTFT* learned that Emilio Estevez acted in a short film produced in his high school. It was an anti-nuclear film entitled, *Meet Mr. Bomb.* He also starred with his father, Martin Sheen, in the production of *Mister Roberts,* at the Burt Reynold's Theatre.

ADDRESSES: AGENT—Andrea Jaffe, Inc., 9229 Sunset Blvd., Suite 401, Los Angeles, CA 90069.

*   *   *

ESTRADA, Erik   1949-

PERSONAL: Full name, Henry Enrique Estrada; born March 16, 1949, in New York, NY; married Peggy; children: Anthony Eric. EDUCATION: Musical Dramatic Academy, NY.

VOCATION: Actor.

CAREER: PRINCIPAL TELEVISION APPEARANCES—Series: Officer Frank "Ponch" Poncherello, *CHiPS,* NBC, 1977-1983.

Episodic: "Engaged to Be Buried," *Hawaii Five-0,* CBS, 1973; "Man in a Trap," *Mannix,* CBS, 1974; *Kojack,* CBS, 1975; "Lord of the Smoking Mirror," *Kolchak: The Night Stalker,* ABC, 1975; "Don't Feed the Pigeons," *Police Woman,* NBC, 1975; "Shadow of Guilt," *Barnaby Jones,* CBS, 1975; "On the Take," *Joe Forrester,* NBC, 1975; *Six Million Dollar Man,* ABC, 1975; "The High Cost of Winning," *Medical Center,* CBS, 1975; *Quest,* NBC, 1976; *Delvecchio,* CBS, 1977; *The Love Boat,* ABC, 1978; also, *Owen Marshall: Counselor at Law; Emergency.*

Guest: *Tonight Show; Dinah!; Mike Douglas; Merv Griffin; Hollywood Squares; Celebrity Name That Tune; Easter Seal Telethon; The Bay City Rollers Meet the Saturday Superstars.*

Movie: *Fire!,* 1977.

FILM DEBUT—*The Cross and the Switchblade,* Ross, 1967. PRINCIPAL FILM APPEARANCES—*Cactus Flower,* Columbia, 1969; *John and Mary,* Twentieth Century-Fox, 1969; *The New Centurions,* Columbia, 1972; *Airport '75,* Universal, 1974; *Midway,*

ERIK ESTRADA

1976; *Trackdown,* United Artists, 1976; also, *Honey Boy; Where's Parcefal; The Repentant; Light Blast.*

PRINCIPAL STAGE APPEARANCES—Austin, *True West,* Cherry Lane Theatre, NY, 1984.

ADDRESSES: OFFICE—Azevedo International, 11350 Ventura Blvd., Studio City, CA 91604.

*   *   *

EVANS, Linda   1942-

PERSONAL: Born November 18, 1942, in Hartford, CT; married John Derek (divorced). EDUCATION: Hollywood High School, Los Angeles.

VOCATION: Actress.

CAREER: PRINCIPAL TELEVISION APPEARANCES—Series: Audra Barkley, *The Big Valley,* ABC, 1965-69; Marty Shaw, *The Hunter,* CBS, 1977; Krystle Grant Jennings Carrington, *Dynasty,* ABC, 1981—; Rita, *Dynasty,* 1985—.

Mini-Series: *Bare Essence,* CBS, 1982; Rose Sinclair, *North and South, Book II,* ABC, 1986.

Movies: *Nowhere to Run,* 1978; *Standing Tall,* 1978; *Kenny Rogers as the Gambler, Part II: The Adventure Continues,* 1983.

Episodic: *Bachelor Father,* CBS; *The Love Boat,* ABC.

FILM DEBUT—*Twilight of Honor,* Metro-Goldwyn-Mayer, 1963. PRINCIPAL FILM APPEARANCES—*The Klansman,* Paramount, 1974; *Avalanche Express,* 1979; *Tom Horn,* Warner Brothers, 1980.

MEMBER: American Federation of Television and Radio Artists, Screen Actors Guild.

ADDRESSES: OFFICE—c/o Aaron Spelling Productions, 1041 N. Formosa Avenue, Los Angeles, CA 90046. AGENT—c/o Mike Greenfield, Charter Management, 9000 Sunset Blvd., Los Angeles, CA 90069.*

*   *   *

EVANS, Michael Jonas   1949-

PERSONAL: Born November 3, 1949, in Salibury, NC; son of Theodore and Anna Sue (Murdock) Evans. EDUCATION: Attended Los Angeles City College; graduate work in production at American Film Institute, 1983.

VOCATION: Actor and writer.

CAREER: PRINCIPAL TELEVISION APPEARANCES—Series: Lionel Jefferson, *All in the Family,* CBS, 1970-75; Lionel Jefferson, *The Jeffersons,* CBS, 1975, 1979-81.

WRITINGS: TELEVISION—*Good Times.*

MICHAEL JONAS EVANS

MEMBER: Academy of Arts and Sciences.

ADDRESSES: OFFICE—P.O. Box 581, Van Nuys, CA 91408. AGENT—Atkins & Associates, 208 S. Beverly Drive, Beverly Hills, CA 90212.

*   *   *

EVERETT, Chad   1937-

PERSONAL: Born Raymon Lee Cramton, June 11, 1937, in South Bend, IN; son of "Ted" Harry Clyde and Virdeen Ruth (Hopper) Cramton; married Brenda Lee Thompson (an actress and writer; professional name, Shelby Grant), 1966; children: Katherine Kerrie, Shannon Kimberly. EDUCATION: Wayne State University, B.A., mass communications; studied acting with Eugene Baker and De Leonard Leone. POLITICS: Republican. RELIGION: Christian. MILITARY: U.S. Naval Reserve.

VOCATION: Actor.

CAREER: PRINCIPAL FILM APPEARANCES—*Claudelle Inglish* (also known as *Young and Eager*), Warner Brothers, 1961; *The Chapman Report*, Warner Brothers/Darryl F. Zanuck, 1962; *Get Yourself a College Girl*, Metro-Goldwyn-Mayer, 1964; *The Singing Nun*, Metro-Goldwyn-Mayer, 1966; *Made in Paris*, Metro-Goldwyn-Mayer, 1966; *Johnny Tiger*, Universal, 1966; *The Last Challenge*, Metro-Goldwyn-Mayer, 1967; *The Impossible Years*, Metro-Goldwyn-Mayer, 1968; *Airplane, II: The Sequel*, Paramount, 1982; the Dutchman, *Fever Pitch*, Metro-Goldwyn-Mayer, 1985.

CHAD EVERETT

PRINCIPAL TELEVISION APPEARANCES—Series: Deputy Del Stark, *The Dakotas*, ABC, 1963; Dr. Joe Gannon, *Medical Center*, CBS, 1969-76; Paul Hagen, *Hagen*, CBS, 1980.

Episodic: *Hawaiian Eye; 77 Sunset Strip; Surfside Six; Lawman; Bronco; The Lieutenant; Redigo; Route 66; Ironside; The Rousters*.

Movies: *Return of the Gunfighter*, 1967; others.

Mini-Series: Maxwell Mercy, *Centennial*, NBC, 1978-79.

AWARDS: Best Actor in the World, Don Quixote Award (Spain); *Photoplay's* Favorite Actor Gold Medal; Emmy Award and Golden Globe Award nominations, for *Medical Center*.

MEMBER: American Federation of Television and Radio Artists, Screen Actors Guild; Muscular Dystrophy Association (vice president).

SIDELIGHTS: RECREATIONS—Breeding thoroughbreds, furniture making, tennis, horseback riding, fishing, and sailing. In his spare moments he also writes poetry and paints.

Chad Everett told *CTFT* that he made his stage debut at age fourteen in a high school play; later, while attending Wayne State University he was a member of a State Department sponsored dramatic group which toured India.

He was the last performer signed to a long-term Hollywood contract when he joined Metro-Goldwyn-Mayer studios in 1964.

Everett hosts the Michelob Chad Everett Tennis Tournament for Special Children and a golf tournament for the American Cancer Society. He has appeared for Project Orbis, Multiple Sclerosis, and many others.

ADDRESSES: OFFICE—19901 Northridge Road, Chatsworth, CA 91311. AGENT—c/o Jack Gilardi, International Creative Management, 8899 Beverly Blvd., Los Angeles, CA 90048.

*   *   *

EYEN, Tom   1941-

PERSONAL: Born August 14, 1941, in Cambridge, OH; son of Abraham and Julia (Farhat) Eyen; married Liza Giraudoux, August 10, 1963; children: Jacque, Christopher, David. EDUCATION: Ohio State University, M.A., English, 1961.

VOCATION: Playwright and director.

CAREER: PRINCIPAL STAGE WORK—Director: At the Theatre of the Eye, 1964— (see plays, produced); *Rachel Lily Rosenbloom (And Don't You Forget It)*, Broadhurst Theatre, NY, 1973.

WRITINGS: PLAYS, PRODUCED—*(When) The Clock Strikes Thirteen*, Cambridge, OH, 1950; *Tour de Four*, Writers Stage, NY, 1963.

At the La Mama Experimental Theatre Club, NY: *Frustrata, the Dirty Little Girl with the Red Paper Rose Stuck in Her Head, Is Demented, The White Whore and Bit Player*, and *My Next Husband Will Be a Beauty*, all 1964; *Can You See a Prince?, The Demented World of Tom Eyen, Why Hanna's Skirt Won't Stay Down*, and *Miss Nefertiti Regrets*, all 1965; *Cinderella Revisited* (children's musi-

TOM EYEN

cal), *Sinderella Revisted* (adult's musical), *Eyen on Eyen*, and *Give My Regards to Off-Off-Broadway*, all 1966; *Court, Sarah B. Divine!* (Part I), *Grand Tenement*, and *November 22*, all 1967; *Why Johnny Comes Dancing Home, The Kama Sutra (An Organic Happening), Who Killed My Bald Sister Sophie?, A Vanity Happening*, and *Alice Through the Looking Glass Lightly*, all 1968; *The Four No Plays, Caution: A Love Story*, and *Eye in New York*, all 1969; *Areatha in the Ice Palace, What Is Making Gilda So Gray, 2008 1/2, Gertrude Stein and Other Great Men*, and *The Women Behind Bars*, all 1974; *The Dirtiest Musical*, 1975; *The Neon Woman*, 1978.

The White Whore and the Bit Player, Mercury Theatre, London, 1970; *The Dirtiest Show in Town*, Duchess Theatre, London, 1971; book and lyrics, *Dreamgirls*, Majestic Theatre, NY, 1981. Also, *The Milliken Breakfast Shows*, 1977-78.

PLAYS, UNPRODUCED—*Kicks*, 1984.

SCREENPLAYS—*The White Whore and the Bit Player*, 1969; *Ava*, 1982.

TELEVISION—*Mary Hartman, Mary Hartman*, 1976-77; *The Bette Midler Special*, 1977; *Neon Woman*, 1978; *Melody of the Glittering Parrot*, 1980; *The Dirtiest Show in Town*, Showtime, 1980.

MEMBER: Harvard Club.

AWARDS: Rockefeller Fellow, 1967; Guggenheim Fellow, 1970; Antoinette Perry Award, 1982, for *Dreamgirls*.

SIDELIGHTS: RECREATION—Scuba diving and sky-diving.

ADDRESSES: AGENT—c/o Bridget Aschenberg, International Creative Management, 40 W. 57th Street, New York, NY 10019.

F

DOUGLAS FAIRBANKS, JR.

FAIRBANKS, Douglas, Jr.   1909-

PERSONAL: Full name, Douglas Elton Fairbanks, Jr.; born December 9, 1909, in New York, NY; son of Douglas Elton (an actor) and Anna Elizabeth (Beth; maiden name, Sully) Fairbanks; married Joan Crawford, 1929 (divorced, 1933); married Mary Lee Epling Hartford, April 22, 1939; children: (second marriage) Daphne, Kay, Victoria, Melissa. EDUCATION: Attended Bovee and Collegiate Military School, New York, Knickerbocker Greys, New York, Harvard Military Academy Los Angeles, and Pasadena Polytechnic School; studied painting and sculpture in London and Paris. MILITARY: U.S. Navy, 1942-46 (achieved rank of Lt. Commander).

VOCATION: Actor, producer, writer, and corporate director.

CAREER: STAGE DEBUT—*Young Woodley,* Los Angeles, CA, 1929. NEW YORK DEBUT—Participant, *A Gala Tribute to Joshua Logan,* Imperial Theatre, March 9, 1975. LONDON DEBUT—

Stephen, *Moonlight Is Silver,* Queen's Theatre, September 19, 1934. PRINCIPAL STAGE APPEARANCES—*Saturday's Children,* Hollywood; Michael Robbins, *The Winding Journey,* Opera House, Manchester, England, 1934; *Here Lies Truth,* England, 1934; *Tonight at 8:30,* Los Angeles, 1940; Biddeford Poole, *The Pleasure of His Company,* in California and at the Royal Alexandra Theatre, Toronto, Canada, December, 1974; Garry Essendine, *Present Laughter,* Eisenhower Theatre, Kennedy Center for the Performing Arts, Washington, DC, 1975; Biddeford Poole, *The Pleasure of His Company,* Phoenix Theatre, London, 1976; also appeared in *The Dummy, Toward the Light, Romeo and Juliet, The Jest,* and *Man in Possession.*

MAJOR TOURS—*Young Woodley,* California, 1929; Professor Henry Higgins, *My Fair Lady,* national, 1968; Biddeford Poole, *The Pleasure of His Company,* toured the U.S. and Canada, 1970-72 (also toured in 1974 after appearance in Canada); *The Secretary Bird,* national, 1973-74; Garry Essendine, *Present Laughter,* national, 1975; also toured in *Out on a Limb* and *Sleuth.*

FILM DEBUT—Title role, *Stephen Steps Out,* Paramount, 1923. PRINCIPAL FILM APPEARANCES—(Silent films) *The Air Mail,* Paramount, 1925; *Wild Horse Mesa,* Paramount, 1925; *Stella Dallas,* Paramount (Goldwyn), 1925; *A Texas Steer,* Paramount, 1925; *Padlocked,* Paramount, 1926; *Broken Hearts of Hollywood,* Paramount, 1926; *Manbait,* Paramount, 1927; *Women Love Diamonds,* Paramount, 1927; *The Brass Band,* Paramount, 1927; *Dead Man's Curves,* Paramount, 1928; *Modern Mothers,* Paramount, 1928; *The Toilers,* Paramount, 1928; *The Power of the Press,* Columbia, 1929; *A Woman of Affairs,* Metro-Goldwyn-Mayer, 1929; *Our Modern Maidens,* Metro-Goldwyn-Mayer, 1929.

(Sound films) *The Barker,* Warner Brothers, 1929; *The Forward Pass,* Warner Brothers, 1929; *The Careless Age,* Warner Brothers, 1929; *Fast Life,* Warner Brothers, 1929; *Show of Shows,* Warner Brothers, 1929.

Party Girl, Tiffany, 1930; *Loose Ankles,* Warner Brothers, 1930; *The Dawn Patrol,* Warner Brothers, 1930; *The Little Accident,* Universal, 1930; *The Way of All Men,* Warner Brothers, 1930; *Sin Flood,* Warner Brothers, 1930; *One Night at Susie's,* Warner Brothers, 1930; Henry, *Outward Bound,* Warner Brothers, 1930; Joe Massara, *Little Caesar,* Warner Brothers, 1930; *Chances,* Warner Brothers, 1931; *I Like Your Nerve,* Warner Brothers, 1931; *Union Depot,* Warner Brothers, 1932; *It's Tough to Be Famous,* Warner Brothers, 1932; *Love Is a Racket,* Warner Brothers, 1932; *Scarlet Dawn,* Warner Brothers, 1932; Bill Keller, *Parachute Jumper,* Warner Brothers, 1933; Joseph Sheridan, *Morning Glory,* RKO, 1933; title role, *The Life of Jimmy Dolan,* Warner Brothers, 1933; *Captured!,* Warner Brothers, 1933; *The Narrow Corner,* Warner Brothers, 1933; Czar Peter, *Catherine the Great,* United Artists (Korda), 1934; *Success at Any Price,* RKO, 1934; Rudolpho,

Mimi, Alliance Pictures, 1935; *Man of the Moment,* Warner Brothers (British), 1936; *The Amateur Gentleman,* United Artists, 1936; *Accused,* United Artists, 1936; *Jump for Glory,* United Artists, 1937; *When Thief Meets Thief,* Universal, 1937; Rupert of Hentzau, *The Prisoner of Zenda,* United Artists (Selznick), 1937; *The Joy of Living,* RKO, 1938; Chick Kirkland, *Having Wonderful Time,* RKO, 1938; *The Rage of Paris,* Universal, 1938; *The Young in Heart,* United Artists, 1938; Ballantine, *Gunga Din,* RKO, 1939; *The Sun Never Sets,* Paramount, 1939; *Rulers of the Sea,* Paramount, 1939.

Green Sea, Universal, 1940; *Safari,* Paramount, 1940; *Angels Over Broadway,* Columbia, 1941; both title roles, *The Corsican Brothers,* United Artists, 1941; title role, *Sinbad the Sailor,* RKO, 1947; *The Exile,* Universal, 1947; *That Lady in Ermine,* Twentieth Century-Fox, 1948; title role, *The Fighting O'Flynn,* Universal, 1949; *State Secret,* Columbia, 1950; *Mr. Drake's Duck,* United Artists, 1951; *Ghost Story,* Universal, 1981.

PRINCIPAL FILM WORK—Producer: *The Amateur Gentleman,* United Artists, 1936; *Accused,* United Artists, 1936; *Jump for Glory,* United Artists, 1937; *Crime Over London,* United Artists, 1937; *Another Man's Poison,* United Artists, 1951; *Chase a Crooked Shadow,* Warner Brothers, 1958; *Ghost Story,* Universal, 1981; others.

PRINCIPAL TELEVISION WORK—Producer: *Douglas Fairbanks Jr., Presents . . . ,* for British television (occasional appearances in this series) seen in U.S. in syndication only, 177 episodes produced between 1952-1957; *The Rheingold Theatre,* for British television; more than 160 half-hour shows; others.

WRITINGS: Titles for silent films, including *The Gaucho,* United Artists, starring Douglas Fairbanks, Sr. Also: screenplays, articles, political essays, short stories.

RECORDINGS: ALBUM—Scenes from *Moonlight Is Silver,* with co-star Gertrude Lawrence.

AWARDS: Honorary Knight of the British Empire (one of seventy Americans knighted after World War II), in recognition of his political and philanthropic activities on behalf of Anglo-American relationships, 1949. Military awards: Silver Star Medal, Legion of Merit with a "V" for valor clasp, Distinguished Service Cross, Legion d'Honneur, Croix de Guerre, with palm; he has been the recipient of several international awards, honors and degrees; Order of the Crown, Belgium; American Image Award, 1976; Award for Contribution to World Understanding and Peace, World Affairs Council, Philadelphia, 1978; Salvation Army, National Brotherhood Award, 1980; Honorary Citizen of Korea; others.

MEMBER: American Museum in Britain (governor); Royal Shakespeare Theatre, Stratford-on-Avon; Edwina Mountbatten Trust (trustee); Ditchley Foundation (board of governors); Denver Center for the Performing Arts (advisory committee); International Cultural Center for Youth, Jerusalem (chairman); British-American Alumni Association; American Friends of the Order of St. John, Jerusalem; Racquet Club (New York); Myopia Hunt Club (honorary member; Hamilton, Massachusetts); Newport Reading Room (Rhode Island); others.

SIDELIGHTS: Douglas Fairbanks has made England his principal home since the early 1950's. In 1955, he was the subject of a biography, *Knight Errant,* by Brian Connell. In 1951, Fairbanks formed his own company, The Dougfair Corporation, through which he pursues all his professional activities.

ADDRESSES: OFFICE—545 Madison Avenue, New York, NY 10022; The Vicarage, 448 N. Lake Way, Palm Beach, FL 33480.

*   *   *

FAIRSERVIS, Elfie   1957-

PERSONAL: Born May 19, 1957, in Sharon, CT; daughter of Dr. Walter A. (an archaeologist) and Jane Bell (a free lance artist; maiden name, Sutherland) Fairservis. EDUCATION: Bennett College, A.A.S., 1977; New York University, B.S., 1980; attended the directing program at Columbia University for three years; studied with Nikos Psacharopoulis at Circle in the Square in New York.

VOCATION: Actress and writer.

CAREER: PRINCIPAL STAGE APPEARANCES—Ursula, *Bye Bye Birdie* and Peaseblossom, *A Midsummer Night's Dream,* both Hyde Park Playhouse; Susan, *Veronica's Room,* Susannah, *Bedroom Farce,* Nancy, *Angel Street,* Princess Kukachin, *Marco Millions,* and Melba Snyder, *Pal Joey,* all at the Sharon Playhouse, CT; Queen Elizabeth, *The Royal Visit,* Country Theatre; Kate, *Off Season* and Dianne, the dog, *A Little More Wine with Lunch,* both No Smoking Playhouse, NY; Rebecca Gibbs, *Our Town,* Columbia University; Andy Lewis, *Independent Study,* Equity Library Theatre, NY; Hippie, Edmund de Muskie, Duke of York, *Dick Deterred,* West Bank Cafe, NY; Mammy Yokum, *L'il Abner,* Prescott Park Arts Festival.

WRITINGS: BOOKS, UNPUBLISHED—(As Elfie Deville) "Revenge Is Sweet."

ELFIE FAIRSERVIS

MEMBER: Merely Players Theatre Company, No Smoking Playhouse.

ADDRESSES: HOME—New York, NY.

*   *   *

FARLEIGH, Lynn   1942-

PERSONAL: Born May 3, 1942, in Bristol, England; daughter of Joseph Sydney and Marjorie Norah (Clark) Farleigh; married Michael Jayston (an actor; divorced). EDUCATION: Attended Guildhall School of Music and Dramatic Art, London, England.

VOCATION: Actress.

CAREER: STAGE DEBUT—*Under Milkwood,* Playhouse, Salisbury, England, 1962. NEW YORK DEBUT—Ruth, *The Homecoming,* Music Box Theatre, 1967. LONDON DEBUT—Helena, *All's Well that Ends Well,* Royal Shakespeare Company, 1968. PRINCIPAL STAGE APPEARANCES—(All London unless otherwise indicated) Amanda, *The Relapse* and Portia, *Julius Caesar,* both at the Aldwych Theatre with the Royal Shakespeare Company, 1968; double bill, *Blim at School* and *Poet of the Anemonies,* Royal Court Theatre, 1969.

Simone, *The Friends,* Round House Theatre, 1970; Beatrice Justice, *Exiles,* Mermaid Theatre, 1970; Monique Combes, *Suzanna Andler,* Aldwych Theatre, 1973; Anne, *Ashes,* Open Space Theatre, 1974; Jennifer Dubedat, *The Doctor's Dilemma,* Mermaid Theatre, 1975; Beryl, *Sex and Kinship in a Savage Society,* Theatre Upstairs, 1975; Charlotte, *A Room with a View,* Prospect Theatre Company, 1975; Viola, *Twelfth Night,* St. George's Theatre, Islington, 1976; Lady Anne, *Richard III,* St. George's Theatre, 1976; Anwar, *The Ascent of Mount Fuji, Almost Free,* and as the title role in *Sovereignty Under Elizabeth,* all at the Hampstead Theatre, 1977; Agnes, *Brand,* Olivier Theatre, 1978; Mrs. Forsythe, *Shout Across the River* and Jane, *The Hang of the Gaol,* both Warehouse Theatre with the Royal Shakespeare Company, 1978; Margaret, *Close of Play,* Lyttleton, 1979.

Simone, *The Workshop,* Oxford Playhouse, 1980, then Hampstead Theatre, 1981; Elizabeth Proctor, *The Crucible,* Comedy Theatre, 1981; *Harvest,* Ambassadors Theatre, 1981; Giant's wife, *Jack and the Beanstalk,* Theatre Royal, Stratford Festival, 1982; Mrs. Alving, *Ghosts,* Shaw Theatre, 1984; *The Man Who Fell in Love with His Wife!,* Lyric Theatre, Hammersmith, 1984; Hermonie, *Winter's Tale,* Lyceum Theatre, 1985; Chorus, *Medea,* Lyric Theatre, Hammersmith, 1986.

MAJOR TOURS—*The Workshop,* England, 1980; *Lady Chatterley's Lover,* 1983; Elizabeth Proctor, *The Crucible,* European tour with the Royal Shakespeare Company, 1985.

FILM DEBUT—*Three into Two Won't Go,* 1968. PRINCIPAL FILM APPEARANCES—*A Phoenix too Frequent; Voices; The Word.*

PRINCIPAL TELEVISION APPEARANCES—Movies and Episodic: *The Rivals; Eyeless in Gaza; Fall of Eagles; Brand; Antony and Cleopatra; Fothergill; Waving to a Train; Dearly Beloved; Let's Run Away to Africa.*

AWARDS: Clarence Derwent Award, 1975, for Charlotte, *A Room with a View.*

LYNN FARLEIGH

SIDELIGHTS: FAVORITE ROLES—Ruth in *The Homecoming,* Elizabeth Proctor in *The Crucible,* and Hermonie in *Winter's Tale.*

Lynn Farleigh informs *CTFT* that she enjoys tennis, swimming, gardening, and "gallery going," when she is not on stage.

ADDRESSES: AGENT—c/o Jeremy Conway, Gagle House, 109 Jemyn Street, London SW1 6MB, England.

*   *   *

FARNSWORTH, Richard

VOCATION: Actor and former stuntman.

CAREER: PRINCIPAL FILM APPEARANCES—*Comes a Horseman,* United Artists, 1978; *Tom Horn,* Warner Brothers, 1980; *Resurrection,* Universal, 1980; *The Legend of the Lone Ranger,* Universal, 1981; *Ruckus,* 1982; *The Grey Fox,* 1982; *The Natural,* Universal, 1984; *Into the Night,* Universal, 1985; *Sylvester,* Columbia, 1985.

PRINCIPAL TELEVISION APPEARANCES—Movies: Matthew, *Anne of Green Gables,* PBS, 1985; *Wild Horses,* CBS, 1985.

SIDELIGHTS: CTFT learned that Richard Farnsworth worked as a stuntman in major films for forty years before turning to acting.

ADDRESSES: AGENT—c/o Diane Davis, Twentieth Century Artists, 3518 Cahuenga Blvd., Suite 316, Los Angeles, CA 90068.*

*   *   *

FARR, Derek   1912-1986

PERSONAL: Born February 7, 1912, in Cheswick, England; died of cancer in London, March 22, 1986; son of Gerald and Vera Eileen (Miers) Farr; married Carole Lynne (divorced); married Muriel Pavlow. EDUCATION: Graduated from the Cranbrook School, Kent, England. MILITARY: British Army, World War II.

VOCATION: Actor.

CAREER: STAGE DEBUT—As a member of the repertory company

at the Barn Theatre, Oxted, Surrey, 1937. LONDON DEBUT—*The Gate Revue*, Ambassadors Theatre, 1939. PRINCIPAL STAGE APPEARANCES—(All London unless otherwise indicated) John Anstruther, *A House in the Square*, St. Martin's Theatre, 1940; Joe, *Fools Rush In*, Fortune Theatre, 1946; Bruce Banning, *Young Wives' Tale*, Savoy Theatre, 1949; Eugene Bazarov, *Spring at Marino*, Arts Theatre, 1951; Stephen Binns, *Adam's Apple*, Royal Brighton Theatre, 1952; Philip Langdon, *The Step Forward*, Strand Theatre, 1952; Edward Bare, *Murder Mistaken*, Ambassadors Theatre, 1952; Dudley, *Trial and Error*, Vaudeville Theatre, 1953; Dr. Alan Beresford, *Dr. Jo*, Royal Brighton Theatre, 1955; George Lawrence, *One Bright Day*, Apollo Theatre, 1956; George Maxwell, *Odd Man In*, St. Martin's Theatre, 1957; Hannibal, *A Fig for Glory*, Royal Court Theatre, Liverpool, 1958; Julian Calvert, *Wolf's Clothing*, Roy Collier, *Signpost to Murder*, both Cambridge, 1962; George, *Every Other Evening*, Phoenix Theatre, 1964; Mr. Blundell, *Wanted—One Body*, Arnaud Theatre, Guildford, 1966; Visitor, *Any Just Cause*, Genee Theatre, East Grinstead, 1967; Sir Lindsay Cooper, *Uproar in the House*, Garrick Theatre, 1967; Henry B. Wymark, *Let Sleeping Wives Lie*, Garrick Theatre, 1967; Gilbert Bodley, *Not Now Darling*, Strand Theatre, 1969.

MAJOR TOURS—Julian Calvert, *Wolf's Clothing*, Australia, and New Zealand, 1960; *Mary, Mary*, Australia, 1963; *Treasure Island*, tour for Mermaid Theatre, 1970-71.

FILM DEBUT—First appearance in 1937. PRINCIPAL FILM APPEARANCES—*Spellbound*, 1945; *Bond Street*, 1946; *Young Wives' Tale*, 1951; *Double Confession*, 1951; *Eight O'Clock Walk*, 1952; *Vicious Circle* (also known as *The Circle of Vikki*), 1953; *Front Page Story*, 1954; *Dam Busters*, 1954; *Bang! You're Dead* (also known as *Game of Danger*), 1954; *Doctor at Large*, 1957; *The Truth About Women*, 1958; *Attempt to Kill*, 1961; *30 Is a Dangerous Age, Cynthia*, 1968; *Reluctant Heroes*, 1971; *Pope Joan*, 1972; also appeared in *The Outsider; Murder without Crime; Town on Trial*.

PRINCIPAL TELEVISION APPEARANCES—Episodic: *The Projected Man*, BBC; *Dixon of Dock Street*, BBC; *The Human Jungle*, BBC; *Inspector Rose*, BBC; *Adam Adamant*, BBC; *Owen, M.D.*, BBC; *The Visitors*, BBC; *Crossroads*, BBC; *We the Accused*, BBC; *Young at Heart*, BBC; *Madge*, BBC; *Partners*, BBC; *Bergerac*, BBC; *Pinkerton's Progress*, BBC; *Frances Durbridge Presents*, BBC; *Coronation Street; Nightingale Boys; The Avengers; The Duchess of Duke Street; Some Mothers Do 'Ave Em; Rumpole of the Bailey; Murder Mistaken; Two Dozen Red Roses; Deadline Midnight; Faraway Music; Zero One; The Saint.* *

* * *

FEINGOLD, Michael 1945-

PERSONAL: Born May 5, 1945, in Chicago, IL; son of Bernard C. and Elsie Feingold. EDUCATION: Attended Columbia University; Yale School of Drama, M.F.A., 1970.

VOCATION: Critic, translator, director.

CAREER: PRINCIPAL STAGE WORK—Director: *Two-Part Inventions*, Circle Repertory, NY, 1976, then Goodman Theatre, Chicago, IL, 1979; *Speakeasy: An Evening Out with Dorothy Parker*, American Place Theatre, NY, 1983.

PRINCIPAL TELEVISION WORK—Play: Director, ''Happy End,'' *America's Musical Theatre*, PBS, 1986.

RELATED CAREER—Literary manager, Yale Repertory, New Haven, CT, 1972-76; artistic director, Theatre-at-Noon, NY, 1975-76; literary director, Guthrie Theatre, Minneapolis, 1977-79; dramaturg, O'Neill Playwrights Center, Watertown, CT; literary manager, American Repertory Theatre, Cambridge, MA, 1980-82.

WRITINGS: PLAYS, TRANSLATIONS—*When We Dead Awaken* (by Henrik Ibsen), 1971; *Happy End* (by Bertolt Brecht and Elisabeth Hauptmann), Brooklyn Academy of Music, Brooklyn, then Martin Beck Theatre, NY, 1972, also at Arena Stage, Washington, DC, 1985; *The Rise and Fall of the City of Mahagonny* (opera libretto by Bertolt Brecht), 1974; *The Bourgeois Gentleman* (play by Moliere), 1974; *Rameau's Nephew* (play by Diderot), 1976; *Force of Habit* (play by Thomas Bernhard), 1976; also opera librettos with music by Offenbach and Donizetti; *The Pretenders*, Guthrie, Minneapolis, MN, 1977; *Lulu* (by Wedekind), American Repertory Theatre, Cambridge, MA, 1983; *Roundheads and Pointheads* (play by Brecht), Classic Theatre, NY, 1985.

LYRICS—*Times and Appetites of Toulouse-Lautrec*, American Place Theatre, NY, 1985.

DRAMA CRITICISM—For the *Village Voice*, New York, since 1970.

RECORDINGS: Lyrics of Kurt Weill Songs sung by Estelle Parsons, Ellen Burstyn, Tammy Grimes, and Paula Laurence.

AWARDS: Guggenheim Fellowship, 1976; National Educational Association Translation Grant, 1986.

ADDRESSES: HOME—749 West End Avenue, New York, NY 10025. AGENT—Helen Merrill, 361 W. 17th Street, New York, NY 10011.

* * *

FELL, Norman 1924-

PERSONAL: Born March 24, 1924. EDUCATION: Attended Temple University; studied acting with Stella Adler.

VOCATION: Actor.

CAREER: PRINCIPAL TELEVISION APPEARANCES—Series: Mike the cabbie, *Joe and Mabel*, CBS, 1956; Det. Meyer Meyer, *87th Precinct*, NBC, 1961-62; Sgt. Charles Wilentz, *Dan August*, ABC, 1970-71; Nathan Davidson, *Needles and Pins*, NBC, 1973; Stanley Roper, *Three's Company*, ABC, 1977-79; Stanley Roper, *The Ropers*, ABC, 1979-80.

Mini-series: Smitty, *Rich Man, Poor Man*, ABC, 1976; *Roots: The Next Generation*, ABC, 1979.

Episodic: *Tom Ewell Show*, CBS.

PRINCIPAL FILM APPEARANCES—*Pork Chop Hill*, United Artists, 1959; *Oceans Eleven*, Warner Brothers, 1960; *Rat Race*, Paramount, 1960; *Inherit the Wind*, United Artists, 1960; *The Graduate*, Embassy, 1967; *Bullitt*, Warner Brothers/Seven Arts, 1968; *If It's Tuesday, This Must Be Belgium*, United Artists, 1969; *Catch-22*, Paramount, 1970; *The End*, United Artists, 1978.

STAGE DEBUT—*Bonds of Interest*, Circle-in-the-Square, NY.

MEMBER: Actors' Equity Association, Screen Actors Guild,

American Federation of Television and Radio Actors.

ADDRESSES: AGENT—Contemporary-Korman Agency, 132 Lasky Drive, Beverly Hills, CA 90212.*

* * *

FIELD, Sally   1946-

PERSONAL: Born in 1946, in Pasadena, CA; married Steve Craig, September, 1968 (divorced, 1975); married Alan Greisman (a producer), December, 1984; children: (first marriage) Peter, Eli. EDUCATION: Studied acting at the Actors Studio, 1973-75.

VOCATION: Actress.

CAREER: FILM DEBUT—*The Way West,* United Artists, 1967. PRINCIPAL FILM APPEARANCES—*Stay Hungry,* United Artists, 1976; *Heroes,* Universal, 1977; *Smokey and the Bandit,* Universal, 1977; *Hooper,* Warner Brothers, 1978; *The End,* United Artists, 1978; title role, *Norma Rae,* Twentieth Century-Fox, 1979; *Beyond the Poseidon Adventure,* Warner Brothers, 1979; *Smokey and the Bandit II,* Universal, 1980; *Back Roads,* Warner Brothers, 1981; *Absence of Malice,* Columbia, 1981; *Kiss Me Goodbye,* Twentieth Century-Fox, 1982; *Places in the Heart,* Tri-Star, 1984; *Murphy's Romance,* Columbia, 1985.

PRINCIPAL TELEVISION APPEARANCES—Series: Francine "Gidget" Lawrence, *Gidget,* ABC, 1965-66; Sister Bertrille, *The Flying Nun,* ABC, 1967-69; Sally Burton, *The Girl with Something Extra,* NBC, 1973.

Movies: *Maybe I'll Come Home in the Spring,* ABC, 1971; *Marriage: Year One,* 1971; *Home for the Holidays,* 1972; *Bridges,* 1976; *Sybil,* NBC, 1976.

Special: *All the Way Home,* 1981.

Photograph by Harry Langdon

AWARDS: Outstanding Lead Actress in a Drama or Comedy Special, Emmy, 1976-77, for *Sybil;* Best Actress, Academy Award, New York Film Critics Award, Golden Globe, National Society of Film Critics Award, Golden Globe, and Cannes Film Festival Award, all 1980, for *Norma Rae;* Best Actress, Academy Award, 1984, for *Places in the Heart.*

MEMBER: Screen Actors Guild, American Federation of Television and Radio Artists.

ADDRESSES: AGENT—c/o Rick Nicita and Mike Ovitz, Creative Artists Agency, 1888 Century Park E., Suite 1400, Los Angeles, CA 90067.

* * *

FIRTH, David   1945-

PERSONAL: Born David Firth Coleman, March 15, 1945, in Bedford, England; son of Ivor Firth and Beatrice (Jenkins) Coleman; married Julia Elizabeth Gould. EDUCATION: Bedford Modern School; Sussex University; studied for the theatre at the Guildhall School of Music.

VOCATION: Actor and singer.

CAREER: STAGE DEBUT—Fyodor, *Notes from the Underground,* N.U.S. Drama Festival, Garrick Theatre, London, January 1967. PRINCIPAL STAGE APPEARANCES—The courier, *1776,* New Theatre (the Alberry), London, 1970; Orlando, *As You Like It* and Mercutio, *Romeo and Juliet,* both Phoenix Theatre, Leicester, England, 1971; Roger, *After Haggerty* and Jo Jo, *Irma La Douce,* both Belgrade Theatre, Coventry, England, 1972; Gawain, *The Green Knight* and *Happy as a Sandbag,* both Phoenix Theatre, Leicester, 1973; Donalbain, *Macbeth* and Yasha, *The Cherry Orchard,* both National Theatre, London, 1973; Lucio, *Measure for Measure,* Old Vic, London, 1973; Attilio, *Saturday, Sunday, Monday,* National Theatre Company, Queen's Theatre, London, 1974; Massingham, *All Good Men,* Young Vic, London, 1975; Parolles, *All's Well That Ends Well* and Lucio, *Measure for Measure,* both Greenwich Theatre, London, 1975; Nickleby, *Nickleby and Me,* Royal Theatre, Stratford, England, 1975; Richard Pershore, *The Chairman,* Globe Theatre, London, 1976; *Side by Side by Sondheim,* Wyndham's Theatre, London, 1977; Courtall, *She Would and If She Could,* Greenwich Theatre, London, 1979; Captain Loveit, *Miss in Her Teens* and Leander, *The Padlock,* both Old Vic, London, 1979.

MAJOR TOURS—Amiens, *As You Like It,* Balthasar, *Much Ado About Nothing,* Helenus, *Troilus and Cressida,* Sordido, *The Revenger's Tragedy,* all with Royal Shakespeare Company, Stratford, London, United States and Europe, 1967-70; James, *Me Times Me,* British Isles, 1972.

PRINCIPAL STAGE WORK—Director, *Purity,* Phoenix Theatre, Leicester, England, 1973.

PRINCIPAL TELEVISION APPEARANCES—*Search for the Nile,* 1971; *Love for Lydia; Raffles; Nanny's Boy; Whodunit.*

ADDRESSES: HOME—One Newry Road, St. Margaret's, Twickenham, Middlesex, England.*

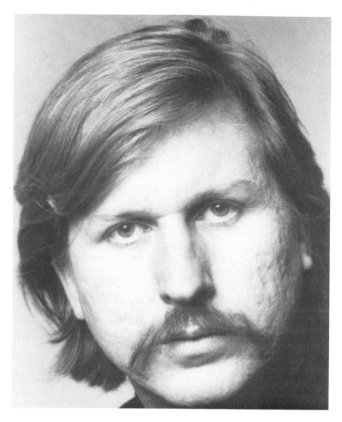

LANNY FLAHERTY

FLAHERTY, Lanny   1942-

PERSONAL: Born July 27, 1942, in Pontotoc, MS; son of Lander (a farmer) and Beryl (Maharrey) Flaherty. EDUCATION: University of Southern Mississippi, B.F.A., 1969; Southern Methodist University, M.F.A., 1972. MILITARY: U.S. Army Military Police Corps, 1963-65.

VOCATION: Actor and writer.

CAREER: STAGE DEBUT—Capulet, *Romeo and Juliet,* Dallas Shakespeare Festival, TX. NEW YORK DEBUT—Scotty, *Sweet Bird of Youth,* Harkness Theatre. PRINCIPAL STAGE APPEARANCES—Broadway: *Requiem for a Heavyweight;* understudy for Slim, Whit, Boss, and Carlson, *Of Mice and Men;* Off Off-Broadway: Hank, *The Other Women,* Judith Anderson Theatre; Owen, *The Pickle,* T.O.M.I. Theatre; regional: Lee, *True West,* Actors Theatre of Louisville, KY, Capitol Repertory; Lennie, *Of Mice and Men,* Actors Theatre of Louisville; Tilden, *Buried Child,* Pittsburgh Public Theatre, PA; governor and hanging judge, *Hot Grog,* Virginia Stage Company.

Also: as Krapp, *Krapp's Last Tape;* Malvolio, *Twelfth Night;* Sir Toby Belch, *Twelfth Night;* Sir Sampson Legend, *Love for Love;* Junius Brutus Booth, *At the Tavern of the Raven;* James Tyrone, *Long Day's Journey into Night;* Hamm, *Endgame;* J. Brown, R.E. Lee, and A. Lincoln, *John Brown's Body;* Victor Velasco, *Barefoot in the Park;* Henry II, *The Lion in Winter;* General St. Pe, *Waltz of the Toreadors;* Vershinen, *Three Sisters.*

Also performed at the Actors Theatre of Louisville's New Play Festival as Mr. Vaughn, *Courtship;* driver, *Summer;* Roundhouse,

Love Suicide; and Moore, *Advice to the Players.* Performed at the Dallas Shakespeare Festival as Gremio, *The Taming of the Shrew;* ghost, *Hamlet;* Pistol, *Merry Wives of Windsor.*

TELEVISION DEBUT—*John Locke,* PBS, Dallas, TX. PRINCIPAL TELEVISION APPEARANCES—Stan, *The Guiding Light;* Big Vinnie Nichols, *As the World Turns;* sheriff, *The Edge of Night.*

PRINCIPAL FILM APPEARANCES—Security guard, *The Prof.*

WRITINGS: PLAYS, PRODUCED—*Showdown at the Adobe Motel,* O'Neill Playwrights Conference, 1979; Hartman Stage Company. PLAYS, UNPRODUCED—"A Birthing at Nubbin Ridge;" "Crisscrosscreeks," 1981; "Cedars Mark the Campground," 1983; "No More Topwaters at Little Owl Creek;" "Whilom."

MEMBER: Actors' Equity Association, Screen Actors Guild, American Federation of Television and Radio Artists, The Dramatists Guild.

AWARDS: CAPS Grant, 1983, for "Cedars Mark the Campground."

ADDRESSES: HOME—New York, NY. AGENT—Sames and Rollnick Associates, 250 W. 57th Street, New York, NY 10107.

*   *   *

FLOOD, Ann

PERSONAL: Born Ann Ott, November 12; daughter of Frank J. and Ann K. (Flood) Ott; married Herbert A. Granath, November 22, 1958; children: Kevin Michael, Brian John, Peter James, Karen Mary.

VOCATION: Actress.

CAREER: PRINCIPAL TELEVISION APPEARANCES—Series: *From These Roots,* 1958-62; Nancy Karr, *The Edge of Night,* CBS, 1962-1975, then ABC, 1975-84; *Matinee Theatre.*

Episodic: *The Cosby Show,* NBC, 1986.

PRINCIPAL STAGE APPEARANCES—Broadway productions: *Kismet,* 1953, and *Holiday for Lovers,* 1958; regional appearances include *Isn't It Romantic?,* Birmingham, AL; O'Neill Playwright Conference, Waterford, CT, 1986.

MEMBER: Actors' Equity Association, Screen Actors Guild, Academy of Television Arts and Sciences.

ADDRESSES: OFFICE—222 E. 44th Street, New York, NY 10017.*

*   *   *

FOGARTY, Jack   1923-

PERSONAL: Born October 23, 1923, in Liverpool, England; son of James and Catherine (Paterson) Fogarty. MILITARY: U.S. Army, World War II.

VOCATION: Actor.

JACK FOGARTY

CAREER: PRINCIPAL TELEVISION APPEARANCES—Episodic: *Studio One; The Defenders; The Nurses; The Guiding Light; Search for Tomorrow; One Life to Live; The Doctors.* On PBS: *Adams Chronicles; Best of Families; On Being Black.*

Movies: *Rage of Angels,* 1983; *The Royal Romance of Charles and Diana,* 1982; *The Equalizer.*

Pilots: Judge Whitehead, *People Versus . . .*

PRINCIPAL STAGE APPEARANCES—Off-Broadway: *No Exit; Hogan's Goat;* Mortimer, *The Fantasticks;* Old Billy Rice, *The Entertainer;* Mr. Reardon, *In Celebration;* the Father, *Scenes Dedicated to My Brother;* also productions of *A Delicate Balance; Gingerbread Lady; Plaza Suite; Little Mary Sunshine; Amorous Flea.*

PRINCIPAL FILM APPEARANCES—*Still of the Night,* Metro-Goldwyn-Mayer, United Artists, 1982; *Tootsie,* Columbia, 1982; *King of Comedy,* Twentieth Century-Fox, 1983; also, *Across the Brooklyn Bridge; Double Take.*

RELATED CAREER—Also employed by the Office of Communication, Archdiocese of New York.

MEMBER: Actors' Equity Association, Screen Actors Guild, American Federation of Television and Radio Artists.

ADDRESSES: HOME—294 Highwood Street, Teaneck, NJ 07666.

FORD, Glen 1916-

PERSONAL: Full name, Gwyllin Samuel Newton Ford, May 1, 1916, in Quebec, Canada; son of Newton and Hannah Ford; married Eleanor Powell, October 23, 1943 (divorced); married second wife, March 27, 1966; children: (first marriage) Peter Newton. MILITARY: U.S. Marine Corps., 1942-45.

VOCATION: Actor.

CAREER: FILM DEBUT—*Heaven with a Barbed Wire Fence,* Twentieth Century Fox, 1939. PRINCIPAL FILM APPEARANCES—*My Son Is Guilty,* 1939; *Convicted Woman,* 1940; *Babies for Sale,* 1940; *Blondie Plays Cupid,* 1940; *Men without Souls,* 1940; *The Lady in Question,* 1940; *So Ends Our Night,* 1941; *Texas,* 1941; *Go West, Young Lady,* 1941; *Flight Lieutenant,* 1942; *The Adventures of Martin Eden,* 1942; *The Desperadoes,* 1943; *Destroyer,* 1943; *Gilda,* 1946; *Gallant Journey,* 1946; *A Stolen Life,* 1946; *Framed,* 1947; *The Mating of Millie,* 1948; *The Return of October,* 1948; *The Loves of Carmen,* 1948; *The Man from Colorado,* 1948; *The Undercover Man,* 1949; *Lust for Gold,* 1949; *The Doctor and the Girl,* 1949; *Mr. Soft Touch,* 1949.

The Flying Missile, 1950; *Follow the Sun,* 1951; *The Secret of Convict Lake,* 1951; *The Green Glove,* 1951; *Young Man with Ideas,* 1952; *Affair in Trinidad,* 1952; *The Man from the Alamo,* 1953; *Terror on a Train,* 1953; *Plunder of the Sun,* 1953; *The Big Heat,* 1953; *Appointment in Honduras,* 1953; *Human Desire,* 1954; *The Americano,* RKO, 1955; *The Violent Men,* Columbia, 1955; *Interrupted Melody,* Metro-Goldwyn-Mayer, 1955; *Blackboard Jungle,* Metro-Goldwyn-Mayer, 1955; *Trial,* Metro-Goldwyn-Mayer, 1955; *Ransom,* Metro-Goldwyn-Mayer, 1956; *The Fastest Gun Alive,* Metro-Goldwyn-Mayer, 1956; *Jubal,* Columbia, 1956; *The Teahouse of the August Moon,* Metro-Goldwyn-Mayer, 1956; *Don't Go Near the Water,* Metro-Goldwyn-Mayer, 1957; *3:10 to Yuma,* Columbia, 1957; *Imitation General,* Metro-Goldwyn-Mayer, 1958; *Cowboy,* Columbia, 1958; *The Sheepman,* Metro-Goldwyn-Mayer, 1958; *Torpedo Run,* Metro-Goldwyn-Mayer, 1958; *It Started with a Kiss,* Metro-Goldwyn-Mayer, 1959; *The Gazebo,* Metro-Goldwyn-Mayer, 1959.

The Four Horseman of the Apocalypse, Metro-Goldwyn-Mayer, 1961; *Cimarron,* Metro-Goldwyn-Mayer, 1961; *Pocketful of Miracles,* United Artists, 1961; *Cry for Happy,* Columbia, 1961; *Experiment in Terror,* Columbia, 1962; *Love Is a Ball,* United Artists, 1963; *The Courtship of Eddie's Father,* Metro-Goldwyn-Mayer, 1963; *Fate Is the Hunter,* Twentieth Century-Fox, 1964; *Advance to the Rear,* Metro-Goldwyn-Mayer, 1964; *Dear Heart,* Warner Brothers, 1965; *The Rounders,* Metro-Goldwyn-Mayer, 1965; *Rage,* Columbia, 1966; *Is Paris Burning?,* Paramount, 1966; *The Last Challenge,* Metro-Goldwyn-Mayer, 1967; *A Time for Killing,* Columbia, 1967; *The Money Trap,* Metro-Goldwyn-Mayer, 1968; *The Day of the Evil Gun,* Metro-Goldwyn-Mayer, 1968; *Heaven with a Gun,* Metro-Goldwyn-Mayer, 1969; *Smith!,* Buena Vista, 1969; *Santee!,* 1973; *Midway,* 1976; *Goodbye and Amen,* 1978; *Superman,* Warner Brothers, 1978; *The Visitor,* 1980; *Happy Birthday to Me and Virus,* 1981; also appeared in *The Redhead and the Cowboy.*

PRINCIPAL TELEVISION APPEARANCES—Series: *Cade's County,* CBS, 1971-72; narrator, *Friends of Man,* syndicated, 1973-74; Rev. Tom Holvak, *The Family Holvak,* NBC, 1975-77; George Caldwell, *Once an Eagle,* NBC, 1976-77; narrator, *When Havoc Struck,* syndicated, 1978.

Specials: narrator, *America,* 1971; *Evening in Byzantium,* 1978.

Movies: *The Brotherhood of the Bell*, 1970; *Cade's County*, 1971; *Police Story*, 1973; *Punch and Jody*, 1974; *The Greatest Gift*, 1975; *The Disappearance of Flight 412*, 1975; *No Margin for Error*, 1978; *The Gift*, 1979.

STAGE DEBUT—*Tom Thumbs Wedding*, 1920. PRINCIPAL STAGE APPEARANCES—Broadway productions: *The Children's Hour*, 1935; *Golden Boy; Broom for a Bride*.

MAJOR TOURS—*Soliloquy*, U.S. cities, 1938.

AWARDS: Number One Box Office Star in America, *Motion Picture Herald-Fame* Poll, 1958.*

*   *   *

FRANCIOSA, Anthony   1928-

PERSONAL: Born Anthony Papaleo, October 25, 1928, in New York, NY; son of Anthony and Jean (Franciosa) Papaleo; married Beatrice Bakalyar, 1952 (divorced, 1957); married Shelley Winters, May 5, 1957 (divorced, 1960); married Judy Balaban, January 1, 1962. EDUCATION: Studied drama with Joseph Geiger; won a scholarship to the Dramatic Workshop, New School for Social Research; studied at the Actors Studio.

VOCATION: Actor.

CAREER: PRINCIPAL FILM APPEARANCES—*A Face in the Crowd*, Warner Brothers, 1957; *This Could Be the Night*, Metro-Goldwyn-Mayer, 1957; *A Hatful of Rain*, Twentieth Century-Fox, 1957; *Wild In the Wind*, Paramount, 1957; *The Long Hot Summer*, Twentieth Century-Fox, 1958; *Naked Maja*, United Artists, 1959; *Career Story on Page One*, 1960; *Go Naked in the World*, 1960; *Senilita*, 1961; *Period of Adjustment*, Metro-Goldwyn-Mayer, 1962; *Rio Conchos*, Twentieth Century-Fox, 1964; *Assault on a Queen*, Paramount, 1966; *A Man Could Get Killed*, Universal, 1966; *The Swinger*, Paramount, 1966; *A Girl Called Fathom*, 1967; *A Man Called Gannon*, Universal, 1968; *The Sweet Ride*, Twentieth Century-Fox, 1968; *In Enemy Country*, 1968; *Across 110th Street*, United Artists, 1972; *The Drowning Pool*, Warner Brothers, 1975; *Firepower*, Associated Film Distributors, 1979; *Death Wish II*, Filmways, 1982.

PRINCIPAL TELEVISION APPEARANCES—Series: Valentine Farrow, *Valentine's Day*, ABC, 1964-65; Jeff Dillon, *The Name of the Game*, 1968-72; Nick Bianco, *Search*, 1972-73; title role, *Matt Helm*, ABC, 1975-76; host, *That's Hollywood*, syndicated, 1976; Cary Maxwell, *Finder of Lost Loves*, ABC, 1984.

Mini-Series: Alex Budde, *The Innocent and the Damned* (also known as *Aspen*), NBC, 1979; Smokey Stephenson, *Wheels*, NBC, 1979.

Movie: *Stagecoach*, CBS, 1986.

PRINCIPAL STAGE APPEARANCES—Broadway production: *End as a Man*, 1953; *Wedding Breakfast*, 1954-55; *A Hatful of Rain*, 1955; also worked with drama groups including Off-Broadway, Inc. and the New York Repertory Theatre.

AWARDS: Golden Globe Award, Best Motion Picture Actor, 1960, for *Career Story on Page One;* Count Volpe Ei Misurata Cup Award, Venice Film Festival.

ADDRESSES: AGENT—Creative Artists Agency, 1888 Century Park E., Suite 1400, Los Angeles, CA 90067.*

*   *   *

FRANCISCUS, James   1934-

PERSONAL: Full name, James Grover Franciscus; born January 31, 1934, in Clayton, MO; son of John Allen and Loraine (Grover) Franciscus; married Kathleen Kent Wellman, March 28, 1960; children: Jaimie, Kellie, Korie, Jolie. EDUCATION: Yale University, B.A., 1957.

VOCATION: Actor and producer.

CAREER: PRINCIPAL TELEVISION APPEARANCES—Series: Detective Jim Halloran, *Naked City*, ABC, 1948-63; Russ Andrews, *The Investigators*, CBS, 1961; John Novak, *Mr. Novak*, NBC, 1963-65; Mike Longstreet, *Longstreet*, ABC, 1971-72; Dr. Benjamin Elliot, *Doc Elliot*, ABC, 1974; James Hunter, *Hunter*, CBS, 1977.

Movie: John F. Kennedy, *Jacqueline Bouvier Kennedy*, 1981; *Elena*, NBC, 1985.

PRINCIPAL FILM APPEARANCES—*The Outsiders*, Universal, 1962; *Youngblood Hawke*, Warner Brothers, 1964; *Hell Boats*, 1968; *Marooned*, Columbia, 1969; *Beneath the Planet of the Apes*, Twentieth Century-Fox, 1969; *Cat O' Nine Tails*, National General, 1971; *The Amazing Dobermans*, Buena Vista, 1976; *Puzzle*, 1977; *Good Guys Wear Black*, 1977; *The Greek Tycoon*, Universal, 1978; *Greed*, 1978; *The Concorde: Airport '79*, Universal, 1979; *City on Fire*, Avco Embassy, 1979; *Killer Fish*, 1979; *Nightkill*, 1980; *Butterfly*, 1980; *White Death*, 1980; *The Courageous*, 1982.

PRINCIPAL FILM WORK—Producer: *Heidi*, Warner Brothers, 1969; *David Copperfield*, 1970; *Jane Eyre*, 1971; *Kidnapped*, American International, 1971; *The Red Pony*, 1973.

RELATED CAREER—Vice president, Omnibus Productions, Inc., Ltd., 1968—.

ADDRESSES: AGENT—International Creative Management, 8899 Beverly Blvd., Los Angeles, CA 90048.*

*   *   *

FRIEDMAN, Bruce Jay   1930-

PERSONAL: Born April 26, 1930, in the Bronx, NY; married Ginger Howard (an interior designer), 1954 (divorced); married Pat O'Donohue, July 3, 1983. EDUCATION: Attended the University of Missouri. MILITARY: U.S. Air Force.

VOCATION: Playwright and novelist.

WRITINGS: PLAYS, PRODUCED—*23 Pat O'Brien Movies*, American Place Theatre, NY, 1966; *Scuba Duba*, New Theatre, NY, 1968, published by Simon & Schuster; *A Mother's Kisses*, 1968; *The Car Lover*, 1968; *Steambath*, Truck and Warehouse Theatre, NY, 1970, published by Knoph, 1971; (with Jacques Levy) *First Offenders*, 1973; *Turtlenecks*, Philadelphia, PA, 1973; *A Foot in the Door*, American Place Theatre, NY, 1979.

SCREENPLAYS—*The Owl and the Pussycat* (based on the play by

William Manhof), Columbia, 1971; (story only) *The Heartbreak Kid,* Twentieth Century-Fox, 1972; *Stir Crazy,* Columbia, 1980; (story, co-screenwriter) *Doctor Detroit,* 1982; (story, co-screenwriter) *Splash,* Buena Vista, 1984.

NOVELS—*Stern,* Simon & Schuster, 1962; *A Mother's Kisses,* Simon & Schuster, 1964; *The Dick,* 1970; *About Harry Towns,* 1974; *The Lonely Guy's Book of Life* (basis for the movie, *The Lonely Guy*), 1982; *Tokyo Woes,* Donald I. Fine, 1985.

SHORT STORIES—*Far From the City of Class and Other Stories,* Frommer Pasmantier, 1963; *Black Angels,* Simon & Schuster, 1966; *Let's Hear It for a Beautiful Guy,* 1984.

ADDRESSES: AGENT—c/o The Lantz Office, 888 Seventh Avenue, New York, NY 10019.

*   *   *

FROST, David   1939-

PERSONAL: Full name, David Paradine Frost; born April 7, 1939, in Tenderdon, England; son of W.J. and Paradine Frost; married Lynne Frederick, January, 1981 (divorced, 1982); married Carina Fitzalan Howard, 1983. EDUCATION: Gonnville and Caius College, University of Cambridge, England, M.A.

VOCATION: Interviewer and writer.

CAREER: PRINCIPAL TELEVISION APPEARANCES—*That Was the Week That Was,* BBC, 1962-63, NBC, 1964-65; *A Degree of Frost,* BBC, 1963; *Not So Much a Program, More of a Way of Life,* BBC, 1964-65; *David Frost at the Phonograph,* 1966; "David Frost's Night Out in London," *ABC Stage 67,* ABC, 1967; *The Frost Report,* 1966-67; *Frost Over England,* 1967; *The Frost Program,* 1966-68, 1972; *Frost on Friday, Frost on Saturday, Frost on Sunday,* 1968-69; *The David Frost Show,* syndicated, 1969-72; *David Frost Review,* 1971-73; *That Was the Year That Was,* 1973; *The Frost Interview,* 1974; *We British,* 1975; *The Sir Harold Wilson Interviews,* 1976-77; *The Crossroads of Civilization,* 1977-78; *The Nixon Interviews,* 1977; *Headliners with David Frost,* NBC, 1978; *Good Morning Britain,* 1983.

PRINCIPAL TELEVISION WORK—Producer, *James A. Michener's Dynasty,* 1976.

PRINCIPAL STAGE APPEARANCES—*An Evening with David Frost,* 1966.

RELATED CAREER—Creator, London Weekend Consortium (with Aidan Crawley), 1967; chairman, David Paradine, Ltd., 1966—; joint deputy chairman, Equity Enterprises, 1973-76; commentator, NBC Current Affairs.

WRITINGS: BOOKS—*That Was the Week That Was,* 1963; *How to Live Under Labour,* 1964; *Talking with Frost,* 1967; *To England with Love,* 1967; *The Presidential Debate,* 1968; *The Americans, Whitman and Frost, I Gave Them a Sword, I Could Have Kicked Myself,* 1982; *Who Wants to Be a Millionaire,* 1983; *David Frost's Book of the World's Worst Decisions,* 1983; *David Frost's Book of Millionaires, Multimillionaires and Really Rich People,* 1984.

AWARDS: Emmy Awards, 1970, 1971; Decorated Order of the British Empire, 1967; Golden Rose of Montreaux Award, 1967; Royal Television Society Award, 1967; Richard Dimbleby Award,

1967; Religious Heritage American Award, 1971; Albert Einstein Award, 1982.

ADDRESSES: OFFICE—46 Egerton Crescent, London SW3, England.*

*   *   *

FUGARD, Athol   1932-

PERSONAL: Born June 11, 1932, in Middleburg, Cape Province, South Africa; son of Harold David and Elizabeth Madalena (Potgeiter) Fugard; married Sheila Mering (a poet, novelist and actress); children: Lisa, Maria. EDUCATION: University of Cape Town.

VOCATION: Playwright, actor, and director.

CAREER: PRINCIPAL STAGE APPEARANCES—Morris, *The Blood Knot,* Sophiatown, South Africa, 1961, Hapstead, England, 1966, Yale Repertory, New Haven, CT, 1985, John Golden Theatre, NY, 1985-86.

PRINCIPAL STAGE WORK—Directed: *Blood Knot,* Hampstead, England, 1966; *The Trials of Brother Jero,* Hampstead, 1966; *The Island, Sizwe Bansi Is Dead,* NY, *Statements After an Arrest Under the Immorality Act,* Royal Court Theatre, London, 1974; *Dimetos,* Edinburgh Festival, 1975, then Comedy Theatre, London, 1976; *Hello and Goodbye,* Riverside Theatre, NY, 1978; *A Lesson from Aloes,* Yale Repertory, New Haven, CT, 1979-80, then ran on Broadway, 1980; *Master Harold . . . and the Boys,* Lyceum, NY, 1982.

PRINCIPAL FILM APPEARANCES—*Meetings with Remarkable Men,* 1979; General Jan Christian Smuts, *Gandhi,* Columbia, 1982; Eugene Marais, *The Guest,* 1984; *The Killing Fields,* Warner Brothers, 1984.

WRITINGS: PLAYS, PRODUCED—*The Cell,* Cape Town, South Africa, 1957; *Klaas and the Devil,* Cape Town, 1957; *No-Good Friday,* Bantu Mews Social Center, Johannesburg, South Africa, 1958; *Nongogo,* South Africa, 1959; *A Place for the Pigs,* South Africa, 1959; *The Cure,* South Africa, 1962-63; *People Are Living There,* 1968; *Hello and Goodbye,* 1969; *Friday's Bread on Monday,* 1970; *Boesman and Lena,* 1970; *Orestes,* 1971; *People Arriving There,* Forum, NY, 1971; *Siswe Bansi Is Dead, The Island,* 1973; *Statements After an Arrest Under the Immorality Act,* Royal Court Theatre, London, 1974; *Dimetos,* Comedy Theatre, London, 1976; *A Lesson from Aloes,* Yale Repertory, New Haven, CT, 1979-80, then NY, 1980; *Master Harold . . . and the Boys,* Lyceum Theatre, NY, 1982; *The Road to Mecca,* Yale Repertory, New Haven, CT, 1984.

SCREENPLAYS—*Boesman and Lena,* 1973; *Marigolds in August,* 1980; *The Guest,* 1984.

TELEVISION—*Millie Miglia,* 1968.

BOOKS—*Tsotsi,* 1960-80; *Note-books,* 1960-77, 1984.

AWARDS: Best Director, Antoinette Perry Award nomination, 1974, for *Sizwe Bansi Is Dead;* Best Play, Antoinette Perry Award nomination, 1980, for *A Lesson from Aloes;* Best Play, New York Drama Critics' Award, 1981, for *A Lesson from Aloes;* Best Play, Drama Desk Award, Antoinette Perry Award, Drama Critics' Circle Award, 1982, for *Master Harold . . . and the Boys;* Best Director,

Drama Critics Circle Award, 1982, for *Master Harold . . . and the Boys;* Honorary D.Litt., 1981, from Natal University, 1983, from Rhodes University, South Africa, 1984, from University of Cape Town; Honorary Doctorate of Fine Arts, 1983, from Yale; Honorary Doctorate of Humane Letters, 1984, from Georgetown.

SIDELIGHTS: CTFT learned Athol Fugard helped create the Serpent Players in Port Elizabeth, South Africa, with whom he has worked and for whom he created *Sizwe Bansi Is Dead* and *The Island.*

ADDRESSES: OFFICE—Box 5090, Walmer, Port Elizabeth, South Africa.

*   *   *

FURTH, George   1932-

PERSONAL: Born George Schweinfurth, December 14, 1932, in Chicago, IL; son of George and Evelyn (Tuelk) Schweinfurth. EDUCATION: Attended Northwestern University and Columbia University. MILITARY: U.S. Navy, 1957-58.

VOCATION: Actor and playwright.

CAREER: NEW YORK DEBUT—Jordan, *A Cook for Mr. General,* The Playhouse, 1961. PRINCIPAL STAGE APPEARANCES—Harley, *Hot Spot,* Majestic Theatre, NY, 1963; in a revue at Upstairs at the Downstairs, NY, 1960; Baby, *Plays for Bleeker Street,* Circle in the Square, NY, 1962; *The Premise,* NY, 1962; Butler, *Tiny Alice,* Los Angeles, 1965; *Tadpole,* New Theatre for Now, Los Angeles, CA, 1973.

PRINCIPAL FILM APPEARANCES—*The Best Man,* United Artists, 1964; *The New Interns,* Columbia, 1964; *A Rage to Live,* United Artists, 1965; *A Very Special Favor,* Universal, 1965; *Games,* Universal, 1967; *Tammy and the Millionaire,* Universal, 1967; *The Cool Ones,* Warner Brothers, 1967; *P.J.,* 1968; *Butch Cassidy and the Sundance Kid,* Twentieth Century-Fox, 1969; *Myra Breckenridge,* Twentieth Century-Fox, 1970; *Sleeper,* United Artists, 1973; *Blazing Saddles,* Warner Brothers, 1974; *Shampoo,* Columbia, 1975; *Oh, God!,* Warner Brothers, 1977; *Hooper,* Warner Brothers, 1978; *Cannonball Run,* Twentieth Century-Fox, 1981; *Young Doctors in Love,* Twentieth Century-Fox, 1982; *Dr. Detroit,* Universal, 1983; *The Man with Two Brains,* Warner Brothers, 1983.

Photograph by Henry Grossman

GEORGE FURTH

PRINCIPAL TELEVISION APPEARANCES—Series: Ensign Beasley, *Broadside,* ABC, 1964-65; Dwayne Witt, *Tammy,* ABC, 1965-66; Hal Dawson, *The Good Guys,* CBS, 1968-69; Frederick Steele, *The Dumplings,* NBC, 1976.

Episodic: Has appeared on numerous television shows.

WRITINGS: PLAYS, PRODUCED—Book, *Company,* Alvin Theatre, NY, 1970, and Her Majesty's Theatre, London, England, 1972; *Twigs,* Broadhurst Theatre, NY, 1971; book, *The Act,* Majestic Theatre, NY, 1977; *The Supporting Cast,* Biltmore Theatre, NY, 1981; *Merrily We Roll Along,* Alvin Theatre, NY, 1982; *Precious Sons,* Longacre Theatre, NY, 1986.

G

GABOR, Zsa Zsa 1919-

PERSONAL: Born Sari Gabor, February 6, 1919, in Budapest, Hungary; daughter of Vilmos and Jolie Gabor; married Burhan Belge (a Turkish diplomat), 1940 (marriage ended, 1941); married Conrad Hilton (a hotel owner), 1942 (divorced, 1948); married George Sanders (an actor), 1949 (marriage ended, 1954); married Herbert Hutmer (an investor), 1964 (divorced, 1966); married Joshua Cosden, Jr., 1966 (divorced, 1967); married Jack Ryan (an inventor), 1975 (divorced, 1976); married Michael O'Hara (a lawyer), 1977 (divorced, 1982); married Felipe de Alba (a lawyer), 1982; children: (second marriage) Francesca.

VOCATION: Actress.

CAREER: PRINCIPAL FILM APPEARANCES—*Lovely to Look At,* Metro-Goldwyn-Mayer, 1952; *We're Not Married,* 1952; June Avril, *Moulin Rouge,* 1952; *The Story of Three Loves,* Metro-Goldwyn-Mayer, 1953; *Lili,* Metro-Goldwyn-Mayer, 1953; *Three Ring Circus,* 1953; *Death of a Scoundrel,* Universal, 1956; *Girl in the Kremlin,* Universal, 1957; *For the First Time,* Metro-Goldwyn-Mayer, 1959; *Boys Night Out,* Metro-Goldwyn-Mayer, 1962; *Picture Mommy Dead,* Embassy, 1966; *Jack of Diamonds,* Metro-Goldwyn-Mayer, 1967; *Won Ton Ton, the Dog Who Saved Hollywood,* Paramount, 1976; *Hollywood Here I Come,* 1980.

PRINCIPAL TELEVISION APPEARANCES—Guest: *Hobby Lobby,* ABC, 1959; *Shindig,* ABC, 1965; *Person to Person,* CBS.

Pilot: Shown on *Sneak Preview,* NBC, 1956.

STAGE DEBUT—Europe. PRINCIPAL STAGE APPEARANCES—*Arsenic and Old Lace,* 1975; *Forty Carats,* 1983.

WRITINGS: BOOKS—*Zsa Zsa's Complete Guide to Men,* 1969; *How to Get a Man, How to Keep a Man, How to Get Rid of a Man,* 1971.

ADDRESSES: AGENT—Robert Hussong Agency, 8721 Melrose Avenue, Suite 108, Los Angeles, CA 90046.*

*　　　*　　　*

GAINES, Charles L. 1942-

PERSONAL: Born January 6, 1942, in Florida; son of Charles Latham (a businessman) and Margaret (Shook) Gaines; married Patricia Ellison (an artist) June 20, 1963; children: Latham, Greta, Shelby. EDUCATION: Attended Washington and Lee University; Birmingham Southern Unversity, B.A.; University of Iowa, M.F.A.

VOCATION: Writer.

WRITINGS: SCREENPLAYS—*Stay Hungry,* United Artists, 1976; *Pumping Iron,* 1977; also, *Pumping Iron: The Women,* Cinecom International, 1985

TELEVISION SCRIPTS—*Summer;* others.

BOOKS, PUBLISHED—*Stay Hungry,* Doubleday, 1972; *Pumping Iron,* Simon and Schuster, 1974; *Staying Hard,* Simon and Schuster, 1975; *Dangler,* Keiran Press, 1976; *Sportselection,* Viking Press, 1984; *Pumping Iron II: The Women,* Viking Press, 1985.

RELATED CAREER—Director, Title III Program, Green Bay, Wisconsin, 1967-69; associate professor of creative writing, New England College, 1970-76.

AWARDS: Emmy Award; two Cine Golden Eagle Awards; finalist nominee, National Book Awards, 1973; others.

ADDRESSES: HOME—Old Post Road, S. Newbury, NH 03272. AGENT—Phoenix Literary Agency, 150 E. 74th Street, New York, NY 10021.

*　　　*　　　*

GALE, John 1929-

PERSONAL: Born August 2, 1929, in Chigwell, Essex, England; son of Frank Haith and Martha Edith (Evans) Gale; married Liselotte Ann Wratten; children: two sons.

VOCATION: Producer.

CAREER: FIRST STAGE WORK—Producer, *Inherit the Wind,* St. Martin's Theatre, London, 1960. PRINCIPAL STAGE WORK—Producer (all West End, London productions): *Candida,* 1960; *On the Brighter Side* and *Caesar and Cleopatra,* both 1961; *Boeing-Boeing* and *Big Fish, Little Fish,* both 1962; *Devil May Care, Windfall, Where Angels Fear to Tread,* and *The Wings of a Dove,* all 1963; *Amber for Anna, The Easter Man, Boeing-Boeing,* and *Present Laughter,* all 1964; *Maigret and the Lady* and *The Platinum Cat,* both 1965; *The Sacred Flame* and *An Evening with George Bernard Shaw,* both 1966; *Minor Murder* and *A Woman of No Importance,* both 1967; *The Secretary Bird* and *Dear Charles,* both 1968; *Highly Confidential, The Young Churchill,* and *The Lionel Touch,* all 1969; *Abelard and Heloise,* 1970; *No Sex Please, We're British,* 1971; *Lloyd George Knew My Father, The Mating Game,* and *Parents' Day,* all 1972; *At the End of the Day, Spring,* and *Betzi,* all 1975; *Out on a Limb,* 1976; *Separate Tables, The Kingfisher, Sextet, Cause Celebre,* and *Shut Your Eyes and Think of England,* all 1977;

Murder Among Friends, 1978; *Under the Greenwood Tree, Can You Hear Me at the Back?, Happy Birthday,* and *Middle Age Spread,* 1979.

RELATED CAREER—President, Society of West End Theatre Managers, 1972-75; chairman of Theatres National Committee, 1979-85; director, Chichester Festival Theatre, 1984—.

MEMBER: Garrick Club, Green Room Club.

SIDELIGHTS: RECREATIONS—Travel and rugby.

ADDRESSES: OFFICE—The Strand Theatre, Aldwych, London WC2, England.

*   *   *

GALLAGHER, Peter

BRIEF ENTRY: Born and raised in Yonkers and Armonk, NY. Actor. Peter Gallagher attended Tufts University, where he majored in Economics. After graduating, he spent several seasons with the Boston Shakespeare Company before moving to New York, where he studied at the Actors Studio with Robert Lewis. Gallagher is one of the many actors, including Treat Williams, John Travolta, Barry Bostwick, and Marilu Henner, who got a start in the long-running Broadway hit, *Grease.* He has been seen in many off Off-Broadway and Off-Broadway productions including *Caligula* and the American premiere of *Another Country.* The actor won the Clarence Derwent award for his brief part as Billy in *The Real Thing,* and was acclaimed for his performance as Moran Evans in *The Corn Is Green.* Gallagher won a *Theatre World* award for his appearance in the short-lived *A Doll's Life,* and he was singled out by the critics as one of the few bright spots in Ray Sharkey's film *The Idolmaker.* Currently, Gallagher can be seen as Edmund in Jonathan Miller's controversial production of *Long Day's Journey into Night.**

*   *   *

GAMMON, James   1940-

PERSONAL: Born April 20, 1940, in Newman, IL; son of Donald (a musician) and Doris Latimer (Toppe) Gammon; married Nancy Jane Kapusta (a producer and theatre administrator), 1972; children: Allison Raye, Amy Sue. EDUCATION: Trained for the stage at the Company of Actors with Lawrence Parke.

VOCATION: Actor.

CAREER: PRINCIPAL FILM APPEARANCES—*Cool Hand Luke,* Warner Brothers, 1967; *Journey to Shiloh,* Universal, 1968; *Fire in the Wind,* Universal; *Thousand Plane Raid,* Metro-Goldwyn-Mayer, 1969; *A Man Called Horse,* Warner Brothers, 1970; *Macho Callahan,* Paramount, 1970; *Macon County Line,* 1974; *The Wild McCullocks,* 1975; *Bobbi Jo and the Outlaw Man,* 1976; *Pom Pom Girls,* Crown, 1976; *Black Oak Conspiracy,* 1977; *The Greatest,* Columbia, 1977; *On the Nickel,* 1980; *Urban Cowboy,* Paramount, 1980; *Any Which You Can,* Warner Brothers, 1980; *Smithereens,* 1982; *Ballad of Gregorio Cortez,* Embassy, 1982; *Vision Quest,* Warner Brothers, 1983; *Sylvester,* Columbia, 1983; *Silverado,* Columbia, 1984; *Silver Bullet,* 1985; *Sylvester,* Columbia, 1985; *Hard Traveling,* 1985; also, *Count Your Bullets.*

PRINCIPAL TELEVISION APPEARANCES—Movies: *Noon Wine,* PBS; *Kansas City Massacre,* 1975; *The Sacketts,* ABC, 1979; *The*

JAMES GAMMON

Big Black Pill (also known as *Joe Dancer*), NBC, 1981; *Rage,* 1980; *American Eagle; M.A.D.D.: Mothers Against Drunk Drivers,* NBC, 1983; *Women of San Quentin,* 1983; *Long, Hot Summer,* 1985.

Episodic: *Cagney and Lacey; The Master; The Waltons; Code R; Hunter; Charlie's Angels; Kaz; Lou Grant; The Mississippi; Murder, She Wrote; Helltown.*

NEW YORK DEBUT—Weston, *Curse of the Starving Class,* Public, 1978. PRINCIPAL STAGE APPEARANCES—Rubin Flood, *The Dark at the Top of the Stairs,* MET Theatre, Los Angeles, CA, 1978; *Middle Class White,* L.A.A.T.; *On the Money,* Victory Theatre, Los Angeles, CA; Baylor, *A Lie of the Mind,* Promenade Theatre, NY, 1985-86.

Also, at the MET Theatre in Los Angeles, CA: *Black Hole in Space; Orpheus Descending; Curse of the Starving Class; Who'll Save the Plow Boy?; The Rainmaker; Cheeseburg; The Dreamcrust; Dark at the Top of the Stairs; Bus Stop.*

RELATED CAREER—Co-founder, MET Theatre, Los Angeles, CA, 1973-83.

MEMBER: Actors' Equity Association, Screen Actors Guild, American Federation of Television and Radio Actors, Academy of Motion Picture Arts and Sciences.

AWARDS: Best Actor, Los Angeles Drama Critics Award, 1974, for *Dark at the Top of the Stairs;* Los Angeles Drama Critics Award,

Continued Excellence, 1975, to the MET Theatre.

ADDRESSES: AGENT—Rickey Barr Agency, 8350 Santa Monica Blvd., Suite 206A, Los Angeles, CA 90069.

* * *

GARDNER, Ava   1922-

PERSONAL: Born December 24, 1922, in Smithfield, NC, daughter of Jonas B. and Mary Elizabeth Gardner; married Mickey Rooney (an actor), January 10, 1942 (divorced May, 1943); married Artie Shaw (a musician), 1945 (divorced, 1946); married Frank Sinatra (a singer and actor), 1951 (divorced). EDUCATION: Attended Atlantic Christian College.

VOCATION: Actress.

CAREER: FILM DEBUT—*We Were Dancing*, 1942. PRINCIPAL FILM APPEARANCES—*Joe Smith, American*, 1942; *Lost Angel*, 1943; *Three Men in White*, Metro-Goldwyn-Mayer, 1943; *Maisie Goes to Reno*, Metro-Goldwyn-Mayer, 1945; *She Went to the Races*, Metro-Goldwyn-Mayer, 1945; *Whistle Stop*, 1946; *The Killers*, 1946; *The Hucksters*, Metro-Goldwyn-Mayer, 1947; *Singapore*, 1947; title role, *One Touch of Venus*, 1948; *The Bribe*, Metro-Goldwyn-Mayer, 1949; *The Great Sinner*, Metro-Goldwyn Mayer, 1949; *East Side, West Side*, Metro-Goldwyn-Mayer, 1949; Julia, *Showboat*, Metro-Goldwyn-Mayer, 1951; *Pandora and the Flying Dutchman*, 1951; *Lone Star*, Metro-Goldwyn-Mayer, 1952; *The Snows of Kilimanjaro*, 1952; *Ride, Vaquero*, Metro-Goldwyn-Mayer, 1952; *Mogambo*, Metro-Goldwyn-Mayer, 1953; *Knights of the Roundtable*, 1953; *The Barefoot Contessa*, 1954; *Bhowani Junction*, Metro-Goldwyn-Mayer, 1956; *The Little Hut*, Metro-Goldwyn-Mayer, 1957; *The Naked Maja*, United Artists, 1959; *On the Beach*, United Artists, 1959.

55 Days at Peking, Allied Artists, 1963; *Night of the Iguana*, Metro-Goldwyn-Mayer, 1964; *The Bible . . . in the Beginning*, Twentieth Century-Fox, 1966; *Mayerling*, Metro-Goldwyn-Mayer, 1969; *The Life and Times of Judge Roy Bean*, National General, 1972; *The Devil's Widow*, American International, 1972; *Earthquake*, Universal, 1974; *Permission to Kill*, Avco Embassy, 1975; *The Bluebird*, Twentieth Century-Fox, 1976; *The Sentinel*, 1976; *The Cassandra Crossing*, Avco Embassy, 1977; *City on Fire*, Avco Embassy, 1978; *The Kidnapping of the President*, 1979; *Priest of Love*, Filmways, 1980; *Regina*, 1982; also appeared in *The Fair Bride*.

PRINCIPAL TELEVISION APPEARANCES—Series: Ruth Sumner, *Knot's Landing*, CBS, 1985.

Mini-Series: Agrippina, *A.D.*, NBC, 1985; *Long Hot Summer*, NBC, 1985.

AWARDS: Best Actress, Academy Award nomination, 1953, for *Mogambo*.

ADDRESSES: AGENT—William Morris Agency, 151 El Camino Drive, Beverly Hills, CA 90212.*

* * *

GARNER, James   1928-

PERSONAL: Born James Scott Bumgarner, April 7, 1928, in Norman, OK; married Lois Clarke; children: Kimberly, Gretta, Scott. EDUCATION: Attended the University of Oklahoma; studied acting at the Herbert Berghof Studios, New York. MILITARY: Merchant Marines, U.S. Army, Korean conflict.

VOCATION: Actor.

CAREER: FILM DEBUT—*Toward the Unknown*, Warner Brothers, 1956. PRINCIPAL FILM APPEARANCES—*Sayonara*, Warner Brothers, 1957; *Shoot-Out at Medicine Bend*, Warner Brothers, 1957; *Darby's Rangers*, Warner Brothers, 1958; *Up Periscope*, Warner Brothers, 1959; *Cash McCall*, Warner Brothers, 1960; *The Children's Hour*, United Artists, 1962; *The Thrill of It All*, Universal, 1963; *Move Over Darling*, Twentieth Century-Fox, 1963; *The Great Escape*, United Artists, 1963; *The Americanization of Emily*, Metro-Goldwyn-Mayer, 1964; *36 Hours*, Metro-Goldwyn-Mayer, 1964; *The Art of Love*, 1965; *A Man Could Get Killed*, Universal, 1966; *Duel at Diablo*, United Artists, 1966; *Mister Buddwing*, Metro-Goldwyn-Mayer, 1966; *Grand Prix*, Metro-Goldwyn-Mayer, 1966; *Hour of the Gun*, United Artists, 1967; *Marlowe*, Metro-Goldwyn-Mayer, 1969; *Support Your Local Sheriff*, United Artists, 1971; *Support Your Local Gunfighter*, United Artists, 1971; *Skin Game*, Warner Brothers, 1971; *They Only Kill Their Masters*, Metro-Goldwyn-Mayer, 1972; *One Little Indian*, Buena Vista, 1973; *Health*, 1979; *The Fan*, 1980; *Victor/Victoria*, Metro-Goldwyn-Mayer/United Artists, 1982; title role, *Murphy's Romance*, Columbia, 1985; also appeared in *Hawaiian Cowboy*.

PRINCIPAL TELEVISION APPEARANCES—Series: Bret Maverick, *Maverick*, ABC, 1957-62; title role, *Nichols*, NBC, 1971-72; Jim Rockford, *The Rockford Files*, NBC, 1974-79; title role, *Bret Maverick*, NBC, 1981-82.

Movies: *The Rockford Files*, NBC, 1974; *The Glitter Dome*, HBO, 1984; *Heartsounds*, ABC, 1984.

Mini-series: *Space*, CBS, 1985.

Episodic: *Young Maverick*, CBS, 1979.

MEMBER: Screen Actors Guild, American Academy of Television and Radio Artists.

AWARDS: Outstanding Lead Actor in a Drama Series, Emmy, 1976, for *The Rockford Files;* military award, Purple Heart.

SIDELIGHTS: Before becoming an actor, James Garner worked as a salesman, an oil field worker, a carpet layer, a lifeguard, and a truck driver. He was also a pace car driver in the Indianapolis 500 in 1975 and 1979.

ADDRESSES: AGENT—Robinson, Lutrell, and Assoc., 141 El Camino Drive, Suite 110, Beverly Hills, CA 90212.*

* * *

GARR, Teri

PERSONAL: Born in Hollywood, CA.

VOCATION: Actress.

CAREER: PRINCIPAL FILM APPEARANCES—*The Conversation*, Paramount, 1974; *Won Ton Ton, The Dog Who Saved Hollywood*, Paramount, 1976; *Oh God!*, Warner Brothers, 1977; *Close En-*

counters of the Third Kind, Columbia, 1979; *Mr. Mike's Mondo Video*, 1979; *The Black Stallion*, United Artists, 1979; *One from the Heart*, Columbia, 1982; *Tootsie*, Columbia, 1982; *The Escape Artist*, Warner Brothers, 1982; *The Sting II*, Universal, 1983; *The Black Stallion Returns*, Metro-Goldwyn-Mayer/United Artists, 1983; *Mr. Mom*, Twentieth Century-Fox, 1983; *Firstborn*, 1984; *After Hours*, Warner Brothers, 1985; *Miracles*, Orion, 1986.

PRINCIPAL TELEVISION APPEARANCES—Movies: *Law and Order*, 1976; *Winter of Our Discontent*, 1983; *Intimate Strangers*, CBS, 1985.

Series: Regular, *The Ken Berry "Wow" Show*, ABC, 1972; Amber, *The Girl with Something Extra*, NBC, 1973-74; regular, *The Sonny and Cher Show*, CBS, 1973-74; regular, *The Sonny Comedy Review*, ABC, 1974.

PRINCIPAL STAGE APPEARANCES—Dancer, *West Side Story*, U.S. cities.

RELATED CAREER—Dancer with the San Francisco Ballet and the Los Angeles Ballet.

MEMBER: Screen Actors Guild, American Federation of Television and Radio Artists.

ADDRESSES: AGENT—c/o Rick Nicita, Creative Artists Agency,

TERI GARR

1888 Century Park E., Suite 1400, Los Angeles, CA 90067; c/o Pat Kingsley, P/M/K, 8436 W. Third Street, Suite 650, Los Angeles, CA 90048.

* * *

GASKILL, William   1930-

PERSONAL: Born June 24, 1930, in Shipley, Yorkshire, England; son of Joseph Linnaeus and Maggie (Simpson) Gaskill. EDUCATION: Graduated from Salt High School, Shipley, and Hertford College, Oxford University.

VOCATION: Director.

CAREER: FIRST STAGE WORK—Director, *The First Mrs. Fraser*, Redcar Theatre, Yorkshire, England, 1954. LONDON DEBUT—Director, *A Resounding Tinkle*, Royal Court Theatre, 1957. PRINCIPAL STAGE WORK—Director: (All London unless otherwise indicated) Assistant director and played role of Quack, *The Country Wife*, Theatre Royal, Stratford, 1955; *The Hawthorn Tree*, Q Theatre, 1955; *Epitaph for George Dillon*, 1958; double bill, *A Resounding Tinkle* and *The Hole*, 1958; *Brixham Regatta*, 1958; *The Deadly Game*, New York, 1958; *The Happy Haven*, 1960; *Richard III*, Stratford-on-Avon, 1961; *Infanticide in the House of Fred Ginger*, 1962; *Baal*, 1963. With the National Theatre of Great Britain: *The Recruiting Officer*, 1963, *Philoctetes*, *The Dutch Courtesan*, also at Chichester Festival, both 1964, *Mother Courage*, 1965, co-director, *Armstrong's Last Goodnight*, also at Chichester Festival, 1965.

With the English Stage Company at the Royal Court Theatre: *Saved*, 1965, *A Chaste Maid in Cheapside*, 1966, co-director, *The Performing Giant*, 1966, *Their Very Own, Golden City*, and *Macbeth*, all 1966, *The Three Sisters*, 1967; *Fill the Stage with Happy Hours* at the Vaudeville Theatre, 1967, *Early Morning*, 1968, *Saved*, *Early Morning*, and *The Double Dealer*, all 1969; "Come," "Go," and "Play," *Beckett 3* (triple bill), Theatre Upstairs, 1970, *Cheek*, 1970, *Man Is Man* and Edward Bond's *Lear*, 1971, *Big Wolf*, 1972, *The Sea*, 1973.

With Joint Stock Theatre Group (co-director with Max Stafford-Clark): *The Speakers*, 1974, *Fanshem*, 1975, *Yesterday's News*, 1976, *A Mad World, My Masters*, 1977, *The Ragged Trousered Philanthropists*, 1978, *An Optimistic Thrust*, 1980, *The Crimes of Vautrin*, 1983.

MAJOR TOURS AND INDEPENDENT PRODUCTIONS—Director: *Hadrian VII*, Hamburg, Germany, 1969; *The Beaux Stratagem*, National Theatre and U.S. tour, 1970; *Measure for Measure*, Exeter, 1972; *Lear*, Munich, Germany, 1973; *Galileo*, Hamburg, Germany, 1973; *Snap*, *The Kitchen*, Brussels, 1974; *Love's Labour's Lost*, Sydney, Australia, 1974; *The Government Inspector*, Edinburgh Festival, 1975; *King Oedipus* and *Oedipus at Colonus*, Dubrovnik, 1976; *The Madras House*, National Theatre, 1977; *The Barber of Seville*, Wales, 1977; *La Boheme*, Wales, 1977; *A Fair Quarrel*, National Theatre, 1979; *The Gorky Brigade*, Royal Court Theatre, 1979; *Touched* and *Tibetan Inroads*, Royal Court Theatre, 1981; *Hamlet*, Sydney, Australia, 1981; *Pericles*, Genoa, Italy, 1982; *She Stoops to Conquer*, London, 1982; *The Entertainer*, New York, 1983; *The Relapse*, London, 1983; *Rents*, London, 1984; *The Way of the World*, Chichester Festival, and London, 1984; *Candida*, Guthrie Theatre, Minneapolis, MN, 1985; *Women Beware Women*, Royal Court Theatre, 1986.

PRINCIPAL TELEVISION WORK—Director, *Zoo Time*, BBC.

SIDELIGHTS: Mr. Gaskill informs *CTFT* that he worked as a male nurse, a baker, and as a factory worker prior to his directing career.

ADDRESSES: OFFICE—124a Leighton Road, London NW5, England.

* * *

GAZZARA, Ben   1930-

PERSONAL: Born August 28, 1930, in New York, NY; son of Antonio and Angelina (Cusumano) Gazzara; married Louise Erickson (divorced); married Janice Rule (divorced); married Elke Kriwat; children (second marriage) one daughter, one stepdaughter. EDUCATION: Attended City College of New York; studied acting at Erwin Piscator's Dramatic Workshop, 1948-49, and the Actors Studio in New York.

VOCATION: Actor.

CAREER: STAGE DEBUT—Micah, *Jezebel's Husband*, Pocono Playhouse, PA, 1952. NEW YORK DEBUT—Jocko De Paris, *End as a Man*, Theatre de Lys, 1953. PRINCIPAL STAGE APPEARANCES—*Day of Grace*, Westport, CT, 1953; Jocko De Paris, *End as a Man*, Vanderbilt Theatre, NY, 1953; Brick, *Cat on a Hot Tin Roof*, Morosco Theatre, NY, 1955; Johnny Pope, *A Hatful of Rain*, Lyceum Theatre, NY, 1955; Joy, *The Night Circus*, Golden Thea-

tre, NY, 1958; *Epitaph for George Dillon*, Playhouse in the Park, Philadelphia, PA, 1959; *The Night Circus*, 1959; *Two for the Seesaw*, 1960; Edmund Darrell, *Strange Interlude*, Hudson Theatre, NY, 1963; Gaston, *Traveller without Luggage*, American National Theatre and Academy (ANTA), 1964; Erie Smith, *Hughie*, First Chicago Center, 1974; Erie Smith, *Hughie* and Leonard Pelican, *Duet*, both Golden Theatre, NY, 1975; George, *Who's Afraid of Virginia Woolf?*, Music Box Theatre, NY, 1976.

MAJOR TOURS—Micah, *Jezebel's Husband*, summer tour, 1952.

FILM DEBUT—*The Strange One*, Columbia, 1957. PRINCIPAL FILM APPEARANCES—*Anatomy of a Murder*, Columbia, 1959; *The Passionate Thief*, 1960; *The Young Doctors*, 1961; *Convicts Four*, 1962; *Conquered City*, American International Pictures, 1965; *A Rage to Live*, United Artists, 1965; *The Bridge at Remagen*, United Artists, 1969; *Husbands*, Columbia, 1970; *Capone*, Twentieth Century-Fox, 1975; *High Velocity*, 1976; *Killing of a Chinese Bookie*, Faces Distributing Corporation, 1976; *High Velocity*, 1977; *Opening Night*, 1977; *Voyage of the Damned*, Avco Embassy, 1977; *Bloodline*, 1978; *They All Laughed*, 1981; *Inchon*, Metro-Goldwyn-Mayer/United Artists, 1982; *Tales of Ordinary Madness*, 1983.

PRINCIPAL TELEVISION APPEARANCES—Series: Detective Sergeant Nick Anerson, *Arrest and Trial*, ABC, 1963-64; Paul Bryan, *Run for Your Life*, NBC, 1965-68.

Movies: *QB VII; An Early Frost*, NBC, 1985; *Letter to Three Wives*, 1985.

Episodic: *Dupont Show of the Month*.

MEMBER: Actors' Equity Association, Screen Actors Guild, American Federation of Television and Radio Artists, Directors Guild of America.

AWARDS: Drama Critics Award, 1953, for *End as a Man; Theatre World* Award, 1953.

ADDRESSES: ATTORNEY—Jay Julien, 1501 Broadway, New York, NY 10036.

* * *

GELBART, Larry   1928-

PERSONAL: Born February 25, 1928, in Chicago, IL; son of Harry and Frieda (Sturner) Gelbart; married Pat Marshall (an actress and singer), November 25, 1956; children: Cathy, Gary, Paul, Adam, Becky. EDUCATION: Attended Chicago and Los Angeles public schools. MILITARY: U.S. Army, 1945-46.

VOCATION: Writer and producer.

CAREER: PRINCIPAL STAGE WORK—Producer, *The Wrong Box*, 1966.

PRINCIPAL TELEVISION WORK—Producer: *M*A*S*H*, CBS, 1972; *Karen*, ABC, 1975; *United States*, NBC, 1980; *AfterM*A*S*H*, CBS, 1983-84.

WRITINGS: RADIO—*Duffy's Tavern*, 1945-48; *Jack Parr Show*, 1947; *Jack Carson*, 1947-48; *Bob Hope*, 1947-51; *Eddie Cantor; Joan Davis; Command Performance; Maxwell House Coffee Time with Danny Thomas*.

BEN GAZZARA

TELEVISION—*The Red Buttons Show*, CBS, 1952-53; *Your Show of Shows*, NBC, 1953-55; *The Pat Boone-Chevy Showroom*, ABC, 1957-60; *M*A*S*H*, CBS, 1972; *Karen*, ABC, 1975; *United States*, NBC, 1980; *AfterM*A*S*H*, CBS, 1983-84. Also wrote for Bob Hope, Art Carney, Celeste Holm, and Patrice Munsel.

SCREENPLAYS—*Notorious Landlady*, Columbia, 1962; *The Thrill of It All*, Universal, 1963; *The Wrong Box*, Columbia, 1966; *Oh, God*, Warner Brothers, 1977; *Oh, God, Book II*, Warner Brothers, 1980; *Movie, Movie*, Warner Brothers, 1981; *Neighbors*, Twentieth Century-Fox, 1981; (with Murray Schisgal) *Tootsie*, Columbia, 1982; (with Charlie Peters) *Blame It on Rio*, Twentieth Century-Fox, 1984; *Jazz Babies* (upcoming).

PLAYS—*My L.A.*, 1950; *The Conquering Hero*, 1960; *A Funny Thing Happened on the Way to the Forum*, 1961; *Jump*, London, 1972; *Sly Fox*, 1976.

BOOKS—*The Conquering Hero*, 1961.

MEMBER: Dramatists Guild, Writers Guild of America, American Society of Composers, Authors and Publishers, Directors Guild of America, Authors League, Motion Picture Academy of Arts and Sciences (board of governors), PEN International.

AWARDS: Emmy Award, Sylvania Award, 1960, for *Art Carney Special;* Antoinette Perry Award, 1962, for *A Funny Thing Happened on the Way to the Forum;* Writers Guild Award, 1972-73, for *M*A*S*H;* Humanities Award, Peabody Award, for *M*A*S*H;* Outstanding Comedy Series, Emmy Award, Writers Guild Award, 1973-74, for *M*A*S*H;* Edgar Allan Poe Award, Writers Guild Award, for *Oh, God;* Writers Guild Award, for *Movie, Movie;* Best Screenplay, Academy Award nomination, 1983, Los Angeles Film Critics Award, New York Film Critics Award, National Society of Film Critcs Award, Best Screenplay, all for *Tootsie.*

ADDRESSES: AGENT—c/o Louis Blau, Loeb and Loeb, 10100 Santa Monica Blvd., Suite 2200, Los Angeles, CA 90067.

*   *   *

GENET, Jean   1910-1986

PERSONAL: Born December 10, 1910, in Paris, France; died of throat cancer, in a hotel in Paris, April 14, 1986; son of Gabrielle Genet.

VOCATION: Novelist, poet, and playwright.

WRITINGS: PLAYS, PRODUCED—*Les Bonnes* (*The Maids*), first produced at Theatre Athenee, Paris, 1947, first U.S. production at the Tempo Playhouse, NY, 1955, many regional U.S. productions, published by Pauvert, translation by Bernard Frechtman, with introduction by Jean-Paul Sartre, 1954; *Haute Surveillance* (*Deathwatch*), first produced at Theatre des Mathurins, Paris, France, 1949, first U.S. production at the Theatre East, NY, 1958, published by Gallimard, 1949, English translation by Bernard Frechtman, Faber, 1961; *Le Balcon* (*The Balcony*), first produced at the London Arts Theatre Club, 1957, first U.S. production at the Circle in the Square, NY, 1960, many U.S. regional productions, including, American Repertory Theatre, Cambridge, MA, 1986, English translation by Bernard Frechtman, Faber, 1957, Grove Press, 1958, revised, edition, 1960; *Les Negres: Clownerie* (*The Blacks: A Clown Show*), first produced at the Theatre de Lutece, Paris, 1959, first U.S. production at St. Mark's Playhouse, NY, 1961, published

by M. Barbezat, 1958, translation by Bernard Frechtman as *The Blacks: A Clown Show*, Grove Press, 1960; *Les Paravents* (*The Screens*), first produced at Schlosspark Theatre, West Berlin, Germany, 1961, first U.S. production at the Chelsea Theatre Company at the Brooklyn Academy of Music, NY, 1971, published by M. Barbezat, 1961, translation by Frechtman, Grove Press, 1962.

NOVELS—*Notre-Dame-des-Fleurs* (*Our Lady of the Flowers*), limited edition published by L'Arbalete, 1943, revised edition by Gallimard, Paris, 1951, translated by Bernard Frechtman, Morihien, Paris, 1949, and with introduction by Jean-Paul Sartre, by Grove Press, 1963; *Miracle de la rose* (*Miracle of the Rose*), Arbaltet, 1946, second edition, 1956, translation by Frechtman, published by Blond, 1965 and Grove Press, 1966; *Querelle de Brest*, privately printed, 1947, translation by Gregory Streathem, Blond, 1966; *Pompes funebres* (*Funeral Rites*), privately printed, 1947, revised edition, 1948, translation by Frecthman, Grove Press, 1969; *Poemes*, privately printed by Arbalete, 1948, second edition, 1962; *Journal du voleur* (*The Thief's Journal*), Gallimard, 1949, translation by Frechtman, Olympia Press, 1954; *Letters to Roger Blin: Reflections on the Theatre*, 1969.

POETRY—*Chants secrets*, privately printed, 1944.

SCREENPLAYS—*Un Chant d'Amour* (*Love Song*); *Mademoiselle*, 1966.

PLAYS ADAPTED TO FILM—*The Balcony*, Continental, 1963; *Deathwatch*, 1965; *The Maids*, AFT, 1975.

SIDELIGHTS: CTFT notes from Jean Genet's published obituaries in *The New York Times* and *Variety* that he was abandoned by his mother and had never known his father. He was raised by peasant foster parents and was sent to a reformatory for thievery. He became a vagabond and was arrested for various crimes, spending time in and out of prisons in Europe. He began writing on brown paper bags while in prison which eventually came to the attention of Jean Cocteau, who helped arrange publication. His writings deal with the darker side of the human spirit, exploring sexual deviance and political power. Many of his plays were censored and his screenplay *Un Chant d'amour*, when shown in New York, led to police action and the closing of the theatre where it was shown. Jean Cocteau dubbed him "the black prince of French literature." Genet himself commented on his work and life, "Abandoned by my family, I found it natural to aggravate this fact by the love of males, and that love by stealing, and stealing by crime, or complicity with crime. Thus I decisively repudiated a world that has repudiated me."*

*   *   *

GIBBS, Marla   1931-

PERSONAL: Full name, Margaret Gibbs; born June 14, 1931; daughter of Douglas Bradley and Ophelia Birdie (Kemp) Gibbs; children: Angela Elayne, Jordan Joseph, Dorian Demetrius. EDUCATION: Cortez Peters Business School, Chicago, 1950-52. RELIGION: Science of the Mind Church.

VOCATION: Actress.

CAREER: PRINCIPAL TELEVISION APPEARANCES—Series: Florence Johnston, *The Jeffersons*, CBS, 1974-1985; title role, *Florence* (short-lived spin-off of *The Jeffersons*), CBS; Mary Jenkins, *227*, 1985—.

Special: Rheba, *You Can't Take It with You.*

MARLA GIBBS

Movie: *Nobody's Child*, CBS, 1986.

RELATED CAREER President, Marla Gibbs Enterprises, Los Angeles, CA, 1978—

NON-RELATED CAREER—Receptionist, Service Bindery, Chicago, IL, 1951-56; addressograph machine operation, Kelly Girls, 1956; switchboard operator, Gotham Hotel, Chicago, IL, 1957; information operator, Department of Street Railways, Chicago, IL, 1957; travel consultant, United Airlines, Detroit, MI, 1963-74; vice-president, Hormar, Inc., Los Angeles, 1978—.

AWARDS: Image Award, National Association for the Advancement of Colored People, 1979-83; Appreciation Award, Los Angeles School District, 1978; Miss Black Culture Pagaent Award, 1977; Outstanding Continuing Performance by a Supporting Actress in a Comedy, Emmy Award nominations, 1981-84.

MEMBER: American Federation of Television and Radio Artists.

SIDELIGHTS: Marla Gibbs was a member of the California State Assembly in 1980.

ADDRESSES: AGENT—c/o Brad Lemack, Lemack and Company, 7060 Hollywood Blvd., Suite 206, Los Angeles, CA 90027.

*   *   *

GIBSON, Henry   1935-

PERSONAL: Born Henry Bateman, September 21, 1935, in Germantown, PA; son of Edmund Albert and Dorothy (Cassidy) Bateman; married Lois Joan Geiger, April 6, 1966; children: Jonathan

David, Charles Alexander, James Bateman. EDUCATION: Catholic University, B.A., drama; was an observer at the Royal Academy of Dramatic Arts, London.

VOCATION: Actor and writer.

CAREER: STAGE DEBUT—Child actor, Mae Desmond Theatre Company, Philadelphia, PA. NEW YORK DEBUT—*My Mother, My Father and Me*, Broadway production, 1962. PRINCIPAL STAGE APPEARANCES—Stock productions in East Coast companies, 1943-57.

PRINCIPAL FILM APPEARANCES—*Charlotte's Web*, Paramount, 1973; *The Long Goodbye*, 1973; *Nashville*, Paramount, 1975; *The Last Remake of Beau Geste*, Universal, 1977; *The Kentucky Fried Movie*, United Film, 1977; *A Perfect Couple*, Twentieth Century-Fox, 1979; *H.E.A.L.T.H.*, 1979; *The Blues Brothers*, Universal, 1980; *The Incredible Shrinking Woman*, Universal, 1981.

PRINCIPAL TELEVISION APPEARANCES—Series: The poet (semi-regular), *The Jack Paar Show*, NBC, 1960-62; Wrongo Starr, *F-Troop*, ABC, 1967; company, *Rowan and Martin's Laugh-In*, NBC, 1968-71.

Episodic: *Fantasy Island*, ABC, 1978.

Movie: *Every Man Needs One*, 1972.

WRITINGS: BOOKS—*A Flower Child's Garden of Verses*, 1970; *Carnival of the Animals*, 1971; *The Only Show on Earth*, 1973.

ARTICLES—In *Environment* and *Quality* magazines.

MEMBER: Academy of Motion Picture Arts and Sciences, National Academy of Television Arts and Sciences, Actor's Fund, 1970—, Keep America Beautiful (advisor, 1967-69); Environmental Defense Fund, Izaak Walton League (honorary president, 1975—), Citizen's Committee on Population Growth and the American Future (1972-75); United Nations Association; National Teach-In, 1970;

ADDRESSES: AGENT—David Shapira and Associates, 15301 Ventura Blvd., Sherman Oaks, CA 91403.*

*   *   *

GILROY, Frank D.   1925-

PERSONAL: Full name Frank Daniel Gilroy; born October 13, 1925 in New York, NY; son of Frank B. (a coffee broker) and Bettina (Vasti) Gilroy; married Ruth Dorothy Gaydos, February 13, 1954; children: Anthony, John, Daniel. EDUCATION: Dartmouth College, B.A. (magna cum laude), 1950; attended Yale School of Drama. MILITARY: U.S. Army, 1943-46.

VOCATION: Playwright, director, and producer.

CAREER: (In addition to writings, below) PRINCIPAL FILM WORK—Producer and director, *Desperate Characters*, Paramount, 1971; director, *From Noon Till Three*, United Artists, 1976; producer and director, *Once in Paris*, Leigh & McLaughlin, 1978; director, *The Gig*, 1985.

WRITINGS: PLAYS, PRODUCED—*The Middle World*, Dartmouth College, 1949; *Who'll Save the Plowboy?*, Phoenix Theatre, NY,

1962; *The Subject Was Roses,* Royale Theatre, NY, 1964; *That Summer—That Fall,* 1967; *The Only Game in Town,* 1968; ''Come Next Tuesday,'' ''Twas Brilling,'' ''So Please Be Kind,'' and ''Present Tense,'' four short plays under the title, *Present Tense,* 1972; *Last Licks,* 1979.

SCREENPLAYS—(With Russell Rouse; adapted from the short story and play by Gilroy) *Fastest Gun Alive,* Metro-Goldwyn-Mayer, 1956; (with Bernie Lay, Jr.) *The Gallant Hours,* United Artists, 1960; (adapted from his own play) *The Subject Was Roses,* Metro-Goldwyn-Mayer, 1968; *The Only Game in Town,* Twentieth Century-Fox, 1969; (adapted from the novel by Paula Fox) *Desperate Characters,* Paramount, 1971; (adapted from his own novel) *From Noon Till Three,* United Artists, 1976; *Once in Paris,* Leigh & McLaughlin, 1978; *The Gig,* 1985.

TELEVISION—Episodic: *Playhouse 90; Omnibus; Studio One; U.S. Steel Hour; Kraft Theatre; LuxVideo.*

BOOKS—*About Those Roses; Or, How Not to Do a Play and Succeed* (journal), Random House, 1965; *Private,* Harcourt, 1970; (with Ruth G. Gilroy) *Little Ego* (juvenile), Simon & Schuster, 1970; *From Noon Till Three: The Possibly True and Certainly Tragic Story of an Outlaw and a Lady Whose Love Knew No Bounds,* Doubleday, 1973.

MEMBER: Dramatists Guild (council member, 1965—; president, 1969-71), Writers Guild.

AWARDS: Best American Play, Obie, 1962, for *Who'll Save the Plowboy?;* Outer Circle Award, Drama Critics Award, and Theatre Club Award, all 1964, for *The Subject Was Roses;* Pulitzer Prize for

Drama and Antoinette Perry Award, 1965, for *The Subject Was Roses.*

ADDRESSES: OFFICE—Dramatists Guild, 234 W. 44th Street, New York, NY 10036.

* * *

GLASER, Paul Michael

PERSONAL: Born March 25, in Cambridge, MA. EDUCATION: Tulane University; Boston University, M.A.

VOCATION: Actor and director.

CAREER: NEW YORK DEBUT—*Hamlet* (a rock musical version), Off-Broadway production, 1968. PRINCIPAL STAGE APPEARANCES—Has appeared in Summer Stock and Off-Broadway.

PRINCIPAL FILM APPEARANCES—as Michael Glaser: Perchik, *Fiddler on the Roof,* United Artists, 1971; *Butterflies Are Free,* Columbia, 1972.

PRINCIPAL TELEVISION APPEARANCES—Series: Det. Dave Starsky, *Starsky and Hutch,* ABC, 1975-79.

Episodic: *Love of Life; Love Is a Many Splendored Thing; Kojak; Toma; The Streets of San Francisco; The Rockford Files; The Sixth Sense; The Waltons.*

Movies: Harry Houdini, *The Great Houdinis,* 1976; *Princess Daisy,* 1983; *Jealousy,* 1984; *Attack on Fear,* CBS, 1984; *Single Bars, Single Women,* ABC, 1984; also appeared in *Trapped Beneath the Sea,* ABC.

PRINCIPAL TELEVISION WORK—Director, *Miami Vice* (episodes), ABC, 1985—.

ADDRESSES: AGENT—Hesseltine-Baker Associates, 165 W. 46th Street, New York, NY 10036; Artists Agency, 10000 Santa Monica Blvd., Suite 305, Los Angeles, CA 90067.*

* * *

GLASS, Ron

PERSONAL: Born July 10, in Evansville, IN; son of Crump and Lethia Glass. EDUCATION: University of Evansville, B.A.

VOCATION: Actor.

CAREER: STAGE DEBUT—At the Tyrone Guthrie Theatre, Minneapolis, MN. PRINCIPAL STAGE APPEARANCES—*Slow Dance on the Killing Ground,* 1972; also appeared in *The House of Atreus* and *The Taming of the Shrew.*

TELEVISION DEBUT—*Sanford and Son,* NBC, 1972. PRINCIPAL TELEVISION APPEARANCES—Series: Det. Ron Harris, *Barney Miller,* ABC, 1975-82; Felix Ungar, *The New Odd Couple,* ABC, 1982-83.

Movies: *Shirts and Skins,* 1973; *Crash,* 1978.

Episodic: *The Streets of San Francisco.*

AWARDS: Medal of Honor Award, University of Evansville.*

Photograph by Ilene Jones

FRANK D. GILROY

GLENN, Scott

PERSONAL: Born in Pittsburgh, PA.

VOCATION: Actor.

CAREER: PRINCIPAL STAGE APPEARANCES—Larry, *Angelo's Wedding,* Circle Repertory Theatre, NY (previews only), 1985; has appeared Off-Broadway in *Fortune in Men's Eyes* and *Long Day's Journey into Night.*

FILM DEBUT—*The Baby Maker,* National General, 1970. PRINCIPAL FILM APPEARANCES—*Apocalypse Now,* United Artists, 1979; *Urban Cowboy,* 1980; *Personal Best,* Warner Brothers, 1982; *The Challenge,* Embassy, 1982; *The Right Stuff,* Warner Brothers, 1983; *The Keep,* Paramount, 1983; *The River,* Universal, 1984; *Wild Geese II,* 1985; *Silverado,* Columbia, 1985.

PRINCIPAL TELEVISION APPEARANCES—Movies: *As Summers Die,* HBO, 1986; *Countdown to Looking Glass.*

MEMBER: Actors' Equity Association, Screen Actors Guild, Actor's Studio.

ADDRESSES: HOME—New York, NY.*

*   *   *

GLOVER, William 1911-

PERSONAL: Born May 6, 1911, in New York, NY; son of William H. (a telegraph executive) and Lily P. (Freir) Glover; married Isobel Cole, October 26, 1936 (divorced, 1971); married Virginia Frey (a public relations executive), August 29, 1985. EDUCATION: Rutgers University, Litt. B., 1932. MILITARY: U.S. Maritime Service, 1944-45.

VOCATION: Theatre critic and writer.

CAREER: City editor *Asbury Park Press,* NJ, 1935-39; news editor Associated Press (AP) news features, 1941-53; theatre writer, AP, 1953—, drama critic, AP, 1960-78; contributor to periodicals and journals.

MEMBER: New York Drama Critic's Circle, American League of Theatre Owners for the Antoinette Perry Awards (nominating committee, 1975-86), New Drama Forum, New York Press Club, New York Academy of Sciences, Sigma Delta Chi, Players Club, Overseas Press Club, NY, New York Reporters Association, Phi Beta Kappa.

ADDRESSES: HOME—Four E. 88th Street, New York, NY 10128.

*   *   *

GOGGIN, Dan 1943-

PERSONAL: Born May 31, 1943, in Alma, MI; son Edward Ralph (a lawyer) and Gretchen Hassig (a teacher; maiden name, Wilson) Goggin. EDUCATION: Attended Manhattan School of Music and the University of Michigan. RELIGION: Roman Catholic.

VOCATION: Writer and composer.

CAREER: NEW YORK DEBUT—Lead singer, *Luther,* St. James

Theatre, NY, 1963. PRINCIPAL STAGE WORK—Musical score writer, *Hark,* NY; musical score writer, *Legend,* NY; musical score writer, *Seven,* NY; musical score writer, *Because We're Decadent,* NY; musical score writer, *Something for Everybody's Mother,* NY; writer and director, *Nunsense,* Cherry Lane Theatre, NY.

MAJOR TOURS—Singer, *Luther,* U.S. and Canadian cities.

MEMBER: Dramatists Guild.

SIDELIGHTS: CTFT learned that Dan Goggin toured for five years with the folk singing duo, "The Saxons."

ADDRESSES: AGENT—c/o Mitch Douglas, International Creative Management, 40 W. 57th Street, New York, NY 10019.

*   *   *

GOLDBERG, Leonard 1934-

PERSONAL: Born January 24, 1934, in New York, NY; son of William and Jean (Smith) Goldberg; married Wendy Howard, November 26, 1972; children: Amanda Erin. EDUCATION: University of Pennsylvania, B.S., 1955. RELIGION: Jewish.

VOCATION: Executive producer.

CAREER: PRINCIPAL TELEVISION WORK—Series: Co-executive producer (with Aaron Spelling) for *The Rookies,* ABC, 1972-76; *Starsky and Hutch,* ABC, 1975-79; *Family,* ABC, 1976-80; *Charlie's Angels,* ABC, 1976-81; *Fantasy Island,* ABC, 1978-84; *Hart to Hart,* ABC, 1979-84; *T. J. Hooker,* ABC, 1982 85, then CBS, 1985—present; also executive producer, *Paper Dolls,* ABC, 1984.

Movies: Co-executive producer: *Brian's Song,* ABC, 1970; *Boy in the Plastic Bubble,* 1976; co-executive producer, *Little Ladies of the Night,* ABC, 1977; co-executive producer, *Paper Dolls,* ABC, 1982; executive producer, *Something About Amelia,* ABC, 1984.

PRINCIPAL FILM WORK—Co-Producer, *California Split,* Columbia, 1974; co-producer, *Baby Blue Marine,* Columbia, 1976; executive producer, *Bad News Bears in Breaking Training,* Paramount, 1977; co-executive producer, *All Night Long,* Universal, 1981; executive producer, *War Games,* Metro-Goldwyn-Mayer/United Artists, 1983.

RELATED CAREER—With research department, ABC, 1956; supervisor of special projects, NBC, 1957-61; in charge of daytime television and overall broadcast coordination with Batton, Barton, Durstine and Osborn advertising agency, 1961-63; manager of programming, ABC, 1963-64; director of programming, ABC, 1964-65; vice-president of daytime programmming, ABC, 1965-66; vice-president of network programming, ABC, 1966-69; vice-president of television production, Screen Gems (now Columbia Television), 1969-72; co-president, Spelling-Goldberg Productions, 1972-76; president and owner, Mandy Productions, 1981—present.

AWARDS: Emmy Ward nomination, Critics Circle Award, Humantas Award (three), Outstanding Service Award from the National Association for Retarded Citizens, all for *Family;* Peabody Award, Image Award of the National Association for the Advancement of Colored People, Film Advisory Board Award of Excellence, all for *Brian's Song;* Outstanding Program, Emmy Award, for *Something About Amelia.*

MEMBER: Producers Association, Hollywood Academy of Television Arts and Sciences, Hollywood Radio and Television Society; also, Cedars Sinai Hospital (board of directors).

SIDELIGHTS: RECREATION—Tennis and basketball.

Leonard Goldberg told *CTFT* ''My favorite production was *Something About Amelia,* which brought the problem of incest to the public's attention and helped thousands of people.''

ADDRESSES: OFFICE—Paramount Studios, 5555 Melrose Avenue, DeMille Building, Room 211, Los Angeles, CA 90038.

*   *   *

GOLDBERG, Whoopi

BRIEF ENTRY: Born and reared in Manhattan's Chelsea disrict. Actress and commedienne. Whoopi Goldberg joined the Helen Rubinstein Children's Theatre of the Hudson Guild when she was eight years old. In the following years, Goldberg had small roles in Broadway productions of *Pippin, Hair,* and *Jesus Christ Superstar.* In 1974, she divorced her husband and moved with her daughter, Alexandria, to San Diego, CA. There she took on the name Whoopi Kushon, but changed it shortly thereafter to Whoopi Goldberg. She prefers to keep her real name private. Goldberg was a founding member of the San Diego Repertory Company where she starred in *Mother Courage and Her Children* and in Marsha Norman's *Getting Out.* She performed with the improvisational group ''Spontaneous Combustion'' and has also earned money in such non-entertainment jobs as a bricklayer and as a mortuary cosmetologist. Goldberg moved to northern California and joined Berkeley's ''Blake Street Hawkeyes'' comedy group, where she began to develop a repertoire of characters. She put them together in a show entitled *The Spook Show.* Goldberg toured throughout the United States and Europe. The director Mike Nichols was at the Manhattan Dance Theatre when the show premiered in New York, and after seeing her performance wrote Goldberg a five page letter telling her that if she were ever interested in performing on Broadway, she should contact him. In 1984, under Nichol's direction, *Whoopi Goldberg* opened on Broadway at the Lyceum Theatre. Goldberg is a movie buff with a particular fondness for 1930's romantic comedies and 1950's horror films. In 1985, she was given the change to make a movie with director Steven Spielberg. Her portrayal of Celie in *The Color Purple* won Goldberg an Academy Award nomination. She is currently working on a new comedy film, *Jumpin' Jack Flash.**

*   *   *

GOLDSMITH, Jerry   1929-

PERSONAL: Full name, Jerrald K. Goldsmith; born February 10, 1929; son of Morris K. (a structural engineer) and Tessa (an artist; maiden name, Rappaport) Goldsmith; divorced first wife, 1971; married Carol Heather Sheinkopf, July 23, 1972; children: (first marriage) Ellen, Carrie, Joel, Jennifer; (second marriage) Aaron. EDUCATION: Studied music with Jakob Gimpel and Mario Castelnuovo-Tedesco.

VOCATION: Composer.

CAREER: FILM DEBUT—Composer, *Black Patch,* 1956. PRINCIPAL FILM WORK—Composer: *City of Fear,* Columbia, 1957; *Face of a Fugitive,* Columbia, 1959; *Studs Lonigan,* United Artists, 1960; *Lonely Are the Brave,* Universal, 1961; *The Spiral Road,* Universal, 1962; *Freud,* Universal, 1962; *The List of Adrian Messenger,*

JERRY GOLDSMITH

Universal, 1963; *Take Her, She's Mine,* Twentieth Century-Fox, 1963; *A Gathering of Eagles,* Universal, 1963; *The Stripper,* Twentieth Century-Fox, 1963; *The Prize,* Metro-Goldwyn-Mayer, 1963; *Lillies of the Field,* United Artists, 1963; *Shock Treatment,* Twentieth Century-Fox, 1964; *Seven Days in May,* Paramount, 1964; *Fate Is the Hunter,* Twentieth Century-Fox, 1964; *Rio Conchos,* Twentieth Century-Fox, 1964; *The Satan Bug,* United Artists, 1965; *In Harm's Way,* Paramount, 1965; *Von Ryan's Express,* Twentieth Century-Fox, 1965; *Morituri,* Twentieth Century-Fox, 1965; (prologue) *The Agony and the Ecstasy,* Twentieth Century-Fox, 1965.

Our Man Flint, Twentieth Century-Fox, 1966; *A Patch of Blue,* Metro-Goldwyn-Mayer, 1966; *Seconds,* Paramount, 1966; *The Trouble with Angels,* Columbia, 1966; *Stagecoach,* Twentieth Century-Fox, 1966; *The Sand Pebbles,* Twentieth Century-Fox, 1966; *Warning Shot,* Paramount, 1967; *The Flim-Flam Man,* Twentieth Century-Fox, 1967; *In Like Flint,* Twentieth Century-Fox, 1967; *The Traveling Executioner,* Metro-Goldwyn-Mayer, 1967; *Planet of the Apes,* Twentieth Century-Fox, 1968; *Hour of the Gun,* United Artists, 1967; *Sebastian,* Paramount, 1968; *Bandolero,* Twentieth Century-Fox, 1968; *The Detective,* Twentieth Century-Fox, 1968; *The Illustrated Man,* Warner Brothers/Seven Arts, 1969; *Justine,* Twentieth Century-Fox, 1969; *100 Rifles,* Twentieth Century-Fox, 1969; *The Chairman,* Twentieth Century-Fox, 1969.

The Ballad of Cable Hogue, Warner Brothers, 1970; *Tora! Tora! Tora!* Twentieth Century-Fox, 1970; *Patton,* Twentieth Century-Fox, 1970; *Rio Lobo,* National General, 1970; *The Wild Rovers,* Metro-Goldwyn-Mayer, 1971; *The Mephisto Waltz,* Twentieth Century-Fox, 1971; *The Last Run,* Metro-Goldwyn-Mayer, 1971;

Escape from the Planet of the Apes, Twentieth Century-Fox, 1971; *The Other*, Twentieth Century-Fox, 1972; *Ace Eli and Rodger of the Skies*, Twentieth Century-Fox, 1973; *Shamus*, Columbia, 1973; *One Little Indian*, Buena Vista, 1973; *Take a Hard Ride*, Twentieth Century-Fox, 1973; *The Don Is Dead*, Universal, 1973; *Papillon*, Allied Artists, 1973; *Break Out*, 1974; *Chinatown*, Paramount, 1974; *The Reincarnation of Peter Proud*, American International, 1975; *The Wind and the Lion*, United Artists/Metro-Goldwyn-Mayer, 1975.

Breakheart Pass, 1976; *The Omen*, Twentieth Century-Fox, 1976; *Ransom*, 1977; *Twilight's Last Gleaming*, Allied Artists, 1977; *Islands in the Stream*, Paramount, 1977; *MacArthur*, Universal, 1977; *Damnation Alley*, Twentieth Century-Fox, 1977; *Coma*, United Artists, 1978; *Capricorn One*, Warner Brothers, 1978; *Magic*, Twentieth Century-Fox, 1978; *Damien—Omen II*, Twentieth Century-Fox, 1978; *The Swarm*, Warner Brothers, 1978; *The Great Train Robbery*, United Artists, 1979; *The Boys from Brazil*, Twentieth Century-Fox, 1979; *Alien*, Twentieth Century-Fox, 1979; *Players*, Paramount, 1979; *Star Trek—The Motion Picture*, Paramount, 1979.

Caboblanco, 1980; *The Salamander*, U.S.-British-Italian, 1981; *The Final Conflict*, Twentieth Century-Fox, 1981; *Outland*, Warner Brothers, 1981; *Raggedy Man*, Universal, 1981; *The Challenge*, Embassy, 1982; *Night Crossing*, Buena Vista, 1982; *The Secret of Nimh*, Metro-Goldwyn-Mayer/United Artists, 1982; *Poltergeist*, Metro-Goldwyn-Mayer/United Artists, 1982; *First Blood*, Orion, 1982; *The Twilight Zone—The Movie*, Warner Brothers, 1983; *Psycho II*, Universal, 1983; *Under Fire*, Orion, 1983; *Gremlins*, Warner Brothers, 1984; *Supergirl*, Warner Brothers, 1984; *Baby*, Buena Vista, 1985; *Runaway*, 1985; *Legend*, 1985; *Explorers*, 1985; *Rambo: First Blood II*, Orion, 1985; *King Solomon's Mines*, 1985; *Link*, 1986; *Poltergeist II—The Other Side*, Metro-Goldwyn-Mayer/United Artists, 1986; *Lionheart: the Children's Crusade* (upcoming).

PRINCIPAL TELEVISION WORK—Composer: *Hallmark Hall of Fame; Playhouse 90; Studio One; The Twilight Zone; Climax; General Electric Theatre; Gunsmoke; Doctor Kildare; The Red Pony; Thriller; The Man from U.N.C.L.E.; QBVII; Babe; Stakeout on Cherry Street; Masada*.

PRINCIPAL CONCERT WORK—Composer: *Christus Apollo*, 1969; *Music for Orchestra*, 1971; a new piece commissioned by Dallas Symphony (upcoming).

PRINCIPAL DANCE WORK—Composer: *A Patch of Blue*, 1970; *Othello*, 1971.

RELATED CAREER—Visiting artist, Berklee College of Music, Boston, MA.

MEMBER: Academy of Motion Picture Arts and Sciences, Broadcast Music Inc. (B.M.I.); Yamaha Artist Program, University of Southern California School of Music (board of advisors); Society for the Preservation of Film Music (board of advisors).

AWARDS: Academy Award, 1976, for *The Omen;* Academy Award nominations: 1962, for *Freud;* 1965, for *A Patch of Blue;* 1966, for *The Sand Pebbles;* 1968, for *Planet of the Apes;* 1970, for *Patton;* 1973, for *Papillon;* 1974, for *Chinatown;* 1975, for *The Wind and the Lion;* for best song, 1976, "Ave Satani," from *The Omen;* 1978, for *The Boys from Brazil;* 1979, for *Star Trek—The Motion Picture;* 1982, for *Poltergeist;* 1983, for *Under Fire.*

Emmy Awards for *The Red Pony, QBVII, Babe,* and *Masada.* Emmy Award nominations: 1960 and 1961, for *Thriller;* 1965 and 1966, for *The Man from U.N.C.L.E.*

Grammy Award nominations for *The Man from U.N.C.L.E., QBVII, The Wind and the Lion, Alien, The Omen,* and *Masada* (two nominations).

Golden Globe Award nominations for *Chinatown, Seven Days in May, The Sand Pebbles, Alien, Star Trek,* and *Under Fire.*

British Film Society Award nominations for *Chinatown, The Wind and the Lion,* and *Alien.* Max Steiner Award in recognition of achievement in scoring and composing motion picture music, National Film Society, 1982.

SIDELIGHTS: Jerry Goldsmith has been a guest conductor for many symphony orchestras including the Unione Musiche di Roma in Italy and the Kurt Granke Orchestra in Munich, West Germany. He has appeared with the Royal Philharmonic, the Glendale Symphony, the U.S. Air Force Band and the San Diego Pops.

ADDRESSES: OFFICE—Laventhol & Horwath, 2049 Century Park E., Suite 3700, Los Angeles, CA 90067. AGENT—c/o David Cohen, Sunshine Talent Agency, 2049 Century Park E., Los Angeles, CA 90067.

*   *   *

GOODSON, Mark   1915-

PERSONAL: Born January 24, 1915, in Sacramento, CA; son of Abraham Ellis and Fannie (Gross) Goodson; married Bluma Neveleff, 1941 (divorced); married Virginia McDavid (divorced); married Suzanne Russell Waddell, August 17, 1972; children: (first marriage) Jill, Jonathan; (second marriage) Marjorie. EDUCATION: University of California at Berkeley, B. A., cum laude, 1937.

VOCATION: Producer and director.

CAREER: PRINCIPAL RADIO WORK—Announcer and disc-jockey, KJBS, San Francisco, CA, 1937-38; announcer, newscaster, and station director, Mutual Broadcasting System, KFRC, San Francisco, 1939; originated and produced game show, *Pop the Question,* KFRC, San Francisco, 1939-40; master of ceremonies, *The Jack Dempsey Sports Quiz,* NY, 1941; *The Answer Man,* NY, 1942; announcer, *Just Plain Bill,* NY, 1942; announcer, *Front Page Farrell,* NY, 1942; voices, *We the People,* NY, 1942; creator, *Appointment with Life,* ABC, NY, 1943; writer and director of dramatic episodes, *Kate Smith Variety Hour,* NY, 1944; director, *The Treasury Salute,* United States Treasury Department bond selling show, 1944-45; producer, *Portia Faces Life,* 1945; master of ceremonies, *Battle of the Boroughs,* WABC, 1945-46; creator, in association with Bill Todman, *Winner Take All,* CBS, 1946; creator, *Stop the Music; Hit the Jackpot.*

PRINCIPAL TELEVISION WORK—Game shows: producer and creator in association with Bill Todman as Goodson-Todman Productions: *What's My Line,* CBS, 1950-1967; *I've Got a Secret,* CBS, 1952-1976; *It's News to Me,* 1951-54; *The Name's the Same,* ABC, 1951-55; *Two for the Money,* NBC, 1953-56, CBS, 1956-57; *Judge for Yourself,* NBC, 1953-54; *To Tell the Truth,* CBS, 1956-1967; *Password,* CBS, 1962-67, then ABC, 1969-1975, then NBC, 1979-1984; *The Price Is Right,* NBC, 1957-1963, ABC, 1963-64, then CBS to present; *The Match Game,* NBC, 1962-69, then CBS,

Photograph by Thomas Neerken

MARK GOODSON

1973-79; *Tattletales*, syndicated, 1974-80; *Concentration*, NBC, 1958-1961; *Family Feud*, ABC, 1977-83.

Series: producer in association with Bill Todman, *Jefferson Drum*, NBC, 1958-59; *The Rebel*, ABC, 1959-1961, then NBC, 1962; *The Richard Boone Repertory Theatre*, NBC, 1963-64; *Branded*, NBC, 1965-66.

NON-RELATED CAREER—Vice president, Ingersoll Newspaper Group.

AWARDS: National Television Award of Great Britain, 1951; Emmys: Best Audience Participation, Quiz or Panel Program, 1953, for *What's My Line,* also 1951 and 1977; Sylvania Award; Phi Beta Kappa.

MEMBER: Academy of Television Arts and Sciences, (president, New York chapter, 1957-58); New York City Center of Music and Drama (board of directors); American Film Institute.

SIDELIGHTS: In an interview with Stephen Steiner for in the January 7, 1978 *TV-Guide*, Mark Goodson talked about his critics: "There's a vast pluralistic society out there and the dial is its weapon. There are millions of people out there who love to watch game shows. One of the prices I pay is that the game show business is essentially without status. I regret it and I resent it. There aren't many people at the Yale Drama School studying game shows. The first thing people ask is, 'Why is somebody as literate and articulate as you in games?' It's like they're saying, 'Why is an engineer picking up garbage?'"

ADDRESSES: OFFICE—375 Park Avenue, New York, NY 10152; 6340 Sunset Blvd., Los Angeles, CA 90028.

*   *   *

GORDON, Gale   1906-

PERSONAL: Born Charles T. Aldrich, Jr., February 2, 1906, in New York, NY.

VOCATION: Actor.

CAREER: STAGE DEBUT—*The Dancers*.

FILM DEBUT—*The Pilgrimage Play*, 1929. PRINCIPAL FILM APPEARANCES—*Rally Round the Flag Boys*, Twentieth Century-Fox, 1959; *Don't Give Up the Ship*, Paramount, 1959; *Visit to a Small Planet*, Paramount, 1960; *All in a Night's Work*, Paramount, 1961; *All Hands on Deck*, Twentieth Century-Fox, 1961; *Speedway*, Metro-Goldwyn-Mayer, 1968.

PRINCIPAL TELEVISION APPEARANCES—Series: Osgood Conklin, *Our Miss Brooks*, CBS, 1952-56; Harvey Box, *The Brothers*, CBS, 1956-58; Bascomb Blecher, *Sally*, NBC, 1958; Uncle Paul, *Pete and Gladys*, CBS, 1960-62; John Wilson, *Dennis the Menace*, CBS, 1962-63; Theodore J. Mooney, *The Lucy Show*, CBS, 1963-68; Harrison Otis Carter, *Here's Lucy*, CBS, 1968-74; will appear on Lucille Ball's new series, ABC, 1986—.

Episodic: *My Favorite Husband*, CBS; *I Love Lucy*, CBS.

PRINCIPAL RADIO WORK—*Flash Gordon*, 1935.

ADDRESSES: HOME—Tub Canyon Farm, Box 126, Borrego Springs, CA 92004.

*   *   *

GRANGER, Farley   1925-

PERSONAL: Born July 1, 1925, in San Jose, CA. MILITARY: U.S. Armed Forces, 1944-46.

VOCATION: Actor.

CAREER: FILM DEBUT—*North Star*, 1943. PRINCIPAL FILM APPEARANCES—*Enchantment*, 1948; *Rope*, 1948; *They Live by Night*, 1949; *Roseanna McCoy*, 1949; *Side Street*, Metro-Goldwyn-Mayer, 1949; *Our Very Own*, 1950; *The Story of Three Loves*, Metro-Goldwyn-Mayer, 1950; *Edge of Doom*, 1950; *I Want You*, 1951; *Strangers on a Train*, 1951; *Behave Yourself*, 1951; *Hans Christian Andersen*, 1952; *Small Town Girl*, Metro-Goldwyn-Mayer, 1953; *Senso the Serpent* (also known as *Wanton Contessa*), 1954; *Naked Street*, United Artists, 1955; *Girl in a Velvet Swing*, Twentieth Century-Fox, 1955; *Arnold*, Cinerama, 1973; *A Man Called Noon*, National General, 1973; *The Prisoner of Zenda*, Universal, 1979; also appeared in *Summer Hurricane; Brass Ring; Arrow Smith; The Heiress; Those Days in the Sun; The Chief of Homicide; The Painter and the Red Head; Call Me Trinity; The Syndicate; A Crime for a Crime*.

PRINCIPAL TELEVISION APPEARANCES—Episodic: *Playhouse of the Stars; U.S. Steel Hour; Producer's Showcase; Climax; Ford Theatre; Playhouse 90; Twentieth Century-Fox Hour; Robert Montgomery Presents; Arthur Murray Dance Party; Wagon Train; Mas-*

querade; Kojak; The Six Million Dollar Man; Ellery Queen; National Repertory Company; One Life to Live.

Movies: *The Widow,* 1976; *The Nine Lives of Jenny Dolan.*

PRINCIPAL STAGE APPEARANCES—*First Impressions,* Broadway production, 1959; Sidney Bruhl, *Deathtrap,* Music Box Theatre, NY, 1981; *Night of 100 Stars,* Radio City Music Hall, NY, 1982; Prior, *Outward Bound,* Apple Corps Theatre, NY, 1984; also appeared in *The Warm Peninsula,* Broadway production; *Advise and Consent,* Broadway production; *The King and I,* Broadway production; *Brigadoon,* Broadway production; *The Seagull,* Broadway production; *The Crucible,* Broadway production; *The Carefree Tree,* Off-Broadway production; *A Month in the Country,* Off-Broadway production.

MEMBER: Actors' Equity Association, Screen Actors Guild, American Federation of Television and Radio Artists.

ADDRESSES: AGENT—William Morris Agency, 1350 Avenue of the Americas, New York, NY 10019.

* * *

GRANT, Cary 1904-

PERSONAL: Born Archibald Alexander Leach, January 18, 1904, in Bristol, England; son of Elias and Elsie (Kingdom) Leach; immigrated to U.S., 1921, became a naturalized citizen, 1942; married Virginia Cherill, February, 1934 (divorced, September, 1934); married Barbara Hutton, July 8, 1942; (divorced, August, 1945); married Betsy Drake (divorced); married Dyan Cannon, July 22, 1965 (divorced); married Barbara Harris, 1981; children: (fourth marriage) Jennifer. EDUCATION: Attended Fairfield Academy, Somerset, England, 1914-19.

VOCATION: Actor and business executive.

CAREER: PRINCIPAL STAGE APPEARANCES—New York productions: *Street Singer, Nikki, Golden Dawn, Polly Boom Boom, Wonderful Night.*

FILM DEBUT—*This Is the Night,* Paramount, 1932. PRINCIPAL FILM APPEARANCES—*Blonde Venus,* 1932; *Madame Butterfly,* 1933; *She Done Him Wrong,* 1933; *I'm No Angel,* 1933; Mock Turtle, *Alice in Wonderland,* Paramount, 1933; *Born to Be Bad,* 1934; *Sylvia Scarlett,* RKO, 1935; *Suzy,* Metro-Goldwyn-Mayer, 1936; *The Awful Truth,* Columbia, 1937; George Kerby, *Topper,* Metro-Goldwyn-Mayer, 1937; *Bringing Up Baby,* 1938; *Holiday,* 1938; *Only Angels Have Wings,* 1939; *In Name Only,* 1939; *Gunga Din,* 1939; *The Philadelphia Story,* Metro-Goldwyn-Mayer, 1940; *The Howards of Virginia,* 1940; *My Favorite Wife,* 1940; *His Girl Friday,* 1940; *Penny Serenade,* 1941; *Suspicion,* 1941; *The Talk of the Town,* 1942; *Once Upon a Honeymoon,* 1942; *Mr. Lucky,* 1943; *Destination Tokyo,* 1943; *Once Upon a Time,* 1944; *None but the Lonely Heart,* 1944; Mortimer, *Arsenic and Old Lace,* 1944; Cole Porter, *Night and Day,* 1946; *The Bachelor and the Bobby Soxer,* 1947; *The Bishop's Wife,* 1947; *Every Girl Should Be Married,* 1948; title role, *Mr. Blandings Builds His Dreamhouse,* 1948; *I Was a Male War Bride,* 1949; *Crisis,* Metro-Goldwyn-Mayer, 1950; *People Will Talk,* 1951; *Room for One More,* 1952; *Monkey Business,* 1952; *Dream Wife,* Metro-Goldwyn-Mayer, 1953; *To Catch a Thief,* Paramount, 1955; *The Pride and the Passion,* United Artists, 1957; *An Affair to Remember,* Twentieth Century-Fox, 1957; *Kiss Them for Me,* Twentieth Century-Fox, 1957; *Houseboat,*

Paramount, 1958; *North by Northwest,* Metro-Goldwyn-Mayer, 1959; *Operation Petticoat,* Universal, 1959; *The Grass Is Greener,* Universal, 1961; *That Touch of Mink,* Universal, 1962; *Charade,* Universal, 1964; *Father Goose,* Universal, 1965; *Walk, Don't Run,* Columbia, 1966; also appeared in *Gambling Ship.*

RELATED CAREER: Director, Faberge Inc.; director, Hollywood Park Inc.; director, Metro-Goldwyn-Mayer; director emeritus, Western Airlines.

MEMBER: Board of Governors, U.S.O.

AWARDS: One of the ten best Money Making Stars in *Motion Picture Herald-Fame* Poll, 1944, 1949; special award for contributions to the film industry, National Academy of Motion Picture Arts and Sciences, 1969; Kennedy Center Honors Medal, 1981.

ADDRESSES: OFFICE—Faberge Inc., 1345 Avenue of the Americas, New York, NY 10019.*

* * *

GRANT, David

BRIEF ENTRY: Full name, David Marshall Grant; born and reared in Westport, CT. Actor and director. David Grant studied with New York City's Juilliard School of Acting for one summer and performed in regional theatre before enrolling in Yale University's School of Drama. At Yale, Grant was seen in such plays as *The Ghost Sonata, Julius Caesar,* and *Tom Jones.* After graduating, the actor performed in two Broadway plays dealing with the horrors of Nazi's during World War II. In the first, marking his Broadway debut, he played the dancer, Rudy, in *Bent.* His return to Broadway was as Gasik in *The Survivor.* Grant has been seen in the television movies *Kent State, Legs,* and as the young Digger Barnes in *Dallas: The Early Years.* His film debut was in the 1979 film *French Postcards,* and he has since been seen in *The Awakening, Happy Birthday Gemini,* and as David Sommers in *American Flyers.* Grant made his directing debut with David Rabe's *Streamers* at the Fig Tree Theatre in Los Angeles.*

* * *

GRASSLE, Karen

PERSONAL: Born in Berkeley, CA; daughter of Gene F. and Frae Ella Grassle. EDUCATION: University of California at Berkeley, B.A.; trained for the stage at the London Academy of Music and Dramatic Art.

VOCATION: Actress and writer.

CAREER: STAGE DEBUT—Lady Mortimer, *Henry IV, Part 1,* Actors Workshop of San Francisco, CA, 1962, for thirty performances. NEW YORK DEBUT—*The Gingham Dog,* Golden Theatre, 1968, for ten perfomances. PRINCIPAL STAGE APPEARANCES—Broadway: *Butterflies Are Free,* 1969-70; *Cymbeline,* New York Shakespeare Festival, Delacorte Theatre, NY 1970; appeared in repertory and stock productions throughout the U.S.

PRINCIPAL TELEVISION APPEARANCES—Series: Caroline Ingalls, *Little House on the Prairie,* NBC, 1974-1982.

Movies: *Battered,* 1978; *Cocaine: One Man's Poison,* 1982.

KAREN GRASSLE

JOHNNY GREEN

FILM DEBUT—*Harry's War*, 1980.

WRITINGS: TELEPLAYS—*Battered* (with Cynthia Lovelace Sears), 1978.

MEMBER: American Federation of Radio and Television Artists, Screen Actors Guild, Writers Guild of America, Actors' Equity Association; National Organization of Women.

AWARDS: Fulbright Fellow, 1965; Public Service Award, Women's Transitional Living Center, Orange County, CA, 1979; American Women in Radio and Television, 1979; Public Service Award, Riverside County Coalition Against Domestic Violence, 1983.

ADDRESSES: HOME—Pacific Palisades, CA. OFFICE— Francis Management, 328 S. Beverly Drive, Beverly Hills, CA 90212.

*   *   *

GREEN, Johnny   1908-

PERSONAL: Born October 10, 1908, in New York, NY; son of Vivian (a builder, developer, and banker) and Irma E. (Jellenik) Green; married Betty Furness, 1937 (divorced, 1943); married Bunny Waters (an actress), November 20, 1943; children: Barbara, Kathe, Kim. EDUCATION: Harvard College, A.B., 1928; studied music with Hans Ebell, Walter Raymond Spalding, Clair Leonard, Edward Ballentyne, Herman Wasserman, and Ignace Hilsberg; studied conducting with Frank Tours. RELIGION: "Jewish/Christian."

VOCATION: Composer, conductor, arranger, and pianist.

CAREER: PRINCIPAL FILM WORK—Composer, conductor, and arranger for Metro-Goldwyn-Mayer from 1942-1949, on such films as *Fiesta*, 1947, *Easter Parade*, 1948, and *The Inspector General*, 1949; general music director and executive in charge of music with Metro-Goldwyn-Mayer for such films as *An American in Paris*, 1951, *Royal Wedding*, 1951; *The Great Caruso*, 1951; *High Society*, 1956; also composed scores for *Raintree Country*, Metro-Goldwyn-Mayer, 1957; *West Side Story*, United Artists, 1961; *Bye, Bye, Birdie*, Columbia, 1963, *Oliver!*, 1968, *They Shoot Horses, Don't They?*, Cinerama, 1969, and *The Strauss Fantasy*.

PRINCIPAL STAGE WORK—Guest Conductor with the Los Angeles Philharmonic, Hollywood Bowl, 1949-84; associate conductor, *The Promenade Concerts;* conductor and commentator, *Symphonies for Youth*, Los Angeles Philharmonic Orchestra, 1959-61; principal pops conductor, San Francisco Symphony Orchestra, 1960-61.

Guest conductor since 1958 with Philadelphia Orchestra, Chicago Symphony, Boston Pops, Ravinia Festival, St. Louis Symphony, Atlanta Symphony, Denver Symphony Orchestra, National Symphony in Washington, DC, and the San Diego Symphony.

RELATED CAREER—Arranger and orchestrator for Guy Lombardo and his Royal Canadians, Cleveland, OH; lecturer, American Film Institute, Beverly Hills, CA, and Washington, DC; guest lecturer, Film Department, University of Southern California School of the Performing Arts; lecturer, artist in residence, Harvard University, 1979.

PRINCIPAL RADIO WORK—Conductor, "Johnny Green, His Piano and Orchestra," 1933-40: *The Packard Hour with Fred Astaire; JELL-O Hour with Jack Benny; The Philip Morris Programs,* 1938-40; *St. Regis Roof; Socony Sketch Book with Christopher Morley.*

WRITINGS: SONGS—"Coquette," "I'm Yours," "Out of Nowhere," "I Wanna Be Loved," "You're Mine, You!" "I Cover the Waterfront," "Easy Come, Easy Go," "The Song of Raintree County," "Body and Soul."

ORCHESTRAL COMPOSITIONS—*Poem for Orchestra,* 1931; *Nightclub,* 1932; *Music for Elizabeth,* 1942; *Fantacia Mexicana,* 1945; *Materia Medica,* 1948; *Raintree County,* 1958, revised, 1966; *Combo,* 1967; *Mine Eyes Have Seen,* 1976.

RECORDINGS: SERIES—*Fred Astaire.*

MEMBER: American Society of Composers, Authors and Publishers (board of directors, 1980—), Songwriters Guild of America (former officer and council member), Academy of Motion Picture Arts and Sciences, Academy of Television Arts and Sciences, American Society of Music Arrangers, American Federation of Musicians.

Also member of Young Musicians Foundation (past-president, chairman of the board, chairman emeritus, 1970), Los Angeles Music Center (board of governors, performing arts council, 1964-71), California Commission on Public Education.

AWARDS: Best Score, Academy Awards: (with Roger Edens) 1948, for *Easter Parade;* 1951, for *An American in Paris;* for the "The Merry Wives of Windsor Overture" portion of *The Metro-Goldwyn-Mayer Concert Hall;* (in collaboration) 1961, for *West Side Story;* 1968, for *Oliver!.* Best Score, Academy Award nominations: 1947, for *Fiesta;* 1951, for *The Great Caruso;* 1956, for *High Society;* 1957, for *Raintree Country;* 1963, for *Bye, Bye, Birdie;* 1969, for *They Shoot Horses, Don't They?;* for *The Strauss Fantasy.*

Songwriters Hall of Fame, American Academy of Popular Music, 1973; Special Citation Award, from the President and Fellows of Harvard College, 1979-80; Grammy Award, for *West Side Story;* Golden Globe Award, for *The Inspector General;* Gold Record Award, for *Oliver!;* Aggie Award, The Songwriters' Guild.

American-Israel Cultural Foundation Award, 1963; Distinguished Alumnus Award, Horace Mann School, NY, 1965; People's Award, City of Los Angeles, 1966; Special Citation, "John Green Week," Los Angeles County, 1973; Special Citation Award, Harvard University Club of Southern California, 1973; honorary degree from Pepperdine University.

ADDRESSES: OFFICE—903 N. Bedford Drive, Beverly Hills, CA 90210. AGENT—c/o Marvin Schofer, International Creative Management, 40 W. 57th Street, New York, NY 10019.

*   *   *

GREENE, Lorne   1915-

PERSONAL: Born February 12, 1915, in Ottawa, Canada; son of Daniel and Dora Greene; married Rita Hands, 1940 (divorced, 1960); married Nancy Deale, December 17, 1961; children: (first marriage) Belinda, Charles (twins); (second marriage) one child. EDUCATION: Queen's University, Canada; studied for the stage at the Neighborhood Playhouse, New York. MILITARY: Royal Canadian Air Force.

VOCATION: Actor.

CAREER: PRINCIPAL TELEVISION APPEARANCES—Series: Ben Cartwright, *Bonanza,* NBC, 1959-73; Wade Griffin, *Griff,* ABC, 1973-74; host and narrator, *Lorne Greene's Last of the Wild,* syndication, 1974-79; Commander Adama, *Battlestar Galactica,* ABC, 1978-80; Battalion Chief Joe Rorchek, *Code Red,* ABC, 1981-82.

Episodic: "Journey to Nowhere," *Philip Morris Playhouse,* CBS, 1953; *Star Stage,* NBC; *Actuality Specials,* NBC; "How the West Was Swung," *Kraft Music Hall,* NBC; *Andy Williams Show; Johnny Cash Show; Sonny and Cher Show.*

Movies: *Destiny of a Spy,* NBC, 1969; *The Harness,* NBC, 1971, *Man on the Outside* (pilot for *Griff*), ABC, 1975; *Nevada Smith,* 1975; *SST: Death Flight.*

Mini-series: *The Moneychangers,* 1976; John Reynolds, *Roots,* ABC, 1977; *The Bastard,* 1978.

Specials: Big Brother, "1984," *Studio One;* narrator, *Tribute to John F. Kennedy; Lorne Greene's American West; Christmas Special with United Nation's Children's Chorus; Lewis and Clark Expedition; Big Cats, Little Cats; Wonderful World of Horses; Swing Out, Sweet Land; Celebration; The Barnum & Bailey Special,* NBC.

PRINCIPAL FILM APPEARANCES—*The Silver Chalice,* 1954; *Tight Spot,* Columbia, 1955; *Autumn Leaves,* Columbia, 1956; *The Hard Man,* 1957; *Peyton Place,* Twentieth Century-Fox, 1957; *Last of the Fast Guns,* Universal, 1958; *Gift of Love,* Twentieth Century-Fox, 1958; *The Buccaneer,* Paramount, 1959; *The Trap,* Paramount, 1959; *Earthquake,* Universal, 1974; *Tidal Wave;* voice, *Heidi's Song,* 1982.

PRINCIPAL STAGE APPEARANCES—Broadway: *The Prescott Proposals,* 1953, *Speaking of Murder,* 1956, *Edwin Booth,* 1958; appeared with the New Play Society, Canada, Earl Grey Players, Toronto, and at the Stratford Shakespeare Festival, Canada. Greene was also founder, director, and actor with the Jupiter Theatre, Toronto.

RELATED CAREER—Founder and director, Academy of Radio Arts, Canada; newscaster, Canadian Broadcasting Corporation.

NON-RELATED CAREER—Program supervisor, advertising agency.

RECORDINGS: ALBUM—*Welcome to the Ponderosa;* narrator, *Peter and the Wolf.* SINGLE—*Ringo.*

AWARDS: Radio and Television Mirror Award, Most Popular Television Star; Variety Club of America, Heart Award; John Swett Award, California Teachers Association; Foreign Press Association Award, Best Performance by an Actor; Order of Canada Award, 1971; Grand Marshal Award, Tournament of Roses Parade, 1981; honorary doctorates: Doctor of Law Degree, Queen's University, 1969; Doctor of Humane Letters, Missouri Valley College, 1981.

MEMBER: Actor's Equity Association, Screen Actors Guild, American Federation of Television and Radio Artists; American Horse Protection Association (vice-chairman), National Wildlife

LORNE GREENE

Foundation (former chairman); Pritikin Research Center (board of directors), American Freedom from Hunger Foundation (former chairman).

SIDELIGHTS: RECREATION—Photography, tennis, bridge, conversation.

Through his publicity release, *CTFT* learned Greene's philosophy of life: "I became aware at an early age of the fact that while the body has its limitations, the mind never reaches its full potential, so I determined to use as much of me as possible for as long as I was alive. I don't feel now that I by any means have reached the ultimate use of my potential, nor do I expect to, but I certainly keep trying. I know that if there is any trick at all to living a reasonably happy life, it will stretch what abilities I have. I have observed over the years that most people who get on in years and still seem to remain youthful do exactly that."

ADDRESSES: AGENT—Michael Levine Public Relations Company, 9123 Sunset Blvd., Los Angeles, CA 90069.

*   *   *

GREGORY, Don   1934-

PERSONAL: Born December 3, 1934, in New York, NY; married Sharon Kaye Romain (a fashion coordinator), June 11, 1981; children: Stephanie, David. EDUCATION: University of Connecticut, B.S., 1955; trained for the stage at the Jeff Corey Acting School and the Actors Mobile Theatre with Bret Warren; also trained at the

Players Ring Acting School with Robert Vaughn. MILITARY: U.S. Army, 1957-59.

VOCATION: Producer.

CAREER: PRINCIPAL STAGE WORK—Producer: *Clarence Darrow,* Helen Hayes Theatre, NY, 1974, then Minskoff Theatre, NY, 1974, and Piccadilly Theatre, London, 1975; *The Best of Everybody,* Studebaker Theatre, Chicago, IL, 1975; *Belle of Amherst,* Longacre Theatre, NY, 1976; *Paul Robeson,* Lunt-Fontanne Theatre, NY, 1977; *My Fair Lady,* Pantages Theatre, Los Angeles, CA, 1980; *Camelot,* New York State Theatre, NY, and Pantages Theatre, Los Angeles, CA, 1980; *Copperfield,* American National Theatre and Academy (ANTA), NY, 1981; *South Pacific,* Dorothy Chandler Pavilion, Los Angles, CA, 1985; *Chaplin* (upcoming), NY.

MAJOR TOURS—Producer: *Paul Robeson; F.D.R.; Camelot; My Fair Lady; Othello,* all U.S. cities.

PRINCIPAL TELEVISION WORK—Producer: *Celebrity Bowling; Celebrity Tennis; Clarence Darrow,* NBC, 1974; *Camelot,* HBO, 1982; also, *Belle of Amherst* and *Paul Robeson,* both PBS.

PRINCIPAL FILM WORK—Producer, *F.D.R.,* International Cinegraph and Aurora Sunrise, 1978.

RELATED CAREER—Former actor; former vice president, Agency for the Performing Arts, responsible for such clients as Harry Belafonte, Red Buttons, Bobby Darin, Frank Gorshin, and Rowan and Martin; senior advisor, Fine Arts Department, University of Connecticut.

DON GREGORY

MEMBER: League of American Theatres and Producers, Producers Group.

SIDELIGHTS: RECREATIONS—Collecting films of the 1930's and 1940's.

Don Gregory shared these thoughts with *CTFT:* ''The pursuit of excellence, the chance to work with some of the most creative people of our time, the opportunity to be part of the ongoing process of theatre and what good theatre can mean to everyone, to leave a legacy of a body of work which would live far beyond me—all this provides the motivation to produce. Regarding causes, the only subjects that interest me are the ones that are not temporary, such as the quest for cures for disease. Political causes in general seem too expedient for me.

''I believe the lack of education is the cause of most of the world's ills.''

ADDRESSES: OFFICE—Sharome Enterprises, Inc., 165 W. 46th Street, New York, NY 10036. AGENT—c/o Tod Harris, Sterling Lord Agency, 660 Madison Avenue, New York, NY 10017.

*   *   *

GREGORY, James   1911-

PERSONAL: Born December 23, 1911, in New York, NY; son of James Gillen and Axennia Theresa (Ekdahl) Gregory; married Ann Catherine Miltner, May 25, 1944. MILITARY: U.S. Naval Reserve, U.S. Marine Corps. Reserve, 1942-45.

VOCATION: Actor.

CAREER: PRINCIPAL STAGE APPEARANCES—Summer stock companies: Deer Lake, PA, 1936, 1937, 1939, Millbrook, NY, 1938, Braddock Heights, MD, 1940, Bucks County Playhouse, New Hope, PA, 1941, Ivy Tower Playhouse, Spring Lake, NJ, 1951. Broadway productions: *Key Largo,* 1939; *Journey to Jerusalem,* 1940; *In Time to Come,* 1941; *Dream Girl,* 1945; *Dead Pigeon,* 1954; *All My Sons,* 1947; *Death of a Salesman,* 1948-49; *Fragile Fox,* 1955; *The Desperate Hours,* 1956-57.

PRINCIPAL FILM APPEARANCES—*The Young Strangers,* Universal, 1957; *Gun Glory,* Metro-Goldwyn-Mayer, 1957; *Nightfall,* Columbia, 1957; *The Big Caper,* United Artists, 1957; *Underwater Warrior,* Metro-Goldwyn-Mayer, 1958; *Al Capone Story,* Allied Artists, 1959; *PT-109,* Warner Brothers, 1963; *A Distant Trumpet,* Warner Brothers, 1964; *Captain Newman M.D.,* Universal, 1964; *Sons of Katie Elder,* Paramount, 1965; *Clam Bake,* United Artists, 1967; *The Secret War of Harry Frigg,* Universal, 1968; *Manchurian Candidate,* United Artists, 1968; *Shoot Out,* Universal, 1971; *The Million Dollar Duck,* Buena Vista, 1971; *Strongest Man in the World,* Buena Vista, 1974; *The Main Event,* Warner Brothers, 1979.

PRINCIPAL TELEVISION APPEARANCES—Series: *Police Story,* CBS, 1952; Barney Rudisky, *The Lawless Years,* NBC, 1959-61; T.R. Scott, *The Paul Lynde Show,* ABC, 1972-73; Inspector Frank Luger, *Barney Miller,* ABC, 1975-82; Nick Hannigan, *Detective School,* ABC, 1979.

Episodic: *Studio One,* CBS; *The Web,* CBS; *Gunsmoke,* CBS.

Movies: *Wait Til Your Mother Gets Home,* 1982, also appeared in five ''Matt Helm'' television movies.

MEMBER: Actors' Equity Association, Screen Actors Guild, American Federation of Television and Radio Artists; Society for the Preservation and Encouragement of Barber Shop Quartet Singing, Hollywood Hackers (singing club).

ADDRESSES: AGENT—International Creative Management, 8899 Beverly Blvd., Los Angeles, CA 90048.

*   *   *

GRIFFIN, Merv   1925-

PERSONAL: Full name, Mervyn Edward Griffin, Jr.; born July 6, 1925 in San Mateo, CA; son of Mervyn Edward and Rita (Robinson) Griffin; married Julann Elizabeth Wright, May 18, 1958 (divorced, 1976); children: Anthony Patrick. EDUCATION: Attended San Francisco State College and Stanford University.

VOCATION: Producer, singer, host, and actor.

CAREER: PRINCIPAL RADIO APPEARANCES—*The Merv Griffin Show,* KFRC, San Francisco, 1945-48.

PRINCIPAL FILM APPEARANCES—*So This Is Love,* Warner Brothers, 1952; *The Boy from Oklahoma,* Warner Brothers, 1955.

PRINCIPAL TELEVISION APPEARANCES—Game, Talk, and Variety Shows: Regular, *The Freddy Martin Show,* NBC, 1951; regular, *Summer Holiday,* CBS, 1954; host, *Look Up and Live,* CBS; vocalist, *The Morning Show,* CBS, 1956; vocalist, *The Robert Q. Lewis Show,* CBS, 1956; host, *Going Places,* CBS, 1957; *Keep Talking,* CBS, ABC, 1959-60; host, *Play Your Hunch,* NBC, 1960-62; substitute host, *The Tonight Show,* NBC, 1962; host, *Talent Scouts,* CBS, 1963; host, *Word for Word,* NBC, 1963; guest host, *Hippodrome,* CBS, 1966; star, *The Merv Griffin Show,* CBS, 1969-72, in syndication, Westinghouse Broadcasting, 1972—.

PRINCIPAL TELEVISION WORK—Producer, *Dance Fever,* Merv Griffin Productions, 1979—; *Wheel of Fortune,* CBS, 1983—.

RELATED CAREER—Vocalist, Freddy Martin's Orchestra, 1948-52; owner, Merv Griffin Productions, Hollywood, CA; owner of three radio stations, 1965—; vice president, director of special promotions, Camelot, Inc.; vice president, American Leisure Corporation, 1981—; director and owner, Teleview Racing Patrol, Inc., Miami, FL.

MEMBER: Bohemian Club (San Francisco); Dr. Armand Hammer United World College of America (trustee).

AWARDS: L.H.D., Pepperdine University, 1981.

ADDRESSES: OFFICE—1541 N. Vine Street, Los Angeles, CA 90028.*

*   *   *

GRIFFITH, Andy   1926-

PERSONAL: Born June 1, 1926, in Mount Airy, NC; son of Carl and Geneva Griffith; married Barbara Edwards (divorced); married Cindi Knight, April 2, 1983; children: (previous marriage) Andy Sam, Dixie Nann. EDUCATION: Attended University of North Carolina at Chapel Hill.

CAREER: NEW YORK DEBUT—*No Time for Sergeants,* 1955. PRINCIPAL STAGE APPEARANCES—Sir Walter Raleigh, *The Lost Colony,* Outdoor Drama, NC; *Destry Rides Again,* NY, 1959.

PRINCIPAL FILM APPEARANCES—*A Face in the Crowd,* Warner Brothers, 1957; *No Time for Sergeants,* Warner Brothers, 1958; *Onionhead,* Warner Brothers, 1958; *Second Time Around,* Twentieth Century-Fox, 1961; *Angel in My Pocket,* Universal, 1969; *Adams of Eagle Lake,* 1975; *The Treasure Chest Murder,* 1975; *Hearts of the West,* United Artists, 1975.

TELEVISION DEBUT—*The Ed Sullivan Show,* CBS, 1954. PRINCIPAL TELEVISION APPEARANCES—Series; Andy Taylor, *The Andy Griffith Show,* CBS, 1960-69; Andy Thompson, *Headmaster,* CBS, 1970-71; Andy Sawyer, *The New Andy Griffith Show,* CBS, 1971; Harry Broderick, *Salvage 1,* ABC, 1978.

Mini-Series: *Washington Behind Closed Doors,* ABC, 1977; Lew Vernor, *Centennial,* NBC, 1978-79.

Movies: *No Time for Sergeants,* 1955; *Go Ask Alice,* 1972; *Savages,* 1974; *Winter Kill,* ABC, 1974; *Hollywood TV Theatre,* 1976; *Deadly Game,* ABC, 1977; *The Girl in the Empty Grave,* 1977; Ash Robinson, *Murder in Texas,* 1981; *Murder in Cowenta County,* 1983; *Fatal Vision,* CBS, 1985; title role, *Matlock,* NBC, 1986; Andy Taylor, *Return to Mayberry,* NBC, 1986; also, *From Here to Eternity; Six Characters in Search of an Author.*

RELATED CAREER—Stand-up comic at the Blue Angel nightclub in NY, 1954, and other clubs across the country.

ANDY GRIFFITH

NON-RELATED CAREER: Teacher, Goldsboro High School, NC.

RECORDINGS: COMEDY—*What It Was Was Football,* 1953.

AWARDS: Tarheel Award, 1961; Distinguished Salesman's Award, Asheville, NC, 1962; Advertising Club of Baltimore, Outstanding Television Personality Award, 1968; Emmy nomination, 1981, for *Murder in Texas.*

ADDRESSES: HOME—North Hollywood, CA; Manteo, NC. OFFICE—c/o Richard O. Linke Associates, Inc., 4445 Cartwright Avenue, Suite 305, North Hollywood, CA 91602. AGENT—William Morris Agency, 151 El Camino, Beverly Hills, CA 90212.

*   *   *

GRODIN, Charles   1935-

PERSONAL: Born April 21, 1935, in Pittsburgh, PA; son of Ted and Lana Grodin; children: Marion. EDUCATION: Attended the University of Miami, FL; studied theatre at the Pittsburgh Playhouse; studied acting with Uta Hagen and Lee Strasberg in New York.

VOCATION: Actor, director, and writer.

CAREER: NEW YORK DEBUT—Robert Pickett, *Tchin-Tchin,* Plymouth Theatre, 1962. PRINCIPAL STAGE APPEARANCES—Perry Littlewood, *Absence of a Cello,* Ambassador Theatre, NY, 1964; Tandy, *Steambath* (previews), Truck and Warehouse Theatre, NY, 1970; George, *Same Time Next Year,* Brooks Atkinson Theatre, NY, 1975; *Night of 100 Stars,* Radio City Music Hall, NY, 1982.

MAJOR TOURS—George, *Same Time Next Year.*

PRINCIPAL STAGE WORK—Director, *Hooray! It's a Glorious Day . . . And All That,* Theatre Four, NY, 1966; director, *Lovers and Other Strangers,* Brooks Atkinson Theatre, NY, 1968; producer and director, *Thieves,* Broadhurst Theatre, NY, 1974; producer and director, *Unexpected Guests,* Little Theatre, NY, 1977.

PRINCIPAL FILM APPEARANCES—*Rosemary's Baby,* Paramount, 1968; *Catch-22,* Paramount, 1970; *The Heartbreak Kid,* Twentieth Century-Fox, 1972; *11 Harrowhouse,* Twentieth Century-Fox, 1974; *King Kong,* Paramount, 1976; *Thieves,* Paramount, 1977; *Heaven Can Wait,* Paramount, 1978; *Real Life,* Paramount, 1979; *Sunburn,* Paramount, 1979; *Seems Like Old Times,* Columbia, 1980; *It's My Turn,* Columbia, 1980; *Great Muppet Caper,* Universal, 1981; *Incredible Shrinking Woman,* Universal, 1981; *The Lonely Guy,* Universal, 1984; *Woman in Red,* Orion, 1984; *Movers and Shakers,* Metro-Goldwyn-Mayer/United Artists, 1985.

PRINCIPAL FILM WORK—Co-producer, *Movers and Shakers,* Metro-Goldwyn-Mayer/United Artists, 1985.

PRINCIPAL TELEVISION APPEARANCES—Frequent guest on talk shows.

PRINCIPAL TELEVISION WORK—Director: *Marlo Thomas* special; *Acts of Love and Other Comedies,* ABC, 1983.

WRITINGS: PLAYS, PRODUCED—(With Maurice Teitelbaum) Book and lyrics, *Hooray! It's a Glorious Day . . . And All That,* Theatre Four, NY, 1966.

SCREENPLAY—*Movers and Shakers.*

TELEVISION—*The Paul Simon Special*, NBC, 1977.

MEMBER: Actors' Equity Association, Screen Actors Guild.

AWARDS: Outer Critics Circle Award, 1975, for *Same Time Next Year;* Actors Fund Award of Merit, 1975; Outstanding Writing in A Comedy-Variety or Music Special, Emmy (shared), 1977-78, for *The Paul Simon Special.**

*   *   *

GROH, David   1941-

PERSONAL: Full name, David Lawrence Groh; born May 21, 1941, in New York, NY; son of Benjamin and Mildred Groh. EDUCATION: Brown University, B.A., 1961; did post graduate work at the London Academy of Music and Dramatic Arts on a Fulbright Scholarship, 1962-63. MILITARY: U.S. Army, 1963-64.

VOCATION: Actor.

CAREER: PRINCIPAL STAGE APPEARANCES—*Chapter Two*, Broadway production, 1978; *Antony and Cleopatra*, Broadway production; *Elizabeth the Queen*, Broadway production; *The Hot L Baltimore*, Off-Broadway production.

PRINCIPAL FILM APPEARANCES—*Change in the Wind*, Cinerama, 1972; *Two Minute Warning*, Universal, 1976; *A Hero Ain't Nothin' but a Sandwich*, 1977.

PRINCIPAL TELEVISION APPEARANCES—Series: Joe Gerard, *Rhoda*, CBS, 1974-77; Don Gardner, *Another Day*, CBS, 1978; D.L. Brock, *General Hospital*, ABC, 1983-85.

Episodic: *Murder, She Wrote*, CBS, 1986.

Movies: *Smash-Up on Interstate 5*, 1976; *Victory at Entebbe*, 1977; *Murder at the Mardi Gras*, 1978; *Child Stealer*, 1979; *Power*, 1979.

MEMBER: Actors' Equity Association, Screen Actors Guild, American Federation of Television and Radio Artists; Phi Beta Kappa.

ADDRESSES: AGENT—Phil Gersh Agency, 222 N. Canon Drive, Beverly Hills, CA 90210.

*   *   *

GUILLAUME, Robert

PERSONAL: Born November 30, in St. Louis, MO; married. EDUCATION: Attended St. Louis University and Washington University.

VOCATION: Actor.

CAREER: PRINCIPAL TELEVISION APPEARANCES—Series: Benson, *Soap*, ABC, 1977-79; Benson Dubois, *Benson*, ABC, 1979-86.

Episodic: *Dinah; Jim Nabor's Show; All in the Family; The Jeffersons; Sanford and Son; Marcus Welby, M.D.*

Specials: *Purlie*, Showtime, 1983; *Mel and Susan Together; Rich Little's Washington Follies.*

PRINCIPAL FILM APPEARANCES—*Seems Like Old Times*, Columbia, 1980.

PRINCIPAL STAGE APPEARANCES—*Carousel; Night of 100 Stars*, Radio City Music Hall, NY, 1982.

MEMBER: American Federation of Television and Radio Artists, Screen Actors Guild.

AWARDS: Outstanding Supporting Actor in a Comedy or Comedy-Variety Series, 1978-79, for *Soap;* Best Actor, Comedy or Comedy-Variety Series, 1984-85, for *Benson.*

ADDRESSES: OFFICE—Robert Guillaume Productions, 1438 N. Gower Street, Suite 567, Los Angeles, CA 90028. AGENT—Charter Management, 9000 Sunset Blvd., Suite 1112, Los Angeles, CA 90069.

*   *   *

GUSTAFSON, Karin   1959-

PERSONAL: Born June 23, 1959, in Miami, FL; daughter of Arland Bennett (a dentist) and Dianne Maredydd (Harrison) Gustafson. EDUCATION: Villanova University, B.A., communication arts major, theatre arts minor, 1981.

VOCATION: Actress and dancer.

CAREER: STAGE DEBUT—Alice in Wonderland, *Alice*, Dade County Theatre, 1966, Miami, FL. PRINCIPAL STAGE APPEAR-

KARIN GUSTAFSON

ANCES—Appeared at the North Carolina Summer Theatre, 1967; Corrie, *Barefoot in the Park,* Thomas Players, PA, 1978; *Cabaret,* Vasey Theatre, 1979; Patsy, *Little Murders,* Villanova Theatre, 1979; Kristen, *A Chorus Line,* University Center, PA, 1980; Chasity, *Anything Goes,* Thomas Theatre, PA, 1981.

PRINCIPAL DANCE APPEARANCES—Sacred Dance Guild of America; Florida Ballet Company.

PRINCIPAL STAGE WORK—Director, *After the Rain,* Radnor, PA, 1975; makeup and special effects, *Frankenstein,* Radnor, PA, 1976; sound, *Jack the Ripper Revue,* New York and Pennsylvania tour, 1979; stage manager, *Picnic,* Temple Theatre, 1980; acting coach and choreographer, St. Thomas Children's Theatre, PA, 1981; director, *A Certain Small Shepherd,* OMGC Children's Theatre, PA, 1982; director, *The Lovers,* Arami Theatre, CA, 1983; set consultant, *Silent Night,* Odyssey Theatre, CA, 1984.

FILM DEBUT—*Taps,* Twentieth Century-Fox, 1981. PRINCIPAL FILM APPEARANCES—*Surf II; Wise Guys,* Metro-Goldwyn-Mayer, 1985; *ARA,* Bulldog Film, 1985.

TELEVISION DEBUT—Head leopard, *Popeye Playhouse,* ABC, Fl, 1967. PRINCIPAL TELEVISION APPEARANCES—*Santa and Son,* CBS, 1981; *Knight Rider,* NBC, 1983; *Dallas,* CBS, 1983; co-host and co-producer, *Sports Power* Santa Fe Communications, branch in Primos, PA, 1984.

RELATED CAREER—Commercial instructor, Kingsley Six, King of Prussia, PA, 1977, 1982, 1984-86; casting director, New Graphic Pictures, Hollywood, CA, 1983-84; acting instructor, career advisor, Entertainment Services Association, 1983-84; performer, The Singing Telegram Company, Eastern PA, 1985-86.

MEMBER: Screen Actors Guild, American Federation of Radio and Television Artists, American Film Institute; National Swedish Historical Society, 1975-86.

SIDELIGHTS: Karin Gustafson told *CTFT,* "Anytime I am not working, I use the time to learn something new and off-beat such as parachuting, snow skiing, and scuba diving, which I now teach. I like to move people and pull them out ot their everyday problems for a while. My favorite role is Corrie in *Barefoot in the Park.*"

H

HACKFORD, Taylor   1944-

PERSONAL: Born December 31, 1944, in Santa Barbara, CA; son of Joseph and Mary (Taylor) Hackford; married Georgie Lowres (divorced, 1972); married Lynne Littman (divorced, 1985); children: (first marriage) Rio; (second marriage) Alexander. EDUCATION: University of Southern California, B.A., international relations.

VOCATION: Producer and director.

CAREER: PRINCIPAL FILM WORK—Director: *Teenage Father* (short), 1978; *The Idolmaker*, United Artists, 1980; *An Officer and a Gentleman*, Paramount, 1982; *Against All Odds*, Columbia, 1984; *White Nights*, Columbia, 1985; *At Play in the Fields of the Lord* (upcoming).

RELATED CAREER—Director, producer, reporter, and writer, KCET, community television of Southern California, Los Angeles, 1970-77; director, producer, and writer, Hackford Littman Films, Los Angeles, CA, 1977-79; director, United Artists Films, Los Angeles, 1979-80; director, Paramount Pictures, Los Angeles, CA, 1983; director, Columbia Pictures, 1983-85.

MEMBER: Directors Guild of America, Writers Guild of America.

AWARDS: Silver Reel Award, San Francisco Film Festival, 1972; Emmy Award, 1974, 1977; Academy Award, 1979, for *Teenage Father*.

SIDELIGHTS: Taylor Hackford was a Peace Corps volunteer in Bolivia between 1968-69.

ADDRESSES: OFFICE—New Visions, Inc., 6311 Romaine Street, Suite 7133, Los Angeles, CA 90038. AGENT—Creative Artists Agency, 1888 Century Park E., Suite 1400, Los Angeles, CA 90067.

*   *   *

HAGGERTY, Dan   1941-

PERSONAL: Born November 19, 1941, in Hollywood, CA; son of Don (an actor) Haggerty; married Diane Rooker; children: Tracey, Tammy.

VOCATION: Actor and animal trainer.

CAREER: PRINCIPAL FILM APPEARANCES—*Easy Rider*, Columbia, 1969; *Wild Country*, Buena Vista, 1971; *Tender Warrior*, 1971; *The Life and Times of Grizzly Adams*, 1976; *The Adventures of*

Frontier Fremont, 1977; *King of the Mountain*, Universal, 1981; also appeared in *Grasslands, Snow Tigers, Where the North Wind Blows*.

PRINCIPAL FILM WORK—Animal trainer for: *Lt. Robin Crusoe, USN*, Buena Vista, 1966; *Monkeys, Go Home!*, Buena Vista, 1967; *The Christmas Tree*, Continental, 1969:

PRINCIPAL TELEVISION APPEARANCES—Series, James "Grizzly" Adams, *The Life and Times of Grizzly Adams*, NBC, 1977-78.

Movie: *Terror Out of the Sky*, 1978.

ADDRESSES: AGENT—David Shapira and Associates, 15301 Ventura Blvd., Sherman Oaks, CA 91403.*

*   *   *

HAGMAN, Larry   1931-

PERSONAL: Born September 21, 1931, in Fort Worth, TX; son of Benjamin and Mary (an actress; maiden name, Martin) Hagman; married Maj Alexsson (a spa designer); children: Heidi, Preston. EDUCATION: Attended Bard College. MILITARY: U.S. Air Force.

VOCATION: Actor and director.

CAREER: STAGE DEBUT—At the Margo Jones Theatre in the Round, Dallas, TX. PRINCIPAL STAGE APPEARANCES—*Taming of the Shrew*, NY; *South Pacific*, London, 1952. In Broadway productions: *God and Kate Murphy*, 1959; Bummy Carwell, *The Nervous Set*, 1959; *The Warm Pennisula*, 1959-60; *The Beauty Part*, 1962-63.

FILM DEBUT—*Ensign Pulver*, Warner Brothers, 1964. PRINCIPAL FILM APPEARANCES—*Fail Safe*, Columbia, 1964; *In Harms Way*, Paramount, 1965; *The Cavern*, Twentieth Century-Fox, 1965; *The Group*, United Artists, 1966; (also director) *Beware! The Blob*, 1972; *Harry and Tonto*, Twentieth Century-Fox, 1974; *Stardust*, Columbia, 1975; *Mother, Jugs and Speed*, 1976; *The Eagle Has Landed*, Columbia, 1977; *S.O.B.*, Paramount, 1981; *Superman*, Warner Brothers, 1982; also appeared in *Three in the Cellar*.

PRINCIPAL TELEVISION APPEARANCES—Series: Ed Gibson, *The Edge of Night*; Captain Tony Nelson, *I Dream of Jeannie*, NBC, 1965-70; Albert Miller, *The Good Life*, NBC, 1971-72; Richard Evans, *Here We Go Again*, ABC, 1973; J.R. Ewing, *Dallas*, CBS, 1978—.

Movies: *The President's Mistress*, 1978; *Last of the Good Guys*, 1978; *Battered*, 1978.

Episodic: *What Really Happened to the Class of '65?*, NBC.

RELATED CAREER: Directed USO shows for the U.S. Air Force in Europe.

MEMBER: Actors' Equity Association, Screen Actors Guild, American Federation of Television and Radio Artists.

ADDRESSES: OFFICE—Lorimar Productions, 10202 W. Washington Blvd., Culver City, CA 90230.

*   *   *

HALL, Peter   1930-

PERSONAL: Born November 22, 1930, in Bury St. Edmunds, Suffolk, England; son of Reginald Edward Arthur and Grace (Pamment) Hall; married Leslie Caron (divorced); married Jacqueline Taylor. EDUCATION: Cambridge University, M.A., 1964.

VOCATION: Director.

CAREER: FIRST STAGE WORK—Director, Cambridge Amateur Dramatic Club, Marlowe Society and University Actors. LONDON DEBUT—Director, Theatre Royal, Windsor, 1953. FIRST NEW YORK STAGE WORK—Director, *The Rope Dancers*, Cort Theatre, 1957. PRINCIPAL STAGE WORK—Director, all at the Arts Theatre, London: *Blood Wedding, The Immoralist, The Lesson, South*, all 1954; *Mourning Becomes Electra, Waiting for Godot, Burnt Flower-Bed, Listen to the Wind*, all 1955; *The Waltz of the Toreadors*, 1956.

Gigi, New Theatre, London, 1956; *Love's Labour's Lost*, Stratford-Upon-Avon, 1956; *Camino Real*, Phoenix Theatre, London, 1957; *The Moon and Sixpence*, Sadler's Wells, 1957; *Cymbeline*, Stratford, 1957; *Cat on a Hot Tin Roof*, London production, 1958; *Twelfth Night, Brouhaha, Shadow of Heroes*, all Stratford, 1958; *Madame De . . . , A Traveler without Luggage, A Midsummer Night's Dream, Coriolanus, The Wrong Side of the Park*, all Stratford, 1959; *Two Gentlemen of Verona, Twelfth Night, Troilus and Cressida*, all Stratford, 1960.

Director, Royal Shakespeare Company, Memorial Theatre, Stratford-Upon-Avon, and Aldwych Theatre, London: *Ondine, Becket, Romeo and Juliet, A Midsummer Night's Dream, The Collection, Troilus and Cressida*, all 1961; "Henry VI, Parts I, II, III and Richard III," under the title *War of the Roses*, 1963; *A Midsummer Night's Dream*, 1963; "Richard II, Henry IV Part I, Henry IV Part II, Henry VI, Edward IV and Richard III," under title *A Cycle of Seven History Plays*, 1964; *The War of the Roses*, 1964; *Eh?*, 1964; *The Homecoming*, London, then New York, 1965; *Moses and Aaron*, Royal Opera House, Covent Garden, London, 1965; *Hamlet, The Government Inspector*, both 1965; *The Magic Flute*, Covent Garden, London, 1966; *Staircase*, 1966; *A Midsummer Night's Dream, Macbeth*, both 1967; *A Delicate Balance, Dutch Uncle, Landscape and Silence*, all 1969; *The Knot Garden*, Covent Garden, London, 1970; *La Calista*, Glyndebourne, 1970; *The Battle of the Shrivings*, Lyric Theatre, London, 1970.

Eugene Onegin, Covent Garden, London, 1971; *Old Times*, London, then New York, 1971; *Tristan and Isolde*, Covent Garden,

1971; *All Over*, Aldwych Theatre, 1972; *Il Ritorno d'Ulisse*, Glyndebourne, 1972; *Alte Zeiten*, Burgtheatre, Vienna, 1972; *Via Galactica*, NY, 1972; *The Marriage of Figaro*, Glyndebourne, 1973; *The Tempest*, National Theatre, London, 1973; *John Gabriel Borkman, Happy Days*, both National Theatre, 1974; *No Man's Land, Hamlet, Judgement*, all National Theatre, 1975; *Tamburlaine the Great, Bedroom Farce*, both National Theatre, 1977; *Don Giovanni*, Glyndebourne, 1977; *Volpone, The Country Wife, The Cherry Orchard, Macbeth, Betrayal*, all National Theatre, 1978; *Cosi Fan Tutte*, Glyndebourne, 1978; *Fidelio*, Glyndebourne, 1979; *Amadeus*, National Theatre, 1979; *Betrayal*, NY, 1980; *Othello*, 1980; *Amadeus*, NY, 1980.

Family Voices, National Theatre, 1981; *A Midsummer Night's Dream*, Glyndebourne, 1982; *The Importance of Being Earnest*, National Theatre, 1982; *Macbeth*, Glyndebourne, then Metropolitan Opera, NY, 1982; *Other Places*, National Theatre, 1982; *Der Ring Des Nibelungen*, Bayreuth, West Germany, 1983; *Jean Seberg*, National Theatre, 1983; *Animal Farm*, National Theatre, 1984; *Coriolanus*, National Theatre, 1984; *Yonadab*, National Theatre, 1985; *Carmen*, Glyndebourne, 1985; *Albert Herring*, Glyndebourne, 1985.

FIRST FILM WORK—*Work Is a Four Letter Word*, 1966. PRINCIPAL FILM WORK—Director: *A Midsummer Night's Dream*, 1969;

PETER HALL

Three into Two Won't Go, 1969; *Perfect Friday,* 1970; *The Home-coming,* AFT Distributing, 1973; also directed *Landscape* and *Akenfield.*

PRINCIPAL TELEVISION WORK—Director, *The War of the Roses,* BBC, 1964.

PRINCIPAL RADIO WORK—Director, *Family Voices,* BBC, 1981.

RELATED CAREER—Director, Oxford Playhouse, 1954-55; director, Arts Theatre, London, 1955-57; founder, International Playwrights' Theatre, 1957; creator and managing director, Royal Shakespeare Company, 1960-68; director, National Theatre of Great Britain, 1973—; artistic director, Glyndebourne Festival Opera, 1984—.

MEMBER: Arts Council of Great Britain, Garrick Club, Athenaeum Club.

AWARDS: Antoinette Perry Award, 1967, for *The Homecoming;* Antoinette Perry Award, 1981, for *Amadeus.* Created Commander of the British Empire, 1963 and Knight of the British Empire, 1977. Honorary degrees: University of York, 1966; Chevalier des Ordres des Arts et des Lettres, 1965; Hamburg University Shakespeare Prize, 1967; University of Reading, 1973; University of Liverpool, 1974; University of Leicester, 1977.

SIDELIGHTS: RECREATIONS—Music.

ADDRESSES: OFFICE—National Theatre, South Bank, London SE1 9PX, England.

* * *

HAMILTON, George   1939-

PERSONAL: Born August 12, 1939, in Memphis, TN; married Alana (divorced). EDUCATION: Attended Hackley Prep School, New York, and Palm Beach High School, Florida.

VOCATION: Actor and producer.

CAREER: FILM DEBUT—*Crime and Punishment, USA,* Allied Artists, 1959. PRINCIPAL FILM APPEARANCES—*Home from the Hill,* 1960; *All the Fine Young Cannibals,* Metro-Goldwyn-Mayer, 1960; *Angel Baby,* Allied Artists, 1961; *Where the Boys Are,* Metro-Goldwyn-Mayer, 1960; *By Love Possessed,* United Artists, 1961; *A Thunder of Drums,* Metro-Goldwyn-Mayer, 1961; *Light in the Piazza,* Metro-Goldwyn-Mayer, 1962; *Two Weeks in Another Town,* Metro-Goldwyn-Mayer, 1962; *The Victors,* Columbia, 1963; *Your Cheatin' Heart,* Metro-Goldwyn-Mayer, 1965; *Viva Maria,* United Artists, 1966; *That Man George,* Allied Artists, 1967; *Doctor, You've Got to Be Kidding!,* Metro-Goldwyn-Mayer, 1967; *Jack of Diamonds,* Metro-Goldwyn-Mayer, 1967; *A Time for Killing* (also known as *The Long Ride Home*), Columbia, 1967; *The Power,* Metro-Goldwyn-Mayer, 1968; *Evel Knievel,* Fanfare, 1972; *The Man Who Loved Cat Dancing,* Metro-Goldwyn-Mayer, 1973; *Once Is Not Enough,* Paramount, 1975; *Love at First Bite,* American International, 1979; *Zorro, the Gay Blade,* Twentieth Century-Fox, 1981.

PRINCIPAL FILM WORK—Co-producer: *Love at First Bite; Zorro, the Gay Blade.*

PRINCIPAL TELEVISION APPEARANCES—Series: Duncan Carlyle, *The Survivors,* ABC, 1969; Jack Brennan, *Paris 7000,* ABC, 1970; Joel Abrigore, *Dynasty,* ABC, 1985-86.

Episodic: *The Adventures of Rin Tin Tin,* ABC; *The Donna Reed Show,* ABC.

Mini-Series: Stephen Bennett, *Roots,* ABC, 1977.

Movie: *Two Fathers' Justice,* NBC, 1985.

PRINCIPAL TELEVISION WORK—Producer: *The Veil; Roots.*

ADDRESSES: AGENT—Contemporary-Korman Artists, 132 Lasky Drive, Beverly Hills, CA 90212.

* * *

HARRINGTON, Pat Jr.   1929-

PERSONAL: Born August 13, 1929, in New York, NY. EDUCATION: Attended Fordham University. MILITARY: U.S. Air Force, 1952-54.

PERSONAL: Actor and comedian.

CAREER: PRINCIPAL TELEVISION APPEARANCES—Series: Regular, *A Couple of Joes,* ABC, 1950; *The Steve Allen Show,* NBC, 1958-61; Pat Hannigan, *The Danny Thomas Show,* CBS, 1959-60; Guido Panzini, *The Jack Paar Show,* NBC, 1959-62; host, *Stump the Stars,* CBS, 1962; Tony Lawrence, *Mr. Deeds Goes to Town,* ABC, 1969-79; Dwayne Schneider, *One Day at a Time,* CBS, 1975-84.

Episodic: Has appeared on many shows, including *Owen Marshall.*

PRINCIPAL FILM APPEARANCES—*The Wheeler Dealers,* Metro-Goldwyn-Mayer, 1963; *Move Over Darling,* Twentieth Century-Fox, 1963; *Easy Come, Easy Go,* Paramount, 1967; *The President's Analyst,* Paramount, 1967; *2000 Years Later,* Warner Brothers/Seven Arts, 1969; *The Candidate,* Warner Brothers, 1972.

RELATED CAREER—Time salesman for NBC, 1954-58; performed in night clubs, 1960-63.

MEMBER: American Federation of Television and Radio Artists, Screen Actors Guild.

AWARDS: Outstanding Supporting Actor in a Comedy, Variety, or Music Series, Emmy, 1983-84, for *One Day at a Time.*

ADDRESSES: OFFICE—CBS Television City, 7800 Beverly Blvd., Los Angeles, CA 90036.*

* * *

HARRIS, Rosemary

PERSONAL: Born September 19, in Ashby, Suffolk, England; daughter of Stafford Berkley and Enid Maude Frances (Campion) Harris; married Ellis Rabb (an actor and director; divorced); married John Ehle (a novelist); children: (second marriage) Jennifer. EDUCATION: Attended the Royal Academy of Dramatic Art in London, 1951-52.

ROSEMARY HARRIS

VOCATION: Actress.

CAREER: STAGE DEBUT—*Winter Sunshine,* Roof Garden Theatre, Bognar Regis, England, 1948. NEW YORK DEBUT—Mabel, *The Climate of Eden,* Martin Beck Theatre, 1952. LONDON DEBUT—The Girl, *The Seven Year Itch,* Aldwych Theatre, 1953. PRINCIPAL STAGE APPEARANCES—With the Bristol Old Vic Company, 1954-55: Beatrice, *Much Ado About Nothing,* Elizabeth Proctor, *The Crucible,* Francoise Piquetot, *Image in the Sun,* Portia, *The Merchant of Venice,* Isabel, *The Enchanted,* Mrs. Golightly, *The Golden Cuckoo,* Hermione, *The Winter's Tale,* 1954-55; Calpurnia, *Julius Caesar,* Dorcas, *The Winter's Tale,* Desdemona, *Othello,* all at the Old Vic, London, 1955; Cressida, *Troilus and Cressida,* Old Vic, London, and Winter Garden Theatre, NY, 1956; Hilde, *Interlock,* American National Theatre and Academy (ANTA), NY, 1958; Jere Halliday, *The Disenchanted,* Coronet Theatre, NY, 1958; with the Group 20 Players, Wellesley, MA: Eliza Doolittle, *Pygmalion,* Beatrice, *Much Ado About Nothing,* Ann Whitefield, *Man and Superman,* and title role, *Peter Pan,* 1958-59.

Lennie, *The Tumbler,* Helen Hayes Theatre, NY, 1960; Constantia, *The Chances* and Panthea, *The Broken Heart,* both at the Chichester Festival, England, 1962; with the Association of Producing Artists (APA) Repertory Theatre in residence at the University of Michigan, 1962-63: Regina, *Ghosts,* Lady Teazle, *School for Scandal,* Virginia, *The Tavern,* the Girl, *We Comrades Three,* Duchess of Gloucester, *Richard III,* and Portia, *The Merchant of Venice;*

Ilyena, *Uncle Vanya,* Chichester Festival, 1963; Ophelia, *Hamlet* and Ileyna, *Uncle Vanya,* both Old Vic, London, 1963; First Woman, *Play,* Old Vic, London, 1964; with APA Repertory Company, University of Michigan, 1964: title role, *Judith,* Natasha, *War and Peace,* Violet, *Man and Superman,* then at the Phoenix Theatre, NY, 1964, and Megara, *Herakles;* Alice, *You Can't Take It with You,* Lyceum Theatre, NY, 1965; Eleanor, *The Lion in Winter,* Ambassador Theatre, NY, 1966; with the APA Repertory Company at the Lyceum Theatre, 1966-67: Gina, *The Wild Duck,* Signora Ponza, *Right You Are,* Natasha, *War and Peace,* Lady Teazle, *School for Scandal,* and Alice, *You Can't Take It with You;* as Karen Nash, Muriel Tate, and Norma Hubley, *Plaza Suite,* Lryic Theatre, London, 1969.

Irene, *Idiot's Delight,* Ahmanson Theatre, Los Angeles, 1970; Anna, *Old Times,* Billy Rose Theatre, NY, 1971; Portia, *The Merchant of Venice* and Blanche, *A Streetcar Named Desire,* both at the Vivian Beaumont Theatre, 1973; Julie Cavendish, *The Royal Family,* Brooklyn Academy of Music, and the Helen Hayes Theatre, NY, 1975; Vida Phillimore, *The New York Idea* and Olga, *The Three Sisters,* both with the Brooklyn Academy of Music Theatre Company, 1977; Natalia, *A Month in the Country,* Williamstown Theatre Festival, 1978; *Home and Beauty,* Kennedy Center for the Performing Arts, Washington, DC, 1979.

Madame Arkadina, *The Seagull,* New York Shakespeare Festival, 1981; Kate, *All My Sons,* Wyndhams Theatre, London, 1981; Lady Utterword, *Heartbreak House,* Haymarket Theatre, London, 1982; Hesione Hushabye, *Heartbreak House,* Circle in the Square, NY, 1983; Barbara Jackson, *A Pack of Lies,* Royale Theatre, NY, 1984; Judith Bliss, *Hay Fever,* Music Box Theatre, then at the Kennedy Center, Eisenhower Theatre, Washington, DC, 1985-86.

MAJOR TOURS—Lucasta Angel, *The Confidential Clerk,* England, 1954; throughout the U.S. with the APA, 1960-62: Lady Teazle, *School for Scandal,* Bianca, *The Taming of the Shrew,* Cecily, *The Importance of Being Earnest,* Gabrielle, *Anatole,* Phoebe, *As You Like It,* Ann Whitefield, *Man and Superman,* Nina and Madame Arkadina, *The Seagull,* Viola, *Twelfth Night,* Titania, *A Midsummer Night's Dream,* and Virginia, *The Tavern.*

FILM DEBUT—*Beau Brummel,* 1954. PRINCIPAL FILM APPEARANCES—*The Shiralee,* 1957; *A Flea in Her Ear,* 1968; *The Boys from Brazil,* Twentieth Century-Fox, 1979; Ann, *A Ploughman's Lunch,* 1983.

PRINCIPAL TELEVISION APPEARANCES—Movies: *Cradle of Willow,* BBC, 1951; *Othello,* BBC and PBS; *The Prince and the Pauper; Twelfth Night; Wuthering Heights;* George Sand, *Notorious Woman;* Bertha Weiss, *Holocaust; Profiles in Courage; To the Lighthouse,* PBS, 1984.

Series: Minerva Chisholm, *The Chisholms,* CBS, 1979-80.

MEMBER: Actors' Equity Association, Screen Actors Guild, American Federation of Television and Radio Artists.

AWARDS: Best Actress, Antoinette Perry Award, 1966, for *The Lion in Winter;* Drama League Award, 1967, for *The Wild Duck;* Best Actress, *Evening Standard* Award, 1969, for *Plaza Suite;* Emmy Award, for *Notorious Woman;* Golden Globe Award, for *Holocaust;* Drama Desk and Outer Critics Circle Awards, Antoinette Perry Award nomination, 1984, for *Pack of Lies.*

ADDRESSES: AGENT—c/o Milton Goldman, International Creative Management, 40 W. 57th Street, New York, NY 10019; c/o Lawrence Evans, International Creative Management, 22 Grafton Street, London, W1, England.

* * *

HARRISON, Gregory   1950-

PERSONAL: Born May 31, 1950, in Avalon, Santa Catalina Island, CA; son of Ed (a ship's captain and poet) Harrison; married Randi Oakes (an actress); children: Emma Lee. EDUCATION: Studied acting at Estelle Harmon Actors Workshop and with Lee Strasberg and Stella Adler in Hollywood. MILITARY: U.S. Army medic.

VOCATION: Actor, producer, and director.

CAREER: PRINCIPAL TELEVISION APPEARANCES—Series: Title role, *Logan's Run*, CBS, 1977-78; Dr. George Alonzo "Gonzo" Gates, *Trapper John, M.D.*, CBS, 1979-85.

Movies: *Trilogy in Terror*, 1975; *The Gathering*, ABC, 1977; *The Best Place to Be*, NBC, 1979; Capt. Bob Lewis, *Enola Gay: The Men, the Mission, the Atomic Bomb*, NBC, 1980; Ben, *The Women's Room*, ABC, 1980; *For Ladies Only*, NBC, 1981; *The Fighter*, CBS, 1983; *Seduced*, CBS, 1985; *Oceans of Fire*, CBS, 1986; *Circus*, CBS, 1986.

Episodic: *The American Sportsman*, ABC, 1981; *Barnaby Jones*, CBS; *M*A*S*H*, CBS.

Photograph by Marc Raboy

GREGORY HARRISON

Mini-Series: Levi Zandt, *Centennial*, NBC, 1979-80.

Plays: Lachie, *The Hasty Heart*, Showtime, 1983.

PRINCIPAL TELEVISION WORK—With partner Franklin R. Levy, formed the Catalina Production Group, Ltd., in 1981, and has produced these television movies: *For Ladies Only*, NBC, 1981; *Thursday's Child*, CBS, 1983; *The Fighter*, CBS, 1983; *Legs*, ABC, 1983; *Samson and Delilah*, ABC, 1984; *Seduced*, CBS, 1985; *Oceans of Fire*, CBS, 1986; *Circus*, CBS, 1986; *Pleasures*, ABC, 1986; also, directed six episodes of *Trapper John, M.D.* Catalina also produced *Journey's End* for Showtime, 1983, and *The Hasty Heart*, also for Showtime.

PRINCIPAL FILM APPEARANCES—*Jim, the World's Greatest*, Universal, 1976; *Fraternity Row*, Paramount, 1977; *Razorback*, Warner Brothers, 1984.

PRINCIPAL STAGE APPEARANCES—Lachie, *The Hasty Heart*, CAST at the Circle Theatre, then Ahmanson Theatre, Los Angeles, 1981-82; Claggart, *Billy Budd*, Los Angeles, 1984; *Picnic*, Ahmanson Theatre, Los Angeles, 1986; *The Promise*, *The Fantasticks*, and *The Subject Was Roses*, all Los Angeles; "The Troubadour," *Festival*, American Conservatory Theatre, San Francisco, 1978-79.

MAJOR TOUR—"The Troubadour," *Festival*, Los Angeles and Washington, DC.

PRINCIPAL STAGE WORK—Producer (as part of Catalina Production Group): *The Hasty Heart*, CAST at-the-Circle Theatre, then Ahmanson Theatre, Los Angeles, 1981-82; *The Orphan's Revenge*, CAST, then Ford's Theatre, Washington, DC, 1982; *Journey's End*, Los Angeles, 1983; *Billy Budd*, Los Angeles, 1984; *Out of Gas on Lover's Leap*, Coast Playhouse, West Hollywood, 1986; *Picnic*, Ahmanson Theatre, Los Angeles, 1986; also, *Women Behind Bars*, *In Trousers*, and *Living Dolls*, all produced in Los Angeles, and Carl Reiner's *Enter Laughing*, Coast Playhouse, West Hollywood.

MEMBER: Screen Actors Guild, American Federation of Television and Radio Artists.

AWARDS: Best New Actor, Dallas Film Festival Award, 1976, for *Fraternity Row;* as part of Catalina Production Group, has won Los Angeles Drama Critics Circle Awards, Drama-Logue Awards, *L.A. Weekly* Awards, and for continuous exceptional achievement in theatre, the Drama-Logue Publisher/Critics Award, 1984.

ADDRESSES: HOME—Sherman Oaks, CA; Santa Barbara, CA. OFFICE—Catalina Production Group, Ltd., 15301 Ventura Blvd., Suite 221, Sherman Oaks, CA 91403. AGENT—Selfman & Others, 2491 Purdue Avenue, Suite 204, Los Angeles, CA 90064.

* * *

HARTMAN, David   1935-

PERSONAL: Born May 19, 1935, in Pawtucket, RI; son of Cyril Baldwin and Fannie Rodman (Downs) Hartman; married Maureen Downey, June, 1974; children: Sean, Brian, Bridget, Conor. EDUCATION: Duke University, B.A., 1956, economics; American Academy of Dramatic Arts, New York, 1961.

VOCATION: Actor, producer, and host.

CAREER: NEW YORK DEBUT—*My Fair Lady,* 1962-63. PRINCIPAL STAGE APPEARANCES—Original cast, *Hello, Dolly!,* NY, 1963-65.

PRINCIPAL FILM APPEARANCES—*The Island at the Top of the World,* Buena Vista, 1974.

PRINCIPAL TELEVISION APPEARANCES—David Sutton, *The Virginian,* NBC, 1968-69; Dr. Paul Hunter, "The New Doctors" segment of *The Bold Ones,* NBC, 1969-73; title role, *Lucas Tanner,* NBC, 1974-75; host, *Good Morning America,* ABC, 1975—.

Movies: *Feminist and the Fuzz,* ABC, 1970; *I Love a Mystery,* 1973; *Miracle on 34th Street,* 1973; also appeared in *Nobody's Perfect; Ballad of Josie.*

PRINCIPAL TELEVISION WORK—Producer: special on photojournalists for ABC-TV; *Birth and Babies,* ABC.

MEMBER: Vice president, Muscular Dystrophy Association of America, 1970—; National Board of Directors, UNICEF, 1980; Board of Directors, Foundation Jr. Blind.

ADDRESSES: OFFICE—c/o Trascott, Alyson & Craig Inc., 222 Cedar Lane, Teaneck, NJ 07666.

*   *   *

HARTMAN, Jan   1938-

PERSONAL: Born May 23, 1938, in Stockholm, Sweden; came to U.S., 1938, naturalized citizen, 1948; son of Robert Schirokauer (a philosopher) and Rita D. (Emanuel) Hartman; married Lorie Selz (a writer and teacher), June 9, 1960; children: Katherine Emanuel, Tanya Elizabeth. EDUCATION: Harvard College, B.A., 1960.

VOCATION: Writer.

WRITINGS: TELEVISION—1963-75: *Feeling Good,* Children's Television Workshop; "Alred Running Wild," *CBS Playhouse;* "The Long Conversation," *Camera Three;* "A Memory of Autumn," *Prudential Onstage;* "The Survivor," *CBS Playhouse;* "Alexander," *ABC Afterschool Special.*

Song of Myself, CBS, 1976; *With All Deliberate Speed,* CBS, 1976; *Bound for Freedom,* NBC, 1976; *The Great Wallendas,* NBC, 1977; "Hewitt's Just Different," *ABC Afterschool Special,* 1978; "Second Sight," *ABC Theatre,* 1978; *The Herman Graebe Story,* CBS, 1979; "The Late Great Me," *ABC Afterschool Special,* 1980.

A Lasting Love, CBS, 1981; "Killing the Goose," *National Television Theatre,* PBS, 1982; "Stix and Stones," *ABC Afterschool Special; The Campbells,* CTV; *The Last Weapon,* CBC; *Pigeon Feathers; The Day the Children Saved the World; The Presidents; Ganesh; The Story of Mother Teresa of Calcutta.*

Mini-series: *Muir: Earth, Planet, Universe,* PBS, 1984-85; *The Manor and the Estate* (upcoming).

Documentary series: *Lamp Unto My Feet,* CBS; *Directions,* ABC; *Look Up and Live,* CBS; *Frontiers of Faith,* NBC.

PLAYS, PRODUCED—*Samuel Hoopes Reading from His Own Works,* Wichita State University, 1963; *The Shadow of the Valley,*

JAN HARTMAN

Lemars, IA, 1964; *The Legend of Daniel Boone,* Harrodsburg, KY, 1964-present; *Antique Masks,* Villanova, PA, 1966; *Freeman, Freeman,* Karamu House, Cleveland, OH; *Final Solutions,* Felt Forum, Madison Square Garden, NY, 1968; *Fragment of a Last Judgment,* Eugene O'Neill Memorial Theatre Foundation, Waterford, CT, 1967; *The American War Crimes Trial,* Long Wharf Theatre, New Haven, CT, 1973; *Flight 981,* St. Clements, NY, 1977; *Abelard and Heloise,* Charlotte Opera House, NC, 1982; *To the Ninth Circle,* Juilliard School of Drama, NY, 1983; *K,* Performance Theater Center, NY, 1983-84; *A Winter Visitor,* Ventura Theatre Company, 1986.

PLAYS, PUBLISHED—"Samuel Hoopes Reading from His Own Works," *Best Short Plays of 1978,* Dramatists Play Service, 1978; *The Shadow of the Valley: Four Contemporary Religious Plays,* Paulist; *Flatboatman,* Dramtists Play Service; *Every Year at the Carnival,* Dramatists Play Service.

SCREENPLAYS—*Hail to the Chief,* Twentieth Century-Fox; *The Cursed Medallion* or *Emily,* Italian International; *Jelly Roll,* Belafonte Enterprises; *The Bauhaus,* NEH.

BOOKS—*Political Theatre, an Anthology,* Bantam; *Elements of Film Writing,* Intext-Crowell; *Joshua,* Popular Library

RELATED CAREER—Resident Playwright, Theatre of the Living Arts, Philadelphia, PA, 1964-65; teacher, Political Theatre, New School, NY, 1969, 1975; contributing editor, *Religious Theatre* magazine; director, founder, Playwights Theatre Project, Circle in the Square, 1967-69; director, founder, Eleventh Hour Productions, 1977; resident playwright, Theatre St. Clements, 1977-78; adjunct professor for Dramatic Writing and Shakespeare, New York University, 1981—present.

MEMBER: PEN, Writers Guild of America, American National Theatre and Academy, Dramatists Guild, Eugene O'Neill Memorial Theatre Foundation.

AWARDS: Writers Guild of America Award nomination, Best Anthology, 1966, 1967, Best Children's Script, 1977; Freedom Foundation Award, 1971, for "Flatboatman," *ABC Directions;* Cine Award, Bronze Plaque Award, Columbus Film Festival, Certificate of Merit Award, Chicago Film Festival, all 1976, for *Bound for Freedom;* Christopher Award, 1976, for *With All Deliberate Speed;* Ohio State Award, 1976, for *Song of Myself;* Emmy Award, Best Writing of Children's Programming, Best Children's Program, 1978, for *Hewitt's Just Different;* Christopher Award, 1979, Emmy Award, 1980, both for "The Late Great Me," *ABC Afterschool Special;* Writers Guild of America Award, Best Radio Play, 1984, for *The Next War;* fellowships and grants: Guggenheim for Playwriting, 1964; New York State Council of the Arts, 1976; National Endowment for the Arts, 1982.

ADDRESSES: HOME—New York, NY. AGENT—c/o Robert A. Freedman Dramatic Agency and Brandt & Brandt Literary Agency, 1501 Broadway, Suite 2310, New York, NY 10036; c/o Robin Lowe, MLR Ltd., 200 Fulham Road, London SW10 9PN, England.

*   *   *

HARTMAN, Lisa

BRIEF ENTRY: Born in Houston, TX. Actress and singer. Lisa Hartman began her career as a singer, recording her first album when she was eighteen. Despite the positive reviews the album received, it was not a commercial hit, and Hartman found herself in Los Angeles, working as an actress. ABC chose her as the title role in *Tabitha,* a spin-off the the 1960's comedy *Bewitched,* but a short run of that series left her doing the guest appearance circuit and a string of television movies, most notably *Where the Ladies Go.* Fame came to her with her portrayal of the drug addicted rock star in the CBS remake of *Valley of the Dolls.* Given the chance to incorporate her singing and acting, Hartman took the role of Ciji Dunne on *Knot's Landing* in 1982. At the end of the season, Hartman wanted to leave the series, and her character was killed. The audience was so disappointed with her absence that the producers brought her back to the show as a new character, Cathy Geary. Hartman was recently seen in the film remake of *Where the Boys Are* and as a Czechoslovakian woman during World War II who is forced to marry, in *The Bride.* Lisa Hartman continues with her singing career and has released three additional albums since her recording debut.*

*   *   *

HASTINGS, Edward   1931-

PERSONAL: Born April 14, 1931, in New Haven, CT; son of Edward Walton (a salesman) and Madeline (Cassidy) Hastings. EDUCATION: Yale University, B.A., 1952; also attended Columbia University, 1955-56; trained for the stage at the Royal Academy of Dramatic Art. MILITARY: U.S. Army, 1953-55.

VOCATION: Director.

CAREER: STAGE DEBUT—Actor, *Stage Shop,* Canton, CT, 1947. FIRST NEW YORK STAGE WORK—Stage manager, *Lady's Not for Burning,* Carnegie Hall Playhouse, 1957, for forty-eight performances. PRINCIPAL STAGE WORK—Stage manager, *Ross,* O'Neill Theatre, NY, 1961; stage manager, *Oliver!,* Imperial Theatre, NY, 1962-64; director: *Our Town,* Mineola, Long Island, NY, 1968; *Shay,* Westport, CT, 1974; *Hot L Baltimore,* Brisbane, Australia, 1975; *Buried Child,* Belgrade, Yugoslavia, 1980; *Macbeth,* Guthrie Theatre, Minneapolis, MN, 1981; *Another Part of the Forest,* Seattle Repertory, WA, 1981; *The Magistrate,* Hartman Theatre, Stamford, CT, 1982; *Arms and the Man,* Denver Center, CO, 1983; *The Margaret Ghost,* Berkeley Repertory, CA, 1984; *The Majestic Kid,* Ashland, OR, 1985; *All My Sons,* Seattle Repertory, WA, 1985.

At American Conservatory Theatre, San Francisco, CA: *Charley's Aunt,* 1966, *Our Town,* 1967, *A Delicate Balance,* 1968, *The Promise,* 1969, *The Relapse,* 1970, *The Time of Your Life,* 1971, *The House of Blue Leaves,* 1972, *Dandy Dick,* 1973, *Family Album,* 1973, *Broadway,* 1974, *Street Scene,* 1975, *General Gorgeous,* 1976, *Valentin and Valentina,* 1977, *All the Way Home,* 1978, *The Fifth of July,* 1979, *Girl of the Golden West,* 1980, *Happy Landings,* 1982, *The Holdup,* 1983, *Dial M for Murder,* 1983, *Angels Fall,* 1984, *Macbeth,* 1985.

MAJOR TOURS—Director: *Oliver!,* U.S. cities, 1964; *Shakespeare's People,* U.S. cities, 1977.

EDWARD HASTINGS

RELATED CAREER—Co-founder and executive director, American Conservatory Theatre, San Francisco, CA, 1965-80, artistic director, 1986—; works-in-progress director, Eugene O'Neill Playwright's Conference, Waterford, CT, 1973, 1974; Squaw Valley Community of Writers, 1974-76; Plays in Progress, American Conservatory Theatre, San Francisco, CA; Asian-American Theatre Company (trustee), San Francisco, CA, 1977-79; consultant, National Foundation for Advancement in Arts, Miami, FL, 1983—.

MEMBER: Society of Stage Directors and Choreographers.

ADDRESSES: OFFICE—American Conservatory Theatre, 450 Geary Street, San Francisco, CA 94102. AGENT—c/o Jerry Hogan, Henderson/Hogan Agency, 405 W. 44th Street, New York, NY 10036.

*   *   *

HASTINGS, Hugh   1917-

PERSONAL: Born January 31, 1917, in Syndey, New South Wales; son of Hugh James and Margaret Williamson Hastings. EDUCATION: Attended Fort Street High School. MILITARY: Royal Navy, World War II.

VOCATION: Actor, pianist, playwright, and theatre director.

CAREER: STAGE DEBUT—Kit, *Cat's Cradle*, Sydney, New South Wales, 1935. LONDON DEBUT—*Sweetest and Lowest*, Ambassadors' Theatre, 1946. PRINCIPAL STAGE APPEARANCES—With Dundee Repertory Company, 1939, and St. Andrews Repertory Company, 1939-40; Rolf, *Touch of the Sun*, New Lindsey, UK, 1952; *Do Look in Revue*, Irving, UK, 1954; *A Matter of Choice Revue*, New Arts, UK, 1966; Father, *A Sense of Detachment*, Royal Court Theatre, London, 1972.

With the Young Vic Company, London, 1974-82: Headwaiter, *Scapino;* Brabantio and Gratiano, *Othello;* Brasset, *Charley's Aunt;* Maingot, *French without Tears;* Willie, *Happy Days;* Araminta Ditch, *All Walks of Leg;* Baptista, *The Taming of the Shrew;* First Witch, *Macbeth.*

Also in *The Portage to San Cristobal of A.H.*, Mermaid Theatre, London; *Her Mother Came Too.*

MAJOR TOURS—*Murder without Crime* and as Duke, *Worm's Eye View*, Arts Council, UK cities, 1947; *Fly Away Peter*, UK cities; *A Matter of Choice*, UK cities, 1966; with the Young Vic Company, toured the United States and Australian and Mexican cities, 1974; *Dead Ringer*, UK cities; *The Vortex*, Cambridge Theatre Company, UK cities.

PRINCIPAL TELEVISION APPEARANCES—*Dad's Army*, BBC; *Scapino*, BBC; *Macbeth*, BBC.

WRITINGS: PLAYS—*Seagulls over Sorrento*, 1949; *Red Dragon*, 1950; *Inner Circle*, 1952; *Touch of the Sun*, 1952; *Pink Elephants*, 1955; *Blood Orange*, 1958; *Scapa!* (also composed music), 1962; *Purple Patch*, 1963; *The Tattoo Parlour*, 1965; *The Boy*, 1973; *An Evening with Walter Pinge*, 1980; *Cross Words*, 1986.

SCREENPLAYS—*Glory at Sea; Crest of the Wave;* (adaptor) *It Started in Paradise.*

HUGH HASTINGS

SIDELIGHTS: RECREATIONS—Theatre and cricket.

ADDRESSES: AGENT—Eric Glass, Ltd., 28 Berkeley Square, London W1 X6 HD, England.

*   *   *

HAVARD, Lezley   1944-

PERSONAL: Born Lezley Morton-Fincham, August 9, 1944, in London, England; daughter of Ernest (a surveyor) and Iris Margaret (a secretary; maiden name, Tobin) Morton-Fincham; married Bernard Havard (a theatrical producer), January 16, 1963; children: Celine, Christiane, Julien.

VOCATION: Playwright.

WRITINGS: PLAYS, PRODUCED—*Only Yesterday*, University of Edmonton, 1976; *Jill*, Citadel Theatre, Edmonton, Canada, 1977; *Hide and Seek*, Citadel Theatre, Edmonton, Canada, 1977, Lennoxville Festival, Quebec, Canada, 1977, Wilbur Theatre, Boston, MA, 1980, Belasco Theatre, NY, 1980, and Peachtree Playhouse, Atlanta, GA, 1981; *Victims*, Windsor, Ontario, Canada, 1979, Whitehorse Theatre, Yukon, Canada, 1979, and Alliance Theatre, Atlanta, GA, 1980; *In the Name of the Father*, Alliance Theatre 1980, *The Actors*, Alliance Theatre, 1981; *In the Bag*, Actors Theatre of Louisville, 1982.

RELATED CAREER—Literary manager, Alliance Theatre, 1980-81.

MEMBER: Dramatists Guild.

AWARDS: Best Full Length Play, National Competition Women-Write-for-Theatre, Playwights Co-Op, Toronto, Canada, 1975, for *Victims;* Best Play, Multi-Cultural Association, Toronto, Canada, 1975, for *Only Yesterday;* Clifford E. Lee Playwriting Award, University of Edmonton, Alberta, Canada, 1976, for *Jill;* Senior Arts Grant, Canada Council for the Arts, 1977.

ADDRESSES: OFFICE—Walnut Street Theatre, Ninth and Walnut Streets, Philadelphia, PA 19146. AGENT—c/o Earl Graham, Graham Agency, 317 W. 45th Street, New York, NY 10036.

*   *   *

HEBERT, Rich   1956-

PERSONAL: Born December 12, 1956, in Quincy, MA; son of William and Ann Hebert. EDUCATION: Boston University, B.F.A., 1979.

VOCATION: Actor.

CAREER: BROADWAY DEBUT—*Rock 'n' Roll, the First 5000 Years,* St. James Theatre, for fourteen performances. PRINCIPAL STAGE APPEARANCES—Off-Broadway: Sam Grey, *Wanted: Dead or Alive,* Panache Theatre; Gus, *110 in the Shade,* York Players; Scott Williams, *Easy Money,* St. Clements Theatre; Walter, *The*

RICH HEBERT

Rimers of Eldritch, Theater of the Changing Space; Chuck, *Dazy,* Manhattan Punchline Theatre.

Regional: Nick, *Baby,* Olney Theatre, MD; John/Judas, *Godspell,* Charles Playhouse, Boston, MA; Shem, *Two by Two,* Shawnee Playhouse, PA; Charlie, *Brigadoon,* Green Mountain Guild, VT; Hornbeck, *Inherit the Wind,* Little Harp, *The Robber Bridegroom,* Riff, *West Side Story,* all Hope Summer Repertory, MI.

MAJOR TOURS—Rum Tum Tugger, *Cats,* U.S. cities.

PRINCIPAL FILM APPEARANCES—M.P. *A Small Circle of Friends,* United Artists, 1980; Businessman, *Altered States,* Warner Brothers, 1980; Student, *Dirty Tricks,* Avco Embassy, 1981; Boston Cop, *Night School,* 1981.

PRINCIPAL TELEVISION APPEARANCES—Mr. Williams, *The New Voice,* PBS; Doctor, *All My Children,* ABC; intern, *The Doctors,* NBC.

MEMBER: Actors' Equity Association, Screen Actors Guild, American Federation of Television and Radio Artists, New York Road Runners Club, Young Mens Christian Association.

ADDRESSES: HOME—New York, NY. AGENT—Triad Artists, 888 Seventh Avenue, New York, NY 10106.

*   *   *

HELD, Dan   1948-

PERSONAL: Born May 20, 1948, in New York, NY; son of Irving (an executive) and Sallee (Honigstien) Held; married Barbara Katarnia (an interior designer), April 30, 1977; children: Vanessa Leigh, Cassandra Lynn. EDUCATION: Hofstra University, B.A., 1971; trained for the stage at the American Musical and Dramatic Academy with Robert Modoca. RELIGION: Jewish.

VOCATION: Director, producer, choreographer, and actor.

CAREER: STAGE DEBUT—Henry Higgins, *My Fair Lady,* Surflight Summer Theatre, 1967, for ten performances. NEW YORK DEBUT—*Baron Rommer,* East Side Playhouse, 1973, for twenty performances. PRINCIPAL STAGE APPEARANCES—Papa Pepe Hernandes, *El Grande De Coca Cola,* Plaza 9 Theatre, NY, 1974-75.

PRINCIPAL STAGE WORK—Director: *Love's Labour's Lost,* Cherry Lane Theatre, NY; *Room Service,* Manhattan Punchline Theatre, NY; *Romeo and Juliet,* Equity Library Theatre, NY; *Reach for the Sky,* Black Theatre Alliance, NY; *Returnings,* ATA Chernuchin, NY; *D,* Manhattan Theatre Club, NY. All with the American Jewish Theatre: *The Man in the Glass Booth; From the Memoirs of Pontius Pilate; The Tenth Man; The Caine Mutiny Court Martial; The Price; Two for the Seesaw.*

Patrick Henry Lake Liquors, American Academy of Dramatic Art; *Scapino,* The Theatre Place; *Last of the Red Hot Lovers,* Harlequin Dinner Theatre; *Follies,* Surflight Summer Theatre; *Mack and Mabel,* Theatre by the Sea; *Rosencruntz and Guildenstern Are Dead,* Adelphi Festival; *Round and Round the Garden, That Championship Season,* both Nassau Repertory; *The Lion in Winter, The Gin Game,* New Jersey Theatre Forum; *Knock, Knock, Let's Get a Divorce,* both New Jersey Shakespeare Festival.

DAN HELD

Opera: *Angel Levine, Gimpel the Fool,* both 92nd Street Young Men's Hebrew Association.

Choreographer: *Berlin to Broadway,* South Jersey Regional Theatre; *Bodo,* Goodspeed Opera House; Hasty Pudding Theatrical, Harvard University, Boston, MA, 1981, 1982; *Fiddler on the Roof,* Hofstra University; *Working,* Montclair State College; *Threepenny Opera,* The Theatre Place; *You're a Good Man Charlie Brown,* Theatre Tonight; *South Pacific,* Lakewood Playhouse; *Jacques Brel Is Alive and Well, Side by Side by Sondheim,* both Nassau Repertory.

RELATED CAREER—Resident director, American Jewish Theatre, NY, 1980—present.

MEMBER: Actors' Equity Association, Society of Stage Directors and Choreographers, Trilogy Theatre (board of directors).

ADDRESSES: HOME—Mount Vernon, NY. AGENT—Shukat Company, 340 W. 55th Street, New York, NY 10019.

*   *   *

HELMOND, Katherine   1934-

PERSONAL: Born July 5, 1934, in Galveston, TX; daughter of Patrick Joseph and Thelma Louise (Malone) Helmond; married David Christian (an artist and writer), June, 1971. RELIGION: Roman Catholic.

VOCATION: Actress and director.

CAREER: PRINCIPAL TELEVISION APPEARANCES—Series: Jessica Tate, *Soap,* ABC, 1977-80; Mona Robinson, *Who's the Boss,* ABC. Episodic: *The Six Million Dollar Man; The Bionic Woman; The F.B.I.;* Emily Dickinson, *Meeting of the Minds.*

Mini-Series: *Pearl.*

Movies: *The Autobiography of Miss Jane Pittman,* 1974; *The Legend of Lizzie Borden,* 1975; *Wanted: The Sundance Woman,* 1976; *Diary of a Teenage Hitchhiker,* 1976; *Honeymoon Hotel,* ABC, 1982; Frances Clooney, *Rosie: The Rosemary Clooney Story,* CBS, 1982; *World War III,* 1982.

PRINCIPAL TELEVISION WORK—Director: *Benson; Who's the Boss.*

PRINCIPAL FILM APPEARANCES—*The Hindenberg,* Universal, 1975; *Baby Blue Marine,* Columbia, 1976; *Family Plot,* Universal, 1976; *Time Bandits,* Embassy, 1981; *Brazil,* Universal, 1985.

PRINCIPAL FILM WORK—Director, *Bankrupt,* American Films International.

STAGE DEBUT—*Stage Door,* Community Theater, Galveston, TX. PRINCIPAL STAGE APPEARANCES—Bananas, *House of Blue Leaves,* NY, 1971; *Great God Brown,* on Broadway, 1973; *Quartermaine's Terms,* San Francisco, 1984; also appeared at Houston Playhouse, TX; Margo Jones Theater, Dallas, TX; Associated

KATHERINE HELMOND

Producing Artists, NY; Trinity Square Repertory, RI; Hartford Stage, CT; Phoenix Repertory, NY.

RELATED CAREER—President, *Taur Can Productions,* Hollywood, CA, 1979—.

MEMBER: Actor's Equity Association, American Federation of Television and Radio Artists, Screen Actors Guild, Directors Guild of America.

AWARDS: Clarence Derwent Award, New York Drama Critics Award, both 1971, for *House of Blue Leaves;* Los Angeles Drama Critics Award, 1972; Emmy Award nominations, Best Actress in a Comedy Series, 1978, 1979, 1980, 1981, all for *Soap;* Golden Globe Award, 1980, for *Soap.*

ADDRESSES: OFFICE—P.O. Box 10029, Beverly Hills, CA 90213. AGENT—William Morris Agency, 151 El Camino Drive, Beverly Hills, CA 90212.

*   *   *

HEMINGWAY, Mariel   1961-

PERSONAL: Born November 21, 1961, in Mill Valley, CA; daughter of John Hadley (a sportsman and writer) and Byra Louise (Whittlesey) Hemingway; married Steven Douglas Crisnan (a restauranteur, writer, and producer), December 9, 1984. EDUCATION: KSVCS High School, Ketchum, Sun Valley, ID; studied for the theatre with Harold Guskin.

VOCATION: Actress and producer.

CAREER: STAGE DEBUT—Charlene Loody, *The Palace of Amateurs,* Dallas, TX, for seventy performances. NEW YORK DEBUT—Lead, *California Dog Fight,* Manhattan Theatre Club, March, 1985, for forty performances.

FILM DEBUT—Kathy, *Lipstick,* Paramount, 1976. PRINCIPAL FILM APPEARANCES—Traccy, *Manhattan,* United Artists, 1979; Chris, *Personal Best,* Warner Brothers, 1982; Dorothy Stratton, *Star '80,* Warner Brothers, 1983; Melo, *Creator,* Universal, 1985; Chris, *The Mean Season,* Orion, 1985.

TELEVISION DEBUT—Movies: Cathy, *I Want to Keep My Baby,* CBS, 1977.

RELATED CAREER—Owner and secretary, Clear Water Pictures, 1986.

AWARDS: Academy Award nomination, Best Supporting Actress, 1979, for *Manhattan.*

SIDELIGHTS: In a note to *CTFT,* Mariel Hemingway expressed the following thoughts on her career and her method of working and growing in this business: "All roles, films, directors, and technicians have something invaluable that they have given me. All are different and unique and uncomparable and I take all these different experiences into my next project."

She is also co-owner with her husband, designer, and menu maker for Sam's Cafe Restaurant, New York.

ADDRESSES: OFFICE—Sam's Cafe, 1406 Third Avenue, New York, NY 10021. AGENT—c/o Ron Myers, Creative Artists Agency, 1888 Century Park E., Los Angeles, CA 90067.

*   *   *

HEMSLEY, Sherman   1938-

PERSONAL: Born February 1, 1938, in Philadelphia, PA. EDUCATION: Attended Philadelphia Academy of Dramatic Arts; studied with Lloyd Richards in New York. MILITARY: U.S. Air Force.

VOCATION: Actor.

CAREER: STAGE DEBUT—Advanced workshop of the Negro Ensemble Company, NY. PRINCIPAL STAGE APPEARANCES—*The People vs. Ranchman,* Off-Broadway production, 1968; Mad Hatter, *Alice in Wonderland,* Off-Broadway production, 1969; Gitlow, *Purlie,* Broadway production, 1970; Gitlow, *Purlie Victorious,* and others with the Theatre XIV Company; *The Blacks,* Society Hill Playhouse; *Norman, Is That You?,* Los Angeles; *Under the Yum-Yum Tree; Death of a Salesman.*

MAJOR TOURS—*Don't Bother Me I Can't Cope,* Toronto, Canada, San Francisco, CA; *The Odd Couple,* Dallas, TX, Chicago, IL; spent several summers with Dalli Mohammed and Shirley Goldenberg's Phoenix Productions, performing children's plays in East Coast cities.

PRINCIPAL TELEVISION APPEARANCES—Series: *Black Book,* Philadelphia television; George Jefferson, *All in the Family,* CBS, 1973-75; George Jefferson, *The Jeffersons,* CBS, 1975-85.

Movie: *Alice in Wonderland,* CBS, 1985.

PRINCIPAL FILM APPEARANCES—*Love at First Bite,* American International, 1979.

MEMBER: Actors' Equity Association, Screen Actors Guild, American Federation of Television and Radio Artists; Vinnette Carrol's Urban Arts Corps.

SIDELIGHTS: Sherman Hemsley worked for eight years for the U.S. Post Office.

ADDRESSES: OFFICE—c/o Kenny Johnston, 6920 Sunset Blvd., Suite 1002, Los Angeles, CA 90028. AGENT—Tobias, Herb, and Associates, 1901 Avenue of the Stars, Suite 840, Los Angeles, CA 90067.*

*   *   *

HENNING, Linda Kaye   1944-

PERSONAL: Born September 16, 1944, in Toluca Lake, CA; daughter of Paul (a television producer) Henning. EDUCATION: Attended San Fernando Valley State College.

VOCATION: Actress.

CAREER: PRINCIPAL STAGE APPEARANCES—*Gypsy; Applause; Damn Yankees; I Do, I Do; Pajama Game; Sugar; Wonderful Town; Fiddler on the Roof; Sound of Music; Vanities; Born Yesterday; Mary, Mary; Bus Stop.*

PRINCIPAL FILM APPEARANCES—*Bye, Bye Birdie,* Columbia, 1963.

PRINCIPAL TELEVISION APPEARANCES—Series: Betty Jo Bradley Elliott, *Petticoat Junction,* CBS, 1963-70.

Episodic: *Happy Days; Mork & Mindy; Double Trouble; Barnaby Jones; Love American Style; Adam 12.*

Pilots: *Kudzu; The Circle; Family.*

Movies: *The Return of the Beverly Hillbillies,* 1981; *The Dog Days of Arthur Kane; Gift of Terror.*

ADDRESSES: OFFICE—9056 Santa Monica Blvd., Suite 201, Los Angeles, CA 90069.*

*   *   *

HERMAN, Jerry   1933-

PERSONAL: Born July 10, 1933, in New York, NY; son of Harry (a summer camp operator) and Ruth (a piano teacher; maiden name, Sachs) Herman. EDUCATION: University of Miami, A.B., 1954;

JERRY HERMAN

also attended Parsons School of Design. RELIGION: Jewish. MILITARY: U.S. Army, 1954-55.

VOCATION: Composer and lyricist.

CAREER: STAGE DEBUT—Og, *Finian's Rainbow,* University of Miami, FL, 1954. CONCERT—*An Evening with Jerry Herman,* Concert Hall, NY, 1974.

WRITINGS: MUSIC AND LYRICS—*I Feel Wonderful,* Theatre de Lys, 1954; *Nightcap,* 1958; *Parade,* 1960; *A to Z,* 1960; *Milk and Honey,* Martin Beck Theatre, NY, 1961; *Madame Aphrodite,* Phoenix Theatre, NY, 1961; *Hello, Dolly!,* St. James Theatre, NY, 1964, then Drury Lane Theatre, London, 1965; *Mame,* Winter Garden Theatre, NY, 1966; *Dear World,* Mark Hellinger Theatre, NY, 1966; *Mack and Mable,* Palace Theatre, NY, 1974; *The Grand Tour,* Palace Theatre, NY, 1978; "Mother of Burlesque" (unproduced), 1979; (wrote some songs) *A Day in Hollywood/A Night in the Ukraine,* John Golden Theatre, NY, 1981; *La Cage Aux Folles,* Palace, NY, 1983; *Jerry's Girls,* St. James Theatre, NY, 1985-86.

RECORDINGS: ALBUM—*Hello, Jerry!,* 1965.

MEMBER: Zeta Beta Tau Fraternity.

AWARDS: Antoinette Perry Award, two Grammy Awards, two Gold Record Awards, 1964, for *Hello, Dolly!;* Antoinette Perry Award nomination, 1966, for *Mame;* Best Lyricist Award, *Variety,* Poll, 1967; Zeta Beta Tau Award, 1968; Antoinette Perry Award, Drama Desk Award, Best Score, 1984, for *La Cage Aux Folles;* also, Iron Arrow Award, University of Miami Honor Society.

SIDELIGHTS: RECREATIONS—Architecture and design.

CTFT has learned Jerry Herman, reportedly, cannot read or write music and plays music by ear into a tape recorder.

ADDRESSES: HOME—55 Central Park West, New York, NY 10023.

*   *   *

HERSEY, David   1939-

PERSONAL: Born November 30, 1939, in Rochester, NY; son of C. Kenneth and Ella (Morgan) Hersey. EDUCATION: Attended Oberlin College.

VOCATION: Lighting designer and actor.

CAREER: STAGE DEBUT—Stage Manager, *Six Characters in Search of an Author,* Martinique Theatre, NY, 1962. FIRST LONDON STAGE WORK—Lighting designer, *She Stoops to Conquer,* Garrick Theatre, 1969. PRINCIPAL STAGE WORK—Actor, stage manager, lighting designer, in over seventy-five productions throughout the United States, 1961-67; lighting supervisor, National Theatre of Great Britain, 1974-84.

Lighting designer for such companies as: Royal Shakespeare Company, Royal Opera, Royal Ballet, Scottish Ballet, Ballet Rambert, London Contemporary Dance, English National Opera, and with companies in Austria, France, Germany, Canada, and Iran.

DAVID HERSEY

Most recently designed shows in London's West End include: *Cats, Starlight Express, Guys and Dolls, Les Miserables, Song and Dance, Marilyn, Evita, The King and I, The Sound of Music, Camelot, The Little Shop of Horrors;* Broadway productions include: *Evita, Merrily We Roll Along, Nicholas Nickleby, Cats;* in Los Angeles, *Evita, Crucifer of Blood, Old Times,* others; at the National Theatre, London: *Guys and Dolls, The Government Inspector;* for the Royal Shakespeare Company in London and Stratford: *Peter Pan, Mother Courage, As You Like It, Nicholas Nickleby.*

RELATED CAREER—Founder, DHA Lighting, Limited.

MEMBER: Association of Lighting Designers (chairman).

AWARDS: Best Lighting Design, Los Angeles Drama Critics Circle Award, 1979, for *Evita;* Best Lighting Design, Drama-Logue Critics Award, 1980, for *The Crucifer of Blood;* Best Lighting Design, Antoinette Perry Award, 1980, for *Evita;* Maharam Foundation Design Award, 1982, for *Nicholas Nickleby;* Best Lighting Design, Antoinette Perry Award, Drama Desk Award, both 1983, for *Cats;* Best Lighting Design, Drama-Logue Critics Award, 1985, for *Old Times.*

SIDELIGHTS: RECREATIONS—Jewelry-making and boating.

ADDRESSES: OFFICE—DHA Lighting Ltd., Seven Bishop's Terrace, London SE11 4UE, England.

*   *   *

HERSHEY, Barbara   1948-

PERSONAL: Born February 5, 1948, in Los Angeles, CA; children: Tom (name legally changed from Free).

VOCATION: Actress.

CAREER: FILM DEBUT—*With Six You Get Eggroll,* National General, 1968. PRINCIPAL FILM APPEARANCES—*Last Summer,* Allied Artists, 1968; *Heaven with a Gun,* Metro-Goldwyn-Mayer, 1968; *The Liberation of L.B. Jones,* Columbia, 1970; *The Baby Maker,* National General, 1970; *The Pursuit of Happiness,* Columbia, 1971; *Boxcar Bertha,* 1971; *Dealing,* Warner Brothers, 1972; *Angela—Love Comes Quietly,* 1972; *The Crazy World of Julius Vrooder,* Twentieth Century-Fox, 1974; *The Last Hard Men,* Twentieth Century-Fox, 1975; *Diamonds,* Avco Embassy, 1975; *A Choice of Weapons,* 1975; Nina Franklin, *The Stuntman,* 1978; *Take This Job and Shove It,* Avco Embassy, 1981; *The Entity,* Twentieth Century-Fox, 1983; *The Right Stuff,* Warner Brothers, 1983; *The Natural,* Tri-Star, 1984; Lee, *Hannah and Her Sisters,* Orion, 1986.

PRINCIPAL TELEVISION APPEARANCES—Series: Kathy Monroe, *The Monroes,* ABC, 1966-67; Karen Holmes, *From Here to Eternity,* NBC, 1980.

Mini-Series: *A Man Called Intrepid,* 1979.

Episodic: *Gidget,* 1965; *The Invaders,* 1967; *Daniel Boone,* 1967; *Bob Hope's Chrysler Theatre,* 1967; *High Chaparral,* 1967; *CBS Playhouse,* 1967; *Love Story,* 1973; *Kung Fu,* 1973.

Movies: *In the Glitter Palace,* 1977; *Just a Little Inconvenience,* 1977; *Sunshine Christmas,* 1977; *Angel on My Shoulder,* 1980, *My Wicked, Wicked Ways: The Legend of Errol Flynn,* CBS, 1985.

ADDRESSES: AGENT—Creative Artists Agency, 1888 Century Park E., Los Angeles, CA 90067.*

*   *   *

HESSEMAN, Howard   1940-

PERSONAL: Born February 27, 1940, in Lebanon, OR; son of George Henry and Edna (Forster) Hesseman. EDUCATION: Attended University of Oregon.

VOCATION: Actor.

CAREER: PRINCIPAL TELEVISION APPEARANCES—Series: Johnny Caravella (Dr. Johnny Fever), *WKRP in Cincinnati,* CBS, 1978-82; Sam Royer, *One Day at a Time,* CBS, 1982-84.

Movies: *The Victim,* 1972; *Hustling,* 1975; *The Amazing Howard Hughes,* 1977; *Tarantulas: The Deadly Cargo,* 1977; *The Comedy Company,* 1978; *The Ghost of Flight 401,* 1978; *In Our Hands,* 1984; *Silence of the Heart,* CBS, 1984; *Heat,* 1986; also appeared in *The Life and Times of Senator Joe McCarthy; Skyward.*

Specials: *Twenty-five Years of Motown,* 1982; *Supernight of Rock & Roll,* 1983; also: *The TV TV Show; You Can't Take It with You.*

PRINCIPAL STAGE APPEARANCES—Company member, The Committee, San Francisco, CA. 1965-75.

PRINCIPAL FILM APPEARANCES—*Petulia,* Warner Brothers/Seven Arts, 1968; *Billy Jack,* Warner Brothers, 1971; *Steelyard Blues,* Warner Brothers, 1973; *Shampoo,* Columbia, 1975; *The Sunshine Boys,* United Artists, 1975; *Jackson County Jail,* 1976; *The Big Bus,*

HOWARD HESSEMAN

Paramount, 1976; *Silent Movie,* Twentieth Century-Fox, 1976; *The Other Side of Midnight,* Twentieth Century-Fox, 1977; *The Jerk,* Universal, 1979; *Private Lessons,* 1980; *Honky Tonk Freeway,* Universal, 1981; *Dr. Detroit,* Universal, 1983; *Police Academy II,* Warner Brothers, 1984; *My Chauffeur,* Crown International, 1986; *Voyage of the Navigator,* 1986.

MEMBER: Screen Actors Guild, American Federation of Television and Radio Artists.

ADDRESSES: AGENT—William Morris Agency, 151 El Camino Drive, Beverly Hills, CA 90212.

*   *   *

HESTON, Charlton   1922-

PERSONAL: Born Charlton Carter, October 6, 1922, in Evanston, IL; son of Russell Whitford and Lilla (Charlton) Carter; married Lydia Clarke, March 17, 1944; children: Fraser Clarke, Holly Ann. EDUCATION: Attended Northwestern University. MILITARY: U.S. Air Force, World War II.

VOCATION: Actor.

CAREER: NEW YORK DEBUT—Proculeuis, *Antony and Cleopatra,* Martin Beck Theatre, 1947. PRINCIPAL STAGE APPEARANCES— *State of the Union* and *The Glass Menagerie,* Thomas Wolfe Memorial Theatre, Ashville, NC, 1947; Glenn Campbell, *Leaf and Bough,* Cort Theatre, NY, 1949; A2, *Cock-a-Doodle-Doo,* Lenox Hill Playhouse, NY, 1949; John Clitherow, *Design for a Stained Glass Window,* Mansfield Theatre, NY, 1950; *The Traitor,* 1952; Doug Roberts, *Mister Roberts,* City Center Theatre, NY, 1956; Kell, *The Tumbler,* Helen Hayes Theatre, NY, 1960; Sir Thomas

More, *A Man for All Seasons,* Mill Run Playhouse, Skokie, IL, 1965; John Proctor, *The Crucible,* Ahmanson Theatre, Los Angeles, 1972; title role, *Macbeth,* Ahmanson Theatre, Los Angeles, 1975; James Tyrone, *Long Days Journey into Night,* Ahmanson Theatre, Los Angeles, 1977; Sir Thomas More, *A Man for All Seasons,* Ahmanson Theatre, Los Angeles, 1979; Sherlock Holmes, *The Crucifer of Blood,* Ahmanson Theatre, Los Angeles, CA, 1980; McLeod, *Detective Story,* Ahmanson Theatre, Los Angeles, 1984; Captain Queeg, *The Caine Mutiny Court Martial,* Queen's Theatre, London, England, 1985.

FILM DEBUT—*Dark City,* 1950. PRINCIPAL FILM APPEARANCES— *The Greatest Show on Earth,* 1952; *The Savage,* 1952; *Ruby Gentry,* 1952; *President's Lady,* 1953; *Pony Express,* 1953; *Arrowhead,* 1953; *Bad for Each Other,* 1953; *Naked Jungle,* 1954; *Secret of the Incas,* 1954; *Far Horizons,* 1955; *Lucy Galland,* 1955; *Private War of Major Benson,* 1955; *The Maverick,* 1956; Moses, *The Ten Commandments,* Paramount, 1957; *The Big Country,* United Artists, 1958; *The Buccaneers,* Paramount, 1959; title role, *Ben Hur,* Metro-Goldwyn-Mayer, 1959; *Wreck of the Mary Deare,* Metro-Golden-Mayer, 1959.

El Cid, 1961; *The Pigeon That Took Rome,* Paramount, 1962; *55 Days at Peking,* Allied Artists, 1963; *Major Dundee,* Columbia, 1965; *The Agony and the Ecstacy,* Twentieth Century-Fox, 1965; *The War Lord,* Universal, 1965; *The Greatest Story Ever Told,* United Artists, 1966; *Khartoum,* United Artists, 1966; *The Battle Horns,* 1968; *Will Penny,* Paramount, 1968; *Planet of the Apes,* Twentieth Century-Fox, 1968; *Number One,* United Artists, 1969.

Title role, *Julius Caesar,* American International, 1970; *Beneath the Planet of the Apes,* Twentieth Century-Fox, 1970; *The Hawaiians,*

CHARLTON HESTON

United Artists, 1970; *The Omega Man*, Warner Brothers, 1971; Skyjacked, Metro-Goldwyn-Mayer, 1972; *Antony and Cleopatra*, 1973; *Soylent Green*, Metro-Goldwyn-Mayer, 1973; *The Three Musketeers*, Twentieth Century-Fox, 1974; *The Four Musketeers*, Twentieth Century-Fox, 1975; *The Last Hard Men*, Twentieth Century-Fox, 1976; *Midway*, 1976; *Two Minute Warning*, Universal, 1976; *Crossed Swords*, Warner Brothers, 1978; *Gray Lady Down*, Universal, 1978; *The Awakening*, Warner Brothers, 1980; *Mother Lode*, 1982.

PRINCIPAL FILM WORK—Director: *Antony and Cleopatra*, 1973; *The Mother Lode*, 1982.

TELEVISION DEBUT—*Julius Caesar*, Studio One, 1949. PRINCIPAL TELEVISION APPEARANCES—Series: Narrator, *F.D.R.*, NBC, 1965; Jason Colby, *Dynasty II: The Colbys*, ABC, 1985—.

Episodic: "Macbeth," "The Taming of the Shrew," "Jane Eyre," "Wuthering Heights," "Of Human Bondage," all on *Studio One*, CBS, 1949-52.

Lux Video Theatre, CBS, 1953; *Philco TV Playhouse*, NBC, 1954; guest host, *The Colgate Variety Hour*, NBC, 1955; *Danger*, CBS, 1955; *Shirley Temple's Storybook*, NBC; *The Dick Cavett Show*, ABC; *Fernwood 2Night*, syndicated; *Dynasty*, 1985.

Mini-Series: *Chiefs*, NBC, 1984.

Movie: *Nairobi Affair*, CBS, 1984.

WRITINGS: BOOKS—*An Actor's Life*, Dutton, 1980.

MEMBER: Screen Actors Guild (president, 1966-71), Actors' Equity Association, American Film Institute (chairman), Los Angeles Theatre Group (trustee), National Council on the Arts, 1967-72, President's Task Force on Arts and Humanities, 1981—;

AWARDS: Best Actor, Academy Award, 1959, for *Ben Hur;* Jean Hersholt Humanitarian of the Year, American Academy of Motion Picture Arts and Sciences, 1978.

ADDRESSES: AGENT—Michael Levine Public Relations, 9123 Sunset Blvd., Los Angeles, CA 90069.

* * *

HILLERMAN, John 1932-

PERSONAL: Full name, John Benedict Hillerman; born December 20, 1932, in Dennison, TX; son of Christopher Benedict and Lenora JoAnn (Medinger) Hillerman. EDUCATION: Attended the University of Texas; studied at at the American Theatre Wing in New York. MILITARY: U.S. Air Force, 1953-57.

VOCATION: Actor.

CAREER: PRINCIPAL TELEVISION APPEARANCES—Series: Simon Brimmer, *The Adventures of Ellery Queen*, NBC, 1975-76; John Elliot, *The Betty White Show*, CBS, 1977-78; Jonathan Quale Higgins III, *Magnum, P.I.*, CBS, 1980—.

Episodic: *The F.B.I.*, ABC; *Mannix*, CBS; *Maude*, CBS; *Kojak*, CBS; *Serpico*, NBC; *Little House on the Prairie*, NBC; *The Love Boat*, ABC; *Soap*, ABC; *Lou Grant*, CBS.

Movies: *The Law*, 1974; *Relentless*, 1977; *Betrayal*, 1978; *Marathon*, 1980; *Young Again*, ABC, 1985.

PRINCIPAL FILM APPEARANCES—*Lawman*, United Artists, 1971; *The Last Picture Show*, Columbia, 1971; *What's Up Doc?*, Warner Brothers, 1972; *Paper Moon*, Paramount, 1973; *Blazzing Saddles*, Warner Brothers, 1974; *Chinatown*, Paramount, 1974; *At Long Last Love*, Twentieth Century-Fox, 1975; *The Day of the Locust*, Paramount, 1975; *Up the Creek*, Orion, 1984.

PRINCIPAL STAGE APPEARANCES—*Lady of the Camellias*, Broadway production; *The Great God Brown*, Broadway production; Off-Broadway and in stock appeared in: *Death of a Salesman, The Lion in Winter, The Little Foxes, Come Blow Your Horn, Caligula, Rhinoceros, The Fourposter, The Lark, The Devil's Disciple*.

MEMBER: Actors' Equity Association, Academy of Motion Picture Arts and Sciences, Screen Actors Guild, American Federation of Television and Radio Artists.

ADDRESSES: OFFICE— 10350 Santa Monica Blvd., Suite 350, Los Angeles, CA 90025.*

* * *

HILLIARD, Harriet
See NELSON, Harriet

* * *

HINES, Gregory 1946-

PERSONAL: Full name, Gregory Oliver Hines; born February 14, 1946, in New York, NY; son of Maurice Robert (a dancer and actor) and Alma Iola (Lawless) Hines; married Pamela Koslow, April 12, 1981; children: Daria, Jessica Koslow, Zachary Evan.

VOCATION: Actor and dancer.

CAREER: STAGE DEBUT—With family group, Hines Kids, 1949-55. PRINCIPAL STAGE APPEARANCES—Performed with family as the Hines Brothers, 1955-63, then as Hines, Hines, and Dad, 1963-73; *The Girl in Pink Tights*, Broadway production, 1954; *Severance*, 1974-77; *Eubie!*, Broadway production, 1978; *Comin' Uptown*, Broadway production, 1980; *Sophisticated Ladies*, Lunt-Fontanne Theatre, NY, 1981, the Shubert Theatre, Los Angeles, 1981; as Bill Robinson, *Parade of Stars Playing the Palace*, Palace Theatre, NY, May 2, 1983; *Night of 100 Stars II*, Radio City Music Hall, February, 1985; also appeared in *Black Broadway; The Last Minstrel Show in New York*.

FILM DEBUT—*Wolfen*, 1981. PRINCIPAL FILM APPEARANCES—*History of the World, Part I*, 1981; *Deal of the Century*, Warner Brothers, 1983; *Muppets Take Manhattan*, Tri-Star, 1984; *The Cotton Club*, Orion, 1984; *White Nights*, Columia, 1985; *Running Scared*, Metro-Goldwyn-Mayer, 1986.

MEMBER: Actors' Equity Association, Screen Actors Guild, American Federation of Television and Radio Artists.

AWARDS: Theater World Award, 1978-79, for *Eubie!;* Antoinette Perry Award nominations, 1979, 1980, 1981; Tor award, Dance Educators of America.

ADDRESSES: AGENT—c/o Rick Nicita, Creative Artists Agency, 1888 Century Park E., Suite 1400, Los Angeles, CA 90067; c/o George Freeman, P/M/K, 8642 W. Third Street, Suite 650, Los Angeles, CA 90048. MANAGER—c/o Fran Sperstein, Brillstein Company, 9200 Sunset Blvd., Suite 428, Los Angeles, CA 90069.*

*   *   *

HOLLIMAN, Earl   1928-

PERSONAL: Born September 11, 1928, in Delhi, LA. EDUCATION: Attended University of Southern California. MILITARY: U.S. Navy.

VOCATION: Actor.

CAREER: PRINCIPAL STAGE APPEARANCES—*A Streetcar Named Desire.*

PRINCIPAL FILM APPEARANCES—*Girls of Pleasure Island,* 1953; *Destination Gobi,* 1953; *East of Sumatra,* 1953; *Devils Canyon,* 1953; *Tennessee Champ,* 1954; *Broken Lance,* 1954; *Bridge of Toko-Ri,* Paramount, 1955; *Big Combo,* Allied Artists, 1955; *I Die a Thousand Times,* 1955; *Forbidden Planet,* Metro-Goldwyn-Mayer, 1956; *Burning Hills,* Warner Brothers, 1956; *Giant,* Warner Brothers, 1956; *The Rainmaker,* Paramount, 1956; *Gunfight at the O.K. Corral,* Paramount, 1957; *Trooper Hook,* United Artists, 1957; *Hot Spell; Last Train from Gun Hill,* 1959; *Visit to a Small Planet,* Paramount, 1960; *Armoured Command,* Allied Artists, 1961; *The Sons of Katie Elder,* Paramount, 1965; *Covenant with Death,* Warner Brothers, 1967; *The Power,* Metro-Goldwyn-Mayer, 1968; *Anzio,* Columbia, 1968; *Smoke,* 1969; *Sharkey's Machine,* Warner Brothers, 1981.

PRINCIPAL TELEVISION APPEARANCES—Series: Sundance, *Hotel de Paree,* CBS, 1959-60; Mitch Guthrie, *The Wide Country,* NBC, 1962-63; Lt. Bill Crowley, *Police Woman,* NBC, 1974-78.

Movies: *Tribes,* 1970; *Cannon,* 1971; *Alexander: The Other Side of Dawn,* 1977; *The Solitary Man,* 1979.

Episodic: *Ironside; Playhouse 90; Kraft Theatre; The F.B.I.; Medical Center; The Rookies.*

MEMBER: Screen Actors Guild, American Federation of Radio and Television Artists, Academy of Motion Picture Arts and Sciences; Actors and Others for Animals (past president).

AWARDS: Golden Globe Award.

ADDRESSES: AGENT—Phil Gersh Agency, 222 N. Canon Drive, Beverly Hills, CA 90210; Creative Artists Agency, 1888 Century Park E., Suite 1400, Los Angeles, CA 90067.*

HOPE, Bob   1903-

PERSONAL: Born Leslie Townes Hope, May 29, 1903, in Eltham, England; moved to Cleveland, OH, 1907; married Dolores Reade, February 19, 1934; children: Linda, Anthony, Kelly, Nora. EDUCATION: Attended public schools in Cleveland.

VOCATION: Comedian and actor.

CAREER: STAGE DEBUT—Dancing act with partner George Byrne, in the Fatty Arbuckle Revue, Cleveland, OH. NEW YORK DEBUT—*Sidewalks of New York,* 1927. PRINCIPAL STAGE APPEARANCES—Broadway: *Ballyhoo,* 1932; *Roberta,* 1933; *Say When,* 1934; *Ziegfield Follies,* 1935; *Red, Hot, and Blue,* 1936; *Smiles,* 1938.

MAJOR TOURS—With the USO, entertained United States armed forces troops in the North Atlantic, Caribbean, Europe, North Africa, the Middle East, Pacific, and Southeast Asia from 1941-72; established an annual Christmas tour to entertain troops overseas, 1941-1972; Christmas tours to United States veterans hospitals, 1972—; college tours: St. Louis University; Central New England College; Rochester Institute of Technology; Austin Peay State University; Indiana State University; University of Alabama; University of Florida; Colgate University; Harvard University; University of Southern California.

Performed Command performances, for the British monarch in London, in 1948, 1954, 1962, 1967, and 1977.

FILM DEBUT—*The Big Broadcast of 1938,* 1938. SHORT FILMS—*Paree, Paree,* 1934; *Going Spanish,* 1934; *The Old Grey Mayor,* 1935; *Watch the Birdie,* 1935; *Double Exposure,* 1935; *Calling All Tars,* 1936; *Shop Talk,* 1936; *Don't Look Now,* 1938.

FEATURE FILMS—*College Swing,* 1938; *Give Me a Sailor,* 1938; *Thanks for the Memory,* 1938; *Never Say Die,* 1939; *Some Like It Hot,* 1939; *The Cat and the Canary,* 1939; *Road to Singapore,* 1940; *The Ghostbreakers,* 1940; *Caught in the Draft,* 1941; *Nothing but the Truth,* 1941; *Road to Zanzibar,* 1941; *Louisiana Purchase,* 1941; *My Favorite Blonde,* 1942; *The Road to Morocco,* 1942; *Star Spangled Rhythm,* 1942; *They Got Me Covered,* 1943; *Let's Face It,* 1943; *Welcome to Britain,* 1943; *The Princess and the Pirate,* 1944; *Road to Utopia,* 1945; *Hollywood Victory Caravan,* 1945; *All Star Bond Rally,* 1945; *Monsieur Beaucaire,* 1946; *My Favorite Brunette,* 1947; *Variety Girl,* 1947; *Where There's Life,* 1947; *Road to Rio,* 1948; *The Paleface,* 1948; *Sorrowful Jones,* 1949; *The Great Lover,* 1949.

Fancy Pants, 1950; *The Lemon Drop Kid,* 1951; *My Favorite Spy,* 1951; *Son of Paleface,* 1952; *Greatest Show on Earth,* 1952; *Road to Bali,* 1953; *Off Limits,* 1953; *Here Come the Girls,* 1953; *Scared Stiff,* 1953; *Casanova's Big Night,* 1954; *The Seven Little Foys,* Paramount, 1955; *That Certain Feeling,* Paramount, 1956, *The Iron Petticoat,* Metro-Goldwyn-Mayer, 1956; *Beau James,* Paramount, 1957; *The Heart of Show Business,* 1957; *Showdown at Ulcer Gulch,* 1958; *Paris Holiday,* United Artists, 1958; *Five Pennies,* 1959; *Alias Jesse James,* United Artists, 1959.

The Facts of Life, United Artists, 1960; *Bachelor in Paradise,* Metro-Goldwyn-Mayer, 1961; *Road to Hong Kong,* 1961; *The Sound of Laughter,* 1963; *Critic's Choice,* Warner Brothers, 1963; *Call Me Bwana,* United Artists, 1963; *A Global Affair,* Metro-Goldwyn-Mayer, 1964; *The Oscar,* 1966; *Hollywood Star Spangled Revue,* 1966; *I'll Take Sweden,* United Artists, 1967; *Boy, Did I Get a Wrong Number,* United Artists, 1967; *Eight on the Lam,* United

BOB HOPE

Artists, 1967; *The Private Navy of Sergeant O'Farrell*, United Artists, 1968; *How to Commit Marriage*, 1969; *Cancel My Reservation*, Warner Brothers, 1972.

PRINCIPAL TELEVISION APPEARANCES—Signed contract with NBC, 1950; has appeared in more than four hundred and seventy five programs and specials.

Movie: *A Nice, Pleasant, Deadly Weekend*, 1986.

RADIO DEBUT—*Capitol Family Hour*, 1932. PRINCIPAL RADIO APPEARANCES—Over one thousand programs including guest appearances.

NON-RELATED CAREER—Dance instructor; clerk; amateur boxer "Packy East;" newspaper reporter.

WRITINGS: BOOKS—*They've Got Me Covered*, 1941; *I Never Left Home*, Simon & Schuster, 1944; *So This Is Peace*, Simon & Schuster, 1946; *Have Tux Will Travel*, Simon & Schuster, 1954; *I Owe Russia $1200*, Doubleday, 1963; *The Last Christmas Show*, as told to Pete Martin, Doubleday, 1974; *Road to Hollywood*, as told to Bob Thomas, Doubleday, 1977; (with Dwayne Newland) *Bob Hope's Confessions of a Hooker—My Lifelong Love Affair with Golf*, Doubleday, 1985.

AWARDS: People to People Award, President Dwight D. Eisenhower; Congressional Gold Medal, President John F. Kennedy; Medal of Freedom, President Lyndon B. Johnson; Medal of Merit, United States Congress; four special awards, the Jean Hersholt award and three special honors, National Academy of Motion Picture Arts and Sciences; National Academy of Television Arts and Sciences (Emmy) award; Decorated Honorary Commander of the Order of the British Empire; initiated into the Entertainment Hall of Fame, 1975; Screen Producers Milestone award; Philadelphia's Poor Richard award; USO Silver Medal of Merit; Murray-Green AFL/CIO award.

NAB Distinguished Service award; Tom Dooley award; Pacem in Terris award; first honorary member of Harvard's Hasty Pudding Theatricals; Father Flanagan award; first American Guild of Variety Artists Entertainer of the Year award; NATO Walt Disney award; International Platform Association's Mark Twain award; Criss award for outstanding contributions in fields of Health, Safety, and National Welfare; Distinguished Public Service award, United States military organizations; Fashion Foundation's Best Dressed award; National Football Foundation Hall of Fame, Distinguished American award.

Will Rogers Humanitarian award; National Entertainment Council, Comedian of the Century award; Golden Ike award; Favorite Male Entertainer of the Year award (five consecutive years); Hollywood Women's Press CLub, Golden Apple award; USO Man of the Year; Congressional Medal of Honor Society, Patriot's award; Touchdown Club's Most Valuable Performer; Thomas White award, United States Air Force; SCOPUS award, American Friends of Hebrew University; Hubert Humphrey award for outstanding contributions to the world of sports; National Association of Television Program Executives, Award of the Year.

Distinguished Communications award, Radio and Television Commission of Southern Baptist Convention; Charles Evans Hughes Gold Medal, National Conference of Christians and Jews; Gold Medal of Merit award, Jewish War Veterans; Maxwell A. Kriendler Memorial award, National Air Force Association; Defense Industry Endowment award and the Order of the Sword, Norton Air Force Base; *Photoplay* Magazine's Bing Crosby award; inducted into California Golf Writer's Hall of Fame; voted 'most admired male in the world' by readers of *Seventeen;* Lifetime Achievement award presented by President Ronald Reagan at the the Kennedy Center Honors, 1986.

Honorary Degrees: Doctor of Humane Letters—Quincy College, IL; Georgetown University; Monmouth College, NJ; Whittier College, CA; Pennsylvania Military College; Southern Methodist University; Miami University, OH; Ohio State University; University of Cincinnati; University of Nevada; California State Colleges; Indiana Univeristy; Mercy College, NJ; John Carroll University, OH; College of the Desert, CA; Baldwin-Wallace College, OH; St. Louis University, MO.

Doctor of Laws: University of Wyoming; Northwestern University, IL; Saint Bonaventure University, NY; Pace College, NY; Pepperdine University; University of Scranton; Western State University, CA.

Doctor of Humanities: Ohio Dominican College; Bowling Green University; Santa Clara University; Wilberforce University, OH; Florida Southern University; Northwood Institute; Norwich University, VT; Bethel College, TN; Utah State University; St. Anselm's College, NH.

Doctor of Fine Arts: Brown University; Jacksonville University.

Doctor of Humane Service, Drury College, MO; Doctor of Humane Humor, Benedictine College, KS; Doctor of International Relations, Salem College, WV; Doctor of Performing Arts, Dakota Weslyan University, SD; Doctor of Public Service, St. Ambrose College, IA; Doctor of Oratorical Science, Central New England College.

SIDELIGHTS: CTFT learned from publicity material submitted by his agent that Bob Hope has helped to provide more than a billion dollars for hospitals, scientific research, the Boy Scouts, the handicapped, and organizations combating many of the world's most debiltating diseases. He sponsored the Bob Hope Vocational High School for the Severly Handicapped in Texas and has lent his energies to Hanukah celebrations, Catholic and Protestant charities, the Urban League, World Hunger Fund, Heart Association, Cancer Society, Lung Association, Diabetes Foundation, Boy's Republic, Parkinson Foundation, Blinded Veterans Association and Sugar Ray Robinson's Youth Foundation.

ADDRESSES: AGENT—Elliott Kozak, 3808 Riverside Drive, Suite 100, Burbank, CA 91505.

*   *   *

HOPKINS, Bo

PERSONAL: Born in Greenville, SC; children: Jane. EDUCATION: Trained for the stage with Uta Hagen and at the Desilu Playhouse Training School. MILITARY: U.S. Army, 1958.

CAREER: FILM DEBUT—*The Wild Bunch,* Warner Brothers, 1969. PRINCIPAL FILM APPEARANCES—*Monte Walsh,* National General, 1970; *The Moonshine War,* Metro-Goldwyn-Mayer, 1970; *The Culpepper Cattle Company,* Twentieth Century-Fox, 1972; *The Getaway,* National General, 1972; *White Lightning,* United Artists, 1973; *The Man Who Loved Cat Dancing,* Metro-Goldwyn-Mayer, 1973; *American Graffiti,* Universal, 1973; *The Nickel Ride,* Twentieth Century-Fox, 1975; *The Day of the Locust,* Paramount, 1975;

BO HOPKINS

Posse, 1975; *The Killer Elite,* United Artists, 1975; *A Small Town in Texas,* American International, 1976; *Tentacles,* 1977; *Midnight Express,* Columbia, 1978; *More American Graffiti,* Universal, 1979; *The Fifth Floor,* 1980; *Mutant* (also known as *Forbidden World*), 1982; *Sweet Sixteen,* Aquarius, 1984; *Night Shadows,* Film Ventures International, 1985; also, *What Comes Around Goes Around.*

PRINCIPAL TELEVISION APPEARANCES—Series: Eldred McCoy, *Doc Elliott,* ABC, 1974; Matthew Blaisdale, *Dynasty,* ABC, 1981.

Episodic: *Mod Squad; The Virginian; Judd for the Defense; Nichols; Gunsmoke; Fantasy Island; Matt Houston; Hotel; Scarecrow and Mrs. King; Fall Guy; Murder, She Wrote.*

Movies: Pretty Boy Floyd, *Kansas City Massacre,* 1975; *Dawn, Portrait of a Teenage Runaway,* 1976; *Thaddeus Rose and Eddie,* CBS, 1978; *Ghost Dancing,* CBS, 1983; also, Captain Daniels, *The Courtmartial of Lt. William Calley; Aspen.*

STAGE DEBUT—*Teahouse of the August Moon.* PRINCIPAL STAGE APPEARANCES—Desilu Studios, Hollywood, CA: *Cat on a Hot Tin Roof, Picnic,* and *Between Two Thieves.*

MEMBER: Screen Actors Guild, American Federation of Television and Radio Artists; Hollywood Celebrity Softball Team.

ADDRESSES: AGENT—c/o Diane Davis, Twentieth Century Artists, 3518 Cahuenga Blvd. W., Suite 316, Los Angeles, CA 90068.

*   *   *

HORNER, Richard   1920-

PERSONAL: Born June 29, 1920, in Portland, OR; son of Godfrey Richard (a plant pathologist) and Ruby (Weller) Horner; married Lynne Stuart (an actress, singer, and producer), December 11, 1959; children: two sons, two daughters. EDUCATION: University of Washington, B.A., 1942. MILITARY: U.S. Navy, 1942-46.

VOCATION: Producer, general manager, and former actor.

CAREER: STAGE DEBUT—John, *John Loves Mary,* Showshop, Canton, CT. PRINCIPAL STAGE APPEARANCES—Nuangola Summer Theatre, Nuangola, PA, 1947.

PRINCIPAL STAGE WORK—Business manager, Playhouse, Windham, NH, 1948; stage manager, *The Curious Savage,* Martin Beck Theatre, NY, 1950; stage manager, *Captain Carvall,* Buffalo, NY, then Cleveland, OH, 1950; company manager, *The Constant Wife,* National Theatre, NY, 1951; business manager, *Paris 90,* Booth Theatre, NY, 1952; company manager, *I've Got Six-Pence,* Ethel Barrymore Theatre, NY, 1953; company manager, *The Martha Graham Dance Company,* Alvin Theatre, NY, 1953; company manager, *The Pajama Game,* St. James Theatre, NY, 1954; company manager, *On Your Toes,* 46th Street Theatre, NY, 1954; company manager, *The Dark Is Light Enough,* American National Theatre and Academy (ANTA), NY, 1955; company manager, *Damn Yankees,* 46th Street Theatre, NY, 1955.

Co-producer (with Justin Sturm), *Debut,* Holiday Theatre, NY, 1956; general manager, *Cranks,* Bijou Theatre, NY, 1956; company manager, *New Girl in Town,* 46th Street Theatre, NY, 1957;

RICHARD HORNER

company manager, *West Side Story*, Winter Garden Theatre, NY, 1957; general manager, *Copper and Brass*, Martin Beck Theatre, NY, 1957; general manager, *Clerambard*, Rooftop Theatre, NY, 1957; general manager, *Blue Denim*, Playhouse Theatre, NY, 1958; general manager, *The Next President*, Bijou Theatre, NY, 1958; company manager, *Goldilocks*, Lunt-Fontanne Theatre, NY, 1958; company manager, *Make a Million*, Playhouse Theatre, NY, 1958; company manager, *Redhead*, 46th Street Theatre, NY, 1959; general manager, *The Geranium Hat*, Orpheum Theatre, NY, 1959; company manager, *Destry Rides Again*, Imperial Theatre, NY, 1959; general manager, *The Nervous Set*, Henry Miller's Theatre, NY, 1959; general manager, *Chic*, Orpheum Theatre, NY, 1959; company manager, *Little Mary Sunshine*, Orpheum Theatre, NY, 1959; company manager, *Fiorello!*, Broadhurst Theatre, NY, 1959; company manager, *Take Me Along*, Shubert Theatre, NY, 1959.

General manager, *Russell Patterson's Sketchbook*, Maidman Theatre, NY, 1960; general manager, *The Crystal Heart*, East 74th Street Theatre, NY, 1960; general manager, *The Cool World*, Eugene O'Neill Theatre, NY, 1960; general manager, *The Jackass*, Barbizon Plaza Theatre, NY, 1960; general manager, *Farewell, Farewell Eugene*, Helen Hayes Theatre, NY, 1960; general manager, *Greenwich Village, U.S.A.*, Sheridan Square Theatre, NY, 1960; general manager, *Face of a Hero*, Eugene O'Neill Theatre, NY, 1960; general manager, *Love and Libel*, Martin Beck Theatre, NY, 1960; general manager, *The Rules of the Game*, Gramercy Arts Theatre, NY, 1960; company manager, *Rhinoceros*, Longacre Theatre, NY, 1961; general manager, *Show Girl*, Eugene O'Neill Theatre, NY, 1961; general manager, *The Tatooed Countess*, Barbizon-Plaza Theatre, NY, 1961; general manager, *Moby Dick*, Madison Avenue

Playhouse, NY, 1961; general manager, *Young Abe Lincoln*, York Playhouse, NY, 1961; company manager, *A Call on Kuprin*, Broadhurst Theatre, NY, 1961; general manager, *The Thracian Horses*, Orpheum Theatre, NY, 1961; general manager, *Sing Muse*, Van Dam Theatre, NY, 1961; general manager, *New Faces of 1962*, Alvin Theatre, NY, 1962; general manager, *The Aspern Papers*, Playhouse Theatre, NY, 1962; general manager, *Isle of Children*, Cort Theatre, NY, 1962; general manager, *The Boys from Syracuse*, Theatre Four, NY, 1963; general manager, *Something More!*, Eugene O'Neill Theatre, NY, 1964; co-producer (with Robert Fletcher and Lester Osterman), *High Spirits*, Alvin Theatre, NY, 1965; general manager, *Fade Out-Fade In*, Mark Hellinger Theatre, NY, 1965; co-producer (with Robert Fletcher), *The Queen and the Rebels*, Theatre Four, NY, 1965.

General manager, *The Office*, Henry Miller's Theatre, NY, 1966; general manager, *Dinner at Eight*, Alvin Theatre, NY, 1966; general manager, *The Flip Side*, Booth Theatre, NY, 1968; producer and general manager, *A Mother's Kisses*, Shubert Theatre, New Haven, CT, then Mechanic Theatre, Baltimore, MD, 1968; general manager, *Hadrian VII*, Helen Hayes Theatre, NY, 1969; general manager, *Norman, Is That You?* Lyceum Theatre, NY, 1970; general manager, *Borstal Boy*, Lyceum Theatre, NY, 1970; producer (with Lester Osterman and Michael Codron), *Butley*, Morosco Theatre, NY, 1972; co-producer (with Lester Osterman and Michael Codron), *Crown Matrimonial*, Helen Hayes Theatre, NY, 1973; co-producer (with Elliot Martin and Lester Osterman), *A Moon for the Misbegotten*, Morosco Theatre, NY, 1973; co-producer (with Lester Osterman), *James Whitmore in Will Rogers' U.S.A.*, Helen Hayes Theatre, NY, 1974; co-producer (with Osterman), *Sizwe Bansi Is Dead/The Island*, Helen Hayes Theatre, NY, 1974; co-producer (with Osterman), *Rodgers and Hart*, NY, 1975; producer, *Doubles*, Ritz Theatre, NY, 1985.

Also producer of: *A Life; The Crucifer of Blood; Passione;* productions at Jones Beach Marine Theatre, Long Island, NY, including: *The Music Man*, 1979; *The Sound of Music*, 1980; *Damn Yankees*, 1981; *Grease, West Side Story*, 1982; produced *Kennedy at Colonus*, Off-Broadway, 1984-85.

Company manager of the touring productions of *Twin Beds*, 1953-54, and *Agnes de Mille Dance Theatre*, 1953-54; also produced the U.S. tours of *Damn Yankees*, 1958, and *Hadrian VII*, 1969.

RELATED CAREER—Partner, general manager, Eugene O'Neill Theatre, NY, 1959; general manager, 46th Street Theatre, 1960; general manager, Alvin Theatre, NY, 1962; president, Richard Horner Associates, 1978—; president, Interative Media Corporation, 1983—.

MEMBER: Stage Directors and Choreographers Workshop Foundation (board member), League of American Producers and Theatre Owners, The Producers Group, Association of Theatrical Press Agents and Managers; New York Athletic Club; American Field Studies (board member).

ADDRESSES: OFFICE—165 W. 46th Street, Suite 710, New York, NY 10036.

*　　*　　*

HOROVITZ, Israel 1939-

PERSONAL: Born March 31, 1939 in Wakefield, MA; son of Julius Charles (a lawyer) and Hazel Rose (Solberg) Horovitz; married

ISRAEL HOROVITZ

second wife, Doris Keefe (divorced); married Gillian Adams, 1981; children: (second marriage) Rachael, Matthew, Adam; (third marriage), Hannah Rebecca, Oliver Adams (twins). EDUCATION: Royal Academy of Dramatic Art, London, M.A., 1963; attended the New School for Social Research, 1963-66; City University of New York, M.A., 1977, Ph.D. candidate.

VOCATION: Playwright and director.

WRITINGS: PLAYS, PRODUCED—*The Comeback,* Suffolk Theatre, Emerson Theatre, Boston, MA, 1957; *The Hanging of Emmanuel,* Il Cafe Cabaret Theatre, South Orange, NJ, 1962; *This Play Is About Me,* Il Cafe Cabaret Theatre, South Orange, NJ, 1963; *The Death of Bernard the Believer,* 1963; *The Simon Street Harvest,* 1964; *Hop, Skip, and Jump,* 1964; *The Killer Dove,* Theatre on the Green, West Orange, NY, 1966; *Line,* Cafe La Mama, Thirteenth Street Theatre, NY, 1967; *The Indian Wants the Bronx,* Astor Place Theatre, NY, 1968; *It's Called the Sugar Plum,* Astor Place Theatre, NY, 1968; *Rats,* Cafe Au Go Go, NY, 1968; *Chiaroscuro,* Spoleto Festival, Italy (also directed), 1968; *The Honest-to-God Schnozzola,* Act IV Theatre, Provincetown, MA, 1968; "Morning," of *Morning, Noon, and Night,* Henry Miller's Theatre, NY, 1968; *Leader,* Gramercy Arts Theatre, NY, 1969.

Acrobats, Mickery Theatre, Amsterdam, 1970; *Clair-Obscur,* Theatre Lucernaire, Paris, 1970; *Dr. Hero* (originally titled *The World's Greatest Play*), Public Theatre, NY, 1971; *Le Premiere,* Theatre de Poche, Paris, 1972 (also directed by Horovitz); *Shooting Gallery,* WPA Theatre, NY, 1973; *The First, The Last, The Middle* (comic triptych), 1974; *Spared,* 1975; *Uncle Snake,* 1975; *The Primary English Class,* Cubicula Theatre, NY, 1975; *The Reason We Eat,* Hartman Theatre, Stamford, CT, 1976; *The Former One-on-One Basketball Champion,* Actors Studio, NY, 1977; *Man with Bags,* Towson State University Theatre, MD, 1977; *Stage Directions,* Actors Studio, NY, 1978; *Cappella,* 1978; *Mackerel,* Gloucester Stage Company, 1978; "Hopscotch," "The 75th," "Alfred the Great," "Our Father's Failing," "Alfred Dies," "Stage Directions," "Spared," all known as *The Wakefield Plays,* 1973-86; "Today, I Am a Fountain Pen," "A Rosen by Any Other

Name," "The Chopin Playoffs," known as *A Trilogy,* NY, 1985-86; also, *The Good Parts; Sunday Runners in the Rain; The Widow's Blind Date; Park Your Car in the Harvard Yard; Henry Lumper; Firebird at Dogtown; Year of the Duck; North Shore Fish.*

SCREENPLAYS—*The Strawberry Statement* (based on the book by James Simon Kumen), Metro-Goldwyn-Mayer, 1970; *Line* (adapted from his play of the same name), Kaleidoscope Films, 1970; *Believe in Me* (originally titled *Speed Is of the Essence*), Metro-Goldwyn-Mayer, 1971; *Camerian Climbing,* 1971; *The Sad-Eyed Girls in the Park,* 1971; *Acrobats* (adapted from his play of the same name), Walker Stuart Productions, 1972; *Author, Author,* Twentieth Century-Fox, 1982; *Henry Lumper* (based on his play); *Light Years* (based on the novel by James Salter).

TELEVISION—Plays: *Play for Trees; Funny Books; Happy; Bartleby the Scrivener* (adapted from Herman Melville story); *A Day with Conrad Green* (adapted from Ring Lardner's story); (with Jules Feiffer) *VD Blues/Play for Germs* (also produced and directed).

BOOKS—(With David Boorshin) *First Season Cappella,* Harper and Row, 1973; *Nobody Loves Me,* 1975; *Spider Poems and Other Writings,* Harper and Row, 1976.

RELATED CAREER—Playwright in residence, Royal Shakespeare Company, London, England, 1965; professor of English and playwright in residence, College of the City of New York, 1968; Fanny Hurst Visiting Playwright, Brandeis University, 1974-76; founder, Gloucester Stage Company, 1979; founding member, Eugene O'Neill Memorial Theatre Foundation.

AWARDS: Best Play, Vernon Rice Award, Drama Desk, Obie, *Jersey Journal* (Jersey City) Award; all 1968, for *Indian Wants the Bronx;* Best Play, Drama Desk Award, 1968, for *It's Called the Sugar Plum;* Best Play, Obie, 1969, for *The Honest-to-God Schnozzola;* Cannes Film Festival Prix de Jury, 1971, for *The Strawberry Statement;* French Critics Prize. 1973, for *Line;* (with Jules Feiffer) Emmy and Christopher awards, for *VD Blues;* fellow, Royal Academy of Dramatic Art, London, 1963; Rockefeller Foundation Fellow in Playwriting, 1967-70; American Academy of Arts and Letters, Literature Award, 1972; Fulbright foundation grant, 1975; Guggenheim fellowship, 1977-78.

MEMBER: International P.E.N, Authors League of America, Dramatist Guild, Players Club.

SIDELIGHTS: Israel Horovitz's plays have been translated into nearly twenty languages and have been produced in Paris, Rome, London, Budapest, Bonn, Berlin, Montreal, Sydney, Frankfurt, Marseilles, Amsterdam and Tokyo.

RECREATION: Teaching, poker, Descartes, chess, guitar, and his children and their friends.

ADDRESSES: AGENT—Writers and Artists Agency, 162 W. 56th Street, New York, NY 10019; Margaret Ramsay, 14a Goodwins Court, London WC2, England.

*   *   *

HORSLEY, Lee

PERSONAL: Born May 15, in Muleshow, TX. EDUCATION: Attended University of North Colorado.

VOCATION: Actor.

CAREER: PRINCIPAL STAGE APPEARANCES—Local productions: *Oklahoma!; Fiddler on the Roof; Lion in Winter.*

PRINCIPAL FILM APPEARANCES—*The Sword and the Sorcerer,* 1982.

PRINCIPAL TELEVISION APPEARANCES—Series: Archie Goodwin, *Nero Wolfe,* NBC, 1981; title role, *Matt Houston,* ABC, 1982-85.

Mini-Series: *Crossings,* 1985; *North and South, Book II,* ABC, 1986.

ADDRESSES: AGENT—Triad, 10,100 Santa Monica Blvd., 16th Floor, Los Angeles, CA 90067.*

*　　*　　*

HORWITZ, Murray   1949-

PERSONAL: Born September 28, 1949, in Dayton, OH; son of Alan S. (a physician) and Charlotte (Vangrov) Horwitz; married Lisa Miller (a singer), September 7, 1974; children: Alexander, Ann. EDUCATION: Kenyon College, A.B., English and Drama, 1970.

VOCATION: Actor and director.

MURRAY HORWITZ

CAREER: STAGE DEBUT—Clown, *Ringling Brothers, Barnum and Bailey Circus,* 1970-72. NEW YORK DEBUT—*An Evening with Sholom Aleichem,* Manhattan Theatre Club, 1975-76. LONDON DEBUT—Co-author, associate director, *Ain't Misbehavin',* Her Majesty's Theatre, 1979.

PRINCIPAL THEATRE APPEARANCES—*An Evening of Sholom Aleichem,* Grendel's Lair, Philadelphia, PA, 1975-76; *The Body Politic,* Chicago, IL, 1979; *An Evening of Yiddish Poetry,* New York Shakespeare Festival, 1980;*The Ballroom,* NY, 1983.

PRINCIPAL THEATRE WORK—Comedy consultant, *Puntila,* Yale Repertory Theatre, New Haven, CT, 1977; co-author, associate director, lyricist, *Ain't Misbehavin,* Longacre Theatre, NY, Plymouth Theatre, NY, Morosco Theatre, NY, London, and Paris, 1978—; director, *Jus' Like Livin',* Chelsea's West Side Theatre, NY, 1979; actor, writer, and director, *Hard Sell,* New York Shakespeare Festival, 1980; writer and director, *Carnegie at Midnight* (ninetieth anniversary celebration), Carnegie Hall, NY, 1981; actor and director, *A Comedy Cabaret with Jonathan Winters,* Kenyon Festival, OH, 1981; writer and director, *While Shubert Slept,* reopening of the Shubert Theatre, New Haven, CT, 1984; writer and director, *This Is Opening Night,* reopening of the State Theatre, Cleveland, OH, 1984; co-author and co-director, *Haarlem Nocturne,* La Mama Experimental Theatre Club, NY, then Latin Quarter Theatre, NY, 1984; also, director, *Ain't Misbehavin,* Stagewest, Alaska Repertory Theatre, and Kansas City Starlight Theatre.

PRINCIPAL CONCERT WORK—Producer, writer, and director, *A Tribute to Stan Kenton,* Kool Jazz Festival, Avery Fisher Hall, NY, 1982.

PRINCIPAL FILM APPEARANCES—Yogurt man, *Night of the Juggler,* Columbia, 1980.

PRINCIPAL TELEVISION WORK—Director: *Guiding Light,* CBS, 1985; *As the World Turns,* CBS, 1985; *Search for Tomorrow,* NBC, 1985-86.

Producer: *The Making of a Song,* Arts and Entertainment Network, 1981; *America, Where It All Happens,* Arts and Entertainment, 1981; *Jazz Comes Home to Newport,* PBS, 1984.

WRITINGS: (In addition to above) CABARET—*Talking Morosco Blues,* Upstairs at O'Neals, NY, 1982-83.

SCREENPLAY—(With others)*Soldier Boy,* Universal, 1982.

MEMBER: Screen Actors Guild, American Guild of Variety Artists, Writers Guild East, Society of Stage Directors and Choreographers, Dramatists Guild, American Society of Composers, Authors and Publishers (ASCAP), Young Playwrights Festival Committee, Foundation of the Dramatists Guild (secretary, 1983—), New York Sheet Music Society, The Player's Club, Project Return Foundation (board, 1978—), Urban League; Society for American Baseball Research.

AWARDS: Excellence in Acting, Paul Newman Award, Kenyon College, 1970; Antoinette Perry Award, Obie Award, New York Drama Critics' Circle Award, Outer Critics' Circle Awards, 1978, all for *Ain't Misbehavin;* ASCAP Songwriting Award, 1981-85.

SIDELIGHTS: SPECIAL INTERESTS—Jazz, Yiddish language and culture.

ADDRESSES: HOME—New York, NY. AGENT—c/o Mitch Douglas and Dick Welch, International Creative Management, 40 W. 57th Street, New York, NY 10019.

*   *   *

HOSKINS, Bob   1942-

PERSONAL: Born October 26, 1942, in Bury St. Edmonds, Suffolk, England; son of Robert and Elsie (Hopkins) Hoskins; married Jane Livesey (divorced). EDUCATION: Attended Stroud Green School, Finsbury Park.

VOCATION: Actor.

CAREER: STAGE DEBUT—Peter, *Romeo and Juliet,* Victoria Theatre, Stoke on Trent, 1969. PRINCIPAL STAGE APPEARANCES—Pinchwife, *The Country Wife,* Century Theatre, London, 1970; *The Baby Elephant,* Theatre Upstairs, London, 1971; Uriah Shelley, *Man Is Man,* Royal Court Theatre, London, 1971; Lenny, *The Homecoming,* title role, *Richard III,* Hull Arts Center, 1971; Bernie the Volt, *Veterans,* Royal Court Theatre, London, 1971; title role, *King Lear,* Dartington Hall, 1972; Sextus Pompeius, *Antony and Cleopatra,* Bankside Globe Theatre, London, 1973; *Geography of a Horse Dreamer,* Royal Court Theatre, London, 1974; Doolittle, *Pygmalion,* Albert Theatre, London, 1974; Touchstone, *As You Like It,* Oxford Playhouse, 1974; Bill Cracker, *Happy End,* Oxford Playhouse, then Lyric Theatre, London, 1974-75; Rocky, *The Iceman Cometh,* Borkov, *Ivanov,* Sergeant, *The Devil's Disciple,* all with the Royal Shakespeare Company, Aldwych Theatre, London, 1976; Jake, *England, England,* Jeannetta Cochrane Theatre, London, 1977; *The World Turned Upside Down,* Joe Veriatio, *Has Washington Legs?,* both Cottesloe Theatre, London, 1978; Nathan Detroit, *Guys and Dolls,* National Theatre, London, 1982.

Also: Marker, *A View from the Bridge,* Hiring, *The Anniversary,* both Century Theatre, London; Menelaus, *The Trojan Woman,* Hull Arts; Doolittle, *Pygmalion,* Albery Theatre, London; Common Man, *A Man for All Seasons,* Manchester 69 Company; Borkov, *Ivanov,* Royal Shakespeare Company, London; Lee, *True West,* National Theatre, London; Bosola, *The Duchess of Malfi,* Manchester Royal Exchange, The Roundhouse Theatre, London.

PRINCIPAL FILM APPEARANCES—Foster, *The National Health,* Virgin Films, 1974; *Royal Flash,* Twentieth Century-Fox, 1975; Big Mac, *Inserts,* United Artists, 1976; Sergeant Williams, *Zulu Dawn,* 1980; Rock and Roll Manager, *Pink Floyd's The Wall,* Metro-Goldwyn-Mayer/United Artists, 1982; Harold Shand, *The Long Good Friday,* Handmade Films/Embassy, 1982; Colonel Perez, *The Honorary Consul* (also known as *Beyond the Limit*), Paramount, 1983; Becker, *Lassiter,* Sunrise Films/Warner Brothers, 1974; Owney Madden, *The Cotton Club,* Zoetrope/Orion, 1984; Spoor, *Brazil,* Handmade, 1985; *Sweet Liberty,* Universal, 1986.

Also: Morrie Mendelsohn, *The Dunero Boys,* Jethro Films; George, *The Woman Who Married Clark Gable,* Set 2 Films.

PRINCIPAL TELEVISION APPEARANCES—Woodbine, *Her Majesty's Pleasure,* BBC, 1972; *Villains on the High Road,* 1972; Sexton, *If There Weren't Any Blacks . . . ,* LWT, 1973; *Softly, Softly,* 1973; Dobbs, *Thick as Thieves,* LWT, 1973; *Schmoedipus,* BBC, 1974; *The Gentle Rebellion,* 1974; *On the Move,* 1975; Arthur Parker, *Pennies from Heaven,* BBC, 1977-78; title role, *Sheppey,* BBC,

1980; Arnie Cole, *Flickers,* ATV, 1980; Iago, *Othello,* BBC, 1981; Eddie Reed, *You Don't Have to Walk to Fly,* LWT, 1982; Joe Grimaldi, "It Must Be Something in the Water," *Omnibus,* BBC; Knocker, *The Villains,* LWT; *And All Who Sail in Her,* BBC; *On the Road,* BBC; *Crown Court,* Granada; *New Scotland Yard,* LWT; *Shoulder to Shoulder,* BBC; "On Brecht," *Omnibus,* BBC; *Three Piece Suit,* BBC; *In the Looking Glass,* BBC; Napoleon, *Penninsular,* BBC; Chorus, *Mycenae and Men,* BBC; *The Beggars Opera,* BBC; Mussolini, *Mussolini and I,* RAI, Italy.

AWARDS: Best Actor, British Academy of Film and Television Arts Award nomination, 1978, for *Pennies from Heaven;* Best Actor, Evening Standard Award, British Academy of Film and Television Arts Award nomination, 1982, for *The Long Good Friday.*

SIDELIGHTS: FAVORITE ROLES—Bernie the Volt, *Veterans;* title role, *Richard III;* title role, *King Lear.* RECREATION—Writing, listening to music, his children.

ADDRESSES: AGENT—Hope and Lyne, Five Milner Place, London N1 1TN, England.

*   *   *

HOWARD, Bart   1915-

PERSONAL: Born Howard Joseph Gustafson, June 1, 1915, in Burlington, IA; son of Harry and Naomi Gustafson. MILITARY: U.S. Army, 1941-46.

VOCATION: Composer and lyricist.

CAREER: PRINCIPAL STAGE WORK—Composer, *Curtain Going Up,* Forrest Theatre, Philadelphia, PA, 1952; composer and lyricist, "My Love Is a Wanderer," *John Murray Anderson's Almanac,* Imperial Theatre, NY, 1953; composer and lyricist, *Fourth Avenue North,* Madison Avenue Playhouse, NY, 1961; adaptor (with Ruth Goetz), *Play on Love,* London, 1969.

PRINCIPAL TELEVISION WORK—Composer, *Imogene Coca Musical,* 1952, *American Musical Theater,* 1961; *Today Show,* NBC, 1965.

RELATED CAREER—Accompanist for Mabel Mercer, 1948-50; master of ceremonies, Blue Angel nightclub, NY, 1950-59.

MEMBER: Dramatists Guild, American Society of Composers, Authors, and Publishers, American Federation of Musicians.

SIDELIGHTS: RECREATION—Cooking, reading Tolstoy.

ADDRESSES: HOME—Box C, North Salem, NY 10560.

*   *   *

HOWLAND, Beth

PERSONAL: Born May 28, in Boston, MA; married Michael J. Pollard (divorced); children: Holly.

VOCATION: Actress.

CAREER: PRINCIPAL STAGE APPEARANCES—New York: *A Tribute to Stephen Sondheim, Bye, Bye Birdie, Twelfth Night, George M!, The Rainmaker, Any Wednesday, A Taste of Honey;* Paula Ritter, *The Torch-Bearers,* Old Globe Theatre, San Diego, CA 1985; *The Unvarnished Truth,* Ahmanson Theatre, Los Angeles, 1985.

PRINCIPAL TELEVISION APPEARANCES—Series: Vera Louise Gorman, *Alice,* CBS, 1976-85.

Episodic: *The Love Boat; Mary Tyler Moore Show; Little House on the Prairie; The Rookies; Cannon; Eight Is Enough.*

Specials: *You Can't Take It with You.*

MEMBER: Actors' Equity Association, American Federation of Television and Radio Artists.

ADDRESSES: AGENT—Baumann, Hiller, and Associates, 9220 Sunset Blvd., Suite 202, Los Angeles, CA 90069.*

*　　*　　*

HULCE, Tom

BRIEF ENTRY: Born in White Water, WI, reared in Michigan. Actor. Tom Hulce studied at the North Carolina School of the Arts and completing his studies, moved to New York City. Within a month of his arrival in New York, Hulce answered an audition advertised in *Variety* and found himself understudying the role of Alan Strang in *Equus.* Hulce didn't have an Equity card, which meant that he shouldn't have been able to perform in the show, but by the time that was discovered, the principal player had left and Hulce had already taken over the role. He made his film debut in James Bridge's *September 30, 1955,* and followed that with the commercially successful *National Lampoon's Animal House.* In 1984, after intense competition, Hulce won the title role in Milos Foreman's *Amadeus.* Hulce had to learn to play the piano in three months' time in order to portray Mozart. His performance won him the Academy Award nomination as Best Actor and Italy's Donatello Award for Best Actor. The actor has appeared in numerous plays and television shows, most notably the title role in the Playwrights Horizon's presentation of *The Rise and Rise of Daniel Rocket,* which was later broadcast on PBS. Hulce made his directorial debut with the musical *Sleep Around Town,* also produced at the Playwrights Horizon. The actor is currently appearing in the film *Echo Park.**

*　　*　　*

HUNT, Linda

VOCATION: Actress.

CAREER: STAGE DEBUT—*Down by the River,* Off-Broadway production, 1975. PRINCIPAL STAGE APPEARANCES—*Elizabeth Dead,* Cubiculo Theatre, NY, 1981; Pope Joan and Louise, *Top Girls,* Newman Theatre at the Public, NY, 1983; Joan of Arc, *Little Victories,* American Place Theatre, NY, 1983; Audrey Wood, *End of the World,* Music Box Theatre, NY, 1984; *Aunt Dan & Lemon,* New York Shakespeare Festival, Public Theatre, 1985; also appeared in *Mother Courage and Her Children; The Tennis Game; Metamorphosis in Miniature; Ah, Wilderness!,* Broadway production.

PRINCIPAL FILM APPEARANCES—*Popeye,* Paramount, 1980; Billy Kwan, *The Year of Living Dangerously,* Metro-Goldwyn-Mayer/United Artists, 1983; *Dune,* Universal, 1984; *The Bostonians,* Almi Pictures, 1984; *Eleni,* CBS Films, 1985; *Silverado,* Columbia, 1985.

MEMBER: Actors' Equity Association, Screen Actors Guild.

AWARDS: Best Supporting Actress, Academy Award, 1983, for *The Year of Living Dangerously.*

ADDRESSES: OFFICE—457 W. 57th Street, New York, NY 10019.*

*　　*　　*

HUNTER, Kim   1922-

PERSONAL: Born Janet Cole, November 12, 1922, in Detroit, MI; daughter of Donald (an engineer) and Grace (Lind) Cole; married William A. Baldwin, February 11, 1944 (divorced, 1946); married Robert Emmett (a writer), December 20, 1951; children: (first marriage) Kathryn Deidre; (second marriage) Sean Robert. EDUCATION: Attended public schools in Miami Beach, FL; studied acting with Charmine Lantaff Camine, Miami Beach, FL; studied acting at the Actors Studio in New York.

VOCATION: Actress.

KIM HUNTER

CAREER: STAGE DEBUT—Penny, *Penny Wise,* for the Miami Women's Club, Miami, FL, 1939. NEW YORK DEBUT—Stella Kowalski, *A Streetcar Named Desire,* Barrymore Theatre, 1947. PRINCIPAL STAGE APPEARANCES—Little Seal, *Petticoat Fever* and Martha, *Angela Is 22,* Old Mill Playhouse, Flat Rock, NC, 1940; defense attorney's secretary, *The Night of January 16th,* Gant Gaither Theatre, Maimi, FL, 1940-41; Cecily, *The Importance of Being Earnest* and Prompter, *Ten Nights in a Barroom,* Theatre of the Fifteen, Coral Gables, FL, 1941; Peggy, *The Women* and Elaine, *Arsenic and Old Lace,* Pasadena Playhouse, 1942-43; title role, *Claudia,* Summer Theatre, Stamford, CT, 1943; Cathy, *Wuthering Heights,* Lake George Playhouse, NY, 1947; Nancy, *Sundown Beach,* Westport Country Playhouse, 1948.

Daisy Sage, *The Animal Kingdom,* Westport Country Playhouse, 1951; Luba, *Darkness at Noon,* Alvin Theatre, NY, 1951; Ruby Hawes, *The Chase,* Playhouse Theatre, NY, 1952; Karen Wright, *The Children's Hour,* Coronet Theatre, NY, 1952; Sylvia Crewes, *The Tender Trap,* Longacre Theatre, NY, 1954; Patty O'Neill, *The Moon Is Blue,* Roosevelt Playhouse, Miami Beach, 1954; Penelope Toop, *See How They Run,* Thalian Hall, Wilmington, NC, 1955; Dunreath Henry, *King of Hearts,* Bucks County Playhouse, PA, 1955; Linda Seton, *Holiday,* Cincinnati Playhouse, 1955; Nora Parker, *Down Came a Blackbird,* John Drew Theatre, East Hampton, NY, 1955; Laura Creech, *I Hear You Singing,* Spa Summer Theatre, Saratoga Springs, NY, 1955; Celia Pope, *A Hatful of Rain,* Playhouse in the Park, Philadelphia, PA, then Pocono Playhouse, PA, 1957; Kate Adams, *This Is Goggle,* McCarter Theatre, Princeton, NJ, then Shubert Theatre, Washington, DC, 1958; Cora Flood, *Dark at the Top of the Stairs,* Tapia Theatre, San Juan, Puerto Rico, 1959, then Ann Arbor MI, 1960; Alma Winemiller, *Summer and Smoke,* Coconut Grove Playhouse, 1959; Lady Torrence, *Orpheus Descending,* Capri Theatre, Atlantic Beach, NY, 1959.

Billie Dawn, *Born Yesterday,* Charlotte Summer Theatre, NC, 1960; Jere Halliday, *The Disenchanted,* Tenthouse Theatre, Highland Park, IL, 1960, Playhouse-in-the-Park Phildelphia, then Coconut Grove Playhouse, Fl, 1960; Rosalind, *As You Like It,* first Witch, *Macbeth,* Helen, *Troilus and Cressida,* all at the Shakespeare Festival Theatre, Stratford, CT, 1961; Julie Sturrock, *Write Me a Murder,* Belasco Theatre, NY, 1961, then O'Hare Inn Theatre, Chicago, 1962; *Come Woo Me!* (scenes from Shakespeare), Library of Congress, Washington, DC, 1963; title role, *Major Barbara,* University of Utah, 1963; Paula Maugham, *Linda Stone Is Brutal,* Bucks County Playhouse, then Olney Theatre, MD, 1964.

Sally Thomas, *Signpost To Murder,* Playhouse-on-the-Mall, Paramus, NJ, 1965; Dowager Empress, *Anastasia,* Otterbein College, OH, 1965; one woman show, *The Human Voice, Before Breakfast,* and Kate's final speech from *The Taming of the Shrew,* White Meadow Lake, NJ, then Indiana State University, 1965; Emily Dickinson, *Come Slowly, Eden,* White Barn, Westport CT, also at the Library of Congress in Washington, DC and Theatre de Lys in NY, 1966; Miss Wilson, *Weekend,* Broadhurst Theatre, NY, 1968; Alma Winemiller, *Eccentricities of a Nightingale,* Long Island Repertory Festival, 1968; Masha, *The Three Sisters,* Long Island Repertory Festival, 1968; Hester, *Hello and Goodbye,* Theatre de Lys, 1968; Carrie Bishop, *The Penny Wars,* Royale Theatre, NY, 1969; title role, *The Prime of Miss Jean Brodie,* Ivoryton Playhouse, CT, then Playhouse-on-the-Mall, Paramus, NJ, then Falmouth Playhouse, 1969.

A Passage to E. M. Forster, staged reading at the McCarter Theatre, NJ, 1971; Mary Haines, *The Women,* 46th Street Theatre, NJ, 1973; Amanda Wingfield, *The Glass Menagerie,* Alliance Theatre, Atlanta, GA, 1973; Eleanor of Aquitane, *The Lion in Winter,* William Patterson College, NJ, 1975; Madame Ranevskaya, *The Cherry Orchard,* Roundabout Theatre, NY, 1976; Miss Madrigal, *The Chalk Garden,* Bucks County Playhouse, PA, 1976; title role, *Elizabeth the Queen,* Studio Arena, Buffalo, NY, 1977; Romaine, *Witness for the Prosecution,* Greenwood, SC, 1977; Barbara, *At the End of Long Island—An Endsummer Daydream,* Eugene O'Neill Theatre Center, Waterford, CT, 1977; Julia, *Semmelweiss,* Studio Arena, Buffalo, NY, 1977; Emily Dickinson, *The Belle of Amherst,* New Jersey Theatre Forum, 1978; narrator, *The Story of Babar,* Plainfield Symphony Orchestra, NJ, 1979.

The Little Foxes, Berkshire Theatre Festival, MA, 1980; Virginia Woolf, *Virginia and Vanessa,* benefit for Charleston House Trust, NY, 1980; Harriet, *To Grandmother's House We Go,* Biltmore Theatre, NY, 1981; *Another Part of the Forest,* Seattle Repertory Theatre, 1981; *When We Dead Awaken,* Open Space Theatre, Seattle, WA, 1982; Mrs. Alving, *Ghosts,* Adelphi University, Long Island, NY, New Globe Theatre, Tarrytown, NY, 1982; Margaret, *Territorial Rites,* American Place Theatre, 1983; Linda Loman, *Death of a Salesman,* Stratford Shakespeare Festival, Ontario Canada, 1983; Big Mama, *Cat on a Hot Tin Roof,* Coconut Grove Playhouse, 1983-84; Emily Dickinson, *The Belle of Amherst,* William Carlos Williams Center, Rutherford, NJ, 1983-84; Vinnie, *Life with Father,* Coconut Grove Playhouse, FL, 1984; Maude, *Sabrina Fair,* Berkshire Theatre Festival, 1984; Mama, *Faulkner's Bicycle,* Yale Repertory Theatre's Winterfest V, 1985, American Theatre Exchange, Joyce Theatre, NY, 1985; Margaret, *Antique Pink,* University of Michigan Theatre Project, 1985; Emily Dickinson, *The Belle of Amherst,* Theatre by the Sea, Portsmouth, NH, 1986.

MAJOR TOURS—Title role, *Claudia,* summer tour, Oneonta, NY, Lake George NY, Lake Placid Club, NY, Detroit Music Hall, 1947; Karen Norwood, *Two Blind Mice,* Washington, DC, Chicago, 1950; Amy, *They Knew What They Wanted,* summer tour, 1952; Catherine, *And Miss Reardon Drinks a Little,* national tour, Baltimore, Detroit, Pittsburgh, Cincinnati, Cleveland, St. Louis, Hollywood, Toronto, Canada, 1971-72; Lydia Cruttwell, *In Praise of Love,* summer tour, 1975.

FILM DEBUT—Leading role, *The Seventh Victim,* RKO, 1943. PRINCIPAL FILM APPEARANCES—*Tender Comrade,* RKO, 1943; *When Strangers Marry* (also known as *Betrayed*), Monogram, 1944; *You Came Along,* Paramount, 1945; *Stairway to Heaven* (also known as *A Matter of Life and Death*), Universal, 1946; *A Canterbury Tale,* Eagle Lion, 1949; Stella Kowalski, *A Streetcar Named Desire,* Warner Brothers, 1951; *Anything Can Happen,* Paramount, 1952; *Deadline U.S.A.,* Twentieth Century-Fox, 1952; *Storm Center,* Columbia, 1956; *Bermuda Affair,* DCA, 1957; *Young Stranger,* Universal, 1957; *Money, Women, and Guns,* Universal, 1958; *Lilith,* Columbia, 1964; Zira, *Planet of the Apes,* Twentieth Century-Fox, 1968; *The Swimmer,* Columbia, 1968; Zira, *Beneath the Planet of the Apes,* Twentieth Century-Fox, 1970; Zira, *Escape from the Planet of the Apes,* Twentieth Century-Fox, 1971; *Dark August,* Raffia First Productions, 1976.

TELEVISION DEBUT—*Actors Studio,* ABC, 1948. PRINCIPAL TELEVISION APPEARANCES—Episodic: *Philco Television Theatre,* NBC; *Ford Theatre,* CBS; *Studio One,* CBS; *Your Show of Shows,* ABC, 1951; *Celanese Playhouse,* ABC; *Lux Theatre,* NBC; *First Person,* CBS, 1953; *Justice,* ABC; *Climax!,* CBS; *Adventure,* ABC; *Kaiser Aluminum Hour,* NBC; *G.E. Theatre,* CBS; *Alcoa*

Hour, NBC; *Goodyear Playhouse*, NBC; *Lamp Unto My Feet*, CBS; the trial scene from "Saint Joan," on *Omnibus*, NBC, 1955; "Requiem for a Heavyweight," "The Comedian," both *Playhouse 90*, CBS; *The Line-Up*, CBS; *Screen Directors Playhouse*, CBS; *Rawhide*, CBS; *Naked City*, ABC, 1961; "Give Us Barabbas," *Hallmark Hall of Fame*, NBC, 1961; *Eleventh Hour*, NBC; *U.S. Steel Hour*, CBS, 1962; *Dick Powell Show*, CBS; *The Nurses*, CBS, 1963; *Adventures in Paradise*, ABC; *Alfred Hitchcock Presents*, CBS, 1964; *Mr. Broadway*, CBS; *The Defenders*, CBS; *Dr. Kildare*, NBC; "Lamp at Midnight," *Hallmark Hall of Fame*, NBC, 1965; *Confidential for Women*, ABC; *Hawk*, ABC; *Mannix*, CBS; *Disney's Wonderful World of Color*, NBC, 1968; *Bonanza*, NBC, 1968; "People Next Door," *CBS Playhouse*, CBS, 1968; "When This You See Remember Me" and "The Prodigal," *NET Playhouse*, 1969.

The Young Lawyers, ABC, 1970; *Bracken's World*, NBC, 1970; "The New Doctors," *The Bold Ones*, NBC, 1970; *Medical Center*, CBS, 1971 and 1974; *Gunsmoke*, CBS, 1971; *Cannon*, CBS, 1971; *Columbo*, NBC, 1971; *Night Gallery*, NBC, 1972; *Owen Marshall, Counselor-at-Law*, ABC, 1972; *Love, American Style*, ABC, 1972; *Young Dr. Kildare*, CBS, 1972; *The Evil Touch*, ABC, 1973; *Mission: Impossible*, CBS, 1973; *The Magician*, NBC, 1973; *Marcus Welby, M.D.*, ABC, 1973; *Hec Ramsey*, NBC, 1973; *Griff*, ABC, 1973; *Police Story*, NBC, 1973; *Ironside* (two episodes), NBC, 1974; "The Impersonation Murder Case," *Wide World of Mystery*, ABC, 1975; *Lucas Tanner*, NBC, 1975; "This Is The Life," *The People Next Door*, ABC, 1975; *Hunter*, CBS, 1976; "Crazy Annie," *Baretta*, ABC, 1976; *The Oregon Trail*, NBC, 1977; *Project U.F.O.*, NBC, 1978; "Stubby Pringle's Christmas," *Hallmark Hall of Fame*, NBC, 1978; *The Rockford Files*, NBC, 1979; *Hot Pursuit*, NBC, 1985; *Private Sessions*, NBC, 1985.

Specials: *Secret of Freedom*, NBC, 1960; two *Plays-of-the-Week*, NTA; *Purex Special for Women*, NBC; *Americans: A Portrait in Verses*, 1962 and 1963; *Russians: Self-Impressions*, CBS, 1963; *The French—They Are So French*, CBS, 1963; *Dial Hot-Line*, ABC, 1970; *In Search of America*, ABC, 1971; *Your Choice for the Oscars*, syndicated, 1975; *200 Years Ago Today*, CBS, 1975; "The Last of the Great Male Chauvinists," *Insight*, NBC, 1975; *F.D.R.'s Last Year*, NBC, 1980; *Skokie*, CBS, 1981; *Scene of the Crime*, NBC, 1984.

Movies: *Unwed Father*, ABC, 1974; *Born Innocent*, NBC, 1974; *Bad Ronald*, ABC, 1974; *Ellery Queen*, NBC, 1975; *This Side of Innocence*, NBC, 1976; *The Golden Gate Murders*, CBS, 1979.

Guest: *Kate Smith Hour*, NBC, 1953; *Person to Person*, CBS, 1957; *The Today Show*, NBC, 1961; *The Jackie Gleason Show*, CBS, 1964 and 1968; *The Tonight Show*, NBC, 1968 and 1971; *The David Frost Show*, ABC, 1970; *What's My Line*, NBC, 1971.

Mini-Series: Ellen Wilson, *Backstairs at the White House*, NBC, 1979; "Three Sovereigns for Sarah," *American Playhouse*, PBS, 1985.

Series: Nola Madison, *The Edge of Night*, ABC, 1979-80.

RECORDINGS: ALBUMS—*From Morning 'Til Night (And a Bag Full of Poems)*, RCA Victor, 1961; *Come, Woo Me!*, Unified Audio Classics, 1964.

WRITINGS: BOOKS—*Kim Hunter—Loose in the Kitchen*, autobiographical cookbook, Domina Books, 1975.

MEMBER: Actors' Equity Association, Screen Actors Guild, American Federation of Television and Radio Artists.

AWARDS: Donaldson Award and *Variety* New York Critics Poll, 1948, for Stella Kowalski, *A Streetcar Named Desire;* Best Supporting Actress, Academy Award, *Look* Magazine Award, Golden Globe, all 1952, for *A Streetcar Named Desire*, 1952; Emmy nominations, 1977, for "Crazy Annie," *Baretta*, 1980, for Nola Madison, *The Edge of Night;* Carbonnell Award (South Florida), 1984, for Big Mama, *Cat on a Hot Tin Roof*.

SIDELIGHTS: RECREATION—Cooking, music, books, and dancing.

ADDRESSES: AGENT—Lionel Larner, Ltd., 850 Seventh Avenue, New York, NY 10019.

*   *   *

HURSEY, Sherry

PERSONAL: Born November 22, in Rutherfordton, NC. EDUCATION: Attended the University of California at Los Angeles.

VOCATION: Actress and singer.

CAREER: TELEVISION DEBUT—*The Rookies*, ABC. PRINCIPAL TELEVISION APPEARANCES—Series: *Number 96* (pilot), NBC, 1985; *Best Friends*, NBC; Debbie Flynn, *Morning Star/Evening Star*, CBS, 1986.

Episodic: *Riptide*, NBC; *Simon & Simon*, CBS; *Rhoda*, CBS; *Happy Days*, ABC; *Family*, ABC; *Mary Tyler Moore Show*, CBS.

SHERRY HURSEY

Movies: *Friendly Fire,* 1979; *Victims,* 1982; *The Prince of Bel Air,* ABC.

Specials: *Girl on the Edge of Town,* 1980; *Member of the Wedding,* NBC.

PRINCIPAL FILM APPEARANCES—*The Avenging; Almost Summer; Corvette Summer.*

PRINCIPAL STAGE APPEARANCES—*In Trousers,* Los Angeles and New York, 1985.

ADDRESSES: PUBLICIST—Sumski, Green & Company, Inc., 8380 Melrose Avenue, Suite 200, Los Angeles, CA 90069.

*   *   *

HURT, John   1940-

PERSONAL: Born January 22, 1940, in Chesterfield, Derbyshire, England; son of Reverend Arnould Herbert (an Anglican minister) and Phyllis (an engineer; maiden name, Massey) Hurt; married Annette Robertson (an actress; divorced); married Marie-Lise

JOHN HURT

Volpeliere-Pierrot (a composer; died January 26, 1983); married Donna-Lynn Laurence, September 6, 1984. EDUCATION: Lincoln School; studied for the theatre at the Royal Academy of Dramatic Art.

VOCATION: Actor.

CAREER: STAGE DEBUT—Mytyl, *The Blue Bird,* 1953. LONDON DEBUT—Knocker White, *Infanticide in the House of Fred Ginger,* Arts Theatre, 1962. PRINCIPAL STAGE APPEARANCES—Lady Bracknell, *The Importance of Being Earnest,* 1954; *Chips with Everything,* Vaudeville Theatre, London, 1962; Len, *The Dwarfs,* Arts Theatre, London, 1963; Hamp, *Hamp,* Edinburgh Festival, 1964; Jones, *Inadmissable Evidence,* Wyndham's Theatre, London, 1965; Malcolm Scrawdyke, *Little Malcolm and His Struggle Against the Eunuchs,* Garrick Theatre, London, 1966; Victor, *Belcher's Luck,* Royal Shakespeare Company (RSC), Aldwych Theatre, London, 1966; Malcolm, *Macbeth,* 1967; Octavious, *Man and Superman,* Gaiety Theatre, Dublin, 1969; Peter, *Ride a Cocked Horse,* Hampstead, 1972; Mick, *The Caretaker,* Mermaid Theatre, London, 1972; Martin, *The Only Street,* Eblana, Edinburgh Festival, King's Head, Islington, 1973; Ruffian, *The Ruffian on the Stair,* and Ben, *The Dumb Waiter,* both at SoHo Poly, London, 1973; Tristan Tzara, *Travesties,* RSC, Aldwych Theatre, London, 1974; Young Man, *The Arrest,* Bristol Old Vic, 1974; Romeo, *Romeo and Juliet,* Coventry, 1973; Donal, *Shadow of a Gunman,* 1978; Trigorin, *The Seagul,* Lyric Theatre, Hammersmith, 1985.

FILM DEBUT—Phil, *The Wild and the Willing,* 1962. PRINCIPAL FILM APPPEARANCES—Richard Rich, *A Man for All Seasons,* Columbia, 1966; *Sinful Davey,* United Artists, 1969; *Before Winter Comes,* Columbia, 1969; *In Search of Gregory,* Universal, 1970; Timothy Evans, *10 Rillington Place,* Columbia, 1971; *Mr. Forbush and the Penguins,* 1971; *The Ghoul,* 1975; *East of Elephant Rock,* 1977; Max, *Midnight Express,* Columbia, 1978; *The Shout,* 1978; voice of Hazel, *Watership Down,* Avco Embassy, 1978; *Midnight Express,* Columbia, 1978; voice of Strider, *Lord of the Rings,* United Artists, 1978; Kane, *Alien,* Twentieth Century-Fox, 1979; John Merrick, *The Elephant Man,* Paramount, 1980; *Heaven's Gate,* United Artists, 1980; *The Disappearance,* 1981; Jesus, *History of the World, Part I,* 1981; *Night Crossing,* Buena Vista, 1982; *Partners,* Paramount, 1982; *The Hit,* 1982; *The Osterman Weekend,* Embassy, 1983; *Champions,* Embassy, 1984; *1984,* 1984; Peter Huninger, *After Darkness,* 1986.

PRINCIPAL TELEVISION APPEARANCES—*Mourtzanos,* 1961; *The Waste Places,* 1967; Quentin Crisp, *The Naked Civil Servant,* 1975; *The Playboy of the Western World,* 1976; Caligula, *I, Claudius,* 1977-78; Raskolnikov, *Crime and Punishment,* 1980; Fool, *King Lear,* 1982; *The Hard Case; Acquit and Hang; Watch Me; I'm a Bird; Menace; The Stone Dance; The Spectre.*

AWARDS: Best Television Actor, British Academy Award, Emmy Award, 1975, for *The Naked Civil Servant;* Best Supporting Actor, British Academy Award, Academy Award nomination, 1978, for *Midnight Express;* Best Actor, British Academy Award, Academy Award nomination, 1980, for *Elephant Man;* Best Actor, *Evening Standard* Award, 1984, for *1984.*

ADDRESSES: AGENT—Leading Artists, 60 St. James Street, London W1, England.

CONTEMPORARY THEATRE, FILM, AND TELEVISION • Volume 3

HYMAN

HUTTON, Lauren   1944-

PERSONAL: Born Mary Laurence Hutton, 1944, in Charleston, SC; daughter of Laurence Hutton (a writer). EDUCATION: Attended University of Florida; Sophia Newcombe College.

VOCATION: Actress and model.

CAREER: FILM DEBUT—*Paper Lion*, United Artists, 1968. PRINCIPAL FILM APPEARANCES—Rita Nebraska, *Little Fauss and Big Halsey*, Paramount, 1970; *Pieces of Dreams*, United Artists, 1970; *The Gambler*, Paramount, 1974; *Gator*, United Artists, 1976; *Welcome to L.A.*, Lion's Gate, 1977; Flo Farmer, *A Wedding*, Twentieth Century-Fox, 1978; *American Gigolo*, Paramount, 1980; *Zorro, the Gay Blade*, Twentieth Century-Fox, 1981; *Paternity*, Paramount, 1981; *Lassiter*, Warner Brothers, 1984; *Once Bitten*, Samuel Goldwyn, 1985; *A Certain Desire*, Worldwide Entertainment Corp., 1986; also appeared in *The Wine and the Music; Excuse Me, My Name Is Rocco Papaleo*, Italian; *Tout Feu Tout Flaimme*, French; *Hectate*, French.

PRINCIPAL TELEVISION APPEARANCES—Movies: *Someone's Watching Me*, 1978; *The Cradle Will Rock*, 1983; *Starflight: The Plane That Couldn't Land*, 1983; *Scandal Sheet*, ABC, 1985.

Series: Leslie H. Hawkewood, *The Rhinemann Exchange*, NBC, 1977.

STAGE DEBUT—*Extremities*, Los Angeles Public Theatre.

RELATED CAREER—Hutton was one of the top fashion models from the 1960's through to the 1980's.

ADDRESSES: AGENT—Creative Artists Agency, 1888 Century Park E., Suite 1400, Los Angeles, CA 90067.*

*   *   *

EARLE HYMAN

Photograph by Foto Tryxve Schoenfelder

HYMAN, Earle   1926-

PERSONAL: Born October 11, 1926, in Rocky Mount, NC; son of Zachariah and Maria Lilly (Plummer) Hyman. EDUCATION: Attended public schools in Brooklyn, NY; studied with Eva Le Gallienne at the American Theatre Wing, and at the Actors Studio in New York.

VOCATION: Actor, director, and teacher.

CAREER: NEW YORK DEBUT—Diaperman, *Three's a Family*, American Negro Theatre, 1943. LONDON DEBUT—Rudolf, *Anna Lucasta*, His Majesty's Theatre, 1947. PRINCIPAL STAGE APPEARANCES—*Run, Little Chillun*, Hudson Theatre, NY, 1943; Rudolf, *Anna Lucasta*, Mansfield Theatre, NY, 1944; Turner Thomas, *Sister Oakes*, Lenox Hill Playhouse, NY, 1949.

Logan, *The Climate of Eden*, Martin Beck Theatre, NY, 1952; Prince of Morocco, *The Merchant of Venice*, City Center Theatre, NY, 1953; title role, *Othello*, Jan Hus Auditorium, NY, 1953; Prince of Morocco, *The Merchant of Venice*, Jan Hus Auditorium, NY, 1955; Pindarus and Soothsayer, *Julius Caesar* and Boatswain, *The Tempest*, both at American Shakespeare Festival, Stratford, CT, 1955; Lieutenant, *No Time for Sergeants*, Alvin Theatre, NY, 1955; title role, *Mister Johnson*, Martin Beck Theatre, NY, 1956;

Melun, *King John*, American Shakespeare Festival, 1956; Dunois, *Saint Joan*, Phoenix Theatre, NY, 1956; voice of the Player King, *Hamlet*, Theatre de Lys, NY, 1957; Vladimir, *Waiting for Godot*, Barrymore Theatre, NY, 1957; Antonio, *The Duchess of Malfi*, Phoenix Theatre, NY, 1957; Prince of Morocco, *The Merchant of Venice* and title role, *Othello*, both American Shakespeare Festival, 1957; Ghost of Laius, *The Infernal Machine*, Phoenix Theatre, NY, 1958; Horatio, *Hamlet*, Philostrate, *A Midsummer's Night Dream*, and Autolycus, *The Winter's Tale*, all American Shakespeare Festival, 1958; Ephraim, *Moon on a Rainbow Shawl*, Royal Court Theatre, London, 1958; Walter Lee, *A Raisin in the Sun*, Adelphi Theatre, London, 1959.

Caliban, *The Tempest* and Alexas, *Antony and Cleopatra*, both American Shakespeare Festival, 1960; *Mister Roberts*, Equity Library Theatre, 1963; title role, in Norwegian, *Othello*, Bergen, Norway, 1963; *The White Rose and the Red*, Shakespeare anthology, Stage 73, NY, 1963; *The Angel in Jonah*, St. Clement's Church, NY, 1966; Captain La Hire, *St. Joan*, Vivian Beaumont Theatre, NY, 1968.

Title role, *Othello*, Repertory Company of St. Louis, MO, 1970; Abioseh Matoseh, *Les Blancs*, Longacre Theatre, NY, 1970; title role, *The Life and Times of J, Walter Smintheus*, Theatre de Lys, NY, 1970; *The Seagull*, Center Stage, Baltimore, MD, 1970; Alex,

Orrin, Theatre de Lys, NY, 1973; Oscar, *The Lady from Dubuque,* 1973; Gayev, *The Cherry Orchard,* Anspacher/Public Theatre, NY, 1973; *House Party,* American Place Theatre, NY, 1973; *Waiting for Godot,* Cincinnati Playhouse in the Park, OH, 1974; title role, *Emperor Jones,* Virginia Museum Theatre, Richmond, VA, 1976; Dr. Winston Gerrard, *As to the Meaning of Words,* Hartman Theatre, Stamford, CT, 1977; chorus leader, *Agamemnon,* Delacorte Theatre, NY, 1977; title role, *Othello,* Roundabout Theatre, NY, 1978; Cicero, *Julius Caesar,* Anspacher/Public Theatre, NY, 1979; Cominius, *Coriolanus,* Anspacher/Public Theatre then Delacorte Theatre, NY, 1979; Ezra Pilgrim, *Remembrance,* Other Stage/Public Theatre, 1979.

Oscar, *The Lady from Dubuque,* Hartford Stage Company, Hartford, CT, 1980; James Tyrone, *Long Day's Journey into Night,* Theatre at St. Peter's Church, NY, 1981, then at the Public Theatre, NY, 1982; *A Doll's House,* Yale Repertory Theatre, New Haven, CT, 1982; Nothenberg and Dr. Jones, *Execution of Justice,* Virginia Theatre, NY, 1986.

MAJOR TOURS—Everett du Shane, *A Lady Passing Fair,* national, 1947; concert reading, *The Worlds of Shakespeare,* national and Carnegie Recital Hall, 1963; *Othello; Emperor Jones; Scenes from Shakespeare,* Norwegian State Travelling Theatre, tour of Scandinavia, 1964.

PRINCIPAL STAGE WORK—Director, *Orrin,* Theatre de Lys, NY, 1973.

FILM DEBUT—*The Bamboo Prison,* 1954. PRINCIPAL FILM APPEARANCES—*The Possession of Joel Delaney,* Paramount, 1972.

PRINCIPAL TELEVISION APPEARANCES—Adam Hezdrel, *The Green Pastures;* Jim, *Huckleberry Finn;* Shepard, *Emmanuel;* Russell Huxtable, *The Bill Cosby Show,* NBC, 1985—.

MEMBER: Actors' Equity Association, Screen Actors Guild, American Federation of Television and Radio Artists.

AWARDS: Theatre World Award, 1955; Norwegian Best Actor of the Year, 1963, for *Emperor Jones;* Hearst's ABC Ace Award, for *Long Day's Journey into Night.*

SIDELIGHTS: Favorite roles: Othello, Mister Johnson. RECREATION: Lauguages, especially Norwegian and the study of Henrik Ibsen.

ADDRESSES: HOME—484 W. 43rd Street, New York, NY 10036.

I

IVES, Burl 1909-

PERSONAL: Born Icle Ivanhoe Ives, June 14, 1909, in Hunt City Township, IL; son of Frank and Cordella Ives; married Helen Peck Ehrlich, 1945 (marriage ended); married Dorothy Koster, 1971; children: (first marriage) Alexander. EDUCATION: Attended Eastern Illinois State Teachers College; Juilliard School of Music.

VOCATION: Actor, singer, and writer.

CAREER: NEW YORK DEBUT—*I Married an Angel*, Shubert Theatre, 1938. PRINCIPAL STAGE APPEARANCES—Tailor's apprentice, *The Boys from Syracuse*, Alvin Theatre, NY, 1938; *Heavenly Express*, National Theatre, NY, 1940; *This Is the Army*, Broadway Theatre, NY, 1942; the traveller, *Sing Out, Sweet Land*, International Theatre, NY, 1944; Squire Hardcastle, *She Stoops to Conquer*, City Center, NY, 1949; Captain Andy, *Show Boat*, City Center, NY, 1954; Big Daddy, *Cat on a Hot Tin Roof*, Morosco Theatre, NY, 1955; Joshua Beene, *Joshua Beene and God*, Dallas Theatre Center, Dallas, TX, 1961; Joshua Leonard Cook, *Dr. Cook's Garden*, Belasco Theatre, NY, 1967; also appeared in *Knickerbocker Holiday* and *The Man Who Came to Dinner*.

MAJOR TOURS—*This Is the Army*, national; Ben Rumson, *Paint Your Wagon*, national, 1952-53; also: tent show tours during the Depression; singer with Evangelistic touring show during the Depression.

FILM DEBUT—*Smoky*, Twentieth Century-Fox, 1946. PRINCIPAL FILM APPEARANCES—Uncle Hiram, *So Dear to My Heart*, RKO Radio (Disney), 1948; *Sierra*, 1950; Sam, *East of Eden*, Warner Brothers, 1955; *The Power and the Prize*, Metro-Goldwyn-Mayer, 1956; Big Daddy, *Cat on a Hot Tin Roof*, Metro-Goldwyn-Mayer, 1958; Ephrain Cabot, *Desire Under the Elms*, Paramount, 1958; Rufus Hannassey, *The Big Country*, United Artists, 1958; *Wind Across the Everglades*, Warner Brothers, 1958; *The Day of the Outlaw*, Security Pictures, 1958; *Our Man in Havana*, Columbia, 1959; *Let No Man Write My Epitaph*, Columbia, 1960; *The Spiral Road*, Universal-International, 1962; Osh Popham, *Summer Magic*, Buena Vista, 1963; *The Brass Bottle*, Universal-International, 1964; *Ensign Pulver*, Warner Brothers, 1964; *Mediterranean Holiday*, Continental, 1964; *P.T. Barnum's Rocket to the Moon*, 1967; *The McMasters*, JayJen Films, 1969; *Baker's Hawk*, 1976; *Just You and Me, Kid*, Columbia, 1979; *Earthbound*, 1981; *The White Dog*, 1982; also appeared in *Up Hill All the Way* and *The Adversaries*.

TELEVISION DEBUT—Subject and interviewee, *Action Autographs*, ABC, 1949. PRINCIPAL TELEVISION APPEARANCES—Series: Semi-regular, *High-Low* (quiz program), NBC, 1957; title role, *O.K. Crackerby*, ABC, 1965-66; Walter Nichols, "The Lawyers,"

originally seen as one-third of the rotating segments on *The Bold Ones*, NBC, 1969-72.

Episodic: *Little House on the Prairie; Night Gallery; Captains and Kings; Sing America; Oddessy; Celebration; On Eagle's Wings.*

Mini-Series: Justin, *Roots*, ABC, 1977-78.

Guest: *Glen Campbell Goodtime Hour; The Johnny Cash Show; Flip Wilson; The Ed Sullivan Show*, others.

BURL IVES

Specials: *The Perry Como Show,* NBC, 1949; voice of Sam the Snowman (narrator), *Rudolph the Red Nosed Reindeer,* CBS; *The Great Easter Bunny.*

WRITINGS: MEMOIR—*The Wayfaring Stranger's Notebook.*

MUSIC BOOKS—*New Guitar Book Methods,* three volumes; *Burl Ives Song Books I and II; Burl Ives Sampler of American Music; The Wayfaring Stranger; Burl Ives Sea Songs; America's Musical Heritage—Song in America.*

RECORDINGS: ALBUMS—*Sing Out, Sweet Land,* original cast recording, Decca; *So Dear to My Heart,* original soundtrack recording, Decca; *Summer Magic,* original soundtrack recording, Buena Vista; *Burl Ives Presents America's Musical Heritage* (seventeen record set), Encyclopedia Britannica Records; *We Americans,* National Geographic Records; *The Children at Christmas,* Salvation Army Records; *Christmas at the White House,* Caedmon Records; *Salute to America,* Xerox Records; *A Day at the Zoo,* Disney/Buena Vista Records; *200 Years Experience* (a nuance of American history), Bert Tenzer Records; *Burl Ives and the Korean Orphans Choir Sings Songs of Faith,* Word Records; *Burl Ives Live in Europe,* Polygram/Polydor Records; *The Wayfaring Stranger,* Columbia Records; *Little White Duck and Other Favorites,* Columbia Records; *Men: Songs for and About,* Decca Records; *Coronation Concert,* Decca Records; *Women: Folk Songs About the Fair Sex,* Decca Records; *The Lonesome Train,* Decca Records; *The Legend That Is Burl Ives,* TeeVee Records; and dozens of others.

AWARDS: Best Supporting Actor, Academy Award, 1958, for *The Big Country;* Lincoln Laureate, State of Illinois; Minnesota Heritage Award; Carl Sandburg Award; National Boy Scouts Award; Crystal Humanitarian Award, given by the Crystal Cathedral; Honorary Doctorate of Law, Fairleigh Dickinson University; Honorary Doctorate in Music, Carl Sandburg College; U.S. Navy "E" Award.

SIDELIGHTS: Interspersed with his work in theatre, film, television, and recordings, Burl Ives has continually appeared in concerts around the United States as well as around the world. As frequently found in the posh concert hall as he is in the folk music arena, he has appeared before Golda Meier in a private audience in Israel, before a United States' president in Alaska and for the Queen of England in a special command performance. His tours have taken him far from the homeland he sings about, New Zealand and Australia having enthusiastically called him back several times.

ADDRESSES: HOME—Montecito, CA. OFFICE—Gemini Gems Music, Inc., 1880 E. Valley Road, Montecito, CA 93108. AGENT—Beakel and Jennings Agency, 427 N. Canon Drive, Suite 205, Beverly Hills, CA 90210.

J

JABLONSKI, Carl 1937-

PERSONAL: Born June 23, 1937, in Gary IN; son of Vincent Stanley (a steelworker) and Sophie Marie (Poplonski) Jablonski. EDUCATION: Trained for the stage at Frances School of the Dance with Frances Brumshagen and Louise Glenn. RELIGION: Roman Catholic. MILITARY: U.S. Army, 1960-62.

VOCATION: Choreographer and director.

CAREER: STAGE DEBUT—Dancer, St. Louis Municipal Opera, 1954-55, for 120 performances. NEW YORK DEBUT—Dancer, Catch a Star, Plymouth Theatre, 1955, for sixty performances. PRINCIPAL STAGE APPEARANCES—Dancer, My Fair Lady, Mark Hellinger Theatre, NY. MAJOR TOURS—Ballet Ho, Paris, France.

PRINCIPAL STAGE WORK—Choreographer, Paris Mes Amours, Paris, 1959; choreographer, Olympia Music Hall, 1959-60; assistant choreographer, Calamity Jane, Dallas, TX, 1963; assistant choreographer, Superman, Broadway, 1966; assistant choreographer, Fade Out, Fade In, Broadway, 1966; choreographer, Once Upon a Mattress, Gigi, On a Clear Day You Can See Forever, all Sacramento, CA, 1974; choreographer, San Diego Youth Ballet, 1977; director, Gypsy, Long Beach Civic Light Opera, CA.

Cabaret and Revues: Mitzi Gaynor's nightclub act, 1966-1968; director, Follies '73, Harrah's, Lake Tahoe, NV, 1973; director for the Jackson Five show, MGM Grand, Las Vegas, NV, 1974; director for Florence Henderson's revue, Riviera, Las Vegas, NV, 1974; director and choreographer, Showboat '75, Opryland, USA, Nashville, TN, 1975; director and choreographer for Florence Henderson's revue, MGM Grand, Las Vegas, NV, 1975; director, Sergio Franchi, MGM Grand, Las Vegas, NV, 1975; director and choreographer, Liberty's Song, I Hear America Singing, Showboat '76, Opryland, USA, 1976; choreographer for Cyd Charisse's revue, 1977; director and co-producer, Good Stuff, Sparks, NV, 1977; director and choreographer for Suzanne Somers' revue, 1980; director and choreographer, Broadway Salutes New York City Opera, NY; choreographer, Happy Birthday Bob (Bob Hope's eightieth birthday celebration), Kennedy Center, Washington, DC; choreographer for Suzanne Somers' revue, Hilton, Las Vegas, NV; choreographer, Glitter; director and choreographer for Jonelle Allen's revue; director and choreographer for Ann Jillian's revues at the, Sands in Atlantic City, NJ, and at the MGM Grand, Las Vegas, NV.

Award shows: Choreographer, Rock Music Awards, 1975, 1976; choreographer, Entertainer of the Year Awards, Las Vegas, NV, 1979.

MAJOR TOURS —Director and choreographer, Country, Music, U.S.A., Soviet Union, 1975; director and choreographer, Donny and Marie, U.S. cities, 1979; director and co-producer, Perry Como Summer Tour, U.S. cities, 1978, 1980; choreographer, Colette, U.S. cities.

FILM DEBUT—Dancer, Reluctant Debutante, Metro-Goldwyn-Mayer, 1958.

TELEVISION DEBUT—Dancer and acrobat, Caesar's Hour, NBC, 1955. PRINCIPAL TELEVISION APPEARANCES—Dancer: The Entertainers, CBS, 1964; Jimmy Dean Show, ABC, 1964-65; Carol Burnett Show, CBS, 1967-73.

PRINCIPAL TELEVISION WORK—Series: Assistant choreographer, Judy Garland Show, CBS, 1963-64; assistant choreographer, Carol Burnett Show, CBS, 1971; choreographer, Diahann Carroll Show, CBS, 1976; choreographer, Rich Little Show, NBC, 1976; Donny and Marie, ABC, 1977-79; director and choreographer, Sha Na Na, syndication, 1979-80; choreographer, Marie, NBC, 1980-81; director, Seven Brides for Seven Brothers, CBS, 1982-83.

Specials: Choreographer, Academy Award Show, 1973; choreographer, NBC Follies (thirteen shows), 1973; choreographer, Monty Hall at Sea World, 1974; director, Emmy Awards, 1974; choreographer, Cotton Club '75, NBC, 1974; choreographer, Lights-Camera-Monty, 1975; choreographer, Fashion Awards, ABC, 1975; choreographer, A Circus of American Music, 1975; choreographer, With Love, 1977; choreographer, Circus of the Stars, 1976; choreographer, People's Choice Awards, 1977; choreographer, Chevy Chase Special, 1977; choreographer, Perry Como Summer Show; choreographer, Singin', Swingin' . . . and All That Jazz!, 1977; choreographer, Bob Hope's 75th Birthday, 1978; choreographer, The Carpenter's Christmas Special, 1978; director, The Road to China, 1979; choreographer, Osmond Family Christmas Show, 1979; director, Broadway Baby, 1980; choreographer, Suzanne Somers Special; director and choreographer, Love Boat Special, ABC; director and choreographer, The Way We Were; choreographer, Love Boat Follies, ABC; director, Loretta Lynn, the Legend; director and choreographer, Face of the 80's; choreographer, All-star Hour, NBC, 1985; director, Bob Hope's Christmas Show.

PRINCIPAL FILM WORK—Choreographer, Goin' Coconuts, 1978.

MEMBER: Professional Dancers Society (president).

AWARDS: Emmy nomination, Best Choreographer, 1974, for NBC Follies.

ADDRESSES: HOME—Oxnard, CA. OFFICE—1973 1/2 Carmen Avenue, Hollywood, CA 90068. AGENT—c/o Aaron Cohen, William Morris Agency, Beverly Hills, CA 90212.

JACKSON, Kate 1949-

PERSONAL: Born October 29, 1949, in Birmingham, AL; daughter of Hogan (a business executive) and Ruth (Shepherd) Jackson; married Andrew Stevens (divorced). EDUCATION: Attended the University of Mississippi; Birmingham Southern University; studied acting at the American Academy of Dramatic Arts in New York.

VOCATION: Actress, director, and model.

CAREER: TELEVISION DEBUT—*Dark Shadows*. PRINCIPAL TELEVISION APPEARANCES—Series: Jill Danko, *The Rookies*, ABC, 1972-76; Sabrina Duncan, *Charlie's Angels*, ABC, 1976-79; Amanda King, *Scarecrow and Mrs. King*, CBS, 1983—.

Episodic: *The Jimmy Stewart Show*.

Movies: *Killer Bees*, 1974; *The Shrine of Lorna Love*; *The Jenny Storm Homicide*.

PRINCIPAL TELEVISION WORK—Director, *Scarecrow and Mrs. King* (episodes); producer, *Topper*, 1979; producer, *Child's Cry*.

PRINCIPAL FILM APPEARANCES—*Thunder and Lightning*, 1977; *Dirty Tricks*, Avco Embassy, 1980; *Making Love*, Twentieth Century-Fox, 1982.

MEMBER: Screen Actors Guild, Directors Guild of America, American Federation of Television and Radio Artists.

KATE JACKSON

SIDELIGHTS: CTFT learned Kate Jackson was once an NBC tour guide and a fashion model, is an avid skier, tennis player and photographer.

ADDRESSES: AGENT—c/o Ron Meyer, Creative Artists Agency, 1888 Century Park E., Suite 1400, Los Angeles, CA 90067.

*   *   *

JAMES, Clifton 1923-

PERSONAL: Born May 29, 1923, in Spokane, WA; son of Harry (a journalist) and Grace (a teacher; maiden name, Dean) James; married Laurie Harper (a writer), May, 1951; children: Mike, Winkie, Hardy, Lynn, Mary. EDUCATION: University of Oregon, B.A., 1950; trained for the stage at the Actors Studio. MILITARY: U.S. Army. POLITICS: Democrat. RELIGION: Protestant.

VOCATION: Actor.

CAREER: PRINCIPAL FILM APPEARANCES—*On the Waterfront*, Columbia, 1954; *The Strange One*, Columbia, 1957; *David and Lisa*, Continental, 1962; *Experiment in Terror*, Columbia, 1962; *The Chase*, Columbia, 1966; *The Happening*, Columbia, 1967; *The Caper of the Golden Bulls*, Embassy, 1967; *Cool Hand Luke*, Warner Brothers, 1967; *Will Penny*, Paramount, 1968; *The Reivers*, National General, 1969; *WUSA*, Paramount, 1970; *Tick . . . Tick . . . Tick*, Metro-Goldwyn-Mayer, 1970; *The Iceman Cometh*, American Film Theatre, 1972; *The New Centurions*, Columbia, 1972; *The Laughing Policeman*, Twentieth Century-Fox, 1973; *Live and Let Die*, United Artists, 1973; *Bank Shot*, United Artists, 1974; *The Last Detail*, Columbia, 1974; *Juggernaut*, United Artists, 1974; *Buster and Billie*, Columbia, 1974; *Rancho DeLuxe*, 1974; *Man with the Golden Gun*, United Artists, 1974.

NEW YORK DEBUT—First Cop, *The Time of Your Life*, City Center, NY, 1955. PRINCIPAL STAGE APPEARANCES—Robert Kensington, *Career*, Seventh Avenue South Playhouse, NY, 1957; wrecking crew boss, *The Cave Dwellers*, Bijou Theatre, NY, 1957; first roustabout, *J.B.*, American National Theatre and Academy (ANTA), NY, 1958; Blick, *The Time of Your Life*, Brussels World's Fair, Belgium, 1958-59; Michaud, in *Sweet Confession*, and *I Rise in Flame Cried the Phoenix*, both Theatre de Lys, NY, 1959; Willie Stark, *All the King's Men*, East 74th Street Theatre, NY, 1959; Clem, *The Long Dream*, Ambassador Theatre, NY, 1960.

Antonio, *Twelfth Night*, Stephano, *The Tempest*, Pompey, *Antony and Cleopatra*, all at American Shakespeare Festival, Stratford, CT, 1960; Ralph Follet, *All the Way Home*, Belasco Theatre, NY, 1960; Brennan Farrell, *Great Day in the Morning*, Henry Miller's Theatre, NY, 1962; Polly Baker, *A Man's a Man*, Masque Theatre, NY, 1962; the carpenter, *Andorra*, Biltmore Theatre, NY, 1963; U.S. Grant, *The Last Days of Lincoln*, Library of Congress, Washington, DC, 1965, then Theater de Lys, NY, 1965; Lawrence Phelps, *The Trial of Lee Harvey Oswald*, ANTA, NY, 1967; title role, *Felix*, Actors Studio, NY, 1972.

MAJOR TOURS—Bottom, *A Midsummer Night's Dream*, New York Shakespeare Festival, U.S. cities, 1964.

CLIFTON JAMES

MEMBER: Actors' Equity Association, Screen Actors Guild, American Federation of Television and Radio Artists, Players Club, University of Oregon Alumni Club.

AWARDS: MILITARY—Silver Star and Purple Heart.

ADDRESSES: HOME—95 Buttonwood Drive, Dix Hills, NY 11746.

*   *   *

JARMUSCH, Jim

BRIEF ENTRY: Born in Akron, OH. Director, writer, composer, and actor. Jim Jarmusch attended Columbia University where he majored in literature with hopes of becoming a writer. In his senior year, he went to Paris where he became intrigued by European cinema and returned to America to enroll in New York University's film school. Jarmusch became friendly with Nicholas Ray, who directed *Rebel without a Cause,* and Nicholas was influential in getting the young director to complete his first film, *Permanent Vacation.* This film won several foreign awards. A director who was working on a major motion picture gave Jarmusch thirty minutes worth of leftover, unused film. Jarmusch was left with an interesting challenge: he could make a half hour film if each scene were photographed in a single shot with no cuts. Jarmusch wrote a script and shot a film entitled *New World,* which won the International Critics' Prize at the Rotterdam Film Festival. Jarmusch wanted to

expand the movie and so, after raising more money, he shot another hour's worth of film, added it to the thirty minutes he already had, and called the completed project *Stranger Than Paradise.* It went on to win the Best Film award from the National Society of Film and the Golden Leopard award at the Locarno Film Festival. Jarmusch was awarded the Camera d'Or as best new director at Cannes. Versatile in many aspects of film, Jarmusch was seen in *Red Italy* and *Fraulein Berlin* and has composed scores for *The State of Things* and *Reverse Angle.* He is currently working on a new film, *Down by Law.**

*   *   *

JOHNSON, Arte 1934-

PERSONAL: Born Arthur Stanton Eric Johnson, January 20, 1934, in Benton Harbor, MI; son of Abraham Lincoln (an attorney) and Edythe MacKenzie (Golden) Johnson; married Gisela Von Busch (a fashion co-ordinator), August 15, 1968. EDUCATION: University of Illinois, B.A., M.A.

VOCATION: Actor.

CAREER: TELEVISION DEBUT—Stanley Schreiber, *It's Always Jan,* CBS, 1955-56. PRINCIPAL TELEVISION APPEARANCES—

ARTE JOHNSON

Series: Bascomb Bleacher, Jr., *Sally,* NBC, 1958; Seaman Shatz, *Hennesey,* CBS, 1959-62; Corporal Lefkowitz, *Don't Call Me Charlie,* NBC, 1962-63; *Rowan and Martin's Laugh-In,* NBC, 1968-71; *Ben Vereen Comin' at Ya,* NBC, 1975.

Episodic: *General Electric True,* CBS; *The Love Boat,* ABC; *Hotel,* ABC.

Guest: *Bobbie Vinton Show; David Frost Review.*

FILM DEBUT—*Miracle in the Rain,* Warner Brothers, 1956. PRINCIPAL FILM APPEARANCES—*The Subterraneans,* Metro-Goldwyn-Mayer, 1960; *The Third Day,* Warner Brothers, 1965; *The President's Analyst,* Paramount, 1967; *Twice in a Lifetime,* 1974; *Bud and Lou,* 1978; *Love at First Bite,* American International, 1979; *The Sacketts,* 1979; *If Things Were Different,* 1980; *Detour by Terror,* 1980.

STAGE DEBUT—*Gentlemen Prefer Blondes.* PRINCIPAL STAGE APPEARANCES—Ben, *No Time for Sergeants.* MAJOR TOURS—*The Foreigner,* U.S. cities, 1986.

MEMBER: Screen Actors Guild, American Federation of Television and Radio Artists; California Special Olympic (board of directors), Pacific Gamefish Foundation.

AWARDS: Outstanding Individual Achievement, Emmy Award, 1968-69, for *Laugh In;* Best Supporting Performer, Academy of Science Fiction Award, 1979, for *Love at First Bite.*

ADDRESSES: AGENT—J. Carter Gibson, 9000 Sunset Blvd., Los Angeles, CA 90069.

*   *   *

JOHNSON, Ben   1918-

PERSONAL: Born June 13, 1918, in Foracre, OK; son of Ben (a rancher) and Ollie Susan (Workman) Johnson; married Carol Jones, August 31, 1941. EDUCATION: Attended Ramona High School, OK. RELIGION: Protestant.

VOCATION: Actor.

CAREER: FILM DEBUT—Horse wrangler, *The Outlaw,* 1941. PRINCIPAL FILM APPEARANCES—Double for Tom Tyler, *Riders of the Rio Grande,* 1943; bit part, *Border Town Gunfighters,* 1943; bit part, *Nevada,* 1944; hack driver, *Naughty Nineties,* 1945; double for Fred MacMurray, *Smoky,* 1946; posse member, *Badman's Territory,* 1946; double for Bill Elliott, *Wyoming,* 1947; double for Bill Elliott, *Gallant Legion,* 1948; double for John Wayne, *Fort Apache,* 1948; posse member, *Three Godfathers,* 1948; Gregg Johnson, *Mighty Joe Young,* Argosy, 1949; Tyree, *She Wore a Yellow Ribbon,* 1949.

Travis Blue, *Wagon Master,* 1950; Travis Tyree, *Rio Grande,* 1950; Ben Shelby, *Fort Defiance,* 1951; Dan Light, *Wild Stallion,* 1952; Chris Calloway, *Shane,* 1953; Frank Mason, *Rebel in Town,* United Artists, 1956; Fargo, *War Drums,* United Artists, 1957; Montana Buriss, *Slim Carter,* Universal, 1957; Tomahawk Thompson, *Fort

BEN JOHNSON

Bowie,* United Artists, 1958; George Bradley, *Ten Who Dared,* Buena Vista, 1960; Bob Amory, *One-Eyed Jacks,* Paramount, 1961; Jim, *Tomboy and the Champ,* Universal, 1961; Plumtree, *Cheyenne Autumn,* Warner Brothers, 1964; stuntman, *War Party,* Twentieth Century-Fox, 1965; Chillum, *Major Dundee,* Columbia, 1965; Jeff Harter, *The Rare Breed,* Universal, 1966; Alex, *Will Penny,* Paramount, 1967; Dave Bliss, *Hang 'em High,* United Artists, 1968; Tector Gorch, *The Wild Bunch,* Warner Brothers, 1969; Short Grub, *The Undefeated,* Twentieth Century-Fox, 1969.

James Pepper, *Chisum,* Warner Brothers, 1970; Jesse Bookbinder, *Something Big,* National General, 1971; Sam the Lion, *The Last Picture Show,* Columbia, 1971; Boland, *Corky,* 1972; Buck Roan, *Junior Bonner,* Cinerama, 1972; Jack Benyon, *The Getaway,* National General, 1972; Mean John Simpson, *Kid Blue,* Twentieth Century-Fox, 1973; Melvin H. Purvis, *Dillinger,* American International, 1973; Jess Taylor, *The Red Pony,* 1973; Will Jesse, *The Train Robbers,* Warner Brothers, 1973; Holly Gibson, *Runaway,* 1973; Dwayne Birdsong, *Blood Sport,* 1973; Amos Fletcher, *The Locusts,* 1974; Harland Tanner, *The Sugarland Express,* Universal, 1974; Pop, *Bite the Bullet,* Columbia, 1975; Martin Hollinger, *Hustle,* Paramount, 1975; Nathan Pearce, *Breakheart Pass,* 1976; Donald McKew, *The Savage Bees,* 1976; Faraday Hollis, *The Greatest,* Columbia, 1977; J.D. Lone Wolf Morales, *Town That Dreaded Sundown,* American International, 1977; Colter, *Gray Eagle,* American International, 1977; Felix Austin, *The Swarm,* Warner Brothers, 1978.

Doc George P. Bogardus, *Wild Times,* 1980; John Strong, *The Hunter,* Paramount, 1980; Carne, *Terror Train,* Twentieth Century-Fox, 1980; Sam Gorch, *Soggy Bottom USA,* 1981; Sam Bellows, *Ruckus,* 1981; Cole Collins, *Tex,* Buena Vista, 1982; Jack Mason, *Red Dawn,* Metro-Goldwyn-Mayer, United Artists, 1984; Burly Cocks, *Champions,* Embassy, 1984; *Wild Horses,* 1985; Jake, *Cherry 2000,* 1985.

PRINCIPAL TELEVISION APPEARANCES—Series: Sleeve, *The Monroes*, ABC, 1966-67.

Episodic: Tex Barton, "Top Gun," *Adventures of Ozzie and Harriet*, ABC, 1958; sheriff, "And the Desert Shall Bloom," *Alfred Hitchcock Presents*, CBS, 1958; Billy Pardee, "Hour After Dawn," *Laramie*, NBC, 1960; John Anderson, "A Head of Hair," CBS, *Have Gun Will Travel*, 1960; Sam Crabbe, "The Race," CBS, *Have Gun Will Travel*, 1961; Del McNabb, "A Long Piece of Mischief," CBS, *Route 66*, 1962; Stan, "The Gamble," NBC, *Bonanza*, 1962; John Bartlett, "The Fifth Bullet," CBS, *Have Gun Will Travel*, 1962; Spinner, "Duel at Shiloh," *The Virginian*, NBC, 1963; Ben Crown, "Quint-Cident," *Gunsmoke*, CBS, 1963; Burt Wade, "March from Camp Tyler," *Bob Hope Presents the Chrysler Theatre*, NBC, 1965; Bill Latigo, "McCord's Way," *Branded*, NBC, 1966; Hogan, "Johnny Moon," *The Virginian*, NBC, 1967; Jed Cooper, "A Vision of Blindness," *The Virginian*, NBC, 1968; Will Parker, "Ride a Northbound Horse," *Wonderful World of Disney*, NBC, 1969; Bellis, "The Deserter," *Bonanza*, NBC, 1969; Kelly James, "Top Hand," *Bonanza*, NBC, 1971; Hannon, "Drago," *Gunsmoke*, CBS, 1971.

Guest: *The Red Fisher Show*, 1979.

Movies: Cap Roundtree, *The Sacketts*, 1979; Black Jack Traven, *The Shadow Riders*, 1982.

Mini-Series: Jim Bridger, *Dream West*, CBS, 1986.

MEMBER: Masquers' Club.

AWARDS: Best Supporting Actor, Academy Award, 1971, for *The Last Picture Show;* New York Critics Award; Golden Globe Award; Peoples Choice Award; British Academy Award; Golden Boot Award; Man of the West Award; Buffalo Bill Award; Hall of Fame Award; Hall of Champions Award; honorary member of the Osage Indian Tribe.

SIDELIGHTS: CTFT learned that Ben Johnson is an honorary deputy sheriff in many states and was honored with "Ben Johnson Day" by the city of Los Angeles in 1984.

ADDRESSES: OFFICE—100 N. Westlake Blvd., Westlake Village, CA 91362. AGENT—Herb Tobias, 1901 Avenue of the Stars, Los Angeles, CA 90067.

*   *   *

JONES, Dean   1933-

PERSONAL: Full name, Dean Carroll Jones; born January 25, 1933, in Morgan City, AL; son of Andrew Guy and Nolia Elizabeth (Wilhite) Jones; married Mae Inez Entwisle, January 1, 1954 (divorced); children: Carol Elizabeth, Deanna Mae. EDUCATION: Attended Asbury College, Wilmore, KY; attended University of California, Los Angeles, 1957. MILITARY: U.S. Navy, 1953.

VOCATION: Actor.

CAREER: PRINCIPAL STAGE APPEARANCES—*There Was a Little Girl*, NY; *Under the Yum Yum Tree*, Broadway production, 1960; Robert, *Company*, Shubert Theatre, NY, 1970.

PRINCIPAL FILM APPEARANCES—*Handle With Care*, Metro-Goldwyn-Mayer, 1958; *Never so Few*, Metro-Goldwyn-Mayer, 1959; *Under the Yum Yum Tree*, Columbia, 1963; *The New Interns*, Columbia, 1964; Zeke Kelso, *That Darn Cat*, Buena Vista, 1965; *Two on a Guillotine*, Warner Brothers, 1965; Mark Garrison, *The Ugly Dachshund*, Buena Vista, 1965; Hank Dussard, *Monkeys Go Home*, Buena Vista, 1967; *Blackbeard's Ghost*, Buena Vista, 1968; Jim Douglas, *The Love Bug*, Buena Vista, 1969; *The $1,000,000 Duck*, Buena Vista, 1971; *Snowball Express*, Buena Vista, 1972; *Mr. Super Invisible*, Buena Vista, 1976; *The Shaggy D.A.*, Buena Vista, 1976; Jim Douglas, *Herbie Goes to Monte Carlo*, Buena Vista, 1977; Charles Colson, *Born Again*, Munger/Capra, Jr., 1978.

PRINCIPAL TELEVISION APPEARANCES—Series: Title role, *Ensign O'Toole*, NBC, 1962-63, then ABC, 1964; host, *What's It All About, World?*, ABC, 1969; Linc McCray, *The Chicago Teddy Bears*, CBS, 1971; Jim Douglas, *Herbie, the Love Bug*, CBS, 1982.

Movies: *When Every Day Was the 4th of July*, NBC, 1978; *The Long Day of Summer*, ABC, 1980.

RECORDINGS: ALBUM—*Company*, original cast recording, Columbia.

SIDELIGHTS: Jones made his professional debut as a blues singer in New Orleans.

ADDRESSES: HOME—Tarzana, CA. AGENT—Contemporary-Korman Artists, Ltd., 132 Lasky Drive, Beverly Hills, CA 90212.*

*   *   *

JOY, Robert   1951-

BRIEF ENTRY: Born in 1951, in Montreal, Canada. Actor and composer. Robert Joy graduated from Newfoundland Memorial University and was a Rhodes Scholar. He came to the United States after finishing school and began to work in regional and Off-Broadway theatre. His Off-Broadway debut was in the 1978 production of *The Diary of Anne Frank*. Other Off-Broadway appearances include *Found a Peanut*, *Lenny and the Heartbreakers*, *Life and Limb* and *Fables for Friends*. His portrayal of Mercutio in *Romeo and Juliet* at the La Jolla, Playhouse, CA, won him a Los Angeles Drama-Logue Award. Joy portrayed Huck in the world premiere of *Big River* at the American Repertory Theatre in Cambridge, MA. His most recent theatre work also marked his Broadway debut, as Simon Bliss in a revival of Noel Coward's *Hay Fever*. On film, Joy has been seen in *Ragtime*, *Atlantic City*, and *Desperately Seeking Susan*, and will have a key role in the upcoming *Adventures of Faustus Bidgood*, which he also co-produced. Joy has composed music for stage, radio, and film, including some of the music for *Faustus Bidgood*.*

*   *   *

JULIA, Raul   1940-

PERSONAL: Born March 9, 1940, in San Juan, Puerto Rico; son of Raul (a restaurateur) and Olga (Arcelay) Julia; married Merel Poloway (a dancer), June 28, 1976; children: Raul Sigmund.

RAUL JULIA

EDUCATION: Attended the University of Puerto Rico; trained for the stage with Wynn Handman.

VOCATION: Actor.

CAREER: NEW YORK DEBUT—Astolfo, *La Vida Es Sueno,* Astor Playhouse, 1964. PRINCIPAL STAGE APPEARANCES— Conrad Birdie, *Bye, Bye Birdie, The Four Poster,* Alfred, *The Happy Time,* title role, *Macbeth,* Rodrigo, *Othello,* all at the Tapia Theatre, San Juan, 1963; the suitor, *The Marriage Proposal,* 1966; Macduff, *Macbeth,* New York Shakespeare Festival, Delacorte Theatre, 1966; Luis, *The Ox Cart,* Greenwich Mews Theatre, NY, 1966; Demetrius, *Titus Andronicus,* Delacorte Theatre, NY, 1967; Cradeau, *No Exit,* Bouwerie Lane Theatre, NY, 1967; Conrad Birdie, *Bye, Bye Birdie,* Dallas, 1967; *A Clerk in the Memorandum,* Anspacher Theater, NY, 1968; *The Hide and Seek Odyssey of Madelain Gimple,* O'Neill Theatre Center, Waterford, CT, 1968; Orson, *Your Own Thing,* Orpheum Theatre, NY, 1968; Chan, *The Cuban Thing,* Henry Miller's Theatre, NY, 1968; Workman, *Paradise Gardens East* and Jesus, *Conrico Was Here to Stay,* Fortune Theatre, NY, 1969; Grand Duke Alexis, Uncas, *Indians,* Arena Stage, Washington, DC, the Brooks Atkinson Theatre, NY, 1969.

Persian Elder, *The Persians,* St. George's Church, NY, 1970; Paco Montoya, *The Castro Complex,* Stairway Theatre, NY, 1970; Consequently Joy, *Pinkville,* St. Clement's Church, NY, 1971; Proteus, *Two Gentlemen of Verona,* New York Shakespeare Festival, Delacorte Theatre, then St. James Theatre, NY, 1971; Osric, *Hamlet,* Delacorte Theatre, 1972; Gabriel Finn, *Via Galactica,* Uris (now Gershwin) Theatre, NY, 1972; Orlando, *As You Like It,* Edmund, *King Lear,* both Delacorte Theatre, NY, 1973; Commissioner, *The Emperor of Late Night Radio,* Other Stage Theatre, NY, 1974; Jaimie Lockhart, *The Robber Bridegroom,* St. Clement's Church, NY, 1974; Charles Wykeham, *Where's Charley?,* Circle in the Square, NY, 1974; Mack the Knife, *The Threepenny Opera,*

Vivian Beaumont Theatre, NY, 1976; Lopatkin, *The Cherry Orchard,* Vivian Beaumont Theatre, NY, 1977; title role, *Dracula,* Baltimore, 1978, then Martin Beck Theatre, NY, 1979; Petruchio, *The Taming of the Shrew,* Delacorte Theatre, NY, 1978; Othello, *Othello,* Delacorte Theatre, 1979; *Betrayal,* Trafalgar Theatre, NY, 1980; Guido Contini, *Nine,* 46th Street Theatre, NY, 1982; *Design for Living,* Circle in the Square, NY, 1984; Sergius, *Arms and the Man,* Circle in the Square, NY, 1985.

MAJOR TOURS—*Illya, Darling,* 1968.

PRINCIPAL FILM APPEARANCES—*Panic in Needle Park,* Twentieth Century Fox, 1971; *Been Down So Long It Looks Like Up to Me,* 1971; *Gumball Rally,* Warner Brothers, 1976; *The Eyes of Laura Mars,* Columbia, 1978; Kalibanos, *Tempest,* 1980; *The Escape Artist,* Orion, 1982; *One from the Heart,* Columbia, 1982; Valentin, *Kiss of the Spider Woman,* Cinecom, 1985; *Compromising Positions,* Paramount, 1985.

PRINCIPAL TELEVISION APPEARANCES—Raphael, *Sesame Street; King Lear, The National Health; McCloud; Love of Life; Aces Up,* 1974; *Death Scream,* 1975; *Overdrawn at the Memory Bank,* PBS, 1984.

AWARDS: Antoinette Perry Award nominations: 1971, for *Two Gentlemen of Verona;* 1974, for *Where's Charley?;* 1976, for *The Threepenny Opera;* 1982, for *Nine.*

ADDRESSES: HOME—New York, NY. AGENT—Triad Artists, 888 Seventh Avenue, New York, NY 10106.

*   *   *

JUMP, Gordon

PERSONAL: Born April 1, in Dayton, OH; married Anna; children: Cindy, Kiva, Maggi-Jo. EDUCATION: Attended Kansas State University.

VOCATION: Actor, writer, and producer.

CAREER: PRINCIPAL TELEVISION APPEARANCES—Series: Arthur Carlson, *WKRP in Cincinnati,* CBS, 1978-82.

Episodic: *Get Smart; Daniel Boone,* NBC; *Mannix,* CBS; *The Mary Tyler Moore Show,* CBS; *Bewitched,* ABC; *Alice,* CBS; *Starsky and Hutch,* ABC; *Soap,* ABC.

Movies: *Ruby and Oswald,* 1978; *Goldie and the Boxer,* 1979; also appeared in *Big Stuffed Dog; The Phantom Rebel; Fawn Story.*

PRINCIPAL FILM APPEARANCES—*Adam at Six A.M.,* National General, 1970; *Conquest of the Planet of the Apes,* Twentieth Century-Fox, 1972; *Trouble Man,* Twentieth Century-Fox, 1972.

PRINCIPAL STAGE WORK—Producer and writer, *High Times.*

RELATED CAREER—Production director, WIBW, Dayton, OH; manager, broadcast services department, WLWD, Dayton, OH.

ADDRESSES: AGENT—Artists Agency, 190 N. Cannon Drive, Beverly Hills, CA 90212.*

K

Photograph by James Hamilton

PAULINE KAEL

KAEL, Pauline 1919-

PERSONAL: Born June 19, 1919, in Sonoma County, CA; daughter of Isaac Paul and Judith (Friedman) Kael; children: Gina James. EDUCATION: Attended University of California at Berkeley.

VOCATION: Writer and film critic.

WRITINGS: BOOKS—*I Lost It at the Movies,* Atlantic Monthly Press, 1965; *Kiss Kiss Bang Bang,* Atlantic Monthly Press, 1968; *Going Steady,* 1970; "Raising Kane," *The Citizen Kane Book,* Limelight Editions, 1971; *Deeper into Movies,* 1973; *Reeling,* 1976; *5001 Nights at the Movies,* Holt, Rinehart, and Winston, 1982;

When the Lights Go Down, Owl Books, 1983; *Taking It All In,* W. Abrahams Books, 1984; *State of the Art,* W. Abrahams Books, 1985; *Spitting Images,* W. Abrahams Books, 1985; *A Guide from A to Z,* Holt, Rinehart, and Winston.

MAGAZINES—Staff writer for *Partisan Review, Vogue, The New Republic, McCall's, The Atlantic, Harpers;* film critic, *New Yorker,* 1968—.

AWARDS: Guggenheim Fellowship, 1964; George Polk Memorial Award for Criticism, 1970; National Book Award, 1974, for *Deeper into the Movies;* Front Page Award, Newswomen's Club, Best Magazine Column, 1974; Front Page Award, Newswomen's Club, Distinguished Journalism, 1983. Honorary degrees from Georgetown University 1972; Columbia College, Chicago, 1972; Smith College, 1973; Kalamazoo College, 1975; Haverford College, 1975; Allegheny College, 1979; School of Visual Arts, 1980; honorary member, Phi Beta Kappa, Radcliffe College, 1982.

ADDRESSES: OFFICE—*New Yorker,* 25 W. 43rd Street, New York, NY 10036.

*   *   *

KAGAN, Diane

PERSONAL: Daughter of Stanley W. (a real estate developer and mayor of Juno Beach, FL) and Natalie B. (a painter) Kagan. EDUCATION: Florida State University, B.A.; trained for the stage at the Martha Graham School of Dance with Martha Graham and at the Stella Adler Conservatory with Stella Adler.

VOCATION: Actress and writer.

CAREER: STAGE DEBUT—Title role, *Rosemary,* Spoleto Festival of Two Worlds, Spoleto, Italy. NEW YORK DEBUT—*The Chinese Prime Minister,* Royale Theatre, 1964. PRINCIPAL STAGE APPEARANCES—Broadway productions: Ellen, *Any Wednesday;* Jane, *Vieux Carre; Never Too Late; A Doll's House,* Thea, *Hedda Gabler.* At Lincoln Center: *Macbeth; Little Black Sheep;* Helen of Troy, *Tiger at the Gates.*

Off-Broadway productions: *The Family,* Chelsea Theatre, NY; *Alive and Well in Argentina,* St. Clements Theatre, NY; *Emma Instigated Me,* American Place Theatre, NY; *Luminosity,* Manhattan Theatre Club, NY; *High Time and on the Rocks,* WPA Theatre, NY; also appeared in *Scenes from Everyday Life; Asylum; The Days and Nights of Beebe Fenstermaker;* and in the title role in *Madame De Sade.*

Regionally, has appeared in *Whose Life Is It Anyway?,* Burt Rey-

DIANE KAGAN

nolds' Jupiter Theatre, FL; Blanche, *Streetcar Named Desire*, Arena Stage, Washington, DC; *Shivaree*, Long Wharf Theatre, New Haven, CT; Viola, *Twelfth Night*, Playhouse in the Park, Cincinnati, OH; *Man on a Fence*, Seattle Repertory, WA; and in these stock productions: *Poor Richard*, Pocono Playhouse; *Here Lies Jeremy Troy; The Whole Ninth Floor.*

TELEVISION DEBUT—Rose Long, *Huey Long*, NBC. PRINCIPAL TELEVISION APPEARANCES—Movies: *The Art of Crime*, NBC, 1975; *A Circle of Children*, CBS, 1977; *Mother Seton*, ABC, 1981; also appeared in "Barn Burning," *American Short Story*, PBS.

Episodic: *The Best of Everything*, ABC; *Andros Targets*, CBS; *Another World*, NBC; *The Edge of Night*, ABC; *Search for Tomorrow.*

WRITINGS: PLAYS—*Marvelous Gray*, O'Neill Playwright's Conference, Waterford, CT, 1982; then Lion Theatre Company, NY; *Man on a Fence*, O'Neill Playwright's Conference.

BOOKS—*Who Won Second Place at Omaha?*, Random House.

MEMBER: Actors' Equity Association, Screen Actors Guild, American Federation of Television and Radio Artists, New Dramatists, Dramatists Guild, Women's Project of the American Place Theatre.

AWARDS: Harvard Playwrights' Fellowship, 1984-85.

SIDELIGHTS: FAVORITE ROLES—Blanche, *Streetcar Named Desire;* Viola, *Twelfth Night.*

ADDRESSES: AGENT—Triad Artists, 888 Seventh Avenue, New York, NY 10106.

*   *   *

KAHN, Madeline   1942-

PERSONAL: Born Madeline Gail Wolfson, September 29, 1942, in Boston, MA; daughter of Bernard B. and Paula (Kahn) Wolfson. EDUCATION: Hofstra University, B.A., 1964.

VOCATION: Actress.

CAREER: PRINCIPAL STAGE APPEARANCES—Revue performer, various Julius Monk reviews, Upstairs at the Downstairs, NY, 1966-67; revue performer, *New Faces of 1968*, NY, 1968; Old Lady, *Candide in Concert*, Philharmonic Hall, NY, 1968; *Promenade*, Promenade Theatre, NY, 1969; Goldie, *Two by Two*, Imperial Theatre, NY, 1970-71; *In the Boom Boom Room*, Vivian Beaumont Theatre, Lincoln Center, NY, 1973; Lily, *On the Twentieth Century*, St. James Theatre, NY, 1978; Madame Arcati, *Blithe Spirit*, Santa Fe Festival Theatre, New Mexico, 1983; Shirley, *What's Wrong with This Picture*, Manhattan Theatre Club, Downstage Theatre, NY, 1985.

FILM DEBUT—Eunice, *What's up, Doc?*, Warner Brothers, 1972. PRINCIPAL FILM APPEARANCES—*Paper Moon*, Paramount, 1973; Lily von Schlump, *Blazing Saddles*, Warner Brothers, 1974; the bride, *Young Frankenstein*, Twentieth Century-Fox, 1974; Kitty O'Kelly, *At Long Last Love*, Twentieth Century-Fox, 1975; *The Adventures of Sherlock Holmes' Smarter Brother*, Twentieth Century-Fox, 1975; *Won-Ton-Ton, the Dog Who Saved Hollywood*, Paramount, 1976; *High Anxiety*, Twentieth Century-Fox, 1977; *The Cheap Detective*, Columbia, 1978; Simon, Warner Brothers, 1980; *Happy Birthday, Gemini*, United Artists, 1980; *The First Family*, Warner Brothers, 1980; *A History of the World, Part I*, Twentieth Century-Fox, 1981; *Yellowbeard*, Orion, 1983; Caroline Houten, *City Heat*, Warner Brothers, 1984; Mrs. White, *Clue*, Paramount, 1985.

PRINCIPAL TELEVISION APPEARANCES—Series: Regular, *Comedy Tonight*, CBS, 1970; title role, *Oh, Madeline*, ABC, 1983.

Guest: *The Carol Burnett Show; Comic Relief*, HBO, 1986, others.

Video: The women, *Scrambled Feet*, 1984.

RECORDINGS: ALBUMS—*Two Revues*, original cast recording; *New Faces of 1968*, original cast recording; *Two by Two*, original cast recording, Columbia; *On the Twentieth Century*, original soundtrack recording; *At Long Last Love*, original cast recording, Twentieth Century-Fox.*

*   *   *

KANALY, Steve   1946-

PERSONAL: Full name Steven Francis Kanaly; born March 14, 1946, in Burbank, CA; son of Lowell Francis and Marjorie Bell (Hinds) Kanaly; married Brent Elizabeth Power, March 27, 1975; children: Quinn Kathryn, Evan Elizabeth. EDUCATION: Attended Pierce College and California State University at Northridge; trained for the stage and film at the Film Industry Workshop and with Victor French and Stella Adler. MILITARY: U.S. Army, 1966-68.

STEVE KANALY

VOCATION: Actor.

CAREER: TELEVISION DEBUT—*Chase*, ABC, 1973. PRINCIPAL TELEVISION APPEARANCES—Series: Ray Krebbs, *Dallas*, CBS, 1978—.

Episodic: *Police Story; The Bionic Woman; Police Woman; The Love Boat; Charlie's Angels; Starsky and Hutch; Fantasy Island; Hotel.*

Movies: *Amelia Earhart*, 1976; *Melvin Purvis G Man*, 1974; *To Find My Son*, 1979; also, *Young Joe, the Forgotten Kennedy; He Wants Her Back*, PBS.

FILM DEBUT—*The Life and Times of Judge Roy Bean*, National General, 1970. PRINCIPAL FILM APPEARANCES—Pretty Boy Floyd, *Dillinger*, American International, 1973; *Sugarland Express*, Universal, 1974; *My Name Is Nobody*, Universal, 1974; *Terminal Man*, Warner Brothers, 1974; Captain Jerome, *The Wind and the Lion*, United Artists/Metro-Goldwyn-Mayer, 1975; *Midway*, 1976; *Big Wednesday*, Warner Brothers, 1978; *Fear in a Handful of Dust*, 1983; *Fleshburn*, Warner Brothers, 1984.

STAGE DEBUT—Slim, *Of Mice and Men*, Will Geer's Theatrical Botanicum, 1975, for twelve performances.

MEMBER: Screen Actors Guild, American Federation of Television and Radio Artists.

AWARDS: Best Supporting Actor, two *Soap Opera Digest* awards, for *Dallas.*

SIDELIGHTS: RECREATIONS—Painting, piano, gardening, tennis, skiing, hunting, fishing and archery.

CTFT learned that Kanaly is the founder and producer of the annual Steve Kanaly Celebrity Ski Classic benefiting the March of Dimes. He is the owner of the Los Desperados Cattle Company.

ADDRESSES: OFFICE—c/o Michael B. Druxman, P.O. Box 8086, Calabasas, CA 91302. AGENT—Paul Kohner Agency, 9169 Sunset Blvd., Los Angeles, CA 90069.

*   *   *

KAPLAN, Gabe   1945-

PERSONAL: Full name, Gabriel Kaplan; born March 31, 1945, in Brooklyn, New York; son of Charles and Dorothy Kaplan.

VOCATION: Actor and comedian.

CAREER: PRINCIPAL FILM APPEARANCES—*Fast Break*, Columbia, 1979; *Nobody's Perfekt*, Columbia, 1981; *Tulips* (Canadian), 1981.

PRINCIPAL TELEVISION APPEARANCES—Series: Gabe Kotter, *Welcome Back, Kotter*, ABC, 1975-79.

Specials: *Gabriel Kaplan Presents the Future Stars.*

Movies: *The Love Boat*, 1976; *Lewis and Clark*, 1981.

Guest: *The Tonight Show; The Merv Griffin Show; The Mike Douglas Show;* others.

RECORDINGS: COMEDY—*Holes and Mellow Rolls*, 1974.

MEMBER: American Federation of Television and Radio Artists, Screen Actors Guild; Cystic Fibrosis Foundation (national chairman, 1977).

ADDRESSES: AGENT—Creative Artists Agency, 1888 Century Park E., Suite 1400, Los Angeles, CA 90067.*

*   *   *

KASARDA, John   1943-

PERSONAL: Born June 8, 1943, in Chicago, IL; married Nora Peterson, April 18, 1979; chidren: Andrei, Kevin. EDUCATION: State University of Iowa, B.A., 1966; Carnegie Institute of Technology, M.F.A., 1968.

VOCATION: Designer and film art designer.

CAREER: FIRST STAGE WORK—Assistant designer, *Two Gentlemen of Verona*, St. James Theatre, NY, 1972.

FIRST FILM WORK—Assistant art director, *The Wiz*, Universal, 1978. PRINCIPAL FILM WORK—Assistant art director, *Eyewitness*, Twentieth Century-Fox, 1981; art director, *The Verdict*, Twentieth Century-Fox, 1982; assistant art director, *Purple Rose of Cairo*, Orion, 1985; assistant art director, *The Money Pit*, Universal, 1986; art director, *Heartburn*, 1986.

PRINCIPAL TELEVISION WORK—Art director, *Death of a Salesman*, CBS, 1985.

MEMBER: United Scenic Artists.

ADDRESSES: OFFICE—2255 Broadway, Room 308, New York, NY 10024.

* * *

KATT, William   1951-

PERSONAL: Born February 16, 1951; son of Bill Williams (an actor) and Barbara Hale (an actress) Katt; married Deborah Kahane, July 22, 1979; children: Clayton Alexander, Emerson Hunter. EDUCATION: Attended Orange Coast College; trained for the stage with the Los Angeles Civic Light Opera Workshop. POLITICS: Democrat. MILITARY: U.S. Air National Guard.

VOCATION: Actor.

CAREER: FILM DEBUT—Tommy Ross, *Carrie*, United Artists, 1976. PRINCIPAL FILM APPEARANCES—*First Love*, UMC Pictures, 1977; *Big Wednesday*, Warner Brothers, 1978; Sundance, *Butch and Sundance, the Early Years*, Twentieth Century-Fox, 1978; *Baby, Secret of a Lost Legend*, Buena Vista, 1985; *House*, New World, 1986.

TELEVISION DEBUT—Young marine, *Night Chase*, 1970. PRINCIPAL TELEVISION APPEARANCES—Series: Ralph Hinkley (Hanley), *Greatest American Hero*, ABC, 1980-82.

Movies: Paul Drake, Jr., *Perry Mason Returns*, NBC, 1985; Paul Drake, Jr., *Perry Mason: The Case of the Notorious Nun*, NBC, 1986.

STAGE DEBUT—Young Fisher, *We Bombed in New Haven*, South Coast Repertory, Orange County, CA, 1969. NEW YORK DEBUT—Serge, *Bon Jour La Bon Jour*, Phoenix Repertory, 1979. PRINCIPAL STAGE APPEARANCES—Rolf, *The Sound of Music*, Dorothy Chandler Pavilion, Los Angeles, CA, 1972; *Cyrano de Bergerac*, 1973; Too Much Johnson, *Shadow Box*, Mark Taper Forum, Los Angeles, CA, 1975.

MAJOR TOURS—Rolf, *The Sound of Music*, U.S. cities, 1972.

AWARDS: Best Actor, Drama Critics Circle Award, 1979, for *Bon Jour La Bon Jour*.

ADDRESSES: AGENT—c/o Todd Smith, Creative Artists Agency, 1888 Century Park E., Suite 1400, Los Angeles, CA 90067.

* * *

KAYE, Danny   1913-

PERSONAL: Born Daniel Kominski, January 18, 1913, in New York, NY; son of Jacob and Clara (Memorovsky) Kominski; married Sylvia Fine, January 3, 1940; children: Dena. EDUCATION: Attended public schools in Brooklyn, NY.

VOCATION: Actor, comedian, singer, and conductor.

CAREER: STAGE DEBUT—*La Vie Paris*, vaudeville revue touring United States and Asia. NEW YORK DEBUT—*Left of Broadway*, Keynote Stage, 1939. PRINCIPAL STAGE APPEARANCES—Cabaret performances at the Dorchester Hotel in London, England; *The Straw Hat Revue*, Ambassador Theatre, NY, 1939; Russell Paxton,

Lady in the Dark, Alvin Theatre, NY, 1941; vaudeville revue at the Palace Theatre, NY, 1941; Jerry Walker, *Let's Face It*, Imperial Theatre, NY, 1941; vaudeville revue at the Palladium, London, 1948; the "Royal Variety" performances, Palladium, London, 1948-52.

Appeared in variety performances: Canadian National Exposition, 1950; Curran Theatre, San Francisco, 1952; Palace Theatre, NY, 1953; Shubert Theatre, Detroit, MI, 1955; Greek Theatre, Los Angeles, 1958; Curran Theatre, San Francisco, 1959; in Sydney and Melbourne, Australia, 1959; Framingham, MA, 1961; Ziegfeld Theatre, NY, 1963.

Noah, *Two by Two*, Imperial Theatre, NY, 1970-71; host, *Opera Laugh-In*, Metropolitan Opera, NY, 1973; also appeared on Broadway in *The Play's the Thing; Death Takes a Holiday*.

MAJOR TOURS—With Abe Lyman's band, throughout United States; for the USO, Vietnam war fronts, 1966.

CONDUCTOR—Benefit concert, New York Philharmonic, 1965; charity concert, London Symphony Orchestra, 1975.

FILM DEBUT—*Up in Arms*, 1944. PRINCIPAL FILM APPEARANCES—*Wonder Man*, 1945; *Kid from Brooklyn*, 1946; *The Secret Life of Walter Mitty*, 1947; *A Song Is Born*, 1947; *The Inspector-General*, 1949; *On the Riviera*, 1951; title role, *Hans Christian Andersen*, 1952; *Knock on Wood*, 1954; *White Christmas*, 1954; *The Court Jester*, Paramount, 1958; title role, *Merry Andrew*, Metro-Goldwyn-Mayer, 1958; *Me and the Colonel*, Columbia, 1958; *The Five Pennies*, Columbia, 1959; *On the Double*, Paramount, 1961; *The Man from the Diner's Club*, Columbia, 1963; *The Madwoman of Chaillot*, Warner Brothers, 1969.

PRINCIPAL TELEVISION APPEARANCES—Series: *The Danny Kaye Show*, CBS, 1963-67.

Movie: *Skokie*, 1981.

Episodic: Dentist, *Bill Cosby Show*, NBC, 1986.

Guest: *John Gary Show*, CBS, 1966; *Dick Clark's Live Wednesday*, NBC, 1978.

Specials: *The Secret Life of Danny Kaye;* "Emperor's New Clothes," *Monday Night Special*, ABC, 1972; *Opera Laugh-In*, 1975; *Pinocchio*, 1976.

MEMBER: Lambs Club.

AWARDS: Special Academy Award, 1954; Outstanding Performance in a Variety or Musical Program or Series, Emmy, 1963-64, for *The Danny Kaye Show;* Peabody, 1963, for *The Danny Kaye Show;* Ambassador-at-Large, United Nations Children's Fund (UNICEF), first award for Distinguished Service from the United Nations Children's Fund; Scopus Laureate, 1977; Wateler Peace Price, Carnegie Foundation, 1981; Honorary Doctor of Humane Letters, Colgate University.

SIDELIGHTS: Danny Kaye's original intention was to enter the medical profession. He is an owner of the Seattle Mariner's baseball team.

ADDRESSES: HOME—Beverly Hills, CA. OFFICE—P.O. Box 750, Beverly Hills, CA 90213.*

KAZAN, Elia 1909-

PERSONAL: Born Elia Kazanjoglou, September 7, 1909, in Constantinople, Turkey; son of George and Athena (Sismanoglou) Kazanjoglou; married Molly Day Thatcher, December 2, 1932 (died); married Barbara Loden (an actress), June 5, 1967 (died); married Frances Rudge, June 28, 1982; children: (first marriage) Judy, Chris, Nick, Katherine. EDUCATION: Williams College, B.A., 1930; Wesleyan University, M.F.A.; Yale University (postgraduate work).

VOCATION: Director, producer, actor, and writer.

CAREER: STAGE DEBUT—Stage manager/understudy, *The Pure in Heart,* Theatre Guild Production, Ford's Theatre, Baltimore, 1932. PRINCIPAL STAGE APPEARANCES—*Men in White,* Broadway production, 1933; Agate, *Waiting for Lefty,* Group Theatre Production on Broadway, 1935; Baum/prisoner, *Till the Day I Die* and Kewpie, *Paradise Lost,* both Group Theatre Production, Longacre Theatre, NY, 1935; Private Harwood (a Texas cowpuncher)/Dr. Frewd, *Johnny Johnson,* Group Theatre Production, 44th Street Theatre, NY, 1936; Eddie Fusseli, *Golden Boy,* Group Theatre Production, Belasco Theatre, NY, 1937; *The Gentle People,* Broadway production, 1939; others.

PRINCIPAL STAGE WORK—Director: *The Skin of Our Teeth,* Broadway production, 1942; *Harriet,* Broadway production, 1943; *Jacobowsky and the Colonel,* Broadway production, 1944; *Deep Are the Roots,* Broadway production, 1945; *All My Sons,* Broadway production, 1947; *A Streetcar Named Desire,* Broadway production, 1947; *Death of a Salesman,* Broadway production, 1949; *Camino Real,* Broadway production, 1953; *Tea and Sympathy,* Broadway production, 1954; *Cat on a Hot Tin Roof,* Broadway production, 1955; *The Dark at the Top of the Stairs,* Broadway production, 1957; *J.B.,* Broadway production, 1958, *Sweet Bird of Youth,* Broadway production, 1959; *After the Fall, But for Whom, Charlie?,* and *The Changeling,* American National Theatre and Academy (ANTA), Washington Square, NY, 1964 (the last three for the inaugural season of the Lincoln Center Repertory Theatre).

PRINCIPAL FILM APPEARANCES—*Blues in the Night,* Warner Brothers, 1941; *City for Conquest,* Warner Brothers, 1941; others.

PRINCIPAL FILM WORK—Director: *A Tree Grows in Brooklyn,* Twentieth Century-Fox, 1945; *Boomerang,* Twentieth Century-Fox, 1947; *Gentleman's Agreement,* Twentieth Century-Fox, 1947; *Pinky,* Twentieth Century-Fox, 1949; *Panic in the Streets,* Twentieth Century-Fox, 1950; *A Streetcar Named Desire,* Warner Brothers, 1951; *Viva Zapata,* Twentieth Century-Fox, 1953; *Man on a Tightrope,* Twentieth Century-Fox, 1953; *On the Waterfront,* Columbia, 1954; *East of Eden,* Warner Brothers, 1954; *Baby Doll,* Warner Brothers, 1956; *A Face in the Crowd,* Warner Brothers, 1957; *Wild River,* Twentieth Century-Fox, 1960; *Splendor in the Grass,* Warner Brothers, 1961; *America, America* (also known as *The Anatolian Smile*), Warner Brothers, 1963; *The Arrangement,* Warner Brothers, 1969; *The Assassins,* 1972; *The Visitors,* 1972; *The Understudy,* 1974; *The Last Tycoon,* Paramount, 1976; *Acts of Love,* 1978; *The Anatolian,* 1982.

Producer: *A Streetcar Named Desire,* Warner Brothers, 1951; *Baby Doll,* Warner Brothers, 1956; *A Face in the Crowd,* Warner Brothers, 1957; *Wild River,* Twentieth Century-Fox, 1960; *Splendor in the Grass,* Warner Brothers, 1961; *America, America,* Warner Brothers, 1963; *The Arrangement,* Warner Brothers, 1969; *The Assassins,* 1972; *The Understudy,* 1974; *Acts of Love,* 1978; *The Anatolian,* 1982.

WRITINGS: FICTION—*America, America,* Stein and Day, 1962; *The Arrangement,* 1968.

SCREENPLAY—*America, America,* Warner Brothers, 1963.

AWARDS: Best Director, Antoinette Perry Award, *J.B.,* 1958; Best Director, Academy Awards, 1947, for *Gentleman's Agreement* and 1954, for *On the Waterfront;* Best Director, Academy Award nominations, 1951, for *A Streetcar Named Desire,* 1955, for *East of Eden,* 1963, for *America, America;* Academy Award nominations, Best Picture and Best Story and Screenplay Written Directly for the Screen, 1963, for *America, America.*

ADDRESSES: OFFICE—432 W. 44th Street, New York, NY 10036.*

*   *   *

KEAL, Anita

PERSONAL: Born Anita Kirshbaum, February 19, in Philadelphia, PA; daughter of Abe (a businessman) and Eva Z. (Acharenko) Kirshbaum; married Morton Wolkowitz (a business executive and producer), December 22, 1951; children: Michael, Ruth. EDUCATION: Syracuse University, B.A., 1951; trained for the stage with Uta Hagen, Allan Miller, and Michael Howard.

VOCATION: Actress.

CAREER: STAGE DEBUT—Mrs. Manningham, *Angel Street,* Pris-

ANITA KEAL

cilla Beach Theatre, MA, 1950, for eight performances. NEW YORK DEBUT—Servant girl, *Private Life of Master Race*, Open State Theatre, 1954, for more than 160 performances. PRINCIPAL STAGE APPEARANCES—Dol Common, *The Alchemist*, White Friars Theatre, NY, 1953; the whore, *Ricky*, Theatrewrights, NY, 1954; Bianca, *Affairs of Anatol*, Directors Theatre, NY, 1955; serving maid, *Brothers Karamazov*, Gate Theatre, NY, 1956; Thea Elvsted, *Hedda Gabler*, Fourth Street Theatre, NY, 1960; Lady Helene, *The Witches Sabbath*, Madison Avenue Playhouse, NY, 1961; Connie, *Yes, My Darling Daughter*, Equity Library Theatre, NY, 1968; Mommy, *The Kindness of Strangers*, Roundabout Theatre, NY, 1968.

Alice, *Play Strindberg*, Impossible Ragtime Theatre, NY, 1975; *My Friend Weissman Is Back*, Chelsea Theatre, NY, 1975; Dot, *You Didn't Have to Tell Me*, Ensemble Studio Theatre, NY, 1976; Lady, *Orpheus Descending*, Morgan's Theatre, NY, 1977; Margo, *A Late Show*, Playwright's Horizons, NY, 1978; Dr. Petrelli, Maggie, and Hilary, *Tribute*, Brooks Atkinson Theatre, NY, 1978; mother, *Getting Out*, Theatre de Lys, NY, 1979; Kitty Cochrane, *Last Summer at Bluefish Cove*, Mainstate Theatre, NY, 1980; Elsie, *Do You Still Believe the Rumor*, ARTC Theatre, NY, 1980; mother, *Farmyard by Kroetz*, Theatre for the New City, 1981; Sylvia Plath, *A Difficult Borning*, ARTC, NY, 1982; Grappina, *The Raspberry Picker*, 92nd Street YWHA Theatre, NY, 1982; Harriet, *Grievances*, Real Stage, 1982; May, *Fish Riding Bikes*, Women's Interart Theatre, NY, 1983; Tasha, *Isn't It Romantic*, Playwrights' Horizons, NY, 1984; Mrs. Horowitz, *Haven*, South Street Theatre, NY, 1985; Lillian, *The Affair*, ARTC, 1985.

Regional: Charlotta, *The Cherry Orchard*, Center Stage, Baltimore, MD, 1975; Tasha, *Isn't It Romantic*, Caldwell Playhouse, NJ, 1984; Maddy, *Family Affair*, Dorset Theatre Festival, 1985.

MAJOR TOURS—Madame Pace, *Six Characters in Search of an Author*, U.S. cities, 1965; Dr. Petrelli, *Tribute*, U.S. cities, 1980.

PRINCIPAL TELEVISION APPEARANCES—Series: Mignon, *Search for Tomorrow*, 1979-81; Trude, *Guiding Light*.

Episodic: *Kojak; Joe Forrester; How to Survive a Marriage; The Doctors; Man Behind the Badge; Seven Lively Arts.*

MEMBER: Actors' Equity Association, Screen Actors Guild, American Federation of Television and Radio Artists; Zeta Phi Eta (National Women's Speech Fraternity).

SIDELIGHTS: RECREATIONS—Playing guitar and singing folk songs.

ADDRESSES: HOME—New York, NY.

*   *   *

KEITH, Penelope

PERSONAL: Born Penelope Hatfield, in Sutton, Surrey, England; daughter of Arthur Walter and Constance Mary (Nutting) Hatfield; married Rodney Timson. EDUCATION: Attended Annecy Convent in Seaford Sussex and at Bayeux; studied acting at the Webber-Douglas Academy of Dramatic Art.

VOCATION: Actress.

CAREER: STAGE DEBUT—Alice Pepper, *The Tunnel of Love,*

PENELOPE KEITH

Civic Theatre, Chesterfield, England, 1959. LONDON DEBUT—Simcox's wife/Lord Mayor's wife, *The Wars of the Roses*, with the Royal Shakespeare Company at the Aldwych Theatre, 1964. PRINCIPAL STAGE APPEARANCES—Big Molly, *Ballad of the False Barman*, Hampstead Theatre, London, 1966; Tiny Cruise-Orb, *Mr. Kilt and the Great I Am*, Hampstead Theatre, London, 1970; Maggie Howard, *Suddenly at Home*, Fortune Theatre, London, 1971; Magdalena, *The House of Bernada Alba* and Ilona, *Catsplay*, both at Greenwich Theatre, London, 1973; Julia, *Fallen Angels*, Palace Theatre, Watford, 1974; Sarah, *The Norman Conquests* (trilogy), Greenwich Theatre, then Globe Theatre, London, 1974; reader, *Sweet Mr. Shakespeare*, Open Air Theatre, Regents Park, London, 1975; Lady Driver, *Donkey's Years*, Globe Theatre, London, 1976; Orinthia, *The Apple Cart*, Chichester Festival, 1977; Orinthia, *The Apple Cart*, Phoenix Theatre, London, 1977; Epifania, *The Millionairess*, Haymarket Theatre, London, 1978; *Moving*, Queens' Theatre, London, 1986; and in the West End, London, productions: *Hobson's Choice*, 1986; *Captain Brassbound's Conversion*, 1986; *Hay Fever*, 1986.

PRINCIPAL FILM APPEARANCES—*Every Home Should Have One* (titled *Think Dirty* in United States), 1970; *Take a Girl Like You*, Columbia, 1970; *Penny Gold.*

PRINCIPAL TELEVISION APPEARANCES—Series: *Kate; The Good Life; To The Manor Born; Executive Stress.*

Teleplays: *Private Lives; The Norman Conquests; Donkey's Years.*

AWARDS: Variety Club and Society of West End Theatre Awards, 1977, for *Donkey's Years.*

SIDELIGHTS: RECREATION—Gardening, bridge, and theatre-going.

ADDRESSES: AGENT—Howes and Prior, 66 Berkeley House, Hay Hill, London W1, England.

*   *   *

KELLEY, DeForest   1920-

PERSONAL: Born January 20, 1920, in Atlanta, GA.

VOCATION: Actor.

CAREER: PRINCIPAL FILM APPEARANCES—*Variety Girl,* Paramount, 1947; *Fear in the Night,* Maxwell Shane Films, 1947; *Canon City,* Eagle Lion, 1948; *Duke of Chicago,* 1950; *House of Bamboo,* Twentieth Century-Fox, 1955; *The Man in the Grey Flannel Suit,* Twentieth Century-Fox, 1956; *Tension at Table Rock,* Universal, 1956; *Gunfight at the O.K. Corral,* Paramount, 1957; *Raintree County,* Metro-Goldwyn-Mayer, 1958; *The Law and Jake Wade,* Metro-Goldwyn-Mayer, 1958; *Warlock,* Twentieth Century-Fox, 1959; *Where Love Has Gone,* Paramount, 1964; *Marriage on the Rocks,* Warner Brothers, 1965; *Johnny Reno,* Paramount, 1966; Dr. Leonard McCoy, *Star Trek: The Motion Picture,* Paramount, 1979; Dr. McCoy, *Star Trek II: The Wrath of Khan,* Paramount, 1982; Dr. McCoy, *Star Trek III: The Search for Spock,* Paramount, 1984; Dr. McCoy, *Star Trek IV: The Voyage Home,* Paramount, 1986.

PRINCIPAL TELEVISION APPEARANCES—Dr. Leonard McCoy, *Star Trek,* NBC, 1966-1969.

ADDRESSES: AGENT—Contemporary-Korman Artists, 132 Lasky Drive, Beverly Hills, CA 90212.*

*   *   *

KELLY, Gene   1912-

PERSONAL: Full name, Eugene Curran Kelly; born August 23, 1912, in Pittsburgh, PA; son of James Patrick Joseph and Harriet Curran (an actress) Kelly; married Betsy Blair (an actress), September 22, 1941 (divorced, 1957); married Jeanne Coyne (an actress), August 6, 1960 (died, 1973); children: (first marriage) Kerry; (second marriage) Timothy, Bridget. EDUCATION: University of Pittsburgh, B.A., 1933. MILITARY: U.S. Naval Air Service, 1944-46.

VOCATION: Actor, dancer, choreographer, and director.

CAREER: DEBUT—As part of a dance act with brother Fred Kelly, Chicago World's Fair, 1934-36. NEW YORK DEBUT—Dancer, *Leave It to Me,* Imperial Theatre, November 21, 1938. PRINCIPAL STAGE APPEARANCES—Revue performer, *Hold Your Hats,* Pittsburgh Playhouse, Pittsburgh, PA, 1938; revue performer, *One For the Money,* 1939; Harry, *The Time of Your Life,* Theatre Guild Production, Booth Theatre, NY, 1939; Joey Evans, *Pal Joey,* Ethel Barrymore Theatre, NY, 1941.

PRINCIPAL STAGE WORK—Dance director, *Hold Your Hats,* Pittsburgh Playhouse, 1938; choreographer, *The Emperor Jones* and a revue, both at the Westport Summer Theatre, Westport, CT, 1938; choreographer, *Green Grow the Lilacs,* Westport Summer Theatre, 1939; dance director, *Billy Rose's Diamond Horseshoe Revue,* NY, 1939-40; choreographer, *Best Foot Forward,* Broadway production, 1941; director, *Flower Drum Song,* St. James Theatre, NY, 1958.

FILM DEBUT—Harry Palmer, *For Me and My Gal,* Metro-Goldwyn-Mayer, 1942. PRINCIPAL FILM APPEARANCES—Vito S. Allesandro, *Pilot No. 5,* Metro-Goldwyn-Mayer, 1942; Alec Howe/Black Arrow, *DuBarry Was a Lady,* Metro-Goldwyn-Mayer, 1943; Eddy Marsh, *Thousands Cheer,* Metro-Goldwyn-Mayer, 1943; Victor, *The Cross of Lorraine,* Metro-Goldwyn-Mayer, 1943; Danny McGuire, *Cover Girl,* Columbia, 1944; Robert Manette, *Christmas Holiday,* Universal, 1944; Joseph Brady, *Anchors Aweigh,* Metro-Goldwyn-Mayer, 1945; *Ziegfeld Follies,* Metro-Goldwyn-Mayer, 1945; Leo Gogarty, *Living in a Big Way,* Metro-Goldwyn-Mayer, 1947; Serafin, *The Pirate,* Metro-Goldwyn-Mayer, 1948; d'Artagnan, *The Three Musketeers,* Metro-Goldwyn-Mayer, 1948; "Slaughter on Tenth Avenue" segment of *Words and Music,* Metro-Goldwyn-Mayer, 1948; Eddie O'Brien, *Take Me Out to the Ball Game,* Metro-Goldwyn-Mayer, 1949; Gabey, *On the Town,* Metro-Goldwyn-Mayer, 1949; Johnny Columbo, *The Black Hand,* Metro-Goldwyn-Mayer, 1949.

Joe D. Ross, *Summer Stock,* Metro-Goldwyn-Mayer, 1950; Jerry Mulligan, *An American in Paris,* Metro-Goldwyn-Mayer, 1951; Icarus Xenophon, *It's a Big Country,* Metro-Goldwyn-Mayer, 1952; Don Lockwood, *Singin' in the Rain,* Metro-Goldwyn-Mayer, 1952; Capt. Jeff Eliot, *The Devil Makes Three,* Metro-Goldwyn-Mayer, 1952; Tommy Albright, *Brigadoon,* Metro-Goldwyn-Mayer, 1954; Lieutenant Bradville, *Crest of the Wave,* Metro-Goldwyn-Mayer, 1954; specialty routine with his brother Fred Kelly, *Deep in My Heart,* Metro-Goldwyn-Mayer, 1955; Ted Riley, *It's Always Fair Weather,* Metro-Goldwyn-Mayer, 1955; the clown/the marine/Sinbad, *Invitation to the Dance,* Metro-Goldwyn-Mayer, 1956; Mike Andrews, *The Happy Road,* Metro-Goldwyn-Mayer, 1957; Barry Nichols, *Les Girls,* Metro-Goldwyn-Mayer, 1957; Noel Airman, *Marjorie Morningstar,* Beachwold/Warner Brothers, 1958.

E.K. Hornbeck, *Inherit the Wind,* United Artists, 1960; Gene Kelly, *Let's Make Love,* Twentieth Century-Fox, 1960; Jerry Benson, *What a Way to Go,* Twentieth Century-Fox, 1964; Andy Miller, *The Young Girls of Rochefort,* Seven Arts/Warner Brothers, 1968; Billy Boylan, *Forty Carats,* Columbia, 1973; co-narrator, *That's Entertainment!,* United Artists, 1974; co-narrator, *That's Entertainment, Part II,* United Artists, 1976; *Viva Knievel,* Warner Brothers, 1977; Danny McGuire, *Xanadu,* Universal, 1980; co-narrator, *That's Dancing!,* Metro-Goldwyn-Mayer/United Artists, 1985.

PRINCIPAL FILM WORK—Choreographer, *Cover Girl,* Columbia, 1944; choreographer, *Anchors Aweigh,* Metro-Goldwyn-Mayer, 1944; choreographer, *Livin' in a Big Way,* Metro-Goldwyn-Mayer, 1947; choreographer, *The Pirate,* 1948; choreographer, "Slaughter on Tenth Avenue" sequence of *Words and Music,* Metro-Goldwyn-Mayer, 1948; choreographer, *Take Me Out to the Ball Game,* Metro-Goldwyn-Mayer, 1949; choreographer and director (with Stanley Donen), *On the Town,* Metro-Goldwyn-Mayer, 1950; choreographer, *An American in Paris,* Metro-Goldwyn-Mayer, 1951; choreographer and director (with Stanley Donen), *Singin' in the Rain,* Metro-Goldwyn-Mayer, 1952; choreographer, *Brigadoon,* Metro-Goldwyn-Mayer, 1954; choreographer, "I Love to Go Swimmin' with Wimmen" sequence from *Deep in My Heart,* Metro-Goldwyn-Mayer, 1955; choreographer and director (with Stanley Donen), *It's Always Fair Weather,* Metro-Goldwyn-Mayer, 1955; choreographer and director, *Invitation to the Dance,* Metro-Goldwyn-Mayer, 1956; producer and director, *The Happy Road,* Metro-Goldwyn-Mayer, 1957; director, *The Tunnel of Love,* Metro-Goldwyn-Mayer, 1958; director, *Gigot,* Seven Arts/Twentieth Century-Fox, 1962; director, *A Guide for the Married Man,* Twentieth Century-Fox, 1967; director, *Hello, Dolly!,* Twentieth Century-Fox, 1969; producer and director, *The Cheyenne Social Club,* National General, 1970.

PRINCIPAL TELEVISION APPEARANCES—Series: Commentator, *The Gillette Summer Sports Reel*, NBC, 1954; Father Chuck O'Malley, *Going My Way*, ABC, 1962-63; host, *The Funny Side*, NBC, 1971.

Episodic: "The Life You Save," on *Schlitz Playhouse of Stars*, CBS, 1957.

Specials: Co-host, *The Academy Awards Presentation*, ABC, 1975.

Mini-Series: *North and South*, ABC, 1986.

WRITINGS: FILMS—Story (with Stanley Donen), *Take Me Out to the Ball Game*, Metro-Goldwyn-Mayer, 1948; screenplay, *Invitation to the Dance*, Metro-Goldwyn-Mayer, 1956.

RECORDINGS: For Me and My Gal, original soundtrack recording, Soundtrack; *The Pirate*, original soundtrack recording, Metro-Goldwyn-Mayer; *Summer Stock*, original soundtrack recording, Metro-Goldwyn-Mayer; *An American in Paris*, original soundtrack recording, Metro-Goldwyn-Mayer; *Singin' in the Rain*, original soundtrack recording, Metro-Goldwyn-Mayer; *Brigadoon*, original soundtrack recording, Metro-Goldwyn-Mayer; *Deep in My Heart*, original soundtrack recording, Metro-Goldwyn-Mayer; *It's Always Fair Weather*, original soundtrack recording, Metro-Goldwyn-Mayer; *Les Girls*, original soundtrack recording, Metro-Goldwyn-Mayer; others.

AWARDS: Best Actor, Academy Award nomination, 1945, for *Anchors Aweigh;* Special Academy Award for "brilliant achievements in the art of choreography on film," 1951; Cecil B. de Mille Award, 1981; Kennedy Center Lifetime Achievement Award, 1982; French Chevalier, Legion of Honor.

ADDRESSES: AGENT—Chasin-Park-Citron Agency, 9255 W. Sunset Blvd., Los Angeles, CA 90069.*

*   *   *

KENDAL, Felicity   1946-

PERSONAL: Born September 25, 1946 in Olton, Warwickshire, England; daughter of Geoffrey and Laura (Liddell) Kendal; married Drewe Henley (divorced); married Michael Rudman. EDUCATION: Attended six convents in India.

VOCATION: Actress.

CAREER: STAGE DEBUT—At age nine months, carried on as the Changeling Boy in *A Midsummer's Night Dream*, 1947. LONDON DEBUT—Carla, *Minor Murder*, Savoy Theatre, 1967. PRINCIPAL STAGE APPEARANCES—Appeared with her parents' theatre company as page boys, Puck, *A Midsummer's Night Dream*, Viola, *Twelfth Night*, Jessica, *The Merchant of Venice*, Ophelia, *Hamlet*, all touring Far East and India; Katherine, *Henry V* and Lika, *The Promise*, both Phoenix Theatre, Leicester, U.K., 1968; Amaryllis, *Back to Methuselah, Part II*, National Theatre at the Old Vic, London, 1969.

Hermia, *A Midsummer's Night Dream*, Hero, *Much Ado About Nothing*, and *The Lord Byron Show*, all Open Air Theatre, Regent's Park, London, 1970; Anne Danby, *Kean*, Oxford Playhouse, 1970, then Globe Theatre, 1971; Juliet, *Romeo and Juliet*, Oxford Playhouse, 1972; Annabella, *'Tis Pity She's a Whore*, Actors Company and at the Edinburgh Festival, Scotland, 1972; Annie, *The Norman*

Conquests, Greenwich Theatre, London, then Globe Theatre, 1974; Vitoshka, *Once Upon a Time*, Little Theatre, Bristol, 1976; Raina, *Arms and the Man*, Greenwich Theatre, London, 1978; Mara, *Clouds*, Duke of York's Theatre, London, 1978; Constanze, *Amadeus*, National Theatre at the Olivier, London, 1979.

Desdemona, *Othello*, National Theatre at the Olivier, London, 1980; Christopher, *On the Razzle* and title role, *The Second Mrs. Tanqueray*, both National Theatre, London, 1981-82; Annie, *The Real Thing*, Strand Theatre, London, 1982-83; Dorothy, *Jumpers*, London; Frances, *Made in Bangkok*, Aldwych Theatre, London, 1986.

PRINCIPAL FILM APPEARANCES—*Shakespeare Wallah*, 1964; *Valentino*, 1976.

PRINCIPAL TELEVISION APPEARANCES—Viola, *Twelfth Night*, 1979; *Edward VII*, BBC; *The Good Life*, BBC; *Solo; The Mistress*.

AWARDS: Most Promising Newcomer, Variety Club, 1974; Best Actress, Variety Club, 1979, for Mara, *Clouds;* Clarence Derwent Award, 1980.

SIDELIGHTS: RECREATIONS—"Holidays in France" and golf.

ADDRESSES: AGENT—Chatto and Linnit Ltd., Prince of Wales Theatre, Coventry Street, London W1, England.

*   *   *

KENNEDY, Arthur   1914-

PERSONAL: Born February 17, 1914, in Worcester, MA; son of Dr. J.T. and Helen (Thompson) Kennedy; married Mary Cheffey. EDUCATION: Attended Worcester Academy and the Carnegie Institute of Technology.

VOCATION: Actor.

CAREER: NEW YORK DEBUT—Bushy, *Richard II*, St. James Theatre, 1937. PRINCIPAL STAGE APPEARANCES—Sir Richard Vernon, *Henry IV, Part I*, St. James Theatre, NY, 1939; Jerry Dorgan, *Life and Death of an American*, Maxine Elliott Theatre, NY, 1939; Smithers, *International Incident*, Barrymore Theatre, NY, 1940; Chris Keller, *All My Sons*, Coronet Theatre, NY, 1947; Biff, *Death of a Salesman*, Morosco Theatre, NY, 1949-1950; Dave Ricks, *See the Jaguar*, Cort Theatre, NY, 1952; John Proctor, *The Crucible*, Martin Beck Theatre, NY, 1953; Lt. Colonel William Edwards, *Time Limit*, Booth Theatre, NY, 1956; Patrick Flannigan, *The Loud Red Patrick*, Ambassador Theatre, NY, 1956; title role, *Becket*, Hudson Theatre, NY, 1961; Walter Franz, *The Price*, Morosco Theatre, NY, 1968; Man, *Veronica's Room*, Music Box Theatre, NY, 1973.

FILM DEBUT—*City for Conquest*, 1940. PRINCIPAL FILM APPEARANCES—*They Died with Their Boots On*, 1941; *High Sierra*, 1941; *Strange Alibi*, 1941; *Knockout*, 1941; *Highway West*, 1943; *Air Force*, 1943; *Devotion*, 1946; *Boomerang*, 1947; *The Window*, 1949; *Chicago Deadline*, 1949; *Champion*, 1949; *The Glass Menagerie*, 1950; *Red Mountain*, 1951; *Bright Victory*, 1951; *Bend of the River*, 1952; *Rancho Notorious*, 1952; *Girl in White*, 1952; *Lusty Men*, 1952; *Man from Laramie*, Columbia, 1955; *Trail*, Metro-Goldwyn-Mayer, 1955; *Naked Dawn*, Universal, 1955; *The Desperate Hours*, Paramount, 1955; *Crashout*, Filmakers, 1955; *Rawhide Years*, Universal, 1956; *Peyton Place*, Twentieth Century-Fox, 1957; *Some Came Running*, Metro-Goldwyn-Mayer, 1959.

Elmer Gantry, United Artists, 1960; the father, *Claudelle Inglish,* Warner Brothers, 1961; *Adventures of a Young Man,* Twentieth Century-Fox, 1962; *Barabbas,* Columbia, 1962; *Lawrence of Arabia,* Columbia, 1962; *Italiano Brava Gente,* Embassy, 1965; *Fantastic Voyage,* Twentieth Century-Fox, 1966; *Stay Away Joe,* Metro-Goldwyn-Mayer, 1968; *A Minute to Pray, a Second to Die,* Cinerama, 1968; *Hail Hero,* National General, 1969; *Shark,* 1969; *My Old Man's Place,* 1972; *The Sentinel,* Universal, 1977.

PRINCIPAL TELEVISION APPEARANCES—Series: Narrator, *F.D.R.,* ABC, 1965; Sheriff Sam Jericho, *Nakia,* ABC, 1974.

Episodic: "People Need People," *Alcoa Premiere,* ABC, 1961; *Dupont Show of the Week,* NBC, 1963; *Espionage,* NBC, 1964.

MEMBER: Actors' Equity Association, Screen Actors Guild.*

*   *   *

KERBOSCH, Roeland   1940-

PERSONAL: Born December 19, 1940, in Amsterdam, Holland. EDUCATION: Graduate, Netherlands Film Academy, Amsterdam, 1962.

VOCATION. Film producer and director.

CAREER: PRINCIPAL FILM WORK—Producer, in Holland: *The Dream; Shots* (documentary); *The Ice-Cream Parlour; Diary from South Africa* (documentary); *Dreamland; More Than a Concert;* has directed many Dutch films.

ADDRESSES: HOME—Keizersgracht 678, 1017ET Amsterdam, Netherlands. AGENT—c/o Sheri Mann Agency, 8480 Beverly Blvd., Los Angeles, 90048.

ROELAND KERBOSCH

KEYSAR, Franklin   1939-

PERSONAL: Born January 22, 1939, in Warren, NH; son of Miles Herman (a mechanic) and Bertha Nellie (a nurse; maiden name, Snelgrove) Keysar. EDUCATION: Boston University, B.F.A., 1962.

VOCATION: Production stage manager.

CAREER: PRINCIPAL STAGE WORK—Production stage manager: *Division Street,* Ambassador Theatre, NY, 1980; *The Floating Light Bulb,* Vivian Beaumont Theatre, NY, 1981; *The Wake of Jamey Foster,* Eugene O'Neill Theatre, 1982; *Solomon's Child,* Little Theatre, NY, 1982; *The Curse of an Aching Heart,* Little Theatre, NY, 1982; *Passion,* Longacre Theatre, NY, 1983; *The Lady and the Clarinet,* Lucille Lortel Theatre, NY, 1983; *The Golden Age,* Jack Lawrence Theatre, NY, 1984; *Joe Egg,* Longacre Theatre, NY, 1985; *Corpse,* Helen Hayes Theatre, NY, 1986; earlier Broadway and Off-Broadway work includes: *Hughie/Duet; Strangers; Gorey Stories; The Shadow Box; Benno Blimpie; Park Your Car in Harvard Yard; Zelda.*

Also production stage manager for seven seasons at the Trinity Square Repertory Company, RI; three seasons at Long Wharf Theatre, New Haven, CT; one season at the Kenyon Theatre Festival, Gambier, OH; ten seasons with the Williamstown Theatre Festival, MA.

MAJOR TOUR WORK—Production stage manager, U.S. cities: *A Chorus Line; American Ballet Theatre.*

ADDRESSES: OFFICE—1257 Park Avenue, New York, NY 10029.

*   *   *

KILTY, Jerome   1922-

PERSONAL: Born June 24, 1922, on the Pala Indian Reservation, CA; son of Harold and Irene (Zellinger) Kilty; married Cavada Humphrey. EDUCATION: Attended Guildhall School of Drama, London, England, 1945-46; Harvard University, B.A., 1949.

VOCATION: Actor, director, writer, and educator.

CAREER: STAGE DEBUT—Walk-on, *Faust* (Max Reinhardt production), California, 1937. NEW YORK DEBUT—Coupler, *The Relapse,* Morosco Theatre, 1950. LONDON DEBUT—Bernard Shaw, *Dear Liar,* Criterion Theatre, 1960. PRINCIPAL STAGE APPEARANCES—King of Navarre, *Love's Labour's Lost* and Gunner, *Misalliance,* both New York City Drama Company at City Center, 1953; Mr. Ringwood, *A Pin to See the Peep Show,* Playhouse Theatre, NY, 1953; Asa McK Gelwicks, *The Frogs of Spring,* Broadhurst Theatre, NY, 1953; Reverend Edgar Spevin, *Quadrille,* Coronet Theatre, NY, 1954; Iago, *Othello,* with the Group 20 Players at the City Center, NY, 1955; Falstaff, *Henry IV, Part I,* City Center, NY, 1955; Benedick, *Much Ado About Nothing* and the Actor, *The Guardsman,* Studebaker Theatre, Chicago, 1957.

Bernard Shaw, *Dear Liar,* Marquee Theatre, NY, 1962; George, *Who's Afraid of Virginia Woolf?,* Piccadilly Theatre, London, 1964; title role, *Falstaff,* American Shakespeare Festival, Stratford, CT, 1966; Robert Browning, *Dear Love,* Alley Theatre, Houston, TX, 1970; Bernard Shaw, *Dear Liar,* Geary Theatre, San Francisco, 1967, then Roundabout Theater, NY, 1977; Walt Whitman, *Two-*

JEROME KILTY

Part Inventions, Goodman Theatre, Chicago, 1978; Trissotin, *Les Femmes Savantes,* California Actors Theatre, Costa Mesa, CA, 1979; title role, *Julius Caesar,* Old Globe Theatre, San Diego, CA, 1979; Arkady Islayev, *A Month in the Country,* Roundabout Theatre, 1979.

Bernard Shaw, *Dear Liar,* Roundabout Theatre, 1982; title role, *The Magistrate,* Hartman Stage Company, CT, 1982; Sir Oliver Surface, *A School for Scandal,* American Repertory Theatre, Cambridge, MA, 1983; the King, *Big River,* American Repertory Theatre, 1984; Phil Hogan, *A Moon for the Misbegotten,* Cort Theatre, NY, 1984; George Riley, *Enter a Free Man,* Perry Street Theatre, NY, 1984; Don Armado, *Love's Labour's Lost,* American Repertory Theatre, 1985; Gonzalo, *The Tempest,* Toby Belch, *Twelfth Night,* and Caesar and Bernard Shaw, *Androcles and the Lion,* all Hartford Stage Company, 1985; Hector Nations, *Foxfire,* Missouri Repertory Company, Kansas City, MO, 1985; Dr. Chebutykin, *The Three Sisters,* Hartman Theatre Company, Boston, MA, 1986.

MAJOR TOURS—Harry Kaye, *Will Success Spoil Rock Hunter,* national, 1955-56; George, *Who's Afraid of Virginia Woolf?,* South Africa, 1963; Robert Browning, *Dear Love,* national, 1971.

PRINCIPAL STAGE WORK—Director: *The Guardsman,* Studebaker Theatre, Chicago, 1957; *The Girl of the Golden West,* Phyllis Anderson Theatre, NY, 1957; (also adapted) *Dear Liar,* Renaissnace Theatre, Berlin, Germany, 1957, Billy Rose Theatre, NY, 1959, Athenee Theatre, Paris, France, 1961, German language version at the Barbizon-Plaza, NY, 1963, Geary Theatre, San Francisco,

1966, Huntington Hartford Theatre, Los Angeles, 1967, French version, Paris, 1974, Italian version, Rome, 1975, Roundabout Theatre, NY, 1982, Theatre de l'Athenee, Paris, 1983, and Teatro Belli Arte, Rome, 1984; *Les Violons Parfois,* Piccadilly Theatre, London, 1962 and Gymnase Theatre, Paris, 1963; *Die Iden des Maerz (The Ides of March),* Renaissance Theatre, Berlin, Germany, 1962, then co-director, Haymarket Theatre, London, 1963; *Saint Joan, Man and Superman,* and *The Ides of March,* all at the Boston Arts Festival, 1964; *Oh, What a Lovely War!* (Italian version), Quirino Theatre, Rome, 1964; *The Ides of March,* Quirino Theatre, 1965; *Antigone,* Amercian Shakespeare Festival, Stratford, CT, 1967; *Long Live Life,* American Conservatory Theatre, 1968; *Possibilities,* Player Theatre, NY, 1968; *Lascio Alle Mie Donne,* Teatro Nuovo, Milan, Italy, 1969; *Mrs. Warren's Profession,* Rome, 1976; *Julius Caesar,* Old Globe Theatre, San Diego, CA, 1979; *Love's Labour's Lost,* Old Globe Theatre, 1980; *Misalliance,* Denver Center Theatre, CO, 1981; *Whistler,* Provincetown Playhouse, NY, 1981; *The Millionairess,* Hartman Theatre Company, 1982; *Love's Labour Lost,* American Repertory Theatre, 1985; *Foxfire,* Missouri Repertory Company, 1985.

WRITINGS: PLAYS—*Dear Liar,* produced on Broadway in New York, London, Paris, Rome, Berlin, 1959—; adaptation of Thornton Wilder novel into German and English language play, *Die Iden des Maerz (The Ides of March),* premiered at the Renaissance Theatre, Berlin, Germany, 1962 (German language version) and at the Haymarket Theatre, London, England, 1963 (English language version); (co-author) revue, *Nymphs and Satires,* Apollo Theatre, London, 1965; *Don't Shoot Mabel, It's Your Husband,* San Francisco, 1967, New York, 1968; *Long Live Life,* American Conservatory Theatre, 1968; adapted works of Robert and Elizabeth Browning, *Dear Love,* Alley Theatre, 1970, Comedy Theatre, London, 1973; translation, *The Little Black Book,* Helen Hayes Theatre, NY, 1972; *Look Away,* Playhouse, NY, 1973; *The Laffing Man,* 1974.

MUSICALS, BOOK—*What the Devil,* 1977; *Barnum,* 1980.

RELATED CAREER—Co-founder, Brattle Theatre, Cambridge, MA, 1948-52; artistic director, director, actor, Group 20 Players, Wellesley, MA, 1955-60; associate director, American Conservatory Theatre, San Francisco, 1966-68; visiting actor and director at the Goodman Theatre, Chicago, Yale Repertory Theatre, New Haven, CT, and Alley Theatre, Houston, TX, 1967-69; visiting professor of drama, University of Oklahoma, 1971, University of Texas, 1972, and University of Kansas, 1973.

MEMBER: Actors' Equity Association, Screen Actors Guild, American Federation of Television and Radio Artists, Dramatists Guild; Players Club.

AWARDS: Berlin Festival Critics Award, 1961, for *Dear Liar;* Baton di Brigadier of France, 1961-62; Paume d'Or of Italy, 1962-63; Stanislavsky Centenary Medal, Moscow, 1963; holder of O'Conner Chair of Literature, Colgate University, 1974.

SIDELIGHTS: Jerome Kilty's favorite roles have been Bernard Shaw in *Dear Liar,* Falstaff, and Tartuffe. He enjoys gardening, reading, and horse racing. He has also appeared in and written for television.

ADDRESSES: OFFICE—P.O. Box, 1074, Weston, CT, 06880.

ALAN KING

KING, Alan　1927-

PERSONAL: Born Irwin Kniberg, December 26, 1927, in Brooklyn, NY; son of Bernard and Minnie (Solomon) Kniberg; married Jeanette Sprung, February 1, 1947; children: Robert, Andrew, Elaine.

VOCATION: Actor, comedian, and producer.

CAREER: PRINCIPAL STAGE APPEARANCES—*The Impossible Years,* Broadway production, 1965; *Something Different,* Broadway production, 1967; *Guys and Dolls,* City Center Theatre, NY.

PRINCIPAL STAGE WORK—Producer: *The Lion in Winter,* Broadway production, 1966; *Dinner at Eight,* Broadway production, 1966; *The Investigation,* Broadway production, 1966.

FILM DEBUT—*Helen Morgan Story,* Warner Brothers, 1957. PRINCIPAL FILM APPEARANCES—*The Anderson Tapes,* Columbia, 1971; *Just Tell Me What You Want,* Warner Brothers, 1980; *Author! Author!,* Twentieth Century-Fox, 1982; *I, The Jury,* 1982; *Cat's Eye,* 1983; *Lovesick,* Warner Brothers, 1983.

PRINCIPAL FILM WORK—Producer: *Happy Birthday, Gemini,* United Artists, 1980; *Lovesick,* 1983.

TELEVISION DEBUT—*The Garry Moore Show,* CBS. PRINCIPAL TELEVISION APPEARANCES—Series: Frequent guest, *That's Life,* ABC, 1968-69; Harry Lee, *Seventh Avenue,* NBC, 1977.

Specials: *ABC Comedy Hour,* ABC, 1972; *Comedy Is King;* one of the most frequent guest hosts, *The Kraft Music Hall,* NBC, 1967-71.

Guest: *The Garry Moore Show; The Ed Sullivan Show; The Perry Como Show; The Bob Hope Show.*

PRINCIPAL TELEVISION WORK—Producer, *The Corner Bar,* ABC, 1972-73; "Executive in Charge of Comedy," *Saturday Night Live with Howard Cosell,* ABC, 1975-76.

CABARET AND CONCERT APPEARANCES—Dominion Theatre, London, 1957; Palace Theatre, NY, 1959; Metropolitan Opera House, NY, 1960; Waldorf-Astoria Hotel, NY; other clubs and halls.

RECORDINGS: COMEDY ALBUMS—*Alan King in Suburbia,* Seeco; *The Best of Alan King,* Seeco.

WRITINGS: BOOKS—*Anybody Who Owns His Own Home Deserves It,* 1962; *Help, I'm a Prisoner in a Chinese Bakery,* 1964; *Is Salami and Eggs Better Than Sex?,* 1985.

ADDRESSES: OFFICE—665 Fifth Avenue, New York, NY 10022. AGENT—William Morris Agency, Inc., 1350 Avenue of the Americas, New York, NY 10036; c/o Lee Solters, Solters-Roskin-Friedman, Inc., 5455 Wilshire Blvd., Suite 2200, Los Angeles, CA 90036.

*　　*　　*

KINZER, Craig　1953-

PERSONAL: Born May 11, 1953, in Evanston, IL; son of David Mathias (the director of Illinois Hospital Association) and Phyllis Jean (a development director; maiden name, Casey) Kinzer. EDUCATION: Northwestern University, B.S., 1976; New York University, M.F.A., 1982.

VOCATION: Director and teacher.

CAREER: FIRST STAGE WORK—Director, *Justine, or the Misfortunes of Virtue,* Body Politic Theatre, Chicago, IL, 1977, for sixteen performances. FIRST NEW YORK STAGE WORK—Director, *The Underpants,* City Stage Company, 1985, for twenty-four performances.

RELATED CAREER—Teacher, Northwestern University, National High School Institute, 1974-85, theatre arts division director, 1983—; assistant artistic director, 1982-85, artistic director, 1985—, City Stage Company, New York, NY.

MEMBER: American Theatre Association.

ADDRESSES: OFFICE—City Stage Company, 136 E. 13th Street, New York, NY 10003.

*　　*　　*

KITT, Eartha　1928-

PERSONAL: Full name Eartha Mae Kitt; born January 26, 1928, in Columbia, South Carolina; daughter of William and Mamie (Reily) Kitt; married William McDonald, June, 1960 (divorced); children: one daughter. EDUCATION: New York School of the Performing Arts.

VOCATION: Singer, dancer, and actress.

CAREER: NEW YORK DEBUT—Dancer with Katherine Dunham Dance Troupe, *Blue Holiday,* Belasco Theatre, May 21, 1945. LONDON DEBUT—Mrs. Gracedew, *The High Bid,* Criterion Theatre, after trying out in Guildford, 1970. PRINCIPAL STAGE APPEARANCES—Dancer with Dunham troupe, *Bal Negre,* Belasco Theatre, NY, 1946; revue performer, *New Faces of 1952,* Royale Theatre, NY, 1952; Teddy Hicks, *Mrs. Patterson,* National Theatre, NY, 1954; Mehitabel, the cat, *Archie and Mehitabel,* Broadway Theatre, NY, 1957; title role, *Jolly's Progress,* Longacre Theatre, NY, 1959; Bunny Novak, *Bunny,* Belgrade Theatre, Coventry, then Criterion Theatre, London, 1972; Sahleem-La-Lume, *Timbuktu,* Mark Hellinger Theatre, NY, 1978; revue performer, *New Faces of 1952* (revival), Equity Library Theatre, NY, 1982.

MAJOR TOURS—Dancer, *Bal Negre,* Katherine Dunham Dance Troup on tour in Europe, 1946-47; Helen of Troy, *Orson Welles' Faust,* France, Germany, Belgium, 1951; Doris W., *The Owl and the Pussycat,* national, 1965-66; *A Musical Jubilee,* national, 1976; Sahleem-La-Lume, *Timbuktu,* 1979-80; Woman of the World, *Blues in the Night,* southern U.S. cities, 1985.

PRINCIPAL FILM APPEARANCES—Revue performer, *New Faces of 1952,* 1954; *Mark of the Hawk,* Universal, 1958; *St. Louis Blues,* 1958; title role, *Anna Lucasta,* United Artists, 1959; *Synanon,* Columbia, 1965; also, *The Saint of Devil's Island.*

PRINCIPAL TELEVISION APPEARANCES—*Kaskade,* Swedish television, 1962; Catwoman, *Batman* (she followed Julie Newmar and Lee Meriwether in the role), ABC, 1968; *Salome, Wingless Victory,* and other dramatic programs as well as numerous appearances on variety shows as a singer.

RECORDINGS: ALBUMS—*New Faces of 1952* original cast recording, RCA Victor; *Mrs. Patterson* original cast recording, RCA Victor; *Down to Eartha,* RCA Victor; *That Bad Eartha,* RCA Victor; *Thursday's Child,* RCA Victor; others.

WRITINGS: AUTOBIOGRAPHY—*Thursday's Child,* 1956; *Alone with Me,* 1976.

AWARDS: Golden Rose of Montreux, 1962, for *Kaskade;* Woman of the Year, National Association of Negro Musicians, 1968.

ADDRESSES: AGENT—International Creative Management, 40 W. 57th Street, New York, NY 10019.*

                    *   *   *

KLEIN, Robert   1942-

PERSONAL: Born February 8, 1942, in the Bronx, NY; son of Benjamin and Frieda (Moskowitz) Klein; married Brenda Boozer (an opera singer), April 29, 1973; children: Alexander Stuart. EDUCATION: Alfred University, B.A., 1962, political science and history; attended Yale School of Drama, 1962-63.

VOCATION: Comedian and actor.

CAREER: STAGE DEBUT—With Second City Theatrical Company, Chicago, 1965. NEW YORK DEBUT—With Second City Theatrical Company, *20,000 Frozen Grenadiers,* Square East Theatre, 1966. PRINCIPAL STAGE APPEARANCES—Small roles, *The Apple Tree,* Shubert Theatre, NY, 1966; revue performer, *New Faces of 1968,*

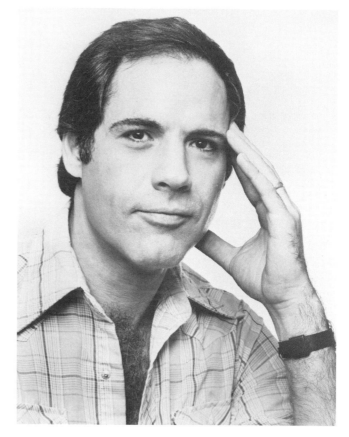

ROBERT KLEIN

Booth Theatre, NY, 1968; Junior, "Morning," Asher, "Noon," and the man, "Night," in the triple bill, *Morning, Noon and Night,* Henry Miller's Theatre, NY, 1968; Vernon Gersch, *They're Playing Our Song,* Imperial Theatre, NY, 1979.

PRINCIPAL FILM APPEARANCES—*The Landlord,* United Artists, 1970; *The Owl and the Pussycat,* Columbia, 1970; *Rivals,* Avco Embassy, 1972; *Hooper,* Warner Brothers, 1978; *The Bell Jar,* Avco Embassy, 1979; *Nobody's Perfeckt,* Columbia, 1981; voice, *The Last Unicorn,* Jensen-Farley, 1982.

PRINCIPAL TELEVISION APPEARANCES—Series: Host, *Comedy Tonight,* CBS, summer, 1970; *Bloopers and Practical Jokes,* NBC, 1984.

Specials for Home Box Office; guest appearances on various shows.

Movies: *Your Place or Mine?,* 1983, CBS; also appeared in *Summer Switch,* ABC; *This Wife for Hire,* ABC; *Poison Ivy,* NBC.

Plays: *Table Settings,* HBO; *Pajama Tops,* Showtime.

Home Video: *Robert Klein: Child of the 50's, Man of the 80's,* Thorne/EMI-HBO, 1984.

CONCERT APPEARANCES—*Annual Robert Klein Reunions,* Carnegie Hall, NY; many comedy concerts.

CABARET AND NIGHT CLUB APPEARANCES—At the Improvisation, Bitter End, Cafe Wha?, all NY, and Los Angeles clubs, 1966-69; others.

PRINCIPAL RADIO WORK—Host, *The Robert Klein Radio Show,* internationally syndicated.

RECORDINGS: COMEDY—*Child of the Fifties,* 1973; *Mind Over Matter,* 1974; *New Teeth,* 1975. MUSIC—*They're Playing Our Song,* original cast recording, Casablanca.

MEMBER: Actors' Equity Association, Screen Actors Guild, American Federation of Television and Radio Artists, American Guild of Variety Artists, Writers Guild.

AWARDS: Best Comedy Albums, Grammy nominations, for *Child of the Fifties* and *Mind Over Matter;* Best Actor in a Musical, Antoinette Perry Award, 1979, for *They're Playing Our Song;* honorary doctorate of humane letters, Alfred University, 1980.

ADDRESSES: AGENT—c/o Hal Ray, William Morris Agency, 151 El Camino Drive, Beverly Hills, CA 90212.

*　　*　　*

KLINE, Kevin   1947-

PERSONAL: Born October 24, 1947, in St. Louis, MO; son of Robert Joseph (a toy and record store owner and singer) and Peggy (Kirk) Kline. EDUCATION: Attended St. Louis Priory and Indian University; trained for the stage at Juilliard School of Drama with Harold Guskin.

VOCATION: Actor.

KEVIN KLINE

CAREER: DEBUT—*The Living Newspaper,* Indiana University, late 60's. NEW YORK DEBUT—Minor roles, *Henry VI, Part I* and *Part II,* and *Richard III,* New York Shakespeare Festival, Delacorte Theatre, 1970. PRINCIPAL STAGE APPEARANCES—Charles Surface, *The School for Scandal,* Vaskal Pepel, *The Lower Depths,* IRA officer, *The Hostage,* Guardiano, *Women Beware Women,* all at the Acting Company, Good Shepherd-Faith Church, NY, 1972; Vershinin, *The Three Sisters,* MacHeath, *The Beggars Opera,* Friar Peter, *Measure for Measure,* all at the Acting Company, NY, 1973; Leandre, *Scapin,* Acting Company, NY, then Billy Rose Theatre, NY, 1973; Jaime Lockhart, *The Robber Bridegroom,* McCarthy, *The Time of Your Life,* both Harkness Theatre, Los Angeles, 1975; Clym Yeobright, *Dance on a Country Grave,* Hudson Guild Theatre, NY, 1977.

The Promise, Bucks County Playhouse, PA, 1977; Bruce Granit, *On the Twentieth Century,* St. James Theatre, NY, 1978; understudy/standby for MacHeath, *The Threepenny Opera,* New York Shakespeare Festival, Vivian Beaumont Theatre, NY, 1978; Paul, *Loose Ends,* Circle in the Square, NY, 1979; Pirate King, *The Pirates of Penzance,* New York Shakespeare Festival, Delacorte Theatre, then Uris (now Gershwin) Theatre, NY, 1980; title role, *Richard III,* New York Shakespeare Festival, Delacorte Theatre, NY, 1983; *Henry V,* Delacorte Theatre, NY, 1984; *Arms and the Man,* Circle in the Square, NY, 1985; title role, *Hamlet,* Public Theatre, NY, 1986.

MAJOR TOURS—Tony Lumpkin, *She Stoops to Conquer,* Tom, *The Knack,* Acting Company, 1974.

FILM DEBUT—Nathan Landau, *Sophie's Choice,* Universal, 1982. PRINCIPAL FILM APPEARANCES—Pirate King, *Pirates of Penzance,* Universal, 1983; *The Big Chill,* Columbia, 1983; *Silverado,* Columbia, 1985; *Violets Are Blue,* Rastar/Columbia, 1986.

PRINCIPAL TELEVISION APPEARANCES—*Search for Tomorrow,* 1976-77; *The Time of Your Life,* PBS.

MEMBER: Actors' Equity Association, Screen Actors Guild.

AWARDS: Best Supporting Actor in a Musical, Antoinette Perry Award, 1978, for *On the Twentieth Century;* Best Actor in a Musical, Antoinette Perry Award, 1980, for *The Pirates of Penzance.*

SIDELIGHTS: RECREATION—Musical composition, travel, sports.

As a graduate of the first class of the Juilliard Drama Center in 1972, Mr. Kline was invited to be one of the founding members of the Acting Company.

ADDRESSES: AGENT—Triad Artists, 888 Seventh Avenue, New York, NY 10106.

*　　*　　*

KLUGMAN, Jack   1922-

PERSONAL: Born April 27, 1922, in Philadelphia, PA; son of Max and Rose Klugman; married Brett Somers, 1966 (separated); children: David, Adam. EDUCATION: Attended Carnegie Institute of Technology; trained for the stage at the American Theatre Wing.

VOCATION: Actor.

CAREER: PRINCIPAL TELEVISION APPEARANCES—Series: Alan

JACK KLUGMAN

Harris, *Harris Against the World*, NBC, 1964-65; Oscar Madison, *The Odd Couple*, ABC, 1970-75; title role, *Quincy*, NBC, 1976-83; *You Again*, NBC, 1986.

Movies: *Fame Is the Name of the Game*, 1966; *The Underground Man*, 1974; *One of My Wives Is Missing*, 1976.

Episodic: *Naked City; Twilight Zone; Alfred Hitchcock Presents; Kraft Theatre; Studio One; U.S. Steel Hour; The Defenders; Playhouse 90; Love Boat; Suspicion; Studio One; Kiss Me, Kate; The Time of Your Life.*

FILM DEBUT—*Timetable*, United Artists, 1956. PRINCIPAL FILM APPEARANCES— *Twelve Angry Men*, United Artists, 1957; *Cry Terror*, Metro-Goldwyn-Mayer, 1958; *The Scarface Mob*, 1962; *Days of Wine and Roses*, Warner Brothers, 1963; *Act One*, Warner Brothers, 1963; *I Could Go on Singing*, United Artists, 1963; *Yellow Canary*, Twentieth Century-Fox, 1963; *Hail, Mafia*, 1965; *The Detective*, Twentieth Century-Fox, 1968; *The Split*, Metro-Goldwyn-Mayer, 1968; *Goodbye, Columbus*, Paramount, 1969; *Who Says I Can't Ride a Rainbow*, Transvue, 1971; *Two Minute Warning*, Universal, 1976.

NEW YORK STAGE DEBUT—*Stevedore*, Equity Library Theatre, 1949. LONDON DEBUT—Oscar Madison, *The Odd Couple*, Queen's Theatre, 1966. PRINCIPAL STAGE APPEARANCES—*Saint Joan*, NY, 1949; *Bury the Dead*, NY, 1950; Frank Bonaparte, *Golden Boy*, American National Theatre and Academy (ANTA), NY, 1952; Citizen/Volscian Servant, *Coriolanus*, Phoenix Theatre, NY, 1954; Carmen, *A Very Special Baby*, Playhouse, NY, 1956; Herbie, *Gypsy*, Broadway, NY, 1959; Caesario Grimaldi, *Tchin-Tchin*,

Plymouth Theatre, NY, 1963; Horse Johnson, *The Sudden and Accidental Re-education of Horse Johnson*, Belasco Theatre, NY, 1968; Oscar Madison, *The Odd Couple*, Maddox Hall, Atlanta, GA, 1972, Miami, FL, Houston, TX, 1973, Plymouth Theatre, NY, 1977; Melbourne, Australia, 1984.

MAJOR TOURS—Dowdy, *Mister Roberts*, U.S. cities, 1950-51; Oscar Madison, *The Odd Couple*, U.S. cities, 1974, U.S. and Canadian cities, 1975; one man show about Lyndon B. Johnson, *Lyndon*, East Coast cities, 1984.

MEMBER: Actors' Equity Association, Screen Actors Guild, American Federation of Television and Radio Artists.

AWARDS: Outstanding Single Performance by an Actor in a Leading Role, Emmy Award, 1964, for "Blacklist," *The Defenders;* Outstanding Continued Performance by an Actor in a Leading Role in a Comedy Series, Emmy Awards, 1970-71 and 1972-73, for *The Odd Couple*.

ADDRESSES: OFFICE—Universal Studios, 100 Universal City Plaza, Universal City, CA 91608; c/o NBC Press Department, 30 Rockefeller Plaza, New York, NY 10020.

*   *   *

KNIGHT, Shirley   1936-

PERSONAL: Born July 5, 1936, in Goessel, KS; daughter of Noel Johnson (an oil company executive) and Virginia (Webster) Knight; married Gene Persson (divorced); married John R. Hopkins (a writer); children: Kaitlin, Sophie. EDUCATION: Attended Phillips University and Wichita University; trained for the stage with Erwin Piscator and Lee Strasberg. POLITICS: Democrat. RELIGION: Protestant.

VOCATION: Actress.

CAREER: STAGE DEBUT—Alison, *Look Back in Anger*, Pasadena Playhouse, CA, 1958. NEW YORK DEBUT—Katherine, *Journey to the Day*, Theatre de Lys, 1963. PRINCIPAL STAGE APPEARANCES—Irina, *The Three Sisters*, Morsoco Theatre, NY, 1964; Lulu, *Dutchman*, Warner Playhouse, Los Angeles, CA, 1965; Jenny Zubitsky, "Better Luck Next Time," and Helen Windsor, "A Walk in Dark Places," *Rooms*, Cherry Lane Theatre, NY, 1966; Constance, *We Have Always Lived in the Castle*, Ethel Barrymore Theatre, NY, 1966; Jean, *And People All Around*, Bristol Old Vic Theatre, England, 1967; Janet, *The Watering Place*, Music Box Theatre, NY, 1969.

Sara Melody, *A Touch of the Poet*, Gardner Centre Theatre, Brighton, England, 1970; title role, *Antigone*, Nottingham Playhouse, Theatre, 1971; *Economic Necessity*, Haymarket Theatre, Leicester, England, 1973; Carla, *Kennedy's Children*, John Golden Theatre, NY, 1975; Blanche, *A Streetcar Named Desire*, McCarter Theatre, Princeton, NJ, 1976; Lt. Lillian Holiday, *Happy End*, Chelsea Theatre Center, NY, 1977; Betty, *Landscape of the Body*, Drake Theatre, Chicago, IL, then Public Theatre, NY, 1977; Dorothea, *A Lovely Sunday for Creve Coeur*, Dock Street Theatre, Charleston, SC, 1978, then Hudson Guild Theatre, NY, 1979; Ruth, *Losing Time*, Manhattan Theatre Club, NY, 1979; Lil, *I Won't Dance*, Sudio Arena, Buffalo, NY, 1980; *Come Back Little Sheba*, Roundabout Theatre, NY, 1984.

FILM DEBUT—*Five Gates to Hell*, Twentieth Century-Fox, 1959. PRINCIPAL FILM APPEARANCES—Reenie Flood, *The Dark at the*

Top of the Stairs, Warner Brothers, 1960; *Sweet Bird of Youth*, Metro-Goldwyn-Mayer, 1962; *House of Women*, Warner Brothers, 1962; *Flight from Ashiya*, United Artists, 1964; *The Group*, United Artists, 1966; *Petulia*, Warner Brothers, 1966; *Dutchman*, Continental, 1967; *The Rain People*, 1969; *The Counterfeit Killer*, Universal, 1970; *Juggernaut*, United Artists, 1974; *Beyond the Poseidon Adventure*, Warner Brothers, 1979; *Endless Love*, Universal, 1981; *The Sender*, Paramount, 1982; also, *Prisoners*.

PRINCIPAL TELEVISION APPEARANCES—Movies: *With Intent to Kill*, CBS, 1984.

AWARDS: Antoinette Perry Award, 1975, for *Kennedy's Children;* honorary doctorate of fine arts, Lake Forest College.

SIDELIGHTS: FAVORITE ROLES—Lulu in *Dutchman* and the lead in *Economic Necessity.* RECREATIONS—Music, philosophy.

ADDRESSES: HOME—Connecticut. AGENT—Lionel Larner, Ltd., 850 Seventh Avenue, New York, NY 10019.

*   *   *

KNOTTS, Don   1924-

PERSONAL: Born July 21, 1924, in Morgantown, WV; son of William Jesse and Elsie (Moore) Knotts; married Kathryn Metz (divorced); married Loralee Czuchna (divorced); children: (first marriage) Karen Ann, Thomas Allen. EDUCATION: West Virginia University, B.A., 1948. MILITARY: U.S. Army, World War II, South Pacific.

DON KNOTTS

VOCATION: Actor.

CAREER: PRINCIPAL TELEVISION APPEARANCES—Series: *Steve Allen Show*, 1959-60; Barney Fife, *Andy Griffith Show*, 1960-65 (with guest appearances afterwards); *The Don Knotts Show*, NBC, 1970-71; Ralph Furley, *Three's Company*, ABC, 1979-84; also *The Garry Moore Show*.

Movie: Barney Fife, *Return to Mayberry*, NBC, 1986.

FILM DEBUT—*No Time for Sergeants*, Warner Brothers, 1958. PRINCIPAL FILM APPEARANCES—*It's a Mad, Mad, Mad, Mad World*, United Artists, 1963; *Move Over Darling*, Twentieth Century-Fox, 1963; *The Incredible Mr. Limpet*, Warner Brothers, 1964; *The Shakiest Gun in the West*, Universal, 1968; *The Ghost and Mr. Chicken*, Universal, 1966; *The Reluctant Astronaut*, Universal, 1967; *The Love God*, Universal, 1969; *How to Frame a Figg*, Universal, 1971; *The Apple Dumpling Gang*, Buena Vista, 1975; *No Deposit, No Return*, 1976; *Gus*, Buena Vista, 1976; *Herbie Goes to Monte Carlo*, Buena Vista, 1977; *Hot Lead, Cold Feet*, 1978; *The Prize Fighter*, 1979; *The Apple Dumpling Gang Rides Again*, Buena Vista, 1979; *Cannonball Run II*, Warner Brothers, 1984; also, *Trails End*.

PRINCIPAL STAGE APPEARANCES—Broadway: *No Time for Sergeants*, 1955-56; *A Good Look at Boney Kern; Last of the Red Hot Lovers; Mind with the Dirty Man*.

RELATED CAREER—Comedian, *Stars and Gripes*, South Pacific Theatre of Operations, U.S. Army.

AWARDS: Outstanding Performance in a Supporting Role by an Actor in a Comedy Series, five Emmy Awards, 1960-61, 1961-62, 1962-63, 1965-66, 1966-67, all for *The Andy Griffith Show*.

ADDRESSES: AGENT—c/o Sherwin Bash, BNB Associates, 804 N. Crescent Drive, Beverly Hills, CA 90210.

*   *   *

KORMAN, Harvey   1927-

PERSONAL: Full name, Harvey Herschel Korman; born February 15, 1927, in Chicago, IL; son of Cyril Raymond and Ellen (Belcher) Korman; married Donna Ehlert, August 27, 1960; children: Maria Ellen, Christopher Peter. EDUCATION: Attended Wright Junior College; attended the Goodman Theatre School in Chicago, 1946-50. MILITARY: U.S. Naval Reserve, 1945-46.

VOCATION: Actor and director.

CAREER: PRINCIPAL TELEVISION APPEARANCES—Comedy and Variety Series: Regular, *The Danny Kaye Show*, CBS, 1964-67; regular, *The Carol Burnett Show*, CBS, 1967-77; three episodes, *The ABC Saturday Comedy Special*, ABC, 1978; regular, *The Tim Conway Show*, CBS, 1980-81; Ed Higgins, *Mama's Family*, NBC (occasional), 1983-84.

PRINCIPAL TELEVISION WORK—Director: Stage sketches for the *Steve Allen Show*, CBS; two episodes, *The Dick Van Dyke Show*, CBS.

PRINCIPAL FILM APPEARANCES—*Lord Love a Duck*, United Artists, 1966; *The Last of the Secret Agents*, Paramount, 1966; *Three Bites of an Apple*, Metro-Goldwyn-Mayer, 1967; *The April Fool's*,

National General, 1969; *Blazing Saddles,* Warner Brothers, 1974; *Huckleberry Finn,* United Artists, 1974; *High Anxiety,* Twentieth Century-Fox, 1978; *Americathon,* United Artists, 1979; *First Family,* Warner Brothers, 1980; *History of the World—Part I,* 1981; *Trail of the Pink Panther,* Metro-Goldwyn-Mayer/United Artists, 1982; *Curse of the Pink Panther,* Metro-Goldwyn-Mayer/United Artists, 1983; *The Long Shot,* Orion, 1986.

AWARDS: Emmys: Outstanding Individual Achievement (special classification), 1969 and 1971, for *The Carol Burnett Show,* Outstanding Achievement by a Performer in Music or Variety, 1972, for *The Carol Burnett Show,* Best Supporting Actor in a Comedy or Variety Continuing Role, 1974, for *The Carol Burnett Show.*

SIDELIGHTS: CTFT learned that Harvey Korman appeared in small roles in Broadway productions and worked in television commercials before his appearance on *The Danny Kaye Show.*

ADDRESSES: AGENT—Singer and Lewak, 10960 Wilshire Blvd., Los Angeles, CA 90024.*

*   *   *

KORVIN, Charles   1907-

PERSONAL: Born Geza Kaiser, November 21, 1907, in Postyen, Hungary; immigrated to United States, 1937; son of Ede (a boatbuilder) and Ernestine (Fische) Kaiser; married Anne Bogy, May 17, 1957. EDUCATION: Real School, Budapest, Hungary; attended University of Paris, the Sorbonne, France, 1932-36. POLITICS: Liberal Socialist (no party affiliation).

CHARLES KORVIN

VOCATION: Actor.

CAREER: STAGE DEBUT—Steven Gay, *Accent on Youth,* Barter Theatre, Abingdon, VA, 1940. NEW YORK DEBUT—Niko, *Dark Eyes,* Biltmore Theatre, 1943. PRINCIPAL STAGE APPEARANCES—Performed at Barter Theatre, Abingdon, VA, 1940-42; *Thunder Rock; Margin for Error; The Time of the Cuckoo.*

MAJOR TOURS—The King of Siam, *The King and I,* U.S. cities; Niko, *Dark Eyes,* U.S. cities, 1944.

FILM DEBUT—Title role, *Enter Arsene Lupin,* Universal, 1944. PRINCIPAL FILM APPEARANCES—*This Love of Ours; Temptation,* 1946; *Berlin Express,* 1948; *The Killer That Stalked New York,* 1950; *Lydia Bailey,* 1952; *Tarzan's Savage Fury,* 1952; *Sangaree,* 1953; *Ship of Fools,* Columbia, 1965; *The Man Who Had Power Over Women,* Avco Embassy, 1970; *Inside Out,* Warner Brothers, 1975.

TELEVISION DEBUT—*Studio One,* CBS. PRINCIPAL TELEVISION APPEARANCES—Series: *Interpol* (52 episodes).

Episodic: *Zorro; Playhouse 90; Theatre Guild on the Air.*

MEMBER: Screen Actors Guild, Actors' Equity Association, American Federation of Television and Radio Artists.

SIDELIGHTS: Charles Korvin informs *CTFT* that he is a "very good cook," and speaks Hungarian, French, Italian, German, and Spanish. He has travelled throughout Europe, the United States, the Near East, Far East, Australia, and North Africa.

ADDRESSES: HOME—(Summer) 137 Ave Des Alouettes, Bois Fleuri, 06410, France; (winter) 7250 Klosters, Switzerland.

*   *   *

KOTLOWITZ, Dan   1957-

PERSONAL: Born March 26, 1957, in New York, NY; son of Robert (a writer) and Carol Naomi (a therapist; maiden name, Liebowitz) Kotlowitz. EDUCATION: Grinnell College, B.A., 1979; University of Wisconsin, M.F.A., 1983.

VOCATION: Lighting designer.

CAREER: FIRST STAGE WORK—Lighting designer, *Birdbath,* Grinnell College, IA, 1977, ten performances. FIRST NEW YORK STAGE WORK—Lighting designer, *On the Town,* Amas Repertory Theatre, 1983, thirty performances. PRINCIPAL STAGE WORK—Lighting designer: *Dry Apricots,* 1980 and *Never Seen Another Butterfly,* 1980, both at the Guthrie Showcase, Minneapolis, MN. At the Milwaukee Repertory, WI: *Today's Special,* 1982; *Countertalk,* 1982; *Fall Guy,* 1982; *A Christmas Carol,* 1982; *The Government Man,* 1983; *American Buffalo,* 1983; *A Kingdom Come,* 1983; *A Christmas Carol,* 1984; *Translations,* 1984; *Miss Lulu Bett,* 1984; *A Woman without Means,* 1985; *A Flea in Her Ear,* 1986.

American Buffalo, 1983, *A Kingdom Come,* 1985, *Twelfth Night,* 1986, all at the Berkeley Repertory; *The Foreigner,* Studio Arena, Buffalo, NY, 1985; *Loud Bang on June the First,* 13th Street Theatre, NY, 1985; *Energumen* and *The Winter's Tale,* both Soho Repertory Theatre, NY, 1985; *Moon,* Cash Performance Space, NY, 1985; *Ladies and Gentleman, Jerome Kern,* Harold Clurman

Theatre, NY, 1985; *The Second Hurricane*, New Federal Theatre, NY, 1985.

WRITINGS: PLAYS—*Gestures*, University of Wisconsin Playwrights' Workshop, 1982.

SIDELIGHTS: FAVORITE WORK—Lighting design for *Peer Gynt*. RECREATIONS—Fishing, sculpting, painting, and saxophone playing.

ADDRESSES: OFFICE—312 W. 48th Street, No. 27, New York, NY 10036.

*   *   *

KOVACS, Laszlo   1933-

PERSONAL: Born May 14, 1933, in Hungary; son of Imre and Juliana Kovacs; married Audrey A. Vaught, March 18, 1984. EDUCATION: Prepared for his work at the Academy of Drama and Motion Picture Arts, Budapest, Hungary, 1956, and with Gyorgy Illes.

VOCATION: Cinematographer.

CAREER: PRINCIPAL FILM WORK—Cinematographer: *Hells Angels on Wheels*, 1967; *The Savage Seven*, American-International, 1968; *Targets*, Paramount, 1968; *Easy Rider*, Columbia, 1969; *That Cold Day in the Park*, Commonwealth United, 1969; *Getting Straight*, Columbia, 1970; *Alex in Wonderland*, Metro-Goldwyn-Mayer, 1970; *Five Easy Pieces*, Columbia, 1970; *The Last Movie*, Universal, 1971; *Marriage of a Young Stockbroker*, Twentieth Century-Fox, 1971; *What's Up, Doc?*, Warner Brothers, 1972; *Pocket Money*, National General, 1972; *The King of Marvin Gardens*, Columbia, 1972; *Paper Moon*, Paramount, 1973; *Huckleberry Finn*, United Artists, 1974; *For Pete's Sake*, Columbia, 1974; *Freebie and the Bean*, Warner Brothers, 1974.

Shampoo, Columbia, 1975; *At Long Last Love*, Twentieth Century-Fox, 1975; *Harry and Walter Go to New York*, Columbia, 1976; *Baby Blue Marine*, Columbia, 1976; (additional photography only) *Close Encounters of the Third Kind*, Columbia, 1977; *New York, New York*, United Artists, 1977; *F.I.S.T.*, United Artists, 1978; *The Last Waltz*, United Artists, 1978; *Paradise Alley*, Universal, 1978; *Butch and Sundance: The Early Years*, Twentieth Century-Fox, 1979; *The Runner Stumbles*, Twentieth Century-Fox, 1979; *Heart Beat*, Warner Brothers, 1980; *The Legend of the Lone Ranger*, EMI, 1981; *Frances*, Universal, 1982; *The Toy*, Columbia, 1982; *Crackers*, Universal, 1982; *Ghostbusters*, Universal, 1983; *Mask*, Universal, 1984; *Legal Eagles*, Universal, 1985.

MEMBER: American Society of Cinematographers, Academy of Motion Picture Arts and Sciences.

ADDRESSES: OFFICE—Skip Nicholson Agency, 13701 Riverside Drive, Suite 314, Sherman Oaks, CA 91423.

*   *   *

KOVE, Martin

PERSONAL: Born March 6, in Brooklyn, NY; married Vivienne.

VOCATION: Actor.

MARTIN KOVE

CAREER: PRINCIPAL TELEVISION APPEARANCES—Series: George Baker, *Code R*, CBS, 1977; Ken Redford, *We've Got Each Other*, CBS, 1977-78; Romeo Slade, *The Edge of Night*, ABC, 1982; Detective Isbecki, *Cagney and Lacey*, CBS, 1982—.

Mini-Series: *Captains and Kings; City of Angels; The Yeagers*.

Movies: *Cry for the Strangers*, 1982; also appeared in *Sky Trap; Donovan's Kid; The Optimist*.

FILM DEBUT—*Little Murders*, Twentieth Century-Fox, 1971. PRINCIPAL FILM APPEARANCES—*Last House on the Left*, 1972; *Savages*, 1974; *The Wild Party*, 1975; *Deathrace 2000*, 1975; *The Four Deuces*, 1975; *Capone*, Twentieth Century-Fox, 1975; *White Line Fever*, Columbia, 1975; *The White Buffalo*, 1977; *Mr. Billion*, Twentieth Century-Fox, 1977; *Seven*, 1979; *Partners*, Paramount, 1982; Kreese, *Karate Kid*, Columbia, 1984; helicopter pilot, *Rambo: First Blood Part II*, Tri-Star, 1985; Kreese, *Karate Kid II* (upcoming).

NEW YORK STAGE DEBUT—*Woyceck*, La Mama, E.T.C., NY. PRINCIPAL STAGE APPEARANCES—Off-Broadway: *Volpone* and *Toyland*; Regional: *Delicate Champions; Poor Bitos; Revengers Tragedy; Man and Superman; Moby Dick*; Stanley, *A Streetcar Named Desire; The Rainmaker*; appeared as Lenny, *Of Mice and Men*, MET Theatre, Los Angeles, CA.

SIDELIGHTS: RECREATION—Tennis, horse training, racketball, skiing, gourmet cooking.

ADDRESSES: AGENT—c/o Joe Freeman, Freeman and Sutton, 8961 Sunset Blvd., Suite 2A, Los Angeles, CA 90069.

KULP, Nancy   1921-

PERSONAL: Full name, Nancy Jane Kulp; born August 28, 1921, in Harrisburg, PA; daughter of Robert Tilden and Marjorie (Snyder) Kulp; married Charles Malcolm Dacus, April 1, 1951. EDUCATION: Florida State University, B.A., journalism, 1943; University of Miami, post-graduate studies, 1950. MILITARY: Women Accepted for Voluntary Emergency Services (WAVES), U.S. Naval Reserve.

VOCATION: Actress.

CAREER: PRINCIPAL FILM APPEARANCES—*The Model and the Marriage Broker*, Twentieth Century-Fox, 1952; *A Star Is Born*, Warner Brothers, 1954; Jenny, the maid, *Sabrina*, Paramount, 1954; Eve's mother, *The Three Faces of Eve*, Twentieth Century-Fox, 1957; Miss Grunecker, *The Parent Trap*, Buena Vista, 1961; nutritionist, *Moon Pilot*, Buena Vista, 1962; *A Wilder Summer*, 1983.

PRINCIPAL TELEVISION APPEARANCES—Series: Pamela Livingston, *The Bob Cumming Show*, NBC, then CBS, then NBC, 1955-59; Jane Hathaway, *The Beverly Hillbillies*, CBS, 1961-71; Mrs. Gruber, *The Brian Keith Show*, NBC, 1973-74.

Episodic: *Lux Video Theatre*, NBC, 1955; *Playhouse 90*, CBS, 1956; *I Love Lucy*, CBS, 1956; *Sanford and Son*, NBC.

PRINCIPAL STAGE APPEARANCES—Aaronetta Gibbs, *Mornings at Seven*, Lyceum Theatre, NY, 1981; *Accent on Youth*, Long Wharf Theatre, New Haven, CT, 1983; also appeared in *Busybody*.

RELATED CAREER—Publicity director, WGBS Radio, 1946-47; continuity director, WTOD Radio, Miami, FL; continuity director and performer, WTVJ Television, Miami, 1949-50.

AWARDS: Outstanding Performance by an Actress in a Supporting Role in a Comedy, Emmy Award nomination, *The Beverly Hillbillies*, 1967.*

L

LAINE, Cleo 1927-

PERSONAL: Born October 28, 1927, in Southall, England; married George Langridge, 1947 (divorced, 1957); married John Philip William Dankworth (a composer and conductor), 1958; children: (first marriage) a son; (second marriage) a son and daughter.

VOCATION: Singer and actress.

CAREER: STAGE DEBUT—Lead, Flesh to a Tiger, Royal Court Theatre, London, 1958. PRINCIPAL STAGE APPEARANCES—Performed in A Midsummer Night's Dream, Valmouth, Women of Troy, title role, Hedda Gabler; Julie, Showboat, 1971; The Seven Deadly Sins, Edinburgh Festival, Scotland and Detroit, MI; title role, Colette, London; A Little Night Music, Michigan Opera Theatre, Detroit; Lady in Waiting, Houston Ballet, TX; The Merry Widow, Detroit, MI; Princess Puffer, The Mystery of Edwin Drood, Delacorte Theatre, NY, 1985, then Imperial Theatre, NY, 1985-86.

CLEO LAINE

Concerts with the Scottish National Orchestra, London Philharmonic, Carnegie Hall, Alice Tully Hall and extensive touring throughout North America, New Zealand, Australia, Japan, Hong Kong, Europe, and Britain.

PRINCIPAL TELEVISION APPEARANCES—Guest: That Was the Week That Was; The Muppet Show; An Evening at the Pops with Cleo Laine; Cleo Laine: Live at Wolftrap; The Tonight Show; Merv Griffin Show; Mike Douglas Show.

RELATED CAREER—Singer, Dankworth Seven (later the John Dankworth Big Band), 1952.

AWARDS: Melody Maker Award, 1956; New Musical Express Top Girl Singer, 1956; Moscow Arts Theatre Award, 1958, for Flesh to a Tiger; International Critics' Poll Award, Downbeat Magazine, 1965; Golden Feather Award, Woman of the Year, 1973; Edison Award, 1974; Variety Club Award, Show Business Personality of the Year, 1977; TV Times Viewers Award, Most Exciting Female singer, 1978; Order of the British Empire, 1978; honorary Doctor of Music, Berklee College of Music, Boston, MA.

SIDELIGHTS: RECREATIONS—Painting.

CTFT learned Cleo Laine began singing at age three.

ADDRESSES: OFFICE—c/o Kurt M. Gebauer, WTS Inc., P.O. Box 239, Hope, NJ 07844.

*　　*　　*

LAMBERT, Christopher 1957-

BRIEF ENTRY: Born Christophe Lambert in New York, NY, 1957; reared in Geneva, Switzerland. Actor. Christopher Lambert's parents wanted him to be financially secure, so they sent him to apprentice at Barclay's Bank and the London Stock Exchange. Lambert lasted at these jobs for several months, but then gave them up to attend the National Conservatory of Dramatic Art in Paris. He was expelled from the Conservatory during his third year there, but landed a small role in the French film Le bar du telephone, which started him in his acting career. La dame de coeur and Legitime violence followed, but it was his performance in the title role of Greystroke: The Legend of Tarzan, Lord of the Apes that secured him a following in England and America. Lambert most recently starred opposite Isabelle Adjani in Subway and with Catherine Deneuve in Paroles et musique.*

*　　*　　*

LANCHESTER, Elsa 1902-

PERSONAL: Born Elsa Sullivan, October 28, 1902, in Lewisham,

London, England; daughter of James and Edith (Lanchester) Sullivan; married Charles Laughton (the actor) February 10, 1929 (died, 1962). EDUCATION: Attended English private schools; studied dance with Raymond Chelsea and Isadora Duncan.

VOCATION: Actress and writer.

CAREER: LONDON DEBUT—*Thirty Minutes in a Street,* Kingway Theatre, 1922. NEW YORK DEBUT—*Payment Deferred,* Lyceum Theatre, 1931. PRINCIPAL STAGE APPEARANCES—Larva, *The Insect Play,* Regent Theatre, London, 1923; Peggy, *The Way of the World,* Lyric, Hammersmith Theatre, London, 1924; Sancho, *The Duenna,* London, 1924; Sophie Binner, *Cobra,* Garrick Theatre, London, 1925; *Riverside Nights,* London, 1926; *Q,* London, 1926; the Kid, *Cautious Campbell,* Royalty Theatre, London, 1927; Rosie Betts, *The Pool,* Everyman Theatre, London, 1927; Mimi Winstock, *Mr. Prohack,* Court Theatre, London, 1927; Anna, *The Outskirts,* Court Theatre, London, 1929; Mary Morgan, *Ten Nights in a Bar-Room,* Gate Theatre, London, 1930; Cedric, *Little Lord Fauntleroy,* London, 1931; Winnie Marble, *Payment Deferred,* St. James Theatre, London, 1931; with the Old Vic-Sadler's Wells company, 1933-34, played Charlotta Ivanova in *The Cherry Orchard,* the Singer in *Henry VIII,* Juliet in *Measure for Measure,* Ariel in *The Tempest,* Miss Prism in *The Importance of Being Earnest,* and Miss Prue in *Love for Love;* title role, *Peter Pan,* Palladium, London, 1936 and subsequent tour; *Martha Jones,* NY, 1937; *The Beachcomber,* NY, 1937; Emmy Baudine, *They Walk Alone,* John Golden Theatre, NY, 1941; member, Turnabout Theatre, Los Angeles, CA, 1941-56.

FILM DEBUT—*The Constant Nymph* (silent version). PRINCIPAL FILM APPEARANCES—*The Private Life of Henry VIII,* 1933; *David Copperfield,* Metro-Goldwyn-Mayer, London, 1935; *Naughty Marietta,* Metro-Goldwyn-Mayer, 1935; title role, *The Bride of Frankenstein,* Universal-London, 1935; *The Ghost Goes West,* United Artists-London, 1936; *Rembrandt,* United Artists-London, 1936; *The Beachcomber,* Mayflower/Paramount, 1938; *Ladies in Retirement,* Columbia, 1941; *Son of Fury,* Twentieth Century-Fox, 1942; *Tales of Manhattan,* Twentieth Century-Fox, 1942; *Forever and a Day,* 1943; *Lassie Come Home,* Metro-Goldwyn-Mayer, 1943; *Passport to Adventure,* 1943; *Witness for the Prosecution,* 1944; *Bell, Book, and Candle,* 1944; *The Spiral Staircase,* 1946; *The Razor's Edge,* 1946; *Northwest Outpost,* 1947; *The Bishop's Wife,* 1947; *The Secret Garden,* Metro-Goldwyn-Mayer, 1949; *Come to the Stable,* 1949; *The Inspector General,* 1949.

Buccaneer's Girl, 1950; *Mystery Street,* Metro-Goldwyn-Mayer, 1950; *Frenchie,* 1950; *Petty Girl,* 1950; *Androcles and the Lion,* 1952; *Dreamboat,* 1952; *Les Miserables,* 1952; *The Girls of Pleasure Island,* 1953; *Hell's Half Acre,* 1954; *Three Ring Circus,* 1954; *The Glass Slipper,* Metro-Goldwyn-Mayer, 1954; *Witness for the Prosecution,* United Artists, 1958; *Honeymoon Hotel,* Metro-Goldwyn-Mayer, 1964; *Mary Poppins,* Buena Vista, 1964; *That Darn Cat,* Buena Vista, 1965; *Easy Come, Easy Go,* Paramount, 1967; *Blackbeard's Ghost,* Buena Vista, 1968; *Rascal,* Buena Vista, 1969; *Me, Natalie,* National General, 1969; *My Dog,* Buena Vista, 1969; *Willard,* Cinerama, 1971; *Arnold,* Cinerama, 1973; *Murder by Death,* 1976.

PRINCIPAL TELEVISION APPEARANCES—Series: Miss Margaret, *The John Forsythe Show,* NBC, 1965-66; Aunt Henrietta, *Nanny and the Professor,* ABC, 1971.

Episodic: *Omnibus,* CBS, ABC; *Schlitz Playhouse of the Stars,* CBS; *I Love Lucy,* CBS; *The Bill Cosby Show,* NBC; *To Catch a Thief,* ABC; *Then Came Bronson,* NBC; *The Lucy Show,* CBS; *Studio One,* CBS.

WRITINGS: AUTOBIOGRAPHY—*Charles Laughton and I,* 1939; *Elsa Lanchester, Herself,* 1983.

AWARDS: Best Supporting Actress, Academy Award nominations, 1949, for *Come to the Stable* and 1958, for *Witness for the Prosecution.*

ADDRESSES: OFFICE—c/o Harold R. Williams, 9405 Brighton Way, Beverly Hills, CA 90210.*

*   *   *

LANDAU, Vivien

PERSONAL: Born Vivien Leventhal, in New York, NY; daughter of Harry (a certified public accountant) and Elizabeth (a ballerina; maiden name, Barany) Leventhal; married Arthur Landau (a chemist) September 3, 1961; children: Jeffrey, Seth, Kevin. EDUCATION: High School of Performing Arts, 1958; City College of New York, B.A., 1962.

VOCATION: Actress.

CAREER: NEW YORK DEBUT—(As Tisa Barunne) Brigette, *Clerembard,* Rooftop Playhouse, NY, 1958. PRINCIPAL STAGE APPEARANCES—(As Tisa Barunne): Vestal Virgin, *The Golden Six,* York Playhouse, NY, 1958; Miss Leighton, *Once in a Lifetime,* York Playhouse, NY, 1963.

(As Vivien Landau) Penelope Ryan, *Happy Birthday, Wanda June,* Hudson Guild Theatre, NY, 1973; title role, *Yerma,* Briarcliff College, 1976; Antigone, *Excepts from Antigone,* Robert Lewis Acting Company, 1978; Ellen Manville, *Luv* and Gittel Mosca, *Two for the Seesaw,* New Jersey Shakespeare Festival, 1979; Duchess Stephanie, *Death Takes a Holiday,* Equity Library Theatre, NY, 1980; Dee Dee Grogan, *Invitation to a March,* Wonderhorse Theatre, NY, 1981; Rhonda McKay, *Wash, Rinse, Spin Dry,* Greeley Street Theatre, NY, 1983; Frances Black, *Light Up the Sky,* New Jersey Shakespeare Festival, 1985.

Stock: Elaine, *Last of the Red Hot Lovers,* La Pino Dinner Theatre, Vista, NY, 1975; Anne Miller, *6 Rms Riv Vw,* Mahopa Farm, NY, 1976; Hannah, Beth, *California Suite,* Fort Salem, NY, 1979.

MAJOR TOURS—U.S. cities: Karen Nash, *Plaza Suite;* Jacqueline, *Boeing-Boeing;* Edna, *Prisoner of Second Avenue;* Miss Casewell, *The Mousetrap;* Fiona, *How the Other Half Loves;* Doris, *The Owl and the Pussycat.*

TELEVISION DEBUT—Celestina, "Sunday Costs Five Pesos," *Wide, Wide World,* 1956. PRINCIPAL TELEVISION APPEARANCES—*The Edge of Night,* ABC; *Love of Life,* CBS; *Search for Tomorrow,* CBS, NBC; *As the World Turns,* CBS.

FILM DEBUT—Salesperson, *They All Laughed,* 1981.

MEMBER: Actors' Equity Association, Screen Actors Guild, American Federation of Television and Radio Artists, Theatre Artists Workshop of Westport.

AWARDS: Best Actress, New Jersey Critics Award, 1979, for *Two for the Seesaw.*

VIVIEN LANDAU

WILLIAM LANDIS

SIDELIGHTS: RECREATIONS—"Avid" skier, feminism.

ADDRESSES: HOME—Mt. Holly Road E., Katonah, NY 10536.

*   *   *

LANDESBERG, Steve

PERSONAL: Born November 23, in New York, NY.

VOCATION: Comedian and actor.

CAREER: STAGE DEBUT—Member, New York Stickball Team (comedy group).

PRINCIPAL TELEVISION APPEARANCES—Series: *Dean Martin Presents the Bobby Darin Amusement Co.,* NBC, 1972; Fred Meyerbach, *Paul Sand in Friends and Lovers,* CBS, 1974-75; Detective Arthur Dietrich, *Barney Miller,* ABC, 1976-82.

Guest: *The Ed Sullivan Show; The Tonight Show, Starring Johnny Carson,* NBC.

ADDRESSES: AGENT—Agency for the Performing Arts, 888 Seventh Avenue, New York, NY 10106.*

*   *   *

LANDIS, William   1921-

PERSONAL: Born May 21, 1921, in Minneapolis, MN; son of Willis Emory (an undertaker and certified public accountant) and

Ann Elizabeth (Lightner) Landis; married Elizabeth E. Engrav (an antique doll dealer), July 12, 1955; children: Liz Anne, Maura, Willie. EDUCATION: Pacific Lutheran College, B.A., 1949; University of Washington, M.A., 1950. MILITARY: U.S. Marine Corps, 1940-41.

VOCATION: Actor, director, manager, and producer.

CAREER: STAGE DEBUT—Bill Dowton, *The Drunkard,* Theatre Mart, Los Angeles, CA, 1944-46, for seven hundred performances. NEW YORK DEBUT—Montano, Duke of Venice, *Othello,* Jan Hus House Theatre, 1954, for fifteen performances. PRINCIPAL STAGE APPEARANCES—Morrell, *Candida,* 1956, Bluntschi, *Arms and the Man,* 1956, Godrey Kneller, *In Good King Charles' Golden Days,* 1957, Charteris, *The Philanderer,* 1958, Bolton, *Never Can Tell,* 1958, Lickcheese, *Widower's Houses,* 1959, Aegisthus, *The Prodigal,* 1960, all at the Downtown Theatre, NY; Manders, *Ghosts* and Mortensagaard, *Rosmersholm,* both at the Fourth Street Theatre, NY, 1961; acted in over thirty roles at the Sharon Playhouse between 1968 and 1981, including Caesar, *Caesar and Cleopatra,* Tarleton, *Misalliance,* Vershinin, *The Three Sisters.*

PRINCIPAL THEATRE WORK—Producer, *The Prodigal,* Downtown Theatre, NY, 1960.

RELATED CAREER—English teacher, Allen Stevenson Lenox School, NY, 1959-81; teacher of drama, speech, and the history of theatre, the Gunnery School, Washington, CT, 1982-86; actor, director, and producer, Sharon Playhouse, 1968-81, managing director, 1973-75, 1978-81.

MEMBER: Actors' Equity Association; Sharon Creative Arts Foundation (president, 1979-80).

SIDELIGHTS: FAVORITE ROLES—Caesar, *Caesar and Cleopatra*, Tarleton, *Misalliance*, Vershinin, *The Three Sisters*.

ADDRESSES: OFFICE—P.O. Box 84, Main Street, Sharon, CT, 06069.

* * *

LANE, Stewart F. 1951-

PERSONAL: Born May 3, 1951, in New York, NY; son of Leonard Charles (a business executive) and Mildred C. (Chesnow) Lane; married Robin Etta Lavin (an actress), May 16, 1981; children: Eliana Constance. EDUCATION: Boston University, B.F.A., 1973.

VOCATION: Producer.

CAREER: PRINCIPAL STAGE WORK—Producer, *The Grand Tour*, Palace Theatre, NY, 1979; associate producer, *West Side Story* (revival), Minskoff Theatre, NY, 1980; co-producer, *Frankenstein*, Palace Theatre, NY, 1981; co-producer, *Can-Can* (revival), Minskoff Theatre, NY, 1981; co-producer, *Woman of the Year*, Palace Theatre, NY, 1981-82; co-producer, *Teaneck Tanzi: The Venus Flytrap*, Nederlander Theatre, NY, 1983; associate producer, *La Cage Aux Folles*, Palace Theatre, NY, 1983—; associate producer, *Lone Star/Private Wars*, NY, 1983.

MAJOR TOURS—*Woman of the Year*, national, 1983.

AWARDS: Best Musical, Antoinette Perry Award nomination, 1981, for *Woman of the Year;* Drama League Critics Award, 1983, for *Teaneck Tanzi: The Venus Flytrap;* Best Musical, Antoinette Perry Award, Outer Critics Circle Award, Drama Desk Award nomination, all 1984, for *La Cage Aux Folles*.

ADDRESSES: OFFICE—Palace Theatre, 1564 Broadway, New York, NY 10036.

STEWART F. LANE

Photograph by Fred Marcus

LANGE, Ted

PERSONAL: Born January 5, in Oakland, CA; son of Ted and Geraldine L. Lange; married Sheryl; children: Ted IV. EDUCATION: Attended San Francisco City College and Merritt Junior College.

VOCATION: Actor.

CAREER: PRINCIPAL TELEVISION APPEARANCES—Series: Junior, *That's My Mama*, ABC, 1974-75; Harvard, *Mr. T and Tina*, ABC, 1976; Bartender Issac Washington, *The Love Boat*, ABC, 1977—.

Episodic: *The Last Detail*.

Specials: American Film Institute's *Salute to James Cagney*.

PRINCIPAL FILM APPEARANCES—*Trick Baby*, 1972; *Wattsax*, 1973; *Blade*, Joesph Green Pictures, 1973; *Larry*, 1974.

NEW YORK DEBUT—*Hair*, 1969. PRINCIPAL STAGE APPEARANCES—*Ain't Supposed to Die a Nautral Death; Dialogue Black and White; Golden Boy; Tell Pharoah; Big Time Buck White;* also, performed with the New Shakespearean Company.

ADDRESSES: OFFICE—Aaron Spelling Productions, Warner Hollywood Studios, 1041 N. Formosa Avenue, Hollywood, CA 90046.*

* * *

LANSING, Robert 1928-

PERSONAL: Born Robert Howell Brown, June 5, 1928, in San Diego, CA; son of Robert George and Alice Lucille (Howell) Brown; married Emily McLaughlin, 1956 (divorced); married Garifalia Hardy, 1969 (divorced); married Anne Cecile Erde Pivar, 1981. MILITARY: U.S. Army, 1946-47. POLITICS: Democrat.

VOCATION: Actor and director.

CAREER: NEW YORK DEBUT—*Stalag 17*, 1951. PRINCIPAL STAGE APPEARANCES—*Charley's Aunt*, City Center, NY, 1953-54; *The Lovers*, 1956; *Cue for Passion*, 1958; *Suddenly Last Summer*, 1958-59; *The Great God Brown*, 1959; *Cut of the Axe*, 1960; *Antony and Cleopatra*, 1967; *Brightower*, 1970; *Finishing Touches*, 1973; *The O'Neill Sea Plays*, Long Wharf Theatre, New Haven, CT, 1977; *Damien* (one man show), PAF Playhouse, Long Island, NY, 1981; *Dance of Death*, Seattle Repertory Theatre, WA, 1981; Benjamin, *The Little Foxes*, Ahmanson Theatre, Los Angeles, 1981; *The Bathers*, Long Wharf Theatre, New Haven, 1984; also appeared in production of *Richard III* and *Cyrano de Bergerac*.

MAJOR TOURS—*Stalag 17*, U.S. cities, 1951-52; *The Little Foxes*, London, 1982.

PRINCIPAL TELEVISION APPEARANCES—Series: Steve Carella, *87th Precinct*, NBC, 1961-62; General Frank Savage, *Twelve O'Clock High*, ABC, 1964-67; Peter Murphy/Mark Wainwright, *The Man Who Never Was*, ABC, 1967; Jack Curtis, *Automan*, ABC, 1984.

Episodic: *Kraft Mystery Theatre*, NBC; *Camera Three*; *U.S. Steel Hour*, ABC; *General Electric Theatre*, CBS; *Star Trek*, NBC;

CONTEMPORARY THEATRE, FILM, AND TELEVISION • Volume 3

LAPOTAIRE

ROBERT LANSING

Twilight Zone, CBS; *Gunsmoke,* CBS; *Bonanza,* NBC; *The Name of the Game,* NBC; *Simon and Simon,* CBS, 1984, 1985; *Hotel,* ABC, 1986; *The Equalizer,* 1986.

PRINCIPAL FILM APPEARANCES—*The 4-D Man,* Universal, 1959; *A Gathering of Eagles,* Universal, 1963; *Under the Yum Yum Tree,* Columbia, 1963; *An Eye for an Eye,* Embassy, 1966; *Namu the Killer Whale,* United Artists, 1966; *The Grissom Gang,* National General, 1971; *Bittersweet Love,* Avco Embassy, 1976; *Scalpel,* 1977; *Life on the Mississippi,* 1980.

MEMBER: Actors' Equity Association, Screen Actors Guild (director, national vice-president), Directors Guild of America, Affiliated Television and Radio Artists; Player's Club, Academy of Magical Arts.

ADDRESSES: HOME—New York, NY. AGENT—Don Buchwald and Associates, Ten E. 44th Street, New York, NY 10017.

*   *   *

LAPOTAIRE, Jane   1944-

PERSONAL: Born December 26, 1944, in Ipswich, Suffolk, England; step-daughter of Yves Lapotaire, daughter of Louise Elise (Burgess) Lapotaire; married Roland Joffe (divorced). EDUCATION: Northgate Grammar School, Ipswich; studied for the theatre at the Bristol Old Vic Theatre School.

VOCATION: Actress.

CAREER: DEBUT—Ruby Birtle, *When We Are Married,* Bristol

Old Vic, England, September, 1965. NEW YORK DEBUT—Title role, *Piaf,* Plymouth Theatre, 1980. PRINCIPAL STAGE APPEARANCES—Vivie, *Mrs. Warren's Profession,* Natasha, *War and Peace,* Ruth, *The Homecoming,* all at Bristol Old Vic, 1965-67; Judith, *The Dance of Death,* Antoinette, *A Flea in Her Ear,* both for the National Theatre, London, 1967; Mincing, later Mrs. Fainall, *The Way of the World,* Tania, *Macrune's Guevara,* Zanche, *The White Devil,* Don Quixote's niece, *The Travails of Sancho Panza,* all for the National Theatre, London, 1969.

Jessica, *The Merchant of Venice,* National Theatre, London, 1970; Lieschen, *The Captain of Koepenick,* National Theatre, London, 1971; Zerbinetta, *Scapino,* Katherina, *The Taming of the Shrew,* Jocasta, *Oedipus,* Isabella, *Measure for Measure,* all with the Young Vic, London, 1970-71; Viola, *Twelfth Night,* Royal Shakespeare Company, Stratford, England, 1974, then at the Aldwych Theatre, London, 1975; Lady Macduff, *Macbeth,* Sonya, *Uncle Vanya,* both with the Royal Shakespeare Company, Stratford, 1974; Rosalind, *As You Like It,* Nottingham Playhouse, England, and Edinburgh Festival, Scotland, 1975; Vera, *A Month in the Country,* Lucy Honeychurch, *A Room with a View,* both with the Royal Shakespeare Company, Albery Theatre, London, 1975; Rosalind, *As You Like It,* Riverside Studios, London, 1976; title role, *The Duchess of Malfi,* Bristol Old Vic, 1976; Rosaline, *Love's Labour's Lost,* Stratford, England, 1978, later at the Aldwych Theatre, London, 1979; Edith Piaf, *Piaf,* The Other Place, London, then the Warehouse Theatre, London, transferring to the Aldwych Theatre, London, 1979; then moving to Wyndham's Theatre, to the Piccadilly Theatre, London, 1980, and to the Plymouth Theatre, NY, 1981.

PRINCIPAL FILM APPEARANCES—Cleopatra, *Antony and Cleopatra,* British, 1971; *Eureka,* British, 1985; also seen in *Lady Jane.*

JANE LAPOTAIRE

237

PRINCIPAL TELEVISION APPEARANCES—(British productions, some seen in U.S. on PBS) *Stocker's Copper; The Other Woman; Marie Curie; The Devil's Crown; Seal Morning;* Lady Macbeth, "*Macbeth*," Cleopatra, "*Antony and Cleopatra*," both part of *The Shakespeare Plays* series; *Piaf,* for Showtime, 1983.

AWARDS: Emmy Award nomination, for *Marie Curie;* Best Actress, London Critics Award, Society of West End Theatres Award, Variety Club Award, Antoinette Perry Award nomination, all 1981, for *Piaf.*

SIDELIGHTS: Jane Lapotaire's favorite roles include Sonya in *Uncle Vanya,* Isabella in *Measure for Measure,* and Viola in *Twelfth Night,* but it has been as Cleopatra and as French singer Edith Piaf that she has become an internationally recognized star.

ADDRESSES: AGENT—William Morris Agency, 147-149 Wardour Street, London W1, England.

* * *

LARROQUETTE, John   1947-

PERSONAL: Born November 25, 1947, in New Orleans, LA; son of John Edgar and Berthalla Oramous (Helmstetter) Larroquette; married Elizabeth Ann Cookson, July 4, 1975; children: Lisa Katherina, Jonathan Preston.

VOCATION: Actor.

JOHN LARROQUETTE

CAREER: PRINCIPAL TELEVISION APPEARANCES—Series: Dr. Paul Herman, *Doctors' Hospital,* NBC, 1975-76; Lt. Bob Anderson, *Baa Baa Black Sheep,* NBC, 1976-78; Assistant D.A. Dan Fielding, *Night Court,* NBC, 1984—;

PRINCIPAL FILM APPEARANCES—*Altered States,* Warner Brothers, 1980; *Stripes,* Columbia, 1981; *Cat People,* Universal, 1982; *Twilight Zone: The Movie,* Warner Brothers, 1983; *Star Trek III: The Search for Spock,* Paramount, 1984; *Choose Me,* Island Alive, 1984; *Summer Rental,* Paramount, 1985.

PRINCIPAL STAGE APPEARANCES—Reverend Hale, *The Crucible, Enter Laughing,* and *Endgame,* all Los Angeles.

RELATED CAREER—Worked as a disc jockey in New Orleans.

AWARDS: Drama League Award, for *Endgame.*

SIDELIGHTS: John Larroquette told *CTFT,* "Life couldn't be better. I'm working on a show I like with people I respect. My family is happy and healthy and we just moved into a new house in Malibu."

ADDRESSES: AGENT—c/o Monique Moss, Michael Levine Public Relations Company, 9123 Sunset Blvd., Los Angeles, CA 90069.

* * *

LASSER, Louise   1941-

PERSONAL: Born 1941, in New York, NY; married Woody Allen (the actor and director), 1966 (divorced). EDUCATION: Attended Brandeis University and the New School for Social Research; studied acting with Sanford Meisner in New York.

VOCATION: Actress.

CAREER: FILM DEBUT—*What's New Pussycat?,* United Artists, 1965. PRINCIPAL FILM APPEARANCES—*What's Up Tiger Lily?,* American International, 1966; *Take the Money and Run,* Cinerama, 1969; *Bananas,* United Artists, 1971; *Such Good Friends,* Paramount, 1971; *Everything You Always Wanted to Know About Sex, But Were Afraid to Ask,* United Artists, 1972; *Slither,* Metro-Goldwyn-Mayer, 1973; *In God We Trust,* Universal, 1980.

PRINCIPAL TELEVISION APPEARANCES—Series: Title role, *Mary Hartman, Mary Hartman,* syndicated, 1976-77; Maggie McBurney, *It's a Living,* ABC, 1981-82.

Episodic: *Masquerade,* ABC.

Movies: *Isn't It Shocking?,* 1973; *The Lie,* 1976; *Just Me and You,* 1978.

Guest: Host, *Saturday Night Live,* NBC.

PRINCIPAL STAGE APPEARANCES—*I Can Get It for You Wholesale,* 1962; *The Third Ear,* 1964; *Henry Sweet Henry,* 1967; *Lime Green/Khaki Blue,* 1969; *The Chinese,* 1970.

ADDRESSES: AGENT—Bret Adams Ltd., 448 W. 44th Street, New York, NY 10036.*

PIPER LAURIE

LAURIE, Piper   1932-

PERSONAL: Born Rosetta Jacobs, January 22, 1932, in Detroit, MI; children: Anne.

VOCATION: Actress.

CAREER: FILM DEBUT—Daughter, *Louisa,* Universal, 1950. PRINCIPAL FILM APPEARANCES—*The Milkman,* Universal, 1950; *Francis Goes to the Races,* Universal, 1951; *The Prince Who Was a Thief,* Universal, 1951; *Son of Ali Baba,* Universal, 1952; *Has Anybody Seen My Gal,* Universal, 1952; *No Room for the Groom,* Universal, 1952; *Mississippi Gambler,* 1953; *Golden Blade,* 1953; *Dangerous Mission,* 1954; *Johnny Dark,* 1954; *Dawn at Socorro,* 1954; *Smoke Signal,* 1955; *Ain't Misbehavin'* Universal, 1955; *Until They Sail,* Metro-Goldwyn-Mayer, 1957; *The Hustler,* Twentieth Century-Fox, 1961; *Carrie,* United Artists, 1976; *Ruby,* 1977; *Tim,* 1979; *Return to Oz,* Buena Vista, 1985; *Children of a Lesser God,* Paramount, 1986.

PRINCIPAL TELEVISION APPEARANCES—Series: Jo Skagska, *Skag,* NBC, 1980.

Episodic: *Robert Montgomery Presents,* CBS; "The Days of Wine and Roses," *Playhouse 90,* CBS; "The Road that Led Afar," *General Electric Theatre,* CBS; *St. Elsewhere,* NBC; "Murder at the Oasis," *Murder She Wrote,* CBS.

Movies: *The Dear Heart;* Magda Goebbels, *The Bunker,* CBS, 1981; *The Life of Margaret Sanger,* PBS; *The Mae West Story,* 1982; *Tender Is the Night,* BBC for Showtime Cable; *Love, Mary,* CBS; *Toughlove,* ABC, 1985.

Mini-Series: Annie, *The Thorn Birds,* ABC.

PRINCIPAL STAGE APPEARANCES—*Rosemary and the Alligators,* off-Broadway; Laura, *The Glass Menagerie,* Broadway revival.

MEMBER: Screen Actors Guild, American Federation of Television and Radio Artists.

AWARDS: Emmy nominations: *The Dear Heart,* CBS; "The Days of Wine and Roses," *Playhouse 90,* CBS; "The Road that Led Afar," *General Electirc Theatre,* CBS; Magda Goebbels, *The Bunker,* CBS, 1981; Annie, *The Thorn Birds,* ABC; *St. Elsewhere,* NBC. Golden Globe Award, for Annie, *The Thorn Birds,* ABC; National Academy of Motion Picture Arts and Sciences Award nominations: 1961, for *The Hustler,* 1976, for *Carrie.*

SIDELIGHTS: Through Piper Laurie's publicity release, *CTFT* learned that since her debut in the film *Louisa,* in which she played Ronald Reagan's daughter, her career has developed in television, theatre, and films. While she was raising her daughter, she temporarily retired from performing, taking up sculpting as a major hobby. When her daughter reached "driving age," Laurie returned to the screen in *Carrie,* and has been active in films and television since her return.

ADDRESSES: OFFICE—c/o Si Litvinoff, 8467 Beverly Blvd., Suite 100, Los Angeles, CA 90048. AGENT—Triad, 10100 Santa Monica Blvd., 16th Floor, Los Angeles, CA 90067.

*   *   *

LAVIN, Linda   1937-

PERSONAL: Born October 15, 1937, in Portland, ME; daughter of David J. and Lucille (Potter) Lavin; married Ron Leibman (an actor; divorced); married Kip Niven; children: (first marriage) Jim, Kate. EDUCATION: Attended the College of William and Mary.

VOCATION: Actress and singer.

CAREER: STAGE DEBUT—White Rabbit, *Alice in Wonderland,* Wayneflete School, Portland, ME, 1942. NEW YORK DEBUT—Izzy, *Oh, Kay!,* East 74th Street Theatre, April 16, 1960. PRINCIPAL STAGE APPEARANCES—Wilma, crying daughter, Fifi of Paris, quiet girl, *A Family Affair,* Billy Rose Theatre, NY, 1962; Barbara, *The Riot Act,* Cort Theatre, NY, 1963; Evelyn, *Kiss Mama,* Actors Playhouse, NY, 1965; revue performer, *Wet Paint,* Renata Theatre, NY, 1965; Victoire, *Hotel Passionato,* New Theatre, NY, 1965; revue performer, *The Mad Show,* East 74th Street Theatre, NY, 1966; Sydney, *It's a Bird . . . It's a Plane . . . It's Superman,* Alvin Theatre, NY, 1966; Beth Nemerov, *Something Different,* Cort Theatre, NY, 1967; Patsy Newquist, *Little Murders,* Circle in the Square, NY, 1969; all the women's roles, *Cop-Out,* Cort Theatre, NY, 1969; Elaine Nevazio, *Last of the Red Hot Lovers,* Eugene O'Neill Theatre, NY, 1969.

In the Beginning Moon and *A Servant of Two Masters,* both at the John Drew Theatre, Easthampton, NY, 1971; Leah, *The Enemy Is Dead,* Bijou Theatre, NY, 1973; courtesan, *The Comedy of Errors,* New York Shakespeare Fesitval, Delacorte Theatre, Central Park, NY, 1975; Tlimpattia, *Dynamite Tonite!,* Yale Repertory, New Haven, CT, 1975; Sonya, *Uncle Vanya,* Globe Theatre, San Diego, CA, 1979; mother, *Six Characters in Search of an Author,* American Repertory Theatre, Cambridge, MA, 1984; Lady Sneerwell, *A School for Scandal,* American Repertory Theatre, Cambridge, MA, then Los Angeles Olympic Arts Theatre Festival, CA, 1985.

Photograph by Greg Gorman

LINDA LAVIN

MAJOR TOURS—*On a Clear Day You Can See Forever,* national.

PRINCIPAL TELEVISION APPEARANCES—Series: Detective Janice Wentworth, *Barney Miller,* ABC, 1975-76; Alice Hyatt, *Alice,* CBS, 1976-1985.

Episodic: *CBS Playhouse; Rhoda; Harry O,* others.

Specials: *The Beggars' Opera; Damn Yankees.*

Movies: *Like Mom, Like Me,* 1978; *The $5.20 an Hour Dream,* 1980; *A Matter of Life and Death,* 1981; *Another Woman's Child,* 1983; *A Place to Call Home,* 1985.

PRINCIPAL TELEVISION WORK—Producer: *Another Woman's Child; A Matter of Life and Death; The $5.20 an Hour Dream; A Place to Call Home.*

Director, episodes of *Alice,* CBS.

RELATED CAREER—President, Big Deal Films, Inc.

RECORDINGS: ALBUMS—*A Family Affair,* original cast recording, United Artists; *The Mad Show,* original cast recording, Columbia; *It's a Bird . . . It's a Plane . . . It's Superman,* original cast recording, Columbia.

MEMBER: Academy of Television Arts and Sciences (board of governors), National Commission of Working Women, Step Families of America.

AWARDS: Best Actress in a Comedy Series, two Golden Globe Awards, two Emmy Award nominations, for *Alice.*

SIDELIGHTS: Lavin's favorite roles include Elaine Navazio in *Last of the Red Hot Lovers,* Patsy Newquist in *Little Murders* by Jules Feiffer and the girl in *Cop-Out.* She enjoys tennis and cooking.

ADDRESSES: OFFICE—Warner Brothers, 4000 Warner Brothers Blvd., Burbank, CA 91505. AGENT—c/o Marty Litke, Litke/Grossbart Agency, 8500 Wilshire Blvd., Suite 506, Beverly Hills, CA 90211; c/o Nan Sumski, Sumski, Green & Co., 8380 Melrose Avenue, Suite 200, Los Angeles, CA 90069.

*   *   *

LEABO, Loi   1935-

PERSONAL: Born September 27, 1935, in Portland, OR.

VOCATION: Choreographer, director, and producer.

CAREER: PRINCIPAL STAGE WORK—Director of these Equity Showcases and Stock productions: *Scandal; The Fantasticks; Any Wednesday; Barefoot in the Park; Born Yesterday; Butterflies Are Free; Nothing to Hide; Bell, Book, and Candle; Generation; Luv; Three Bags Full; The Odd Couple; The Grass Harp.* Choreographer of these Equity Showcases and Stock productions: *Funny Girl; Oklahoma!; Brigadoon; Finian's Rainbow; King and I; Half-a-Sixpence; Carnival; Destry; The Great Waltz; La Traviata; The Pearl Fishers; Romeo and Juliet.*

LOI LEABO

Broadway productions: Dance captain, *Oklahoma!, Brigadoon,* both at New York City Center; assistant choreographer, *The Birds;* dancer: *Music Man; King and I; 110 in the Shade; Brigadoon; Oklahoma!; Destry;* corps de ballet, Metropolitan Opera Company, NY.

PRINCIPAL FILM WORK—Producer, *Landscapes of the Mind.*

RELATED CAREER—Co-producer, Theatre Seven (Equity Stock productions), Massachusetts and Rhode Island; producer and director, J.C. Penney Company, Internal Communications Department, 1970-78; client services, producer, Comart Aniforms, NY, 1979-81; vice-president, producer, Nicholodeon Productions, Inc., 1981—.

MEMBER: Society of Stage Directors and Choreographers, Actors' Equity Association, Screen Actors Guild, American Guild of Musical Artists.

ADDRESSES: OFFICE—30 Greenwich Avenue, Suite 1A, New York, NY 10011.

*   *   *

LEARY, David   1939-

PERSONAL: Born August 8, 1939, in Brooklyn, NY; son of Elizabeth Frances McKechnie; married Ellen Tovatt; children: Deborah, Rebecca, Daniel. EDUCATION: Attended City College of New York.

VOCATION: Actor.

CAREER: STAGE DEBUT—*Shoot Anything That Moves,* Off-Broadway production, 1969. PRINCIPAL STAGE APPEARANCES—Manager, emcee, *Piaf,* Plymouth Theatre, NY, 1981; Sergeant Karn, *Sus,* Hudson Guild Theatre, NY, 1983; standby Bob, *Home Front,* Royale Theatre, NY, 1985; Anton Gorbunov, *Before the Dawn,* American Place Theatre, NY, 1985; also appeared in *Emigres; Plough and the Stars,* Lincoln Center; *The National Health,* Circle in the Square; *Butley;* title role, *Macbeth,* Mercer-O'Casey Theatre; *Bloodknot,* Manhattan Theatre Club; Charley Now, *Da,* Broadway production; Edgar, *The Lady from Dubuque,* Broadway production; standby Dysart, *Equus,* Broadway production.

Regional: Lawrence Vail, *Once in a Lifetime,* and Hovstad, *An Enemy of the People,* both Arena Stage, Washington, DC; Bentham, *Juno and the Paycock,* Father Declan, *A Pagan Place,* Chaplain, *National Health,* Defense, *Arturo Ui,* all at the Long Wharf Theatre, New Haven, CT; Hildy Johnson, *The Front Page,* Actor's Theatre of Lousiville, KY; Donald, *The Philantropist,* Goodman Theatre, Chicago, IL; Aubrey Piper, *Show Off,* Claudius, *Hamlet,* both at the Philadelphia Drama Guild; Constable, *Henry V,* Gary, *Rooted,* both at the Hartford Stage Company, CT; Le Bret, *Cyrano de Bergerac,* Tesman, *Hedda Gabler, The Birthday Party,* and *St. Joan,* all at the Williamstown Theatre Festival, MA; *Julius Caesar* and *Antony and Cleopatra,* both with the American Shakespeare Festival, Stratford, CT; Reg, *Butley,* Coconut Grove Playhouse, FL.

PRINCIPAL TELEVISION APPEARANCES—Episodic: *The Equalizer; As the World Turns; Ryan's Hope; Guiding Light; One Life to Live; Search for Tomorrow; You Are There,* CBS; *Theatre Beat,* KCET; *Best of Families,* NET.

Movies: *Kojak: The Belarus File,* CBS, 1985.

DAVID LEARY

Mini-Series: *Kennedy,* NBC.

PRINCIPAL FILM APPEARANCES—*Piaf;* voice over, *Taps,* Twentieth Century-Fox, 1981.

MEMBER: Actors' Equity Association, Screen Actors Guild, American Federation of Television and Radio Artists, Players Club, Friars Club.

ADDRESSES: AGENT—c/o Neal Altman, Abrams Artists, 420 Madison Avenue, New York, NY 10017; Triad, 888 Seventh Avenue, Suite 1602, New York, NY 10106.

*   *   *

LEE, Irving Allen   1948-

PERSONAL: Born November 21, 1948, in New York, NY; son of Allan Ezekiel (a minister) and Ruth Juliet (Green) Lee. EDUCATION: Boston University, B.A., 1971. POLITICS: Democrat. RELIGION: Christian.

VOCATION: Actor and director.

CAREER: STAGE DEBUT—Judas, *Godspell,* Ford's Theatre, Washington, DC, 1972, for 832 performances. NEW YORK DEBUT—Leading player, *Pippin,* Imperial Theatre, 1974, for four hundred performances. PRINCIPAL STAGE APPEARANCES—Player King, *Rockabye Hamlet,* Minskoff Theatre, NY, 1975; male leads, *Ain't*

CONTEMPORARY THEATRE, FILM, AND TELEVISION • *Volume 3*

IRVING ALLEN LEE

Misbehavin', Longacre Theatre, NY, 1978; James Lincoln, *A Broadway Musical*, Lunt-Fontaine Theatre,NY, 1978; Daddy Johann Sebastian Brubeck, *Sweet Charity*, Minskoff Theatre, NY, 1986.

TELEVISION DEBUT—Calvin Stoner, *The Edge of Night*, ABC, 1978. PRINCIPAL TELEVISION APPEARANCES—Dr. Evan Cooper, *Ryan's Hope*, ABC, 1986.

MEMBER: Actors' Equity Association, Society of Stage Directors and Choreographers.

SIDELIGHTS: RECREATIONS—Writing poetry, refinishing wooden antiques.

Irving Lee wrote *CTFT*, "I decided on a career in theater—after years of training for the ministry—as the best possible alternative use of my communication skills. I wanted to influence the community of man, to which I feel very much connected, and to aspire to actualizing its highest potential and aspirations."

ADDRESSES: AGENT—c/o Dorothy Scott, Marje Fields, Inc., 165 W. 46th Street, Suite 1205, New York, NY 10036.

*   *   *

LEIGH, Janet   1927-

PERSONAL: Born Jeanette Helen Morrison, July 6, 1927, in Mercedes, CA; married John K. Carlyle, 1942 (annulled, 1942); married Stanley Reames (a bandleader), 1946 (divorced, 1948); married Tony Curtis (an actor), 1951 (divorced, 1963); married

Robert Brant (a stockbroker), 1964; children: (third marriage) Kelly Lee, Jamie Leigh.

VOCATION: Actress.

*CAREER:*FILM DEBUT—*The Romance of Rosey Ridge*, Metro-Goldwyn-Mayer, 1947. PRINCIPAL FILM APPEARANCES—*If Winter Comes*, Metro-Goldwyn-Mayer, 1947; *Hills of Home*, Metro-Goldwyn-Mayer, 1948; Dorothy Feiner, *Words and Music*, Metro-Goldwyn-Mayer, 1948; *Acts of Violence*, Metro-Goldwyn-Mayer, 1948; Meg March, *Little Women*, Metro-Goldwyn-Mayer, 1949; *That Forsythe Woman*, Metro-Goldwyn-Mayer, 1949; *The Doctor and the Girl*, Metro-Goldwyn-Mayer, 1949; *The Red Danube*, Metro-Goldwyn-Mayer, 1949; *Holiday Affair*, RKO, 1949.

Strictly Dishonorable, Metro-Goldwyn-Mayer, 1951; *Angels in the Outfield*, Metro-Goldwyn-Mayer, 1951; *Two Tickets to Broadway*, RKO, 1951; Rosa Szabo, *It's a Big Country*, Metro-Goldwyn-Mayer, 1952; *Just This Once*, Metro-Goldwyn-Mayer, 1952; *Scaramouche*, Metro-Goldwyn-Mayer, 1952; *Fearless Fagan*, Metro-Goldwyn-Mayer, 1952; *The Naked Spur*, Metro-Goldwyn-Mayer, 1953; *Confidentially Connie*, Metro-Goldwyn-Mayer, 1953; *Houdini*, Paramount, 1953; *Walking My Baby Back Home*, Universal, 1953; *Prince Valiant*, Twentieth Century-Fox, 1954; *Living It Up*, Paramount, 1954; *The Black Shield of Falworth*, Universal 1954; *Rogue Cop*, Metro-Goldwyn-Mayer, 1954; Ivy Conrad, *Pete Kelly's Blues*, Warner Brothers, 1955; Eileen Sherwood, *My Sister Eileen*, Columbia, 1955; *Safari*, Columbia, 1956; *Jet Pilot*, Universal, 1957; *Touch of Evil*, Universal, 1958; *The Vikings*, United Artists, 1958; *The Perfect Furlough*, Universal, 1958.

Who Was That Lady? Columbia, 1960; Marion Crane, *Psycho*, Paramount, 1960; guest star, *Pepe*, Columbia, 1960; *The Manchurian Candidate*, United Artists, 1962; Rosie, *Bye, Bye Birdie*, Columbia, 1963; *Wives and Lovers*, Paramount, 1963; *Three on a Couch*, Columbia, 1966; Susan Harper, *Harper*, Warner Brothers, 1966; *Kid Rodelo*, Paramount, 1966; *An American Dream*, Warner Brothers, 1966; *Hello Down There*, Paramount, 1968; *Grand Slam*, Paramount, 1968; *The Deadly Dream*, 1971; *One Is a Lonely Number*, Metro-Goldwyn-Mayer, 1972; *Night of the Lepus*, Metro-Goldwyn-Mayer, 1972; *Boardwalk*, Atlantic Releasing, 1979; *The Fog*, Avco Embassy, 1980.

PRINCIPAL TELEVISION APPEARANCES—Movies: *The Monk*, 1969; *Honeymoon with a Stranger*, 1969; *House on Greenapple Road*, 1970; also appeared in *World Series Murders; Death's Head*.

RECORDINGS: ALBUM—*Bye, Bye Birdie*, original soundtrack recording, Victor.

AWARDS: Best Supporting Actress, Academy Award nomination, 1960, for *Psycho*.

ADDRESSES: AGENT—Contemporary-Korman Agency, 132 Lasky Drive, Beverly Hills, CA 90212.*

*   *   *

LEONARD, Sheldon   1907-

PERSONAL: Born Sheldon Bershad, February 22, 1907; son of Frank and Anna (Levitt) Bershad; married Frances Bohr, June 28, 1931; children: Andrea, Stephen W.EDUCATION: Syracuse University, B.A., 1929.

VOCATION: Actor, producer, and director.

CAREER: PRINCIPAL STAGE APPEARANCES—*Kiss the Boys Goodbye*, Broadway production, 1938.

PRINCIPAL FILM APPEARANCES—Sam Church, *Another Thin Man*, Metro-Goldwyn-Mayer, 1939; *Tall, Dark and Handsome*, Twentieth Century-Fox, 1941; *Rise and Shine*, Twentieth Century-Fox, 1941; Tito Ralph, *Tortilla Flat*, Metro-Goldwyn-Mayer, 1942; Slip Moran, *Lucky Jordan*, Paramount, 1942; *Somewhere in the Night*, Twentieth Century-Fox, 1946; *Her Kind of Man*, Warner Brothers, 1946; Nick, *It's a Wonderful Life*, RKO, 1946; *The Gangster*, Warner Brothers, 1947; *Sinbad the Sailor*, RKO, 1947; *If You Knew Susie*, RKO, 1948; *My Dream Is Yours*, Warner Brothers, 1949; *Take One False Step*, Universal-International, 1949; *The Iroquois Trail*, 1950; *Here Come the Nelsons*, 1952; *Young Man with Ideas*, Metro-Goldwyn-Mayer, 1952; *Stop, You're Killing Me*, Warner Brothers, 1953; *Diamond Queen*, 1953; *Money from Home*, 1953; Harry, the Horse, *Guys and Dolls*, Metro-Goldwyn-Mayer, 1955; Chicago mobster, *Pocketful of Miracles*, United Artists, 1961.

PRINCIPAL TELEVISION APPEARANCES—Series: Danny's masseur, *Make Room for Daddy*, ABC, 1953; Sam Marco, *The Duke*, NBC, 1954; Phil Brokaw, *The Danny Thomas Show*, CBS, 1959-61; Eddic Smith, *Big Eddie*, CBS, 1975.

Episodic: *Damon Runyon Theatre*, CBS; *General Electric Theatre*, CBS; *Jeweler's Showcase*.

Guest: *Jimmy Durante Show*.

Movies: *Top Secret*, 1978.

PRINCIPAL TELEVISION WORK—Producer and director, *The Danny Thomas Show*, CBS. 1959-61; executive producer, *The Andy Griffith Show*, CBS, 1960-68; executive producer, *The Dick Van Dyke Show*, CBS, 1961-66; executive producer, *Gomer Pyle, U.S.M.C.*, CBS, 1964-70; executive producer, *I Spy*, NBC, 1965-68; executive producer, *My World and Welcome to It*, NBC, 1969-70; directed episodes of *The Real McCoys*.

AWARDS: Emmy Awards: Best Direction for Half Hour or Less, 1956, for "Danny's Comeback" episode of *The Danny Thomas Show;* Outstanding Directorial Achievement in Comedy, 1960-61, for *The Danny Thomas Show;* Outstanding Comedy Series, 1969-70, for *My World and Welcome to It*. Directors Guild of America Award; Sylvania Award; four nominations for Director of the Year by the Directors Guild of America.

ADDRESSES: OFFICE—Sheldon Leonard Productions, 315 S. Beverly Drive, Beverly Hills, CA 90212.*

*   *   *

LERNER, Alan Jay   1918-1986

PERSONAL: Born August 31, 1918, in New York, NY; died of throat cancer, June 14, 1986, in New York, NY, son of Joseph J. and Edith (Adelson) Lerner; married Ruth Boyd; married Marion Bell (a singer and actress); married Nancy Olsen (an actress); married Micheline Mussellin Posso di Bergo; married Karen Gundersson; married Sandra Payne; married Nina Bushkin; married Liz Robertson (an actress), August, 1981. EDUCATION: Attended Bedales in England; attended Choate; attended Harvard University.

VOCATION: Playwright, lyricist, producer, and director.

CAREER: PRINCIPAL STAGE WORK—Producer, *On a Clear Day You Can See Forever*, Lunt-Fontanne Theatre, NY, 1965; director, *Dance a Little Closer*, Minskoff Theatre, NY, 1983.

WRITINGS: MUSICAL PLAYS—*The Life of the Party*, Detroit, 1942; *What's Up?*, 1943; *The Day Before Spring*, Broadway production, NY, 1945; *Brigadoon*, Broadway production, NY, 1947; *Love Life*, 46th Street Theatre, NY, 1948; *Paint Your Wagon*, Shubert Theatre, NY, 1951; *My Fair Lady*, Mark Hellinger Theatre, NY, 1956; *Camelot*, Majestic Theatre, NY, 1960; *On a Clear Day You Can See Forever*, Lunt-Fontanne Theatre, NY, 1965; *Coco*, Mark Hellinger Theatre, NY, 1969; *Lolita*, 1971; *Gigi*, Broadway production, NY, 1973; *Music! Music!*, Broadway production, NY, 1974; *1600 Pennsylvania Avenue*, Broadway production, NY, 1976; *Carmelina*, St. James Theatre, NY, 1979; *Dance a Little Closer*, Minskoff Theatre, NY, 1983; lyrics featured in *Mighty Fine Music*, TOMI Theatre, NY, 1983.

MAJOR TOUR—Book, *Gene Kelly's Salute to Broadway*, 1975.

SCREENPLAYS AND/OR LYRICS—Script only, *An American in Paris*, Metro-Goldwyn-Mayer, 1951; lyrics only, *A Royal Wedding*, Metro-Goldwyn-Mayer, 1951; script and lyrics, *Gigi*, Metro-Goldwyn-Mayer, 1958; script and lyrics, *The Little Prince*, Paramount, 1974; also: *Brigadoon*, Metro-Goldwyn-Mayer, 1954; *My Fair Lady*, Warner Brothers, 1964; *Camelot*, Warner Brothers/Seven Arts, 1967, *Paint Your Wagon*, Paramount, 1969; *On a Clear Day You Can See Forever*, Paramount, 1970.

MUSICAL FILMS, UNPRODUCED—Script and lyrics, "Huckleberry Finn."

AUTOBIOGRAPHY—*The Street Where I Live*.

RECORDINGS: *Brigadoon*, original cast recording, Victor; *Paint Your Wagon*, original cast recording, RCA Victor; *My Fair Lady*, original cast recording, Columbia; *Camelot*, original cast recording, Columbia; *On a Clear Day You Can See Forever*, original cast recording, Victor; *Coco*, original cast recording, ABC-Paramount Records; *Gigi*, original cast recording, RCA; *Carmelina*, Original Cast Records; *An American in Paris*, original soundtrack recording, Metro-Goldwyn-Mayer; *Brigadoon*, original soundtrack recording, Metro-Goldwyn-Mayer; *A Royal Wedding*, original soundtrack recording, Metro-Goldwyn-Mayer; *Gigi*, original soundtrack recording, Metro-Goldwyn-Mayer; *My Fair Lady*, original soundtrack recording, Columbia; *Camelot*, original soundtrack recording, Warner Brothers; *Paint Your Wagon*, original soundtrack recording, Paramount; *On a Clear Day You Can See Forever*, original soundtrack recording, Columbia.

Collected lyrics: *Alan Jay Lerner Revisited*, Painted Smiles Records; *Lyrics by Lerner* (some performed by Lerner himself), DRG Records; *Kurt Weill Revisited, Volumes I and II*, Painted Smiles Records; *Burton Lane Revisited*, Painted Smiles Records.

AWARDS: New York Drama Critics Circle Award, 1947, for *Brigadoon;* Best Story and Screenplay, Academy Award, 1951, for *An American in Paris;* Best Song, Academy Award, 1951, for "Too Late Now," from *A Royal Wedding;* Antoinette Perry Award, New York Drama Critics Circle Award, Donaldson Award, all 1956, for *My Fair Lady;* Best Screenplay (based on material from another medium) and Best Song (title song), Academy Award, both 1958, for *Gigi;* Antoinette Perry Award nomination, 1960, for *Camelot;*

Best Screenplay (based on material from another medium), Academy Award nomination, 1964, for *My Fair Lady;* Antoinette Perry Award nomination, Grammy Award, 1965, for *On a Clear Day You Can See Forever;* Antoinette Perry Award nomination, 1969, for *Coco;* Original Song Score and/or Adaptation, Antoinette Perry Award, 1973, for *Gigi;* Original Song Score and/or Adaptation, Original Song Score and/or Adaptation, Academy Award, 1974, for *The Little Prince;* Best Song, Academy Award, 1974, for the title song from *The Little Prince;* Antoinette Perry Award nomination, 1983, for *Dance a Little Closer;* Choate Alumni Seal.

MEMBER: Dramatists Guild of America (president, 1958-62); President's Committee for the Cultural Center (Kennedy Center) in Washington, DC, 1962; elected to Songwriter's Hall of Fame, NY, 1971.

SIDELIGHTS: RECREATION—Tennis and boating.

Alan Jay Lerner worked with some of the most creative theatrical practitioners of the twentieth century. Most of his works (*The Day Before Spring, Brigadoon, Paint Your Wagon, My Fair Lady, Camelot, Gigi,* and *The Little Prince*) were written with the composer Frederick Loewe. *Love Life* was written with composer Kurt Weill; *1600 Pennsylvania Avenue* with Leonard Bernstein; *A Royal Wedding, On a Clear Day You Can See Forever* and *Carmelina* were written with Burton Lane; *Coco* was written with Andre Previn. Lerner also wrote a version of *On a Clear Day . . . ,* then titled *I Picked a Daisy,* with Richard Rodgers.

Lerner appeared at the YMHA series in New York City, *Lyrics and Lyricists,* discussing and performing his own works, on December 12, 1971.*

*   *   *

LESTER, Richard   1932-

PERSONAL: Born January 19, 1932, in Philadelphia, PA; married Deirdre Vivian Smith (a choreographer), August 28, 1956; children: Dominic, Claudia. EDUCATION: University of Pennsylvania, B.A., 1951.

VOCATION: Director, producer, and composer.

CAREER: PRINCIPAL FILM WORK—Director and composer, *The Running, Jumping and Standing Still Film,* 1959; director: *It's Trad, Dad,* 1961; *Mouse on the Moon,* 1963; *A Hard Day's Night,* 1964; *The Knack,* United Artists, 1964; *Help,* United Artists, 1965; *A Funny Thing Happened on the Way to the Forum,* United Artists, 1966; *How I Won the War,* United Artists, 1967; *Petulia,* Warner Brothers, 1968; *Bed Sitting Room,* United Artists, 1969; *The Three Musketeers,* Twentieth Century-Fox, 1973; *Juggernaut,* United Artists, 1974; *The Four Musketeers,* Twentieth Century-Fox, 1974; *Royal Flash,* Twentieth Century-Fox, 1975; *Robin and Marian,* Columbia, 1976; *The Ritz,* Warner Brothers, 1977; (producer only) *Superman,* Warner Brothers, 1978; *Butch and Sundance, the Early Years,* Twentieth Century-Fox, 1979; *Superman II,* Warner Brothers, 1981; *Superman III,* Warner Brothers, 1983; *Finders Keepers,* Warner Brothers, 1984.

RELATED CAREER—Music editor, assistant director, then director, CBS television, Philadelphia, PA, 1951-54; director and composer, ITV, London, 1955-57, producer, 1958-59; scriptwriter, CBC television, Canada, 1957; director, Courtyard Films, Ltd., 1967—.

AWARDS: Best Director, Rio de Janiero Film Festival, 1965, for *Help!;* Best Director, Tehran Film Festival, 1974, for *Juggernaut.*

ADDRESSES: OFFICE—Twickenham Studios, St. Margarets, Middlesex, England. AGENT—Creative Artists Agency, 1888 Century Park E., Los Angeles, CA 90067.

*   *   *

LEVIN, Peter

PERSONAL: Born Daniel Levin, in Trenton, NJ; son of Max (a merchant) and Katherine (Klempner) Levin; married Audrey Davis (a writer). EDUCATION: Carnegie-Mellon University, B.F.A., 1954; trained for the stage at the Webber-Douglas School of Drama, London, and with Lee Strasberg.

VOCATION: Actor and director.

CAREER: NEW YORK DEBUT—Peter, *The Diary of Anne Frank,* Cort Theatre, 1955. PRINCIPAL STAGE APPEARANCES—Orlando, *As You Like It,* Octavius Caesar, *Julius Caesar,* Horatio, *Hamlet,* all with San Diego Shakespeare Festival, CA, 1960; Parritt, *The Iceman Cometh,* Arena Stage, Washington, DC, 1960; Orlando, *As You Like It,* APA Shakespeare Festival, Princeton, NJ, 1961.

PRINCIPAL STAGE WORK—Director: *Hardware Poets,* Playhouse Theatre, NY, 1962-66; *Real Inspector Hound* and *A Memory of Two Mondays,* both Guildhall School, London; *Hamlet,* U.S. cities; *You Never Can Tell,* Arlington Heights, then Chicago, IL; *The Show Off,* Long Wharf Theatre, New Haven, CT, 1975.

PRINCIPAL TELEVISION WORK—Movies: Director—"The Other Woman," *ABC Playbreak,* 1973; "Heart in Hiding," *ABC Playbreak,* 1974; *The Comeback Kid,* 1979; *Rape and Marriage,* 1980; *Palmerstown, USA,* 1980; *Washington Mistress,* 1981; *The Marra Collins Story,* 1980; *Royal Romance of Charles and Diana,* CBS, 1982; *A Doctor's Story,* 1983; *A Reason to Live,* 1984; *Call to Glory,* 1985; *J.F.K.,* 1985; *Between Darkness and Dawn,* 1985; "Ashes of Mrs. Reasoner," *Hollywood Television Theatre;* "The Madness of God," *Theatre in America,* PBS.

Series: Director—*Lou Grant; Family; Paper Chase; Call to Glory; Ryan's Four; Fame; Cagney and Lacey; James at 15; Trauma Center; Love Is a Many Splendored Thing; Beacon Hill; Best of Families.*

Pilots: Director, *Knot's Landing.*

MEMBER: Actors' Equity Association, Directors Guild of America, Academy of Television Arts and Sciences.

AWARDS: Emmy Award nomination, 1980, for *Lou Grant;* Fullbright Scholarship, Norman Apell Award; Webber Cup; Shakespeare Cup, 1954-55.

ADDRESSES: AGENT—c/o Ken Gross, Robinson-Weintraub-Gross, 8428 Melrose Place, Suite C, Los Angeles, CA 90069.

*   *   *

LEVY, David   1913-

PERSONAL: Born January 2, 1913, in Philadelphia, PA; son of Benjamin (an accountant) and Lillian (Potash) Levy; married Lucile Alva Wilds, July 25, 1941 (divorced, 1970); children: Lance,

Linda. EDUCATION: Wharton School, University of Pennsylvania, B.S., economics, 1934, M.B.A., 1935. POLITICS: Independent Republican. MILITARY: U.S. Naval Reserve, 1944-46.

VOCATION: Producer and writer.

CAREER: PRINCIPAL TELEVISION WORK—Creator and producer, *The Addams Family,* ABC, 1964-66; executive producer, *The Double Life of Henry Phyfe,* ABC, 1966; producer, *The Pruitts of Southampton,* ABC, 1966-67; creative consultant, *Name That Tune,* for Ralph Edwards Productions, 1974-81; co-creator and executive producer, *Face the Music,* 1980-81; creative consultant, *The New You Asked for It,* 1981.

RELATED CAREER—With Young & Rubicam, NY: advertising copy-writer, 1938, vice-president, 1950-59, associate director of radio and television department, 1958-59; vice-president in charge of network programs and talent, NBC, NY, 1959-61; executive producer, Filmways Television Productions, Los Angeles, from 1964; executive producer, Goodson-Todman Productions, Los Angeles, 1968-69; executive vice-president in charge of television activities, Four Star International, Inc., 1970-72; producer, Paramount Television, 1972-73; member of faculty, California State University, Northridge, 1973-74; 1976-79.

WRITINGS: TELEVISION SCRIPTS—For: *Bonanza; Dr. Kildare; The Dick Powell Show; Bat Masterson; Klondike; The Americans; Outlaws; The Chameleons; The Gods of Foxcroft House; Goodyear-Alcoa Theatre; Robert Montgomery Presents;* others.

NOVELS—*The Chameleons,* Dodd, 1964; *The Gods of Foxcroft,* Arbor House, 1970; *The Network Jungle,* Major Books, 1976.

POETRY—*Against the Stream,* Outposts, 1970. Also short stories to magazines such as *Collier's* and *Good Housekeeping.*

AWARDS: Distinguished Service Award, Caucus for Producers, Writers, and Directors, 1984.

MEMBER: Writers Guild of America, Producers Guild (secretary, 1979-80); Caucus for Producers, Writers, and Directors (secretary, 1974—; executive director, 1978—).

SIDELIGHTS: David Levy worked as chief of the radio section, War Finance Division of the United States Treasury Department and consultant to the Secretary of the Treasury, from 1944-46 while serving in the Naval Reserves. Between 1952 and 1956 he was senior adviser for Logos Ltd. Citizens for Eisenhower-Nixon and was their director of radio-television in 1956.

ADDRESSES: HOME—214 1/2 S. Spalding Drive, Beverly Hills, CA 90212.

*   *   *

LEVY, Jonathan F.   1935-

PERSONAL: Born February 20, 1935; son of Milton Jerome (a lawyer) and Sylvia (a teacher; maiden name, Narins) Levy; married Geraldine Carro (a journalist), November 24, 1968; children: Catherine Sylvia. EDUCATION: Harvard College, A.B., 1956; Columbia University, M.A., Ph.D., 1966. RELIGION: Jewish. MILITARY: U.S. Army.

VOCATION: Writer.

WRITINGS: PLAYS—Translation, *Turandot,* 1964; Libretto, *Boswell's Journals,* Alice Tully Hall, NY, 1972; *Marco Polo,* Phoenix Theatre, NY, 1977; libretto translation, *Wild Rose,* Brooklyn Academy of Music, 1978, Belwin Mills, 1986; *Charlie the Chicken,* Manhattan Theatre Club, published in the *Best Short Plays of 1983,* 1983.

RELATED CAREER—Playwright in Residence, Manhattan Theatre Club, NY, 1983-78; teacher, State University of New York at Stony Brook, 1979—; literary advisor, Manhattan Theatre Club, NY, 1982—; visiting scholar, Harvard University, MA, 1985—.

AWARDS: Charlotte Chorpenning Award, Outstanding Playwright for Children, 1979.

ADDRESSES: OFFICE—Department of Theatre Arts, State University of New York at Stony Brook, Stony Brook, NY 11794. AGENT—Susan Schulman, 454 W. 44th Street, New York, NY 10036.

*   *   *

LEWIS, Daniel E.   1944-

PERSONAL. Born July 12, 1944, in New York, NY; son of Jerome (a tool and dye maker) and Louise (an x-ray technician; maiden name, Lavria) Lewis; married Jane Zarrington (a choreographer), December 13, 1980. EDUCATION: Trained for the stage at the Juilliard School of Performing Arts.

VOCATION: Choreographer, dancer, director, and teacher.

CAREER: PRINCIPAL STAGE WORK—Dancer: Yiddish Theater, NY, 1960-64; *A Choreographic Offering, Legend, Psalm, The Winged, Comedy, The Unsung,*Jose Limon Dance Company, Asia, Europe, South America, Union of Soviet Socialists Republics, U.S., 1962-74; Daniel Lewis Dance Company, 1981; Ruth Currier Company; Felix Fibich Company; Stuart Hodes Company; Sofie Maslow Company; David Wood Company; Norman Waler Company; Charles Weidman Company; Anna Sokolow Company; American Dance Theater; The Juilliard Dance Ensemble.

Director: Batsheva Company, Israel, 1969; Repertory Dance Theater of Salt Lake City, UT, 1969; Royal Swedish Ballet, 1970, 1971, 1973; Royal Danish Ballet, 1972; Alvin Ailey American Dance Theater, 1972; American Ballet Theatre, 1969, 1970; National Ballet of Canada, 1968; Danzahoy Caracus, 1980; The National Ballet School of Toronto, 1985; Dance Kern Holland, 1985.

Choreographer: Individual dances—"The Minding of the Flesh Is Death," Juilliard School, NY, 1967; "My Echo, My Shadow and Me," Contemporary Dance System, 1972; "Irving the Terrific," Lincoln Center Student Programs, NY, 1972; "And First They Slaughtered Angels," New York State Council of the Arts, 1974; "Cabbagepatch," University of California at Los Angeles, 1976; "Proliferation," 1976; "Life and Other Things," 1978; "Mostly Beethoven," 1979; "There's Nothing Here of Me but Me," Amherst College, MA, 1980; "Beethoven Duet," University of Calgary, 1980; "Open Book," 1981; "Moments," 1982; "To Doris and Charles," Portland State College, OR, 1982; "Textured Lighting," 1984; "Atomic Ambiance," 1985; "Women," 1985; "Mind Over Matter," 1985.

Choreographer: Productions—*Dido and Aeneur,* Dallas Civic Opera, TX, 1971; *Aiada,* Houston Grand Opera, TX, 1978; *Feathertop* and *Le Rossignol,* American Opera Center, Lincoln Center, NY, 1980; *The Tempest* and *Nefertiti,* Amherst College, MA, 1977; *Crisp,* INTAR, NY, 1981.

PRINCIPAL TELEVISION WORK—Dancer: *And David Wept,* CBS; *Lamp unto My Feet; Camera Three;* others.

RELATED CAREER—Teacher: Juilliard School, NY, 1967—; Amherst College, 1974-80; New York University, 1977—; London Contemporary Dance School, 1976-83; University of California at Los Angeles, 1970-71; Movimento in Mexico City, 1980-81; University of Calgary, Canada, 1984.

Artistic director and choreographer of Daniel Lewis Dance, 1972—; director and administrator, National Ballet School of Canada, 1984-85; program director and administrator, Bennington College, summer dance, 1985.

WRITINGS: BOOKS—*The Illustrated Dance Technique of Jose Limon,* Harper and Row, 1984.

MEMBER: Society of Stage Directors and Choreographers, American Guild of Musical Artists.

ADDRESSES: HOME—260 W. 22nd Street, New York, NY 10011. AGENT—Pentalle, 104 Franklin Street, New York, NY 10013.

* * *

LEWIS, Shari   1934-

PERSONAL: Born Shari Hurwitz, January 17, 1934, in New York, NY; daughter of Abraham B. (an educator and magician) and Ann (a music coordinator; maiden name, Ritz) Hurwitz; married Stan Lewis (marriage ended); married Jeremy Tarcher (a television producer), March 15, 1958; children: Mallory Jessica. EDUCATION: High School of Music and Arts, NY; attended Columbia University, 1951; studied acting with Sanford Meisner at the Neighborhood Playhouse.

VOCATION: Ventriloquist, puppeteer, and conductor.

CAREER: PRINCIPAL TELEVISION APPEARANCES—Series: *Facts 'n Fun,* WRCA, 1953; *Kartoon Club,* 1954; *Shari and Her Friends,* 1955; *Shariland,* 1956; *Hi, Mom,* 1957; *The Shari Lewis Show,* 1960-62; *Shari at Six,* BBC, 1968-76; *The Shari Show,* syndicated, 1976-77.

Specials: *Once upon an Evening with Shari Lewis,* CBC, 1978; *Shari's Christmas Concert,* 1983.

PRINCIPAL TELEVISION WORK—Writer, producer, and performer, *A Picture of Us,* NBC, 1971.

PRINCIPAL STAGE APPEARANCES—Dancer with Zachary Solov, Music Tent, Lambertville, NJ; Royal Command performances, London, 1970, 1973, 1978; conductor of over fifty symphony orchestras, including the National Symphony at the Kennedy Center, Washington, DC, Pittsburgh Symphony, and the National Arts Centre Orchestra of Canada.

WRITINGS: BOOKS—*The Shari Lewis Puppet Book,* Citadel, 1958, revised edition published as *Making Easy Puppets,* Dutton, 1967; *Fun with Kids,* Doubleday, then McFadden/Bartell, 1960; (with Lillian Oppenheimer) *Folding Paper Puppets,* Stein and Day, 1962;

SHARI LEWIS

(with Oppenheimer) *Folding Paper Toys,* Stein and Day, 1963; *Dear Shari,* Stein and Day, 1963; (with Oppenheimer) *Folding Paper Masks,* Dutton, 1965.

"Headstart" series, McGraw-Hill, all with Jacquelyn Reinach: *The Headstart Book of Looking and Listening,* 1966; *The Headstart Book of Thinking and Imagining,* 1966; *The Headstart Book of Knowing and Naming,* 1966; *The Headstart Book of Be Nimble and Be Quick,* 1968.

The Tell-It-Make-It Book, J.P. Tarcher, 1972; (with father, Abraham B. Hurwitz) *Magic for Non-Magicians,* J.P. Tarcher, 1975; *The Kids-Only Club Book,* J.P. Tarcher, 1976; *How Kids Can Really Make Money,* Holt, 1979; *Spooky Stuff* (4 volumes), Holt, 1979; *Impossible--Unless You Know How,* Holt, 1979; *Toy Store-in-a-Book,* Holt, 1979; *Magic Show-in-a-Book,* Holt, 1980; *Secrets, Signs, Signals and Codes,* Holt, 1980; *Things Kids Collect,* Holt, 1981; *The Do It Better Book,* Holt, 1981; (with Lan O'Kun) *One-Minute Bedtime Stories* (illustrated by Art Cummings), Doubleday, 1982; (with Jacquelyn Reinach) *Lamb Chop's Play Along Storybook* (with J. Reinach), Scholastic, 1983; *Abracadabra! Magic and Other Tricks,* World Almanac/Ballantine, 1984; *One Minute Animal Stories,* Doubleday, 1984; *One Minute Favorite Fairy Tales,* Doubleday, 1985; *One Minute Bible Stories, Old Testament,* Doubleday, 1986; *One Minute Bible Stories, New Testament,* Doubleday, 1987.

RECORDINGS: Shari in Storyland, RCA Victor; *Fun in Shariland,* RCA Camden; *Hi, Kids!,* Golden; *Give Your Child a Headstart,* RCA Camden; *One-Minute Bedtime Stories,* Polygram; video cassettes, Metro-Goldwyn-Mayer/United Artists: *Have I Got a Story for You; You Can Do It; Kooky Classics; One-Minute Bedtime Stories,* Worldvision.

AWARDS: Emmy Awards: Best Local Program, Outstanding Female Personality, 1957; Best Children's Show, Outstanding Female Personality, 1958, 1959; Outstanding Children's Entertainer, 1972-73. Peabody Award, 1960; Monte Carlo International Television Award, 1961; Radio-Television Mirror Award, 1960; Kennedy Center Award, Excellence in the Arts for Young People, 1983.

ADDRESSES: AGENT—c/o GTA, Inc., 3128 Cavendish, Los Angeles, CA 90064.

* * *

LIBERACE 1919-

PERSONAL: Born Wladziu Valentino Liberace, May 16, 1919, in West Allis, WI; son of Salvatore and Francis Liberace. EDUCATION: Attended Wisconsin College of Music.

VOCATION: Pianist, concert artist, actor, and composer.

CAREER: DEBUT—With the Chigago Symphony Orchestra, 1935.

FILM DEBUT—*Sincerely Yours,* Warner Brothers, 1955. PRINCIPAL FILM APPEARANCES—*When the Boys Meet the Girls,* Metro-Goldwyn-Mayer, 1965; Counsel Starker, *The Loved One,* Metro Goldwyn-Mayer, 1965.

TELEVISION DEBUT—Concert artist, KLAC, Los Angeles, 1951. PRINCIPAL TELEVISION APPEARANCES—Series: *Liberace,* NBC, 1952, then in syndication, 1953-55, then ABC, 1958-59, and then CBS, 1969.

Episodic: Shandal, *Batman,* ABC; *Hotel,* ABC, 1985; *Another World,* NBC, 1985, 1986.

Guest: *The Ed Sullivan Show,* others.

CONCERT AND NIGHTCLUB APPEARANCES—Carnegie Hall, NY, 1953; Madison Square Garden, NY, 1954; other clubs and halls around the world.

WRITINGS: BOOKS—*Liberace Cooks,* 1970; *Liberace,* 1973; *The Wonderful Private World of Liberace,* Harper & Row, 1986.

AWARDS: Twice recipient of the Emmy Award; Entertainer of the Year Award, 1973.

ADDRESSES: AGENT—c/o Burt Taylor, Agency for the Performing Arts, 9000 Sunset Blvd., Los Angeles, CA 90069.*

* * *

LIGHT, Judith

BRIEF ENTRY: Born in Trenton, NJ. Actress. The only child of an accountant and a former model, Judith Light graduated from a private school at age sixteen and attended Carnegie Tech in Pittsburgh, graduating in 1970 with a drama degree. Light spent four-and-one half years working in repertory in Seattle and Milwaukee until she landed a small role in Joseph Papp's New York production of *A Doll's House.* Roles in *Guys and Dolls* and on television's *Kojak* followed, and she portrayed Stella in *A Streetcar Named Desire* in Toronto, but she was on the verge of giving up acting when she auditioned for and won a role as a regular on ABC's daytime serial, *One Life to Live.* Her character, Karen Wolek, a doctor's wife

turned afternoon prostitute who reformed but spent most of the time on the verge of returning to her former life, became a popular staple of the show from 1977 to 1982. Light received two daytime Emmy awards and two Soapy Awards. She currently plays Angela Bower on ABC's prime-time series, *Who's the Boss.**

* * *

LINDEN, Hal 1931-

PERSONAL: Born Harold Lipshitz, March 20, 1931, in New York, NY; son of Charles and Frances (Rosen) Lipshitz; married Frances Martin. EDUCATION: City College of New York, B.B.A., 1952; studied voice with Lou McCollogh and John Mace; studied acting with Paul Mann and Lloyd Richards at the America Theatre Wing. MILITARY: U.S. Army Special Services.

VOCATION: Actor and singer.

CAREER: STAGE DEBUT—In chorus, *Mr. Wonderful,* Cape Cod Melody Tent, Hyannis, MA, 1955. NEW YORK DEBUT—Jeff Moss, *Bells Are Ringing* (replacing Sydney Chaplin) Shubert Theatre, 1958. PRINCIPAL STAGE APPEARANCES—Chuck, *Strip for Action,* Shubert Theatre, New Haven, CT, 1956; *Angel in the Pawnshop,* Playhouse-in-the-Park, Philadelphia, PA, 1960; Matt, *Wildcat,* Alvin Theatre, NY, 1960; *On a Clear Day You Can See Forever,* 1960; Pinky Harris, *Wish You Were Here,* summer stock, 1961; Jeff Moss, *Bells Are Ringing,* summer stock, 1961; Billy Crocker, *Anthing Goes,* Orpheum Theatre, NY, 1962; Sid Sorokin, *The Pajama Game,* summer stock, 1963; Dick, *Something More,* Eugene O'Neill Theatre, NY, 1964; *Subways Are for Sleeping,* 1965; No Face, *Illya Darling,* Mark Hellinger Theatre, NY, 1967;

HAL LINDEN

The Devil, *The Apple Tree,* Shubert Theatre, NY, 1967; Yissel Fishbein, *The Education of H*Y*M*A*N K*A*P*L*A*N,* Alvin Theatre, NY, 1968; Ernest, *The Love Match,* Ahmanson Theatre, Los Angeles, 1968; Mayer Rothschild, *The Rothschilds,* Lunt-Fontanne Theatre, NY, 1969; Charlie, *Three Men on a Horse,* Lyceum Theatre, NY, 1969.

Title role, *The Sign in Sidney Brustein's Window,* Longacre Theatre, NY, 1972; Ben, *The Enclave,* Washington Theatre Club, Washington, DC, 1973; Sid Sorokin, *The Pajama Game,* Lunt-Fontanne Theatre, NY, 1973; *Night of 100 Stars,* Radio City Music Hall, NY, 1982; *Room Service,* Kennedy Center for the Performing Arts, 1983; also appeared in *Kismet.*

MAJOR TOURS—Jeff Moss, *Bells Are Ringing,* 1959.

FILM DEBUT—*Bells Are Ringing,* 1959. PRINCIPAL FILM APPEARANCES—*When You Comin' Back Red Ryder,* Columbia, 1979.

PRINCIPAL TELEVISION APPEARANCES—Series: Host, *Animals, Animals, Animals,* ABC; title role, *Barney Miller,* ABC, 1975-1982; host, *FYI,* ABC; Alexander Blacke, *Blacke's Magic,* NBC, 1986—.

Movies: *Father Figure,* CBS, 1980; *Starflight,* ABC, 1983; *The Other Woman,* CBS, 1983; Jack Warner, *My Wicked Wicked Ways,* CBS, 1985.

Specials: *The Hal Linden Special,* ABC; *Hal Linden's Big Apple,* ABC; *I Do! I Do!,* RKO/Nederlander, Entertainment Channel, cable, 1983; *The Best of Everything,* 1983.

AWARDS: Antoinette Perry Award, 1970, for Mayer Rothschild, *The Rothschilds.*

SIDELIGHTS: Before turning to acting, Hal Linden was a professional musician, playing saxophone with the Sammy Kaye and Bobby Sherwood orchestras.

ADDRESSES: MANAGER—Paul Tush, 119 W. 57th Street, New York, NY 10019.

*   *   *

LINDLEY, Audra

PERSONAL: Daughter of Bert (an actor) and Bessie (an actress; maiden name, Fisher) Lindley; married James Whitmore (an actor); children: John, Elizabeth, Alice, William, Bert. EDUCATION: Attended the Max Reinhardt Workshop. POLITICS: Democrat.

VOCATION: Actress.

CAREER: PRINCIPAL STAGE APPEARANCES—*Take Her She's Mine,* Broadway; *A Case of Libel,* Broadway; *Spofford,* Broadway; *Fire,* Broadway, 1966; *The Magnificent Yankee,* Washington, DC; *On Golden Pond,* Fifth Avenue Theatre, NY, 1981; *Elba,* Manhattan Theatre Club; *In the Sweet Bye 'n Bye,* Washington, DC, 1984; *The Chic Life,* summer stock, 1984; Molly Egan, *Handy Dandy,* Syracuse Stage, Syracuse, NY, 1984, then Empire State Institute for the Performing Arts, Albany, NY, 1985; *Long Days Journey into Night,* Citadel Theatre, Canada, 1984; *Death of a Salesman,* Citadel Theatre, 1984.

MAJOR TOURS—*Handy Dandy,* 1985.

PRINCIPAL FILM APPEARANCES—*Taking Off,* Universal, 1971; *The Heartbreak Kid,* Twentieth Century-Fox, 1972; *When You Comin' Back Red Ryder,* Columbia, 1979; *Cannery Row,* Metro-Goldwyn-Mayer, United Artists, 1982; *Best Friends,* Warner Brothers, 1982; *Desert Hearts,* Samuel Goldwyn, 1986.

PRINCIPAL TELEVISION APPPEARANCES—Series: Liz Matthews, *Another World,* NBC; Amy Fitzgerald, *Bridget Loves Bernie,* CBS, 1972-73; Janet Scott, *Doc,* CBS, 1976; Lillian, *Fay,* NBC, 1976; Helen Roper, *Three's Company,* ABC, 1977-79; Helen Roper, *The Ropers,* ABC, 1979-80.

Movies: *The Love Boat,* 1976; *Pearl; Canterbury Ghost,* BBC; *Revenge of the Stepford Wives,* 1980; *The Day the Bubble Burst,* 1982.

MEMBER: Actors' Equity Association, Screen Actors Guild, American Federation of Television and Radio Artists.

AWARDS: Golden Globe award nominations, for *Bridget Loves Bernie,* and *Three's Company;* Best Performer of the 1983-84 season, Citadel Theatre, Canada; Straw Hat award, 1984, for *The Chic Life.*

ADDRESSES: AGENT—c/o Marcie Glenn, International Creative Management, 8899 Beverly Blvd., Los Angeles, CA 90048. OFFICE—9000 Sunset Blvd., Suite 1115, Los Angeles, CA 90069.

*   *   *

LINKLETTER, Art   1912-

PERSONAL: Full name, Arthur Gordon Linkletter, July 17, 1912, in Moose Jaw, Saskatchewan, Canada; son of Fulton John and Mary (Metzler) Linkletter; married Lois Foerster, November 25, 1935; children: Jack, Dawn, Robert (died), Sharon, Diane (died). EDUCATION: San Diego State College, B.A., 1934.

VOCATION: Television broadcaster, writer, and producer.

CAREER: PRINCIPAL RADIO WORK—Program director, KGB, San Diego, CA, 1934; radio director, *California International Exposition,* San Diego, 1935; radio director, *Texas Centennial Exposition,* Dallas, 1936; radio director, *San Francisco World's Fair,* 1937-39; co-host and staff writer, *People Are Funny,* NBC, from 1942; host, *House Party,* CBS, from 1944.

PRINCIPAL TELEVISION WORK—Host and executive producer, *Life with Linkletter,* ABC, 1950-52; host, executive producer, and writer, *People Are Funny,* NBC, 1954-1961; host, *Inside Beverly Hills,* NBC, 1955; *Art Linkletter's House Party,* CBS, 1955-70; *Ford Startime,* NBC, 1959; substitute host, *The Tonight Show,* NBC, 1962; host, *The Art Linkletter Show,* CBS, 1963; host, executive producer, and writer, *Salute to Baseball,* NBC, 1965; host, *Hollywood Talent Scouts,* CBS, 1965-66; host, *Art Linkletter's Secret World of Kids,* NBC.

RELATED CAREER: President, Linkletter Productions; co-owner, John Gruedel Radio Productions; chairman, Linkletter Enterprises.

WRITINGS: BOOKS—*People Are Funny,* 1953; *Kids Say the Darndest Things,* 1957; *The Secret World of Kids,* 1959; *Confessions of a Happy Man,* 1961; *Kids Still Say the Darndest Things,* 1961; *A Child's Garden of Misinformation,* 1965; *I Wish I'd Said That,* 1968; *Linkletter Down Under,* 1969; *Oops,* 1969; *Drugs at My*

Door Step, 1973; *Women Are My Favorite People*, 1974; *How to Be a Super Salesman*, 1974; *Yes, You Can!*, 1979; *I Didn't Do It Alone*, 1979; *Public Speaking for Private People*, 1980.

STAGE SCRIPTS—*Cavalcade of the Golden West*, 1940; *Cavalcade of America*, 1941.

ADDRESSES: OFFICE—8500 Wilshire Blvd., Beverly Hills, CA 90211.*

* * *

LINVILLE, Larry   1939-

PERSONAL: Full name, Larry Lavon Linville; born September 29, 1939, in Ojai, CA; son of Harry Lavon and Fay Pauline (Kennedy) Linville; children: Kelly Leigh. EDUCATION: Attended University of Colorado, 1957-59; studied for the theatre at the Royal Academy of Dramatic Art, London, England, 1959-61.

VOCATION: Actor and writer.

CAREER: PRINCIPAL STAGE APPEARANCES—In repertory, U.S. cities, 1961-68; *More Stately Mansions*, Broadway production, 1968.

PRINCIPAL FILM APPEARANCES—*Kotch*, Cinerama Releasing Corp., 1972.

PRINCIPAL TELEVISION APPEARANCES—Series: Major Frank Burns, *M*A*S*H*, CBS, 1972-77; Major General Kevin Kelley, *Grandpa Goes to Washington*, NBC, 1978-79; Lyle Block, *Checking In*, CBS, 1981; Randy Bigelow, *Herbie, the Love Bug*, CBS, 1982.

Movies: *Grandpa Goes to Washington*, NBC, 1978.

WRITINGS: SCREENPLAY—*Ragwing*, 1975.

MEMBER: Actors' Equity Association, American Federation of Television and Radio Artists, Screen Actors Guild, Writers Guild of America.

ADDRESSES: AGENT—David Shapira & Associates, 15301 Ventura Blvd., Sherman Oaks, CA 91403.*

* * *

LITTLE, Rich   1938-

PERSONAL: Full name, Richard Caruthers Little; born November 26, 1938, in Ottawa, Ontario, Canada; son of Lawrence Peniston and Elizabeth Maud (Wilson) Little; married Jeanne E. Worden, October 16, 1971. EDUCATION: Lisgar Collegiate, Ottawa, B.A., 1957.

VOCATION: Actor, comedian, and impressionist.

CAREER: TELEVISION DEBUT—Guest, *The Judy Garland Show*, CBS, 1964. PRINCIPAL TELEVISION APPEARANCES—Series: Stan Parker, *Love on a Rooftop*, ABC, 1966-71; regular, *The John Davidson Show*, ABC, 1969; regular, *ABC Comedy Hour*, ABC, 1972; regular, *The Julie Andrews Hour*, ABC, 1972-73; host, *The Rich Little Show*, NBC, 1976; host, *You Asked for It*, syndication, 1981-83.

Guest: *On Broadway Tonight*, CBS, 1965; *The Barbara McNair Show*, syndication; *The David Frost Show*, syndication; guest host, *Operation: Entertainment*, ABC, 1968; *Love, American Style*, ABC.

AWARDS: Entertainer of the Year Award, 1974.

ADDRESSES: AGENT—c/o Frank Rio, Triad Artists, 10100 Santa Monica Blvd., 16th Floor, Los Angeles, CA 90067.*

* * *

LO BIANCO, Tony   1936-

PERSONAL: Born October 19, 1936, in New York, NY.

VOCATION: Actor and director.

CAREER: PRINCIPAL STAGE APPEARANCES—*The Royal Hunt of the Sun*, American National Theatre and Academy (ANTA), NY, 1965; *The Office*, Broadway production, 1966; *The Rose Tattoo*, City Center, then Broadway run, NY, 1966; *Yankees 3 Detroit 0 Top of the Seventh*, Off-Broadway production, 1975; Eddie, *A View from the Bridge*, Long Wharf Theatre, New Haven, CT, 1981, then Ambassador Theatre, NY, 1983.

Earlier Broadway productions include *The Goodbye People* and *90 Day Mistress*. Also seen Off-Broadway in *Oh Dad, Poor Dad, Mama's Hung You in the Closet and I'm Feelin' So Sad*, *The Zoo Story*, *Tartuffe*, *The Threepenny Opera*, *Answered the Flute*, *Camino Real*, *Journey to the Day*, *Nature of the Crime*, and *Incident at Vichy*.

PRINCIPAL FILM APPEARANCES—Ray Fernandez, *The Honeymoon Killers*, Cinerama Releasing Corp., 1970; *The French Connection*, Twentieth Century-Fox, 1971; *The Seven-Ups*, Twentieth Century-Fox, 1973; *F.I.S.T.*, United Artists, 1978; *Blood Brothers*, Warner Brothers, 1979; *The Conspiracy*, CAC Productions, 1985.

PRINCIPAL FILM WORK—Director, *Too Scared to Scream*, Paramount, 1985.

PRINCIPAL TELEVISION APPEARANCES—Series: Lt. Alex Ascoli, *Jessie*, ABC, 1984.

Episodic: Tony Calabrese, *Police Story*, NBC, 1973-75; *Love of Life*.

Movies: *The Story of Jacob and Joseph*, 1974; *Welcome Home, Bobby*, 1986; also appeared in *Hidden Faces*.

Pilot: *Pals*, NBC, 1981.

AWARDS: Obie Award, 1976, for *Yanks 3 Detroit 0 Top of the Seventh*.

ADDRESSES: AGENT—c/o Ed Limato, William Morris Agency, 151 El Camino Drive, Beverly Hills, CA 90212.*

* * *

LOPEZ, Priscilla   1948-

PERSONAL: Born February 26, 1948, in the Bronx, NY; daughter of Francisco and Laura (Candelaria) Lopez; married Vincent

Fanuele, January 16, 1972. EDUCATION: Studied for the theatre at the Performing Arts High School in New York.

VOCATION: Actress.

CAREER: PRINCIPAL STAGE APPEARANCES—*Breakfast at Tiffany's,* Broadway production, 1966; revue performer, *What's a Nice Country Like You Doing in a Place Like This,* Off-Broadway production, 1973; Morales, *A Chorus Line,* New York Shakespeare Festival, Public Theatre, NY, 1975, then Shubert Theatre, NY; *A Day in Hollywood/A Night in the Ukraine,* John Golden Theatre, NY, 1980-81; Lisa, *Key Exchange,* Orpheum Theatre, NY, 1982; Joy/Shirley, *Buck,* American Place Theatre, NY, 1983; Terry, *Extremities,* Westside Arts Center/Cheryl Crawford Theatre, NY, 1983; Norina, *Non-Pasquale,* New York Shakespeare Festival, Delacorte Theatre, August-September, 1983. Earlier Broadway appearances include: *Henry, Sweet Henry; Lysistrata; Company; Her First Roman; The Boy Friend; Pippin.*

PRINCIPAL STAGE WORK—Special assistant to Tommy Tune for *Nine,* Forty-Sixth Street Theatre, NY, 1982-83.

PRINCIPAL FILM APPEARANCES—*Cheaper to Keep Her,* 1980.

PRINCIPAL TELEVISION APPEARANCES—Series: Sister Agnes, *In the Beginning,* CBS, 1978.

AWARDS: Obie Award, 1975, for *A Chorus Line;* Antoinette Perry Award nomination, 1976, for *A Chorus Line;* Antoinette Perry Award, 1980, for *A Day in Hollywood/A Night in the Ukraine.*

ADDRESSES: AGENT—William Morris Agency, 1350 Avenue of the Americas, New York, NY 10019.*

*   *   *

LOREN, Sophia   1934-

PERSONAL: Born Sofia Villani Scicolone, September 20, 1934, in Rome, Italy; daughter of Riccardo (a construction engineer) and Romilda (Villani) Scicolone; married Carlo Ponti (a film producer) September 17, 1957; children: Carlo, Jr., Eduardo. EDUCATION: Scuole Magistrali Superiori, Naples, Italy.

VOCATION: Actress.

CAREER: PRINCIPAL FILM APPEARANCES—As Sofia Scicolone: Extra, *Quo Vadis,* Metro-Goldwyn-Mayer, 1950; extra, *Cuori Sul Mare (Hearts at Sea),* Cine-Albatross, 1950; extra, *Il Voto (The Vote),* A.R.A. Films, 1950; extra, *Le Sei Moglie di Barbarlu (Bluebeard's Seven Wives),* Golden Film Production, 1950; extra, *Io Sono il Capatz,* Jolly Films, 1950; extra, *Milana Miliardaria,* Mambretti Productions, 1951; extra, *Anna,* Archway, 1951; extra, *Il Mago per Forza,* Amati-Mambretti, 1951; extra, *Il Sogno di Zorro (Zorro's Dream)* I.C.S. Productions, 1951.

As Sofia Lazzaro: Bit part, *E' arrivato L'Accordatore (The Tuner Has Arrived),* Itala/Titanus, 1951; extra, *Era Lui . . . Si, Si (It's Him . . . Yes, Yes),* Italian Amati, 1951.

As Sophia Loren: Bit part, *La Favorita,* M.A.S. Productions, 1952; Barbara, *Africa Sotto I Mari (Africa Under the Seas),* Gala Films, 1952; Elvira, *La Tratta Delle Bianche* (also known as *Girls Marked for Danger* or *The White Slave Trade*), Excelsa/Ponti-De Laurentiis, 1952; title role (acting only) *Aida,* Eagle Films, 1953; Sisina,

Neapolitan Fantasy, Archway, 1953; *Ci Troviamo in Galleria (We'll Meet in the Gallery),* Athene-Enic Production, 1953; the model, *Our Times* (also known as *Anatomy of Love*), Lux/Cines, 1953; *La Domenica Della Buona Genti (Good Folks' Sunday),* Trionfalcine Production, 1953; lead role, *Il Paese dei Campanella,* Valentina Films, 1953; Anna, *Un Giorno in Pretura (A Day in Court),* Excelsa/Documento, 1953; Cleopatra/Nisca, *Two Nights with Cleopatra,* Excelsa-Rosa Production, 1953; lead role, *Pellegrini D'Amore (Pilgrim of Love),* Pisorno Production, 1953; Honoria, *Attila, the Hun,* Archway, 1953; the ballerina, *Miseria e Nobilita (Poverty and Nobility),* Excelsa, 1954; Sofia, *Gold of Naples* (also known as *Every Day's a Holiday*), Gala Films, 1954; Nives Mongolini, *Woman of the River,* Columbia, 1954; Lina, *Too Bad She's Bad,* Gala, 1954.

Agnese, *The Sign of Venus,* Gala, 1955; Carmela, *The Miller's Wife,* Gala, 1955; Donna Sofia, *Scandal in Sorrento,* Gala, 1955; Antoinette, *Lucky to Be a Woman,* Intercontinental Films, 1955; Juana, *The Pride and the Passion,* United Artists, 1957; Phaedra, *Boy on a Dolphin,* Twentieth Century-Fox, 1957; Dita, *Legend of the Lost,* United Artists, 1957; Anna, *Desire Under the Elms,* Paramount, 1958; Cinzia Zaccardi, *Houseboat,* Paramount-Scribe, 1958; Stella, *The Key,* Columbia, 1958; Rose Bianco, *Black Orchid,* Paramount, 1959; Kay, *That Kind of Woman,* Paramount, 1959.

Angela Rossini, *Heller in Pink Tights,* Paramount, 1960; Lucia Curcio, *It Started in Naples,* Paramount, 1960; Princess Olympia, *A Breath of Scandal* (also known as *Olympia*), Paramount, 1960; Epifania Parerga, *The Millionairess,* Twentieth Century-Fox, 1960; Cesira, *Two Women,* Gala Films, 1961; Chimene, *El Cid,* Rank Organization, 1961; Catherine Huebscher, *Madame* (also known as *Madame Sans-Gene*), Embassy/Twentieth Century-Fox, 1961; Zoe, "The Raffle," sketch in *Boccaccio '70,* Embassy/Twentieth Century-Fox, 1961; Lisa Macklin, *Five Miles to Midnight,* United Artists, 1962; Johanna, *The Condemned of Altona,* Twentieth Century-Fox, 1962; Adelina/Anna/Mara, *Yesterday, Today, and Tomorrow,* Embassy/Paramount, 1963; Lucilla, *The Fall of the Roman Empire,* Rank, 1964; Filumena Marturano, *Marriage, Italian Style,* Embassy/Paramount, 1964; Nora, *Operation Crossbow,* Metro-Goldwyn-Mayer/Carlo Ponti, 1965; title role, *Lady L,* Metro-Goldwyn-Mayer, 1965; title role, *Judith,* Paramount, 1965.

Yasmin Azir, *Arabesque,* Rank/Universal, 1966; Natascha, *A Countess from Hong Kong,* Rank/Universal, 1966; Isabella, *Cinderella, Italian Style* (also known as *More Than a Miracle* or *Happily Every After*) Metro-Goldwyn-Mayer, 1967; Maria, *Ghosts, Italian Style* or *Three Ghosts,* Metro-Goldwyn-Mayer, 1967; Giovanna, *Sunflower,* Avco Embassy, 1969; Valeria Billi, *The Priest's Wife,* Warner Brothers, 1970; Maddalena, *Lady Liberty,* Warner Brothers/United Artists, 1971; Sister Germana, *White Sister,* Columbia-Warner, 1971; Aldonza/Dulcinea, *Man of La Mancha,* United Artists, 1972; Adriana De Mauro, *The Voyage,* United Artists, 1973; Teresa Leoni, *Verdict,* Les Films Concordia, 1974; title role, *Angela,* 1977; *The Cassandra Crossing,* Avco Embassy, 1977; *A Special Day,* Cinema Five, 1977; *Brass Target,* United Artists, 1978; *Firepower,* Associated Film Distributors, 1979.

PRINCIPAL TELEVISION APPEARANCES—Movies: Romilda Villani and the title character, *Sophia Loren: Her Own Story,* 1980; *Aurora,* NBC, 1984.

Episodic: "Softly, Softly," *30 Minute Theatre; Rivals of Sherlock Holmes; Fantasy Island.*

Specials: *Profile of Sophia Loren; From Rome with Love; Sophia.*

RECORDINGS: Original soundtrack recording, *Man of La Mancha,* United Artists; *Peter Sellers and Sophia Loren,* Angel Records.

AWARDS: Best Actress, Buenos Aires Festival Award, 1956, for *Too Bad, She's Bad;* Best Actress, Japanese Academy Award, 1958, for *The Key;* Venice Festival Award, David Di Donatello Award (Italy), Victoire Popularity Award, (France), all 1959, for *Black Orchid;* Best Actress, Academy Award, David Di Donatello Award, Cannes Festival Award, New York Critic Award, Cork Festival Award, Japanese Academy Award, Belgian Academy Award, Golden Owl Award, Show Buiness Illustrated, Golden Globe Award, Trofeo Cinelandia Award (Spain), Ohio Critics Award, Victoire Popularity Award, Sole D'Oro Popularity Award (Italy), Bambi Popularity Award (West Germany), Prix Uilenspigoel Award (Belgium), 1961, Grand Prix Europa Award, British Film Academy Award, Golden Laurel Award (Chile), Victoire Popularity Award, Fungo D'Oro Popularity Award (Italy), all 1961, for *Two Women.*

Best Actress, Rapallo Festival Award (Italy), 1961, for *Heller in Pink Tights;* Best Actress, Prix Uilenspigoel Award, American Legion Popularity Award, Bambi Popularity Award, Bravo Popularity Award (West Germany), Victoire Popularity Award, Snosiki Popularitry Award (Finland), Premio Triunfo Award, Bengal Film Journalists Association Award (India), all 1962; Bambi Popularity Award, Bravo Popularity Award, Snosiki Popularity Award, all 1963; Bambi Popularity Award, Bravo Popularity Award, Snosiki Popularity Award, all 1964.

Best Actress, David di Donatello Award, Golden Globe Award, all 1964, for *Yesterday, Today, and Tomorrow;* Best Actress, Academy Award nomination, 1965, for *Marriage, Italian Style;* Bambi Popularity Award, Snosiki Popularity Award, Bravo Popularity Award, Texas Cinema Exhibitors Popularity Award, all 1966; Bengal Film Journalists Association, Bambi Popularity Award, Bravo Popularity Award, all 1967; Ramo d'Oro Award, Box-Office Favorite Medal Award (Italy), Bambi Popularity Award, Bravo Popularity Award, all 1968, for *More Than a Miracle;* Best Foreign Actress Diploma Award, U.S.S.R., 1969, for *Marriage, Italian Style;* David di Donatello Award, 1970, for *Sunflower;* Bengal Film Journalists Association Award, Premio Stadio Popularity Award (Italy), 1971; Helene Curtis Award, 1972; Simpatia Popularity Award (Italy), Rudolph Valentino Screen Services Award (Italy), 1973; David di Donatello Award, 1974, for *The Journey.*

In addition to the above, Sophia Loren has won Best Actress awards at the Cannes Film Festival and Cork Festival, been named Best Actress by Japan, Belgium, Spain, France and Italy for *Two Women,* and has been voted the most popular actress on three continents by more individual polls, critics polls and various film societies than any other actress.

ADDRESSES: HOME—Geneva, Switzerland. OFFICE—c/o Champion Film, One Piazza Aracoeli, Roma, Italy.

*   *   *

LORING, Gloria   1946-

PERSONAL: Born Gloria Jean Goff, December 10, 1946, in New York, NY; daughter of Gerald Louis (a musician and salesman) and Dorothy Ann (Tobin) Goff; married Alan Thicke, July 22, 1970 (divorced, 1986); children: Brennan Todd, Robin Alan.

VOCATION: Actress and singer.

GLORIA LORING

CAREER: TELEVISION DEBUT—Singer, *Merv Griffin Show,* 1967. PRINCIPAL TELEVISION APPEARANCES—Liz Chandler, *Days of Our Lives,* NBC, 1980—.

RECORDINGS: ALBUMS—Produced *A Shot in the Dark* for the Juvenile Diabetes Foundation, 1985; has recorded several albums of her own.

WRITINGS: BOOKS—*Days of Our Lives Celebrity Cookbook,* Volume I, 1981, Volume II, 1983; *Living the Days of Our Lives,* 1985. SONGS—Composed themes for *Differ'nt Strokes,* NBC, 1979-85, ABC, 1985—, and *Facts of Life,* NBC, 1979—.

AWARDS: Humanitarian Award, 1983, and International Parents of the Year Award, 1984, both from Juvenile Diabetes Foundation.

ADDRESSES: OFFICE—14755 Ventura Blvd., Suite 477, Sherman Oaks, CA 91403. AGENT—The Craig Agency, 8485 Melrose Place, Suite E, Los Angeles, CA 90069.

*   *   *

LOUIS, Tobi   1940-

PERSONAL: Born April 14, 1940, in Madison, WI. EDUCATION: American Academy of Dramatic Arts, teaching certificate, 1958; New York University, B.A., 1960, M.A., 1963; also attended the New School, NY; studied at Martha Graham and Katherine Dunham schools of dance and with Lee Strasberg, Horton Foote, and Sharon Thie.

VOCATION: Writer and actor.

CAREER: STAGE DEBUT—Jo, *Little Women,* Barbizon Plaza Theatre, NY, for ten performances. PRINCIPAL STAGE APPEARANCES—In stock, regional, and off-Broadway theaters.

FILM DEBUT—Extra, *Fourteen Hours,* Twentieth Century-Fox, 1951.

TELEVISION DEBUT—First woman, *The Old Lady Shows Her Medals,* Theater Guild. PRINCIPAL TELEVISION APPEARANCES—*Irving Mansfield/Betsy Arnell Game Show,* ABC; *U.S. Steel Hour,* CBS.

WRITINGS: PLAYS—*Cry of a Summer Night,* first produced at the Actors Playhouse, NY, 1965; *Sounds of Laughter,* first produced at the Actors Playhouse, NY, 1965; *Time Is a Thief,* O'Neill Theater Foundation, CT, and at New Dramatists, NY; *Fantasy,* O'Neill Theater Foundation, CT, and Playbox Theatre, NY; *Solitude, Frenzy and the Revolution,* Farleigh Dickinson University, NY, and O'Neill Theater Foundation at the Manhattan Theater Club, NY; *The Insides of Orchid Price,* Hunter College, NY, and Old Burney Theater, NY; *Take a Chance,* New Dramatists, NY, 1985.

AWARDS: John Golden Playwriting Fellowship and Columbia Film Writers Workshop Award, both for *Orchid Price;* CBS Television Writers Workshop Award, for *Cry of a Summer Night.*

MEMBER: Actor's Equity Association, Dramatists Guild, O'Neill Theater Association, New Dramatists, PEN, Columbia Films Writers Workshop, CBS Television Writers Workshop.

SIDELIGHTS: Tobi Louis wrote *CTFT,* "I'm a very private person with a great love for animals. If I weren't a writer, I'd be a veternarian."

ADDRESSES: HOME—New York, NY.

* * *

LOUISE, Tina   1938-

PERSONAL: Born February 11, 1938, in New York, NY. EDUCATION: Attended Miami University; studied for the theatre at the Neighborhood Playhouse in New York as well as at the Actors Studio with Lee Strasberg.

VOCATION: Actress.

CAREER: NEW YORK DEBUT—Chorus, *Two's Company,* Alvin Theatre, 1952. PRINCIPAL STAGE APPEARANCES—*The Fifth Season,* Broadway production, 1953; *John Murray Anderson's Almanac,* Broadway production, 1953; Appassionata von Climax, *Li'l Abner,* St. James Theatre, NY, 1956; Gloria Currie, *Fade Out, Fade In,* Mark Hellinger Theatre, NY, 1964.

FILM DEBUT—Griselda, *God's Little Acre,* United Artists, 1958. PRINCIPAL FILM APPEARANCES—*Day of the Outlaw,* United Artists, 1959; *For Those Who Think Young,* United Artists, 1964; *The Wrecking Crew,* Columbia, 1969; *The Good Guys and the Bad Guys,* Warner Brothers, 1969; *How to Commit Marriage,* Cinerama, 1969; *The Happy Ending,* United Artists, 1969; *The Stepford Wives,* Columbia, 1975; *O.C. and Stiggs,* 1985; *Dog Day.*

TELEVISION DEBUT—*Studio One.* PRINCIPAL TELEVISION APPEARANCES—Series: *Jan Murray Time,* NBC, 1955; Ginger Grant, *Gilligan's Island,* CBS, 1964-67; Julie Grey, *Dallas,* CBS, 1978; Taylor Chapin, *Rituals,* syndicated, 1984-85.

Episodic: *Mannix; Ironside; Kung Fu; Police Story; Kojak; Matt Houston; Fantasy Island; Love Boat; Marcus Welby; Cannon; Chips; Blacke's Magic; Simon and Simon.*

Movies: *Nightmare in Badham County* (also known as *Nightmare*), ABC, 1976; *Look What's Happened to Rosemary's Baby* (retitled *Rosemary's Baby II*), ABC, 1976; *SST Death Flight* (retitled *SST: Disaster in the Sky*), ABC, 1977; *Friendship, Secrets, and Lies,* NBC, 1979; *The Day the Women Got Even,* NBC, 1980; *Advice to the Lovelorn,* NBC, 1981; *Indian Summer,* 1986.

ADDRESSES: HOME—Beverly Hills, CA.

* * *

LOY, Myrna   1905-

PERSONAL: Born Myrna Williams, August 2, 1905, in Raidersburg, MT; daughter of David Frankin (a rancher) and Della (Johnson) Williams; married Arthur Hornblow, Jr. (a producer), 1936 (divorced, 1942); married John Hertz, Jr., 1942 (divorced, 1945); married Gene Markey (a writer), 1946 (divorced, 1950), married Howland Sargeant, 1952 (divorced, 1960); children: (third marriage) Melinda, James. EDUCATION: Westlake School for Girls.

VOCATION: Actress.

CAREER: STAGE DEBUT—Chorus dancer, Graumann's Chinese Theatre, Hollywood, CA, 1925. NEW YORK DEBUT—Mrs. Morehead, *The Women,* Broadway, 1973. PRINCIPAL STAGE APPEARANCES—*Good Housekeeping;* the woman, *Don Juan in Hell; The Marriage-Go-Round; Relatively Speaking.*

MAJOR TOURS—Lead, *There Must Be a Pony,* pre-Broadway tour, 1962; *Dear Love,* tour, 1970; Ethel Banks, *Barefoot in the Park,* tour.

FILM DEBUT—*What Price Beauty?* 1925. PRINCIPAL FILM APPEARANCES—Senator's mistress, *Ben Hur,* Metro-Goldwyn-Mayer, 1925; chorus, *Pretty Ladies,* Metro-Goldwyn-Mayer, 1925; chorus, *Cave Man,* Warner Brothers, 1926; *The Gilded Highway,* Warner Brothers, 1926; *Why Girls Go Back Home,* Warner Brothers, 1926; native girl, *Across the Pacific,* Warner Brothers, 1926; Borgia spy, *Don Juan,* Warner Brothers, 1926; negro spy, *Ham and Eggs at the Front,* Warner Brothers, 1927; *The Climbers,* Warner Brothers, 1927; *Simple Sis,* Warner Brothers, 1927; showgirl, *The Jazz Singer,* Warner Brothers, 1927; lead role, *Bitter Apples,* Warner Brothers, 1927; title role, *The Girl from Chicago,* Warner Brothers, 1927; *If I Were Single,* Warner Brothers, 1928; *Heart of Maryland,* Warner Brothers, 1928; *Beware of Married Men,* Warner Brothers, 1928; *Turn Back the Hours,* 1928; *Crimson City* (first oriental role), Warner Brothers, 1928; *Pay as You Enter,* Warner Brothers, 1928; Slinky, *State Street Sadie* (part-talkie), Warner Brothers, 1928; gangster's moll, *The Midnight Taxi,* Warner Brothers, 1928; dancer/slave girl, *Noah's Ark,* Warner Brothers, 1928; *Fancy Baggage,* Warner Brothers, 1929 (all the above silent or part-talkies).

Azuri, *The Desert Song,* Warner Brothers, 1929; Indian mystery woman, *The Black Watch,* Fox, 1929; gypsy adventuress, *The*

Squall, Warner Brothers, 1929; southern belle, *Hardboiled Rose*, Warner Brothers, 1929; native girl, *Evidence*, Warner Brothers, 1929; Floradora Sextette/Chinese Fantasy sequence, *The Show of Shows*, Warner Brothers, 1929; a Mexican, *The Great Divide*, Warner Brothers, 1930; *The Jazz Cinderella*, Chesterfield, 1930; *Cameo Kirby*, Fox, 1930; native belle, *Isle of Escape*, Warner Brothers, 1930; *Under the Texas Moon*, Warner Brothers, 1930; *Cock o' the Walk*, Sono Art-World Wide, 1930; *Bride of the Regiment*, Warner Brothers, 1930; *The Last of the Duanes*, Fox, 1930; Kara, the "firefly," *The Truth About Youth*, Warner Brothers, 1930; harem girl, *Renegades*, Fox, 1930; *Rogue of the Rio Grande*, Sono Art-World Wide, 1930; *The Devil to Pay*, United Artists, 1930; *Naughty Flirt*, Warner Brothers, 1931; *Body and Soul*, Fox, 1931; Morgan Le Faye, *A Connecticut Yankee*, Fox, 1931; *Hush Money*, Fox, 1931; *Transatlantic*, Fox, 1931; *Skyline*, Fox, 1931; *Rebound*, RKO, 1931; *Consolation Marriage*, RKO, 1931; Joyce, *Arrowsmith*, United Artists, 1931.

Emma, Metro-Goldwyn-Mayer, 1932; *The Wet Parade*, Metro-Goldwyn-Mayer, 1932; Becky Sharp, *Vanity Fair*, Hollywood Exchange, 1932; *The Woman in Room 13*, Metro-Goldwyn-Mayer, 1932; *New Morals for Old*, Metro-Goldwyn-Mayer, 1932; Countess Valentine, *Love Me Tonight*, Paramount, 1932; half-caste, *Thirteen Women*, RKO, 1932; Fah Lo See (Fu Manchu's daughter), *The Mask of Fu Manchu*, Metro-Goldwyn-Mayer, 1932; Cecilia Henry, *The Animal Kingdom*, RKO, 1932; *Topaze*, RKO, 1933; *The Barbarian*, Metro-Goldwyn-Mayer, 1933; title role, *The Prizefighter and the Lady* (also known as *Every Woman's Man*), Metro-Goldwyn-Mayer, 1933; *When Ladies Meet*, Metro-Goldwyn-Mayer, 1933; *Penthouse*, Metro-Goldwyn-Mayer, 1933; *Night Flight*, Metro-Goldwyn-Mayer, 1933; Laura Hudson, *Men in White*, Metro-Goldwyn-Mayer, 1934; Eleanor, *Manhattan Melodrama*, Metro-Goldwyn-Mayer, 1934; Nora Charles, *The Thin Man*, Metro-Goldwyn-Mayer, 1934; *Stamboul Quest*, Metro-Goldwyn-Mayer, 1934; title role, *Evelyn Prentice*, Metro-Goldwyn-Mayer, 1934; *Broadway Bill*, Columbia, 1934; Sheila Mason, *Wings in the Dark*, Paramount, 1934; Vivian Palkmer, *Whipsaw*, Metro-Goldwyn-Mayer, 1935.

Linda Sanford, *Wife vs. Secretary*, Metro-Goldwyn-Mayer, 1936; *Petticoat Fever*, Metro-Goldwyn-Mayer, 1936; Billie Burke, *The Great Ziegfeld*, Metro-Goldwyn-Mayer, 1936; title role, *To Mary with Love*, Twentieth Century-Fox, 1936; Connie Allenbury, *Libeled Lady*, Metro-Goldwyn-Mayer, 1936; Nora Charles, *After the Thin Man*, Metro-Goldwyn-Mayer, 1936; Katie O'Shea, *Parnell*, Metro-Goldwyn-Mayer, 1937; *Double Wedding*, Metro-Goldwyn-Mayer, 1937; *Manproof*, Metro-Goldwyn-Mayer, 1938; Ann Barton, *Test Pilot*, Metro-Goldwyn-Mayer, 1938; Alma Harding, *Too Hot to Handle*, Metro-Goldwyn-Mayer, 1938; *Lucky Night*, Metro-Goldwyn-Mayer, 1939; Lady Edwina Esketh, *The Rains Came*, Twentieth Century-Fox, 1939; Nora Charles, *Another Thin Man*, Metro-Goldwyn-Mayer, 1939.

I Love You Again, Metro-Goldwyn-Mayer, 1940; *Third Finger, Left Hand*, Metro-Goldwyn-Mayer, 1940; *Love Crazy*, Metro-Goldwyn-Mayer, 1941; Nora Charles, *Shadow of the Thin Man*, Metro-Goldwyn-Mayer, 1941; Nora Charles, *The Thin Man Goes Home*, Metro-Goldwyn-Mayer, 1944; *So Goes My Love*, Universal, 1946; Milly Stephenson, *The Best Years of Our Lives*, RKO, 1946; Margaret, *The Bachelor and the Bobby Soxer*, RKO, 1947; Nora Charles, *Song of the Thin Man*, Metro-Goldwyn-Mayer, 1947; unbilled guest appearance, *The Senator Was Indiscreet*, Universal, 1947; Muriel Blandings, *Mr. Blandings Builds His Dream House*, RKO, 1948; mother, *The Red Pony*, Republic, 1949; *That Dangerous Age*, Korda, 1949.

Mrs. Lillian Gilbreth, *Cheaper by the Dozen*, Twentieth Century-Fox, 1950; *This Be Sin*, United Artists, 1950; Mrs. Lillian Gilbreth, *Belles on Their Toes*, Twentieth Century-Fox, 1952; *The Ambassador's Daughter*, United Artists, 1956; *Lonelyhearts*, United Artists, 1958; Martha Eaton, *From the Terrace*, Twentieth Century-Fox, 1960; Aunt Bea, *Midnight Lace*, Universal, 1960; *The April Fools*, National General, 1969; *Airport 1975*, Universal, 1974; *The End*, United Artists, 1978; *Just Tell Me What You Want*, Warner Brothers, 1980.

PRINCIPAL TELEVISON APPEARANCES—Episodic: *General Electric Theatre; Family Affair; The Virginians; Ironside; Columbo.*

Movies: *Do Not Fold, Spindle or Mutilate*, 1971; *Death Takes a Holiday*, 1971; *The Couple Takes a Wife*, 1972; *Indict and Convict*, 1973; *The Elevator*, 1974; *It Happened at Lakewood Manor*, 1977; also, *Summer Solstice.*

Specials: *Meet Me in St. Louis; Minerva; Happy Birthday.*

Guest: *The George Gobel Show; The Perry Como Show; The June Allyson Show;* others.

AWARDS: One of the Ten Best Money Making Stars, *Motion Picture Herald-Fame* Poll Award, 1937, 1938.

ADDRESSES: OFFICE—229 S. Orange Drive, Los Angeles, CA 90036. AGENT—The Lantz Office Inc., 9255 Sunset Blvd., Suite 509, Los Angeles, CA 90069.

*   *   *

LUDLAM, Charles   1943-

PERSONAL: Born April 12, 1943, in Floral Park, NY; son of Joseph William and Marjorie (Braun) Ludlam. EDUCATION: Hofstra University, B.A., 1965.

VOCATION: Actor, playwright, director, and producer.

CAREER: NEW YORK DEBUT—Peeping Tom, *The Life of Lady Godiva*, 17th Street Studio, 1967. LONDON DEBUT—Baron Khanazar von Bluebeard, *Bluebeard*, Open Space Theatre, 1971. PRINCIPAL STAGE WORK—Producer, director, and actor, *Big Hotel*, 17th Street Studio, NY.

With the Ridiculous Theatrical Company at the 17th Street Studio, NY: actor and director, *Conquest of the Universe/When Queens Collide*, 1967; actor and director, *Turds in Hell*, 1968; actor and director, *The Grand Tarot*, 1969; actor and director, *Bluebeard*, 1970; actor and director, *Eunuchs of the Forbidden City*, 1971.

Paw Hatfield, *Corn*, 13th Street Theatre, NY, 1972; Marguerite Gautier, *Camille, A Tearjerker*, 13th Street Theatre, NY, 1973; Buck Armstrong, *Hot Ice* and Marguerite Gautier, *Camille*, both Evergreen Theatre, NY, 1974; producer and director of puppet play, *Professor Bedlam's Punch and Judy*, Evergreen Theatre, NY, 1974; producer, director, and portrayed Carlton Stone, Jr., *Stage Blood*, Evergreen Theatre, NY, 1974; Baron Khanazar von Bluebeard, *Bluebeard*, Evergreen Theatre, NY, 1975; producer, director, and actor, *Caprice*, Provincetown Playhouse, NY, 1976; director, *Der Ring Gott Farblonjet*, Truck and Warehouse, NY, 1977.

Revivals at One Sheridan Square, Ridiculous Theatrical Company: actor, director, and producer, *Stage Blood*, 1978; *Camille*, 1978;

actor, producer, and director, *The Ventriloquist's Wife*, 1978; actor, producer, and director, *The Enchanted Pig*, 1979; actor, producer, and director, *A Christmas Carol*, 1979; actor and director, *Women Behind Bars*, 1980; actor, producer, and director, *The Mystery of Irma Vep*, 1984-86; producer and director, *Salammbo*, 1986.

MAJOR TOURS—European tours, 1971 and 1973.

RELATED CAREER—Associate adjunct professor and playwright in residence, Yale University, 1982-83.

WRITINGS: PLAYS, PRODUCED—At the Ridiculous Theatrical Company, Evergreen Theatre, One Sheridan Square: *Big Hotel,* 1967; *Conquest of the Universe/When Queens Collide,* 1967; (with Bill Vehr) *Turds in Hell,* 1968; *The Grand Tarot,* 1969; *Bluebeard,* 1970; *Eunuchs of the Forbidden City,* 1971; *Corn,* 13th Street Theatre, 1971; *Camille, A Tearjerker,* 1972; *Hot Ice,* 1973; *Professor Bedlam's Punch and Judy,* 1974; *Stage Blood,* 1974; *Bluebeard,* 1975; *Caprice,* Provincetown Playhouse, 1976; book, *Der Ring Got Farblonjet,* 1977; *The Ventriloquist's Wife,* 1978; *The Enchanted Pig,* 1979; *A Christmas Carol,* 1979; *Women Behind Bars,* 1980; *Irma Vep,* 1985; *Salammbo,* 1986.

RELATED CAREER—Co-founder, The Ridiculous Theatrical Company, NY, 1967.

AWARDS: Village Voice Off-Broadway (Obie) Award 1969, for founding the Ridiculous Theatrical Company; Guggenheim Fellowship in Playwriting, 1979; *Village Voice* Off-Broadway (Obie) Awards, 1972, for Paw Hatfield, *Corn,* and 1973, for title role, *Camille.*

SIDELIGHTS: RECREATION—Puppetry and horticulture.

Charles Ludlam has appeared on stage since his childhood. He founded a theatre in Northport, Long Island at the age of seventeen and produced plays by August Strindberg, Eugene O'Neill and others. His favorite roles include Camille and Bluebeard.

ADDRESSES: HOME—55 Morton Street, New York, NY 10014. OFFICE—Ridiculous Theatrical Company, One Sheridan Square, New York, NY 10014.*

M

MacARTHUR, James   1937-

PERSONAL: Born December 8, 1937, in Los Angeles, CA; adopted son of Charles and Helen (an actress; maiden name Hayes) MacArthur; married Melody Patterson (an actress; divorced); children: Charles, Mary.

VOCATION: Actor.

CAREER: STAGE DEBUT—*The Corn Is Green*, Olney Theatre, MD, 1945. PRINCIPAL STAGE APPEARANCES—*Life with Father*, 1953; *Invitation to a March*, Broadway, 1960.

PRINCIPAL FILM APPEARANCES—*The Young Stranger*, Universal, 1957; *The Light in the Forest*, Buena Vista, 1958; *The Third Man on the Mountain*, Buena Vista, 1959; *Kidnapped*, Buena Vista, 1960; *The Swiss Family Robinson*, Buena Vista, 1960; *The Interns*, Columbia, 1962; *Spencer's Mountain*, 1963; *Cry of Battle*, Allied Artists, 1963; *The Truth About Spring*, 1965; *The Bedford Incident*, Columbia, 1965; *Ride Beyond Vengence*, Columbia, 1966; *The Love-Ins*, Columbia, 1967; *Hang 'em High*, United Artists, 1968; *The Angry Breed*, 1968.

PRINCIPAL TELEVISION APPEARANCES—Series: Detective Danny Williams, *Hawaii Five-O*, CBS, 1968-80.

ADDRESSES: AGENT—Contemporary-Korman, 132 Lasky Drive, Beverly Hills, CA 90212.*

*   *   *

MACCHIO, Ralph

PERSONAL: Born on Long Island, NY.

VOCATION: Actor.

CAREER: PRINCIPAL FILM APPEARANCES—*Up the Academy*, Warner Brothers, 1980; title role, *The Karate Kid*, Columbia, 1984; *Teachers*, Metro-Goldwyn-Mayer/United Artists, 1985; *Crossroads*, Columbia, 1986; *The Karate Kid II*, Columbia, 1986.

PRINCIPAL TELEVISION APPEARANCES—Series: Jeremy Andretti, *Eight Is Enough*, ABC, 1980-81.

Movies: *Journey to Survival; Dangerous Company*, 1982; *The Three Wishes of Billy Grier*, ABC, 1984.

PRINCIPAL STAGE APPEARANCES—*Cuba and His Teddy Bear*, Public Theatre, NY, 1986.

ADDRESSES: AGENT—Writers & Artists Agency, 11726 San Vicente Boulevard, Suite 300, Los Angeles, CA 90049.*

*   *   *

MacMURRAY, Fred   1908-

PERSONAL: Full name, Frederick Martin MacMurray; born August 30, 1908, in Kankakee, IL; son of Frederick and Maleta (Martin) MacMurray; married Lillian Lamont, June 19, 1936 (divorced); married June Haver, June 28, 1954. EDUCATION: Attended Carroll College, WI, 1925-26.

VOCATION: Actor and musician.

CAREER: PRINCIPAL STAGE APPEARANCES—Member of a comedy stage band; *Three's a Crowd* (revue) NY, 1934; *Roberta*, NY, 1934.

FILM DEBUT—*Grand Old Girl*, 1935. PRINCIPAL FILM APPEARANCES—*Gilded Lily*, 1935; *Hands Across the Table*, 1935; *The Bride Comes Home*, 1935; *Alice Adams*, 1935; *Trail of the Lonesome Pine*, 1936; *Beyond Suspicion*, 1936, *Maid of Salem*, 1937; *Exclusive*, 1937; *True Confession*, 1937; *Men with Wings*, 1938; *Coconut Grove*, 1938; *Sing You Sinners*, 1938; *Cafe Society*, 1939; *Invitation to Happiness*, 1939; *Honeymoon in Bali* (also known as *My Love for Yours*), 1939; *Never a Dull Moment*, 1943; *Double Indemnity*, 1944; *Murder He Says*, 1945; *Pardon My Past*, 1945; *Smoky*, 1946; *Suddenly It's Spring*, 1947; *The Egg and I*, 1947; *Singapore*, 1947; *A Miracle Can Happen*, 1947; *Miracle of the Bells* 1948; *Don't Trust Your Husband* (also known as *An Innocent Affair*) 1948; *Family Honeymoon*, 1948.

Car 99, 1950; *Callaway Went Thataway*, Metro-Goldwyn-Mayer, 1951; *Millionaire for Christy*, 1951; *Fair Wind for Java*, 1953; *The Moonlighter*, 1953; *Caine Mutiny*, 1954; *Pushover*, 1954; *Woman's World*, 1954; *The Far Horizons*, 1955; *At Gunpoint*, Allied Artists, 1955; *The Rains of Rachipur*, Twentieth Century-Fox, 1955; *There's Always Tomorrow*, Universal, 1956; *Gun for a Coward*, Universal, 1957; *Quantez*, Universal, 1957; *Good Day for a Hanging*, Columbia, 1958; *The Shaggy Dog*, Buena Vista, 1959; *Face of a Fugitive*, Columbia, 1959; *The Oregon Trail*, Twentieth Century-Fox, 1959.

The Apartment, United Artists, 1960; *The Absent Minded Professor*, Buena Vista, 1961; *Bon Voyage*, Buena Vista, 1962; *Son of Flubber*, Buena Vista, 1963; *Kisses for My President*, Warner Brothers, 1964; *Follow Me Boys*, Buena Vista, 1966; *The Happiest Millionaire*, Buena Vista, 1967; *Charlie and the Angel*, Buena Vista, 1972; *The Swarm*, Warner Brothers, 1978.

PRINCIPAL TELEVISION APPEARANCES—Series: Steve Douglas, *My Three Sons,* ABC, 1960-65, then CBS, 1965-72.

Episodic: *The U.S. Steel Hour.*

RELATED CAREER—Orchestra musician, Chicago, Los Angeles, 1925-29; vaudeville circuit, 1929-34.

ADDRESSES: AGENT—Chasin-Park-Citron, 9255 Sunset Blvd., Los Angeles, CA 90069.*

*   *   *

MacRAE, Gordon   1921-1986

PERSONAL: Born March 12, 1921, in East Orange, NJ; died of cancer, January 24, 1986, in Lincoln, NE; married Sheila Stevens, 1941 (divorced); married Elizabeth Lambert Schrafft, 1967; children: (first marriage) Meredith, Heather, W. Gordon, Bruce; (second marriage) Amanda. MILITARY: U.S. Armed Forces, World War II.

VOCATION: Singer and actor.

CAREER: STAGE DEBUT—Performed at the Millpond Playhouse, in Roslyn, NY, 1941. PRINCIPAL STAGE APPEARANCES—*Three to Make Ready,* musical revue, Broadway, 1946; *I Do, I Do* (replaced Robert Preston), Broadway, 1967; performed as a singer with the Harry James Band, 1939-40 and with the Horace Heidt Band, 1940-42; appeared in Las Vegas clubs and hotels as well as major performing arenas with first wife, Sheila.

FILM DEBUT—*The Big Punch,* Warner Brothers, 1948. PRINCIPAL FILM APPEARANCES—*Look for the Silver Lining,* Warner Brothers, 1949; *Backfire,* Warner Brothers, 1950; *The Daughter of Rose O'Grady,* 1950; *The Return of the Frontiersman,* 1950; *Tea for Two,* 1950; *The West Point Story,* 1950; *On Moonlight Bay,* 1951; *Starlift,* 1951; *About Face,* 1952; *By the Light of the Silvery Moon,* 1953; *Desert Song,* 1953; *Three Sailors and a Girl,* 1953; *Oklahoma!,* Magna, 1955, then Twentieth Century-Fox, 1956; *Carousel,* Twentieth Century-Fox, 1956; *The Best Things in Life Are Free,* Twentieth Century-Fox, 1956; *The Pilot,* 1979.

PRINCIPAL TELEVISION APPEARANCES—Series: Host, *The Railroad Hour,* 1950; host, *The Colgate Comedy Hour,* NBC, 1954-55; *The Gordon MacRae Show,* NBC, 1956.

Episodic: *Lux Video Theatre,* NBC, 1956-57; *The Revlon Revue,* CBS, 1960; *The Voice of Firestone,* NBC, 1960.

RECORDINGS: Recorded for Capitol Records 1948-59; "Hair of Gold, Eyes of Blue," "It's Magic," "Rambling Rose," "So in Love," "I've Grown Accustomed to Her Face," "The Secret."

AWARDS: Star of the Season award, March of Dimes, 1968.

MEMBER: National Council on Alcoholism (national honorary chairman).

SIDELIGHTS: A child actor on radio, Gordon MacRae played Wee Willie MacRae and became the juvenile soloist with the Ray Bolger revue. At the 1939-40 Worlds Fair, he won an amateur singing contest and performed for two weeks with the Harry James Band. MacRae worked as a page at NBC before joining the Horace Heidt Band for two years.*

MADONNA

BRIEF ENTRY: Full name, Madonna Louise Ciccone; born in Bay City, MI. Singer, actress, and dancer. Madonna's second album, *Like a Virgin,* her film *Desperately Seeking Susan,* and her highly publicized wedding to actor Sean Penn have made her one of the biggest stars of the mid 1980's and a household name. After studying ballet, modern dance, and jazz at the University of Michigan, she moved to New York where she worked with the Alvin Ailey American Dance Theatre and with Pearl Lang. Madonna auditioned as a singer and dancer with French disco singer Patrick Hernandez and she was flown to Paris, given a vocal coach, dance instructor, an apartment, a chauffeur, and was told she would be famous. When nothing happened after several months, she returned to New York where she joined a band called "The Breakfast Club." With them she learned to play guitar, keyboards, and drums, and began to write her own songs. She played the nightclub circuit for a while with "The Breakfast Club" but then left the band to pursue a career on her own. She cut a demonstration tape called "Everybody" and took it to nightclubs in New York, persuading the disc jockeys to play it. At one popular club, The Danceteria, the song became a favorite. "Everybody" came to the attention of an executive of Sire Records, who signed Madonna to a recording contract. Her first album, *Madonna* hit the charts in 1983, and she had several hit singles from it. *Like a Virgin* followed in 1984, and became one of the best selling albums of 1984 and 1985. Madonna is currently completing her next film, *Shanghi Suprise,* which co-stars her husband.*

*   *   *

MAFFETT, Debbie

PERSONAL: Born November 9, in Cut-n-Shoot, TX. EDUCATION: Larmar University, B.A., 1980.

DEBBIE MAFFETT

VOCATION: Actress, singer, television hostess, and spokesperson.

CAREER: TELEVISION DEBUT—Extra, *Days of Our Lives.* PRINCIPAL TELEVISION APPEARANCES—Series: Hostess, *PBS Latenight;* hostess, *Epcot Magazine;* co-host, *P.M. Magazine,* Los Angeles, CA.

Specials: *Bobby Vinton Special;* host, *National Rollerskating Championships,* 1985.

RELATED CAREER—Singer, Main Room, Sahara Hotel, Las Vegas, NV; talent instructor, *Instant Karate,* Video Tape, Video Reel Company, 1986; founder, California Cameos, Inc.

AWARDS: Miss America, 1983; National Council of Physical Fitness Award, national spokesperson for rollerskating.

ADDRESSES: HOME—Toluca Lake, CA. AGENT—Sumski, Green & Company, 8380 Melrose Avenue, Suite 200, Los Angeles, CA 90069.

*   *   *

MAJORS, Lee   1940-

PERSONAL: Born April 23, 1940, in Wyandotte, MI; married Farrah Fawcett (an actress) July 28, 1973 (divorced). EDUCATION: Graduate Eastern Kentucky State College; studied acting with Estelle Harmon at Metro-Goldwyn-Mayer Studios.

VOCATION: Actor and producer.

CAREER: PRINCIPAL TELEVISION APPEARANCES—Series: Heath Barkley, *The Big Valley,* ABC, 1965-69; Roy Tate, *The Virginian,* NBC, 1970-71; Jess Brandon, *Owen Marshall, Counselor at Law,* ABC, 1971-74; Colonel Steve Austin, *The Six Million Dollar Man,* ABC, 1974-78; Colt Seavers, *The Fall Guy,* ABC, 1981-85.

Movies: *The Ballad of Andy Crocker,* 1969; *Weekend of Terror,* 1970; *The Six Million Dollar Man,* 1973; *Just a Little Convenience,* 1977; *Francis Gary Powers: The U-2 Incident,* 1977; *The Cowboy and the Ballerina,* CBS, 1984; also appeared in *High Noon Part II—The Return of Will Kane.*

Episodic: *Gunsmoke,* CBS; *The Bionic Woman,* NBC; *Alias Smith and Jones,* ABC; *Bracken's World,* NBC.

PRINCIPAL TELEVISION WORK—Executive producer, *The Cowboy and the Ballerina,* CBS, 1984.

FILM DEBUT—*Will Penny,* Paramount, 1968. PRINCIPAL FILM APPEARANCES—*The Liberation of L.B. Jones,* Columbia, 1970; *Killer Fish,* 1979.

MEMBER: American Federation of Television and Radio Artists; Academy of Motion Picture Arts and Sciences.

SIDELIGHTS: CTFT learned that Lee Majors turned down an an offer from the St. Louis Cardinals baseball team in his final year at college to pursue an acting career.

ADDRESSES: AGENT—Traubner & Flynn, 1849 Sawtell Blvd., Suite 500, Los Angeles, CA 90025.*

MANCHESTER, Joe   1932-

PERSONAL: Born March 17, 1932; son of Samuel Eli (an orthodox cantor) and Dora (a real estate agent; maiden name, Markman) Manchester. EDUCATION: Carnegie-Mellon University, B.F.A., 1954; New York School of Law, L.L.B., 1960.

VOCATION: Writer and producer.

WRITINGS: PLAYS—*The Deadly Game,* NY, 1959; *Run, Thief Run!,* Dramatists Play Service, 1963; *Balloon Shot,* Dramatists Play Service, 1964; *The Secret Life of Walter Mitty,* Samuel French, 1964; *Except for Susie Finkel,* Samuel French, 1972.

SCREENPLAYS—*The Deadly Game,* 1982.

ADDRESSES: OFFICE—P.O. Box 42, Waterford, CT 06385.

*   *   *

MANDEL, Howie

BRIEF ENTRY: Born in Toronto, Canada. Actor and comedian. Howie was ejected from three high schools because of his "sense of humor," which included hiring a contractor to build an extension on the resource center of one school. He received a high school equivalency diploma, and shortly thereafter decided to become a millionaire. His first job was in a carpet store. He used the money earned at this job to open his own novelty business and became the Canadian distributor of the infamous "Flasher" doll. On one novelty-buying trip to Los Angeles, Mandel performed at the Comedy Store and impressed George Foster, a producer, who signed him to fifteen segments of the syndicated television show, *Make Me Laugh.* He appeared in the film *Funny Farm* with Eileen Brennan and was a regular on the television programs *The Shape of Things* and *Laugh Trax,* before establishing himself as Dr. Wayne Fiscus on NBC's critically acclaimed *St. Elsewhere.* In addition to this role, Mandel will be seen in two new movies, *A Fine Mess* and *Bobo the Dog Boy.* His comedy show, *The Watusi Tour* was filmed for HBO and was recorded for release as an album. Mandel can be heard as the voices of Animal, Skeeter, and Bunson Honeydew on the children's television program *Jim Henson's Muppets, Babies, and Monsters,* as Gizmo in the film *Gremlins* and as Omni, the robot, in the upcoming film *Once Upon a Star.**

*   *   *

MANKOFSKY, Isidore   1931-

PERSONAL: Born September 22, 1931, in New York, NY; married Chris Ludwig (a photographer), November, 1972. EDUCATION: Trained at the Brooks Institute of Photography, 1955-56. MILITARY: U.S. Air Force, 1951-55.

VOCATION: Cinematographer.

CAREER: PRINCIPAL FILM WORK—Director of Photography: *My Summer Vacation,* 1973; *Scream, Blackula, Scream,* 1973; *Trick Baby,* 1973; *Homebodies,* 1974; *The Ultimate Thrill* (also known as *The Ultimate Chase*), 1974; *The Muppet Movie,* Associated Film Distributors, 1979; *Somewhere in Time,* Universal, 1980; *The Jazz Singer,* Associated Film Distributors, 1980; also, *Say Yes; Better Off Dead; Suzanne.*

PRINCIPAL TELEVISION WORK—Movies: Director of Photography—

ISIDORE MANKOFSKY

Goldie and the Boxer, 1979; *Midnight Lace*, 1980; *Escape*, 1980; *Jacqueline Bouvier Kennedy*, 1981; *Forbidden Love*, 1982; *In the Custody of Strangers*, 1982; *Quarterback Princess*, 1983; *Night Partners*, 1983; *The Other Woman*, 1983; *Hobson's Choice*, 1983; *Silence of the Heart*, CBS, 1984; *The Burning Bed*, NBC, 1984; *Ewok Movie II*, ABC, 1985; also, *Murder Among Friends; Jillian, Portrait of a Showgirl; Race Against Time*.

Mini-Series: *Captains and Kings*, NBC, 1976; *Aspen* (also known as *The Innocent and the Damned*), NBC, 1977; also, *Testimony of Two Men*.

Pilots: *Misfits of Science*, NBC, 1985; *Brothers*, Showtime.

RELATED CAREER—Cameraman, Encyclopedia Britannica Films, 1957-66; owner, director of photography, I AM Films, Inc., 1966—.

MEMBER: Society of Motion Picture and Television Engineers, American Society of Cinematographers.

ADDRESSES: AGENT—Grace Lyons Management, 204 S. Beverly Drive, Suite 102, Beverly Hills, CA 90212.

*   *   *

MANOFF, Dinah

PERSONAL: Born January 25, in New York, NY; daughter of Arnold and Lyova (the actress, Lee Grant; maiden name, Rosenthal) Manoff.

VOCATION: Actress.

CAREER: PRINCIPAL STAGE APPEARANCES—Daughter, *I Ought to Be in Pictures*, Neil Simon Theatre, NY, 1980; Jill, *Gifted Children*, Jewish Repertory Theatre, NY, 1983; young Ellie Greenwich, *Leader of the Pack*, Ambassador Theatre, NY, 1985; others.

PRINCIPAL FILM APPEARANCES—Marty, *Grease*, Paramount, 1978; *Ordinary People*, Paramount, 1980; *I Ought to Be in Pictures*, Twentieth Century-Fox, 1982.

PRINCIPAL TELEVISION APPEARANCES—Series: Elaine Lefkowitz, *Soap*, ABC, 1978-79.

Movies: *For Ladies Only*, 1981; *The Seduction of Gina*, 1984; *Flight Number 90: Disaster on the Potomac*, 1984; Theresa, *Classified Love*, CBS, 1986.

AWARDS: Antoinette Perry Award, Theatre World Award, both 1980, for *I Ought to Be in Pictures*.

ADDRESSES: OFFICE—c/o Bill Evans, 165 W. 46th Street, Suite 914, New York, NY 10036. AGENT—Triad Agency, 888 Seventh Avenue, Suite 1602, New York, NY 10019.*

*   *   *

MANTEGNA, Joe   1947-

PERSONAL: Born November 13, 1947, in Chicago, IL; son of Joe Anthony (an insurance salesman) and Mary Ann (a shipping clerk; maiden name, Novelli) Mantegna; married Arlene Urhel, December 3, 1975. EDUCATION: Attended Morton Junior College; trained for the stage at the Goodman School of Drama.

VOCATION: Actor.

CAREER: STAGE DEBUT—Berger, *Hair*, Shubert Theatre, Chicago, IL, 1969, for four hundred performances. NEW YORK DEBUT—Emilio and a trucker, *Working*, 46th Street Theater, 1978, for forty performances. PRINCIPAL STAGE APPEARANCES—Judas, *Godspell*, Studebaker Theatre, Chicago, IL, 1972; Decker, *Bleacher Bums*, Organic Theatre, Chicago, IL, 1977; Rocky Roma, *Glengarry Glen Ross*, Golden Theatre, NY, 1984; also, Michael, *Mattress*, La Mama Theatre, Los Angeles, CA; Corvino, *Volpone*, various parts, *Sirens of Titan*, Gomez, *The Wonderful Ice Cream Suit*, and Jack Rolf, *Cops*, all at the Organic Theatre, Chicago, IL; John, *A Life in the Theatre*, Goodman Theatre, Chicago, IL.

MAJOR TOURS—Berger, *Hair*, Chicago, IL, Cincinnati, OH, Pittsburgh, PA, 1971; Duke, *Huckleberry Finn* and Jack Rackam, *Bloody Bess*, both European cites; Rocky Roma, *Glengarry Glen Ross*, San Francisco and Los Angeles, CA, 1985.

FILM DEBUT—Dr. Bruce Fleckstein, *Compromising Positions*, Paramount, 1985. PRINCIPAL FILM APPEARANCES--Art Shirk, *The Money Pit*, Universal, 1986; Pete Petersen, *Offbeat*, Buena Vista, 1986.

TELEVISION DEBUT—Juan One, *Soap*, ABC, 1982. PRINCIPAL TELEVISION APPEARANCES—Pilots: *Bigshots in America*, NBC; *Open All Night*, ABC; *The Outlaws*, ABC; *Now We're Cooking*, CBS.

Specials: *Bleacher Bums*, PBS.

JOE MANTEGNA

Movies: *Elvis*, 1979.

Episodic: *Greatest American Hero*, CBS; *Making a Living*, ABC; *Bosom Buddies*, ABC; *Archie Bunker's Place*, CBS; *Simon and Simon*, CBS; *Magnum P.I.*, CBS.

RELATED CAREER: Teacher, Columbia College, Chicago, IL, 1976-77.

WRITINGS: PLAYS, PRODUCED—*Bleacher Bums*, Organic Theatre, Chicago, IL, then American Place Theatre, NY, 1977, published by Samuel French, 1977; *Leonardo*, Lee Strasberg Institute, Los Angeles, CA.

AWARDS: Joseph Jefferson Award, New York Dramatists Guild Award, 1979, for *Bleacher Bums;* Emmy Award, 1980, for *Bleacher Bums;* Antoinette Perry Award, Drama Desk Award, Joseph Jefferson Award, 1984, for *Glengarry Glen Ross*.

ADDRESSES: AGENT—Bauman, Hiller, and Strain, 250 W. 57th Street, New York, NY 10107.

* * *

MARKS, Jack R.   1935-

PERSONAL: Born February 28, 1935, in New York, NY; son of Louis and Molly (Stengel) Marks; divorced; children: Sam.

VOCATION: Actor.

CAREER: STAGE DEBUT—Speed, *The Odd Couple*, Beef 'n' Boards Theatre, Louisville, KY, 1961. PRINCIPAL STAGE APPEARANCES—Traveler, *The Queen and the Rebels*, Plymouth Theatre, NY; Gravedigger, *Hamlet* and Snug and understudy Bottom, *A Midsummer Night's Dream*, both Vivian Beaumont Theatre, Lincoln Center, NY; Henchman, *Goose and Tom-Tom*, Sergeant Wall, *The Basic Training of Pavlo Hummell*, Apothecary, *Mary Stuart*, all at the New York Shakespeare Festival, Public Theatre, NY; Bennie Davis, *Getting Out*, Theatre de Lys, NY; Inspector Rough, *Angel Street*, Perry Street Theatre, NY; Goldberg, *The Birthday Party*, Jewish Repertory, NY; Tarzan, *Tarzan and the Boy*, New Federal Theatre, NY; Father, *The Carpenters*, Westside YMCA, NY.

Baron, *Becket*, Elder, *Oedipus the King*, and Commissioner of Education, *The Government Inspector*, all at the Guthrie Theatre, Minneapolis, MN; the Salesman, *The Rose Tattoo*, Long Wharf Theatre, New Haven, CT; Constable Simms, *Oh Boy*, Goodspeed Opera House, East Haddam, CT; Dan Roche, *A Touch of the Poet*, Yale Repertory Theatre, New Haven, CT; Shamraev, *The Seagull*, Syracuse Stage, Syracuse, NY; Ned Buntline, *Indians*, Buffalo Studio Arena, NY; Stockbroker, *Steambath*, New Jersey Shakespeare Festival, Madison, NJ; Narrator, *A Christmas Carol*, Ford's Theatre, Washington, DC; Horace Vandergelder, *The Matchmaker*, Williamstown Theatre Festival, MA; actor, *Swan Song* and Father, *The Marriage Proposal*, both at the California Actors Theatre, Los Gatos, CA; Oscar Hubbard, *The Little Foxes*, Stage West, West Springfield, MA; Estrada and Parke, *Lady, Be Good!*, North Shore Music Theatre; Mitch, *A Streetcar Named Desire*, Purdue University, IA.

PRINCIPAL FILM APPEARANCES—*Annie Hall*, United Artists, 1977; *Eyes of Laura Mars*, Columbia, 1978; *Blood Brothers*, Warner Brothers, 1979; *Ragtime*, Paramount, 1981; *Friday the 13th Part Two*, Paramount, 1981.

PRINCIPAL TELEVISION APPEARANCES—Series: Leon Matthews, *The Doctors*.

Episodic: *Kojak*, CBS; *Adams Chronicles*, PBS; *American Parade*, CBS, 1984.

Movies: *In the Case of Milligan; Living Together; Mundo Real; The Molders of Troy*.

MEMBER: Actors' Equity Association, Screen Actors Guild.

ADDRESSES: HOME—361 E. Tenth Street, New York, NY 10009.

* * *

MARSH, Jean   1934-

PERSONAL: Full name Jean Lyndsey Torren Marsh; born July 1, 1934, in London, England; daughter of Henry Charles John and Emmeline Susannah Nightingale Poppy (Bexley) Marsh; married Jon Devon Roland Pertwee, April 2, 1955 (divorced, 1960).

VOCATION: Actress and writer.

CAREER: NEW YORK DEBUT—*Much Ado About Nothing*, 1959. PRINCIPAL STAGE APPEARANCES—Broadway: *Travesties*, 1975; *The Importance of Being Earnest*, 1977; *Too True to Be Good*, 1977; *My Fat Friend*, 1979; *Whose Life Is It Anyway?*, 1979; *Blithe Spirit*.

Eliza Doolittle, *Pygmalion*, Trinity Square Repertory Company, Providence, RI, 1983.

PRINCIPAL FILM APPEARANCES—Octavia, *Cleopatra*, Twentieth Century-Fox, 1963; *The Limbo Line*, 1969; *Frenzy*, Universal, 1972; *Dark Places*, 1977; *The Eagle Has Landed*, Columbia, 1977; *The Changeling*, 1979.

PRINCIPAL TELEVISION APPEARANCES—Series: Rose, *Upstairs, Downstairs*, BBC/PBS; Roz Keith, *Nine to Five*, ABC, 1982-83.

Specials: *The Grover Monster*, 1975; *A State Dinner with Queen Elizabeth II*, 1976; *Mad About the Boy: Noel Coward—A Celebration*, 1976.

Plays: *Habeas Corpus; Uncle Vanya; Twelfth Night; Pygmalion; On the Rocks Theatre*.

Movie: *The Corsican Brothers*, CBS, 1985.

WRITINGS: TELEVISION—(Co-author and co-creator) *Upstairs, Downstairs*.

AWARDS: Most Outstanding New Actress, 1972; Outstanding Lead Actress in a Drama Series, Emmy Award, 1974-75, for *Upstairs, Downstairs*.

ADDRESSES: HOME—The Pheasant, Chinnor Hill, Oxfordshire OX9 4BN, England.*

*   *   *

MARSHALL, E.G.   1910-

PERSONAL: Born June 18, 1910, in Owatonna, MN; son of Charles G. and Hazel Irene (Cobb) Marshall; married Helen Wolf, April 26, 1939 (divorced, 1953); children: Jill, Degen. EDUCATION: Attended Carlton College, 1930; attended the University of Minnesota, 1932.

VOCATION: Actor.

CAREER: STAGE DEBUT—Touring repertory, *The Oxford Players*, 1933. NY DEBUT—Henry Onstott, *Prologue to Glory*, Federal Theatre Project, Ritz Theatre, September 19, 1938. PRINCIPAL STAGE APPEARANCES—*The Big Blow*, Federal Theatre Project, Ritz Theatre, NY, 1938; Humphrey Crocker, *Jason*, Hudson Theatre, NY, 1942; Mr. Fitzpatrick, *The Skin of Our Teeth*, Plymouth Theatre, NY, 1942; Gramp Maple, *The Petrified Forest*, New Amsterdam Roof, NY, 1943; Brigadier, *Jacobowsky and the Colonel*, Martin Beck Theatre, NY, 1944; Dave, *Beggars Are Coming to Town*, Coronet Theatre, NY, 1945; Sims, *Woman Bites Dog*, Belasco Theatre, NY, 1946; Willie Oban, *The Iceman Cometh*, Martin Beck Theatre, NY, 1946; Judas, *Dear Judas*, Playhouse Theatre, Ogunquit, ME, 1947; Finlay Decker, *The Survivors*, Playhouse Theatre, NY, 1948.

Ernest Bruni, *The Gambler*, Lyceum Theatre, NY, 1952; Reverend John Hale (later John Proctor), *The Crucible*, Martin Beck Theatre, NY, 1953; Brennan, *Red Roses for Me*, Booth Theatre, NY, 1955; Ferrante, *Queen After Death*, Phoenix Theatre, NY, 1956; Vladimir, *Waiting for Godot*, John Golden Theatre, NY, 1956; Ephraim Cabot, *Desire Under the Elms*, Studebaker Theatre, Chicago, IL, 1956; Walter Rafferty, *The Gang's All Here*, Ambassador Theatre, NY, 1959; Oscar Hubbard, *The Little Foxes*, Vivian Beaumont

Theatre, Lincoln Center, NY, 1967; Benjamin Hubbard, *The Little Foxes*, Ethel Barrymore Theatre, NY, 1967; Sam Nash/Jesse Kiplinger/Roy Hubley, *Plaza Suite*, Plymouth Theatre, NY, 1969 (replacing George C. Scott).

The Imaginary Invalid, Walnut Street Theatre, Philadelphia, 1971; title role, *Macbeth*, Virginia Museum Theatre, Richmond, VA, 1973; revue performer, *Nash at Nine*, Helen Hayes Theatre, NY, 1973; Halvard Solnes, *The Master Builder*, Long Wharf Theatre, New Haven, CT, 1973; Phillip Hammer, *The Sponsor*, Peachtree Playhouse, Atlanta, GA, 1975; Walter F. Bickmore, *Old Movies*, National Theatre Production, Cottesloe, England, 1977; Walter Martin, *The Gin Game*, John Golden Theatre, NY, 1977 (replacing Hume Cronyn); title role, *John Gabriel Borkman*, Circle in the Square, NY, 1980-81; Father Tim Farley, *Mass Appeal*, York Theatre Company, Church of the Heavenly Rest, NY, 1984; Mr. Hardcastle, *She Stoops to Conquer*, Roundabout Triplex Theatre, NY, 1984; Matthew Harrison Brady, *Inherit the Wind*, Paper Mill Playhouse, Milburn, NJ, 1984-85.

FILM DEBUT—Attendant at morgue, *The House on 92nd Street*, Twentieth Century-Fox, 1945. PRINCIPAL FILM APPEARANCES—*Thirteen Rue Madeleine*, Twentieth Century-Fox, 1946; Rayska, *Call Northside 777*, Twentieth Century-Fox, 1948; Lt. Cdr. Challee, *The Caine Mutiny*, Columbia, 1954; *Pushover*, Columbia, 1954; *The Bamboo Prison*, 1954; *Broken Lance*, Twentieth Century-Fox, 1954; *The Silver Chalice*, Warner Brothers, 1955; Dr. Sigman, *The Left Hand of God*, Twentieth Century-Fox, 1955; *The Scarlet Hour*, Paramount, 1955; Juror Number Four, *Twelve Angry Men*, United Artists, 1957; Walter, *The Bachelor Party*, United Artists, 1957; D.A. Horn, *Compulsion*, Twentieth Century-Fox, 1959; *Town without Pity*, United Artists, 1961; *The Chase*, Columbia, 1966; *The Bridge at Remagen*, United Artists, 1968; *The Pursuit of Happiness*, Columbia, 1970; *Tora! Tora! Tora!*, Twentieth Century-Fox, 1970; *Interiors*, United Artists, 1978; *Superman, II*, Warner Brothers, 1981; *Creepshow*, Warner Brothers, 1983.

PRINCIPAL TELEVISION APPEARANCES—Series: Lawrence Preston, *The Defenders*, CBS, 1961-1965; Dr. David Craig, *The New Doctors*, segment of *The Bold Ones*, NBC, 1969-70. Dr. David Craig, *The New Doctors*, NBC, 1969-73.

Episodic: *Kraft Television Theatre*, NBC, 1947-58; *Chevrolet Tele-Theatre*, NBC, 1948-50; *Short Short Dramas*, NBC, 1952-53; *Campbell Soundstage*, NBC, 1952-54; *Police Story*, CBS, 1952; *Ponds Theatre*, ABC, 1955; *Suspense*, CBS, 1964.

Movies: *Vampire*, 1979; *Disaster on the Coastliner*, 1979; *The Winter of Our Discontent*, 1983.

Specials: *The Little Foxes; Clash by Night; The Plot to Kill Stalin; The Shrike*, English, 1960.

AWARDS: Emmy, 1963, for *The Defenders*.

SIDELIGHTS: RECREATIONS—Writing and cycling.

ADDRESSES: AGENT—William Morris Agency, 1350 Avenue of the Americas, New York, NY 10019.*

*   *   *

MARVIN, Lee   1924-

PERSONAL: Born February 19, 1924, in New York, NY; son of

Lamont W. and Courtenay D. Marvin; married Pamela Feeley, October 18, 1970. MILITARY: U.S. Marine Corps, World War II.

VOCATION: Actor.

CAREER: FILM DEBUT—*You're in the Navy Now,* 1951. PRINCIPAL FILM APPEARANCES—*Diplomatic Courier,* 1952; *We're Not Married,* 1952; *Eight Iron Men,* 1952; *Down Among the Sheltering Palms,* 1953; *The Stranger Wore a Gun,* 1953; *The Big Heat,* 1953; *Gun Fury,* 1953; *The Wild One,* 1954; *The Caine Mutiny,* 1954; *Gorilla at Large,* 1954; *The Raid,* 1954; *Bad Day at Black Rock,* 1954; *Life in the Balance,* 1955; *Violent Saturday,* 1955; *Not as a Stranger,* 1955; *Pete Kelly's Blues,* 1955; *I Died a Thousand Times,* 1955; *The Rack,* Metro-Goldwyn-Mayer, 1956; *Shack Out on 101,* 1955; *Attack!,* United Artists, 1958.

The Killers, Universal, 1964; *Ship of Fools,* Columbia, 1965; *Cat Ballou,* Columbia, 1965; *The Professionals,* Columbia, 1966; *The Dirty Dozen,* Metro-Goldwyn-Mayer, 1967; *Point Blank,* Metro-Goldwyn-Mayer, 1967; *Sergeant Ryker,* Universal, 1968; *Paint Your Wagon,* Paramount, 1969; *Monte Walsh,* National General, 1970; *Pocket Money,* National General, 1972; *Prime Cut,* National General, 1972; *The Iceman Cometh,* AFT Distributing, 1973; *The Emperor of the North,* Twentieth Century-Fox, 1973; *The Spikes Gang,* United Artists, 1974; *The Klansman,* Paramount, 1974; *Great Scout and Cathouse Thursday,* American International, 1976; *Shout at the Devil,* American International, 1976; *Death Hunt,* Twentieth Century-Fox, 1981; *Gorky Park,* Orion, 1983.

PRINCIPAL TELEVISION APPEARANCES—Series: Lt. Frank Ballinger, *M Squad,* NBC, 1957-60.

Episodic: *Rebound,* ABC, 1952; *The Doctor,* NBC, 1952; *Center Stage,* ABC, 1954; "People Need People," *Alcoa Premiere,* ABC, 1961; *Treasury Men in Action,* NBC; *TV Readers Digest,* ABC; *Kraft Suspense Theatre,* NBC.

Movies: *The Dirty Dozen: The Next Mission.*

AWARDS: Best Actor, Academy Award, Berlin Film Festival Award, British Academy Award, all 1965, for *Cat Ballou;* Spanish Silver Film Award, 1970.

ADDRESSES: AGENT—Mishkin Agency, 9255 Sunset Blvd., Los Angeles, CA 90069; c/o Paul Wasserman, Mahoney/Wasserman, 117 N. Robertson Blvd., Los Angeles, CA 90048.*

*   *   *

MASON, Ethelmae

PERSONAL: Born Ethelmae Barker, in Binghamton, NY; daughter of Archibald C. and Freida B. Barker; married Harold Mason (a singer, actor, and music publisher), June 25, 1960. EDUCATION: Trained for the stage at the Tri-Cities Opera, Binghampton, NY, and the Chautauqua Association, NY.

VOCATION: Actress, writer, and singer.

CAREER: STAGE DEBUT—Marcelline, *Marriage of Figaro,* Syracuse Symphony, Syracuse, NY, 1963, for four performances. NEW YORK DEBUT—Mrs. Herring, *Albert Herring,* Hunter College Theater, 1974, for three performances. PRINCIPAL STAGE APPEARANCES—Rachel, *Pantagleize,* Brooklyn College, NY, 1973; Maria Luisa, *The Penitents,* Aspen Music Festival, CO, 1975;

ETHELMAE MASON

Buttercup, *H.M.S. Pinafore,* Ruth, *Pirates of Penzance,* Katisha, *The Mikado,* Queen of the Fairy Dames, *Iolanthe,* Carruthers, *Yeomen of the Guard,* Hannah, *Ruddigore,* all Eastside Playhouse, NY, 1976-83; Shakespearean Lady, *Shakespeare and the Indians,* State University of New York, Purchase, NY, 1983.

MAJOR TOURS—Theatre for Young Audiences, New York State cities, 1958-60.

FILM DEBUT—Nurse Pierson, *Endless Love,* Polygram, 1981. PRINCIPAL FILM APPEARANCES—Singer, *So Fine,* Warner Brothers, 1983; secretary, *Muppet's Take Manhattan,* Jim Henson Productions, 1984.

TELEVISION DEBUT—Princess, *Magic Cottage,* 1950.

RELATED CAREER—Roberson Memorial Center, Binghamton, NY, 1955-60; Juilliard School, NY, 1970-77.

MEMBER: Actors' Equity Association, Screen Actors Guild, American Federation of Television and Radio Artists, American Guild of Musical Artists, New York State Opera League (secretary, 1956-58).

ADDRESSES: HOME—484 W. 43rd Street, Apt. 38A, New York, NY 10036.

*   *   *

MASON, Marshall W.   1940-

PERSONAL: Born February 24, 1940, in Amarillo, TX; son of Marvin Marshall and Lorraine Chrisman (Hornsby) Marshall; mar-

MARSHALL W. MASON

ried Zita Litvinas (deceased). EDUCATION: Attended Northwestern University; studied for the theatre at the Actors Studio.

VOCATION: Director and former actor.

CAREER: STAGE DEBUT—Malvolio, *Twelfth Night,* Eagles Mere, PA, 1959. PRINCIPAL STAGE APPEARANCES—Claudius, *Hamlet,* Circle Repertory Company, NY, 1979; Malvolio, *Twelfth Night,* Circle Repertory Company, NY, 1980.

PRINCIPAL STAGE WORK—Director: *The Wild Duck, The Trojan Women, Cat on a Hot Tin Roof,* all at Northwestern University, 1959; *Medea, An Evening of Love, The Clown, The Rue Garden,* all at Cafe Cino, NY, 1962; assistant director, *One Way Pendulum,* Phoenix Theatre, NY, 1962; *Little Eyolf,* Actor's Playhouse, NY, 1964; *Home Free,* Off-Broadway, 1965; *Home Free* and *The Madness of Lady Bright,* Mercury Theatre, London, 1968.

In July, 1969, became artistic director of the Circle Repertory Company, NY and directed: *The Hot L Baltimore* and *When We Dead Awaken,* both 1973; *Battle of Angels* and *The Sea Horse,* both 1974; *Harry Outside* and *The Mound Builders,* both 1975; *Knock Knock, Serenading Louie,* co-director, *Mrs. Murray's Farm, The Farm,* and *A Tribute to Lili Lamont,* all 1976; *My Life* and *Ulysses in Traction,* 1977; *The Fifth of July* and *In the Recovery Lounge,* both 1978; *Winter Signs* and *Talley's Folly,* both 1979; *Childe Byron* and *A Tale Told,* both 1981; *Richard II,* 1982; *Angels Fall* and *Full Hook-Up,* 1983; *Talley and Son,* 1985; *The Mound Builders* and *Caligula,* 1986.

Also directed: *Come Back, Little Sheba,* Queens Playhouse, NY,

1974; (supervisor) *Gemini,* Little Theatre, NY, 1977; *Murder at the Howard Johnson's,* John Golden Theatre, NY, 1979; *Slugger,* PAF Playhouse, NY, 1979; *Talley's Folly,* John Golden Theatre, NY, 1980; *The Fifth of July,* New Apollo Theatre, NY, 1980; *Foxfire,* Tyrone Guthrie Theatre, Minneapolis, MN, 1981; *Angels Fall,* Longacre Theatre, NY, 1982; *The Great Grandson of Jedediah Kohler,* Entermedia Theatre, NY, 1982; *Passion,* Longacre Theatre, NY, 1983; *As Is,* Lyceum Theatre, NY, 1985; *Picnic,* Ahmanson Theatre, Los Angeles, 1986; also: *Talley's Folly,* London; productions at the Mark Taper Forum, Los Angeles and the Academy Festival Theatre, Lakewood, IL.

PRINCIPAL TELEVISION WORK—Director: *Kennedy's Children,* 1982; *The Fifth of July,* Showtime, 1983.

AWARDS: Best Director, Obie Awards, for *Hot L Baltimore, Battle of Angels, The Mound Builders, Serenading Louie,* and *Knock Knock;* Antoinette Perry Award nominations, for *Knock, Knock, Talley's Folly, The Fifth of July;* Drama Desk Award; Margo Jones Award; Outer Critics Circle Award; *Theatre World* Award; Shubert Foundation Award; Arts and Business Council Award for the Circle Repertory's consistent searching out and producing work by new American talent.

SIDELIGHTS: RECREATION—Archaeology and travel.

Mason relinquished the position of artistic director of the Circle Repertory in 1980 to allow himself the freedom of directing in other venues.

ADDRESSES: HOME—165 Christopher Street, New York, NY 10014. OFFICE—Circle Repertory Company, 161 Avenue of the Americas, New York, NY 10013.

*   *   *

MATHESON, Tim   1947-

PERSONAL: Born December 31, 1947, in Glendale, CA. EDUCATION: Attended California State University.

VOCATION: Actor.

CAREER: PRINCIPAL FILM APPEARANCES—*Divorce, American Style,* Columbia, 1967; *Yours, Mine and Ours,* United Artists, 1968; *How to Commit Marriage,* Cinerama, 1969; *Magnum Force,* Warner Brothers, 1973; *Impulse,* 1974; *Almost Summer,* 1978; *National Lampoon's Animal House,* Universal, 1978; *Dreamer,* Twentieth Century-Fox, 1979; *The Apple Dumpling Gang Rides Again,* Buena Vista, 1979; *1941,* Universal, 1979; *A Little Sex,* Universal, 1982; *To Be or Not to Be,* Twentieth Century-Fox, 1983; *Up the Creek,* Orion, 1984; *Impulse,* Twentieth Century-Fox, 1984; *Fletch,* Universal, 1985.

PRINCIPAL TELEVISION APPEARANCES—Series: Roddy Miller, *Window on Main Street,* CBS, 1961-62; Jim Horn, *The Virginian,* NBC, 1969-70; Griff King, *Bonanza,* NBC, 1972-73; Quentin Beaudine, *The Quest,* NBC, 1976; Rick Tucker, *Tucker's Witch,* CBS, 1982-83.

Movies: *Lock, Stock, and Barrel,* 1970; *Hitched,* 1971; *Owen Marshall, Counselor-at-Law,* 1971; *Remember When,* 1974; *The Last Day,* 1975; *The Runaway Barge,* 1975; *The Quest,* 1976; *Mary White,* 1977; Bo, *Bus Stop,* cable, 1982; *Classmates,* HBO, 1984.

Episodic: *Amazing Stories,* NBC, 1986.

STAGE DEBUT—Austin, *True West,* Cherry Lane Theatre, NY, 1984.

ADDRESSES: AGENT—Agency for the Performing Arts, 9000 Sunset Blvd., Suite 315, Los Angeles, CA 90069.*

* * *

MAUCERI, John 1945-

PERSONAL: Born September 12, 1945; son of Gene B. (a physician) and Mary E. Mauceri; married Betty Weiss (an arts consultant), June 15, 1968; children: Benjamin Robert. EDUCATION: Yale University, B.A., 1967, Master of Philosophy, 1969.

VOCATION: Conductor, music supervisor, and producer.

CAREER: STAGE DEBUT—Music supervisor and director, *Candide,* Brooklyn Academy of Music, Brooklyn, NY, then Broadway Theatre, NY, 1973. LONDON DEBUT—Music supervisor, *On Your Toes,* Palace Theatre, 1984. PRINCIPAL STAGE WORK—Music supervisor and director, *On Your Toes,* Virginia Theatre, NY, 1982; producer, music supervisor, and director, *Song and Dance,* Royale Theatre, NY, 1985.

MAJOR TOURS—Associate producer, music supervisor, and director, *On Your Toes,* Miami, New Orleans, and Texas, 1984.

CONDUCTOR—Opera: La Scala, Milan; Metropolitan Opera, NY; Santa Fe Opera, NM; Covent Garden, UK; English National Opera, UK; New York City Opera; Scottish Opera, Welsh National Opera; New Orleans Opera, LA; Washington Opera; San Francisco Opera.

JOHN MAUCERI

Orchestral: American Symphony; Israel Philharmonic; San Francisco Symphony; Los Angeles Philharmonic; Boston Pops; National Symphony; Baltimore Symphony; London Symphony; London Philharmonic Hall.

TELEVISION DEBUT—Music supervisor and director, *Leonard Bernstein's Mass,* 1973. PRINCIPAL TELEVISION WORK—Host, *Live from Lincoln Center,* CBS Cable, 1980, 1982; *Live from the Kennedy Center,* PBS, 1981, 1982.

RELATED CAREER—Consultant for music theater and director of orchestras, John F. Kennedy Center for the Performing Arts, Washington, DC, 1982—present; music director, American Symphony Orchestra, 1984—present.

RECORDINGS: Candide, original cast album, 1983; *On Your Toes,* original cast album, 1983; *Candide,* New York City Opera, 1985.

WRITINGS: TELEVISION—Series: *Classical Music,* CBS Cable, 1982.

AWARDS: Antoinette Perry Award, Outer Critics Circle Award, Drama Desk Award, 1982, all for *On Your Toes;* Distinguished Alumni Award, Yale University, 1985.

ADDRESSES: AGENT—c/o Ronald Wilford, Columbia Artists Management, 165 W. 57th Street, New York, NY 10019.

* * *

MAXWELL, Wayne F., Jr

PERSONAL: Son of Wayne F. and Esther (Faust) Maxwell. EDUCATION: University of Tulsa, B.A.; trained for the stage at the Theatre Studio with Curt Conway. POLITICS: Republican. RELIGION: Methodist.

VOCATION: Actor.

CAREER: STAGE DEBUT—Senya, *Listen Professor,* Tulsa Little Theater, Tulsa, OK, 1945, for thirty-five performances. NEW YORK DEBUT—Chiron, *Titus Andronicus,* New York Shakespeare Festival. LONDON DEBUT—*Whitman Portrait,* West End production. PRINCIPAL STAGE APPEARANCES—Frankie Scruggs, *Legend,* Broadway production; *Two by Jack Dunphy,* American National Theatre and Academy (ANTA), NY; *A Whitman Portrait,* Gramercy Arts, NY; Nick, *Long Voyage Home,* Mermaid Theatre, NY; *Picture in the Hallway,* Greenwich Mews Theatre, NY; Alvin, *Kataki,* St. Mark's Place Theatre, NY; Riccardo, *Dog in a Manger,* Cooper Union Theatre, NY; *Gallery,* Troupe Theatre, NY; *In White America,* West End Players, NY; Father Angelo, *The Beheading,* Lincoln Center Library, NY.

Regional: Werth, *Quail Southwest,* Carnegie Mellon Theatre, Pittsburgh, PA; *March to the Sea,* Hyde Park Playhouse, NY; *Night of the Dunce,* Alley Theatre, Houston, TX; *Last Meeting of the Knights of the White Magnolias,* Arena Stage, Washington, DC; Pish Tush, *The Mikado;* Dr. Caius, *Merry Wives of Windsor;* Sycamore and Kolenkov, *You Can't Take It with You; Oh, What a Lovely War;* Paravacini, *The Mousetrap;* Dromio, *Comedy of Errors;* Tom, *Glass Menagerie;* Goldberg, *Birthday Party;* Muelady, *The Hostage;* Shelby Marcus, *Best Man.*

MAJOR TOURS—*A Whitman Portrait,* U.S. cities; *The Front Page,* Los Angeles and other U.S. cities; *John Dos Passos USA,* U.S. cities; *Matchmaker,* U.S. cites.

WAYNE F. MAXWELL, JR.

FILM DEBUT—*Stardust Memories,* United Artists, 1979. PRINCI-PAL FILM APPEARANCES—Headwaiter, *Hair,* United Artists, 1979; German general, photographer, *Zelig,* Warner Brothers, 1983.

TELEVISION DEBUT—McNabe, "Stover at Yale," *Omnibus,* CBS, 1957. PRINCIPAL TELEVISION APPEARANCES—Peter, *Naked City,* ABC; *Our Story,* WNET; *American Parade; Davy Crockett.*

MEMBER: Actors' Equity Association, Screen Actors Guild, American Federation of Television and Radio Artists.

ADDRESSES: HOME—441 Fourteenth Street, Brooklyn, NY 11215.

*   *   *

McGILLIS, Kelly

BRIEF ENTRY: Born in Newport, CA. Actress. Kelly McGillis has stated in several interviews that she does not consider herself to be "the typical Hollywood beauty." She was overweight as a girl, and feels that she lacks the subtlety of a glamorous actress. When critics reviewed her performance in *Witness,* however, they claimed she was comparable to past starlets such as Lauren Bacall, Ingrid Bergman, and Joan Crawford. McGillis dropped out of high school but studied acting first at the Pacific Conservatory of Performing Arts and then at Juilliard in New York. While in her fourth and final year at Juilliard she was cast as the young lover in *Reuben, Reuben.* Refusing to leave Juilliard and made to adhere to the school's strick

rules regarding class attendance, McGillis flew to filming locations on weekends to shoot her scenes. She has appeared on stage with the New York Shakespeare Festival and played opposite Christopher Plummer in *Peccidillo.* She appeared on television on several daytime serials and in a made for television movie. Her latest film appearance is as Charlotte Blackwood in *Top Gun* and she is currently filming *Made in Heaven.**

*   *   *

McGOVERN, Elizabeth   1961-

PERSONAL: Born July 18, 1961, in Evanston, IL. EDUCATION: Attended Juilliard.

VOCATION: Actress.

CAREER: STAGE DEBUT—*To Be Young, Gifted, and Black,* Thea-tre Off Park, NY, 1981. PRINCIPAL STAGE APPEARANCES—*Hotel Play;* Lea, *My Sister in This House,* Second Stage, NY, 1981-82; *Major Barbara,* Alaska Repertory Company, 1982; Margaret Church, *Painting Churches,* Lambs Theatre, NY, 1983-84; Viola, *Twelfth Night,* Huntington Theatre, Boston, 1984; Carol, *The Hitch-Hiker,* WPA Theatre, NY, 1985; *A Map of the World,* Public Theatre, NY, 1985.

PRINCIPAL FILM APPEARANCES—*Ordinary People,* Paramount, 1980; Evelyn Nesbit Thaw, *Ragtime,* Paramount, 1981; *Lovesick,* Warner Brothers, 1983; *Racing with the Moon,* Paramount, 1984; *Once Upon a Time in America,* Warner Brothers, 1984.

AWARDS: *Theatre World* Award, 1981-82, for *My Sister in This House.*

ADDRESSES: AGENT—Writers and Artists Agency, 11726 San Vicente Blvd., Suite 300, Los Angeles, CA 90049.*

*   *   *

McGUIRE, Dorothy   1918-

PERSONAL: Full name, Dorothy Hackett McGuire; born June 14, 1918, in Omaha, NE; daughter of Thomas Johnson and Isabelle (Flaherty) McGuire; married John Swope, July 18, 1943; children: two. EDUCATION: Ladywood Convent in Indianapolis, IN; at-tended Omaha Junior College; attended Pine Manor in Wellesley, MA.

VOCATION: Actress.

CAREER: STAGE DEBUT—*A Kiss for Cinderella,* Community Theatre, Omaha, NE, 1930. NEW YORK DEBUT—Understudy, *Stop-Over,* Lyceum Theatre, 1938. PRINCIPAL STAGE APPEAR-ANCES—Emily (understudy), *Our Town,* Morosco Theatre, NY, 1938; Helena, *Swingin' the Dream,* City Center Theatre, NY, 1939; Dora, *Medicine Show,* New Yorker Theatre, NY, 1940; Ada, *Kind Lady,* Playhouse Theatre, NY, 1940; Claudia Naughton, *Claudia,* Booth Theatre, NY, 1941; The Actress, *Legends and Lovers,* Plymouth Theatre, NY, 1951; Elizabeth Willard, *Winesburg, Ohio,* National Theatre, NY, 1958; Hannah Jelkes, *Night of the Iguana,* Ahmanson Theatre, Los Angeles, 1975; Hannah Jelkes, *Night of the Iguana,* Circle in the Square, NY, 1976; *Cause Celebre,* Ahmanson Theatre, Los Angeles, 1979; Lavinia, *Another Part of the Forest,* Center Theatre Group/Ahmanson Theatre, Los Angeles, 1982.

DOROTHY McGUIRE

MAJOR TOURS—Portia, *My Dear Children*, 1939; Kitty, *The Time of Your Life*, 1940; *Dear Ruth*, USO tour, 1945; *Tonight at 8:30*, 1947; Alma Winemiller, *Summer and Smoke*, 1950.

FILM DEBUT—Title role, *Claudia*, 1943. PRINCIPAL FILM APPEARANCES—*A Tree Grows in Brooklyn*, 1945; *The Enchanted Cottage*, 1945; *The Spiral Staircase*, 1946; *Claudia and David*, 1946; *Gentleman's Agreement*, 1947; *Mister 880*, 1950; *Callaway Went Thataway*, Metro-Goldwyn-Mayer, 1951; *I Want You*, 1951; *Invitation*, Metro-Goldwyn-Mayer, 1951; *Make Haste to Live*, 1954; *Three Coins in the Fountain*, 1954; *Trial*, Metro-Goldwyn-Mayer, 1955; *Friendly Persuasion*, Allied Artists, 1956; *Old Yeller*, Buena Vista, 1958; *This Earth Is Mine*, Universal, 1959; *The Remarkable Mr. Pennypacker*, Twentieth Century-Fox, 1959; *A Summer Place*, Warner Brothers, 1959; *Dark at the Top of the Stairs*, Warner Brothers, 1960; *The Swiss Family Robinson*, Buena Vista, 1960; *Susan Slade*, Warner Brothers, 1961; *Summer Magic*, Buena Vista, 1963; *The Greatest Story Ever Told*, United Artists, 1965; *Flight of Doves*, Columbia, 1971; voice, *Jonathan Livingston Seagull*, Paramount, 1973.

PRINCIPAL TELEVISION APPEARANCES—Series: Marmee March, *Little Women*, NBC, 1979.

Episodic: "The Philadelphia Story," *Best of Broadway*, CBS, 1954; *U.S. Steel Hour*, ABC, 1954; *Lux Video Theatre*, CBS, 1954; *Climax*, CBS, 1954 and 1956; *Playhouse 90; The Love Boat*, 1984; *St. Elsewhere*, NBC, 1985; *The Young and the Restless*, CBS, 1985; *Hotel*, ABC, 1985.

Mini-Series: Mary Jordache, *Rich Man, Poor Man, Book I*, ABC, 1976.

Movie: *Runaways*, 1975; Marmee March, *Little Women*, NBC,

1978; *Ghost Dancing*, ABC, 1983; *Darkness to Dawn*, 1985; *Geisha*, 1985.

PRINCIPAL RADIO WORK—Series: *Big Sister*, 1937.

Specials: Ophelia, *Hamlet*, 1951.

MEMBER: Actors' Equity Association, Screen Actors Guild, American Federation of Television and Radio Artists.

AWARDS: New York Drama Critics Circle, 1941, for Claudia Naughton, *Claudia;* Best Actress, National Board of Review, 1955.

SIDELIGHTS: RECREATION—Writing and swimming.

ADDRESSES: OFFICE—P.O. Box 25940, Los Angeles, CA 90025.

*   *   *

McKEAN, Michael

PERSONAL: Born October 17, in New York, NY; son of Gilbert and Ruth McKean; married Susan; children: Colin Russell. EDUCATION: New York University, studied for the theatre at the Carnegie Institute of Technology.

VOCATION: Actor.

CAREER. MAJOR TOUR—*The Credibility Gap.*

PRINCIPAL FILM APPEARANCES—*1941*, Universal, 1979; *Used Cars*, 1980; *This Is Spinal Tap*, Embassy, 1984; *D.A.R.Y.L*, Paramount, 1985; Mr. Green, *Clue*, 1985.

PRINCIPAL TELEVISION APPEARANCES—Series: Lenny Kosnowski, *Laverne and Shirley*, ABC, 1976-83.

Episodic: *The Goodtime Girls; More Than Friends; American Bandstand; The TV Show.*

Movies: Pete Newly, *Classified Love*, CBS, 1986.

RECORDINGS: ALBUM—(With David Lander) *Lenny and the Squigtones.*

ADDRESSES: AGENT—Triad Agency, 10100 Santa Monica Blvd., 16th Floor, Los Angeles, CA 90067.*

*   *   *

McLAUGHLIN, Emily

PERSONAL: Born December 1, in White Plains, NY; married Jeffrey Hunter (an actor; deceased); married Robert Lansing (divorced); children: Robert. EDUCATION: Middlebury College, B.A., American Literature.

VOCATION: Actress.

CAREER: PRINCIPAL STAGE APPEARANCES—*The Lovers*, Broadway production; *Troilus and Cressida*, Off-Broadway production.

MAJOR TOUR—*Plaza Suite*, U.S. and Canadian cities.

PRINCIPAL TELEVISION APPEARANCES—Series: Jessie Brewer, *General Hospital*, ABC, 1983—.

Special: *The Eleventh Hour.*

MEMBER: American Federation of Television and Radio Artists, Actors' Equity Association.

ADDRESSES: HOME—Van Nuys, CA. OFFICE—ABC Television, 1330 Avenue of the Americas, New York, NY 10019.*

*   *   *

McNICHOL, James

PERSONAL: Son of Carollyne McNichol.

VOCATION: Actor and singer.

CAREER: TELEVISION DEBUT—*Family Affair,* CBS, 1966. PRINCIPAL TELEVISION APPEARANCES—Series: Jack, *The Fitzpatricks,* CBS, 1977-78; Vince Butler, *California Fever,* CBS, 1979; host, *Hollywood Teen,* ABC; Josh Clayton, *General Hospital,* ABC.

Movies: *Smokey Bites the Dust; Night Warning; Safe Harbour; Escape from El Diablo;* ''First the Egg,'' *ABC After School Special; Champions: A Love Story; Blinded by the Light,* CBS.

PRINCIPAL STAGE APPEARANCES—Danny Zuko, *Grease,* Turn of the Century Theatre, Los Angeles, CA.

RELATED CAREER—Singer, musician, *Secret Service Band.*

SIDELIGHTS: RECREATIONS—Surfing, skiing, tennis, equestrian sports, and carpentry.

James McNichol is the founder of Coast to Coast Data Computer Company.

ADDRESSES: AGENT—Sumski, Green & Company, 8380 Melrose Avenue, Suite 200, Los Angeles, CA 90069.

JAMES McNICHOL

KRISTY McNICHOL

McNICHOL, Kristy   1962-

PERSONAL: Born September 9, 1962, in Los Angeles, CA; daughter of Carollyne McNichol.

VOCATION: Actress.

CAREER: TELEVISION DEBUT—At age seven, performing in commercials. PRINCIPAL TELEVISION APPEARANCES—Series: Patricia Apple, *Apple's Way,* CBS, 1974-75; Letitia ''Buddy'' Lawrence, *Family,* ABC, 1976-80.

Episodic: *Love, American Style,* ABC; *The Bionic Woman,* NBC.

Movies: *Like Mom, Like Me,* 1978; *Summer of My German Soldier,* 1978; *My Old Man; Love, Mary,* CBS, 1986; *Women of Valor,* CBS, 1986.

Guest: *People,* CBS, 1978; *Dick Clark's Live Wednesday,* NBC, 1978.

Specials: *Challenge of the Network Stars.*

PRINCIPAL FILM APPEARANCES—*The End,* United Artists, 1978; *Little Darlings,* Paramount, 1980; *The Night the Lights Went Out in Georgia,* Avco Embassy, 1981; *Only When I Laugh,* Columbia, 1981; *The Pirate Movie,* Twentieth Century-Fox, 1982; *The White Dog,* 1982; *Just the Way You Are,* Metro-Goldwyn-Mayer/United Artists, 1984; *Dream Lover,* Metro-Goldwyn-Mayer/United Artists, 1986.

AWARDS: Photoplay's Gold Medal Award, 1976; Emmy Awards: outstanding continuing performance by a supporting actress in a drama, *Family*, 1977 and 1979;

ADDRESSES: HOME—Studio City, CA. AGENT—William Morris Agency, 151 El Camino Drive, Beverly Hills, CA 90212.

*　　*　　*

MEACHAM, Anne   1925-

PERSONAL: Born July 21,1925, in Chicago, IL; daughter of Florus David and Virginia (Foster) Meacham. EDUCATION: Attended University of Rochester; attended Yale School of Drama; studied acting at the Neighborhood Playhouse.

VOCATION: Actress.

CAREER: STAGE DEBUT—Mrs. Brown, *Claudia*, Bridgeton, ME, 1946. NEW YORK DEBUT—Ensign Jane Hilton, *The Long Watch*, Lyceum Theatre, 1952. PRINCIPAL STAGE APPEARANCES—Violante, *Ondine*, 46th Street Theatre, NY, 1954; Lorna, *Golden Boy*, Arena Stage, Washington, DC, 1954; Aurora, *The Immortal Husband*, Theatre de Lys, NY, 1955; Gertrude Wentworth, *Eugenia*, Ambassador Theatre, NY, 1957; Romaine, *Witness for the Prosecution*, Arena Stage, Washington, DC, 1957; Catherine Holly, *Suddenly Last Summer*, York Playhouse, NY, 1958; Lizzie Borden, *The Legend of Lizzie*, 54th Street Theatre, 1959.

Jere Halliday, *The Disenchanted*, Arena Stage, Washington, DC,

ANNE MEACHAM

1960; Hedda, *Hedda Gabler*, Fourth Street Theatre, NY, 1960; Adela Quested, *A Passage to India*, Ambassador Theatre, NY, 1962; Maria, *School for Scandal*, Violet, *The Tavern*, Dorcas, *A Penny for a Song*, all with the Association of Producing Artists at the University of Michigan, Ann Arbor, 1962; Elma, *As You Desire Me* and Monica Claverton-Ferry, *The Elder Statesman*, both Milwaukee, WI, 1963; Nina, *The Seagull* and Elizabeth Proctor, *The Crucible*, both part of Eva Le Gallienne's National Repertory Theatre, Belasco Theatre, 1964; Dienaeria, *The Wives*, Stage 73, NY, 1965; Vinnie Dickinson, *Come Slowly, Eden*, White Barn Theatre, Westport, CT, 1966; Penelope Gray, *Elizabeth the Queen*, City Center Theatre, NY, 1966; Gertrude, *Rosencrantz and Guildenstern Are Dead*, Alvin Theatre, NY, 1967; Countess Aurelia, *The Madwoman of Chaillot*, Cincinnati Playhouse in the Park, OH, 1968; *Knights of the Round Table* and *Little Eyolf*, both Artists Theatre, Southhampton, NY, 1968; Madame Acardina, *The Seagull*, Hartford Stage Company, CT, 1968; Miriam, *In the Bar of a Tokyo Hotel*, Eastside Playhouse, NY, 1969; Barinin, *Edith Stein*, Arena Stage, Washington, DC, 1969.

Louise, *Fathers Day*, Washington Theatre Club, Washington, DC, 1971; Gwendolyn, *The Importance of Being Earnest* and Julie, *The Royal Family*, both Goodman Theatre, Chicago, 1972; title role, *The Latter Days of a Celebrated Soubrette*, Central Arts, NY, 1974; Nurse Boyd, *A Destiny with Half Moon Street*, Coconut Grove Playhouse, Coconut Grove, FL, 1983; Eleanor of Aquitane, *The Lion in Winter*, Clarence Brown Theatre, University of Tennessee, 1986.

MAJOR TOURS—Penny, *The Fatal Weakness*, national, 1947; Elsie Fraser, *The First Mrs. Fraser*, 1948; Laura Bateman, *Masquerade*, national, 1952-53; with Eve Le Gallienne's National Repertory Theatre tour: Lady India, *Ring Round the Moon*, Nina, *The Seagull*, and Elizabeth Procter, *The Crucible*, 1963-64.

PRINCIPAL FILM APPEARANCES—*Lilith*, Columbia, 1964; *Dear Dead Delilah*, 1971; *Seizure*, 1974.

PRINCIPAL TELEVISION APPEARANCES—Series: Louise, *Another World*.

Episodic: *Playhouse 90; Dr. Kildare; The Virginian; Therese Raquin*, PBS.

AWARDS: Clarence Derwent Award, 1952, for Ensign Jane Hilton, *The Long Watch;* Obies, *Village Voice*, 1958, for Catherine Holly, *Suddenly Last Summer* and 1960, for Hedda, *Hedda Gabler*.

ADDRESSES: HOME—New York, NY. AGENT—Barry Agency, 165 W. 46th Street, New York, NY 10036.

*　　*　　*

MEADE, Julia

PERSONAL: Born December 17, in Boston, MA; daughter of Adam (a businessman) and Caroline (an actress, maiden name, Meade) Kunze; married O. Worsham Rudd, Jr. (an artist), May 17, 1952; children: Caroline, Alice. EDUCATION: Attended Yale University School of Drama.

VOCATION: Actress.

CAREER: TELEVISION DEBUT—*Fashions on Parade*, Dumont, 1949. PRINCIPAL TELEVISION APPEARANCES—Series: *Julia*

Meade's News You Can Use; Family Health News; Your Hit Parade, NBC, CBS.

Guest: *Password; The Match Game; To Tell the Truth*, CBS; *The Tonight Show*, NBC.

Episodic: *Playhouse 90*, CBS; *Search for Tomorrow; Ryan's Hope; My Little Love*.

FILM DEBUT—Marie, *Pillow Talk*, Universal, 1959. PRINCIPAL FILM APPEARANCES—*Tammy Tell Me True*, Universal, 1961; *Zotz*, Columbia, 1962.

NEW YORK DEBUT—Jessica, *Tender Trap*, Longacre Theatre, 1954. PRINCIPAL STAGE APPEARANCES—*Double in Hearts*, John Golden Theatre, NY, 1956; *Roman Candle*, Cort Theatre, NY, 1959; *Mary, Mary*, Helen Hayes Theatre, NY, 1962; *The Front Page*, Barrymore Theatre, NY, 1969.

Stock: *Wait Until Dark; Tea and Sympathy; Once More with Feeling; The Pajama Game; Bells Are Ringing; Plain and Fancy; Do I Hear a Waltz; A Little Night Music; Send Me No Flowers; Everything in the Garden; She Loves Me; The Reluctant Debutante*, Caldwell Playhouse, Boca Raton, FL.

MAJOR TOURS—*Mary, Mary*, U.S. cities.

AWARDS: Sarah Siddons Award, for *Mary, Mary*.

ADDRESSES: HOME—New York, NY.

*   *   *

MELNICK, Daniel 1932-

PERSONAL: Born April 21, 1932, in New York, NY; children: Peter. EDUCATION:New York University.

VOCATION: Producer.

CAREER: PRINCIPAL FILM WORK—Producer: *Straw Dogs*, 1971; *That's Entertainment!*, United Artists, 1975; *The Sunshine Boys*, United Artists, 1975; *The Wind and the Lion*, United Artists, 1975; *Network*, United Artists, 1976; *The Goodbye Girl*, Warner Brothers, 1977; *Midnight Express*, Columbia, 1978; *China Syndrome*, Columbia, 1979; *Ice Castles*, Columbia, 1979; *California Suite*, Columbia, 1978; *And Justice for All*, Columbia, 1979; *Chapter Two*, Columbia, 1979; *Kramer vs. Kramèr*, Columbia, 1979; *All That Jazz*, Twentieth Century-Fox, 1979; *Altered States*, Warner Brothers, 1980; *Footloose*, Paramount, 1984.

PRINCIPAL TELEVISION WORK—Producer: Specials—*Death of a Salesman; The Ages of Man*.

Series: *East Side/West Side*, CBS, 1963-64; *N.Y.P.D.*, ABC, 1967-69.

RELATED CAREER—Staff producer, CBS; producer of children's theater, Circle in the Square, NY; vice-president of programming, ABC Television Network; partner, Talent Associates.

AWARDS: Emmy Awards, for *Death of a Salesman* and *The Ages of Man*.

ADDRESSES: OFFICE—4000 Warner Blvd., Burbank, CA 91505.

MEPPEN, Adrian Joseph 1940-

PERSONAL: Born April 11, 1940, in New York, NY; son of Morris and Adele Meppen; married Arlene Widelitz, June 15, 1963; children: Roberta, Michelle, Sara. EDUCATION: City College of New York, B.A., 1962; Columbia University, M.S., 1963. MILITARY: U.S. Army, 1963-64.

VOCATION: Writer.

CAREER: Reporter, *Newsday*, Garden City, Long Island, NY, 1964-66; reporter, *Wall Street Journal*, 1966-67; reporter and writer, *The New York Times*, 1967-69; producer and writer, WCBS television news, 1969—; adjunct instructor of broadcast journalism, City College of New York, 1974-79.

WRITINGS: BOOKS—*Broadcast News: Writing, Reporting and Production*, McMillan, 1983.

MEMBER: Writers Guild of America, East (vice president, 1985-87).

ADDRESSES: OFFICE—WCBS Television News, 518 W. 57th Street, New York, NY 10019.

*   *   *

MESSICK, Don 1926-

PERSONAL: Full name Donald E. Messick; born September 7, 1926; son of Binford Earl (a housepainter) and Lena Birch (Hughes)

DON MESSICK

Messick; married Helen (a shopkeeper), October 10, 1953; children: Timothy, Charles. EDUCATION: Graduated from Nanticoke High School, MD, 1943; trained for the stage at the William Ramsay Street School of Acting, Baltimore, MD. MILITARY: U.S. Army.

VOCATION: Actor.

CAREER: PRINCIPAL TELEVISION WORK—Cartoon voice of: Ruff, Professor Gismo, and narrator, *Ruff 'n' Reddy,* NBC, 1959; Boo-Boo Bear and Ranger Smith, *Yogi Bear Show,* 1960; Astro, *The Jetsons,* ABC, 1962; title role, *Scooby Doo,* 1969; Nobody and Sparerib, *Dingbat and the Creeps;* Henry Jeckyll-Hyde and Ruckus, *Bailey's Comets;* Push-me Pull-you, Chee Chee, and Nico, *The Adventures of Dr. Doolittle;* Harvey and Chili Dog, *Sabrina, The Teen-Age Witch;* Hot Dog, *Archie;* Pixie Mouse, *Huckleberry Hound;* Mr. Twiddle, *Wally Gator;* So-so, *Peter Potamus;* Dr. Benton Quest, *Jonny Quest;* Shag Rugg, *Hillbilly Bears;* title role, *Ricochet Rabbit;* Falcon 7, *Birdman;* Multi-man, *Impossibles;* title role, *Precious Pupp.*

Mumbly, *Lt. Mumbly;* Aramis, *The Three Musketeers;* Muttley and Pat Pending, *Wacky Races;* Hoppy and Smirky, *Around the World in 79 Days;* Dum Dum, Pockets, Snoozy, and Zippy, *Perils of Penelope Pitstop;* Muttley, Zilly, Klunk, Pigeon, and narrator, *Dick Dastardly and Muttley and Their Flying Machines;* Sebastien and Bleep, *Josie and the Pussycats;* Chu Chu, *Chan Clan;* Jonas and Pegasus, *These Are the Days;* Scramble, *Wheelie and the Chopper Bunch;* Spot, *Hong Kong Phooey;* Sinestro and Scarecrow, *Challenge of the Superfriends;* Bamm Bamm, *Flintstones;* Gleep, Gloop, and Zok, *Herculoids;* Toad, *The Drak Pack;* Mr. Hoofnagel and Officer Growler, *The Get-Along Gang;* Crunch and Rondu, *Mighty Orbots;* Ratchet and Gears, *Transformers;* Pupooch, *The Paw Paws;* Boo Boo, Ranger Smith, Muttley, *Yogi's Funtastic Treasure Hunt;* Papa Smurf and Azrael, *Smurfs,* 1981—.

PRINCIPAL TELEVISION APPEARANCES—*The Buffalo Billy Show,* WCBS, NY, 1950; Wally Wooster, *The Duck Factory,* NBC, 1984.

PRINCIPAL RADIO APPEARANCES—WBOC, Salsbury, MD, 1941-43; Raggedy Andy, *The Raggedy Ann Show,* 1946.

MEMBER: Pacific Pioneer Broadcasters (charter member), Screen Actors Guild, American Federation of Television and Radio Artists.

SIDELIGHTS: Don Messick told *CTFT* that he began his career as a performer at age thirteen when he developed his own act as a ventriloquist in rural Maryland.

ADDRESSES: HOME—Santa Barbara, CA. AGENT—Charles H. Stern Agency, 9220 Sunset Blvd., Los Angeles, CA 90069.

*   *   *

MILES, Sarah   1941-

PERSONAL: Born December 31, 1941, in Ingatestone, England; daughter of John (an engineer) and Vanessa Miles; married Robert Bolt (a playwright), 1967 (divorced, 1975); children: Thomas. EDUCATION: Studied for the theatre at the Royal Academy of Dramatic Art, London.

VOCATION: Actress.

CAREER: LONDON DEBUT—*Dazzling Prospect,* Globe Theatre, 1961. PRINCIPAL STAGE APPEARANCES—(All London unless

otherwise noted) Anna Brierly, *Kelly's Eye,* Royal Court Theatre, 1963; *The Recruiting Officer, Hayfever* and as Abigail Williams, *The Crucible,* all with the National Theatre Company, Old Vic, 1964-65; Marina Oswald, *The Silence of Lee Harvey Oswald,* Hampstead Theatre, 1966; woman, *World War 2 1/2,* New Theatre, 1966; Mary, Queen of Scots, *Vivat! Vivat Regina!* Chichester Festival, Chichester, England, 1967, then Piccadilly Theatre, 1970; title role, *Saint Joan,* Ahmanson Theatre, Los Angeles, 1970; Sabina, *The Skin of Our Teeth,* Ahmanson Theatre, Los Angeles, 1974; one woman show, *Sarah Miles Is Me,* American Conservatory Theatre, San Francisco, 1978; also appeared in *The Reluctant Debutant* and *The Moon Is Blue,* in repertory at the Connaught Theatre, Worthing.

FILM DEBUT—*Term of Trial,* Romulus Films, 1962. PRINCIPAL FILM APPEARANCES—*The Servant,* Elstree/Springbok Films, 1963; *The Ceremony,* United Artists, 1963; *Those Magnificent Men in Their Flying Machines,* Twentieth Century-Fox, 1965; *I Was Happy Here* (also known as *Time Lost and Time Remembered*), Partisan Films, 1965; *Blow Up,* Metro-Goldwyn-Mayer, 1966; title role, *Ryan's Daughter,* Metro-Goldwyn-Mayer, 1970; title role, *Lady Caroline Lamb,* EMI/GEC/Pulsar/Video Cinemtographica Films, 1972; *The Hireling,* Columbia, 1973; *The Man Who Loved Cat Dancing,* Metro-Goldwyn-Mayer, 1973; *The Sailor Who Fell from Grace with the Sea,* 1976; *The Big Sleep,* United Artists, 1978; *Venom,* Paramount, 1982; *Ordeal by Innocence,* 1984; also appeared in: *Steaming; Six-Sided Triangle.*

PRINCIPAL TELEVISION APPEARANCES—Movies: *Great Expectations,* 1974; Jennifer Blackwood, *James Michener's Dynasty,* 1976.

AWARDS: Best Actress, Academy Award nomination, 1970, for *Ryan's Daughter.*

ADDRESSES: AGENT—William Morris Agency, 147-149 Wardour Street, London W1V 3TB, England.*

*   *   *

MILITELLO, Anne E.   1957-

PERSONAL: Born April 29, 1957, in Buffalo, NY; daughter of George J. (a barber) and E. Patricia (a payroll clerk; maiden name, Pollina) Militello. EDUCATION: Attended the State University of New York at Buffalo; trained in stage design at the Polakov Studio and the Forum of Stage Design.

VOCATION: Lighting designer.

CAREER: FIRST STAGE WORK—Lighting designer, *Josephine the Mouse Singer,* Magic Theatre, San Francisco, CA, 1980, for thirty-six performances. FIRST NEW YORK STAGE WORK—Lighting designer, *After Stardrive,* La Mama Experimental Theatre Club (ETC), 1981, for thirty-six performances. FIRST LONDON STAGE WORK—Lighting designer, *Aladin,* Commonwealth Institute, 1983, for fourteen performances.

PRINCIPAL STAGE WORK—Lighting designer: *Hurrah for the Bridge,* La Mama ETC, NY, 1981; *Why Hanna's Skirt Won't Stay Down,* Theatre of Big Dreams, NY, 1981; *The Unseen Hand,* Provincetown Playhouse, NY, 1982; *Starburn* and *MUD,* both Theatre for the New City, NY, 1983; *Sarita,* Intar Theatre, NY, 1983; *To Heaven in a Swing,* American Place Theatre, NY, 1984; *The Dog Lady/Cuban Swimmer,* Intar Theatre, NY, 1984; *Imagination Dead Imagine,* Performing Garage Theatre, NY, 1984; *The*

Photograph by McKitterick

ANNE E. MILITELLO

Danube, American Place Theatre, NY, 1984; *Rapmaster Ronnie*, Village Gate Theatre, NY, 1984; *Four Corners*, American Place Theatre, NY, 1985; *Conduct of Life*, Theatre for the New City, NY, 1985; *Flow My Tears, the Policeman Said*, Boston Shakespeare Company, MA, 1985; *A Lie of the Mind*, Promenade Theatre, NY, 1985—.

MAJOR TOURS—Lighting designer: *Aladin*, European cities, 1982; *Ghost Sonata*, Italian cities, 1982.

MEMBER: International Association of Lighting Designers.

AWARDS: Sustained Excellence in Lighting Design, Obie Award, 1984.

ADDRESSES: AGENT—c/o George Lane, William Morris Agency, 1350 Avenue of the Americas, New York, NY 10019.

*   *   *

MILKIS, Edward Kenneth   1931-

PERSONAL: Born July 16, 1931, in Los Angeles, CA; son of Sam and Minnie (Satnick) Milkis; married Marcia; children: Steven, Gary, Charles. EDUCATION: Attended Los Angeles City College, 1949-50; attended University of Southern California, 1952-56.

VOCATION: Producer.

CAREER: PRINCIPAL FILM WORK—Co-producer, *Silver Streak*, Twentieth Century-Fox, 1976; co-producer, *Foul Play*, Paramount, 1978; co-producer, *The Best Little Whorehouse in Texas*, Universal, 1982.

PRINCIPAL TELEVISION WORK—Associate producer, *Star Trek*, NBC, 1966-69; *Petrocelli*, NBC, 1974-76; executive producer, *Laverne and Shirley*, ABC, 1977-83; executive producer, *Angie*, ABC, 1979-80; *Joanie Loves Chiachi*, ABC, 1982-83; *Bosom Buddies*, ABC, 1980-82.

RELATED CAREER—Film shipper, assistant film editor, ABC Television, Hollywood, CA, 1952; assistant film editor, Walt Disney Productions, Metro-Goldwyn-Mayer, Los Angeles, 1954-60; film editor, Metro-Goldwyn-Mayer, 1960-65; executive post production, Paramount Television, 1969-72; partner, Miller-Milkis Productions, 1972—; partner, Milkins-Milkis-Boyett Productions, 1979—.

MEMBER: Academy of Motion Picture Arts and Sciences, Academy of Television Arts and Sciences, Directors Guild of America, Film Editors Guild.

ADDRESSES: HOME—5451 Marathon Street, Hollywood, CA 90038. OFFICE—5555 Melrose Avenue, Hollywood, CA 90038.*

*   *   *

MILLAND, Ray   1905-1986

PERSONAL: Full name Reginald Truscott-Jones; born January 3, 1905, in Neath Glamorganshire, Wales; died of cancer in Torrance, CA, March 10, 1986; married Muriel (Mal) Weber (a showgirl) 1932; children: one son (died, 1981). MILITARY: Household Cavalry (Guards of the Royal Family).

VOCATION: Actor, director, and writer.

CAREER: PRINCIPAL FILM APPEARANCES—*Ambassador Bill*, Metro-Goldwyn-Mayer, 1930; *The Bachelor Father*, Metro-Goldwyn-Mayer, 1931; *Blonde Crazy*, Metro-Goldwyn-Mayer, 1931; *Just a Gigolo*, Metro-Goldwyn-Mayer, 1932; *Polly of the Circus*, Metro-Goldwyn-Mayer, 1932; *Bought*, Metro-Goldwyn-Mayer, 1932; *Payment Deferred*, Metro-Goldwyn-Mayer, 1932; *Orders Is Orders*, British, 1933; *This Is the Life*, British, 1933; *Bolero*, Paramount, 1934; *One Hour Late*, Paramount, 1934; *We're Not Dressing*, Paramount, 1934; *The Glass Key*, Paramount, 1935; *The Gilded Lady*, Paramount, 1935; *Four Hours to Kill*, Paramount, 1936; *Alias Mary Dow*, Paramount, 1936; *The Big Broadcast of 1937*, Paramount, 1936; *Three Smart Girls*, Paramount, 1937; *Bulldog Drummond Escapes*, Paramount, 1937; *Easy Living*, Paramount, 1937; *Ebb Tide*, Paramount, 1937; *Wise Girl*, Paramount, 1937; *Beau Geste*, Paramount, 1939; *French without Tears*, British, 1939; *Everything Happens at Night*, Paramount, 1939; *Hotel Imperial*, Paramount, 1939; *Men with Wings*, Paramount, 1939.

Hostile Witness, Paramount, 1940; *Till We Meet Again*, Paramount, 1940; *Arise My Love*, Paramount, 1940; *Irene*, Paramount, 1940; *Doctor Takes a Wife*, Paramount, 1940; *I Wanted Wings*, Paramount, 1941; *The Lady Has Plans*, 1942; *Reap the Wild Wind*, Paramount, 1942; *Are Husbands Necessary?*, 1942; *The Major and the Minor*, 1942; *The Crystal Ball*, 1943; *Forever and a Day*, 1943; *Ministry of Fear*, Paramount, 1944; *The Uninvited*, Paramount, 1944; *Lady in the Dark*, 1944; *Kitty*, Paramount, 1945; *Lost Weekend*, Paramount, 1945; *The Well Groomed Bride*, Paramount, 1946; *California*, 1946; *The Imperfect Lady*, 1947; *The Trouble with Women*, 1947; *Golden Earrings*, Paramount, 1947; *The Big Clock*, 1948; *Wings Over Honolulu*, 1948; *Sealed Verdict*, 1948; *So Evil My Love*, 1948; *Alias Nick Beal*, Paramount, 1949; *It Happens Every Spring*, Paramount, 1949.

A *Life of Her Own*, 1950; *Copper Canyon*, Paramount, 1950; *Woman of Distinction*, 1950; *Circle of Danger*, 1951; *Night into Morning*, Paramount, 1951; *Rhubarb*, 1951; *Close to My Heart*, Paramount, 1951; *Something to Live For*, Paramount, 1952; *Bugles in the Afternoon*, Paramount, 1952; *The Thief*, 1952; *Jamaica Run*, Paramount, 1953; *Let's Do It Again*, Paramount, 1953; *Dial M for Murder*, 1954; *The Girl on the Red Velvet Swing*, Twentieth Century-Fox, 1955; *A Man Alone*, Republic Pictures, 1955; *Lisbon*, Republic Pictures, 1956; *Three Brave Men*, Twentieth Century-Fox, 1957; *The River's Edge*, Twentieth Century-Fox, 1957; *The Safecracker*, 1958.

Premature Burial, American International, 1962; *Panic in Year Zero*, American International, 1962; *The Man With X-Ray Eyes*, American International, 1962; *Love Story*, Paramount, 1970; *The Thing with Two Heads*, American International, 1971; *Frogs*, American International, 1972; *Terror in the Wax Museum*, American International, 1973; *The House in Nightmare Park*, American International, 1973; *Gold*, Allied Artists, 1974; *Escape to Witch Mountain*, Buena Vista, 1975; *The Last Tycoon*, Paramount, 1977; *Oil*, 1977; *Blackout*, 1978; *Game for Vultures*, American International, 1978; *Oliver's Story*, Paramount, 1978; *Slavers*, German, 1978; *Battlestar Galactica*, Universal, 1979; *Survival Run*, 1980; *The Sea Serpent*, 1984.

PRINCIPAL FILM WORK—Director: *Hostile Witness*, 1940; *A Man Alone*, Republic Pictures, 1955; *Lisbon*, Republic Pictures, 1956; *The Safecracker*, 1958; *Panic in Year Zero*, American International, 1962.

PRINCIPAL TELEVISION APPEARANCES—Series: Professor Ray McNutley, *The Ray Milland Show*, CBS, 1953-55; Roy Markham, *Markham*, CBS, 1959-60.

Episodic: *General Electric Theatre; Suspicion; Suspense; The Du-Pont Show of the Month; Seventh Avenue; The Love Boat.*

Mini-Series: Duncan Calderwood, *Rich Man Poor Man Book I*, ABC, 1976-77; *The Dream Merchants.*

Movies: *The Royal Romance of Charles and Diana*, 1982; *Cave In!*, 1983; *Starflight One*, 1983; *The Gold Key*, 1985.

NEW YORK DEBUT—*Hostile Witness*, 1966. PRINCIPAL STAGE APPEARANCES—*Lady from the Sea*, England; *The Plaything*, England.

MAJOR TOURS—*The Woman in Room 13*, England; *Hostile Witness*, U.S. cities.

WRITINGS: AUTOBIOGRAPHY—*Wide-Eyed in Babylon*, 1974.

AWARDS: Best Actor, Academy Award, New York Film Critic's Award, Cannes Film Festival Citation, Golden Globe Award, all 1945, for *Lost Weekend*.

SIDELIGHTS: CTFT learned from the obituary published in *Variety* Wednesday, March 12, 1986, that Ray Milland was an excellent marksman. He did some "trick shooting" for the 1929 film *The Informer* after the original marksman was killed in an accident. He then changed his name from "Spike Milland to Raymond Milland" and pursued his acting career. He later reflected, "I didn't choose acting, it chose me. I just fell into it—a matter of being in the right place at the wrong time."*

MILLER, Richard   1930-

PERSONAL: Born March 15, 1930; son of Maurice Entler (a teacher) and Lillian (Reed) Miller; married Teresa Robinson (a singer in the Metropolitan Opera Chorus). EDUCATION: American University, B.A., 1953; Columbia University, M.F.A., 1957.

VOCATION: Actor.

CAREER: PRINCIPAL STAGE APPEARANCES—Broadway: Billy the Kid, *Indians;* Forward Sailor, *Illya Darling;* Renaldi, *Funny Girl;* standby, *Superman;* Dr. Baxter, *Baker Street;* understudy, Fagin, *Oliver!;* Fletcher, *Wonderful Town.* Off-Broadway: Toby Higgins, *Rise and Fall of the City of Mahogonny.*

Stock: John Dickinson, *1776;* Polpoch, *Marat/Sade;* Chuch, *Hatful of Rain;* Lindstrom, *Mr. Roberts;* Carnes, *Oklahoma!;* Gremio, *Kiss Me, Kate;* Ford, *Merry Wives of Windsor;* Laudisi, *Right You Are If You Think You Are;* Chic Clark, *My Sister, Eileen;* Gentleman Caller, *Glass Menagerie;* Hercule, *Can-Can;* Macduff, *Macbeth;* President, *Madwoman of Chaillot;* Jumelle, *Reclining Figure;* Smokey, *Damn Yankees;* Sheriff, *Finian's Rainbow;* Postman, *Most Happy Fella;* Benny Southstreet, *Guys and Dolls;* Rabbi, *Fiddler on the Roof;* Keeny, *Funny Girl;* Bellerose and DeGuiche, *Send for Cyrano.*

PRINCIPAL TELEVISION APPEARANCES—*Linda and Harry*, PBS.

AWARDS: Fulbright Fellowship, Paris, 1953.

ADDRESSES: HOME—222 W. 83rd Street, New York, NY 10024.

*   *   *

MILLER, Thomas L.   1940-

PERSONAL: Full name Thomas Lee Miller; born August 31, 1940, in Milwaukee, WI; son of Edward Allan and Shirley Annette (Plous) Miller.

VOCATION: Producer and writer.

CAREER: PRINCIPAL FILM WORK—Co-producer, *The Best Little Whorehouse in Texas*, Universal, 1982.

PRINCIPAL TELEVISION WORK—Executive producer, *Bosom Buddies*, ABC, 1980-81; *Foul Play*, ABC, 1981.

RELATED CAREER: Director of Development, Twentieth Century-Fox Television, 1967-68; vice president of development, Paramount Television, 1968-72; partner, Miller-Milkis-Boyett Productions, Inc., 1972—.

WRITINGS: TELEVISION—(Also co-creator) *Love, American Style*, ABC, 1967-74; *Nanny and the Professor*, ABC, 1970-71; *Me and the Chimp*, CBS, 1972; *Sweepstakes*, NBC-TV, 1979; *Out of the Blue*, ABC, 1979.

MEMBER: Writers Guild of America West, Academy of Motion Picture Arts and Sciences, Academy of Television Arts and Sciences, Producers Guild of America.

ADDRESSES: OFFICE—Writers Guild of America West, 8955 Beverly Blvd., Los Angeles, CA 90048.*

MILLS, Donna

PERSONAL: Born December 11, in Chicago, IL. EDUCATION: University of Illinois.

VOCATION: Actress.

CAREER: STAGE DEBUT—As a dancer in Chicago, IL. PRINCIPAL STAGE APPEARANCES—*Don't Drink the Water,* NY, c. 1967.

FILM DEBUT—*The Incident,* 1967. PRINCIPAL FILM APPEARANCES—*Play Misty for Me,* Universal, 1971; others.

PRINCIPAL TELEVISION APPEARANCES—Series: *The Secret Storm; Love Is a Many Splendored Thing;* Jane Miller, *The Good Life,* NBC, 1971-72; Abby, *Knots Landing,* CBS, 1979—.

Episodic: *Dan August,* ABC; *Lancer,* CBS.

Mini-Series: *Bare Essence,* NBC, 1983.

Movies: *The Bait,* 1973; *The Hunted Lady,* 1977; *Fire!,* 1977; *Doctor's Private Lives,* 1978; *Superdome,* 1978; *Hanging by a Thread,* 1979; *Waikiki,* 1980; *He's Not Your Son,* CBS, 1984; *Woman on the Run.*

ADDRESSES: AGENT—c/o Mike Greenfield, Charter Management, 9000 Sunset Blvd., Suite 1112, Los Angeles, CA 90069.*

*   *   *

MILLS, Hayley   1946-

PERSONAL: Full name, Hayley Catherine Rose Vivian Mills; born April 18, 1946, in London, England; daughter of John (an actor) and Mary Hayley (an actress and writer; maiden name, Bell) Mills; married Roy Boulting (a producer), 1971 (divorced, 1977); children: (first marriage) Crispian; (with Leigh Lawson) Jason Lawson. EDUCATION: Attended Elmhurst Ballet School, Camberly, Surrey, England.

VOCATION: Actress.

CAREER: FILM DEBUT—Gillie, *Tiger Bay,* Continental Films, 1959. PRINCIPAL FILM APPEARANCES—Title role, *Pollyanna,* Buena Vista, 1960; Sharon McKendrick/Susan Evers, *The Parent Trap,* Buena Vista, 1961; *Whistle Down the Wind,* Pathe-American, 1962; Mary Grant, *In Search of the Castaways,* Buena Vista, 1962; Nancy Carey, *Summer Magic,* Buena Vista, 1963; *The Chalk Garden,* Universal, 1964; Nikky Ferris, *The Moonspinners,* Buena Vista, 1964; title role, *The Truth About Spring,* Universal, 1965; Patti Randall, *That Darn Cat,* Buena Vista, 1965; *Sky West and Crooked,* Rank Films, 1965; *The Trouble with Angels,* Columbia, 1966; Little Mermaid, *The Daydreamer,* Embassy Pictures, 1966; *The Family Way,* Warner Brothers, 1966; title role, *Gypsy Girl,* Continental Films, 1967; *Africa, Texas Style,* Paramount, 1967; *Pretty Polly,* Universal, 1968; *A Matter of Innocence,* Universal, 1968; *Twisted Nerve,* British Lion Films, 1968; *Take a Girl Like You,* Columbia, 1970; *Endless Night,* British Lion/EMI Films, 1971; *Mr. Forbush and the Penguins,* 1971; Belle Adams, *Deadly Strangers,* 1974; *The Kingfisher Caper,* 1975; *What Changed Charley Farthing?,* Patina-Hidalgo Films, 1975; also appeared in *The Diamond Hunters* and *Mother Superior.*

STAGE DEBUT—Title role, *Peter Pan,* New Victoria Theatre,

London, 1969. PRINCIPAL STAGE APPEARANCES—Hedvig, *The Wild Duck,* Criterion Theatre, London, 1970; Rose Trelawney, *Trelawney of the Wells,* Prince of Wales Theatre, London, 1972; Alison Ames, *A Touch of Spring,* Comedy Theatre, London, 1975; Mrs. de Winter, *Rebecca,* Arnaud Theatre, Guildford, 1977; Gwendolyn Fairfax, *The Importance of Being Earnest,* Chichester Festival, 1979; *The Summer Party,* 1980; Sally, *Talley's Folley,* 1982; also appeared as Irene in *The Three Sisters.*

PRINCIPAL TELEVISION APPEARANCES—Mini-Series: Tilly Grant, *The Flame Trees of Thika,* PBS, 1982.

Movies: *Silhouette;* sequel to *The Parent Trap,* 1986.

Guest: *The Danny Kaye Show, The Ed Sullivan Show, Disneyland,* others.

Special: *The Art of Disney,* NBC, 1981.

RECORDINGS: ALBUMS—*In Search of the Castaways,* Buena Vista; *Summer Magic,* original soundtrack recording, Buena Vista Records; *The Daydreamer,* original soundtrack recording, Columbia.

SINGLES—*Let's Get Together; Johnny Jingo; Ding Ding Ding; Teen Street.*

AWARDS: Best Actress, Silver Bear from the Berlin Film Festival, 1959, for *Tiger Bay;* Variety Clubs of Great Britain and honorary Academy Award (miniature statuette) both 1960, for *Pollyanna;* British Academy Award, Golden Globe, and voted "Number One Star of Tomorrow" in the United States and Canada, all 1962, for *In Search of the Castaways.*

SIDELIGHTS: RECREATION—Swimming, tennis, riding, and skiing.

ADDRESSES: AGENT—International Creative Management, 388 Oxford Street, London, W1, England.*

*   *   *

MILLS, Juliet   1941-

PERSONAL: Born November 21, 1941, in London, England; daughter of John (an actor) and Mary Hayley (an actress and writer; maiden name Bell) Mills; married Russell Alquist, Jr., 1961 (divorced); married Michael Miklenda (an architect; divorced); married Maxwell Caulfield (an actor), 1981; children: (first marriage) Sean Ryan; (second marriage) Melissa. EDUCATION: Attended Elmhurst Ballet School, Camberly, Surrey, England.

VOCATION: Actress.

CAREER: LONDON DEBUT—Alice, *Alice Through the Looking Glass,* Chelsea Palace Theatre, December, 1955. NEW YORK DEBUT—Pamela Harrington, *Five Finger Exercise,* Music Box Theatre, November, 1959. PRINCIPAL STAGE APPEARANCES—Pamela Harrington, *Five Finger Exercise,* Comedy Theatre, London, 1958; Wendy, *Peter Pan,* Scala Theatre, London, 1960; Kitty, *The Glad and Sorry Season,* Piccadilly Theatre, London, 1962; Titania, *A Midsummer Night's Dream,* Royal Shakespeare Company, Aldwych Theatre, London, 1963; Gilda, *Alfie,* Morosco Theatre, NY, 1964; *The Knack,* Los Angeles, 1964; title role, *Lady Windermere's Fan,* Phoenix Theatre, London, 1966; Kate Hardcastle, *She Stoops to Conquer,* Garrick Theatre, London, 1969; Susy Hendrix, *Wait Until Dark,* Alcazar Theatre, San Francisco, 1979;

Mrs. Kemble, *The Elephant Man*, Royal Poinsiana Playhouse, Palm Beach, FL, 1980; Catherine Sloper, *The Heiress*, Nottingham Playhouse, Nottingham, England, 1980; member of the company of the Mirror Repertory Company, Theatre at St. Peter's Church, NY, 1983—.

MAJOR TOURS—*The Mousetrap*, United States tour, 1976.

FILM DEBUT—At age eleven weeks, *In Which We Serve*, Rank/Two Cities, 1942. PRINCIPAL FILM APPEARANCES—*So Well Remembered*, RKO Alliance, 1947; *The October Man*, 1947; *The History of Mr. Polly*, GFD/Two Cities, 1949; Tansy, *No, My Darling Daughter*, 1961; *Twice Around the Daffodils*, Anglo Amalgamated Films, 1962; *Carry on Sailor*, Anglo Amalgamated Films, 1963; *Nurse on Wheels*, Anglo Amalgamated Films, 1963; *Carry on, Jack*, Anglo Amalgamated Films, 1964; *The Rare Breed*, Universal, 1966; *Oh, What a Lovely War!* Paramount, 1969; *Avanti!*, United Artists/Mirisch Corporation, 1972; *Beyond the Door*, U.S.-Italian co-production, 1982; also: *Wings of War; The Second Power; The Last Melodrama*.

PRINCIPAL TELEVISION APPEARANCES—Series: Phoebe Figalilly (Nanny), *Nanny and the Professor*, ABC, 1970-71.

Films: *Wings of Fire*, 1967; *The Challengers*, 1969; *Letters from Three Lovers*, 1973; Mrs. Cabe, *QB VII*, ABC, 1974; *Alexander: The Other Side of Dawn*, 1977; *The Cracker Factory*, 1979; also appeared in *Mr. Dickens of London, Mrs Miniver, The Morning After*, others.

Mini-Series: *Once an Eagle*.

AWARDS: Outstanding Single Performance by a Supporting Actress in a Comedy or Drama Special, Emmy, 1974-75, for *QB VII*.

SIDELIGHTS: RECREATION—Cooking, skating, riding, tennis.

ADDRESSES: AGENT—Crouch Associates, 59 Frith Street, London W1, England.*

*   *   *

MITCHUM, Robert   1917-

PERSONAL: Full name, Robert Charles Duran Mitchum; born August 6, 1917, in Bridgeport, CT; son of James (a railroad worker) and Anne Mitchum; married Dorothy Spencer, March 16, 1940; children: Petrine, Jim, Chris.

VOCATION: Actor.

CAREER: FILM DEBUT—*Hoppy Serves a Writ* (in the William Boyd "Hopalong Cassidy" series), United Artists, 1943.

PRINCIPAL FILM APPEARANCES—*The Leather Burners*, United Artists, 1943; *Border Patrol*, United Artists, 1943; *Follow the Band*, Universal, 1943; *Colt Comrades*, United Artists, 1943; Horse, *The Human Comedy*, Metro-Goldwyn-Mayer, 1943; *We've Never Been Licked*, Wanger/Universal, 1943; *Beyond the Last Frontier*, Republic, 1943; *Bar 20*, United Artists, 1943; *The Lone Star Trail*, Universal, 1943; *False Colors*, United Artists, 1943; *Dancing Masters*, Twentieth Century-Fox, 1943; *Riders of the Deadline*, United Artists, 1943; *Cry Havoc*, Metro-Goldwyn-Mayer, 1943; *Gung Ho!*, Universal, 1943; *Johnny Doesn't Live Here Anymore*, Monogram, 1944; *When Strangers Marry*, Monogram, 1944; *The Girl Rush*, RKO, 1944; Bob Gray, *Thirty Seconds Over Tokyo*, Metro-Goldwyn-Mayer, 1944; *Nevada*, RKO, 1944; *West of the Pecos*, RKO, 1944; Lieutenant Walker, *The Story of G.I. Joe*, United Artists, 1945; *Till the End of Time*, RKO, 1946; *Undercurrent*, Metro-Goldwyn-Mayer, 1946; *The Locket*, RKO, 1946; *Pursued*, Warner Brothers, 1947; Sgt. Peter Keeley, *Crossfire*, RKO, 1947; *Out of the Past*, RKO, 1947; *Rachel and the Stranger*, RKO, 1948; *Blood on the Moon*, RKO, 1948; *The Red Pony*, Republic, 1949; *The Big Steal*, RKO, 1949; *Holiday Affair*, RKO, 1949.

Where Danger Lives, RKO, 1950; *My Forbidden Past*, RKO, 1951; *His Kind of Woman*, RKO, 1951; *The Racket*, RKO, 1951; *Macao*, RKO, 1952; *One Minute to Zero*, RKO, 1952; *The Lusty Men*, RKO, 1952; *Angel Face*, RKO, 1952; *White Witch Doctor*, Twentieth Century-Fox, 1953; *Second Chance*, RKO, 1953; *She Couldn't Say No*, RKO, 1954; Matt Chandler, *River of No Return*, Twentieth Century-Fox, 1954; *Track of the Cat*, Warner Brothers, 1954; Lucas Marsh, *Not as a Stranger*, United Artists, 1955; Preacher, *The Night of the Hunter*, United Artists, 1955; *Man with a Gun*, United Artists, 1955; *Foreign Intrigue*, United Artists, 1956; *Bandido*, United Artists, 1956; Corporal Allison, U.S.M.C., *Heaven Knows, Mr. Allison*, Twentieth Century-Fox, 1957; *Fire Down Below*, Columbia, 1957; Captain Murrell, *The Enemy Below*, Twentieth Century-Fox, 1957; *Thunder Road*, United Artists, 1958; *The Hunters*, Twentieth Century-Fox, 1958; *The Angry Hills*, Metro-Goldwyn-Mayer, 1959; *The Wonderful Country*, United Artists, 1959.

Home from the Hill, Metro-Goldwyn-Mayer, 1960; *The Night Fighters*, United Artists, 1960; *The Grass Is Greener*, Universal, 1960; Paddy Carmody, *The Sundowners*, Warner Brothers, 1960; *The Last Time I Saw Archie*, United Artists, 1961; *Cape Fear*, Universal, 1962; Brigadier General Norman Cota, *The Longest Day*, Twentieth Century-Fox, 1962; Jerry Ryan, *Two for the Seesaw*, United Artists, 1962; *The List of Adrian Messenger*, Universal, 1963; *Rampage*, Warner Brothers, 1963; *Man in the Middle*, Twentieth Century-Fox, 1964; *What a Way to Go!*, Twentieth Century-Fox, 1964; *Mr. Moses*, United Artists, 1965; *El Dorado*, Paramount, 1967; *Anzio*, Columbia, 1968; *Villa Rides*, Paramount, 1968; *Five Card Stud*, Paramount, 1968; Albert, *Secret Ceremony*, Universal, 1969; *Young Billy Young*, United Artists, 1969; *The Good Guys and the Bad Guys*, Warner Brothers, 1969.

Ryan's Daughter, Metro-Goldwyn-Mayer, 1970; *Going Home*, Metro-Goldwyn-Mayer, 1971; *The Wrath of God*, Metro-Goldwyn-Mayer, 1972; *The Friends of Eddie Coyle*, Paramount, 1973; *The Yakuza*, Warner Brothers, 1975; Philip Marlowe, *Farewell, My Lovely*, Avco Embassy, 1975; *Midway*, Universal, 1976; *The Last Tycoon*, Paramount, 1977; *The Amsterdam Kill*, Columbia, 1978; Philip Marlowe, *The Big Sleep*, United Artists, 1978; *Matilda*, American-International, 1978; Coach, *That Championship Season*, Cannon, 1982; *Maria's Lovers*, Cannon, 1984; *The Ambassador*, Cannon, 1985; *Breakthrough*, 1985.

PRINCIPAL TELEVISION APPEARANCES—Movies: *The Winds of War*, ABC, 1983; William Randolph Hearst, *The Hearst and Davies Affair*, ABC, 1985; *Reunion at Fairborough*, HBO, 1985.

AWARDS: Best Supporting Actor, Academy Award nomination, 1945, for *The Story of G.I. Joe*.

ADDRESSES: AGENT—c/o Tom Chasin, Gersh Agency, 222 N. Canon Drive, Suite 204, Beverly Hills, CA 90210.*

MARY ANN MOBLEY

MOBLEY, Mary Ann   1937-

PERSONAL: Born February 17, 1937; daughter of Robert (a lawyer) and Mary Moore (an insurance executive; maiden name, Farish) Mobley; married Gary Ennis Collins (an actor and television host), October 24, 1967; children: Mary Clancy Collins. EDUCATION: University of Mississippi, B.A., 1958; trained for the stage with Lee Strasberg and Wynn Handman. RELIGION: Methodist.

VOCATION: Actress and singer.

CAREER: STAGE DEBUT—Sarah Brown, *Guys and Dolls,* Boston, MA, 1960. NEW YORK DEBUT—Ingenue lead, *Nowhere to Go but Up,* Winter Garden Theatre, 1962. PRINCIPAL STAGE APPEAR-ANCES—Julie, *Oklahoma!,* North Shore Music Theatre, Beverly, MA, 1960; Meg, *Brigadoon,* Cape Cod Music Tent, MA, 1960; Sarah, *Guys and Dolls,* North Shore Music Theatre, 1961, Cape Cod Music Tent, 1961, and Anaheim, CA, 1962; Sally Bowles, *Cabaret,* Sacramento, CA, 1969; Tuptim, *The King and I,* Sacramento, CA, 1970; Dolly Gallagher Levi, *Hello, Dolly!,* Sacramento, CA, 1971; Daisy, *On a Clear Day You Can See Forever,* Ft. Worth, TX, 1972; Sally Bowles, *Cabaret,* Ft. Worth, TX, 1973; Sharon, *Finian's Rainbow,* Sacramento, CA, 1975; Katie "Babe" Williams, *The Pajama Game,* Sacramento, CA, 1976; Sally Bowles, *Cabaret,* Cleveland, OH, 1979.

FILM DEBUT—Lead, *Get Yourself a College Girl,* Metro-Goldwyn-Mayer, 1964. PRINCIPAL FILM APPEARANCES—*Girl Happy,* Metro-Goldwyn-Mayer, 1965; *Harum Scarum,* Metro-Goldwyn-Mayer, 1965; *Young Dillinger,* Allied Artists, 1965; *Three on a Couch,* Columbia, 1966; *The King's Pirate,* Universal, 1967; *For Singles*

Only, Columbia, 1968; *Smokey and the Bandit, Part II,* Universal, 1980.

TELEVISION DEBUT—Featured singer, *Be My Guest,* CBS, 1960. PRINCIPAL TELEVISION APPEARANCES—Series: Mrs. Drummond, *Diff'rent Strokes,* NBC.

Episodic: "Who Killed Julie Greer?," *The Dick Powell Show,* NBC, 1962; *Fantastic Journey; My Dog, the Thief; Fantasy Island; Ironside; Police Woman; Police Story; Love, American Style; Matt Houston; Wonderful World of Disney; Man Trap; Tales of the Unexpected; The Sixth Sense; General Hospital; The Love Boat; Vega$; Whew.*

Guest: *The Tonight Show; Mike Douglas Show; Merv Griffin Show; Dinah Shore Show; John Davidson Show; The Match Game; Keep Talking; All Star Secrets; Cross Wits; Make Me Laugh; Beat the Clock; Scribble; Body Language; To Tell the Truth; Card Sharks; Disco Fever.*

Specials: *Third Annual Collegiate Cheerleading Championships; 1984 Olympics; March of Dimes Telethon; The Miss America Pageant.*

Movies: *Istanbul Express,* 1967; *The Girl on the Late, Late Show,* 1974; *Flying High,* 1978; *Earthbound,* 1981.

MEMBER: Rape Prevention Treatment Center, Santa Monica Hospital (advisory board); Boy Scouts of America, Los Angeles Area Counsel (advisory board); Scouting for the Handicapped; Sarah Isom Center for Women's Studies, University of Mississippi (regional advisory council).

AWARDS: Miss America, 1959.

ADDRESSES: OFFICE—c/o Ernst and Whinney, 185 Century Park E., Suite 2200, Los Angeles, CA 90067. AGENT—International Creative Management, 8899 Beverly Blvd., Los Angeles, CA 90048.

*   *   *

MONK, Meredith   1942-

PERSONAL: Born November 20, 1942, in New York, NY; daughter of Theodore Glen (an executive) and Audrey Lois (a singer; maiden name, Marsh) Monk. EDUCATION: Sarah Lawrence College, B.A.; trained for the stage with with Robert Joffrey, Mia Slavenska, Mary Anthony, Allan Wayne, Judith Dunn, and Jeannette Loverri.

VOCATION: Actress, choreographer, composer, director, and singer.

CAREER: STAGE DEBUT—Performer, *Scrouse,* Actors Playhouse, NY, 1961, for twelve performances. LONDON DEBUT—Performer, composer, director, *Juice* and *Education of the Girlchild,* Place Theatre, 1972, for fourteen performances. PRINCIPAL STAGE APPEARANCES—Performer and choreographer, *Break,* Washington Square Galleries, 1964; creator, composer, performer, and director, *Juice,* Guggenheim Museum, 1969; creator, composer, performer, and director, *Quarry,* La Mama, 1976; creator, composer, performer, and director, *The Games,* Brooklyn Academy of Music, 1984.

Photograph by Jack Mitchell

MEREDITH MONK

MAJOR TOURS—As a creator, performer, director, and composer, has toured France and England, 1972; Italy, France, and Holland, 1975; Japan, Germany, France, and Italy, 1982.

FILM DEBUT—Director, and performer, *16 Millimeter Earrings,* 1966. PRINCIPAL FILM WORK—Director: *Children,* 1967; *Ballbearing,* 1968; *Quarry,* 1976; *Ellis Island,* Greenwich Films, 1981.

TELEVISION DEBUT—Choreographer and performer, *New Voices in the Arts,* PBS, 1964. PRINCIPAL TELEVISION WORK—Director and performer, *Paris,* KCTA, Minneapolis, MN, 1982; director and performer, *Turtle Dreams,* WGBH, Boston, 1983.

RELATED CAREER—Instructor, New York University, 1972, 1975, 1978; instructor, Godard College, 1971, 1975; artistic director, The House Foundation for the Arts, 1968—.

WRITINGS: PLAYS— In addition to above: *Vessel; Recent Ruins.* PERIODICALS—"Notes on the Voice," *Painted Bride Quarterly,* 1984; "Digging for Quarry," *Village Voice,* 1985.

AWARDS: Guggenheim Fellowship, 1972, 1982; Brandeis Creative Arts Award, 1974; Obie Award, 1972, for *Vessel;* Obie Award, 1976, for *Quarry;* Villager Award, 1979, for *Recent Ruins;* Villager Award, 1983 for *Turtle Dreams;* Obie Award, Sustained Achievement, 1985.

MEMBER: American Society of Composers and Publishers, National Theatre of the Kennedy Center (board of directors), American Music Center, The Kitchen (board of directors).

ADDRESSES: OFFICE—The House Foundation for the Arts, 325 Spring Street, New York, NY 10013.

*   *   *

MONTALBAN, Ricardo   1920-

PERSONAL: Born November 25, 1920, in Mexico City, Mexico; son of Jenaro and Ricarda Montalban; married Georgianna Young (an actress), 1944; children: Mark, Victor, Laura, Anita.

VOCATION: Actor.

CAREER: PRINCIPAL FILM APPEARANCES—(English language) *Fiesta,* Metro-Goldwyn-Mayer, 1947; *On an Island with You,* Metro-Goldwyn-Mayer, 1948; *The Kissing Bandit,* Metro-Goldwyn-Mayer, 1948; Jose O'Rourke, *Neptune's Daughter,* Metro-Goldwyn-Mayer, 1949; *Border Incident,* Metro-Goldwyn-Mayer, 1949; Rodriguez, *Battleground,* Metro-Goldwyn-Mayer, 1949; *Mystery Street,* Metro-Goldwyn-Mayer, 1950; *Right Cross,* Metro-Goldwyn-Mayer, 1950; *Two Weeks with Love,* Metro-Goldwyn-Mayer, 1950; *Mark of the Renegade,* Universal, 1951; *Across the Wide Missouri,* Metro-Goldwyn-Mayer, 1951; *My Man and I,* Metro-Goldwyn-Mayer, 1952; *Sombrero,* Metro-Goldwyn-Mayer, 1952; *Latin Lovers,* Metro-Goldwyn-Mayer, 1953; *The Saracen Blade,* Metro-Goldwyn-Mayer, 1954; *A Life in the Balance,* Twentieth Century-Fox, 1955; *Three for Jamie Dawn,* Allied Artists, 1956; Nakamura, *Sayonara,* Warner Brothers, 1957.

Let No Man Write My Epitaph, Columbia, 1960; *Hemingway's*

RICARDO MONTALBAN

Adventures of a Young Man, Twentieth Century-Fox, 1962; *The Reluctant Saint,* Davis-Royal Films International, 1962; *Love Is a Ball,* United Artists, 1963; *Cheyenne Autumn,* Warner Brothers, 1964; *The Money Trap,* Metro-Goldwyn-Mayer, 1966; *Madame X,* Universal, 1966; Father Clementi, *The Singing Nun,* Metro-Goldwyn-Mayer, 1966; *The Train Robbers,* Warner Brothers, 1967; *Sol Madrid,* Metro-Goldwyn-Mayer, 1968; *Blue,* Paramount, 1968; *Sweet Charity,* Universal, 1969; *Escape from the Planet of the Apes,* Twentieth Century-Fox, 1971; *Conquest of the Planet of the Apes,* Twentieth Century-Fox, 1972; *Joe Panther,* 1976; *Won Ton Ton, the Dog Who Saved Hollywood,* Paramount, 1976; Khan, *Star Trek II: The Wrath of Khan,* Paramount, 1982; *Cannonball Run, II,* Twentieth Century-Fox, 1983.

Also appeared in films in Mexico from 1941 through 1946.

PRINCIPAL TELEVISION APPEARANCES—Series: Mr. Roarke, *Fantasy Island,* ABC, 1978-84; Zachary Powers, *Dynasty II: The Colbys,* ABC, 1985—.

Episodic: Nine starring appearances between 1953 and 1961 on *The Loretta Young Show,* NBC; *Hollywood Summer Theatre,* CBS, 1956; "The Massacre at Wounded Knee," *The Great Adventure,* CBS, 1964; Khan, *Star Trek,* NBC; Zachary Powers, *Dynasty,* ABC.

Movies: *The Pigeon,* 1969; *The Aquarians,* 1970; *Fireball Forward,* 1972; *The Mark of Zorro,* 1974; *McNaughton's Daughter,* 1976; *Fantasy Island,* 1977; *Return to Fantasy Island,* 1977.

Mini-Series: *How the West Was Won,* ABC, 1978.

AWARDS: Outstanding Single Performance by a Supporting Actor in a Comedy or Drama Series, Emmy, 1978, for *How the West Was Won.*

ADDRESSES: AGENT—William Morris Agency, 151 El Camino Drive, Beverly Hills, CA 90212; Brokaw Company, 9255 Sunset Blvd., Suite 706, Los Angeles, CA 90069.

*   *   *

MONTEFIORE, David 1944-

PERSONAL: Born January 2, 1944, in London, England; son of Hirsh Laib (a cantor and opera singer) and Rachel (a school teacher; maiden name, Fortleman) Montefiore; married April Evans (an opera singer), January 5, 1975. EDUCATION: University of Maryland, B.A.; trained in voice at La Scala and Juilliard School of Music. MILITARY: U.S. Air Force.

VOCATION: Actor and opera singer.

CAREER: STAGE DEBUT—*The Jewish Gypsy,* Town Hall, NY, 1983, for ninety performances. PRINCIPAL STAGE APPEARANCES—Opera roles: Nemorino; Edgardo; Alfredo, the Duke of Mantua; Werther; *Israel in Egypt,* St. Cecelia Chorus, Carnegie Hall, NY; *The Magic Flute,* Rome Festival; *Cosi Fan Tutte,* Rome Festival, 1983; Alfredo, *La Traviata,* Haifa Symphony, Israel, 1985; Captain Macheath, *The Beggar's Opera,* NY, 1985; The Rabbi, *A Match Made in Heaven,* Yiddish Musical Theatre, NY, 1985.

MEMBER: American Guild of Musical Artists, Actors' Equity Association, Hebrew Actors Union, English Speaking Union, Vietnam Veterans of America; Jewish Minister Cantors Association.

DAVID MONTEFIORE

ADDRESSES: AGENT—Robert M. Gewald, 58 W. 58th Street, New York, NY 10019.

*   *   *

MONTGOMERY, Elizabeth 1933-

PERSONAL: Born April 15, 1933, in Los Angeles, CA; daughter of Robert (an actor) and Elizabeth Bryan (Allen) Montgomery; married Frederick Gallatin Cammann, 1954 (divorced, 1955); married Gig Young (an actor), 1957 (divorced, 1963); married William Asher (a producer), 1963 (divorced, 1974); children: (third marriage) William, Jr., Robert, Rebecca Elizabeth. EDUCATION: Studied for the theatre at the American Academy of Dramatic Arts, New York.

VOCATION: Actress.

*CAREER:*NEW YORK DEBUT—Janet Colby, *Late Love,* National Theatre, 1953.

PRINCIPAL FILM APPEARANCES—Margaret Landsdowne, *The Court-Martial of Billy Mitchell,* United Artists, 1955; *Johnny Cool,* United Artists, 1963; *Who's Been Sleeping in My Bed?,* Paramount, 1964.

PRINCIPAL TELEVISION APPEARANCES—Series: *Robert Montgomery Presents,* NBC, as a summer repertory player in 1953, 1954, and 1956; Samantha Stephens (also Cousin Serena), *Bewitched,* ABC, 1964-72.

Episodic: *Studio One,* CBS, 1955; "Mr. Lucifer," *Alcoa Premiere;* ABC, 1963; *Twilight Zone;* numerous other guest appearances.

Movies: *A Case of Rape,* 1974; title role, *Mrs. Sundance,* 1974; title role, *The Legend of Lizzie Borden*, 1975; Judith, *Dark Victory*, 1976; *The Awakening Land*, 1978; title role, *Jennifer: A Woman's Story*, 1979; *Missing Pieces*, 1983; *Second Sight: A Love Story*, 1985.

AWARDS: Most Promising Newcomer, Daniel Blum *Theatre World* Award, 1953.

ADDRESSES: HOME—Beverly Hills, CA.*

*   *   *

MOORE, Demi

PERSONAL: Born Demi Guynes, November 11, in Roswell, NM; daughter of Danny and Virginia Guynes; married Freddy Moore (a songwriter and musician). EDUCATION: Trained for the stage with Zina Provendie.

VOCATION: Actress.

CAREER: PRINCIPAL TELEVISION APPEARANCES—Series: Jackie Templeton, *General Hospital*, ABC.

Episodic: *Kaz*, CBS; *Vega$*, ABC; *W.E.B.*

Plays: *Bedrooms*, HBO.

PRINCIPAL FILM APPEARANCES—*Young Doctors in Love*, Twentieth Century-Fox, 1982; *Blame It on Rio*, 1984; *No Small Affair*, Columbia, 1984; Julianna "Jules" Van Patten, *St. Elmo's Fire*, Columbia, 1985; *Choices*, 1986; *Greetings from Nantucket*, Warner Brothers, 1986; *About Last Night . . .*, Tri-Star, 1986; *Wisdom*, Twentieth Century-Fox, 1987; also appeared in *Parasite*.

RELATED CAREER—Fashion model.

ADDRESSES: AGENT—Andrea Jaffee, Inc., 9229 Sunset Blvd., Suite 401, Los Angeles, CA 90069.

DEMI MOORE

RITA MORENO

MORENO, Rita   1931-

PERSONAL: Born Rosa Dolores Alverio, December 11, 1931, in Humacao, Puerto Rico; married Leonard Gordon.

VOCATION: Actress and dancer.

CAREER: NEW YORK STAGE DEBUT—Angelina, *Skydrift*, Belasco Theatre, 1945. LONDON DEBUT—Ilona Ritter, *She Loves Me*, Lyric Theatre, 1964. PRINCIPAL STAGE APPEARANCES—Iris Parodus Brustein, *The Sign in Sidney Brustein's Window*, Longacre Theatre, NY, 1964; Sharon Falconer, *Gantry*, George Abbott Theatre, NY, 1970; Elaine Navazio, *Last of the Red Hot Lovers*, Eugene O'Neill Theatre, NY, 1970; Shoplifter, *Detective Story*, Shubert Theatre, Philadelphia, PA, 1973; Staff Nurse Norton, *The National Health*, Long Wharf Theatre, New Haven, CT, 1973-74, then Circle in the Square, NY, 1974; Googie Gomez, *The Ritz*, Longacre Theatre, NY, 1975; Serafina, *The Rose Tattoo*, Long Wharf Theatre, New Haven, CT, 1977; Louise, *Wally's Cafe*, Brooks Atkinson Theatre, NY, 1981; Olive, *The New Odd Couple*, Broadhurst Theatre, NY, 1985.

FILM DEBUT—*So Young, So Bad*, 1950. PRINCIPAL FILM APPEARANCES—*Singin' in the Rain*, Metro-Goldwyn-Mayer, 1952; *The King and I*, Twentieth Century-Fox, 1956; *Summer and Smoke*, Paramount, 1962; Anita, *West Side Story*, United Artists, 1961; *Carnal Knowledge*, 1971; *The Ritz*, Warner Brothers, 1976; *Happy Birthday, Gemini*, 1980; *The Four Seasons*, Universal, 1981.

PRINCIPAL TELEVISION WORK—Series: Violet Newstead, *9 to 5*, ABC, 1982-83; *The Electric Company*.

Episodic: *The Rockford Files*, NBC.

Guest: *The Muppet Show*, syndicated.

AWARDS: Best Supporting Actress, Academy Award, 1961, for *West Side Story;* Antoinette Perry Award, 1975, for *The Ritz;* Outstanding Continuing or Single Performance by a Supporting Actress in Variety or Music, Emmy, 1976-77, for *The Muppet Show;* Outstanding Lead Actress for a Single Appearance in a Drama or Comedy Series, 1977-78, for "The Paper Palace," *The Rockford Files;* also received a Grammy Award.

ADDRESSES: AGENT—William Morris Agency, 151 El Camino, Beverly Hills, CA, 90212.

*   *   *

MORGAN, Harry   1915-

PERSONAL: Born Harry Bratsburg, April 10, 1915, in Detroit, MI; married Eileen; children: Chris, Charles, Paul, Daniel. EDUCATION: University of Chicago.

VOCATION: Actor.

CAREER: PRINCIPAL STAGE APPEARANCES—*The Gentle People,* NY, 1939; *My Heart's in the Highlands,* NY, 1939; *Thunder Rock,* NY, 1939; *Night Music; Night Before Christmas;* others.

PRINCIPAL FILM APPEARANCES—Mouthy, *To the Shores of Tripoli,* Twentieth Century-Fox, 1942; *The Loves of Edgar Allan Poe,* Twentieth Century-Fox, 1942; *Orchestra Wives,* Twentieth Century-Fox, 1942; Bleecker, *Dragonwyck,* Twentieth Century-Fox, 1946; *From This Day Forward,* Twentieth Century-Fox, 1946; *The Saxon Charm,* Universal, 1948; *Moonrise,* Republic, 1948; *Appointment with Danger,* Paramount, 1949.

The Highwayman, Allied Artists, 1951; *The Well,* Cardinal/Harry M. Popkin Pictures, 1951; *When I Grow Up,* Eagle-Lion Classics, 1951; *Stop, You're Killing Me,* Warner Brothers, 1951; *The Blue Veil,* RKO, 1951; *Bend of the River,* Universal, 1952; *Scandal Sheet,* Columbia, 1952; *My Six Convicts,* Columbia, 1952; *Boots Malone,* Columbia, 1952; William Fuller, *High Noon,* United Artists, 1952; Morgan, *What Price Glory?,* Twentieth Century-Fox, 1952; *Arena,* Metro-Goldwyn-Mayer, 1953; *Torch Song,* Metro-Goldwyn-Mayer, 1953; Chummy, *The Glenn Miller Story,* Universal, 1954; *About Mrs. Leslie,* Paramount, 1954; *The Forty-Niners,* 1955; *The Far Country,* Universal, 1955; *Not as a Stranger,* United Artists, 1955; Sergeant Bible, *Strategic Air Command,* Paramount, 1955; *Backlash,* Universal, 1956.

Judge, *Inherit the Wind,* United Artists, 1960; *John Goldfarb, Please Come Home,* Twentieth Century-Fox, 1964; *What Did You Do in the War, Daddy?,* United Artists, 1966; *Support Your Local Sheriff,* United Artists, 1969; *Charley and the Angel,* Buena Vista, 1972; *Snowball Express,* Buena Vista, 1972; *The Apple Dumpling Gang,* Buena Vista, 1975; *The Greatest,* Columbia, 1977; *The Cat from Outer Space,* Buena Vista, 1977; others.

PRINCIPAL TELEVISION APPEARANCES—Series: Pete Porter, *December Bride,* CBS, 1954-61; Pete Porter, *Pete and Gladys,* CBS, 1960-62; repertory actor on the anthology series: *The Richard Boone Show,*, NBC, 1963-64; Seldom Jackson, *Kentucky Jones,* NBC, 1964-65; Officer Bill Gannon, *Dragnet,* NBC, 1967-70; Chief Deputy D.A. "Staff" Stafford, *The D.A.,* NBC, 1071-72; Doc Amos Googan, *Hec Ramsay,* NBC, 1972-74; Col. Sherman Potter, *M*A*S*H,* CBS, 1975-83; Col. Sherman Potter, *After-M*A*S*H,* CBS, 1983-84; Leonard Blacke, *Blacke's Magic,* NBC, 1986—.

Episodic: *Love, American Style,* ABC; others.

ADDRESSES: OFFICE—Public Relations, NBC Television, 3000 W. Alameda Avenue, Burbank, CA 91523.*

*   *   *

MORITA, Noriyuki "Pat"

VOCATION: Actor and comedian.

*CAREER:*PRINCIPAL FILM APPEARANCES— Second laundryman, *Thoroughly Modern Millie,* Universal, 1967; *Savannah Smiles,* 1982; *Jimmy the Kid,* 1983; *The Karate Kid,* Columbia, 1984; *The Karate Kid II,* Columbia, 1986.

PRINCIPAL TELEVISION APPEARANCES—Series: Barney, *The Queen and I,* CBS, 1969; Ah Chew, *Sanford and Son,* NBC, 1974-75; Arnold, *Happy Days,* ABC, 1975-76 and 1982-83; Taro Takahashi, *Mr. T. and Tina,* ABC, 1976; Arnold, *Blansky's Beauties,* ABC, 1977.

Episodic: *M*A*S*H,* CBS; *The Love Boat,* ABC; *Magnum, P.I.,* CBS; others.

Movies: *The Vegas Strip War,* NBC, 1984.

CABARET—Opening act for such performers as Johnny Mathis, Ella Fitzgerald, Glen Campbell before becoming headliner in Las Vegas and clubs.

ADDRESSES: AGENT—Contemporary-Korman Artists Ltd., 132 Lasky Drive, Beverly Hills, CA 90212.*

*   *   *

MOSES, Charles Alexander   1923-

PERSONAL: Born March 1, 1923, in Chicago, IL; son of Harry Marcus (an insurance executive) and Rose (Kieferstein) Moses; married Paola Toninato, 1955 (divorced); married Sharon Stelmok (divorced); children: Edward, Howard, Richard. EDUCATION: Northwestern University, B.A., 1945; Antioch University, Los Angeles, M.A., 1985. POLITICS: Democrat. RELIGION: Jewish. MILITARY: U.S. Army Air Force, 1942-43.

VOCATION: Writer, public relations director, and film executive.

CAREER: PRINCIPAL FILM WORK—Advertising and publicity director, Orion Pictures; New York domestic and foreign advertising and publicity director, Universal Pictures; advertising and public relations director, Sinatra Enterprises; publicity director, Bel Air Productions; European advertising and publicity supervisor, RKO Radio Pictures; European advertising and publicity director, United Artists; European advertising and publicity supervisor, Eagle Lion Films; editor, *Motion Picture Daily;* editor, *Motion Picture Herald.*

WRITINGS: SCREENPLAYS—*Frankenstein 1970; Department Store.*

TELEVISION—*Abigail; The Callers.*

BOOKS—*Demon Ground.*

PLAYS—(Book) *Daddy.*

MEMBER: Publicists Guild of America (president, 1961-66), Academy of Motion Picture Arts and Sciences, Academy of Television Arts and Sciences; Southern California Society for Psychical Research, London Society for Psychical Research; Los Angeles Democratic County Committee (1964-66, 1982-84).

SIDELIGHTS: Charles Moses told *CTFT* that he is an international authority in the field of parapsychology and has traveled extensively in the United States and abroad to lecture and appear on television and radio shows.

ADDRESSES: OFFICE—3219 W. Alameda Avenue, Burbank, CA 91505.

*   *   *

MULL, Martin   1943-

PERSONAL: Born 1943, in Chicago, IL; married Sandra Baker. EDUCATION: Graduate of the Rhode Island School of Design.

VOCATION: Actor, comedian, and singer.

CAREER: PRINCIPAL FILM APPEARANCES—*FM,* Universal, 1978; *My Bodyguard,* Twentieth Century-Fox, 1980; *Serial,* Paramount, 1980; *Take This Job and Shove It,* Avco Embassy, 1981; Colonel Mustard, *Clue,* 1985.

PRINCIPAL TELEVISION APPEARANCES—Series: Garth Gimble, *Mary Hartman, Mary Hartman,* syndicated, 1976-77; Barth Gimble, *Fernwood 2-Night,* syndicated, 1977; Barth Gimble, *America 2-Night,* syndicated, 1978; Martin Crane, *Domestic Life,* CBS, 1984.

Guest: *Soundstage;* others.

Special: *The History of White People in America,* HBO.

RELATED CAREER: Nightclub singer and comedian.

RECORDINGS: COMEDY ALBUMS—*I'm Everyone I've Ever Loved,* MCA; *Sex and Violins.*

ADDRESSES: AGENT—Agency for the Performing Arts, 9000 Sunset Blvd., Suite 315, Los Angeles, CA 90069.*

*   *   *

MURPHY, Ben   1942-

PERSONAL: Born March 6, 1942, in Jonesboro, AR; son of Patrick Henry and Nadine (Steele) Murphy. EDUCATION: Attended Loras College, 1960-61; attended Loyola University, 1961-62; attended University of the Americas, 1962-63; University of Illinois, B.A., political science, 1965.

VOCATION: Actor.

CAREER: PRINCIPAL STAGE APPEARANCES—Summer stock.

FILM DEBUT—*The Graduate,* Embassy, 1967. PRINCIPAL FILM APPEARANCES—*Yours, Mine, and Ours,* United Artists, 1968; *The Thousand Plane Raid,* United Artists, 1969; *Sidecar Racers,* Universal, 1975.

PRINCIPAL TELEVISION APPEARANCES—Series: Joe Sample, *The Name of the Game,* NBC, 1968-71; Jed "Kid" Curry (Thaddeus Jones), *Alias Smith and Jones,* ABC, 1971-73; S. Michael (Mike) Murdoch, *Griff,* ABC, 1973-74; Sam Casey, *Gemini Man,* NBC, 1976; Will Chisholm, *The Chisholms,* CBS, 1979-80; Patrick Sean Flaherty, *Lottery,* NBC, 1983-84; *Berringers,* CBS, 1984.

Episodic: *Scarecrow and Mrs. King,* CBS, 1985.

Mini-Series: *The Winds of War,* 1983.

Movies: *Wild Bill Hickock; Runaway,* 1973; *Heat Wave,* 1974; *This Is the West That Was,* 1974; *Bridger,* 1976; *Hospital Fire; The Cradle Will Fall,* 1983.

ADDRESSES: AGENT—William Morris Agency, 151 El Camino Drive, Beverly Hills, CA 90212.*

N

NABORS, Jim   1933-

PERSONAL: Born June 12, 1933, in Sylacauga, AL; son of Fred Nabors.EDUCATION: University of Alabama.

VOCATION: Actor and singer.

CAREER: PRINCIPAL FILM APPEARANCES—*The Best Little Whorehouse in Texas,* Universal, 1982; *Stroker Ace,* Universal, 1983; *Cannonball II,* Twentieth Century-Fox, 1983.

PRINCIPAL TELEVISION APPEARANCES—Series: Gomer Pyle, *The Andy Griffith Show,* CBS, 1963-64; title role, *Gomer Pyle, U.S.M.C.,* CBS, 1964-69; *The Jim Nabors Hour,* CBS, 1969-71.

Episodic: *The Rookies,* ABC; others.

Movies: *Return to Mayberry,* NBC, 1986.

JIM NABORS

Guest: *The Steve Allen Show,* ABC, 1961; season-opener guest, *The Carol Burnett Show,* CBS, 1967-78; *The Redd Foxx Show,* ABC, 1977-78; others.

CABARET—The Horn, Santa Monica, CA; *Jim Nabors Polynesian Extravaganza,* Honolulu, HI, 1979-81; headliner in Las Vegas and Lake Tahoe resort hotels; others.

RECORDINGS: ALBUMS—*Old Religion,* Ranwood; *Town and Country,* Ranwood; *Sincerely,* Ranwood; *I See God,* Ranwood; *Lord's Prayer,* Columbia; *Man of La Mancha* (with Marilyn Horne and others), Columbia; others.

AWARDS: Five gold albums; one platinum album.

ADDRESSES: AGENT—c/o Tom Illius, William Morris Agency, 151 El Camino Drive, Beverly Hills, CA 90212.

* * *

NAMATH, Joe   1943-

PERSONAL: Full name, Joseph William Namath; born May 31, 1943, in Beaver Falls, PA; son of John Andrew and Rose (Juhasz) Namath; married; children: one daughter. EDUCATION: University of Alabama.

VOCATION: Actor, broadcaster, former professional football player.

CAREER: DEBUT—Hal Carter, *Picnic,* summer stock, 1979. PRINCIPAL STAGE APPEARANCES—Abner, *Li'l Abner,* 1980; Joe Hardy, *Damn Yankees,* Jones Beach Marine Theatre, NY, 1981; *The Caine Mutiny Court Martial,* Circle in the Square, NY, 1983; Joe/Josephine, *Sugar,* Atlantic City, NJ, 1984.

FILM DEBUT—*Norwood,* Paramount, 1970. PRINCIPAL FILM APPEARANCES—*C.C. & Company,* Avco Embassy, 1970; *The Last Rebel,* 1971; *Avalanche Express,* 1979.

PRINCIPAL TELEVISION APPEARANCES—Series: Joe Casey, *The Waverly Wonders,* NBC, 1978.

Guest: Talk show appearances, frequent guest host of *The Tonight Show with Johnny Carson,* NBC; guest host, *The Nashville Palace,* NBC.

Movies: *Marriage Is Alive and Well,* 1980; *All American Pie.*

RELATED CAREER—Quarterback, New York Jets, 1965-77; quarterback, Los Angeles Rams, 1977-78; co-owner, Joe Namath Instructional Football Camp, Dudley, MA.

WRITINGS: AUTOBIOGRAPHY—*Namath—A Matter of Style.*

AWARDS: Sporting News American Football League Rookie of the Year, 1965; American Football League All-Star Team, 1968 and 1972; Most Valuable Player, Super Bowl, 1969; Dodge Man of the Year, New York Jets; Alabama Sports Hall of Fame, 1981; Hickock Belt for Professional Athlete of the Year; George Halas Most Courageous Athlete Award; holder of record for most yards passed in one season.

ADDRESSES: OFFICE—c/o James C. Walsh, 300 E. 51st Street, New York, NY 10022. AGENT—The Lantz Office, 888 Seventh Avenue, New York, NY 10016.*

* * *

NARDINO, Gary   1935-

PERSONAL: Born August 26, 1935, in Garfield, NJ; son of Louis and Phyllis (Iacovino) Nardino; married Florence Peluso, May 1, 1965; children: Caroline, Gary Charles Frank, Teresa. EDUCATION: Seton Hall University, B.S. and B.A. MILITARY: U.S. Army, 1957-59.

VOCATION: Producer.

CAREER: PRINCIPAL FILM WORK—Executive producer, *Star Trek III: The Search for Spock,* Paramount, 1984; producer, *Fire with Fire,* Paramount, 1986.

PRINCIPAL TELEVISION WORK—Producer, *Brothers,* Showtime Cable, 1982—; executive producer, *Chameleon,* 1986; president, Television Production division, Paramount Pictures Corp., 1977-83; president, Gary Nardino Productions, Paramount Pictures Corp., 1983—, series produced during this time include *Happy Days, Laverne and Shirley, Blansky's Beauties, Joanie Loves Chachi,* and *Mork and Mindy.*

RELATED CAREER—Agent, William Morris Agency, NY, 1959-61; agent, Frank Cooper Associates, NY, 1961-64; senior vice-president, head of television department, Ashley-Famous Agency (now International Creative Management), NY, 1964-76; senior vice-president, head of television department, William Morris Agency, NY, 1976-77.

MEMBER: Academy of Television Arts and Sciences, Hollywood Radio and Television Society (president, 1981-83); Alpha Kappa Psi.

AWARDS: Man of the Year, WAIF, Inc., 1983; Producers Guild of America Television Man of the Year; B'nai B'rith Sword of Truth; honorary doctorate from Seton Hall.

ADDRESSES: OFFICE—5555 Melrose Avenue, Los Angeles, CA 90038.

* * *

NEAL, Patricia   1926-

PERSONAL: Born January 20, 1926, in Packard, KY; daughter of William Burdette and Eura Mildred (Petrey) Neal; married Roald Dahl, July 2, 1953 (divorced); children: Olivia (died, 1962), Tessa Sophia, Theo Mathew, Ophelia Magdalene, Lucy. EDUCATION: Attended Northwestern University.

PATRICIA NEAL

VOCATION: Actress.

CAREER: FILM DEBUT—*John Loves Mary,* Warner Brothers, 1948. PRINCIPAL FILM APPEARANCES—Dominique, *The Fountainhead,* Warner Brothers, 1949; *It's a Great Feeling,* Warner Brothers, 1949; *The Hasty Heart,* Warner Brothers, 1950 *Bright Leaf,* Warner Brothers, 1950; *Three Secrets,* Warner Brothers, 1950; *The Breaking Point,* Warner Brothers, 1950; Mary Stuart, *Operation Pacific,* Warner Brothers, 1951; *Raton Pass,* Warner Brothers, 1951; *Diplomatic Courier,* Twentieth Century-Fox, 1951; *The Day the Earth Stood Still,* Twentieth Century-Fox, 1951; *Weekend with Father,* Universal, 1951; *Washington Story,* Metro-Goldwyn-Mayer, 1952; *Something for the Birds,* Twentieth Century-Fox, 1952; *Stranger from Venus,* Princess Pictures, 1954; Marcia Jeffries, *A Face in the Crowd,* Warner Brothers, 1957; 2-E, *Breakfast at Tiffany's,* Paramount, 1961; Alma Brown, *Hud,* Paramount, 1963; *Psyche 59,* Columbia, 1964; Lt. Maggie Haynes, *In Harm's Way,* Paramount, 1965; mother, *The Subject Was Roses,* Metro-Goldwyn-Mayer, 1968; *The Night Digger,* Metro-Goldwyn-Mayer, 1971; *Baxter!,* National General, 1973; *Happy Mother's Day . . . Love, George,* Cinema V, 1973; *Widow's Nest,* 1976; *The Passage,* United Artists, 1979; *Ghost Story,* Universal, 1981.

PRINCIPAL TELEVISION APPEARANCES—Episodic: *Espionage,* NBC, 1964; *Little House on the Prairie,* NBC.

Mini-Series: *The Bastard,* 1978; *All Quiet on the Western Front,* 1979.

Movies: Olivia Walton, *The Homecoming—A Christmas Story,* CBS, 1971; *Shattered Vows,* NBC, 1984.

NEW YORK DEBUT—Regina Hubbard, *Another Part of the Forest,* 1946. PRINCIPAL STAGE APPEARANCES—*The Children's Hour,* NY, 1952; *A Roomful of Roses,* NY, 1955; *Suddenly Last Summer,* NY, 1958; *The Miracle Worker,* 1960.

MEMBER: Actors' Studio, Pi Beta Phi, Phi Beta.

AWARDS: Best Actress, New York Critics Award, 1946, for

Another Part of the Forest; Best Actress, Antoinette Perry Award, Donaldson Award, 1947, for *Another Part of the Forest;* Best Actress, Academy Award, 1963 for *Hud;* Best Actress, Academy Award nomination, 1968, for *The Subject Was Roses.*

SIDELIGHTS: *CTFT* learned that Patricia Neal lectures extensively with an autobiographical speech titled, "An Unquiet Life," and is preparing an autobiography to be published by Simon and Schuster.

ADDRESSES: AGENT—c/o Clifford Stevens, STE, 888 Seventh Avenue, New York, NY 10019.

* * *

NEIL, Julian   1952-

PERSONAL: Born July 29, 1952, in New York, NY. EDUCATION: New York University, School of the Arts, B.F.A., 1973; studied at the New York University Film School and with Warren Robertson at the Warren Robertson Theatre Workshop in New York.

VOCATION: Director and writer.

CAREER: PRINCIPAL STAGE WORK—Director: *Luv,* Hyde Park Playhouse, NY; *You Can't Take It with You,* Naples Summer Theatre, ME; *Killing Game,* Davis Center of Performing Arts, NY; *Hustlers with Worn Out Shoes,* Davis Center of Performing Arts, NY, then New York Shakespeare Festival, Public Theatre; *Josie,* Southern Connecticut State College, New Haven, CT; *Crashing of Moses Flying-By,* West Chester University, West Chester, PA; *Waiting for Godot, The Cocktail Party, Look Back in Anger,* all three at Somerville Theatre, NJ; *Welcome Home,* New York Stageworks New Works Festival, 1982; *Jackalopes,* Poets Theatre, NY, 1982; *Family and Friend,* Lincoln Center/Circle Repertory Company, NY; *Mysteries of the Bridal Night,* Lincoln Center, NY; *Running Time,* Circle Repertory Directors Lab Festival, 1984; *An Evening with Joan Crawford,* Orpheum Theatre, NY; *Nuyoricans: Bicultural Nomads,* Third Latin/American Popular Theatre Festival, and Theatro Four/Museo Del Barrio.

PRINCIPAL TELEVISION APPEARANCES—*The Catlins,* WTBS, Atlanta, GA; *The Guiding Light,* CBS; *As the World Turns,* CBS.

WRITINGS: PLAYS—*An Evening with Joan Crawford* (co-author with the company), produced at Orpheum Theatre, NY; *Nuyoricans: Bicultural Nomads* (co-author with Sandy Esteves and Lucky Cienfuegos), produced at Third Latin/American Popular Theatre Festival and Theatro Four/Museo Del Barrio; *Jackalopes* (co-author with Elinor Naven), Poets Theatre Festival, NY, 1982.

MEMBER: Society of Stage Directors and Choreographers, Directors Guild of America, Actors' Equity Association, Screen Actors Guild, American Federation of Radio and Television Artists.

ADDRESSES: HOME—416 W. 20th Street, New York, NY 10011.

* * *

NELSON, Craig T.

VOCATION: Actor and writer.

CAREER: PRINCIPAL FILM APPEARANCES—*And Justice for All,* Columbia, 1979; *The Formula,* United Artists, 1980; *Where the Buffalo Roam,* 1980; *Private Benjamin,* Warner Brothers, 1980;

Steve Freeling, *Poltergeist,* Metro-Goldwyn-Mayer/United Artists, 1982; *The Osterman Weekend,* Twentieth Century-Fox, 1983; *All the Right Moves,* Twentieth Century-Fox, 1983; *Silkwood,* Twentieth Century-Fox, 1984; Steve Freeling, *Poltergeist II: The Other Side,* Metro-Goldwyn-Mayer/United Artists, 1986.

PRINCIPAL FILM WORK—Producer: *American Still,* fifty-two half-hour films on American artists.

PRINCIPAL TELEVISION APPEARANCES—Series: Host, *Heroes: Made in the U.S.A.,* syndicated, 1986—.

Episodic: *The Mary Tyler Moore Show,* CBS; *How the West Was Won,* ABC, 1978; *Charlie's Angels,* ABC; *Wonder Woman,* CBS, 1978.

Movies: *Diary of a Teenage Hitchhiker,* 1979; *Rage,* 1980.

PRINCIPAL STAGE WORK—Harold "Okie," Peterson, *Friends,* Manhattan Theatre Club, 1983-84.

WRITINGS: TELEVISION—*The Lohman and Barkley Show,* Los Angeles; *The Tim Conway Show; The Alan King Special.*

ADDRESSES: AGENT—Writers & Artists Agency, 11726 San Vicente Blvd., Suite 300, Los Angeles, CA 90049.*

* * *

NELSON, Harriet   1914-
(Harriet Hilliard)

PERSONAL: Born Harriet Hilliard, July 18, 1914, in Des Moines, IA; daughter of Roy R. and Hazel Dell (McNutt) Hilliard; married Ozzie Nelson (a bandleader and actor) October 8, 1935; children: David Ozzie, Eric Hilliard (died, 1985). EDUCATION: Attended St. Agnes Academy.

VOCATION: Actress and singer.

CAREER: PRINCIPAL STAGE APPEARANCES—*The Marriage Go-Round; The Impossible Years; State Fair; Ozzie and Harriet.*

PRINCIPAL FILM APPEARANCES—As Harriet Hilliard: Connie Martin, *Follow the Fleet,* RKO, 1936; *Cocoanut Grove,* Paramount, 1938; *She's My Everything,* 1938; *Sweetheart of the Campus,* Columbia, 1941; *Canal Zone,* 1942; *Hi, Buddy!,* Universal, 1943; *The Falcon Strikes Back,* RKO, 1943; *Swingtime Johnny,* Universal, 1944. As Harriet Nelson, *Here Come the Nelsons,* 1952.

PRINCIPAL TELEVISION APPEARANCES—As herself, *The Adventures of Ozzie and Harriet,* ABC, 1952-66; *Love, American Style,* ABC; as herself, *Ozzie's Girls,* ABC, 1973.

Movies: *Smashup on Interstate 5,* 1976.

PRINCIPAL RADIO WORK—*The Joe Penner Show; Believe It or Not; The Bob Ripley Show; The Feg Murray Show; Seeing Stars; The Red Skelton Show; The Adventures of Ozzie and Harriet,* ABC, 1944-52.

RECORDINGS: As Harriet Hilliard, for Brunswick, Vocalian, Victor, and Blue Bird labels, some with husband Ozzie Nelson's band.

AWARDS: Woman of the Year in the field of Entertainment, *Los*

Angeles Times; Best Husband-Wife Team in television, voted by readers of *Television Radio-Mirror* for seven consecutive years, 1953-60; Genii Award, Radio and Television Women of Southern California, 1960; National Family Week Radio Citation by International Council on Christian Family life, 1947.

ADDRESSES: AGENT—Bauman and Hiller, 9220 Sunset Blvd.,. Suite 322, Los Angeles, CA 90069.*

*   *   *

NELSON, Rick   1940-1985

PERSONAL: Full name, Eric Hilliard Nelson; born May 8, 1940, in Teaneck, NJ; died in an airplane crash in Texas, December 31, 1985; son of Ozzie (a bandleader, singer, and actor) and Harriet (a singer and actress; maiden name, Hilliard) Nelson; married Kristin Harmon in 1963 (divorced); children: Tracy, Eric and Matthew (twins), Gunnar. EDUCATION: Attended Hollywood High School.

VOCATION: Singer and actor.

CAREER: FILM DEBUT—As himself, *Here Come the Nelsons,* 1952. PRINCIPAL FILM APPEARANCES—*The Story of Three Loves,* Metro-Goldwyn-Mayer, 1953; Colorado Ryan, *Rio Bravo,* Warner Brothers, 1959; *The Wackiest Ship in the Army,* Columbia, 1960; *Love and Kisses,* Universal, 1965.

TELEVISION DEBUT—As himself, *The Adventures of Ozzie and Harriet,* ABC, 1952-66. PRINCIPAL TELEVISION APPEARANCES—Host, *Malibu U,* ABC, 1967; guest, *Dick Clark's Live Wednesday,* NBC, 1978; guest host, *Saturday Night Live,* NBC; other guest appearances.

Movies: Principal, *High School, U.S.A.,* 1984.

RECORDINGS: SINGLES—"A Teenager's Romance," Verve Records, 1957; "Poor Little Fool," Imperial Records, 1958; "Hello Mary Lou," Imperial Records, 1961; "It's Up to You," Imperial Records; "For You," Decca Records; "She Belongs to Me," Decca, 1969; "Garden Party," Decca, 1972; "I'm Walking," "Be-Bop Baby," "Stood Up," "Believe What You Say," "Travelin' Man," "Young World," "Teenage Idol," "Fools Rush In," others; also recorded for MCA.

SIDELIGHTS: Rick Nelson made many concert appearances in his singing career, including an historic Madison Square Garden appearance in 1972, at which he sang his new material when his audience wanted to hear his earlier work. The song "Garden Party" is about that concert. His musical career embraced a variety of styles including hard rock and country-style music. When his airplane crashed on New Year's Eve, 1985, it killed him, his fiancee, Helen Blair, and members of Rick Nelson's Stone Canyon Band. He was the younger brother of actor-director David Nelson.*

*   *   *

NELSON, Tracy

BRIEF ENTRY: Daughter of Rick and Kristin (Harmon) Nelson. Actress. Tracy Nelson is carrying on the acting tradition of her family. Her father was the singer and actor Rick Nelson; she is the niece of David Nelson, a director, and the actor Mark Harmon, and granddaughter of one of television's most famous couples, Ozzie and Harriet Nelson. Her maternal grandmother, Elyse Knox, was a

film star in the 1940's and her maternal grandfather is former professional football great Tom Harmon. Tracy Nelson began taking dancing lessons when she was four years old and she entered Bard College with thoughts of becoming a professional dancer. A six-week special course in drama that she took in a college in northern England impressed her, and when she returned to America, she auditioned for and won the part of Jennifer DeNuccio in the CBS series *Square Pegs.* She followed this with the role of Angela Timini in ABC's *Glitter* and was seen in several television movies. Although she is currently gaining critical acclaim for her role as the daughter in *Down and Out in Beverly Hills,* it is not her first major film. Nelson portrayed the youngest daughter in *Yours, Mine, and Ours* when she was four years old.*

*   *   *

NEWMAN, Barry   1938-

PERSONAL: Full name Barry Foster Newman; born November 7, 1938, in Boston, MA; son of Carl Henry and Sarah (Ostrovsky) Newman. EDUCATION: Brandeis University, 1958.

VOCATION: Actor.

CAREER: PRINCIPAL FILM APPEARANCES—*City on Fire,* Avco Embassy, 1979.

PRINCIPAL TELEVISION APPEARANCES—Series: Tony Petrocelli, *Petrocelli,* NBC, 1974-76.

Movies: *Sex and the Married Woman,* 1977.

Mini-Series: Jeff MacDonald, *Fatal Vision,* NBC, 1985.

Play: *King Crab,* 1980.

AWARDS: Best Actor, Academy of Television Arts and Sciences nomination, for *Petrocelli;* Best Actor, Golden Globe, for, *Petrocelli.*

ADDRESSES: AGENT—Artists Agency, 190 N. Canon Drive, Beverly Hills, CA 90210.*

*   *   *

NEWMAN, Paul   1925-

PERSONAL: Born January 26, 1925, in Cleveland, OH; son of Arthur S. and Theresa (Fetzer) Newman; married Jacqueline Witte, December, 1949 (divorced); married Joanne Woodward (an actress), January 1958; children: (first marriage) Scott (died), Susan, Stephanie; (second marrige) Elinor, Melissa, Clea. EDUCATION: Kenyon College, B.A. 1949; attended Yale University School of Drama, 1951. MILITARY: U.S. Navy Reserve, 1943-46.

VOCATION: Actor, director, and producer.

CAREER: PRINCIPAL STAGE APPEARANCES—Broadway: *Picnic,* 1953-54; *The Desperate Hours,* 1955; Chance Wayne, *Sweet Bird of Youth,* 1959; *Baby Want a Kiss,* 1964.

PRINCIPAL FILM APPEARANCES—*The Silver Chalice,* Warner Brothers, 1955; *The Rack,* Metro-Goldwyn-Mayer, 1956; *Somebody Up There Likes Me,* Metro-Goldwyn-Mayer, 1957; *Until They Sail,* Metro-Goldwyn-Mayer, 1957; *The Helen Morgan Story,*

PAUL NEWMAN

Warner Brothers, 1957; *The Long Hot Summer*, Twentieth Century-Fox, 1958; *Brick, Cat on a Hot Tin Roof*, Metro Goldwyn-Mayer, 1958; *The Left Handed Gun*, Warner Brothers, 1958; *Rally 'Round the Flag Boys!*, Twentieth Century-Fox, 1959; *The Young Philadelphians*, Warner Brothers, 1959.

From the Terrace, Twentieth Century-Fox, 1960; *Exodus*, United Artists, 1960; *The Hustler*, Twentieth Century-Fox, 1961; Chance Wayne, *Sweet Bird of Youth*, Metro-Goldwyn-Mayer, 1962; *Adventures of a Young Man*, Twentieth Century-Fox, 1962; *Hud*, Paramount, 1963; *A New Kind of Love*, Paramount, 1963; *The Prize*, Metro-Goldwyn-Mayer, 1963; *The Outrage*, Metro-Goldwyn-Mayer, 1964; *What a Way to Go!*, Twentieth Century-Fox, 1964; *Lady L*, Metro-Goldwyn-Mayer, 1966; *Torn Curtin*, Universal, 1966; *Harper*, Warner Brothers, 1966; *Hombre*, Twentieth Century-Fox, 1967; *Cool Hand Luke*, Warner Brothers-Seven Arts, 1967; *The Secret War of Harry Frigg*, Universal, 1968; *Winning*, Universal, 1969; Butch Cassidy, *Butch Cassidy and the Sundance Kid*, Twentieth Century-Fox, 1969; *WUSA*, Paramount, 1969.

Sometimes a Great Notion, Universal, 1971; *Pocket Money*, National General, 1972; *The Life and Times of Judge Roy Bean*, National General, 1972; *The Mackintosh Man*, Warner Brothers, 1973; *The Sting*, Universal, 1973; *The Towering Inferno*, Twentieth Century-Fox, 1974; *The Drowning Pool*, Warner Brothers, 1975; *Buffalo Bill and the Indians*, United Artists, 1976; *Slap Shot*, Universal, 1977; *Quintet*, Twentieth Century-Fox, 1979; *When Time Ran Out*, Warner Brothers, 1980; *Fort Apache, the Bronx*, Twentieth Century-Fox, 1981; *Absence of Malice*, Columbia, 1981;

The Verdict, Twentieth Century-Fox, 1982; *Harry and Son*, Orion Pictures, 1984.

PRINCIPAL FILM WORK—Producer and director, *Rachel, Rachel*, Warner Brothers-Seven Arts, 1968; Producer, *Winning*, Universal, 1969; producer, *WUSA*, Paramount, 1969; co-director (with Richard Colla), *Sometimes a Great Notion*, Universal, 1971; producer, *Pocket Money*, National General, 1972; producer, *The Life and Times of Judge Roy Bean*, National General, 1972; producer, *The Mackintosh Man*, Warner Brothers, 1973; producer, *The Sting*, Universal, 1973; director, *The Effect of Gamma Rays on Man-in-the-Moon Marigolds*, Twentieth Century-Fox, 1973; producer, *The Towering Inferno*, Twentieth Century-Fox, 1974; producer, *The Drowning Pool*, Warner Brothers, 1975; producer, *Buffalo Bill and the Indians*, United Artists, 1976; producer, *Slap Shot*, Universal, 1977; director and co-producer, *Harry and Son*, Orion Pictures, 1984.

PRINCIPAL TELEVISION APPEARANCES—Episodic: *Kraft Television Theatre*, NBC, 1952; "One for the Road," *The Web*, CBS, 1953; *Danger*, CBS, 1954; "Our Town," *Producers Showcase*, NBC, 1955; "Army Game," *The Kaiser Aluminum Hour*, NBC, 1956; "Bang the Drum Slowly," *U.S. Steel Hour*, CBS, 1956; *Appointment with Adventure*, CBS, 1956; also appeared as Billy the Kid, *Philco TV Playhouse*, NBC, and in the *Goodyeur TV Playhouse*, NBC.

Guest: *Hollywood and the Stars*, NBC; *The David Frost Show*, syndicated; *The Tonight Show*, NBC.

PRINCIPAL TELEVISION WORK—Director, *The Shadow Box*, 1979.

RELATED CAREER—Formed First Artists Production Company, Ltd. in 1969.

WRITINGS: SCREENPLAY—(Co-writer) *Harry and Son*, Orion Pictures, 1984.

AWARDS: Best Actor, Academy Award nominations, 1958, for *Cat on a Hot Tin Roof*, 1961, for *The Hustler*, 1963, for *Hud*, 1967, for *Cool Hand Luke*, 1981, for *Absence of Malice*, and 1982, for *The Verdict;* Golden Globe Award, World Film Favorite Male, 1967, for *Hud;* Best Motion Picture Producer, Producers Guild of America, and Best Director, New York Film Critics, both 1968, for *Rachel, Rachel;* Harvard University, Hasty Pudding Theatrical, Man of the Year, 1968.

SIDELIGHTS: In addition to his film career, Paul Newman is a professional race car driver.

ADDRESSES: AGENT—Creative Artists, 1888 Century Park E., Los Angeles, CA 90067.

*   *   *

NICHOLSON, Jack   1937-

PERSONAL: Born April 22, 1937, in Neptune, NJ; son of John (a sign painter) and Ethel May Nicholson; married Sandra Knight, 1961 (divorced 1966); children: Jennifer.

VOCATION: Actor, director, writer, and producer.

CAREER: STAGE DEBUT—*Tea and Sympathy*, Los Angeles, CA.

FILM DEBUT—*The Cry Baby Killer*, Allied Artists, 1958. PRINCI-PAL FILM APPEARANCES—*Too Young to Love*, Rank/Welback, 1959; Wilbur Force, *The Little Shop of Horrors*, Filmgroup/Cor-man, 1960; *The Wild Ride*, Filmgroup, 1960; *Studs Lonigan*, United Artists, 1960; *The Raven*, American International Pictures/Alta Vista, 1963; Lieutenant Andre Duvalier, *The Terror*, American International Pictures/Filmgroup, 1963; *Ensign Pulver*, Warner Brothers, 1964; *Back Door to Hell*, Twentieth Century-Fox, 1964; *Ride the Whirlwind*, Twentieth Century-Fox, 1966; *Flight to Fury*, Feature Films, 1966; *The Shooting*, Twentieth Century-Fox, 1967; *The St. Valentine's Day Massacre*, Twentieth Century-Fox, 1967; Poet, *Hell's Angels on Wheels*, American International Pictures, 1967; *Rebel Rousers*, Four Star Excelsior, 1967 (released 1970); Stoney, *Psych-Out*, American International Pictures, 1968; *Easy Rider*, Columbia, 1969.

Tad, *On a Clear Day You Can See Forever*, Paramount, 1970; *Five Easy Pieces*, Columbia, 1970; *Carnal Knowledge*, Avco Embassy, 1971; *King of Marvin Gardens*, Columbia, 1971; *A Safe Place*, Columbia, 1971; *The Last Detail*, Columbia, 1973; *Chinatown*, Paramount, 1974; *Tommy*, Columbia, 1975; *The Passenger*, United Artists/Metro-Goldwyn-Mayer, 1975; *The Fortune*, Columbia, 1975; *One Flew Over the Cuckoo's Nest*, United Artists, 1975; *The Missouri Breaks*, Warner Brothers, 1976; *The Last Tycoon*, Para-mount, 1977; *Goin' South*, Paramount, 1978; *The Shining*, Warner Brothers, 1980; *The Postman Always Rings Twice*, Paramount, 1981; *Reds*, Warner Brothers, 1981; *The Border*, 1982; *Terms of Endearment*, Paramount, 1983; *Prizzi's Honor*, ABC Motion Pic-tures, 1985; *Heartburn*, Paramount, 1986.

PRINCIPAL FILM WORK—Producer, *Ride the Whirlwind*, Twenti-eth Century-Fox, 1965; producer, *The Shooting*, Twentieth Cen-tury-Fox, 1967; producer, *Head*, Columbia, 1968; producer and director, *Drive, He Said*, Columbia, 1971; director, *Goin' South*, Paramount, 1978.

WRITING: SCREENPLAYS—*Ride the Whirlwind*, Twentieth Cen-tury-Fox, 1965; *Flight to Fury*, Feature Films, 1966; *The Trip*, American-International, 1967; *Head*, Columbia, 1968; *Drive, He Said*, Columbia, 1971.

AWARDS: Best Supporting Actor, Academy Award nomination, 1969, for *Easy Rider;* Best Actor, Academy Award nomination, 1970, for *Five Easy Pieces;* Best Actor, Academy Award nomina-tion, Cannes Film Festival Prize, 1973, for *The Last Detail;* Best Actor, Academy Award nomination, New York Film Critics Circle, both 1974, for *Chinatown;* Best Actor, Academy Award, Golden Globe, and New York Film Critics Circle, 1975, all for *One Flew Over the Cuckoo's Nest;* Best Supporting Actor, Academy Award nomination, 1981, for *Reds;* Best Supporting Actor, 1983, for *Terms of Endearment;* Best Actor, Academy Award nomination, 1985, for *Prizzi's Honor;* also awards from National Society of Film Critics and the British Film Society.

SIDELIGHTS: Nicholson began his career in the cartoon department of Metro-Goldwyn-Mayer.

ADDRESSES: AGENT—Sandy Bressler and Associates, 15760 Ventura Blvd., Suite 1730, Encino, CA 91436.

*   *   *

NIELSEN, Leslie   1926-

PERSONAL: Born February 11, 1926, in Regina, Saskatchewan,

Canada. EDUCATION: Studied acting at the Neighborhood Play-house in New York.

VOCATION: Actor.

CAREER: PRINCIPAL FILM APPEARANCES—*The Vagabond King*, Paramount, 1956; Commander Adams, *Forbidden Planet*, Metro-Goldwyn-Mayer, 1956; *Ransom!*, Metro-Goldwyn-Mayer, 1956; *The Opposite Sex*, Metro-Goldwyn-Mayer, 1956; *Hot Summer Night*, Metro-Goldwyn-Mayer, 1957; *Tammy and the Bachelor*, Universal, 1957; *Night Train to Paris*, Twentieth Century-Fox, 1964; *Harlow*, Paramount, 1965; *Dark Intruder*, Universal, 1965; *Beau Geste*, Universal, 1965; *Gunfight in Abilene*, Universal, 1967; *The Reluctant Astronaut*, Universal, 1967; *Rosie*, Universal, 1967; *Counterpoint*, Universal, 1967; *Dayton's Devils*, Commonwealth United, 1969; *How to Commit Marriage*, Cinerama, 1969; *Change of Mind*, Cinerama, 1969; *The Resurrection of Zachary Wheeler*, Gold Key Entertainment, 1971; *The Poseidon Adventure*, Twentieth Century-Fox, 1972; *Viva, Knievel*, Warner Brothers, 1977; *City on Fire*, Avco Embassy, 1979; the doctor, *Airplane!*, Paramount, 1980; *Wrong Is Right*, 1982; *Creepshow*, Warner Brothers, 1983.

PRINCIPAL TELEVISION APPEARANCES—Series: Lt. Price Adams, *The New Breed*, ABC, 1961-62; Dr. Vincent Markham, *Peyton Place*, ABC, 1965; Sam Danforth, *The Protectors*, NBC, 1969-70; John Bracken, *Bracken's World*, NBC, 1970; host, *The Explorers*, syndication, 1972-73; Det. Frank Drebin, *Police Squad*, ABC, 1982; Buddy Fox, *Shaping Up*, ABC, 1984.

Episodic: *Lights Out,*, NBC; *Man Behind the Badge*, CBS; *Short Short Dramas*, NBC; *Studio One*, CBS; *Sure as Fate*, CBS; *Tales of Tomorrow*, ABC; *Kraft Television Theatre; Philco TV Playhouse*, NBC; *Robert Montgomery Presents*, NBC; *Pulitzer Prize Play-house*, ABC; *Suspense*, CBS; *Danger*, CBS; *Justice*, NBC; *Death of a Salesman;* Francis Marion, "Swamp Fox," *Wonderful World of Walt Disney*, NBC; *Ben Casey*, ABC; *The Wild, Wild West*, CBS; *The Virginian*, NBC; *The Loner*, CBS; *What Really Happened to the Class of '65?*, NBC, 1978.

Mini-Series: Ike Hoover, *Backstairs at the White House*, NBC, 1979.

Movie: *Blade in Hong Kong*, CBS, 1985.

RELATED CAREER: Announcer for Canadian radio stations; actor on New York radio and in summer stock.

SIDELIGHTS: Nielsen's 1971 film, *The Resurrection of Zachary Wheeler*, while intended for commercial theatrical release, was never seen in theatres. Shot on video-tape, it was immediately sold for television presentation.

ADDRESSES: AGENT—The Artists Agency, 10000 Santa Monica Blvd., Suite 305, Los Angeles, CA 90067.*

*   *   *

NORTON-TAYLOR, Judy

PERSONAL: Born January 29, in Santa Monica, CA; daughter of Harry Vincent and Constance (Glazebrook) Norton-Taylor.

VOCATION: Actress.

CAREER: PRINCIPAL TELEVISION APPEARANCES—Series: Mary Ellen Walton Willard, *The Waltons*, CBS, 1972-81.

JUDY NORTON-TAYLOR

Movies: Mary Ellen Walton, *The Homecoming—A Christmas Story*, CBS, 1971; *Valentine*, ABC, 1979; *Valentine's Day: A Love Story*, NBC, 1982; Mary Ellen Walton Willard, *Mother's Day on Walton Mountain*, NBC, 1982; *A Day of Thanks*, NBC, 1982.

Episodic: *The Love Boat*, ABC, 1981.

PRINCIPAL STAGE APPEARANCES—With the Stable Players, 1969-71; title role, *Cinderella*, Pittsburg Civic Light Opera, 1981; title role, *Annie Get Your Gun*, Lutcher Theatre, TX, 1983; Libby, *I Ought to Be in Pictures*, Country Squire Dinner Theatre, TX, and Mickey Rooney Dinner Theatre, Los Angeles, 1983; Katia, *Spring at Marino* and Augusta, *Perfect Pitch*, both at Ivoryton Playhouse, CT, 1984; *Times of Your Life*, Sheraton Lakeview Theatre, 1985.

Additional stock credits: *Just Roomies; Wait Until Dark; The Leaving; My Son Sam; Somebody Up There Likes Me; I Love You with All My Heart, Sherri Willis; Vanities; Broadway Review; Pirate's Island; The Rainmaker; Come Back, Little Sheba*.

PRINCIPAL FILM APPEARANCES—*Hotel*, Warner Brothers, 1967.

MEMBER: Actors' Equity Association, Screen Actors Guild, American Federation of Television and Radio Artists.

ADDRESSES: OFFICE—135 Screenland Drive, Burbank, CA 91505. AGENT—Exclusive Artists Agency, 2501 W. Burbank Blvd., Suite 304, Burbank, CA 91505.

*   *   *

NOVELLO, Don   1943-

PERSONAL: Born January 1, 1943, in Ashtabula, OH; son of Augustine J. (a physician) and Eleanor (Finnerty) Novello; married.

EDUCATION: University of Dayton, B.A., 1964. RELIGION: Roman Catholic.

VOCATION: Writer, comedian, and producer.

CAREER: PRINCIPAL TELEVISION APPEARANCES—*The Smothers Brothers Comedy Hour*, NBC, 1975; *Saturday Night Live*, NBC, 1978-80.

PRINCIPAL FILM APPEARANCES—Father Guido Sarducci, *Gilda Live*, Warner Brothers, 1980.

PRINCIPAL TELEVISION WORK—Producer, *SCTV Comedy Network*, NBC, 1982.

WRITINGS: TELEVISION—*The Smothers Brothers Comedy Hour*, NBC, 1975; *Van Dyke & Company*, NBC, 1976; *Saturday Night Live*, NBC, 1978-80.

REVUE—(With Gilda Radner, Lorne Michaels, and others)*Gilda Radner—Live from New York*, Winter Garden Theatre, NY, 1979.

SCREENPLAYS—(With Gilda Radner, Lorne Michaels, and others) *Gilda Radner—Live from New York*, Warner Brothers, 1980.

BOOKS—(Under pseudonym Laszlo Toth)*The Laszlo Letters: The Amazing, Real-Life Actual Correspondence of Lazlo Toth, American!*, Workman Publishing, 1977.

ARTICLES—In *Playboy, Rolling Stone* and *The Washington Post.*

RECORDINGS: COMEDY ALBUM—*Father Guido Sarducci: Live at St. Douglas Convent*, Warner Brothers, 1980.

MEMBER: Writers Guild of America, Screen Actors Guild, American Federation of Television and Radio Artists; Cavalier's Club.

SIDELIGHTS: Much of Novello's career, both performing and writing, has been under the assumed character name, Father Guido Sarducci.

ADDRESSES: OFFICE—c/o Workman Publishing Company, One W. 39th Street, New York, NY 10018.*

*   *   *

NUNN, Trevor   1940-

PERSONAL: Full name, Trevor Robert Nunn; born January 14, 1940, in Ipswich, England; son of Robert Alexander and Dorothy May (Piper) Nunn; married Janet Suzman (an actress), 1969; children: one. EDUCATION: Attended Northgate Grammar School, Ipswich; Downing College, Cambridge; studied directing as a trainee at the Belgrade Theatre, Coventry, England.

VOCATION: Director.

CAREER: PRINCIPAL STAGE WORK—Director: *The Caucasian Chalk Circle, A View from the Bridge*, and *Peer Gynt*, all at Belgrade Theatre, Coventry, England.

With the Royal Shakespeare Company: *The Thwarting of Baron Bolligrew*, Aldwych Theatre, London, 1965; *Henry IV, Parts I and II*, Stratford-upon-Avon, 1966; *Henry V*, Aldwych Theatre, London, 1966; *The Revengers Tragedy*, Stratford-upon-Avon, 1966, then Aldwych Theatre, 1966; *Tango*, Aldwych Theatre, London,

1966; *The Taming of the Shrew,* Stratford-upon-Avon, 1967, then Aldwych Theatre, London, 1967; *The Relapse,* Aldwych Theatre, London, 1967; *King Lear,* Stratford-upon-Avon, 1968; *Much Ado About Nothing,* Stratford-upon-Avon, 1968, then Aldwych Theatre, London, 1968; *The Winter's Tale,* Stratford-upon-Avon, 1969, then Aldwych Theatre, 1969; *Henry VIII,* Stratford-upon-Avon, 1969, then Aldwych Theatre, 1969.

Hamlet, Stratford-upon-Avon, 1970; "Roman Season," Stratford-upon-Avon, 1972, then Aldwych Theatre, London, 1973: *Antony and Cleopatra, Coriolanus, Julius Caesar, Titus Andronicus; Macbeth,* Stratford-upon-Avon, 1974, then Aldwych Theatre, London, 1974; *Hedda Gabler,* Aldwych Theatre, London, 1975; *Romeo and Juliet,* Stratford-upon-Avon, 1976; *The Winter's Tale,* Stratford-upon-Avon, 1976; *The Comedy of Errors,* Stratford-upon-Avon, 1976, then Aldwych Theatre, 1976; *King Lear,* Stratford-upon-Avon, 1976, then Aldwych Theatre, 1976; *Macbeth,* The Other Place, Stratford-upon-Avon, 1976, then Aldwych Theatre, London, 1976; *The Alchemist,* The Other Place, Stratford-upon-Avon, 1977, then Aldwych Theatre, London, 1977; *As You Like It,* Stratford-upon-Avon, 1977, then Aldwych Theatre, London, 1977; *Every Good Boy Deserves Favour,* Royal Festival Hall, London, 1977; *Macbeth,* Warehouse Theatre, London, 1977; *The Three Sisters,* Aldwych Theatre, London, 1978; *The Merry Wives of Windsor,* Stratford-upon-Avon, 1979, then Aldwych Theatre, 1979; *The Three Sisters,* The Other Place, Stratford-upon-Avon, 1979, then Aldwych Theatre, London, 1979.

Once in a Lifetime, Aldwych Theatre, London, 1979, then Piccadilly Theatre, London, 1980; *Juno and the Paycock,* 1980; *The Life and Times of Nicholas Nickleby,* Aldwych Theatre, London, 1980, then Plymouth Theatre, NY, 1981; *All's Well That Ends Well,* Stratford-upon-Avon, 1981, then Martin Beck Theatre, NY, 1982; *Cats,* New London Theatre, London, 1981, then Winter Garden Theatre, NY, 1982; *Henry IV, Parts I and II,* Stratford-upon-Avon, 1981, then Aldwych Theatre, London, 1982; *Starlight Express,* Apollo Theatre, London, 1984; *Les Miserables,* Palace Theatre, London, 1985; *The Life and Times of Nicholas Nickleby,* Stratford-upon-Avon, 1985; *Chess,* London, 1986.

MAJOR TOURS—*Hedda Gabler,* U.S. and Australia, 1975; *Cats,* Los Angeles, CA, Vienna, Austria, Tokyo, Japan, Hamburg, Germany, 1982—.

PRINCIPAL TELEVISION WORK—Director: *Antony and Cleopatra,* BBC, 1975; *Comedy of Errors,* BBC, 1976; *Every Good Boy Deserves Favour,* BBC, 1978; *Macbeth,* 1978; *Shakespeare Workshops Word of Mouth,* 1979; *The Three Sisters,* 1982; *Peter Pan,* 1982.

PRINCIPAL FILM WORK—Director: *Hedda,* 1975; *Lady Jane,* 1984.

RELATED CAREER: Associate director, Royal Shakespeare Company, 1964; artistic director, Royal Shakespeare Company, 1968—; joint artistic director, Royal Shakespeare Company, 1978—; chief executive officer, Royal Shakespeare Company.

Photograph by Michael Le Poer Trench

TREVOR NUNN

WRITINGS: PLAY ADAPTATIONS—*Hedda Gabler,* 1975.

TELEVISION—*Shakespeare Workshops Word of Mouth,* 1979.

SCREENPLAY—*Hedda,* 1974.

AWARDS: Best Director, London Theatre Critics, 1966, for *The Revenger's Tragedy* and 1969, for *The Winter's Tale;* Society of Film and Television Arts, 1976, for *Antony and Cleopatra;* Best Director, Sydney Edwards Award, 1977-78, for *Once in a Lifetime;* Best Director, *Evening Standard,* Drama Award, Antoinette Perry Award, New York Drama Critics Circle, and Society of West End Theatres, all 1982, for *The Life and Adventures of Nicholas Nickleby;* honorary Litt.D., Warwick, 1982; honorary M.A., Newcastle upon Tyne, 1982; named Commander of the British Empire (C.B.E.), 1978.

ADDRESSES: OFFICE—Barbican Centre, Silk Street, London EC2, England.

O

O'BRIEN, Margaret 1937-

PERSONAL: Born Angela Maxine O'Brien, January 15, 1937, in San Diego, CA; daughter of Lawrence (a circus performer) and Gladys (Flores) O'Brien; married Harold R. Allen, Jr. (an artist), August 8, 1959 (divorced, 1968); married Roy T. Thorsen, June 8, 1974; children: (second marriage) Mara Tolene.

VOCATION: Actress.

CAREER: FILM DEBUT—(As Maxine O'Brien)*Babes on Broadway,* Metro-Goldwyn-Mayer, 1941. PRINCIPAL FILM APPEARANCES—Title role, *Journey for Margaret,* Metro-Goldwyn-Mayer, 1942; *Doctor Gillespie's Criminal Case,* Metro-Goldwyn-Mayer, 1943; *Thousands Cheer,* Metro-Goldwyn-Mayer, 1943; *Lost Angel,* Metro-Goldwyn-Mayer, 1943; *Madame Curie,* Metro-Goldwyn-Mayer, 1943; Adele, *Jane Eyre,* Twentieth Century-Fox, 1944; *The Canterville Ghost,* Metro-Goldwyn-Mayer, 1944; "Tootie" Smith, *Meet Me in St. Louis,* Metro-Goldwyn-Mayer, 1944; *Music for Millions,* Metro-Goldwyn-Mayer, 1944; *Our Vines Have Tender Grapes,* Metro-Goldwyn-Mayer, 1945; *Bad Bascomb,* Metro-Goldwyn-Mayer, 1946; *Three Wise Fools,* Metro-Goldwyn-Mayer, 1946; *The Unfinished Dance,* Metro-Goldwyn-Mayer, 1947; *Tenth Avenue Angel,* Metro-Goldwyn-Mayer, 1947; *Big City,* Metro-Goldwyn-Mayer, 1948; Beth March, *Little Women,* Metro-Goldwyn-Mayer, 1949; *The Secret Garden,* Metro-Goldwyn-Mayer, 1949; *Her First Romance,* Columbia, 1951; *Glory,* RKO, 1956; Della Southby, *Heller in Pink Tights,* Paramount, 1960; also, *Annabelle Lee; Diabolic Wedding.*

PRINCIPAL STAGE APPEARANCES—*Barefoot in the Park, Under the Yum Yum Tree, A Thousand Clowns,* all in summer stock or summer tour productions.

PRINCIPAL TELEVISION APPEARANCES—Episodic: *Perry Mason,* CBS, 1963; *Bob Hope Presents the Chrysler Theatre,* NBC, 1964; *Combat,* ABC, 1967; *Ironside,* NBC, 1968; *Love, American Style,* ABC, 1968; *Adam-12,* NBC, 1971; *Marcus Welby, M.D.,* ABC, 1972; others.

WRITINGS: AUTOBIOGRAPHY—*My Diary.*

AWARDS: "Best Child Actress," honorary Academy Award (a miniature statuette was presented), 1944; voted one of the ten best money-making stars, *Motion Picture Herald-Fame* Poll, 1945-46.

SIDELIGHTS: Margaret O'Brien has served as civilian aide to the Secretary of the Army for Southern California from 1979 to the present. She is a collector of Peruvian and Spanish art. In 1977, the money which she earned as a child star was turned over to her, having been held in trust for her during her career. It is reported that

in 1945, at the age of nine, she was earning $2,500 dollars per week.

ADDRESSES: AGENT—Mark Levin Associates, 328 S. Beverly Drive, Suite E, Beverly Hills, CA 90212.*

*   *   *

O'CONNOR, Donald 1925-

PERSONAL: Full name, Donald David Dixon O'Connor; born August 28, 1925, in Chicago, Il.; son of John Edward (a circus strong man) and Effie Irene (a circus acrobat; maiden name, Crane) O'Connor; married Gwendolyn Carter (an actress), 1944 (divorced, 1954); married Gloria Noble, November, 1956; children: (first marriage) Donna, (second marriage) Alicia, Donald Frederick, Kevin. MILITARY: U.S. Armed Services, 1943.

VOCATION: Actor, singer, and dancer.

CAREER: STAGE DEBUT—Vaudeville sketch with family. NEW YORK DEBUT—Albert Peterson, *Bring Back Birdie,* Martin Beck Theatre, 1981. PRINCIPAL STAGE APPEARANCES—*Sons of Fun,* Syracuse, NY; vaudeville, 1940-41; Captain Andy Hawks, *Show Boat,* Minksoff Theatre, NY, 1984.

FILM DEBUT—Mike Beebe, *Sing You Sinners,* Paramount, 1938. PRINCIPAL FILM APPEARANCES—*Sons of the Legion,* Paramount, 1938; *Men with Wings,* Paramount, 1938; *Tom Sawyer, Detective,* Paramount, 1938; *Unmarried,* Paramount, 1939; *Death of a Champion,* Paramount, 1939; *Million Dollar Legs,* Paramount, 1939; *Night Work,* Paramount, 1939; *On Your Toes,* Warner Brothers, 1939; *Beau Geste,* Paramount, 1939; *Private Buckaroo,* Universal, 1942; *What's Cooking?,* 1942; *Give Out, Sisters,* Universal, 1942; *Get Hep to Love,* Universal, 1942; *When Johnny Comes Marching Home,* Universal, 1942; *Strictly in the Groove,* Universal, 1943; *It Comes Up Love,* Universal, 1943; *Mr. Big,* Universal, 1943; *Top Man,* Universal, 1943; *Chip Off the Old Block,* Universal, 1944; *This Is the Life,* Universal, 1944; *Follow the Boys,* Universal, 1944; *The Merry Monahans,* Universal, 1944; *Bowery to Broadway,* Universal, 1944; *Patrick the Great,* Universal, 1945; *Something in the Wind,* Universal, 1947; *Are You with It?,* Universal, 1948; *Feudin', Fussin' and a-Fightin',* Universal, 1948; *Yes Sir, That's My Baby,* Universal, 1949; Peter Sterling, *Francis,* Universal, 1949.

Curtain Call at Cactus Creek, Universal, 1950; *The Milkman,* Universal, 1950; *Double Crossbones,* Universal, 1950; Peter Stirling, *Francis Goes to the Races,* Universal, 1951; Cosmo, *Singin' in the Rain,* Metro-Goldwyn-Mayer, 1952; Peter Sterling, *Francis Goes to West Point,* Universal, 1952; Kenneth, *Call Me Madam,* Twentieth Century-Fox, 1953; title role, *I Love Melvin,* Metro-Goldwyn-

Mayer, 1953; Peter Stirling, *Francis Covers the Big Town,* Universal, 1953; *Walking My Baby Back Home,* Universal, 1953; Peter Stirling, *Francis Joins the WACs,* Universal, 1954; Tim, *There's No Business Like Show Business,* Twentieth Century-Fox, 1954; Peter Stirling, *Francis in the Navy,* Universal, 1955; *Anything Goes,* Paramount, 1956; title role, *The Buster Keaton Story,* Paramount, 1957.

Cry for Happy, Columbia, 1961; *The Wonders of Alladin,* Metro-Goldwyn-Mayer, 1961; *That Funny Feeling,* Universal, 1965; *That's Entertainment!,* United Artists, 1974; *That's Entertainment, Part II,* United Artists, 1976; *The Big Fix,* Universal, 1979; singer, *Ragtime,* Paramount, 1981; *Pandemonium,* 1982.

PRINCIPAL TELEVISION APPEARANCES—Series: *Colgate Comedy Hour,* NBC, 1951-54; *The Donald O'Connor Texaco Show,* NBC, 1954-55.

Guest: Master of Ceremonies, *Academy Awards Presentation,* March 25, 1954; guest host, *The Tonight Show,* NBC, 1962; season premiere, *The Judy Garland Show,* 1963.

Episodic: *The Love Boat,* ABC; *Hotel,* ABC.

Specials: Hermes, "Olympus 7-0000," *ABC Stage '67,* 1967; *Alice in Wonderland,* CBS, 1985.

RECORDINGS: ALBUMS—*Singin' in the Rain,* original soundtrack, Metro-Goldwyn-Mayer; *Call Me Madam,* original soundtrack; *There's No Business Like Show Business,* original soundtrack, Decca; *Anything Goes,* original soundtrack, Decca; *Olympus 7-0000,* original soundtrack, Command Records; *Bring Back Birdie,* original cast, Original Cast Recordings; others.

AWARDS: Best Male Star of a Regular Series, Emmy Award, 1953; voted Best Television Performance, *Motion Picture Daily* Poll, 1953.*

*   *   *

O'NEAL, Tatum 1963-

PERSONAL: Born November 5, 1963, in Los Angeles, CA; daughter of Ryan (an actor) and Joanna (an actress; professional name, Moore) O'Neal; children: (by John McEnroe) Kevin Jack.

VOCATION: Actress.

CAREER: FILM DEBUT—*Paper Moon,* Paramount, 1973. PRINCIPAL FILM APPEARANCES—*The Bad News Bears,* Paramount, 1976; *Nickelodeon,* Columbia, 1976; title role, *International Velvet,* United Artists, 1978; *Little Darlings,* Paramount, 1980; *Circle of Two,* 1981; *Certain Fury,* New World, 1984.

AWARDS: Best Supporting Actress, Academy Award, *Paper Moon,* 1973.

ADDRESSES: AGENT—International Creative Management, 8899 Beverly Blvd., Los Angeles, CA 90048.*

*   *   *

ONTKEAN, Michael 1950-

PERSONAL: Born 1950, in Canada; son of Leonard (an actor) and

Muriel (an actress; maiden name, Cooper) Ontkean. EDUCATION: Attended University of New Hampshire.

VOCATION: Actor.

CAREER: PRINCIPAL FILM APPEARANCES—*The Peace Killers,* 1971; *Pick Up on 101,* 1972; *Necromancy,* Cinerama, 1972; *Hot Summer Weekend; Slap Shot,* Universal, 1977; *Voices,* United Artists, 1979; *Willie and Phil,* Twentieth Century-Fox, 1980; *Making Love,* Twentieth Century-Fox, 1982; *Just the Way You Are,* Metro-Goldwyn-Mayer/United Artists, 1984.

PRINCIPAL TELEVISION APPEARANCES—Series: Officer Willie Gillis, *The Rookies,* ABC, 1972-74.

Movies: *The Blood of Others,* HBO, 1984; *Kids Don't Tell,* CBS, 1985.

ADDRESSES: AGENT—Triad, 888 Seventh Avenue, 1602, New York, NY 10106.*

*   *   *

O'SULLIVAN, Maureen 1911-

PERSONAL: Born May 17, 1911, in Roscommon, Ireland; daughter of Charles Joseph and Mary Lovatt (Fraser) O'Sullivan; married John Villiers Farrow (died); married James E. Cushing, August, 1983; children: six (including Mia Farrow). EDUCATION: Attended Convent of the Sacred Heart in London, Dublin, and Paris.

VOCATION: Actress.

CAREER: PRINCIPAL FILM APPEARANCES—Jane, *Tarzan the Ape Man,* Metro-Goldwyn-Mayer, 1932; *Skyscraper Souls,* Metro-Goldwyn-Mayer, 1932; *Strange Interlude,* Metro-Goldwyn-Mayer, 1932; *Payment Deferred,* Metro-Goldwyn-Mayer, 1932; *Tugboat Annie,* Metro-Goldwyn-Mayer, 1933; *The Thin Man,* Metro-Goldwyn-Mayer, 1934; *Barretts of Wimpole Street,* Metro-Goldwyn-Mayer, 1934; Jane, *Tarzan and His Mate,* Metro-Goldwyn-Mayer, 1934; *David Copperfield,* Metro-Goldwyn-Mayer, 1934; *Woman Wanted,* Metro-Goldwyn-Mayer, 1935; *The Flame Within,* Metro-Goldwyn-Mayer, 1935; *Anna Karenina,* Metro-Goldwyn-Mayer, 1935; *The Bishop Misbehaves* (also known as *The Bishop's Misadventures*), Metro-Goldwyn-Mayer, 1935; *Cardinal Richelieu,* 1935; Jane, *Tarzan Escapes,* Metro-Goldwyn-Mayer, 1936; *The Voice of Bugle Ann,* Metro-Goldwyn-Mayer, 1936; *The Devil Doll,* Metro-Goldwyn-Mayer, 1936; *My Dear Miss Aldrich,* Metro-Goldwyn-Mayer, 1937; *Between Two Women,* Metro-Goldwyn-Mayer, *A Day at the Races,* Metro-Goldwyn-Mayer, 1937; *A Yank at Oxford,* Metro-Goldwyn-Mayer, 1937; *Hold That Kiss,* Metro-Goldwyn-Mayer, 1938; *Port of Seven Seas,* Metro-Goldwyn-Mayer, 1938; *Spring Madness,* Metro-Goldwyn-Mayer, 1938; Jane, *Tarzan Finds a Son,* Metro-Goldwyn-Mayer, 1939.

Pride and Prejudice, Metro-Goldwyn-Mayer, 1940; *Maisie Was a Lady,* Metro-Goldwyn-Mayer, 1940; Jane, *Tarzan's Secret Treasure,* Metro-Goldwyn-Mayer, 1941; Jane, *Tarzan's New York Adventure,* Metro-Goldwyn-Mayer, 1942; *The Big Clock,* 1948; *Bonzo Goes to College,* 1952; *All I Desire,* 1953; *Mission Over Korea,* 1953; *Duffy of San Quentin,* 1954; *The Steel Cage,* 1954; *Never Too Late,* Warner Brothers, 1965; *Hannah and Her Sisters,* Orion, 1986; *Peggy Sue Gets Married,* 1986.

TELEVISION DEBUT—1942. PRINCIPAL TELEVISION APPEAR-

ANCES—Episodic: *Playhouse 90*, CBS; *Alcoa Presents*, ABC; *Guiding Light*, 1984; *Search for Tomorrow*, 1985; also *Screen Gems*.

Movie: *The Crooked Hearts*, 1972.

STAGE DEBUT—Nancy Fallon, *A Roomful of Roses*, Drury Lane Theatre, Chicago, IL, 1961. NEW YORK DEBUT—Edith Lambert, *Never Too Late*, Playhouse Theatre, 1962. PRINCIPAL STAGE APPEARANCES—Edith Lambert, *Never Too Late*, Nottingham Playhouse, UK; Nettie Cleary, *The Subject Was Roses*, Helen Hayes Theatre, NY, 1965; Marian Plummer, *The 5:07*, Royal Poinciana Playhouse, Palm Beach, FL, 1967; Daisy Brady, *Keep It in the Family*, Plymouth Theatre, NY, 1967; leads, *You Know I Can't Hear You When the Water's Running*, Coconut Grove Playhouse, Miami, FL, 1968; Donna Lucia D'Alvadorez, *Charley's Aunt*, Brooks Atkinson Theatre, NY, 1970; Mrs. Grant, *The Front Page*, Ethel Barrymore Theatre, NY, 1970; Eleanor Hunter, *No Sex, Please, We're British*, Ritz Theatre, NY, then London, 1973; Amanda Wingfield, *The Glass Menagerie*, Cohoes Music Hall, 1977; *Pygmalion*, Ahmanson Theatre, Los Angeles, CA, 1978; Esther Crampton, *Morning's at Seven*, Lyceum Theatre, NY, 1980.

MAJOR TOURS—Edith Lambert, *Never Too Late*, U.S. cities, 1965; Nettie Cleary, *The Subject Was Roses*, U.S. cities, 1966-67; *The Pleasure of His Company*, U.S. cities, 1971; *Sabrina Fair*, 1975.

MEMBER: Actors' Equity Association, Screen Actors Guild; Social Service Auxiliary.

SIDELIGHTS: RECREATIONS—Painting and acting.

ADDRESSES: AGENT—c/o Milton Goldman, International Creative Management, 40 W. 57th Street, New York, NY 10019.

*   *   *

OVERTON, Rick

PERSONAL: Born in Forest Hills, NY. EDUCATION: Farleigh Dickinson College, B.A.; studied comedy with J.J. Barry and Marty Friedberg.

VOCATION: Actor and comedian.

CAREER: FILM DEBUT—Thurman Flicker, *Young Doctors in Love*, Twentieth Century-Fox, 1982. PRINCIPAL FILM APPEARANCES—*Airplane II: The Sequel*, Paramount, 1982; *Beverly Hills*

RICK OVERTON

Cop, Paramount, 1984; Googie, *Gung Ho*, Paramount, 1986; *Odd Jobs*, Tri-Star, 1986.

PRINCIPAL TELEVISION APPEARANCES—*Laugh-Off*, HBO, 1980; *Sixth Annual Comedians Special*, HBO; *Road Comics*, HBO-Cinemax.

Plays: "Popular Neurotics," *American Playhouse*, PBS, 1982.

RELATED CAREER—One half of the comedy team Overton and Sullivan.

AWARDS: Showtime Comic of the Month Award, February, 1986.

ADDRESSES: AGENT—Sumski, Green & Company, 8380 Melrose Avenue, Suite 200, Los Angeles, CA 90069.

P-Q

PALMER, Lilli 1914-1986

PERSONAL: Born Lillie Marie Peiser, May 24, 1914, in Poznan, Poland; daughter of Alfred (a surgeon) and Rose (an actress) Peiser; died of cancer in Los Angeles, CA, January 27, 1986; married Rex Harrison, 1943 (divorced, 1957); married Carlos Thompson (an author and actor); children: (first marriage) Carey.

VOCATION: Actress and writer.

CAREER: FILM DEBUT—1935. PRINCIPAL FILM APPEARANCES—*The Secret Agent*, 1936; *Chamber of Horrors*, 1940; *Thunder Rock*, 1942; *Cloak and Dagger*, 1946; *Notorious Gentleman*, 1946; *Beware of Pity*, 1947; *My Girl Tisa*, 1948; *Body and Soul*, 1948; *No Minor Vices*, Metro-Goldwyn-Mayer, 1948; *Her Man Gilbey*, 1948; *The Wicked City*, 1950; *The Long Dark Hall*, 1951; *The Counterfeit Traitor*, Paramount, 1952; *The Four Poster*, 1952; *Main Street to Broadway*, Metro-Goldwyn-Mayer, 1953; *But Not for Me*, Paramount, 1959; *Conspiracy of Hearts*, 1960; *The Pleasure of His Company*, Paramount, 1961; *Adorable Julia*, See-Art, 1964; *Operation Crossbow*, Metro-Goldwyn-Mayer, 1965; *Jack of Diamonds*, Metro-Goldwyn-Mayer, 1967; *Oedipus the King*, Universal, 1967; *The High Commissioner*, Cinerama, 1968; *Hard Contract*, 1969; *The House That Screamed*, American International, 1970; *Murders in the Rue Morgue*, American International, 1971; *The Boys from Brazil*, Twentieth Century-Fox, 1978.

Also appeared in: *Gentle Sex; English without Tears; Silent Barrier; Sunday in Vienna; Command Performance; The Man with Ten Faces; The Girl Must Live; Is Anna Anderson Anastasia; The Flight of the White Stallions; Le tonnerre de dieu; Le Voyage dupere; Marquis de sade; La residencia; What the Peeper Saw; The Holcroft Covenant.*

STAGE DEBUT—In Berlin, 1932. PRINCIPAL STAGE APPEARANCES—Broadway: *Caesar and Cleopatra*, 1949; *Venus Observed*, 1952; *Love of Four Colonels*, 1952.

PRINCIPAL TELEVISION APPEARANCES—Episodic: "Twentieth Century," Ford Theatre, CBS, 1950; title role, "The Trial of Anne Boleyn," *Omnibus*, CBS, 1952; "The Man in Possession," *U.S. Steel Hour*, ABC, 1954.

Mini-Series: *Peter the Great*, 1986.

WRITINGS: BOOKS—*Change Lobsters and Dance*, 1975; *The Red Raven*, 1979.

AWARDS: Best Actress, Venice International Film Festival Award, 1952, for *The Four Poster*.*

PARIS, Jerry 1925-1986

PERSONAL: Born July 25, 1925, in San Francisco, CA; died of a brain tumor in Los Angeles, CA, March 31, 1986; divorced; children: two sons and a daughter. EDUCATION: Attended New York University and University of California at Los Angeles; trained for the stage with the Actors Studio. MILITARY: U.S. Navy.

VOCATION: Actor, director, producer, and writer.

CAREER: PRINCIPAL TELEVISION APPEARANCES—Artie, *Those Whiting Girls*, CBS, 1957; Agent Martin Flaherty, *The Untouchables*, ABC, 1959-60; Major Willie Williston, *Steve Canyon*, NBC, then ABC, 1959-60; Tim Rourke, *Michael Shayne*, NBC, 1960-61; Jerry Helper, *The Dick Van Dyke Show*, CBS, 1961-1966.

PRINCIPAL TELEVISION WORK—Series: Directed episodes of *That Girl*, ABC, 1966-71; *The Dick Van Dyke Show*, CBS, 1964; *The Partridge Family*, ABC, 1970-74; *Love, American Style*, ABC, 1969-74; *The Odd Couple*, ABC, 1970-83; producer and directed episodes of *Happy Days*, ABC, 1974-84.

Movies: Directed—*The Feminist and the Fuzz*, ABC, 1970; *Evil Roy Slade*, 1971; *How to Break Up a Happy Divorce*, 1976; *Make Me an Offer*, 1980; also directed *The Beanes of Boston*.

PRINCIPAL FILM APPEARANCES—*Cyrano de Bergerac*, 1950; *Call Me Mister*, 1951; *The Wild One*, 1954; *The Caine Mutiny Court Martial*, 1954; *Marty*, United Artists, 1955; *The View from Pompey's Head*, Twentieth Century-Fox, 1955; *Good Morning Miss Dove*, 1955; *D-Day: The Sixth of June*, Twentieth Century-Fox, 1958; *Zero Hour*, Paramount, 1957; *The Lady Takes a Flyer*, Universal, 1958; *The Naked and the Dead*, Warner Brothers, 1958; *The Great Imposter*, Universal, 1961; also appeared in *Outrage*.

PRINCIPAL FILM WORK—Co-writer and associate producer, *The Caretakers*, United Artists, 1963; director of all the following: *Don't Raise the Bridge, Lower the River*, Columbia, 1968; *Never a Dull Moment*, Buena Vista, 1968; *How Sweet It Is*, National General, 1968; *Viva Max*, Commonwealth United, 1969; *The Grasshopper*, National General, 1970; *The Star Spangled Girl*, 1971; *Leo and Loree*, 1980; *Police Academy 2, Their First Assignment*, Warner Brothers, 1985; *Police Academy 3, Back in Training*, Warner Brothers, 1986.

PRINCIPAL STAGE APPEARANCES—*Medea; Anna Christie.*

MAJOR TOURS—*The Front Page.*

AWARDS: Emmy Award, Outstanding Directorial Achievement in Comedy, 1964, for *The Dick Van Dyke Show*.*

PARSONS, Estelle 1927-

PERSONAL: Born November 20, 1927, in Lynn, MA; daughter of Eben and Elinor (Mattson) Parsons; married Richard Gehman (divorced). EDUCATION: Oak Grove School for Girls, Vassalboro, ME, 1945; Connecticut College for Women, B.A., 1949; attended Boston University Law School, 1949-50.

VOCATION: Actress.

CAREER: NEW YORK DEBUT—Girl reporter, *Happy Hunting,* Majestic Theatre, 1956. PRINCIPAL STAGE APPEARANCES—Appeared in two of Julius Monk's revues, 1958; *Nightcap at the Showplace,* NY, 1958; Cleo, *The Most Happy Fella,* North Shore Music Festival, Beverly, MA, 1958; *Demi-Dozen,* and *Pieces of Eight* (revues), Upstairs at the Downstairs, NY, 1959.

Ollie, *Beg, Borrow, or Steal,* Martin Beck Theatre, 1960; Mrs. Coaxer, *The Threepenny Opera,* Theatre de Lys, 1960; Mrs. Peachum, *The Threepenny Opera,* Los Angeles, CA, San Francisco, CA, 1960; Nellie Forbush, *South Pacific,* Chautauqua, NY, 1961; Lasca, *The Automobile Graveyard,* 41st Street Theatre, NY, 1961; *Put It in Writing* (revue), Royal Poinciana Playhouse, FL, 1962; Lula Roca, *Hey You, Light Man!,* Theatre by the Sea, Mantunuck, RI, 1962; Mrs. Dally, *Mrs. Dally Has a Lover,* Cherry Lane Theatre, NY, 1962; Lizzie, *Next Time I'll Sing to You,* Phoenix Theatre, NY, 1963; Gertrude Eastman-Cuevas, *In the Summer House,* Little Fox Theatre, NY, 1964; Felicia, *Ready When You Are, C.B.,* Brooks Atkinson Theatre, NY, 1964.

Major Barbara, and *Summer of the Seventeeth Doll,* Cincinnati Playhouse in the Park, OH, 1965; Mrs. Goldman, *Suburban Tragedy,* and Shirley, *Princess Rebecca Birnbaum,* both one-acts in *Monopoly,* Stage 73 Theatre, NY, 1965; Laureen, *Malcolm,* Shu-

bert Theatre, NY, 1966; Doris, *The East Wind,* Vivian Beaumont Theatre, Lincoln Center, NY, 1967; Virginia, *Galileo,* Vivian Beaumont Theatre, Lincoln Center, NY, 1967; member of the Yale Repertory Theatre company, 1967-68; Myrtle, *The Seven Descents of Myrtle,* Barrymore Theatre, NY, 1968; *Honor and Offer,* Cincinnati Playhouse in the Park, OH, 1968; Janice Krieger, *A Way of Life,* American National Theatre and Academy (ANTA), NY, 1969; Aase, *Peer Gynt,* Delacorte Theatre, NY, 1969.

Leocadia Begbick, *Mahagonny,* Anderson Theatre, NY, 1970; Catherine Reardon, *And Miss Reardon Drinks a Little,* Morosco Theatre, NY, 1971; Milly, *People Are Living There,* Forum Theatre, NY, 1971; *Oh Glorious Tintinnabulation,* Actors Studio, NY, 1974; Mert, *Mert and Phil,* Vivian Beaumont Theatre, Lincoln Center, NY, 1974; *The Norman Conquests;* Edna Wrath, *The Reason We Eat,* Hartman Theatre, Stamford, CT, 1976; Dede Cooper, *Ladies at the Alamo,* Martin Beck Theatre, NY, 1977; title role, *Miss Margarida's Way,* Public Theatre, NY, then Ambassador Theatre, NY, 1977; *Man Is Man,* Yale Repertory Theatre, New Haven, CT, 1978; Martha, *Who's Afraid of Virginia Woolf?,* Buffalo Studio Arena, Buffalo, NY, 1978; Ruth, *Pirates of Penzance,* Uris (now Gershwin) Theatre, NY, 1982; adapted, co-directed, and performed *Orgasmo Adulto Escapes from the Zoo,* Public Theatre, NY, 1983.

MAJOR TOURS—Elizabeth Dale, *A Sense of Humor,* western U.S. cities, 1983-84.

PRINCIPAL STAGE WORK—Director: *Voices,* St. Clements Theatre, NY, 1978; *Antony and Cleopatra,* Interart Theatre, NY, 1979.

PRINCIPAL FILM APPEARANCES—*Ladybug, Ladybug,* 1964; Blanche, *Bonnie and Clyde,* Warner Brothers, 1967; *Rachel, Rachel,* Warner Brothers, 1968; *Don't Drink the Water,* Avco Embassy, 1969; *Strangers; Watermelon Man,* Columbia, 1970; *I Never Sang for My Father,* Columbia, 1970; *Two People,* Universal, 1973; *For Pete's Sake,* 1974.

PRINCIPAL TELEVISION APPEARANCES—Episodic: *The Gambling Heart,* 1964; *The Nurses; The Verdict Is Yours; Faith for Today.*

Mini-Series: Bess Truman, *Backstairs at the Whitehouse,* NBC, 1979.

PRINCIPAL TELEVISION WORK—Commentator, production assistant, feature producer, and writer, *Today Show,* NBC.

MEMBER: Actors' Equity Association, Screen Actors Guild, American Federation of Radio and Television Artists, Actors Studio.

AWARDS: Best Supporting Actress, 1967, for *Bonnie and Clyde.*

SIDELIGHTS: Estelle Parsons has been selected by Joseph Papp to direct a company of young New York City actors and actresses in Shakespearean roles, in an effort to introduce schoolchildren to theatre.

ADDRESSES: HOME—New York, NY. AGENT—William Morris Agency, 1350 Sixth Avenue, New York, NY 10036.

*   *   *

PATINKIN, Mandy 1952-

PERSONAL: Born November 30, 1952, in Chicago, IL; son of Lester and Doris (Sinton) Patinkin; married Kathryn Grody, June

ESTELLE PARSONS

15, 1980. EDUCATION: Attended University of Kansas, 1970-72; studied for the theatre at the Juilliard School of Music, 1972-74.

VOCATION: Actor.

CAREER: PRINCIPAL STAGE APPEARANCES—With the New York Shakespeare Festival between 1975-81, including such roles as Hotspur, *Henry IV, Part I*, and the title role in *Hamlet*. Performed in *Rebel Women, Leave It to Beaver Is Dead*, and *Savages*, all at the Hudson Guild Theatre, NY; Che, *Evita*, Broadway Theatre, NY, 1979; *The Shadow Box*, Morosco Theatre, NY, 1980; George, *Sunday in the Park with George*, Booth Theatre, NY, 1984; Buddy, "*Follies*" *in Concert*, Avery Fisher Hall, NY, 1985.

PRINCIPAL FILM APPEARANCES—*French Postcards*, Paramount, 1979; *The Big Fix*, Universal, 1979; *The Last Embrace*, United Artists, 1979; *Night of the Juggler*, 1980; *Ragtime*, Paramount, 1981; *Daniel*, 1983; *Yentl*, United Artists, 1983; *Maxie*, Orion, 1985.

PRINCIPAL TELEVISION APPEARANCES—Episodic and Specials: *That Thing on ABC; That Second Thing on ABC; Taxi; Midnight Special*.

Movies: *Charleston*, 1979; *Streets of Gold; Sparrow*.

Plays: Buddy, "*Follies*" *in Concert*, PBS, 1986; George, *Sunday in the Park with George*, cable, 1986.

RECORDINGS: ALBUMS—*Evita*, original cast recording; *Sunday in the Park with George*, original cast recording, RCA Red Seal; "*Follies*" *in Concert*, original cast recording.

MEMBER: Actors' Equity Association, Screen Actors Guild, American Federation of Television and Radio Artists.

AWARDS: Best Actor in a Musical, Antoinette Perry Award, 1980, for *Evita;* Best Actor in a Musical, Antoinette Perry Award nomination, 1985, for *Sunday in the Park with George*.

ADDRESSES: AGENT—Triad, 888 Seventh Avenue, 1602, New York, NY 10019.*

* * *

PAUL, Kent 1936-

PERSONAL: Born December 30, 1936, in Beatrice, NE; son of Otto Emil (manager for a men's clothing store) and Evelyn Louise (systems analyst at a hospital for the mentally retarded; maiden name, Kuhn) Paul. EDUCATION: Harvard, A.B., 1958; graduate, Neighborhood Playhouse School of Theatre, NY, 1961.

VOCATION: Director and producer.

CAREER: STAGE DEBUT—Director, *Mrs. Dally Has a Lover* (one-act version), Cincinnati Playhouse in the Park, 1966. PRINCIPAL STAGE WORK—Director: *Silent Night, Lonely Night* and *A Clearing in the Woods*, Theatre of the Riverside Church, NY, 1966; *Blythe Spirit*, Barter Theatre, Abdingdon, VA, 1967; *The Homecoming*, Center Stage, Baltimore, MD, 1967; *The Square* (U.S. premiere), New York Shakespeare Festival, 1968; *Fireworks* (world premiere), Village South Theatre, NY, 1969; *A Hatful of Rain*, Equity Library Theatre, NY, 1969; *Mary, Mary*, Friars

Dinner Theatre, Minneapolis, MN, 1970; *The False Confessions*, Equity Library Theatre, NY, 1970.

(Assistant director) *Mary Stuart*, Repertory Theatre of Lincoln Center, NY, 1971; *The Lady's Not for Burning*, Long Warf Theatre, New Haven, CT, 1971; *Forty Carats* and *Jacques Brel Is Alive and Well and Living in Paris*, Woodstock Playhouse, Woodstock, NY, 1971; *A Moon for the Misbegotten*, Loeb Drama Center, Cambridge, MA, 1971; *The Hunter*, New York Shakespeare Festival, NY, 1972; *Dear Antoine* (U.S. premiere), Loeb Drama Center, 1972; *Bound East for Cardiff, The Long Voyage Home, In the Zone* and *A Memory of Two Mondays*, all at Cincinnati Playhouse in the Park, 1972; *The Hostage*, Duke University, Durham, NC, 1972; *The Beaux Stratagem*, Stanford University, Stanford, CA, 1973; *Studs Edsel* (New York premiere), Ensemble Studio Theatre, NY, 1974.

The Drapes Come, Theatre at Noon, NY, 1975; *Anna Christie*, Theatre by the Sea, Portsmouth, NH, 1975; *Ah! Wilderness*, Southern Methodist University, Dallas, TX, 1976; *Vanities*, Milwaukee Repertory Theatre, WI, 1976; *Ladyhouse Blues*, A Contemporary Theatre, Seattle, WA, 1976; *Hedda Gabler*, Alliance Theatre, Atlanta, GA, 1976; *Blithe Spirit*, Cohoes Music Hall, Cohoes, NY, 1976; *The Lion in Winter*, Westchester Rockland Regional Theatre, NY, 1977; *Our Town* and *Judas* (first version), both at Pacific Conservatory of the Performing Arts, Santa Maria, CA, 1977; *Judas* (second version) and *The Alcestiade* (U.S. premiere), both at Pacific Conservatory of the Performing Arts Theaterfest, Solvang/Santa Maria, CA, 1978; *The Days Between*, Playhouse Repertory Company, NY, 1979.

Peking Man, Center for Theatre Studies, Columbia University, NY, 1980; *Death of a Salesman*, Theatre by the Sea, Portsmouth, NH, 1980; *Brecht on Brecht*, American Jewish Theatre, 92nd Street YMHA, NY, 1981; *Long Day's Journey into Night*, National Theatre of Iceland, 1981; *Journey to Gdansk* (four short plays, U.S. premiere), Westside Mainstage, NY, 1981; *A Streetcar Named Desire*, Theatre by the Sea, Portsmouth, 1982; *Accounts* (U.S. premiere), Hudson Guild Theatre, NY, 1983; *Tomorrow's Monday* (New York premiere), Circle Repertory Company, NY, 1983; *The Double Bass*, New Theatre of Brooklyn, 1984; *Miss Julie*, Theatre of the Open Eye, NY, 1985; *The Bone Ring* (New York premiere), Theatre of the Open Eye, NY, 1986.

Associate producer, Cincinnati Playhouse in the Park, 1964-66; producer, *The Neighborhood Playhouse at Fifty: A Celebration*, Shubert Theatre, NY, 1978.

PRINCIPAL STAGE APPEARANCES—With the Champlain Shakespeare Festival, Burlington, VT, 1961; with the Great Lakes Shakespeare Festival, Lakewood, OH, 1962 and 1963.

PRINCIPAL FILM WORK—Produced documentary, *Sanford Meisner: The Theatre's Best Kept Secret*, Columbia, 1984.

RELATED CAREER—Adjunct professor of directing, Columbia University, 1980; media panelist, National Endowment for the Humanities, 1983.

MEMBER: Society of Stage Directors and Choreographers. Actors' Equity Association.

ADDRESSES: HOME—155 E. 93rd Street, New York, NY 10128.

PAUL, Steven   1958-

PERSONAL: Born May 16, 1958, in New York, NY; son of Hank and Dorothy (Kosker) Paul.

VOCATION: Actor, producer, writer, and director.

CAREER: STAGE DEBUT—*Lemon Sky,* 1970. PRINCIPAL STAGE APPEARANCES—Paul, *Happy Birthday Wanda June,* Edison Theatre, NY, 1970; *Burning,* Public Theatre, NY, 1976. MAJOR TOURS—*Oliver,* National tour, 1969.

FILM DEBUT—Paul, *Happy Birthday Wanda June,* Columbia, 1970. PRINCIPAL FILM APPEARANCES—*The Kremlin Letter,* Twentieth Century-Fox, 1970; *Falling in Love Again,* 1980; *Slapstick (Of Another Kind),* International Film Marketing, 1984.

PRINCIPAL FILM WORK—Screenwriter, producer, and director, *Falling in Love Again,* 1980; writer (story) *Never Too Young to Die;* producer, *Emanon;* writer (story) *Melissa;* screenwriter, producer, director, *Slapstick (Of Another Kind),* 1984.

TELEVISION DEBUT—Bobby, *A Visiting Angel,* CBS, 1968. PRINCIPAL TELEVISION APPEARANCES—Special: Georgie Gillis, *Whatever Happened to Dobie Gillis?,* CBS, 1977.

Episodic: *Another World; Secret Storm; Kraft Music Hall; A Comedy Tonight; Isis; To Tell the Truth.*

RELATED CAREER—President, Paul Entertainment Company.

MEMBER: Actors' Equity Association, American Federation of Radio and Television Artists, Screen Actors Guild.

SIDELIGHTS: Mr. Paul has plans to finance and produce four films in 1986 through his company, Paul Entertainment.

ADDRESSES: OFFICE—8776 Sunset Blvd., Los Angeles, CA 90069.

*   *   *

PAULSEN, Pat   1927-

PERSONAL: Born July 6, 1927, in South Bend, WA; son of Norman Inge and Irene (Fadden) Paulsen; married Betty Jane Cox; children: Tersea, Montgomery, Justin. EDUCATION: City College of San Francisco. MILITARY: U.S. Marine Corps, 1945-46.

VOCATION: Actor, comedian, writer, and producer.

CAREER: TELEVISION DEBUT—*The Steve Allen Show.* PRINCIPAL TELEVISION APPEARANCES—Series: *The Smothers Brothers Comedy Hour,* CBS, 1967-69, 1970, 1975; *Summer Smothers Brothers Show,* CBS, 1968; *Pat Paulsen's Half a Comedy Hour,* ABC, 1970; *Joey and Dad,* CBS, 1975.

Episodic: *Hollywood Talent Scouts,* CBS, 1965; *Love, American Style; Mouse Factory; Too Close for Comfort; Get Smart; The Wild Wild West; The Tonight Show.*

FILM DEBUT—*Where Were You When The Lights Went Out,* Metro-Goldwyn-Mayer, 1968. PRINCIPAL FILM APPEARANCES—*Harper Valley P.T.A.,* 1978; *Night Patrol,* New World, 1985; *Blood Suckers from Outer Space.*

PRINCIPAL STAGE APPEARANCES—Over a period of fifteen years, has appeared in dinner and other theatres in works ranging from

STEVEN PAUL   **PAT PAULSEN**

Greater Tuna and *Play It Again Sam*, to *The Fantastiks* and *The Odd Couple*.

RELATED CAREER—Owner of the Cherry County Playhouse, Traverse City, MI.

WRITINGS: TELEVISION—Comedy writer for several television shows.

AWARDS: Special Classification of Outstanding Individual Achievement, Emmy, for 1967-68 season.

MEMBER: Actors' Equity Association, Screen Actors Guild, American Federation of Radio and Television Artists; National Kidney Foundation (honorary chairman).

SIDELIGHTS: Pat Paulsen owns the Pat Paulsen Vineyards in Cloverdale, California.

In 1968, he ran for president of the United States.

ADDRESSES: OFFICE—P.O. Box 1547, Lafayette, CA 94549.

*   *   *

PAYMER, David

PERSONAL: Born in Long Island, NY; son of Marv (a pianist and musical director) and Edythe (a travel agent) Paymer. EDUCATION: University of Michigan, B.A.

VOCATION: Actor.

DAVID PAYMER

CAREER: TELEVISION DEBUT—Thief, *Barney Miller*, ABC. PRINCIPAL TELEVISION APPEARANCES—Series: Chino, *Days of Our Lives*, NBC; manager of Hamburger Haven, *Diff'rent Strokes*, NBC, 1978-85; Myslesky, *The Paper Chase*, Showtime; Todd Feldberg, *Cagney and Lacey*, CBS, 1982—.

Episodic: *Happy Days*, ABC; *Hill Street Blues*, NBC; *Taxi*, ABC; *Lou Grant*, CBS.

Movies: *Love, Mary*, CBS, 1985; *Pleasures*, ABC, 1986.

FILM DEBUT—Cabdriver, *The In-Laws*, Warner Brothers, 1979. PRINCIPAL FILM APPEARANCES—Attorney, *Irreconcilable Differences*, Warner Brothers, 1984; editor, *Perfect*, Columbia, 1985; scientist, *Howard the Duck*, Universal, 1986; *The Creeps*, Tri-Star, 1986; exterminator, *Extremities* (upcoming).

PRINCIPAL STAGE APPEARANCES—Sonny Latieri, *Grease*, Royale Theatre, NY.

MAJOR TOURS—Sonny Latieri, *Grease*, U.S. cities.

RELATED CAREER—Acting teacher, Film Actors Workshop, Los Angeles, CA.

ADDRESSES: AGENT—Sumski, Green & Company, 8380 Melrose Avenue, Suite 200, Los Angeles, CA 90069.

*   *   *

PEARSON, Sybille   1937-

PERSONAL: Born Sybille Weiss, January 25, 1937, in Prague, Czechoslavakia; daughter of Frederick (a physician) and Gertrude (a writer; maiden name, Loesener) Weiss; married Frederick Weber, February 18, 1957 (divorced, 1958); married Anthony G. Pearson (an organizational psychologist), August 12, 1966; children: (first marriage) Matthew; (second marriage) Sean. EDUCATION: Attended the High School of the Performing Arts, New York and City College of New York.

VOCATION: Writer.

WRITINGS: PLAYS, PRODUCED—*Sally and Marsha*, Yale Repertory, New Haven, CT, 1980, then Manhattan Theatre Club, NY, 1982; wrote the book (with Richard Maltby composing music and David Shire writing lyrics) *Baby*, Ethel Barrymore Theatre, NY, 1983-84.

MEMBER: Women's Project of the American Place Theatre, League of Professional Women in Theatre, Playwrights Unit of the Manhattan Theatre Club, Dramatists Guild.

AWARDS: Rockefeller Grant, 1981.

ADDRESSES: AGENT—c/o Luis Sanjurjo, International Creative Management, 40 W. 57th Street, New York, NY 10019.

*   *   *

PELIKAN, Lisa

PERSONAL: Daughter of Robert G. (an international economist) and Helen L. (a psychologist; maiden name, Biren) Pelikan. EDUCATION: Attended Juilliard School of Drama.

LISA PELIKAN

VOCATION: Actress.

CAREER: TELEVISION DEBUT—"The Country Girl," *Hallmark Hall of Fame,* NBC, 1974. PRINCIPAL TELEVISION APPEARANCES—Mini-Series: *The Best of Families,* PBS, 1977; Lucy Scanlon, *Studs Lonigan,* NBC, 1979; *The Last Convertible,* NBC, 1979.

Movies: *Valley Forge,* 1975; *I Want to Keep My Baby,* CBS, 1976; *Perfect Gentlemen,* 1978; *True Grit: A Further Adventure,* 1978; *The Women's Room,* 1980; *The Best Little Girl in the World,* 1981; *A Bunny's Tale,* ABC, 1985.

FILM DEBUT—Young Julia, *Julia,* Twentieth Century-Fox, 1977. PRINCIPAL FILM APPEARANCES—Title role, *Jennifer,* Arista, 1978; Anne, *L'Homme en Colere,* Cinevideo, Films Ariane, 1979; Dr. Jo Miller, *The House of God,* United Artists, 1979; Violet, *Swing Shift,* Warner Brothers, 1984.

NEW YORK DEBUT—Wendla, *Spring's Awakening,* Circle Repertory Company, 1975. PRINCIPAL STAGE APPEARANCES—*The Elephant in the House,* Circle Repertory, NY, 1975; *Dynamo,* Syracuse Stage, NY, 1976; *Romeo and Juliet,* Circle in the Square, NY, 1977; *The Butterfingers Angel,* Syracuse Stage, NY, 1978; *The American Clock,* Spoleto Festival, SC, then Harold Clurman Theatre, NY, 1980; *The Diviners,* Circle Repertory, NY, 1980; *The Midnight Visitor,* Shaliko Company, NY, 1981.

AWARDS: Best Actress, International Science Fiction and Horror Film Festival Award, 1979, for *Jennifer.*

ADDRESSES: AGENT—c/o Hildy Gottlieb, International Creative Management, 8899 Beverly Blvd., Los Angeles, CA 90048.

PENN, Sean   1960-

PERSONAL: Born August 17, 1960, in California; son of Leo (a director) and Eileen (an actress; maiden name, Ryan) Penn; married Madonna (a singer and actress), August 17, 1985. EDUCATION: Attended Santa Monica High School; studied professionally at the Loft Studio and with Peggy Feury.

VOCATION: Actor.

CAREER: STAGE DEBUT—*Earthworms,* Group Repertory Theatre, Los Angeles, CA. NEW YORK DEBUT—James, *Heartland,* Century Theatre, 1981, for twenty-nine performances. PRINCIPAL STAGE APPEARANCES—*The Girl on the Via Flaminia,* Gene Dynarski Theatre, Hollywood, California; George "Spanky" Farrell, *Slab Boys,* Playhouse Theatre, NY, 1983.

PRINCIPAL STAGE WORK—Director, *Terrible Jim Fitch,* Group Repertory Theatre, Los Angeles.

FILM DEBUT—Alex Dwyer, *Taps,* Twentieth Century-Fox, 1981. PRINCIPAL FILM APPEARANCES—Jeff Spicoli, *Fast Times at Ridgemont High,* Universal, 1982; Mick O'Brien, *Bad Boys,* Universal, 1983; *Crackers,* Universal, 1984; *Racing with the Moon,* Paramount, 1984; Andrew Daulton Lee, *The Falcon and the Snowman,* Orion, 1985; *At Close Range,* Orion, 1986; *Shanghai Surprise,* 1986.

TELEVISION DEBUT—*Barnaby Jones,* CBS, 1979. PRINCIPAL TELEVISION APPEARANCES—Movies: *Concrete Cowboys,* CBS, 1979; *Hellinger's Law,* 1981; *The Killing of Randy Webster,* 1981.

SIDELIGHTS: Sean Penn worked as an apprentice with the Group

Photograph by Joyce Rudolph. © Orion Pictures Corp.

SEAN PENN

Repertory Theatre in Los Angeles, working backstage in a variety of duties; he also assisted director and actor Pat Hingle.

ADDRESSES: OFFICE—1900 Avenue of the Stars, Suite 2200, Los Angeles, CA. AGENT—Creative Artists Agency, 1888 Century Park E., Los Angeles, CA.

*   *   *

PEPPARD, George   1928-

PERSONAL: Born October 1, 1928, in Detroit, MI; married Helen Davies (divorced); married Elizabeth Ashley (divorced); married Sherry Boucher (divorced); married Alexis Adams (an artist), 1984; children: (first marriage) Bradford, Julie; (second marriage) Christian. EDUCATION: Carnegie Mellon University, B.F.A. MILITARY: U.S. Marine Corps.

VOCATION: Actor and writer.

CAREER: FILM DEBUT—*The Strange One*, Columbia, 1957. PRINCIPAL FILM APPEARANCES—*Pork Chop Hill*, United Artists, 1959; *Home from the Hill*, Metro-Goldwyn-Mayer, 1960; *The Subterraneans*, Metro-Goldwyn-Mayer, 1960; *Breakfast at Tiffany's*, Paramount, 1961; *How the West Was Won*, Metro-Goldwyn-Mayer, 1962; *The Victors*, Columbia, 1963; *The Carpetbaggers*, Paramount, 1964; *The Third Day*, Warner Brothers, 1965; *Operation Crossbow*, Metro-Goldwyn-Mayer, 1965; *The Blue Max*, Twentieth Century-Fox, 1966; *Tobruk*, United Artists, 1967; *Rough Night in Jericho*, Universal, 1967; *P.J.*, Universal, 1968; *What's So Bad About Feeling Good*, Universal, 1968; *House of Cards*, Universal, 1969; *Pendulum*, Columbia, 1969; *Cannon for Cordoba*, United Artists, 1970; *The Executioner*, Columbia, 1970; *One More Train to*

GEORGE PEPPARD

Rob, Universal, 1971; *The Groundstar Conspiracy*, Universal, 1972; *Newman's Law*, Universal, 1974; *Damnation Alley*, Twentieth Century-Fox, 1977; *Five Days from Home*, 1978; *Battle Beyond the Stars*, 1980; *Race to the Yankee Zephyr*, 1981; also, *Your Ticket Is No Longer Valid*.

PRINCIPAL FILM WORK—Director and producer, *Five Days from Home*, 1978.

PRINCIPAL TELEVISION APPEARANCES—Series: Thomas Banacek, *Banacek*, NBC, 1972-74; Dr. Jake Goodwin, *Doctors' Hospital*, NBC, 1975-76; Colonel John "Hannibal" Smith, *The A-Team*, NBC, 1983—.

Movies: *Suspicion*, NBC; *The Bravos*, 1971; *The Sam Sheppard Murder Trial; Crisis in Mid-Air*, 1979; *Torn Between Two Lovers*, 1979.

Episodic: "Bang the Drum Slowly," *U.S. Steel Hour*, CBS, 1956; "Little Moon of Alban," *Hallmark Hall of Fame*, NBC, 1959; *Alfred Hitchcock Presents; Matinee Theatre; Alcoa Hour; Goodyear Television Playhouse; Studio One*.

STAGE DEBUT—Pittsburgh Playhouse. PRINCIPAL STAGE APPEARANCES—*Girls of Summer; The Pleasure of His Company*, NY.

WRITINGS: SCREENPLAYS—*Five Days from Home*, 1978.

SIDELIGHTS: CTFT learned George Peppard worked as a mason, construction laborer, fencing instructor, and radio announcer in Braddock, PA, prior to entering show business.

ADDRESSES: OFFICE—P.O. Box 1643, Beverly Hills, CA 90210.

*   *   *

PERRINE, Valerie   1943-

PERSONAL: Born September 3, 1943, in Galveston, TX; daughter of Kenneth and Renee (McGinley) Perrine. EDUCATION: Studied at the University of Arizona, 1961.

VOCATION: Actress.

CAREER: FILM DEBUT—*Slaughterhouse Five*, Universal, 1972. PRINCIPAL FILM APPEARANCES—*The Last American Hero*, Twentieth Century-Fox, 1973; Mrs. Lenny Bruce, *Lenny*, United Artists, 1974; Carlotta Monterey, *W.C. Fields and Me*, Universal, 1976; *Mr. Billion*, Twentieth Century-Fox, 1977; *The Electric Horseman*, Columbia, 1979; *Can't Stop the Music*, Associated Film Distributors, 1980; *Superman II*, Warner Brothers, 1981; *Agency*, Canadian, 1981; *The Border*, Warner Brothers, 1982; Pamela, *Water*, Handmade Films, 1986.

PRINCIPAL TELEVISION APPEARANCES—Movies: *The Couple Takes a Wife*, 1972; *Ziegfeld: The Man and His Women*, 1978; *When Your Lover Leaves*.

AWARDS: Best Actress from the Cannes Film Festival, Best Supporting Actress from the New York Film Critics Circle, Actress of the Year Award from the United Motion Pictures Association, and Most Promising Newcomer to Leading Film Roles from the British Academy of Motion Picture Arts and Sciences, all 1975, for *Lenny*.

MEMBER: Screen Actors Guild, American Federation of Television and Radio Artists.

SIDELIGHTS: Perrine worked as a show girl in Las Vegas prior to her film debut.

ADDRESSES: AGENT—Agency for the Performing Arts, 9000 Sunset Blvd., Suite 315, Los Angeles, CA 90069.*

*   *   *

PESCOW, Donna

PERSONAL: Born March 24, in Brooklyn, NY. EDUCATION: Studied for the theatre at the American Academy of Dramatic Arts.

VOCATION: Actress.

CAREER: STAGE DEBUT—Touring production of Ah! Wilderness, 1975.

FILM DEBUT—Annette, Saturday Night Fever, Paramount, 1977.

PRINCIPAL TELEVISION APPEARANCES—Series: title role, Angie, ABC; Lynn, All My Children, ABC, 1984.

Movie: Rainbow, 1984.

ADDRESSES: AGENT—Kohner-Levy Agency, 9169 Sunset Blvd., Los Angeles, CA 90069.*

*   *   *

PETERS, Bernadette   1948-

PERSONAL: Born Bernadette Lazzara, February 28, 1948, in Ozone Park, Long Island, NY; daughter of Peter and Marguerite (Maltese) Lazzara. EDUCATION: Attended Quintano School for Young Professionals.

VOCATION: Actress.

CAREER: STAGE DEBUT—Tessie, The Most Happy Fella, City Center, NY, 1959. PRINCIPAL STAGE APPEARANCES—Cinderella, The Penny Friend, Stage 73, NY, 1966; understudy, The Girl in the Freudian Slip, Booth Theatre, NY, 1967; Bettina, Johnny No-Trump, Cort Theatre, NY, 1967; Alice, Curley McDimple, Bert Wheeler Theatre, NY, 1967; Josie Cohan, George M!, Palace Theatre, NY, 1968; Ruby, Dames at Sea, Bouwerie Lane Theatre, NY, 1968; Gelsomin, La Strada, Lunt-Fontanne Theatre, NY, 1969; Consuelo, Nevertheless They Laugh, Lambs Club, NY, 1971; Hildy, On the Town, Imperial Theatre, NY, 1971; Dorine, Tartuffe, Walnut Street Theatre, Philadelphia, PA, 1972; Mabel Normand, Mack and Mable, Majestic Theatre, NY, 1974; Sally and Marsha, Manhattan Theatre Club, NY, 1982; Sunday in the Park with George, Booth Theatre, NY, 1984-85; Song and Dance, Royale Theatre, 1985-86.

PRINCIPAL FILM APPEARANCES—The Longest Yard, Paramount, 1974; Silent Movie, Twentieth Century-Fox, 1976; Vigilante Force, United Artists, 1976; W.C. Fields and Me, Universal, 1976; The Jerk, Universal, 1979; Tulips, 1980; Pennies from Heaven, United Artists, 1981; Heartbeeps, Universal, 1981; Annie, Columbia, 1982.

PRINCIPAL TELEVISION APPEARANCES—Series: Charlotte Drake, All's Fair, CBS, 1976-77.

Guest: The Carol Burnett Show, CBS, 1970-75.

Specials: The Martian Chronicles, 1980; George M!; Once Upon a Mattress.

RECORDINGS: ALBUMS—Bernadette Peters, MCA, 1980; Now Playing, MCA, 1981; Sunday in the Park with George, RCA, 1984; Song and Dance, 1986.

AWARDS: Drama Desk Award, 1968, for Dames at Sea; Theatre World Award, 1968, for George M!; Antoinette Perry Award nominations, 1971, for On the Town and 1974, for Mack and Mable; Best Actress, Golden Globe Award, 1981, for Pennies from Heaven; Antoinette Perry Award nomination, 1985, for Sunday in the Park with George; Best Actress in a Musical, Antoinette Perry Award, 1986, for Song and Dance.

ADDRESSES: AGENT—Agency for the Performing Arts, 9000 Sunset Blvd., Los Angeles, CA 90069.

*   *   *

PETERS, Jon   1947-

PERSONAL: Born 1947, in Van Nuys, CA.

VOCATION: Producer.

CAREER: PRINCIPAL FILM WORK—Producer: A Star Is Born, Warner Brothers, 1976; The Eyes of Laura Mars, Columbia, 1978; The Main Event, Warner Brothers, 1979; Die Laughing, Warner Brothers, 1980; Caddyshack, Warner Brothers, 1980; Six Weeks, Universal, 1982; D.C. Cab, Universal, 1983; Visionquest, 1984; The Color Purple, Universal, 1985.

RELATED CAREER—Formed Jon Peters Organization, 1980; joined with Peter Guber and Neil Bogart to form the Boardwalk Company.

SIDELIGHTS: Peters owned and operated a hairdressing business prior to producing films.

ADDRESSES: OFFICE—Guber-Peters, 4000 Warner Blvd., Burbank, CA 90024.*

*   *   *

PETERSEN, William L.

BRIEF ENTRY: Born in Evanston, IL. Actor. Described as the all-American boy with an angry violence lurking beneath the surface, William Petersen has impressed critics who praise his ability to bring out the darker side of a character and still hold the sympathy of an audience. His performances as Stanley Kowalski in A Streetcar Named Desire and Jack Henry Abbott in In the Belly of the Beast have established for him an important reputation in American theatre. Petersen is one of the new breed of actors who is committed to both stage and screen. His films include To Live and Die in L.A. and The Red Dragon. The actor is one of the founding members of Innisfere, a theatre company that was formed during the Chicago theatre renaissance of the seventies. When Innisfere disbanded, some of its members, including Petersen, formed the Remains Theatre, which became the avant-garde theatre of the renaissance and still continues to produce plays today. He is also a founding member of a Chicago-based film development company, High Horse, which recently bought rights to the novel, The Soloist.*

PFEIFFER, Michelle

BRIEF ENTRY: Reared in Santa Ana, CA. Actress. The daughter of a heating and air conditioning executive and his wife, Michelle Pfeiffer attended Fountain Valley High School. She enrolled at Golden West College but soon left it to attend Whitley College for court reporting. When that didn't work out, Pfeiffer found herself working in a supermarket. At the urging of her friends, she entered a beauty contest and, although she didn't win, she was persuaded by one judge to join an acting class. As a result, Pfeiffer was cast in two short-lived television series, *Delta House* and *B.A.D. Cats,* in addition to numerous episodic appearances. She had roles in two feature films, *Charlie Chan and the Curse of the Dragon* and *Hollywood Nights,* but her big break came when she was cast as the ingenue in the film *Grease II.* Since then she has played a wide variety of characters from Al Pacino's cocaine addicted wife in *Scarface* to a maiden who turns into a hawk by day in *Ladyhawke.* She has most recently been seen in the spy thriller *Into the Night,* co-starring Jeff Goldblum.*

*   *   *

PICKLES, Christina

PERSONAL: Born in Great Britain; daughter of Wilfred (an actor) Pickles. EDUCATION: Trained for the stage at the Royal Academy of Dramatic Art.

VOCATION: Actress

CAREER: PRINCIPAL STAGE APPEARANCES—With the Association of Producing Artists (A.P.A.) Repertory Company, NY: *You Can't Take It with You, War and Peace, A School for Scandal,* and *Pantegleize; Sherlock Holmes,* Royal Shakespeare Company, NY; *Cloud 9,* Los Angeles, CA.

Also appeared at the Long Wharf Theatre, New Haven, CT; American Shakespeare Festival, Stratford, CT; Williamstown Theatre Festival, MA; Manhattan Theatre Club, NY.

PRINCIPAL TELEVISION APPEARANCES—Helen Rosenthal, *St. Elsewhere,* NBC, 1983—.

AWARDS: Emmy Award nomination, 1983, for *St. Elsewhere.*

ADDRESSES: AGENT—J. Michael Bloom, Ltd., 400 Madison Avenue, New York, NY 10017 or 9200 Sunset Blvd., Los Angeles, CA 90069.

*   *   *

PIERCE, Paula Kay   1942-

PERSONAL: Born Paula Kay Hasslocher, October 1, 1942 in Rio de Janeiro; daughter of Paulo Germano (a diplomat) and Olga (a dancer, singer, and teacher; maiden name, Balabanoff) Hasslocher; married George Adams Pierce, 1964 (divorced, 1969); married Jan Barry Crumb (a writer), 1970; children: (second marriage) Chris, Nikolai. EDUCATION: Fairleigh Dickinson University, B.A., 1964; Hunter College, M.A., theatre, 1968; City University of New York, Ph.D., theatre, 1972.

VOCATION: Director and producer.

CAREER: PRINCIPAL STAGE WORK—Director: *Antigone,* Hunter

PAULA KAY PIERCE

College, 1968; various children's plays, Brooklyn College, 1971; *Munro,* Brooklyn College, 1971; *Warplay,* Brooklyn College, 1972; *Winning Hearts and Minds,* New York Shakespeare Festival, Anspacher Theatre, NY, 1972; *A Slight Ache,* AIM Theatre, NY, 1974; *The Dragon,* Big Apple Theatre parks tour, Manhattan, Brooklyn, Staten Island, 1974; *April Off Atlantic Avenue,* Big Apple Theatre, NY, 1975; *American Fourth of July,* Lincoln Center Out-of-Doors series, NY, 1975; *The Merchant of Venice,* Big Apple Theatre, NY, 1976; *It's Only Temporary,* Gate Theatre, NY; *The Hot L Baltimore* and *The Three Sisters,* both at Bell & Barter Theatre, NY, 1977; *The Coach,* Gene Frankel Theatre, NY, 1979.

The following were all directed by Pierce and produced by the Eccentric Circles Theatre: *96 A,* St. Malachy's, NY, 1980; *Nirvana Manor,* Actor's Outlet, NY, 1981; *Burnscape,* Actor's Outlet, NY, 1983; *Love Games,* Eighteenth Street Playhouse, NY, 1984; *Dancing to Dover* and *Dance of the Mayfly,* both at Eighteenth Street Playhouse, NY, 1985.

Also directed: *Oh, Baby!,* Actor's Outlet, NY, 1983; *Rachel's Gifts,* South Street Theatre, NY, 1985.

RELATED CAREER—Founder, artistic director, producer, and manager, Eccentric Circles Theatre, NY, 1980—present; theatre critic, feature writer, *Educational Theatre Journal, Backstage, Show Business, NY Daily Mirror;* narrator for television documentaries; theatre critic on cable television.

MEMBER: Society of Stage Directors and Choreographers, Dramatists Guild.

SIDELIGHTS: As the founder of Eccentric Circles Theatre, Ms. Pierce states that it is a non-profit company dedicated to new

American plays written by women, directed by women, with emphasis on strong performing roles for women, especially over the age of thirty-five.

ADDRESSES: HOME—Montclair, NJ. OFFICE—400 W. 43rd Street, Suite 4N, New York, NY 10036.

*   *   *

PISCOPO, Joe 1951-

PERSONAL: Full name, Joseph Charles Piscopo; born June 17, 1951, in Passaic, NJ; son of Joseph and Edith I. (LaMagna) Piscopo; married Nancy Jones, December 1, 1973 (divorced); children: Joseph.

VOCATION: Comedian and actor.

CAREER: PRINCIPAL TELEVISION APPEARANCES—Series: *Saturday Night Live,* NBC, 1980-84.

Specials: *Comic Relief,* HBO, 1986.

PRINCIPAL STAGE APPEARANCES—Numerous appearances in regional theatres and dinner theatres in the South and Northeast.

PRINCIPAL FILM APPEARANCES—*Johnny Dangerously,* 1984; *Wise Guys,* Metro-Goldwyn-Mayer, 1986.

PRINCIPAL RADIO APPEARANCES—*Joe Piscopo at Large,* 1983—.

NIGHT CLUB APPEARANCES—Stand up comic, improvisation and comic strip clubs, NY, 1976-80.

WRITINGS: BOOKS—*The Piscopo Tapes.*

AWARDS: Father of the Year, National Father's Day Committee, 1983.

ADDRESSES: OFFICE—c/o NBC Press Relations, 30 Rockefeller Plaza, New York, NY 10020.*

*   *   *

PLACE, Mary Kay 1947-

PERSONAL: Born September, 1947, in Tulsa, OK; daughter of Bradley E. Place. EDUCATION: University of Tulsa, 1969.

VOCATION: Actress and singer.

CAREER: PRINCIPAL FILM APPEARANCES—*Bound for Glory,* United Artists, 1977; *New York, New York,* United Artists, 1977; *More American Graffiti,* Universal, 1979; *Starting Over,* Paramount, 1979; *Private Benjamin,* Warner Brothers, 1980; *Modern Problems,* Twentieth Century-Fox, 1981; *Waltz Across Texas,* Jastrow-Archer Productions, 1982; Meg, *The Big Chill,* Columbia, 1983; voice over, *Terms of Endearment,* Paramount, 1983; mother, *Smooth Talk,* Spectrafilms, 1986.

PRINCIPAL TELEVISION APPEARANCES—Series: Loretta Haggers, *Mary Hartman, Mary Hartman* (later called *Fernwood Forever),* syndication, 1976-77.

Episodic: *All in the Family,* CBS; *The Mary Tyler Moore Show,* CBS; Loretta Haggers, *Fernwood 2-Nite,* syndication, 1977.

Guest: *Saturday Night Live,* NBC; *The Tonight Show with Johnny Carson,* NBC; *The John Denver Special;* others.

PRINCIPAL STAGE APPEARANCES—Cary Davis, *Juno's Swans,* Second Stage Theatre, NY, 1985.

RECORDINGS: ALBUMS—*New York, New York,* original soundtrack recording, United Artists; *Aimin' to Please;* others.

AWARDS: Outstanding Continuing Performance by a Supporting Actress in a Comedy Series, Emmy Award, 1976-77, for *Mary Hartman, Mary Hartman.*

ADDRESSES: AGENT—Century Artists, 9744 Wilshire Blvd., Suite 206, Beverly Hills, CA 90212.*

*   *   *

PONTI, Carlo 1913-

PERSONAL: Born December 11, 1913, in Milan, Italy; married second wife, Sophia Loren (an actress), by proxy in 1957 and again in 1966; children: Carlo, Jr., Eduardo. EDUCATION: University of Milan, 1934.

VOCATION: Film producer.

CAREER: PRINCIPAL FILM WORK—*Little Old World,* in Milan; produced "Toto" pictures, i.e. *Toto Horsehunting,* Lux Film, Rome; *A Dog's Life; The Knight Has Arrived; The Outlaw; Romanticism; Sensuality; Europe 1951; Toto in Color; The Three Corsairs; An American in Rome; The Last Lover.*

Anna, Archway-Lux, 1951; *The White Slave Trade,* Excelsa, Ponti-DiLaurentiis, 1952; *A Day in Court,* Excelsa/Documento, 1953; *Attila, the Hun,* Archway-Lux, 1953; *Gold of Naples* (also known as *Every Day's a Holiday),* Gala Films, 1954; *The Woman of the River,* Columbia, 1954; *The Miller's Wife,* Titanus, 1955; *War and Peace,* Paramount, 1956; *The Black Orchid,* Paramount, 1959; *That Kind of Woman,* Paramount, 1959; *Heller in Pink Tights,* Paramount, 1960; *A Breath of Scandal,* Paramount, 1960; *Two Women,* Gala Films, 1961; *Boccaccio '70,* Embassy/Twentieth Century-Fox, 1961; *The Condemned of Altona,* Twentieth Century-Fox, 1962; *Yesterday, Today and Tomorrow,* Embassy/Paramount, 1963; *Marriage, Italian Style,* Embassy/Paramount, 1964; *Operation Crossbow,* Metro-Goldwyn-Mayer, 1965; *Lady L,* Metro-Goldwyn-Mayer, 1965; *Cinderella, Italian Style* (also known as *More Than a Miracle),* Metro-Goldwyn-Mayer, 1967; *Ghosts, Italian Style* (also known as *Three Ghosts),* Metro-Goldwyn-Mayer, 1967; *The Girl and the General,* Metro-Goldwyn-Mayer, 1967; *Sunflower,* Avco Embassy, 1969; *The Best House in London,* Metro-Goldwyn-Mayer, 1969.

The Priest's Wife, Warner Brothers, 1970; *Lady Liberty,* Warner Brothers, 1971; *White Sister,* Columbia/Warner Brothers, 1971; *The Voyage,* United Artists/Champion, 1973; *What?* Avco Embassy, 1973; *Verdict,* Les Films Concordia, 1974; *Andy Warhol's Frankenstein,* Bryanston, 1974; *The Passenger,* United Artists/ Metro-Goldwyn-Mayer, 1975; *The Cassandra Crossing,* Avco Embassy, 1977; *A Special Day,* Cinema 5, 1977; others.

ADDRESSES: OFFICE—One Piazza D'Aracoeli, Roma, Italy.*

PORTER, Eric   1928-

PERSONAL: Born April 8, 1928, in London, England; son of Richard John and Phoebe Elizabeth (Spall) Porter. EDUCATION: Attended elementary school in London, England; attended Wimbledon Technical College. MILITARY: Royal Air Force, 1946-47.

VOCATION: Actor.

CAREER: STAGE DEBUT—*Twelfth Night,* Shakespeare Memorial Theatre Company, Cambridge, England, 1945. LONDON DEBUT—Dunois' page, *Saint Joan,* King's Theatre, Hammersmith, 1946. NEW YORK DEBUT—Burgomaster, *The Visit,* Lunt-Fontanne Theatre, 1958. PRINCIPAL STAGE APPEARANCES—(All London unless otherwise noted) Member of the Shakespeare Memorial Theatre Company, Stratford-upon-Avon, for one season, 1945; joined the Travelling Repertory Theatre Company, 1945; Dillan, *In Time to Come,* King's Theatre, Hammersmith, 1946; played two seasons with Sir Barry Jackson's Company at Birmingham Repertory Theatre, 1948-50.

Jones, *The Silver Box* and Messenger, *Thor, with Angels,* both Lyric Theatre, Hammersmith, 1951; Solyoni, *The Three Sisters,* Aldwych Theatre, 1951; Jeff Smith, *The Same Sky* and Bolingbroke, *Richard III,* both Lyric Theatre, Hammersmith, 1952; Boy, *Under the Sycamore,* Aldwych Theatre, 1952; Fainall, *The Way of the World* and Reynault, *Venice Preserv'd,* both Lyric Theatre, Hammersmith, 1953; Becket, *Murder in the Cathedral* and Father Browne, *The Living Room,* both Bristol Old Vic, 1954. With the Old Vic Company: Banquo, *Macbeth,* 1955; Navarre, *Love's Labour's Lost,* 1955; Christopher Sly, *The Taming of the Shrew,* 1955; Bolingbroke, *Richard II,* 1955; Jacques, *As You Like It,* 1955; King Henry, *Henry IV, Parts I and II,* 1955. With the Bristol Old Vic Company: Horace Van der Gelder, *The Matchmaker,* 1956; title role, *Uncle Vanya,* 1956; title role, *Volpone,* 1956; title role, *King Lear,* 1956. Appeared as Vadim Romanoff, *Romanoff and Juliet,* Picadilly Theatre, 1956; Herr Compass, *A Man of Distinction,* Edinburgh Festival, then Princess Theatre, London, 1957; Burgomaster, *Time and Again* (re-titled *The Visit*), Theatre Royal, Brighton, 1957; Rosmer, *Rosmersholm,* Royal Court Theatre, 1959, then Comedy Theatre, 1960.

With the Shakespeare Memorial Theatre, Stratford-upon-Avon (later renamed Royal Shakespeare Company): Malvolio, *Twelfth Night,* 1960; Duke of Milan, *The Two Gentlemen of Verona,* 1960; Ulysses, *Troilus and Cressida,* 1960; Leontes, *The Winter's Tale,* 1960; Ferdinand, *The Duchess of Malfi,* 1960; Lord Chamberlain, *Ondine,* 1960; Duke of Buckingham, *Richard III,* 1961; Thomas Becket, *Becket,* then at the Globe Theatre, London, 1961; title role, *Macbeth,* 1962; Iachimo, *Cymbeline,* 1962; Pope Pius XII, *The Representative,* 1963; Bolingbroke, *Richard II,* 1964; King Henry, *Henry IV, Parts I and II,* 1964; Chorus, *Henry V,* 1964; Earl of Richmond, *Richard III,* 1964; Barabas, *The Jew of Malta,* 1965; Shylock, *The Merchant of Venice,* 1965; Chorus, *Henry V,* 1965; Ossip, *The Government Inspector,* 1966; King Lear, *King Lear,* 1968; title role, *Dr. Faustus,* 1968.

Paul Thomsen, *My Little Boy, My Big Girl,* Fortune Theatre, 1969; title role, *The Protagonist,* Gardner Center, Brighton, 1971; Mr. Darling/Captain Hook, *Peter Pan,* Gardner Center, Brighton, 1971; Malvolio, *Twelfth Night,* St. George's Theatre, Islington, 1976.

MAJOR TOURS—With Sir Donald Wolfit's Company, Britain and Canada, 1947-48; Burgomaster, *The Visit,* England, 1957; Jansen, *The Coast of Coromandel,* England, 1959; title role, *Dr. Faustus,* Royal Shakespeare Company tour of U.S., 1969.

PRINCIPAL FILM APPEARANCES—*The Fall of the Roman Empire,* Paramount, 1964; *The Pumpkin Eater,* Royal International, 1964; *The Heroes of Telemark,* Columbia, 1965; *Kaleidoscope,* Warner Brothers, 1966; *The Lost Continent,* Twentieth Century-Fox, 1968; *Hands of the Ripper,* 1971; *Nicholas and Alexandra,* Columbia, 1971; *Anthony and Cleopatra,* 1973; *The Day of the Jackal,* Universal, 1973; *Hitler: The Last Ten Days,* 1973; *The Belstone Fox,* 1973; *Callan,* 1974; *Hennessy,* American International, 1975; *The Thirty-Nine Steps,* 1978.

TELEVISION DEBUT—Dunois' page, *Saint Joan,* 1945. PRINCIPAL TELEVISION APPEARANCES—(British television) Title role, *Cyrano de Bergerac;* Soames Forsyte, *The Forsyte Saga;* Alanbrook, *Churchill and the Generals;* Polonius, *Hamlet; Separate Tables; The Statue and the Rose; Why Didn't They Ask Evans?; Tolstoy; Macbeth 1970; When We Were Married; The Glittering Prizes; The Canal Children; The Winslow Boy; Anna Karenina; The Crucible; The Sinbin; Neville Chamberlain; Churchill: The Wilderness Years; A Shilling Life; Little Lord Fauntleroy; The Jewel in the Crown.*

AWARDS: Best Actor, *Evening Standard* Drama Award, 1959, for *Rosmersholm;* Television Actor of the Year, Guild of Television Producers and Directors Award, 1967.

ADDRESSES: AGENT—London Management Ltd., 235-241 Regent Street, London W1, England.*

*   *   *

POTTER, Dennis   1935-

PERSONAL: Born May 17, 1935, in Forest of Dean, Gloucester, England; son of Walter Edward and Margaret Constance (Wale) Potter; married Margaret Morgan. EDUCATION: Attended New College, Oxford University.

VOCATION: Writer.

WRITINGS: PLAYS, PRODUCED—*Vote, Vote, Vote for Nigel Barton,* 1968; *Son of Man,* 1969; *Only Make Believe,* 1974; *Brimstone and Treacle,* 1977; *Sufficient Carbohydrate,* Hampstead Theatre, London, 1983.

TELEVISION MINI-SERIES—*Pennies from Heaven,* BBC, 1978; *Blue Remembered Hills,* BBC, 1979; *Blade on the Feather, Rain on the Roof,* and *Cream in My Coffee* (trilogy), ITV, 1980; also, *Traitor; Paper Roses.*

SERIES—*Casanova.*

TELEPLAYS—*The Confidence Courses,* BBC; *Stand Up Nigel Barton,* BBC, 1965; *Vote, Vote, Vote for Nigel Barton,* BBC, 1966; *Almost Cinderella,* BBC, 1966; *Son of Man,* 1969; *Lay Down Your Arms,* 1970; *Follow the Yellow Brick Road,* BBC, 1972; *Only Make Believe,* BBC, 1973; *Joe's Ark,* BBC, 1974; *Schmoedipus,* BBC, 1974; *Late Call,* BBC, 1975; *Double Dare,* BBC, 1976; *Where Adam Stood,* BBC, 1976; *Brimstone and Treacle,* BBC, 1976.

SCREENPLAYS—*Pennies from Heaven,* United Artists, 1981; *Gorky Park,* Orion, 1983; *Dreamchild,* Universal, 1985.

NOVELS—*The Glittering Coffin,* 1960; *The Changing Forest,* 1962; *Hide and Seek,* 1973.

RELATED CAREER—Television critic, *The Sunday Times,* from 1976.

MEMBER: Writers Guild of Great Britain.

AWARDS: Writer of the Year, Writers Guild Award, 1966; Best Writer, British Academy of Film and Television Arts, 1980, for *Blue Remembered Hills.*

ADDRESSES: HOME—Morecambe Lodge, Duxmere, Ross-on-Wye, Herefordshire, England. OFFICE—c/o Writers Guild of Great Britain, 430 Edgware Road, London W2, England.*

* * *

POTTS, Nancy

VOCATION: Costume designer.

CAREER: FIRST NEW YORK STAGE WORK—Costume design, *Right You Are (If You Think You Are),* Phoenix Theatre, 1964. FIRST LONDON STAGE WORK—Costume design, *Hair,* Shaftsbury Theatre, 1968. PRINCIPAL STAGE WORK—Costume designer: *The Tavern,* NY, 1964; *Scapin,* NY, 1964; *Impromptu at Versailles,* NY, 1964; *The Lower Depths,* NY, 1964; *Man and Superman,* NY, 1964; *War and Peace,* NY, 1965; *Judith,* NY, 1965; *You Can't Take It with You,* NY, 1965; *The School for Scandal,* NY, 1966; *We Comrades Three,* NY, 1966; *The Wild Duck,* NY, 1967; *Pantagleize,* NY, 1967; *The Show-Off,* NY, 1967; *Exit the King,* NY, 1968; *The Cherry Orchard,* NY, 1968; *The Cocktail Party,* NY, 1968; *The Misanthrope,* NY, 1968; *Horseman, Pass By,* NY, 1969; *Cock-a-Doodle Dandy,* NY, 1969; *Hamlet,* NY, 1969; *La Strada,* NY, 1969.

Harvey, NY, 1970; *The Criminals,* NY, 1970; *The Persians,* NY, 1970; *Early Morning,* NY, 1970; *The School for Wives,* NY, 1971; *The Grass Harp,* NY, 1971; *The Selling of the President,* NY, 1972; *Don Juan,* NY, 1972; *Rainbow,* NY, 1972; *Medea,* NY, 1973; *Detective Story,* Philadelphia, 1973; *A Streetcar Named Desire,* NY, 1973; *Veronica's Room,* NY, 1973; *Chemin de Fer,* NY, 1973; *Holiday,* NY, 1973; *Who's Who in Hell,* NY, 1974; *The Rules of the Game,* NY, 1974; *Edward II,* NY, 1975; *The Time of Your Life,* NY, 1975; *Porgy and Bess,* NY, 1976; *The New York Idea,* NY, 1977; *The Three Sisters,* NY, 1977; *The Play's the Thing,* NY, 1978; *King Lear,* NY, 1978; *The Most Happy Fella,* NY, 1979; *I Ought to Be in Pictures,* NY, 1979.

The Philadelphia Story, Vivian Beaumont Theatre, NY, 1980-81; *Children of a Lesser God,* Longacre Theatre, NY, 1980-82; *Einstein and the Polar Bear,* Cort Theatre, NY, 1981; *Lolita,* Brooks Atkinson Theatre, NY, 1981; *The Curse of An Aching Heart,* Little Theatre, NY, 1982; *Do Patent Leather Shoes Really Reflect Up?,* Alvin Theatre, NY, 1982; *Hedda Gabler,* Hartman Theatre, Stamford, CT, 1982; *You Can't Take It with You,* Plymouth Theatre, 1983; *Porgy and Bess,* Radio City Music Hall, 1983.

MAJOR TOURS—*Children of a Lesser God,* national, 1980-83; *I Ought to Be in Pictures,* national, 1980-81.

ADDRESSES: OFFICE—c/o Theatrical Costume Worker's Union, 218 W. 40th Street, New York, NY 10018.*

* * *

POUL, Alan Mark 1954-

PERSONAL: Surname pronounced "pool"; born May 1, 1954, in Philadelphia, PA.

VOCATION: Producer, writer, and lyricist.

CAREER: PRINCIPAL FILM WORK—Associate producer, *Mishima,* premiere at Cannes Film Festival, 1985; producer, *Tight Connection (Has Anybody Seen My Love),* Bob Dylan rock video, 1985; associate producer, *Light of Day* (upcoming); lyricist, *Round Eyes* (upcoming), Warner Brothers, 1986.

PRINCIPAL STAGE WORK—Lyricist, *Vagabond Stars,* Berkshire Theatre Festival, 1978, Jewish Repertory Theatre, 1982; lyricist, *Ladies in Waiting,* Civic Theatre, Chicago, 1982; director, lyricist, *New Tunes,* Manhattan Theatre Club, NY, 1983; story, book, *Casanova '85,* Seibu Theatre, Japan, 1985; director, text, Japanese section, *Robert Wilson's the Civil warS,* premiere Austin, TX, 1986; lyricist, *Orphan Train,* currently in development.

PRINCIPAL TELEVISION WORK—Lyricist, *The Dollmaker,* ABC, 1984.

RELATED CAREER—Visiting professor of Japanese Cinema, Yale University, 1981; news correspondent, Tokyo Broadcasting System, 1983.

ADDRESSES: HOME—New York, NY. AGENT—Luis Sanjurjo, International Creative Management, 40 W. 57th Street, New York, NY 10019.

* * *

PREMINGER, Otto 1906-1986

PERSONAL: Born December 5, 1906, in Vienna, Austria; died of cancer in New York, NY, April 23, 1986; son of Marc (a lawyer) and Josefa Preminger; married Marion Mill (marriage ended); married Mary Gardner (divorced, 1960); married Patricia Hope Bryce, March, 1960; children: (third marriage) Victoria and Mark (twins); Erik Kirkland (son of Gypsy Rose Lee). EDUCATION: L.L.D., University of Vienna.

VOCATION: Director, producer, actor, and lawyer.

CAREER: DEBUT—Lysander, *A Midsummer Night's Dream,* Max Reinhardt Company, Vienna, Austria, 1930. PRINCIPAL STAGE APPEARANCES—With Max Reinhardt troupe, Theatre-in-Josefstadt, Vienna.

PRINCIPAL STAGE WORK—Director, with Max Reinhardt troupe, Vienna, 1935-40; director, *Margin for Error,* Broadway production, NY, 1939; producer and director, *The Moon Is Blue,* Henry Miller's Theatre, NY, 1951; director, *Critic's Choice,* Morosco Theatre, NY, 1960; also, director, *Full Circle,* Broadway production; director, *A Midsummer Night's Dream,* Broadway production; *Outward Bound,* Broadway production.

PRINCIPAL FILM APPEARANCES—Major Diessen, *The Pied Piper,* Twentieth Century-Fox, 1942; *They Got Me Covered,* Paramount, 1943; *Margin for Error,* 1943; Oberst von Scherbach, *Stalag 17,* Paramount, 1953; *Hollywood on Trial,* 1977.

PRINCIPAL FILM WORK—Director (and producer as indicated): *Die Grosse Liebe,* 1932; *Under Your Spell,* Twentieth Century-Fox, 1936; *Danger—Love at Work,* Twentieth Century-Fox, 1937; *Margin for Error,* Twentieth Century-Fox, 1943; *In the Meantime, Darling,* Twentieth Century-Fox, 1944; and producer, *Laura,* Twentieth Century-Fox, 1944; *A Royal Scandal,* Twentieth Century-Fox, 1945; and producer, *Fallen Angel*, Twentieth Century-Fox, 1945; *Centennial Summer*, Twentieth Century-Fox, 1946; *Forever Amber*, Twentieth Century-Fox, 1947; *Daisy Kenyon*, Twentieth Century-Fox, 1947; and producer, *That Lady in Ermine* (replacing Ernst Lubitsch), Twentieth Century-Fox, 1948; *The Fan*, Twentieth Century-Fox, 1949; *Whirlpool*, Twentieth Century-Fox, 1949.

Where the Sidewalk Ends, Twentieth Century-Fox, 1950; *The Thirteenth Letter*, Twentieth Century-Fox, 1951; *Angel Face*, RKO, 1952; and producer, *The Moon Is Blue*, United Artists, 1953; *River of No Return*, Twentieth Century-Fox, 1954; and producer, *Carmen Jones*, Twentieth Century-Fox, 1954; *The Court Martial of Billy Mitchell*, Warner Brothers, 1955; and producer, *The Man with the Golden Arm*, United Artists, 1956; and producer, *Saint Joan*, United Artists, 1957; *Bonjour Tristesse*, Columbia, 1958; and producer, *Porgy and Bess* (replacing Rouben Mamoulian), Columbia, 1959; and producer, *Anatomy of a Murder*, Columbia, 1959; and producer, *Exodus*, United Artists, 1960; *Advise and Consent*, Columbia, 1962; *The Cardinal*, Columbia, 1963; and producer, *In Harm's Way*, Paramount, 1965; *Bunny Lake Is Missing*, Columbia, 1965; and producer, *Hurry Sundown*, Paramount, 1967; *Skidoo*, Paramount, 1968; and producer, *Tell Me That You Love Me, Junie Moon*, Paramount, 1970; and producer, *Such Good Friends*, Paramount, 1971; *Rosebud*, United Artists, 1975; and producer, *The Human Factor*, Bryanston, 1975.

WRITINGS: AUTOBIOGRAPHY—*Preminger*, Doubleday, 1977.

AWARDS: Best Director, Academy Award nominations, 1944, for *Laura* and 1963, for *The Cardinal;* Best Picture (as producer), Academy Award nomination, 1959, for *Anatomy of a Murder.**

*   *   *

PRESCOTT, Ken   1948-

PERSONAL: Born Ken Ploss, December 28, 1948, in Omaha, NE; son of Kenneth H. (a business executive) and Marie E. (Broszies) Ploss; married Ginger Prince (an actress), July 7, 1975. EDUCATION: University of Omaha, two years; University of Utah, two years; studied dance with the Joffrey Ballet, Luigi, Phil Black, Matt Mattox, Bob Audy, David Howard, and Martha Graham. MILITARY: U.S. Air Force.

VOCATION: Actor, dancer, choreographer, and director.

CAREER: PRINCIPAL STAGE APPEARANCES—Broadway productions: *No No Nanette; Lorelei;* understudy, *Follies;* Billy Lawlor, *42nd Street; The Tap Dance Kid.*

Dinner theatres: Lt. Cable, *South Pacific;* Horace, *Goldiggers of 1633;* Will, *Oklahoma!;* Peter, *No Sex Please, We're British;* Bobby, *The Boyfriend;* Billy, *Anything Goes;* Tony, *West Side Story;* Joey, *Pal Joey;* Michael, *I Do, I Do.*

Stock productions: Huck Haines, *Roberta;* Matt, *The Fantasticks;* Sid, *Half a Sixpence;* leading man, *Lullaby of Broadway.*

MAJOR TOURS—Phillipe, *New Moon;* Will, *Oklahoma!;* understudy to Ben, *Follies*, California company; *Best Little Whorehouse in Texas.*

PRINCIPAL STAGE WORK—Director and choreographer: *George M!*, National tour; *Goldiggers of 1633, Cheerful Little Earful, West Side Story, The Boyfriend, Pal Joey*, all Golden Apple Dinner

KEN PRESCOTT

Theatre, Naples, FL; *Damn Yankees* and *Oklahoma!*, both Once Upon a Stage Dinner Theatre; *Dames at Sea*, Port Charlotte Dinner Theatre, FL; *George M!*, Naples Dinner Theatre, FL.; *I Do, I Do*, Saugatuck Barn Theatre, MI; *Roberta, Cole, Pal Joey*, all Brunswick Music Theatre, ME; *Thé Boyfriend*, Breckenridge Theatre, St. Louis, MO; *Lullaby of Broadway*, Milwaukee Melody Top, WI.

PRINCIPAL FILM APPEARANCES—*Saturday Night Fever*, Paramount, 1977; *The Goodbye Girl*, Warner Brothers, 1977; *Zelig*, Warner Brothers, 1983.

PRINCIPAL TELEVISION APPEARANCES—*Another World*, NBC; leading man, *The Best of Burlesque*, cable.

RELATED CAREER—Assistant professor of dance, California State University; teacher, Florida State Ballet Company; teacher, jazz ballet, Florida State University; teacher, jazz ballet, Lexington Ballet Company.

MEMBER: Actors' Equity Association, American Federation of Radio and Television Artists, Screen Actors Guild, Society of Stage Directors and Choreographers.

ADDRESSES: HOME—746 Ninth Avenue, New York, NY 10036. AGENT—c/o Dorothy Scott, Marje Fields Agency, 165 W. 46th Street, New York, NY 10036.

*   *   *

PRINCE, Jonathan   1958-

PERSONAL: Born August 16, 1958, in Los Angeles, CA; son of Martin Harry (an optometrist) and Gayle Lee (a special education teacher; maiden name, Schlanger) Prince. EDUCATION: Harvard University, B.A., 1980. RELIGION: Jewish.

VOCATION: Actor, producer, and writer.

CAREER: STAGE DEBUT—Ottavio, *Scapino,* Loeb Theatre, Cambridge, MA, 1976. PRINCIPAL STAGE APPEARANCES—Speed, *Two Gentlemen of Verona,* Harvard Yard Theatre, Cambridge, MA, 1976; herald, *Marat/Sade,* Loco Theatre, 1977; Basilo, *The Marriage of Figaro,* Loeb Theatre, 1978; the boy, *Purgatory,* Theatre West, Los Angeles, CA, 1978; Sir Joseph Porter, *H.M.S. Pinafore,* Loeb Theatre, 1979; Mercutio, *Romeo and Juliet,* Hasty Pudding Theatre, Cambridge, MA, 1979; player, *Story Theatre,* Loeb Theatre, 1980; Eddie, *Runaways,* Richard Sheperd Theatre, Los Angeles, CA, 1980-81.

FILM DEBUT—Stu, *The Incredible Shrinking Woman,* Universal, 1978. PRINCIPAL FILM APPEARANCES—*Halloween II,* Universal, 1981; *Private School,* Universal, 1983; *Private Resort,* 1985.

TELEVISION DEBUT—Leo Samuels, *Mr. Merlin,* CBS, 1981-82. PRINCIPAL TELEVISION APPEARANCES—Series: Danny, *Alice,* CBS, 1984-85.

Episodic: *Secrets of Midland Heights,* CBS, 1980; *Open All Night,* ABC, 1982; *Sara; Hotel.*

Movies: *Pray TV,* 1982; *It's My Tomorrow Too.*

PRINCIPAL TELEVISION WORK—(With Joshua Goldstein) Co-creator, writer, and producer *What's Hot, What's Not* (pilot), 1984-85.

RELATED CAREER—(With Goldstein) Co-producer, Frog on a Rock Productions, Los Angeles, CA.

WRITINGS: SCREENPLAYS—(With Joshua Goldstein): *The Sky's the Limit,* Warner Brothers, 1985; *The Fine Touch,* Metro-Goldwyn-Mayer, 1985.

PILOTS—(With Goldstein) Co-writer, *Amigos,* 1985; *Uncle Bob,* 1986.

MEMBER: Screen Actors Guild, American Federation of Television and Radio Artists, Writers Guild of America.

SIDELIGHTS: FAVORITE ROLE—Mercutio, *Romeo and Juliet.*

ADDRESSES: OFFICE—c/o Via Com, 10900 Wilshire Blvd., Seventh Floor, Los Angeles, CA 90024. AGENT—Triad Artists, 10100 Santa Monica Blvd., Los Angeles, CA 90067.

*   *   *

PROSKY, Robert   1930-

PERSONAL: Born December 13, 1930, in Philadelphia, PA; son of Joseph (a grocer) and Helen Prosky; married Ida Hove (an anthropologist), June 4, 1960; children: Stefan, John, Andrew. EDUCATION: Attended Temple University; trained for the stage at the American Theatre Wing. MILITARY: U.S. Air Force.

VOCATION: Actor.

JONATHAN PRINCE

ROBERT PROSKY

CAREER: STAGE DEBUT—*Mrs. Gibbon's Boys,* Bucks County Playhouse, PA, 1955. NEW YORK DEBUT—Landlord, *Moonchildren,* for fifteen performances. PRINCIPAL STAGE APPEARANCES—Has acted on stage for over twenty-three years and in more than 135 roles at the Arena Stage in Washington, DC, including Stage Manager, *Our Town;* Matthew Harrison Brady, *Inherit the Wind;* title role, *Gallileo;* Willie Loman, *Death of a Salesman.*

Alfieri, *A View from the Bridge,* Ambassador Theatre, NY, 1983; Shelly Levene, *Glengarry Glen Ross,* Goodman Theatre, Chicago, IL, 1984, then John Golden Theatre, NY, 1984; also appeared in *A Delicate Balance* and *Hamlet* at the Guthrie Theatre, Minneapolis, MN.

MAJOR TOURS—Stage Manager, *Our Town* and Matthew Harrison Brady, *Inherit the Wind,* Soviet Union.

PRINCIPAL FILM APPEARANCES—*Thief,* United Artists, 1981; *Hanky Panky,* Columbia, 1982; *The Keep,* Paramount, 1983; *The Lords of Discipline,* Paramount, 1983; *Christine,* Columbia, 1983; *The Natural,* Tri-Star, 1984.

PRINCIPAL TELEVISION APPEARANCES—Series: Sergeant Stanislaus Jablonski, *Hill Street Blues,* NBC, 1984—.

Movies: *Into Thin Air,* CBS, 1985.

AWARDS: Antoinette Perry Award nomination, 1984, for *Glengarry Glen Ross.*

SIDELIGHTS: RECREATIONS—Furniture and home restoration, flying, stamp and coin collecting, photography, golf, tennis, bowling, travel, sailing, and fishing.

Robert Prosky told *CTFT* that his summer home in Cape May Point, NJ, is in the National Historic Register and has been traced back to 1876.

ADDRESSES: AGENT—Smith-Freedman and Associates, 123 N. Vincente Blvd., Beverly Hills, CA 90211.

*   *   *

PRYOR, Richard   1940-

PERSONAL: Born December 1, 1940, in Peoria, IL; son of Leroy and Gertude (Thomas) Pryor; children: Elizabeth, Ann, Richard, Rain, Renee. MILITARY: U.S. Army, 1958-60.

VOCATION: Actor, comedian, and writer.

CAREER: PRINCIPAL FILM APPEARANCES—Piano Man, *Lady Sings the Blues,* Paramount, 1972; *Hit,* Paramount, 1973; *Wattstax,* Columbia, 1973; *Bingo Long and the Traveling All Stars and Motor Kings,* Universal, 1976; *Silver Streak,* Twentieth Century-Fox, 1976; *Greased Lightning,* Warner Brothers, 1977; *Which Way Is Up?,* Universal, 1977; *Blue Collar,* Universal, 1978; Tin Man, *The Wiz,* Universal, 1978; *California Suite,* Columbia, 1978; *Wholly Moses,* Columbia, 1980; *In God We Trust,* Universal, 1980; *Stir Crazy,* Columbia, 1980; *Bustin' Loose,* Universal, 1981; *Live on Sunset Strip,* Columbia, 1982; *Some Kind of Hero,* Paramount, 1982; *The Toy,* Columbia, 1982; *Brewster's Millions,* Universal, 1985; title role, *Jo Jo Dancer: Your Life Is Calling You,* Columbia, 1986; *Critical Condition* (upcoming).

PRINCIPAL FILM WORK—Producer, *Bustin' Loose,* Universal, 1981; director, *The Toy,* Columbia, 1982.

PRINCIPAL TELEVISION APPEARANCES—Series: *The Richard Pryor Show,* NBC, 1977; *Pryor's Place* (children's show).

Guest: *The Ed Sullivan Show,* CBS; *The Merv Griffin Show,* CBS; *The Tonight Show with Johnny Carson,* NBC; *On Broadway Tonight,* CBS; guest host, *Saturday Night Live,* NBC; others.

WRITINGS: SCREENPLAYS—(With Mel Brooks) *Blazing Saddles,* Warner Brothers, 1974; *Lily,* 1974; *Adios, Amigos,* 1976; *The Bingo Long Traveling All-Stars and Motor Kings,* Universal, 1976; *Car Wash,* Universal, 1977; *Silver Streak,* Twentieth Century-Fox, 1977; *Greased Lightning,* Warner Brothers, 1977; *Which Way Is Up?,* Universal, 1977; *Blue Collar,* Universal, 1978; *Stir Crazy,* Columbia, 1980.

TELEVISION—(Co-author) *The Lily Tomlin Special,* 1973; also shows for Flip Wilson.

RECORDINGS: COMEDY ALBUMS—*That Nigger's Crazy,* Reprise, 1974; *Bicentennial Nigger,* Warner Brothers, 1976; *Here and Now,* Warner Brothers; *Is It Something I Said?,* Reprise; *Wanted,* Warner Brothers; *Greatest Hits,* Warner Brothers.

MEMBER: National Academy of Recording Arts and Sciences, Writers Guild of America.

AWARDS: Emmy Award, 1973, for *The Lily Tomlin Special;* American Academy of Humor Award, 1974, for *Lily;* American Writers Guild Award and American Academy of Humor Award, both 1974, for *Blazing Saddles;* Best Comedy Album, Grammy Award, also certified gold and platinum albums, 1974, for *That Nigger's Crazy;* Best Comedy Album, Grammy Award, 1976, for *Bicenntenial Nigger.*

SIDELIGHTS: Richard Pryor made his professional debut as a drummer at the age of seven. He is the owner of Richard Pryor Enterprises, Inc., in Los Angeles, organized in 1975.

ADDRESSES: AGENT—Ramone Harvey, 801 W. Mount Drive, Los Angeles, CA 90069.*

*   *   *

QUESENBERY, Whitney   1954-

PERSONAL: Born August 31, 1954, in Boston, MA; daughter of William Doyle (a writer) and Marilyn Resnick (a librarian) Quesenbery. EDUCATION: Bryn Mawr College, B.A., 1976; studied at the National Theatre Institute, 1975.

VOCATION: Lighting designer.

CAREER: PRINCIPAL STAGE WORK—Lighting design: *Contemporary Mythmakers,* touring company, 1983; *Tintypes,* Cortland Repertory Company, Cortland, NY, 1983; *Who'll Save the Ploughboy,* Equity Library Theatre, NY, 1983; Berkshire Ballet tour, 1983-84; *Africanus Instructus,* Lenox Arts Center, Stockbridge, MA, 1984; *Dr. Selavy's Magic Theatre,* Lenox Arts Center, NY, 1984; *Shoot Me While I'm Happy,* Goodman Theatre, Chicago, IL, 1985; Rebecca Kelly Dance Company tour, 1985; *Frankenstein,* City Stage Company, NY, 1985; *Tatterdemalion,* Douglas Fairbanks Theatre, NY, 1985; *La Traviata, Barbe Bleu, Der Freischutz,* and *Cosi-Fan Tutti,* all Bronx Opera, NY, 1985.

MEMBER: United Scenic Artists, Local 829.

ADDRESSES: HOME—27 Third Avenue, Brooklyn, NY 11217.

R

RABE, David 1940-

PERSONAL: Born March 10, 1940, in Dubuque, IA; son of William and Ruth (McCormick) Rabe; married Elizabeth Pan (divorced); married Jill Clayburgh (an actress); children: (second marriage) one son. EDUCATION: Loras College, B.A.; Villanova University, M.A.

VOCATION: Writer.

WRITINGS: PLAYS, PRODUCED—*The Basic Training of Pavlo Hummel,* New York Shakespeare Festival, 1971; *Sticks and Bones,* New York Shakespeare Festival, 1971; *The Orphan,* New York Shakespeare Festival, 1973; *In the Boom Boom Room,* Lincoln Center, NY, 1974; *Burning,* 1974; *Streamers,* 1976; *Goose and Tomtom,* 1976; *Hurlyburly,* Promenade Theatre, NY, 1984, then Ethel Barrymore Theatre, NY, 1984-85.

FILMS, PRODUCED—*I'm Dancing As Fast As I Can.*

AWARDS: Obie Award, Drama Desk Award, Variety Critics Poll, all 1971, for *The Basic Training of Pavlo Hummel;* Best Play, Antoinette Perry Award, Outer Critics Circle Award, New York Drama Critics Citation, all 1971, for *Sticks and Bones.*

ADDRESSES: AGENT—Ellen Neuwald, 905 West End Avenue, New York, NY 10025.

* * *

RADNER, Gilda 1946-

PERSONAL: Born June 28, 1946, in Detroit, MI; married G.E. Smith (a musician; divorced); married Gene Wilder (an actor), September 18, 1984. EDUCATION: University of Michigan. RELIGION: Jewish.

VOCATION: Actress, writer, and comedienne.

CAREER: DEBUT—With Second City Improvisational Theatre, Toronto, Canada. NEW YORK DEBUT—*National Lampoon Show,* Village Gate Theatre, NY, 1975. PRINCIPAL STAGE APPEARANCES—*Godspell,* Canada; *Gilda Radner—Live from New York,* Winter Garden Theatre, NY, 1979; *Lunch Hour,* Ethel Barrymore Theatre, NY, 1980.

PRINCIPAL FILM APPEARANCES—*First Family,* Warner Brothers, 1980; *Gilda Live,* Warner Brothers, 1980; *Hanky Panky,* Columbia, 1982; *It Came from Hollywood,* Paramount, 1982; *The Woman in Red,* Orion, 1984; *Movers and Shakers,* Metro-Goldwyn-Mayer, 1985; *Haunted Honeymoon,* Orion, 1986.

PRINCIPAL TELEVISION APPEARANCES—Series: a Not Ready for Prime Time Player, *Saturday Night Live,* NBC, 1975-80; CBC programs including an original rock opera, *Jack;* guest appearances on other shows.

PRINCIPAL RADIO APPEARANCES—*National Lampoon Radio Hour.*

WRITINGS: RADIO SCRIPTS—*National Lampoon Radio Hour.*

REVUE—(With Lorne Michaels and Don Novello) *Gilda Radner—Live from New York,* Winter Garden Theatre, NY, 1979.

SCREENPLAY—(With Lorne Michaels and Don Novello) *Gilda Live,* Warner Brothers, 1980.

MEMBER: Actors' Equity Association, American Federation of Television and Radio Artists, Screen Actors Guild.

AWARDS: Outstanding Continuing or Single Performance by a Supporting Actress in a Variety or Music, Emmy, 1977-78, for *Saturday Night Live;* Antoinette Perry nomination, 1980, for *Lunch Hour.*

ADDRESSES: OFFICE—9200 Sunset Blvd., Suite 428, Los Angeles, CA 90069.*

* * *

RAFKIN, Alan 1928-

PERSONAL: Born July 23, 1928, in New York, NY; son of Victor and Til (Bernstein) Rafkin; children: Dru, Leigh Ann. EDUCATION: Syracuse University, B.S., 1950. POLITICS: Democrat. RELIGION: Jewish. MILITARY: U.S. Army.

VOCATION: Director and former actor.

CAREER: PRINCIPAL TELEVISION APPEARANCES—*The Robert Q. Lewis Show,* CBS, 1950-51, 1955; daytime shows, CBS.

PRINCIPAL TELEVISION WORK—Director: *Verdict Is Yours,* CBS, 1960; *The Mary Tyler Moore Show,* CBS, 1970-71; *Love, American Style,* ABC, 1970-71; *Sanford and Son,* NBC, 1972; *The Bob Newhart Show,* CBS, 1972-73; *Rhoda,* CBS, 1973; *M*A*S*H,* CBS, 1976-77; *Laverne and Shirley,* ABC, 1977; others.

ADDRESSES: OFFICE—c/o ABC Press Relations, 1330 Avenue of the Americas, New York, NY 10019.*

RATZENBERGER, John

PERSONAL: Born April 6, in Bridgeport, CT; married Georgia Karamitros (a hair stylist). EDUCATION: Attended Sacred Heart University.

VOCATION: Actor, comedian, and writer.

CAREER: TELEVISION DEBUT—*Goliath Awaits.* PRINCIPAL TELEVISION APPEARANCES—Series: Clifford Clavin, *Cheers,* NBC, 1982—.

Episodic: *Wizards and Warriors,* CBS, 1983; "The Good Soldier," *Masterpiece Theatre,* PBS.

FILM DEBUT—*The Ritz,* Warner Brothers, 1976. PRINCIPAL FILM APPEARANCES—*Superman,* Warner Brothers, 1978; *The Empire Strikes Back,* Twentieth Century-Fox, 1980; *Outland,* Warner Brothers, 1981; *Reds,* Paramount, 1981; *Firefox,* Warner Brothers, 1982; *Gandhi,* Columbia, 1982; *Protocol,* Warner Brothers, 1984; *The Falcon and the Snowman,* Orion, 1985.

STAGE DEBUT—*Summer and Smoke,* Sacred Heart University. PRINCIPAL STAGE APPEARANCES—*Luv,* Stowe Playhouse, VT; *West Side Story; Waiting for Godot.*

RELATED CAREER—Co-writer, director, and actor, *Sal's Meat Market,* touring comedy troupe, British and European cities.

WRITINGS: TELEVISION—*Friends in Space,* ITV, Great Britain; *Crown Court,* ITV, Great Britain; *The Golden Dreamboat.*

RECORDINGS: SINGLE—*Do the Jog,* Great Britain, 1979.

MEMBER: Screen Actors Guild, American Federation of Television and Radio Artists; American Farmland Trust, World Wildlife Foundation, National Resource Defense Council.

AWARDS: British Government Grant Award, for *Sal's Meat Market.*

SIDELIGHTS: RECREATIONS—Sailing, hiking, karate, and studying world history.

ADDRESSES: HOME—San Fernando Valley, CA. AGENT— Sumski, Green & Company, 8380 Melrose Avenue, Suite 200, Los Angeles, CA 90069.

*   *   *

RAYBURN, Gene   1917-

PERSONAL: Born Eugene Rubessa, December 22, 1917, in Christopher, IL; son of Milan and Mary (Hikec) Rubessa; married Helen Ticknor, January 1, 1940; children: Lynn. EDUCATION: Attended Knox College, Galesburg, IL. MILITARY: U.S. Air Force.

VOCATION: Actor and game show host.

CAREER: PRINCIPAL STAGE APPEARANCES—Albert Peterson, *Bye Bye Birdie,* Shubert Theatre, NY, 1961; Buddy, *Come Blow Your Horn,* NY, 1962.

PRINCIPAL TELEVISION APPEARANCES—Game Shows: Panelist, *The Name's the Same,* ABC, 1953-55; host, *Make the Connection,*

NBC, 1955; host, *Dough-Re-Mi,* NBC, 1958-61; host, *Play Your Hunch;* host, *Tic Tac Dough;* host, *Match Game,* NBC, 1962-69, CBS, 1973-79, NBC, 1983-84; host, *Match Game PM,* syndication, 1975-82; *Amateur's Guide to Love.*

Variety: Regular, *Steve Allen's Tonight Show,* NBC 1953-59; regular, *The Steve Allen Show,* NBC, 1956-59; announcer, *Steve Allen presents The Steve Lawrence-Eydie Gorme Show,* NBC, 1958; *Helluva Town;* others.

Episodic: *Robert Montgomery Presents,* NBC, 1956.

PRINCIPAL RADIO WORK—*Rayburn and Finch Show,* WNEW-AM, 1946-53; *Monitor,* WNBC-AM, 1961-73.

MEMBER: American Federation of Television and Radio Artists (board of directors, and past president, New York City Local; trustee of pension and welfare fund); Wianno Club; Canadian Club of New York; Centerville Beach Club (Massachusetts).

ADDRESSES: OFFICE—c/o Goodson-Todman Productions, 375 Park Avenue, New York, NY 10022.*

*   *   *

REDFORD, Robert   1937-

PERSONAL: Born August 18, 1937, in Santa Barbara, CA; married Lola Van Wangemen. EDUCATION: Attended the University of Colorado and Pratt Institute, NY; studied at the American Academy of Dramatic Arts, NY.

VOCATION: Actor and director.

CAREER: PRINCIPAL STAGE APPEARANCES—Broadway: *Tall Story,* 1959; *The Highest Tree,* 1960; *Sunday in New York,* 1961; Paul Bratter, *Barefoot in the Park,* 1963.

ROBERT REDFORD

PRINCIPAL FILM APPEARANCES—*Warhunt*, 1961; *Situation Hopeless, but Not Serious*, Paramount, 1965; *Inside Daisy Clover*, Warner Brothers, 1966; *The Chase*, Columbia, 1966; *This Property Is Condemned*, Paramount, 1966; Paul Bratter, *Barefoot in the Park*, Paramount, 1967; *Downhill Racer*, Paramount, 1967; the Sundance Kid, *Butch Cassidy and the Sundance Kid*, Twentieth Century-Fox, 1969; *Big Fauss and Little Halsey*, 1970; *Tell Them Willy Boy Is Here*, Universal, 1970; title role, *Jeremiah Johnson*, Warner Brothers, 1972; *The Hot Rock*, Twentieth Century-Fox, 1972; *The Candidate*, Warner Brothers, 1972; *The Way We Were*, Columbia, 1973; Jay Gatsby, *The Great Gatsby*, Paramount, 1974; title role, *The Great Waldo Pepper*, Universal, 1975; *Three Days of the Condor*, Paramount, 1975; *All the President's Men*, Warner Brothers, 1976; *A Bridge Too Far*, United Artists, 1977; *The Electric Horseman*, Columbia, 1979; title role, *Brubaker*, Twentieth Century-Fox, 1980; Roy Hobbs, *The Natural*, Tri-Star Pictures, 1984; *Out of Africa*, Columbia, 1985; Tom Logan, *Legal Eagles*, Universal, 1986.

PRINCIPAL FILM WORK—Director, *Ordinary People*, Paramount, 1980; producer, *The Natural*, 1984.

AWARDS: Best Director, Academy Award, Golden Globe Award, both 1981, for *Ordinary People*.

SIDELIGHTS: Robert Redford is the owner of the ski resort Sundance, in Provo, Utah.

ADDRESSES: AGENT—Roger & Cowan, 122 E. 42nd Street, New York, NY 10168.

*   *   *

REED, Donna   1921-1986

PERSONAL: Born Donna Belle Mullenger, January 27, 1921, in Denison, IA; died of complications from pancreatic cancer, in Beverly Hills, CA, January 14, 1986; daughter of William R. and Hazel Mullenger; married William Tuttle, January 30, 1943 (divorced, 1944); married Anthony I. Owen, June 15, 1945 (divorced, 1972) married Grover Asmus (retired U.S. Army colonel), 1975; children: (second marriage) Anthony R., Timothy G., Mary Anne, (adopted) Penny Jane. EDUCATION: Attended Los Angeles City College, 1938-40.

VOCATION: Actress.

CAREER: FILM DEBUT—(As Donna Adams) *The Get-Away*, Metro-Goldwyn-Mayer, 1941. PRINCIPAL FILM APPEARANCES—*The Bugle Sounds*, Metro-Goldwyn-Mayer, 1941; *The Courtship of Andy Hardy*, Metro-Goldwyn-Mayer, 1941; *Shadow of the Thin Man*, Metro-Goldwyn-Mayer, 1941; *Babes on Broadway*, Metro-Goldwyn-Mayer, 1941; *Calling Dr. Gillespie*, Metro-Goldwyn-Mayer, 1942; *Apache Trail*, Metro-Goldwyn-Mayer, 1942; *Dr. Gillespie's Criminal Case*, 1942; *Mokey*, Metro-Goldwyn-Mayer, 1942; *Eyes in the Night*, Metro-Goldwyn-Mayer, 1942; *The Human Comedy*, Metro-Goldwyn-Mayer, 1943; *Thousands Cheer*, Metro-Goldwyn-Mayer, 1943; *See Here, Private Hargrove*, Metro-Goldwyn-Mayer, 1943; *The Man from Down Under*, Metro-Goldwyn-Mayer, 1943; *Mrs. Parkington*, 1944; *Gentle Annie*, Metro-Goldwyn-Mayer, 1944; *Picture of Dorian Gray*, Metro-Goldwyn-Mayer, 1944; *They Were Expendable*, Metro-Goldwyn-Mayer, 1945; *Faithful in My Fashion*, Metro-Goldwyn-Mayer, 1946; *It's a Wonderful Life*, RKO, 1946; *Green Dolphin Street*, Metro-Goldwyn-Mayer, 1947; *Beyond Glory*, 1947; *Chicago Deadline*, 1948.

Scandal Sheet, 1951; *Saturday's Hero*, Columbia, 1951; *Hangman's Noose*, Columbia, 1952; *Barbarossa*, Columbia, 1952; *Raiders of the Seven Seas*, 1952; *Trouble Along the Way*, 1953; *The Caddy*, 1953; *Gun Fury*, 1953; Alma, *From Here to Eternity*, Columbia, 1953; *The Last Time I Saw Paris*, Metro-Goldwyn-Mayer, 1954; *The Far Horizons*, 1954; *Three Hours to Kill*, 1954; *They Rode West*, 1954; *Ransom*, Metro-Goldwyn-Mayer, 1955; *The Benny Goodman Story*, Universal, 1956; *Beyond Mombasa*, Columbia, 1957; *The Whole Truth*, Columbia, 1958; *Pepe*, Columbia, 1960; "Yellow-Headed Summer" (unreleased), 1974.

PRINCIPAL TELEVISION APPEARANCES—Series: Donna Stone, *The Donna Reed Show*, ABC, 1958-66; replaced Barbara Bel Geddes as Miss Ellie, *Dallas*, CBS, 1984.

Movies: *The Love Boat*, ABC; *The Best Place to Be*, 1979.

AWARDS: Named Princess Young Victory, Flathead Indian Tribes, 1952; Best Supporting Actress, Academy Award, 1954, for Alma, *From Here to Eternity*.

SIDELIGHTS: Donna Reed was co-chairwoman of the Beverly Hills chapter of Another Mother for Peace in 1970.*

*   *   *

REED, Oliver   1938-

PERSONAL: Full name, Robert Oliver Reed; born February 13, 1938, in Wimbledon, England; son of Peter (a journalist) and Marcia (Andrews) Reed; married Katherine Byrne, 1960 (divorced, 1970); children: Mark Thurloe, Sarah. MILITARY: British Army.

VOCATION: Actor.

CAREER: PRINCIPAL FILM APPEARANCES—*Beat Girl*, 1959; *The Angry Silence*, British Lion, 1960; *The League of Gentlemen*, Rank/Allied Film Makers, 1960; *The Rebel* (also known as *Call Me Genius*), Associated British, 1960; *Two Faces of Dr. Jekyll* (also known as *House of Fright*), American International, 1961; *Sword of Sherwood Forest*, Columbia, 1961; *Curse of the Werewolf*, Universal International/Hammer Films, 1961; *No Love for Johnnie*, Rank/Five Star, 1961; *Pirates of Blood River*, Hammer Films, 1961; *Paranoiac*, Universal International/Hammer Films, 1963; *Scarlet Blade* (also known as *The Crimson Blade*), Columbia, 1964; *The Damned* (also known as *These Are the Damned*), Columbia 1965; *Masquerade*, United Artsts/Novus, 1965; *The Party's Over*, Allied Artists, 1966; *The System* (also known as *The Girl-Getters*) American International Pictures, 1966; *Brigand of Kandahar*, Columbia, 1966; *The Trap*, 1966; *The Jokers*, United Artists, 1967; *The Shuttered Room*, Warner Brothers/Seven Arts, 1968; *I'll Never Forget What's 'is Name*, Regional, 1968; Bill Sykes, *Oliver!*, Columbia, 1968; *The Assassination Bureau*, Paramount, 1969; *Hannibal Brooks*, United Artists, 1969.

Women in Love, United Artists, 1970; *Take a Girl Like You*, Columbia, 1970; *The Lady in the Car with Glasses and a Gun*, Columbia 1971; *The Hunting Party*, United Artists, 1971; *Zero Population Growth*, Saggitarius Films, 1971; *The Devils*, Warner Brothers, 1971; *Sitting Target*, Metro-Goldwyn-Mayer, 1972; *Triple Echo*, Altura Films, 1973; *Blue Blood*, Mallard-Impact Quadrant, 1973; *The Three Musketeers*, Twentieth Century-Fox, 1974; *Tommy*, Columbia, 1975; *The Four Musketeers*, Twentieth Century-Fox, 1975; *Ten Little Indians*, Avco Embassy, 1975; *Royal Flash*, Twentieth Century-Fox, 1975; Ben, *Burnt Offerings*, United

Artists, 1976; *The Great Scout and Cathouse Thursday,* American-International, 1976; *Tomorrow Never Comes,* Canadian, 1977; *The Prince and the Pauper* (also known as *Crossed Swords*), Warner Brothers, 1978; *The Big Sleep,* United Artists, 1978; *The Class of Miss MacMichael,* Brut/Kettledrum, 1978.

Dr. Heckle and Mr. Hype, 1980; *Lion of the Desert,* United Film Distributors, 1981; *Condorman,* Buena Vista, 1981; *Venom,* Paramount, 1982; *Deathbite* (also known as *Spasms*) Canadian, 1983; *The Sting II,* Universal, 1983; *Two of a Kind,* Twentieth Century-Fox, 1983.

Also: *His and Hers; Bulldog Breed; Curse of Captain Clegg; Fury Rides the Wind; Dirty Weekend; Revolver; Sell Out; Assault on Paradise; The Broad; Death in Persepolis; The Great Question; Second Chance.*

MEMBER: White Elephant Club (England).

AWARDS: Named Master of Arts and Sciences; Musketeer of France.

ADDRESSES: AGENT—International Creative Management, 8899 Beverly Blvd., Los Angeles, CA 90048.*

* * *

REEVE, Christopher   1952-

PERSONAL: Born September 25, 1952, in New York, NY; son of Franklin D. and Barbara (Johnson) Reeve; children: Matthew. EDUCATION: Cornell University, B.A.; trained for the stage at the Juilliard School and Herbert Berghof Studios with Uta Hagen, Marian Seldes, and Austin Pendleton.

VOCATION: Actor.

CAREER: PRINCIPAL FILM APPEARANCES—*Gray Lady Down,* Universal, 1978; Clark Kent/title role, *Superman,* Warner Brothers, 1978; *Somewhere in Time,* Universal, 1980; Clark Kent/title role, *Superman II,* Warner Brothers, 1981; *Deathtrap,* Warner Brothers, 1982; *Monsignor,* Twentieth Century-Fox, 1982; Clark Kent/title role, *Superman III,* Warner Brothers, 1983; *The Bostonians,* Almi Pictures, 1984; Edgar Anscombe, *The Aviator,* Metro-Goldwyn-Mayer/United Artists, 1985.

PRINCIPAL STAGE APPEARANCES—Boothbay Playhouse, ME; Williamstown Theatre, MA; San Diego Shakespeare Festival; Loeb Drama Center; *A Matter of Gravity,* 1976; *My Life,* 1977; *Fifth of July,* Broadway, NY, 1980; *The Greeks,* Williamstown Theatre Festival, MA, 1981; *The Aspern Papers,* West End, London, 1984; *The Marriage of Figaro,* Circle in the Square, NY, 1985.

MAJOR TOURS—*Irregular Verb to Love,* U.S. cities.

PRINCIPAL TELEVISION APPEARANCES—*Love of Life; Enemies; The American Revolution; Anna Karenina,* 1985.

MEMBER: Actors' Equity Association (council), Motion Picture Academy of Arts and Sciences; Players Club, Actors Fund of America; Soaring Society of America, Save the Children (honorary chairman), Special Olympics, American Cancer Society, American Medical Association (advisor to council on teenage alchoholism), Save the Theaters.

AWARDS: British Academy Award, 1979 for *Superman;* United States Jaycees Award, Ten Outstanding Young Americans, 1981; Circle K Humanitarian Award, 1984.

SIDELIGHTS: RECREATION—Sailing, skiing, glider-pilot, and piano.

ADDRESSES: AGENT—International Creative Management, 8899 Beverly Blvd., Los Angeles, CA 90048.

* * *

REGINA, Paul   1956-

PERSONAL: Born October 25, 1956, in Brooklyn, NY; son of Paul Joseph (a tradesman) and Patricia (an Internal Revenue Service worker; maiden name, Manjarrez) Regina. EDUCATION: Attended Patchogue Medford High School, NY; trained for the stage with Mira Rostova, Gordan Hunt, Tracy Roberts, John Sarno, John Strasberg, Sabra Jones, Gail Ross, Barbara Beebe, and Harvey Lembeck.

VOCATION: Actor.

CAREER: TELEVISION DEBUT—Mike, *Police Woman,* CBS, 1976. PRINCIPAL TELEVISION APPEARANCES—Series: Joe Pizo, *Joe and Valerie,* NBC, 1978-79; Don Carlos de la Vega (Zorro, Jr.), *Zorro and Son,* CBS, 1983; Cliff Waters, *Brothers,* Showtime, 1983—.

Episodic: *T.J. Hooker; Devlin Connection; Tucker's Witch; Powers of Mathew Star; Voyagers; Gimme a Break; Cassie and Company; Benson; Here's Boomer; A Single Life; Hagen; The Baxters; Hardy Boys; Police Woman.*

PAUL REGINA

Movies: *The Choice,* 1981; *A Long Way Home,* CBS, 1981; *The Renegades,* 1982; *The Awakening of Candra,* 1983; *Adam,* NBC, 1983; also appeared in *The Gangster Chronicles.*

NEW YORK DEBUT—Moishe, townsperson, *The World of Sholom Alecheim,* Roundabout Theatre, 1976, for eighty performances. PRINCIPAL STAGE APPEARANCES—*Grease,* Broadway production; *A Hundred Percent Alive,* Westwood Playhouse, Los Angeles; *Mississippi Blue,* Los Angeles Actors Theatre; *Two Outs Bottom of the Ninth,* McCadden Place Theatre, Los Angeles; *Wrestlers,* Cast Theatre, Los Angeles.

FILM DEBUT—Mickey, *A Change of Seasons,* Twentieth Century-Fox, 1980.

MAJOR TOURS—*Grease,* U.S. cities.

MEMBER: Adam Walsh Child Resource Center.

AWARDS: Los Angeles Drama Critics Circle nomination, for *Two Outs Bottom of the Ninth*.

ADDRESSES: AGENT—J. Michael Bloom, 400 Madison Avenue, New York, NY 10017.

*   *   *

REILLY, Charles Nelson   1931-

PERSONAL: Born January 13, 1931, in New York, NY; son of Charles Joseph and Signe Elvera (Nelson) Reilly. EDUCATION: Attended the University of Connecticut; studied acting at the Herbert Berghof Studio with Uta Hagen and Herbert Berghof; studied singing with Keith Davis.

VOCATION: Actor and director.

CAREER: STAGE DEBUT—The detective, *Broken Dishes,* Metropolitan Players, Tiverton, RI, 1950. NEW YORK DEBUT—*Best Foot Forward,* Equity Library Theatre production at the Lenox Hill Playhouse, 1956. PRINCIPAL STAGE APPEARANCES—Performed in stock productions at the Newport Casino, RI, Starlight Theatre, Kansas City, MO, Playhouse on the Mall, Paramus, NJ, Woodstock Playhouse, NY, and the Theatre by the Sea, Mantunuck, RI, all between 1951-64.

Virgil Cicero Tubbs, *The Saintliness of Margery Kempe,* York Playhouse, NY, 1959; *Fallout* (revue) and *Lend an Ear* (revue), both at the Renata Theatre, NY, 1959; *The Billy Barnes Revue,* Carnegie Hall Playhouse, NY, 1959; *Parade* (revue), Players Theatre, NY, 1960; *The Inspector General,* Equity Library Theatre, NY, 1960; Mr. Henkel, Albert Peterson (understudy), and Mr. MacAfee, *Bye, Bye Birdie,* Martin Beck Theatre, NY, 1960; Bud Frump, *How to Succeed in Business without Really Trying,* 46th Street Theatre, NY, 1961; Cornelius Hackl, *Hello, Dolly!,* St. James Theatre, NY, 1964; Roger Summerhill, *Skyscraper,* Lunt-Fontanne Theatre, NY, 1965; Sidney Lipton, *God's Favorite,* Eugene O'Neill Theatre, NY, 1974; *Charlotte,* 1980; *Bye, Bye Birdie,* Burt Reynolds Theatre, Jupiter, FL, 1983.

CABARET—Performed at the Showplace, 1958; *Nightcap* (revue); teamed with Eileen Brennan, in *Brennan and Reilly.*

PRINCIPAL STAGE WORK—Director: *The Belle of Amherst,* NY, 1976, then London, 1977; *Paul Robeson,* 1978; *Break a Leg,* NY,

1979; *Under the Ilex,* Repertory Theatre of St. Louis, MO, 1982, then Long Wharf Theatre, New Haven, CT, 1983; *Prisoner of Second Avenue,* Burt Reynolds Theatre, Jupiter, FL, 1984.

FILM DEBUT—*A Face in the Crowd,* Warner Brothers, 1957. PRINCIPAL FILM APPEARANCES—*Two Tickets to Paris,* Columbia, 1962; *The Tiger Makes Out,* Columbia, 1967; *Cannonball Run II,* Warner Brothers, 1984.

PRINCIPAL TELEVISION APPEARANCES—Series: Regular, *Talent Scouts,* CBS, 1962-63; regular, *The Steve Lawrence Show,* CBS, 1965; Claymore Gregg, *The Ghost and Mrs. Muir,* NBC, 1968-69, ABC, 1970; regular, *Dean Martin Presents,* NBC, 1970; Rendy Robinson, *Arnie,* CBS, 1971-72.

Variety: *The Sid Caesar Show; The Ed Sullivan Show; The Gold Diggers; The Peter Marshall Variety Show,* syndicated, 1976.

Game Shows: Panelist, *It Pays to Be Ignorant,* syndicated, 1973-74; panelist, *Match Game, Hollywood Squares.*

Children's Shows: Hoo Doo, *Lidsville;* voice, *The Wind in the Willows,* ABC, 1985.

RELATED CAREER: Founder and teacher, The Faculty drama school, Los Angeles, CA.

MEMBER: Actors' Equity Association, American Federation of Television and Radio Artists, Screen Actors Guild.

AWARDS: Antoinette Perry Award, 1961, for Bud Frump, *How to Succeed in Business without Really Trying;* New York Drama Critic's Circle award, 1964, for Cornelius Hackl, *Hello, Dolly!;* Antoinette Perry nomination, 1965, for *Skyscraper;* Emmy nomination, for *The Ghost and Mrs. Muir*.

SIDELIGHTS: Charles Nelson Reilly worked as a mail clerk, hospital orderly, usher, stock boy, and at other jobs while pursuing his performing career.

ADDRESSES: AGENT—William Morris Agency, 1350 Avenue of the Americas, New York, NY 10019.*

*   *   *

REYNOLDS, Debbie   1932-

PERSONAL: Full name, Mary Frances Reynolds; born April 1, 1932, in El Paso, TX; daughter of Raymond F. (a carpenter for the Southern Pacific Railroad) and Maxene Reynolds; married Eddie Fisher (a singer and actor) September 26, 1955 (divorced, 1959); married Harry Karl (a shoe magnate and producer) November 25, 1960 (divorced, 1973); married third husband, 1985; children: (first marriage) Carrie Frances, Todd Emmanuel; (step-children from second marriage) Denise, Harrison, Tina Marie. EDUCATION: Attended John Burroughs High School, Burbank, CA.

VOCATION: Actress and singer.

CAREER: PRINCIPAL STAGE APPEARANCES—*Stars of Tomorrow,* Bliss-Hayden Theatre, Los Angeles, 1952; title role, *Irene,* Majestic Theatre, NY, 1973; *The Debbie Reynolds Show,* London Palladium, 1975; Annie Oakley, *Annie Get Your Gun,* Los Angeles and San Francisco, 1977; Tess Harding, *Woman of the Year,* Palace Theatre, NY, 1983; also nightclub appearances since 1961.

FILM DEBUT—*The Daughter of Rosie O'Grady,* Warner Brothers, 1950. PRINCIPAL FILM APPEARANCES—Helen Kane, *Three Little Words,* Metro-Goldwyn-Mayer, 1950; *Two Weeks with Love,* Metro-Goldwyn-Mayer, 1950; *Mr. Imperium,* Metro-Goldwyn-Mayer, 1951; Kathy Selden, *Singin' in the Rain,* Metro-Goldwyn-Mayer, 1952; *Skirts Ahoy,* Metro-Goldwyn-Mayer, 1952; *I Love Melvin,* Metro-Goldwyn-Mayer, 1953; *The Affairs of Dobie Gillis,* Metro-Goldwyn-Mayer, 1953; *Give the Girl a Break,* Metro-Goldwyn-Mayer, 1953; title role, *Susan Slept Here,* RKO, 1953; *Athena,* Metro-Goldwyn-Mayer, 1954; *Hit the Deck,* Metro-Goldwyn-Mayer, 1955; *The Tender Trap,* Metro-Goldwyn-Mayer, 1955; Jane Hurley, *The Catered Affair,* Metro-Goldwyn-Mayer, 1956; *Bundle of Joy,* RKO, 1956; Tammy Tartleton, *Tammy and the Bachelor,* Universal, 1957; *This Happy Feeling,* Universal, 1958; *The Mating Game,* Metro-Goldwyn-Mayer, 1959; *Say One for Me,* Twentieth Century-Fox, 1959; *It Started with a Kiss,* Metro-Goldwyn-Mayer, 1959; *The Gazebo,* Metro-Goldwyn-Mayer, 1959.

Peggy Brown, *The Rat Race,* Paramount, 1960; *The Pleasure of His Company,* Paramount, 1961; *The Second Time Around,* Paramount, 1963; Lilith Prescott, *How the West Was Won,* Metro-Goldwyn-Mayer, 1963; *My Six Loves,* Paramount, 1963; Mary McKellaway, *Mary, Mary,* Warner Brothers, 1963; title role, *The Unsinkable Molly Brown,* Metro-Goldwyn-Mayer, 1964; title role, *Goodbye, Charlie,* Twentieth Century-Fox, 1964; Soeur Sourire, *The Singing Nun,* Metro-Goldwyn-Mayer, 1966; *Divorce, American Style,* Columbia, 1967; *How Sweet It Is,* National General Pictures, 1968; *What's the Matter with Helen?,* United Artists, 1971; *That's Entertainment!,* United Artists, 1974; *That's Entertainment, Part II,* United Artists, 1976.

PRINCIPAL TELEVISION APPEARANCES—Series: Debbie Thompson, *The Debbie Reynolds Show* (later called *Debbie*), NBC, 1969-70.

Guest: First telecast guest, *The Joey Bishop Show,* ABC, April 17, 1967; opening program guest, *Pat Paulsen's Half a Comedy Hour,* ABC, January 22, 1970; *The Carol Burnett Show;* others.

WRITINGS: AUTOBIOGRAPHY—*If I Knew Then,* 1963.

RECORDINGS: ALBUMS—*Two Weeks with Love,* original soundtrack recording, Metro-Goldwyn-Mayer; *Singin' in the Rain,* original soundtrack recording, Metro-Goldwyn-Mayer; *Hit the Deck,* original soundtrack recording, Metro-Goldwyn-Mayer; *Bundle of Joy,* original soundtrack recording, Victor; *Tammy and the Bachelor,* original soundtrack recording, Coral; *The Unsinkable Molly Brown,* original soundtrack recording, Metro-Goldwyn-Mayer; *The Singing Nun,* original soundtrack recording, Metro-Goldwyn-Mayer; *Irene,* original cast recording, Columbia; others.

SINGLES—"Tammy;" "Aba Daba Honeymoon."

AWARDS: Miss Burbank, 1948; Las Vegas Entertainer of the Year Award; Best Actress, Academy Award nomination, 1964, for *The Unsinkable Molly Brown;* "Tammy" and "Aba Daba Honeymoon" both became gold records.

SIDELIGHTS: During high school, Debbie Reynolds appeared with

DEBBIE REYNOLDS

the Burbank Youth Symphony. She is the head of Harmon Productions in Los Angeles.

ADDRESSES: OFFICE—Raymax Productions, 6514 Lankershim Blvd., North Hollywood, CA 91606. AGENT—c/o Ed Micone, International Creative Management, 40 W. 57th Street, New York, NY 10019.

*   *   *

REYNOLDS, Gene   1925-

PERSONAL: Born in 1925; married Bonnie Jones.

VOCATION: Producer, director, and actor.

CAREER: PRINCIPAL FILM APPEARANCES—*Thank You, Jeeves,* Twentieth Century-Fox, 1936; young Dion O'Leary, *In Old Chicago,* Twentieth Century-Fox, 1937; Tony Ponessa, *Boy's Town,* Loew's, Inc., 1938; *They Shall Have Music,* United Artists, 1939; the kid, *Eagle Squadron,* Universal, 1942; Larry, *The Country Girl,* Paramount, 1954; C.I.C. officer, *The Bridges at Toko-ri,* Paramount, 1954; *Diane,* Metro-Goldwyn-Mayer, 1955.

PRINCIPAL TELEVISION WORK—Series: Executive producer, *The Ghost and Mrs. Muir* (pilot), NBC, 1968; executive producer, *Room 222,* ABC, 1969-74; executive producer, *Anna and the King,* CBS, 1972; executive producer, *Roll Out,* CBS, 1973-74; producer and director, *M*A*S*H,* CBS, 1972-76; executive producer, *Karen,* ABC, 1975; executive producer, *Lou Grant,* CBS, 1977-82.

Movie: Producer and director, *People Like Us,* 1976.

Photograph by Harry Langdon

MEMBER: Directors Guild of America.

AWARDS: Emmy Awards: Outstanding New Series, 1969-70, for *Room 222;* Outstanding Comedy Series, 1973-74, for *M*A*S*H;* Outstanding Directing in a Comedy Series, 1974-75, for ''O.R.'' *M*A*S*H;* Outstanding Directing in a Comedy Series, 1975-76, for ''Welcome to Korea'' *M*A*S*H;* Outstanding Drama Series, 1978-79 and 1979-80, for *Lou Grant.* Director's Guild of America Awards for Television Comedy; Peabody Award, for *M*A*S*H.*

ADDRESSES: HOME—Los Angeles, CA.*

* * *

REYNOLDS, Jonathan   1942-

PERSONAL: Born February 13, 1942, in Fort Smith; son of Donald Worthington (a newspaper publisher) and Edith (Remick) Reynolds; married Charlotte Kirk (a real estate agent), June 10, 1978; children: Frank, Edward. EDUCATION: Denison University, Granville, OH, B.F.A., 1965; studied for the theatre at the London Academy of Music and Dramatic Art, 1965-67; also studied acting with Alvina Krause and William O. Brasmer.

VOCATION: Writer and former actor.

CAREER: STAGE DEBUT—Minor role and Guildenstern (understudy), *Rosenkrantz and Guildenstern are Dead,* Broadway Theatre, NY, 1967. PRINCIPAL STAGE APPEARANCES—*Coriolanus,* New York Shakespeare Festival, NY, 1968; (others).

WRITINGS: PLAYS, PRODUCED—*Yanks 3, Detroit 0, Top of the Seventh* and *Rubbers,* American Place Theatre, NY, 1976; *Tunnel Fever,* American Place Theatre, NY, 1979; *Geniuses,* Playwright's Horizons, NY, 1982-83, Arena Stage, Washington, DC, 1984, Philadelphia, 1985, and Public Theatre, Los Angeles, 1985; *Fighting International Fat,* Playwright's Horizons, NY, 1985. PLAYS, PUBLISHED—*Yanks 3, Detroit 0, Top of the Seventh,* in *Best Short Plays of 1977.*

TELEVISION—Talent coordinator and writer, *The David Frost Show;* talent coordinator and writer, *The Dick Cavett Show.*

MEMBER: Dramatists Guild, Writers Guild, Screen Actors Guild, Actors' Equity Association.

AWARDS: Rockefeller Foundation Fellowship, 1976.

ADDRESSES: HOME—New York, NY. AGENT—Flora Roberts, Inc. 157 W. 57th Street, New York, NY 10019.

* * *

RHODES, Nancy   1946-

PERSONAL: Born July 5, 1946, in Chambersburg, PA; daughter of Harry Merriweather (an aviation cost estimator) and Alice Leidig (a pre-school director and puppeteer; maiden name, Ryder) Rhodes. EDUCATION: Ohio University, B.F.A., 1968; New York University, M.F.A., 1973.

VOCATION: Director, producer, actress, and teacher.

CAREER: STAGE DEBUT—Kim Macafee, *Bye Bye Birdie,* Chambersburg Community Theatre, Chambersburg, PA, 1963, for eight

performances. NEW YORK DEBUT—Director, *American Gothics,* Roundabout Theatre, 1972, for twenty-five performances. PRINCIPAL STAGE WORK—Director, *An Evening of Russian Theatre,* Roundabout Theatre, NY, 1971; *The Lover* and *Box and Box,* both Roundabout Theatre, 1972; director, *Middle of the Night,* Kagan Theatre, NY, 1974; director, *Common Garden Variety* and director, *Mine!,* both Interart, NY, 1974; director, *One Short Day at the Jamboree,* Town Hall, NY, 1974; producing director, *New Plays by Women Writers,* Westbeth Playwrights Collective, NY, 1974-75; director, *Scapin,* Geva Theatre, Rochester, NY, 1977.

Director, all at the Encompass Music Theatre, NY: *The Mother of Us All,* 1976; *The Yellow Wallpaper,* 1976; *The Tender Land,* 1977; *He Who Gets Slapped,* 1978; *Hear Their Voices, Women Founders of the American Theatre, 1910-1946,* 1978; *Regina,* 1978; *Fantasies Take Flight,* 1979; *The Wise Woman,* 1979; *Postcard from Morocco,* 1979; *Elizabeth and Essex,* 1980; *Der Vampyr,* 1980.

Director, *Transatlantic,* Trenton, NJ, 1981; director, *The Abduction from the Seraglio,* Lake George Opera Festival, Glen Falls, NY, 1981; director, *The Adventures of Friar Tuck,* Eugene O'Neill Composers Conference, Waterford, CT, 1981; director, *Tartuffe,* San Francisco Opera, CA, 1981; director, *The Monkey Opera,* Brooklyn Academy of Music, NY, 1982; director, *Death in Venice,* Gota Lejon Theatre, Stockholm, Sweden, 1983-84; director, *The Fantasticks,* Hartt Opera Theatre, West Hartford, CT, 1985; director and producer, *Lord Byron,* Alice Tully Hall, Lincoln Center, NY, 1985.

MAJOR TOURS—Writer and director, *Miss Jane's Parlour,* Rotterdam, Den Haag, Utrecht, Amsterdam, Netherlands, 1982.

NANCY RHODES

RELATED CAREER—Teacher, Pratt Institute, 1976-81; director and casting, Roundabout Theatre, NY, 1971-73; teacher, Manhattan School of Music, 1984—; co-artistic director, New York Opera Repertory Theatre, 1984—; American representative, International Theatre Institute, 1983-87.

MEMBER: American Directors Institute (advisory council), League of Professional Theatre Women, Society of Stage Directors and Choreographers (executive board, 1982-83), American Guild of Musical Artists, National Music Theatre Network.

AWARDS: Soho Weekly News Award, Excellence in the Creative Arts, 1977, for *The Mother of Us All.*

ADDRESSES: OFFICE—New York Opera Repertory Theatre, 180 W. 93rd Street, Suite 1H, New York, NY 10025. AGENT—c/o Barbara Eubanks, Associate Artistic Entertainment, 782 West End Avenue, Suite 32, New York, NY 10025.

*   *   *

RICE, Peter   1928-

PERSONAL: Born September 13, 1928, in Simla, India; son of Cecil Morrish and Ethel (Blacklaw) Rice; married Pat Albeck. EDUCATION: Attended St. Dunstan's College, Reigate, Surrey and the Royal College of Art.

VOCATION: Designer.

CAREER: FIRST STAGE WORK—Designer, *Sex and Seraphim,* Watergate Theatre, England, 1951. PRINCIPAL STAGE WORK—Designer, with the Old Vic Theatre Company, London, *Time Remembered,* 1954; *The Taming of the Shrew, The Winter's Tale, Much Ado About Nothing,* all 1956; *Living for Pleasure,* 1958; *A Day in the Life Of . . . ,* 1958; *On the Avenue, Toad of Toad Hall, The Lord Chamberlain Regrets,* all 1961; *Castle in Sweden,* double bill, *Talking to You* and *Across the Board on Tomorrow Morning, Rule of Three,* all 1962; *Madigan's Lock, The Wood of the Whispering,* both 1963; *Mr. Whatnot,* 1964; *Pickwick,* London and New York, 1965; *As You Like It,* 1965; *The Two Character Play,* 1967; *The Duel,* 1968; *Ann Veronica, On a Foggy Day, His, Hers and Theirs,* all 1969; *The Happy Apple, Flint, Oedipus Now,* all 1972; *Say Goodnight to Grandma,* 1973; *The Vortex,* 1975.

With the Greenwich Theatre Company: *Heaven and Hell, Miss Julie,* both 1976; *The Admirable Crichton, Singles, Pinch-Me-Not, The Bells of Hell, Shut Your Eyes and Think of England,* all 1977; *Don Juan, An Audience Called Edouard, See How They Run,* also at the Royal Exchange Theatre, Manchester, *Murder Among Friends,* all 1978; *Semi-Detached, The Passing-Out Parade, I Sent a Letter to Me Love,* all 1979.

At the Chichester Festival: *The Farmer's Wife, The Beaux Stratagem, Heartbreak House; An Italian Straw Hat,* all 1966; *Arms and the Man* and *The Proposal,* both 1970.

Also: *Move Over Mrs. Markham,* Ambassador Theatre, London, 1971.

RELATED CAREER—Designed operas and ballets for Aldeburgh, Convent Garden, Glyndebourne, Sadler's Wells and abroad.

ADDRESSES: HOME—Four Western Terrace, London W6, England.*

RICHARDS, Evan

PERSONAL: Son of Normand Richards (a hair designer) and Diana Darrin (an actress).

VOCATION: Actor.

CAREER: PRINCIPAL TELEVISION APPEARANCES—Series: Frankie, *Mama Malone,* CBS, 1984.

Movies: *One Cooks, The Other Doesn't,* CBS, 1984; *Moonlight,* 1984; *Two Kinds of Love,* CBS, 1985.

PRINCIPAL FILM APPEARANCES—*Altered States,* Warner Brothers, 1980; *Twilight Zone: The Movie,* Warner Brothers, 1983; Max Whiteman, *Down and Out in Beverly Hills,* Touchstone, 1986.

PRINCIPAL STAGE APPEARANCES—*Blue Denim,* Catalina Theatre, CA; title role, *Oliver,* San Bernadino Civic Light Opera; young David, *Copperfield,* American National Theatre and Academy (ANTA), NY; *Evita,* Shubert, NY; *Table Settings,* Los Angeles Matrix Theatre, CA.

SIDELIGHTS: RECREATIONS—Playing piano, dancing, singing, composing, making costumes, and creating character make-ups.

ADDRESSES: AGENT—c/o Abrams, Harris and Goldberg, 9220 Sunset Blvd., Suite 101B, Los Angeles, CA 90069. PUBLICIST—Sumski, Green & Company, 8380 Melrose Avenue, Suite 200, Los Angeles, CA 90069.

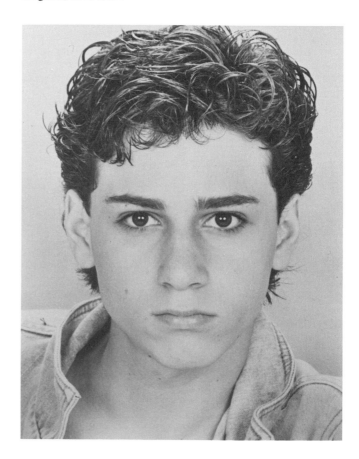

EVAN RICHARDS

RICHARDSON, Ian   1934-

PERSONAL: Born April 7, 1934, in Edinburgh, Scotland; son of John and Margaret (Drummond) Richardson; married Maroussia Frank. EDUCATION: Attended Tynecastle School, Edinburgh; trained for the stage at the College of Dramatic Art, Glasgow.

VOCATION: Actor.

CAREER: LONDON DEBUT—Count Malatesti, *The Duchess of Malfi*, Aldwych Theatre, 1960. NEW YORK DEBUT—Antipholus of Ephesus, *The Comedy of Errors*, State Theatre, 1964. PRINCIPAL STAGE APPEARANCES—Title role, *Hamlet*, John Worthing, *The Importance of Being Earnest*, Adolph, *Creditors*, all with the Birmingham Repertory Company, 1958; Arragon, *The Merchant of Venice*, Sir Andrew Aguecheek, *Twelfth Night*, both Shakespeare Memorial Theatre Company, Stratford-Upon-Avon, 1960.

With the Royal Shakespeare Company: Don John, *Much Ado About Nothing*, 1961; Oberon, *A Midsummer Night's Dream*, Tranio, *The Taming of the Shrew*, Antipholus of Ephesus, *The Comedy of Errors*, all 1962; Doctor, *The Representative*, Herod, *The Miracles*, Southwark Cathedral, 1963; Edmund, *King Lear*, Herald, *Marat/Sade*, Aldwych Theatre, London, Ithamore, *The Jew of Malta*, Ford, *The Merry Wives of Windsor*, all 1964; Antipholus of Syracuse, *The Comedy of Errors*, Eino Silakka, *Squire Puntila and His Servant Matti*, Aldwych Theatre, London, 1965, Marat, *Marat/Sade*, Aldwych Theatre, London, then Martin Beck Theatre, NY, 1965.

Chorus, *Henry V*, Vendice, *The Revenger's Tragedy*, 1966; title role, *Coriolanus*, Vendice, *The Revenger's Tragedy*, Bertram, *All's Well That Ends Well*, Malcolm, *Macbeth*, all 1967, with the last two repeated at the Aldwych Theatre, London, 1968; Cassius, *Julius Caesar*, Ford, *The Merry Wives of Windsor*, both 1968; title role, *Pericles*, Ford, *The Merry Wives of Windsor*, Vendice, *The Revenger's Tragedy*, all 1969; Angelo, *Measure for Measure*, Buckingham, *Richard III*, Proteus, *The Two Gentlemen of Verona*, Prospero, *The Tempest*, all 1970; Tom Wrench, *Trelawny of the Wells*, Sadler's Wells Theatre, then Prince of Wales' Theatre, London, 1972.

With the Royal Shakespeare Company, Stratford-Upon-Avon: alternated (with Richard Pasco) roles of Richard II and Bolingbroke, *Richard II*, 1973-74, then at the Brooklyn Academy of Music, NY, 1974; Berowne, *Love's Labours' Lost*, 1973; Shalimov, *Summerfolk*, Stratford, then Brooklyn Academy of Music, NY, Ernst Scholz, *The Marquis of Keith*, Iachimo, *Cymbeline*, also at the Aldwych Theatre, London, all 1974; Berowne, *Love's Labor's Lost*, also at the Aldwych Theatre, London, Ford, *The Merry Wives of Windsor*, title role, *Richard III*, all 1975.

Henry Higgins, *My Fair Lady*, St. James Theatre, London, 1976; Jack Tanner, *Man and Superman*, 1977; Doctor, *The Millionairess*, Shaw Festival, Niagra on the Lake, Canada, 1977; Mercutio, *Romeo and Juliet*, Khlestakov, *The Government Inspector*, David Garrick, *The Undisputed Monarch of the English Stage*, all Old Vic, London, 1979.

MAJOR TOURS—Antipholus of Ephesus, *The Comedy of Errors*, Edmund, *King Lear*, European and Soviet cities, 1964; with the Royal Shakespeare Company, Japanese cities, 1970.

PRINCIPAL FILM APPEARANCES—*The Darwin Adventure*, Twentieth Century-Fox, 1972; *Man of La Mancha*, United Artists, 1972; *Brazil*, Universal, 1986.

IAN RICHARDSON

TELEVISION DEBUT—*As You Like It*, BBC, 1962. PRINCIPAL TELEVISION APPEARANCES—*Private Shulz; Mistral's Daughter;* Nehru, *Mountbatten; Star Quality; Monsignor Quixote.*

AWARDS: James Bride Gold Medal Award, 1957.

SIDELIGHTS: FAVORITE ROLES—Richard II, Cassius, Prospero, Richard III, Berowne. RECREATIONS—Music, cine-photography.

ADDRESSES: AGENT—London Management, 235-241 Regent Street, London W1A 2JT, England.

*　　*　*　　*　*

RICHARDSON, Patricia   1951-

PERSONAL: Born February 23, 1951, in Bethesda, MD; daughter of Lawrence Baxter (a retired naval officer and corporate executive) and Elizabeth (Howard) Richardson; married Raymond Baker (an actor), June 20, 1982; children: Henry. EDUCATION: Southern Methodist University, B.F.A., 1972.

VOCATION: Actress.

CAREER: NEW YORK DEBUT—Chorus, *Gypsy*, Music Box Theatre. PRINCIPAL STAGE APPEARANCES—Understudy Louise, *Gypsy*, Music Box Theatre, NY; Janice, *Loose Ends*, Circle in the Square, NY; Collard Darnell, *The Wake of Jamie Foster*, Eugene O'Neill Theatre, NY; Sally Chisum, *The Collected Works of Billy the Kid*, Nameless Theatre, NY; Lisa, *The Frequency*, WPA

PATRICIA RICHARDSON

Theatre, NY; Joanne, *Vanities*, Chelsea Westside Theatre, NY; Ovidia, *The Coroner's Plot*, Ronda, *Hooters*, Jenny, *Company*, multiple roles, *Fables for Friends*, all at the Playwright's Horizons, NY; Elain Rutledge, *The Miss Firecracker Contest*, Manhattan Theatre Club, NY.

Cordelia, *King Lear*, Bob Hope Theatre, Dallas, TX; Childie, *The Killing of Sister George*, Asolo State Theatre, FL; Ginny, *Relatively Speaking*, Tanglewood, MA; Gwendolyn, *The Importance of Being Earnest*, Curley's Wife, *Of Mice and Men*, Tracy Lord, *The Philadelphia Story*, all with the Peterborough Players; Collard Darnell, *The Wake of Jamie Foster*, Hartford Stage Company, CT; Hilda Manney, *Room Service*, Gwen Landis, *Fifth of July*, both at the Cincinnati Playhouse, OH; Lucia Rismondi, *About Face*, Yale Repertory, New Haven, CT.

MAJOR TOURS—Joanne, *Vanities*, Ford Theatre, Washington, DC, American Conservatory Theatre, San Francisco, CA, and Fisher Theatre, Detroit, MI.

PRINCIPAL FILM APPEARANCES—*Gas*, Paramount, 1981; Mrs. Azure, *You Better Watch Out*, Azure Productions.

PRINCIPAL TELEVISION APPEARANCES—Series: Beth, *Double Trouble*, NBC.

Episodic: *The Doctors*, NBC; "A Piece of the Rock," *Love, Sidney*, NBC.

ADDRESSES: AGENT—c/o Jeff Hunter, Triad Artists, 888 Seventh Avenue, New York, NY 10106.

RICHARDSON, Tony   1928-

PERSONAL: Born June 5, 1928, in Shipley, Yorkshire, England; son of C.A. and Elsie (Campion) Richardson; married Vanessa Redgrave, April 29, 1962 (divorced); children: Natasha Jane. EDUCATION: Attended Ashville College, Harrogate and Wadham College, Oxford.

VOCATION: Director and producer.

CAREER: FIRST STAGE WORK—Director, Oxford University Dramatic Society, 1949-51: *The Duchess of Malfi; Peer Gynt; Romeo and Juliet; King John.* FIRST NEW YORK STAGE WORK—Director, *Look Back in Anger*, Lyceum Theatre, 1957.

PRINCIPAL STAGE WORK—Director: *The Country Wife*, Royal Theatre, Stratford, England, 1955; With the English Stage Company, Royal Court Theatre: *Look Back in Anger, Cards of Identity*, both 1956, *The Member of the Wedding, The Entertainer, The Chairs, The Making of Moo*, all 1957; *The Entertainer*, Palace Theatre, NY, 1957; *Requiem for a Nun*, NY, 1957; *The Chairs* and *The Lesson*, Phoenix Theatre, NY, 1958; *The Entertainer*, Royale Theatre, NY, 1958; *Flesh to a Tiger*, 1958; *Pericles*, Shakespeare Memorial, Stratford upon Avon, 1958; *Requiem for a Nun*, John Golden Theatre, NY, 1959; *Othello*, Memorial, Stratford, 1959; *Orpheus Descending*, 1959; *Look After Lulu*, 1959.

A Taste of Honey, Lyceum Theatre, NY, 1960; *The Changeling*, NY, 1961; *Luther*, NY, Paris, Holland, and Edinburgh Festival, 1961; *A Midsummer Night's Dream*, 1962; *Semi-Detached*, 1962; *Natural Affection*, Booth Theatre, NY, 1963; *Arturo Ui*, Lunt-Fontanne Theatre, NY, 1963; *The Milk Train Doesn't Stop Here Any More*, Brooks Atkinson Theatre, NY, 1963; *The Seagull*, 1964; *St. Joan of the Stockyards*, 1964; *Hamlet*, Lunt-Fontanne Theatre, NY, 1969; *The Threepenny Opera*, 1972; *I, Claudius*, 1972; *Antony and Cleopatra*, 1973; *The Lady from the Sea*, Circle in the Square, NY, 1976; *As You Like It*, Long Beach Festival, 1979; *Toyer*, Kennedy Center, Washington, DC, 1981; *Dreamhouse*, Los Angeles, CA, 1983.

PRINCIPAL FILM WORK—Director: *Momma Don't Allow; Look Back in Anger*, Warner Brothers, 1959; *The Entertainer*, Continental, 1960; *Saturday Night and Sunday Morning*, Continental, 1961; *A Taste of Honey*, Continental, 1962; *The Loneliness of the Long Distance Runner*, 1962; *Tom Jones*, Lopert, 1963; *The Loved One*, Metro-Goldwyn-Mayer, 1965; *The Charge of the Light Brigade*, United Artists, 1968; *Laughter in the Dark*, Lopert, 1969; *Hamlet*, Columbia, 1970; *A Delicate Balance*, American Film Theatre, 1973; *Joseph Andrews*, 1977; *A Death in Canaan*, 1978; *The Border*, 1982; *Hotel New Hampshire*, Orion, 1984.

PRINCIPAL TELEVISION WORK—Director: *Othello*, BBC; *The Gambler*, BBC.

RELATED CAREER—Associate artistic director, the English Stage Company, 1955-57.

AWARDS: Best Director, Academy Award, 1963, for *Tom Jones*.

ADDRESSES: OFFICE—1478 N. Kings Road, Los Angeles, CA 90069.

RIEHLE, Richard   1948-

PERSONAL: Born May 12, 1948, in Menomonee Falls, WI; son of Herbert John (an assistant postmaster) and Mary Margaret (a nurse; maiden name, Walsh) Riehle. EDUCATION: University of Notre Dame, B.A., 1970; University of Minnesota, M.F.A., 1971; trained for the stage at the John Fernald Academy of Dramatic Art.

VOCATION: Actor and director.

CAREER: STAGE DEBUT—Judge, *Andersonville Trial,* Meadowbrook Theatre, Rochester, MI, 1971. NEW YORK DEBUT—Melia, Dolson, Cop, *Execution of Justice,* Virginia Theatre, 1986, for nineteen performances. PRINCIPAL STAGE APPEARANCES—Nathan Detroit, *Guys and Dolls,* Tiger Brown, *Threepenny Opera,* both at the Ledges Playhouse; Pinky Hartman, *Front Page,* Joseph, *Judas,* James Larabee, *Sherlock Holmes,* Frank Strang, *Equus,* Phil Hogan, *Moon for the Misbegotten,* Rufe Phelps, *Knights of the White Magnolia,* all at the Pacific Conservatory of the Performing Arts Theatre, CA; Brabantio, *Othello,* Gremio, *Taming of the Shrew,* Toby Belch, *Twelfth Night,* Posso, *Waiting for Godot,* Walter Morley, *Artichoke,* Captain Boyle, *Juno and the Paycock,* Sir George Thunder, *Wild Oats,* all at the Oregon Shakespeare Festival, Medford, OR; Virgil Blessing, *Bus Stop,* Jaspar Fidget, *The Country Wife,* Hardcastle, *She Stoops to Conquer,* all at the Intiman Theatre, Seattle, WA.

Mr. Gill, *The Showoff,* Doc Baugh, *Cat on a Hot Tin Roof,* Bill Whitmore, *Ballad of Soapy Smith,* Schwartz, *Front Page,* all at the Seattle Repertory Company, WA; Capulet, *Romeo and Juliet,* Colorado Shakespeare Festival; Peter Quince, *A Midsummer Night's Dream,* Meadowbrook Theatre, Rochester, MI; Touchstone, *As You Like It,* Solvang Summerfest, CA; Solyony, *The Three Sisters,* Guthrie Other Place, Minneapolis, MN; Baptista, *The Taming of the*

Shrew, Arizona Theatre Company; Dr. Gibbs, *Our Town,* Banquo, *Macbeth,* both at the American Conservatory Theatre, San Francisco, CA; Harry Brock, *Born Yesterday,* Phil Romano, *That Championship Season,* McMurphy, *One Flew Over the Cuckoo's Nest,* all at the Boarshead Theatre, MI; Leon, *Return of Pinocchio,* Hans, *Through the Leaves,* both at the Empty Space Theatre, Seattle, WA; Joshua, Cathy, *Cloud Nine,* Lee, *True West,* both at A Contemporary Theatre, Seattle, WA; Michael James, *Playboy of the Western World,* Berkeley Repertory, CA; Count Gregor, *Fools,* Thurston Wheelis, *Greater Tuna,* both with the Alaska Repertory; Dudard, *Rhinoceros,* Chaplain de Stugumber, *St. Joan,* Host of the Garter, *Merry Wives of Windsor,* and Fezziwig, *A Christmas Carol,* all at the Guthrie Theatre, Minneapolis, 1986-87.

FILM DEBUT—*Rooster Cogburn,* Universal, 1974. PRINCIPAL FILM APPEARANCES—Bartender, *Joy Ride,* American International, 1976; *The Duchess and the Dirtwater Fox,* Twentieth Century-Fox, 1976; *Twice in a Lifetime,* 1985.

TELEVISION DEBUT—Tom, *The Other Side of Hell,* CBS, 1977. PRINCIPAL TELEVISION APPEARANCES—Specials: "The Trial of Paul Robeson," *Black Perspectives,* 1975.

Movies: *Escape from Hell,* 1977; Joe Kennedy, *The Forgotten Kennedy,* 1977.

Episodic: "Riding High," *Hot Pursuit,* NBC, 1984.

MEMBER: Actors' Equity Association, Screen Actors Guild, American Federation of Television and Radio Artists.

SIDELIGHTS: Richard Riehle told *CTFT* that he speaks fluent German, which he learned by studying in Innsbruck and Salzburg, Austria.

ADDRESSES: AGENT—Amy Wright Representatives, 136 E. 57th Street, New York, NY 10022.

*   *   *

RIGG, Diana   1938-

PERSONAL: Born July 20, 1938, in Doncaster, Yorkshire, England; daughter of Louis and Beryl (Helliwell) Rigg; married Menachem Gueffen (an artist; divorced); married Archie Stirling (a businessman); children (second marriage) Rachel. EDUCATION: Attended Fulneck Girls School, Pudsey; studied at the Royal Academy of Dramatic Art, London.

VOCATION: Actress.

CAREER: STAGE DEBUT—Natella Abashwili, *The Caucasian Chalk Circle,* Royal Academy of Dramatic Art production at the Theatre Royal, York Festival, 1957. LONDON DEBUT—Second Ondine and Violanta, *Ondine,* Aldwych Theatre, 1961. NEW YORK DEBUT—Cordelia, *King Lear,* and Adriana, *The Comedy of Errors,* in repertory, New York State Theatre, 1964. PRINCIPAL STAGE APPEARANCES—Appeared in repertory in Chesterfield and York, England, 1957-58; with the Royal Shakespeare Company at the Aldwych Theatre, London: Phillipe Trincante, *The Devils,* Gwendolen, *Becket,* and Bianca, *The Taming of the Shrew,* all 1961, and Madame de Touruel, *The Art of Seduction,* 1962; with the Royal Shakespeare Company, Stratford-on-Avon: Helena, *Midsummer Night's Dream,* Bianca, *The Taming of the Shrew,* Lady Macduff, *Macbeth,* Adriana, *The Comedy of Errors,* and Cordelia, *King Lear,*

RICHARD RIEHLE

all 1962; Monica Stettler, *The Physicists,* Aldwych Theatre, 1963; Helena, *Midsummer Night's Dream,* Stratford-on-Avon, Aldwych Theatre, 1963; Cordelia, *King Lear,* Aldwych Theatre, 1964; Viola, *Twelfth Night,* Stratford-on-Avon, 1966.

Heloise, *Abelard and Heloise,* Wyndham's Theatre, London, 1970, then Brooks Atkinson Theatre, NY, 1971; with the National Theatre of Great Britain: Dottie, *Jumpers;* Lady Macbeth, *Macbeth,* 1972; Celimene, *The Misanthrope,* 1973; Eliza Doolittle, *Pygmalion,* Albery Theatre, 1974; Celimene, *The Misanthrope,* Old Vic Theatre, then in a Broadway production, 1975; Governor's Wife, *Phaedra Britannica,* Old Vic Theatre, 1975; Ilona, *The Guardsman,* National Theatre, 1978; Ruth Carson, *Night and Day,* Phoenix Theatre, London, 1978; Rita, *Little Eyolf,* Lyric Theatre, Hammersmith, London, 1985; Cleopatra, *Antony and Cleopatra,* Chichester Festival, 1985.

MAJOR TOURS—Helena, *A Midsummer Night's Dream,* tour of English provinces, 1963; Adriana, *The Comedy of Errors* and Cordelia, *King Lear,* international tour sponsored by the British Council, Europe, USSR, and the United States, 1964-65.

PRINCIPAL FILM APPEARANCES—*The Assassination Bureau,* Paramount, 1969; *On Her Majesty's Secret Service,* United Artists, 1969; *Julius Caesar,* American International Pictures, 1970; *The Hospital,* United Artists, 1971; *Theatre of Blood,* United Artists, 1973; *A Little Night Music,* 1978; *The Great Muppet Caper,* Univeral, 1981; *Evil Under the Sun,* Universal, 1982.

TELEVISION DEBUT—Adriana, *The Comedy of Errors,* BBC, 1964. PRINCIPAL TELEVISION APPEARANCES—Series: Emma Peel, *The Avengers,* ABC, 1966-68.

Movies: *In This House of Brede,* 1975; also appeared in *Married Alive; Three Piece Suite.*

Plays: Regan, *King Lear,* PBS, 1983.

Episodic: Lady Dedlock, "Bleak House," *Masterpiece Theatre,* PBS, 1986.

WRITINGS: MEMOIR—*No Turn Unstoned.*

AWARDS: Antoinette Perry Award nominations, 1971, for *Abelard and Heloise* and 1975, for *The Misanthrope.*

ADDRESSES: AGENT—John Redway Ltd, 16 Berners Street, London W1, England.*

*   *   *

RIKER, William R.   1923-

PERSONAL: Born June 8, 1923; married Sigrid W., October 4, 1983; children: Rick, Robin, Van. EDUCATION: Syracuse University, B.S., 1949. MILITARY: U.S. Army Air Force, 1942-45.

VOCATION: Actor.

CAREER: TELEVISION DEBUT—*Studio One,* CBS. PRINCIPAL TELEVISION APPEARANCES—*Kraft Theater,* NBC; *Milton Berle Show,* NBC; *Jimmy Durante Show,* NBC; *The Trap,* CBS; *You Are There,* CBS; *The Web,* CBS; *Martin Kane,* NBC; *One Man's Family,* NBC; *Robert Montgomery Presents,* NBC; *Andy Williams Show,* NBC; *J.R.R. Tolkien; One Life to Live; Another World; Search for Tomorrow; Edge of Night; All My Children; Dallas.*

Movies: *Muggable Mary, Street Cop,* NBC, 1982.

Specials: *The Great American Fourth of July and Other Tragedies,* PBS.

PRINCIPAL FILM APPEARANCES—Wilfred, *Female Animal,* Universal, 1958; Dr. Kaltenbach, *Games,* Universal, 1967; Dr. Meyer, *Such Good Friends,* Paramount, 1971; Carlton Smyth, *Lady Liberty,* United Artists, 1972; Mr. Blackman, *Audrey Rose,* United Artists, 1977; Mr. Jordan, *Chapter Two,* Columbia, 1979.

STAGE DEBUT—*Accent on Youth,* Fayetteville Country Playhouse, NY. PRINCIPAL STAGE APPEARANCES—*Philadelphia Story, Arsenic and Old Lace,* both at the Fayetteville Country Playhouse, NY; *Harvey,* Elitch Gardens, CO; David Slater, *Moon Is Blue,* Aspen Playhouse, CO; the Colonel, *La Ronde,* Sheridan Whiteside, *The Man Who Came to Dinner,* and Shylock, *Merchant of Venice,* all with the Nomad Players, CO; Willie, *Sunshine Boys,* Allenberry Playhouse, PA; Max, *The Day the Whores Came Out to Play Tennis,* Pappa, *Clash By Night,* both at the IRT, NY; Pat, *The Hostage,* Geva Theatre, Rochester, NY; Candy, *Of Mice and Men,* American Stage Festival; Uncle Willie, *Philadelphia Story* and *Born Yesterday,* both Pennsylvania Stage Company, Allentown, PA; Squire Cayce, *The Freak,* WPA Theatre, NY; Senator Hedges, Judge Murdoch, *Nuts,* Birmingham, MI; Fitz, *Crossing the Bar,* Constable, *Our Town,* both Center Stage Company, Baltimore, MD.

MEMBER: Actors' Equity Association, Screen Actors Guild, American Federation of Television and Radio Artists.

ADDRESSES: AGENT—Don Buchwald, Ten E. 44th Street, New York, NY 10017.

*   *   *

RILEY, Jack   1935-

PERSONAL: Born December 30, 1935, in Cleveland, OH; son of John A. and Agnes C. (Corrigan) Riley; married Ginger Lawrence, May 18, 1974; children: Jamie, Brian. EDUCATION: John Carroll University, B.S., 1961. MILITARY: U.S. Army, 1958-61.

VOCATION: Actor and writer.

CAREER: PRINCIPAL TELEVISION APPEARANCES—Series: Wally Frick, *Occasional Wife,* NBC, 1966-67; Mr. Carlin, *The Bob Newhart Show,* CBS, 1972-78; *Keep on Truckin',* ABC, 1975.

Episodic: *Mary Tyler Moore Show,* CBS, 1972; *Barney Miller,* ABC, 1979; *Diff'rent Strokes,* NBC, 1979; *Hart to Hart,* ABC, 1980; *The Love Boat,* ABC, 1980.

PRINCIPAL FILM APPEARANCES—*Catch 22,* Paramount, 1970; *McCabe and Mrs. Miller,* Warner Brothers, 1971; *The Long Goodbye,* 1972; *California Split,* Columbia, 1974; *The World's Greatest Lover,* Twentieth Century-Fox, 1977; *High Anxiety,* Twentieth Century-Fox, 1978; *Butch and Sundance—The Early Years,* Twentieth Century-Fox, 1979; *History of the World, Part I,* 1981; *Frances,* Universal, 1982; *To Be or Not to Be,* Twentieth Century-Fox, 1983; *Finders Keepers,* Warner Brothers, 1984.

PRINCIPAL STAGE APPEARANCES—*Small Craft Warnings,* West Coast premier, 1975.

RELATED CAREER—Instructor of comedy acting, Sherwood Oaks

College; member, "Rolling Along of 1960," Department of the Army Traveling Show, 1960; voice over in numerous commercials.

WRITINGS: TELEVISION—*The Mort Sahl Show,* 1967; *The Don Rickles Show,* 1968; commercials for Blore & Richman, Los Angeles, 1966-84.

MEMBER: Screen Actors Guild, Actors' Equity Association, Writers Guild of America, Academy of Motion Picture Arts and Sciences, American Federation of Television and Radio Artists, Academy of Television Arts and Sciences.

ADDRESSES: AGENT—The Artists Agency, 10,000 Santa Monica Blvd., Los Angeles, CA 90067.*

*   *   *

RILEY, Larry

PERSONAL: Born June 21; son of George C. Bass and Corine C. Riley; children: Larry M., Jr. EDUCATION: Memphis State University, M.F.A.; trained for the stage at the Goodman Theatre School, Chicago, with Patrick Henery. RELIGION: Baptist.

VOCATION: Actor.

CAREER: STAGE DEBUT—Judge, *The Blacks,* Memphis State University, TN, 1971. NEW YORK DEBUT—Leading Player, *Pippin,* Minskoff Theatre. PRINCIPAL STAGE APPEARANCES—Wally, *I Love My Wife,* Longacre Theatre, NY, 1978; Frances, *Night and Day,* American National Theatre and Academy (ANTA), NY, 1979; the Conductor, *Frimbo,* Grand Central Station Theatre, NY, 1980; Lawrence, *Shakespeare's Cabaret,* Bijou Theatre, NY, 1981; C.J. Memphis, *A Soldier's Play,* Theatre Four, NY, 1981-82; Larry, *Maybe I'm Doing It Wrong,* Astor Place Theatre, NY, 1982; Curtis Taylor, *Dreamgirls,* Shubert Theatre, Los Angeles, CA, 1983; also: Robinson, *Amerika,* Music Theatre Lab, NY; Larry, *Styne After Styne* and Silky, *Sidewalkin',* both Manhattan Theatre Club, NY.

Regional: Valere, *Doctor in Spite of Himself,* David, *Way Back When,* Clay, *The Dutchman,* all Center Stage, Baltimore, MD; Rip, *A Crowd of People,* the Phaedra, *Tomorrow,* Nat Baker, *Workin',* both Chicago Free Street Theatre, IL; the Butterfly, *Three Mean Fairy Tales,* Kennedy Center, Washington, DC; Teshembe, *To Be Young, Gifted, and Black,* Goodman Theatre, Chicago; Larry, *August 6th 1945,* C.J. Memphis, *A Soldier's Play,* Mark Taper Forum, Los Angeles, 1982.

MAJOR TOURS—Leading Player, *Pippin,* U.S. cities; Curtis Taylor, Jr. *Dreamgirls,* U.S. cities, 1983-84.

FILM DEBUT—Boardwalk, *Crackers,* Universal, 1984. PRINCIPAL FILM APPEARANCES—C.J. Memphis, *A Soldier's Story,* Columbia, 1984.

TELEVISION DEBUT—Calvin Barnes, *The Doctors,* NBC. PRINCIPAL TELEVISION APPEARANCES—Series: Detective Garrison, *One Life to Live,* ABC; Vernon Tucker, *Hill Street Blues,* NBC.

Movies: Steve Kelsey, *Muggable Mary, Street Cop,* NBC, 1982.

MEMBER: Actors' Equity Association, Screen Actors Guild, American Federation of Television and Radio Artists, American Guild of Variety Artists.

LARRY RILEY

ADDRESSES: AGENT—Triad, 888 Seventh Avenue, Suite 1602, New York, NY 10106.

*   *   *

ROBERTS, Marilyn

PERSONAL: Born October 30; daughter of Alec and Grace (McKay) Roberts. EDUCATION: San Francisco State College, B.A.; trained for the stage with John Stix and David Sorin Collyer. RELIGION: Movement of Spiritual Inner Awareness.

VOCATION: Actress.

CAREER: STAGE DEBUT—Barbara Allen, *Dark of the Moon,* San Francisco State College Theatre, CA, 1958. NEW YORK DEBUT—General understudy, *Telemachus Clay,* Writers Stage, 1963. LONDON DEBUT—Mrs. Loop, *Futz,* Mercury Theatre, 1967. PRINCIPAL STAGE APPEARANCES—Nora, *A Clearing in the Woods,* San Francisco Theatre Company, CA, 1958; Dixie Evans, *The Big Knife,* San Francisco, CA, 1958; Mrs. Loop, *Futz,* Theatre de Lys, NY, 1969; Marie, Queen Marie Antoinette, *Tom Paine,* Stage 73, NY, 1969.

Rain Octaine, *Massachusetts Trust,* Brandeis Festival; various roles, *The Eighth Wonder,* Brooklyn Bridge Centennial, NY; Roller Skater, *Split Lip,* Theatre in Space; Mrs. Malloy, *The Matchmaker,* Erie Playhouse, PA; Vera Charles, *Auntie Mame,* Sheila Broadbent, *The Reluctant Debutante,* both Moline Theatre; Lily Thepary, *The Class,* Writers' Stage, NY; Lois, *Why Tuesday Never Has a Blue Monday,* Bobo Society, *Times Square,* Rosemary, *A Rat's Mass,* Richest Girl, *The Richest Girl in the World Finds Happiness,* all La Mama E.T.C.; mother, *Mert and Phil,* New York Shakespeare

MARILYN ROBERTS

Festival; Musetta Stone, *The Blonde Leading the Blonde*, Theatre for the New City; stand-up comic, *The Seth Allen Show*, Playboy Club, NY; Taffy, *Taffy's Taxi*, Beverly Hills Playhouse, CA; Jenny Diver, *The Threepenny Opera*, Odyssey Theatre.

FILM DEBUT—Mrs. Loop, *Futz*, American International, 1969. PRINCIPAL FILM APPEARANCES—Tony's blonde, *Looking for Mr. Goodbar*, Paramount, 1977; *Skateboard*, Universal, 1978.

TELEVISION DEBUT—"Ted's Moment of Glory," *Mary Tyler Moore Show*, CBS.

MEMBER: Actors' Equity Association (western advisory board, 1977-81), Screen Actors Guild, American Federation of Television and Radio Artists; Theatre Gym, Westbeth Artists.

AWARDS: North American Senior Dance Champion (with Gary Castre, three times).

SIDELIGHTS: CTFT learned that Marilyn Roberts is also a roller-skating champion.

ADDRESSES: OFFICE—463 West Street, New York, NY 10014.

*   *   *

ROBERTS, Pernell

PERSONAL: Born May 18, in Waycross, GA; married Kara Knack; children: Christopher. EDUCATION: Attended the University of Maryland. MILITARY: U.S. Marine Corps.

VOCATION: Actor.

CAREER: STAGE DEBUT—*The Man Who Came to Dinner*, Olney Theatre, MD. NEW YORK DEBUT—*Tonight in Samarkand*, Broadway production, 1953. PRINCIPAL STAGE APPEARANCES—As a member of the resident company at the Arena Stage in Washington, DC; *A Clearing in the Woods*, Broadway production; *Macbeth*, NY, 1955; *Gone with the Wind*, Los Angeles Civic Light Opera.

MAJOR TOURS—*The King and I*, national tour.

PRINCIPAL TELEVISION APPEARANCES—Series: Adam Cartwright, *Bonanza*, NBC, 1959-65; Dr. John "Trapper John" McIntyre, *Trapper John M.D.*, CBS, 1979-85.

Episodic: *Vega$*, ABC; *Hotel*, ABC.

Guest: *Hollywood Screen Test*, ABC.

Mini-Series: *Captains and the Kings*, 1976.

Movies: Charlie Cobb, *Nice Night for a Hanging; High Noon Part II—The Return of Will Kane*.

FILM DEBUT—*Desire Under the Elms*, Paramount, 1958. PRINCIPAL FILM APPEARANCES—*The Sheepman*, Metro-Goldwyn-Mayer, 1958; *Ride Lonesome*, 1959; *The Magic of Lassie*, 1978.

AWARDS: Drama Desk Award, 1955, for *Macbeth*.

ADDRESSES: OFFICE—c/o CBS Entertainment 51 W. 52nd Street, New York, NY 10019.*

*   *   *

ROBERTSON, Cliff   1925-

PERSONAL: Full name, Clifford Parker Robertson; born September 9, 1925, in La Jolla, CA; son of Clifford and Andree Robertson; married Cynthia Stone, 1957 (divorced); married Dina Merrill (an actress), 1966; children: (first marriage) Stephanie; (second marriage) Heather.

VOCATION: Actor, director, and writer.

CAREER: PRINCIPAL STAGE APPEARANCES—*Mr. Roberts;* Matthew Anderson, *Late Love*, National Theatre, NY, 1953; *The Lady and the Tiger; The Wisteria Trees;* Val Xavier, *Orpheus Descending*, NY, 1957.

PRINCIPAL STAGE WORK—Director, *The V.I.P.'s*, 1981.

FILM DEBUT—Alan, *Picnic*, Columbia, 1955. PRINCIPAL FILM APPEARANCES—Burt Hanson, *Autumn Leaves*, Columbia, 1956; *The Girl Most Likely*, Universal, 1957; *The Naked and the Dead*, Warner Brothers, 1958; *Gidget*, Columbia, 1959; *Battle of the Coral Sea*, Columbia, 1959; *As the Sea Rages*, Columbia, 1960; *All in a Night's Work*, Paramount, 1961; *The Big Show*, Twentieth Century-Fox, 1961; *Underworld, U.S.A.*, Columbia, 1962; Dr. John Paul Otis, *The Interns*, Columbia, 1962; *My Six Loves*, Paramount, 1963; John F. Kennedy, *PT-109*, Warner Brothers, 1963; *Sunday in New York*, Metro-Goldwyn-Mayer, 1963; *The Best Man*, United Artists, 1964; *633 Squadron*, United Artists, 1964; *Up from the Beach*, Twentieth Century-Fox, 1965; *Love Has Many Faces*, Columbia, 1965; *Masquerade*, United Artists, 1965.

The Honey Pot, United Artists, 1966; title role, *Charly,* Cinerama/Selmur Films, 1968; *The Devil's Brigade,* United Artists, 1968; *Too Late the Hero,* Cinerama, 1970; *The Great Northfield, Minnesota Raid,* Universal, 1972; *J.W. Coop,* Columbia, 1972; *Man on a Swing,* Paramount, 1974; Higgins, *Three Days of the Condor,* Paramount, 1975; *Midway,* Universal/Mirisch Corporation, 1976; *Shoot,* Avco Embassy, 1976; Fowler, "Morning, Winter and Night" (abandoned in production), Xanadu Films, 1977; *Class,* Orion Films, 1983; *Brainstorm,* Metro-Goldwyn-Mayer/United Artists, 1983; *Star '80,* Warner Brothers, 1983; *Charly II,* Selmur Films, 1984; also *Shaker Run.*

PRINCIPAL FILM WORK—Director: *J.W. Coop,* Columbia, 1972; "Morning, Winter and Night," Xanadu Films, 1977; *Charly II,* Selmur Films, 1984.

PRINCIPAL TELEVISION APPEARANCES—Series: Dr. Michael Ranson, *Falcon Crest,* CBS, 1983-84.

Episodic: *Short, Short Dramas,* NBC, 1953; *Treasury Men in Action,* ABC, 1954; *Philco TV Playhouse,* 1955; *Robert Montgomery Presents,* NBC, 1954; "The Two Worlds of Charlie Gordon," *The U.S. Steel Hour; Alcoa Theatre,* NBC; *Studio One,* CBS; *Alcoa Premiere,* ABC; "The Game," *Bob Hope Presents the Chrysler Theatre,* NBC, 1965.

Movies: Philip Nolan, *Man without a Country,* 1973.

Mini-Series: *The Key to Rebecca,* syndicated, 1985; also, *Washington, Behind Closed Doors.*

WRITINGS: PLAYS—*The V.I.P.'s,* 1981.

AWARDS: Best Actor, Academy Award, 1969, for *Charly.*

ADDRESSES: AGENT—International Creative Management, 40 W. 57th Street, New York, NY 10019.*

*   *   *

ROBERTSON, Joel   1950-

PERSONAL: Born December 19, 1950; son of Bernard Arthur (a career U.S. Army officer) and Rosealeen Delores (a registered nurse; maiden name, Hall) Robertson; married Roseanne Germer (a ballet dancer), June 26, 1981.

VOCATION: Actor, dancer, and singer.

CAREER: STAGE DEBUT—Tybalt, *Romeo and Juliet,* Theatre at Monmouth, ME, 1970. NEW YORK DEBUT—Fyedka, *Fiddler on the Roof,* New York State Theatre, 1981, for fifty-six performances. PRINCIPAL STAGE APPEARANCES—Ronnie, *Getting Out,* Theatre de Lys, NY, 1979; Phil, *Snapshot,* Hudson Guild, NY, 1979; *Cats,* Winter Garden, 1983-84.

MAJOR TOURS—Fyedka, *Fiddler on the Roof,* Boston, Philadelphia, Washington, DC, Chicago, Detroit, San Francisco, Minneapolis, Seattle, 1980-83.

ADDRESSES: AGENT—Roxy Horen Allen Management, 1650 Broadway, Suite 1119, New York, NY 10019.

LAILA ROBINS

ROBINS, Laila   1959-

PERSONAL: Born March 14, 1959, in St. Paul, MN; daughter of Janis (a research chemist) and Brigita (Suarcs) Robins. EDUCATION: University of Wisconsin, B.A.; Yale School of Drama, M.F.A.

VOCATION: Actress.

CAREER: STAGE DEBUT—Solveig, *Peer Gynt,* Williamstown Theatre Festival, MA, 1984, for nine performances. NEW YORK DEBUT—Annie, *The Real Thing,* Plymouth, 1984, for 216 performances. PRINCIPAL STAGE APPEARANCES—Stepdaughter, *Six Characters in Search of an Author,* American Repertory Theatre, Cambridge, MA, 1984; Evna, *Undiscovered Country,* Williamstown Theatre Festival, MA, 1985; sweet young girl, *La Ronde,* Williamstown Theatre Festival, MA, 1985.

FILM DEBUT—Marty Ellis, *A Walk on the Moon,* Midwest, 1985.

ADDRESSES: AGENT—c/o Sam Cohn, International Creative Management, 40 W. 57th Street, New York, NY 10019.

*   *   *

RODDENBERRY, Gene   1921-

PERSONAL: Born Eugene Wesley Roddenberry, August 19, 1921, in El Paso, TX; son of Eugene Edward and Caroline Glen (Golemon) Roddenberry; married Majel Leigh Hudec, August 6, 1969; children: Darleen, Dawn Alison, Eugene Wesley, Jr. EDUCATION: Los Angeles City College, A.A.; also attended University of Miami, Columbia University, and University of Southern California. MILITARY: U.S. Army Air Force, 1941-45.

VOCATION: Producer and writer.

CAREER: PRINCIPAL FILM WORK—Producer: *Pretty Maids All in a Row,* Metro-Goldwyn-Mayer, 1971; *Star Trek: The Motion Picture,* Paramount 1979; *Star Trek II: The Wrath of Khan,* Paramount, 1982; executive consultant, *Star Trek III: The Search for Spock,* Paramount, 1984; creator, *Star Trek IV: The Voyage Home,* Paramount, 1986.

PRINCIPAL TELEVISION WORK—Producer, *The Lieutenant,* NBC, 1960-61; producer and creator: *Star Trek,* NBC, 1966-69; *Genesis II,* 1973; *The Questor Tapes,* 1974; *Planet Earth,* 1974; *Spectre,* 1977.

RELATED CAREER: President, Norway Production, Inc., 1962—.

NON-RELATED CAREER—Pilot, Pan American World Airways, 1945-49; sergeant, Los Angeles Police Department, 1949-53.

WRITINGS: SCREENPLAYS—*Pretty Maids All in a Row,* 1971.

TELEVISION—Various television shows between 1953-62, including: *Goodyear Theatre; The Kaiser Aluminum Hour; Chevron Theatre; Four Star Theatre; Dragnet; The Jane Wyman Theatre; Naked City; Have Gun, Will Travel; Star Trek; Spectre.*

BOOKS—*The Making of Star Trek,* Ballantine, 1968; *The Questor Tapes,* Ballantine, 1974, Aeonian, 1975; *Star Trek: The Motion Picture,* Simon and Schuster, 1979, Pocket, 1980.

MEMBER: Writers Guild of America, Television Academy of Arts and Sciences (past member of the executive council); Explorers

GENE RODDENBERRY

Club; Bel-Air Country Club, La Costa Country Club; Association for Professional Law Enforcement, American Civil Liberties Union.

AWARDS: Writers Guild of America Award for writing and production; National Academy of Television Arts and Sciences Awards; Star in his honor placed in the Hollywood Walk of Fame, 1985; Distinguished Flying Cross, Air Medal; honorary degrees: D.H.L., Emerson College, Boston, MA, 1973 and Doctor of Science, Clarkson College, NY, 1981.

ADDRESSES: OFFICE—Paramount Pictures, 5451 Marathon Street, Hollywood, CA 90038. AGENT—Leonard Maizlish, 9255 Sunset Blvd., Los Angeles, CA 90069.

*   *   *

ROGERS, Ginger   1911-

PERSONAL: Born Virginia Katherine McMath, July 16, 1911, in Independence, MO; daughter of William Eddins (an electrcial engineer) and Lela Emogene (a scriptwriter, reporter and critic; maiden name, Owens) McMath; married Jack Edward Culpepper (a vaudevillean known as Jack Pepper), 1929 (divorced, 1931); married Lew Ayres (an actor), 1934 (divorced, 1941); married Jack Bridges, 1943 (divorced, 1949); married Jacques Bergerac (an actor), 1953 (divorced, 1957); married William Marshall (a producer), 1961 (divorced, 1972); children: (stepson) Michael Marshall.

VOCATION: Dancer and actress.

CAREER: STAGE DEBUT—Dancer, *Ginger and Her Redheads,* vaudeville, 1925. NEW YORK DEBUT—In vaudeville, Brooklyn Paramount Theatre, 1931. LONDON DEBUT—Mame Dennis, *Mame,* Drury Lane Theatre, 1969.

PRINCIPAL STAGE APPEARANCES—In vaudeville: *The Original John Held, Jr. Girl,* 1926; with husband Jack Culpepper as *Ginger and Pepper,* 1928-31. On the legitimate stage: Babs Green, *Top Speed,* 46th Street Theatre, NY, 1929; Molly Gray, *Girl Crazy,* Alvin Theatre, NY, 1930; Valerie King/Ruth Gage, *Love and Let Love,* Plymouth Theatre, NY, 1951; Tess Jackson, *The Pink Jungle,* Alcazar Theatre, San Francisco, then Shubert Theatre, Boston, 1959; *More Perfect Union,* California, 1963; Mrs. Dolly Gallagher Levi, *Hello, Dolly!,* St. James Theatre, NY, 1965; Stage Manager, *Our Town,* Ida Green Communications Center, Sherman, TX, 1972.

MAJOR TOURS—Gillian Holroyd, *Bell, Book and Candle,* stock tour, 1958 and 1962; Mrs. Dolly Gallagher Levi, *Hello, Dolly!,* national tour, 1967; also, Annie Oakley, *Annie Get Your Gun;* title role, *The Unsinkable Molly Brown;* Natalya, *Tovarich;* title role, *Coco;* others.

FILM DEBUT—*Campus Sweethearts* (two-reel short), Radio Pictures, 1929. PRINCIPAL FILM APPEARANCES—*A Night in a Dormitory* (two-reel short), Pathe, 1929; *A Day of a Man of Affairs* (one-reel short), Columbia, 1929; Ann Vaughn, *Young Man of Manhattan,* Paramount, 1930; Polly Rockwell, *Queen High,* Paramount, 1930; Ellen Saunders, *The Sap from Syracuse,* Paramount, 1930; secretary, *Office Blues* (one-reel short), Paramount, 1930; Mary Brennan, *Follow the Leader,* Paramount, 1930; Doris Blake, *Honor Among Lovers,* Paramount, 1931; Baby Face, *The Tip-Off,* RKO-Pathe, 1931; Sally, *Suicide Fleet,* RKO-Pathe, 1931; Honey, *Carnival Boat,* RKO-Pathe, 1932; *Hollywood on Parade, Number One* (short), Paramount-Publix, 1932; Ruth, *The Tenderfoot,* First

National/Vitaphone, 1932; *Screen Snapshots* (short), Columbia, 1932; Marie Morgan, *The Thirteenth Guest*, Monogram, 1932; Jessie King, *Hat Check Girl*, Fox, 1932; Alice Brandon, *You Said a Mouthful*, First National/Vitaphone, 1932.

Anytime Annie, *Forty Second Street*, Warner Brothers/Vitaphone, 1933; *Hollywood on Parade, Number Nine* (short), Paramount Publix, 1933; Flip Daly, *Broadway Bad*, Fox, 1933; Fay Fortune, *Gold Diggers of 1933*, Warner Brothers/Vitaphone, 1933; Glory Eden (the "Purity Girl of the Air"), *Professional Sweetheart*, RKO-Pathe, 1933; Patricia Morgan, *A Shriek in the Night*, Allied Films, 1933; Molly Gilbert, *Don't Bet on Love*, Universal, 1933; Dorothy, *Sitting Pretty*, Paramount, 1933; Honey Hale, *Flying Down to Rio*, RKO-Pathe, 1933; Marje Harris, *Chance at Heaven*, RKO-Radio, 1933; Mary Carroll, *Rafter Romance*, RKO-Radio, 1934; Cecelia (Pony) Ferris, *Finishing School*, RKO-Radio, 1934; Peggy, *Twenty Million Sweethearts*, First National/Vitaphone, 1934; Madge Rountree, *Change of Heart*, Fox, 1934; Lilly Lander, *Upperworld*, Warner Brothers, 1934; Mimi Glossop, *The Gay Divorcee*, RKO-Radio, 1934; Sylvia Dennis, *Romance in Manahattan*, RKO-Radio, 1934.

Countess Scharwenka, *Roberta*, RKO-Radio, 1935; Donna Martin, *Star of Midnight*, RKO-Radio, 1935; Dale Tremont, *Top Hat*, RKO-Radio, 1935; Carol Corliss (Cora Colfax), *In Person*, RKO-Radio, 1935; Sherry Martin, *Follow the Fleet*, RKO-Radio, 1936; Penelope (Penny) Carroll, *Swing Time*, RKO-Radio, 1936; Linda Keene, *Shall We Dance*, RKO-Radio, 1937; Jean Maitland, *Stage Door*, RKO-Radio, 1937; *Holiday Greetings* (short), 1937; Teddy Shaw, *Having Wonderful Time*, RKO-Radio, 1938; Frances Brent (Francey La Roche), *Vivacious Lady*, RKO-Radio, 1938; Amanda Cooper, *Carefree*, RKO-Radio, 1938; Irene (Foote) Castle, *The Story of Vernon and Irene Castle*, RKO-Radio, 1939; Polly Parrish, *Bachelor Mother*, RKO-Radio, 1939; Mary Gray, *Fifth Avenue Girl*, RKO-Radio, 1939.

Ellie May Adams, *Primrose Path*, RKO-Radio, 1940; Jean Newton, *Lucky Partners*, RKO-Radio, 1940; title role, *Kitty Foyle*, RKO-Radio, 1940; Janie, *Tom, Dick and Harry*, RKO-Radio, 1941; title role, *Roxie Hart* (also known as *Chicago*), Twentieth Century-Fox, 1942; Diane, *Tales of Manhattan*, Twentieth Century-Fox, 1942; Susan Applegate, *The Major and the Minor*, Paramount, 1942; Katie O'Hara, *Once Upon a Honeymoon*, RKO-Radio, 1942; Jo, *Tender Comrade*, RKO-Radio, 1943; *Show Business at War; The March of Time: Issue Number Ten, Volume IX* (short), Twentieth Century-Fox, 1943; *Battle Stations* (short), Twentieth Century-Fox, 1943-44; Liza Elliott, *Lady in the Dark*, Paramount, 1944; Mary Marshall, *I'll Be Seeing You*, Selznick/United Artists, 1944; Irene Malvern, *Weekend at the Waldorf*, Metro-Goldwyn-Mayer, 1945; Arlette, *Heartbeat*, RKO-Radio, 1946; Dolly Payne Todd Madison, *Magnificent Doll*, Universal-International/Hallmark, 1946; Victor Stafford, *It Had to Be You*, Columbia, 1947; Dinah Barkley, *The Barkleys of Broadway*, Metro-Goldwyn-Mayer, 1949.

Terry Scott, *Perfect Strangers*, Warner Brothers, 1950; Marsha Mitchell, *Storm Warning*, Warner Brothers, 1950; Abigail Furnival, *The Groom Wore Spurs*, Universal International, 1951; Ramona, *We're Not Married*, Twentieth Century-Fox, 1952; Edwina Fulton, *Monkey Business*, Twentieth Century-Fox, 1952; Gloria, *Dreamboat*, Twentieth Century-Fox, 1952; Beatrice Page, *Forever Female*, Paramount, 1953; Lottie, *Black Widow*, Twentieth Century-Fox, 1954; "Johnny" Victor, *Beautiful Stranger* (also known as *Twist of Fate*), British Lion/United Artists, 1954; Sherry Conley, *Tight Spot*, Columbia, 1955; Rose Gilray, *The First Travelling Saleslady*, RKO-Radio, 1956; Nancy Fallon, *Teenage Rebel*, Twentieth Century-Fox, 1956; Mildred Turner, *Oh, Men! Oh,*

Women!, Twentieth Century-Fox, 1957; Mama Jean, *Harlow*, Magna Pictures/Electronovision, 1965; Madame Rinaldi, *The Confession* (also known as *Quick, Let's Get Married*, also known as *Seven Different Ways*), Adrian Weiss Productions, 1964-71; *That's Entertainment!*, United Artists, 1974; *That's Dancing!*, United Artists, 1984.

PRINCIPAL TELEVISION APPEARANCES—Episodic: "Shadow Play," *Producer's Showcase*, NBC, 1954; *Dick Powell's Zane Gray Theatre*, CBS, 1958; *The DuPont Show with June Allyson*, CBS, 1960; *Ginger Rogers Show* (pilot), 1961; *The Red Skelton Show*, CBS, 1962; "Terror Island," *Bob Hope Presents the Chrysler Theatre*, NBC, 1965; *The Ed Sullivan Show; The Hollywood Palace;* others.

Specials: *Three by Coward; Red Peppers; Still Life; The Ginger Rogers Special*, 1958; *Carissima*, BBC, 1959; *Bob Hope's Potomac Madness*, 1960; *The Bell Telephone Hour: The Songs of Irving Berlin*, NBC, 1962; Queen, *Rodgers and Hammerstein's Cinderella*, CBS, 1965; several Perry Como specials; others.

WRITINGS: BOOKS—Foreword to reissue of Irene Castle's memoirs, *Castles in the Air*, Da Capo Books, 1980.

AWARDS: Best Actress, Academy Award, 1940, *Kitty Foyle;* voted one of the ten best money-making stars in motion pictures by the *Motion Picture Herald-Fame* Poll, 1935 and 1937.

ADDRESSES: OFFICE—Thunderbird Country Club, Rancho Mirage, CA 92270. AGENT—International Creative Management, 40 W. 57th Street, New York, NY 10019.*

*   *   *

ROGERS, Wayne   1933-

PERSONAL: Born April 7, 1933, in Birmingham, AL; children: Laura, Billy. EDUCATION: Princeton University, B.A., 1954; studied acting with Sanford Meisner and dance with Martha Graham at the Neighborhood Playhouse in New York. MILITARY: U.S. Navy.

VOCATION: Actor.

CAREER: PRINCIPAL TELEVISION APPEARANCES—Luke Perry, *Stagecoach West*, ABC, 1961; Captain John "Trapper John," McIntyre, *M*A*S*H*, CBS, 1972-75; Jake Axminster, *City of Angels*, NBC, 1976; Dr. Charley Michaels, *House Calls*, CBS, 1979-82; also appeared in *The Edge of Night*.

Movies: *Attack on Terror: The F.B.I. vs. the Ku Klux Klan*, 1975; *It Happened One Christmas*, 1977; Greer, *He's Fired, She Hired*, CBS, 1984; *Lady from Yesterday*, CBS, 1985.

FILM DEBUT—*Odds Against Tomorrow*, 1959. PRINCIPAL FILM APPEARANCES—*The Glory Guys*, United Artists, 1965; *Chamber of Horrors*, Warner Brothers, 1966; *Cool Hand Luke*, Warner Brothers, 1967; *Pocket Money*, National General, 1972; *Once in Paris*, Leigh & McLaughlin, 1978.

PRINCIPAL STAGE APPEARANCES—*Misalliance; Bus Stop; Under the Yum Yum Tree*.

ADDRESSES: AGENT—William Morris Agency, 151 El Camino Drive, Beverly Hills, CA 90212.*

ROLLE, Esther

PERSONAL: Born November 8, in Pompano Beach, FL. EDUCA-
TION: Attended Hunter College.

VOCATION: Actress.

CAREER: NEW YORK DEBUT—Felicity Trollop Pardon, *The
Blacks,* St. Mark's Playhouse, 1962. LONDON DEBUT—Cannibal,
God Is a (Guess What?), with the Negro Ensemble Company at the
Aldwych Theatre, during World Theatre season, 1969. PRINCIPAL
STAGE APPEARANCES—*Blues for Mister Charlie,* American Na-
tional Theatre and Academy (ANTA), 1964; *The Amen Corner,*
Ethel Barrymore Theatre, NY, 1965; Ellie, *Happy Ending* and
Clubwoman, *Day of Absence,* and St. Mark's Playhouse, NY, 1965;
with the Arena Stage, Washington, DC, season, 1966-67; Pearl
Cunningham, *Summer of the Seventeenth Doll,* Negro Ensemble
Company at St. Mark's Playhouse, NY, 1968; Cannibal, *God Is a
(Guess What?),* Mrs. Beverly, *String,* and Katy Jones, *Contribu-
tion,* all Negro Ensemble Company at St. Mark's Playhouse, 1969;
Song of the Lusitanian Bogey, Aldwych Theatre, London, 1969;
Alice Sugar, *Man Better Man,* St. Mark's Playhouse, 1969.

First Operator and Aide, *Day of Absence,* St. Mark's Playhouse,
1970; revue, *Akokwe (Initiation),* 1970; *The Blacks,* Theatre Com-
pany of Boston, 1970; Market Wife, *The Dream on Monkey
Mountain,* Mark Taper Forum, Los Angeles, 1970, then St. Mark's
Playhouse, NY, 1971; Maybelle Johnson, *Rosalee Pritchett,* Faye,
Ride a Black Horse, both St. Mark's Playhouse, 1971; Shouter
woman, *A Ballet Behind the Bridge,* St. Mark's Playhouse, 1972;
Miss Maybell, *Don't Play Us Cheap,* Ethel Barrymore Theatre,
NY, 1972; Mother, *The Newlyweds,* Jacksonville, FL, 1976; Lady
Macbeth, *Macbeth,* New Federal Theatre, NY, 1977.

Horowitz and Mrs. Washington, John Golden Theatre, NY, 1980;
The River Niger, Newark, NJ, 1983; Lena, *Raisin in the Sun,*
Repertory Theatre of St. Louis, 1984; also appeared Off-Broadway
in *The Crucible* and *Black Girl.*

MAJOR TOURS—*The Skin of Our Teeth,* Scandinavia; *Black Nativity,* Australia and New Zealand; *Purlie,* national.

PRINCIPAL FILM APPEARANCES—*Cleopatra Jones,* Warner
Brothers, 1973.

PRINCIPAL TELEVISION APPEARANCES—Series: *One Life to Live;*
Florida Evans, *Maude,* CBS, 1972-74; Florida Evans, *Good Times,*
CBS, 1974-77 and 1978-79.

Episodic: *Darkroom,* ABC, 1981; also, *N.Y.P.D; Like It Is.*

Movies: *Summer of My German Soldier,* NBC, 1978.

MEMBER: Actors' Equity Association, American Federation of
Television and Radio Artists, Screen Actors Guild.

AWARDS: Emmy Award, Best Supporting Actress in a Limited
Series or Special, 1978-79, for *Summer of My German Soldier;*
among the winners of the first annual Mother's Day Award from the
National Organization of Women, 1978.*

*   *   *

ROONEY, Mickey   1922-

PERSONAL: Born Joe Yule, Jr., September 23, 1922, in Brooklyn,
NY; son of Joe (a vaudeville performer) and Nell (a vaudeville
performer; maiden name, Carter) Yule; married Ava Gardner (an
actress) January 10, 1942 (divorced May, 1943); married Betty Jane
Rase, September 30, 1944 (divorced, 1947); married Martha Vickers
(an actress), June 3, 1949 (divorced, 1951); married Elaine Mahn-
ken, 1952 (divorced, 1959); married Barbara Thomason, 1959
(died, 1966); married Carolyn Hockett, 1969 (divorced); married
Janice Darlene Chamberlain (a singer), 1978; children: (second
marriage) Mickey Rooney, Jr. (Joe, Jr.), Timothy; (third marriage)
Theodore; (fifth marriage) Kelly Ann, Kerry, Kyle, Kimmy Sue.
MILITARY: U.S. Army during World War II.

VOCATION: Actor.

CAREER: PRINCIPAL STAGE APPEARANCES—*Sugar Babies,* Mark
Hellinger Theatre, NY, 1979.

MAJOR TOURS—In vaudeville, as Joe Yule, Jr., and later as Mickey
Rooney with his family and, in 1932, with Sid Gold; *Sugar Babies,*
1983—.

PRINCIPAL FILM APPEARANCES—As Mickey McGuire: *Mickey's
Big Idea, Mickey's Movie, Not to Be Trusted, Orchids and Ermine,
The King,* others, 1926-32.

As Mickey Rooney: *Information Kid,* Universal, 1932; *Fast Com-
panions,* Universal, 1932; *My Pal the King,* Universal, 1932; *Beast
of the City,* Metro-Goldwyn-Mayer, 1932; *The Big Cage,* Univer-
sal, 1933; *The Life of Jimmy Dolan,* Warner Brothers, 1933; *The
Bowery,* United Artists, 1933; *Broadway to Hollywood,* Metro-
Goldwyn-Mayer, 1933; *The Big Chance,* Arthur Greenblatt, 1933;
The Chief, Metro-Goldwyn-Mayer, 1933; *Lost Jungle* (serial),
Mascot, 1934; *Beloved,* Universal, 1934; *I Like It That Way,*
Universal, 1934; *Love Birds,* Universal, 1934; Blackie at age 12,
Manhattan Melodrama, Metro-Goldwyn-Mayer, 1934; boy swim-
mer, *Chained,* Metro-Goldwyn-Mayer, 1934; Jerry, *Upperworld,*
Warner Brothers, 1934; *Half a Sinner,* Universal, 1934; *Blind Date,*
Columbia, 1934; *Death on the Diamond,* Metro-Goldwyn-Mayer,
1934; *County Chairman,* Fox, 1935; *The Healer,* Monogram, 1935;
Puck, *A Midsummer Night's Dream,* Warner Brothers, 1935; *Reck-
less,* Metro-Goldwyn-Mayer, 1935; *Riffraff,* Metro-Goldwyn-Mayer,
1935; *Little Lord Fauntleroy,* United Artists, 1936; *The Devil Is a
Sissy,* Metro-Goldwyn-Mayer, 1936; *Down the Stretch,* Warner
Brothers, 1936.

Dan, *Captains Courageous,* Metro-Goldwyn-Mayer, 1937; Andy
Hardy, *A Family Affair,* Metro-Goldwyn-Mayer, 1937; *The Hoosier
Schoolboy,* Monogram, 1937; *Slave Ship,* Twentieth Century-Fox,
1937; jockey, *Thoroughbreds Don't Cry,* Metro-Goldwyn-Mayer,
1937; *Live, Love and Learn,* Metro-Goldwyn-Mayer, 1937; *Love Is
a Headache,* Metro-Goldwyn-Mayer, 1938; Andy Hardy, *Judge
Hardy's Children,* Metro-Goldwyn-Mayer, 1938; *You're Only
Young Once,* Metro-Goldwyn-Mayer, 1938; *Hold That Kiss,* Metro-
Goldwyn-Mayer, 1938; *Lord Jeff,* Metro-Goldwyn-Mayer, 1938;
title role, *Loves Finds Andy Hardy,* Metro-Goldwyn-Mayer, 1938;
Whitey Marsh, *Boy's Town,* Metro-Goldwyn-Mayer, 1938; Andy
Hardy, *Out West with the Hardys,* Metro-Goldwyn-Mayer, 1938;
Stablemates, Metro-Goldwyn-Mayer, 1938; Huck, *The Adventures
of Huckleberry Finn,* Metro-Goldwyn-Mayer, 1939; Andy Hardy,
The Hardy's Ride High, Metro-Goldwyn-Mayer, 1939; title role,
Andy Hardy Gets Spring Fever, Metro-Goldwyn-Mayer, 1939;
Mickey Moran, *Babes in Arms,* Metro-Goldwyn-Mayer, 1939;
Andy Hardy, *Judge Hardy and Son,* Metro-Goldwyn-Mayer, 1939.

Title role, *Young Tom Edison,* Metro-Goldwyn-Mayer, 1940; title role, *Andy Hardy Meets a Debutante*, Metro-Goldwyn-Mayer, 1940; *Strike Up the Band*, Metro-Goldwyn-Mayer, 1940; title role, *Andy Hardy's Private Secretary*, Metro-Goldwyn-Mayer, 1941; Whitey Marsh, *Men of Boy's Town*, Metro-Goldwyn-Mayer, 1941; title role, *Life Begins for Andy Hardy*, Metro-Goldwyn-Mayer, 1941; *Babes on Broadway*, Metro-Goldwyn-Mayer, 1941; title role, *The Courtship of Andy Hardy*, Metro-Goldwyn-Mayer, 1942; *A Yank at Eton*, Metro-Goldwyn-Mayer, 1942; title role, *Andy Hardy's Double Life*, Metro-Goldwyn-Mayer, 1942; Homer Macauley, *The Human Comedy*, Metro-Goldwyn-Mayer, 1943; Danny Churchill, Jr., *Girl Crazy*, Metro-Goldwyn-Mayer, 1943; *Thousands Cheer*, Metro-Goldwyn-Mayer, 1943; title role, *Andy Hardy's Blonde Trouble*, Metro-Goldwyn-Mayer, 1944; Mi Taylor, *National Velvet*, Metro-Goldwyn-Mayer, 1944; title role, *Love Laughs at Andy Hardy*, Metro-Goldwyn-Mayer, 1946; *Killer McCoy*, Metro-Goldwyn-Mayer, 1947; Lorenz Hart, *Words and Music*, Metro-Goldwyn-Mayer, 1948; *The Big Wheel*, United Artists, 1949;

Quicksand, United Artists, 1950; *The Fireball*, Twentieth Century-Fox, 1950; *He's a Cockeyed Wonder*, Columbia, 1950; *My Outlaw Brother*, Eagle Lion Classics, 1951; *The Strip*, Metro-Goldwyn-Mayer, 1951; *Sound Off*, Columbia, 1952; *Off Limits*, Paramount, 1953; *A Slight Case of Larceny*, Metro-Goldwyn-Mayer, 1953; *Drive a Crooked Road*, Columbia, 1954; *The Atomic Kid*, Republic, 1954; Mike Forney, *The Bridges at Toko-Ri*, Paramount, 1954; *The Twinkle in God's Eye*, Republic, 1955; *The Bold and the Brave*, RKO, 1956; *Francis in the Haunted House*, Universal, 1956; *Magnificent Roughnecks*, Allied Artists, 1956; *Operation Mad Ball*, Columbia, 1957; title role, *Baby Face Nelson*, United Artists, 1957; title role, *Andy Hardy Comes Home*, Metro-Goldwyn-Mayer, 1958; *A Nice Little Bank That Should Be Robbed*, Twentieth Century-Fox, 1958; *The Last Mile*, United Artists, 1959.

Platinum High School, Metro-Goldwyn-Mayer, 1960; *The Private Lives of Adam and Eve*, Universal, 1960; *King of the Roaring '20's: The Story of Arnold Rothstein*, Allied Artists, 1961; Mr. Yunioshi, *Breakfast At Tiffany's*, Paramount, 1961; *Everything's Ducky*, Columbia, 1961; Army, *Requiem for a Heavyweight*, Columbia, 1962; Ding Bell, *It's a Mad, Mad, Mad, Mad World*, United Artists, 1963; *The Secret Invasion*, United Artists, 1964; *How to Stuff a Wild Bikini*, American International Pictures, 1965; *24 Hours to Kill*, Seven Arts, 1965; *Ambush Bay*, United Artists, 1966; *The Extraordinary Seaman*, Metro-Goldwyn-Mayer, 1968; *Skidoo*, Paramount, 1968; *The Devil in Love*, Warner Brothers/Seven Arts, 1968; *The Comic*, Columbia, 1969; *80 Steps to Terror*, 1969; *Billy Bright*, 1969.

The Cockeyed Cowboys of Calico County, Universal, 1970; *B.J. Presents; That's Entertainment!*, United Artists, 1974; *Pete's Dragon*, Buena Vista, 1977; *The Magic of Lassie*, Jack Wrather Films, 1978; *The Domino Principle*, Avco Embassy, 1979; *The Black Stallion*, United Artists, 1979; *Arabian Adventure*, Associated Film Distributors, 1979.

PRINCIPAL TELEVISION APPEARANCES—Series: Mickey Mulligan, *The Mickey Rooney Show* (also known as *Hey Mulligan*), NBC, 1954-55; Mickey Grady, *Mickey*, ABC, 1964-65; host, *NBC Follies*, NBC, 1973; Oliver Nugent, *One of the Boys*, NBC, 1982.

Episodic: *Celanese Theatre*, ABC, 1952; *The Revlon Review*, CBS, 1960; *The Jackie Gleason Show*, CBS, 1961; *The Judy Garland Show*, CBS, 1963; panelist, *Laughs for Sale*, ABC, 1963; *The Hollywood Palace*, ABC, January 4, 1964; *Shindig*, ABC, 1966; "The Comedian," *Playhouse 90*, CBS; George M. Cohan, "The Seven Little Foys," *Bob Hope Presents the Chrysler Theatre*, NBC.

Specials: Title role, *Pinocchio*, October 13, 1957; *A Year at the Top*, CBS, 1977.

Movies: Jack Thum, *Leave 'em Laughing*, 1981; Bill Sackter, *Bill*, 1981; Bill Sackter, *Bill: On His Own*, 1983.

RECORDINGS: ALBUMS—*Pinocchio*, original television cast recording, Columbia; *Girl Crazy*, original soundtrack recording, Metro-Goldwyn-Mayer Records; *Sugar Babies*, original cast recording.

WRITINGS: AUTOBIOGRAPHY—*I.E.*, 1965.

AWARDS: Special Academy Award, 1938; Academy Award nominations: Best Actor, 1939, for *Babes in Arms;* Best Actor, 1943, for *The Human Comedy;* Best Supporting Actor, 1956, for *The Bold and the Brave*. Outstanding Actor in a Limited Series or Special, Emmy Award, 1981-82, for *Bill*.

SIDELIGHTS: Rooney was voted among the first ten money-making stars in the *Motion Picture Herald-Fame* Poll, from 1938 to 1942.

ADDRESSES: AGENT—Ruth Webb Enterprises, 7500 Devista Drive, Los Angeles, CA 90046.*

*   *   *

ROSS, Alex

PERSONAL: EDUCATION: University of Wisconsin, B.S., political science; also received certificate from the Paris Institute of Political Science.

VOCATION: Producer.

CAREER: PRINCIPAL FILM WORK—Producer: *Drive-In*, Columbia, 1976; *Big Wednesday* (executive producer), Warner Brothers, 1978; *I Wanna Hold Your Hand*, Universal, 1978; *Norma Rae*, Twentieth Century-Fox, 1979; *Nothing in Common*, Tri-Star, 1985.

PRINCIPAL TELEVISION WORK—Producer: Pilots—*Norma Rae*, 1981; *Just Us Kids*, 1982.

MEMBER: Hollywood Women's Coalition, Hollywood Women's Political Committee (board of directors).

ADDRESSES: HOME—Los Angeles, CA. OFFICE—c/o Nothing in Common, Raleigh Studios, 650 N. Bronson, Hollywood, CA 90009.

*   *   *

ROSS, Katharine   1943-

PERSONAL: Born January 29, 1943, in Los Angeles, CA; married Sam Elliot (an actor). EDUCATION: Attended Santa Rosa College; studied acting at the San Francisco Actor's Workshop.

VOCATION: Actress.

CAREER: PRINCIPAL STAGE APPEARANCES—*The Devil's Disciple, The Balcony*, both San Francisco Actors Workshop, 1962; *King Lear*, University of California at Los Angeles.

PRINCIPAL TELEVISION APPEARANCES—Series: Francesca, *Dynasty II: The Colbys,* ABC, 1985.

Episodic: *Ben Casey,* ABC; *The Bob Hope Chrysler Theatre,* NBC; *The Virginian,* NBC; *Wagon Train,* ABC; *Kraft Mystery Theatre,* NBC.

Movies: *The Longest Hundred Miles* (also known as *Escape from Bataan*), 1967; *The Shadow Riders,* 1982; *Secrets of a Mother and Daughter,* 1983; also appeared in *Doctor's at Work; The Road West.*

PRINCIPAL FILM APPEARANCES—*Shenandoah,* Universal, 1965; *Mister Buddwing,* Metro-Goldwyn-Mayer, 1966; *Games,* Universal, 1967; *The Graduate,* Embassy, 1967; *Hellfighters,* Universal, 1969; *Butch Cassidy and the Sundance Kid,* Twentieth Century-Fox, 1969; *Fools,* Cinerama, 1970; *Tell Them Willie Boy Is Here,* Universal, 1970; *They Only Kill Their Masters,* Metro-Goldwyn-Mayer, 1972; *The Stepford Wives,* Columbia, 1975; *Voyage of the Damned,* Avco Embassy, 1977; *The Betsy,* Allied Artists, 1978; *The Swarm,* Warner Brothers, 1978; *The Legacy,* Universal, 1979; *The Final Countdown,* United Artists, 1980; *Wrong Is Right,* Columbia, 1982.

AWARDS: Golden Globe Award, 1968.

ADDRESSES: AGENT—International Creative Management, 8899 Beverly Blvd., Los Angeles, CA 90048.*

* * *

ROSS, Marion

PERSONAL: Born October 25, in Albert Lea, MN; children: Jim, Ellen. EDUCATION: Attended San Diego Stage College.

VOCATION: Actress.

CAREER: NEW YORK DEBUT—*Edwin Booth.* PRINCIPAL STAGE APPEARANCES—At the Globe Theatre, San Diego, CA; La Jolla Summer Theatre, La Jolla, CA.

MAJOR TOURS—*Shelves; Barefoot in the Park; Forever Female; Chapter Two; Time of the Cuckoo,* La Mirada, 1986.

PRINCIPAL FILM APPEARANCES—*Grand Theft Auto,* 1977.

PRINCIPAL TELEVISION APPEARANCES—Series: Kathleen, *Life with Father,* CBS, 1953-55; *Paradise Bay,* 1965-66; Marion Cunningham, *Happy Days,* ABC, 1974-84; Emily Stubing, *Love Boat,* ABC, 1985-86.

Episodic: Baglady, *Glitter,* 1985; *Hotel.*

Movies: Edith, *Blithe Spirit,* CBS; *Dinner at Eight; The Story of Barbara Hallberg; Pearl,* 1978; *Skyward,* 1980; *Sins of the Father,* NBC; *Survival of Dana,* CBS; *The Burning,* ABC.

Specials: "Which Mother Is Mine?," *ABC Afterschool Special,* ABC; *The History of White People in America,* HBO.

AWARDS: Two Emmy Award nominations, for *Happy Days.*

ADDRESSES: OFFICE—Marion Ross Enterprises, Inc., 14159 Riverside Drive, Sherman Oaks, CA 91423. AGENT—Barbara Best, 14159 Riverside Drive, Suite 101, Sherman Oaks, CA 91423.

MARION ROSS

* * *

ROTHSCHILD, Ami   1959-

PERSONAL: Born April 8, 1959, in Newark, NJ; daughter of David E. (a businessman) and Carolyn L. (a sculptress) Rothschild. EDUCATION: Trinity College, Hartford, CT, B.A., psychology, 1981; studied for the theatre at the Terry Schreiber Studio in New York with Schreiber, Bob Smith, Carol Reynolds, and Chuck Jones; at the Strasberg Institute with Irma Saundry and Charles Laughton; at the Circle in the Square with Terese Hayden, and at the Actor's Lab with John Stix; also attended the American Academy of Dramatic Art.

VOCATION: Actress.

CAREER: STAGE DEBUT—Grocer, *Arturo Ui,* Williamstown Theatre Festival, Williamstown, MA, 1979, for four weeks. NEW YORK DEBUT—Eighth, *The Line,* Raft Theatre, 1982, for seven performances. PRINCIPAL STAGE APPEARANCES—Title role, *Mary Poppins,* Hampton Playhouse, Hampton, NH, 1983; Sophie Cerny, *The Great Sebastians,* Hampton Playhouse, 1984; Dvorl, *The Golem,* Tyson Studio, NY, 1984; Jane, *Becoming Strangers,* 13th Street Repertory Theatre, NY, 1985; Lea/understudy, *My Sister in This House,* The Second Stage Company, Promenade Theatre, New York, 1985; also: Young Girl, *The Matchmaker,* Williamstown Theatre Festival; Dawn, *The Best Little Whorehouse in Texas,* Burlicutie, *Red, Hot & Burlesque,* and Mrs. Fisher, *Squabbles,* all Hampton Playhouse; Bonnie, *Anything Goes,* Bianca/Lois, *Kiss Me, Kate,* Velma, *Birdbath,* and woman, *Veronica's Room* all at Trinity College.

AMI ROTHSCHILD

PRINCIPAL FILM APPEARANCES—*Islands,* and *Two Friends,* both for the New York University film school.

PRINCIPAL TELEVISION APPEARANCES—*As the World Turns,* CBS, 1985.

MEMBER: Actors' Equity Association, Screen Actors Guild, American Federation of Television and Radio Artists; Threshold Theatre Company.

ADDRESSES: HOME—New York, NY.

* * *

ROUNDTREE, Richard   1942-

PERSONAL: Born July 9, 1942, in New Rochelle, NY; son of John and Kathryn Roundtree. EDUCATION: Southern Illinois University.

VOCATION: Actor.

CAREER: PRINCIPAL STAGE APPEARANCES—*Man, Better Man, Mau Mau Room, Kongi's Harvest,* all with the Negro Ensemble Company, NY.

MAJOR TOURS—Jack, *The Great White Hope,* Philadelphia, PA.

PRINCIPAL FILM APPEARANCES—*What Do You Say to a Naked Lady?,* United Artists, 1970; John Shaft, *Shaft,* Metro-Goldwyn-Mayer, 1971; John Shaft, *Shaft's Big Score,* Metro-Goldwyn-Mayer, 1972; John Shaft, *Shaft in Africa,* Metro-Goldwyn-Mayer,

1973; *Charley One-Eye,* Paramount, 1973; *Earthquake,* Universal, 1974; *Diamonds,* Avco Embassy, 1975; Friday, *Man Friday,* Avco Embassy, 1976; *Escape to Athena,* Associated Film Distributors, 1979; *An Eye for an Eye,* Embassy, 1981; *The Winged Serpent* (also known as *Q*), 1982; *Inchon,* Metro-Goldwyn-Mayer/United Artists, 1982; *The Graduates of Malibu High,* 1985; *Parachute to Paradise.*

PRINCIPAL TELEVISION APPEARANCES—Series: *Search for To-morrow;* John Shaft, *Shaft,* CBS, 1973-74.

Mini-Series: Sam Bennett, *Roots,* ABC, 1977-78.

Guest: *The Merv Griffin Show; The Dean Martin Show; The New Yorkers; Inside Bedford-Stuyvesant.*

Movie: *Firehouse,* ABC, 1972.

RECORDINGS: ALBUMS—*The Man from Shaft.* SINGLE—"Street Brother."

SIDELIGHTS: Before becoming an actor, Roundtree was a clothing salesman turned model, moving from the floor at Barney's Men's Shop in New York City to the pages and covers of *Ebony Fashion Fair* magazine.*

* * *

RUBIN, Mann   1927-

PERSONAL: Born December 11, 1927, in New York, NY; son of Samuel (a dentist) and Agusta (Wolfe) Rubin; married Jane Smith (a model and teacher), December 20, 1957; children: Richard, Kenneth, Jamie. EDUCATION: New York University, B.A., 1952. MILITARY: U.S. Air Force, 1945-47.

VOCATION: Writer.

CAREER: SCREENPLAYS, PRODUCED—*The Best of Everything,* Twentieth Century-Fox, 1959; *Brainstorm,* Warner Brothers, 1965; *An American Dream,* Warner Brothers, 1966; *Warning Shot,* Paramount, 1967; *The First Deadly Sin,* Filmways, 1981.

TELEVISION SCRIPTS—For *Philco Playhouse, Playhouse 90, Studio One, T. J. Hooker, The Paper Chase; A Step in Time,* 1972.

Movies: *See the Man Run,* 1972; others.

AWARDS: Edgar Awards (Mystery Writers of America), Best Mystery Television Episode, 1972, for *A Step in Time,* and Best Television Mystery Movie, 1973, for *See the Man Run.*

MEMBER: Writers Guild of America West, Motion Picture Academy of Arts and Sciences, Mystery Writers of America, P.E.N., Television Academy of Arts and Sciences.

SIDELIGHTS: Mann Rubin has been at work on an untitled play about Alger Hiss and Whitaker Chambers as well as a screen adaptation of Richard Yates' *The Easter Parade.* Since finishing college in 1952 he has been an active free-lance screen and television writer with over two hundred television scripts to his credit.

Rubin informed the publishers that he likes " . . . Edwin Arlington Robinson's adage that writers live in a kind of spiritual kindergarten, where they run around trying to spell out the meaning of life, but always with the wrong set of blocks. That's the category I fit into. I'm always in search of that one idea, the one story or vision that can communicate my personal truth to someone else. It's a quest that never seems to reach a finish line. I like the challenge and perpetual restlessness it creates in my mind.''

ADDRESSES: HOME—11975 Foxboro Drive, Los Angeles, CA 90049. OFFICE—9507 Santa Monica Blvd., Beverly Hills, CA 90210. AGENT—Irv Schechter & Associates Agency, 9300 Wilshire Blvd., Suite 410, Beverly Hills, CA 90212.

*   *   *

RUSSELL, Kurt   1951-

PERSONAL: Full name, Kurt Von Vogel Russell; born March 17, 1951, in Springfield, MA; son of Bing Oliver and Louis Julia (Crone) Russell; married Season Hubley (an actress) March 17, 1979 (divorced). MILITARY: California Air Naval Guard.

VOCATION: Actor.

CAREER: PRINCIPAL FILM APPEARANCES—*The Absent-Minded Professor*, Buena Vista, 1961; Whitey, *Follow Me, Boys!*, Buena Vista, 1966; *The Horse in the Grey Flannel Suit*, Buena Vista, 1968; *Charley and the Angel*, Buena Vista, 1972; *Superdad*, Buena Vista, 1974; *Used Cars*, 1980; *Escape from New York*, Avco Embassy, 1981; *The Fox and the Hound*, Buena Vista, 1981; *The Thing*, Universal, 1982; *Silkwood*, Twentieth Century-Fox, 1983; *Swing Shift*, Warner Brothers, 1984; *The Mean Season*, Orion, 1985; Reno Williams, *The Best of Times*, Universal, 1986; *Big Trouble in Little China*, Twentieth Century-Fox, 1986.

PRINCIPAL TELEVISION APPEARANCES—Title role, *The Travels of Jaimie McPheeters*, ABC, 1963-64; Bo, *The New Land*, ABC, 1974; Morgan Beaudine, *The Quest*, NBC, 1976.

Movie: Elvis Presley, *Elvis*, 1979.

MEMBER: Screen Actors Guild, American Federation of Television and Radio Artists; Professional Baseball Players Association; Stuntman's Association; World Championship Class Modified Stock (1959 Race of Champions), Las Vegas.

AWARDS: Five acting awards; ten baseball awards; one golf championship; numerous auto racing trophies.

SIDELIGHTS: Russell was a professional baseball player from 1971-73.

ADDRESSES: AGENT—William Morris Agency, 151 El Camino Drive, Beverly Hills, CA 90212.*

*   *   *

RYDELL, Mark   1934-

PERSONAL: Born March 23, 1934, in New York, NY; son of Sidney and Evelyn Rydell; children: Christopher, Amy. EDUCATION: Studied acting with Sanford Meisner at the Neighborhood Playhouse in New York; also at the Actors Studio.

VOCATION: Director, producer, and actor.

CAREER: PRINCIPAL STAGE APPEARANCES—*Seagulls Over Sorrento*, NY.

PRINCIPAL FILM APPEARANCES—*Crime in the Streets*, Allied Artists, 1965; *The Long Goodbye*, Altman, 1973.

PRINCIPAL FILM WORK—Director: *The Fox*, Claridge, 1968; *The Reivers*, National General, 1969; (also producer) *The Cowboys*, Warner Brothers, 1972; (also producer) *Cinderella Liberty*, Twentieth Century-Fox, 1974; *Harry and Walter Go to New York*, Columbia, 1976; *The Rose*, Twentieth Century-Fox, 1979; *On Golden Pond*, Universal, 1981; *The River*, Universal, 1984.

PRINCIPAL TELEVISION APPEARANCES—*As the World Turns*, CBS, for six years.

PRINCIPAL TELEVISION WORK—Director: *Ben Casey*, ABC, 1965; *I Spy*, NBC, 1966; *Gunsmoke*, CBS, 1967; others.

MEMBER: Directors Guild of America, Actors Studio (board of directors).

SIDELIGHTS: With Sydney Pollack, Rydell is a principal partner in the film and television production company, Sanford Productions.

ADDRESSES: AGENT—William Morris Agency, 151 El Camino Drive, Beverly Hills, CA 90212.*

S

SAINT, Eva Marie 1924-

PERSONAL: Born July 4, 1924 in Newark, NJ; daughter of John Merle and Eva Marie (Rice) Saint; married Jeffery Hayden, October 27, 1951; children: Darrell, Laurette. EDUCATION: Bowling Green State University, B.A., 1946; studied at the Actors Studio in New York.

VOCATION: Actress.

CAREER: FILM DEBUT—*On the Waterfront*, Columbia, 1954. PRINCIPAL FILM APPEARANCES—*That Certain Feeling*, Paramount, 1956; *Raintree County*, Metro-Goldwyn-Mayer, 1957; *A Hatful of Rain*, Twentieth Century-Fox, 1957; *North by Northwest*, Metro-Goldwyn-Mayer, 1959; *Exodus*, United Artists, 1960; *All Fall Down*, Metro-Goldwyn-Mayer, 1962; *36 Hours*, Metro-Goldwyn-Mayer, 1965; *The Sandpiper*, Metro-Goldwyn-Mayer, 1965; *The Russians Are Coming, the Russians Are Coming*, United Artists, 1966; *Grand Prix*, Metro-Goldwyn-Mayer, 1966; *The Stalking Moon*, 1969; *Loving*, Columbia, 1970; *Cancel My Reservation*, Warner Brothers, 1972.

PRINCIPAL TELEVISION APPEARANCES—Series: Claudia Barbour Roberts, *One Man's Family*, NBC, 1950-52.

Episodic: *Goodyear TV Playhouse*, NBC; "Last Chance," *The Web*, CBS, 1953; "Our Town," *Producers' Showcase*, NBC, 1955; *Taxi*, ABC, 1978; *Moonlighting*, ABC, 1986.

Movies: *The Macahans*, 1976; *A Christmas to Remember*, 1978; *When Hell Was in Session*, 1980; *The Best Little Girl in the World*, 1981; *Splendor in the Grass*, 1981; *Fatal Vision*, NBC, 1984; *The Last Days of Patton*, CBS, 1985.

PRINCIPAL STAGE APPEARANCES—*The Trip to Bountiful*, 1953; *Mr. Roberts*, Alvin Theatre, 1954; *First Monday in October*, 1979.

AWARDS: Outer Critics Circle Award, New York Drama Critics Award, both 1953, for *The Trip to Bountiful;* Academy Award, Best Supporting Actress, 1955, for *On the Waterfront.*

ADDRESSES: AGENT—Agency for the Performing Arts, 9000 Sunset Blvd., Suite 315, Los Angeles, CA 90069; Diamond Artists, Ltd., 119 W. 57th Street, New York, NY 10019.*

*   *   *

ST. JOHN, Jill 1940-

PERSONAL: Born August 19, 1940, in Los Angeles, CA; married Neil Durbin, 1957 (divorced, 1959); married Lance Reventlow, 1960 (divorced, 1963); married Jack Jones, 1967 (divorced, 1969). EDUCATION: Attended the University of California at Los Angeles.

VOCATION: Actress.

CAREER: FILM DEBUT—*A Christmas Carol*, 1948. PRINCIPAL FILM APPEARANCES—*The Remarkable Mr. Pennypacker*, Twentieth Century-Fox, 1950; *Summer Love*, Universal International, 1958; *Holiday for Lovers*, 1959; *The Roman Spring of Mrs. Stone*, Warner Brothers, 1961; *Tender Is the Night*, Twentieth Century-Fox, 1962; *Come Blow Your Horn*, Paramount, 1963; *Who's Minding the Store*, 1963; *Who's Been Sleeping in My Bed*, Paramount, 1964; *Honeymoon Hotel*, Metro-Goldwyn-Mayer, 1964; *The Oscar*, Embassy, 1966; *The Liquidator*, Metro-Goldwyn-Mayer, 1966; *Banning*, Universal, 1967; *Eight on the Lam*, United Artists, 1967; *Tony Rome*, Twentieth Century-Fox, 1967; *Diamonds Are Forever*, United Artists, 1971; *The Concrete Jungle*, 1982.

PRINCIPAL TELEVISION APPEARANCES—Series: Deanna Kincaid, *Emerald Point, N.A.S.*, CBS, 1983-84.

Episodic: *Big Valley*, ABC; *Dupont Theatre; Fireside Theatre.*

Movies: *Fame Is the Name of the Game*, 1969; *Foreign Exchange*, 1969.

PRINCIPAL RADIO APPEARANCES—Sharon Barbour, *One Man's Family.*

RELATED CAREER—Co-owner, Smith-St. John Ltd.

SIDELIGHTS: Jill St. John began work at age six and by age sixteen had appeared in more than one thousand radio shows and fifty television programs.

ADDRESSES: OFFICE—McCart-Oreck-Barrett, 9200 Sunset Blvd., Suite 1009, Los Angeles, CA 90069.*

*   *   *

SARANDON, Susan 1946-

PERSONAL: Born Susan Abigail Tomalin, October 4, 1946, in New York, NY; daughter of Phillip Leslie and Lenora Marie (Criscione) Tomalin; married Chris Sarandon (an actor), September 16, 1967 (divorced); children: Eva Maria Livia Amurri. EDUCATION: Catholic University, B.A., drama and English, 1968.

VOCATION: Actress.

CAREER: PRINCIPAL STAGE APPEARANCES—*A Coupla White Chicks Sittin' Around Talkin'*, New York Shakespeare Festival, Public Theatre, NY, 1980; Marjorie, *Extremities*, Westside Arts Center, NY, 1982-83.

PRINCIPAL FILM APPEARANCES—*Walk Away; Madden; Joe*, Cannon, 1970; Mary Beth, *The Great Waldo Pepper*, Universal, 1975; Janet Weiss, *The Rocky Horror Picture Show*, Twentieth Century-Fox, 1975; *Lovin' Molly*, Columbia, 1974; *The Front Page*, Columbia, 1976; *Dragon Fly*, American International, 1976; *The Other Side of Midnight*, Twentieth Century-Fox, 1977; *Pretty Baby*, Paramount, 1978; *King of the Gypsies*, Paramount, 1978; *Loving Couples*, Twentieth Century-Fox, 1980; *Atlantic City*, Paramount, 1981; *Tempest*, Columbia, 1982; *The Hunger*, Metro-Goldwyn-Mayer/United Artists, 1983; *The Buddy System*, Twentieth Century-Fox, 1984; *Compromising Positions*, Paramount, 1985.

PRINCIPAL TELEVISION APPEARANCES—Episodic: *Calucci's Department*, CBS, 1973; *Search for Tomorrow;* others.

Movies: *F. Scott Fitzgerald and "The Last of the Belles,"* 1974; *Women of Valor*, CBS, 1986.

Mini-Series: *A.D.*, NBC, 1985; Edda, *Mussolini*, 1985.

MEMBER: Actors' Equity Association, Screen Actors Guild, American Federation of Television and Radio Artists, Academy of Motion Pictures Arts and Sciences; National Organization of Women, Amnesty International, American Civil Liberties Union, Performing Artists for Nuclear Disarmament, Madre.

AWARDS: Best Actress, Canada, Best Actress, Academy Award nomination, 1981, both for *Atlantic City;* Best Actress, Venice Film Festival, 1982, for *Tempest*.

ADDRESSES: AGENT—William Morris Agency, Inc., 1350 Avenue of the Americas, New York, NY 10019.

*   *   *

SAVIOLA, Camille

PERSONAL: Born in New York, NY; daughter of Michael and Mary (d'Esopo) Saviola. EDUCATION: Attended the High School of Music and Art and the City College of New York.

VOCATION: Actress, composer, writer, and comedienne.

CAREER: PRINCIPAL STAGE APPEARANCES—Diane, *The Zinger*, P.A.F. Playhouse, NY; mother, Rainbeam, *Rainbow*, Orpheum Theatre, NY; Diva, mother, *Starmites*, Ark Theatre Company, NY; Irene, the bag lady, *Dementos;* Atina, Evil Queen of the Galaxy, *Battle of the Giants*, City Center, NY; Mama Maddalena, *Nine*, 46th Street Theatre, NY, 1983; Connie Janick, *Spook House*, Circle Repertory, NY, 1984; *A Vaudeville*, Manhattan Theatre Club, NY, 1984; Diva Rita, *The Road to Hollywood*, Production Company, NY, 1984.

MAJOR TOURS—Mother, Acid Queen, *Tommy, a Rock Opera*, U.S. cities; Saraghina, *Nine*, U.S. cities.

PRINCIPAL FILM APPEARANCES—Doris, *The Dogs of War*, United Artists, 1981; woman at party, *Broadway Danny Rose*, Orion, 1984; Olga, *The Purple Rose of Cairo*, Orion, 1985.

CAMILLE SAVIOLA

PRINCIPAL TELEVISION APPEARANCES—Estella, *Jacobo Timerman: Prisoner without a Name, Cell without a Number*, NBC, 1983; *Merv Griffin Show*, 1984; *Remington Steele*, ABC, 1984; Mrs. Carlucci, *All My Children*, ABC; *Live at Five*, NBC, NY.

WRITINGS: PLAYS, PRODUCED—(With Peter Dallas) One woman show, *A Vaudeville*.

SONGS—"Keep on Shakin' That Thing."

RECORDINGS: SINGLE—"Keep on Shakin' That Thing," Tropique Records.

MEMBER: Actors' Equity Association, American Federation of Television and Radio Artists, Screen Actors Guild, Dramatists Guild.

ADDRESSES: AGENT—Dulcina Eisen, 154 E. 61st Street, New York, NY 10021.

*   *   *

SCHALLERT, William   1922-

PERSONAL: Full name, William Joseph Schallert; born July 6, 1922, in Los Angeles, CA; son of Edwin Francis and Elza Emily (Baumgarten) Schallert; married Rosemarie Diann Waggner, February 26, 1949; children: William Joseph, Edwin G., Mark M., Brendan C. EDUCATION: University of California at Los Angeles, B.A., 1946; studied with Sanford Meisner. MILITARY: U.S. Army, 1942-44; U.S. Army Air Force, 1944-45.

VOCATION: Actor.

CAREER: PRINCIPAL TELEVISION APPEARANCES—Series: Mr. Pomfritt, *The Many Loves of Dobie Gillis*, CBS, 1959-63; Martin Lane, *The Patty Duke Show*, ABC, 1963-66; Carson Drew, *The Hardy Boys Mysteries*, ABC, 1977-78; Carson Drew, *The Nancy Drew Mysteries*, ABC, 1977-78; Reverend John March, *Little Women*, NBC, 1979.

Movies: *Ike, the War Years*, 1978; *Blind Ambition*, 1979; *Voyeurs*, 1983.

PRINCIPAL FILM APPEARANCES—*Lonely Are the Brave*, Universal, 1962; *The Trial of the Catonsville Nine*, 1971; *Twilight Zone—The Movie*, Warner Brothers, 1983.

PRINCIPAL STAGE APPEARANCES—*The Trial of the Catonsville Nine*, Off-Broadway production, 1971.

RELATED CAREER—Co-founder, owner, Circle Theatre, Hollywood, CA 1947-50.

MEMBER: Screen Actors Guild (president, 1979-83), Motion Picture and Television Fund (trustee), Academy of Motion Picture Arts and Sciences (board of governors, 1977-79), American Society of Composers, Authors, and Publishers; Permanent Charities Committee, Entertainment Industry, 1975—.

AWARDS: Obie Award, 1971, for *The Trial of the Catonsville Nine*.

ADDRESSES: OFFICE—Freedman Kinzelberg and Broder, 1801 Avenue of the Stars, Suite 911, Los Angeles, CA 90067.*

*   *   *

SCHLARTH, Sharon

PERSONAL: EDUCATION: State University of New York, B.F.A.; trained for the stage with Ernie Martin, Michael Shurtleff, and Warren Robertson.

VOCATION: Actress.

CAREER: PRINCIPAL STAGE APPEARANCES—Mildred, *Fahrenheit 451*, Colony Studio, Los Angeles, CA, 1979; Samantha, *Uncommon Women and Others*, Callboard Theatre, Los Angeles, CA, 1980; Curley's Wife, *Of Mice and Men*, La Mama, Los Angeles, CA, 1980; Muffet, Carter, Leilah, and Susie, *Uncommon Women and Others*, Los Angeles Stage Company, CA, 1981; Betty Blue, *Hoagy, Bix and Bunkhaus*, Mark Taper Forum, Los Angeles, CA, 1981; Anna, *Anna Christie*, Actors Federal Theatre, NY, 1982; Ludmyla, *The Bathers* and Laurel, *The Early Girl*, both New Dramatists, NY, 1982; May, *Fool for Love* and Beth, *Full Hookup*, Circle Repertory, NY, 1983; Jacquenetta, *Love's Labor's Lost*, Circle Repertory, NY, 1984.

Regional: *Rhino Fat from Red Dog Notes*, Studio Arena, Buffalo, NY, 1982; Jackie, *Hot L Baltimore*, Michael C. Rockefeller Theatre; Ismene, *Antigone*, Marvel Theatre; Fran, *Shay*, Fachel, *Ludlow Fair*, and Diana, *Ring 'Round the Moon*, all Arena Studio, Washington, DC; Nancy, *Oliver!*, Carousel Theatre; Charity, *Sweet Charity*, Aldonza, *Man of La Mancha*, Joan, *Dames at Sea*, all Springside Inn.

MAJOR TOURS—May, *Fool for Love*, Circle Repertory, Japanese cities, 1985.

PRINCIPAL TELEVISION APPEARANCES—Series: Lois Carney, *Loving*, ABC; Rachel Jolene, *The Young and the Restless*, CBS.

Episodic: *Omnibus*, BBC, Los Angeles, CA; Pamela, *Skeleton Key*, PBS; *Variety Club Telethon*, PBS; *As the World Turns*, CBS.

PRINCIPAL FILM APPEARANCES—Postgirl, *Fade to Black*, 1980; Linda Regan, *Doorman*, 1984; *Mangia!*, 1985.

MEMBER: Actors' Equity Association, Screen Actors Guild, American Federation of Television and Radio Artists, Circle Repertory Company.

AWARDS: Outstanding Performer, State University of New York.

ADDRESSES: HOME—New York, NY.

*   *   *

SCHRODER, Ricky   1970-

PERSONAL: Born April 3, 1970, on Staten Island, NY; son of Dick (a district manager with New York Telephone) and Diane Schroder.

VOCATION: Actor.

CAREER: PRINCIPAL TELEVISION APPEARANCES—Series: Ricky Stratton, *Silver Spoons*, NBC, 1982—.

RICKY SCHRODER

333

Movies: Title role, *Little Lord Fauntleroy*, CBS, 1980; *Two Kinds of Love*, CBS, 1983; *A Reason to Live*, NBC, 1985; *Hansel and Gretel*.

Specials: *The Jimmy McNichol Special; Doug Henning's World of Magic; An Orchestra Is a Team, Too; Walt Disney's Tenth Anniversary Special; Battle of the Network Stars; Circus of the Stars; Missing, Have You Seen This Person?; S.O.S., Secrets of Surviving.*

FILM DEBUT—*The Champ*, United Aritists, 1979. PRINCIPAL FILM APPEARANCES—*The Last Flight of Noah's Ark*, Buena Vista, 1980; *The Earthling*, Filmways, 1981.

AWARDS: Best New Male Star, Golden Globe Award, 1979, for *The Champ*.

SIDELIGHTS: CTFT learned from his agent that Ricky Schroder began his career at age three months doing television commercials and by the time he was eight years old he had appeared in over fifty television commercials and countless print advertisements.

ADDRESSES: AGENT—Jeff Ballard, 4814 Lemona Avenue, Sherman Oaks, CA 91403.

* * *

SCHULL, Rebecca

PERSONAL: EDUCATION: New York University, B.A.; trained for the stage with Michael Howard and David Craig and at the Stanislavski Studio in Dublin, Ireland.

VOCATION: Actress.

CAREER: PRINCIPAL STAGE APPEARANCES—Nursemaid, *Herzl*, Broadway production; Clara, *Golda*, Broadway production; Jane, *Mary Stuart*, Public Theatre, NY; Clara, *On Mt. Chimborazo*, Dodger Theatre, Brooklyn Academy of Music; Fefu, *Fefu and Her Friends*, American Place Theatre, NY; Matchmaker, *Balzaminov's Wedding*, Theatre Off Park, NY; Ana A., *Exiles*, INTAR, NY; Ruchelaya, *Before She Is Even Born*, T.N.C. Theatre, NY; Madame, *My Sister in This House*, New Dramatists Theatre, NY; Duchess of Gloucester, *Richard II*, Yale Repertory, New Haven, CT; Nitetis, chorus, *The Greeks*, Hartford Stage Company, CT; Polina, *The Seagull*, Pittsburgh Public, PA; Meg, *The Hostage*, Geva, Rochester, NY; Adelle, *Separations*, Arena Stage, Washington, DC.

Agnes, *A Delicate Balance*, Dublin, Ireland, 1975; *Journey into the Whirlwind*, Focus Theatre, Trinity College, Dublin, Ireland, 1983; also in Dublin performed as Mrs. Borkman in *John Gabriel Borkman* and as the Lady in *The Lady of Larkspur Lotion*.

PRINCIPAL TELEVISION APPEARANCES—Series: Cousin Twyla, *One Life to Live;* Harriet, *The Guiding Light.*

Episodic: Mrs. Wood, *Nurse*, CBS.

Movies: Anne, *A Private Battle*, CBS; Maya, *Yulya*, PBS.

PRINCIPAL FILM APPEARANCES—Secretary of Agriculture, *The Soldier*, 1982; mother, *16 Down*.

MEMBER: Actors' Equity Association, Screen Actors Guild, American Federation of Television and Radio Artists.

SEGAL, George 1934-

PERSONAL: Born February 13, 1934, in New York, NY; married Marion Sobol. EDUCATION: Columbia University, B.A., 1955.

VOCATION: Actor.

CAREER: STAGE DEBUT—*Don Juan*, Circle in the Square Downtown, NY. PRINCIPAL STAGE APPEARANCES—*The Iceman Cometh*, Circle in the Square, NY, 1956; *Antony and Cleopatra*, New York Shakespeare Festival; Ollie, *Leave It to Jane*, Sheridan Square Playhouse, NY, 1959; *The Premise*, Off-Broadway production, NY, 1960; *Rattle of a Simple Man*, Broadway production, NY, 1963; *The Knack*, Broadway production, NY, 1964; Maish Resnick, *Requiem for a Heavyweight*, Dallas, TX, then Martin Beck Theatre, NY, 1985.

PRINCIPAL FILM APPEARANCES—*The Young Doctors*, United Artists, 1961; *The Longest Day*, Twentieth Century-Fox, 1962; *Act One*, Warner Brothers, 1963; *The New Interns*, Columbia, 1964; *Invitation to a Gunfighter*, United Artists, 1964; *Ship of Fools*, Columbia, 1965; *King Rat*, Columbia, 1965; *The Lost Command*, Columbia, 1966; Nick, *Who's Afraid of Virginia Woolf?*, Warner Brothers, 1966; *The Quiller Memorandum*, Twentieth Century-Fox, 1966; *The St. Valentine's Day Massacre*, Twentieth Century-Fox, 1967; *Bye Bye Braverman*, Warner Brothers/Seven Arts, 1968; *No Way to Treat a Lady*, Paramount, 1968; *The Southern Star*, Columbia, 1969; *The Bridge at Remagen*, United Artists, 1969.

The Girl Who Couldn't Say No, Twentieth Century-Fox, 1970; *Loving*, Columbia, 1970; *The Owl and the Pussycat*, Columbia, 1970; *Where's Poppa?*, United Artists, 1970; *Born to Win*, United Artists, 1971; *Hot Rock*, Twentieth Century-Fox, 1972; *A Touch of Class*, Avco Embassy, 1973; *Blume in Love*, Warner Brothers, 1973; *The Terminal Man*, Warner Brothers, 1974; *California Split*, Columbia, 1974; *The Black Bird*, Columbia, 1975; *Russian Roulette*, Avco Embassy, 1976; *The Duchess and Dirtwater Fox*, Twentieth Century-Fox, 1976; *Fun with Dick and Jane*, Columbia, 1977; *Rollercoaster*, Universal, 1977; *Who Is Killing the Great Chefs of Europe?*, Warner Brothers, 1978; *Lost and Found*, Columbia, 1979; *The Last Married Couple in America*, Universal, 1980; *Carbon Copy*, Embassy, 1981; *Stick*, Universal, 1985.

PRINCIPAL TELEVISION APPEARANCES—Movies: *Death of a Salesman; Of Mice and Men; The Desperate Hours; The Cold Room*, cable, 1984; *Not My Kid*, CBS, 1985; *Killing 'em Softly*, 1986.

RECORDINGS: ALBUM—*Leave It to Jane*, original cast recording, Strand Records; *The Yama Yama Man;* others.

AWARDS: Best Supporting Actor, Academy Award nomination, 1966, for *Who's Afraid of Virginia Woolf?*

SIDELIGHTS: Segal worked as a janitor, ticket-taker, soft-drink salesman, and as an usher and understudy at the Circle in the Square Theatre, in New York.

ADDRESSES: OFFICE—c/o Wallin-Simon-Black & Company, 1350 Avenue of the Americas, New York, NY 10019.*

SUSAN SEIDELMAN

Photograph by Andy Schwartz. © Orion Pictures Corp.

SEIDELMAN, Susan   1952-

PERSONAL: Born December 11, 1952, in Philadelphia, PA. EDUCATION: Drexel University, B.A.; New York University, M.F.A.

VOCATION: Director and producer.

CAREER: PRINCIPAL FILM WORK—Director and producer, *Smithereens*, New Line Cinema, 1982; director, *Desperately Seeking Susan*, Orion, 1984.

MEMBER: Directors Guild of America.

ADDRESSES: AGENT—c/o Brenda Beckett, Sandford-Beckett Agency, 1015 Gayley Avenue, Suite 301, Los Angeles, CA 90024.

*   *   *

SELBY, Nicholas   1925-

PERSONAL: Born September 13, 1925, in Holborn, London, England; married Kathleen Rayner. EDUCATION: Attended the Central School of Speech and Drama, 1948-50, London. MILITARY: British Armed Forces, World War II.

VOCATION: Actor.

CAREER: STAGE DEBUT—Gordon, *Dangerous Corner*, for ENSA near Preston, England, 1943. LONDON DEBUT—Bernardo, *Aunt Edwina*, Fortune Theatre, 1959. NEW YORK DEBUT—James Larrabee, *Sherlock Holmes*, with the Royal Shakespeare Company, Broadhurst Theatre, 1974. PRINCIPAL STAGE APPEARANCES—(All London unless otherwise stated) Spent nine years in repertory at Liverpool, Birmingham, Coventry, York, Guildford, Hornchurch, and Cambridge, 1946-55; with the English Stage Company at the Royal Court Theatre: Ben, *The Dumb Waiter*, Sullivan, *The Naming*

of *Murderer's Rock*, Hardrader, *The Happy Haven*, Vengerovich, *Platnov*, all 1960; Bluntschli, *Arms and the Man*, Pembroke Theatre, Croydon, 1960; Joesph Engleman, *Masterpiece*, Royality Theatre, 1961; Surrey, *That's Us*, Royal Court Theatre, 1961; Mosbie, *Arden of Faversham*, for the English Stage Company at the Arts Theatre, Cambridge, 1961; Lord Byron, *An Elegance of Rebels*, Liverpool, 1962; Richard Warboys, *Rockets in Ursa Major*, Mermaid Theatre, 1962.

Joined the Royal Shakespeare Company as associate artist, performed at the Stratford Memorial Theatre, and the Aldwych Theatre, London: Antonio, *The Tempest*, Casca, *Julius Caesar*, Winchester, *Henry VI*, all Stratford Memorial Theatre, 1963; Lord Chief Justice, *Henry IV, Part II*, Stratford Memorial Theatre, 1964; Reverend Mort, *Eh?*, Aldwych Theatre, 1964; Duke Solinus, *The Comedy of Errors*, French King, *Henry V*, and The Great Muheim, *The Meteor*, all Aldwych Theatre, 1965; Squire Blackheart, *The Thwarting of Baron Bolligrew*, Aldwych Theatre, 1965 and 1966; Junius Brutus, *Coriolanus*, Duke, *The Revenger's Tragedy*, Capulet, *Romeo and Juliet*, all Stratford Memorial Theatre, 1967; Lafeu, *All's Well that Ends Well*, Aldwych Theatre, also Paris, France, 1968; Camillo, *The Winter's Tale*, Hippolito, *Women Beware Women*, and Lord Chamberlain, *Henry VIII*, all Stratford, 1969; Camillo, Lord Chamberlain, and Erwin, *The Plebeians Rehearse the Uprising*, Aldwych Theatre, 1970; Owen Lamb, *West of Suez*, Royal Court Theatre and at Cambridge Theatre, 1971.

Foot, *After Magritte*, Birdboot, *The Real Inspector Hound*, God Ra, *Caesar and Cleopatra*, and Garry Essendine, *Present Laughter*, Birmingham Repertory Company, all 1972; Carter, *Captain Oate's Left Sock*, Theatre Upstairs, London, 1973; Eric, *The Houseboy*, Open Space Theatre, 1973; Asquith, *Cries from Casement*, for the Royal Shakespeare Theatre at The Place, 1973; Cominius, *Coriolanus*, Aldwych Theatre, 1973; James Larrabee, *Sherlock Holmes*, Aldwych Theatre, then Kennedy Center, Washington, DC, 1973; Almirante de Castilla, *The Bewitched*, Aldwych Theatre, 1974; Lord Milton, *The Fool*, Royal Court Theatre, 1975; Max, *Anatol*, Open Space Theatre, 1976; Nestor, *Troilus and Cressida*, Young Vic Theatre Company, at the National Theatre, 1976.

With the National Theatre Company of Great Britain: Meander, *Tamburlaine the Great*, Olivier Theatre, 1976; Captain, *Tales from the Vienna Woods*, 1977; First Avocatore, *Volpone*, also at the Hippodrome Theatre, Bristol, 1977; Quack, *The Country Wife*, 1977; the Dean, *Brand*, 1978; Duncan, *Macbeth*, 1978; Lord Froth, *The Double Dealer*, 1978; William Scantlebury, *Strife*, 1978; the Professor, *The Fruits of Enlightment*, 1979; Duke Frederick, *As You Like It*, 1979; Baron Von Sweiten, *Amadeus*, 1979; Lodovico, *Othello*, 1980.

PRINCIPAL FILM APPEARANCES—*A Midsummer Night's Dream*, Columbia, 1962; *Macbeth*, Columbia, 1971.

PRINCIPAL TELEVISION APPEARANCES—Since 1956, has appeared in over one hundred programs and broadcasts.

SIDELIGHTS: RECREATION—Music, books, and architecture.

ADDRESSES: AGENT—John Cadell Ltd., Two Southwood Lane, London N6 5EE, England.*

TOM SELLECK

SELLECK, Tom   1945-

PERSONAL: Born January 29, 1945, in Detroit, MI. EDUCATION: Attended the University of Southern California.

VOCATION: Actor.

CAREER: PRINCIPAL TELEVISION APPEARANCES—Series: Lance White, *The Rockford Files*, NBC, 1979-80; Tom Magnum, *Magnum P.I.*, CBS, 1980—.

Episodic: *Braken's World*, NBC.

Movies: *The Concrete Cowboys*, CBS, 1979; *The Sacketts*, 1979; *Shadow Riders*, 1982; *Divorce Wars: A Love Story*, 1982.

PRINCIPAL FILM APPEARANCES—*Myra Breckenridge*, Twentieth Century-Fox, 1970; *The Seven Minutes*, Twentieth Century-Fox, 1971; *Daughters of Satan*, United Artists, 1972; *Midway*, 1976; *Coma*, United Artists, 1978; *High Road to China*, Warner Brothers, 1983; title role, *Lassiter*, Warner Brothers, 1984; *Runaway*, 1985.

AWARDS: Outstanding Lead Actor in a Drama Series, Emmy and Golden Globe, 1984, for *Magnum P.I.*

ADDRESSES: OFFICE—c/o Press Information CBS Entertainment, 51 W. 52nd Street, New York, NY 10019. AGENT—Esmee Chandlee, 9021 Melrose Avenue, Suite 207, Los Angeles, CA 90069.

*   *   *

SELZER, Julie

VOCATION: Producer and casting director.

CAREER: PRINCIPAL TELEVISION WORK—Producer, *Fame*,

Metro-Goldwyn-Mayer Television, syndicated; *Players*, Metro-Goldwyn-Mayer Television, syndicated.

PRINCIPAL FILM WORK—Producer: *Whoopee Boys*, Paramount; *Grease II*, Paramount, 1982; *Flashdance*, Paramount, 1983; *Heart Like a Wheel*, Twentieth Century-Fox, 1983; *Making the Grade*, Metro-Goldwyn-Mayer/United Artists, 1984.

RELATED CAREER: Casting director, Catalina Productions, responsible for: *Livin' Dolls; In Trousers; Stryder; Enter Laughing*.

ADDRESSES: AGENT—c/o Michael Menchel, Creative Artists Agency, 1888 Century Park E., Suite 1400, Los Angeles, CA 90067.

*   *   *

SHATNER, William   1931-

PERSONAL: Born March 22, 1931, in Montreal, Canada; son of Joseph and Anne Shatner; married Gloria Rand, August 12, 1956 (divorced, 1969); married Marcy Lafferty, October 20, 1973; children: 3 daughters. EDUCATION: McGill University, B.A., 1952.

VOCATION: Actor.

CAREER: PRINCIPAL TELEVISION APPEARANCES—Series: Captain James T. Kirk, *Star Trek*, NBC, 1966-69; Jeff Cable, *Barbary Coast*, ABC, 1975-76; title role, *T.J. Hooker*, ABC, 1982-84, CBS, 1984—.

Mini-Series: *Testimony of Two Men*, 1976; *How the West Was Won*, 1978; *The Bastard*, 1978; *Little Women*, 1978.

Guest: *$20,000 Pyramid*, 1976; *$25,000 Pyramid*, 1976; *Hollywood Squares*, 1976; *$20,000 Pyramid*, 1977; *Dinah!*, *Mike Douglas Show*, *Merv Griffen*, *Liar's Club*, *Tattletales*, *American Sportsman*, all 1977; *Match Game*, *Celebrity Bowling*, *Rhyme and Reason*, *Masquerade Party*, *To Tell the Truth*, *Celebrity Sweepstakes*, *Cross Wits*, all 1978; *Midday Live*, *The Tonight Show*, *The Parkinson Show*, *Multi-Coloured Swapshop*, *Clapperboard*, all 1979; *52nd Annual Academy Awards Show*, *The Toni Tenille Show*, *Merv Griffin*, *Kidsworld*, *Over Easy*, 1980; *John Davidson Show*, *Hour Magazine*, 1981; *AM Los Angeles*, *Merv Griffin*, 1982; *Tom Cottle: Up Close*, *The Tonight Show*, *Entertainment Tonight*, *Eye on LA*, *The Emmy Awards*, *The Alan Thicke Show*, *Worldvision*, *7 on Location*, *PM Magazine*, *AM Los Angeles*, *Merv Griffin Show*, *Toys for Tots*, *Christmas Lane Parade*, *Good Morning America*, 1983; *Good Morning America*, *Golden Globes*, 1984.

Movies: *The Revolution of Antonio De Leon*, 1972; *Incident on a Dark Street*, NBC, 1972; *Go Ask Alice*, ABC, 1972; *Horror at 37,000 Feet*, CBS, 1972; *Pioneer Woman*, ABC, 1973; *Indict and Convict*, ABC, 1973; *Pray for the Wildcats*, ABC, 1974; *In Old San Francisco*, 1975; *American Enterprise: The Land*, 1975; *Oregon Trail*, 1976; *Crash*, 1978; *Disaster on the Coastliner*, 1979; *The Babysitter*, 1980; *Trick Eyes*, NBC, 1984; *Secrets of a Married Man*, NBC, 1984.

Specials: *Benjamin Franklin: The Statesman*, CBS, 1975; *Us Against the World*, 1979; *Battle of the Network Stars*, 1982; *Prime Time*, NBC, 1983; *I Love TV Test*, 1983; *TV's Censored Bloopers*, NBC, 1983; *Battle of the Network Stars*, 1983; *World of Tomorrow*, 1984.

WILLIAM SHATNER

Episodic: *Circle Theater*, 1956; "All Summer Long," *Goodyear Playhouse*, NBC, 1956; "School for Wives," and "Oedipus Rex," *Omnibus*, ABC, 1956; "Gwyneth," *Kaiser Aluminum Hour*, NBC, 1956; "The Deadly Silence," *Kaiser Aluminum Hour*, CBS, 1957; "The Glass Eye," *Alfred Hitchcock Presents*, 1957; "The Defender," "The Deaf Heart," "No Deadly Medicine," all *Studio One*, CBS, 1957; "Medic," and "The Velvet Trap," *Kraft Theatre*, NBC, 1958; "Walk with a Stranger," "Man in Hiding," "Old Marshalls Never Die,"all *U.S. Steel Hour*, CBS, 1958; "Time of Hanging," *Climax*, CBS, 1958; "A Town Has Turned to Dust," *Playhouse 90*, CBS, 1958; "The Indestructable Mr. Gore," *Sunday Showcase*, NBC, 1959.

"Mother May I Go Out To Swim?," *Alfred Hitchcock Presents*, 1960; "The Story of a Gunfighter," *Robert Herridge Theatre*, 1960; "The Scarlet Pimpernel," *Family Clasics*, CBS, 1960; "Nick of Time," *Twilight Zone*, CBS, 1960; "Starfall," *Outlaws*, NBC, 1960; "The Promise," *Alcoa Premiere*, ABC, 1960; "The Hungry Glass," and "The Grim Reaper," *Thriller*, NBC, 1961; "Admitting Service," *Dr. Kildare*, NBC, 1961; "Killer Instinct," *The Defenders*, CBS, 1961; "Portrait of a Painter," "Neither Stick Nor Sword," CBS, 1962; "The Invisible Badge," *The Defenders*, NBC, 1962; "Cruel Hook," *The Defenders*, CBS, 1963; "A Difference of Years," and "A Question of Mercy," *The Nurses*, CBS, 1963; "Colossus," *Dick Powell Theater*, NBC, 1963; "Million Dollar Hospital," *Alcoa Premiere*, ABC, 1963; "Five," and "Cameo," *77 Sunset Strip*, ABC, 1963; "Nightmare at 20,000 Feet," *Twilight Zone*, CBS, 1963; "We Build Our Houses with

Their Backs to the Sea," *Route 66*, CBS, 1963; "Dragon in the Den," *Channing*, ABC, 1963; "Winner of Their Springs," *Ben Casey*, 1963.

"Cold Hands, Warm Heart," *Outer Limits*, ABC, 1964; "Onward and Upward," *Arrest and Trial*, ABC, 1964; "Who Killed Carrie Cornell," *Burke's Law*, ABC, 1964; "Uncivil War," *The Defenders*, CBS, 1964; "Project Strigas Affair," *The Man from U.N.C.L.E.*, NBC, 1964; "The Shattered Glass," *Bob Hope Crysler Theatre*, NBC, 1964; "He Stuck in His Thumb," *The Reporter*, 1964; "Act of Violence," *The Doctors and the Nurses*, 1965; "Whipping Boy," *The Defenders*, CBS, 1965; "The Cape," *Lamp Unto My Feet*, CBS, 1965; "The Claim," *The Virginian*, NBC, 1965; "Locusts Have No King," *Insight*, CBS, 1965; "Stranger in the Mirror," *The Fugitive*, ABC, 1965.

"A Time to Kill," *Big Valley*, ABC, 1966; "The Encroachment," "A Patient Lost," "Whatever Happened to all the Sunshine and Roses," "A Taste of Crow," "Out of a Concrete Tower," all *Dr. Kildare*, NBC, 1966; "Wind Fever," *Bob Hope Chrysler Theatre*, NBC, 1966; *Suspense Theater*, 1966; "Quaker Girl," *Gunsmoke*, CBS, 1966; "Shadow Game," *CBS Playhouse*, CBS, 1969; "Black Jade," *The Virginian*, NBC, 1969; "The Discovery," *Norman Corwin Presents*, 1969; "Tarot," *The Name of the Game*, NBC, 1970; "The Shattered Idol," *Paris 7000*, ABC, 1970; "Little Jerry Jessup," *Ironside*, NBC, 1970; "The Combatants," *Medical Center*, CBS, 1970; "Antennea of Death," *The FBI*, ABC, 1970; "The Glory Shouter," *The Name of the Game*, NBC, 1970.

"Walls Are Waiting," *Ironside*, NBC, 1971; "One American," *Men at Law*, CBS, 1971; "Encore," *Mission: Impossible*, CBS, 1971; "The Armegeddon Contract," *Cade's County*, CBS, 1971; "You Don't Have to Kill to Get Rich, But it Helps," *Hawaii Five-0*, 1972; "Cocaine," *Mission: Impossible*, CBS, 1972, "Five Will Get You Six," *Owen Marshall, Counselor at Law*, 1972; "Heartbeat for Yesterday," *Marcus Welby, M.D.*, ABC, 1972; "To Catch a Dead Man," *Barnaby Jones*, CBS, 1973; "Search for a Whisper," *Mannix*, CBS, 1973; "Ten Kilos to Nowhere," *Police Surgeon*, Canada, 1973; "Kiss the World Goodbye," *The Collaborators*, Canada, 1973; "Illusion of the Queens Gambit," *The Magician*, NBC, 1974; "Burning Bright," *The Six Million Dollar Man*, ABC, 1974; "A Small Execution," *Kung Fu*, ABC, 1974; "The Chief," *Ironside*, NBC, 1974; "Smack," *Police Woman*, NBC, 1974; "Love Mabel," *Police Story*, NBC, 1974; "Baptism of Fire," *Amy Prentiss*, NBC, 1974; "Hunting Ground," *The Rookies*, ABC, 1975; "Edge of Evil," *Petrocelli*, NBC, 1975; "Fade into Murder," *Columbo*, NBC, 1976; "Bad Apple," *Police Surgeon*, NBC, 1978; *Kodiak*, 1978; *Anyone for Tennyson*, PBS, 1978.

Mork and Mindy, ABC, 1981; *Fridays*, ABC, 1981; *Madame's Place*, 1983; *Foul-Ups Bleeps and Blunders*.

PRINCIPAL FILM APPEARANCES—*The Brothers Karamazov*, Metro-Goldwyn-Mayer, 1958; *The Explosive Generation*, United Artists, 1961; *Judgement at Nuremburg*, United Artists, 1962; *The Intruder*, Pathe American, 1962; *The Outrage*, Metro-Goldwyn-Mayer, 1964; *Incubus*, Independent Theatrical Films, 1966; *Shame*, Theatrical Movie Release, 1969; *Impulse*, Conquedor, 1972; *Big Bad Mama*, New World, 1974; *Dead of the Night*, Europix, 1974; *The Devil's Rain*, Bryanston, 1975; narrator, *Mysteries of the Gods*, *Whale of a Tale*, Luckers, 1977; *Kingdom of the Spiders* Dimension, 1978; James T. Kirk, *Star Trek: The Motion Picture*, Paramount, 1979; *The Kidnapping of the President*, Theatrical, 1979; *Visiting Hours*, Theatrical, 1980; James T. Kirk, *Star Trek II: The Wrath of Khan*, Paramount, 1982; *Airplane II*, Paramount, 1982; James T.

Kirk, *Star Trek III: The Search for Spock,* Paramount, 1984; *Star Trek IV: The Voyage Home,* Paramount, 1986.

STAGE DEBUT—Title role, *Tom Sawyer,* Montreal, Canada, 1952. NEW YORK DEBUT—Usumcasme, *Tamburlaine the Great,* Winter Garden Theatre, 1956. PRINCIPAL STAGE APPEARANCES—Montreal Playhouse, 1952-53; Canadian Repertory Theatre, Ottawa, Canada, 1952-53; Young Lord, *Measure for Measure,* Lucentio, *The Taming of the Shrew,* Chorus, *Oedipus Rex,* all Stratford Shakespeare Festival, Ontario, Canada, 1954; Lucius, *Julius Caesar,* Gratiano, *The Merchant of Venice,* Chorus, *King Oedipus,* all Stratford Shakespeare Festival, Ontario, Canada, 1955; Fenton, *The Merry Wives of Windsor,* Duke of Glouchester, *Henry V,* all Stratford Shakespeare Festival, Ontario, Canada, 1956; Robert Lomax, *The World of Suzie Wong,* Broadhurst Theatre, NY, 1958; Paul Sevigne, *A Shot in the Dark,* Booth Theatre, NY, 1961; Tom, *Remote Asylum,* Ahmanson Theatre, Los Angeles, CA, 1971; *Arsenic and Old Lace,* 1973; *Tricks of the Trade,* 1977; *Otherwise Engaged,* Los Angeles, CA, 1978.

MAJOR TOURS—*An Evening with William Shatner,* U.S. cities, 1976; *Deathtrap,* U.S. cities, 1980.

MEMBER: Actors' Equity Association, Screen Actors Guild, American Federation of Television and Radio Artists.

AWARDS: Tyrone Guthrie Award, 1956; Theatre World Award, 1958.

SIDELIGHTS: RECREATION—Riding, archery, photography, and writing.

ADDRESSES: AGENT—William Morris Agency, 151 El Camino, Beverly Hills, CA 90212.

*   *   *

SHAYE, Robert   1939-

PERSONAL: Born March 3, 1939; son of Max (an artist) and Dorothy Shaye; married Eva; children: Katja, Juno. EDUCATION:

ROBERT SHAYE

University of Michigan, B.B.A., 1959; Columbia University School of Law, L.L.B., 1964; also studied at the Sorbonne in Paris and the University of Stockholm.

VOCATION: Producer.

CAREER: FIRST FILM WORK—Producer, *Stunts,* New Line Cinema, 1978. PRINCIPAL FILM WORK—Producer with New Line Cinema: *Polyester,* 1981; *The First Time,* 1982; *Alone in the Dark,* 1983; *Nightmare on Elm Street,* 1984; *Nightmare 2, Freddy's Revenge,* 1985; *Critters,* 1986.

RELATED CAREER—Founder and president, New Line Cinema Corporation.

MEMBER: Friars Club, New York Bar and New York State Bar Association.

AWARDS: Film Image Award; Fulbright Scholarship, 1964-66; Diploma of Merit in Copyrights, University of Stockholm, 1966.

ADDRESSES: OFFICE—c/o New Line Cinema, 575 Eighth Avenue, New York, NY 10018.

*   *   *

SHENA, Lewis   1948-

PERSONAL: Born Lewis Pshena, December 14, 1948; son of Martin (a garment cutter) and Toby (a secretary; maiden name, Berger) Pshena. EDUCATION: State University of New York at Buffalo, B.A., 1970; New York University, M.A., 1972.

VOCATION: Director, designer, and stage manager.

CAREER: FIRST STAGE WORK—Assistant stage manager, *Knight of the Burning Pestle,* State University of New York at Buffalo, NY, 1967, for five performances. FIRST NEW YORK STAGE WORK—Stage manager, *Vermin,* Playbox Theatre, 1970, for eighteen performances. LONDON DEBUT--Intern, *Street Theatre,* Interspace Theatre Company, 1968, for ten performances. PRINCIPAL THEATRE WORK—Stage manager for Manhattan Theatre Club, NY, Playwright's Horizons, NY, Hudson Guild, NY, Theatre Dance Collection, Eleo Pomare Dance Company, Maria Alba Spanish Dance Company, Eglevsky Ballet, Jennifer Mullen and the Works, Chelsea Theatre Center, Laurel Theatre Productions.

Director: *The Hot L Baltimore, Third Child, The Skin of Our Teeth,* all State University of New York at Buffalo; *Through the Looking Glass,* Haas Theatre, NY; *St. Joan,* St. John's Episcopal Church, NY; *Come Blow Your Horn,* Stagelights II Theatre, NY; *The Investigation of J.T.,* Playwrights' Horizons, NY; *Playing with Fire,* Spectrum Theatre, NY; *Hooks and Eyes,* St. Clement's Theatre, NY; *Ballad of Raintree County,* Puerto Rican Traveling Theatre, NY; *Dolorosa Sanchez,* New Dramatists Theatre, NY; *Full Circle,* Collective Actors Theatre, NY; *The Collector,* Greenwich Mews Theatre, NY.

Also directed summer stock and dinner theatre productions at the Millbrook Playhouse, Tibbits Opera House, Fort Totten Little Theatre and Spotlight Productions including: *The Knack; Thurber Carnival; The Mousetrap; The Apple Tree; God's Favorite; Sound of Music; You Can't Take It with You; You Know I Can't Hear You When the Water's Running; Carousel; Life with Father; Fiddler on the Roof; Sunshine Boys; Night of January 16; Jesse and the Bandit Queen; Same Time Next Year.*

Also directed the operas: *Trouble in Tahiti, The Wandering Scholar, The Brute,* all at State University of New York at Buffalo, 1969; *The Turn of the Screw,* State University of New York at Buffalo, 1970; *The Marriage of Figaro,* Opera Camerata, 1978; *Cosi Fan Tutte,* Opera Camerata, 1979; *The Barber of Seville,* Richmond Opera Company, 1980; *Don Giovanni,* Opera Camerata, 1980; *Rigoletto,* Opera Camerata, 1981; *Abduction from the Seraglio,* Opera Camerata, 1982; *The Medium,* Texas Woman's University, 1985.

Designer: Costumes, *A Slight Ache* and *The Basement,* Manhattan Theatre Club, NY; costume and set decoration, *Ceremonies in Dark Old Men,* Hudson Guild Theatre, NY.

PRINCIPAL TELEVISION WORK—Director, *The Boor* and *The Marriage Proposal,* cable, 1975.

RELATED CAREER—Instructor, Occupation Day Care Center, 1970-71; dramatics instructor, Lorge School, 1974-75; adjunct assistant professor of English and Drama, LaGuardia Community College, 1977-84; visiting lecturer in acting and directing, Texas Women's University, 1984-85; artistic director and general manager, The Millbrook Playhouse, 1985.

MEMBER: Society of Stage Directors and Choreographers, Actors Studio Directors Unit, Actors' Equity Association, American Theatre Association, Professional Staff Congress.

ADDRESSES: HOME—484 W. 43rd Street, Apt. 23P, New York, NY 10036.

*   *   *

SHIELDS, Brooke 1965-

BRIEF ENTRY: Born May 31, 1965, in New York, NY; daughter of Frank and Teri Shields. Model and actress. Brooke Shields has become one of the most recognized personalities in the world today through her career as model and actress. She began her modeling career at age eleven months, when photographer Francesco Scavullo used her as an Ivory Snow baby. Her career continued throughout her childhood and she was seen in Simplicity pattern books and in advertisments for Breck shampoo, Carter's pajamas, Colgate toothpaste, and Band-Aids, and for the stores J.C. Penny and Sears. Shields was cast in her first film, a low budget horror movie, at age ten, but it was her portrayal of Violet, the child prostitute in Louis Malle's controversial film *Pretty Baby,* made the following year, that caused a sensation. Since then, the young actress has starred in nine feature films, including *Endless Love, The Blue Lagoon,* and *Just You and Me, Kid.* Although critics have not been overwhelming in their praise of Shields' acting talent, she continues to work at establishing a reputation for herself as a serious and intelligent actress. She is currently attending Princeton University and is a member of its musical theatre group, "Triangle."*

*   *   *

SHORE, Dinah 1917-

PERSONAL: Full name, Frances Rose Shore; born March 1, 1917, in Winchester, TN; daughter of S.A. and Anna (Stein) Shore; married George Montgomery, December 5, 1943 (divorced, 1962); married Maurice Smith, May 26, 1963 (divorced, 1964); children: (first marriage) Melissa Ann, John David. EDUCATION: Vanderbilt University, B.A., 1939.

VOCATION: Singer and television hostess.

CAREER: TELEVISION DEBUT—*Toast of the Town,* CBS. PRINCIPAL TELEVISION APPEARANCES—Series: *Dinah Shore Show,* NBC, 1951-57; *The Chevy Show,* NBC, 1956; *Dinah Shore Chevy Show,* 1956-63; *Like Hep,* 1970-71; *Dinah's Place,* NBC, 1970-74; *Dinah!,* CBS, 1974-79; *Dinah and Her New Best Friends,* CBS, 1976; *Dinah and Friends,* 1979-81.

Guest: "The Nashville Sound," *Kraft Music Hall,* NBC;

Specials: *Dinah Shore* specials, 1964-65, 1969; *Dinah Shore Invitational* (golf), NBC, 1986.

PRINCIPAL FILM APPEARANCES—*Thank Your Lucky Stars,* 1943; *Till the Clouds Roll By,* 1946; *Make Mine Music,* 1946; *Follow the Boys,* 1963.

PRINCIPAL RADIO APPEARANCES—Singer, WNEW, NY, 1938; singer, NBC, 1938; singer, *Chamber Music Society of Lower Basin Street,* 1940; singer, *Eddie Cantor Program,* 1941; *General Foods Program,* 1943; singer, *Procter and Gamble Program.*

MAJOR TOURS—Singer at European sites with the USO.

WRITINGS: BOOKS—*Someone's in the Kitchen with Dinah,* 1971.

AWARDS: Radio and Motion Picture *Daily* Poll Award, *World Telegram-Scripps-Howard* Poll Award, 1940; Favorite Female Vocalist in Records, *Billboard,* 1947; Favorite Female Vocalist in Radio, *Billboard,* 1949; Best Popular Female Vocalist, *Daily Fame's* Annual Poll Radio Award, 1941-61; Best Female Vocalist for Radio and Television, Michael Award, 1950, 1951, 1952; Best Female Vocalist, *Radio-TV Daily* Award, 1949, 1956; One of the Most Admired Women in the World, Gallup Poll Award, 1958-61, six Emmy Awards, 1954-59; *Los Angeles Times* Award, Woman of the Year, 1957; Best Female Singer, Radio, *TV-Radio Mirror* Magazine Award, 1952, 1953, 1956, 1957, 1958; Television's Best Musical Variety Show, *TV-Radio Mirror* Magazine Award, 1956, 1958, 1959; Peabody Television Award, 1957; Best Female Vocalist, *Fame's* Critics' Poll Award, 1958, 1963; Hollywood Foreign Press Association's Golden Globe Award, 1959.*

*   *   *

SHUE, Larry 1946-1985

PERSONAL: Born July 23, 1946, in New Orleans, LA; died in a plane crash in Weyers Cove, VA, September 23, 1985; son of Percy Howard (an educator and service organization administrator) and Marguerite Dolores (a Spanish teacher; maiden name, Wilson) Shue; married Linda Faye Wilson (an actress) September 7, 1968 (divorced, 1977). EDUCATION: Illinois Wesleyan University, B.F.A., 1968. MILITARY: U.S. Army, 1969-72.

VOCATION: Playwright and actor.

CAREER: PRINCIPAL STAGE APPEARANCES—Zlapoot, *Confrontation,* New Playwrights' Theatre, Hollywood, CA, 1969; actor with the Elden Bruch Repertory Theatre, Oshkosh, WI, 1969; Tevye, *Fiddler on the Roof* and Malvolio, *Twelfth Night,* both Harlequin Dinner Theatre, Atlanta, GA, 1977; Billis, *South Pacific,*

Atlanta Theatre of the Stars, GA, 1977; *Lakeboat,* Long Wharf Theatre, New Haven, CT, 1982; Donny, *American Buffalo,* Berkeley Repertory Theatre, CA, 1983; *The Foreigner,* NY, 1984; *The Mystery of Edwin Drood,* Delacorte Theatre, NY, 1985.

Appearing at the Milwaukee Repertory Theatre, 1977-85: Gale, *Miss Lulu Bett;* Farquhar, *The Recruiting Officer;* Chichikov, *Dead Souls;* Vicomte de Trivelin, *Have You Anything to Declare?;* third son, *Tomodoachi;* The Presser, *L'Atelier;* Hermann Schmidt, *The Fuhrer Is Still Alive;* Joe Litko, *Lakeboat;* Gus, *High Times;* Willum Cubbert, *The Nerd;* George Herrick, *Fridays;* Beckersteth, *Namesake;* Senator Philetus Sawyer, *Fighting Bob.*

Also appeared at Theatre X, Milwaukee, 1980.

MAJOR TOURS—Pablo Gonzales, *A Streetcar Named Desire,* Tilden, *Buried Child,* with the Milwaukee Repertory Company in Japanese cities, 1983.

PRINCIPAL FILM APPEARANCES—*A Common Confusion; The Hungry Leaves.*

PRINCIPAL TELEVISION APPEARANCES—*One Life to Live,* ABC.

WRITINGS: PLAYS, PRODUCED—*My Emperor's New Clothes,* Illinois Wesleyan University, 1968; *Siliascoles,* Illinois Wesleyan University, 1968; *Grandma Duck Is Dead,* Milwaukee Repertory Theatre, 1979; *The Nerd,* Milwaukee Repertory Theatre, 1981, Royal Exchange Theatre Company, Manchester, England, 1982; *Wenceslas Square,* Milwaukee Repertory Company Studio, 1982, Midwest Playwrights Program, St. Paul, MN, 1983; *The Foreigner,* Milwaukee Repertory Theatre, 1983, NY, 1984-85.

PLAYS, PUBLISHED—*Grandma Duck Is Dead,* Dramatists Play Service, 1984; *The Foreigner,* Dramatists Play Service, 1984.

AWARDS: First Army Entertainment Contest, 1970; Eddie Fox Award for Dramtic Excellence, 1971; Best Actor in a Non-Musical, Atlanta Circle of Drama Critics Award, 1977, for *Twelfth Night;* Best Actor in a Musical, Atlanta Circle of Drama Critics Award, 1977, for *Fiddler on the Roof;* two Obie Awards; two New York Drama Critics Awards.

SIDELIGHTS: CTFT learned that Larry Shue trained with the Waseda Theatre Company in Toga-mura, Japan in 1980.

*   *   *

SIGNORET, Simone   1921-1985

PERSONAL: Born Simone Kaminken, March 25, 1921, in Weisbaden, Germany; died in Normandy, France, September 30, 1985; married Yves Alegret (a director, divorced); married Yves Montand (an actor and singer), 1951; children: (first marriage) Catherine.

VOCATION: Actress.

CAREER: FILM DEBUT—*Les Visiteurs du Soer.* PRINCIPAL FILM APPEARANCES—*Casque d'Or,* 1951; *Les Diaboliques,* 1955; *Room at the Top,* Continental, 1959; *Adua,* 1961; *Term of Trial,* Warner Brothers, 1963; *Is Paris Burning?,* Paramount, 1966; *Ship of Fools,* Columbia, 1965; *The Sleeping Car Murder,* Seven Arts, 1966; *The Deadly Affair,* Columbia, 1967; *Games,* Universal, 1967; *The Seagull,* Warner Brothers/Seven Arts, 1968; *L'aveu,* 1970; *L'Armee des ombres,* 1971; *Le Chat,* 1971; *Rude journee pour la*

Reine Rosa, 1977; *La chair de l'orchidee,* 1975; *La vie devant soi,* 1976; *Madame Rosa,* Atlantic, 1978; *Le siyet,* 1978; *L'Adolescente,* 1978; *Chere inconnue,* 1980; *I Sent a Letter to My Love,* 1981; *L'Etoile du Nord,* 1982; *Guy de Maupussant,* 1982; also appeared in *Les Demos a l'aube; Dedee d'Anvers; Maneges; Le couple ideal; La ronde; Therese Raquin; Macadam; L'Impasse des deux Anges; La mort en de jardin; Les sorcieres de Salem; Le Jour et l'heure; Compartiment Lueuers; Judith Therpouve; Dragees au poivre.*

PRINCIPAL STAGE APPEARANCES—Lady Macbeth, *Macbeth,* Royal Court, London, 1966; also: *The Crucible; The Little Foxes.*

PRINCIPAL TELEVISION APPEARANCES—"A Small Rebellion," *Bob Hope Presents the Chrysler Theatre,* NBC, 1966.

AWARDS: Best Actress, Academy Award, 1959, for *Room at the Top;* Outstanding Performance by an Actress in a Leading Role in a Drama, Emmy Award, 1965-66, for "A Small Rebellion," *Bob Hope Presents the Chrysler Theatre.**

*   *   *

SILLIPHANT, Stirling

PERSONAL: Son of Leigh and Ethel (Noaker) Silliphant; married Tiana DuLong (an actress), July 4, 1974; children: Stirling. EDUCATION: University of Southern California, A.B., 1938. MILITARY: U.S. Navy, 1942-45.

VOCATION: Writer and producer.

CAREER: PRINCIPAL TELEVISION WORK—Writer, *Naked City,* ABC, 1958-63; writer and co-creator, *Route 66,* CBS, 1960-64; writer, *The Chrysler Theatre,* NBC; writer, *Alfred Hitchcock Presents,* NBC; writer, *G.E. Theatre,* ABC; writer, *Longstreet,* ABC, 1971-72.

Movies: Executive producer and writer, *A Time for Love,* NBC, 1973; executive producer and writer, *The First Thirty-Six Hours of Dr. Durant,* ABC, 1975; writer, *Death Scream,* ABC, 1975; executive producer and writer, *Salem's Lot,* CBS, 1979; writer, *Golden Gate,* ABC, 1981; executive producer and writer, *Fly Away Home,* ABC, 1981; also executive producer and writer, *Pearl,* ABC.

Mini-Series: Writer, *Space,* CBS, 1985; producer and writer, *Mussolini: The Untold Story,* NBC, 1985.

PRINCIPAL FILM WORK—Producer, *The Joe Louis Story,* United Artists, 1953; producer and writer, *Five Against the House,* Columbia, 1955; writer, *Huk,* United Artists, 1956; writer, *Nightfall,* Columbia, 1957; writer, *Damn Citizen,* Universal, 1958; writer, *Lineup,* Columbia, 1958; writer, *Village of the Damned,* Metro-Goldwyn-Mayer, 1961; executive producer and writer, *The Slender Thread,* Paramount, 1966; writer, *In the Heat of the Night,* United Artists, 1967; producer and writer, *Charly,* Cinerama, 1968; producer and writer, *Marlowe,* Metro-Goldwyn-Mayer, 1969.

Producer and writer, *A Walk in the Spring Rain,* Columbia, 1970; writer, *Liberation of L.B. Jones,* Columbia, 1970; writer, *Murphy's War,* Paramount, 1971; executive producer, *Shaft,* Metro-Goldwyn-Mayer, 1971; executive producer, *Shaft's Big Score,* Metro-Goldwyn-Mayer, 1972; writer, *The New Centurions,* Columbia, 1972; writer, *The Poseidon Adventure,* Twentieth Century-Fox, 1972; executive producer and writer, *Shaft in Africa,* Metro-Gold-

STIRLING SILLIPHANT

CATHY SILVERS

wyn-Mayer, 1973; writer, *The Towering Inferno*, Twentieth Century-Fox, 1974; writer, *The Killer Elite*, United Artists, 1975; writer, *The Enforcer*, Warner Brothers, 1976; writer, *Telefon*, Metro-Goldwyn-Mayer, 1977; writer, *The Swarm*, Warner Brothers, 1978; writer, *Circle of Iron*, Avco Embassy, 1979; writer, *When Time Ran Out*, Warner Brothers, 1980.

WRITINGS: SCREENPLAYS AND TELEVISION—As above.

BOOKS—*The Steel Tiger*, Ballantine (reissued), 1985; *Bronze Bell*, Ballantine, 1985; *Maracaibo*, Ballantine, 1985; *Silver Star*, Ballantine, 1986; also *Pearl*, Dell; *The Slender Thread*, Signet.

MEMBER: Writers Guild of America West, Mystery Writers Association, Authors Guild.

AWARDS: Best Screenplay, Academy Award, Golden Globe, 1967, for *In the Heat of the Night;* Best Screenplay, Golden Globe, 1968, for *Charly;* Edgar Allan Poe Award, Mystery Writers Association.

ADDRESSES: AGENT—c/o Bill Haber, Creative Artists Agency, 1888 Century Park E., Suite 1400, Los Angeles, CA 90048.

*   *   *

SILVERS, Cathy   1961-

PERSONAL: Full name, Catherine Silvers; born in 1961, in New York, NY; daughter of Phil (an actor) and Evelyn (a psychologist) Silvers. EDUCATION: Graduated from Beverly Hills High School.

VOCATION: Actress.

CAREER: TELEVISION DEBUT-Jenny Piccolo, *Happy Days*, ABC, 1980-83. PRINCIPAL TELEVISION APPEARANCES—Series: Molly Dobbs, *Foley Square*, CBS, 1985—.

Episodic: *The Paper Chase*, CBS; *The Love Boat*, ABC; *Punky Brewster*, NBC.

Pilots: *Tender Loving Care; Sam;* voice of Nurse Kitty, *Animal Hospital*.

PRINCIPAL FILM WORK—Voice of Marie Dodo Bird, *Follow That Bird*, 1985.

PRINCIPAL STAGE APPEARANCES—*House of Blue Leaves*, college production.

SIDELIGHTS: RECREATIONS—Gymnastics, skiing, and needlepoint.

ADDRESSES: AGENT—Sumski, Green & Company, 8380 Melrose Avenue, Suite 200, Los Angeles, CA 90069.

*   *   *

SIMMONS, Jean   1929-

PERSONAL: Born January 31, 1929, in London, England; married Stewart Granger (divorced); married Richard Brooks (a director and writer). EDUCATION: Attended the Aida Foster School.

VOCATION: Actress.

CAREER: FILM DEBUT—*Mr. Emmanuel*, 1941. PRINCIPAL FILM APPEARANCES—*Kiss the Boys Goodbye*, 1941; *Give Us the Moon*,

1944; *Way to the Stars*, 1945; *Caesar and Cleopatra*, 1945; *Sports Day*, 1946; *Black Narcissus*, 1946; *Great Expectations*, 1946; *Hungry Hill*, 1947; *Hamlet*, 1948; *The Woman in the Hall*, 1949; *Adam and Evalyn*, 1949; *Blue Lagoon*, 1949.

Trio, 1950; *So Long at the Fair*, 1950; *Cage of Gold*, 1950; *The Clouded Yellow*, 1951; *Androcles and the Lion*, 1952; *Angel Face*, 1953; *Young Bess*, Metro-Goldwyn-Mayer, 1953; *Affair with a Stranger*, 1953; *The Actress*, 1953; *The Robe*, Twentieth Century-Fox, 1954; *She Couldn't Say No*, 1954; *A Bullet Is Waiting*, 1954; *The Egyptian*, 1954; *Desiree*, 1954; *Footsteps in the Fog*, Columbia, 1955; *Guys and Dolls*, Metro-Goldwyn-Mayer, 1955; *Hilda Crane*, Twentieth Century-Fox, 1956; *This Could Be the Night*, Metro-Goldwyn-Mayer, 1957; *Until They Sail*, Metro-Goldwyn-Mayer, 1957; *Home Before Dark*, Warner Brothers, 1958.

Spartacus, Universal, 1960; *The Grass Is Greener*, Universal, 1960; *Elmer Gantry*, United Artists, 1960; *All the Way Home*, Paramount, 1963; *Mr. Buddwing* (also known as *Woman without a Face*), Metro-Goldwyn-Mayer, 1966; *Divorce, American Style*, Columbia, 1967; *Rough Night in Jericho*, Universal, 1967; *The Happy Ending*, Universal, 1969.

PRINCIPAL TELEVISION APPEARANCES—Mini-Series: *The Thorn Birds*, ABC, 1983.

AWARDS: Voted one of the top ten British money-making stars in *Motion Picture Herald-Fame* Poll, 1950-51; Academy Award nomination, 1969, for *The Happy Ending;* Outstanding Supporting Actress in a Limited Series, Emmy Award, 1983, for *The Thorn Birds*.

ADDRESSES: AGENT—Morgan Maree, 6363 Wilshire Blvd., Los Angeles, CA 90048.*

*   *   *

SLADE, Julian 1930-

PERSONAL: Born May 28, 1930, in London; son of George Penkivil and Mary Albinia Alice (Carnegie) Slade. EDUCATION: Attended Eton and Trinity College, Cambridge; trained for the stage at Bristol Old Vic Drama School.

VOCATION: Composer, author, and actor.

CAREER: STAGE DEBUT—Flunkey, *The Prodigious Snob*, Theatre Royal, Bristol, England, 1951. LONDON DEBUT—Musician, *The Two Gentlemen of Verona*, Old Vic, 1952.

WRITINGS: MUSICALS—(With James Cairncross and Dorothy Reynolds) *Christmas in King Street*, London, 1952; composer, *The Duenna, Love for Love, She Stoops to Conquer*, all with the Bristol Old Vic, 1953; incidental music composer, *The Merchant of Venice*, Shakespeare Memorial Theatre, Stratford, 1953; incidental music composer, *The Comedy of Errors*, Arts Theatre, London, 1956.

(All with Dorothy Reynolds) Composer: *The Merry Gentleman*, 1953; *Salad Days*, 1954, revived in 1976; *Free as Air*, 1957; *Hooray for Daisy*, 1959; *Follow That Girl*, 1960; *Wildest Dreams*, 1960; *Vanity Fair*, Theatre Royal, Bristol, 1966; *Sixty Thousand Nights*, Theatre Royal, Bristol, 1966.

Composer, lyricist, and writer, *Nutmeg and Ginger*, Cheltenham, 1963; adaptor, *The Pursuit of Love*, Bristol, 1967; composer, *As You*

Like It, Bristol, 1967; composer, *A Midsummer Night's Dream*, Regent's Park, London, 1970; composer, *Much Ado About Nothing*, Regent's Park, 1970; adaptor and composer, *Winnie the Pooh*, Phoenix Theatre, London, 1970; composer and lyricist, *Trelawny of the Wells*, 1972; writer, lyricist and composer, *Out of Bounds*, Bristol, 1973; (with Gyles Brandretts) writer and composer, *A.A. Milne*, 1982; composer, *Dear Brutus*, 1985.

MAJOR TOURS—(With Dorothy Reynolds) Composer, *Salad Days*, Paris, U.S., Canada, South Africa, Australia, New Zealand, Scandinavia.

TELEVISION—Composer, *Love in a Cold Climate*, 1980; composer and adaptor, *Salad Days*, 1982.

SIDELIGHTS: RECREATIONS—Drawing, going to the theatre and cinema.

Julian Slade told *CTFT* that *Salad Days* ran for 2,288 performances in London before its revival there in 1976.

ADDRESSES: OFFICE—Three Priory Walk, London SW10, England.

*   *   *

SMITH, Alexis 1921-

PERSONAL: Born June 8, 1921, in Penticton, Canada; married Craig Stevens (an actor). EDUCATION: Attended Los Angeles City College.

VOCATION: Actress.

CAREER: NEW YORK DEBUT—Phyllis Rogers Stone, *Follies*, Winter Garden Theatre, 1971. PRINCIPAL STAGE APPEARANCES—Phyllis Rogers Stone, *Follies*, Shubert Theatre, Century City, CA, 1972; Sylvia (Mrs. Howard Fowler), *The Women* (revival), 46th Street Theatre, NY, 1973; Rosemary Sydney, *Summer Brave*, American National Theatre and Academy (ANTA), 1975; Lila Halliday, *Sunset*, Studio Arena Theatre, Buffalo, NY, 1977; Lila Halliday, *Platinum*, Mark Hellinger Theatre, NY, 1978.

MAJOR TOURS—Miss Mona, *Best Little Whorehouse in Texas*, national, 1982-83; Vera, *Pal Joey*, national, 1983.

FILM DEBUT—*The Lady with Red Hair*, 1940. PRINCIPAL FILM APPEARANCES—*Smiling Ghost*, 1940; *Dive Bomber*, 1941; *Steel Against the Sky*, 1941; *Gentleman Jim*, 1942; *Thank Your Lucky Stars*, Warner Brothers, 1943; *The Constant Nymph*, 1943; *The Adventures of Mark Twain*, 1944; *The Doughgirls*, 1944; *Conflict*, 1945; *Rhapsody in Blue*, 1945; *The Horn Blows at Midnight*, 1945; *One More Tomorrow*, 1946; *Night and Day*, 1946; *Of Human Bondage*, 1946; *Stallion Road*, 1947; *The Two Mrs. Carrolls*, 1947; *Woman in White*, 1948; *Decision of Christopher Blake*, 1948; *Whiplash*, 1948; *South of St. Louis*, 1949; *Any Number Can Play*, 1949; *One Last Fling*, 1949; *Undercover Girl*, 1950; *Wyoming Mail*, 1950; *Montana*, 1950; *Here Comes the Groom*, 1951; *Cave of the Outlaws*, 1951; *The Turning Point*, 1952; *Split Second*, 1953; *Sleeping Tiger*, 1954; *The Eternal Sea*, Republic Pictures, 1955; *Beau James*, 1957; *The Young Philadelphians*, Warner Brothers, 1959; *Once Is Not Enough*, Paramount, 1975; *The Little Girl Who Lives Down the Lane*, American International, 1977; *Casey's Shadow*, Columbia, 1978; also appeared in *La Troite*.

PRINCIPAL TELEVISION APPEARANCES—Series: Lady Jessica Montford, *Dallas*, CBS, 1984-85.

Episodic: *Stage 7*, CBS, 1955; *The Love Boat*, ABC.

Mini-Series: *A Death in California*, ABC, 1985.

MEMBER: Actors' Equity Association, Screen Actors Guild, American Federation of Television and Radio Artists.

AWARDS: Star of Tomorrow, 1943; Antoinette Perry Award, 1971, for *Follies.**

*   *   *

SMOTHERS, Dick   1939-

PERSONAL: Born 1939; son of Thomas B. and Ruth Smothers; children: Susan, Dick, Steven. EDUCATION: Attended San Jose State College.

VOCATION: Comedian and singer.

CAREER: PRINCIPAL TELEVISION APPEARANCES—Series: Co-star, *The Smothers Brothers Show*, CBS, 1965-66; co-star, *The Smothers Brothers Comedy Hour*, CBS, 1967-69, ABC, 1970, then NBC, 1975; Ryan Fitzpatrick, *Fitz and Bones*, NBC, 1981.

PRINCIPAL FILM APPEARANCES—*The Silver Bears*, Columbia, 1978.

PRINCIPAL STAGE APPEARANCES—*I Love My Wife*, Broadway, 1978-79.

CABARET—Nightclub appearances with brother, Tom, as The Smothers Brothers at Harrah's Lake Tahoe and the Riveria, Las Vegas.*

*   *   *

SMOTHERS, Tom   1937-

PERSONAL: Born 1937; son of Thomas B. and Ruth S. Smothers; children: Tom. EDUCATION: Attended San Jose State College.

VOCATION: Comedian and singer.

CAREER: PRINCIPAL TELEVISION APPEARANCES—Series: Co-star, *The Smothers Brothers Show*, CBS, 1965-66; co-star, *The Smothers Brothers Comedy Hour*, CBS, 1967-69, ABC, 1970, then NBC, 1975; Bones Howard, *Fitz and Bones*, NBC, 1981.

PRINCIPAL FILM APPEARANCES—*The Silver Bears*, Columbia, 1978; *Pandemonium*, 1982.

PRINCIPAL STAGE APPEARANCES—*I Love My Wife*, Broadway, 1978-79.

CABARET—Nightclub appearances with brother, Dick, as The Smothers Brothers at Harrah's Lake Tahoe and the Riveria, Las Vegas.*

SNOW, Donna

PERSONAL: Married Peter Webster (an actor), September, 1982. EDUCATION: University of Washington, B.A.; trained for the stage at the American Conservatory Theatre School, San Francisco, CA.

VOCATION: Actress.

CAREER: STAGE DEBUT—Katarina, *The Master Builder*, American Conservatory Theatre, San Francisco, CA, 1977. NEW YORK DEBUT—Young woman, *Private Scenes*, Production Company, 1985, for fifty performances. PRINCIPAL STAGE APPEARANCES—At the American Conservatory Theatre, San Francisco, CA: Young girl, *The National Health;* Bibi, *Hotel Paradiso;* Luella, *The Day Roosevelt Died;* Mrs. Nicholson, *Waiting for Godiva;* understudy Irene, *Crucifer of Blood;* Birdie and Sara, *An Evening with Lillian Hellman.*

Birdie, *Another Part of the Forest*, Seattle Repertory, WA; Helena, *All's Well That Ends Well*, Folger Theatre, Washington, DC; Marianne, *Tartuffe* and Sorel, *Hayfever*, Pittsburgh Public Theatre; Belle, *A Christmas Carol*, Ford's Theatre, Washington, DC; Ann, *All My Sons*, Stage West; Helena, *A Midsummer Night's Dream* and Catherine, *The Foreigner*, Sudio Arena, Buffalo, NY; Firelei, *Out of the Night*, Off-Broadway production.

MAJOR TOURS—Alais, *Lion in Winter*, Sybil, *Private Lives*, both with the Long Wharf Theatre Company, U.S. cities, 1980-81.

TELEVISION DEBUT—Paula Davidson, *Mickey Spillane's Mike Hammer*, CBS, 1985.

DONNA SNOW

RELATED CAREER: Voice instructor, Temple University, Philadelphia, 1978-79, American Conservatory Theatre, San Francisco, Circle in the Square Theatre School, New York, NY, 1982-83.

AWARDS: Phi Beta Kappa Scholarship, University of Washington.

ADDRESSES: AGENT—ADM Associated, Inc., 165 W. 46th Street, Suite 1109, New York, NY 10036.

*   *   *

SOMERS, Suzanne   1946-

PERSONAL: Born October 16, 1946, in San Bruno, CA; divorced first husband; married Alan Hamel (a manager); children: (first marriage) one son. EDUCATION: Attended Lone Mountain School and San Francisco College for Women; trained for the stage with Charles Conrad.

VOCATION: Actress and singer.

CAREER: PRINCIPAL TELEVISION APPEARANCES—Series: Chrissy Snow, *Three's Company*, ABC, 1977-81.

Episodic: *Mantrap; Lotsa Luck; One Day at a Time; Rockford Files; Starsky and Hutch.*

Mini-Series: Gina Germaine, *Hollywood Wives*, ABC, 1985.

Game Shows: *Anniversary Show; High Rollers.*

Guest: *Tonight Show; Phil Donahue.*

SUZANNE SOMERS

PRINCIPAL FILM APPEARANCES—*Yesterday's Hero; Bullitt*, Warner Brothers, 1968; *Daddy's Gone a Hunting*, National General, 1969; *Fools*, Cinerama, 1970; girl in the white Thunderbird, *American Graffitti*, 1973; *Magnum Force*, Warner Brothers, 1973; *Nothing Personal*, 1980.

PRINCIPAL STAGE APPEARANCES—Stock: *Guys and Dolls; Annie Get Your Gun; Sound of Music; The Boyfriend.*

CABARET—"Moulin Rouge," Las Vegas Hilton, NV; and at the MGM Grand, Las Vegas, NV and Sands Hotel, Atlantic City, NJ.

MAJOR TOURS—USO, Pacific Theatres of Operation.

RELATED CAREER—Fashion model; television commercial actress.

WRITINGS: POETRY—*Touch Me*, Workman, 1973.

ADDRESSES: PUBLICIST—Michael Levine, 9123 Sunset Blvd., Los Angeles, CA 90069.

*   *   *

SOMMER, Elke   1941-

PERSONAL: Born Elke Schletz, November 5, 1941, in Berlin Germany, immigrated to Britain, 1956; married Joe Hyams, 1964. EDUCATION: Attended the University of Erlangen, West Germany.

VOCATION: Actress.

CAREER: PRINCIPAL FILM APPEARANCES—European films, 1958-60: *Friend of the Jaguar; Traveling Luxury; Heaven and Cupid; Ship of the Dead.* U.S. films: *Don't Bother to Knock*, 1960; *The Victors*, Columbia, 1963; *The Prize*, Metro-Goldwyn-Mayer, 1963; *A Shot in the Dark*, United Artists, 1964; *The Art of Love*, 1965; *Four Kinds of Love*, 1965; *The Oscar*, Embassy, 1966; *Frontier Hellcat*, Columbia, 1966; *The Money Trap*, Metro-Goldwyn-Mayer, 1966; *Boy, Did I Get the Wrong Number*, United Artists, 1966; *The Venetian Affair*, Metro-Goldwyn-Mayer, 1967; *Deadlier Than the Male*, Universal, 1967; *The Corrupt Ones*, Warner Brothers, 1967; *The Wicked Dreams of Paula Schultz*, United Artists, 1968; *They Came to Rob Las Vegas*, Warner Brothers, 1969; *The Wrecking Crew*, Columbia, 1969; *Percy*, Metro-Goldwyn-Mayer, 1971; *Zeppelin*, Warner Brothers, 1971; *Baron Blood*, American International, 1972; *Ten Little Indians*, Avco Embassy, 1975; *The Net*, 1975; *Lisa and the Devil*, 1976; *The Swiss Conspiracy*, 1979; *The Double Maguffin*, 1979; *The Prisoner of Zenda*, Universal, 1979; *Lily in Love*, New Line Cinema, 1985.

PRINCIPAL TELEVISION APPEARANCES—Movies: *Top of the Hill*, 1980.

Mini-Series: *Peter the Great*, 1985.

Guest: *Celebrity Challenge of the Sexes*, CBS, 1978; *Fernwood 2-Night*, 1978.

PRINCIPAL STAGE APPEARANCES—*The Milliken Breakfast Show*, 1980; *Born Yesterday*, Europe; *Seascape*, Chicago; *Cactus Flower*.

AWARDS: The Peking Medallion, 1967, for *The Corrupt Ones;* Best Actress, Silver Bambi Award (Germany).

ADDRESSES: OFFICE—c/o George Durgom, 9255 Sunset Blvd., Los Angeles, CA 90069.*

SOUL, David   1943-

PERSONAL: Born August 28, 1943, in Chicago, IL; married Karen Carlson (an actress).

VOCATION: Actor.

CAREER: TELEVISION DEBUT—The hooded "mystery" singer, *Merv Griffin Show*, 1966. PRINCIPAL TELEVISION APPEARANCES— Series: Joshua Bolt, *Here Come The Brides*, ABC, 1968-70; Ted Warrick, *Owen Marshall, Counselor at Law*, ABC, 1974; Detective Ken Hutchinson (Hutch), *Starsky and Hutch*, ABC, 1975-79; Rick Blaine, *Casablanca*, NBC, 1983; Roy Champion, *The Yellow Rose*, NBC, 1983-84.

Guest: *The Streets of San Francisco*, ABC; *Cannon*, CBS; *Medical Center*, CBS; *The Rookies*, ABC; *Ironside*, NBC; *Star Trek*, NBC; *McMillan and Wife*, NBC; *Dan August*, CBS; *Circle of Fear*, NBC.

Movies: *The Disappearance of Flight 412*, 1974; *Movin' On*, 1974; *Little Ladies of the Night*, 1977; *Salem's Lot*, 1979.

Mini-Series: *The Key to Rebecca*, Taft Entertainment, 1985; *The Manions of America*, syndicated (upcoming).

PRINCIPAL FILM APPEARANCES—*Johnny Got His Gun*, Marketing & Distribution Company, 1971; *Magnum Force*, Warner Brothers, 1973; *Dog Pound Shuffle*, 1975.

MEMBER: Screen Actors Guild, American Federation of Television and Radio Artists.

ADDRESSES: AGENT—William Morris Agency, 151 El Camino Drive, Beverly Hills, CA 90212.*

*   *   *

SPACEK, Sissy   1950-

PERSONAL: Full name Mary Elizabeth Spacek; born December 25, 1950, in Quitman, TX; daughter of Edwin A. and Virginia Spacek; married Jack Fisk, 1974; children: Schuyler Elizabeth. EDUCATION: Attended Lee Strasberg Theater Institute.

VOCATION: Actress.

CAREER: FILM DEBUT—*Prime Cut*, National General, 1972. PRINCIPAL FILM APPEARANCES—*Ginger in the Morning*, 1972; *Badlands*, Warner Brothers, 1974; title role, *Carrie*, United Artists, 1976; *Three Women*, Twentieth Century-Fox, 1977; *Welcome to L.A.*, Lion's Gate, 1977; *Heart Beat*, Warner Brothers, 1980; Loretta Lynn, *Coal Miner's Daughter*, Universal, 1980; *Raggedy Man*, Universal, 1981; *Missing*, Universal, 1982; voice of brain, *The Man with Two Brains*, Warner Brothers, 1983; *The River*, Universal, 1984; Marie, *Marie*, Metro-Goldwyn-Mayer, 1985; *Violets Are Blue*, Rastar/Columbia, 1986.

PRINCIPAL TELEVISION APPEARANCES—Movies: *The Girls of Huntington House*, 1973; *The Migrants*, 1973; *Katherine*, 1975; *Verna: USO Girl*, 1978.

Episodic: *The Waltons* (two segments), CBS; guest host, *Saturday Night Live*, 1977.

MEMBER: Screen Actors Guild.

AWARDS: Best Actress, National Society of Film Critics Award, Academy Award nomination, both 1976, for *Carrie;* Best Actress, New York Film Critics Award, 1977, for *Three Women;* Best Actress, New York Film Critics Award, Los Angeles Film Critics Award, Golden Globe, National Society of Film Critics Award, Academy Award, all 1980, for *Coal Miner's Daughter;* Album of the Year, Country Music Association Award, 1980 for *Coal Miner's Daughter* (vocals by Spacek); Best Actress, Academy Award nomination, 1982, for *Missing;* Best Actress, Academy Award nomination, 1984, for *The River*.

ADDRESSES: AGENT—Creative Artists Agency 1888 Century Park E., Los Angeles, CA 90067.

*   *   *

SPELLING, Aaron   1928-

PERSONAL: Born April 22, 1928, in Dallas, TX; son of David and Pearl (Wall) Spelling; married Carole Gene Marer, November 23, 1968; children: Victoria, Randall. EDUCATION: Studied at the Sorbonne, University of Paris, France, 1945-46; Southern Methodist University, B.A., 1950. MILITARY: U.S. Army Air Force, 1942-45.

VOCATION: Producer.

CAREER: PRINCIPAL TELEVISION WORK—Producer: *Dick Powell's Zane Grey Theatre*, CBS, 1956-62; *Honey West*, ABC, 1965-66; *Smothers Brothers Show*, CBS, 1965-66; *Dick Powell Show*, NBC, 1961-63; *Danny Thomas Hour*, NBC, 1967-68; *Burke's Law*, ABC, 1963-66; *Mod Squad*, ABC, 1968-73; *The Rookies*, ABC, 1972-76; *Starsky and Hutch*, ABC, 1975-79; *Family*, ABC, 1976-80; *Charlie's Angels*, ABC, 1976-81; *The Beach Bums*, ABC; *The Love Boat*, ABC, 1977—; *Vega$*, ABC, 1978-81; *Fantasy Island*, ABC, 1978-84; *Hart to Hart*, ABC, 1979-84; *The B.A.D. Cats*, ABC, 1980; *Aloha Paradise*, ABC, 1981-83; *Dynasty*, ABC, 1981—; *Strike Force*, ABC, 1981-82; *Hotel*, ABC, 1983—.

Photograph by Harry Langdon

AARON SPELLING

Movies: *The Legend of Valentino*, 1975; *The Boy in the Plastic Bubble*, 1976; *One of My Wives Is Missing*, 1976; *Little Ladies of the Night*, 1977; *The Users*, 1978; *Murder Can Hurt You*, 1980; *The Best Little Girl in the World*, 1981; *Sizzle*, 1981; *Matt Houston*, 1982; *Masserit and the Brain*, 1982; *Wild Women of Charity Gulch*, 1982; *Don't Go to Sleep*, 1982; *Shooting Stars*, 1983; *Hotel*, 1983.

PRINCIPAL FILM WORK—Executive producer, *Mr. Mom*, Twentieth Century-Fox, 1983.

MEMBER: Writers Guild of America, Producers Guild of America, Hollywood Radio and Television Society, Hollywood Television Academy of Arts and Sciences; the Caucus, Friars Club, Big Brothers of America.

AWARDS: Eugene O'Neill Awards, 1947, 1948; Writers Guild Award, 1962; Man of the Year Award, Publicists of America, 1971; National Association for the Advancement of Colored People Image Award, 1970, 1971, 1973, 1975; B'nai B'rith Man of the Year Award, 1972; military: Purple Heart with oak leaf cluster and Bronze Star Medal.

ADDRESSES: OFFICE—Aaron Spelling Productions, 1041 N. Formosa, Los Angeles, CA 90046.

* * *

STACK, Robert   1919-

PERSONAL: Full name, Robert Langford Stack; born January 13, 1919, in Los Angeles, CA; son of James Langford and Elizabeth (Wood) Stack; married Rosemarie Bowe, January 23, 1956; children: Elizabeth, Charles. EDUCATION: Attended the University of Southern California, 1937-38. MILITARY: Served in the U.S. Armed Forces, World War II.

VOCATION: Actor and producer.

CAREER: PRINCIPAL FILM APPEARANCES—*First Love*, 1939; *When the Daltons Rode*, 1940; *Mortal Storm*, Metro-Goldwyn-Mayer, 1940; *A Little Bit of Heaven*, 1941; *Nice Girl*, 1941; *Badlands of Dakota*, 1941; *To Be or Not to Be*, 1942; *Eagle Squadron*, 1942; *Men of Texas*, 1942; *Fighter Squadron*, 1948; *Date with Judy*, Metro-Goldwyn-Mayer, 1948.

Miss Tatlock's Millions, 1950; *Mr. Music*, 1951; *The Bullfighter and the Lady*, 1951; *My Outlaw Brother*, 1951; *Bwana Devil*, 1952; *War Paint*, 1953; *Conquest of Cochise*, 1953; *Sabre Jet*, 1953; *Iron Glove*, 1954; *The High and the Mighty*, 1954; *House of Bamboo*, Twentieth Century-Fox, 1955; *Good Morning Miss Dove*, Twentieth Century-Fox, 1955; *Great Day in the Morning*, 1956; *Written on the Wind*, Universal, 1956; *John Paul Jones' Last Voyage*, Metro-Goldwyn-Mayer, 1959.

Killers of Killimanjaro, Columbia, 1960; *The Caretakers*, United Artists, 1963; *The Corrupt Ones*, Warner Brothers, 1967; *Story of a Woman*, Universal, 1970; *1941*, Universal, 1979; *Airplane!*, Paramount, 1980; *Uncommon Valor*, Paramount, 1983; *Big Trouble*, 1984.

PRINCIPAL TELEVISION APPEARANCES—Series: Elliot Ness, *The Untouchables*, ABC, 1959-1963; Dan Farrell, *The Name of the Game*, NBC, 1968-71; Captain Linc Evers, *Most Wanted*, ABC, 1976-77; Captain Frank Murphy, *Strike Force*, ABC, 1981-82.

ROBERT STACK

Episodic: Elliot Ness "The Untouchables," *Westinghouse Desilu Playhouse*, ABC, 1959; *Pantomime Quiz; Bob Hope Presents the Chrysler Theatre*, NBC.

Mini-Series: *Hollywood Wives*, ABC, 1985.

RELATED CAREER: Co-producer, *The Untouchables*, ABC, 1959-1963; president, Langford Productions, 1959—.

AWARDS: Best Supporting Actor, Academy Award nomination, 1956, for *Written on the Wind;* Outstanding Performance by an Actor in a Series, Emmy Award, 1959-60, for *The Untouchables*.

ADDRESSES: AGENT—Camden Artists, 409 N. Camden Drive, Suite 202, Beverly Hills, CA 90210.

* * *

STAMOS, John

BRIEF ENTRY: Actor and musician. John Stamos made his acting debut as Blackie on ABC's daytime serial *General Hospital*, and he received so much audience reaction that the producers signed him to a two year contract. Stamos' work on *General Hospital* was rewarded with two Soapy Awards, a Youth in Film Award, and as the youngest actor every to receive one, a daytime Emmy nomination for Best Supporting Actor. Since leaving *General Hospital*, Stamos has co-starred in two prime-time series, as Gino Minelli in *Dreams* and as Matthew Willows in *You, Again?* His feature film debut was *Never Too Young to Die*. Stamos is a singer, guitarist, drummer, and composer. In his spare time, he sometimes tours with the Beach Boys as the group's drummer.*

*   *   *

STANLEY, Kim   1921-

PERSONAL: Born Patricia Reid, February 11, 1921, in Tularosa, NM; daughter of J.T. (a physician) and Ann (Miller) Reid; married Bruce Hall (divorced); married Curt Conway (divorced); married Alfred Ryder. EDUCATION: Attended Texas State University and University of New Mexico; trained for the stage at the Actors Studio with Lee Strasberg and Elia Kazan.

VOCATION: Actress.

CAREER: STAGE DEBUT—Stock companies, Louisville, KY, and Pompton Lakes, NJ. LONDON DEBUT—Maggie, Cat on a Hot Tin Roof, Comedy Theatre, 1958. PRINCIPAL STAGE APPEARANCES—Iris, The Dog Beneath the Skin, Carnegie Recital Hall, NY, 1948; Him, Provincetown Playhouse, NY, 1949; Yes Is for a Very Young Man, Cherry Lane Theatre, NY, 1949; tite role, Saint Joan, Equity Library Theatre, NY, 1949; Felisa, Monteserrat, Fulton Theatre, NY, 1949; Adela, The House of Bernarda Alba, American National Theatre and Academy (ANTA), NY, 1951; Anna Reeves, The Chase, Playhouse Theatre, NY, 1952; Millie Owens, Picnic, Music Box Theatre, NY, 1953; Georgette Thomas, The Traveling Lady, Playhouse Theatre, NY, 1954; Mrs. Theodore Herzl, The Great Dreamer, Madison Square Garden, NY, 1954; Cherie, Bus Stop, Music Box Theatre, NY, 1955; Virginia, A Clearing in the Woods, Belasco Theatre, NY, 1957; Sara Melody, A Touch of the Poet, Helen Hayes Theatre, NY, 1958; Les de Lonval, Cheri, Morosco Theatre, NY, 1959; Elizabeth von Ritter, A Far Country, Music Box Theatre, NY, 1961; Sue Barker, Natural Affection, Booth Theatre, NY, 1963; Masha, The Three Sisters, Actors Studio, then Morosco Theatre, NY, 1964, then Aldwych Theatre, London, 1965.

FILM DEBUT—The Goddess, Columbia, 1958. PRINCIPAL FILM APPEARANCES—Seance on a Wet Afternoon, Artixo, 1964; Frances, Universal, 1982; The Right Stuff, Warner Brothers, 1983.

PRINCIPAL TELEVISION APPEARANCES—Episodic: Sure as Fate, CBS; Danger, CBS; Goodyear TV Playhouse, NBC; title role, "Joan of Arc," Omnibus, CBS; Clash by Night; The Traveling Lady; title role, "Cleopatra," You Are There; "A Cardinal Act of Mercy," Ben Casey, ABC, 1963.

AWARDS: New York Drama Critics Award, 1953, for Picnic; Donaldson Award, New York Drama Critics Poll Award, 1955, for Bus Stop; Emmy Award, 1963 for "A Cardinal Act of Mercy," Ben Casey.

ADDRESSES: AGENT—Robert Lantz Agency, 9255 Sunset Blvd., Los Angeles, CA 90069.*

*   *   *

STANWYCK, Barbara   1907-

PERSONAL: Born Ruby Stevens, July 16, 1907, in New York, NY; married Frank Fay, 1928 (marriage ended); married Robert Taylor, May 14, 1939.

VOCATION: Actress.

CAREER: FILM DEBUT—Locked Door, 1929. PRINCIPAL FILM

APPEARANCES—Ladies of Leisure, 1930; Night Nurse, 1931; Ten Cents a Dance, Columbia, 1931; Bitter Tea of General Yen, 1933; Brief Moment, 1933; Woman in Red, 1935; Annie Oakley, 1935; The Plough and the Stars, 1936; His Brother's Wife, Metro-Goldwyn-Mayer, 1936; Stella Dallas, 1937; Mad Miss Manton, 1938; Union Pacific, 1939; Lorna, Golden Boy, 1939; Meet John Doe, 1941; Ball of Fire, 1941; The Great Man's Lady, 1942; The Gay Sisters, 1942; Double Indemnity, 1944; My Reputations, 1945; Two Mrs. Carrolls, 1946; Christmas in Connecticut, 1946; The Bride Wore Boots, 1947; Strange Love of Martha Ivars, 1947; Cry Wolf, 1948; The Other Love, 1948; B.F.'s Daughter, Metro-Goldwyn-Mayer, 1949; Sorry Wrong Number, 1949; File on Thelma Jordan, 1949; The Lady Gambles, 1949; The Lie, 1949; East Side, West Side, Metro-Goldwyn-Mayer, 1949; The Furies, 1949.

No Man of Her Own, 1950; To Please a Lady, Metro-Goldwyn-Mayer, 1950; The Man in the Cloak, Metro-Goldwyn-Mayer, 1951; Clash by Night, 1951; Jeopardy, Metro-Goldwyn-Mayer, 1952; Titanic, 1952; All I Desire, 1953; Blowing Wild, 1953; The Moonlighter, 1953; Executive Suite, Metro-Goldwyn-Mayer, 1954; Witness to Murder, 1955; Violent Men, Columbia, 1955; Escape to Burma, RKO, 1955; Cattle Queen of Montana, 1956; There's Always Tomorrow, Universal, 1956; Maverick Queen, Republic, 1956; These Wilder Years, Metro-Goldwyn-Mayer, 1956; Crime of Passion, United Artists, 1957; Trooper Hook, United Artists, 1957; Forty Guns, Twentieth Century-Fox, 1957; Walk on the Wild Side, Columbia, 1962; Roustabout, Paramount, 1964; The Night Walker, Universal, 1965.

PRINCIPAL TELEVISION APPEARANCES—Series: The Barbara Stanwyck Theatre, NBC, 1960-61; Victoria Barkley, The Big Valley, ABC, 1965-69; Constance Colby, Dynasty II: The Colbys, ABC, 1985—.

Guest: The Jack Benny Show, CBS; Zane Grey Theatre, CBS; Alcoa Theatre, NBC; Goodyear Theatre, NBC; Ford Theatre, ABC.

Movies: The Letters, 1973.

Mini-Series: The Thorn Birds, ABC, 1983.

AWARDS: Outstanding Performance by an Actress in a Series, Emmy Award, 1960-61, for The Barbara Stanwyck Show; Outstanding Lead Actress in a Limited Series, Emmy Award, 1982-83, for The Thorn Birds; Special Academy Award, 1982.

SIDELIGHTS: Barbara Stanwyck began her performing career as a chorus girl in New York and moved into a dramatic show called Burlesque, produced by Arthur Hopkins.

ADDRESSES: AGENT—A. Morgan Maree and Associates, Inc., 6363 Wilshire Blvd., Los Angeles, CA 90048.

*   *   *

STEELE, Tommy   1936-

PERSONAL: Born Thomas Hicks, December 17, 1936, in Bermondsey, London, England; son of Thomas Walter and Elizabeth Ellen (Bennett) Hicks; married Ann Donoughue. EDUCATION: Attended Bacon's School for Boys, Bermondsey, London, England.

VOCATION: Actor and singer.

CAREER: STAGE DEBUT—In a variety show, Empire Theatre, Sunderland, England, 1956. LONDON DEBUT—Royal Variety

Performance, Dominion Theatre, 1957. NEW YORK DEBUT—Arthur Kipps, *Half-a-Sixpence*, Broadhurst Theatre, 1965. PRINCIPAL STAGE APPEARANCES—Buttons, *Cinderella*, Coliseum Theatre, London, 1958; Tony Lumpkin, *She Stoops to Conquer*, Old Vic Theatre, London, 1960; Arthur Kipps, *Half-a-Sixpence*, Cambridge Theatre, 1963; *Royal Variety Performance*, 1963; Truffaldino, *The Servant of Two Masters*, Queen's Theatre, 1968; title role, *Dick Whittington*, Palladium Theatre, 1969; *Meet Me in London*, Las Vegas, NV, then Adelphi Theatre, London, 1971; in a variety show at the Palladium Theatre, 1973; title role, *Hans Andersen*, Palladium Theatre, 1974, and in revival, 1977; *An Evening with Tommy Steele*, Prince of Wales Theatre, 1979; Don Lockwood, *Singin' in the Rain*, Palladium Theatre, 1983.

MAJOR TOURS—*The Tommy Steele Anniversary Show*, 1976.

FILM DEBUT—*Kill Me Tomorrow*, British, 1957. PRINCIPAL FILM APPEARANCES—*The Tommy Steele Story* (also known as *Rock Around the World*), British, 1957; *It's All Happening* (also known as *The Dream Maker*), 1964; *The Happiest Millionaire*, 1967; Og, *Finian's Rainbow*, Warner Brothers/Seven Arts, 1968; Arthur Kipps, *Half-a-Sixpence*, Paramount, 1969; *Where's Jack*, British, 1969; also appeared in *The Duke Wore Jeans; Tommy the Toreador; Light Up the Sky*.

TELEVISION DEBUT—*Off The Record*, 1956. PRINCIPAL TELEVISION APPEARANCES—Series: *Quincy's Quest*, BBC, 1979; *The Tommy Steele Hour*.

Specials: *Tommy Steele Spectaculars; Richard Whittington Esquire; Tommy Steele in Search of Charlie Chaplin; Tommy Steele and a Show; Twelfth Night*.

Guest: *Ed Sullivan Show; Gene Kelly Show; Perry Como Show*.

RECORDINGS: ALBUMS—*My Life, My Song*, musical autobiography, 1974.

SINGLE—"Rock with the Caveman," 1955.

WRITINGS: BOOKS—*Quincy*, 1981; *The Final Run*, 1983.

MUSIC—Composer, *My Life, My Song*, 1974.

AWARDS: Order of the British Empire for his service to the theatre, 1979.

ADDRESSES: AGENT—Talent Artists Ltd., 37 Hill Street, London W1X 8JY, England.

*   *   *

STEIGER, Rod   1925-

PERSONAL: Born April 14, 1925, in Westhampton, NY; married Claire Bloom (divorced). EDUCATION: Studied acting at the American Theatre Wing and the Dramatic Workshop of the Actors Studio in New York. MILITARY: U.S. Navy.

VOCATION: Actor.

CAREER: PRINCIPAL STAGE APPEARANCES—*Night Music*, American National Theatre and Academy (ANTA).

FILM DEBUT—*Teresa*, Metro-Goldwyn-Mayer, 1950. PRINCIPAL FILM APPEARANCES—Charlie, *On the Waterfront*, 1954; *The Big*

Knife, United Artists, 1955; *The Court Martial of Billy Mitchell*, Warner Brothers, 1955; Jud, *Oklahoma!*, Twentieth Century-Fox, 1956; *Jubal*, Columbia, 1956; *The Harder They Fall*, 1956; *Back from Eternity*, Universal, 1956; *Run of the Arrow*, Universal, 1957; *Unholy Wife*, Universal, 1957; *Cry Terror*, Metro-Goldwyn-Mayer, 1958; *Al Capone*, Allied Artists, 1959.

Seven Thieves, Twentieth Century-Fox, 1960; *The Mark*, Continental, 1962; *Reprieve*, Allied Artists, 1962; *13 West Street*, Columbia, 1962; *Hands Upon the City*, 1963; *The Time of Indifference*, Continental, 1964; *The Loved One*, Metro-Goldwyn-Mayer, 1965; *The Pawnbroker*, Allied Artists-Landau, 1965; *In the Heat of the Night*, United Artists, 1967; *The Girl and the General*, Metro-Goldwyn-Mayer, 1967; *No Way to Treat a Lady*, Paramount, 1968; *And There Came a Man*, Brandon, 1968; *The Illustrated Man*, Warner Brothers/Seven Arts, 1969; *Three into Two Won't Go*, Universal, 1969.

Waterloo, Paramount, 1971; *Happy Birthday Wanda June*, 1971; *Duck! You Sucker*, United Artists, 1972; *The Lolly-Madonna Wars*, Metro-Goldwyn-Mayer, 1974; *Lucky Luciano*, Avco Embassy, 1975; *Hennessy*, American International, 1976; *W.C. Fields and Me*, Universal, 1978; *The Amityville Horror*, American International, 1979; *The Lion of the Desert*, United Film Distributors, 1981; *Cattle Annie and Little Britches*, Universal, 1981; *The Chosen*, Twentieth Century-Fox, 1982; *The Naked Face*.

PRINCIPAL TELEVISION APPEARANCES—Episodic: *Danger*, CBS; title role, "Marty," *Goodyear TV Playhouse*, NBC, 1953; *Kraft Television Theatre; Philco TV Playhouse*, NBC; *Sure as Fate*, CBS.

NON-RELATED CAREER: Civil service employee.

AWARDS: Best Actor, Academy Award, 1967, for *In the Heat of the Night*.

ADDRESSES: AGENT—Creative Artists Agency, 1888 Century Park E., Suite 1400, Los Angeles, CA 90067.*

*   *   *

STEVENS, Andrew   1955-

PERSONAL: Born Andrew Stephens, June 10, 1955, in Memphis, TN; son of Noble Herman and Stella (the actress; maiden name, Eggleston) Stephens; married Kate Jackson (divorced). EDUCATION: Attended Immaculate Heart College, Los Angeles, CA, 1973-74; attended West Los Angeles College and Los Angeles Valley College, 1974-75; Antioch University, 1985-87; studied acting with Lee Strasberg, David Craig, Vincent Chase, and Robert Easton. POLITICS: Democrat.

VOCATION: Actor and producer.

CAREER: PRINCIPAL TELEVISION APPEARANCES—Series: Andrew Thorpe, *Oregon Trail*, NBC, 1977; Ted Rorchek, *Code Red*, ABC, 1981-82; Lt. Glenn Matthews, *Emerald Point N.A.S.*, CBS, 1983-84.

Movies: *The Oregon Trail*, 1975; *The Werewolf of Woodstock*, 1975; *The Last Survivors*, 1975; *Secrets*, 1977; *Women at West Point*, CBS, 1978; *Topper*, 1979; *Miracle on Ice*, 1981; *Code Red*, 1981; *Forbidden Love*, CBS, 1982; *Journey's End*, Showtime, 1983; *Circus*, CBS, 1986.

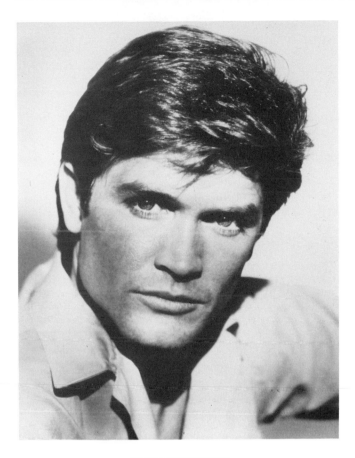

ANDREW STEVENS

Mini-Series: *Once an Eagle*, NBC, 1977; *The Bastard*, Operation Prime Time, 1978; *The Rebels*, Operation Prime Time, 1979; *Beggarman, Thief*, NBC, 1979; *Hollywood Wives*, ABC, 1985.

Episodic: *Murder, She Wrote*, CBS, 1984; *Hotel*, ABC, 1984; *Love Boat*, ABC, 1984; also appeared in *Adam 12*, NBC; *Apple's Way*, CBS; *The Quest*, ABC; *Police Story*, CBS; *Shazam; Pumper One*.

PRINCIPAL FILM APPEARANCES—*Shampoo*, Columbia, 1975; *Vigilante Force*, United Artists, 1976; *Massacre at Central High*, 1976; *Day of the Animals*, 1977; *Las Vegas Lady*, Crown International, 1977; *The Boys in Company C*, Columbia, 1978; *The Fury*, Twentieth Century-Fox, 1978; *Death Hunt*, Twentieth Century-Fox, 1981; *The Seduction*, Embassy, 1982; *Ten to Midnight*, Canon, 1983; *Fire in Eden*, 1986; *The Attic*, 1986.

PRINCIPAL STAGE APPEARANCES—Paul Bratter, *Barefoot in the Park*, Burt Reynold's Dinner Theatre, Jupiter, FL, 1980; Lt. Raleigh, *Journey's End*, Los Angeles, 1982; Mark Dolson, *Mass Appeal*, Old Globe Theatre, San Diego, CA, 1983; title role, *Billy Budd*, Los Angeles, 1984; Jimmy Zoole, *P.S. Your Cat Is Dead*, Los Angeles, 1985.

RELATED CAREER—Owner, executive producer, King Cod Productions, Los Angeles, CA.

RECORDINGS: *Helpless in Love*, Warner/Curb, 1978; *The Party's Not Over*, Warner/Curb, 1979.

MEMBER: Actors' Equity Association, Screen Actors Guild, Ameri-

can Federation of Television and Radio Artists, ASCAP; Studio Transportation Drivers-Teamster's Union, local 399 (honorary).

SIDELIGHTS: Andrew Stevens is co-owner of Butterbean Electric Company, Memphis, TN.

ADDRESSES: OFFICE—King Cod, Inc., c/o Laventhol & Horwath, 2049 Century Park E., Suite 3700, Los Angeles, CA 90067.

*   *   *

STEVENS, Connie   1938-

PERSONAL: Born Concerta Ann Ingolia, August 8, 1938, in New York, NY; daughter of Peter and Eleanore (McGinley) Ingolia; married Maurice Elias (divorced); married Eddie Fisher (singer and actor, divorced); children: (second marriage) Joely, Tricia Leigh. EDUCATION: Attended Sacred Heart Academy and the Hollywood Professional School.

VOCATION: Singer and actress.

CAREER: STAGE DEBUT—*Finians Rainbow*, Hollywood Repertory Theatre, Los Angeles, CA. NEW YORK DEBUT—*Star Spangled Girl*, Broadway, 1967. PRINCIPAL STAGE APPEARANCES—*The Wizard of Oz*, Carousel Theatre, Southern California; *Any Wednesday*, Melodyland, Anaheim, CA.

CABARET—Performed in Las Vegas at the Flamingo Hotel, Sands Hotel, Hilton International Hotel, and Desert Inn, between 1969-76.

MAJOR TOURS—Toured with Bob Hope annual U.S.O. Christmas show around the world, 1969.

PRINCIPAL FILM APPEARANCES—*Eighteen and Anxious*, Republic, 1957; *Young and Dangerous*, Twentieth Century-Fox, 1957; *Dragstrip Riot*, American International, 1958; *Rock-a-Bye Baby*, Paramount, 1958; *Parrish*, Warner Brothers, 1961; *Susan Slade*, Warner Brothers, 1961; *Palm Springs Weekend*, Warner Brothers, 1963; *Cruise A-Go-Go*, 1963; *The Grissom Gang*, National General, 1971; *Scorchy*, 1976; *Grease 2*, Paramount, 1982. Also, *Last Generation*.

PRINCIPAL TELEVISION APPEARANCES—Series: Cricket Blake, *Hawaiian Eye*, ABC, 1959-63; Wendy Conway, *Wendy and Me*, ABC, 1964-65; *Kraft Music Hall Presents the Des O'Connor Show*, NBC, 1971.

Episodic: *The Bob Hope Show; The Red Skelton Show; The Perry Como Show; Spotlight; Rowan and Martin's Laugh-In; Hotel; Murder, She Wrote*

Movies: *Mister Jericho*, 1969; *Call Her Mom*, ABC, 1972; *Playmates*, 1972; *Cole Porter in Paris; The Sex Symbol*, 1974.

Specials: *Englebert Humperdinck; Tom Jones; Harry's Battles*.

RECORDINGS: SINGLES—"Kookie, Kookie, Lend Me Your Comb"; "16 Reasons"; "What Did You Make Me Cry For"; "From Me to You"; "They're Jealous of Me"; "A Girl Never Knows."

SIDELIGHTS: Connie Stevens began her show business career as a member of the Three Debs singing group in Los Angeles.*

STEVENS, Emily Favella

PERSONAL: Born Amelia Del Carmen, in Mexico City, Mexico. EDUCATION: Attended Los Angeles City College; University of California, Los Angeles, 1944, where she studied cinematography; studied for the theatre at the Goodman Theatre School, Chicago, studying set design with Jan Scott.

VOCATION: Actress, designer, and producer.

CAREER: NEW YORK DEBUT—*The Enchanted,* Circle in the Square, 1950. PRINCIPAL STAGE APPEARANCES—Summer Stock, Plymouth, MA, and Woodstock, NY; Antigone, *The Infernal Machine,* first sprite, *Don Perlimplin and Belisa,* both Villetta Studio Players, Woodstock, NY, 1945; Esther, *The Red Velvet Goat* and *The Gallows Man,* Villetta Studio Players, both 1946; Columbine, *Aria Da Capo,* the Art Institute, Woodstock, NY, 1946; *Don Perlimplin and Belisa,* the Art Institute, Woodstock, 1947.

Alice in Wonderland, Laura Wingfield, *The Glass Menagerie,* woman, *Riders to the Sea,* Columbine, *Aria Da Capo,* first sprite, *Don Perlimplin and Belisa,* all with the Loft Players, Maverick Theatre, Woodstock.

Amata, Circle in the Square, NY, 1950; *Bonds of Interest,* Mordeen, *Burning Bright,* both Circle in the Square, 1951; Miss Rosemary, *Summer and Smoke,* Circle in the Square, 1952; Nellie Ewell, *Summer and Smoke,* Academy of Music, Philadelphia, 1952; also *Yerma* and *American Gothic,* both Circle in the Square.

MAJOR TOURS—Laura Wingfield, *The Glass Menagerie,* the Catskill Mountain resorts with the Loft Players.

PRINCIPAL STAGE WORK—Lighting designer, *The Infernal Machine,* Villetta Studio Players, 1945; production designer, *Ten Nights in a Bar Room,* Villetta Studio Players, 1946; prop designer, *Alice in Wonderland,* Loft Players; set and costume designer, *Riders to the Sea* and *In the Shadow of the Glen* (double bill), Loft Players; production designer, *A Ribbon of Smoke,* Loft Players; set designer, *Dark of the Moon,* Circle in the Square, NY, 1950; sets designer, *The Enchanted,* Circle in the Square, NY.

Co-producer (for the Villetta Theatre), *The Infernal Machine, Don Perlimplin and Belisa, The Red Velvet Goat, The Gallows Man, Mr. Sleeman Is Coming, Ten Nights in a Bar Room, Aria Da Capo;* co-producer *(for the Loft Players), Alice in Wonderland, The Glass Menagerie, Angel Street, The Beautiful People, Riders to the Sea* and *In the Shadow of the Glen, A Ribbon of Smoke, A Phoenix Too Frequent, Aria Da Capo, Don Perlimplin and Belisa;* summer tour, *The Glass Menagerie* and *The Voice of the Turtle;* co-producer (for Circle in the Square), *Dark of the Moon, The Enchanted, Amata, Bonds of Interest, Burning Bright, American Gothic, The Grass Harp, Yerma, Summer and Smoke, Orpheus and Eurydice, Ah, Wilderness!, The Girl on the Via Flaminia* (the last play also on Broadway, 48th Street Theatre, 1954); co-producer, *Suddenly Last Summer;* producer, *Candied House;* producer and director, *Elizabethan Rendezvous,* Roanoke Island, NC.

Producer, Circle in the Square Sunday Concerts, featuring: Lillian Hellman, Tennessee Williams, Dylan Thomas, Dorothy Parker, Gore Vidal, Alexander Schneider, Oscar Brand; producer, Circle in the Square Saturday Night Jazz Concerts; producer, Circle in the Square Children Shows.

RELATED CAREER—In addition to the above credits, Stevens has appeared in several motion pictures (including a bit part in *The Ten*

Commandments) and television shows, apprenticed as a script supervisor for Paramount, Universal, Parthenon, and Federal Films, served as associate producer and story consultant for an Hispanic series, worked as a consultant to Bob Banner Productions for an Ernest Hemingway television special, 1974, written a medical cassette series as well as lectured and taught at a number of professional and educational institutions including the American Academy of Dramatic Arts and the American Cultural Center in Madrid, Spain.

She served, for a time, on the Council for the Arts on the North Shore, Long Island, NY, where she taught and directed.

MEMBER: Actors' Equity Association, Screen Actors Guild, Writers Guild West, Dramatists Guild.

SIDELIGHTS: Emily (sometimes known as Emilie) Favella Stevens has been credited by Stuart W. Little in his book, *Off-Broadway* (Coward, McCann & Geoghegan, Inc., NY, 1972) with being among the founders (and one of the original members of the board of directors) of the Circle in the Square, one of the three theatres which, historically, gave birth to the Off-Broadway movement of the 1950's. Elaborating on this, in a letter to *CTFT,* Stevens comments that she ''was largely responsible for the post-war renaissance and stature of Off-Broadway.'' She goes on to remark that the inclusion of Jose Quintero in the original ''circle'' was due to her invitation to him, an old school-chum from California. She claims to be ''the'' founder of the Villetta Players and the Loft Players, both in Woodstock, the two groups which, critics and historians acknowledge, became the Circle in the Square. In addition to her work with these three companies, cited above, she also functioned as stage manager, technical director and, for Circle in the Square, as company manager.

ADDRESSES: OFFICE—Larkmont, P.O. Box 424, Sea Cliff, NY 11579.

*   *   *

STUART, Lynne   1930-

PERSONAL: Born September 30, 1930, in Lakeland, FL; married Richard Horner (a producer and general manager), 1959; children: Lindsey, Randall, Robin; (stepdaughter) Anne. EDUCATION: Attended Tampa University.

VOCATION: Producer, actress, singer, and dancer.

CAREER: PRINCIPAL STAGE APPEARANCES—Standby for Lalume, *Kismet,* Ziegfeld Theatre, NY, 1953-55; standby for Judy Holliday, *Bells Are Ringing,* NY, 1958; Ruth, *High Spirits,* Alvin Theatre, NY, 1965; standby for Ann Miller, *Anything Goes,* NY, 1973; standby for Mary Martin, *I Do, I Do,* 46th Street Theatre, NY, 1978.

PRINCIPAL STAGE WORK—Associate producer, *A Life,* Morosco Theatre, NY, 1981; co-executive director, *Hamlet* and *Henry IV, Part I,* American Shakespeare Festival, Stratford, CT, 1982; co-producer, *Blood Moon,* Actors and Directors Theatre, NY, 1983; co-producer, *Kennedy at Colonus,* 47th Street Theatre, NY, 1984; co-producer, *Doubles,* Ritz Theatre, NY, 1985.

PRINCIPAL TELEVISION APPEARANCES—Hostess, WTVT Television, CBS, Tampa, FL, 1957-58.

LYNNE STUART

RELATED CAREER—Production assistant, KNXT Television, Los Angeles, CA, 1950-51; executive assistant, CBS Television, NY, 1952-53; president, Interactive Media Corporation, 1983— ; vice president, Richard Horner Associates; officer, Horner/Stuart Enterprises.

RECORDINGS: VIDEOCASSETTE—Producer: *Philip Pearlstein Draws the Artist's Model,* 1985; *Stories from the Little Stone House,* 1986.

MEMBER: League of American Theatre Owners and Producers, The Producers Group, National Academy of Television Arts and Sciences, American Federation of Musicians; Ziegfeld Club; National Organization of Women, Women's Political Caucus; honorable withdrawal from Actors' Equity Association, Screen Actors Guild, American Federation of Television and Radio Artists, and American Guild of Variety Artists; Catholics for a Free Choice.

ADDRESSES: OFFICE—Richard Horner Associates, 165 W. 46th Street, Suite 710, New York, NY 10036.

*   *   *

SVENSON, Bo   1941-

PERSONAL: Born February 13, 1941, in Sweden, immigrated to United States, 1958; son of Birger Ragnar and Lola Iris Viola (Johansson) Svenson; married Lise Hartmann-Berg, December 30, 1966; children: Pia, Maja. EDUCATION: Attended the University of Meiji, 1960-63; University of California at Los Angeles, 1970-74. MILITARY: U.S. Marine Corps, 1959-65.

VOCATION: Actor.

CAREER: PRINCIPAL FILM APPEARANCES—*Maurie,* National General, 1973; *The Great Waldo Pepper,* Universal, 1975; *Part II:*

Walking Tall, American International, 1975; *The Breaking Point,* 1975; *Special Delivery,* American International, 1976; *Final Chapter: Walking Tall,* American International, 1976; *Our Man in Mecca,* 1977; *Son of the Sheik,* 1978; *Snow Beast,* 1978; *Gold of the Amazon,* 1978; *North Dallas Forty,* Paramount, 1979.

NON-RELATED CAREER—Professional race car driver; professional hockey player; holder third degree black belt in Judo.

AWARDS: Far East heavy weight division champion, 1961.

ADDRESSES: AGENT—Agency for Performing Arts, 888 Seventh Avenue, 10106.*

*   *   *

SWAYZE, Patrick

BRIEF ENTRY: Born in Houston, TX; son of Patsy Swayze (a choreographer). Actor and dancer. Patrick Swayze learned to dance from his mother, who choreographed the film *Urban Cowboy,* when he was a young child. In an effort to escape the teasing of his peers because of his dancing ability, he joined the football team in high school and went on to receive a gymnastics scholarship to San Jacinto College in Houston. Swayze dropped out of school after a year and worked for a while as Prince Charming in Walt Disney World. From there he moved on to a ballet company in Buffalo, NY, and, in the hopes of becoming a major dancer, went to New York City to study dance with the Harkness and Joffrey ballet schools. Although he won a position with the Field Ballet, Swayze was forced to give up ballet dancing professionally due to an aggravated knee injury from his high school football days. He supported himself by working as a carpenter in New York until he landed the role of Danny Zuko in the Broadway production of *Grease.* He moved to Los Angeles hoping to break into films, and there he worked as a house renovator until his film debut in *Skatetown U.S.A.* He has gained fame for his role in the movie *Youngblood* and as Orry Main in the television mini-series *North and South, Books I and II.**

*   *   *

SWIFT, Allen   1924-

PERSONAL: Born Ira Stadlen, January 16, 1924, in New York, NY; son of Max (an attorney) and Sallie (Jacobson) Stadlen; married Vivienne Chassler, June 22, 1943 (divorced, 1958); married Lenore Cohen (an actress), November 11, 1961; children: Lewis J. Stadlen. EDUCATION: Graduated from the High School of Music and Art, New York. MILITARY: U.S. Army Air Force, World War II.

VOCATION: Actor and writer.

CAREER: PRINCIPAL STAGE APPEARANCES—Television commentator, *How to Make a Man,* Brooks Atkinson, NY; Papa Glockenspiel, *The Student Gypsy or the Prince of Liederkrantz,* 54th Street Theatre, NY; Catlan, *My Old Friends,* 22 Steps Theatre, NY; Morris Applebaum, *Checking Out,* Longacre Theatre, NY; Ed Mosher, *The Iceman Cometh,* Lunt-Fontanne Theatre, NY; the drunk, *The Bar Room Monks* and president of the university, *Portrait of the Artist as a Young Man,* both Martinique Theatre, NY; Ponce Packard, *A Month of Sundays,* Theatre de Lys, NY; Max Silverman, *The Goodbye People,* PAF Playhouse, Huntington, Long Island, NY; Ed Mosher, *The Iceman Cometh,* American National Theatre, Washington, DC.

CABARET—The Palace, the Paramount, the Strand, all NY; the London Palladium.

ALLEN SWIFT

PRINCIPAL TELEVISION APPEARANCES—Series: Voices of Howdy Doody, Mr. Bluster, Dilly Dally, Flub-a-dub, *Howdy Doody Show;* Captain Allen Swift (host), *Popeye.*

Episodic: Sam Finster, *Kate and Allie.*

Guest: *The Tonight Show; Mike Douglas Show; Bob Hope; Eddie Cantor.*

Cartoon voices for characters on: *Popeye; Mighty Mouse; Herman the Mouse; Tom and Jerry; Under Dog; The King and Odie; Tooter the Turtle.*

PRINCIPAL FILM APPEARANCES—Maurice Venice, *Seize the Day;* voice of General Eisenhower, *The Longest Day,* Twentieth Century-Fox, 1962.

RELATED CAREER—Playwright, magician, hypnotist, and psychic entertainer.

MEMBER: International Brotherhood of Magicians.

ADDRESSES: OFFICE—Allen Swift, Inc., 888 Seventh Avenue, New York, NY 10106.

*   *   *

SWIT, Loretta   1937-

PERSONAL: Born November 4, 1937, in Passaic, NJ. EDUCATION: Studied at the American Academy of Dramatic Arts with Gene Frankel.

VOCATION: Actress.

CAREER: PRINCIPAL TELEVISION APPEARANCES—Series: Major Margaret "Hot Lips" Houlihan, *M*A*S*H,* CBS, 1972-83.

Episodic: *Gunsmoke,* CBS; *Mannix,* CBS; *Hawaii Five-O,* CBS; *Mission: Impossible,* CBS; *The Doctors,* CBS; *Cade's County,* CBS.

Movies: *Secrets and Lies,* 1972; *Shirts/Skins,* 1973; *Valentine,* 1979; *Mirror, Mirror,* 1979; *The Walls Came Tumbling Down,* 1980; Cagney, *Cagney and Lacey,* CBS, 1981; *Games Mother Never Taught You,* 1982; *First Affair,* 1983; *The Execution,* NBC, 1985; also appeared in *Coffeeville.*

Specials: *Bob Hope Christmas Special.*

PRINCIPAL FILM APPEARANCES—*Stand Up and Be Counted,* Columbia, 1972; *Freebie and the Bean,* Warner Brothers, 1974; *Race with the Devil,* Twentieth Century-Fox, 1975; *S.O.B.,* Paramount, 1981; *Beer,* Orion, 1985.

PRINCIPAL STAGE APPEARANCES—*Any Wednesday; Same Time Next Year,* Broadway.

MAJOR TOURS—*Mame,* national tour, one year.

MEMBER: Actors' Equity Association, Screen Actors Guild, American Federation of Television and Radio Artists.

AWARDS: Emmy Awards, Outstanding Supporting Actress in a Comedy Series, 1979 and 1981, for *M*A*S*H.*

ADDRESSES: AGENT—William Morris Agency, 151 El Camino Drive, Beverly Hills, CA 90212.*

*   *   *

SWOPE, Tracy Brooks

PERSONAL: Born February 20, in New York, NY; daughter of Herbert Bayard, Jr. (a producer, director, and critic) and Margaret (an actress; maiden name, Hayes) Swope. EDUCATION: Graduated from the High School of the Performing Arts, New York, and the Masters School, Dobbs Ferry, NY; trained for the stage at the Neighborhood Playhouse and the American Academy of Dramatic Art with Mira Rostova.

VOCATION: Actress.

CAREER: STAGE DEBUT—*The Odd Couple,* Peterborough Players, NH, 1968. NEW YORK DEBUT—Victoria Wendredge, *Woman Is My Idea,* Belasco Theatre, 1969. PRINCIPAL STAGE APPEARANCES—*A Little Family Business,* Martin Beck Theatre, NY, 1982; also appeared in *Children in the Rain,* Cherry Lane Theatre, NY; *A Midsummer Night's Dream* and *Sabrina Fair,* both Dartmouth Summer Theatre, NH; *Hot L Baltimore,* Playhouse in the Park, Cincinnati, OH; Trina, *Forty Carats,* stock production.

MAJOR TOURS—Trina, *Forty Carats,* U.S. cities.

TELEVISION DEBUT—Alison, *Me,* PBS, 1974. PRINCIPAL TELEVISION APPEARANCES—Series: Liz, *Where the Heart Is,* CBS; Christie, *Another World,* NBC; Vanessa, *General Hospital,* ABC.

TRACY BROOKS SWOPE

SYLVIA SYMS

Episodic: *Charlie's Angels; Starsky and Hutch; Love Boat; Baretta; Rafferty; Dog and Cat; Serpico; Partridge Family; Love, American Style; United States; Voyagers; Mickey Spillane's Mike Hammer; A-Team; Hardcastle and McCormick.*

Movies: *Terror on the Fortieth Floor,* 1974; *The Night That Panicked America,* 1975; *Revenge for a Rape,* 1976; *Crisis in Sun Valley,* 1978; *The Ultimate Imposter,* 1979; *Secret War of Jackie's Girls,* NBC, 1980; also appeared in *A Very Dangerous Love.*

Mini-Series: Liz Baynor, *The Last Convertible,* NBC, 1981.

FILM DEBUT—Toby, *Hard to Hold,* Universal, 1983. PRINCIPAL FILM APPEARANCES—*To Live and Die in L.A.,* Metro-Goldwyn-Mayer/United Artists, 1985; *Happy New Year,* Columbia, 1986.

MEMBER: American Civil Liberties Union, Actors for Animals.

AWARDS: Most Promising New Actress, Straw Hat Award, for *Forty Carats.*

ADDRESSES: AGENT—The Artists' Agency, 10000 Santa Monica Blvd., Suite 305, Los Angeles, CA 90067; Leaverton-Sames Associates, 1650 Broadway, New York, NY 10019.

*   *   *

SYMS, Sylvia   1934-

PERSONAL: Born 1934, in London, England; daughter of Edwin (a trade unionist and civil servant) and Daisy (Hale) Syms; married Ed Ney (a company director), June 8, 1956; children: Beatrice, Benja-

min. EDUCATION: Attended the Convent of Ladies of Mary; trained for the stage at the Royal Academy of Dramatic Art.

VOCATION: Actress.

CAREER: STAGE DEBUT—*The Apple Cart,* Theatre Royal, Haymarket. PRINCIPAL STAGE APPEARANCES—Understudy, assistant stage manager, *Charley's Aunt,* London; maid, understudy Mai, *A Doll's House,* Lyric Theatre, Hammersmith; juvenile leads in weekly repertory in Bath, England; *A Kind of Folly,* Duchess Theatre, London, 1954.

Beginning in 1956, leading roles in: *Dual Marriageway,* Phoenix Theatre, London; *Peter Pan,* Scala Theatre, London; *Much Ado About Nothing* and *Boswell's Life of Johnson,* both Edinburgh Festival, Scotland; *Not Now Darling,* and *House Guest,* both Savoy Theatre, London; *Dead Ringer,* Duke of York's Theatre; *The Vortex,* 1984; *Entertaining Mr. Sloane,* Royal Exchange, Manchester, 1985; also appeared in *The Rivals; The Holiday; Dance of Death; The Heiress; Monique; Thieves Carnival; Odd Girl Out; The Beaux Strategem; The Ideal Husband; The Innocents; A Doll's House; In Praise of Love; Black Chiffon; Ghosts; Gert and Daisy.*

FILM DEBUT—*My Teenage Daughter,* 1955. PRINCIPAL FILM APPEARANCES—*The Birthday Present,* 1956; *No Time for Tears,* 1956; *Woman in a Dressing Gown,* Warner Brothers, 1957; *The Moonraker,* 1957; *Ice Cold in Alex,* 1957; *No Tree in the Street,* Seven Arts, 1958; *Bachelor of Hearts,* 1958; *Ferry to Hong Kong,* Twentieth Century-Fox, 1959; *Conspiracy of Hearts,* 1959; *Expresso Bong,* 1960; *Virgins of Rome,* 1960; *Flame in the Streets,* 1961; *The World of Suzie Wong,* Paramount, 1961; *Victim,* 1961; *The Punch and Judy Men,* 1962; *The Quare Fellow,* 1963; *The World Ten Times Over,* 1963; *East of Sudan,* 1964; *The Big Job,*

1965; *Operation Crossbow*, Metro-Goldwyn-Mayer, 1965; *Hostile Witness*, 1966; *The Image Makers*, 1967; *Danger Route*, United Artists, 1968; *Run Wild, Run Free*, Columbia, 1969; *The Desperadoes*, Columbia, 1969; *Asylum*, Cinerama, 1972; *The Tamarind Seed*, Avco Embassy, 1974; *There Goes the Bride*, 1980.

PRINCIPAL TELEVISION APPEARANCES—Series: *My Good Woman*, ITV, 1972-73; *The Movie Quiz*, BBC, 1972-73.

Episodic and Specials: *The Romantic Young Lady*, BBC, 1954; *The Devil's Disciple*, BBC, 1954; *The Powder Magazine*, BBC, 1954; *Climbing for Glory*, BBC, 1955; *Terminus*, BBC, 1955; *Bat Out of Hell*, BBC, 1960; *Love Story*, ITV, 1964; *The Saint*, ITV, 1967; *Danger Man*, ITV, 1967; *Something to Declare*, ITV, 1967; *The Human Jungle*, ITV, 1968; *Armchair Theatre*, ITV, 1969; *Clutterbuck*, BBC, 1970; *The Adventurer*, ITV, 1971; *Mike and Bernie Music Show*, ITV, 1972; *Give Us a Clue*, ITV, 1975; *Murder Will Out*, ITV, 1976; *Nancy Astor*, ITV, 1982; *Sorry Darling*, ITV, 1983; *A Murder Is Announced*, BBC, 1984; *Murder at Lynch Cross*, ITV, 1985.

PRINCIPAL RADIO APPEARANCES—Series: *Little Dorrit*.

Dramas for BBC: *Love's Labour's Lost; Point of Departure; Equal Terms; Dead Reckoning; Love Story; Justine*.

MEMBER: Actors Centre.

AWARDS: Best Actress in Films, Variety Club, 1958; Most Popular Foreign Actress, Spanish award, 1966; British Academy Award nomination, 1974, for *The Tamarind Seed*; Best Actress, *Manchester Evening News* Award, 1985, for *Entertaining Mr. Sloane*.

ADDRESSES: OFFICE—Crighton Services, 121A Strathville Road, London, SW18, England. AGENT—Barry Brown, 47 West Square, Southwark, London SE11, England.

T

TASCA, Jules 1938-

PERSONAL: Born December 10, 1938; son of Edward Michael (an electronics technician) and Mary Tasca; married Beatrice Hartranft (a tennis professional), January 23, 1962; children: Edward, Jennifer, Joel. EDUCATION: Pennsylvania State University, B.A., 1961; Villanova University, M.A., 1963; Heed University, D.F.A., 1982. MILITARY: U.S. Army.

VOCATION: Writer.

WRITINGS: PLAYS, PRODUCED—The Mind with the Dirty Man, Mark Taper Forum, Los Angeles, CA, 1973; Chip Off Olympus, NY; productions of published plays at the following theatres: The Pheasant Run Playhouse, Chicago, IL.; The Mark Taper Forum, Los Angeles, CA; Huntington Hartford, Los Angeles, CA; Union Plaza Hotel, Las Vegas, NV; Triangle, NY.

PLAYS, PUBLISHED—Tear Along the Dotted Line, Dramatic Publishing; Subject to Change, Samuel French; Tadpole, Dramatists Play Service; The Mind with the Dirty Man, Samuel French; Chip Off Olympus, Samuel French; Five One Act Plays by Mark Twain, Samuel French; Susan B., Dramatic Publishing, 1983; Alive and Kicking, Dramatic Publishing; The Amazing Einstein, Dramatic Publishing, 1984; The Necklace and Other Stories, Samuel French, 1984; The Lion, the Witch and the Wardrobe, Dramatic Publishing, 1985; Will (adaptation of short stories by Robert Louis Stevenson), Baker's Plays, 1985; Sire DeMaletroit's Door, Dramatic Publishing, 1985.

SCREENPLAYS—Frisbee, E.J. Productions, NY.

TELEVISION—Hal Linden Special, CBS, 1979.

RELATED CAREER—Teacher: Villanova University, 1965, Pennsylvania State University, 1970, Beaver College, 1972, 1984.

MEMBER: Dramatists Guild, Authors League of America, Writers Guild.

AWARD: First Prize Award, P.A.R.T. Theatreworks National Playwrighting Contest, NY, 1983.

ADDRESSES: AGENT—c/o Charles Hunt, Fifi Oscard Agency, 19 W. 44th Street, New York, NY 10036.

*　　*　　*

TAYBACK, Vic

PERSONAL: Born Victor Tabback, January 6, in New York, NY; son of Najeeb James and Helen (Hanood) Tabback; married Sheila McKay Barnard, 1962; children: Christopher. EDUCATION: Attended Glendale Community College; studied at the Frederick A. Speare School of Radio and Television Broadcasting. MILITARY: U.S. Navy.

VOCATION: Actor.

CAREER: PRINCIPAL TELEVISION APPEARANCES—Series: Captain Barney Marcus, Griff, ABC, 1973-74; Lieutenant Gubbins, Khan, CBS, 1975; Mel Sharples, Alice, CBS, 1976-85.

Episodic: Fantasy Island, ABC.

Movies: Portrait of a Stripper, 1979.

PRINCIPAL FILM APPEARANCES—Mel Sharples, Alice Doesn't Live Here Anymore, Warner Brothers, 1975.

PRINCIPAL STAGE APPEARANCES—Stalag 17.

RELATED CAREER—Co-founder, Company of Angels Theatre, Los Angeles, CA.

ADDRESSES: OFFICE—c/o CBS Entertainment 7800 Beverly Blvd., Los Angeles, CA 90036.*

*　　*　　*

TAYLOR, Hiram 1952-

PERSONAL: Born February 29, 1952, in Mobile, AL; son of Robert Edwin (a forest ranger) and Willonese Sarah (a postmistress; maiden name, Caraway) Taylor. EDUCATION: Syracuse University, M.A., 1975.

VOCATION: Actor, choreographer, designer, director, and writer.

CAREER: PRINCIPAL STAGE WORK—Director: Solo for Two, Direct Theatre, NY, then Circle Repertory Company, NY, 1975; assistant director and choreographer, Ceremonies in Dark Old Men, Hudson Guild Theatre, NY, 1975; Babette, Bel Canto Opera Company, 1976; Teasers, Quaigh Theatre, NY, 1978; Warm Bodies, Art and Design Theatre, NY, 1979; Villa Serena, 28th Street Playhouse, NY, 1980; Six Women on a Stage, Minskoff Theatre, NY, 1980; also directed Sally's Gone She Left Her Name, Harold Clurman Theatre, NY.

Regional: Macbeth; The Balcony; Madwoman of Chaillot; The Lion in Winter; Death of a Salesman; Oklahoma!; Mame; The Boy Friend; I Do! I Do!; Dames at Sea; The King and I; Camelot; Vanities.

HIRAM TAYLOR

RELATED CAREER—Teacher of Playwriting, Syracuse University; acting teacher, New York, NY.

WRITINGS: PLAYS, PRODUCED—*Mobile,* Mobile Community Theatre, AL; *Members,* Syracuse University, 1974, also produced in New Orleans, LA, Syracuse, NY, and New York, NY; *Movie Buff,* Actors Playhouse, NY, 1976-77; *Teasers,* Quaigh Theatre, NY, 1978; *Thief in the Night,* Amsterdam, Netherlands; *Buddies* (with Rof Barnes), Colonades Theatre, NY, 1985.

MEMBER: Society of Stage Directors and Choreographers, Actors' Equity Association, Dramatists Guild, American Society of Composers, Artists, and Producers.

AWARDS: Bultman Playwriting Award, Syracuse University, 1974, for *Members;* Best Director, Best Production, Direct Theatre Director's Festival Award, 1975, for *Solo for Two.*

ADDRESSES: HOME—Forty First Avenue, New York, NY 10003.

*   *   *

TAYLOR, Renee

PERSONAL: Born March 19; married Joseph Bologna (an actor, comedian, and writer), 1965.

VOCATION: Actress and writer.

CAREER: PRINCIPAL FILM APPEARANCES—*The Errand Boy,* Paramount, 1961; *The Detective,* Twentieth Century-Fox, 1968; *The Producers,* Embassy, 1968; *Lovers and Other Strangers,* Cinerama, 1970; *A New Leaf,* Paramount, 1971; *Made for Each*

Other, Twentieth Century-Fox, 1971; *Last of the Red Hot Lovers,* Paramount, 1972.

PRINCIPAL TELEVISION APPEARANCES—Series: *Jack Paar Show,* NBC, 1959-62; Annabelle, *Mary Hartman, Mary Hartman,* syndicated, 1977-78.

Episodic: *On Broadway Tonight,* CBS.

Specials: *Acts of Love and Other Comedies,* ABC, 1973; *Paradise,* 1979.

PRINCIPAL STAGE APPEARANCES—*Lovers and Other Strangers,* Brooks Atkinson Theatre, NY, 1968; *It Had to Be You,* Marilyn Monroe Theatre, Los Angeles, 1985.

WRITINGS: PLAYS—(With Joseph Bologna) *Lovers and Other Strangers* (four one-acts), Brooks Atkinson Theatre, NY, 1968, published by Samuel French, 1968; *It Had to Be You,* Marilyn Monroe Theatre, Los Angeles, 1985.

SCREENPLAYS—(With Joseph Bologna) *Lovers and Other Strangers,* Cinerama, 1970; (with Joseph Bologna) *Made for Each Other,* Twentieth Century-Fox, 1971; *The Witch of Naples.*

TELEVISION—Series: (Contributor) *Calucci's Department,* CBS, 1973; *The Great American Dream Machine,* PBS.

Specials: *Benny,* PBS, 1971; *Acts of Love and Other Comedies,* ABC, 1973; *Paradise.*

AWARDS: Outstanding Writing Achievement in Comedy, Variety, or Music (Special), Emmy Award, 1972-73, for *Acts of Love and Other Comedies.*

ADDRESSES: AGENT—c/o Catherine Moyers, Guttman and Pam, 120 El Camino Drive, Suite 1094, Beverly Hills, CA 90212.*

*   *   *

TAYLOR, Rip

PERSONAL: Born Charles Elmer Taylor, in Washington, DC; son of Elmer (a musician) and Betty (an internal revenue service employee) Taylor; married Rusty Rowe (divorced). EDUCATION: Attended George Washington University.

VOCATION: Comedian and actor.

CAREER: STAGE DEBUT—Comic, Cliquot Club, Atlantic City, NJ. PRINCIPAL STAGE APPEARANCES—Nightclubs: Beverly Hotel, Catskill Mountains, NY; Dunes Hotel, Las Vegas, NV, 1963; *Hello America,* Desert Inn, Las Vegas, NV; *Judy Garland Show,* Copacabana, NY; *Funny Farm,* Aladdin Hotel, Las Vegas, NV; *Folies Bergere,* Tropicana Hotel, Las Vegas, NV; Sahara Hotel, Las Vegas, NV; also appeared in the play *The Student Prince,* Kenley Players, OH.

MAJOR TOURS—Headlined with Carol Lawrence and Debbie Reynolds.

PRINCIPAL TELEVISION APPEARANCES—*Ed Sullivan Show,* 1963; *The Beautiful Phyllis Diller Show; The $1.98 Beauty Show; Hollywood Squares; Break the Bank.*

Series: *The Dean Martin Show; Down to Earth.*

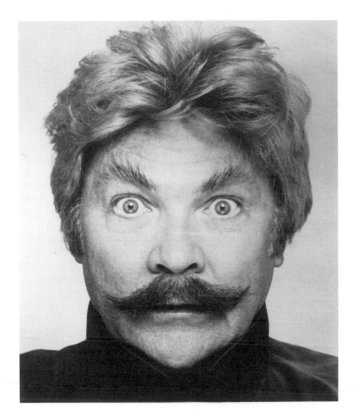

RIP TAYLOR

VICTORIA TENNANT

PRINCIPAL FILM APPEARANCES—*I'd Rather Be Rich*, Universal, 1964.

RELATED CAREER—President, Taylor-Made, Inc.

AWARDS: Best Lounge Act of the Year, three City of Las Vegas awards; Outstanding Opening Act of the Year, *Atlantic City* magazine award, 1985.

SIDELIGHTS: Rip Taylor wrote to *CTFT,* "I like being a second banana and I definitely don't want to be a big star. This way I get all the laughs and work constantly. I have absolutely no responsibility."

ADDRESSES: AGENT—c/o Ed Micone, International Creative Management, 40 W. 57th Street, New York, NY 10019. PUBLICIST—Sterling-Winters, 2040 Avenue of the Stars, Fourth Floor, Los Angeles, CA 90067.

*   *   *

TENNANT, Victoria   1950-

PERSONAL: Born September 30, 1950, in London, England; daughter of Cecil (an agent and producer) and Irina (a prima ballerina; maiden name, Baronova) Tennant. EDUCATION: Trained for the ballet at the Elmhurst Ballet School and for the stage at the Central School of Speech and Drama, London.

VOCATION: Actress.

CAREER: FILM DEBUT—Title role, *The Ragman's Daughter,*

Twentieth Century-Fox, 1971. PRINCIPAL FILM APPEARANCES—*Nullpunkt,* German, 1979; Betty, Carol, *A Stranger's Kiss,* Orion, 1982; *All of Me,* Universal, 1983; *The Holcroft Covenant,* Thorn-EMI, 1984.

TELEVISION DEBUT—Episodic: *Tales of the Unexpected,* 1981; *Dempsey,* NBC, 1983.

Movies: *Chiefs,* CBS, 1983; *Under Siege,* CBS, 1985.

Specials: *George Burns Comedy Theatre,* CBS, 1985.

MEMBER: Screen Actors Guild, British Actors' Equity.

SIDELIGHTS: FAVORITE ROLES—Betty, Carol, *A Stranger's Kiss.*

Victoria Tennant told *CTFT* that she speaks fluent French and Italian.

ADDRESSES: AGENT—Duncan Heath Associates, 162 Wardour Street, London W1, England; Creative Artists Agency, 1888 Century Park E., Los Angeles, CA 90067.

*   *   *

THEUS, B. J.   1947-

PERSONAL: Born October 19, 1947, in Abilene, KS; son of Charles Ralph (a marketing executive) and Betty Lou (Wagener) Theus; married Suzanne Bedgood (an actress, dancer and choreographer), February 13, 1971 (divorced). EDUCATION: East Texas State University, B.S., commerce, 1972; trained for the stage at Los

Angeles Theatre Center and for film at CBS Film Industry Workshop with Paul Baker. POLITICS: Republican. RELIGION: Pentecostal. MILITARY: U.S. Navy, 1967-69; National Guard, 1977; U.S. Army Reserves, 1977—.

VOCATION: Actor and writer.

CAREER: STAGE DEBUT—Santa Claus, *Santa Claus Comes to School,* French Elementary School, Beaumont, TX, 1952. PRINCIPAL STAGE APPEARANCES—At the Dallas Theatre Center, TX: Sailor, *The Hairy Ape,* Bobby, *Plays for Family Living,* Lee Harvey Oswald, *Jack Ruby, All American Boy,* Charles Manson, *Painted Black,* Archie Kramer, *Summer and Smoke,* police detective, *The Happy Hunter,* spear carrier, *Hadrian VII,* Sir William Davison, *Mary Stuart,* Clay Wingate, *John Brown's Body,* Reverend John Hale, *The Crucible.*

Andy Hobart, *Star Spangled Girl,* Toby Company Productions, Dallas, TX, 1974; Biff, *Death of a Salesman* and Starbuck, *The Rainmaker,* both Dallas Repertory, 1975; Teddy, *When You Comin' Back Red Ryder?,* Hollywood Actors Theatre, Los Angeles, CA, 1980; autistic boyfriend, *Heal Thyself, It's Friday,* American Legion Theatre, Liberty, TX, 1983; Otto, *Smile a Crooked Smile,* American Legion Theatre, Liberty, TX, 1984; also appeared as Albert Amundson, *A Thousand Clowns,* University Players, Commerce, TX; Presbyterian boyfriend, *The Peter Marshall Story,* King's Supper Club, Dallas, TX.

MAJOR TOURS—*Caine Mutiny Court Martial,* Kennedy Center,

B.J. THEUS

Photograph by Bongiovanni

Washington, DC and Henry Fonda Theatre, Los Angeles, CA, 1986.

FILM DEBUT—Captain Ben Evers, *A Torn Page of Glory,* 1974. PRINCIPAL FILM APPEARANCES—*Private Benjamin,* Warner Brothers, 1983; Clem, *Bad Girls II,* Planet, 1984; *Pray for Death,* Cannon, 1985; *Ten Speed; Dracula Killing Me Softly.*

TELEVISION DEBUT—Billy Joe, *Bozo the Clown,* 1951. PRINCIPAL TELEVISION APPEARANCES—Series: Mark Jensen, *General Hospital,* ABC, 1983-84.

Episodic: *The Highwayman,* Dallas, TX, 1975; *Diff'rent Strokes,* ABC, 1983; camerman, *Rituals,* 1985.

MEMBER: Actors' Equity Association, Screen Actors Guild, American Federation of Television and Radio Artists.

ADDRESSES: HOME—1016 Briarcliff, Arlington TX. OFFICE—6565 Sunset Blvd., Suite 218, Los Angeles, CA 90028; 1501 Broadway, Suite 2907, New York, NY 10036.

* * *

THOMAS, Danny 1914-

PERSONAL: Born Amos Jacobs, January 6, 1914, in Deerfield, MI; son of Charles and Margaret Christen (Simon) Jacobs; married Rose Marie Cassanti, January 15, 1936; children: Margaret Julia (Marlo), Theresa Cecelia, Charles Anthony. EDUCATION: Attended Christian Brothers College, Memphis, TN.

VOCATION: Actor, entertainer, and producer.

CAREER: CABARET: Master of ceremonies, 5100 Club, Chicago, IL, 1940-43; entertained at the Oriental Theatre, Chicago, 1943; La Martinque night club, New York, 1943-44; Roxy Theatre, NY, 1948; Ciro's, Hollywood, CA, 1949; Palladium, London, England; Chicago Theatre; Chez Paree night club, Chicago, 1945-46.

MAJOR TOURS—Toured overseas Eastern Theatre of Operations, World War II; toured with Marlene Dietrich and Company; toured Pacific Area of Operations, World War II.

PRINCIPAL RADIO WORK—Began in 1934; developed his own show in Chicago, 1940; with Fanny Brice, 1944.

PRINCIPAL TELEVISION APPEARANCES—Series: Danny Williams, *Make Room for Daddy,* ABC, 1953-1964; *The Danny Thomas Hour,* NBC, 1967-68; *Make Room for Granddaddy,* ABC, 1970-71; Dr. Jules Bedford, *The Practice,* NBC, 1976-77; Dr. Benjamin Douglas, *I'm a Big Girl Now,* ABC, 1980-81.

Specials: *Danny Thomas Specials,* 1964-68.

Guest: *All Star Revue,* NBC, 1950-52.

PRINCIPAL TELEVISION WORK—Producer: *Danny Thomas Specials,* Thomas-Leonard Productions, 1964-68; *The Danny Thomas Hour,* Thomas-Spelling Productions, NBC, 1967-68.

FILM DEBUT—*The Unfinished Dance,* 1946. PRINCIPAL FILM APPEARANCES—*The Big City,* 1947; *Call Me Mister,* 1948; *I'll See You in My Dreams,* 1951; *The Jazz Singer,* 1952.

AWARDS: Best Actor Starring in a Regular Series, Emmy Award, 1954, for *Make Room for Daddy;* NCCJ, 1957; Layman's Award, America Medical Association; Better World Award, Ladies Auxillary, Veterans of Foriegn Wars, 1972; Michelango Award, Boys Town of Italy, 1973; award from the Governor of Ohio, 1975; entertainment award, White House Correspondents, 1975; Humanitarian Award, Lions International, 1975; Father Flanagan-Boys Town Award, 1981; Murray-Green-Meany Award, AFL-CIO, 1981; Hubert H. Humphrey Award, Touchdown Club, 1981; American Education Award, 1984; Humantarian Award, Variety Clubs International, 1984; nominated for Nobel Peace Prize, 1980-81; decorated Knight of Malta; Knight Commander with Star Knights of Holy Sepulchre, Pope Paul VI, Roman Catholic; L.H.D., Belmont Abbey, International College, Springfield, MA, 1970; LL.D., Loyola University.

SIDELIGHTS: Danny Thomas is the founder of St. Jude Children's Research Hospital, Memphis, TN.*

*   *   *

THOMAS, Marlo   1943-

PERSONAL: Full name Margaret Julia Thomas; born November 21, 1943, in Detroit, MI; daughter of Danny (the actor and entertainer) and Rose Marie (Cassanti) Thomas; married Phil Donahue (television host and author) May 22, 1980. EDUCATION: Attended the University of Southern California.

VOCATION: Actress and producer.

CAREER: PRINCIPAL STAGE APPEARANCES—*Thieves,* Broadway, 1974; Corrie Bratter, *Barefoot in the Park,* London, *Social Security,* Barrymore Theatre, NY, 1986; also appeared in summer stock in United States.

PRINCIPAL TELEVISION APPEARANCES—Series: Stella Barnes, *The Joey Bishop Show,* NBC, 1961-62; Ann Marie, *That Girl,* ABC, 1966-71.

Specials: *Free to Be . . . You and Me,* ABC, 1974.

Movies: *It Happened One Christmas,* 1977; *Consenting Adults,* ABC, 1985; *Nobody's Child,* CBS, 1986.

PRINCIPAL TELEVISION WORK—Producer, *Free to Be . . . You and Me,* ABC, 1974.

PRINCIPAL FILM APPEARANCES—Title role, *Jenny,* Cinerama, 1970; *Thieves,* Paramount, 1977.

RECORDINGS: ALBUM—*Free to Be . . . You and Me.*

WRITINGS: BOOKS—*Free to Be . . . You and Me,* children's book.

AWARDS: Most Promising Newcomer, *Fame* and *Photoplay* polls; George Foster Peabody Award; Tom Paine Award, Emergency Civil Liberties Commission; Emmy Award, Outstanding Children's Special (as producer), 1973-74, for *Free to Be . . . You and Me.*

ADDRESSES: AGENT—c/o Michael Ovitz, Creative Artists Agency, 1888 Century Park E., Suite 1400, Los Angeles, CA 90067.*

THORNE, Angela   1939-

PERSONAL: Born January 25, 1939, in Karachi; daughter of William H.A. (a doctor) and Sylvia (a teacher; maiden name, Leslie) Thorne; married Peter David Penris-Jones (an actor) September 22, 1967; children: Rupert William, Laurence David. EDUCATION: Trained for the stage at the Guild Hall Drama School.

VOCATION: Actress.

CAREER: STAGE DEBUT—Green Goddess, *Mango Leaf Magic,* Mobile Theatre, UK, 1961. LONDON DEBUT—Gloria Clandon, *You Never Can Tell,* Theatre Royal, Haymarket, 1966. PRINCIPAL STAGE APPEARANCES—Julia, *The Rivals,* 1966, Lady Diana, *Ring 'Round the Moon,* 1967, Portia, *Merchant of Venice,* 1969, all at the Theatre Royal, Haymarket; Io, *Prometheus Bound,* Mermaid Theatre, London, 1971; Esther van Homrigh, *Yahoo,* Duke of York's Theatre, London, 1976; Mrs. Thatcher, *Anyone for Denis,* Whitehall Theatre, London, 1981.

MAJOR TOURS—Olivia, *Twelfth Night,* Prospect Theatre Company, Hong Kong Festival, Soviet Union, Helsinki, Finland, 1972.

FILM DEBUT—Berry Smith, *Oh, What a Lovely War!,* Paramount, 1969.

TELEVISION DEBUT—Virginia, *Canterville Ghost,* ATY, 1965. PRINCIPAL TELEVISION APPEARANCES—Marjorie, *To the Manor Born,* BBC, 1985; Alice, *Paying Guests,* BBC, 1985; Harriet

ANGELA THORNE

Farrington, *Farrington of the F.O.*, ATY, 1985-86.

AWARDS: Comedy Performance of the Year Award nomination, 1981, for *Anyone for Denis*.

ADDRESSES: AGENT—Michael Whitehall Ltd., 125 Gloucester Road, London SW7, England.

*   *   *

THURSTON, Todd   1956-

PERSONAL: Born May 29, 1956, in Baltimore, MD; son of William B. (an aerospace contracts manager) and Virginia Lois (an aerospace security manager; maiden name, Francis) Thurston. EDUCATION: University of Washington, B.F.A., 1979.

VOCATION: Actor.

CAREER: STAGE DEBUT—Harry, *My Fair Lady*, Dallas Summer Musicals, TX, 1981, for thirty-two performances. NEW YORK DEBUT—Kodaly, *She Loves Me*, Equity Library Theatre, 1985, for thirty-two performances. PRINCIPAL STAGE APPEARANCES—Levi, *Joseph and the Amazing Technicolor Dreamcoat*, Phil, *They're Playing Our Song*, both North Shore Music Theatre; Joe Hardy, *Damn Yankees*, Music Theatre of Wichita, KS; Grobert, *Carnival*, Bernie, *Sexual Perversity in Chicago*, both Berkshire Theatre Festival, NY; Rutledge, *1776*, Pacific College of the Performing

TODD THURSTON

Arts; Simon, *Caucasian Chalk Circle*, Arthur, *Ah, Wilderness!*, both Glenn Hughes Playhouse, Seattle, WA; principal, *Hey, Big Spender!*, Indiana Repertory, Indianapolis; Neil, *Fiorello!*, Goodspeed Opera House, East Haddam, CT.

PRINCIPAL TELEVISION APPEARANCES—Episodic: *As the World Turns*, CBS; *The Doctors*, NBC.

Movies: *Stone Pillow*, CBS; *The Lost Honor of Katherine Beck*, CBS.

ADDRESSES: HOME—New York, NY.

*   *   *

TISCH, Steve

PERSONAL: Full name, Steven E. Tisch. EDUCATION: Attended Tufts University.

VOCATION: Producer.

CAREER: PRINCIPAL FILM WORK—Producer: *Outlaw Blues*, Warner Brothers, 1977; *Risky Business*, Tisch/Avnet Productions, Warner Brothers, 1983; *Deal of the Century*, Tisch/Avnet Productions, Warner Brothers, 1983; *Soul Man*, New World, 1986.

PRINCIPAL TELEVISION WORK—Movies: Producer—*No Other Love*, 1979; *Homeward Bound*, 1980; *Prime Suspect*, 1982; *Something So Right*, 1982; *Burning Bed*, 1984; *Silence of the Heart*, 1984.

Series: Producer—*Call to Glory*, ABC, 1984-85.

RELATED CAREER—Formed production company with Jon Avnet, Tisch/Avnet Productions, 1977, now defunct; formed Steve Tisch Co., 1985—; served as executive assistant to Peter Guber, Columbia Pictures; worked during school breaks for John Avildsen and Fred Weintraub.

ADDRESSES: OFFICE—Steve Tisch Company, 515 N. Robertson Blvd., Los Angeles, CA 90048.

*   *   *

TODD, Richard   1919-

PERSONAL: Full name, Richard Palethorpe-Todd; born June 11, 1919, in Dublin, Ireland; son of Andrew William and Marvil (Agar-Daly) Palethorpe-Todd; married Catherine Grant-Bogle (divorced); married Virginia Mailer. EDUCATION: Attended Shrewsbury School; trained for the stage at the Italia Conti School. MILITARY: King's Own Yorkshire Light Infantry and later, Parachute Regiment.

VOCATION: Actor and producing manager.

CAREER: STAGE DEBUT—Curio, *Twelfth Night*, Open Air Theatre, Regent's Park, London, 1936. PRINCIPAL STAGE APPEARANCES—With the Dundee Repertory Company, 1938; Lord Goring, *An Ideal Husband*, Strand Theatre, 1965; Nicholas Randolph, *Dear Octopus*, Haymarket Theatre, London, 1967; *The Hollow Crown* and *Pleasure and Repentance*, Royal Shakespeare Company, 1974; Martin Dysart, *Equus*, Australian National Theatre Company, Perth, Australia, 1975; Duke of Bristol, *On Approval*, Johannesburg, South Africa, 1976; Frank, *This Happy Breed*,

Arnaud Theatre, Guildford, U.K., 1980; *The Business of Murder*, Mayfair Theatre, London, 1984-85.

MAJOR TOURS—Lord Goring, *An Ideal Husband*, South African cities, 1965; formed Triumph Theatre Productions in 1970 and has toured with it in many productions including: Comte, *The Marquise*, U.S. cities, 1972; Andrew Wyke, *Sleuth*, Australian and New Zealand, 1972-73, U.S., Canadian cities, 1974, 1976; John, *Miss Adams Will Be Waiting*, 1975; Sebastian Crutwell, *In Praise of Love*, 1977.

FILM DEBUT—*For Them That Trespass*, 1948. PRINCIPAL FILM APPEARANCES—Lachie, *The Hasty Heart*, 1949; *Stage Fright*, 1950; *Portrait of Clare*, 1951; *Lightning Strikes Twice*, Warner Brothers, 1951; *The Sword and the Rose*, Buena Vista, 1953; title role, *Rob Roy, the Highland Rouge*, Buena Vista, 1954; *The Dam Busters*, 1954; Peter Marshall, *A Man Called Peter*, Twentieth Century-Fox, 1955; Sir Walter Raleigh, *The Virgin Queen*, Twentieth Century-Fox, 1955; *D-Day, the Sixth of June*, Twentieth Century-Fox, 1956; Dunois, *Saint Joan*, United Artists, 1957; *Battle Hell*, DCA Distributors, 1957; Ward, *Chase a Crooked Shadow*, Warner Brothers, 1958; Daniel, *This Naked Earth*, Twentieth Century-Fox, 1958; *The Longest Day*, Twentieth Century-Fox, 1962; *Never Let Go*, Continental, 1963; also appeared in *Robin Hood*, *Yangtze Incident*, and *The Long, the Short, and the Tall*.

PRINCIPAL TELEVISION APPEARANCES—Charles Bulman, *Boy Dominic*, Yorkshire Television, 1974; *Jenny's War*, 1985; also *Wuthering Heights*.

MEMBER: Army and Navy Club.

SIDELIGHTS: FAVORITE ROLES—Martin Dysart, *Equus*. RECREATIONS—Shooting and farming.

ADDRESSES: HOME—Chinham Farm, Faringdon, Oxon, England.*

*   *   *

TOWERS, Constance   1933-

PERSONAL: Born May 20, 1933, in Whitefish, MT; daughter of Harry J. and Ardath L. (Reynolds) Towers; married Eugene C. McGrath (divorced); married John Gavin, September 8, 1974; children: (first marriage) Michael Ford, Maureen; (second marriage) Cristina, Maria. EDUCATION: Trained at the Juilliard School for music and for the stage at the American Academy of Dramatic Arts with David La Grant, Carl Pitzer, Lyn Masters, David Craid and Carlos Noble.

VOCATION: Actress and singer.

CAREER: STAGE DEBUT—Sarah Brown, *Guys and Dolls*, Civic Light Opera Company, Los Angeles, CA, 1960. NEW YORK DEBUT—Title role, *Anya*, Ziegfeld Theatre, 1965. PRINCIPAL STAGE APPEARANCES—Julie, *Showboat*, New York State Theatre, NY, 1966; Julie Jordan, *Carousel*, City Center Theatre, NY, 1966; Maria Rainer, *The Sound of Music*, 1967; Marie, *Dumas and Son*, Civic Light Opera, Los Angeles, CA, 1967; Anna Leonowens, *The King and I*, City Center Theatre, NY, 1968; Vivian Whitney, *The Engagement Baby*, Helen Hayes Theatre, NY, 1970; Maria, *The Sound of Music*, Jones Beach Marina, NY, 1971; Kitty Fremont, *Ari*, Mark Hellinger Theatre, NY, 1971; Anna, *The King and I*, Jones Beach Marina, NY, 1972; Agnes, *I Do! I Do!*, Chateau de Ville, Saugus, MA, 1972; Anna, *The King and I*, State Fair Music

Hall, Dallas, TX, 1973; Eliza Doolittle, *My Fair Lady*, Indianapolis, IN, 1973; Maria, *The Sound of Music*, Pittsburgh Civic Light Opera, PA, 1973; title role, *Mame*, Springfield, MO, 1973; Eleanor Hilliard, *The Desperate Hours*, Arlington Park, IL, 1973; *Oh Coward!*, Westport Country Playhouse, CT, 1974; *Rodgers and Hart*, Westwood, CA, then Detroit Civic Light Opera, MI, 1975; Anna, *The King and I*, Uris Theatre, NY, 1977; Maria, *The Sound of Music*, Jones Beach Theatre, NY, 1980.

MAJOR TOURS—U.S. cities: *Camelot*, 1962; *Oh Coward!*, 1974; Anna, *The King and I*, 1976.

FILM DEBUT—*Horse Soldiers*, United Artists, 1959. PRINCIPAL FILM APPEARANCES—*Sergeant Rutledge*, Warner Brothers, 1960; *Shock Corridor*, Allied Artists, 1963; *Fate Is the Hunter*, Twentieth Century-Fox, 1964; *Naked Kiss*, Allied Artists, 1964; *Sylvester*, Columbia, 1985; also, *The Spy*.

TELEVISION DEBUT—*The Ed Sullivan Show*, 1957. PRINCIPAL TELEVISION APPEARANCES—Series: *Love Is a Many Splendored Thing*; *Capitol*.

Guest: *The Johnny Carson Show*; *Once in Her Life*; *Bob Hope Specials*; *The Tony Awards*; *Mike Douglas Show*.

Episodic: *Hawaii Five-0*.

SIDELIGHTS: FAVORITE ROLES—Maria, *The Sound of Music*; Julie, *Showboat*. RECREATIONS—Needlepoint, swimming, painting, and tennis.

ADDRESSES: AGENT—Burton Moss Agency, 113 N. San Vincente Blvd., Suite 202, Beverly Hills, CA 90211.*

*   *   *

TOWNSEND, Robert   1957-

PERSONAL: Born February 6, 1957; son of Robert and Shirley (Jenkins) Townsend. EDUCATION: Attended Illinois State University and Hunter College.

VOCATION: Actor, producer, director, and writer.

CAREER: NEW YORK DEBUT—Calvin, *Take It from the Top*, Henry Street Settlement, 1979, for twenty performances. PRINCIPAL STAGE APPEARANCES—Charley Soul, *Bones*, Riverside Church, NY, 1980.

FILM DEBUT—Lester, *Streets of Fire*, Universal, 1983. PRINCIPAL FILM APPEARANCES—Corporal Ellis, *Soldier's Story*, Columbia, 1983; Jerome, *American Flyers*, Warner Brothers, 1984; Dwight, *Odd Jobs*, Tri-Star, 1984; Manny Espanoza, *Ratboy*, Warner Brothers, 1985.

SIDELIGHTS: Robert Townsend wrote *CTFT* that he has recently completed a forthcoming untitled feature film of which he is the writer, producer, and director.

ADDRESSES: AGENT—c/o Patricia Hacker, Leading Artists Agency, 445 N. Bedford Drive, Beverly Hills, CA 90212. PUBLICIST—Guttman and Pam, 120 El Camino Drive, Beverly Hills, CA 90212.

ROBERT TOWNSEND

*   *   *

TRAVANTI, Daniel J.

PERSONAL: Full name, Daniel John Travanti; born in Kenosha, WI; son of John and Elvira (DeAngelis) Travanti. EDUCATION: University of Wisconsin, B.A.; Loyola Marymount, Los Angeles, M.A.; attended Yale School of Drama, 1961-62.

VOCATION: Actor.

CAREER: PRINCIPAL STAGE APPEARANCES—*Othello; The Taming of the Shrew; Who's Afraid of Virginia Woolf?; Twigs.*

PRINCIPAL TELEVISION APPEARANCES—Series: Captain Frank Furillo, *Hill Street Blues,* NBC, 1981—.

Movies: *Adam,* 1983; *A Case of Libel; Murrow.*

Episodic: The FBI, ABC; *The Mod Squad,* ABC; *Barnaby Jones,* CBS; *Kojak,* CBS; *Hart to Hart,* ABC; *Knots Landing,* CBS.

AWARDS: Outstanding Lead Actor in a Drama Series, Emmy Awards, 1981 and 1982, for *Hill Street Blues;* Foreign Press Golden Globe Award, 1981, for *Hill Street Blues;* General Motors Fellow, Phi Beta Kappa, University of Wisconsin, 1958-61; Woodrow Wilson Fellow, Yale School of Drama, 1961-62.

ADDRESSES: OFFICE—c/o MTM, 4024 Radford Avenue, Studio City, CA 91604. AGENT—c/o Toni Howard, William Morris Agency, 151 El Camino Drive, Beverly Hills, CA 90212.

TUCKER, Forrest Meredith   1919-

PERSONAL: Born February 12, 1919, in Plainfield, IN; son of Forrest A. and Doris P. (Heringlake) Tucker; married Marilyn Johnson, March 28, 1950 (died July, 1960); married Marilyn Fisk, October 23, 1961; children: (first marriage) Pamela Brooke; (second marriage) Cynthia, Forrest Sean. EDUCATION: Attended George Washington University. MILITARY: U.S. Army, Second Lieutenant, Signal Corps, 1942-45.

VOCATION: Actor.

CAREER: PRINCIPAL STAGE APPEARANCES—*The Confidence Game,* Drury Lane Theatre, Chicago, IL, 1975-76.

MAJOR TOURS—*The Music Man,* National tour, 1958; *Plaza Suite,* 1971-72; *That Championship Season,* National tour, 1972-73.

FILM DEBUT—*The Westerner,* 1939. PRINCIPAL FILM APPEARANCES—*The Howards of Virginia,* 1940; *Keeper of the Flame,* Metro-Goldwyn-Mayer, 1942; *The Yearling,* Metro-Goldwyn-Mayer, 1946; *Never Say Goodbye,* 1946; *Rock Island Trail,* 1950; *Sands of Iwo Jima,* 1950; *Warpath,* 1951; *Oh Susannah,* 1951; *Crosswinds,* 1951; *The Fighting Coast Guard,* 1951; *Wild Blue Yonder,* 1951; *Flaming Feather,* 1951; *Bugles in the Afternoon,* 1952; *Hoodlum Empire,* 1952; *Ride the Man Down,* 1952; *Hurricane Smith,* 1952; *Montana Belle,* 1952; *Pony Express,* 1953; *Laughing Anne,* 1953; *Trouble in the Glen,* 1953; *Jubliee Trail,* 1954; *San Antone,* 1954; *Flight Nurse,* 1954; *Rage at Dawn,* RKO, 1955; *Vanishing American,* Republic, 1955; *Finger Man,* Allied Artists, 1955; *Night Freight,* Allied Artists, 1955; *Paris Follies of 1956,* Allied Artists, 1956; *Break in the Circle,* Twentieth Century-Fox, 1956; *Auntie Mame,* Warner Brothers, 1958; *Counterplot,* United Artists, 1959; *The Night They Raided Minsky's,* United Artists, 1968; *Barquero,* United Artists, 1970; *The Wild McCullocks,* American International, 1975.

PRINCIPAL TELEVISION APPEARANCES—Series: *Crunch and Des,* NBC, 1956; Sergeant Morgan O'Rourke, *F Troop.* ABC, 1965-67; Mr. Callahan, *Dusty's Trail,* syndicated, 1973.

Guest: *Kaiser Aluminum Hour.*

Movies: *The Incredible Rocky Mountain Race,* 1977; *Blood Feud,* 1983.

AWARDS: Star of Tomorrow, 1952.

MEMBER: Screen Actors Guild, American Federation of Television and Radio Artists; Masquers Club (director), Los Angeles; Players Club; Lambs Club; Friars Club, New York; Variety International American Stage Golfing (director, London).*

*   *   *

TURELL, Saul   1920-1986

PERSONAL: Born in 1920; died of cancer in New Rochelle, NY, April 10, 1986; married; children: two sons and one daughter. MILITARY: U.S. Army, World War II.

VOCATION: Producer, director, writer, and film executive.

CAREER: PRINCIPAL TELEVISION WORK—Series: Writer, producer, and director, *Silents Please,* ABC, 1957-61; writer, producer, *The Big Moment,* NBC, 1957.

Movies: Producer (with David Wolper), *The Legend of Valentino,* NBC, 1975; producer (with Wolper), *Hollywood: The Golden Years,* NBC.

PRINCIPAL FILM WORK—Writer and director, *The Love Goddesses,* Continental, Paramount, 1965; writer and director, *Paul Robeson: Tribute to an Artist;* producer and director, *The Great Chase* and *Museum;* writer, producer, and director, *The Art of Film* (film series).

RELATED CAREER—Creator, writer, and editor (with Charles Dolan), Sterling Films, 1946, (later Sterling Communications, presently Manhattan Cable); president, Janus Films, 1965-1986; teacher, New York University Film School, 1974-81.

AWARDS: George Eastman Award, 1973; Best Documentary, Academy Award, 1980, for *Paul Robeson: Tribute to an Artist.**

*   *   *

TWIGGY   1949-

PERSONAL: Born Leslie Hornby, September 19, 1949, in London, England; daughter of William Norman and Helen (Reeman) Hornby; married Michael Whitney (an actor; deceased); children: Carly.

VOCATION: Actress, singer, model, writer, and producer.

CAREER: PRINCIPAL STAGE APPEARANCES—*Cinderella,* London; *Captain Beaky Presents,* London; *Funny Face,* New York, 1983; *My One and Only,* St. James Theatre, New York, Los Angeles, CA, 1984-85.

MAJOR TOURS—*Funny Face,* National tour, 1983.

FILM DEBUT—*The Boy Friend,* Metro-Goldwyn-Mayer, 1971. PRINCIPAL FILM APPEARANCES—*W,* 1974; *There Goes the Bride,* 1979; *The Blues Brothers,* Universal, 1980; *Doctor and the Devils,* Twentieth Century-Fox, 1985; *Club Paradise,* Warner Brothers, 1986.

PRINCIPAL TELEVISION APPEARANCES—Music shows: *Twiggy,* BBC; *Twiggy and Friends,* BBC; *Juke Box,* United States; *Pygmalion,* BBC.

Guest: *Hanna-Barbera Happy Hour,* NBC, 1978.

RELATED CAREER—Professional model, 1966-76; director and manager, Twiggy Enterprises Ltd., 1966—.

RECORDINGS: ALBUMS—*Here I Go Again; Twiggy, Get the Name Right.*

WRITINGS: BOOKS—*Twiggy: An Autobiography,* 1975.*

U

ULLMANN, Liv 1939-

PERSONAL: Born December 16, 1939, in Tokyo, Japan; daughter of Norwegian parents; married Hans Stang (divorced); children: one daughter by Ingmar Bergman (the film and stage director). EDUCATION: Studied acting in London for eight months.

VOCATION: Actress.

CAREER: STAGE DEBUT—*Diary of Anne Frank,* Stavanger, Norway. PRINCIPAL STAGE APPEARANCES Nora, *A Doll's House,* Vivian Beaumont Theatre, Lincoln Center, NY; *Anna Christie,* Imperial Theatre, NY, 1977; title role, *I Remember Mama,* Royale Theatre, 1979; Mrs. Alving, *Ghosts,* Brooks Atkinson Theatre, 1982; *Old Times,* London, England, then Los Angeles, CA, 1985; *Mother Courage,* Norway, 1986.

FILM DEBUT—*Persona,* Lopert, 1967. PRINCIPAL FILM APPEARANCES—*Hour of the Wolf,* Lopert, 1968; *Shame,* Lopert, 1969; *The Passion of Anna,* United Artists, 1970; *The Night Visitor,* UMC Pictures, 1971; *Pope Joan* (also known as *The Devil's Imposter*),

British, 1972; *The Emigrants,* Warner Brothers, 1972; *The New Land,* Warner Brothers, 1973; *Lost Horizon,* Columbia, 1973; *40 Carats,* Columbia, 1973; *Cries and Whispers,* New World Pictures, 1973; *Scenes from a Marriage,* Cinema, 1974; *Zandy's Bride,* Warner Brothers, 1974; *The Abdication,* Warner Brothers, 1974; *Face to Face,* Paramount, 1976; *A Bridge Too Far,* United Artists, 1977; *The Serpents Egg,* Paramount, 1978; *Autumn Sonata,* New World Pictures, 1979; *The Wild Duck,* RKR Releasing, 1985; *Bay Boy,* Orion, 1986.

WRITINGS: AUTOBIOGRAPHY—*Changing,* 1978; *Choices,* 1984.

AWARDS: Six Best Actress awards, National Society of Film Critics and New York Film Critics; Best Actress, New York Film Critics Award, 1973, for *Cries and Whispers;* Official Goodwill Ambassador, UNICEF, 1980; Dag Hammarskjold award, 1986.

ADDRESSES: AGENT—Paul Kohner-Michael Levy Agency, 9169 Sunset Blvd., Los Angeles, CA 90069.

*   *   *

UNGER, Deborah 1953-

PERSONAL: Born July 2, 1953, in Philadelphia, PA; daughter of James Frances (a retired Army officer) and Virginia Emma (Garlach) Unger. EDUCATION: University of Pittsburgh, B.A., 1974; Florida State University, M.A., 1975; M.F.A. (at Asolo State Theatre), 1977; trained for the stage at the Asolo Theatre School, Sarasota, FL.

VOCATION: Actress.

CAREER: STAGE DEBUT—Ms. Akins, *Send Me No Flowers,* Naples Dinner Theatre, Naples, FL, 1977, for thirty-two performances. NEW YORK DEBUT—Shawna, *Street Corner Time,* Grande Finale Theatre, 1978, for ten performances. PRINCIPAL STAGE APPEARANCES—Chorus, *The Elixir of Love,* Off-Broadway production; singing waitress, *AFTRA Showcase,* Nat Horne Theatre, NY; Ethel and chorus, *Seesaw,* Equity Library Theatre, NY; Doto, *A Phoenix Too Frequent,* Tyson Studio, NY; various roles, *On the Air,* Van Buren Theatre, NY; mother, Becky, *The Rise of David Levinsky,* American Jewish Theatre, NY.

Regional: At the Asolo Theatre, Sarasota, FL: Florrie Mangle, *Look Homeward Angel,* Estelle St. Pe, *Waltz of the Toreadors,* Laurette Sincee, *Another Part of the Forest,* Ethel Toffelmier, *The Music Man,* Moll Makepeace, *My Love to Your Wife,* Orange girl and Sister Marthe, *Cyrano De Bergerac,* and Janis Joplin, *Buried Alive in the Blues;* also nun and party person, *The Sound of Music,* Naples Dinner Theatre, FL; singer, *Funny Girl,* Little Theatre on the Square, IL.

LIV ULLMANN

DEBORAH UNGER

Photograph by Susan Cook. Martha Swope Assoc.

SHARI UPBIN

PRINCIPAL TELEVISION APPEARANCES—Episodic: *All My Children; One Life to Live; Ryan's Hope; The Guiding Light.*

PRINCIPAL FILM APPEARANCES—*One Trick Pony,* Warner Brothers, 1980; *Ragtime,* Paramount, 1981; *The Fan,* Paramount, 1981; *Tootsie,* Columbia, 1982; *Without a Trace,* Twentieth Century-Fox, 1983.

MEMBER: Actors' Equity Association, Screen Actors Guild, American Federation of Television and Radio Artists.

ADDRESSES: HOME—169 W. 80th Street, New York, NY 10024.

*   *   *

UPBIN, Shari   1941-

PERSONAL: Born Shari Kiesler, June 28, 1941, in New York, NY; daughter of Al (a writer and financier) and Rae (a teacher; maiden name, Drucker) Kiesler; married Hal J. Upbin, May 29, 1960; children: Edward, Elyse, Danielle. EDUCATION: Trained for the stage at the American Theatre Wing. RELIGION: Jewish.

VOCATION: Director, producer, former actress.

CAREER: STAGE DEBUT—Dinah, *Philadelphia Story,* Legion Star Playhouse, Ephrata, PA, 1959. PRINCIPAL STAGE APPEARANCES—

Appeared in regional theatre productions of *Last of the Red Hot Lovers, Dracula,* and *Prisoner of Second Avenue.*

PRINCIPAL STAGE WORK—Director of regional theatre productions, including *Cabaret, Fiddler on the Roof, Oliver!, Life with Father, Side by Side by Sondheim;* director, *A Matter of Opinion,* Players Theatre NY; producer, *One Mo' Time,* Village Gate Theatre, NY, 1979-83; assistant director, *Julius Caesar* and *Coriolanus,* Public Theatre, NY, 1980; producer and director, *Vincent,* Theatre of the Open Eye, NY, 1981; producer, *Bojangles;* producer, *Captain America* (upcoming).

TELEVISION DEBUT—Tap dancer, *Startime Kids,* 1950.

RELATED CAREER—Co-founder, Queen's Playhouse, NY, 1976; teacher, children's theatre, NJ, 1978; master teacher of tap dancing, 1981-84.

MEMBER: Actors' Equity Association, Society of Stage Directors and Choreographers, Villagers Barn Theatre (president), Franklin Arts Council (board of trustees).

AWARDS: Best Director, New Jersey Theatre Critics Award, 1979, for *Side by Side by Sondheim.*

SIDELIGHTS: RECREATIONS—Designing stylized make-up, weight lifting, teaching acting to children.

ADDRESSES: OFFICE—Shari Upbin Productions, 234 W. 44th Street, New York, NY 10036.

URICH, Robert   1946-

PERSONAL: Born December 19, 1946, in Toronto, OH; married Heather Menzies; children: two. EDUCATION: Florida State University, B.A., radio and television communications; Michigan State University, M.A., communications management.

VOCATION: Actor.

CAREER: STAGE DEBUT—*Lovers and Other Strangers,* Pheasant Run Playhouse. PRINCIPAL STAGE APPEARANCES—*The Hasty Heart,* Burt Reynolds Theatre, Jupiter, FL, 1983, then Kennedy Center for the Performing Arts, Washington, DC, 1983; numerous plays at the Ivanhoe Theatre, Chicago, IL.

PRINCIPAL FILM APPEARANCES—*Magnum Force,* Warner Brothers, 1973; *Endangered Species,* Metro-Goldwyn-Mayer/United Artists, 1982; *The Ice Pirates,* Metro-Goldwyn-Mayer/United Artists, 1984; *Turk 182!,* Twentieth Century-Fox, 1985.

PRINCIPAL TELEVISION APPEARANCES—Series: Bob Sanders, *Bob & Carol & Ted & Alice,* ABC, 1973; Officer Jim Street, *S.W.A.T.,* ABC, 1975-76; Peter Campbell, *Soap,* ABC, 1977; Paul Thurston, *Tabitha,* ABC, 1977-78; Dan Tanna, *Vega$,* ABC, 1978-81; Robert Gavilan, *Gavilan,* NBC, 1982-83; title role, *Spenser for Hire,* ABC, 1985—.

Movies: *Bunco,* 1977; *Leave Yesterday Behind,* 1978; *When She Was Bad,* 1979; *Invitation to Hell,* ABC, 1984; *His Mistress,* ABC, 1984; *Scandal Sheet,* ABC, 1985; *Young Again,* ABC, 1985; *The Defiant Ones.*

Episodic: *The FBI; The Love Boat; Gunsmoke; Kung Fu; Marcus Welby, M.D.; The Billy Crystal Comedy Hour; Fighting Back.*

Mini-Series: *Princess Daisy; Mistral's Daughter; Amerika.*

RELATED CAREER: Account executive, WGN radio, Chicago, prior to acting career.

AWARDS: Best Actor, Golden Globe Award nomination, 1980-81;

ROBERT URICH

People's Choice Award, 1980; Best Actor, Bravo Award, Germany, 1980.

ADDRESSES: AGENT—The Blake Agency Ltd., 409 N. Camden Drive, Beverly Hills, CA 90210.

V

VALENTINE, Karen 1947-

PERSONAL: Born May 25, 1947, in Sebastopol, CA.

VOCATION: Actress.

CAREER: PRINCIPAL FILM APPEARANCES—Forever Young, Forever Free, South African, 1976; Hot Lead and Cold Feet, 1978; The North Avenue Irregulars, 1979.

PRINCIPAL TELEVISION APPEARANCES—Series. Alice Johnson, Room 222, ABC, 1969-74; My Friend Tony, NBC, 1969; Karen Angelo, Karen, ABC, 1975.

Guest: Hollywood Squares; Laugh-In; The Bold Ones; The Sonny and Cher Show.

Movies: Gidget Grows Up, 1970; The Daughters of Joshua Cabe, 1972; Coffee, Tea, or Me?, 1973; The Girl Who Came Gift Wrapped, 1974; The Love Boat, 1976; Having Babies, 1976; Murder at the World Series, 1977; Return to Fantasy Island, 1977; Go West Young Girl, 1978; America 2100, 1978; Only the Pretty Girls Die, 1980; Muggable Mary: Street Cop, 1982; Children in the Crossfire, NBC, 1984; Annabelle Grier, He's Fired, She's Hired, CBS, 1984; A Fighting Choice, ABC, 1986.

Special: Host, Our Time, NBC, 1985.

AWARDS: Outstanding Performance by an Actress in a Supporting Role in a Comedy, Emmy, 1970, for Room 222.

ADDRESSES: HOME—Sherman Oaks, CA. AGENT—International Creative Management, 8899 Beverly Blvd., Los Angeles, CA 90048.*

*   *   *

VAN DEVERE, Trish 1943-

PERSONAL: Born March 19, 1943, in Tenafly, NJ; married George C. Scott (the actor and director). EDUCATION: Attended Ohio Wesleyan University.

VOCATION: Actress.

CAREER: PRINCIPAL STAGE APPEARANCES—Sly Fox, Broadway, 1977; Tricks of the Trade, Broadway, 1978;

PRINCIPAL FILM APPEARANCES—Where's Poppa, United Artists, 1970; The Last Run, Metro-Goldwyn-Mayer, 1971; One Is a Lonely Number, 1972; The Day of the Dolphin, Avco Embassy, 1973; The Savage Is Loose, Campbell Devon, 1974; Movie Movie, Warner Brothers, 1979; The Changeling, Canadian, 1979; The Hearse, 1980; Uphill All the Way, 1985; also appeared in Fifty-Two Pickup.

PRINCIPAL TELEVISION APPEARANCES—Mini-Series: Mayflower—The Pilgrim's Adventure.

Episodic: Hardcastle and McCormick, ABC, 1984.

Movie: All God's Children, ABC, 1980.*

*   *   *

VAN DYKE, Dick 1925-

PERSONAL: Born December 13, 1925, in West Plains, MO; married Marjorie Willett, February 12, 1948; children: Christian, Barry, Stacey, Carrie Beth. MILITARY: U.S. Air Force, World War II.

VOCATION: Comedian, actor, singer, and writer.

CAREER: NEW YORK DEBUT—The Girls Against the Boys, Broadway, 1959. PRINCIPAL STAGE APPEARANCES—Bye Bye Birdie, Broadway, 1960-61.

CABARET—With Philip Erickson, The Merry Mutes, Eric and Van, pantomime act, 1947-53.

PRINCIPAL FILM APPEARANCES—Bye Bye Birdie, Columbia, 1963; What a Way to Go, Twentieth Century-Fox, 1964; Mary Poppins, Buena Vista, 1965; Art of Love, 1965; Lieutenant Robin Crusoe, U.S.N., Buena Vista, 1966; Divorce American Style, Columbia, 1967; Fitzwilly, United Artists, 1967; Chitty, Chitty, Bang, Bang, United Artists, 1968; The Comic, Columbia, 1969; Some Kind of Nut, United Artists, 1969; Cold Turkey, United Artists, 1971; The Morning After, 1974; The Runner Stumbles, Twentieth Century Fox, 1979.

PRINCIPAL TELEVISION APPEARANCES—Series: Master of ceremonies, The Music Shop, Atlanta; master of ceremonies, The Dick Van Dyke Show, New Orleans, LA; host, Morning Show, CBS, 1955; Host, CBS Cartoon Theatre, CBS, 1956; regular, The Andy Williams Show, ABC, 1958; regular, Pantomime Quiz, ABC, 1958-59; emcee, Laugh Line, NBC, 1959; Rob Petrie, The Dick Van Dyke Show, CBS, 1961-66; Dick Preston, The New Dick Van Dyke Show, CBS, 1971-74; Van Dyke and Company, NBC, 1976; regular, The Carol Burnett Show, CBS, 1977.

Episodic: "Trap for a Stranger," U.S. Steel Hour, CBS, 1957-58.

Movie: Strong Medicine, syndicated, 1986.

Play: "Breakfast with Les and Bess," *American Playhouse,* PBS.

WRITINGS: BOOKS—*Faith Hope and Hilarity,* 1970.

AWARDS: Theatre World, 1960, for *Bye Bye Birdie;* Antoinette Perry (Tony) Award, Best Musical Comedy Actor, 1961, for *Bye Bye Birdie;* Emmy awards: Outstanding Continued Performance by an Actor in Series, 1964, for *The Dick Van Dyke Show,* Outstanding Comedy Series, 1966, for *The Dick Van Dyke Show,* Outstanding Continued Performance by an Actor, 1966, for *The Dick Van Dyke Show.*

ADDRESSES: AGENT—William Morris Agency, 151 El Camino Drive, Beverly Hills, CA 90212.*

*   *   *

van ITALLIE, Jean-Claude   1936-

PERSONAL: Born May 25, 1936, in Brussels, Belgium; son of Hugo Ferdinand and Marthe Mathilde Caroline (Levy) van Itallie. EDUCATION: Harvard University, A.B., 1958.

VOCATION: Playwright.

CAREER: PRINCIPAL STAGE WORK—Playwrighting activities include principal playwright with the Open Theatre, NY, 1963-70; playwright in residence, McCarter Theatre, Princeton, NJ, 1972-76.

RELATED CAREER—Visiting Mellon professor, Amherst College, MA, 1976; teacher: Naropa Institute, University of Colorado, Boulder, 1974-76, also, Princeton University, Columbia University, New York University, and Yale University School of Drama.

WRITINGS: PLAYS, PRODUCED—*War,* Playwrights Unit, Vandam, NY, 1963, then Cafe La Mama, 1966; plays written for the Open Theatre, Cafe La Mama, and others include *Almost Like Being, I'm Really Here, Pavane,* 1964; *The Hunter and the Bird,* 1965; "Interview," "T.V.," and "Motel," trilogy comprising *America Hurrah,* Pocket Theatre, NY, 1966, then Royal Court, London, 1967; *The Serpent,* Teatro degli Arte, Rome, Italy, 1968, then Open Theatre, NY; (with Sharon Thie) *Thoughts on the Instant of Greeting a Friend on the Street,* Open Theatre, NY, 1968; (with Megan Terry and Sam Shepard) *Nightwalk,* 1973; (with Richard Peaslee) *The King of the United States,* 1974; (with Richard Peaslee) *The Fable,* 1975; *Naropa, Bag Lady,* Theatre for the New City, NY, 1979; *The Traveler,* Mark Taper Forum, Los Angeles, CA, 1986; also wrote *Early Warnings,* Manhattan Theatre Club, NY; *Mystery Play,* Cherry Lane, NY; *Tibetan Book of the Dead,* Cafe La Mama, NY.

Also made new English translations of: *The Seagull,* McCarter Theatre, Princeton, NJ, Manhattan Theatre Club, NY, and Public Theatre, NY, 1975; *The Cherry Orchard,* Public, NY, and Vivien Beaumont Theatre, NY, 1977; *Three Sisters,* Manhattan Theatre Club, NY, American Repertory Theatre, Cambridge, MA, 1979; *Uncle Vanya,* Cafe La Mama Annex, NY, 1980; *The Balcony,* American Repertory Theatre, Cambridge, MA, 1986.

TELEVISION PLAYS—*Everything's OK with the Forbushers,* 1970; *The Serpent; Pavane; Almost Like Being; Picasso, a Biography,* PBS.

Photograph by Jerry Vezzso

JEAN-CLAUDE van ITALLIE

AWARDS: Vernon Rice Drama Desk Award, Jersey City Critics Award, Outer Circle Critics Award, all 1966, for *America Hurrah;* Obie Award, 1968, for *The Serpent;* two Guggenheim fellowships; grants and fellowships from Creative Artists Public Service program, National Endowment for the Arts, Ford Foundation, and Rockefeller Foundation; honorary doctorate from Kent State University.

SIDELIGHTS: RECREATIONS—Farming and "sitting still."

ADDRESSES: OFFICE—Box Seven, Charlemont, MA, 01339.

*   *   *

VAUGHN, Robert   1932-

PERSONAL: Born Francis Vaughn, November 22, 1932, in New York, NY; son of Walter and Marcella Vaughn; married Linda Staab, 1974; children: Caitlin, Cassidy. EDUCATION: Los Angeles State College, B.A., theatre arts, M.A., theatre arts, 1956; University of Southern California, Ph.D., communications, 1970. RELIGION: Roman Catholic. POLITICS: Democrat.

VOCATION: Actor.

CAREER: PRINCIPAL FILM APPEARANCES—*Hell's Crossroads,* Republic, 1957; *No Time to Be Young,* Columbia, 1957; *Unwed Mother,* Allied Artists, 1958; *Brass Target,* United Artists, 1958; *Good Day for Hanging,* Columbia, 1959; *The Young Philadelphians,* Warner Brothers, 1959; *The City Jungle,* 1959; *The Magnificent Seven,* United Artists, 1960; *The Big Show,* Twentieth Century-Fox, 1961; *The Caretakers,* United Artists, 1963; *To Trap a Spy,* Metro-Goldwyn-Mayer, 1966; *The Spy with My Face,* Metro-Goldwyn-

Mayer, 1966; *One Spy Too Many*, Metro-Goldwyn-Mayer, 1966; *The Venetian Affair*, Metro-Goldwyn-Mayer, 1967; *How to Steal the World*, Metro-Goldwyn-Mayer, 1967; *Bullitt*, Warner Brothers, 1968; *The Bridge at Remagen*, United Artists, 1969; *If It's Tuesday, This Must Be Belgium*, United Artists, 1969.

The Mind of Mr. Soames, Columbia, 1970; *Julius Caesar*, American International Pictures; *The Statue*, Cinerama, 1971; *The Clay Pidgeon*, Metro-Goldwyn-Mayer, 1971; *The Towering Inferno*, Twentieth Century-Fox, 1974; *Starship Invasions*, Warner Brothers, 1978; title role, *F.D.R.*, International Cinegraph and Aurora Sunrise, 1978; *Battle Beyond the Stars*, 1980; *Virus*, 1980; *Cuba Crossing*, 1980; *Hanger 18*, 1980; *S.O.B.*, Paramount, 1981; *Superman III*, Warner Brothers, 1983.

PRINCIPAL TELEVISION APPEARANCES—Series: Captain Ray Rambridge, *The Lieutenant*, NBC, 1963-64; Napoleon Solo, *The Man from U.N.C.L.E.*, NBC, 1964-68; Harry Rule, *The Protectors*, syndicated, 1972-73; Harlan Adams, *Emerald Point, N.A.S.*, CBS, 1983-84.

Episodic: *General Electric True; Telephone Time; Hart to Hart; Murder, She Wrote*, CBS, 1985; "Face to Face," *The Hitchhiker*, HBO, 1985; *Stingray*, NBC, 1986.

Mini-Series: Charles Desmond, *Captains and Kings*, NBC, 1976-77; Morgan Wendall, *Centennial*, NBC, 1978-79; President Woodrow Wilson, *Backstairs at the White House*, NBC, 1979; *Washington: Behind Closed Doors*, ABC, 1979; *The Blue and the Grey*, NBC, 1984; *Evergreen*, NBC, 1985.

Movies: Harry Truman, *The Man from Independence* (play), 1974; *The Greatest Heroes of the Bible*, 1978; *The Rebels*, 1979; *The Gossip Columnist*, 1980; *International Airport*, ABC, 1985; *Private Sessions*, NBC, 1985.

PRINCIPAL STAGE APPEARANCES—*End as a Man*; title role, *Hamlet*, Pasadena Playhouse, CA; *F.D.R.* (one man play), 1978; Henry Drummond, *Inherit the Wind*, Paper Mill Playhouse, Milburn, NJ, 1984-85.

WRITINGS: BOOKS—*Only Victims*, 1972.

MEMBER: Screen Actors Guild, American Federation of Television and Radio Artists; American Academy of Political and Social Sciences, California Democratic Committee.

AWARDS: Outstanding Continuing Performance by a Supporting Actor in a Drama Series, Emmy, 1977-78, for *Washington: Behind Closed Doors;* Best Supporting Actor, Academy Award, 1959, for *The City Jungle*.

ADDRESSES: AGENT—International Creative Management, 8899 Beverly Blvd., Los Angeles, CA 90048.*

*   *   *

VERDON, Gwen   1925-

PERSONAL: Born January 13, 1925, in Culver City, CA; daughter of Joseph William and Gertrude (Standring) Verdon; married Bob Fosse (divorced); trained for the dance with her mother and E. Belcher, Carmelita Marrachi, and Jack Cole.

VOCATION: Actress, singer, and dancer.

CAREER: PRINCIPAL STAGE APPPEARANCES—Gambling dancer, *Bonanza Bound*, Shubert Theatre, Philadelphia, PA, 1947; assistant choreographer, *Magdalena*, Ziegfeld Theatre, NY, 1948; dancer, *Alive and Kicking Revue*, Winter Garden Theatre, NY, 1950; Claudine, *Can-Can*, Shubert Theatre, NY, 1953; Lola, *Damn Yankees*, 46th Street Theatre, NY, 1955; Anna Christie, *New Girl in Town*, 46th Street Theatre, NY, 1957; Essie Whimple, *Redhead*, 46th Street Theatre, NY, 1959; Charity Hope Valentine, *Sweet Charity*, Palace Theatre, NY, 1966; Helen Giles, *Children! Children!*, Ritz Theatre, NY, 1972; *Milliken's Breakfast Show Revue*, Waldorf-Astoria, NY, 1973; Lola, *Damn Yankees*, Westbury Music Fair, Long Island, NY, 1974; Roxie Hart, *Chicago*, 46th Street Theatre, NY, 1975.

MAJOR TOURS—Essie Whimple, *Redhead*, national, 1960.

PRINCIPAL FILM APPEARANCES—*On the Riviera*, 1951; *David and Bathsheba*, 1951; *Meet Me After the Show*, 1951; *Mississippi Gambler*, 1953; *Damn Yankees*, Warner Brothers, 1958; *Cotton Club*, Orion, 1984; *Cocoon*, Twentieth Century-Fox, 1985.

PRINCIPAL TELEVISION APPEARANCES—Episodic: *M*A*S*H; Fame; All Is Forgiven; Trapper John, M.D.; The Equalizer; Magnum P.I.; Webster*.

Movies: *Legs*, 1983.

Pilots: *Community Center*, 1984.

RELATED CAREER—Production supervisor, *Dancin* tour, 1979-80.

AWARDS: Antoinette Perry Awards, 1954, for *Can-Can*, 1956, for *Damn Yankees*, 1958, for *New Girl in Town*, and 1959, for *Redhead*.

GWEN VERDON

SIDELIGHTS: FAVORITE ROLES—Charity, Roxie Hart, Essie Whimple.

ADDRESSES: AGENT—c/o Jerry Martin, William Morris Agency, 151 El Camino Drive, Beverly Hills, CA 90212; Shapiro, Taxon and Kopell, 111 W. 40th Street, New York, NY 10018.

*   *   *

VIDAL, Gore   1925-

PERSONAL: Full name, Eugene Luther Gore Vidal; born October 3, 1925, in West Point, NY; son of Eugene L. (director of Air Commerce under Franklin D. Roosevelt) and Nina (Gore) Vidal. EDUCATION: Attended Phillips Exeter Academy. POLITICS: Democrat. MILITARY: U.S. Army, 1943-46.

VOCATION: Dramatic author and novelist.

WRITINGS: PLAYS—*A Visit to a Small Planet: A Comedy Akin to a Vaudeville,* first produced on Broadway at the Booth Theatre, 1957; *The Best Man: A Play of Politics,* first produced on Broadway at the Morosco Theatre, 1960; (adapted from the play by Friedrich Durrenmatt) *Romulus: A New Comedy,* first produced on Broadway at the Music Box Theatre, 1962; *Weekend,* first produced in New Haven, CT, 1968, first produced on Broadway at the Broadhurst Theatre, 1968; *An Evening with Richard Nixon,* first produced at the Shubert Theatre in New York, 1972.

SCREENPLAYS—*The Catered Affair,* Metro-Goldwyn-Mayer, 1956; *I Accuse,* Metro-Goldwyn-Mayer, 1958; (with Robert Hamer) *The Scapegoat,* Metro-Goldwyn-Mayer, 1959; (with Tennessee Williams) *Suddenly Last Summer,* Columbia, 1959; (based on the play of the same title) *The Best Man,* United Artists, 1964; (with Francis Ford Coppola) *Is Paris Burning?,* Paramount, 1966; *The Last of the Mobile Hotshots,* Warner Brothers, 1970.

TELEVISION PLAYS—*Barn Burning; Dark Possession; A Man and Two Gods; Smoke; Visit to a Small Planet; The Death of Billy the Kid; Dr. Jekyll and Mr. Hyde; A Sense of Justice; Summer Pavilion; The Turn of the Screw; The Contrast; Stage Door; A Farewell to Arms; Honor; Portrait of a Ballerina; The Indestructible Mr. Gore; Dear Arthur.*

MINI-SERIES—*Dress Gray,* NBC, 1986.

BOOKS—*Williwaw,* Dutton, 1946, reprinted by New American Library, 1968; *In a Yellow Wood,* Dutton, 1947; *The City and the Pillar,* Dutton, 1948, revised edition, 1965; *The Season of Comfort,* Dutton, 1949; *A Search for the King,* Dutton, 1950; *Dark Green, Bright Red,* Dutton, 1950, reprinted by New American Library, 1968; *The Judgment of Paris,* Dutton, 1952, revised edition by Little, Brown, 1965; *Messiah,* Dutton, 1954, revised edition by Little, Brown, 1965; *Three: Williwaw, A Thirsty Evil: Seven Short Stories,* New American Library, 1962; *Julian,* Little, Brown, 1964; *Washington DC,* Little, Brown, 1967; *Myra Breckinridge,* Little, Brown, 1968; *Two Sisters: A Novel in the Form of a Memoir,* Little, Brown, 1970; *Burr,* Random House, 1973; *Myron,* Random House, 1974; *1876,* Random House, 1976; *Kalki,* Random House, 1978; *Creation,* Random House, 1981; *Duluth,* Random House, 1983; *Lincoln,* Random House, 1984.

Essays: *Rocking the Boat,* Little, Brown, 1962; *Sex, Death and Money,* Bantam, 1968; *Relections upon a Sinking Ship,* Little, Brown, 1969; *Matters of Fact and Fiction: Essays, 1973-76* Ran-

dom House, 1977; *The Second American Revolution and Other Essays,* Random House, 1982.

Other writings: *A Thirsty Evil: Seven Short Stories,* Zero Press, 1956; editor, *Best Television Plays,* Ballantine, 1965; *Homage to Daniel Shays: Collected Essays, 1952-1972,* Random House, 1972, published as *On Our Own Now,* Panther, 1976; (with others) *Great American Families,* Norton, 1977; (with Robert J. Stanton) *Views from a Window: Conversations with Gore Vidal,* Lyle Stuart, 1980.

RELATED CAREER—Drama critic, *Reporter Magazine,* 1959; president, Edgewater Publishing Company; founder, *The Hyde Park Townsman* newspaper, 1960.

MEMBER: Athenaeum, London.

SIDELIGHTS: Gore Vidal told *CTFT* that he appeared in the film of Fellini's *Roma,* as himself in several episodes of *Mary Hartman, Mary Hartman,* and narrated the television documentary *Vidal in Venice.* He is a frequent guest on talk and discussion television programs. He also ran for the U.S. Congress in 1960 as a Democratic-Liberal.

ADDRESSES: HOME—Los Angeles, CA; Ravello, Italy. AGENT—c/o Owen Laster, William Morris Agency, 1350 Avenue of the Americas, New York, NY 10019.

*   *   *

VIGODA, Abe   1921-

PERSONAL: Born February 24, 1921, in New York, NY; son of Samuel and Lena (Moses) Vigoda; married Beatrice Schy, February 25, 1968; children: Carol. EDUCATION: Studied acting at the Theatre School of Dramatic Arts at the American Theatre Wing.

VOCATION: Actor.

CAREER: PRINCIPAL STAGE APPEARANCES—*Marat-Sade,* Broadway, 1967; *The Man in the Glass Booth,* Broadway, 1968; *Inquest,* Broadway, 1970; *Tough to Get Help,* Broadway, 1972.

PRINCIPAL FILM APPEARANCES—*The Godfather, Part 1,* Paramount, 1972; *The Godfather, Part 2,* Paramount, 1973; *The Don Is Dead,* Universal, 1973; *Newman's Law,* Universal, 1974; *The Cheap Detective,* Columbia, 1978.

PRINCIPAL TELEVISION APPEARANCES—Series: Detective Phil Fish, *Barney Miller,* ABC, 1975-77; Detective Phil Fish, *Fish,* ABC, 1977-78.

MEMBER: Actors' Equity Association, American Federation of Television and Radio Artists, Screen Actors Guild.

AWARDS: Outstanding Continuing Performance by a Supporting Actor in a Comedy Series, Emmy nominations, 1975-76, 1976-77, both for *Barney Miller;* Outstanding Lead Actor in a Comedy Series, Emmy nomination, 1976-77, for *Fish.*

ADDRESSES: AGENT—Contemporary-Korman Artists Ltd., 132 Lasky Drive, Beverly Hills, CA 90212.*

W

WAGNER, Lindsay 1949-

PERSONAL: Born June 22, 1949, in Los Angeles, CA; daughter of Bill Nowels and Marilyn Louise (Thrasher) Wagner; married Michael Brandon, December, 1976 (divorced); married Henry King, 1981. EDUCATION: Attended the University of Oregon, 1967.

VOCATION: Actress.

CAREER: PRINCIPAL TELEVISION APPEARANCES—Series: Jaime Sommers, *The Six Million Dollar Man*, ABC, 1975; Jaime Sommers, *The Bionic Woman*, ABC, 1976-77; NBC, 1977-78; Dr. Jessie Hayden, *Jessie*, ABC, 1984.

Movies: *The Two Worlds of Jennie Logan*, 1979; *The Incredible Journey of Dr. Meg Laurel*, 1979; *Jessie*, ABC, 1984; *Passions*, CBS, 1984; *Young Again*, ABC, 1984; *The Other Lover*, CBS, 1985.

Mini-Series: *Scruples*, 1980.

PRINCIPAL FILM APPEARANCES—*Two People*, Universal, 1973; *The Paper Chase*, Twentieth Century-Fox, 1973; *Second Wind*, 1976; *Martin's Day*, Metro-Goldwyn-Mayer/United Artists, 1985.

RELATED CAREER—Acting teacher, Childrens Founders School, Los Angeles, CA.

AWARDS: Outstanding Lead Actress in a Drama Series, Emmy, 1977, for *The Bionic Woman*.

ADDRESSES: AGENT—Ron Samuels Enterprises, 9046 Sunset Blvd., Suite 208, Los Angeles, CA 90069.*

*   *   *

WAGNER, Robert 1930-

PERSONAL: Born February 10, 1930, in Detroit, MI; married Natalie Wood, 1957 (divorced, 1962); married Marian Donnen (divorced); remarried Wood, 1972 (died, 1981); children: (second marriage) Kate; (third marriage) Courtney.

VOCATION: Actor and producer.

CAREER: FILM DEBUT—*Halls of Montezuma*, 1950. PRINCIPAL FILM APPEARANCES—*The Frogmen*, 1951; *Let's Make It Legal*,

1951; *With a Song in My Heart*, 1952; *What Price Glory*, 1952; *Stars and Stripes Forever*, 1952; *The Silver Whip*, 1953; *Titanic*, 1953; *Beneath the Twelve Mile Reef*, 1953; *Prince Valiant*, Twentieth Century-Fox, 1954; *Broken Lance*, 1954; *White Feather*, Twentieth Century-Fox, 1955; *Kiss Before Dying*, 1956; *Between Heaven and Hell*, Twentieth Century-Fox, 1956; *The Mountain*, Paramount, 1956; *The True Story of Jesse James*, 1957; *Stopover Tokyo*, Twentieth Century-Fox, 1957; *The Hunters*, Twentieth Century-Fox, 1958; *In Love and War*, 1958; *Say One for Me*, Twentieth Century-Fox, 1959.

All the Fine Young Cannibals, Metro-Goldwyn-Mayer, 1960; *Sail a Crooked Ship*, Columbia, 1962; *The Longest Day*, Twentieth Century-Fox, 1962; *The War Lover*, Columbia, 1962; *The Condemned of Altoona*, Twentieth Century-Fox, 1963; *Harper*, Warner Brothers, 1966; *Banning*, Universal, 1967; *The Biggest Bundle of Them All*, Metro-Goldwyn-Mayer, 1968; *Don't Just Stand There*, Universal, 1968; *Winning*, Universal, 1969; *The Affair*, 1973; *Towering Inferno*, Twentieth Century-Fox, 1974; *Midway*, 1976; *The Concord—Airport '79*, 1979; *Curse of the Pink Panther*, Metro-Goldwyn-Mayer/United Artists, 1983.

PRINCIPAL TELEVISION APPEARANCES—Series: Alexander Mundy, *It Takes a Thief*, ABC, 1968-70; Pete Ryan, *Switch*, CBS, 1975-78; Jonathan Hart, *Hart to Hart*, 1979-84; J.G. Culver, *Lime Street*, ABC, 1985.

Movies: *Fame Is the Name of the Game*, 1966; *How I Spent My Summer Vacation*, 1967; *City Beneath the Sea*, 1970; *Madame Sin*, 1971; *Cable Car Murder (Crosscurrent)*, 1971; Brick, *Cat on a Hot Tin Roof*, 1976; *Critical List*, 1978; *Pearl*, 1978; *There Must Be a Pony*, ABC (upcoming); also, *Runaway Bay; The Ox-Bow Incident; Gun in His Hand; And Man Created Vanity; The Enemy on the Beach*.

Episodic: *Streets of San Francisco*.

Special: *S.O.S.: Secrets of Surviving*, NBC, 1984.

PRINCIPAL TELEVISION WORK—Producer: *Madame Sin*, 1971; *Fame Is the Name of the Game*, 1966; *Cable Car Murder (Crosscurrent)*, 1971; *Cat on a Hot Tin Roof*, 1976; *Critical List*, 1978; *Pearl*, 1978; *There Must Be a Pony*, ABC (upcoming); also, *Runaway Bay; The Ox-Bow Incident; Gun in His Hand; And Man Created Vanity; The Enemy on the Beach*.

RELATED CAREER: President, R.J. Productions.

ADDRESSES: AGENT—William Morris Agency, 151 El Camino Drive, Beverly Hills, CA 90212.*

WAGNER, Robin 1933-

PERSONAL: Full name, Robin Samuel Anton Wagner; born August 31, 1933, in San Francisco, CA; son of Jens Otto and Phyllis Edna Catherine (Smith-Spurgeon) Wagner; married Joyce Marie Workman (divorced); children: Kurt, Leslie, Christie. EDUCATION: Attended California School of Fine Arts. RELIGION: Roman Catholic.

VOCATION: Designer.

CAREER: FIRST STAGE WORK—Scenic designer, *Don Pasquale, Amahl and the Night Visitors* and *Zanetto,* all Golden Gate Opera Workshop, San Francisco, CA, 1953. FIRST NEW YORK STAGE WORK—Decor design, *And the Wind Blows,* St. Mark's Playhouse, 1959. FIRST LONDON STAGE WORK—Designer, *Hair,* Shaftesbury Theatre, London, 1968. PRINCIPAL STAGE WORK—Scenic designer: *Contemporary Dancers Wing* and *Tea and Sympathy,* for the Theatre Arts Colony, San Francisco, CA, 1954; *The Immoralist* and *Dark of the Moon,* Encore Theatre, San Francisco, CA; *Waiting for Godot,* 1957, *The Miser,* 1958, *The Ticklish Acrobat,* 1958, and *The Plaster Bambino,* 1959, all with the Actors Workshop, San Francisco, CA; decor and costume designer, *The Filling Station,* San Francisco Ballet Company, CA, 1958; decor design, *The Guardsman,* Sacramento Civic Ballet, CA, 1958; designed for a season of musical productions in Sacramento, CA.

Off-Broadway: *The Prodigal, Between Two Thieves, Borak,* 1960; *A Worm in Horseradish,* 1961; *Entertain a Ghost, The Days and Nights of Beebe Fenstermaker, The Playboy of the Western World,* all for the Irish Players, 1962; *Cages, In White America, The Burning,* 1963; *The White Rose and the Red,* 1964.

Dark of the Moon, Galileo, 1964, *A View from the Bridge, An Evening's Frost,* 1965, *The Condemned of Altoona,* 1966, all Arena Stage, Washington, DC.

Broadway: *Galileo, The Trial of Lee Harvey Oswald, A Certain Young Man,* 1967; *Hair, Lovers and Other Strangers, The Cuban Thing, The Great White Hope, Promises, Promises,* 1968; *The Watering Place, My Daughter, Your Son,* 1969; *Gantry, Mahagonny, The Engagement Baby,* 1970; *Lenny, Jesus Christ Superstar, Inner City,* 1971; *Sugar, Lysistrata,* 1972; *Seesaw, Full Circle,* 1973; *Mack and Mabel, Sergeant Pepper's Lonely Hearts Club Band on the Road,* 1974; *A Chorus Line,* 1975; *On the Twentieth Century,* 1977; *Ballroom, Comin' Uptown,* 1979.

One Night Stand, Nederlander Theatre, NY, 1980 (closed in previews); *Forty-Second Street,* Winter Garden, then Majectic Theatre, NY, 1980—; *Dream Girls,* Imperial Theatre, NY, 1981-85; *Merlin,* Mark Hellinger Theatre, NY, 1983.

Also: *Love Match,* Los Angeles, CA, 1967; *Promises, Promises,* London, 1969; The Rolling Stones Tour of America, 1975; *The Red Devil Battery Sign,* Boston, MA, 1975; *Les Troyens,* Vienna State Opera, 1976; *Hamlet Connotations,* American Ballet Theatre, NY, 1976; *A Chorus Line,* London, 1977; *Julius Caesar,* Stratford, CT, 1978; *West Side Story,* Hamburg, Germany, 1978; *Mahalia,* Hartford Theatre Company, Stamford, CT, 1981, then Hartman Theatre, Stamford, CT, 1982.

PRINCIPAL FILM WORK—Designer, *Glory Boy,* 1970.

AWARDS: Antoinette Perry Award, Drama Desk Award, two New York Critics Circle Awards, Lumen Award, three Joseph Maharam Awards.

ADDRESSES: OFFICE—Robin Wagner Studio, 890 Broadway, New York, NY 10003.*

*   *   *

WALKEN, Christopher 1943-

PERSONAL: Born March 31, 1943, in Astoria, Queens, NY; son of Paul Walken. EDUCATION: Attended Hofstra University; studied with Wynn Handman and at the Actors Studio in New York.

VOCATION: Actor and dancer.

CAREER: NEW YORK DEBUT—(As Ronnie Walken) David, *J.B.,* American National Theatre and Academy (ANTA), NY, 1959. PRINCIPAL STAGE APPEARANCES—(As Ronnie Walken), Clayton "Dutch" Miller, *Best Foot Forward,* Stage 73 Theatre, NY, 1963; chorus (as Ronnie Walken), *High Spirits,* Alvin, 1964; one of the Killers, *Baker Street,* Broadway Theatre, NY, 1965; Philip, King of France, *The Lion in Winter,* Ambassador Theatre, NY, 1966; Claudio, *Measure for Measure,* Delacorte Theatre, 1966; Jack Hunter (The Sailor), *The Rose Tattoo,* City Center, NY, 1966; Unknown Soldier, *The Unknown Soldier and His Wife,* Vivian Beaumont Theatre, NY, 1967; Achilles, *Iphigenia in Aulis,* Circle in the Square, NY, 1967; at the Shakespeare Festival in Stratford, Ontario, played Romeo in *Romeo and Juliet,* Lysander in *A Midsummer Night's Dream,* and Felton in *The Three Musketeers,* all summer, 1968; at the San Diego Shakespeare Festival, appeared in *Julius Caesar,* and in *The Chronicles of Hell,* 1969.

Alan, *Lemon Sky,* Playhouse, NY, then Ivanhoe, Chicago, 1970; appeared in *Scenes from American Life,* Forum Theatre, NY, 1971; Thoreau, *The Night Thoreau Spent in Jail,* Goodman Theatre, Chicago, 1971; Posthumus Leonatus, *The Tale of Cymbeline,* Delacorte Theatre, NY, 1971; title role, *Caligula,* Yale Repertory Theatre, New Haven, CT, 1971-72; Georg, *The Judgement,* American Place Theatre, NY, 1972; appeared at the Long Wharf Theatre, New Haven, CT, 1972-73; Sintsov, *Enemies,* Vivian Beaumont Theatre, NY, 1972; appeared as Jack Clitheroe, *The Plough and the Stars,* 1973; appeared as Bassanio, *Merchant of Venice,* 1973; Achilles, *Troilus and Cressida,* Mitzi E. Newhouse Theatre, NY, 1973; Antonio, *The Tempest,* 1974; title role, *Macbeth,* 1974; title role, *Hamlet,* Seattle Repertory, 1974; title role, *Kid Champion,* Anspacher Theatre, NY, 1975; Chance Wayne, *Sweet Bird of Youth,* Brooklyn Academy of Music, then Rebehak Harkness Theatre, NY, 1975, then Academy Festival Theatre, Chicago, 1976; Gregers Werle, *The Wild Duck,* Yale Repertory, New Haven, CT, 1978.

Hurlyburly, Promenade Theatre, then Ethel Barrymore Theatre, NY, 1984-85; *House of Blue Leaves,* Mitzi Newhouse Theatre, NY, 1986.

Also appeared in productions of *The Seagull, Miss Julie,* and *West Side Story.*

FILM DEBUT—*The Anderson Tapes,* Columbia, 1971. PRINCIPAL FILM APPEARANCES—*Next Stop, Greenwich Village,* 1976; *Roseland,* Cinema Shares, 1977; *Santa Fe--1936; The Sentinel,* Universal, 1977; *Annie Hall,* United Artists, 1977; *The Deer Hunter,* Universal, 1979; *Heaven's Gate,* United Artists, 1980; *The Dogs of War,* United Artists, 1981; *Pennies from Heaven,* United Artists, 1981; *Brainstorm,* Metro-Goldwyn-Mayer/United Artists, 1983; *The Dead Zone,* Paramount, 1983; *A View to a Kill,* Metro-Goldwyn-Mayer/United Artists, 1985; *At Close Range,* Orion, 1986.

MEMBER: Actors' Equity Association, Screen Actors Guild.

AWARDS: Clarence Derwent, 1966, for *The Lion in Winter;* Theatre World's Most Promising Personality, 1966-67, for *The Rose Tattoo;* Joseph Jefferson and Obie 1970-71, for *Kid Champion;* Best Supporting Actor, New York Film Critics, 1978, for *The Deer Hunter;* Best Supporting Actor, Academy Award, 1979, for *The Deer Hunter*.

ADDRESSES: AGENT—Sue Mengers, International Creative Management, 8899 Beverly Blvd., Los Angeles, CA 90048.

*   *   *

WALKER, Nancy   1921-

PERSONAL: Born Anna Myrtle Swoyer, May 10, 1921, in Philadelphia, PA; daughter of Dewey Stewart (a comedian known as Dewey Barto) and Myrtle (Lawler) Swoyer; married Gar Moore (divorced); married David Craig, January 29, 1951; children: Miranda. EDUCATION: Attended Bentley School and the Professional Children's School.

VOCATION: Actress and singer.

CAREER: STAGE DEBUT—Blind date, *Best Foot Forward,* Barrymore Theatre, NY, 1941. PRINCIPAL STAGE APPEARANCES—Hilda, *On the Town,* Adelphi Theatre, NY, 1944, then in summer stock, 1950; Yetta Samovar, *Barefoot Boy with Cheek,* Martin Beck Theatre, NY, 1947; Lily Malloy, *Look, Ma, I'm Dancin',* Adelphi Theatre, NY, 1948; *Along Fifth Avenue Revue,* Broadhurst Theatre, NY, 1949; Shirley Harris, *A Month of Sundays,* Shubert Theatre, Boston, MA, 1952; Gladys, *Pal Joey,* Broadhurst Theatre, NY, 1952; *Phoenix '55 Revue,* NY, 1953; Julia Starbuck, *Fallen Angels,* Playhouse Theatre, NY, 1956; Katey O'Shea, *Copper and Brass,* Martin Beck Theatre, NY, 1957; Ruth, *Wonderful Town,* City Center Theatre, NY, 1958; *The Girls Against the Boys Revue,* Alvin Theatre, NY, 1959.

Kay Cram, *Do-Re-Mi,* St. James Theatre, NY, 1960; Libby Hirsch, *Dear Me, the Sky Is Falling* and Julia Starbuck, *Fallen Angels,* both stock productions, 1966; *Bell, Book, and Candle,* Westbury Music Fair, Westbury, NY, 1967; Charlotta Ivanovna, *The Cherry Orchard* and Julia, *The Cocktail Party,* both APA Phoenix, Lyceum Theatre, NY, 1968; Domina, *A Funny Thing Happened on the Way to the Forum,* Ahmanson Theatre, Los Angeles, CA, 1971; *Sondheim: A Musical Tribute,* Shubert Theatre, NY, 1973.

MAJOR TOURS—Moll, *Roaring Girl,* U.S. cities, 1951; Ellen Manville, *Luv,* U.S. cities, 1966.

PRINCIPAL STAGE WORK—Director: *UTBU,* Helen Hayes Theatre, NY, 1966; *Fallen Angels,* 1966.

PRINCIPAL TELEVISION APPEARANCES—Series: Emily Turner, *Family Affair,* CBS, 1970-71; Mildred, *McMillan and Wife,* 1971-76; Ida Morgenstern, *The Mary Tyler Moore Show,* CBS, 1970-74 (guest appearances); Ida Morgenstern, *Rhoda,* CBS, 1974-76; Nancy Kitteridge, *The Nancy Walker Show,* ABC, 1976; Nancy Blansky, *Blansky's Beauties,* ABC, 1977.

Variety: *Mary Tyler Moore Hour,* CBS, 1979.

FILM DEBUT—Blind date, *Best Foot Forward,* 1943. PRINCIPAL FILM APPEARANCES—*Girl Crazy,* 1943; *Broadway Rhythm,* 1944; *Meet the People,* 1944; *Stand Up and Be Counted,* Columbia, 1972; *The World's Greatest Athlete,* Buena Vista, 1973; *Forty Carats,* Columbia, 1973; *Murder by Death,* 1976; *Won Ton Ton: The Dog Who Saved Hollywood,* Paramount, 1976.

PRINCIPAL FILM WORK—Director, *Can't Stop the Music,* Associated Film Distributors, 1980.

PRINCIPAL RADIO APPEARANCES—Serial: *The Lady Next Door*.

ADDRESSES: OFFICE—3702 Eureka Drive, Studio City, CA, 91604.

*   *   *

WALSTON, Ray   1924-

PERSONAL: Born November 2, 1924, in New Orleans, LA; son of Harry and Mittie (Kimball) Walston; married Ruth Calvert (a printer and reporter).

VOCATION: Actor.

CAREER: STAGE DEBUT—Buddy, *High Tor,* Houston Community Players, TX, 1938. NEW YORK DEBUT—Attendant, *Hamlet,* Columbus Circle Theatre, 1945. LONDON DEBUT—Luther Billis, *South Pacific,* Drury Lane Theatre, 1951. PRINCIPAL STAGE APPEARANCES—Petruchio, *The Taming of the Shrew,* Community Players, Houston, TX, 1939; Morgan Evans, *The Corn Is Green* and Hadrian, *You Touched Me,* both Playhouse, Cleveland, OH, 1943; Schwartz of the Daily News, *Front Page,* Royale Theatre, NY, 1946; Sam Phelphs, *Three Indelicate Ladies,* Shubert Theatre, New Haven, CT, 1947; one of the townspeople, *The Survivors,* Playhouse Theatre, NY, 1948; Drugger, *The Alchemist,* Davis, *Moon of the Caribbees,* Male Cricket and Telegrapher, *The Insect Comedy,* all City Center, NY, 1948; Mr. Kramer, *Summer and Smoke,* Music Box Theatre, NY, 1948; Ratcliff, *Richard III,* Booth Theatre, NY, 1949; Rodla Gibbons, *Mrs. Gibbons' Boys,* Music Box Theatre, NY, 1949; telephone man, *The Rat Race,* Barrymore Theatre, NY, 1949.

The Temptation of Maggie Haggerty, Cambridge, MA, 1952; Mac, *Me and Juliet,* Majestic Theatre, NY, 1953; Captain Jona, *House of Flowers,* Alvin Theatre, NY, 1954; Applegate, *Damn Yankees,* 46th Street Theatre, NY, 1955; Michael Haney, *Who Was That Lady I Saw You With?,* Martin Beck Theatre, NY, 1958; Eddie, *Agatha Sue, I Love You,* Henry Miller's Theatre, NY, 1966; Sir Lucius O'Trigger, *The Rivals,* Walnut Street Theatre, Philadelphia, PA, 1972; Walter Burns, *The Front Page,* Playhouse Theatre, Cleveland, OH, 1973; Mr. Applegate, *Damn Yankees,* Westbury Music Fair, Long Island, NY, 1974; *Gala Tribute to Joshua Logan,*

RAY WALSTON

Imperial Theatre, NY, 1975; Colonel Kincaid, *The Last Meeting of the Knights of White Magnolia,* Cleveland Playhouse, OH, 1976; Trissotin, *The Learned Ladies,* Cleveland Playhouse, OH, 1978.

MAJOR TOURS—Luther Billis, *South Pacific,* national, 1950-51; Applegate, *Damn Yankees,* national, 1956-57, 1974; Steward, *Canterbury Tales,* national, 1969-70; *The Drunkard,* national, 1974; leading male roles, *You Know I Can't Hear You When the Water's Running,* national, 1975; also Felix, *The Odd Couple,* Fagin, *Oliver!*

FILM DEBUT—*Kiss Them for Me,* Twentieth Century-Fox, 1957. PRINCIPAL FILM APPEARANCES—Luther Billis, *South Pacific,* Twentieth Century-Fox, 1958; Devil, *Damn Yankees,* Warner Brothers, 1958; *Say One for Me,* Twentieth Century-Fox, 1959; *The Apartment,* United Artists, 1960; *Portrait in Black,* Universal, 1960; *Convicts Four,* 1962; *Who's Minding the Store?,* 1963; *Wives and Lovers,* Paramount, 1963; *Kiss Me Stupid,* 1964; *Caprice,* Twentieth Century-Fox, 1967; Mad Jack Duncan, *Paint Your Wagon,* Paramount, 1969; *The Sting,* Universal, 1973; Poopdeck Pappy, *Popeye,* Paramount, 1980; *Fast Times at Ridgemont High,* 1982; *O.C.and Stiggs,* 1985; *RAD,* 1986.

PRINCIPAL TELEVISION APPEARANCES—Series: Uncle Martin, *My Favorite Martian,* CBS, 1963-66; *Fast Times,* 1986.

Episodic: *Silver Spoons,* NBC.

Movie: *For Love or Money,* CBS, 1984.

Specials: "The Fall of the House of Usher," *Play of the Week,* NBC.

MEMBER: Actors' Equity Association, Screen Actors Guild, American Federation of Television and Radio Artists; Lambs Club, Players Club, Magic Club.

AWARDS: Best Supporting Actor, Clarence Derwent Award and Variety Drama Critics Poll Award, both 1948, for *Summer and Smoke;* Antoinette Perry Award, 1955, for *Damn Yankees.*

ADDRESSES: OFFICE—423 S. Rexford Drive, Suite 205, Beverly Hills, CA 90212.

* * *

WANAMAKER, Sam   1919-

PERSONAL: Born June 14, 1919, in Chicago, IL; son of Morris and Molly (Bobele) Wanamaker; married Charlotte Holland. EDUCATION: Trained for the stage at the Goodman Theatre School. MILITARY: U.S. Army, 1943-46.

VOCATION: Actor, director, and producer.

CAREER: FIRST STAGE WORK—Actor and director in summer stock productions, Chicago, IL, 1936-39. NEW YORK DEBUT—Lester Freed, *Cafe Crown,* Cort Theatre, 1942. LONDON DEBUT—Bernie Dodd, director, *Winter Journey,* St. James Theatre, 1952. PRINCIPAL STAGE APPEARANCES—Actor and director, Globe Shakespearean Theatre Group, Chicago; Chicago Civic Repertory Theatre, IL, 1938; Kirichenko, *Counterattack,* Windsor Theatre, 1943; Mac Sorrell, *This, Too, Shall Pass,* Belasco Theatre, NY, 1946; Jimmy Masters, *Joan of Lorraine,* Alvin Theatre, NY, 1946; directed and portrayed Matt Cole, *Goodbye, My Fancy,* Morosco Theatre, NY, 1948; producer (with Jack Hylton) and portrayed Jim Downs, *The Shrike,* Princes' Theatre, London, 1953; producer (with Ralph Birch), director, and portrayed Charles Castle, *The Big Knife,* Duke of York's Theatre, London, 1954; producer (with Jack de Leon), director, and portrayed Laurent, *The Lovers,* Winter Garden Theatre, NY, 1955; director (with Jack Minster) and portrayed Bill Starbuck, *The Rainmaker,* Golder's Green Theatre, London, then St. Martin's Theatre, London, 1956; directed and portrayed Polo Pope, *A Hatful of Rain,* Princes' Theatre, London, 1957.

Directed and acted at the New Shakespeare Theatre, Liverpool in the following plays: *A View from the Bridge, Tea and Sympathy, Finian's Rainbow, One More River, Cat on a Hot Tin Roof, The Potting Shed, Reclining Figure, King of Hearts, Bus Stop,* and *The Rose Tatoo.*

Iago, *Othello,* Shakespeare Memorial Theatre Company, Stratford Upon Avon, 1959; Dr. Joseph Breuer, *A Far Country,* Music Box Theatre, NY, 1961; title role, *Macbeth,* Goodman Theatre, Chicago, IL, 1964.

PRINCIPAL STAGE WORK—Director, *Purple Dust,* Royal Theatre, Glasgow, 1953; director, *Foreign Field,* Royal Theatre, Birmingham, 1953; director, *The Soldier and the Lady,* Wimbledon, 1954; director, *The World of Sholom Aleichem,* Embassy Theatre, London, 1955; director, *The Threepenny Opera,* Royal Court Theatre,

London, 1956; director, *Ding Dong Bell,* summer theatres, 1961; director, *King Priam,* Coventry Festival, then Covent Garden, London, 1962; director, *King Priam,* Covent Garden, London, 1962; co-producer and director, *Children from Their Games,* Morosco Theatre, NY, 1963; director, *A Case of Libel,* Longacre Theatre, NY, 1963; director, *A Murderer Among Us,* Morosco Theatre, NY, 1964; director, *War and Peace,* Opera House, Sydney, Australia, 1973; director, *Ice Break,* Tippeh Opera, Covent Garden, London, 1976.

PRINCIPAL FILM APPEARANCES—*Taras Bulba,* United Artists, 1962; *Those Magnificent Men in Their Flying Machines,* Twentieth Century-Fox, 1956; *Death on the Nile,* Paramount, 1978; *From Hell to Victory,* 1979; *Private Benjamin,* Warner Brothers, 1980; *The Competition,* Columbia, 1980; *Irreconcilable Differences,* Warner Brothers, 1984; also appeared in *Give Us This Day; The Aviator; Raw Deal.*

PRINCIPAL TELEVISION APPEARANCES—Series: *Berringer's,* ABC, 1984.

Movies: *Heart Sounds,* ABC, 1984; also appeared in *The Wilderness Years; Family Business; Ghost Writer; Blind Love.*

Episodic: *Hawaii Five-0; Return of the Saint.*

RELATED CAREER—Artistic director, New Shakespeare Theatre, Liverpool, UK, 1957; director, Southwark Summer Festival, 1974; director, Shakespeare Birthday Celebration, 1974.

ADDRESSES: OFFICE—Shakespeare Globe Centre, Bear Gardens, Southwark, London SE1, England. AGENT—William Morris Agency, 151 El Camino Drive, Beverly Hills, CA 90212.

*   *   *

WARD, Fred

BRIEF ENTRY: Born in San Diego, CA. Actor. Three days after his high school graduation, Fred Ward decided to join the Air Force. After his enlistment was finished, he moved to New York to become an actor. His many and varied job experiences from that time to his first major film role in *Escape from Alcatraz* have undoubtedly helped him win such roles as an American Indian union activist in *Silkwood,* as the troubled astronaut Gus Grissom in *The Right Stuff,* and the title role in *Remo Williams: The Adventure Begins.* Once in New York, Ward enrolled at the Herbert Berghof Studios and worked as a janitor and construction worker. After a brief film appearance in *No Available Witness,* he moved to Florida where he loaded trucks. From there he went to New Orleans where he worked in a barrel factory and as a bowling alley short order cook. Moving back west, he joined an experimental theatre company in San Francisco and appeared in several critically acclaimed avant-garde plays while working as a crop picker and a contruction worker on the Bay Area Rapid Transit (BART) system. He also worked as a logger in Northern California and Alaska. He moved to Europe and became involved with the Mask and Mime Theatre where he was spotted by director Roberto Rossellini, who cast him in several films. He headed back to San Francisco, where he won a name for himself as part of Sam Shepard's Magic Theatre. His last job before his break in films was selling jewelry on the street.*

WARRICK, Ruth   1916-

PERSONAL: Born June 29, 1916, in St. Joseph, MO; daughter of Frederick R., Jr., and Annie L. (Scott) Warrick; married Erik Rolf (divorced); married Carl Neubert (divorced); married Robert McNamara (divorced); married L. Jarvis Cushing, Jr. (divorced). EDUCATION: Attended University of Missouri at Kansas City; trained for the stage with Antoinette Perry and Brock Pemberton.

VOCATION: Actress.

CAREER: STAGE DEBUT—University of Missouri, 1937. NEW YORK DEBUT—*The Thorntons,* Provincetown Playhouse, 1956. PRINCIPAL STAGE APPEARANCES—Sister of the dead soldier, *Bury the Dead,* Center Community Theatre, Kansas City, MO, 1937; Margo Wendice, *Dial M for Murder,* 1955; Mary Spain, *Miss Lonelyhearts,* Music Box Theatre, NY, 1957; Dolores Dixon, *Single Man at a Party,* Theatre Marquee, NY, 1959; Essie, *Take Me Along,* Shubert Theatre, NY, 1960; Anna Leonowens, *The King and I,* Music Fair, Toronto, Canada, 1960; Martha, *Who's Afraid of Virginia Woolf?,* Los Angeles, CA, 1965; Mary Tyrone, *Long Day's Journey into Night,* Los Angeles, CA, 1966; Agnes, *The Secret Life of Walter Mitty,* Las Palmas Theatre, Los Angeles, CA, 1966; Mrs. Frodo and Anastasia, *Any Resemblance to Persons Living or Dead,* Gate Theatre, NY, 1971; Mrs. John Tarleton, *Misalliance,* Roundabout Theatre, NY, 1972; Emily Doon, *Conditions of Agreement,* 1972; Emmeline Marshall, *Irene,* Minskoff Theatre, NY, 1973-74; *Roberta,* Westbury Music Fair, Long Island, NY, 1976.

RUTH WARRICK

MAJOR TOURS—Anna, *The King and I*, U.S. cities, 1961; Martha, *Who's Afraid of Virginia Woolf?*, Los Angeles, CA, 1965; Mary Tyrone, *Long Day's Journey into Night*, U.S. cities, 1965.

FILM DEBUT—Mrs. Kane, *Citizen Kane*, RKO, 1942. PRINCIPAL FILM APPEARANCES—*Journey into Fear*, 1942; *The Iron Major*, 1943; *Forever and a Day*, 1943; *Guest in the House*, 1944; *China Sky*, 1945; *The Great Bank Robbery*, 1969; *How to Steal the World*, Metro-Goldwyn-Mayer, 1968.

TELEVISION DEBUT—1949. PRINCIPAL TELEVISION APPEARANCES—Series: Ellie Banks, *Father of the Bride*, CBS, 1961-62; Hannah Cord, *Peyton Place*, ABC, 1965-67; Phoebe Tyler Wallingford, *All My Children*, ABC; *As the World Turns*.

Episodic: "Return to Vienna," *Campbell Soundstage*, NBC, 1952; *Your Play Time*, CBS, 1954.

WRITINGS: AUTOBIOGRAPHY—*The Confessions of Phoebe Tyler*.

RECORDINGS: ALBUM—*Phoebe Tyler Regrets*.

SIDELIGHTS: FAVORITE ROLES—Anna, *The King and I*; Martha, *Who's Afraid of Virginia Woolf?* RECREATIONS—Swimming, skin-diving, walking, music, metaphysics, and political activism.

ADDRESSES: OFFICE—c/o ABC Press Relations, 1330 Avenue of the Americas, New York, NY 10019.

*   *   *

WASHINGTON, Denzel

BRIEF ENTRY: Born in Mt. Vernon, NY. Actor. The son of a minister, Denzel Washington attended a private high school and went on to college at Fordham University in the Bronx, where he completed a major in journalism and a minor in political science. After completing school, he moved to California where he studied acting at the American Conservatory Theatre in San Francisco. While on the west coast, Washington did several films and plays, but his biggest role came when he portrayed Malcolm X in *When the Chicken Comes Home to Roost*, for which he was awarded the prestigious Audelco Award. He landed a role in the New York production of *A Soldier's Play* and went on to tour with that play and also appeared in the film version, *A Soldier's Story*. He was recently seen in director Sidney Lumet's film *Power* and portrays Dr. Chandler in the NBC series *St. Elsewhere*.*

*   *   *

WATERSTON, Sam   1940-

PERSONAL: Full name Samuel Atkinson Waterston; born November 15, 1940, in Cambridge, MA; son of George Chychele (a teacher and director) and Alice Tucker (Atkinson) Waterston; married second wife, Lynn Louisa Woodruff, January 26, 1976; children: (first marriage) James S., Graham C.; (second marriage) Elizabeth P., Katherine B. EDUCATION: Yale University, B.A., 1962; also studied at the Sorbonne, Paris, 1960-61, with John Berry of the American Actors Workshop.

VOCATION: Actor.

CAREER: STAGE DEBUT—Page, *Antigone*. NEW YORK STAGE DEBUT—*Oh Dad, Poor Dad . . .*, 1963. PRINCIPAL STAGE APPEARANCES— Broadway: *The Paisley Convertible*, 1966; *Halfway up the Tree*, 1967; *Indians*, 1969; *Hay Fever*, 1970; *The Trial of the Catonsville Nine*, 1971; *A Meeting by the River*, 1972; *Much Ado About Nothing*, 1972; *A Doll's House*, 1975; *Hamlet*, 1975; *Lunch Hour*, 1980; *Benefactors*, 1985-86.

Off-Broadway: *Thistle in My Bed*, 1963; *The Knack*, 1964; *Fitz and Biscuit*, 1966; *La Turista*, 1967; *Posterity for Sale*, 1967; *Red Cross*, 1968; *Muzeeka*, 1968; *Spitting Image*, 1969; *The Brass Butterfly*, 1970; *And I Met a Man*, 1970; *Waiting for Godot*, 1978; *Chez Nous*, 1979; *Gardenia*, 1982; *Three Sisters*, 1982.

New York Shakespeare Festival, NY: *As You Like It*, 1963; *Ergo*, 1968; *Henry IV, Part I* and *Part II*, 1968; *Cymbeline*, 1971; *Hamlet*, 1972; *Much Ado About Nothing*, 1972; *The Tempest*, 1974.

Regional: *Eh?*, Playhouse in the Park, Cincinnati, OH, 1967; *Rosencrantz and Guildenstern are Dead*, Williamstown Theater Festival, MA, 1969; *Operation Sidewinder*, Williamstown Theater Festival, MA, 1969; *A Meeting by the River*, Mark Taper Forum, Los Angeles, CA, 1972; *Volpone*, Mark Taper Forum, Los Ange-

SAM WATERSTON

les, CA, 1972; *Uncle Vanya*, San Diego, CA, 1979; *Enemies*, Williamstown Theater Festival, MA, 1982; *Traveler in the Dark*, American Repertory Theater, 1984.

MAJOR TOURS—*Oh Dad, Poor Dad . . .*, 1963; *The Knack*, 1965.

FILM DEBUT—*The Plastic Dome of Norma Jean*, 1965. PRINCIPAL FILM APPEARANCES—*Fitzwilly*, United Artists, 1967; *Generation*, Avco Embassy, 1969; *Three*, United Artists, 1969; *Mahoney's Estate*, 1970; *Savages*, 1970; *The Great Gatsby*, Paramount, 1974; *Journey into Fear*, 1974; *Rancho Deluxe*, United Artists, 1975; *Dandy*, 1975; *Capricorn One*, Warner Brothers, 1978; *Eagles Wing*, 1978; *Sweet William*, 1978; *Interiors*, United Artists, 1979; *Hopscotch*, 1980; *Heaven's Gate*, United Artists, 1980; *The Killing Fields*, Warner Brothers, 1984; *Warning Sign*, Twentieth Century-Fox, 1985; *Hannah and Her Sisters*, Orion, 1986; *Just Between Friends*, Orion, 1986; *Something in Common* (upcoming); *Flagrant Desire* (upcoming).

TELEVISION DEBUT—Pound, *Camera Three*, CBS, 1964. PRINCIPAL TELEVISION APPEARANCES—Series: Title role, *Oppenheimer*, PBS, 1981; Quentin E. Deverill, *Q.E.D.*, CBS, 1982.

Episodic or Specials: *American One Act Plays*, 1965; *Robert Lowell*, 1966; *The Good Lieutenant*, 1967; *Much Ado About Nothing*, CBS, 1973; *The Glass Menagerie*, CBS, 1973; *Love Lives On*, 1985; *Steven Spielberg's Amazing Stories*, NBC, 1985.

Movies: *Reflections of a Murder*, 1974; *Friendly Fire*, 1979; *Games Mother Never Taught You*, 1982; *Dempsey*, 1983; *In Defense of Kids*, 1983; *Finnegan, Begin Again*, HBO, 1985; *Love Lives On*, ABC, 1985; *The Gold Crew*, 1985.

MEMBER: Actor' Equity Association, Screen Actors Guild.

AWARDS: Obie Award, Drama Desk Award, Best Actor, 1972, for *Much Ado About Nothing;* Golden Globe Award nominations (two), 1974, for *The Great Gatsby;* Golden Globe Award nomination, 1981, for *Oppenheimer*.

ADDRESSES: HOME—CT. AGENT—Gerald Siegal Public Relations, 1650 Broadway, New York, NY 10019.

*   *   *

WAXMAN, Al   1934-

PERSONAL: Born 1934, in Toronto, Canada; son of Aaron (a furrier) and Toby Waxman; married Sara Shapiro (a columnist and author), 1968; children: Toby (a daughter), Adam. EDUCATION: University of Western Ontario, B.A.; trained at the Neighborhood Playhouse, with Lee Strasberg, and at the London School of Film Technique.

VOCATION: Actor, writer, producer, and director.

CAREER: PRINCIPAL TELEVISION APPEARANCES—Series: Larry King, *King of Kensington*, CBS, 1975-80; Lt. Bert Samuels, *Cagney and Lacey*, CBS, 1982—.

Episodic: *Ben Casey*, ABC.

AL WAXMAN

Movies: *The Winnings of Frankie Walls*, CBC, 1980.

PRINCIPAL FILM WORK—Actor and producer, *Tviggy*, Columbia; writer, producer, and director, *The Crowd Inside;* director, *My Business Is My Pleasure*, 1970's; drug dealer, *Atlantic City*, Paramount, 1981; also appeared in *Class of 1984*, *Double Negative*, and *Tulips*.

PRINCIPAL STAGE APPEARANCES—With the Wimbledon Repertory Company, London, England.

RADIO DEBUT—Ogre, pirate, *Doorway to Fairyland*, Toronto, Canada.

PRINCIPAL TELEVISION WORK—Director: *Night Heat*, CBS; in Canada: *Sidestreet; Phoenix Team; Quentin Durgens; The Littlest Hobo; Danger Bay; Edison Twins.*

MEMBER: Screen Actors Guild, American Federation of Television and Radio Artists, Association of Canadian Television and Radio Artists.

AWARDS: Association of Canadian Television and Radio Artists (ACTRA) Award, Canadian Television, 1976, for *King of Kensington;* ACTRA Award, 1980, for *The Winnings of Frankie Walls;* honorary lieutenant, New York City Police Department, 1986.

ADDRESSES: PUBLICIST—Sumski, Green & Company, 8380 Melrose Avenue, Suite 200, Los Angeles, CA 90069.

WAYNE, Patrick   1939-

PERSONAL: Born July 15, 1939, in Los Angeles, CA; son of John (an actor) and Josephine (Saenz) Wayne; married Peggy Hunt, December 11, 1965 (divorced, 1978); children: Michael, Melanie, Anthony. EDUCATION: Loyola University, B.S. RELIGION: Roman Catholic. MILITARY: U.S. Coast Guard.

VOCATION: Actor.

CAREER: PRINCIPAL FILM APPEARANCES—*The Long Grey Line*, Columbia, 1955; *Mister Roberts*, Warner Brothers, 1955; *The Young Land*, Columbia, 1955; *The Searchers*, Warner Brothers, 1956; *The Alamo*, United Artists, 1960; *The Comancheros*, Twentieth Century-Fox, 1961; *McLintock!*, United Artists, 1963; *Cheyenne Autumn*, Warner Brothers, 1964; *Shenandoah*, Universal, 1965; *The Green Berets*, Warner Brothers/Seven Arts, 1968; *Big Jake*, National General, 1971; *The Deserter*, Paramount, 1971; *Beyond Atlantis*, 1973; *The Bears and I*, Buena Vista, 1974; *Mustang Country*, 1976; *The People That Time Forgot*, American International, 1977; *Sinbad and the Eye of the Tiger*, Columbia, 1977; *Texas Detour*, 1978; *Eye for an Eye*, Embassy, 1981; also appeared in *King Gun; The New Spartans*.

PRINCIPAL TELEVISION APPEARANCES—Series: Howdy Lewis, *The Rounders*, ABC, 1966-67; Lew Armitage, *Shirley*, NBC, 1979-80; host, *The Monte Carlo Show*.

PATRICK WAYNE

Episodic: *Charlie's Angels; The Love Boat; Fantasy Island; Police Woman; Marcus Welby, M.D.; Love, American Style; Twelve O'Clock High; Have Gun Will Travel; Branded; Mr. Adam and Eve; McCloud; Voyage to the Bottom of the Sea; The F.B.I.*

Movies: *Sole Survivor*, 1969; *Flight to Holocaust*, 1977; *Yesterday's Child*, 1977; *The Last Hurrah*, 1977; *Three on a Date*, 1978.

Specials: *The Grizzley Adams Special*.

Pilots: *Suzie Mahoney*, CBS.

STAGE DEBUT—Charlie Bickle, *Here Lies Jeremy Troy*, Country Dinner Playhouse, Dallas, TX, 1982, for eighty performances. PRINCIPAL STAGE APPEARANCES—*Arsenic and Old Lace*, Burt Reynolds Dinner Theatre, FL; *My Three Angels*, Fiesta Dinner Theatre, San Antonio, TX.

SIDELIGHTS: RECREATIONS—Racketball and swimming.

ADDRESSES: HOME—Toluca Lake, CA. OFFICE—9570 Wilshire Blvd., Suite 400, Beverly Hills, CA 90212. AGENT—c/o David Shapira, 15301 Ventura Blvd., Suite 345, Los Angeles, CA 91403.

*   *   *

WEAVER, Dennis   1924-

PERSONAL: Born June 4, 1924, in Joplin, MO; son of Walter and Lenna Weaver; married Gerry Stowell, October 20, 1945; children: Rick, Robby, Rusty. EDUCATION: Joplin Junior College, one year; University of Oklahoma, B.F.A., 1948; studied acting at the Actors Studio in New York, 1949-50. MILITARY: U.S. Naval Reserve, Air Corp. RELIGION: Lay minister, Self-Realization Fellowship Church.

VOCATION: Actor.

CAREER: PRINCIPAL FILM APPEARANCES—*Dragnet*, 1954; *The Bridges at Toko-Ri*, Paramount, 1955; *Ten Wanted Men*, Columbia, 1955; *Seven Angry Men*, Allied Artists, 1955; *The Gallant Hours*, United Artists, 1960; *Touch of Evil*, Universal, 1960; *Duel at Diablo*, United Artists, 1966; *Way, Way Out*, Twentieth Century-Fox, 1966; *Gentle Giant*, Paramount, 1967; *A Man Called Sledge*, Columbia, 1971; *What's the Matter with Helen?*, United Artists, 1971; *Batangas*.

PRINCIPAL TELEVISION APPEARANCES—Series: Chester Goode, *Gunsmoke*, CBS, 1955-64; title role, *Kentucky Jones*, NBC, 1964-65; Tom Wedloe, *Gentle Ben*, CBS, 1967-69; title role, *McCloud*, NBC, 1970-77; Detective Sargent Daniel Stone, *Stone*, ABC, 1979-80; Rear Admiral Thomas Mallory, *Emerald Point, N.A.S.*, CBS, 1983-84; also host, *Country Top 20*.

Movies: *The Great Man's Whiskers*, Universal, NBC, 1969; *Duel*, 1971; *McCloud*, 1971; *Forgotten Man*, 1971; *Rolling Man*, 1973; *Terror on the Beach*, 1973; *Female Artillery*, 1973; *Intimate Strangers*, 1977; *Pearl*, ABC, 1978; *Ishi: The Last of His Tribe*, NBC, 1978; *The Islander*, CBS, 1978; *Amber Waves*, ABC, 1979; *The Ordeal of Patty Hearst*, 1979; *The Ordeal of Dr. Mudd*, 1979; *The Day the Loving Stopped*, ABC, 1981; *Cocaine: One Man's Seduction*, 1983; *Going for the Gold: The Bill Johnson Story*, CBS, 1985; Wyshner, *A Winner Never Quits*, ABC, 1986.

DENNIS WEAVER

Episodic: "Dungeon," *Playhouse 90;* "Burst of Fire" *Climax;* "The Price Is Wrong," *Police Story,* NBC, 1977.

Mini-Series: R. J. Poteet, "The Longhorns," *Centennial,* NBC, 1978.

Guest: *National Academy of Television Arts and Sciences, Emmy Awards Presentations,* 1958; *Hee-Haw; The Flip Wilson Show; The Sonny & Cher Comedy Hour; The Cher Show; The Big Event; A Country Christmas,* CBS; *The Tonight Show,* NBC; *Dinah Shore Show; Tony Tenille Show; American Bag; 50 Years of Country Gold; New Country from Old Country; Dean Martin's Roast.*

PRINCIPAL STAGE APPEARANCES—*Come Back Little Sheba,* Broadway production, 1950; Stanley Kowalski, *A Streetcar Named Desire,* Circle Theatre, Los Angeles, CA; also appeared in *The Big Knife, Stalag 17, The Glass Menagerie, The Ticklish Acrobat,* in Los Angeles, on off-Broadway, or in summer stock.

MAJOR TOURS—*Come Back Little Sheba,* National tour, 1951.

CONCERT APPEARANCES—"An Evening with Dennis Weaver & Family."

RELATED CAREER—Formed music publishing company, Rajamaya Music; organized the Dennis Weaver Actor's Workshop, served as director of the Workshop and directed *Quadrivium,* which played at the Hollywood Repertory Theatre in Los Angeles.

WRITINGS: SONGS—Wrote country songs for his own recording label (Jeremiah) and for Christy Lane (former country music New Female Artist of the Year).

TELEVISION—Wrote scenes and songs for *Amber Waves,* ABC, 1979.

RECORDINGS: ALBUMS—*Calhoun; The World Needs Country Music,* Jeremiah label.

MEMBER: Screen Actors Guild (president, 1973-74), American Federation of Radio and Television Artists, Actors' Equity Association, Directors Guild of America; founder and president, L.I.F.E. (Love Is Feeding Everyone), food distribution program.

AWARDS: Best Supporting Actor, Emmy, 1958-59, for Chester, *Gunsmoke,* CBS; inducted into the Cowboy Hall of Fame, for professional film and television work, 1981; also Most Versatile Man (athletic honor), University of Oklahoma.

SIDELIGHTS: From his publicity release, *CTFT* learned that leaving the series *Gunsmoke,* was one of the biggest decisions of Dennis Weaver's career, "I wanted to grow as an actor, to create, to expand. From the standpoint of money and security it could not be beat. But money should be a means rather than an end. In addition, I just couldn't make one character my whole life's work." Weaver also states that his most challenging role to date was his performance in *Cocaine: One Man's Seduction.*

ADDRESSES: HOME—Calabasas Park, CA. AGENT—Reflections, Inc., 8961 Sunset Blvd., Suite D, Second Floor, Los Angeles, CA 90069.

*   *   *

WEAVER, Sigourney   1949-

PERSONAL: Born 1949, in New York, NY; daughter of Sylvester "Pat" (former president of NBC) and Elizabeth (an actress; maiden name, Inglish) Weaver. EDUCATION: Attended Stanford University; Yale University School of Drama.

CAREER: STAGE DEBUT—*The Constant Wife,* 1974. PRINCIPAL STAGE APPEARANCES—*Titanic,* 1976; *Das Lusitania Songspiel;* Prudence, *Beyond Therapy,* Phoenix Theatre, 1981; Darlene, *Hurlyburly,* Goodman Theatre, Chicago, IL, 1984, Promenade Theatre, NY, then Ethel Barrymore Theatre, NY, 1984; *The Marriage of Bette and Boo,* New York Shakespeare Festival, Public Theatre, 1985.

FILM DEBUT—*Alien,* Twentieth Century-Fox, 1979. PRINCIPAL FILM APPEARANCES—*Eyewitness,* Twentieth Century-Fox, 1981; *The Year of Living Dangerously,* Metro-Goldwyn-Mayer/United Artists, 1983; *Deal of the Century,* Warner Brothers, 1983; *Ghostbusters,* Columbia, 1984; *A Woman or Two,* 1986; *Aliens,* 1986.

MEMBER: Actors' Equity Association, Screen Actors Guild.

AWARDS: Best Supporting Actress, Academy Award nomination, 1984, for *Ghostbusters.*

*ADDRESSES:*HOME—New York, NY. AGENT—International Creative Management, 40 W. 57th Street, New York, NY 10019.*

WEBER, Carl   1925-

PERSONAL: Born August 7, 1925, in Dortmund, Germany; son of Carl M. (a manufacturer) and Hedwig (Graeve) Weber; married Marianne Rossi (an actress), November 29, 1961. EDUCATION: Attended Heidelberg University.

VOCATION: Director, writer, and teacher.

CAREER: STAGE DEBUT—Feste, *Twelfth Night,* Stadttheater, Heidelberg, Germany, 1949. FIRST NEW YORK STAGE WORK—Director, *Cyrano de Bergerac,* Repertory Theatre of Lincoln Center, 1968. FIRST LONDON STAGE WORK—Young Man, *Mother Courage,* Palace Theatre, 1956. PRINCIPAL STAGE WORK—Director: *The Day of the Great Scholar Wu,* Berliner Ensemble, Germany, 1955; *Private Life of the Master Race,* Berliner Ensemble, 1957.

Die Hose, Deutsches, Berlin, 1961; *Threepenny Opera,* Aarhus, Denmark, 1963; *Mother Courage,* Luebeck, 1960; *Caucasian Chalk Circle,* Actors Workshop, San Francisco, CA, 1963; *Country Wife,* Front Street Theatre, Memphis, TN, 1964; *Chicken Soup with Barley,* Schaubuehne, Berlin, 1966; *The Birdlovers,* National Theatre, Oslo, Norway, 1966; *A Man Is a Man,* Aalborg, Denmark, 1967; *Enrico IV,* Yale Repertory, New Haven, CT, 1968; *Caucasian Chalk Circle,* Asian Theatre Institute, New Delhi, India, 1968; *The Miser,* Repertory Theatre of Lincoln Center, NY, 1968.

Naechtliche Huldigung, Schauspielhaus Zuerich, Switzerland, 1970; *Die Hose,* Schauspeilhaus, Hamburg, 1970; *Soldaten,* Kammerspiele, Munich, 1970; *Ride Across Lake Constance,* Repertory Theatre of Lincoln Center, NY, 1972; *Kaspar* and *The Waterhen,* Brooklyn Academy of Music, NY, 1973; *The Entertainer,* McCarter Theatre, Princeton, NJ, 1973; *The Resistible Rise of Arturo Ui,* Arena Stage, Washington, DC, 1974; *Julius Caesar,* Arena, Washington, DC, 1975; *JoAnne,* Theatre at Riverside Church, NY, 1976; *Lincoln,* Brooklyn Academy of Music, NY, 1976; *Heaven and Earth,* Off-Center Theatre, NY, 1977; *Scenes from Country Life,* Perry Street Theatre, NY, 1978; *Starluster,* American Place Theatre, NY, 1979; *They Are Dying Out,* Yale Repertory, New Haven, CT, 1979.

Fueherbunker, American Place Theatre, NY, 1981; *The Broken Pitcher,* Martinique Theatre, NY, 1981; *The Resistible Rise of Arturo Ui,* Bad Staattestheater, Karlsruhe, 1982; *Happy End,* New York University Second Avenue Theatre, NY, 1984; *Arden of Faversham,* Little Theatre, Stanford, CA, 1986.

MAJOR TOUR WORK—Assistant director, Berliner Ensemble: Poland, 1952, Paris, 1954, 1958, London, 1956, Moscow, Leningrad, 1957, Prague, 1958, Stockholm, Helsinki, 1959.

FIRST TELEVISION WORK—Director, *Laughter in Mexico,* Fernsehfunk, Berlin, 1957. PRINCIPAL TELEVISION WORK—Director, *The Countess,* Fernsehfunk, Berlin; writer, narrator, ''Brecht and Handke,'' *Camera Three,* CBS.

RELATED CAREER—Master teacher of directing, Tisch School of the Arts, NY, 1966-84; visiting professor and director: Carnegie Mellon University, Pittsburgh, PA, 1961, Stanford University, 1963-64, University of California, 1966, Canadian National Theatre School, Montreal, 1965, Temple Universtiy, 1981, professor of drama, Stanford University, CA, 1984.

WRITINGS: PLAYS, PRODUCED—(With Peter Palitzsuh) *The Day of the Great Scholar Wu,* Berliner Ensemble, Germany, 1955.

BOOKS—Editor and translator, *Hamletmachine and Other Texts for the Stage,* by Heiner Muller, Performing Arts Journal Publications, 1984.

MEMBER: Society of Stage Directors and Choreographers (board of directors, 1980—), International Brecht Society.

AWARDS: Obie Award, 1973, for *Kaspar.*

ADDRESSES: OFFICE—Department of Drama, Stanford University, Stanford, CA, 94305. AGENT—c/o Howard Rosenstone, Three E. 48th Street, New York, NY 10017.

*   *   *

WEITZENHOFFER, Max   1939-

PERSONAL: Born October 30, 1939, in Oklahoma City, OK; son of Aaron M. and Clara (Rosenthal) Weitzenhoffer; married Fran (an art historian). EDUCATION: Oklahoma State University, B.F.A., 1963.

MAX WEITZENHOFFER

VOCATION: Producer.

CAREER: PRINCIPAL STAGE WORK—Co-producer: *Going Up,* John Golden Theatre, NY, 1976; *Dracula,* Martin Beck Theatre, 1977; *Harold and Maude,* Martin Beck Theatre, 1980; *Pump Boys and Dinettes,* Princess Theatre, NY, 1982; *The Good Parts,* Astor Place Theatre, NY, 1982; *Three Guys Naked from the Waist Down,* Minetta Lane Theatre, NY, 1985; *Blood Knot,* John Golden Theatre, 1985-86; *Song and Dance,* Royal Theatre, NY, 1985—; was also associated with *Sleuth, Equus; The Elephant Man; Rose; Timbuktu!; Mass Appeal; Passion; Bedroom Farce; Piaf; Tickles by Tucholsky.*

RELATED CAREER—General manager, La Jolla Playhouse, CA, 1963-67.

MEMBER: League of American Producers and Theatre Owners, Circle Repertory Theatre (board of directors), Actors' Equity Association, Players Club.

ADDRESSES: OFFICE—1040 Madison Avenue, New York, NY 10021.

*　　*　　*

WELCH, Raquel 1940-

PERSONAL: Born Raquel Tejada, September 5, 1940, in Chicago, IL; daughter of Armand and Josepha (Hall) Tejada; married James Westley Welch, May 8, 1959 (divorced); married Patrick Curtis (divorced); married Andre Weinfeld, (producer and director), July, 1980; children: (first marriage) Damon, Tahnee. EDUCATION: Attended San Diego State College.

VOCATION: Actress, singer, producer, and writer.

CAREER: PRINCIPAL STAGE APPEARANCES—*Woman of the Year,* Palace Theatre, NY, 1981.

CABARET—*Raquel Welch: Live in Concert,* Sands Hotel, Atlantic City, NJ, 1985, tour of U.S. and Europe, 1985-86.

FILM DEBUT—*A Swingin' Summer,* United Screen Artists, 1963. PRINCIPAL FILM APPEARANCES—*Roustabout,* Paramount, 1964; *A House Is Not a Home,* Embassy, 1964; *Fantastic Voyage,* Twentieth Century-Fox, 1966; *Shoot Louder . . . I Don't Understand,* Italian, 1966; *One Million Years B.C.,* Twentieth Century-Fox, 1967; *Fathom,* Twentieth Century-Fox, 1967; *Bedazzaled,* Twentieth Century-Fox, 1967; *The Biggest Bundle of Them All,* Metro-Goldwyn-Mayer, 1968; *The Queens,* Royal, 1968; *Bandolero,* Twentieth Century-Fox, 1968; *Lady in Cement,* Twentieth Century-Fox, 1968; *100 Rifles,* Twentieth Century-Fox, 1969; *Flare Up,* Metro-Goldwyn-Mayer, 1969.

The Magic Christian, Commonwealth United, 1970; *Myra Breckinridge,* Twentieth Century-Fox, 1970; *Hannie Caulder,* British, 1972; *Kansas City Bomber,* Metro-Goldwyn-Mayer, 1972; *Fuzz,* United Artists, 1972; *The Last of Sheila,* 1973; *The Three Musketeers,* Twentieth Century-Fox, 1974; *The Four Musketeers,* Twentieth Century-Fox, 1974; *The Wild Party,* American Interna-

RAQUEL WELCH

Photograph by Andre Weinfeld

tional, 1975; *Mother, Jugs, and Speed,* 1976; *Crossed Swords,* Warner Brothers, 1978; *Story of Walks Far Woman,* 1981.

RELATED CAREER—Owner, producer, Raquel Welch Productions, Inc.

PRINCIPAL TELEVISION APPEARANCES—Guest: Billboard girl, *The Hollywood Palace,* ABC, 1964; *The Muppet Show,* syndication, 1979.

WRITINGS: BOOKS—*Raquel: The Raquel Welch Total Beauty and Fitness Program,* Fawcett/Columbine, 1986.

MEMBER: Actors' Equity Association, Screen Actors Guild.

AWARDS: Golden Globe, 1974, for *The Three Musketeers.*

SIDELIGHTS: From Raquel Welch's publicity releases, *CTFT* learns that she is planning to record an album of her show *Raquel: Live in Concert,* this year. She is now writing film treatments and stories for her own production company which plans to produce her adaptation of *Forever Amber* with Twentieth Century-Fox.

ADDRESSES: OFFICE—Raquel Welch Productions, 146 Central Park West, New York, NY 10023.

WELD, Tuesday 1943-

PERSONAL: Born Susan Ker Weld, August 27, 1943, in New York, NY; daughter of Lathrop Motley and Aileen (Ker) Weld; married Claude Harz, October, 1965 (divorced, 1971); married Dudley Moore (an actor), September 20, 1975 (divorced); children: (first marriage) Natasha; (second marriage) Patrick. EDUCATION: Attended Hollywood Professional School.

VOCATION: Actress.

CAREER: PRINCIPAL TELEVISION APPEARANCES—Series: Thalia Menninger, *The Many Loves of Dobie Gillis,* CBS, 1959-60.

Movies: *Reflections of a Murder,* 1974; Zelda Fitzgerald, *F. Scott Fitzgerald in Hollywood,* 1976; *Winter of Our Discontent,* 1983; *Scorned and Swindled,* CBS, 1984; Also, *The Crucible.*

Episodic: *Cimarron Strip,* CBS; *Playhouse 90,* CBS; *Kraft Theatre,* NBC; *Alcoa Theatre,* ABC; *Climax,* CBS; *Ozzie and Harriet,* ABC; *77 Sunset Strip,* ABC; *The Millionaire,* CBS; *Tab Hunter Show,* NBC; *Zane Grey Theatre,* CBS; *Follow the Sun,* ABC; *Bus Stop,* ABC; *The Dick Powell Show,* NBC; *Adventures in Paradise,* ABC; *Naked City,* ABC; *Eleventh Hour,* NBC; *DuPont Show of the Month,* ABC; *The Greatest Show on Earth,* ABC; *Mr. Broadway,* CBS; *The Fugitive,* ABC.

FILM DEBUT—*Rock, Rock, Rock,* 1956. PRINCIPAL FILM APPEARANCES—*Rally Round the Flag Boys!,* Twentieth Century-Fox, 1959; *The Five Pennies,* Columbia, 1959; *The Private Lives of Adam and Eve,* Universal, 1960; *Because They're Young,* Columbia, 1960; *High Time,* Twentieth Century-Fox, 1960; *Sex Kittens Go to College,* Allied Artists, 1960; *Return to Peyton Place,* Twentieth Century-Fox, 1961; *Wild in the Country,* Twentieth Century-Fox, 1961; *Bachelor Flat,* Twentieth Century-Fox, 1961; *Soldier in the Rain,* Allied Artists, 1963; *The Cincinnati Kid,* Metro-Goldwyn-Mayer, 1965; *I'll Take Sweden,* United Artists, 1965; *Lord Love a Duck,* United Artists, 1966; *Pretty Poison,* Twentieth Century-Fox, 1968.

I Walk the Line, Columbia, 1970; *A Safe Place,* Columbia 1971; *Play It as It Lays,* Universal, 1972; *Who'll Stop the Rain,* United Artists, 1978; *Looking for Mr. Goodbar,* Paramount, 1977; *Serial,* Paramount, 1980; *Thief,* United Artists, 1981; *Author! Author!,* Twentieth Century-Fox, 1982; *Once Upon a Time in America,* Warner Brothers, 1984.*

*   *   *

WELLES, Orson 1915-1985

PERSONAL: Full name, George Orson Welles; born May 6, 1915, in Kenosha, WI; died of an apparent heart attack in Hollywood, CA, on October 10, 1985; son of Richard Head (an inventor and manufacturer) and Beatrice (a concert pianist; maiden name, Ives) Welles; married Virginia Nicholson (an actress), December 20, 1934 (divorced, 1940); married Rita Hayworth (an actress), September 7, 1942 (divorced); married Countess Paola Mori Girlalco (an actress), May 8, 1955; children: (first marriage) Christopher (a daughter); (second marriage) Rebecca; (third marriage) Beatrice. EDUCATION: Graduated from the progressive Todd School for Boys, Woodstock, IL.

VOCATION: Director, actor, and writer.

CAREER: PRINCIPAL FILM WORK—Producer, director, writer, and portrayed Charles Foster Kane, *Citizen Kane,* RKO, 1941; producer, director, and writer, *The Magnificent Ambersons,* RKO, 1942; producer, writer, and portrayed Colonel Haki, *Journey into Fear,* RKO, 1943; uncredited director and portrayed Cagliostro, *Black Magic,* 1944; director and actor, *The Stranger,* 1946; director, producer, and played title role, *Macbeth,* Republic, 1948; director, *The Lady from Shanghai,* 1948; producer, director, writer, and played title role, *Othello,* Universal, 1955; director and played title role, *Mr. Arkadin* (retitled *The Confidential Report*), British, 1955; director, writer, and actor, *Touch of Evil,* Universal, 1958; producer, director, and writer, *The Trial,* 1963.

FILM DEBUT—*The Hearts of Age,* 1934. PRINCIPAL FILM APPEARANCES—(In addition to above) Rochester, *Jane Eyre,* Twentieth Century-Fox, 1944; the Great Orsino, *Follow the Boys,* Metro-Goldwyn-Mayer, 1944; *Tomorrow Is Forever,* 1946; Harry Lime, *The Third Man,* 1949; Cesare Borgia, *Prince of Foxes,* 1949; Khan, *The Black Rose,* 1950; *Trent's Last Case,* 1952; Napoleon, 1952; *Trouble in the Glen,* 1953; *Three Cases of Murder,* Associate Artists, 1955; Father Mapple, *Moby Dick,* Warner Brothers, 1956; *The Long Hot Summer,* Twentieth Century-Fox, 1958; *The Roots of Heaven,* Twentieth Century-Fox, 1958; Clarence Darrow, *Compulsion,* Twentieth Century-Fox, 1959; King Saul, *David and Goliath,* Allied Artists, 1961; *Ferry to Hong Kong,* Twentieth Century-Fox, 1961; Robert Fulton, *Austerlitz,* 1961; *The Tartars,* Metro-Goldwyn-Mayer, 1962; *The VIPs,* Metro-Goldwyn-Mayer, 1963; *Lafayette,* Maco, 1964; *Is Paris Burning,* Paramount, 1966; Cardinal Wolsey, *A Man for All Seasons,* Columbia, 1966; *Tepepa,* 1966; Falstaff, *Chimes at Midnight,* 1966; *Casino Royale,* Columbia, 1967; *The Sailor from Gibralter,* Lopert, 1967; *Oedipus the King,* Universal, 1968; *I'll Never Forget Whats'is Name,* Regional, 1968; Mr. Clay, *The Immortal Story,* Altura Films, 1969; *House of Cards,* Universal, 1969; *The Southern Star,* Columbia, 1969.

Start the Revolution without Me, Warner Brothers, 1970; *The Kremlin Letter,* Twentieth Century-Fox, 1970; *Catch-22,* Paramount, 1970; *The Battle of Nerveta,* American International, 1971; *Waterloo,* Paramount, 1971; *A Safe Place,* Columbia, 1971; *Malpertius,* 1971; *Necromancy,* Cinerama, 1972; *Ten Days Wonder,* Levitt-Pickman, 1972; co-writer and played Long John Silver, *Treasure Island,* National General, 1972; *Get to Know Your Rabbit,* Warner Brothers, 1972; *F for Fake,* 1973; *Voyage of the Damned,* Avco Embassy, 1977; *Filming Othello,* 1978; *The Muppet Movie,* Associated, 1979; J.P. Morgan, *Nikola Tesla,* 1979; *Going for Broke,* 1980; *Butterfly,* 1981; also *Where Is Parsifal; Man Who Saw Tomorrow; Is It You?*

Narrator: *Duel in the Sun,* 1946; *King of Kings,* Metro-Goldwyn-Mayer, 1961; *Bugs Bunny Superstar; The Late Great Planet Earth; Genocide.*

Unfinished films: *Too Much Johnson,* Mercury, 1938; *Don Quixote,* 1950; *The Deep,* 1967; *The Other Side of the Wind,* 1970; *The Making of "The Trial,"* 1981; *King Lear; It's All True; The Dreamers; The Big Brass Ring; The Cradle Will Rock.*

STAGE DEBUT—*Jew Suss,* Dublin Gate, Ireland, 1931. PRINCIPAL STAGE APPEARANCES—(In addition to those listed below with director and producer credits) Mercutio, *Romeo and Juliet,* 1933; *Five Kings,* 1939; *The Unthinking Lobster,* 1950; *King Lear,* 1956; also: *The Barretts of Wimpole Street; Candida; Panic; Ten Million Ghosts; Time Runs.*

PRINCIPAL STAGE WORK—Producer (with John Houseman): *Macbeth*, Lafayette Theater, Harlem, NY, 1936; *Horse Eats Hat*, Maxine Elliott Theater, NY, 1936.

Producer and actor, with the Mercury Theatre, 1937-38: *Julius Caesar, The Shoemaker's Holiday*, as Captain Shotover in *Heartbreak House; Too Much Johnson; Danton's Death*.

Director: *The Second Hurricane; The Cradle Will Rock*, 1937; *Native Son; Around the World in 80 Days*, 1946; *The Lady in Ice; Rhinoceros*, London, 1960.

Director and actor: *Doctor Faustus*, 1937; *Mercury Wonder Show; Othello; Moby Dick*, 1955; *Moby Dick Rehearsed; Chimes at Midnight*, Ireland, 1960.

MAJOR TOURS—*Mercury Wonder Show*, 1943.

PRINCIPAL RADIO WORK—Narrator, *The Shadow*, 1935; producer, director, actor, and narrator, "The War of the Worlds," *Mercury Theatre on the Air*, 1938; producer, director, actor, and narrator, *Hello Americans;* writer, *The Free Company Presents . . . His Honor, the Mayor*, CBS, April 6, 1941; also, narrator, *March of Time*, NBC; *The Orson Welles Show; Suspense; Cavalcade of America; Streamlined Shakespeare; America's Hour; First Person Singular; Campbell Playhouse; Five Kings*.

PRINCIPAL TELEVISION APPEARANCES—Series: *The Orson Welles Sketchbook*, BBC; *Around the World with Orson Welles*, BBC; *Orson Welles Great Mysteries;* director and actor, *The Orson Welles Show; Marty Feldman Comedy Machine*, ABC, 1972; host, *Scene of the Crime*, 1984; voice of Robin Masters, *Magnum P. I.*, CBS, 1981-85.

Episodic and Specials: "King Lear," *Omnibus*, CBS, 1953; as himself, *I Love Lucy;* "Twentieth Century," *Ford Star Jubilee*, CBS, 1956; writer, director, and narrator, "The Fountain of Youth," *Colgate Theatre*, CBS, 1958; *The Man Who Came to Dinner*, 1973; "Magnificent Monsters of the Deep," *Survival-Anglia, Ltd.*, NBC, 1976; *Moonlighting*, ABC, 1985.

Movies: *It Happened One Christmas*, 1977.

WRITINGS: SCREENPLAYS—(In addition to film work mentioned above) *Monsieur Verdoux*, United Artists, 1947.

PLAYS—(In addition to plays mentioned above) Author of libretto for the ballet *The Lady in Ice*, 1953; also: *Marching Song; Bright Lucifer*.

BOOKS—Compiler, *Invasion from Mars, Interplanetary Stories: Thrilling Adventures in Space*, Dell, 1949; (with others) *The Lives of Harry Lime*, News of the World, 1952; *Mr. Arkadin*, Crowell, 1956.

OTHER—Co-Author and narrator of adaptions of novels for radio and recordings. Author of column "Orson Welles' Almanac," for the *New York Post*, 1945.

RECORDINGS: Satirical Political Recordings, 1972.

AWARDS: Claire M. Senie Plaque from the Drama Study Club, 1938; (co-winner with Herman Mankiewicz), Academy Award, Best Screenplay, 1941, for *Citizen Kane;* Golden Palm Award, Cannes Film Festival Award, 1956, for *Othello;* Grand Prize,

Brussels Film Festival, 1958, for *Touch of Evil*, co-winner, Best Actor, Cannes Film Festival, 1959, for *Compulsion; Citizen Kane* chosen as "best film in motion picture history" by international film critics in polls taken in 1962 and 1972; Twentieth Anniversary Special Prize from the Cannes Film Festival, 1966 for *Chimes at Midnight;* Honorary Academy Award, 1970; Grammy Award, 1972, for *Satirical Political Recordings;* Life Achievement Award, American Film Institute, 1974; Legion of Honor Award, France, 1982; D.W. Griffith Award, Directors Guild of America, 1984.

SIDELIGHTS: The critically acclaimed director, writer, and actor Orson Welles was a child prodigy who wrote poetry, painted, studied the violin, put on Shakespearean plays, and played Madama Butterfly's child at the Chicago opera—all before he was ten.

Welles toured Ireland after his high school graduation and while there became a member of the Gate Players troupe for a short period of time. From Ireland he travelled to Morocco, where he spent time polishing scripts and stories he had written. Soon afterwards, he returned to America and burst onto the New York theatrical scene in his early twenties with such unorthodox productions as his so-called "voodoo Macbeth," set in Haiti and using an all-black cast, and a modern-dress version of *Julius Caesar*, which he turned into a parable against Fascism. When the WPA's Federal Theatre Project, for whom Welles had worked up to that point, banned his production of Marc Blitzstein's leftist musical drama *The Cradle Will Rock* and locked the cast out of the theatre, he and his associate John Houseman rented a theatre of their own, where the actors, prohibited by Equity from performing the work on stage, read it from the audience. Welles and Houseman then formed their own company, the Mercury Theatre.

In addition to stage work, the Mercury Theatre also presented radio programs. On Halloween Eve, 1938, Welles' radio dramatization of the Mercury Theatre's *The War of the Worlds* caused a nationwide panic. Done as a fake new broadcast, the show was so realistic that many listeners thought New Jersey had really been invaded by Martians.

After a disastrous attempt to produce his play, *Five Kings*, Welles moved the Mercury Theatre to Hollywood to try his hand at the movie industry. Welles' first film, *Citizen Kane*, "is now fabled," according to his *New York Times* obituary, "for its use of flashback, deep-focus photography, sets with ceilings, striking camera angles, and imaginative sounds and cutting." International critics' polls conducted in 1962, 1972, and 1982 by the British magazine *Sight and Sound* selected *Kane* as the greatest film of all time. Ironically, it was a commercial flop in its first release, largely because of pressure from publisher William Randolph Hearst, on whom the title character was in large part based. Such was Hearst's influence on the public that bad reviews of *Kane* in his newspapers kept moviegoers away from the film. "Rosebud," the title character's dying words in the film and the name of his boyhood sled, has become a household word (the original sled was purchased at auction for $61,000 by director Steven Spielberg).

Even though his next film, *The Magnificent Ambersons*, which he wrote, produced, and directed, was cut heavily by the studio (RKO) over Welles' objections, it, too, is now ranked among the great works of cinema history. Among his later films, *Touch of Evil*, released in 1958, and *Chimes at Midnight*, 1966, in particular, are regarded as masterpieces, but Welles' directorial career after *Kane* and *Ambersons* was marred by an inability to get financial backing because of his reputation of a perfectionist (although he remained in great demand as an actor). Some of his most ambitious film projects were never made or, like his version of *Don Quixote,* begun but never completed.*

*   *   *

WHELCHEL, Lisa

PERSONAL: Born in Fort Worth, TX; daughter of Jenny French.

VOCATION: Actress.

CAREER: PRINCIPAL TELEVISION APPEARANCES—Series: Blair Warner, *Facts of Life,* NBC, 1979—.

Episodic: *Family,* ABC; *The Mary Tyler Moore Show,* CBS; *The Love Boat,* ABC; *Diff'rent Strokes,* NBC.

Movies: *Skyward,* 1980; *Twirl,* 1981.

PRINCIPAL FILM APPEARANCES—*The Magician of Lublin,* 1979; *The Double McGuffin,* 1979.

RECORDINGS: ALBUM—*All Because of You,* Nissi, 1986.

LISA WHELCHEL

ADDRESSES: PUBLICIST—Michael Levine, 967 N. La Cienega Blvd., Los Angeles, CA 90069.

*   *   *

WHITE, Betty   1924-

PERSONAL: Born January 17, 1924, in Oak Park, IL; married Allen Ludden, 1963 (deceased).

VOCATION: Actress.

CAREER: PRINCIPAL TELEVISION APPEARANCES—Series: Elizabeth, *Life with Elizabeth,* syndication, 1953-55; Vicki Angel, *Date with the Angels,* ABC, 1957-58; *The Betty White Show,* 1958; regular, *The Jack Parr Show,* 1959-62; Sue Ann Nivens, *The Mary Tyler Moore Show,* CBS, 1973-77; Joyce Whitman, *The Betty White Show,* CBS, 1977-78; hostess, *Just Men,* syndication, 1982; Ellen Jackson, *Mama's Family,* NBC, 1983-84; Rose, *The Golden Girls,* NBC, 1985—.

Guest: Panelist, *Make the Connection,* NBC, 1955; panelist, *Match Game P.M.,* syndicated, 1975; panelist, *Liars Club,* syndicated, 1976-78; *The Peter Marshall Variety Show,* 1976; also, *Hollywood on Television; The Carol Burnett Show.*

Mini-Series: *The Best Place to Be,* 1979; *The Gossip Columnist,* 1980.

PRINCIPAL FILM APPEARANCES—*Advise and Consent,* Columbia, 1962.

PRINCIPAL STAGE APPEARANCES—Summer stock: *Guys and Dolls; Take Me Along; The King and I; Who Was That Lady?; Critics Choice; Bells Are Ringing; Hello, Dolly!*

MEMBER: American Federation of Television and Radio Artists; American Humane Association, Greater Los Angeles Zoo Association; Morris Animal Foundation (president emeritus).

AWARDS: Los Angeles Area Emmy, 1952; Outstanding Continuing Performance by a Supporting Actress in a Comedy Series, Emmy awards, 1975 and 1976, for *The Mary Tyler Moore Show;* Daytime Emmy, 1982, for *Just Men.*

SIDELIGHTS: Betty White began her career on radio appearing in *The FBI, The Great Gildersleeve,* and *Blondie.*

ADDRESSES: AGENT—William Morris Agency, 151 El Camino Drive, Beverly Hills, CA 90212.

*   *   *

WIDDOES, James   1953-

PERSONAL: Born November 15, 1953, in Pittsburgh, PA; son of William Pierce (a real estate salesman) and Barbara (an arts administrator; maiden name, Landauer) Widdoes; married Brooks Hendrie (a retailer), December 29, 1979; children: Charles Landauer, Sumner Dickinson. EDUCATION: New York University School of the Arts, B.F.A., 1976.

JAMES WIDDOES

WIDMARK, Richard   1914-

PERSONAL: Born December 26, 1914, in Sunrise, MN; son of Carl H. and Ethel Mae (Barr) Widmark; married Ora Jane Hazlewood, April 5, 1942; children: Ann. EDUCATION: Lake Forest College, B.A., 1938.

VOCATION: Actor.

CAREER: PRINCIPAL STAGE APPEARANCES—*Kiss and Tell*, Broadway, 1943; *Get Away Old Man*, Broadway, 1943; *Trio*, Broadway, 1944; *Kiss Them for Me*, Broadway, 1944; *Dunnigan's Daughter*, Broadway, 1945; *Dream Girl*, Broadway, 1946-47. In summer stock: *The Bo Tree*, 1939; *Joan of Lorraine*, 1947.

PRINCIPAL FILM APPEARANCES—*Kiss of Death*, 1947; *Street with No Name*, 1948; *Yellow Sky*, 1948; *Roadhouse*, 1948; *Cry of the City*, 1948; *Down to the Sea in Ships*, 1949; *Night in the City*, 1949; *No Way Out*, 1949; *Slattery's Hurricane*, 1949.

Panic in the Streets, Twentieth Century-Fox, 1950; *Halls of Montezuma*, 1950; *The Frogman*, 1950; *Red Skies of Montana*, 1952; *Don't Bother to Knock*, 1952; *O. Henry's Full House*, 1952; *My Pal Gus*, 1952; *Destination Gobi*, 1953; *Pickup on South Street*, 1953; *Take the High Ground*, 1953; *Hell and High Water*, 1954; *Broken Lance*, 1954; *Prize of Gold*, 1955; *The Cobweb*, 1955; *Backlash*, 1956; *The Last Wagon*, 1956; *Run for the Sun*, United Artists, 1956; *Saint Joan*, United Artists, 1957; *Warlock*, Twentieth Century-Fox, 1959; *Kingdom of Man*, 1959.

VOCATION: Actor.

CAREER: TELEVISION DEBUT—Hoover, *Delta House*, ABC, 1979. PRINCIPAL TELEVISION APPEARANCES—Series: Brad Lincoln, *Park Place*, CBS, 1980-81; Stan Pembroke, *Charles in Charge*, CBS, 1984-85.

Episodic: *Remington Steel*, NBC, 1983; *Simon and Simon*, CBS, 1985; *George Burns' Comedy Week*, CBS, 1985; *My Town*, ABC, 1985.

Pilots: *Back Together*, CBS, 1983.

FILM DEBUT—Hoover, *National Lampoon's Animal House*, Universal 1977.

STAGE DEBUT—*The New Amen Show*, Diners Playhouse, Lexington, KY, 1974, for forth-eight performances. NEW YORK DEBUT— Frank Lippencott, *Wonderful Town*, Equity Library Theatre, 1977, for over fifty performances. PRINCIPAL STAGE APPEARANCES— Mike Conner, *The Philadelphia Story*, Megaw Theatre, Los Angeles, CA, 1980; Charlie, *Charlie's Aunt*, La Mirada Civic Theatre, Los Angeles, CA, 1982; *Is There Life After High School?*, Barrymore Theatre, NY, 1982.

AWARDS: Theatre World Award, 1983, for *Is There Life After High School?*

ADDRESSES: AGENT—c/o Phyllis Carlyle, Abrams Artists and Associates, Ltd., 420 Madison Avenue, New York, NY 10017.

RICHARD WIDMARK

The Alamo, United Artists, 1960; *Judgement at Nuremberg,* United Artists, 1961; *How the West Was Won,* Metro-Goldwyn-Mayer, 1962; *Cheyenne Autumn,* 1963; *Bedford Incident,* 1964; *The Long Ships,* Columbia, 1964; *Alvarez Kelly,* 1965; *The Way West,* United Artists, 1967; *Madigan,* Universal, 1968; *Patch,* 1968; *The Moonshine War,* 1969; *Death of a Gunfighter,* Universal, 1969.

When the Legends Die, Twentieth Century-Fox, 1972; *Murder on the Orient Express,* Paramount, 1974; *To the Devil a Daughter,* 1975; *The Sellout,* 1975; *Twilight's Last Gleaming,* Allied Artists, 1977; *The Domino Principle,* Avco Embassy, 1977; *Rollercoaster,* Universal, 1977; *Coma,* United Artists, 1978; *The Swarm,* Warner Brothers, 1978.

Bear Island, British-Canadian, 1980; *Hanky Panky,* Columbia, 1982; *The Final Option,* Metro-Goldwyn-Mayer/United Artists, 1983; *Against All Odds,* Columbia, 1984.

PRINCIPAL TELEVISION APPEARANCES—Series: Sergeant Dan Madigan, *Madigan,* NBC, 1972-73.

Movies: *Vanished,* 1970; *Benjamin Franklin,* 1974; *Mr. Horn,* 1978; *All God's Children,* 1980; *Blackout,* HBO, 1985.

RELATED CAREER—Instructor in drama, Lake Forest College, 1936-38; president, Heath Productions, 1955—; vice-president, Widmark Cattle Enterprises, 1957—.

MEMBER: Actors' Equity Association, Screen Actors Guild, American Federation of Television and Radio Artists; Hope for Hearing (director); Phi Pi Epsilon; Washington Country Club, Connecticut; Coffee House, New York; Valley Club, Montecito, CA.

ADDRESSES: AGENT—International Creative Management, 8899 Beverly Blvd., Los Angeles, CA 90048.

*   *   *

WIEMER, Robert   1938-

PERSONAL: Full name Robert Ernest Wiemer; born January 30, 1938, in Detroit, MI; son of Carl Ernest (a fireman) and Marion (an executive; maiden name, Israelian) Wiemer; married Rhea Dale McGeath, June 14, 1958; children: Robert Marshall, Whitney Kershaw. EDUCATION: Ohio Wesleyan University, B.A., 1959. MILITARY: U.S. Air Force, 1960-64.

VOCATION: Producer, director, and writer.

CAREER: FIRST TELEVISION WORK—Series: Executive producer, writer, and director, *Big Blue Marble,* 1977-83. PRINCIPAL TELEVISION WORK—Movies: Producer, writer, and director, *My Seventeenth Summer,* 1978; producer and director, *Witch's Sister,* 1979; producer, director, and writer, *Do Me a Favor,* 1980; producer, director, and writer, *Anna to the Infinite Power,* 1982.

PRINCIPAL FILM WORK—Writer, producer, and director, *Somewhere, Tomorrow,* Comworld, 1984.

RELATED CAREER—Child actor, Jam Handy Organization, Detroit, MI, 1946-48; independent film producer, 1956-60; director of

ROBERT WIEMER

documentary operations, WCBS-TV, New York, NY, 1964-67; independent producer of television, theatrical, and business films, New York, NY, 1967-72; executive producer of motion pictures and television, International Telephone and Telegraph, New York, NY, 1973—; president, Tigerfilm, Inc., New York, NY, 1984—; board of directors, Princeton American Communicatons, Inc., Princeton, NJ, 1985—; president, Blue Marble Company, Inc., Telemontage, Inc., Alphaventure Music, Inc., Betaventure Music, Inc.

WRITINGS: BOOKS—*Somewhere, Tomorrow* (novelization of his film), Silhouette-Harlequin, 1986.

MEMBER: National Academy of Television Arts and Sciences, Film Producers Association, American Women in Radio and Television, National Association of Television Programming Executives, New Jersey Broadcasters Association.

AWARDS: Peabody Award, for *Big Blue Marble;* Film Outstanding Producer, Producers Association Award; CINE Awards, 1974, 1976, 1977, 1979; Best Children's Informational Series, Emmy Award, 1979, for *Big Blue Marble.*

ADDRESSES: OFFICE—Tigerfilm, 204 E. 60th Stret, New York, NY 10022.

*   *   *

WILBUR, Richard   1921-

PERSONAL: Born March 1, 1921, in New York, NY; son of Lawrence Lazear and Helen Ruth (Purdy) Wilbur; married Charlotte

Ward. EDUCATION: Amherst College, A.B., 1942; Harvard University, M.A., 1947.

VOCATION: Poet, critic, translator, and teacher.

CAREER: FIRST STAGE WORK—Translator, *Le Misanthrope,* Poets' Theatre, Cambridge, MA, 1955. PRINCIPAL STAGE WORK— Lyricist (with Dorothy Parker and John La Touche), *Candide,* Martin Beck Theatre, NY, 1956, then Saville Theatre, London, 1959, and revived in New York, 1974; translator, *Tartuffe,* Lincoln Center Repertory, NY, Stratford Shakespeare Festival, Ontario, Canada, and National Theatre, London; translator, *The School for Wives,* Phoenix Theatre, NY, 1971; translator, *The Learned Ladies,* Williamstown Festival, MA, 1977; translator, *Andromache,* University of Maryland, Baltimore, MD, 1981.

RELATED CAREER—Teacher: Harvard University, 1950-54, Wellesley College, 1954-57, Wesleyan University, Middletown, CT, 1957-77, writer in residence, Smith College, 1977-86.

WRITINGS: PLAYS, PRODUCED—(With William Schuman) *On Freedom's Ground,* Statue of Liberty Centennial, New York Philharmonic, NY, 1986.

PLAYS, PUBLISHED—Translator: *Moliere: Four Comedies,* 1982; *Andromache,* 1982.

BOOKS—*The Beautiful Changes and Other Poems,* 1947; *Ceremony and Other Poems,* 1950; *Things of This World,* 1956; *Advice to a Prophet,* 1961; *Loudmouse,* 1963; *Walking to Sleep,* 1969.

MEMBER: Dramatists Guild, PEN, American Academy, National Institute of Arts and Letters, American Academy of Arts and Sciences, American Academy of Arts and Letters (president, 1974-76), Academy of American Poets (chancellor).

Photograph by Clemens Kalischer

RICHARD WILBUR

AWARDS: Guggenheim Fellowship, 1952, 1963; Prix de Rome Award, American Society of Arts and Letters, 1954; National Book Award, 1956; Pulitzer Prize, 1956, for *Things of This World;* Millay Prize Award, 1956; Ford Foundation Fellowship, 1960; Bollingen Translation Prize Award, 1963; Brandeis Creative Arts Award, 1971; honorary degrees from Lawrence College, Washington University, 1964, Amherst, 1967.

SIDELIGHTS: RECREATIONS—Tennis, herb gardening, and walking.

ADDRESSES: OFFICE—Dodwells Road, Cummington, MA 01026.

*   *   *

WILLIAMS, Cara

PERSONAL: Born Bernice Kamiat, in New York, NY. EDUCATION: Attended Hollywood Professional School.

VOCATION: Comedienne and actress.

CAREER: PRINCIPAL FILM APPEARANCES—*Something for the Boys,* Twentieth Century-Fox, 1944; *Boomerang,* 1947; *Meet Me in Las Vegas,* Metro-Goldwyn-Mayer, 1956; *The Defiant Ones,* United Artists, 1958; *Never Steal Anything Small,* Universal, 1959; *The Man from the Diners Club,* Columbia, 1963; *Doctors' Wives,* Columbia, 1971.

PRINCIPAL TELEVISION APPEARANCES—Series: Cara Bridges/Wilton, *The Cara Williams Show,* CBS, 1964-65; Gladys Porter, *Pete and Gladys,* CBS, 1960-62; Mae, *Rhoda,* CBS, 1974-75.

Episodic: *Alfred Hitchcock Presents; Desilu Playhouse; The Jackie Gleason Show; Henry Fonda Special.*

SIDELIGHTS: Cara Williams began her career as a child actress with Twentieth Century-Fox studios.

ADDRESSES: AGENT—Fred Amsel & Associates, 215 S. La Cienega Blvd., Suite 200, Beverly Hills, CA 90211.*

*   *   *

WILLIAMS, Cindy   1947-

PERSONAL: Born August 22, 1947, in Van Nuys, CA. EDUCATION: Attended Los Angeles City College.

VOCATION: Actress.

CAREER: FILM DEBUT—*The Blob,* Paramount, 1958. PRINCIPAL FILM APPEARANCES—*Gas-s-s-s,* 1970; *Drive, He Said,* Columbia, 1971; *The Christian Licorice Store,* National General, 1971; *Beware the Blob,* 1972; *Travels with My Aunt,* Metro-Goldwyn-Mayer, 1972; *American Graffiti,* Universal, 1973; *The Conversation,* Paramount, 1974; *Mr. Ricco,* United Artists, 1975; *The First Nudie Musical,* Paramount, 1976; *More American Graffiti,* Universal, 1979; *Uforia,* Universal, 1985.

TELEVISION DEBUT—*Room 222*, ABC. PRINCIPAL TELEVISION APPEARANCES—Series: Shirley Feeney, *Laverne & Shirley*, ABC, 1976-83.

Pilot: *Joanna*, NBC, 1985.

Movies: *The Migrants*, 1974.

Episodic: *The Funny Side*, NBC, 1971; *The Neighbors; Barefoot in the Park*, ABC, 1971; *My World and Welcome To It*, NBC, 1972; *Love American Style*, ABC; *Nanny and the Professor*, ABC; *The Bobby Sherman Show—Getting Together*, ABC; *Happy Days*, ABC.*

*   *   *

WILLIAMS, John T.   1932-

PERSONAL: Born February 8, 1932, in New York, NY; EDUCATION: Attended Juilliard School of Music.

VOCATION: Conductor and composer.

CAREER: PRINCIPAL FILM WORK—Composer: *I Passed for White*, 1960; *Because They're Young*, Columbia, 1960; *The Secret Ways*, Universal, 1961; *Bachelor Flat*, Twentieth Century-Fox, 1961; *Black Sunday*, American International, 1961; *Diamond Head*, Columbia, 1963; *Gidget Goes to Rome*, Columbia, 1963; *The Killers*, Universal, 1964; *None but the Brave*, Warner Brothers, 1965; *John Goldfarb, Please Come Home*, Twentieth Century-Fox, 1965; *The Rare Breed*, Universal, 1966; *How to Steal a Million*, Twentieth Century-Fox, 1966; *The Plainsman*, Universal, 1966; *Not With My Wife, You Don't*, Warner Brothers, 1966; *Penelope*, Metro-Goldwyn-Mayer, 1966; *A Guide for the Married Man*, Twentieth Century-Fox, 1967; *Ftizwilly*, United Artists, 1967; *Valley of the Dolls*, 1967; *Daddy's Gone A-Hunting*, National General, 1969; *Goodbye Mr. Chips*, Metro-Goldwyn-Mayer, 1969; *The Reivers*, National General, 1969.

Jane Eyre, 1971; musical director, *Fiddler on the Roof*, United Artists, 1971; *The Cowboys*, Warner Brothers, 1972; *Images*, Columbia, 1972; *Pete 'n' Tillie*, Universal, 1972; *The Poseidon Adventure*, Twentieth Century-Fox, 1972; *Tom Sawyer*, United Artists, 1973; music supervisor, *The Long Goodbye*, 1973; (with Paul Williams) *The Man Who Loved Cat Dancing*, Metro-Goldwyn-Mayer, 1973; *The Paper Chase*, Twentieth Century-Fox, 1973; (with Paul Williams) *Cinderella Liberty*, Twentieth Century-Fox, 1974; *Conrack*, Twentieth Century-Fox, 1974; *The Sugarland Express*, Universal, 1974; *Earthquake*, Universal, 1974; *The Towering Inferno*, Twentieth Century-Fox, 1974; *The Eiger Sanction*, Universal, 1975; *Jaws*, Universal, 1975; *Family Plot*, Universal, 1976; *The Missouri Breaks*, 1976; *Midway*, 1976; *Star Wars*, Twentieth Century-Fox, 1977; *Close Encounters of the Third Kind*, Columbia, 1977; *Raggedy Ann and Andy*, Twentieth Century-Fox, 1977; *The Fury*, Twentieth Century-Fox, 1978; *Jaws II*, Universal, 1978; *Superman*, Warner Brothers, 1978; *Meteor*, American International, 1979; *Quintet*, Twentieth Century-Fox, 1979; *Dracula*, Universal, 1979; *1941*, Universal, 1979.

Empire Strikes Back, Twentieth Century-Fox, 1980; *Raiders of the Lost Ark*, Paramount, 1981; *Heartbeeps*, Universal, 1981; *Monsignor*, Twentieth Century-Fox, 1982; *Yes Georgio*, Metro-Goldwyn-Mayer, 1982; *E.T. The Extra-Terrestrial*, Universal, 1982;

Return of the Jedi, Twentieth Century-Fox, 1983; *Indiana Jones and the Temple of Doom*, Paramount, 1984.

PRINCIPAL TELEVISION WORK—Composer: *Once Upon a Savage Night; Sergeant Ryker*, 1968; *Heidi*, 1968; *Jane Eyre*, 1972.

RELATED CAREER—Conductor and music director, Boston Pops Orchestra, 1980-84.

AWARDS: Grammy Awards: 1976, for *The Secret Ways;* 1976, for *Jaws;* 1977, for *Star Wars;* 1982, for *Raiders of the Lost Ark*. Academy Award, Best Arrangement, 1971, for *Fiddler on the Roof;* (with Paul Williams) Best Song, Academy Award nomination, 1973, for "(You're So) Nice to Be Around," from *Cinderella Liberty;* Emmy Award, 1972, for *Jane Eyre;* Golden Globe Award, 1978.

ADDRESSES: OFFICE—c/o Boston Symphony, 301 Massachusettes Avenue, Boston, MA 02115.*

*   *   *

WILLIAMS, Paul   1940-

PERSONAL: Full name, Paul Hamilton Williams; born September 19, 1940, in Omaha, NE; son of Paul Hamilton (an architectural engineer) and Bertha Mae (Burnside) Williams; married Katie; children: Christopher Cole.

VOCATION: Composer, singer, and actor.

CAREER: PRINCIPAL FILM APPEARANCES—*The Loved One*, Metro-Goldwyn-Mayer, 1965; *The Chase*, Columbia, 1966; *Planet of the Apes*, Twentieth Century-Fox, 1968; *Watermelon Man*, Columbia, 1970; *The Phantom of the Paradise*, Twentieth Century-Fox, 1974; *Smokey and the Bandit*, Universal, 1977; *The Cheap Detective*, Columbia, 1978; *Stone Cold Dead*, Canadian, 1980; *Smokey and the Bandit II*, Universal, 1980.

PRINCIPAL TELEVISION APPEARANCES—Hosted four shows of *Midnight Special*, NBC; co-host, *The Mike Douglas Show*.

Guest: *Merv Griffin Show; The Tonight Show; Jonathan Winters Show; The Muppet Show*.

Movie: *The Night They Saved Christmas*, ABC, 1984.

WRITINGS: SONGS—In collaboration with Roger Nichols: "We've Only Just Begun," 1970, "Rainy Days and Mondays," 1971, "An Old Fashioned Love Song," 1972, "Family of Man," 1972, "Let Me Be the One," 1972, "Evergreen," 1976 (also with Barbra Streisand); also with Nichols: "Out in the Country," "Cried Like a Baby," "Talk It Over in the Morning." (With composer Michel Colombier) "Wings," a cantata. (With composer John Williams) "(You're So) Nice to Be Around."

FILM SCORES—*The Getaway*, National General, 1972; (with John Williams) *The Man Who Loved Cat Dancing*, Metro-Goldwyn-Mayer, 1972; (with John Williams) *Cinderella Liberty*, Twentieth Century-Fox, 1973; (with Kenny Ascher) *The Phantom of the Paradise*, Twentieth Century-Fox, 1974; *Day of the Locust*, Paramount, 1975; *Bugsy Malone*, Paramount, 1976; (with Kenny Ascher) *A Star Is Born*, Warner Brothers, 1976; (with Charles Fox)

One on One, Warner Brothers, 1977; *The End,* United Artists, 1978; (with Kenny Ascher) *The Muppet Movie,* Associated Film Distribution, 1979; *Agatha,* Warner Brothers, 1979; (with Jerry Goldsmith) *The Secret of Nihm,* Metro-Goldwyn-Mayer, 1982.

TELEVISION—Theme songs for movie *No Place to Run,* 1972, and series *The Love Boat,* ABC, 1977—, *McLean Stevenson Show,* NBC, 1976-77, *It Takes Two,* ABC, 1982-83, and special *Emmet Otter's Jug Band Christmas,* ABC, 1980; wrote songs and served as musical supervisor for *Sugar Time!,* ABC, 1977-78.

RELATED CAREER—President, Hobbitron Enterprises, 1973—; Associate, A & M Records, 1970-77.

RECORDINGS: ALBUMS—*Just an Old-Fashioned Love Song,* A & M Records, 1971; *Life Goes On,* A & M Records, 1972; *A Little Bit of Love,* A & M Records, 1974; *Here Comes Inspiration,* A & M Records, 1974; *Ordinary Fools,* A & M Records, 1975; *Classics,* A & M Records, 1977; *A Little on the Windy Side,* Portrait Records, 1979; *Crazy for Loving You,* Firstline Records, 1981.

AWARDS: (With John Williams) Best Song, Academy Award nomination, 1973, for "(You're So) Nice to Be Around," from *Cinderella Liberty;* Best Original Motion Picture Score, Academy Award nomination, 1974, for *Phantom of the Paradise;* (with Kenny Ascher) Best Original Motion Picture Score, Golden Globe, 1976, for *A Star Is Born;* (with Barbra Streisand) Best Song, Academy Award, 1976, Golden Globe and Grammy Award, both 1977, all for "Evergreen," from *A Star Is Born.*

MEMBER: American Society of Composers, Authors and Publishers, National Academy of Recording Arts and Sciences.

SIDELIGHTS: CTFT learned that Paul Williams began his career in film studios as a set painter and stunt parachutist.

ADDRESSES: HOME—Santa Barbara, CA. OFFICE—Tugboat Productions, Lazy Creek Ranch, 4570 Encino Avenue, Encino, CA 91316.*

*   *   *

WILLIAMS, Robin   1952-

PERSONAL: Born July 21, 1952, in Edinburgh, Scotland; moved to United States, 1953; son of Robert Williams and his wife; married Valerie Velardi, June 4, 1978. EDUCATION: Attended Marin College, CA; Claremont Men's College, CA; Juilliard School of Music and Drama.

VOCATION: Comedian and actor.

CAREER: PRINCIPAL CABARET APPEARANCES—The Holy City Zoo, San Francisco, CA; The Boadinghouse, San Francisco, CA; The Comedy Store, Los Angeles, CA; Intersection, San Francisco, CA; The Great American Music Hall, San Francisco, CA; The Ice House, Los Angeles; The Improvisation, Los Angeles.

TELEVISION DEBUT—*Laugh In,* NBC, 1978. PRINCIPAL TELEVISION APPEARANCES—Series: Mork, *Mork & Mindy,* ABC, 1978-82.

Guest: *The Richard Pryor Show,* NBC, 1977; *America 2-Night,* syndicated, 1978; *The Alan Hamel Show; Ninety Minutes Live; The Great American Laugh Off.*

Specials: *Robin Williams Live,* HBO, 1985; co-host, *Academy Awards Show,* 1986; co-host *Comic Relief* (a fund raiser for the homeless), HBO, 1986.

PRINCIPAL FILM APPEARANCES—*The Last Laugh;* title role, *Popeye,* Paramount, 1980; title role, *The World According to Garp,* Warner Brothers, 1982; *The Survivors,* Columbia, 1983; *Moscow on the Hudson,* Columbia, 1984; *Best of Times,* Universal, 1986; *Club Paradise,* Warner Brothers, 1986.

RECORDINGS: COMEDY ALBUMS—*Reality, What a Concept,* 1979; *Throbbing Python of Love,* 1979.

AWARDS: Best Comedy Album, Grammy, 1979, for *Reality, What a Concept;* other awards include the Golden Apple, Hollywood Women's Press Club, Golden Globe, People's Choice Award, all for his work on *Mork & Mindy.*

ADDRESSES: AGENT—International Creative Management, 8899 Beverly Blvd., Los Angeles, CA 90048.*

*   *   *

WILLIS, Bruce   1955-

BRIEF ENTRY: Born March 19, 1955, in Germany; son of David and Marlene Willis. Actor. Bruce Willis and his family moved to New Jersey from Germany when he was two years old. He attended Penns Grove High School and after graduation worked for a period at the DuPont plant in a neighboring town. His first entertainment venture was as second harmonica player in a band called "Loose Goose," and as sponsor of the band's performance in a local movie house, for which he formed a promotion company called Night Owl Promotions. He attended Montclair State College in New Jersey where he performed in such plays as *Cat on a Hot Tin Roof,* but quit school after a small part in the play *Heaven and Earth* in Manhattan came his way. He was a member of Barbara Contardi's First Amendment Comedy Theatre and was seen in such plays as *Railroad Bill* and *Bayside Boys.* He supplemented his career by doing Levi's 501 Jeans commercials and as a bartender at Kamikaze, a New York nightclub. His portrayal of Eddie in Sam Shepard's *Fool for Love* gained him acclaim, and his role as David Addison on ABC's *Moonlighting* is bringing him fame.*

*   *   *

WILSON, Flip   1933-

PERSONAL: Full name, Clerow Wilson; born December 8,1933, in Jersey City, NJ; married; children: four. MILITARY: U.S. Air Force, 1950-54.

VOCATION: Comedian and actor.

CAREER: PRINCIPAL TELEVISION APPEARANCES—Series: *The Flip Wilson Show*, NBC, 1970-74; host, *People Are Funny*, NBC, 1984; title role, *Charlie & Co.*, CBS, 1985—.

Episodic: *That's Life*, ABC, 1969; *Sammy and Company*, syndicated; *Love, American Style*, ABC; *Rowan & Martin's Laugh In*, NBC; guest host, *The Big Show*, NBC, 1980.

Specials: Appeared in his own specials, 1974-76; *Pinocchio*, 1976.

PRINCIPAL FILM APPEARANCES—*Uptown Saturday Night*, Warner Brothers, 1974; *Skatetown, U.S.A.*, 1979; *The Fish That Saved Pittsburgh*, United Artists, 1979.

RECORDINGS: COMEDY ALBUMS—*Cowboys and Colored People*, 1967; *Flippin'* 1968; *Flip Wilson, You Devil You*, 1968.

AWARDS: Won a Grammy for best comedy record; Outstanding Writing Achievement in Variety or Music, Emmy, 1971, for *The Flip Wilson Show*.*

*   *   *

WILSON, Lanford   1937-

PERSONAL: Born April 13, 1937, in Lebanon, MO; son of Ralph Eugene and Violetta Careybelle (Tate) Wilson. EDUCATION: Attended University of Chicago and San Diego State University.

VOCATION: Playwright.

WRITINGS: PLAYS, PRODUCED—*So Long at the Fair*, Caffe Cino, NY, 1963; *Home Free, No Trespassing, Sandcastle, The Madness of Lady Bright*, all 1964; *Ludlow Fair, Balm in Gilead, This Is the Rill Speaking, Days Ahead, Sex Is Between Two People*, all 1965; *The Gingham Dog, The Rimers of Eldritch, Wandering*, all 1966; *Wandering Days Ahead*, 1967; *Lemon Sky*, 1969; *Serenading Louie, The Great Nebula in Orion*, both 1970; *The Hot L Baltimore, The Family Continues*, both 1972; *The Mound Builders*, 1975; *Fifth of July*, 1978; *Brontasaurus*, 1978; *Talley's Folly*, 1979; *A Tale Told*, 1981; *Angels Fall*, 1982; translation of Chekov's *The Three Sisters*, 1984.

TELEVISION PLAYS—*This Is the Rill Speaking*, 1967; *The Sandcastle; Stoop; The Migrants; Taxi!; Fifth of July*, 1982.

MEMBER: Dramatists Guild, Circle Repertory Company (founder and resident playwright).

AWARDS: Vernon Rice Award, 1966-67; Obie Award, 1972, 1975; Outer Critics Circle Award, Drama Critics Circle Award, 1973, 1980; Pulitzer Prize Award, 1980, for *Talley's Folly*.

ADDRESSES: OFFICE—P.O. Box 891, Sag Harbor, NY 11963; Circle Repertory Company, 161 Sixth Avenue, New York, NY 10014.

*   *   *

WINFREY, Ophra

BRIEF ENTRY: Born in Kosciusko, MI. Talkshow hostess and actress. Ophra Winfrey's show, *AM Chicago*, captured the top spot in the ratings when she took over in January, 1984, and has remained there ever since. Her portrayal of Sophia in Steven Spielberg's *The Color Purple* caused a sensation and won her an Academy Award nomination. Winfrey, with her grandmother's help, began reading at the age of two and a half and by age three she was giving Easter and Christmas speeches in church. Her parents separated when she was a young girl and she became a "troubled child" until her father, who had moved to Nashville, won custody of her. At sixteen, she won an Elks Club oratorical contest that gave her a full scholarship to Tennessee State University, where she earned a B.A. in speech and drama. While in college, Winfrey was a reporter for a Nashville radio station and at WTVF-TV, where she became an anchorwoman at age nineteen. She moved to Baltimore to WJZ-TV and served as a reporter and co-anchorwoman on the evening news. She later became the co-host of the station's morning show, *People Are Talking*, before moving to *AM Chicago*.*

*   *   *

WINKLER, Irwin   1931-

PERSONAL: Born May 28, 1931, in New York, NY; son of Sol and Anna Winkler. EDUCATION: New York University, B.A., 1955.

VOCATION: Producer.

CAREER: PRINCIPAL FILM WORK—Co-Producer (all with Robert Chartoff): *Double Trouble*, Metro-Goldwyn-Mayer, 1967; *Point Blank*, Metro-Goldwyn-Mayer, 1967; *The Split*, Metro-Goldwyn-Mayer, 1968; *Leo the Last*, United Artists, 1969; *They Shoot Horses, Don't They*, Cinerama, 1969; *The Strawberry Statement*, Metro-Goldwyn-Mayer, 1970; *The Gang That Couldn't Shoot Straight*, Metro-Goldwyn-Mayer, 1971; *Believe in Me*, Metro-Goldwyn-Mayer, 1971; *The New Centurions*, Columbia, 1972; *The Mechanic*, United Artists, 1972; *Up the Sandbox*, National General, 1972; *S*P*Y*S*, Twentieth Century-Fox, 1974; *Busting*, United Artists, 1974; *Peeper*, Twentieth Century-Fox, 1975; *The Gambler*, Paramount, 1975; *Breakout*, 1975; *Rocky*, United Artists, 1976; *Nickelodeon*, Columbia, 1976; *New York, New York*, United Artists, 1977; *Valentino*, 1977; *Comes a Horseman*, United Artists, 1978; *Uncle Joe Shannon*, United Artists, 1978; *Rocky II*, United Artists, 1979; *Raging Bull*, United Artists, 1980; *True Confessions*, United Artists, 1981; *Rocky III*, Metro-Goldwyn-Mayer/United Artists, 1982; *Author! Author!*, Twentieth Century-Fox, 1982; *The Right Stuff*, Warner Brothers, 1983; *Rocky IV*, Metro-Goldwyn-Mayer/United Artists, 1985; *'Round Midnight*, 1986.

AWARDS: (Shared with Robert Chartoff) Best Picture, Academy Award, 1976, for *Rocky;* (shared with Robert Chartoff) Best Picture, Academy Award nomination, 1980, for *Raging Bull*.

ADDRESSES: OFFICE—Chartoff-Winkler Productions, Inc., 10125 W. Washington Blvd., Culver City, CA 90230.

*   *   *

WITT, Paul Junger   1941-

PERSONAL: Born March 20, 1941, in New York, NY; son of Jacob Malcomb and Helen Lawrence (Junger) Witt; children: Christopher,

Anthony, Genvieve. EDUCATION: University of Virginia, B.A., Fine Arts, 1963.

VOCATION: Television producer and director.

CAREER: Associate producer and director with Screen Gems, 1965-67, then producer and director with Screen Gems, 1968-71; producer, Spelling/Goldberg Productions, 1972-73; president and executive producer, Danny Thomas Productions, 1973-74; founder and executive producer, Witt, Thomas, Harris Productions, 1976-81; television shows produced include *Soap,* ABC; *Benson,* ABC, *Hail to the Chief,* ABC; *Golden Girls,* NBC.

MEMBER: Directors Guild of America, Writers Guild of America.

ADDRESSES: OFFICE—1438 N. Gower Street, Hollywood, CA 90028.

*　　*　　*

WOLDIN, Judd   1925-

PERSONAL: Born May 30, 1925, in Somerville, NJ; son of Jacob (a businessman) and Gertrude (Balinky) Woldin; married Estelle Pustilnik (an actress, professionally known as Anna Rayne; divorced); children: Donna Ruta, John Jacob, Mark Andrew, Daniel

JUDD WOLDIN

Rakhal. EDUCATION: Rutgers University, B.A., M.A.; trained for the stage at the Broadcast Music Incorporated Theatre Workshop with Lehman Engel. POLITICS: Independent. RELIGION: Jewish.

VOCATION: Composer, lyricist, librettist, choreographer, and jazz pianist.

CAREER: FIRST STAGE WORK—Dance arranger, *The Beast in Me,* Plymouth Theatre, NY, 1960. PRINCIPAL STAGE WORK—Composer, *Raisin,* 46th Street Theatre, NY, 1973, for over eight hundred performances; composer and librettist, *King of Schnorrers,* Harold Clurman Theatre, NY, 1979; composer and librettist, *Lorenzo,* George Street Playhouse, New Brunswick, NJ, 1982.

MAJOR TOUR WORK—Composer, *Raisin,* national, 1975-76.

FIRST FILM WORK—Composer, *Railway with a Heart of Gold.* PRINCIPAL FILM WORK—Composer, *Nobody Ever Died of Old Age;* composer, *Poppycock.*

WRITINGS: PLAYS, PUBLISHED—Musicals: *Raisin,* Samuel French; *King of Schnorrers,* Samuel French.

RECORDINGS: ALBUM—*Raisin,* original cast recording.

MEMBER: Dramatists Guild, Broadcast Music Incorporated, Songwriters Guild, American Federation of Musicians.

AWARDS: Best Musical, Antoinette Perry Award and Best Original Cast Album, Grammy Award, both 1973, for *Raisin;* New Jersey Council of the Arts Grant, 1980.

SIDELIGHTS: Judd Woldin wrote *CTFT,* "I became involved in theatre accidently, when Don Elliott asked me to write dance music for his jazz musical, *The Beast in Me.*"

ADDRESSES: HOME—310 Greenwich Street, 39C, New York, NY 10013.

*　　*　　*

WOODWARD, Joanne   1930-

PERSONAL: Born February 27, 1930, in Thomasville, GA; daughter of Wade and Elinor (Trimmer) Woodward; married Paul Newman (the actor, producer, and director) January 29, 1958; children: Elinor Terese, Melissa Stewart, Clea Olivia. EDUCATION: Attended Lousiana State University; studied at the Neighborhood Playhouse Drama School and at the Actors Studio. POLITICS: Democrat. RELIGION: Episcopalian.

VOCATION: Actress.

CAREER: STAGE DEBUT—Understudy, *Picnic,* 1953. PRINCIPAL STAGE APPEARANCES—*Baby Want a Kiss,* 1964; *Candide,* Circle in the Square, NY, 1982; *The Lovers,* NY.

FILM DEBUT—*Count Three and Pray,* Columbia, 1955. PRINCIPAL FILM APPEARANCES—*Kiss Before Dying,* 1956; title role, *The Three Faces of Eve,* Twentieth Century-Fox, 1957; *No Down Payment,* Twentieth Century-Fox, 1957; *The Long Hot Summer,* Twentieth Century-Fox, 1958; *Rally 'Round the Flag Boys,* Twenti-

JOANNE WOODWARD

Photograph by Harry Langdon

eth Century-Fox, 1958; *The Fugitive Kind*, United Artists, 1960; *From the Terrace*, Twentieth Century-Fox, 1960; *Paris Blues*, United Artists, 1961; *The Stripper*, Twentieth Century-Fox, 1963; *A New Kind of Love*, Paramount, 1963; *A Big Hand for the Little Lady*, Warner Brothers, 1966; *A Fine Madness*, Warner Brothers, 1966; title role, *Rachel, Rachel*, Warner Brothers/Seven Arts, 1968; *Winning*, Universal, 1969; *WUSA*, Paramount, 1970; *They Might Be Giants*, Universal, 1971; *The Effect of Gamma Rays on Man-in-the-Moon Marigolds*, Twentieth Century-Fox, 1972; *Summer Wishes, Winter Dreams*, Columbia, 1973; *The Drowning Pool*, Warner Brothers, 1975; *The End*, United Artists, 1978; *Harry and Son*, Orion Pictures, 1984.

PRINCIPAL TELEVISION APPEARANCES—Episodic: *Streets of L.A.; The Alcoa Hour*, NBC; *Kraft Television Theatre*, NBC; *Ponds Theatre*, ABC; *Star Tonight*, ABC; *The Web*, CBS.

Movies: *Sybil*, NBC, 1976; *Come Back Little Sheba*, 1977; *See How She Runs*, 1978; *Crisis at Central High*, 1979; *The Shadow Box*, 1980; *Do You Remember Love*, 1985; also appeared in *All the Way Home*.

Specials: Narrator, *Angel Dust*, 1981;

MEMBER: Actors' Equity Association, Screen Actors Guild, American Federation of Television and Radio Artists.

AWARDS: Best Actress, Academy Award, 1957, for *The Three Faces of Eve;* Best Actress, Academy Award nomination, 1968, for *Rachel, Rachel;* Emmy Award, 1978, for *See How She Runs*.

ADDRESSES: AGENT—c/o Toni Howard, William Morris Agency, 151 El Camino Drive, Beverly Hills, CA 90212.

*   *   *

WORTH, Irene   1916-

PERSONAL: Born June 23, 1916, in Nebraska. EDUCATION: University of California at Los Angeles, B. Education, 1937; trained with the stage with Elsie Fogarty.

VOCATION: Actress.

CAREER: STAGE DEBUT—Fenella, *Escape Me Never*, U.K. cities, 1942. NEW YORK DEBUT—Cecily Harden, *The Two Mrs. Carrolls*, Booth Theatre, 1943. LONDON DEBUT—Elsie, *The Time of Your Life*, Lyric Theatre, Hammersmith, 1946. PRINCIPAL STAGE AP-PEARANCES—*This Way to the Tomb*, Embassy Theatre, London, 1946; Anabelle Jones, *Love Goes to Press*, Duchess Theatre, London, 1946; Donna Pascuala, *Drake's Drum*, Embassy Theatre, London, 1946; Illona, *The Play's the Thing*, Lyric Theatre, Hammersmith, then St. James's Theatre, London, 1947; Olivia Brown, *Love in Idleness* and title role, *Iris*, both Q Theatre, London, 1947; Mary Dalton, *Native Son* and title role, *Lucrece*, both Bolton's Theatre, London, 1948; Eileen Perry, *Edward My Son*, Lyric Theatre, Hammersmith, 1948; Lady Fortrose, *Home Is To-Morrow*, Cambridge Theatre, London, 1948; Olivia Raines, *Champagne for Delilah*, New Theatre, London, 1949; Delia Coplestone, *The Cocktail Party*, Edinburgh Festival, Scotland, 1949, then Henry Miller's Theatre, NY, 1950.

With the Old Vic Company, London: Desdemona, *Othello*, Berlin Festival, 1951, Helena, *A Midsummer Night's Dream*, Catherine de Vausselles, *The Other Heart*, both 1951-52, Lady Macbeth, *Macbeth*, and Portia, *The Merchant of Venice*, both 1953.

Helena, *All's Well That Ends Well*, Queen Margaret, *Richard III*, Shakespeare Festival Theatre, Stratford, Ontario, Canada, 1953; Frances Farrar, *A Day by the Sea*, Haymarket Theatre, London, 1953; Argia, *The Queen and the Rebels*, Midland Theatre Company, Coventry, U.K., 1955; Alcestis, *A Life in the Sun*, Edinburgh Festival, 1955; Argia, *The Queen and the Rebels*, Haymarket Theatre, London, 1955; Marcelle, *Hotel Paradiso*, Winter Garden Theatre, NY, 1956; title role, *Mary Stuart*, Phoenix Theatre, NY, 1957; Sara Callifer, *The Potting Shed*, Globe Theatre, London, 1958; title role, *Mary Stuart*, Assembly Hall, Edinburgh Festival, Old Vic, London, 1958; Rosaling, *As You Like It*, Stratford Shakespeare Festival, Ontario, Canada, 1959.

Albertine Prine, *Toys in the Attic*, Hudson Theatre, NY, 1960; Marquise de Merteuil, *The Art of Seduction*, Royal Shakespeare Company, Aldwych Theatre, London, 1962; Lady Macbeth, *Macbeth*, and Goneril, *King Lear*, both with the Royal Shakespeare Company, Stratford-upon-Avon, U.K., 1962; Goneril, *King Lear*, Aldwych Theatre, London, 1962; Doktor Mathilde von Aahnd, *The Physicists*, Aldwych Theatre, London, 1963; Clodia Pulcher, *The*

Ides of March, Haymarket Theatre, London, 1963; Goneril, *King Lear,* New York State Theatre, NY, 1964; title role, *Tiny Alice,* Billy Rose Theatre, NY, 1964; Hilde Latymer, *A Song at Twilight,* Queen's London, 1966; Anne Hilgay, "Shadows of the Evening," Anna-Mary Conklin, "Come into the Garden, Maud," both part of *Suite in Three Keys,* London, 1966; Io, *Prometheus Bound,* Yale University, New Haven, CT, 1967; Hesione Hushabye, *Heartbreak House,* Chichester Festival, U.K., then Lyric Theatre, London, 1967; Jocasta, *Oedipus,* Old Vic, London, 1968.

Title role, *Tiny Alice,* Aldwych Theatre, London, 1970; title role, *Hedda Gabler,* Stratford, Ontario, Canada, 1970; Dora Lang, *Notes on a Love Affair,* Globe Theatre, London, 1972; Irina Arkadina, *The Seagull,* Chichester, U.K., 1973, then Greenwich, 1974; Mrs. Alving, *Ghosts* and Gertrude, *Hamlet,* Chichester, U.K., 1974; Princess Kosmonopolis, *Sweet Bird of Youth,* Brooklyn Academy, NY, then Harkness Theatre, NY, 1975; Lina, *Misalliance,* Lake Forest, IL, 1976; Mme. Ranevskaya, *The Cherry Orchard,* Lincoln Center, NY, 1977; Kate, *Old Times,* Lake Forest, IL, 1977; *After the Season,* Lake Forest, IL, 1978; Winnie, *Happy Days,* Public and Newman Theatres, NY, 1979.

Miss Ella Rentheim, *John Gabriel Borkman,* Circle in the Square, NY, 1980-81; Miss Madrigal, *The Chalk Garden,* Roundabout Stage One, NY, 1982; Isabel Hastings Hoyt, *The Golden Age,* Jack Lawrence Theatre, NY, 1984.

MAJOR TOURS—Ilona Szabo, *The Play's the Thing,* U.K. cities, 1946; *Return Journey,* U.K. cities, 1947; Lady Fortrose, *Home Is To-Morrow,* U.K. cities, 1948; Helena, *A Midsummer Night's Dream* and Catherine de Vausselles, *The Other Heart,* both South African cities, 1953; Goneril, *King Lear,* European, Soviet and Canadian cities, 1964; *Men and Women of Shakespeare,* South American cities and U.S. universities, 1966.

PRINCIPAL FILM APPEARANCES—Leonie, *Orders to Kill,* 1958; *The Scapegoat,* Metro-Goldwyn-Mayer, 1959; *King Lear,* 1971; *Nicholas and Alexandra,* Columbia, 1971; *Rich Kids,* United Artists, 1979; *Eyewitness,* Twentieth Century-Fox, 1981; *Deathtrap,* Warner Brothers, 1982.

TELEVISION DEBUT—1949. PRINCIPAL TELEVISION APPEARANCES—Plays: Stella, *The Lake;* Ellida Wangel, *The Lady from the Sea,* 1953; *Candida; The Duchess of Malfi; Antigone,* 1955; Clytemnestra, *Prince Orestes,* 1959; Rose Fish, *Variations on a Theme,* 1966; also, *The Way of the World; The Displaced Person.*

Movie: *Forbidden,* HBO, 1985.

PRINCIPAL RADIO APPEARANCES—*The Cocktail Party,* 1951; *Major Barbara; All's Well That Ends Well; The Queen and the Rebels,* 1954; *The Merchant of Venice,* 1958; *Rosmersholm,* 1959; *Duel of Angels,* 1964.

AWARDS: *Daily Mail* National Television Award, 1953-54; Best Actress, British Academy Award, 1958, for *Orders to Kill;* Antoinette Perry Award, 1965, for *Tiny Alice;* Outstanding Actress, Whitbread Anglo-American Award, 1967; Antoinette Perry Award, Jefferson Award, both 1975, for *Sweet Bird of Youth;* honorary Commander of the British Empire.

SIDELIGHTS: RECREATIONS—Music, piano.

ADDRESSES: AGENT—c/o Milton Goldman, International Creative Management, 40 W. 57th Street, New York, NY 10019.*

WRIGHT, Teresa　1918-

PERSONAL: Born October 27, 1918, in New York, NY; daughter of Arthur and Martha (Espy) Wright; married Niven Busch (divorced); married Robert Woodruff Anderson (divorced). EDUCATION: Attended Columbia High School, Maplewood, NJ.

VOCATION: Actress.

CAREER: STAGE DEBUT—Grazia, *Death Takes a Holiday.* NEW YORK DEBUT—*Our Town,* Henry Miller's Theatre, 1938. PRINCIPAL STAGE APPEARANCES—Daughter, *The Vinegar Tree,* 1938; understudy Emily, *Our Town,* Washington, DC, 1938; Blossom Trexel, *Susan and God,* Wharf Theatre, Provincetown, MA, 1938; played a season of stock at Tanworth, NH, 1939; Mary *Life with Father,* Empire Theatre, NY, 1939; Linnea Ecklund, *Salt of the Earth,* Shubert Theatre, New Haven, CT, 1952; *Bell, Book and Candle,* Sombrero Playhouse, Phoenix, AZ, 1953; Georgie Elgin, *The Country Girl,* Vancouver, Canada, 1953; *The Heiress,* Palm Springs, CA, 1954; Lizzie Curry, *The Rainmaker,* La Jolla Playhouse, CA, 1954; Cora Flood, *The Dark at the Top of the Stairs,* Music Box Theatre, NY, 1957; Katherine Butler Hathaway, *The Locksmith,* U.S. cities, 1965. Alice, *I Never Sang for My Father,* Longacre Theatre, NY, 1968; Mary Hallen, *Who's Happy Now?,* Village South Theatre, NY, 1969.

A Passage to E.M. Forster, Theatre de Lys, NY, 1970; Mary Tyrone, *Long Day's Journey into Night,* Hartford Stage Company, CT, 1971; Beatrice, *The Effect of Gamma Rays on Man-in-the-Moon Marigolds,* Shubert Theatre, New Haven, CT, 1972; Linda Loman, *Death of a Salesman,* Walnut Theatre, Philadelphia, PA, 1974; *The Knight of the Burning Pestle* and Lily Miller, *Ah, Wilderness!,* Long Wharf Theatre, New Haven, CT, 1974; Linda Loman, *Death of a Salesman,* Circle in the Square, NY, 1975; Lily Miller, *Ah, Wilderness!,* Circle in the Square, NY, 1977; *The Master Builder,* Eisenhower Theatre, Kennedy Center, Washington, DC, 1977; *All the Way Home,* Hartford, CT, 1977; appeared at the Cleveland Playhouse, 1978-79.

Cora Swanson, *Morning's at Seven,* Lyceum Theatre, NY, 1980, then in a London production, then at the Center Theatre Group/Ahmanson Theatre, Los Angeles, CA, 1981; Emily, *Wings,* Old Globe Theatre, San Diego, CA, 1983.

MAJOR TOURS—Rebecca, Emily, *Our Town,* summer tour, 1938; Mary McKellaway, *Mary, Mary,* U.S. cities, 1962; Pamela Pew-Picket, *Tchin-Tchin,* U.S. cities, 1963;

FILM DEBUT—Alexandra, *The Little Foxes,* 1941. PRINCIPAL FILM APPEARANCES—*Mrs. Miniver,* Metro-Goldwyn-Mayer, 1942; Eleanor Gehrig, *Pride of the Yankees,* 1942; *Shadow of a Doubt,* 1943; *Casanova Brown,* 1944; *The Best Years of Our Lives,* 1946; *Trouble with Women,* 1947; *Pursued,* 1947; *Imperfect Lady,* 1947; *Enchantment,* 1948; *The Capture,* 1950; *The Men,* 1950; *Something to Live For,* 1952; *California Conquest,* 1952; *Steel Trap,* 1952; *The Actress,* Metro-Goldwyn-Mayer, 1953; *Count the Hours,* 1953; *Track of the Cat,* 1954; *Hail, Hero!,* National General, 1969; *The Happy Ending,* 1969; *Roseland,* Cinema Shares, 1977; *Somewhere in Time,* Universal, 1980.

PRINCIPAL TELEVISION APPEARANCES—Episodic: *Dupont Show of the Week,* NBC; *Ford Theatre,* NBC; *Four Star Playhouse,* CBS; "Love Is Eternal," *General Electric Theatre,* CBS; "Trap for a Stranger," *U.S. Steel Hour,* ABC; *Lux Video Theatre; Playhouse 90.*

Movies: Annie Sullivan, *The Miracle Worker;* title role, *The Louella Parsons Story; The Margaret Bourke-White Story; Big Deal in Laredo.*

AWARDS: Best Supporting Actress, Academy Award, 1942, for *Mrs. Miniver.*

ADDRESSES: AGENT—Lantz Office, 888 Seventh Avenue, New York, NY 10019.

*   *   *

WYATT, Jane   1910-

PERSONAL: Born August 10, 1910, in New York, NY; daughter of Christopher Billopp and Euphemia (Waddington) Wyatt; married Edgar Ward, 1935; children: Christopher, Michael. EDUCATION: Barnard College; studied for the theatre as an apprentice at the Berkshire Playhouse, Stockbridge, Massachusetts.

VOCATION: Actress.

CAREER: PRINCIPAL STAGE APPEARANCES—Understudy, *Tradewinds,* NY; understudy, *The Vinegar Tree,* NY, 1930; *Give Me Yesterday,* NY; *The Tadpole,* NY; *The Mad Hopes,* NY, 1932; *Evensong,* NY, 1933; *Dinner at Eight,* NY, 1933; *The Joyous Season,* 1934; *The Bishop Misbehaves,* NY, 1935; *Night Music,* 1940; *Conquest,* NY; Nina Denery, *The Autumn Garden,* Coronet Theatre, NY, 1951.

FILM DEBUT—*One More River,* Universal, 1934; Estella, *Great Expectations,* Universal, 1934; *We're Only Human,* RKO, 1936; *Luckiest Girl in the World,* Universal, 1936; Sondra, *Lost Horizon,* Columbia, 1937; *Girl from God's Country,* Republic, 1940; *Hurricane Smith,* Republic, 1941; *Weekend for Three,* RKO, 1941; *Kisses for Breakfast,* Warner Brothers, 1941; *The Navy Comes Through,* RKO, 1942; *Army Surgeon,* RKO, 1942; *Buckskin Frontier,* United Artists, 1943; *The Kansan,* United Artists, 1943; Aggie Hunter, *None but the Lonely Heart,* RKO, 1944; *Strange Conquest,* Universal, 1946; *The Bachelor's Daughters,* United Artists, 1946; Mrs. Harvey, *Boomerang,* Twentieth Century-Fox, 1947; Jane, *Gentlemen's Agreement,* Twentieth Century-Fox, 1947; *Pitfall,* United Artists, 1948; *No Minor Vices,* Metro-Goldwyn-Mayer, 1948; *Bad Boy,* Allied Artists, 1949; *Canadian Pacific,* Twentieth Century-Fox, 1949; Mary Morgan, *Task Force,* Warner Brothers, 1949.

Our Very Own, RKO, 1950; *House by the River,* Republic, 1950; *My Blue Heaven,* Twentieth Century-Fox, 1950; *The Man Who Cheated Himself,* Twentieth Century-Fox, 1950; *Criminal Lawyer,* Columbia, 1951; *Interlude,* Universal, 1957; *The Two Little Bears,* Twentieth Century-Fox, 1961; *Never Too Late,* Warner Brothers, 1965; *Treasure of Matacumbe,* Buena Vista, 1976; *Star Trek IV: The Voyage Home,* Paramount, 1986.

TELEVISION DEBUT—*Robert Montgomery Presents,* NBC, 1952. PRINCIPAL TELEVISION APPEARANCES—Series: Margaret Anderson, *Father Knows Best,* CBS, 1954-55; NBC, 1955-58; CBS, 1958-1960; hostess and moderator, *Confidential for Women.*

Episodic: *Bob Hope Presents The Chrysler Theatre,* NBC; *The Virginian,* NBC; *Wagon Train,* ABC; *United States Steel Hour;* Bell

Telephone Hour, NBC; *Kraft Music Hall,* NBC; "Katherine," *Hollywood TV Theatre;* Spock's mother, *Star Trek,* NBC, 1968-69; premier episode, *Love, American Style,* ABC, 1969; *The Ghost and Mrs. Muir,* ABC, 1970; *Here Come the Brides,* ABC; *Alias Smith and Jones,* ABC; *Fantasy Island,* ABC; Mrs. Aushlander, *St. Elsewhere,* NBC.

Movies: *Tom Sawyer,* 1973; *Amelia Earhart,* 1976; *A Love Affair: The Eleanor and Lou Gehrig Story,* 1978; *Superdome,* 1978; *The Nativity,* 1978; *The Millionaire,* 1978. Also: *My Father, My Mother;* Margaret Anderson, *Father Knows Best Reunion.*

AWARDS: Emmy Awards: Best Continuing Performance by an Actress in a Leading Role in a Dramatic or Comedy Series, 1957, Best Actress in a Leading Role (Continuing Character) in a Comedy Series, 1958-59, Outstanding Performance by an Actress in a Series (Lead or Support), 1959-60, all for *Father Knows Best.*

ADDRESSES: HOME—Los Angeles, CA. AGENT—William Morris Agency, 151 El Camino Drive, Beverly Hills, CA 90212.

*   *   *

WYMAN, Jane   1914-

PERSONAL: Born Sarah Jane Fulks, January 4, 1914, in St. Joseph, MO; daughter of R.D. (a politician) and Emma (Reise) Fulks; married Myron Futterman, 1937 (divorced, 1938); married Ronald Reagan, 1940 (divorced, 1948); Fred Karger (a bandleader), 1952 (divorced, 1954); remarried Karger, 1961; children: (second marriage) Michael, Maureen. EDUCATION: Attended University of Missouri, 1935.

VOCATION: Actress.

CAREER: FILM DEBUT—*Golddiggers of 1937,* Warner Brothers, 1936. PRINCIPAL FILM APPEARANCES—Girl at party, *My Man Godfrey,* Universal, 1936; chorus, *King of Burlesque,* Twentieth Century-Fox, 1936; *Smart Blonde,* Warner Brothers, 1936; *Stage Struck,* Warner Brothers, 1936; *The King and the Chorus Girl,* Warner Brothers, 1937; *Ready, Willing, and Able,* Warner Brothers, 1937; *Slim,* Warner Brothers, 1937; *The Singing Marine,* Warner Brothers, 1937; *Public Wedding,* Warner Brothers, 1937; *Mr. Dodd Takes the Air,* Warner Brothers, 1937; *The Spy Ring,* Universal, 1938; *He Couldn't Say No,* Warner Brothers, 1938; *Wide Open Faces,* Columbia, 1938; "Happy" Lane, *The Crowd Roars,* Metro-Goldwyn-Mayer, 1938; *Brother Rat,* Warner Brothers, 1938; *Fools for Scandal,* Warner Brothers, 1938; *Tailspin,* Twentieth Century-Fox, 1939; *Private Detective,* Warner Brothers, 1939; *The Kid from Kokomo,* Warner Brothers, 1939; *Torchy Plays with Dynamite,* Warner Brothers, 1939; *Kid Nightingale,* Warner Brothers, 1939.

Brother Rat and a Baby, Warner Brothers, 1940; *An Angel from Texas,* Warner Brothers, 1940; *Flight Angels,* Warner Brothers, 1940; *My Love Came Back,* Warner Brothers, 1940; *Tugboat Annie Sails Again,* Warner Brothers, 1940; *Gambling on the High Seas,* Warner Brothers, 1940; *Honeymoon for Three,* Warner Brothers, 1941; *Bad Men of Missouri,* Warner Brothers, 1941; *You're in the Army Now,* Warner Brothers, 1941; *The Body Disappears,* Warner Brothers, 1941; *Larceny, Inc.,* Warner Brothers, 1942; *My Favorite Spy,* RKO, 1942; *Footlight Serenade,* Twentieth Century-Fox, 1942; *Princess O'Rourke,* Warner Brothers, 1943; *Make Your Own*

Bed, Warner Brothers, 1944; *Crime by Night,* Warner Brothers, 1944; *The Doughgirls,* Warner Brothers, 1944; *Hollywood Canteen,* Warner Brothers, 1944; Helen St. James, *The Lost Weekend,* Paramount, 1945; *One More Tomorrow,* Warner Brothers, 1946; Gracie Harris, *Night and Day,* Warner Brothers, 1946; Ma Baxter, *The Yearling,* Metro-Goldwyn-Mayer, 1946; *Cheyenne,* Warner Brothers, 1947; *Magic Town,* RKO, 1947; Belinda McDonald, *Johnny Belinda,* Warner Brothers, 1948; *A Kiss in the Dark,* Warner Brothers, 1948; *The Lady Takes a Sailor,* Warner Brothers, 1949; *It's a Great Feeling,* Warner Brothers, 1949.

Eve Gill, *Stage Fright,* Warner Brothers, 1950; Laura, *The Glass Menagerie,* Warner Brothers, 1950; *Three Guys Named Mike,* Metro-Goldwyn-Mayer, 1951; Emmadel Jones, *Here Comes the Groom,* Paramount, 1951; *The Blue Veil,* RKO, 1951; *Starlift,* Warner Brothers, 1951; *The Will Rogers Story,* Warner Brothers, 1952; Carolina Hill, *Just for You,* Paramount, 1952; *Let's Do It Again,* Warner Brothers, 1953; Selina Peake, *So Big,* Warner Brothers, 1953; Helen Phillips, *Magnificent Obsession,* Universal, 1954; Lucy, *Lucy Gallant,* Paramount, 1955; *All That Heaven Allows,* Universal, 1955; *Miracle in the Rain,* Warner Brothers, 1956; *Holiday for Lovers,* Twentieth Century-Fox, 1959; Aunt Polly, *Pollyana,* Buena Vista, 1960; Katie Willard, *Bon Voyage,* Buena Vista, 1962; *How to Commit Marriage,* 1969.

PRINCIPAL TELEVISION APPEARANCES—Hostess and star, *Fireside Theatre* (later known as *Jane Wyman's Fireside Theatre,* and finally *The Jane Wyman Show*), NBC, 1955-58; *General Electric Theatre,* CBS; Angela, *Falcon Crest,* CBS, 1981—.

AWARDS: Best Actress, Academy Award, 1948, for *Johnny Belinda;* Best Actress, Academy Award nominations, 1946, for *The Yearling,* 1951, for *The Blue Veil,* 1954, for *Magnificent Obsession.*

SIDELIGHTS: Ms. Wyman was voted one of the top ten money-making stars in the *Motion Picture Herald-Fame* poll in 1954.

ADDRESSES: OFFICE—Lorimar Productions, 3970 Overland Avenue, Culver City, CA 90230.*

Y

YANEZ, Michael

PERSONAL: Born September 30; son of Victor and Rachel (Sanchez) Yanez; married Diane Lux (a translator), July 27, 1985. EDUCATION: Attended Gavalin College and Monterey Peninsula College; trained for the stage at Herbert Berghof Studios with Ed Morehouse and at Video Associates with J. Henderson.

VOCATION: Actor.

CAREER: STAGE DEBUT—Moor, *Man of La Mancha,* Barnyard Theatre, Carmel, CA, 1978, for forty performances. NEW YORK DEBUT—Primative Shamon, *Heart Drops from the Great Space,* New Vic Theatre, 1981, for twenty-four performances. PRINCIPAL STAGE APPEARANCES—Regionally and at dinner theatre, 1978-80: Title role, *The Man with a Flower in His Mouth;* Julio Valveras, *Paint Your Wagon,* Captain Sanjar, *The Apple Tree;* Tajomaru, *Rashomon;* Aztec Warrior, *La Virgen Del Tepeyac,* El Teatro Campesino (stock).

Futuro, *La Chefa,* Henry Street Settlement, New Federal Theatre, NY, 1982; Yogi, *The Inscrutable West,* 28th Street Playhouse, NY, 1982; Freddy, *Vina,* Intar II, NY, 1983; Tonto, *Does a Tiger Wear a Necktie?,* Actors Outlet Theatre, NY, 1983; Raffy, *The Beautiful LaSalles,* Wonder Horse Theatre, NY, 1984; War and chorus, *Peace,* Divine Theatre, NY, 1985.

TELEVISION DEBUT—Punk, *The New Show,* NBC, 1984.

MEMBER: American Federation of Television and Radio Artists.

ADDRESSES: HOME—513 E. Fifth Street, New York, NY 10005.

* * *

YELLEN, Linda 1949-

PERSONAL: Born July 13, 1949, in New York, NY; daughter of Seymour (a pharmacist) and Bernice Hannah (an actress and singer; maiden name, Mittleman) Yellen. EDUCATION: Barnard College, B.A., 1969; Columbia University, M.F.A., 1972, Ph.D., 1974.

VOCATION: Director, producer, and writer.

MICHAEL YANEZ

LINDA YELLEN

CAREER: PRINCIPAL TELEVISION WORK—Producer, *Mayflower: The Pilgrims' Adventure,* 1979; producer, *Playing for Time,* 1980; producer, *Hardhat and Legs,* 1980; executive producer and co-author, *The Royal Romance of Charles and Diana,* CBS, 1982; producer, director, and co-writer, *Prisoner without a Name, Cell without a Number,* NBC, 1985; producer, *Second Serve: The Renee Richards Story,* CBS, 1985.

PRINCIPAL FILM WORK—Producer and director: *Looking Up,* 1978, *Prospera; Come Out, Come Out.*

RELATED CAREER—Lecturer, Barnard College; lecturer, Yale University; assistant professor, City University of New York.

MEMBER: Directors Guild of America (executive council), Writers Guild of America, Academy of Television Arts and Sciences.

AWARDS: Best Dramatic Special, Emmy Award, Peabody Award, and Christopher Award for Excellence in Television, all 1980, for *Playing for Time;* Peabody Award, Writers Guild Award, both 1985, for *Prisoner without a Name, Cell without a Number.*

ADDRESSES: OFFICE—421 Hudson Street, Suite 303, New York, NY 10014. AGENT—c/o Leonard Hirshan, William Morris Agency, 151 El Camino Drive, Beverly Hills, CA 90069.

YOUNG, Roger   1942-

PERSONAL: Born May 13, 1942, in Champaign, IL; son of Lester E. (a pilot) and Irma (a secretary) Young. EDUCATION: University of Illinois, B.S., 1965.

VOCATION: Director.

CAREER: PRINCIPAL TELEVISION WORK—Director, *Lou Grant.*

Movies: *Bitter Harvest,* 1981; *Innocent Love,* 1982; *Dreams Don't Die,* 1982; *Gulag,* HBO, 1985; also, *Into Thin Air, Under Siege.*

Pilots: *Magnum, P.I.; Hardcastle and McCormick; Dick and Tracy.*

PRINCIPAL FILM WORK—Director, *Lassiter,* Warner Brothers, 1984.

AWARDS: Outstanding Direction in a Drama, Emmy Award, 1979, for "Cop," *Lou Grant;* Directors Guild Award, 1980, 1981; Christopher Award, 1981; Ace Award, 1985.

ADDRESSES: AGENT—Broder-Kurland-Webb, 8439 Sunset Blvd., Hollywood, CA 90069.

Z

ZIEMBA, Karen 1957-

PERSONAL: Born November 12, 1957, in St. Joseph, MI; daughter of Oscar Hugo (an investment broker) and Barbara Marie (Heidt) Ziemba; married William Tatum (an actor), 1984. EDUCATION: Akron University, B.A.

VOCATION: Actress, dancer, and singer.

CAREER: STAGE DEBUT—Solo dancer, *Reflections,* Ohio Ballet, E.J. Thomas Performing Arts Hall, Akron, OH, 1977. NEW YORK DEBUT—Singer, *Radio City Music Hall Revue,* 1982. PRINCIPAL STAGE APPEARANCES—*Seesaw,* Off-Broadway production, 1981; Hilary, *A Chorus Line,* Shubert Theatre, NY, 1982; Peggy Sawyer, *42nd Street,* Majestic Theatre, NY, 1983-84.

MAJOR TOURS—Cassie, Maggie, Diana, *A Chorus Line,* Houston, Atlanta, Fort Lauderdale, Philadelphia, Las Vegas.

ADDRESSES: AGENT—June Henry, 119 W. 57th Street, New York, NY 10019.

KAREN ZIEMBA

ZIMBALIST, Efrem, Jr. 1923-

PERSONAL: Born November 30, 1923, in New York, NY; son of Efrem (a violinist) and Alma (an opera singer; maiden name, Gluck) Zimbalist; married Emily McNair, 1945 (died, 1950); married Loranda Stephanie Spalding, 1956 (divorced); remarried Loranda Spalding, 1972; children: (first marriage) Nancy, Efrem, III; (second marriage) Stephanie (the actress). EDUCATION: Yale University; studied for the theatre at the Neighborhood Playhouse in New York. MILITARY: U.S. Army, World War II, five years in Europe and U.S.

VOCATION: Actor and producer.

CAREER: STAGE DEBUT—*The Rugged Path,* NY, 1945. PRINCIPAL STAGE APPEARANCES—*Henry VIII, Androcles and the Lion, What Every Woman Knows,* and *Yellow Jack,* all with the American Repertory Theatre, NY, 1946-47; *Hedda Gabler,* 1948; *Fallen Angels,* 1955-56.

PRINCIPAL STAGE WORK—Producer: *The Medium* and *The Telephone,* NY, 1947; *The Consul,* Barrymore Theatre, NY, 1950.

FILM DEBUT—*House of Strangers,* Twentieth Century-Fox, 1950. PRINCIPAL FILM APPEARANCES—*Bombers B-52,* Warner Brothers, 1957; *Band of Angels,* Warner Brothers, 1957; *The Deep Six,* Warner Brothers, 1958; *Violent Road,* Warner Brothers, 1958; Vincent Bryant, *Too Much, Too Soon,* Warner Brothers, 1958; *Home Before Dark,* Warner Brothers, 1958; *The Crowded Sky,* Warner Brothers, 1960; *A Fever in the Blood,* Warner Brothers, 1961; Arthur Winner, *By Love Possessed,* United Artists, 1961; *The Chapman Report,* Warner Brothers, 1962; *The Reward,* Twentieth Century-Fox, 1965; William Mansfield, *Harlow,* Electronovision, 1965; *Wait Until Dark,* Warner Brothers/Seven Arts, 1967; *Airport 1975,* Universal, 1974.

PRINCIPAL TELEVISION APPEARANCES—Series: Stuart Bailey, *Conflict,* ABC, 1957; Stuart Bailey, *77 Sunset Strip,* ABC, 1958-1964; Inspector Lewis Erskine, *The F.B.I.,* ABC, 1965-1974.

Episodic: Dandy Jim Buckley, *Maverick,* ABC, 1957-60; Steele's mentor, *Remington Steele,* NBC, 1984-85. Also: *Philco Playhouse, Goodyear Playhouse, U.S. Steel Hour;* numerous specials and guest appearances.

RECORDINGS: Sang "Adeste Fideles," on the Warner Brothers Christmas Album, *We Wish You a Merry Christmas,* 1959.

SIDELIGHTS: After the death of his first wife in 1950, Zimbalist gave up his career and worked as his father's assistant at the Curtis Institute of Music in Philadelphia for two years. He returned to the stage with a stock company in Hammonton, New Jersey in 1954.

AWARDS: For his producing work: New York Critics Award, Pulitzer Prize, 1950, for *The Consul;* Purple Heart.

EFREM ZIMBALIST, JR.

ADDRESSES: AGENT—The Agency, 10351 Santa Monica Blvd., Los Angeles, CA 90025.

*   *   *

ZINDEL, Paul   1936-

PERSONAL: Born May 15, 1936, in Staten Island, NY; son of Paul (a policeman) and Betty (a practical nurse; maiden name, Frank) Zindel; married Bonnie Hildebrand (a former chemistry teacher, now a screenwriter); children: David Jack, Elizabeth Claire. EDUCATION: Wagner College, B.S., 1958.

VOCATION: Playwright.

WRITINGS: PLAYS, PRODUCED—*Dimensions of Peacocks*, NY, 1959; *Euthanasia and the Endless Hearts*, NY, 1960; *A Dream of Swallows*, NY, 1962; *The Effect of Gamma Rays on Man-in-the-Moon Marigolds*, Alley Theatre, Houston, TX, 1964; Mercer-O'Casey Theatre, NY, 1970; *And Miss Reardon Drinks a Little*, Morosco Theatre, NY, 1971; *The Secret Affairs of Mildred Wild*, NY, 1972; *Ladies at the Alamo*, Actors Studio, NY, 1975 then at the Martin Beck Theatre, NY, 1977.

TELEVISION—Plays: *The Effect of Gamma Rays on Man-in-the-Moon Marigolds;* PBS, 1966; *Let Me Hear You Whisper*, 1969.

Movie: *Alice in Wonderland*, CBS, 1985.

SCREENPLAYS—*Up the Sandbox*, National General, 1972; *The*

Photograph by Jeff Peters

PAUL ZINDEL

Effect of Gamma Rays on Man-in-the-Moon Marigolds, Twentieth Century-Fox, 1973; *Mame*, Warner Brothers, 1974; *Maria's Lovers*, Cannon, 1984; *Runaway Train*, Cannon, 1985.

BOOKS—*The Pigman; My Darling, My Hamburger; I Never Loved Your Mind.*

AWARDS: Pulitzer Prize for Drama, New York Drama Critics Award, Drama Desk Award, all 1971, for *The Effect of Gamma Rays on Man-in-the-Moon Marigolds.*

ADDRESSES: AGENT—Curtis Brown, Ltd., Ten Astor Place, New York, NY 10003.

*   *   *

ZWICK, Edward   1952-

PERSONAL: Born October 8, 1952, in Chicago, IL; son of Allen and Ruth Ellyn (Reich) Zwick; married Lynn Liberty Godshall (a writer), October 24, 1982. EDUCATION: Harvard University, B.A., 1974; American Film Institute Center for Advanced Film Studies, M.F.A., 1976.

VOCATION: Writer, producer and director.

CAREER: FIRST TELEVISION WORK—Writer, *Family*, ABC, 1976. PRINCIPAL TELEVISION WORK—Writer, producer, and director, *Family*, ABC; director, *Paper Dolls*, ABC; director, *Hang It All*, ABC; writer, producer and director, *Special Bulletin*, NBC.

PRINCIPAL FILM WORK—Director, *About Last Night . . . ,* Tri-Star, 1986.

RELATED CAREER—Editor and feature writer, *The New Republic* magazine and *Rolling Stone* magazine, 1972-74.

WRITINGS: NON-FICTION—*Literature and Liberalism,* E.P. Dutton, 1975.

AWARDS: Humanitas Prize Award, 1980, for *Family;* Directors Guild Award, Writers Guild Award, two Emmy Awards, Humanitas Prize Award, all 1983, for *Special Bulletin.*

ADDRESSES: AGENT—c/o Jeffrey Berg, International Creative Management, 8899 Beverly Blvd., Los Angeles, CA 90048.

Cumulative Index

To provide continuity with *Who's Who in the Theatre*, this index interfiles references to *Who's Who in the Theatre*, 1st-17th Editions, and *Who Was Who in the Theatre* with references to *Contemporary Theatre, Film, and Television*, Volumes 1-3.

References in the index are identified as follows:

CTFT and volume number—*Contemporary Theatre, Film, and Television*, Volumes 1-3
WWT and edition number—*Who's Who in the Theatre*, 1st-17th Editions
WWasWT—*Who Was Who in the Theatre*

G

S

443

U